COLLINS
PAPERBACK
SPANISH
DICTIONARY

COLLINS
PAPERBACK
SPANISH
DICTIONARY
SPANISH▶ENGLISH   ENGLISH▶SPANISH

HarperCollins*Publishers*

second edition/segunda edición 1995

© **HarperCollins Publishers 1995**
© **William Collins Sons & Co. Ltd. 1989**

HarperCollins Publishers
P.O. Box, Glasgow G4 0NB, Great Britain
ISBN 0 00 470208 5 (Paperback)
ISBN 0 00 470730 3 (College)

Grijalbo Mondadori S.A.
Aragón 385, Barcelona 08013
ISBN 84 253 2792

Jeremy Butterfield • Mike Gonzalez • Gerry Breslin

contributors to second edition/colaboradores en la segunda edición
Teresa Alvarez García • Brian Steel
Ana Cristina Llompart • José Miguel Galván Déniz

editorial staff/redacción
Megan Thomson
Val McNulty • Irene Lakhani • Sharon Hunter
Tracy Lomas • Claire Evans • Jane Horwood

series editor/colección dirigida por
Lorna Sinclair Knight
editorial management/dirección editorial
Vivian Marr

Typeset by Morton Word Processing Ltd, Scarborough

*Printed in Great Britain by
HarperCollins Manufacturing, Glasgow*

ÍNDICE DE MATERIAS   CONTENTS

INTRODUCCIÓN

Si quieres aprender inglés o profundizar en los conocimientos ya adquiridos, si quieres leer o estudiar textos ingleses o conversar con personas de habla inglesa, acabas de escoger el compañero de trabajo ideal para poder hacerlo, ya estés en el instituto o en la universidad, seas turista, administrativo u hombre/mujer de negocios. Este diccionario, totalmente práctico y al día, abarca una gran parte del vocabulario cotidiano, del relacionado con el mundo de los negocios, de la actualidad, de la administración burocrática y del turismo. Como en todos nuestros diccionarios, hemos hecho hincapié en la lengua contemporánea y en las expresiones idiomáticas.

CÓMO USAR EL DICCIONARIO

Más abajo tienes las explicaciones necesarias para entender cómo está presentada la información en tu diccionario. Nuestro objetivo es darte la mayor información posible sin sacrificar por ello la claridad.

Las entradas

Éstos son los elementos que pueden componer una entrada cualquiera del diccionario:

Transcripción fonética

Ésta aparece inmediatamente después del lema (así denominamos a la palabra cabeza del artículo) y entre corchetes [ ]. Al igual que la mayor parte de los diccionarios actuales, hemos optado por el sistema denominado "alfabeto fonético internacional". En la página xiv encontrarás una lista completa de los caracteres utilizados en este sistema.

Información gramatical

Todas las voces incluidas en el diccionario pertenecen a una determinada categoría gramatical: sustantivo, verbo, adjetivo, pronombre, artículo, conjunción, abreviatura. Los sustantivos pueden ir en singular o en plural y, en español, pueden ser masculinos o femeninos. Los verbos pueden ser transitivos, intransitivos y en español también pronominales (o reflexivos). La categoría gramatical de cada voz aparece en *cursiva*, inmediatamente después de la transcripción fonética.

A menudo una misma palabra puede funcionar con distintas categorías gramaticales. Por ejemplo **deber** puede ser verbo o sustantivo, el término inglés **public** puede ser sustantivo o adjetivo. Incluso un mismo verbo como **importar** o como el inglés **to work** a veces será transitivo y a veces intransitivo, dependiendo de su significado. Para que te resulte más fácil encontrar la categoría gramatical que buscas, en el caso de que haya varias dentro de una misma entrada, y para que la presentación sea más clara, aquéllas aparecen separadas por rombos negros ♦.

Acepciones

La mayor parte de las palabras tienen más de un sentido. Así por ejemplo

crucero puede ser, entre otros, un tipo de barco o un tipo de viaje turístico, y según la acepción que busquemos la traducción varía: "cruise ship" en el primer caso y "cruise" en el segundo. Otras palabras se traducen de forma distinta según el contexto: **bajo** puede traducirse por "low", pero también por "small, short" si se trata de una persona, "ground" si es de un piso etc. Para que puedas escoger la traducción más indicada para cada acepción o contexto hemos incorporado indicaciones de uso o significado, que aparecen entre paréntesis y en *cursiva*. Así figuran los anteriores ejemplos en el diccionario:

crucero *nm* (*NAUT: barco*) cruise ship; (: *viaje*) cruise

bajo *adj* (...) low; (*piso*) ground; (*de estatura*) small, short ...

De la misma forma, muchas voces tienen un sentido distinto según el contexto en el que se usen. Así por ejemplo, **giro** puede ser un movimiento, pero tiene un significado específico en gramática y finanzas. Con la incorporación de indicaciones de campo semántico (tales como LINGÜÍSTICA y COMERCIO en este caso), resulta más fácil saber cuál es la acepción que necesitamos. La mayoría de dichas acepciones aparecen abreviadas para ganar espacio:

giro *nm* (*movimiento*) turn, revolution; (*LING*) expression; (*COM*) draft

Puede verse la lista completa de las abreviaturas que hemos utilizado en la página xii.

Traducciones

La mayor parte de las palabras españolas tienen su traducción al inglés y viceversa, como en los ejemplos que acabamos de ver. Sin embargo hay ocasiones en las que no hay un equivalente exacto en la lengua término, fundamentalmente por razones socio-culturales. En este caso hemos dado una traducción aproximada (que suele ser en realidad un equivalente cultural) y lo indicamos con el signo ≈. Este es el caso de **A road**, cuyo equivalente en español peninsular es "carretera nacional", o de **dual carriageway**, que equivale a "autovía": no se trata de traducciones propiamente dichas, puesto que ambos sistemas de carreteras son diferentes.

A road *n* (*BRIT AUT*) ≈ carretera nacional

dual carriageway *n* (*BRIT*) ≈ autovía

A veces es imposible encontrar incluso un equivalente aproximado, como en el caso de los platos o tradiciones regionales, por lo que se hace necesario dar una explicación en lugar de la traducción. Así ocurre, por ejemplo, con:

ceilidh *n baile con música y danzas tradicionales escocesas o irlandesas*

Como puede verse, la explicación o glosa aparece en *cursiva*, para mayor claridad.

Así mismo, a menudo no se puede traducir palabra por palabra. Aunque **machine** se traduce normalmente por "máquina", **washing machine** es en realidad "lavadora". De la misma forma, la traducción al inglés de

hormiguero es "ant's nest", pero en la expresión **aquello era un hormiguero** la traducción será "it was swarming with people". Es en este tipo de situaciones en las que tu diccionario te será más útil, pues es muy completo en compuestos nominales, frases y expresiones idiomáticas.

Niveles lingüísticos

En español, sabemos instintivamente cuándo usar **eso son tonterías** y cuándo **eso son chorradas**. Sin embargo, a la hora de intentar comprender a alguien que está hablando en inglés o bien de expresarnos nosotros mismos en esa lengua, adquiere una importancia especial saber si una palabra es coloquial o no. Así pues, hemos marcado las palabras o expresiones inglesas que no suelen utilizarse más que en una situación familiar con la indicación (*col*) y aquéllas con las que hay que tener especial cuidado (pues pueden sonar muy vulgares a los oídos de mucha gente) con el signo de admiración (*col!*). No hemos añadido la indicación (*fam*) a la traducción inglesa cuando ésta tiene el mismo nivel que la palabra que se traduce pero a las traducciones que pueden resultar vulgares siempre las sigue el signo de admiración entre paréntesis (*!*).

Palabras clave

Algunas voces especialmente importantes o complejas en ambas lenguas requieren un tratamiento especial dentro del diccionario: verbos como **hacer** o **estar** en español, o **to have** o **to do** en inglés. Por ello, aparecen en un cuadro y bajo la denominación de "palabra clave", y como comprobarás, se ha hecho un análisis más profundo de ellas, pues son elementos básicos de la lengua.

Información de tipo cultural

Los artículos que aparecen separados del texto principal por dos líneas, una abajo y otra arriba, explican diversos aspectos de la cultura en países de habla española e inglesa, como la política, la educación, medios de comunicación y fiestas nacionales.

Nuevo orden alfabético en español

Tras la decisión tomada por la Real Academia Española en conjunción con las Academias hispanoamericanas, CH y LL ya no aparecen como letras independientes en este diccionario. Así por ejemplo **chapa** o **lluvia** se encuentran bajo la C y la L respectivamente. Conviene recordar que palabras como **cacha** y **callar** también han cambiado de lugar y ahora aparecen tras **cacerola** y **calizo**.

INTRODUCTION

You may be starting Spanish for the first time, or you may wish to extend your knowledge of the language. Perhaps you want to read and study Spanish books, newspapers and magazines, or perhaps simply have a conversation with Spanish speakers. Whatever the reason, whether you're a student, a tourist or want to use Spanish for business, this is the ideal book to help you understand and communicate. This modern, user-friendly dictionary gives priority to everyday vocabulary and the language of current affairs, business, computing and tourism, and, as in all Collins dictionaries, the emphasis is firmly placed on contemporary language and expressions.

HOW TO USE THE DICTIONARY

Below you will find an outline of how information is presented in your dictionary. Our aim is to give you the maximum amount of detail in the clearest and most helpful way.

Entries

A typical entry in your dictionary will be made up of the following elements:

Phonetic transcription

Phonetics appear in square brackets immediately after the headword. They are shown using the International Phonetic Alphabet (IPA), and a complete list of the symbols used in this system can be found on page xiv. The pronunciation given is for Castilian Spanish except where a word is solely used in Latin America, when we give the Latin American pronunciation. A further guide to the differences in types of Spanish pronunciation is given on page xiv.

Grammatical information

All words belong to one of the following parts of speech: noun, verb, adjective, adverb, pronoun, article, conjunction, preposition, abbreviation. Nouns can be singular or plural and, in Spanish, masculine or feminine. Verbs can be transitive, intransitive, reflexive or impersonal. Parts of speech appear in *italics* immediately after the phonetic spelling of the headword. The gender of the translation also appears in *italics* immediately following the key element of the translation, except where this is a regular masculine singular noun ending in "o", or a regular feminine singular noun ending in "a".

Often a word can have more than one part of speech. Just as the English word **chemical** can be an adjective or a noun, the Spanish word **conocido** can be an adjective ("(well-)known") or a noun ("acquaintance"). In the same way the verb **to walk** is sometimes transitive, ie it takes an object ("to walk the dog") and sometimes intransitive, ie it doesn't take an object ("to walk to school"). To help you find the meaning you are looking for quickly and for clarity of presentation, the different part of speech categories are separated by a black lozenge ♦.

Meaning divisions

Most words have more than one meaning. Take, for example, **punch** which can be, amongst other things, a blow with the fist or an object used for making holes. Other words are translated differently depending on the context in which they are used. The transitive verb **to put on**, for example, can be translated by "ponerse", "encender" etc depending on *what* it is you are putting on. To help you select the most appropriate translation in every context, entries are divided according to meaning. Each different meaning is introduced by an "indicator" in *italics* and in brackets. Thus, the examples given above will be shown as follows:

punch n (*blow*) golpe m, puñetazo; (*tool*) punzón m

put on vt (*clothes, lipstick etc*) ponerse; (*light etc*) encender

Likewise, some words can have a different meaning when used to talk about a specific subject area or field. For example **bishop**, which in a religious context means a high-ranking clergyman, is also the name of a chess piece. To show English speakers which translation to use, we have added "subject field labels" in capitals and in brackets, in this case (*CHESS*):

bishop n obispo; (*CHESS*) alfil m

Field labels are often shortened to save space. You will find a complete list of abbreviations used in the dictionary on page xii.

Translations

Most English words have a direct translation in Spanish and vice versa, as shown in the examples given above. Sometimes, however, no exact equivalent exists in the target language. In such cases we have given an approximate equivalent, indicated by the sign ≈. An example is **British Rail**, the Spanish equivalent of which is "RENFE". There is no exact equivalent since the bodies in the two countries are quite different:

British Rail (BR) n ≈ RENFE f (*SP*)

On occasion it is impossible to find even an approximate equivalent. This may be the case, for example, with the names of types of food:

fabada nf *bean and sausage stew*

Here the translation (which doesn't exist) is replaced by an explanation. For increased clarity the explanation, or "gloss", is shown in *italics*.

It is often the case that a word, or a particular meaning of a word, cannot be translated in isolation. The translation of **Dutch**, for example, is "holandés/esa". However, the phrase **to go Dutch** is rendered by "pagar cada uno lo suyo". Even an expression as simple as **washing powder** needs a separate translation since it translates as "detergente (en polvo)", not "polvo para lavar". This is where your dictionary will prove to be particularly informative and useful since it contains an abundance of compounds, phrases and idiomatic expressions.

Levels of formality and familiarity

In English you instinctively know when to say **I'm broke** or **I'm a bit short of cash** and when to say **I don't have any money**. When you are trying to understand someone who is speaking Spanish, however, or when you yourself try to speak Spanish, it is important to know what is polite and what is less so, and what you can say in a relaxed situation but not in a formal context. To help you with this, on the Spanish-English side we have added the label (*fam*) to show that a Spanish meaning or expression is colloquial, while those meanings or expressions which are vulgar are given an exclamation mark (*fam!*), warning you they can cause serious offence. Note also that on the English-Spanish side, translations which are vulgar are followed by an exclamation mark in brackets.

Keywords

Words labelled in the text as KEYWORDs, such as **have** and **do** or their Spanish equivalents **tener** and **hacer**, have been given special treatment because they form the basic elements of the language. This extra help will ensure that you know how to use these complex words with confidence.

Cultural information

Entries which appear separated from the main text by a line above and below them explain aspects of culture in Spanish and English-speaking countries. Subject areas covered include politics, education, media and national festivals.

Spanish alphabetical order

In 1994 the **Real Academia Española** and the Spanish American language academies jointly decided to stop treating CH and LL as separate letters in Spanish, thereby bringing it into line with European spelling norms. This means that **chapa** and **lluvia** will be filed in letters C and L respectively. Of course, it should also be remembered that words like **cancha** and **callar**, with **ch** and **ll** in the middle of the words, will also have changed places alphabetically, now being found after **cáncer** and **cáliz** respectively. Spanish however still has one more letter than English with Ñ treated separately, between N and O.

ABREVIATURAS

ABBREVIATIONS

abreviatura	**ab(b)r**	abbreviation
adjetivo, locución adjetiva	**adj**	adjective, adjectival phrase
administración, lengua administrativa	**ADMIN**	administration
adverbio, locución adverbial	**adv**	adverb, adverbial phrase
agricultura	**AGR**	agriculture
alguien	**algn**	
América Latina	**AM**	Latin America
anatomía	**ANAT**	anatomy
arquitectura	**ARQ, ARCH**	architecture
astrología, astronomía	**ASTRO**	astrology, astronomy
el automóvil	**AUT(O)**	the motor car and motoring
aviación, viajes aéreos	**AVIAT**	flying, air travel
biología	**BIO(L)**	biology
botánica, flores	**BOT**	botany
inglés británico	**BRIT**	British English
química	**CHEM**	chemistry
	CINE	cinema
lengua familiar (! vulgar)	**col (!)**	colloquial usage (! particularly offensive)
comercio, finanzas, banca	**COM(M)**	commerce, finance, banking
informática	**COMPUT**	computing
conjunción	**conj**	conjunction
construcción	**CONSTR**	building
compuesto	**cpd**	compound element
cocina	**CULIN**	cookery
economía	**ECON**	economics
electricidad, electrónica	**ELEC**	electricity, electronics
enseñanza, sistema escolar	**ESCOL**	schooling, schools
España	**ESP**	Spain
especialmente	**esp**	especially
exclamación, interjección	**excl**	exclamation, interjection
femenino	**f**	feminine
lengua familiar (! vulgar)	**fam (!)**	colloquial usage (! particularly offensive)
ferrocarril	**FERRO**	railways
uso figurado	**fig**	figurative use
fotografía	**FOTO**	photography
(verbo inglés) del cual la partícula es inseparable	**fus**	(phrasal verb) where the particle is inseparable
generalmente	**gen**	generally
geografía, geología	**GEO**	geography, geology
geometría	**GEOM**	geometry
informática	**INFORM**	computing
invariable	**inv**	invariable
irregular	**irreg**	irregular
lo jurídico	**JUR**	law
América Latina	**LAM**	Latin America
gramática, lingüística	**LING**	grammar, linguistics
literatura	**LIT**	literature
masculino	**m**	masculine
matemáticas	**MAT(H)**	mathematics
medicina	**MED**	medical term, medicine
masculino/femenino	**m/f**	masculine/feminine

lo militar, ejército	**MIL**	military matters
música	**MUS**	music
sustantivo, nombre	**n**	noun
navegación, náutica	**NAUT**	sailing, navigation
sustantivo no empleado en el plural	**no pl**	collective (uncountable) noun, not used in plural
sustantivo numérico	**num**	numeral noun
complemento	**obj**	(grammatical) object
	o.s.	oneself
peyorativo	**pey, pej**	derogatory, pejorative
fotografía	**PHOT**	photography
fisiología	**PHYSIOL**	physiology
plural	**pl**	plural
política	**POL**	politics
participio de pasado	**pp**	past participle
prefijo	**pref**	prefix
preposición	**prep**	preposition
pronombre	**pron**	pronoun
psicología, psiquiatría	**PSICO, PSYCH**	psychology, psychiatry
tiempo pasado	**pt**	past tense
ferrocarril	**RAIL**	railways
religión, lo eclesiástico	**REL**	religion, church service
	sb	somebody
enseñanza, sistema escolar	**SCOL**	schooling, schools
singular	**sg**	singular
España	**SP**	Spain
	sth	something
subjuntivo	**subjun**	subjunctive
sujeto	**su(b)j**	(grammatical) subject
sufijo	**suff**	suffix
tauromaquia	**TAUR**	bullfighting
también	**tb**	also
teatro	**TEAT**	
técnica, tecnología	**TEC(H)**	technical term, technology
telecomunicaciones	**TELEC, TEL**	telecommunications
	THEAT	theatre
imprenta, tipografía	**TIP, TYP**	typography, printing
televisión	**TV**	television
sistema universitario	**UNIV**	universities
inglés norteamericano	**US**	American English
verbo	**vb**	verb
verbo intransitivo	**vi**	intransitive verb
verbo pronominal	**vr**	reflexive verb
verbo transitivo	**vt**	transitive verb
zoología, animales	**ZOOL**	zoology
marca registrada	®	registered trademark
indica un equivalente cultural	≈	introduces a cultural equivalent

SPANISH PRONUNCIATION

Consonants

b	[b]	<u>b</u>om<u>b</u>a	see notes on *v* below
	[ß]	la<u>b</u>or	
c	[k]	<u>c</u>aja	*c* before *a*, *o* or *u* is pronounced as in *c*at
ce, ci	[θe, θi]	<u>c</u>ero	*c* before *e* or *i* is pronounced as in *th*in
		<u>c</u>ielo	and as *s* in *s*in in Latin America and parts
	[se, si][1]	vo<u>c</u>ero	of Spain
		noti<u>c</u>iero	
ch	[tʃ]	<u>ch</u>iste	*ch* is pronounced as *ch* in *ch*air
d	[d]	<u>d</u>anés	at the beginning of a word or after *l* or *n*,
	[ð]	ciu<u>d</u>a<u>d</u>	*d* is pronounced as in English. In any other position it is like *th* in *the*
g	[g]	gafas	*g* before *a*, *o* or *u* is pronounced as in *g*ap,
		guerra	if at the beginning of a word or after *n*. In
	[ɣ]	paga	other positions the sound is softened
ge, gi	[xe, xi]	<u>g</u>ente	*g* before *e* or *i* is pronounced similar to *ch*
		<u>g</u>irar	in Scottish lo*ch*
h		<u>h</u>aber	*h* is always silent in Spanish
j	[x]	<u>j</u>ugar	*j* is pronounced like *ch* in Scottish lo*ch*
ll	[ʎ]	ta<u>ll</u>e	*ll* is pronounced like the *lli* in mi*lli*on
ñ	[ɲ]	ni<u>ñ</u>o	*ñ* is pronounced like the *ni* in o*ni*on
q	[k]	<u>q</u>ue	*q* is pronounced as *k* in *k*ing
r, rr	[r]	quita<u>r</u>	*r* is always pronounced in Spanish, unlike
	[rr]	ga<u>rr</u>a	the silent *r* in dance*r*. *rr* and *r* at the beginning of a word are trilled, like a Scottish *r*
s	[s]	quizá<u>s</u>	*s* is usually pronounced as in pa*s*s, but
		i<u>s</u>la	before *b*, *d*, *g*, *l*, *m* or *n* it is pronounced as in ro*s*e
v	[b]	<u>v</u>ía	*v* is pronounced something like *b*. At the
	[ß]	di<u>v</u>idir	beginning of a word or after *m* or *n* it is pronounced as *b* in *b*oy. In any other position it is pronounce with the lips in position to pronounce *b* of *b*oy, but not meeting
w	[b]	<u>w</u>áter	pronounced either like Spanish *b*, or like
	[w]	<u>w</u>hiskey	English *w*
z	[θ]	tena<u>z</u>	*z* is pronounced as *th*in *th*in and as *s* in
	[s][1]	i<u>z</u>ada	*s*in in Latin America and parts of Spain
	[ks]	tó<u>x</u>ico	*x* is pronounced as in to*x*in except in
	[s]	<u>x</u>enofobia	informal Spanish or at the beginning of a word

f, *k*, *l*, *m*, *n*, *p* and *t* are pronounced as in English.

[1]Only shown in Latin American entries.

Vowels

a	[a]	p*a*ta	not as long as *a* in f*a*r. When followed by a consonant in the same syllable (i.e. in a closed syllable), as in am*a*nte, the *a* is short, as in b*a*t
e	[e]	m*e*	like *e* in th*e*y. In a closed syllable, as in g*e*nte, the *e* is short as in p*e*t
i	[i]	p*i*no	as in m*ea*n or mach*i*ne
o	[o]	l*o*	as in l*o*cal. In a closed syllable, as in c*o*ntrol, the *o* is short as in c*o*t
u	[u]	l*u*nes	as in r*u*le. It is silent after *q*, and in *gue*, *gui*, unless marked *güe*, *güi* e.g. antig*ü*edad, when it is pronounced like *w* in *w*olf

Semivowels

i, y	[j]	b*i*en h*i*elo *y*unta	pronounced like *y* in *y*es
u	[w]	h*u*evo f*u*ente antig*ü*edad	unstressed *u* between consonant and vowel is pronounced like *w* in *w*ell. See also notes on *u* above

Dipthongs

ai, ay	[ai]	b*ai*le	as *i* in r*i*de
au	[au]	*au*to	as *ou* in sh*ou*t
ei, ey	[ei]	bu*ey*	as *ey* in gr*ey*
eu	[eu]	d*eu*da	both elements pronounced independently [e] + [u]
oi, oy	[oi]	h*oy*	as *oy* in t*oy*

Stress

The rules of stress in Spanish are as follows:

(a) when a word ends in a vowel or in *n* or *s*, the second last syllable is stressed: pat*a*ta, pat*a*tas, c*o*me, c*o*men

(b) when a word ends in a consonant other than *n* or *s*, the stress falls on the last syllable: par*e*d, habl*a*r

(c) when the rules set out in a and b are not applied, an acute accent appears over the stressed vowel: com*ú*n, geograf*í*a, ingl*é*s

In the phonetic transcription, the symbol ['] precedes the syllable on which the stress falls.

In general, we give the pronunciation of each entry in square brackets after the word in question.

PRONUNCIACIÓN INGLESA

Vocales y diptongos

	Ejemplo inglés	*Ejemplo español/explicación*
[ɑː]	f<u>a</u>ther	Entre *a* de p*a*dre y *o* de n*o*che
[ʌ]	b<u>u</u>t, c<u>o</u>me	*a* muy breve
[æ]	m<u>a</u>n, c<u>a</u>t	Con los labios en la posición de *e* en p*e*na y luego se pronuncia el sonido *a* parecido *a* la *a* de c*a*rro
[ə]	fath<u>er</u>, <u>a</u>go	Vocal neutra parecida a una *e* u *o* casi muda
[əː]	b<u>ir</u>d, h<u>ear</u>d	Entre *e* abierta, y *o* cerrada, sonido alargado
[ɛ]	g<u>e</u>t, b<u>e</u>d	Como en p*e*rro
[ɪ]	<u>i</u>t, b<u>i</u>g	Más breve que en s*i*
[iː]	t<u>ea</u>, s<u>ee</u>	Como en f*i*no
[ɔ]	h<u>o</u>t, w<u>a</u>sh	Como en t*o*rre
[ɔː]	s<u>aw</u>, <u>a</u>ll	Como en p*o*r
[u]	p<u>u</u>t, b<u>oo</u>k	Sonido breve, más cerrado que b*u*rro
[uː]	t<u>oo</u>, y<u>ou</u>	Sonido largo, como en *u*no
[aɪ]	fl<u>y</u>, h<u>igh</u>	Como en fr*ai*le
[au]	h<u>ow</u>, h<u>ou</u>se	Como en p*au*sa
[ɛə]	th<u>ere</u>, b<u>ea</u>r	Casi como en v*ea*, pero el sonido *a* se mezcla con el indistinto [ə]
[eɪ]	d<u>ay</u>, ob<u>ey</u>	*e* cerrada seguida por una *i* débil
[ɪə]	h<u>ere</u>, h<u>ear</u>	Como en man*ía*, mezclándose el sonido *a* con el indistinto [ə]
[əu]	g<u>o</u>, n<u>o</u>te	[ə] seguido por una breve *u*
[ɔɪ]	b<u>oy</u>, <u>oi</u>l	Como en v*oy*
[uə]	p<u>oor</u>, s<u>ure</u>	*u* bastante larga más el sonido indistinto [ə]

Consonantes

	Ejemplo inglés	Ejemplo español/explicación
[b]	<u>b</u>ig, lo<u>bb</u>y	Como en tum<u>b</u>an
[d]	men<u>ded</u>	Como en con<u>d</u>e, an<u>d</u>ar
[g]	<u>g</u>o, <u>g</u>et, bi<u>g</u>	Como en <u>g</u>rande, <u>g</u>ol
[dʒ]	<u>g</u>in, <u>judge</u>	Como en la <u>ll</u> andaluza y en <u>G</u>eneralitat (catalán)
[ŋ]	si<u>ng</u>	Como en ví<u>n</u>culo
[h]	<u>h</u>ouse, <u>h</u>e	Como la <u>j</u>ota hispanoamericana
[j]	<u>y</u>oung, <u>y</u>es	Como en <u>y</u>a
[k]	<u>c</u>ome, mo<u>ck</u>	Como en <u>c</u>aña, Es<u>c</u>ocia
[r]	<u>r</u>ed, t<u>r</u>ead	Se pronuncia con la punta de la lengua hacia atrás y sin hacerla vibrar
[s]	<u>s</u>and, ye<u>s</u>	Como en ca<u>s</u>a, <u>s</u>esión
[z]	ro<u>s</u>e, <u>z</u>ebra	Como en de<u>s</u>de, mi<u>s</u>mo
[ʃ]	<u>sh</u>e, ma<u>ch</u>ine	Como en <u>ch</u>ambre (francés), ro<u>x</u>o (portugués)
[tʃ]	<u>ch</u>in, ri<u>ch</u>	Como en <u>ch</u>ocolate
[v]	<u>v</u>alley	Como en f, pero se retiran los dientes superiores vibrándolos contra el labio inferior
[w]	<u>w</u>ater, <u>wh</u>ich	Como en la <u>u</u> de h<u>u</u>evo, p<u>u</u>ede
[ʒ]	vi<u>s</u>ion	Como en <u>j</u>ournal (francés)
[θ]	<u>th</u>ink, my<u>th</u>	Como en re<u>c</u>eta, <u>z</u>apato
[ð]	<u>th</u>is, <u>th</u>e	Como en la <u>d</u> de habla<u>d</u>o, verda<u>d</u>

p, f, m, n, l, t iguales que en español

El signo * indica que la r final escrita apenas se pronuncia en inglés británico cuando la palabra siguiente empieza con vocal. El signo ['] indica la sílaba acentuada.

Por regla general, la pronunciación viene dada entre corchetes después de cada entrada léxica. Sin embargo, allí donde la entrada es un compuesto de dos o más palabras separadas, cada una de las cuales es objeto de entrada en alguna otra parte del diccionario, la pronunciación de cada palabra se encontrará en su correspondiente posición alfabética.

SPANISH VERB FORMS

1 Gerund *2* Imperative *3* Present *4* Preterite *5* Future *6* Present subjunctive *7* Imperfect subjunctive *8* Past participle *9* Imperfect

acertar *2* acierta *3* acierto, aciertas, acierta, aciertan *6* acierte, aciertes, acierte, acierten

acordar *2* acuerda *3* acuerdo, acuerdas, acuerda, acuerdan *6* acuerde, acuerdes, acuerde, acuerden

advertir *1* advirtiendo *2* advierte *3* advierto, adviertes, advierte, advierten *4* advirtió, advirtieron *6* advierta, adviertas, advierta, advirtamos, advirtáis, adviertan *7* advirtiera *etc*

agradecer *3* agradezco *6* agradezca *etc*

aparecer *3* aparezco *6* aparezca *etc*

aprobar *2* aprueba *3* apruebo, apruebas, aprueba, aprueban *6* apruebe, apruebes, apruebe, aprueben

atravesar *2* atraviesa *3* atravieso, atraviesas, atraviesa, atraviesan *6* atraviese, atravieses, atraviese, atraviesen

caber *3* quepo *4* cupe, cupiste, cupo, cupimos, cupisteis, cupieron *5* cabré *etc* *6* quepa *etc* *7* cupiera *etc*

caer *1* cayendo *3* caigo *4* cayó, cayeron *6* caiga *etc* *7* cayera *etc*

calentar *2* calienta *3* caliento, calientas, calienta, calientan *6* caliente, calientes, caliente, calienten

cerrar *2* cierra *3* cierro, cierras, cierra, cierran *6* cierre, cierres, cierre, cierren

COMER *1* comiendo *2* come, comed *3* como, comes, come, comemos, coméis, comen *4* comí, comiste, comió, comimos, comisteis, comieron *5* comeré, comerás, comerá, comeremos, comeréis, comerán *6* coma, comas, coma, comamos, comáis, coman *7* comiera, comieras, comiera, comiéramos, comierais, comieran *8* comido *9* comía, comías, comía, comíamos, comíais, comían

conocer *3* conozco *6* conozca *etc*

contar *2* cuenta *3* cuento, cuentas, cuenta, cuentan *6* cuente, cuentes, cuente, cuenten

costar *2* cuesta *3* cuesto, cuestas, cuesta, cuestan *6* cueste, cuestes, cueste, cuesten

dar *3* doy *4* di, diste, dio, dimos, disteis, dieron *7* diera *etc*

decir *2* di *3* digo *4* dije, dijiste, dijo, dijimos, dijisteis, dijeron *5* diré *etc*
6 diga *etc* *7* dijera *etc* *8* dicho

despertar *2* despierta *3* despierto, despiertas, despierta, despiertan *6* despierte, despiertes, despierte, despierten

divertir *1* divirtiendo *2* divierte *3* divierto, diviertes, divierte, divierten *4* divirtió, divirtieron *6* divierta, diviertas, divierta, divirtamos, divirtáis, diviertan *7* divirtiera *etc*

dormir *1* durmiendo *2* duerme *3* duermo, duermes, duerme, duermen *4* durmió, durmieron *6* duerma, duermas, duerma, durmamos, durmáis, duerman *7* durmiera *etc*

empezar *2* empieza *3* empiezo, empiezas, empieza, empiezan *4* empecé *6* empiece, empieces, empiece, empecemos, empecéis, empiecen

entender *2* entiende *3* entiendo, entiendes, entiende, entienden *6* entienda, entiendas, entienda, entiendan

ESTAR *2* está *3* estoy, estás, está, están *4* estuve, estuviste, estuvo, estuvimos, estuvisteis, estuvieron *6* esté, estés, esté, estén *7* estuviera *etc*

HABER *3* he, has, ha, hemos, han *4* hube, hubiste, hubo, hubimos, hubisteis, hubieron *5* habré *etc* *6* haya *etc* *7* hubiera *etc*

HABLAR *1* hablando *2* habla, hablad *3* hablo, hablas, habla, hablamos, habláis, hablan *4* hablé, hablaste, habló, hablamos, hablasteis, hablaron *5* hablaré, hablarás, hablará, hablaremos, hablaréis, hablarán *6* hable, hables, hable, hablemos, habléis, hablen *7* hablara, hablaras, hablara, habláramos, hablarais, hablaran *8* hablado *9* hablaba, hablabas, hablaba, hablábamos, hablabais, hablaban

hacer *2* haz *3* hago *4* hice, hiciste, hizo, hicimos, hicisteis, hicieron *5* haré *etc* *6* haga *etc* *7* hiciera *etc* *8* hecho

instruir *1* instruyendo *2* instruye *3* instruyo, instruyes, instruye, instruyen *4* instruyó, instruyeron *6* instruya *etc* *7* instruyera *etc*

ir *1* yendo *2* ve *3* voy, vas, va, vamos, vais, van *4* fui, fuiste, fue, fuimos, fuisteis, fueron *6* vaya, vayas, vaya, vayamos,

vayáis, vayan *7* fuera *etc 8* iba, ibas, iba,
íbamos, ibais, iban

jugar *2* juega *3* juego, juegas, juega,
juegan *4* jugué *6* juegue *etc*

leer *1* leyendo *4* leyó, leyeron *7* leyera *etc*

morir *1* muriendo *2* muere *3* muero,
mueres, muere, mueren *4* murió,
murieron *6* muera, mueras, muera,
muramos, muráis, mueran *7* muriera *etc*
8 muerto

mostrar *2* muestra *3* muestro, muestras,
muestra, muestran *6* muestre, muestres,
muestre, muestren

mover *2* mueve *3* muevo, mueves, mueve,
mueven *6* mueva, muevas, mueva,
muevan

negar *2* niega *3* niego, niegas, niega,
niegan *4* negué *6* niegue, niegues,
niegue, neguemos, neguéis, nieguen

ofrecer *3* ofrezco *6* ofrezca *etc*

oír *1* oyendo *2* oye *3* oigo, oyes, oye, oyen
4 oyó, oyeron *6* oiga *etc 7* oyera *etc*

oler *2* huele *3* huelo, hueles, huele, huelen
6 huela, huelas, huela, huelan

parecer *3* parezco *6* parezca *etc*

pedir *1* pidiendo *2* pide *3* pido, pides, pide,
piden *4* pidió, pidieron *6* pida *etc*
7 pidiera *etc*

pensar *2* piensa *3* pienso, piensas, piensa,
piensan *6* piense, pienses, piense,
piensen

perder *2* pierde *3* pierdo, pierdes, pierde,
pierden *6* pierda, pierdas, pierda,
pierdan

poder *1* pudiendo *2* puede *3* puedo,
puedes, puede, pueden *4* pude, pudiste,
pudo, pudimos, pudisteis, pudieron
5 podré *etc 6* pueda, puedas, pueda,
puedan *7* pudiera *etc*

poner *2* pon *3* pongo *4* puse, pusiste, puso,
pusimos, pusisteis, pusieron *5* pondré
etc 6 ponga *etc 7* pusiera *etc 8* puesto

preferir *1* prefiriendo *2* prefiere *3* prefiero,
prefieres, prefiere, prefieren *4* prefirió,
prefirieron *6* prefiera, prefieras, prefiera,
prefiramos, prefiráis, prefieran
7 prefiriera *etc*

querer *2* quiere *3* quiero, quieres, quiere,
quieren *4* quise, quisiste, quiso,
quisimos, quisisteis, quisieron *5* querré
etc 6 quiera, quieras, quiera, quieran
7 quisiera *etc*

reír *2* ríe *3* río, ríes, ríe, ríen *4* rio, rieron
6 ría, rías, ría, riamos, riáis, rían *7* riera
etc

repetir *1* repitiendo *2* repite *3* repito,

repites, repite, repiten *4* repitió,
repitieron *6* repita *etc 7* repitiera *etc*

rogar *2* ruega *3* ruego, ruegas, ruega,
ruegan *4* rogué *6* ruegue, ruegues,
ruegue, roguemos, roguéis, rueguen

saber *3* sé *4* supe, supiste, supo, supimos,
supisteis, supieron *5* sabré *etc 6* sepa *etc*
7 supiera *etc*

salir *2* sal *3* salgo *5* saldré *etc 6* salga *etc*

seguir *1* siguiendo *2* sigue *3* sigo, sigues,
sigue, siguen *4* siguió, siguieron *6* siga
etc 7 siguiera *etc*

sentar *2* sienta *3* siento, sientas, sienta,
sientan *6* siente, sientes, siente, sienten

sentir *1* sintiendo *2* siente *3* siento,
sientes, siente, sienten *4* sintió, sintieron
6 sienta, sientas, sienta, sintamos,
sintáis, sientan *7* sintiera *etc*

SER *2* sé *3* soy, eres, es, somos, sois, son
4 fui, fuiste, fue, fuimos, fuisteis, fueron
6 sea *etc 7* fuera *etc 9* era, eras, era,
éramos, erais, eran

servir *1* sirviendo *2* sirve *3* sirvo, sirves,
sirve, sirven *4* sirvió, sirvieron *6* sirva
etc 7 sirviera *etc*

soñar *2* sueña *3* sueño, sueñas, sueña,
sueñan *6* sueñe, sueñes, sueñe, sueñen

tener *2* ten *3* tengo, tienes, tiene, tienen
4 tuve, tuviste, tuvo, tuvimos, tuvisteis,
tuvieron *5* tendré *etc 6* tenga *etc*
7 tuviera *etc*

traer *1* trayendo *3* traigo *4* traje, trajiste,
trajo, trajimos, trajisteis, trajeron
6 traiga *etc 7* trajera *etc*

valer *2* val *3* valgo *5* valdré *etc 6* valga *etc*

venir *2* ven *3* vengo, vienes, viene, vienen
4 vine, viniste, vino, vinimos, vinisteis,
vinieron *5* vendré *etc 6* venga *etc*
7 viniera *etc*

ver *3* veo *6* vea *etc 8* visto *9* veía *etc*

vestir *1* vistiendo *2* viste *3* visto, vistes,
viste, visten *4* vistió, vistieron *6* vista *etc*
7 vistiera *etc*

VIVIR *1* viviendo *2* vive, vivid *3* vivo,
vives, vive, vivimos, vivís, viven *4* viví,
viviste, vivió, vivimos, vivisteis,
vivieron *5* viviré, vivirás, vivirá,
viviremos, viviréis, vivirán *6* viva,
vivas, viva, vivamos, viváis, vivan
7 viviera, vivieras, viviera, viviéramos,
vivierais, vivieran *8* vivido *9* vivía,
vivías, vivía, vivíamos, vivías, vivían

volver *2* vuelve *3* vuelvo, vuelves, vuelve,
vuelven *6* vuelva, vuelvas, vuelva,
vuelvan *8* vuelto

VERBOS IRREGULARES EN INGLÉS

present	pt	pp	present	pt	pp
arise	arose	arisen	eat	ate	eaten
awake	awoke	awoken	fall	fell	fallen
be (am, is, are; being)	was, were	been	feed	fed	fed
			feel	felt	felt
bear	bore	born(e)	fight	fought	fought
beat	beat	beaten	find	found	found
become	became	become	flee	fled	fled
befall	befell	befallen	fling	flung	flung
begin	began	begun	fly	flew	flown
behold	beheld	beheld	forbid	forbad(e)	forbidden
bend	bent	bent	forecast	forecast	forecast
beset	beset	beset	forget	forgot	forgotten
bet	bet, betted	bet, betted	forgive	forgave	forgiven
			forsake	forsook	forsaken
bid (at auction, cards)	bid	bid	freeze	froze	frozen
			get	got	got, (US) gotten
bid (say)	bade	bidden	give	gave	given
bind	bound	bound	go (goes)	went	gone
bite	bit	bitten	grind	ground	ground
bleed	bled	bled	grow	grew	grown
blow	blew	blown	hang	hung	hung
break	broke	broken	hang (execute)	hanged	hanged
breed	bred	bred			
bring	brought	brought	have	had	had
build	built	built	hear	heard	heard
burn	burnt, burned	burnt, burned	hide	hid	hidden
			hit	hit	hit
burst	burst	burst	hold	held	held
buy	bought	bought	hurt	hurt	hurt
can	could	(been able)	keep	kept	kept
cast	cast	cast	kneel	knelt, kneeled	knelt, kneeled
catch	caught	caught			
choose	chose	chosen	know	knew	known
cling	clung	clung	lay	laid	laid
come	came	come	lead	led	led
cost	cost	cost	lean	leant, leaned	leant, leaned
cost (work out price of)	costed	costed			
			leap	leapt, leaped	leapt, leaped
creep	crept	crept			
cut	cut	cut	learn	learnt, learned	learnt, learned
deal	dealt	dealt			
dig	dug	dug	leave	left	left
do (3rd person: he/she/it does)	did	done	lend	lent	lent
			let	let	let
			lie (lying)	lay	lain
			light	lit, lighted	lit, lighted
draw	drew	drawn	lose	lost	lost
dream	dreamed, dreamt	dreamed, dreamt	make	made	made
			may	might	—
drink	drank	drunk	mean	meant	meant
drive	drove	driven	meet	met	met
dwell	dwelt	dwelt	mistake	mistook	mistaken

present	pt	pp	present	pt	pp
mow	mowed	mown, mowed	spend	spent	spent
must	(had to)	(had to)	spill	spilt, spilled	spilt, spilled
pay	paid	paid			
put	put	put	spin	spun	spun
quit	quit, quitted	quit, quitted	spit	spat	spat
			spoil	spoiled, spoilt	spoiled, spoilt
read	read	read			
rid	rid	rid	spread	spread	spread
ride	rode	ridden	spring	sprang	sprung
ring	rang	rung	stand	stood	stood
rise	rose	risen	steal	stole	stolen
run	ran	run	stick	stuck	stuck
saw	sawed	sawed, sawn	sting	stung	stung
say	said	said	stink	stank	stunk
see	saw	seen	stride	strode	stridden
seek	sought	sought	strike	struck	struck
sell	sold	sold	strive	strove	striven
send	sent	sent	swear	swore	sworn
set	set	set	sweep	swept	swept
sew	sewed	sewn	swell	swelled	swollen, swelled
shake	shook	shaken			
shear	sheared	shorn, sheared	swim	swam	swum
shed	shed	shed	swing	swung	swung
shine	shone	shone	take	took	taken
shoot	shot	shot	teach	taught	taught
show	showed	shown	tear	tore	torn
shrink	shrank	shrunk	tell	told	told
shut	shut	shut	think	thought	thought
sing	sang	sung	throw	threw	thrown
sink	sank	sunk	thrust	thrust	thrust
sit	sat	sat	tread	trod	trodden
slay	slew	slain	wake	woke, waked	woken, waked
sleep	slept	slept			
slide	slid	slid	wear	wore	worn
sling	slung	slung	weave	wove	woven
slit	slit	slit	weave *(wind)*	weaved	weaved
smell	smelt, smelled	smelt, smelled	wed	wedded, wed	wedded, wed
sow	sowed	sown, sowed	weep	wept	wept
speak	spoke	spoken	win	won	won
speed	sped, speeded	sped, speeded	wind	wound	wound
			wring	wrung	wrung
spell	spelt, spelled	spelt, spelled	write	wrote	written

NÚMEROS

NUMBERS

Spanish	Number	English
uno (un, una)*	1	one
dos	2	two
tres	3	three
cuatro	4	four
cinco	5	five
seis	6	six
siete	7	seven
ocho	8	eight
nueve	9	nine
diez	10	ten
once	11	eleven
doce	12	twelve
trece	13	thirteen
catorce	14	fourteen
quince	15	fifteen
dieciséis	16	sixteen
diecisiete	17	seventeen
dieciocho	18	eighteen
diecinueve	19	nineteen
veinte	20	twenty
veintiuno(-un, -una)*	21	twenty-one
veintidós	22	twenty-two
treinta	30	thirty
treinta y uno(un, una)*	31	thirty-one
treinta y dos	32	thirty-two
cuarenta	40	forty
cincuenta	50	fifty
sesenta	60	sixty
setenta	70	seventy
ochenta	80	eighty
noventa	90	ninety
cien(ciento)**	100	a hundred, one hundred
ciento uno(un, una)*	101	a hundred and one
ciento dos	102	a hundred and two
ciento cincuenta y seis	156	a hundred and fifty-six
doscientos(as)	200	two hundred
trescientos(as)	300	three hundred
quinientos(as)	500	five hundred
mil	1,000	a thousand
mil tres	1,003	a thousand and three
dos mil	2,000	two thousand
un millón	1,000,000	a million

* 'uno' (+ 'veintiuno' etc) agrees in gender (but not number) with its noun: treinta y una personas; the masculine form is shortened to 'un' unless it stands alone: veintiún caballos, veintiuno.

** 'ciento' is used in compound numbers, except when it multiplies: ciento diez, but cien mil. 'Cien' is used before nouns: cien hombres, cien casas.

NÚMEROS

NUMBERS

primero(primer, primera), 1°, 1er/1ª, 1era	first, 1st
segundo(a), 2°/2ª	second, 2nd
tercero(tercer, tercera), 3°, 3er/3ª, 3era	third, 3rd
cuarto(a), 4°/4ª	fourth, 4th
quinto(a)	fifth, 5th
sexto(a)	sixth, 6th
séptimo(a)	seventh
octavo(a)	eighth
noveno(a); nono(a)	ninth
décimo(a)	tenth
undécimo(a)	eleventh
duodécimo(a)	twelfth
decimotercio(a)	thirteenth
decimocuarto(a)	fourteenth
decimoquinto(a)	fifteenth
decimosexto(a)	sixteenth
decimoséptimo(a)	seventeenth
decimoctavo(a)	eighteenth
decimonono(a)	nineteenth
vigésimo(a)	twentieth
vigésimo primero(a)	twenty-first
vigésimo segundo(a)	twenty-second
trigésimo(a)	thirtieth
trigésimo primero(a)	thirty-first
trigésimo segundo(a)	thirty-second
cuadragésimo(a)	fortieth
quincuagésimo(a)	fiftieth
sexagésimo(a)	sixtieth
septuagésimo(a)	seventieth
octogésimo(a)	eightieth
nonagésimo(a)	ninetieth
centésimo(a)	hundredth
centésimo primero(a)	hundred-and-first
milésimo(a)	thousandth

LA HORA

THE TIME

¿qué hora es?	*what time is it?*

es la una
son las cuatro
medianoche, las doce de la noche
la una (de la madrugada)

it's one o'clock
it's four o'clock
midnight
one o'clock (in the morning), one (a.m.)

la una y cinco
la una y diez
la una y cuarto *or* quince
la una y veinticinco

five past one
ten past one
a quarter past one, one fifteen
twenty-five past one, one twenty-five

la una y media *or* treinta
las dos menos veinticinco, la una treinta y cinco
las dos menos veinte, la una cuarenta
las dos menos cuarto, la una cuarenta y cinco
las dos menos diez, la una cincuenta
mediodía, las doce (de la mañana)
las dos (de la tarde)

las siete (de la tarde)

half-past one, one thirty
twenty-five to two, one thirty-five
twenty to two, one forty
a quarter to two, one forty-five
ten to two, one fifty
twelve o'clock, midday, noon
two o'clock (in the afternoon), two (p.m.)
seven o'clock (in the evening), seven (p.m.)

¿a qué hora?	*at what time?*

a medianoche
a las siete
a las una

at midnight
at seven o'clock
at one o'clock

en veinte minutos
hace diez minutos

in twenty minutes
ten minutes ago

LA FECHA

THE DATE

hoy
mañana
pasado mañana
ayer
antes de ayer, anteayer
la víspera
el día siguiente

today
tomorrow
the day after tomorrow
yesterday
the day before yesterday
the day before, the previous day
the next *or* following day

la mañana	morning
la tarde	evening
esta mañana	this morning
esta tarde	this evening
esta tarde	this afternoon
ayer por la mañana	yesterday morning
ayer por la tarde	yesterday evening
mañana por la mañana	tomorrow morning
mañana por la tarde	tomorrow evening
en la noche del sábado al domingo	during Saturday night, during the night of Saturday to Sunday
vendrá el sábado	he's coming on Saturday
los sábados	on Saturdays
todos los sábados	every Saturday
el sábado pasado	last Saturday
el sábado que viene, el próximo sábado	next Saturday
del sábado en ocho días	a week on Saturday
del sábado en quince días	a fortnight *or* two weeks on Saturday
de lunes a sábado	from Monday to Saturday
todos los días	every day
una vez a la semana	once a week
una vez ala mes	once a month
dos veces a la semana	twice a week
hace una semana *o* ocho días	a week ago
hace quince días	a fortnight *or* two weeks ago
el año pasado	last year
dentro de dos días	in two days
dentro de ocho días *o* una semana	in a week
dentro de quince días	in a fortnight *or* two weeks
el mes que viene, el próximo mes	next month
el año que viene, el próximo año	next year
¿a qué o a cuántos estamos?	*what day is it?*
el 1/24 octubre de 1996	the 1st/24th of October 1996, October 1st/24th 1996
en 1996	in 1996
mil novecientos noventa y cinco	nineteen ninety-five
44 a. de J.C.	44 BC
14 d. de J.C.	14 AD
en el (siglo) XIX	in the nineteenth century
en los años treinta	in the thirties
érase una vez ...	once upon a time ...

Español-Inglés
Spanish-English

A a

A, a [a] *nf* (*letra*) A, a; **A de Antonio** A for Andrew (*BRIT*) o Able (*US*).

═══════════════ *PALABRA CLAVE*

a [a] (*a+el* = *al*) *prep* **1** (*dirección*) to; **fueron** ~ **Madrid/Grecia** they went to Madrid/ Greece; **me voy** ~ **casa** I'm going home
2 (*distancia*): **está** ~ **15 km de aquí** it's 15 kms from here
3 (*posición*): **estar** ~ **la mesa** to be at table; **al lado de** next to, beside; ~ **la derecha/izquierda** on the right/left; *V tb* **puerta**
4 (*tiempo*): ~ **las 10/**~ **medianoche** at 10/midnight; ¿~ **qué hora?** (at) what time?; ~ **la mañana siguiente** the following morning; ~ **los pocos días** after a few days; **estamos** ~ **9 de julio** it's the 9th of July; ~ **los 24 años** at the age of 24; **ocho horas al día** eight hours a day; **al año/**~ **la semana** (*AM*) a year/ week later
5 (*manera*): ~ **la francesa** the French way; ~ **caballo** on horseback; ~ **oscuras** in the dark; ~ **rayas** striped; **le echaron** ~ **patadas** they kicked him out
6 (*medio, instrumento*): ~ **lápiz** in pencil; ~ **mano** by hand; **cocina** ~ **gas** gas stove
7 (*razón*): ~ **30 ptas el kilo** at 30 pesetas a kilo; ~ **más de 50 kms por hora** at more than 50 kms per hour; **poco** ~ **poco** little by little
8 (*dativo*): **se lo di** ~ **él** I gave it to him; **se lo compré** ~ **él** I bought it from him
9 (*complemento directo*): **vi al policía** I saw the policeman
10 (*tras ciertos verbos*): **voy** ~ **verle** I'm going to see him; **empezó** ~ **trabajar** he

started working o to work; **sabe** ~ **queso** it tastes of cheese
11 (*+infin*): **al verle, le reconocí inmediatamente** when I saw him I recognized him at once; **el camino** ~ **recorrer** the distance we (*etc*) have to travel; ¡~ **callar!** keep quiet!; ¡~ **comer!** let's eat!
12 (*a+que*): ¡~ **que llueve!** I bet it's going to rain!; ¿~ **qué viene eso?** what's the meaning of this?; ¿~ **que sí va a venir?** he IS coming, isn't he?; ¿~ **que no lo haces? –** ¡~ **que sí!** bet you don't do it! – yes, I WILL!

═══════════════

A. *abr* (*ESCOL: = aprobado*) pass.
AA *nfpl abr = Aerolíneas Argentinas*.
AA EE *abr* (= *Asuntos Exteriores*): **Min. de AA EE** ≈ FO (*BRIT*).
ab. *abr* (= *abril*) Apr.
abad, esa [a'βað, 'ðesa] *nm/f* abbot/abbess.
abadía [aßa'ðia] *nf* abbey.
abajo [a'ßaxo] *adv* (*situación*) (down) below, underneath; (*en edificio*) downstairs; (*dirección*) down, downwards; ~ **de** *prep* below, under; **el piso de** ~ the downstairs flat; **la parte de** ~ the lower part; ¡~ **el gobierno!** down with the government!; **cuesta/río** ~ downhill/downstream; **de arriba** ~ from top to bottom; **el** ~ **firmante** the undersigned; **más** ~ lower o further down.
abalance [aßa'lanθe] *etc vb V* **abalanzarse**.
abalanzarse [aßalan'θarse] *vr*: ~ **sobre** o **contra** to throw o.s. at.
abalear [aßale'ar] *vt* (*AM fam*) to shoot.
abalorios [aßa'lorjos] *nmpl* (*chucherías*)

trinkets.

abanderado [aßande'raðo] *nm* standard bearer.

abandonado, a [aßando'naðo, a] *adj* derelict; (*desatendido*) abandoned; (*desierto*) deserted; (*descuidado*) neglected.

abandonar [aßando'nar] *vt* to leave; (*persona*) to abandon, desert; (*cosa*) to abandon, leave behind; (*descuidar*) to neglect; (*renunciar a*) to give up; (*INFORM*) to quit; ~**se** *vr*: ~**se a** to abandon o.s. to; ~**se al alcohol** to take to drink.

abandono [aßan'dono] *nm* (*acto*) desertion, abandonment; (*estado*) abandon, neglect; (*renuncia*) withdrawal, retirement; **ganar por** ~ to win by default.

abanicar [aßani'kar] *vt* to fan.

abanico [aßa'niko] *nm* fan; (*NAUT*) derrick; **en** ~ fan-shaped.

abanique [aßa'nike] *etc vb V* **abanicar**.

abaratar [aßara'tar] *vt* to lower the price of ♦ *vi*, ~**se** *vr* to go *o* come down in price.

abarcar [aßar'kar] *vt* to include, embrace; (*contener*) to comprise; (*AM*) to monopolize; **quien mucho abarca poco aprieta** don't bite off more than you can chew.

abarque [a'ßarke] *etc vb V* **abarcar**.

abarrotado, a [aßarro'taðo, a] *adj* packed; ~ **de** packed *o* bursting with.

abarrote [aßa'rrote] *nm* packing; ~**s** *nmpl* (*AM*) groceries, provisions.

abarrotería [aßarrote'ria] *nf* (*AM*) grocery store.

abarrotero, a [aßarro'tero, a] *nm/f* (*AM*) grocer.

abastecedor, a [aßasteθe'ðor, a] *adj* supplying ♦ *nm/f* supplier.

abastecer [aßaste'θer] *vt*: ~ (**de**) to supply (with).

abastecimiento [aßasteθi'mjento] *nm* supply.

abastezca [aßas'teθka] *etc vb V* **abastecer**.

abasto [a'ßasto] *nm* supply; (*abundancia*) abundance; **no dar** ~ **a algo** not to be able to cope with sth.

abatible [aßa'tißle] *adj*: **asiento** ~ tip-up seat.

abatido, a [aßa'tiðo, a] *adj* dejected, downcast; **estar muy** ~ to be very depressed.

abatimiento [aßati'mjento] *nm* (*depresión*) dejection, depression.

abatir [aßa'tir] *vt* (*muro*) to demolish; (*pájaro*) to shoot *o* bring down; (*fig*) to

depress; ~**se** *vr* to get depressed; ~**se sobre** to swoop *o* pounce on.

abdicación [aßðika'θjon] *nf* abdication.

abdicar [aßði'kar] *vi* to abdicate; ~ **en algn** to abdicate in favour of sb.

abdique [aß'ðike] *etc vb V* **abdicar**.

abdomen [aß'ðomen] *nm* abdomen.

abdominal [aßðomi'nal] *adj* abdominal ♦ *nm*: ~**es** (*DEPORTE*) abdominals; (*ANAT*) abdominals, stomach muscles.

abecedario [aßeθe'ðarjo] *nm* alphabet.

abedul [aße'ðul] *nm* birch.

abeja [a'ßexa] *nf* bee; (*fig*: *hormiguita*) hard worker.

abejorro [aße'xorro] *nm* bumblebee.

aberración [aßerra'θjon] *nf* aberration.

aberrante [aße'rrante] *adj* (*disparatado*) ridiculous.

abertura [aßer'tura] *nf* = **apertura**.

abertzale [aßer'tʃale] *adj*, *nm/f* Basque nationalist.

abeto [a'ßeto] *nm* fir.

abierto, a [a'ßjerto, a] *pp de* **abrir** ♦ *adj* open; (*fig*: *carácter*) frank.

abigarrado, a [aßiɣa'rraðo, a] *adj* multicoloured; (*fig*) motley.

abismal [aßis'mal] *adj* (*fig*) vast, enormous.

abismar [aßis'mar] *vt* to humble, cast down; ~**se** *vr* to sink; (*AM*) to be amazed; ~**se en** (*fig*) to be plunged into.

abismo [a'ßismo] *nm* abyss; **de sus ideas a las mías hay un** ~ our views are worlds apart.

abjurar [aßxu'rar] *vt* to abjure, forswear ♦ *vi*: ~ **de** to abjure, forswear.

ablandar [aßlan'dar] *vt* to soften up; (*conmover*) to touch; (*CULIN*) to tenderize ♦ *vi*, ~**se** *vr* to get softer.

abnegación [aßneɣa'θjon] *nf* self-denial.

abnegado, a [aßne'ɣaðo, a] *adj* self-sacrificing.

abobado, a [aßo'ßaðo, a] *adj* silly.

abobamiento [aßoßa'mjento] *nm* (*asombro*) bewilderment.

abocado, a [aßo'kaðo, a] *adj*: **verse** ~ **al desastre** to be heading for disaster.

abochornar [aßotʃor'nar] *vt* to embarrass; ~**se** *vr* to get flustered; (*BOT*) to wilt; ~**se de** to get embarrassed about.

abofetear [aßofete'ar] *vt* to slap (in the face).

abogacía [aßoɣa'θia] *nf* legal profession; (*ejercicio*) practice of the law.

abogado, a [aßo'ɣaðo, a] *nm/f* lawyer; (*notario*) solicitor; (*asesor*) counsel; (*en tribunal*) barrister, advocate, attorney (*US*); ~ **defensor** defence lawyer *o* attorney (*US*); ~ **del diablo** devil's advocate.

abogar [aβo'ɣar] *vi*: ~ **por** to plead for; (*fig*) to advocate.

abogue [a'βoɣe] *etc vb* V **abogar**.

abolengo [aβo'lengo] *nm* ancestry, lineage.

abolición [aβoli'θjon] *nf* abolition.

abolir [aβo'lir] *vt* to abolish; (*cancelar*) to cancel.

abolladura [aβoʎa'ðura] *nf* dent.

abollar [aβo'ʎar] *vt* to dent.

abominable [aβomi'naβle] *adj* abominable.

abominación [aβomina'θjon] *nf* abomination.

abonado, a [aβo'naðo, a] *adj* (*deuda*) paid(-up) ♦ *nm/f* subscriber.

abonar [aβo'nar] *vt* to pay;(*deuda*) to settle; (*terreno*) to fertilize; (*idea*) to endorse; ~**se** *vr* to subscribe; ~ **dinero en una cuenta** to pay money into an account, credit money to an account.

abono [a'βono] *nm* payment; fertilizer; subscription.

abordable [aβor'ðaβle] *adj* (*persona*) approachable.

abordar [aβor'ðar] *vt* (*barco*) to board; (*asunto*) to broach; (*individuo*) to approach.

aborigen [aβo'rixen] *nm/f* aborigine.

aborrecer [aβorre'θer] *vt* to hate, loathe.

aborrezca [aβo'rreθka] *etc vb* V **aborrecer**.

abortar [aβor'tar] *vi* (*malparir*) to have a miscarriage; (*deliberadamente*) to have an abortion.

aborto [a'βorto] *nm* miscarriage; abortion.

abotagado, a [aβota'ɣaðo, a] *adj* swollen.

abotonar [aβoto'nar] *vt* to button (up), do up.

abovedado, a [aβoβe'ðaðo, a] *adj* vaulted, domed.

abr. *abr* (= *abril*) Apr.

abrace [a'βraθe] *etc vb* V **abrazar**.

abrasar [aβra'sar] *vt* to burn (up); (*AGR*) to dry up, parch.

abrazadera [aβraθa'ðera] *nf* bracket.

abrazar [aβra'θar] *vt* to embrace, hug; ~**se** *vr* to embrace, hug each other.

abrazo [a'βraθo] *nm* embrace, hug; **un** ~ (*en carta*) with best wishes.

abrebotellas [aβreβo'teʎas] *nm inv* bottle opener.

abrecartas [aβre'kartas] *nm inv* letter opener.

abrelatas [aβre'latas] *nm inv* tin (*BRIT*) o can (*US*) opener.

abrevadero [aβreβa'ðero] *nm* watering place.

abreviar [aβre'βjar] *vt* to abbreviate;

(*texto*) to abridge; (*plazo*) to reduce ♦ *vi*: **bueno, para** ~ well, to cut a long story short.

abreviatura [aβreβja'tura] *nf* abbreviation.

abridor [aβri'ðor] *nm* (*de botellas*) bottle opener; (*de latas*) tin (*BRIT*) o can (*US*) opener.

abrigar [aβri'ɣar] *vt* (*proteger*) to shelter; (*suj: ropa*) to keep warm; (*fig*) to cherish; ~**se** *vr* to take shelter, protect o.s (*de* from); (*con ropa*) to cover (o.s.) up; ¡**abrígate bien!** wrap up well!

abrigo [a'βriɣo] *nm* (*prenda*) coat, overcoat; (*lugar protegido*) shelter; **al** ~ **de** in the shelter of.

abrigue [a'βriɣe] *etc vb* V **abrigar**.

abril [a'βril] *nm* April.

abrillantar [aβriʎan'tar] *vt* (*pulir*) to polish; (*fig*) to enhance.

abrir [a'βrir] *vt* to open (up); (*camino etc*) to open up; (*apetito*) to whet; (*lista*) to head ♦ *vi* to open; ~**se** *vr* to open (up); (*extenderse*) to open out; (*cielo*) to clear; ~ **un negocio** to start up a business; **en un** ~ **y cerrar de ojos** in the twinkling of an eye; ~**se paso** to find o force a way through.

abrochar [aβro'tʃar] *vt* (*con botones*) to button (up); (*zapato, con broche*) to do up; ~**se** *vr*: ~ **los zapatos** to tie one's shoelaces.

abrogación [aβroɣa'θjon] *nf* repeal.

abrogar [aβro'ɣar] *vt* to repeal.

abrumador, a [aβruma'ðor, a] *adj* (*mayoría*) overwhelming.

abrumar [aβru'mar] *vt* to overwhelm; (*sobrecargar*) to weigh down.

abrupto, a [a'βrupto, a] *adj* abrupt; (*empinado*) steep.

absceso [aβs'θeso] *nm* abscess.

absentismo [aβsen'tismo] *nm* (*de obreros*) absenteeism.

absolución [aβsolu'θjon] *nf* (*REL*) absolution; (*JUR*) acquittal.

absoluto, a [aβso'luto, a] *adj* absolute; (*total*) utter, complete; **en** ~ *adv* not at all.

absolver [aβsol'βer] *vt* to absolve; (*JUR*) to pardon; (: *acusado*) to acquit.

absorbente [aβsor'βente] *adj* absorbent; (*interesante*) absorbing, interesting; (*exigente*) demanding.

absorber [aβsor'βer] *vt* to absorb; (*embeber*) to soak up; ~**se** *vr* to become absorbed.

absorción [aβsor'θjon] *nf* absorption; (*COM*) takeover.

absorto, a [aβ'sorto, a] *pp de* **absorber** ♦ *adj*

absorbed, engrossed.

abstemio, a [aßs'temjo, a] *adj* teetotal.

abstención [aßsten'θjon] *nf* abstention.

abstendré [aßsten'dre] *etc vb* V **abstenerse.**

abstenerse [aßste'nerse] *vr*: ~ **(de)** to abstain *o* refrain (from).

abstenga [aßs'tenga] *etc vb* V **abstenerse.**

abstinencia [aßsti'nenθja] *nf* abstinence; (*ayuno*) fasting.

abstracción [aßstrak'θjon] *nf* abstraction.

abstracto, a [aß'strakto, a] *adj* abstract; **en** ~ in the abstract.

abstraer [aßstra'er] *vt* to abstract; ~**se** *vr* to be *o* become absorbed.

abstraído, a [aßstra'iðo, a] *adj* absentminded.

abstraiga [aßs'traiɣa] *etc*, **abstraje** [aßs'traxe] *etc*, **abstrayendo** [aßstra'jendo] *etc vb* V **abstraer.**

abstuve [aßs'tuße] *etc vb* V **abstenerse.**

absuelto [aß'swelto] *pp de* **absolver.**

absurdo, a [aß'surðo, a] *adj* absurd; **lo** ~ **es que** ... the ridiculous thing is that ... ♦ *nm* absurdity.

abuchear [aßutʃe'ar] *vt* to boo.

abucheo [aßu'tʃeo] *nm* booing; **ganarse un** ~ (*TEAT*) to be booed.

abuela [a'ßwela] *nf* grandmother; **¡cuéntaselo a tu** ~**!** (*fam!*) do you think I was born yesterday? (*fam*); **no tener/ necesitar** ~ (*fam*) to be full of o.s./blow one's own trumpet.

abuelita [aßwe'lita] *nf* granny.

abuelo [a'ßwelo] *nm* grandfather; (*antepasado*) ancestor; ~**s** *nmpl* grandparents.

abulense [aßu'lense] *adj* of Ávila ♦ *nm/f* native *o* inhabitant of Ávila.

abulia [a'ßulja] *nf* lethargy.

abúlico, a [a'ßuliko, a] *adj* lethargic.

abultado, a [aßul'taðo, a] *adj* bulky.

abultar [aßul'tar] *vt* to enlarge; (*aumentar*) to increase; (*fig*) to exaggerate ♦ *vi* to be bulky.

abundancia [aßun'danθja] *nf*: **una** ~ **de** plenty of; **en** ~ in abundance.

abundante [aßun'dante] *adj* abundant, plentiful.

abundar [aßun'dar] *vi* to abound, be plentiful; ~ **en una opinión** to share an opinion.

aburguesarse [aßurɣe'sarse] *vr* to become middle-class.

aburrido, a [aßu'rriðo, a] *adj* (*hastiado*) bored; (*que aburre*) boring.

aburrimiento [aßurri'mjento] *nm* boredom, tedium.

aburrir [aßu'rrir] *vt* to bore; ~**se** *vr* to be

bored, get bored; ~**se como una almeja** *u* **ostra** to be bored stiff.

abusar [aßu'sar] *vi* to go too far; ~ **de** to abuse.

abusivo, a [aßu'sißo, a] *adj* (*precio*) exorbitant.

abuso [a'ßuso] *nm* abuse; ~ **de confianza** betrayal of trust.

abyecto, a [aß'jekto, a] *adj* wretched, abject.

A.C. *abr* (= *Año de Cristo*) A.D.

a/c *abr* (= *al cuidado de*) c/o; (= *a cuenta*) on account.

acá [a'ka] *adv* (*lugar*) here; **pasearse de** ~ **para allá** to walk up and down; **¡vente para** ~**!** come over here!; **¿de cuándo** ~**?** since when?

acabado, a [aka'ßaðo, a] *adj* finished, complete; (*perfecto*) perfect; (*agotado*) worn out; (*fig*) masterly ♦ *nm* finish.

acabar [aka'ßar] *vt* (*llevar a su fin*) to finish, complete; (*consumir*) to use up; (*rematar*) to finish off ♦ *vi* to finish, end; (*morir*) to die; ~**se** *vr* to finish, stop; (*terminarse*) to be over; (*agotarse*) to run out; ~ **con** to put an end to; ~ **mal** to come to a sticky end; **esto acabará conmigo** this will be the end of me; ~ **de llegar** to have just arrived; **acababa de hacerlo** I had just done it; ~ **haciendo** *o* **por hacer algo** to end up (by) doing sth; **¡se acabó!** (*¡basta!*) that's enough!; (*se terminó*) it's all over!; **se me acabó el tabaco** I ran out of cigarettes.

acabóse [aka'ßose] *nm*: **esto es el** ~ this is the limit.

acacia [a'kaθja] *nf* acacia.

academia [aka'ðemja] *nf* academy; (*ESCOL*) private school; V *tb* **colegio.**

académico, a [aka'ðemiko, a] *adj* academic.

acaecer [akae'θer] *vi* to happen, occur.

acaezca [aka'eθka] *etc vb* V **acaecer.**

acallar [aka'ʎar] *vt* (*silenciar*) to silence; (*calmar*) to pacify.

acalorado, a [akalo'raðo, a] *adj* (*discusión*) heated.

acalorarse [akalo'rarse] *vr* (*fig*) to get heated.

acampada [akam'paða] *nf*: **ir de** ~ to go camping.

acampanado, a [akampa'naðo, a] *adj* flared.

acampar [akam'par] *vi* to camp.

acanalado, a [akana'laðo, a] *adj* (*hierro*) corrugated.

acanalar [akana'lar] *vt* to groove; (*ondular*) to corrugate.

acantilado [akanti'laðo] *nm* cliff.

acaparador, a [akapara'ðor, a] *nm/f* monopolizer.

acaparar [akapa'rar] *vt* to monopolize; (*acumular*) to hoard.

acápite [a'kapite] *nm* (*AM*) paragraph; **punto ~** full stop, new paragraph.

acaramelado, a [akarame'laðo, a] *adj* (*CULIN*) toffee-coated; (*fig*) sugary.

acariciar [akari'θjar] *vt* to caress; (*esperanza*) to cherish.

acarrear [akarre'ar] *vt* to transport; (*fig*) to cause, result in; **le acarreó muchos disgustos** it brought him lots of problems.

acaso [a'kaso] *adv* perhaps, maybe ♦ *nm* chance; **¿~ es mi culpa?** (*AM fam*) what makes you think it's my fault?; **(por) si ~** (just) in case.

acatamiento [akata'mjento] *nm* respect; (*de la ley*) observance.

acatar [aka'tar] *vt* to respect; (*ley*) to obey, observe.

acatarrarse [akata'rrarse] *vr* to catch a cold.

acaudalado, a [akauða'laðo, a] *adj* well-off.

acaudillar [akauði'ʎar] *vt* to lead, command.

acceder [akθe'ðer] *vi* to accede, agree; **~ a** (*INFORM*) to access.

accesible [akθe'siβle] *adj* accessible; **~ a** open to.

accésit, *pl* **accésits** [ak'θesit, ak'θesits] *nm* consolation prize.

acceso [ak'θeso] *nm* access, entry; (*camino*) access road; (*MED*) attack, fit; (*de cólera*) fit; (*POL*) accession; (*INFORM*) access; **~ aleatorio/directo/secuencial o en serie** (*INFORM*) random/direct/ sequential o serial access; **de ~ múltiple** multi-access.

accesorio, a [akθe'sorjo, a] *adj* accessory ♦ *nm* accessory; **~s** *nmpl* (*AUTO*) accessories, extras; (*TEAT*) props.

accidentado, a [akθiðen'taðo, a] *adj* uneven; (*montañoso*) hilly; (*azaroso*) eventful ♦ *nm/f* accident victim.

accidental [akθiðen'tal] *adj* accidental; (*empleo*) temporary.

accidentarse [akθiðen'tarse] *vr* to have an accident.

accidente [akθi'ðente] *nm* accident; **por ~** by chance; **~s** *nmpl* unevenness *sg*, roughness *sg*.

acción [ak'θjon] *nf* action; (*acto*) action, act; (*TEAT*) plot; (*COM*) share; (*JUR*) action, lawsuit; **capital en acciones** share capital; **~ liberada/ordinaria/preferente** fully-paid/ordinary/preference share.

accionamiento [akθjona'mjento] *nm* (*de máquina*) operation.

accionar [akθjo'nar] *vt* to work, operate; (*INFORM*) to drive.

accionista [akθjo'nista] *nm/f* shareholder.

acebo [a'θeβo] *nm* holly; (*árbol*) holly tree.

acechanza [aθe'tʃanθa] *nf* = **acecho.**

acechar [aθe'tʃar] *vt* to spy on; (*aguardar*) to lie in wait for.

acecho [a'θetʃo] *nm*: **estar al ~ (de)** to lie in wait (for).

acedera [aθe'ðera] *nf* sorrel.

aceitar [aθei'tar] *vt* to oil, lubricate.

aceite [a'θeite] *nm* oil; (*de oliva*) olive oil; **~ de hígado de bacalao** cod-liver oil.

aceitera [aθei'tera] *nf* oilcan.

aceitoso, a [aθei'toso, a] *adj* oily.

aceituna [aθei'tuna] *nf* olive.

aceitunado, a [aθeitu'naðo, a] *adj* olive *cpd*; **de tez aceitunada** olive-skinned.

acelerador [aθelera'ðor] *nm* accelerator.

acelerar [aθele'rar] *vt* to accelerate; **~se** *vr* to hurry.

acelga [a'θelɣa] *nf* chard, beet.

acendrado, a [aθen'draðo, a] *adj*: **de ~ carácter español** typically Spanish.

acendrar [aθen'drar] *vt* to purify.

acento [a'θento] *nm* accent; (*acentuación*) stress; **~ cerrado** strong o thick accent.

acentuar [aθen'twar] *vt* to accent; to stress; (*fig*) to accentuate; (*INFORM*) to highlight.

acepción [aθep'θjon] *nf* meaning.

aceptación [aθepta'θjon] *nf* acceptance; (*aprobación*) approval.

aceptar [aθep'tar] *vt* to accept; to approve.

acequia [a'θekja] *nf* irrigation ditch.

acera [a'θera] *nf* pavement (*BRIT*), sidewalk (*US*).

acerado, a [aθe'raðo, a] *adj* steel; (*afilado*) sharp; (*fig: duro*) steely; (: *mordaz*) biting.

acerbo, a [a'θerβo, a] *adj* bitter; (*fig*) harsh.

acerca [a'θerka]: **~ de** *adv* about, concerning.

acercar [aθer'kar] *vt* to bring o move nearer; **~se** *vr* to approach, come near.

acerico [aθe'riko] *nm* pincushion.

acero [a'θero] *nm* steel; **~ inoxidable** stainless steel.

acerque [a'θerke] *etc vb V* **acercar.**

acérrimo, a [a'θerrimo, a] *adj* (*partidario*) staunch; (*enemigo*) bitter.

acertado, a [aθer'taðo, a] *adj* correct; (*apropiado*) apt; (*sensato*) sensible.

acertar [aθer'tar] *vt* (*blanco*) to hit; (*solución*) to get right; (*adivinar*) to guess

♦ *vi* to get it right, be right; ~ **a** to manage to; ~ **con** to happen *o* hit on.
acertijo [aθer'tixo] *nm* riddle, puzzle.
acervo [a'θerßo] *nm* heap; ~ **común** undivided estate.
achacar [atʃa'kar] *vt* to attribute.
achacoso, a [atʃa'koso, a] *adj* sickly.
achantar [atʃan'tar] *vt* (*fam*) to scare, frighten; ~**se** *vr* to back down.
achaque [a'tʃake] *etc vb* V **achacar** ♦ *nm* ailment.
achatar [atʃa'tar] *vt* to flatten.
achicar [atʃi'kar] *vt* to reduce; (*humillar*) to humiliate; (*NAUT*) to bale out; ~**se** (*ropa*) to shrink; (*fig*) to humble o.s.
achicharrar [atʃitʃa'rrar] *vt* to scorch, burn.
achicoria [atʃi'korja] *nf* chicory.
achinado, a [atʃi'naðo, a] *adj* (*ojos*) slanting; (*AM*) half-caste.
achique [a'tʃike] *etc vb* V **achicar.**
acholado, a [atʃo'laðo, a] *adj* (*AM*) half-caste.
achuchar [atʃu'tʃar] *vt* to crush.
achuchón [atʃu'tʃon] *nm* shove; **tener un** ~ (*MED*) to be poorly.
achuras [a'tʃuras] *nf* (*AM CULIN*) offal.
aciago, a [a'θjaɣo, a] *adj* ill-fated, fateful.
acicalar [aθika'lar] *vt* to polish; (*adornar*) to bedeck; ~**se** *vr* to get dressed up.
acicate [aθi'kate] *nm* spur; (*fig*) incentive.
acidez [aθi'ðeθ] *nf* acidity.
ácido, a ['aθiðo, a] *adj* sour, acid ♦ *nm* acid; (*fam: droga*) LSD.
acierto [a'θjerto] *etc vb* V **acertar** ♦ *nm* success; (*buen paso*) wise move; (*solución*) solution; (*habilidad*) skill, ability; (*al adivinar*) good guess; **fue un** ~ **suyo** it was a sensible choice on his part.
aclamación [aklama'θjon] *nf* acclamation; (*aplausos*) applause.
aclamar [akla'mar] *vt* to acclaim; to applaud.
aclaración [aklara'θjon] *nf* clarification, explanation.
aclarar [akla'rar] *vt* to clarify, explain; (*ropa*) to rinse ♦ *vi* to clear up; ~**se** *vr* (*suj: persona: explicarse*) to understand; (*fig: asunto*) to become clear; ~**se la garganta** to clear one's throat.
aclaratorio, a [aklara'torjo, a] *adj* explanatory.
aclimatación [aklimata'θjon] *nf* acclimatization.
aclimatar [aklima'tar] *vt* to acclimatize; ~**se** *vr* to become *o* get acclimatized; ~**se a algo** to get used to sth.

acné [ak'ne] *nm* acne.
acobardar [akoßar'ðar] *vt* to daunt, intimidate; ~**se** *vr* (*atemorizarse*) to be intimidated; (*echarse atrás*): ~**se (ante)** to shrink back (from).
acodarse [ako'ðarse] *vr*: ~ **en** to lean on.
acogedor, a [akoxe'ðor, a] *adj* welcoming; (*hospitalario*) hospitable.
acoger [ako'xer] *vt* to welcome; (*abrigar*) to shelter; ~**se** *vr* to take refuge; ~**se a** (*pretexto*) to take refuge in; (*ley*) to resort to.
acogida [ako'xiða] *nf* reception; refuge.
acoja [a'koxa] *etc vb* V **acoger.**
acojonante [akoxo'nante] *adj* (*ESP fam*) tremendous.
acolchar [akol'tʃar] *vt* to pad; (*fig*) to cushion.
acólito [a'kolito] *nm* (*REL*) acolyte; (*fig*) minion.
acometer [akome'ter] *vt* to attack; (*emprender*) to undertake.
acometida [akome'tiða] *nf* attack, assault.
acomodado, a [akomo'ðaðo, a] *adj* (*persona*) well-to-do.
acomodador, a [akomoða'ðor, a] *nm/f* usher(ette).
acomodar [akomo'ðar] *vt* to adjust; (*alojar*) to accommodate; ~**se** *vr* to conform; (*instalarse*) to install o.s.; (*adaptarse*) to adapt o.s.; **¡acomódese a su gusto!** make yourself comfortable!
acomodaticio, a [akomoða'tiθjo, a] *adj* (*pey*) accommodating, obliging; (*manejable*) pliable.
acompañamiento [akompaɲa'mjento] *nm* (*MUS*) accompaniment.
acompañante, a [akompa'ɲante, a] *nm/f* companion.
acompañar [akompa'ɲar] *vt* to accompany, go with; (*documentos*) to enclose; **¿quieres que te acompañe?** do you want me to come with you?; ~ **a algn a la puerta** to see sb to the door *o* out; **le acompaño en el sentimiento** please accept my condolences.
acompasar [akompa'sar] *vt* (*MUS*) to mark the rhythm of.
acomplejado, a [akomple'xaðo, a] *adj* neurotic.
acomplejar [akomple'xar] *vt* to give a complex to; ~**se** *vr*: ~**se (con)** to get a complex (about).
acondicionado, a [akondiθjo'naðo, a] *adj* (*TEC*) in good condition.
acondicionador [akondiθjona'ðor] *nm* conditioner.
acondicionar [akondiθjo'nar] *vt* to get

ready, prepare; (*pelo*) to condition.
acongojar [akongo'xar] *vt* to distress,
grieve.
aconsejable [akonse'xaßle] *adj* advisable.
aconsejar [akonse'xar] *vt* to advise,
counsel; ~**se** *vr*: ~**se con** *o* **de** to consult.
acontecer [akonte'θer] *vi* to happen,
occur.
acontecimiento [akonteθi'mjento] *nm*
event.
acontezca [akon'teθka] *etc vb V* **acontecer**.
acopiar [ako'pjar] *vt* (*recoger*) to gather;
(*COM*) to buy up.
acopio [a'kopjo] *nm* store, stock.
acoplador [akopla'ðor] *nm*: ~ **acústico**
(*INFORM*) acoustic coupler.
acoplamiento [akopla'mjento] *nm*
coupling, joint.
acoplar [ako'plar] *vt* to fit; (*ELEC*) to
connect; (*vagones*) to couple.
acoquinar [akoki'nar] *vt* to scare; ~**se** *vr* to
get scared.
acorazado, a [akora'θaðo, a] *adj* armour-
plated, armoured ♦ *nm* battleship.
acordar [akor'ðar] *vt* (*resolver*) to agree,
resolve; (*recordar*) to remind; ~**se** *vr* to
agree; ~**se (de algo)** to remember (sth).
acorde [a'korðe] *adj* (*MUS*) harmonious; ~
con (*medidas etc*) in keeping with ♦ *nm*
chord.
acordeón [akorðe'on] *nm* accordion.
acordonado, a [akorðo'naðo, a] *adj* (*calle*)
cordoned-off.
acorralar [akorra'lar] *vt* to round up,
corral; (*fig*) to intimidate.
acortar [akor'tar] *vt* to shorten; (*duración*)
to cut short; (*cantidad*) to reduce; ~**se** *vr*
to become shorter.
acosar [ako'sar] *vt* to pursue relentlessly;
(*fig*) to hound, pester; ~ **a algn a**
preguntas to pester sb with questions.
acoso [a'koso] *nm* relentless pursuit; (*fig*)
hounding; ~ **sexual** sexual harassment.
acostar [akos'tar] *vt* (*en cama*) to put to
bed; (*en suelo*) to lay down; (*barco*) to
bring alongside; ~**se** *vr* to go to bed; to
lie down.
acostumbrado, a [akostum'braðo, a] *adj*
(*habitual*) usual; **estar** ~ **a (hacer) algo** to
be used to (doing) sth.
acostumbrar [akostum'brar] *vt*: ~ **a algn a**
algo to get sb used to sth ♦ *vi*: ~ **(a hacer**
algo) to be in the habit (of doing sth);
~**se** *vr*: ~**se a** to get used to.
acotación [akota'θjon] *nf* (*apunte*)
marginal note; (*GEO*) elevation mark; (*de*
límite) boundary mark; (*TEAT*) stage
direction.

acotar [ako'tar] *vt* (*terreno*) to mark out;
(*fig*) to limit; (*caza*) to protect.
acotejar [akote'xar] *vt* (*AM*) to put in
order, arrange.
ácrata ['akrata] *adj, nm/f* anarchist.
acre ['akre] *adj* (*sabor*) sharp, bitter; (*olor*)
acrid; (*fig*) biting ♦ *nm* acre.
acrecentar [akreθen'tar] *vt* to increase,
augment.
acreciente [akre'θjente] *etc vb V*
acrecentar.
acreditado, a [akreði'taðo, a] *adj* (*POL*)
accredited; (*COM*): **una casa acreditada** a
reputable firm.
acreditar [akreði'tar] *vt* (*garantizar*) to
vouch for, guarantee; (*autorizar*) to
authorize; (*dar prueba de*) to prove; (*COM*:
abonar) to credit; (*embajador*) to
accredit; ~**se** *vr* to become famous;
(*demostrar valía*) to prove one's worth;
~**se de** to get a reputation for.
acreedor, a [akree'ðor, a] *adj*: ~ **a** worthy
of ♦ *nm/f* creditor; ~ **común/diferido/con**
garantía (*COM*) unsecured/deferred/
secured creditor.
acribillar [akrißi'ʎar] *vt*: ~ **a balazos** to
riddle with bullets.
acrimonia [akri'monja], **acritud** [akri'tuð]
nf acrimony.
acrobacia [akro'ßaθja] *nf* acrobatics; ~
aérea aerobatics.
acróbata [a'kroßata] *nm/f* acrobat.
acta ['akta] *nf* certificate; (*de comisión*)
minutes *pl*, record; ~ **de nacimiento/de**
matrimonio birth/marriage certificate;
~ **notarial** affidavit; **levantar** ~ (*JUR*) to
make a formal statement *o* deposition.
actitud [akti'tuð] *nf* attitude; (*postura*)
posture; **adoptar una** ~ **firme** to take a
firm stand.
activar [akti'ßar] *vt* to activate; (*acelerar*) to
speed up.
actividad [aktißi'ðað] *nf* activity; **estar en**
plena ~ to be in full swing.
activo, a [ak'tißo, a] *adj* active; (*vivo*)
lively ♦ *nm* (*COM*) assets *pl*; ~ **y pasivo**
assets and liabilities; ~ **circulante/fijo/**
inmaterial/invisible (*COM*) current/fixed/
intangible/invisible assets; ~ **realizable**
liquid assets; ~**s congelados** *o*
bloqueados frozen assets; **estar en** ~
(*MIL*) to be on active service.
acto ['akto] *nm* act, action; (*ceremonia*)
ceremony; (*TEAT*) act; **en el** ~
immediately; **hacer** ~ **de presencia**
(*asistir*) to attend (formally).
actor [ak'tor] *nm* actor; (*JUR*) plaintiff.
actora [ak'tora] *adj*: **parte** ~ prosecution;

(*demandante*) plaintiff.

actriz [ak'triθ] *nf* actress.

actuación [aktwa'θjon] *nf* action; (*comportamiento*) conduct, behaviour; (*JUR*) proceedings *pl*; (*desempeño*) performance.

actual [ak'twal] *adj* present(-day), current; **el 6 del** ~ the 6th of this month.

actualice [aktwa'liθe] *etc vb V* **actualizar**.

actualidad [aktwali'ðað] *nf* present; ~**es** *nfpl* news *sg*; **en la** ~ nowadays, at present; **ser de gran** ~ to be current.

actualización [aktwaliθa'θjon] *nf* updating, modernization.

actualizar [aktwali'θar] *vt* to update, modernize.

actualmente [aktwal'mente] *adv* at present; (*hoy día*) nowadays.

actuar [ak'twar] *vi* (*obrar*) to work, operate; (*actor*) to act, perform ♦ *vt* to work, operate; ~ **de** to act as.

actuario, a [ak'twarjo] *nm/f* clerk; (*COM*) actuary.

acuarela [akwa'rela] *nf* watercolour.

acuario [a'kwarjo] *nm* aquarium; **A**~ (*ASTRO*) Aquarius.

acuartelar [akwarte'lar] *vt* (*MIL: alojar*) to quarter.

acuático, a [a'kwatiko, a] *adj* aquatic.

acuchillar [akutʃi'ʎar] *vt* (*TEC*) to plane (down), smooth.

acuciar [aku'θjar] *vt* to urge on.

acuclillarse [akukli'ʎarse] *vr* to crouch down.

ACUDE [a'kuðe] *nf abr* = *Asociación de Consumidores y Usuarios de España*.

acudir [aku'ðir] *vi* to attend, turn up; ~ **a** to turn to; ~ **en ayuda de** to go to the aid of; ~ **a una cita** to keep an appointment; ~ **a una llamada** to answer a call; **no tener a quién** ~ to have nobody to turn to.

acuerdo [a'kwerðo] *etc vb V* **acordar** ♦ *nm* agreement; (*POL*) resolution; ~ **de pago respectivo** (*COM*) knock-for-knock agreement; **A**~ **general sobre aranceles aduaneros y comercio** (*COM*) General Agreement on Tariffs and Trade; **tomar un** ~ to pass a resolution; **¡de** ~**!** agreed!; **de** ~ **con** (*persona*) in agreement with; (*acción, documento*) in accordance with; **de común** ~ by common consent; **estar de** ~ (*persona*) to agree; **llegar a un** ~ to come to an understanding.

acueste [a'kweste] *etc vb V* **acostar**.

acullá [aku'ʎa] *adv* over there.

acumular [akumu'lar] *vt* to accumulate,

collect.

acunar [aku'nar] *vt* to rock (to sleep).

acuñar [aku'ɲar] *vt* (*moneda*) to mint; (*frase*) to coin.

acuoso, a [a'kwoso, a] *adj* watery.

acupuntura [akupun'tura] *nf* acupuncture.

acurrucarse [akurru'karse] *vr* to crouch; (*ovillarse*) to curl up.

acurruque [aku'rruke] *etc vb V* **acurrucarse**.

acusación [akusa'θjon] *nf* accusation.

acusado, a [aku'saðo, a] *adj* (*JUR*) accused; (*marcado*) marked; (*acento*) strong.

acusar [aku'sar] *vt* to accuse; (*revelar*) to reveal; (*denunciar*) to denounce; (*emoción*) to show; ~ **recibo** to acknowledge receipt; **su rostro acusó extrañeza** his face registered surprise; ~**se** *vr*: ~**se (de)** to confess (to).

acuse [a'kuse] *nm*: ~ **de recibo** acknowledgement of receipt.

acústico, a [a'kustiko, a] *adj* acoustic ♦ *nf* (*de una sala etc*) acoustics *pl*; (*ciencia*) acoustics *sg*.

ADA ['aða] *nf abr* (*ESP*: = *Ayuda del Automovilista*) ≈ AA, RAC (*BRIT*), AAA (*US*).

adagio [a'ðaxjo] *nm* adage; (*MUS*) adagio.

adalid [aða'lið] *nm* leader, champion.

adaptación [aðapta'θjon] *nf* adaptation.

adaptador [aðapta'ðor] *nm* (*ELEC*) adapter.

adaptar [aðap'tar] *vt* to adapt; (*acomodar*) to fit; (*convertir*): ~ (**para**) to convert (to).

adecentar [aðeθen'tar] *vt* to tidy up.

adecuado, a [aðe'kwaðo, a] *adj* (*apto*) suitable; (*oportuno*) appropriate; **el hombre** ~ **para el puesto** the right man for the job.

adecuar [aðe'kwar] *vt* (*adaptar*) to adapt; (*hacer apto*) to make suitable.

adefesio [aðe'fesjo] *nm* (*fam*): **estaba hecha un** ~ she looked a sight.

a. de J.C. *abr* (= *antes de Jesucristo*) B.C.

adelantado, a [aðelan'taðo, a] *adj* advanced; (*reloj*) fast; **pagar por** ~ to pay in advance.

adelantamiento [aðelanta'mjento] *nm* advance, advancement; (*AUTO*) overtaking.

adelantar [aðelan'tar] *vt* to move forward; (*avanzar*) to advance; (*acelerar*) to speed up; (*AUTO*) to overtake ♦ *vi* (*ir delante*) to go ahead; (*progresar*) to improve; (*tb*: ~**se** *vr*: *tomar la delantera*) to go forward, advance; ~**se a algn** to get ahead of sb; ~**se a los deseos de algn** to anticipate sb's wishes.

adelante [aðe'lante] *adv* forward(s),

onward(s), ahead ♦ *excl* come in!; **de hoy en** ~ from now on; **más** ~ later on; (*más allá*) further on.

adelanto [aðe'lanto] *nm* advance; (*mejora*) improvement; (*progreso*) progress; (*dinero*) advance; **los** ~**s de la ciencia** the advances of science.

adelgace [aðel'ɣaθe] *etc vb V* **adelgazar**.

adelgazar [aðelɣa'θar] *vt* to thin (down); (*afilar*) to taper ♦ *vi* to get thin; (*con régimen*) to slim down, lose weight.

ademán [aðe'man] *nm* gesture; **ademanes** *nmpl* manners; **en** ~ **de** as if to.

además [aðe'mas] *adv* besides; (*por otra parte*) moreover; (*también*) also; ~ **de** besides, in addition to.

ADENA [a'ðena] *nf abr* (*ESP*: = *Asociación para la Defensa de la Naturaleza*) *organization for nature conservation*.

adentrarse [aðen'trarse] *vr*: ~ **en** to go into, get inside; (*penetrar*) to penetrate (into).

adentro [a'ðentro] *adv* inside, in; **mar** ~ out at sea; **tierra** ~ inland ♦ *nm*: **dijo para sus** ~**s** he said to himself.

adepto, a [a'ðepto, a] *nm/f* supporter.

aderece [aðe'reθe] *etc vb V* **aderezar**.

aderezar [aðere'θar] *vt* (*ensalada*) to dress; (*comida*) to season.

aderezo [aðe'reθo] *nm* dressing; seasoning.

adeudar [aðeu'ðar] *vt* to owe; ~**se** *vr* to run into debt; ~ **una suma en una cuenta** to debit an account with a sum.

a.D.g. *abr* (= *a Dios gracias*) D.G. (= *Deo gratias*: thanks be to God).

adherirse [aðe'rirse] *vr*: ~ **a** to adhere to; (*fig*) to follow.

adhesión [aðe'sjon] *nf* adhesion; (*fig*) adherence.

adhesivo, a [aðe'siβo, a] *adj* adhesive ♦ *nm* sticker.

adhiera [a'ðjera] *etc*, **adhiriendo** [aði'rjendo] *etc vb V* **adherirse**.

adicción [aðik'θjon] *nf* addiction.

adición [aði'θjon] *nf* addition.

adicional [aðiθjo'nal] *adj* additional; (*INFORM*) add-on.

adicionar [aðiθjo'nar] *vt* to add.

adicto, a [a'ðikto, a] *adj*: ~ **a** (*droga etc*) addicted to; (*dedicado*) devoted to ♦ *nm/f* supporter, follower; (*toxicómano etc*) addict.

adiestrar [aðjes'trar] *vt* to train, teach; (*conducir*) to guide, lead; ~**se** *vr* to practise; (*enseñarse*) to train o.s.

adinerado, a [aðine'raðo, a] *adj* wealthy.

adiós [a'ðjos] *excl* (*para despedirse*) goodbye!, cheerio!; (*al pasar*) hello!

aditivo [aði'tiβo] *nm* additive.

adivinanza [aðiβi'nanθa] *nf* riddle.

adivinar [aðiβi'nar] *vt* (*profetizar*) to prophesy; (*conjeturar*) to guess.

adivino, a [aði'βino, a] *nm/f* fortune-teller.

adj *abr* (= *adjunto*) encl.

adjetivo [aðxe'tiβo] *nm* adjective.

adjudicación [aðxuðika'θjon] *nf* award; (*COM*) adjudication.

adjudicar [aðxuði'kar] *vt* to award; ~**se** *vr*: ~**se algo** to appropriate sth.

adjudique [aðxu'ðike] *etc vb V* **adjudicar**.

adjuntar [aðxun'tar] *vt* to attach, enclose.

adjunto, a [að'xunto, a] *adj* attached, enclosed ♦ *nm/f* assistant.

adminículo [aðmi'nikulo] *nm* gadget.

administración [aðministra'θjon] *nf* administration; (*dirección*) management; ~ **pública** civil service; **A**~ **de Correos** General Post Office.

administrador, a [aðministra'ðor, a] *nm/f* administrator; manager(ess).

administrar [aðminis'trar] *vt* to administer.

administrativo, a [aðministra'tiβo, a] *adj* administrative.

admirable [aðmi'raβle] *adj* admirable.

admiración [aðmira'θjon] *nf* admiration; (*asombro*) wonder; (*LING*) exclamation mark.

admirar [aðmi'rar] *vt* to admire; (*extrañar*) to surprise; ~**se** *vr* to be surprised; **se admiró de saberlo** he was amazed to hear it; **no es de** ~ **que ...** it's not surprising that ...

admisible [aðmi'siβle] *adj* admissible.

admisión [aðmi'sjon] *nf* admission; (*reconocimiento*) acceptance.

admitir [aðmi'tir] *vt* to admit; (*aceptar*) to accept; (*dudas*) to leave room for; **esto no admite demora** this must be dealt with immediately.

admón. *abr* (= *administración*) admin.

admonición [aðmoni'θjon] *nf* warning.

ADN *nm abr* (= *acido desoxirribonucleico*) DNA.

adobar [aðo'βar] *vt* (*preparar*) to prepare; (*cocinar*) to season.

adobe [a'ðoβe] *nm* adobe, sun-dried brick.

adocenado, a [aðoθe'naðo, a] *adj* (*fam*) mediocre.

adoctrinar [aðoktri'nar] *vt* to indoctrinate.

adolecer [aðole'θer] *vi*: ~ **de** to suffer from.

adolescente [aðoles'θente] *nm/f* adolescent, teenager ♦ *adj* adolescent, teenage.

adolezca [aðoˈleθka] *etc vb V* **adolecer.**
adonde [aˈðonde] *adv* (to) where.
adónde [aˈðonde] *adv* = **dónde.**
adondequiera [aðondeˈkjera] *adv* wherever.
adopción [aðopˈθjon] *nf* adoption.
adoptar [aðopˈtar] *vt* to adopt.
adoptivo, a [aðopˈtiβo, a] *adj* (*padres*) adoptive; (*hijo*) adopted.
adoquín [aðoˈkin] *nm* paving stone.
adorar [aðoˈrar] *vt* to adore.
adormecer [aðormeˈθer] *vt* to put to sleep; ~**se** *vr* to become sleepy; (*dormirse*) to fall asleep.
adormezca [aðorˈmeθka] *etc vb V* **adormecer.**
adormilarse [aðormiˈlarse] *vr* to doze.
adornar [aðorˈnar] *vt* to adorn.
adorno [aˈðorno] *nm* adornment; (*decoración*) decoration.
adosado, a [aðoˈsaðo, a] *adj* (*casa*) semidetached.
adquiera [aðˈkjera] *etc vb V* **adquirir.**
adquirir [aðkiˈrir] *vt* to acquire, obtain.
adquisición [aðkisiˈθjon] *nf* acquisition; (*compra*) purchase.
adrede [aˈðreðe] *adv* on purpose.
Adriático [aðˈrjatiko] *nm*: **el (Mar)** ~ the Adriatic (Sea).
adscribir [aðskriˈβir] *vt* to appoint; **estuvo adscrito al servicio de** ... he was attached to ...
adscrito [aðˈskrito] *pp de* **adscribir.**
aduana [aˈðwana] *nf* customs *pl*; (*impuesto*) (customs) duty.
aduanero, a [aðwaˈnero, a] *adj* customs *cpd* ♦ *nm/f* customs officer.
aducir [aðuˈθir] *vt* to adduce; (*dar como prueba*) to offer as proof.
adueñarse [aðweˈɲarse] *vr*: ~ **de** to take possession of.
adulación [aðulaˈθjon] *nf* flattery.
adular [aðuˈlar] *vt* to flatter.
adulterar [aðulteˈrar] *vt* to adulterate ♦ *vi* to commit adultery.
adulterio [aðulˈterjo] *nm* adultery.
adúltero, a [aˈðultero, a] *adj* adulterous ♦ *nm/f* adulterer/adulteress.
adulto, a [aˈðulto, a] *adj, nm/f* adult.
adusto, a [aˈðusto, a] *adj* stern; (*austero*) austere.
aduzca [aˈðuθka] *etc vb V* **aducir.**
advenedizo, a [aðβeneˈðiθo, a] *nm/f* upstart.
advenimiento [aðβeniˈmjento] *nm* arrival; (*al trono*) accession.
adverbio [aðˈβerβjo] *nm* adverb.
adversario, a [aðβerˈsarjo, a] *nm/f*

adversary.
adversidad [aðβersiˈðað] *nf* adversity; (*contratiempo*) setback.
adverso, a [aðˈβerso, a] *adj* adverse; (*suerte*) bad.
advertencia [aðβerˈtenθja] *nf* warning; (*prefacio*) preface, foreword.
advertir [aðβerˈtir] *vt* (*observar*) to notice; (*avisar*): ~ **a algn de** to warn sb about o of.
Adviento [aðˈβjento] *nm* Advent.
advierta [aðˈβjerta] *etc*, **advirtiendo** [aðβirˈtjendo] *etc vb V* **advertir.**
adyacente [aðjaˈθente] *adj* adjacent.
aéreo, a [aˈereo, a] *adj* aerial; (*tráfico*) air *cpd*.
aerobic [aeˈroβik] *nm* aerobics *sg*.
aerodeslizador [aeroðesliθaˈðor] *nm* hovercraft.
aerodinámico, a [aeroðiˈnamiko, a] *adj* aerodynamic.
aeródromo [aeˈroðromo] *nm* aerodrome.
aerograma [aeroˈɣrama] *nm* airmail letter.
aeromodelismo [aeromoðeˈlismo] *nm* model aircraft making, aeromodelling.
aeromozo, a [aeroˈmoso, a] *nm/f* (*AM*) flight attendant, air steward(ess).
aeronáutico, a [aeroˈnautiko, a] *adj* aeronautical.
aeronave [aeroˈnaβe] *nm* spaceship.
aeroplano [aeroˈplano] *nm* aeroplane.
aeropuerto [aeroˈpwerto] *nm* airport.
aerosol [aeroˈsol] *nm* aerosol, spray.
a/f *abr* (= *a favor*) in favour.
afabilidad [afaβiliˈðað] *nf* affability, pleasantness.
afable [aˈfaβle] *adj* affable, pleasant.
afamado, a [afaˈmaðo, a] *adj* famous.
afán [aˈfan] *nm* hard work; (*deseo*) desire; **con** ~ keenly.
afanar [afaˈnar] *vt* to harass; (*fam*) to pinch; ~**se** *vr*: ~**se por** to strive to.
afanoso, a [afaˈnoso, a] *adj* (*trabajo*) hard; (*trabajador*) industrious.
AFE [ˈafe] *nf abr* (= *Asociación de Futbolistas Españoles*) ≈ F.A.
afear [afeˈar] *vt* to disfigure.
afección [afekˈθjon] *nf* affection; (*MED*) disease.
afectación [afektaˈθjon] *nf* affectation.
afectado, a [afekˈtaðo, a] *adj* affected.
afectar [afekˈtar] *vt* to affect, have an effect on; (*AM: dañar*) to hurt; **por lo que afecta a esto** as far as this is concerned.
afectísimo , a [afekˈtisimo, a] *adj* affectionate; ~ **suyo** yours truly.
afectivo, a [afekˈtiβo, a] *adj* affective.
afecto, a [aˈfekto, a] *adj*: ~ **a** fond of; (*JUR*)

subject to ♦ *nm* affection; **tenerle** ~ **a algn** to be fond of sb.

afectuoso, a [afek'twoso, a] *adj* affectionate.

afeitar [afei'tar] *vt* to shave; ~**se** *vr* to shave.

afeminado, a [afemi'naðo, a] *adj* effeminate.

aferrar [afe'rrar] *vt* to moor; (*fig*) to grasp ♦ *vi* to moor; ~**se** *vr* (*agarrarse*) to cling on; ~**se a un principio** to stick to a principle; ~**se a una esperanza** to cling to a hope.

affmo., a. *abr* (= *afectísimo, a*) Yours.

Afganistán [afɣanis'tan] *nm* Afghanistan.

afgano, a [af'ɣano, a] *adj, nm/f* Afghan.

afiance [a'fjanθe] *etc vb V* **afianzar**.

afianzamiento [afjanθa'mjento] *nm* strengthening; security.

afianzar [afjan'θar] *vt* to strengthen, secure; ~**se** *vr* to steady o.s.; (*establecerse*) to become established.

afiche [a'fitʃe] *nm* (*AM*) poster.

afición [afi'θjon] *nf*: ~ **a** fondness o liking for; **la** ~ the fans *pl*; **pinto por** ~ I paint as a hobby.

aficionado, a [afiθjo'naðo, a] *adj* keen, enthusiastic; (*no profesional*) amateur ♦ *nm/f* enthusiast, fan; amateur.

aficionar [afiθjo'nar] *vt*: ~ **a algn a algo** to make sb like sth; ~**se** *vr*: ~**se a algo** to grow fond of sth.

afilado, a [afi'laðo, a] *adj* sharp.

afilador [afila'ðor] *nm* (*persona*) knife grinder.

afilalápices [afila'lapiθes] *nm inv* pencil sharpener.

afilar [afi'lar] *vt* to sharpen; ~**se** *vr* (*cara*) to grow thin.

afiliación [afilja'θjon] *nf* (*de sindicatos*) membership.

afiliado, a [afi'ljaðo, a] *adj* subsidiary ♦ *nm/f* affiliate.

afiliarse [afi'ljarse] *vr* to affiliate.

afín [a'fin] *adj* (*parecido*) similar; (*conexo*) related.

afinar [afi'nar] *vt* (*TEC*) to refine; (*MUS*) to tune ♦ *vi* to play/sing in tune.

afincarse [afin'karse] *vr* to settle.

afinidad [afini'ðað] *nf* affinity; (*parentesco*) relationship; **por** ~ by marriage.

afirmación [afirma'θjon] *nf* affirmation.

afirmar [afir'mar] *vt* to affirm, state; (*sostener*) to strengthen; ~**se** *vr* (*recuperar el equilibrio*) to steady o.s.; ~**se en lo dicho** to stand by what one has said.

afirmativo, a [afirma'tiβo, a] *adj* affirmative.

aflicción [aflik'θjon] *nf* affliction; (*dolor*)

grief.

afligir [afli'xir] *vt* to afflict; (*apenar*) to distress; ~**se** *vr*: ~**se (por** o **con** o **de)** to grieve (about o at); **no te aflijas tanto** you must not let it affect you like this.

aflija [a'flixa] *etc vb V* **afligir**.

aflojar [aflo'xar] *vt* to slacken; (*desatar*) to loosen, undo; (*relajar*) to relax ♦ *vi* (*amainar*) to drop; (*bajar*) to go down; ~**se** *vr* to relax.

aflorar [aflo'rar] *vi* (*GEO, fig*) to come to the surface, emerge.

afluencia [aflu'enθja] *nf* flow.

afluente [aflu'ente] *adj* flowing ♦ *nm* (*GEO*) tributary.

afluir [aflu'ir] *vi* to flow.

afluya [a'fluja] *etc*, **afluyendo** [aflu'jendo] *etc vb V* **afluir**.

afmo., a. *abr* (= *afectísimo, a suyo, a*) Yours.

afónico, a [a'foniko, a] *adj*: **estar** ~ to have a sore throat; to have lost one's voice.

aforar [afo'rar] *vt* (*TEC*) to gauge; (*fig*) to value.

aforo [a'foro] *nm* (*TEC*) gauging; (*de teatro etc*) capacity; **el teatro tiene un** ~ **de 2,000** the theatre can seat 2,000.

afortunado, a [afortu'naðo, a] *adj* fortunate, lucky.

afrancesado, a [afranθe'saðo, a] *adj* francophile; (*pey*) Frenchified.

afrenta [a'frenta] *nf* affront, insult; (*deshonra*) dishonour (*BRIT*), dishonor (*US*), shame.

afrentoso, a [afren'toso, a] *adj* insulting; shameful.

África ['afrika] *nf* Africa; ~ **del Sur** South Africa.

africano, a [afri'kano, a] *adj, nm/f* African.

afrontar [afron'tar] *vt* to confront; (*poner cara a cara*) to bring face to face.

afuera [a'fwera] *adv* out, outside; **por** ~ on the outside; ~**s** *nfpl* outskirts.

ag. *abr* (= *agosto*) Aug.

agachar [aɣa'tʃar] *vt* to bend, bow; ~**se** *vr* to stoop, bend.

agalla [a'ɣaʎa] *nf* (*ZOOL*) gill; ~**s** *nfpl* (*MED*) tonsillitis *sg*; (*ANAT*) tonsils; **tener** ~**s** (*fam*) to have guts.

agarradera [aɣarra'ðera] *nf* (*AM*), **agarradero** [aɣarra'ðero] *nm* handle; ~**s** *npl* pull *sg*, influence *sg*.

agarrado, a [aɣa'rraðo, a] *adj* mean, stingy.

agarrar [aɣa'rrar] *vt* to grasp, grab; (*AM*) to take, catch ♦ *vi* (*planta*) to take root; ~**se** *vr* to hold on (tightly); (*meterse uno con otro*) to grapple (with each other);

agarrársela con algn (*AM*) to pick on sb;
agarró y se fue (*esp AM fam*) he upped
and went.

agarrotar [aɣarro'tar] *vt* (*lío*) to tie tightly;
(*persona*) to squeeze tightly; (*reo*) to
garrotte; ~**se** *vr* (*motor*) to seize up;
(*MED*) to stiffen.

agasajar [aɣasa'xar] *vt* to treat well, fête.

agave [a'ɣaβe] *nf* agave.

agazapar [aɣaθa'par] *vt* (*coger*) to grab
hold of; ~**se** *vr* (*agacharse*) to crouch
down.

agencia [a'xenθja] *nf* agency; ~ **de
créditos/publicidad/viajes** credit/
advertising/travel agency; ~
inmobiliaria estate agent's (office) (*BRIT*),
real estate office (*US*); ~ **de matrimonios**
marriage bureau.

agenciar [axen'θjar] *vt* to bring about; ~**se**
vr to look after o.s.; ~**se algo** to get hold
of sth.

agenda [a'xenda] *nf* diary; ~ **telefónica**
telephone directory.

agente [a'xente] *nm* agent; (*de policía*)
policeman; ~ **femenino** policewoman; ~
acreditado (*COM*) accredited agent; ~ **de
bolsa** stockbroker; ~ **inmobiliario** estate
agent (*BRIT*), realtor (*US*); ~ **de negocios**
(*COM*) business agent; ~ **de seguros**
insurance broker; ~ **de viajes** travel
agent; ~**s sociales** social partners.

ágil ['axil] *adj* agile, nimble.

agilidad [axili'ðað] *nf* agility, nimbleness.

agilizar [axili'θar] *vt* to speed up.

agitación [axita'θjon] *nf* (*de mano etc*)
shaking, waving; (*de líquido etc*) stirring;
agitation.

agitar [axi'tar] *vt* to wave, shake; (*líquido*)
to stir; (*fig*) to stir up, excite; ~**se** *vr* to
get excited; (*inquietarse*) to get worried
o upset.

aglomeración [axlomera'θjon] *nf*: ~ **de
tráfico/gente** traffic jam/mass of people.

aglomerar [axlome'rar] *vt*, ~**se** *vr* to crowd
together.

agnóstico, a [aɣ'nostiko, a] *adj, nm/f*
agnostic.

ag.º *abr* = **ag.**

agobiante [aɣo'βjante] *adj* (*calor*)
oppressive.

agobiar [aɣo'βjar] *vt* to weigh down;
(*oprimir*) to oppress; (*cargar*) to burden;
sentirse agobiado por to be
overwhelmed by.

agobio [a'ɣoβjo] *nm* (*peso*) burden; (*fig*)
oppressiveness.

agolpamiento [aɣolpa'mjento] *nm* crush.

agolparse [aɣol'parse] *vr* to crowd

together.

agonía [aɣo'nia] *nf* death throes *pl*; (*fig*)
agony, anguish.

agonice [aɣo'niθe] *etc vb V* **agonizar**.

agonizante [aɣoni'θante] *adj* dying.

agonizar [aɣoni'θar] *vi* (*tb:* **estar
agonizando**) to be dying.

agorero, a [aɣo'rero, a] *adj* ominous ♦ *nm/f*
soothsayer; **ave agorera** bird of ill omen.

agostar [aɣo'star] *vt* (*quemar*) to parch;
(*fig*) to wither.

agosto [a'ɣosto] *nm* August; (*fig*) harvest;
hacer su ~ to make one's pile.

agotado, a [aɣo'taðo, a] *adj* (*persona*)
exhausted; (*acabado*) finished; (*COM*)
sold out; (: *libros*) out of print; (*pila*) flat.

agotador, a [aɣota'ðor, a] *adj* exhausting.

agotamiento [aɣota'mjento] *nm*
exhaustion.

agotar [aɣo'tar] *vt* to exhaust; (*consumir*)
to drain; (*recursos*) to use up, deplete;
~**se** *vr* to be exhausted; (*acabarse*) to run
out; (*libro*) to go out of print.

agraciado, a [aɣra'θjaðo, a] *adj* (*atractivo*)
attractive; (*en sorteo etc*) lucky.

agraciar [aɣra'θjar] *vt* (*JUR*) to pardon;
(*con premio*) to reward; (*hacer más
atractivo*) to make more attractive.

agradable [aɣra'ðaβle] *adj* pleasant, nice.

agradar [aɣra'ðar] *vt, vi* to please; ~**se** *vr* to
like each other.

agradecer [aɣraðe'θer] *vt* to thank; (*favor
etc*) to be grateful for; **le agradecería me
enviara ...** I would be grateful if you
would send me ...; ~**se** *vr*: **¡se agradece!**
much obliged!

agradecido, a [aɣraðe'θiðo, a] *adj* grateful;
¡muy ~! thanks a lot!

agradecimiento [aɣraðeθi'mjento] *nm*
thanks *pl*; gratitude.

agradezca [aɣra'ðeθka] *etc vb V* **agradecer**.

agrado [a'ɣraðo] *nm*: **ser de tu** *etc* ~ to be
to your *etc* liking.

agrandar [aɣran'dar] *vt* to enlarge; (*fig*) to
exaggerate; ~**se** *vr* to get bigger.

agrario, a [a'ɣrarjo, a] *adj* agrarian, land
cpd; (*política*) agricultural, farming
cpd.

agravante [aɣra'βante] *adj* aggravating
♦ *nf* complication; **con la** ~ **de que ...**
with the further difficulty that ...

agravar [aɣra'βar] *vt* (*pesar sobre*) to make
heavier; (*irritar*) to aggravate; ~**se** *vr* to
worsen, get worse.

agraviar [aɣra'βjar] *vt* to offend; (*ser
injusto con*) to wrong; ~**se** *vr* to take
offence.

agravio [a'ɣraβjo] *nm* offence; wrong;

(JUR) grievance.

agraz [a'ɣraθ] nm (uva) sour grape; **en ~** (fig) immature.

agredir [aɣre'ðir] vt to attack.

agregado [aɣre'ɣaðo] nm aggregate; (persona) attaché; (profesor) assistant professor.

agregar [aɣre'ɣar] vt to gather; (añadir) to add; (persona) to appoint.

agregue [a'ɣreɣe] etc vb V **agregar**.

agresión [aɣre'sjon] nf aggression; (ataque) attack.

agresivo, a [aɣre'siβo, a] adj aggressive.

agreste [a'ɣreste] adj (rural) rural; (fig) rough.

agriar [a'ɣrjar] vt (fig) to (turn) sour; **~se** vr to turn sour.

agrícola [a'ɣrikola] adj farming cpd, agricultural.

agricultor, a [aɣrikul'tor, a] nm/f farmer.

agricultura [aɣrikul'tura] nf agriculture, farming.

agridulce [aɣri'ðulθe] adj bittersweet; (CULIN) sweet and sour.

agrietarse [aɣrje'tarse] vr to crack; (la piel) to chap.

agrimensor, a [aɣrimen'sor, a] nm/f surveyor.

agringado, a [aɣrin'gaðo, a] adj gringolike.

agrio, a ['aɣrjo, a] adj bitter.

agronomía [aɣrono'mia] nf agronomy, agriculture.

agrónomo, a [a'ɣronomo, a] nm/f agronomist, agricultural expert.

agropecuario, a [aɣrope'kwarjo, a] adj farming cpd, agricultural.

agrupación [aɣrupa'θjon] nf group; (acto) grouping.

agrupar [aɣru'par] vt to group; (INFORM) to block; **~se** vr (POL) to form a group; (juntarse) to gather.

agua ['aɣwa] nf water; (NAUT) wake; (ARQ) slope of a roof; **~s** nfpl (de joya) water sg, sparkle sg; (MED) water sg, urine sg; (NAUT) waters; **~s abajo/arriba** downstream/upstream; **~ bendita/ destilada/potable** holy/distilled/drinking water; **~ caliente** hot water; **~ corriente** running water; **~ de colonia** eau de cologne; **~ mineral (con/sin gas)** (fizzy/ non-fizzy) mineral water; **~s jurisdiccionales** territorial waters; **~s mayores** excrement sg; **~ pasada no mueve molino** it's no use crying over spilt milk; **estar con el ~ al cuello** to be up to one's neck; **venir como ~ de mayo** to be a godsend.

aguacate [aɣwa'kate] nm avocado (pear).

aguacero [aɣwa'θero] nm (heavy) shower, downpour.

aguachirle [aɣwa'tʃirle] nm (bebida) slops pl.

aguado, a [a'ɣwaðo, a] adj watery, watered down ♦ nf (AGR) watering place; (NAUT) water supply; (ARTE) watercolour.

aguafiestas [aɣwa'fjestas] nm/f inv spoilsport.

aguafuerte [aɣwa'fwerte] nf etching.

aguaitar [aɣwai'tar] vt (AM) to watch.

aguanieve [aɣwa'njeβe] nf sleet.

aguantable [aɣwan'taβle] adj bearable, tolerable.

aguantar [aɣwan'tar] vt to bear, put up with; (sostener) to hold up ♦ vi to last; **~se** vr to restrain o.s.; **no sé cómo aguanta** I don't know how he can take it.

aguante [a'ɣwante] nm (paciencia) patience; (resistencia) endurance; (DEPORTE) stamina.

aguar [a'ɣwar] vt to water down; (fig): **~ la fiesta a algn** to spoil sb's fun.

aguardar [aɣwar'ðar] vt to wait for.

aguardentoso, a [aɣwarðen'toso, a] adj (pey: voz) husky, gruff.

aguardiente [aɣwar'ðjente] nm brandy, liquor.

aguarrás [aɣwa'rras] nm turpentine.

aguce [a'ɣuθe] etc vb V **aguzar**.

agudeza [aɣu'ðeθa] nf sharpness; (ingenio) wit.

agudice [aɣu'ðiθe] etc vb V **agudizar**.

agudizar [aɣuði'θar] vt to sharpen; (crisis) to make worse; **~se** vr to worsen, deteriorate.

agudo, a [a'ɣuðo, a] adj sharp; (voz) high-pitched, piercing; (dolor, enfermedad) acute.

agüe ['aɣwe] etc vb V **aguar**.

agüero [a'ɣwero] nm: **buen/mal ~** good/ bad omen; **ser de buen ~** to augur well; **pájaro de mal ~** bird of ill omen.

aguerrido, a [aɣe'rriðo, a] hardened; (fig) experienced.

aguijar [aɣi'xar] vt to goad; (incitar) to urge on ♦ vi to hurry along.

aguijón [aɣi'xon] nm sting; (fig) spur.

aguijonear [aɣixone'ar] vt = **aguijar**.

águila ['aɣila] nf eagle; (fig) genius.

aguileño, a [aɣi'leɲo, a] adj (nariz) aquiline; (rostro) sharp-featured.

aguinaldo [aɣi'naldo] nm Christmas box.

aguja [a'ɣuxa] nf needle; (de reloj) hand; (ARQ) spire; (TEC) firing-pin; **~s** nfpl (ZOOL) ribs; (FERRO) points.

agujerear [aɣuxere'ar] *vt* to make holes in; (*penetrar*) to pierce.

agujero [aɣu'xero] *nm* hole; (*COM*) deficit.

agujetas [aɣu'xetas] *nfpl* stitch *sg*; (*rigidez*) stiffness *sg*.

aguzar [aɣu'θar] *vt* to sharpen; (*fig*) to incite; ~ **el oído** to prick up one's ears.

aherrumbrarse [aerrum'brarse] *vr* to get rusty.

ahí [a'i] *adv* there; (*allá*) over there; **de ~ que** so that, with the result that; ~ **llega** here he comes; **por ~** (*dirección*) that way; ¡**hasta ~ hemos llegado!** so it has come to this!; ¡~ **va!** (*objeto*) here it comes!; (*individuo*) there he goes!; ~ **donde le ve** as sure as he's standing there.

ahijado, a [ai'xaðo, a] *nm/f* godson/daughter.

ahijar [ai'xar] *vt*: ~ **algo a algn** (*fig*) to attribute sth to sb.

ahínco [a'inko] *nm* earnestness; **con ~** eagerly.

ahíto, a [a'ito, a] *adj*: **estoy ~** I'm full up.

ahogado, a [ao'ɣaðo, a] *adj* (*en agua*) drowned; (*emoción*) pent-up; (*grito*) muffled.

ahogar [ao'ɣar] *vt* (*en agua*) to drown; (*asfixiar*) to suffocate, smother; (*fuego*) to put out; ~**se** *vr* (*en agua*) to drown; (*por asfixia*) to suffocate.

ahogo [a'oɣo] *nm* (*MED*) breathlessness; (*fig*) distress; (*problema económico*) financial difficulty.

ahogue [a'oɣe] *etc vb V* **ahogar**.

ahondar [aon'dar] *vt* to deepen, make deeper; (*fig*) to go deeply into ♦ *vi*: ~ **en** to go deeply into.

ahora [a'ora] *adv* now; (*hace poco*) a moment ago, just now; (*dentro de poco*) in a moment; ~ **voy** I'm coming; ~ **mismo** right now; ~ **bien** now then; **por ~** for the present.

ahorcado, a [aor'kaðo, a] *nm/f* hanged person.

ahorcar [aor'kar] *vt* to hang; ~**se** *vr* to hang o.s.

ahorita [ao'rita], **ahoritita** [aori'tita] *adv* (*esp AM: fam*) right now.

ahorque [a'orke] *etc vb V* **ahorcar**.

ahorrar [ao'rrar] *vt* (*dinero*) to save; (*esfuerzos*) to save, avoid; ~**se** *vr*: ~**se molestias** to save o.s. trouble.

ahorrativo, a [aorra'tiβo, a] *adj* thrifty.

ahorro [a'orro] *nm* (*acto*) saving; (*frugalidad*) thrift; ~**s** *nmpl* savings.

ahuecar [awe'kar] *vt* to hollow (out); (*voz*) to deepen ♦ *vi*: ¡**ahueca!** (*fam*) beat it!

(*fam*); ~**se** *vr* to give o.s. airs.

ahueque [a'weke] *etc vb V* **ahuecar**.

ahumar [au'mar] *vt* to smoke, cure; (*llenar de humo*) to fill with smoke ♦ *vi* to smoke; ~**se** *vr* to fill with smoke.

ahuyentar [aujen'tar] *vt* to drive off, frighten off; (*fig*) to dispel.

AI *nf abr* (= *Amnistía Internacional*) AI.

aimara [ai'mara], **aimará** [aima'ra] *adj, nm/f* Aymara.

aindiado, a [aindi'aðo, a] *adj* (*AM*) Indian-like.

airado, a [ai'raðo, a] *adj* angry.

airar [ai'rar] *vt* to anger; ~**se** *vr* to get angry.

aire ['aire] *nm* air; (*viento*) wind; (*corriente*) draught; (*MUS*) tune; ~**s** *nmpl*: **darse ~s** to give o.s. airs; **al ~ libre** in the open air; ~ **acondicionado** air conditioning; **tener ~ de** to look like; **estar de buen/mal ~** to be in a good/bad mood; **estar en el ~** (*RADIO*) to be on the air; (*fig*) to be up in the air.

airear [aire'ar] *vt* to ventilate; (*fig: asunto*) to air; ~**se** *vr* to take the air.

airoso, a [ai'roso, a] *adj* windy; draughty; (*fig*) graceful.

aislado, a [ais'laðo, a] *adj* (*remoto*) isolated; (*incomunicado*) cut off; (*ELEC*) insulated.

aislante [ais'lante] *nm* (*ELEC*) insulator.

aislar [ais'lar] *vt* to isolate; (*ELEC*) to insulate; ~**se** *vr* to cut o.s. off.

ajar [a'xar] *vt* to spoil; (*fig*) to abuse; ~**se** *vr* to get crumpled; (*fig: piel*) to get wrinkled.

ajardinado, a [axarði'naðo, a] *adj* landscaped.

ajedrez [axe'ðreθ] *nm* chess.

ajenjo [a'xenxo] *nm* (*bebida*) absinth(e).

ajeno, a [a'xeno, a] *adj* (*que pertenece a otro*) somebody else's; ~ **a** foreign to; ~ **de** free from, devoid of; **por razones ajenas a nuestra voluntad** for reasons beyond our control.

ajetreado, a [axetre'aðo, a] *adj* busy.

ajetrearse [axetre'arse] *vr* (*atarearse*) to bustle about; (*fatigarse*) to tire o.s. out.

ajetreo [axe'treo] *nm* bustle.

ají [a'xi] *nm* chil(l)i, red pepper; (*salsa*) chil(l)i sauce.

ajiaco [axi'ako] *nm* (*AM*) potato and chil(l)i stew.

ajilimoje [axili'moxe] *nm* sauce of garlic and pepper; ~**s** *nmpl* (*fam*) odds and ends.

ajo ['axo] *nm* garlic; ~ **porro** *o* **puerro** leek; (**tieso**) **como un ~** (*fam*) snobbish; **estar**

en el ~ to be mixed up in it.
ajorca [a'xorka] *nf* bracelet.
ajuar [a'xwar] *nm* household furnishings
pl; (*de novia*) trousseau; (*de niño*) layette.
ajustado, a [axus'taðo, a] *adj* (*tornillo*)
tight; (*cálculo*) right; (*ropa*) tight(-
fitting); (*DEPORTE: resultado*) close.
ajustar [axus'tar] *vt* (*adaptar*) to adjust;
(*encajar*) to fit; (*TEC*) to engage; (*TIP*) to
make up; (*apretar*) to tighten; (*concertar*)
to agree (on); (*reconciliar*) to reconcile;
(*cuenta*) to settle ♦ *vi* to fit.
ajuste [a'xuste] *nm* adjustment; (*COSTURA*)
fitting; (*acuerdo*) compromise; (*de
cuenta*) settlement; (*INFORM*) patch.
al [al] = **a + el**; *V* **a**.
ala ['ala] *nf* wing; (*de sombrero*) brim;
(*futbolista*) winger; ~ **delta** hang-glider;
andar con el ~ **caída** to be downcast;
cortar las ~**s a algn** to clip sb's wings;
dar ~ **a algn** to encourage sb.
alabanza [ala'ßanθa] *nf* praise.
alabar [ala'ßar] *vt* to praise.
alacena [ala'θena] *nf* cupboard (*BRIT*),
closet (*US*).
alacrán [ala'kran] *nm* scorpion.
ALADI [a'laði] *nf abr* = *Asociación
Latinoamericana de Integración*.
alado, a [a'laðo, a] *adj* winged.
ALALC [a'lalk] *nf abr* (= *Asociación
Latinoamericana de Libre Comercio*)
LAFTA.
alambicado, a [alambi'kaðo, a] *adj*
distilled; (*fig*) affected.
alambicar [alambi'kar] *vt* to distil.
alambique [alam'bike] *etc vb V* **alambicar**
♦ *nm* still.
alambrada [alam'braða] *nf*, **alambrado**
[alam'braðo] *nm* wire fence; (*red*) wire
netting.
alambre [a'lambre] *nm* wire; ~ **de púas**
barbed wire.
alambrista [alam'brista] *nm/f* tightrope
walker.
alameda [ala'meða] *nf* (*plantío*) poplar
grove; (*lugar de paseo*) avenue,
boulevard.
álamo ['alamo] *nm* poplar; ~ **temblón**
aspen.
alano [a'lano] *nm* mastiff.
alarde [a'larðe] *nm* show, display; **hacer** ~
de to boast of.
alardear [alarðe'ar] *vi* to boast.
alargador [alarɣa'ðor] *nm* extension cable
o lead.
alargar [alar'ɣar] *vt* to lengthen, extend;
(*paso*) to hasten; (*brazo*) to stretch out;
(*cuerda*) to pay out; (*conversación*) to spin

out; ~**se** *vr* to get longer.
alargue [a'larɣe] *etc vb V* **alargar**.
alarido [ala'riðo] *nm* shriek.
alarma [a'larma] *nf* alarm; **voz de** ~
warning note; **dar la** ~ to raise the
alarm.
alarmante [alar'mante] *adj* alarming.
alarmar [alar'mar] *vt* to alarm; ~**se** *vr* to
get alarmed.
alavés, esa [ala'ßes, esa] *adj* of Álava
♦ *nm/f* native *o* inhabitant of Álava.
alazán [ala'θan] *nm* sorrel.
alba ['alßa] *nf* dawn.
albacea [alßa'θea] *nm/f* executor/executrix.
albaceteño, a [alßaθe'teɲo, a] *adj* of
Albacete ♦ *nm/f* native *o* inhabitant of
Albacete.
albahaca [al'ßaka] *nf* (*BOT*) basil.
Albania [al'ßanja] *nf* Albania.
albañal [alßa'ɲal] *nm* drain, sewer.
albañil [alßa'ɲil] *nm* bricklayer; (*cantero*)
mason.
albarán [alßa'ran] *nm* (*COM*) invoice.
albarda [al'ßarða] *nf* packsaddle.
albaricoque [alßari'koke] *nm* apricot.
albedrío [alße'ðrio] *nm*: **libre** ~ free will.
alberca [al'ßerka] *nf* reservoir; (*AM*)
swimming pool.
albergar [alßer'ɣar] *vt* to shelter;
(*esperanza*) to cherish; ~**se** *vr* (*refugiarse*)
to shelter; (*alojarse*) to lodge.
albergue [al'ßerɣe] *etc vb V* **albergar** ♦ *nm*
shelter, refuge; ~ **de juventud** youth
hostel.
albis ['alßis] *adv*: **quedarse en** ~ not to
have a clue.
albóndiga [al'ßondiɣa] *nf* meatball.
albor [al'ßor] *nm* whiteness; (*amanecer*)
dawn.
alborada [alßo'raða] *nf* dawn; (*diana*)
reveille.
alborear [alßore'ar] *vi* to dawn.
albornoz [alßor'noθ] *nm* (*de los árabes*)
burnous; (*para el baño*) bathrobe.
alboroce [alßo'roθe] *etc vb V* **alborozar**.
alborotar [alßoro'tar] *vi* to make a row ♦ *vt*
to agitate, stir up; ~**se** *vr* to get excited;
(*mar*) to get rough.
alboroto [alßo'roto] *nm* row, uproar.
alborozar [alßoro'θar] *vt* to gladden; ~**se** *vr*
to rejoice, be overjoyed.
alborozo [alßo'roθo] *nm* joy.
albricias [al'ßriθjas] *nfpl*: ¡~! good news!
álbum, *pl* **álbums** *o* **álbumes** ['alßum] *nm*
album.
albumen [al'ßumen] *nm* egg white,
albumen.
alcabala [alka'ßala] *nf* (*AM*) roadblock.

alcachofa [alka'tʃofa] *nf* (globe) artichoke; (*TIP*) golf ball; (*de ducha*) shower head.
alcahueta [alka'weta] *nf* procuress.
alcahuete [alka'wete] *nm* pimp.
alcalde, esa [al'kalde, alkal'desa] *nm/f* mayor(ess).
alcaldía [alkal'dia] *nf* mayoralty; (*lugar*) mayor's office.
álcali ['alkali] *nm* (*QUÍMICA*) alkali.
alcance [al'kanθe] *etc vb* V **alcanzar** ♦ *nm* (*MIL, RADIO*) range; (*fig*) scope; (*COM*) adverse balance, deficit; **estar al/fuera del ~ de algn** to be within/beyond one's reach; (*fig*) to be within one's powers/over one's head; **de gran ~** (*MIL*) long-range; (*fig*) far-reaching.
alcancía [alkan'θia] *nf* money box.
alcanfor [alkan'for] *nm* camphor.
alcantarilla [alkanta'riʎa] *nf* (*de aguas cloacales*) sewer; (*en la calle*) gutter.
alcanzar [alkan'θar] *vt* (*algo: con la mano, el pie*) to reach; (*alguien: en el camino etc*) to catch up (with); (*autobús*) to catch; (*suj: bala*) to hit, strike ♦ *vi* (*ser suficiente*) to be enough; **~ algo a algn** to hand sth to sb; **alcánzame la sal, por favor** pass the salt please; **~ a hacer** to manage to do.
alcaparra [alka'parra] *nf* (*BOT*) caper.
alcatraz [alka'traθ] *nm* gannet.
alcayata [alka'jata] *nf* hook.
alcázar [al'kaθar] *nm* fortress; (*NAUT*) quarter-deck.
alce ['alθe] *etc vb* V **alzar**.
alcista [al'θista] *adj* (*COM, ECON*): **mercado ~** bull market; **la tendencia ~** the upward trend ♦ *nm* speculator.
alcoba [al'koβa] *nf* bedroom.
alcohol [al'kol] *nm* alcohol; **no bebe ~** he doesn't drink (alcohol).
alcoholemia [alkoo'lemia] *nf* blood alcohol level; **prueba de la ~** breath test.
alcoholice [alko'liθe] *etc vb* V **alcoholizarse**.
alcohólico, a [al'koliko, a] *adj, nm/f* alcoholic.
alcoholímetro [alko'limetro] *nm* Breathalyser ®, drunkometer (*US*).
alcoholismo [alko'lismo] *nm* alcoholism.
alcoholizarse [alkoli'θarse] *vr* to become an alcoholic.
alcornoque [alkor'noke] *nm* cork tree; (*fam*) idiot.
alcotana [alko'tana] *nf* pickaxe; (*DEPORTE*) ice-axe.
alcurnia [al'kurnja] *nf* lineage.
alcuza [al'kusa] *nf* (*AM*) cruet.
aldaba [al'daβa] *nf* (door) knocker.
aldea [al'dea] *nf* village.

aldeano, a [alde'ano, a] *adj* village *cpd* ♦ *nm/f* villager.
ale ['ale] *excl* come on!, let's go!
aleación [alea'θjon] *nf* alloy.
aleatorio, a [alea'torjo, a] *adj* random, contingent; **acceso ~** (*INFORM*) random access.
aleccionador, a [alekθjona'ðor, a] *adj* instructive.
aleccionar [alekθjo'nar] *vt* to instruct; (*adiestrar*) to train.
aledaño, a [ale'ðaɲo, a] *adj*: **~ a** bordering on ♦ *nmpl* outskirts.
alegación [aleɣa'θjon] *nf* allegation.
alegar [ale'ɣar] *vt* (*dificultad etc*) to plead; (*JUR*) to allege ♦ *vi* (*AM*) to argue; **~ que** ... to give as an excuse that ...
alegato [ale'ɣato] *nm* (*JUR*) allegation; (*escrito*) indictment; (*declaración*) statement; (*AM*) argument.
alegoría [aleɣo'ria] *nf* allegory.
alegrar [ale'ɣrar] *vt* (*causar alegría*) to cheer (up); (*fuego*) to poke; (*fiesta*) to liven up; **~se** *vr* (*fam*) to get merry *o* tight; **~se de** to be glad about.
alegre [a'leɣre] *adj* happy, cheerful; (*fam*) merry, tight; (*licencioso*) risqué, blue.
alegría [ale'ɣria] *nf* happiness; merriment; **~ vital** joie de vivre.
alegrón [ale'ɣron] *nm* (*fig*) sudden joy.
alegue [a'leɣe] *etc vb* V **alegar**.
alejamiento [alexa'mjento] *nm* removal; (*distancia*) remoteness.
alejar [ale'xar] *vt* to move away, remove; (*fig*) to estrange; **~se** *vr* to move away.
alelado, a [ale'laðo, a] *adj* (*bobo*) foolish.
alelar [ale'lar] *vt* to bewilder.
aleluya [ale'luja] *nm* (*canto*) hallelujah.
alemán, ana [ale'man, ana] *adj, nm/f* German ♦ *nm* (*lengua*) German.
Alemania [ale'manja] *nf* Germany; **~ Occidental/Oriental** West/East Germany.
alentador, a [alenta'ðor, a] *adj* encouraging.
alentar [alen'tar] *vt* to encourage.
alergia [a'lerxja] *nf* allergy.
alero [a'lero] *nm* (*de tejado*) eaves *pl*; (*de foca, DEPORTE*) flipper; (*AUTO*) mudguard.
alerta [a'lerta] *adj inv, nm* alert.
aleta [a'leta] *nf* (*de pez*) fin; (*de ave*) wing; (*de coche*) mudguard.
aletargar [aletar'ɣar] *vt* to make drowsy; (*entumecer*) to make numb; **~se** *vr* to grow drowsy; to become numb.
aletargue [ale'tarɣe] *etc vb* V **aletargar**.
aletear [alete'ar] *vi* to flutter; (*ave*) to flap its wings; (*individuo*) to wave one's arms.

alevín [ale'βin] nm fry, young fish.
alevosía [aleβo'sia] nf treachery.
alfabetización [alfaβetiθa'θjon] nf:
campaña de ~ literacy campaign.
alfabeto [alfa'βeto] nm alphabet.
alfajor [alfa'xor] nm (ESP: polvorón) cake
eaten at Christmas time.
alfalfa [al'falfa] nf alfalfa, lucerne.
alfaque [al'fake] nm (NAUT) bar, sandbank.
alfar [al'far] nm (taller) potter's workshop;
(arcilla) clay.
alfarería [alfare'ria] nf pottery; (tienda)
pottery shop.
alfarero [alfa'rero] nm potter.
alféizar [al'feiθar] nm window-sill.
alférez [al'fereθ] nm (MIL) second
lieutenant; (NAUT) ensign.
alfil [al'fil] nm (AJEDREZ) bishop.
alfiler [alfi'ler] nm pin; (broche) clip; (pinza)
clothes peg (BRIT) o pin (US); ~ de
gancho (AM) safety pin; prendido con
~es shaky.
alfiletero [alfile'tero] nm needle case.
alfombra [al'fombra] nf carpet; (más
pequeña) rug.
alfombrar [alfom'brar] vt to carpet.
alfombrilla [alfom'briʎa] nf rug, mat.
alforja [al'forxa] nf saddlebag.
alforza [al'forθa] nf pleat.
algarabía [alɣara'βia] nf (fam) gibberish;
(griterío) hullabaloo.
algarada [alɣa'raða] nf outcry; hacer o
levantar una ~ to kick up a tremendous
fuss.
Algarbe [al'ɣarβe] nm: el ~ the Algarve.
algarroba [alɣa'rroβa] nf carob.
algarrobo [alɣa'rroβo] nm carob tree.
algas ['alɣas] nfpl seaweed sg.
algazara [alɣa'θara] nf din, uproar.
álgebra ['alxeβra] nf algebra.
álgido, a ['alxiðo, a] adj icy; (momento etc)
crucial, decisive.
algo ['alɣo] pron something; (en frases
interrogativas) anything ♦ adv somewhat,
rather; por ~ será there must be some
reason for it; es ~ difícil it's a bit
awkward.
algodón [alɣo'ðon] nm cotton; (planta)
cotton plant; ~ de azúcar candy floss
(BRIT), cotton candy (US); ~ hidrófilo
cotton wool (BRIT), absorbent cotton
(US).
algodonero, a [alɣoðo'nero, a] adj cotton
cpd ♦ nm/f cotton grower ♦ nm cotton
plant.
algoritmo [alɣo'ritmo] nm algorithm.
alguacil [alɣwa'θil] nm bailiff; (TAUR)
mounted official.

alguien ['alɣjen] pron someone, somebody;
(en frases interrogativas) anybody.
alguno, a [al'ɣuno, a] adj (delante de nm:
algún) some; (después de n): no tiene
talento alguno he has no talent, he
hasn't any talent ♦ pron (alguien)
someone, somebody; algún que otro
libro some book or other; algún día iré
I'll go one o some day; sin interés alguno
without the slightest interest; alguno
que otro an occasional one; algunos
piensan some (people) think; alguno de
ellos one of them.
alhaja [a'laxa] nf jewel; (tesoro) precious
object, treasure.
alhelí [ale'li] nm wallflower, stock.
aliado, a [a'ljaðo, a] adj allied.
alianza [a'ljanθa] nf (POL etc) alliance;
(anillo) wedding ring.
aliar [a'ljar] vt to ally; ~se vr to form an
alliance.
alias ['aljas] adv alias.
alicaído, a [alika'iðo, a] adj (MED) weak;
(fig) depressed.
alicantino, a [alikan'tino, a] adj of Alicante
♦ nm/f native o inhabitant of Alicante.
alicatar [alika'tar] vt to tile.
alicate(s) [ali'kate(s)] nm(pl) pliers pl; ~ de
uñas nail clippers.
aliciente [ali'θjente] nm incentive;
(atracción) attraction.
alienación [aljena'θjon] nf alienation.
aliento [a'ljento] etc vb V alentar ♦ nm
breath; (respiración) breathing; sin ~
breathless; de un ~ in one breath; (fig)
in one go.
aligerar [alixe'rar] vt to lighten; (reducir) to
shorten; (aliviar) to alleviate; (mitigar) to
ease.
alijo [a'lixo] nm (NAUT) unloading;
(contrabando) smuggled goods.
alimaña [ali'maɲa] nf pest.
alimentación [alimenta'θjon] nf (comida)
food; (acción) feeding; (tienda) grocer's
(shop); ~ continua (en fotocopiador etc)
stream feed.
alimentador [alimenta'ðor] nm: ~ de papel
sheet-feeder.
alimentar [alimen'tar] vt to feed; (nutrir) to
nourish; ~se vr: ~se (de) to feed (on).
alimenticio, a [alimen'tiθjo, a] adj food cpd;
(nutritivo) nourishing, nutritious.
alimento [ali'mento] nm food; (nutrición)
nourishment; ~s nmpl (JUR) alimony sg.
alimón [ali'mon]: al ~ adv jointly,
together.
alineación [alinea'θjon] nf alignment;
(DEPORTE) line-up.

alineado, a [aline'aðo, a] adj (TIP): **(no)** ~ (un)justified; ~ **a la izquierda/derecha** ranged left/right.

alinear [aline'ar] vt to align; (TIP) to justify; ~**se** vr to line up; ~**se en** to fall in with.

aliñar [ali'ɲar] vt (CULIN) to dress.

aliño [a'liɲo] nm (CULIN) dressing.

alisar [ali'sar] vt to smooth.

aliso [a'liso] nm alder.

alistamiento [alista'mjento] nm recruitment.

alistar [ali'star] vt to recruit; ~**se** vr to enlist; (inscribirse) to enrol; (AM: prepararse) to get ready.

aliviar [ali'βjar] vt (carga) to lighten; (persona) to relieve; (dolor) to relieve, alleviate.

alivio [a'liβjo] nm alleviation, relief; ~ **de luto** half-mourning.

aljibe [al'xiβe] nm cistern.

allá [a'ʎa] adv (lugar) there; (por ahí) over there; (tiempo) then; ~ **abajo** down there; **más** ~ further on; **más** ~ **de** beyond; **¡**~ **tú!** that's your problem!

allanamiento [aʎana'mjento] nm (AM POLICÍA) raid, search; ~ **de morada** housebreaking.

allanar [aʎa'nar] vt to flatten, level (out); (igualar) to smooth (out); (fig) to subdue; (JUR) to burgle, break into; (AM POLICÍA) to raid, search; ~**se** vr to fall down; ~**se a** to submit to, accept.

allegado, a [aʎe'ɣaðo, a] adj near, close ♦ nm/f relation.

allende [a'ʎende] adv on the other side ♦ prep: ~ **los mares** beyond the seas.

allí [a'ʎi] adv there; ~ **mismo** right there; **por** ~ over there; (por ese camino) that way.

alma ['alma] nf soul; (persona) person; (TEC) core; **se le cayó el** ~ **a los pies** he became very disheartened; **entregar el** ~ to pass away; **estar con el** ~ **en la boca** to be scared to death; **lo siento en el** ~ I am truly sorry; **tener el** ~ **en un hilo** to have one's heart in one's mouth; **estar como** ~ **en pena** to suffer; **ir como** ~ **que lleva el diablo** to go at breakneck speed.

almacén [alma'θen] nm (depósito) warehouse, store; (MIL) magazine; (AM) grocer's shop, foodstore, grocery store (US); (grandes) **almacenes** nmpl department store sg; ~ **depositario** (COM) depository.

almacenaje [almaθe'naxe] nm storage; ~ **secundario** (INFORM) backing storage.

almacenamiento [almaθena'mjento] nm (INFORM) storage; ~ **temporal en disco** disk spooling.

almacenar [almaθe'nar] vt to store, put in storage; (INFORM) to store; (proveerse) to stock up with.

almacenero [almaθe'nero] nm warehouseman; (AM) grocer, shopkeeper.

almanaque [alma'nake] nm almanac.

almeja [al'mexa] nf clam.

almenas [al'menas] nfpl battlements.

almendra [al'mendra] nf almond.

almendro [al'mendro] nm almond tree.

almeriense [alme'rjense] adj of Almería. ♦ nm/f native o inhabitant of Almería.

almiar [al'mjar] nm haystack.

almíbar [al'miβar] nm syrup.

almidón [almi'ðon] nm starch.

almidonado, a [almiðo'naðo, a] adj starched.

almidonar [almiðo'nar] vt to starch.

almirantazgo [almiran'taθɣo] nm admiralty.

almirante [almi'rante] nm admiral.

almirez [almi'reθ] nm mortar.

almizcle [al'miθkle] nm musk.

almizclero [almiθ'klero] nm musk deer.

almohada [almo'aða] nf pillow; (funda) pillowcase.

almohadilla [almoa'ðiʎa] nf cushion; (TEC) pad; (AM) pincushion.

almohadillado, a [almoaði'ʎaðo, a] adj (acolchado) padded.

almohadón [almoa'ðon] nm large pillow.

almorcé [almor'θe], **almorcemos** [almor'θemos] etc vb V **almorzar**.

almorranas [almo'rranas] nfpl piles, haemorrhoids (BRIT), hemorrhoids (US).

almorzar [almor'θar] vt: ~ **una tortilla** to have an omelette for lunch ♦ vi to (have) lunch.

almuerce [al'mwerθe] etc vb V **almorzar**.

almuerzo [al'mwerθo] etc vb V **almorzar** ♦ nm lunch.

aló [a'lo] excl (esp AM TELEC) hello!

alocado, a [alo'kaðo, a] adj crazy.

alojamiento [aloxa'mjento] nf lodging(s) (pl); (viviendas) housing.

alojar [alo'xar] vt to lodge; ~**se en** to stay at; (bala) to lodge in.

alondra [a'londra] nf lark, skylark.

alpaca [al'paka] nf alpaca.

alpargata [alpar'ɣata] nf espadrille.

Alpes ['alpes] nmpl: **los** ~ the Alps.

alpinismo [alpi'nismo] nm mountaineering, climbing.

alpinista [alpi'nista] nm/f mountaineer, climber.

alpino, a [al'pino, a] *adj* alpine.
alpiste [al'piste] *nm* (*semillas*) birdseed; (*AM fam*: *dinero*) dough; (*fam*: *alcohol*) booze.
alquería [alke'ria] *nf* farmhouse.
alquilar [alki'lar] *vt* (*suj*: *propietario*: *inmuebles*) to let, rent (out); (: *coche*) to hire out; (: *TV*) to rent (out); (*suj*: *alquilador*: *inmuebles, TV*) to rent; (: *coche*) to hire; "*se alquila casa*" "house to let (*BRIT*) o to rent (*US*)".
alquiler [alki'ler] *nm* renting, letting; hiring; (*arriendo*) rent; hire charge; **de ~** for hire; **~ de automóviles** car hire.
alquimia [al'kimja] *nf* alchemy.
alquitrán [alki'tran] *nm* tar.
alrededor [alreðe'ðor] *adv* around, about; **~es** *nmpl* surroundings; **~ de** *prep* around, about; **mirar a su ~** to look (round) about one.
Alsacia [al'saθja] *nf* Alsace.
alta ['alta] *nf* (certificate of) discharge; **dar a algn de ~** to discharge sb; **darse de ~** (*MIL*) to join, enrol; (*DEPORTE*) to declare o.s. fit.
altanería [altane'ria] *nf* haughtiness, arrogance.
altanero, a [alta'nero, a] *adj* haughty, arrogant.
altar [al'tar] *nm* altar.
altavoz [alta'βoθ] *nm* loudspeaker; (*amplificador*) amplifier.
alteración [altera'θjon] *nf* alteration; (*alboroto*) disturbance; **~ del orden público** breach of the peace.
alterar [alte'rar] *vt* to alter; to disturb; **~se** *vr* (*persona*) to get upset.
altercado [alter'kaðo] *nm* argument.
alternar [alter'nar] *vt* to alternate ♦ *vi*, **~se** *vr* to alternate; (*turnar*) to take turns; **~ con** to mix with.
alternativo, a [alterna'tiβo, a] *adj* alternative; (*alterno*) alternating ♦ *nf* alternative; (*elección*) choice; **alternativas** *nfpl* ups and downs; **tomar la alternativa** (*TAUR*) to become a fully-qualified bullfighter.
alterno, a [al'terno, a] *adj* (*BOT, MAT*) alternate; (*ELEC*) alternating.
alteza [al'teθa] *nf* (*tratamiento*) highness.
altibajos [alti'βaxos] *nmpl* ups and downs.
altillo [al'tiʎo] *nm* (*GEO*) small hill; (*AM*) attic.
altiplanicie [altipla'niθje] *nf*, **altiplano** [alti'plano] *nm* high plateau.
altisonante [altiso'nante] *adj* high-flown, high-sounding.
altitud [alti'tuð] *nf* altitude, height; **a una**

~ de at a height of.
altivez [alti'βeθ] *nf* haughtiness, arrogance.
altivo, a [al'tiβo, a] *adj* haughty, arrogant.
alto, a ['alto, a] *adj* high; (*persona*) tall; (*sonido*) high, sharp; (*noble*) high, lofty; (*GEO, clase*) upper ♦ *nm* halt; (*MUS*) alto; (*GEO*) hill; (*AM*) pile ♦ *adv* (*estar*) high; (*hablar*) loud, loudly ♦ *excl* halt!; **la pared tiene 2 metros de ~** the wall is 2 metres high; **en alta mar** on the high seas; **en voz alta** in a loud voice; **las altas horas de la noche** the small (*BRIT*) o wee (*US*) hours; **en lo ~ de** at the top of; **pasar por ~** to overlook; **~s y bajos** ups and downs; **poner la radio más ~** to turn the radio up; **¡más ~, por favor!** louder, please!
altoparlante [altopar'lante] *nm* (*AM*) loudspeaker.
altramuz [altra'muθ] *nm* lupin.
altruismo [al'truismo] *nm* altruism.
altura [al'tura] *nf* height; (*NAUT*) depth; (*GEO*) latitude; **la pared tiene 1.80 de ~** the wall is 1 metre 80 (cm) high; **a esta ~ del año** at this time of the year; **estar a la ~ de las circunstancias** to rise to the occasion; **ha sido un partido de gran ~** it has been a terrific match.
alubia [a'luβja] *nf* French bean, kidney bean.
alucinación [aluθina'θjon] *nf* hallucination.
alucinante [aluθi'nante] *adj* (*fam*: *estupendo*) great, super.
alucinar [aluθi'nar] *vi* to hallucinate ♦ *vt* to deceive; (*fascinar*) to fascinate.
alud [a'luð] *nm* avalanche; (*fig*) flood.
aludir [alu'ðir] *vi*: **~ a** to allude to; **darse por aludido** to take the hint; **no te des por aludido** don't take it personally.
alumbrado [alum'braðo] *nm* lighting.
alumbramiento [alumbra'mjento] *nm* lighting; (*MED*) childbirth, delivery.
alumbrar [alum'brar] *vt* to light (up) ♦ *vi* (*iluminar*) to give light; (*MED*) to give birth.
aluminio [alu'minjo] *nm* aluminium (*BRIT*), aluminum (*US*).
alumnado [alum'naðo] *nm* (*UNIV*) student body; (*ESCOL*) pupils *pl*.
alumno, a [a'lumno, a] *nm/f* pupil, student.
alunice [alu'niθe] *etc vb V* **alunizar**.
alunizar [aluni'θar] *vi* to land on the moon.
alusión [alu'sjon] *nf* allusion.
alusivo, a [alu'siβo, a] *adj* allusive.
aluvión [alu'βjon] *nm* (*GEO*) alluvium; (*fig*) flood; **~ de improperios** torrent of abuse.
alvéolo [al'βeolo] *nm* (*ANAT*) alveolus; (*fig*)

network.

alza ['alθa] *nf* rise; (*MIL*) sight; ~**s fijas/
graduables** fixed/adjustable sights; **al** *o*
en ~ (*precio*) rising; **jugar al** ~ to
speculate on a rising *o* bull market;
cotizarse *o* **estar en** ~ to be rising.

alzado, a [al'θaðo, a] *adj* (*gen*) raised;
(*COM: precio*) fixed; (: *quiebra*) fradulent;
por un tanto ~ for a lump sum ♦ *nf* (*de
caballos*) height; (*JUR*) appeal.

alzamiento [alθa'mjento] *nm* (*aumento*)
rise, increase; (*acción*) lifting, raising;
(*mejor postura*) higher bid; (*rebelión*)
rising; (*COM*) fraudulent bankruptcy.

alzar [al'θar] *vt* to lift (up); (*precio, muro*) to
raise; (*cuello de abrigo*) to turn up; (*AGR*)
to gather in; (*TIP*) to gather; ~**se** *vr* to get
up, rise; (*rebelarse*) to revolt; (*COM*) to go
fraudulently bankrupt; (*JUR*) to appeal;
~**se con el premio** to carry off the prize.

a.m. *abr* (*AM*: = *ante meridiem*) a.m.

ama ['ama] *nf* lady of the house; (*dueña*)
owner; (*institutriz*) governess; (*madre
adoptiva*) foster mother; ~ **de casa**
housewife; ~ **de cría** *o* **de leche** wet-
nurse; ~ **de llaves** housekeeper.

amabilidad [amaβili'ðað] *nf* kindness;
(*simpatía*) niceness.

amabilísimo, a [amaβi'lisimo, a] *adj
superlativo de* **amable**.

amable [a'maβle] *adj* kind; nice.

amaestrado, a [amaes'traðo, a] *adj*
(*animal*) trained; (: *en circo etc*)
performing.

amaestrar [amaes'trar] *vt* to train.

amagar [ama'ɣar] *vt, vi* to threaten.

amago [a'maɣo] *nm* threat; (*gesto*)
threatening gesture; (*MED*) symptom.

amague [a'maɣe] *etc vb V* **amagar**.

amainar [amai'nar] *vt* (*NAUT*) to lower,
take in; (*fig*) to calm ♦ *vi*, ~**se** *vr* to drop,
die down; **el viento amaina** the wind is
dropping.

amalgama [amal'ɣama] *nf* amalgam.

amalgamar [amalɣa'mar] *vt* to
amalgamate; (*combinar*) to combine,
mix.

amamantar [amaman'tar] *vt* to suckle,
nurse.

amancebarse [amanθe'βarse] *vr* (*pareja*) to
live together.

amanecer [amane'θer] *vi* to dawn; (*fig*) to
appear, begin to show ♦ *nm* dawn; **el niño
amaneció afiebrado** the child woke up
with a fever.

amanerado, a [amane'raðo, a] *adj*
affected.

amanezca [ama'neθka] *etc vb V* **amanecer**.

amansar [aman'sar] *vt* to tame; (*persona*)
to subdue; ~**se** *vr* (*persona*) to calm
down.

amante [a'mante] *adj*: ~ **de** fond of ♦ *nm/f*
lover.

amanuense [ama'nwense] *nm* (*escribiente*)
scribe; (*copista*) copyist; (*POL*) secretary.

amañar [ama'ɲar] *vt* (*gen*) to do skilfully;
(*pey: resultado*) to alter.

amaño [a'maɲo] *nm* (*habilidad*) skill; ~**s**
nmpl (*TEC*) tools; (*fig*) tricks.

amapola [ama'pola] *nf* poppy.

amar [a'mar] *vt* to love.

amargado, a [amar'ɣaðo, a] *adj* bitter;
embittered.

amargar [amar'ɣar] *vt* to make bitter; (*fig*)
to embitter; ~**se** *vr* to become
embittered.

amargo, a [a'marɣo, a] *adj* bitter.

amargor [amar'ɣor] *nm* (*sabor*) bitterness;
(*fig*) grief.

amargue [a'marɣe] *etc vb V* **amargar**.

amargura [amar'ɣura] *nf* = **amargor**.

amarillento, a [amari'ʎento, a] *adj*
yellowish; (*tez*) sallow.

amarillismo [amari'ʎismo] *nm* (*de prensa*)
sensationalist journalism.

amarillo, a [ama'riʎo, a] *adj, nm* yellow.

amarra [a'marra] *nf* (*NAUT*) mooring line;
~**s** *nfpl* (*fig*) protection *sg*; **tener buenas**
~**s** to have good connections; **soltar** ~**s**
to set off.

amarrar [ama'rrar] *vt* to moor; (*sujetar*) to
tie up.

amartillar [amarti'ʎar] *vt* (*fusil*) to cock.

amasar [ama'sar] *vt* to knead; (*mezclar*) to
mix, prepare; (*confeccionar*) to concoct.

amasijo [ama'sixo] *nm* kneading; mixing;
(*fig*) hotchpotch.

amateur ['amatur] *nm/f* amateur.

amatista [ama'tista] *nf* amethyst.

amazacotado, a [amaθako'taðo, a] *adj*
(*terreno, arroz etc*) lumpy.

amazona [ama'θona] *nf* horsewoman.

Amazonas [ama'θonas] *nm*: **el (Río)** ~ the
Amazon.

ambages [am'baxes] *nmpl*: **sin** ~ in plain
language.

ámbar ['ambar] *nm* amber.

Amberes [am'beres] *nm* Antwerp.

ambición [ambi'θjon] *nf* ambition.

ambicionar [ambiθjo'nar] *vt* to aspire to.

ambicioso, a [ambi'θjoso, a] *adj*
ambitious.

ambidextro, a [ambi'ðekstro, a] *adj*
ambidextrous.

ambientación [ambjenta'θjon] *nf* (*CINE, LIT
etc*) setting; (*RADIO etc*) sound effects *pl*.

ambientador [ambjenta'ðor] *nm* air freshener.

ambientar [ambjen'tar] *vt* (*gen*) to give an atmosphere to; (*LIT etc*) to set.

ambiente [am'bjente] *nm* (*tb fig*) atmosphere; (*medio*) environment; (*AM*) room.

ambigüedad [ambiɣwe'ðað] *nf* ambiguity.

ambiguo, a [am'biɣwo, a] *adj* ambiguous.

ámbito ['ambito] *nm* (*campo*) field; (*fig*) scope.

ambos, as ['ambos, as] *adj pl, pron pl* both.

ambulancia [ambu'lanθja] *nf* ambulance.

ambulante [ambu'lante] *adj* travelling, itinerant; (*biblioteca*) mobile.

ambulatorio [ambula'torio] *nm* state health-service clinic.

ameba [a'meßa] *nf* amoeba.

amedrentar [ameðren'tar] *vt* to scare.

amén [a'men] *excl* amen; ~ **de** *prep* besides, in addition to; **en un decir** ~ in the twinkling of an eye; **decir** ~ **a todo** to have no mind of one's own.

amenace [ame'naθe] *etc vb V* **amenazar.**

amenaza [ame'naθa] *nf* threat.

amenazar [amena'θar] *vt* to threaten ♦ *vi*: ~ **con hacer** to threaten to do.

amenidad [ameni'ðað] *nf* pleasantness.

ameno, a [a'meno, a] *adj* pleasant.

América [a'merika] *nf* (*continente*) America, the Americas; (*EEUU*) America; (*Hispanoa~*) Latin *o* South America; ~ **del Norte/del Sur** North/South America; ~ **Central/Latina** Central/Latin America.

americanismo [amerika'nismo] *nm* Americanism.

americano, a [ameri'kano, a] *adj, nm/f* (*V América*) American; Latin *o* South American ♦ *nf* coat, jacket.

americe [ame'riθe] *etc vb V* **amerizar.**

amerindio, a [ame'rindjo, a] *adj, nm/f* Amerindian, American Indian

amerizaje [ameri'θaxe] *nm* (*AVIAT*) landing (on the sea).

amerizar [ameri'θar] *vi* (*AVIAT*) to land (on the sea).

ametralladora [ametraʎa'ðora] *nf* machine gun.

amianto [a'mjanto] *nm* asbestos.

amigable [ami'ɣaßle] *adj* friendly.

amígdala [a'miɣðala] *nf* tonsil.

amigdalitis [amiɣða'litis] *nf* tonsillitis.

amigo, a [a'miɣo, a] *adj* friendly ♦ *nm/f* friend; (*amante*) lover; ~ **de lo ajeno** thief; ~ **corresponsal** penfriend; **hacerse** ~**s** to become friends; **ser** ~ **de** to like, be fond of; **ser muy** ~**s** to be close friends.

amigote [ami'ɣote] *nm* mate (*BRIT*), buddy.

amilanar [amila'nar] *vt* to scare; ~**se** *vr* to get scared.

aminorar [amino'rar] *vt* to diminish; (*reducir*) to reduce; ~ **la marcha** to slow down.

amistad [amis'tað] *nf* friendship; ~**es** *nfpl* friends.

amistoso, a [ami'stoso, a] *adj* friendly.

amnesia [am'nesja] *nf* amnesia.

amnistía [amnis'tia] *nf* amnesty.

amnistiar [amni'stjar] *vt* to amnesty, grant an amnesty to.

amo ['amo] *nm* owner; (*jefe*) boss.

amodorrarse [amoðo'rrarse] *vr* to get sleepy.

amolar [amo'lar] *vt* to annoy.

amoldar [amol'dar] *vt* to mould; (*adaptar*) to adapt.

amonestación [amonesta'θjon] *nf* warning; **amonestaciones** *nfpl* marriage banns.

amonestar [amone'star] *vt* to warn; to publish the banns of.

amoniaco [amo'njako] *nm* ammonia.

amontonar [amonto'nar] *vt* to collect, pile up; ~**se** *vr* (*gente*) to crowd together; (*acumularse*) to pile up; (*datos*) to accumulate; (*desastres*) to come one on top of another.

amor [a'mor] *nm* love; (*amante*) lover; **hacer el** ~ to make love; ~ **interesado** cupboard love; ~ **propio** self-respect; **por (el)** ~ **de Dios** for God's sake; **estar al** ~ **de la lumbre** to be close to the fire.

amoratado, a [amora'taðo, a] *adj* purple, blue with cold; (*con cardenales*) bruised.

amordace [amor'ðaθe] *etc vb V* **amordazar.**

amordazar [amorða'θar] *vt* to muzzle; (*fig*) to gag.

amorfo, a [a'morfo, a] *adj* amorphous, shapeless.

amorío [amo'rio] *nm* (*fam*) love affair.

amoroso, a [amo'roso, a] *adj* affectionate, loving.

amortajar [amorta'xar] *vt* (*fig*) to shroud.

amortice [amor'tiθe] *etc vb V* **amortizar.**

amortiguador [amortiɣwa'ðor] *nm* shock absorber; (*parachoques*) bumper; (*silenciador*) silencer; ~**es** *nmpl* (*AUTO*) suspension *sg*.

amortiguar [amorti'ɣwar] *vt* to deaden; (*ruido*) to muffle; (*color*) to soften.

amortigüe [amor'tiɣwe] *etc vb V* **amortiguar.**

amortización [amortiθa'θjon] *nf* redemption; repayment; (*COM*) capital allowance.

amortizar [amorti'θar] *vt* (*ECON: bono*) to redeem; (: *capital*) to write off; (: *préstamo*) to pay off.

amoscarse [amos'karse] *vr* to get cross.

amosque [a'moske] *etc vb* V **amoscarse.**

amotinar [amoti'nar] *vt* to stir up, incite (to riot); ~**se** *vr* to mutiny.

amparar [ampa'rar] *vt* to protect; ~**se** *vr* to seek protection; (*de la lluvia etc*) to shelter.

amparo [am'paro] *nm* help, protection; **al** ~ **de** under the protection of.

amperímetro [ampe'rimetro] *nm* ammeter.

amperio [am'perjo] *nm* ampère, amp.

ampliable [am'pljaßle] *adj* (*INFORM*) expandable.

ampliación [amplja'θjon] *nf* enlargement; (*extensión*) extension.

ampliar [am'pljar] *vt* to enlarge; to extend.

amplificación [amplifika'θjon] *nf* enlargement.

amplificador [amplifika'ðor] *nm* amplifier.

amplificar [amplifi'kar] *vt* to amplify.

amplifique [ampli'fike] *etc vb* V **amplificar.**

amplio, a ['ampljo, a] *adj* spacious; (*falda etc*) full; (*extenso*) extensive; (*ancho*) wide.

amplitud [ampli'tuð] *nf* spaciousness; extent; (*fig*) amplitude; ~ **de miras** broadmindedness; **de gran** ~ far-reaching.

ampolla [am'poʎa] *nf* blister; (*MED*) ampoule.

ampolleta [ampo'ʎeta] *nf* (*AM*) (light) bulb.

ampuloso, a [ampu'loso, a] *adj* bombastic, pompous.

amputar [ampu'tar] *vt* to cut off, amputate.

amueblar [amwe'ßlar] *vt* to furnish.

amuleto [amu'leto] *nm* (lucky) charm.

amurallar [amura'ʎar] *vt* to wall up *o* in.

anacarado, a [anaka'raðo, a] *adj* mother-of-pearl *cpd*.

anacardo [ana'karðo] *nm* cashew (nut).

anaconda [ana'konda] *nf* anaconda.

anacronismo [anakro'nismo] *nm* anachronism.

ánade ['anaðe] *nm* duck.

anagrama [ana'ɣrama] *nm* anagram.

anales [a'nales] *nmpl* annals.

analfabetismo [analfaße'tismo] *nm* illiteracy.

analfabeto, a [analfa'ßeto, a] *adj, nm/f* illiterate.

analgésico [anal'xesiko] *nm* painkiller, analgesic.

analice [ana'liθe] *etc vb* V **analizar.**

análisis [a'nalisis] *nm inv* analysis; ~ **de costos-beneficios** cost-benefit analysis; ~ **de mercados** market research; ~ **de sangre** blood test.

analista [ana'lista] *nm/f* (*gen*) analyst; (*POL, HISTORIA*) chronicler; ~ **de sistemas** (*INFORM*) systems analyst.

analizar [anali'θar] *vt* to analyse.

analogía [analo'xia] *nf* analogy; **por** ~ **con** on the analogy of.

analógico, a [ana'loxico, a] *adj* analogue.

análogo, a [a'naloɣo, a] *adj* analogous, similar.

ananá(s) [ana'na(s)] *nm* pineapple.

anaquel [ana'kel] *nm* shelf.

anaranjado, a [anaran'xaðo, a] *adj* orange (-coloured).

anarquía [anar'kia] *nf* anarchy.

anarquismo [anar'kismo] *nm* anarchism.

anarquista [anar'kista] *nm/f* anarchist.

anatematizar [anatemati'θar] *vt* (*REL*) to anathematize; (*fig*) to curse.

anatemice [anate'miθe] *etc vb* V **anatemizar.**

anatomía [anato'mia] *nf* anatomy.

anca ['anka] *nf* rump, haunch; ~**s** *nfpl* (*fam*) behind *sg*; **llevar a algn en** ~**s** to carry sb behind one.

ancestral [anθes'tral] *adj* (*costumbre*) age-old.

ancho, a ['antʃo, a] *adj* wide; (*falda*) full; (*fig*) liberal ♦ *nm* width; (*FERRO*) gauge; **le viene muy** ~ **el cargo** (*fig*) the job is too much for him; **ponerse** ~ to get conceited; **quedarse tan** ~ to go on as if nothing had happened; **estar a sus anchas** to be at one's ease.

anchoa [an'tʃoa] *nf* anchovy.

anchura [an'tʃura] *nf* width; (*extensión*) wideness.

anchuroso, a [antʃu'roso, a] *adj* wide.

anciano, a [an'θjano, a] *adj* old, aged ♦ *nm/f* old man/woman ♦ *nm* elder.

ancla ['ankla] *nf* anchor; **levar** ~**s** to weigh anchor.

ancladero [ankla'ðero] *nm* anchorage.

anclar [an'klar] *vi* to (drop) anchor.

andadas [an'daðas] *nfpl* (*aventuras*) adventures; **volver a las** ~ to backslide.

andaderas [anda'ðeras] *nfpl* baby-walker *sg*.

andadura [anda'ðura] *nf* gait; (*de caballo*) pace.

Andalucía [andalu'θia] *nf* Andalusia.

andaluz, a [anda'luθ, a] *adj, nm/f* Andalusian.

andamio [an'damjo] *nm*, **andamiaje** [anda'mjaxe] *nm* scaffold(ing).

andanada [anda'naða] *nf (fig)* reprimand;
soltarle a algn una ~ to give sb a rocket.
andante [an'dante] *adj:* **caballero** ~ knight
errant.
andar [an'dar] *vt* to go, cover, travel ♦ *vi* to
go, walk, travel; (*funcionar*) to go, work;
(*estar*) to be ♦ *nm* walk, gait, pace; ~**se** *vr*
(*irse*) to go away *o* off; ~ **a pie/a**
caballo/en bicicleta to go on foot/on
horseback/by bicycle; ¡**anda!** (*sorpresa*)
go on!; **anda en** *o* **por los 40** he's about
40; **¿en qué andas?** what are you up to?;
andamos mal de dinero/tiempo we're
badly off for money/we're short of time;
~**se por las ramas** to beat about the
bush; **no** ~**se con rodeos** to call a spade
a spade (*fam*); **todo se andará** all in good
time; **anda por aquí** it's round here
somewhere; ~ **haciendo algo** to be doing
sth.
andariego, a [anda'rjeɣo, a] *adj* fond of
travelling.
andas ['andas] *nfpl* stretcher *sg*.
andén [an'den] *nm* (*FERRO*) platform;
(*NAUT*) quayside; (*AM: acera*) pavement
(*BRIT*), sidewalk (*US*).
Andes ['andes] *nmpl:* **los** ~ the Andes.
andinismo [andin'ismo] *nm* (*AM*)
mountaineering, climbing.
andino, a [an'dino, a] *adj* Andean, of the
Andes.
Andorra [an'dorra] *nf* Andorra.
andrajo [an'draxo] *nm* rag.
andrajoso, a [andra'xoso, a] *adj* ragged.
andurriales [andu'rrjales] *nmpl* out-of-the-
way place *sg*, the sticks; **en esos** ~ in
that godforsaken spot.
anduve [an'duße], **anduviera** [andu'ßjera]
etc vb V **andar**.
anécdota [a'nekðota] *nf* anecdote, story.
anegar [ane'ɣar] *vt* to flood; (*ahogar*) to
drown; ~**se** *vr* to drown; (*hundirse*) to
sink.
anegue [a'neɣe] *etc vb V* **anegar**.
anejo, a [a'nexo, a] *adj* attached ♦ *nm* (*ARQ*)
annexe.
anemia [a'nemja] *nf* anaemia.
anestesia [anes'tesja] *nf* anaesthetic; ~
general/local general/local anaesthetic.
anestesiar [aneste'sjar] *vt* to anaesthetize
(*BRIT*) anesthetize (*US*).
anestésico [anes'tesiko] *nm* anaesthetic.
anexar [anek'sar] *vt* to annex; (*documento*)
to attach; (*INFORM*) to append.
anexión [anek'sjon] *nf*, **anexionamiento**
[aneksjona'mjento] *nm* annexation.
anexionar [aneksjo'nar] *vt* to annex; ~**se**
vr: ~ **un país** to annex a country.

anexo, a [a'nekso, a] *adj* attached ♦ *nm*
annexe.
anfetamina [anfeta'mina] *nf*
amphetamine.
anfibio, a [an'fiβjo, a] *adj* amphibious ♦ *nm*
amphibian.
anfiteatro [anfite'atro] *nm* amphitheatre;
(*TEAT*) dress circle.
anfitrión, ona [anfi'trjon, ona] *nm/f*
host(ess).
ángel ['anxel] *nm* angel; ~ **de la guarda**
guardian angel; **tener** ~ to have charm.
Ángeles ['anxeles] *nmpl:* **los** ~ Los
Angeles.
angélico, a [an'xeliko, a], **angelical**
[anxeli'kal] *adj* angelic(al).
angina [an'xina] *nf* (*MED*): ~ **de pecho**
angina; **tener** ~**s** to have a sore throat *o*
throat infection.
anglicano, a [angli'kano, a] *adj, nm/f*
Anglican.
anglicismo [angli'θismo] *nm* anglicism.
anglosajón, ona [anglosa'xon, 'xona] *adj,
nm/f* Anglo-Saxon.
Angola [an'gola] *nf* Angola.
angoleño, a [ango'leɲo, a] *adj, nm/f*
Angolan.
angosto, a [an'gosto, a] *adj* narrow.
anguila [an'gila] *nf* eel; ~**s** *nfpl* slipway *sg*.
angula [an'gula] *nf* elver, baby eel.
ángulo ['angulo] *nm* angle; (*esquina*)
corner; (*curva*) bend.
angustia [an'gustja] *nf* anguish.
angustiar [angus'tjar] *vt* to distress,
grieve; ~**se** *vr* to be distressed (*por* at, on
account of).
anhelante [ane'lante] *adj* eager; (*deseoso*)
longing.
anhelar [ane'lar] *vt* to be eager for; to long
for, desire ♦ *vi* to pant, gasp.
anhelo [a'nelo] *nm* eagerness; desire.
anhídrido [a'niðriðo] *nm:* ~ **carbónico**
carbon dioxide.
anidar [ani'ðar] *vt* (*acoger*) to take in,
shelter ♦ *vi* to nest; (*fig*) to make one's
home.
anilina [ani'lina] *nf* aniline.
anilla [a'niʎa] *nf* ring; **(las)** ~**s** (*DEPORTE*)
the rings.
anillo [a'niʎo] *nm* ring; ~ **de boda** wedding
ring; ~ **de compromiso** engagement
ring; **venir como** ~ **al dedo** to suit to a
tee.
ánima ['anima] *nf* soul; **las** ~**s** the Angelus
(bell) *sg*.
animación [anima'θjon] *nf* liveliness;
(*vitalidad*) life; (*actividad*) bustle.
animado, a [ani'maðo, a] *adj* (*vivo*) lively;

(*vivaz*) animated; (*concurrido*) bustling; (*alegre*) in high spirits; **dibujos ~s** cartoon *sg*.

animador, a [anima'ðor, a] *nm/f* (*TV*) host(ess) ♦ *nf* (*DEPORTE*) cheerleader.

animadversión [animaðßer'sjon] *nf* ill-will, antagonism.

animal [ani'mal] *adj* animal; (*fig*) stupid ♦ *nm* animal; (*fig*) fool; (*bestia*) brute.

animalada [anima'laða] *nf* (*gen*) silly thing (to do *o* say); (*ultraje*) disgrace.

animar [ani'mar] *vt* (*BIO*) to animate, give life to; (*fig*) to liven up, brighten up, cheer up; (*estimular*) to stimulate; **~se** *vr* to cheer up, feel encouraged; (*decidirse*) to make up one's mind.

ánimo ['animo] *nm* soul, mind; (*valentía*) courage ♦ *excl* cheer up!; **cobrar** ~ to take heart; **dar ~(s) a** to encourage.

animoso, a [ani'moso, a] *adj* brave; (*vivo*) lively.

aniñado, a [ani'ɲaðo, a] *adj* (*facción*) childlike; (*carácter*) childish.

aniquilar [aniki'lar] *vt* to annihilate, destroy.

anís [a'nis] *nm* (*grano*) aniseed; (*licor*) anisette.

aniversario [anißer'sarjo] *nm* anniversary.

Ankara [an'kara] *nf* Ankara.

ano ['ano] *nm* anus.

anoche [a'notʃe] *adv* last night; **antes de ~** the night before last.

anochecer [anotʃe'θer] *vi* to get dark ♦ *nm* nightfall, dark; **al ~** at nightfall.

anochezca [ano'tʃeθka] *etc vb V* **anochecer**.

anodino, a [ano'ðino, a] *adj* dull, anodyne.

anomalía [anoma'lia] *nf* anomaly.

anonadado, a [anona'ðaðo, a] *adj* stunned.

anonimato [anoni'mato] *nm* anonymity.

anónimo, a [a'nonimo, a] *adj* anonymous; (*COM*) limited ♦ *nm* (*carta*) anonymous letter; (: *maliciosa*) poison-pen letter.

anorak [ano'rak], *pl* **anoraks** *nm* anorak.

anorexia [ano'reksja] *nf* anorexia.

anormal [anor'mal] *adj* abnormal.

anotación [anota'θjon] *nf* note; annotation.

anotar [ano'tar] *vt* to note down; (*comentar*) to annotate.

anquilosado, a [ankilo'saðo, a] *adj* (*fig*) stale, out of date.

anquilosamiento [ankilosa'mjento] *nm* (*fig*) paralysis, stagnation.

ansia ['ansja] *nf* anxiety; (*añoranza*) yearning.

ansiar [an'sjar] *vt* to long for.

ansiedad [ansje'ðað] *nf* anxiety.

ansioso, a [an'sjoso, a] *adj* anxious;

(*anhelante*) eager; **~ de** *o* **por algo** greedy for sth.

antagónico, a [anta'ɣoniko, a] *adj* antagonistic; (*opuesto*) contrasting.

antagonista [antaɣo'nista] *nm/f* antagonist.

antaño [an'taɲo] *adv* long ago.

Antártico [an'tartiko] *nm*: **el (océano) ~** the Antarctic (Ocean).

Antártida [an'tartiða] *nf* Antarctica.

ante ['ante] *prep* before, in the presence of; (*encarado con*) faced with ♦ *nm* suede; **~ todo** above all.

anteanoche [antea'notʃe] *adv* the night before last.

anteayer [antea'jer] *adv* the day before yesterday.

antebrazo [ante'ßraθo] *nm* forearm.

antecámara [ante'kamara] *nf* (*ARQ*) anteroom; (*antesala*) waiting room; (*POL*) lobby.

antecedente [anteθe'ðente] *adj* previous ♦ *nm*: **~s** *nmpl* (*profesionales*) background *sg*; **~s penales** criminal record; **no tener ~s** to have a clean record; **estar en ~s** to be well-informed; **poner a algn en ~s** to put sb in the picture.

anteceder [anteθe'ðer] *vt* to precede, go before.

antecesor, a [anteθe'sor, a] *nm/f* predecessor.

antedicho, a [ante'ðitʃo, a] *adj* aforementioned.

antelación [antela'θjon] *nf*: **con ~** in advance.

antemano [ante'mano]: **de ~** *adv* beforehand, in advance.

antena [an'tena] *nf* antenna; (*de televisión etc*) aerial.

anteojeras [anteo'xeras] *nfpl* blinkers (*BRIT*), blinders (*US*).

anteojo [ante'oxo] *nm* eyeglass; **~s** *nmpl* (*esp AM*) glasses, spectacles.

antepasados [antepa'saðos] *nmpl* ancestors.

antepecho [ante'petʃo] *nm* guardrail, parapet; (*repisa*) ledge, sill.

antepondré [antepon'dre] *etc vb V* **anteponer**.

anteponer [antepo'ner] *vt* to place in front; (*fig*) to prefer.

anteponga [ante'ponɣa] *etc vb V* **anteponer**.

anteproyecto [antepro'jekto] *nm* preliminary sketch; (*fig*) blueprint; (*POL*): **~ de ley** draft bill.

antepuesto, a [ante'pwesto, a] *pp de* **anteponer**.

antepuse [ante'puse] *etc vb V* **anteponer**.

anterior [ante'rjor] *adj* preceding, previous.

anterioridad [anterjori'ðað] *nf*: **con ~ a** prior to, before.

anteriormente [anterjor'mente] *adv* previously, before.

antes ['antes] *adv* sooner; (*primero*) first; (*con prioridad*) before; (*hace tiempo*) previously, once; (*más bien*) rather ♦ *prep*: **~ de** before ♦ *conj*: **~ (de) que** before; **~ bien** (but) rather; **dos días ~** two days before *o* previously; **mucho/poco ~** long/shortly before; **~ muerto que esclavo** better dead than enslaved; **tomo el avión ~ que el barco** I take the plane rather than the boat; **cuanto ~, lo ~ posible** as soon as possible; **cuanto ~ mejor** the sooner the better.

antesala [ante'sala] *nf* anteroom.

antiadherente [antiaðe'rente] *adj* non-stick.

antiaéreo, a [antia'ereo, a] *adj* anti-aircraft.

antialcohólico, a [antial'koliko, a] *adj*: **centro ~** (*MED*) detoxification unit.

antibalas [anti'ßalas] *adj inv*: **chaleco ~** bulletproof jacket.

antibiótico [anti'ßjotiko] *nm* antibiotic.

anticiclón [antiθi'klon] *nm* (*METEOROLOGÍA*) anti-cyclone.

anticipación [antiθipa'θjon] *nf* anticipation; **con 10 minutos de ~** 10 minutes early.

anticipado, a [antiθi'paðo, a] *adj* (in) advance; **por ~** in advance.

anticipar [antiθi'par] *vt* to anticipate; (*adelantar*) to bring forward; (*COM*) to advance; **~se** *vr*: **~se a su época** to be ahead of one's time.

anticipo [anti'θipo] *nm* (*COM*) advance; *V tb* **anticipación**.

anticonceptivo, a [antikonθep'tißo, a] *adj, nm* contraceptive; **métodos ~s** contraceptive devices.

anticongelante [antikonxe'lante] *nm* antifreeze.

anticonstitucional [antikonstituθjo'nal] *adj* unconstitutional.

anticuado, a [anti'kwaðo, a] *adj* out-of-date, old-fashioned; (*desusado*) obsolete.

anticuario [anti'kwarjo] *nm* antique dealer.

anticuerpo [anti'kwerpo] *nm* (*MED*) antibody.

antidemocrático, a [antiðemo'kratiko, a] *adj* undemocratic.

antideportivo, a [antiðepor'tißo, a] *adj* unsporting.

antideslumbrante [antiðeslum'brante] *adj* (*INFORM*) anti-dazzle.

antidoping [anti'ðopin] *adj inv* anti-drug.

antídoto [an'tiðoto] *nm* antidote.

antidroga [anti'ðroɣa] *adj inv* anti-drug; **brigada ~** drug squad.

antiestético, a [anties'tetiko, a] *adj* unsightly.

antifaz [anti'faθ] *nm* mask; (*velo*) veil.

antigás [anti'gas] *adj inv*: **careta ~** gasmask.

antigualla [anti'ɣwaʎa] *nf* antique; (*reliquia*) relic; **~s** *nfpl* old things.

antiguamente [antiɣwa'mente] *adv* formerly; (*hace mucho tiempo*) long ago.

antigüedad [antiɣwe'ðað] *nf* antiquity; (*artículo*) antique; (*rango*) seniority.

antiguo, a [an'tiɣwo, a] *adj* old, ancient; (*que fue*) former; **a la antigua** in the old-fashioned way.

antihigiénico, a [anti'xjeniko, a] *adj* unhygienic.

antihistamínico, a [antista'miniko, a] *adj, nm* antihistamine.

antiinflacionista [antinflaθjo'nista] *adj* anti-inflationary, counter-inflationary.

antillano, a [anti'ʎano, a] *adj, nm/f* West Indian.

Antillas [an'tiʎas] *nfpl*: **las ~** the West Indies, the Antilles; **el mar de las ~** the Caribbean Sea.

antílope [an'tilope] *nm* antelope.

antimonopolios [antimono'poljos] *adj inv*: **ley ~** anti-trust law.

antinatural [antinatu'ral] *adj* unnatural.

antiparras [anti'parras] *nfpl* (*fam*) specs.

antipatía [antipa'tia] *nf* antipathy, dislike.

antipático, a [anti'patiko, a] *adj* disagreeable, unpleasant.

Antípodas [an'tipoðas] *nfpl*: **las ~** the Antipodes.

antiquísimo, a [anti'kisimo, a] *adj* ancient.

antirreglamentario, a [antirreɣlamen 'tarjo, a] *adj* (*gen*) unlawful; (*POL etc*) unconstitutional.

antirrobo [anti'rroßo] *adj inv*: (*dispositivo*) **~** (*para casas etc*) burglar alarm; (*para coches*) car alarm.

antisemita [antise'mita] *adj* anti-Semitic ♦ *nm/f* anti-Semite.

antiséptico, a [anti'septiko, a] *adj, nm* antiseptic.

antiterrorista [antiterro'rista] *adj* antiterrorist; **la lucha ~** the fight against terrorism.

antítesis [an'titesis] *nf inv* antithesis.

antojadizo, a [antoxa'ðiθo, a] *adj*

capricious.

antojarse [anto'xarse] *vr* (*desear*): **se me antoja comprarlo** I have a mind to buy it; (*pensar*): **se me antoja que** I have a feeling that.

antojo [an'toxo] *nm* caprice, whim; (*rosa*) birthmark; (*lunar*) mole; **hacer a su** ~ to do as one pleases.

antología [antolo'xia] *nf* anthology.

antonomasia [antono'masja] *nf*: **por** ~ par excellence.

antorcha [an'tortʃa] *nf* torch.

antro ['antro] *nm* cavern; ~ **de corrupción** (*fig*) den of iniquity.

antropófago, a [antro'pofaxo, a] *adj, nm/f* cannibal.

antropología [antropolo'xia] *nf* anthropology.

antropólogo, a [antro'poloxo, a] *nm/f* anthropologist.

anual [a'nwal] *adj* annual.

anualidad [anwali'ðað] *nf* annuity, annual payment; ~ **vitalicia** life annuity.

anuario [a'nwarjo] *nm* yearbook.

anudar [anu'ðar] *vt* to knot, tie; (*unir*) to join; ~**se** *vr* to get tied up; **se me anudó la voz** I got a lump in my throat.

anulación [anula'θjon] *nf* annulment; cancellation; repeal.

anular [anu'lar] *vt* to annul, cancel; (*suscripción*) to cancel; (*ley*) to repeal ♦ *nm* ring finger.

anunciación [anunθja'θjon] *nf* announcement; **A**~ (*REL*) Annunciation.

anunciante [anun'θjante] *nm/f* (*COM*) advertiser.

anunciar [anun'θjar] *vt* to announce; (*proclamar*) to proclaim; (*COM*) to advertise.

anuncio [a'nunθjo] *nm* announcement; (*señal*) sign; (*COM*) advertisement; (*cartel*) poster; (*TEAT*) bill; ~**s por palabras** classified ads.

anverso [am'berso] *nm* obverse.

anzuelo [an'θwelo] *nm* hook; (*para pescar*) fish hook; **tragar el** ~ to swallow the bait.

añadido [aɲa'ðiðo] *nm* addition.

añadidura [aɲaði'ðura] *nf* addition, extra; **por** ~ besides, in addition.

añadir [aɲa'ðir] *vt* to add.

añejo, a [a'ɲexo, a] *adj* old; (*vino*) vintage; (*jamón*) well-cured.

añicos [a'ɲikos] *nmpl*: **hacer** ~ to smash, shatter; **hacerse** ~ to smash, shatter.

añil [a'ɲil] *nm* (*BOT, color*) indigo.

año ['aɲo] *nm* year; ¡**Feliz A**~ **Nuevo!** Happy New Year!; **tener 15** ~**s** to be 15

(years old); **los** ~**s 80** the eighties; ~ **bisiesto/escolar** leap/school year; ~ **fiscal** fiscal *o* tax year; **estar de buen** ~ to be in good shape; **en el** ~ **de la nana** in the year dot; **el** ~ **que viene** next year.

añoranza [aɲo'ranθa] *nf* nostalgia; (*anhelo*) longing.

añorar [aɲo'rar] *vt* to long for.

añoso, a [a'ɲoso, a] *adj* ancient, old.

aovado, a [ao'βaðo, a] *adj* oval.

aovar [ao'βar] *vi* to lay eggs.

apabullar [apaβu'ʎar] *vt* (*lit, fig*) to crush.

apacentar [apaθen'tar] *vt* to pasture, graze.

apacible [apa'θiβle] *adj* gentle, mild.

apaciente [apa'θjente] *etc vb V* **apacentar**.

apaciguar [apaθi'ɣwar] *vt* to pacify, calm (down).

apacigüe [apa'θiɣwe] *etc vb V* **apaciguar**.

apadrinar [apaðri'nar] *vt* to sponsor, support; (*REL*) to act as godfather to.

apagado, a [apa'ɣaðo, a] *adj* (*volcán*) extinct; (*color*) dull; (*voz*) quiet; (*sonido*) muted, muffled; (*persona*: *apático*) listless; **estar** ~ (*fuego, luz*) to be out; (*radio, TV etc*) to be off.

apagar [apa'ɣar] *vt* to put out; (*color*) to tone down; (*sonido*) to silence, muffle; (*sed*) to quench; (*INFORM*) to toggle off; ~**se** *vr* (*luz, fuego*) to go out; (*sonido*) to die away; (*pasión*) to wither; ~ **el sistema** (*INFORM*) to close *o* shut down.

apagón [apa'ɣon] *nm* blackout, power cut.

apague [a'paɣe] *etc vb V* **apagar**.

apaisado, a [apai'saðo, a] *adj* (*papel*) landscape *cpd*.

apalabrar [apala'βrar] *vt* to agree to; (*obrero*) to engage.

Apalaches [apa'latʃes] *nmpl*: (**Montes**) ~ Appalachians.

apalear [apale'ar] *vt* to beat, thrash; (*AGR*) to winnow.

apañado, a [apa'ɲaðo, a] *adj* (*mañoso*) resourceful; (*arreglado*) tidy; (*útil*) handy.

apañar [apa'ɲar] *vt* to pick up; (*asir*) to take hold of, grasp; (*reparar*) to mend, patch up; ~**se** *vr* to manage, get along; **apañárselas por su cuenta** to look after number one (*fam*).

apaño [a'paɲo] *nm* (*COSTURA*) patch; (*maña*) skill; **esto no tiene** ~ there's no answer to this one.

aparador [apara'ðor] *nm* sideboard; (*escaparate*) shop window.

aparato [apa'rato] *nm* apparatus; (*máquina*) machine; (*doméstico*) appliance; (*boato*) ostentation; (*INFORM*)

device; ~ **de facsímil** facsimile
(machine), fax; ~ **respiratorio**
respiratory system; ~**s de mando** (AVIAT
etc) controls.
aparatoso, a [apara'toso, a] adj showy,
ostentatious.
aparcamiento [aparka'mjento] nm car
park (BRIT), parking lot (US).
aparcar [apar'kar] vt, vi to park.
aparear [apare'ar] vt (objetos) to pair,
match; (animales) to mate; ~**se** vr to form
a pair; to mate.
aparecer [apare'θer] vi, ~**se** vr to appear;
apareció borracho he turned up drunk.
aparejado, a [apare'xaðo, a] adj fit,
suitable; **ir** ~ **con** to go hand in hand
with; **llevar** o **traer** ~ to involve.
aparejador, a [aparexa'ðor, a] nm/f (ARQ)
quantity surveyor.
aparejar [apare'xar] vt to prepare; (caballo)
to saddle, harness; (NAUT) to fit out, rig
out.
aparejo [apa'rexo] nm preparation; (de
caballo) harness; (NAUT) rigging; (de
poleas) block and tackle.
aparentar [aparen'tar] vt (edad) to look;
(fingir): ~ **tristeza** to pretend to be sad.
aparente [apa'rente] adj apparent;
(adecuado) suitable.
aparezca [apa're θka] etc vb V **aparecer**.
aparición [apari'θjon] nf appearance; (de
libro) publication; (fantasma) spectre.
apariencia [apa'rjenθja] nf (outward)
appearance; **en** ~ outwardly, seemingly.
aparque [a'parke] etc vb V **aparcar**.
apartado, a [apar'taðo, a] adj separate;
(lejano) remote ♦ nm (tipográfico)
paragraph; ~ **(de correos)** post office
box.
apartamento [aparta'mento] nm
apartment, flat (BRIT).
apartamiento [aparta'mjento] nm
separation; (aislamiento) remoteness;
(AM) apartment, flat (BRIT).
apartar [apar'tar] vt to separate; (quitar) to
remove; (MINERALOGÍA) to extract; ~**se** vr
(separarse) to separate, part; (irse) to
move away; (mantenerse aparte) to keep
away.
aparte [a'parte] adv (separadamente)
separately; (además) besides ♦ prep: ~ **de**
apart from ♦ nm (TEAT) aside;
(tipográfico) new paragraph; **"punto y ~"**
"new paragraph".
apasionado, a [apasjo'naðo, a] adj
passionate; (pey) biassed, prejudiced
♦ nm/f admirer.
apasionante [apasjo'nante] adj exciting.

apasionar [apasjo'nar] vt to arouse
passion in; ~**se** vr to get excited; **le
apasiona el fútbol** she's crazy about
football.
apatía [apa'tia] nf apathy.
apático, a [a'patiko, a] adj apathetic.
apátrida [a'patriða] adj stateless.
Apdo. nm abr (= Apartado (de Correos))
P.O. Box.
apeadero [apea'ðero] nm halt, stopping
place.
apearse [ape'arse] vr (jinete) to dismount;
(bajarse) to get down o out; (de coche) to
get out, alight; **no** ~ **del burro** to refuse
to climb down.
apechugar [apetʃu'xar] vi: ~ **con algo** to
face up to sth.
apechugue [ape'tʃuxe] etc vb V **apechugar**.
apedrear [apeðre'ar] vt to stone.
apegarse [ape'xarse] vr: ~ **a** to become
attached to.
apego [a'pexo] nm attachment, devotion.
apegue [a'pexe] etc vb V **apegarse**.
apelación [apela'θjon] nf appeal.
apelar [ape'lar] vi to appeal; ~ **a** (fig) to
resort to.
apelativo [apela'tißo] nm (LING)
appellative; (AM) surname.
apellidar [apeʎi'ðar] vt to call, name; ~**se**
vr: **se apellida Pérez** her (sur)name's
Pérez.
apellido [ape'ʎiðo] nm surname.

In the Spanish-speaking world most people
use two **apellidos**, the first being their
father's first surname, and the second their
mother's first surname: eg the children of
Juan García López, married to Carmen
Pérez Rodríguez would have as their
surname García Pérez. Married women
retain their own surname(s) and
sometimes add their husband's first
surname on to theirs: eg Carmen Pérez de
García. She could also be referred to as (la)
Señora de García. In Latin America it is
usual for the second surname to be
shortened to an initial in correspondence
eg: Juan García L.

apelmazado, a [apelma'θaðo, a] adj
compact, solid.
apelotonar [apeloto'nar] vt to roll into a
ball; ~**se** vr (gente) to crowd together.
apenar [ape'nar] vt to grieve, trouble; (AM:
avergonzar) to embarrass; ~**se** vr to
grieve; (AM) to be embarrassed.
apenas [a'penas] adv scarcely, hardly
♦ conj as soon as, no sooner.

apéndice [a'pendiθe] *nm* appendix.
apendicitis [apendi'θitis] *nf* appendicitis.
Apeninos [ape'ninos] *nmpl* Apennines.
apercibimiento [aperθiβi'mjento] *nm* (*aviso*) warning.
apercibir [aperθi'βir] *vt* to prepare; (*avisar*) to warn; (*JUR*) to summon; (*AM*) to notice, see; ~**se** *vr* to get ready; ~**se de** to notice.
aperitivo [aperi'tiβo] *nm* (*bebida*) aperitif; (*comida*) appetizer.
apero [a'pero] *nm* (*AGR*) implement; ~**s** *nmpl* farm equipment *sg*.
apertura [aper'tura] *nf* (*gen*) opening; (*POL*) openness, liberalization; (*TEAT etc*) beginning; ~ **de un juicio hipotecario** (*COM*) foreclosure.
aperturismo [apertu'rismo] *nm* (*POL*) (policy of) liberalization.
apesadumbrar [apesaðum'brar] *vt* to grieve, sadden; ~**se** *vr* to distress o.s.
apestar [apes'tar] *vt* to infect ♦ *vi*: ~ **(a)** to stink (of).
apestoso, a [apes'toso, a] *adj* (*hediondo*) stinking; (*asqueroso*) sickening.
apetecer [apete'θer] *vt*: *¿***te apetece una tortilla?** do you fancy an omelette?
apetecible [apete'θiβle] *adj* desirable; (*comida*) tempting.
apetezca [ape'teθka] *etc vb V* **apetecer**.
apetito [ape'tito] *nm* appetite.
apetitoso, a [apeti'toso, a] *adj* (*gustoso*) appetizing; (*fig*) tempting.
apiadarse [apja'ðarse] *vr*: ~ **de** to take pity on.
ápice ['apiθe] *nm* apex; (*fig*) whit, iota; **ni un** ~ not a whit; **no ceder un** ~ not to budge an inch.
apicultor, a [apikul'tor, a] *nm/f* beekeeper, apiarist.
apicultura [apikul'tura] *nf* beekeeping.
apiladora [apila'ðora] *nf* (*para máquina impresora*) stacker.
apilar [api'lar] *vt* to pile *o* heap up; ~**se** *vr* to pile up.
apiñado, a [api'ɲaðo, a] *adj* (*apretado*) packed.
apiñar [api'ɲar] *vt* to crowd; ~**se** *vr* to crowd *o* press together.
apio ['apjo] *nm* celery.
apisonadora [apisona'ðora] *nf* (*máquina*) steamroller.
aplacar [apla'kar] *vt* to placate; ~**se** *vr* to calm down.
aplace [a'plaθe] *etc vb V* **aplazar**.
aplanamiento [aplana'mjento] *nm* smoothing, levelling.
aplanar [apla'nar] *vt* to smooth, level;

(*allanar*) to roll flat, flatten; ~**se** *vr* (*edificio*) to collapse; (*persona*) to get discouraged.
aplaque [a'plake] *etc vb V* **aplacar**.
aplastar [aplas'tar] *vt* to squash (flat); (*fig*) to crush.
aplatanarse [aplata'narse] *vr* to get lethargic.
aplaudir [aplau'ðir] *vt* to applaud.
aplauso [a'plauso] *nm* applause; (*fig*) approval, acclaim.
aplazamiento [aplaθa'mjento] *nm* postponement.
aplazar [apla'θar] *vt* to postpone, defer.
aplicación [aplika'θjon] *nf* application; (*esfuerzo*) effort; **aplicaciones de gestión** business applications.
aplicado, a [apli'kaðo, a] *adj* diligent, hard-working.
aplicar [apli'kar] *vt* (*gen*) to apply; (*poner en vigor*) to put into effect; (*esfuerzos*) to devote; ~**se** *vr* to apply o.s.
aplique [a'plike] *etc vb V* **aplicar** ♦ *nm* wall light *o* lamp.
aplomo [a'plomo] *nm* aplomb, self-assurance.
apocado, a [apo'kaðo, a] *adj* timid.
apocamiento [apoka'mjento] *nm* timidity; (*depresión*) depression.
apocarse [apo'karse] *vr* to feel small *o* humiliated.
apocopar [apoko'par] *vt* (*LING*) to shorten.
apócope [a'pokope] *nf* apocopation; **gran es** ~ **de grande** "gran" is the shortened form of "grande".
apócrifo, a [a'pokrifo, a] *adj* apocryphal.
apodar [apo'ðar] *vt* to nickname.
apoderado [apoðe'raðo] *nm* agent, representative.
apoderar [apoðe'rar] *vt* to authorize, empower; (*JUR*) to grant (a) power of attorney to; ~**se** *vr*: ~**se de** to take possession of.
apodo [a'poðo] *nm* nickname.
apogeo [apo'xeo] *nm* peak, summit.
apolillado, a [apoli'ʎaðo, a] *adj* moth-eaten.
apolillarse [apoli'ʎarse] *vr* to get moth-eaten.
apología [apolo'xia] *nf* eulogy; (*defensa*) defence.
apoltronarse [apoltro'narse] *vr* to get lazy.
apoplejía [apople'xia] *nf* apoplexy, stroke.
apoque [a'poke] *etc vb V* **apocar**.
apoquinar [apoki'nar] *vt* (*fam*) to cough up, fork out.
aporrear [aporre'ar] *vt* to beat (up).
aportación [aporta'θjon] *nf* contribution.

aportar [apor'tar] *vt* to contribute ♦ *vi* to reach port.

aposentar [aposen'tar] *vt* to lodge, put up.

aposento [apo'sento] *nm* lodging; (*habitación*) room.

apósito [a'posito] *nm* (*MED*) dressing.

apostar [apos'tar] *vt* to bet, stake; (*tropas etc*) to station, post ♦ *vi* to bet.

aposta(s) [a'posta(s)] *adv* on purpose.

apostatar [aposta'tar] *vi* (*REL*) to apostatize; (*fig*) to change sides.

a posteriori [aposte'rjori] *adv* at a later date *o* stage; (*LÓGICA*) a posteriori.

apostilla [apos'tiʎa] *nf* note, comment.

apóstol [a'postol] *nm* apostle.

apóstrofo [a'postrofo] *nm* apostrophe.

apostura [apos'tura] *nf* neatness, elegance.

apoteósico, a [apote'osiko, a] *adj* tremendous.

apoyar [apo'jar] *vt* to lean, rest; (*fig*) to support, back; ~**se** *vr*: ~**se en** to lean on.

apoyo [a'pojo] *nm* support, backing.

apreciable [apre'θjaßle] *adj* considerable; (*fig*) esteemed.

apreciación [apreθja'θjon] *nf* appreciation; (*COM*) valuation.

apreciar [apre'θjar] *vt* to evaluate, assess; (*COM*) to appreciate, value ♦ *vi* (*ECON*) to appreciate.

aprecio [a'preθjo] *nm* valuation, estimate; (*fig*) appreciation.

aprehender [apreen'der] *vt* to apprehend, detain; (*ver*) to see, observe.

aprehensión [apreen'sjon] *nf* detention, capture.

apremiante [apre'mjante] *adj* urgent, pressing.

apremiar [apre'mjar] *vt* to compel, force ♦ *vi* to be urgent, press.

apremio [a'premjo] *nm* urgency; ~ **de pago** demand note.

aprender [apren'der] *vt, vi* to learn; ~ **a conducir** to learn to drive; ~**se** *vr*: ~**se algo** to learn sth (off) by heart.

aprendiz, a [apren'diθ, a] *nm/f* apprentice; (*principiante*) learner, trainee; ~ **de comercio** business trainee.

aprendizaje [aprendi'θaxe] *nm* apprenticeship.

aprensión [apren'sjon] *nm* apprehension, fear.

aprensivo, a [apren'sißo, a] *adj* apprehensive.

apresar [apre'sar] *vt* to seize; (*capturar*) to capture.

aprestar [apres'tar] *vt* to prepare, get ready; (*TEC*) to prime, size; ~**se** *vr* to get ready.

apresto [a'presto] *nm* (*gen*) preparation; (*sustancia*) size.

apresurado, a [apresu'raðo, a] *adj* hurried, hasty.

apresuramiento [apresura'mjento] *nm* hurry, haste.

apresurar [apresu'rar] *vt* to hurry, accelerate; ~**se** *vr* to hurry, make haste; **me apresuré a sugerir que** ... I hastily suggested that ...

apretado, a [apre'taðo, a] *adj* tight; (*escritura*) cramped.

apretar [apre'tar] *vt* to squeeze, press; (*mano*) to clasp; (*dientes*) to grit; (*TEC*) to tighten; (*presionar*) to press together, pack ♦ *vi* to be too tight; ~**se** *vr* to crowd together; ~ **la mano a algn** to shake sb's hand; ~ **el paso** to quicken one's step.

apretón [apre'ton] *nm* squeeze; ~ **de manos** handshake.

aprieto [a'prjeto] *etc vb V* **apretar** ♦ *nm* squeeze; (*dificultad*) difficulty, jam; **estar en un** ~ to be in a jam; **ayudar a algn a salir de un** ~ to help sb out of trouble.

a priori [apri'ori] *adv* beforehand; (*LÓGICA*) a priori.

aprisa [a'prisa] *adv* quickly, hurriedly.

aprisionar [aprisjo'nar] *vt* to imprison.

aprobación [aproßa'θjon] *nf* approval.

aprobado [apro'ßaðo] *nm* (*nota*) pass mark.

aprobar [apro'ßar] *vt* to approve (of); (*examen, materia*) to pass ♦ *vi* to pass.

apropiación [apropja'θjon] *nf* appropriation.

apropiado, a [apro'pjaðo, a] *adj* appropriate.

apropiarse [apro'pjarse] *vr*: ~ **de** to appropriate.

aprovechado, a [aproße't ʃaðo, a] *adj* industrious, hardworking; (*económico*) thrifty; (*pey*) unscrupulous.

aprovechamiento [aproßetʃa'mjento] *nm* use, exploitation.

aprovechar [aproße'tʃar] *vt* to use; (*explotar*) to exploit; (*experiencia*) to profit from; (*oferta, oportunidad*) to take advantage of ♦ *vi* to progress, improve; ~**se** *vr*: ~**se de** to make use of; (*pey*) to take advantage of; ¡**que aproveche!** enjoy your meal!

aprovisionar [aproßisjo'nar] *vt* to supply.

aproximación [aproksima'θjon] *nf* approximation; (*de lotería*) consolation prize.

aproximadamente [aproksimaða'mente] *adv* approximately.

aproximado, a [aproksi'maðo, a] *adj* approximate.

aproximar [aproksi'mar] *vt* to bring nearer; **~se** *vr* to come near, approach.

apruebe [a'prweße] *etc vb V* **aprobar**.

aptitud [apti'tuð] *nf* aptitude; *(capacidad)* ability; **~ para los negocios** business sense.

apto, a ['apto, a] *adj (apropiado)* fit, suitable *(para* for, to); *(hábil)* capable; **~/no ~ para menores** *(CINE)* suitable/ unsuitable for children.

apuesto, a [a'pwesto, a] *etc vb V* **apostar** ♦ *adj* neat, elegant ♦ *nf* bet, wager.

apuntador [apunta'ðor] *nm* prompter.

apuntalar [apunta'lar] *vt* to prop up.

apuntar [apun'tar] *vt (con arma)* to aim at; *(con dedo)* to point at *o* to; *(anotar)* to note (down); *(datos)* to record; *(TEAT)* to prompt; **~se** *vr (DEPORTE: tanto, victoria)* to score; *(ESCOL)* to enrol; **~ una cantidad en la cuenta de algn** to charge a sum to sb's account; **~se en un curso** to enrol on a course; **¡yo me apunto!** count me in!

apunte [a'punte] *nm* note; *(TEAT: voz)* prompt; *(: texto)* prompt book.

apuñalar [apuɲa'lar] *vt* to stab.

apurado, a [apu'raðo, a] *adj* needy; *(difícil)* difficult; *(peligroso)* dangerous; *(AM)* hurried, rushed; **estar en una situación apurada** to be in a tight spot; **estar ~ to** be in a hurry.

apurar [apu'rar] *vt (agotar)* to drain; *(recursos)* to use up; *(molestar)* to annoy; **~se** *vr (preocuparse)* to worry; *(esp AM: darse prisa)* to hurry.

apuro [a'puro] *nm (aprieto)* fix, jam; *(escasez)* want, hardship; *(vergüenza)* embarrassment; *(AM)* haste, urgency.

aquejado, a [ake'xaðo, a] *adj:* **~ de** *(MED)* afflicted by.

aquejar [ake'xar] *vt (afligir)* to distress; **le aqueja una grave enfermedad** he suffers from a serious disease.

aquel, aquella, aquellos, as [a'kel, a'keʎa, a'keʎos, as] *adj* that; *(pl)* those.

aquél, aquélla, aquéllos, as [a'kel, a'keʎa, a'keʎos, as] *pron* that (one); *(pl)* those (ones).

aquello [a'keʎo] *pron* that, that business.

aquí [a'ki] *adv (lugar)* here; *(tiempo)* now; **~ arriba** up here; **~ mismo** right here; **~ yace** here lies; **de ~ a siete días** a week from now.

aquietar [akje'tar] *vt* to quieten (down), calm (down).

Aquisgrán [akis'ɣran] *nm* Aachen, Aix-la-Chapelle.

A.R. *abr (= Alteza Real)* R.H.

ara ['ara] *nf (altar)* altar; **en ~s de** for the sake of.

árabe ['araße] *adj* Arab, Arabian, Arabic ♦ *nm/f* Arab ♦ *nm (LING)* Arabic.

Arabia [a'raßja] *nf* Arabia; **~ Saudí** *o* **Saudita** Saudi Arabia.

arábigo, a [a'raßixo, a] *adj* Arab, Arabian, Arabic.

arácnido [a'rakniðo] *nm* arachnid.

arado [a'raðo] *nm* plough.

aragonés, esa [araxo'nes, esa] *adj, nm/f* Aragonese ♦ *nm (LING)* Aragonese

arancel [aran'θel] *nm* tariff, duty; **~ de aduanas** (customs) duty.

arandela [aran'dela] *nf (TEC)* washer; *(chorrera)* frill.

araña [a'raɲa] *nf (ZOOL)* spider; *(lámpara)* chandelier.

arañar [ara'ɲar] *vt* to scratch.

arañazo [ara'ɲaθo] *nm* scratch.

arar [a'rar] *vt* to plough, till.

araucano, a [arau'kano, a] *adj, nm/f* Araucanian.

arbitraje [arßi'traxe] *nm* arbitration.

arbitrar [arßi'trar] *vt* to arbitrate in; *(recursos)* to bring together; *(DEPORTE)* to referee ♦ *vi* to arbitrate.

arbitrariedad [arßitrarje'ðað] *nf* arbitrariness; *(acto)* arbitrary act.

arbitrario, a [arßi'trarjo] *adj* arbitrary.

arbitrio [ar'ßitrjo] *nm* free will; *(JUR)* adjudication, decision; **dejar al ~ de algn** to leave to sb's discretion.

árbitro [ar'ßitro] *nm* arbitrator; *(DEPORTE)* referee; *(TENIS)* umpire.

árbol ['arßol] *nm (BOT)* tree; *(NAUT)* mast; *(TEC)* axle, shaft.

arbolado, a [arßo'laðo, a] *adj* wooded; *(camino)* tree-lined ♦ *nm* woodland.

arboladura [arßola'ðura] *nf* rigging.

arbolar [arßo'lar] *vt* to hoist, raise.

arboleda [arßo'leða] *nf* grove, plantation.

arbusto [ar'ßusto] *nm* bush, shrub.

arca ['arka] *nf* chest, box; **A~ de la Alianza** Ark of the Covenant; **A~ de Noé** Noah's Ark.

arcada [ar'kaða] *nf* arcade; *(de puente)* arch, span; **~s** *nfpl* retching *sg*.

arcaico, a [ar'kaiko, a] *adj* archaic.

arce ['arθe] *nm* maple tree.

arcén [ar'θen] *nm (de autopista)* hard shoulder; *(de carretera)* verge.

archiconocido, a [artʃikono'θiðo, a] *adj* extremely well-known.

archipiélago [artʃi'pjelaxo] *nm*

archipelago.
archisabido, a [artʃisa'ßiðo, a] *adj*
extremely well-known.
archivador [artʃißa'ðor] *nm* filing cabinet;
~ **colgante** suspension file.
archivar [artʃi'ßar] *vt* to file (away);
(*INFORM*) to archive.
archivo [ar'tʃißo] *nm* archive(s) (*pl*);
(*INFORM*) file, archive; **A~ Nacional**
Public Record Office; **~s policíacos**
police files; **nombre de** ~ (*INFORM*)
filename; ~ **maestro** (*INFORM*) master
file; ~ **de transacciones** (*INFORM*)
transactions file.
arcilla [ar'θiʎa] *nf* clay.
arco ['arko] *nm* arch; (*MAT*) arc; (*MIL, MUS*)
bow; (*AM DEPORTE*) goal; ~ **iris** rainbow.
arcón [ar'kon] *nm* large chest.
arder [ar'ðer] *vt* to burn; ~ **sin llama** to
smoulder; **estar que arde** (*persona*) to
fume.
ardid [ar'ðið] *nm* ruse.
ardiente [ar'ðjente] *adj* ardent.
ardilla [ar'ðiʎa] *nf* squirrel.
ardor [ar'ðor] *nm* (*calor*) heat, warmth; (*fig*)
ardour; ~ **de estómago** heartburn.
ardoroso, a [arðo'roso, a] *adj* passionate.
arduo, a ['arðwo, a] *adj* arduous.
área ['area] *nf* area; (*DEPORTE*) penalty
area; ~ **de excedentes** (*INFORM*) overflow
area.
ARENA [a'rena] *nf abr* (*El Salvador: POL*)
= *Alianza Republicana Nacionalista*.
arena [a'rena] *nf* sand; (*de una lucha*) arena.
arenal [are'nal] *nm* (*arena movediza*)
quicksand.
arenga [a'renga] *nf* (*fam*) sermon.
arengar [aren'gar] *vt* to harangue.
arengue [a'renge] *etc vb V* **arengar**.
arenillas [are'niʎas] *nfpl* (*MED*) stones.
arenisca [are'niska] *nf* sandstone; (*cascajo*)
grit.
arenoso, a [are'noso, a] *adj* sandy.
arenque [a'renke] *nm* herring.
arepa [a'repa] *nf* (*AM*) corn pancake.
arete [a'rete] *nm* earring.
argamasa [arɣa'masa] *nf* mortar, plaster.
Argel [ar'xel] *n* Algiers.
Argelia [ar'xelja] *nf* Algeria.
argelino, a [arxe'lino, a] *adj, nm/f* Algerian.
Argentina [arxen'tina] *nf*: (**la**) ~ **the**
Argentine, Argentina.
argentino, a [arxen'tino, a] *adj*
Argentinian; (*de plata*) silvery ♦ *nm/f*
Argentinian.
argolla [ar'ɣoʎa] *nf* (large) ring; (*AM: de
matrimonio*) wedding ring.
argot [ar'ɣo] *nm, pl* **argots** [ar'ɣo, ar'ɣos]

slang.
argucia [ar'ɣuθja] *nf* subtlety, sophistry.
argüir [ar'ɣwir] *vt* to deduce; (*discutir*) to
argue; (*indicar*) to indicate, imply;
(*censurar*) to reproach ♦ *vi* to argue.
argumentación [arɣumenta'θjon] *nf* (line
of) argument.
argumentar [arɣumen'tar] *vt, vi* to argue.
argumento [arɣu'mento] *nm* argument;
(*razonamiento*) reasoning; (*de novela etc*)
plot; (*CINE, TV*) storyline.
arguyendo [arɣu'jendo] *etc vb V* **argüir**.
aria ['arja] *nf* aria.
aridez [ari'ðeθ] *nf* aridity, dryness.
árido, a ['ariðo, a] *adj* arid, dry; **~s** *nmpl*
dry goods.
Aries ['arjes] *nm* Aries.
ariete [a'rjete] *nm* battering ram.
ario, a ['arjo, a] *adj* Aryan.
arisco, a [a'risko, a] *adj* surly; (*insociable*)
unsociable.
aristocracia [aristo'kraθja] *nf* aristocracy.
aristócrata [aris'tokrata] *nm/f* aristocrat.
aristocrático, a [aristo'kratiko, a] *adj*
aristocratic.
aritmética [arit'metika] *nf* arithmetic.
aritmético, a [arit'metiko, a] *adj*
arithmetic(al) ♦ *nm/f* arithmetician.
arma ['arma] *nf* arm; **~s** *nfpl* arms; ~
blanca blade, knife; (*espada*) sword; ~
de fuego firearm; **~s cortas** small arms;
rendir las ~s to lay down one's arms; **ser
de ~s tomar** to be somebody to be
reckoned with.
armada [ar'maða] *nf* armada; (*flota*) fleet; *V
tb* **armado**.
armadillo [arma'ðiʎo] *nm* armadillo.
armado, a [ar'maðo, a] *adj* armed; (*TEC*)
reinforced.
armador [arma'ðor] *nm* (*NAUT*) shipowner.
armadura [arma'ðura] *nf* (*MIL*) armour;
(*TEC*) framework; (*ZOOL*) skeleton;
(*FÍSICA*) armature.
armamentista [armamen'tista],
armamentístico, a [armamen'tistiko, a]
adj arms *cpd*.
armamento [arma'mento] *nm* armament;
(*NAUT*) fitting-out.
armar [ar'mar] *vt* (*soldado*) to arm;
(*máquina*) to assemble; (*navío*) to fit out;
~la, ~ **un lío** to start a row; **~se** *vr*: **~se
de valor** to summon up one's courage.
armario [ar'marjo] *nm* wardrobe.
armatoste [arma'toste] *nm* (*mueble*)
monstrosity; (*máquina*) contraption.
armazón [arma'θon] *nf o m* body, chassis;
(*de mueble etc*) frame; (*ARQ*) skeleton.
Armenia [ar'menja] *nf* Armenia.

armería [arme'ria] *nf* (*museo*) military museum; (*tienda*) gunsmith's.
armiño [ar'miɲo] *nm* stoat; (*piel*) ermine.
armisticio [armis'tiθjo] *nm* armistice.
armonía [armo'nia] *nf* harmony.
armónica [ar'monika] *nf* harmonica; V *tb* **armónico.**
armonice [armo'niθe] *etc vb* V **armonizar.**
armónico, a [ar'moniko, a] *adj* harmonic.
armonioso, a [armo'njoso, a] *adj* harmonious.
armonizar [armoni'θar] *vt* to harmonize; (*diferencias*) to reconcile ♦ *vi* to harmonize; ~ **con** (*fig*) to be in keeping with; (*colores*) to tone in with.
arnés [ar'nes] *nm* armour; **arneses** *nmpl* harness *sg.*
aro ['aro] *nm* ring; (*tejo*) quoit; (*AM*: *pendiente*) earring; **entrar por el** ~ to give in.
aroma [a'roma] *nm* aroma.
aromático, a [aro'matiko, a] *adj* aromatic.
arpa ['arpa] *nf* harp.
arpegio [ar'pexjo] *nm* (*MUS*) arpeggio.
arpía [ar'pia] *nf* (*fig*) shrew.
arpillera [arpi'ʎera] *nf* sacking, sackcloth.
arpón [ar'pon] *nm* harpoon.
arquear [arke'ar] *vt* to arch, bend; ~**se** *vr* to arch, bend.
arqueo [ar'keo] *nm* (*gen*) arching; (*NAUT*) tonnage.
arqueología [arkeolo'xia] *nf* archaeology.
arqueológico, a [arkeo'loxiko, a] *adj* archaeological.
arqueólogo, a [arke'oloɣo, a] *nm/f* archaeologist.
arquero [ar'kero] *nm* archer, bowman; (*AM DEPORTE*) goalkeeper.
arquetipo [arke'tipo] *nm* archetype.
arquitecto, a [arki'tekto, a] *nm/f* architect; ~ **paisajista** *o* **de jardines** landscape gardener.
arquitectónico, a [arkitek'toniko, a] *adj* architectural.
arquitectura [arkitek'tura] *nf* architecture.
arrabal [arra'ßal] *nm* suburb; ~**es** *nmpl* outskirts.
arrabalero, a [arraßa'lero, a] *adj* (*fig*) common, coarse.
arracimarse [arraθi'marse] *vr* to cluster together.
arraigado, a [arrai'ɣaðo, a] *adj* deep-rooted; (*fig*) established.
arraigar [arrai'ɣar] *vt* to establish ♦ *vi*, ~**se** *vr* to take root; (*persona*) to settle.
arraigo [a'rraiɣo] *nm* (*raíces*) roots *pl*; (*bienes*) property; (*influencia*) hold; **hombre de** ~ man of property.

arraigue [a'rraiɣe] *etc vb* V **arraigar.**
arrancada [arran'kaða] *nf* (*arranque*) sudden start.
arrancar [arran'kar] *vt* (*sacar*) to extract, pull out; (*arrebatar*) to snatch (away); (*pedazo*) to tear off; (*página*) to rip out; (*suspiro*) to heave; (*AUTO*) to start; (*INFORM*) to boot; (*fig*) to extract ♦ *vi* (*AUTO, máquina*) to start; (*ponerse en marcha*) to get going; ~ **información a algn** to extract information from sb; ~ **de** to stem from.
arranque [a'rranke] *etc vb* V **arrancar** ♦ *nm* sudden start; (*AUTO*) start; (*fig*) fit, outburst.
arras ['arras] *nfpl* pledge *sg*, security *sg.*
arrasar [arra'sar] *vt* (*aplanar*) to level, flatten; (*destruir*) to demolish.
arrastrado, a [arras'traðo, a] *adj* poor, wretched.
arrastrador [arrastra'ðor] *nm* (*en máquina impresora*) tractor.
arrastrar [arras'trar] *vt* to drag (along); (*fig*) to drag down, degrade; (*suj: agua, viento*) to carry away ♦ *vi* to drag, trail on the ground; ~**se** *vr* to crawl; (*fig*) to grovel; **llevar algo arrastrado** to drag sth along.
arrastre [a'rrastre] *nm* drag, dragging; (*DEPORTE*) crawl; **estar para el** ~ (*fig*) to have had it; ~ **de papel por fricción/por tracción** (*en máquina impresora*) friction/tractor feed.
array [a'rrai] *nm* (*INFORM*) array; ~ **empaquetado** (*INFORM*) packed array.
arrayán [arra'jan] *nm* myrtle.
arre ['arre] *excl* gee up!
arrear [arre'ar] *vt* to drive on, urge on ♦ *vi* to hurry along.
arrebañar [arreßa'ɲar] *vt* (*juntar*) to scrape together.
arrebatado, a [arreßa'taðo, a] *adj* rash, impetuous; (*repentino*) sudden, hasty.
arrebatar [arreßa'tar] *vt* to snatch (away), seize; (*fig*) to captivate; ~**se** *vr* to get carried away, get excited.
arrebato [arre'ßato] *nm* fit of rage, fury; (*éxtasis*) rapture; **en un** ~ **de cólera** in an outburst of anger.
arrebolar [arreßo'lar] *vt* to redden; ~**se** *vr* (*enrojecer*) to blush.
arrebujar [arreßu'xar] *vt* (*objetos*) to jumble together; ~**se** *vr* to wrap o.s. up.
arrechar [arre'tʃar] (*AM*) *vt* to arouse, excite; ~**se** *vr* to become aroused.
arrechucho [arre'tʃutʃo] *nm* (*MED*) turn.
arreciar [arre'θjar] *vi* to get worse; (*viento*) to get stronger.

arrecife [arre'θife] *nm* reef.

arredrar [arre'ðrar] *vt* (*hacer retirarse*) to drive back; ~**se** *vr* (*apartarse*) to draw back; ~**se ante algo** to shrink away from sth.

arreglado, a [arre'ɣlaðo, a] *adj* (*ordenado*) neat, orderly; (*moderado*) moderate, reasonable.

arreglar [arre'ɣlar] *vt* (*poner orden*) to tidy up; (*algo roto*) to fix, repair; (*problema*) to solve; ~**se** *vr* to reach an understanding; **arreglárselas** (*fam*) to get by, manage.

arreglo [a'rreɣlo] *nm* settlement; (*orden*) order; (*acuerdo*) agreement; (*MUS*) arrangement, setting; (*INFORM*) array; **con** ~ **a** in accordance with; **llegar a un** ~ to reach a compromise.

arrellanarse [arreʎa'narse] *vr* to sprawl; ~ **en el asiento** to lie back in one's chair.

arremangar [arreman'gar] *vt* to roll up, turn up; ~**se** *vr* to roll up one's sleeves.

arremangue [arre'mange] *etc vb V* **arremangar.**

arremeter [arreme'ter] *vt* to attack, assault; ~ **contra algn** to attack sb.

arremetida [arreme'tiða] *nf* assault.

arremolinarse [arremoli'narse] *vr* to crowd around, mill around; (*corriente*) to swirl, eddy.

arrendador, a [arrenda'ðor, a] *nm/f* landlord/lady.

arrendamiento [arrenda'mjento] *nm* letting; (*el alquilar*) hiring; (*contrato*) lease; (*alquiler*) rent.

arrendar [arren'dar] *vt* to let; to hire; to lease; to rent.

arrendatario, a [arrenda'tarjo, a] *nm/f* tenant.

arreos [a'rreos] *nmpl* harness *sg*, trappings.

arrepentido, a [arrepen'tiðo, a] *nm/f* (*POL*) reformed terrorist.

arrepentimiento [arrepenti'mjento] *nm* regret, repentance.

arrepentirse [arrepen'tirse] *vr* to repent; ~ **de (haber hecho) algo** to regret (doing) sth.

arrepienta [arre'pjenta] *etc*, **arrepintiendo** [arrepin'tjendo] *etc vb V* **arrepentirse.**

arrestar [arres'tar] *vt* to arrest; (*encarcelar*) to imprison.

arresto [a'rresto] *nm* arrest; (*MIL*) detention; (*audacia*) boldness, daring; ~ **domiciliario** house arrest.

arriar [a'rrjar] *vt* (*velas*) to haul down; (*bandera*) to lower, strike; (*un cable*) to pay out.

arriate [a'rrjate] *nm* (*BOT*) bed; (*camino*) road.

═══════════ *PALABRA CLAVE*

arriba [a'rriβa] *adv* **1** (*posición*) above; **desde** ~ from above; ~ **del todo** at the very top, right on top; **Juan está** ~ Juan is upstairs; **lo** ~ **mencionado** the aforementioned; **aquí/allí** ~ up here/ there; **está hasta** ~ **de trabajo** (*fam*) he's up to his eyes in work (*fam*)
2 (*dirección*) up, upwards; **más** ~ higher *o* further up; **calle** ~ up the street
3: **de** ~ **abajo** from top to bottom; **mirar a algn de** ~ **abajo** to look sb up and down
4: **para** ~: **de 5000 pesetas para** ~ from 5,000 pesetas up(wards); **de la cintura (para)** ~ from the waist up
♦ *adj*: **de** ~: **el piso de** ~ the upstairs flat (*BRIT*) *o* apartment; **la parte de** ~ the top *o* upper part
♦ *prep*: ~ **de** (*AM*) above; ~ **de 200 dólares** more than 200 dollars
♦ *excl*: ¡~! up!; ¡**manos** ~! hands up!; ¡~ **España!** long live Spain!

arribar [arri'βar] *vi* to put into port; (*esp AM*: *llegar*) to arrive.

arribista [arri'βista] *nm/f* parvenu(e), upstart.

arribo [a'rriβo] *nm* (*esp AM*) arrival.

arriendo [a'rrjendo] *etc vb V* **arrendar** ♦ *nm* = **arrendamiento.**

arriero [a'rrjero] *nm* muleteer.

arriesgado, a [arrjes'ɣaðo, a] *adj* (*peligroso*) risky; (*audaz*) bold, daring.

arriesgar [arrjes'ɣar] *vt* to risk; (*poner en peligro*) to endanger; ~**se** *vr* to take a risk.

arriesgue [a'rrjesɣe] *etc vb V* **arriesgar.**

arrimar [arri'mar] *vt* (*acercar*) to bring close; (*poner de lado*) to set aside; ~**se** *vr* to come close *o* closer; ~**se a** to lean on; (*fig*) to keep company with; (*buscar ayuda*) to seek the protection of; **arrímate a mí** cuddle up to me.

arrinconado, a [arrinko'naðo, a] *adj* forgotten, neglected.

arrinconar [arrinko'nar] *vt* to put in a corner; (*fig*) to put on one side; (*abandonar*) to push aside.

arriscado, a [arris'kaðo, a] *adj* (*GEO*) craggy; (*fig*) bold, resolute.

arroba [a'rroβa] *nf* (*peso*) 25 pounds; **tiene talento por** ~**s** he has loads *o* bags of talent.

arrobado, a [arro'βaðo, a] *adj* entranced, enchanted.

arrobamiento [arroßa'mjento] *nm* ecstasy.
arrobar [arro'ßar] *vt* to enchant; ~**se** *vr* to be enraptured; (*místico*) to go into a trance.
arrodillarse [arroði'ʎarse] *vr* to kneel (down).
arrogancia [arro'ɣanθja] *nf* arrogance.
arrogante [arro'ɣante] *adj* arrogant.
arrojar [arro'xar] *vt* to throw, hurl; (*humo*) to emit, give out; (*COM*) to yield, produce; ~**se** *vr* to throw *o* hurl o.s.
arrojo [a'rroxo] *nm* daring.
arrollador, a [arroʎa'ðor, a] *adj* crushing, overwhelming.
arrollar [arro'ʎar] *vt* (*enrollar*) to roll up; (*suj: inundación*) to wash away; (*AUTO*) to run over; (*DEPORTE*) to crush.
arropar [arro'par] *vt* to cover (up), wrap up; ~**se** *vr* to wrap o.s. up.
arrostrar [arros'trar] *vt* to face (up to); ~**se** *vr*: ~**se con algn** to face up to sb.
arroyo [a'rrojo] *nm* stream; (*de la calle*) gutter; **poner a algn en el** ~ to turn sb onto the streets.
arroz [a'rroθ] *nm* rice; ~ **con leche** rice pudding.
arrozal [arro'θal] *nm* paddy field.
arruga [a'rruɣa] *nf* fold; (*de cara*) wrinkle; (*de vestido*) crease.
arrugar [arru'ɣar] *vt* to fold; to wrinkle; to crease; ~**se** *vr* to get wrinkled; to get creased.
arrugue [a'rruɣe] *etc vb V* **arrugar**.
arruinar [arrwi'nar] *vt* to ruin, wreck; ~**se** *vr* to be ruined.
arrullar [arru'ʎar] *vi* to coo ♦ *vt* to lull to sleep.
arrumaco [arru'mako] *nm* (*caricia*) caress; (*halago*) piece of flattery.
arrumbar [arrum'bar] *vt* (*objeto*) to discard; (*individuo*) to silence.
arrurruz [arru'rruθ] *nm* arrowroot.
arsenal [arse'nal] *nm* naval dockyard; (*MIL*) arsenal.
arsénico [ar'seniko] *nm* arsenic.
arte ['arte] *nm* (*gen m en sg y siempre f en pl*) art; (*maña*) skill, guile; **por** ~ **de magia** (as if) by magic; **no tener** ~ **ni parte en algo** to have nothing whatsoever to do with sth; ~**s** *nfpl* arts; **Bellas A**~**s** Fine Art *sg*; ~**s y oficios** arts and crafts.
artefacto [arte'fakto] *nm* appliance; (*ARQUEOLOGÍA*) artefact.
arteria [ar'terja] *nf* artery.
arterial [arte'rjal] *adj* arterial; (*presión*) blood *cpd*.
arterio(e)sclerosis [arterjo(e)skle'rosis] *nf inv* hardening of the arteries,

arteriosclerosis.
artesa [ar'tesa] *nf* trough.
artesanía [artesa'nia] *nf* craftsmanship; (*artículos*) handicrafts *pl*.
artesano, a [arte'sano, a] *nm/f* artisan, craftsman/woman.
ártico, a ['artiko, a] *adj* Arctic ♦ *nm*: **el (océano) Á**~ the Arctic (Ocean).
articulación [artikula'θjon] *nf* articulation; (*MED, TEC*) joint.
articulado, a [artiku'laðo, a] *adj* articulated; jointed.
articular [artiku'lar] *vt* to articulate; to join together.
articulista [artiku'lista] *nm/f* columnist, contributor (to a newspaper).
artículo [ar'tikulo] *nm* article; (*cosa*) thing, article; (*TV*) feature, report; ~ **de fondo** leader, editorial; ~**s** *nmpl* goods; ~**s de marca** (*COM*) proprietary goods.
artífice [ar'tifiθe] *nm* artist, craftsman; (*fig*) architect.
artificial [artifi'θjal] *adj* artificial.
artificio [arti'fiθjo] *nm* art, skill; (*artesanía*) craftsmanship; (*astucia*) cunning.
artillería [artiʎe'ria] *nf* artillery.
artillero [arti'ʎero] *nm* artilleryman, gunner.
artilugio [arti'luxjo] *nm* gadget.
artimaña [arti'maɲa] *nf* trap, snare; (*astucia*) cunning.
artista [ar'tista] *nm/f* (*pintor*) artist, painter; (*TEAT*) artist, artiste.
artístico, a [ar'tistiko, a] *adj* artistic.
artritis [ar'tritis] *nf* arthritis.
arveja [ar'ßexa] *nf* (*AM*) pea.
Arz. *abr* (= *Arzobispo*) Abp.
arzobispo [arθo'ßispo] *nm* archbishop.
as [as] *nm* ace; ~ **del fútbol** star player.
asa ['asa] *nf* handle; (*fig*) lever.
asado [a'saðo] *nm* roast (meat); (*AM*: *barbacoa*) barbecue.
asador [asa'ðor] *nm* (*varilla*) spit; (*aparato*) spit roaster.
asadura(s) [asa'ðura(s)] *nf(pl)* entrails *pl*, offal *sg*; (*CULIN*) chitterlings *pl*.
asaetar [asae'tar] *vt* (*fig*) to bother.
asalariado, a [asala'rjaðo, a] *adj* paid, wage-earning, salaried ♦ *nm/f* wage earner.
asaltador, a [asalta'ðor, a], **asaltante** [asal'tante] *nm/f* assailant.
asaltar [asal'tar] *vt* to attack, assault; (*fig*) to assail.
asalto [a'salto] *nm* attack, assault; (*DEPORTE*) round.
asamblea [asam'blea] *nf* assembly; (*reunión*) meeting.

asar [a'sar] *vt* to roast; ~ **al horno/a la parrilla** to bake/grill; ~**se** *vr* (*fig*): **me aso de calor** I'm roasting; **aquí se asa uno vivo** it's boiling hot here.

asbesto [as'ßesto] *nm* asbestos.

ascendencia [asθen'denθja] *nf* ancestry; **de ~ francesa** of French origin.

ascender [asθen'der] *vi* (*subir*) to ascend, rise; (*ser promovido*) to gain promotion ♦ *vt* to promote; ~ **a** to amount to.

ascendiente [asθen'djente] *nm* influence ♦ *nm/f* ancestor.

ascensión [asθen'sjon] *nf* ascent; **la A~** the Ascension.

ascenso [as'θenso] *nm* ascent; (*promoción*) promotion.

ascensor [asθen'sor] *nm* lift (*BRIT*), elevator (*US*).

ascético, a [as'θetiko, a] *adj* ascetic.

ascienda [as'θjenda] *etc vb V* **ascender.**

asco ['asko] *nm*: **el ajo me da ~** I hate *o* loathe garlic; **hacer ~s de algo** to turn up one's nose at sth; **estar hecho un ~** to be filthy; **poner a algn de ~** to call sb all sorts of names *o* every name under the sun; **¡qué ~!** how revolting *o* disgusting!

ascua ['askwa] *nf* ember; **arrimar el ~ a su sardina** to look after number one; **estar en ~s** to be on tenterhooks.

aseado, a [ase'aðo, a] *adj* clean; (*arreglado*) tidy; (*pulcro*) smart.

asear [ase'ar] *vt* (*lavar*) to wash; (*ordenar*) to tidy (up).

asechanza [ase'tʃanθa] *nf* trap, snare.

asediar [ase'ðjar] *vt* (*MIL*) to besiege, lay siege to; (*fig*) to chase, pester.

asedio [ase'ðjo] *nm* siege; (*COM*) run.

asegurado, a [aseɣu'raðo, a] *adj* insured.

asegurador, a [aseɣura'ðor, a] *nm/f* insurer.

asegurar [aseɣu'rar] *vt* (*consolidar*) to secure, fasten; (*dar garantía de*) to guarantee; (*preservar*) to safeguard; (*afirmar, dar por cierto*) to assure, affirm; (*tranquilizar*) to reassure; (*tomar un seguro*) to insure; ~**se** *vr* to assure o.s., make sure.

asemejarse [aseme'xarse] *vr* to be alike; ~ **a** to be like, resemble.

asentado, a [asen'taðo, a] *adj* established, settled.

asentar [asen'tar] *vt* (*sentar*) to seat, sit down; (*poner*) to place, establish; (*alisar*) to level, smooth down *o* out; (*anotar*) to note down ♦ *vi* to be suitable, suit.

asentimiento [asenti'mjento] *nm* assent, agreement.

asentir [asen'tir] *vi* to assent, agree.

aseo [a'seo] *nm* cleanliness; ~**s** *nmpl* toilet *sg* (*BRIT*), restroom *sg* (*US*), cloakroom *sg*.

aséptico, a [a'septiko, a] *adj* germ-free, free from infection.

asequible [ase'kißle] *adj* (*precio*) reasonable; (*meta*) attainable; (*persona*) approachable.

aserradero [aserra'ðero] *nm* sawmill.

aserrar [ase'rrar] *vt* to saw.

asesinar [asesi'nar] *vt* to murder; (*POL*) to assassinate.

asesinato [asesi'nato] *nm* murder; assassination.

asesino, a [ase'sino, a] *nm/f* murderer, killer; (*POL*) assassin.

asesor, a [ase'sor, a] *nm/f* adviser, consultant; (*COM*) assessor, consultant; ~ **administrativo** management consultant.

asesorar [aseso'rar] *vt* (*JUR*) to advise, give legal advice to; (*COM*) to act as consultant to; ~**se** *vr*: ~**se con** *o* **de** to take advice from, consult.

asesoría [aseso'ria] *nf* (*cargo*) consultancy; (*oficina*) consultant's office.

asestar [ases'tar] *vt* (*golpe*) to deal; (*arma*) to aim; (*tiro*) to fire.

aseverar [aseße'rar] *vt* to assert.

asfaltado, a [asfal'taðo, a] *adj* asphalted ♦ *nm* (*pavimento*) asphalt.

asfalto [as'falto] *nm* asphalt.

asfixia [as'fiksja] *nf* asphyxia, suffocation.

asfixiar [asfik'sjar] *vt* to asphyxiate, suffocate.

asga ['asɣa] *etc vb V* **asir.**

así [a'si] *adv* (*de esta manera*) in this way, like this, thus; (*aunque*) although; (*tan pronto como*) as soon as; ~ **que** so; ~ **como** as well as; ~ **y todo** even so; **¿no es ~?** isn't it?, didn't you? *etc*; ~ **de grande** this big; **¡~ sea!** so be it!; ~ **es la vida** such is life, that's life.

Asia ['asja] *nf* Asia.

asiático, a [a'sjatiko, a] *adj*, *nm/f* Asian, Asiatic.

asidero [asi'ðero] *nm* handle.

asiduidad [asiðwi'ðað] *nf* assiduousness.

asiduo, a [a'siðwo, a] *adj* assiduous; (*frecuente*) frequent ♦ *nm/f* regular (customer).

asiento [a'sjento] *etc vb V* **asentar, asentir** ♦ *nm* (*mueble*) seat, chair; (*de coche, en tribunal etc*) seat; (*localidad*) seat, place; (*fundamento*) site; ~ **delantero/trasero** front/back seat.

asierre [a'sjerre] *etc vb V* **aserrar.**

asignación [asiɣna'θjon] *nf* (*atribución*)

assignment; (*reparto*) allocation; (*COM*) allowance; ~ **(semanal)** pocket money; ~ **de presupuesto** budget appropriation.

asignar [asiɣ'nar] *vt* to assign, allocate.

asignatura [asiɣna'tura] *nf* subject; (*curso*) course; ~ **pendiente** (*fig*) matter pending.

asilado, a [asi'laðo, a] *nm/f* refugee.

asilo [a'silo] *nm* (*refugio*) asylum, refuge; (*establecimiento*) home, institution; ~ **político** political asylum.

asimilación [asimila'θjon] *nf* assimilation.

asimilar [asimi'lar] *vt* to assimilate.

asimismo [asi'mismo] *adv* in the same way, likewise.

asintiendo [asin'tjendo] *etc vb V* **asentir.**

asir [a'sir] *vt* to seize, grasp; ~**se** *vr* to take hold; ~**se a** *o* **de** to seize.

asistencia [asis'tenθja] *nf* presence; (*TEAT*) audience; (*MED*) attendance; (*ayuda*) assistance; ~ **social** social *o* welfare work.

asistente, a [asis'tente, a] *nm/f* assistant ♦ *nm* (*MIL*) orderly ♦ *nf* daily help; **los** ~**s** those present; ~ **social** social worker.

asistido, a [asis'tiðo, a] *adj* (*AUTO*: *dirección*) power-assisted; ~ **por ordenador** computer-assisted.

asistir [asis'tir] *vt* to assist, help ♦ *vi*: ~ **a** to attend, be present at.

asma ['asma] *nf* asthma.

asno ['asno] *nm* donkey; (*fig*) ass.

asociación [asoθja'θjon] *nf* association; (*COM*) partnership.

asociado, a [aso'θjaðo, a] *adj* associate ♦ *nm/f* associate; (*COM*) partner.

asociar [aso'θjar] *vt* to associate; ~**se** *vr* to become partners.

asolar [aso'lar] *vt* to destroy.

asolear [asole'ar] *vt* to put in the sun; ~**se** *vr* to sunbathe.

asomar [aso'mar] *vt* to show, stick out ♦ *vi* to appear; ~**se** *vr* to appear, show up; ~ **la cabeza por la ventana** to put one's head out of the window.

asombrar [asom'brar] *vt* to amaze, astonish; ~**se** *vr*: ~**se (de)** (*sorprenderse*) to be amazed (at); (*asustarse*) to be frightened (at).

asombro [a'sombro] *nm* amazement, astonishment.

asombroso, a [asom'broso, a] *adj* amazing, astonishing.

asomo [a'somo] *nm* hint, sign; **ni por** ~ by no means.

asonancia [aso'nanθja] *nf* (*LIT*) assonance; (*fig*) connection; **no tener** ~ **con** to bear no relation to.

asorocharse [asoro'tʃarse] *vr* (*AM*) to get mountain sickness.

aspa ['aspa] *nf* (*cruz*) cross; (*de molino*) sail; **en** ~ X-shaped.

aspaviento [aspa'ßjento] *nm* exaggerated display of feeling; (*fam*) fuss.

aspecto [as'pekto] *nm* (*apariencia*) look, appearance; (*fig*) aspect; **bajo ese** ~ from that point of view.

aspereza [aspe'reθa] *nf* roughness; (*de fruta*) sharpness; (*de carácter*) surliness.

áspero, a ['aspero, a] *adj* rough; sharp; harsh.

aspersión [asper'sjon] *nf* sprinkling; (*AGR*) spraying.

aspersor [asper'sor] *nm* sprinkler.

aspiración [aspira'θjon] *nf* breath, inhalation; (*MUS*) short pause; **aspiraciones** *nfpl* aspirations.

aspiradora [aspira'ðora] *nf* vacuum cleaner, Hoover ®.

aspirante [aspi'rante] *nm/f* (*candidato*) candidate; (*DEPORTE*) contender.

aspirar [aspi'rar] *vt* to breathe in ♦ *vi*: ~ **a** to aspire to.

aspirina [aspi'rina] *nf* aspirin.

asquear [aske'ar] *vt* to sicken ♦ *vi* to be sickening; ~**se** *vr* to feel disgusted.

asquerosidad [askerosi'ðað] *nf* (*suciedad*) filth; (*dicho*) obscenity; (*truco*) dirty trick.

asqueroso, a [aske'roso, a] *adj* disgusting, sickening.

asta ['asta] *nf* lance; (*arpón*) spear; (*mango*) shaft, handle; (*ZOOL*) horn; **a media** ~ at half mast.

astado, a [as'taðo, a] *adj* horned ♦ *nm* bull.

asterisco [aste'risko] *nm* asterisk.

asteroide [aste'roiðe] *nm* asteroid.

astigmatismo [astiɣma'tismo] *nm* astigmatism.

astilla [as'tiʎa] *nf* splinter; (*pedacito*) chip; ~**s** *nfpl* firewood *sg.*

astillarse [asti'ʎarse] *vr* to splinter; (*fig*) to shatter.

astillero [asti'ʎero] *nm* shipyard.

astringente [astrin'xente] *adj, nm* astringent.

astro ['astro] *nm* star.

astrología [astrolo'xia] *nf* astrology.

astrólogo, a [as'troloɣo, a] *nm/f* astrologer.

astronauta [astro'nauta] *nm/f* astronaut.

astronave [astro'naße] *nm* spaceship.

astronomía [astrono'mia] *nf* astronomy.

astronómico, a [astro'nomiko, a] *adj* (*tb fig*) astronomical.

astrónomo, a [as'tronomo, a] *nm/f*

astronomer.

astroso, a [as'troso, a] adj (desaliñado) untidy; (vil) contemptible.

astucia [as'tuθja] nf astuteness; (destreza) clever trick.

asturiano, a [astu'rjano, a] adj, nm/f Asturian.

Asturias [as'turjas] nfpl Asturias; **Príncipe de** ~ crown prince.

astuto, a [as'tuto, a] adj astute; (taimado) cunning.

asueto [a'sweto] nm holiday; (tiempo libre) time off; **día de** ~ day off; **tarde de** ~ (trabajo) afternoon off; (ESCOL) half-holiday.

asumir [asu'mir] vt to assume.

asunción [asun'θjon] nf assumption.

asunto [a'sunto] nm (tema) matter, subject; (negocio) business; **¡eso es** ~ **mio!** that's my business!; ~**s exteriores** foreign affairs; ~**s a tratar** agenda sg.

asustadizo, a [asusta'ðiθo, a] adj easily frightened.

asustar [asus'tar] vt to frighten; ~**se** vr to be/become frightened.

atacante [ata'kante] nm/f attacker.

atacar [ata'kar] vt to attack.

atadura [ata'ðura] nf bond, tie.

atajar [ata'xar] vt (gen) to stop; (ruta de fuga) to cut off; (discurso) to interrupt ♦ vi to take a short cut.

atajo [a'taxo] nm short cut; (DEPORTE) tackle.

atalaya [ata'laja] nf watchtower.

atañer [ata'ɲer] vi: ~ **a** to concern; **en lo que atañe a eso** with regard to that.

ataque [a'take] etc vb V **atacar** ♦ nm attack; ~ **cardíaco** heart attack.

atar [a'tar] vt to tie, tie up; ~ **la lengua a algn** (fig) to silence sb.

atardecer [ataɾðe'θer] vi to get dark ♦ nm evening; (crepúsculo) dusk.

atardezca [atar'ðeθka] etc vb V **atardecer**.

atareado, a [atare'aðo, a] adj busy.

atascar [atas'kar] vt to clog up; (obstruir) to jam; (fig) to hinder; ~**se** vr to stall; (cañería) to get blocked up; (fig) to get bogged down; (en discurso) to dry up.

atasco [a'tasko] nm obstruction; (AUTO) traffic jam.

atasque [a'taske] etc vb V **atascar**.

ataúd [ata'uð] nm coffin.

ataviar [ata'ßjar] vt to deck, array; ~**se** vr to dress up.

atavío [ata'ßio] nm attire, dress; ~**s** nmpl finery sg.

ateísmo [ate'ismo] nm atheism.

atemorice [atemo'riθe] etc vb V **atemorizar**.

atemorizar [atemori'θar] vt to frighten, scare; ~**se** vr to get frightened o scared.

Atenas [a'tenas] nf Athens.

atención [aten'θjon] nf attention; (bondad) kindness ♦ excl (be) careful!, look out!; **en** ~ **a esto** in view of this.

atender [aten'der] vt to attend to, look after; (TEC) to service; (enfermo) to care for; (ruego) to comply with ♦ vi to pay attention; ~ **a** to attend to; (detalles) to take care of.

atendré [aten'dre] etc vb V **atenerse**.

atenerse [ate'nerse] vr: ~ **a** to abide by, adhere to.

atenga [a'tenga] etc vb V **atenerse**.

ateniense [ate'njense] adj, nm/f Athenian.

atentado [aten'taðo] nm crime, illegal act; (asalto) assault; (terrorista) attack; ~ **contra la vida de algn** attempt on sb's life; ~ **golpista** (POL) attempted coup.

atentamente [atenta'mente] adv: **le saluda** ~ Yours faithfully.

atentar [aten'tar] vi: ~ **a** o **contra** to commit an outrage against.

atento, a [a'tento, a] adj attentive, observant; (cortés) polite, thoughtful; **su atenta (carta)** (COM) your letter.

atenuante [ate'nwante] adj: **circunstancias** ~**s** extenuating o mitigating circumstances ♦ nmpl: ~**s** extenuating o mitigating circumstances.

atenuar [ate'nwar] vt to attenuate; (disminuir) to lessen, minimize.

ateo, a [a'teo, a] adj atheistic ♦ nm/f atheist.

aterciopelado, a [aterθjope'laðo, a] adj velvety.

aterido, a [ate'riðo, a] adj: ~ **de frío** frozen stiff.

aterrador, a [aterra'ðor, a] adj frightening.

aterrar [ate'rrar] vt to frighten; (aterrorizar) to terrify; ~**se** vr to be frightened; to be terrified.

aterrice [ate'rriθe] etc vb V **aterrizar**.

aterrizaje [aterri'θaxe] nm landing; ~ **forzoso** forced landing.

aterrizar [aterri'θar] vi to land.

aterrorice [aterro'riθe] etc vb V **aterrorizar**.

aterrorizar [aterrori'θar] vt to terrify.

atesorar [ateso'rar] vt to hoard, store up.

atestado, a [ates'taðo, a] adj packed ♦ nm (JUR) affidavit.

atestar [ates'tar] vt to pack, stuff; (JUR) to attest, testify to.

atestiguar [atesti'ɣwar] vt to testify to, bear witness to.

atestigüe [ates'tiɣwe] etc vb V **atestiguar**.

atiborrar – atribución

atiborrar [atißo'rrar] *vt* to fill, stuff; ~**se** *vr* to stuff o.s.

atice [a'tiθe] *etc vb* V **atizar**.

ático ['atiko] *nm* attic; ~ **de lujo** penthouse flat.

atienda [a'tjenda] *etc vb* V **atender**.

atildar [atil'dar] *vt* to criticize; (*TIP*) to put a tilde over; ~**se** *vr* to spruce o.s. up.

atinado, a [ati'naðo, a] *adj* correct; (*sensato*) sensible.

atinar [ati'nar] *vi* (*acertar*) to be right; ~ **con** *o* **en** (*solución*) to hit upon; ~ **a hacer** to manage to do.

atípico, a [a'tipiko, a] *adj* atypical.

atiplado, a [ati'plaðo, a] *adj* (*voz*) high-pitched.

atisbar [atis'ßar] *vt* to spy on; (*echar ojeada*) to peep at.

atizar [ati'θar] *vt* to poke; (*horno etc*) to stoke; (*fig*) to stir up, rouse.

atlántico, a [at'lantiko, a] *adj* Atlantic ♦ *nm*: **el (océano) A~** the Atlantic (Ocean).

atlas ['atlas] *nm* atlas.

atleta [at'leta] *nm/f* athlete.

atlético, a [at'letiko, a] *adj* athletic.

atletismo [atle'tismo] *nm* athletics *sg*.

atmósfera [at'mosfera] *nf* atmosphere.

atmosférico, a [atmos'feriko, a] *adj* atmospheric.

atol(e) [a'tol(e)] *nm* (*AM*) cornflour drink.

atolladero [atoʎa'ðero] *nm*: **estar en un** ~ to be in a jam.

atollarse [ato'ʎarse] *vr* to get stuck; (*fig*) to get into a jam.

atolondrado, a [atolon'draðo, a] *adj* scatterbrained.

atolondramiento [atolondra'mjento] *nm* bewilderment; (*insensatez*) silliness.

atómico, a [a'tomiko, a] *adj* atomic.

atomizador [atomiθa'ðor] *nm* atomizer.

átomo ['atomo] *nm* atom.

atónito, a [a'tonito, a] *adj* astonished, amazed.

atontado, a [aton'taðo, a] *adj* stunned; (*bobo*) silly, daft.

atontar [aton'tar] *vt* to stun; ~**se** *vr* to become confused.

atorar [ato'rar] *vt* to obstruct; ~**se** *vr* (*atragantarse*) to choke.

atormentar [atormen'tar] *vt* to torture; (*molestar*) to torment; (*acosar*) to plague, harass.

atornillar [atorni'ʎar] *vt* to screw on *o* down.

atorón [ato'ron] *nm* (*AM*) traffic jam.

atosigar [atosi'ɣar] *vt* to harass.

atosigue [ato'siɣe] *etc vb* V **atosigar**.

atrabiliario, a [atraßi'ljarjo, a] *adj* bad-tempered.

atracadero [atraka'ðero] *nm* pier.

atracador, a [atraka'ðor, a] *nm/f* robber.

atracar [atra'kar] *vt* (*NAUT*) to moor; (*robar*) to hold up, rob ♦ *vi* to moor; ~**se** *vr* (*hartarse*) to stuff o.s.

atracción [atrak'θjon] *nf* attraction.

atraco [a'trako] *nm* holdup, robbery.

atracón [atra'kon] *nm*: **darse** *o* **pegarse un** ~ **(de)** (*fam*) to pig out (on).

atractivo, a [atrak'tißo, a] *adj* attractive ♦ *nm* attraction; (*belleza*) attractiveness.

atraer [atra'er] *vt* to attract; **dejarse** ~ **por** to be tempted by.

atragantarse [atraɣan'tarse] *vr*: ~ **(con algo)** to choke (on sth); **se me ha atragantado el chico ese/el inglés** I don't take to that boy/English.

atraiga [a'traiɣa] *etc*, **atraje** [a'traxe] *etc vb* V **atraer**.

atrancar [atran'kar] *vt* (*con tranca, barra*) to bar, bolt.

atranque [a'tranke] *etc vb* V **atrancar**.

atrapar [atra'par] *vt* to trap; (*resfriado etc*) to catch.

atraque [a'trake] *etc vb* V **atracar**.

atrás [a'tras] *adv* (*movimiento*) back(wards); (*lugar*) behind; (*tiempo*) previously; **ir hacia** ~ to go back(wards); to go to the rear; **estar** ~ to be behind *o* at the back.

atrasado, a [atra'saðo, a] *adj* slow; (*pago*) overdue, late; (*país*) backward.

atrasar [atra'sar] *vi* to be slow; ~**se** *vr* to remain behind; (*llegar tarde*) to arrive late.

atraso [a'traso] *nm* slowness; lateness, delay; (*de país*) backwardness; ~**s** *nmpl* arrears.

atravesado, a [atraße'saðo, a] *adj*: **un tronco** ~ **en la carretera** a tree trunk lying across the road.

atravesar [atraße'sar] *vt* (*cruzar*) to cross (over); (*traspasar*) to pierce; (*período*) to go through; (*poner al través*) to lay *o* put across; ~**se** *vr* to come in between; (*intervenir*) to interfere.

atraviese [atra'ßjese] *etc vb* V **atravesar**.

atrayendo [atra'jendo] *vb* V **atraer**.

atrayente [atra'jente] *adj* attractive.

atreverse [atre'ßerse] *vr* to dare; (*insolentarse*) to be insolent.

atrevido, a [atre'ßiðo, a] *adj* daring; insolent.

atrevimiento [atreßi'mjento] *nm* daring; insolence.

atribución [atrißu'θjon] *nf* (*LIT*) attribution; **atribuciones** *nfpl* (*POL*) functions; (*ADMIN*)

responsibilities.
atribuir [atriβu'ir] *vt* to attribute;
(*funciones*) to confer.
atribular [atriβu'lar] *vt* to afflict, distress.
atributo [atri'βuto] *nm* attribute.
atribuya [atri'βuja] *etc*, **atribuyendo**
[atriβu'jendo] *etc vb V* **atribuir**.
atril [a'tril] *nm* lectern; (*MUS*) music stand.
atrincherarse [atrintʃe'rarse] *vr* (*MIL*) to
dig (o.s.) in; ~ **en** (*fig*) to hide behind.
atrio ['atrjo] *nm* (*REL*) porch.
atrocidad [atroθi'ðað] *nf* atrocity, outrage.
atrofiado, a [atro'fjaðo, a] *adj* (*extremidad*)
withered.
atrofiarse [atro'fjarse] *vr* (*tb fig*) to
atrophy.
atronador, a [atrona'ðor, a] *adj* deafening.
atropellar [atrope'ʎar] *vt* (*derribar*) to
knock over *o* down; (*empujar*) to push
(aside); (*AUTO*) to run over *o* down;
(*agraviar*) to insult; ~**se** *vr* to act hastily.
atropello [atro'peʎo] *nm* (*AUTO*) accident;
(*empujón*) push; (*agravio*) wrong;
(*atrocidad*) outrage.
atroz [a'troθ] *adj* atrocious, awful.
A.T.S. *nm/f abr* (= *Ayudante Técnico
Sanitario*) nurse.
atto., a. *abr* (= *atento, a*) Yours faithfully.
attrezzo [a'treθo] *nm* props *pl*.
atuendo [a'twendo] *nm* attire.
atufar [atu'far] *vt* (*suj: olor*) to overcome;
(*molestar*) to irritate; ~**se** *vr* (*fig*) to get
cross.
atún [a'tun] *nm* tuna, tunny.
aturdir [atur'ðir] *vt* to stun; (*suj: ruido*) to
deafen; (*fig*) to dumbfound, bewilder.
atur(r)ullar [atur(r)u'ʎar] *vt* to bewilder.
atusar [atu'sar] *vt* (*cortar*) to trim; (*alisar*)
to smooth (down).
atuve [a'tuβe] *etc vb V* **atenerse**.
audacia [au'ðaθja] *nf* boldness, audacity.
audaz [au'ðaθ] *adj* bold, audacious.
audible [au'ðiβle] *adj* audible.
audición [auði'θjon] *nf* hearing; (*TEAT*)
audition; ~ **radiofónica** radio concert.
audiencia [au'ðjenθja] *nf* audience; (*JUR*)
high court; (*POL*): ~ **pública** public
inquiry.
audífono [au'ðifono] *nm* hearing aid.
audiovisual [auðjoβi'swal] *adj* audiovisual.
auditivo, a [auði'tiβo, a] *adj* hearing *cpd*;
(*conducto, nervio*) auditory.
auditor [auði'tor] *nm* (*JUR*) judge-
advocate; (*COM*) auditor.
auditoría [auðito'ria] *nf* audit; (*profesión*)
auditing.
auditorio [auði'torjo] *nm* audience; (*sala*)

auditorium.
auge ['auxe] *nm* boom; (*clímax*) climax;
(*ECON*) expansion; **estar en** ~ to thrive.
augurar [auɣu'rar] *vt* to predict; (*presagiar*)
to portend.
augurio [au'vurjo] *nm* omen.
aula ['aula] *nf* classroom.
aullar [au'ʎar] *vi* to howl, yell.
aullido [au'ʎiðo] *nm* howl, yell.
aumentar [aumen'tar] *vt* to increase;
(*precios*) to put up; (*producción*) to step
up; (*con microscopio, anteojos*) to magnify
◊ *vi*, ~**se** *vr* to increase, be on the
increase.
aumento [au'mento] *nm* increase; rise.
aún [a'un] *adv* still, yet.
aun [a'un] *adv* even.
aunque [a'unke] *conj* though, although,
even though.
aúpa [a'upa] *excl* up!, come on!; (*fam*): **una
función de** ~ a slap-up do; **una paliza de**
~ a good hiding.
aupar [au'par] *vt* (*levantar*) to help up; (*fig*)
to praise.
aura ['aura] *nf* (*atmósfera*) aura.
aureola [aure'ola] *nf* halo.
auricular [auriku'lar] *nm* earpiece,
receiver; ~**es** *nmpl* headphones.
aurora [au'rora] *nf* dawn; ~ **boreal(is)**
northern lights *pl*.
auscultar [auskul'tar] *vt* (*MED: pecho*) to
listen to, sound.
ausencia [au'senθja] *nf* absence.
ausentarse [ausen'tarse] *vr* to go away;
(*por poco tiempo*) to go out.
ausente [au'sente] *adj* absent ◊ *nm/f*
(*ESCOL*) absentee; (*JUR*) missing person.
auspiciar [auspi'sjar] *vt* (*AM*) to back,
sponsor.
auspicios [aus'piθjos] *nmpl* auspices;
(*protección*) protection *sg*.
austeridad [austeri'ðað] *nf* austerity.
austero, a [aus'tero, a] *adj* austere.
austral [aus'tral] *adj* southern ◊ *nm*
monetary unit of Argentina (*1985-1991*).
Australia [aus'tralja] *nf* Australia.
australiano, a [austra'ljano, a] *adj, nm/f*
Australian.
Austria ['austrja] *nf* Austria.
austriaco, a [aus'trjako, a], **austríaco, a**
[aus'triako, a] *adj, nm/f* Austrian.
autenticar [autenti'kar] *vt* to authenticate.
auténtico, a [au'tentiko, a] *adj* authentic.
autentificar [autentifi'kar] *vt* to
authenticate.
autentique [auten'tike] *etc vb V* **autenticar**.
auto ['auto] *nm* (*coche*) car; (*JUR*) edict,
decree; (*: orden*) writ; ~**s** *nmpl* (*JUR*)

proceedings; (: *acta*) court record *sg*; ~
de comparecencia summons, subpoena;
~ **de ejecución** writ of execution.

autoadhesivo, a [autoaðe'siβo, a] *adj* self-
adhesive; (*sobre*) self-sealing.

autoalimentación [autoalimenta'θjon] *nf*
(*INFORM*): ~ **de hojas** automatic paper
feed.

autobiografía [autoβjoɣra'fia] *nf*
autobiography.

autobús [auto'βus] *nm* bus (*BRIT*),
(passenger) bus (*US*).

autocar [auto'kar] *nm* coach; ~ **de línea**
intercity coach.

autocomprobación [autokomproβa'θjon]
nf (*INFORM*) self-test.

autóctono, a [au'toktono, a] *adj* native,
indigenous.

autodefensa [autoðe'fensa] *nf* self-
defence.

autodeterminación [autoðetermina'θjon]
nf self-determination.

autodidacta [autoði'ðakta] *adj* self-taught
♦ *nm/f*: **ser un(a)** ~ to be self-taught.

autoescuela [autoes'kwela] *nf* driving
school.

autofinanciado, a [autofinan'θjaðo, a] *adj*
self-financing.

autogestión [autoxes'tjon] *nf* self-
management.

autógrafo [au'toɣrafo] *nm* autograph.

automación [automa'θjon] *nf*
= **automatización**.

autómata [au'tomata] *nm* automaton.

automáticamente [auto'matikamente] *adv*
automatically.

automatice [automa'tiθe] *etc vb V*
automatizar.

automático, a [auto'matiko, a] *adj*
automatic ♦ *nm* press stud.

automatización [automatiθa'θjon] *nf*: ~ **de**
fábricas factory automation; ~ **de**
oficinas office automation.

automatizar [automati'θar] *vt* to automate.

automotor, triz [automo'tor, 'triz] *adj*
self-propelled ♦ *nm* diesel train.

automóvil [auto'moβil] *nm* (motor) car
(*BRIT*), automobile (*US*).

automovilismo [automoβi'lismo] *nm*
(*DEPORTE*) (sports) car racing.

automovilista [automoβi'lista] *nm/f*
motorist, driver.

automovilístico, a [automoβi'listiko, a] *adj*
(*industria*) car *cpd*.

autonomía [autono'mia] *nf* autonomy; (*ESP*
POL) autonomy, self-government;
(: *comunidad*) autonomous region.

autonómico, a [auto'nomiko, a] *adj* (*ESP*

POL) relating to autonomy, autonomous;
gobierno ~ autonomous government.

autónomo, a [au'tonomo, a] *adj*
autonomous; (*INFORM*) stand-alone,
offline.

autopista [auto'pista] *nf* motorway (*BRIT*),
freeway (*US*).

autopsia [au'topsja] *nf* autopsy.

autor, a [au'tor, a] *nm/f* author; **los ~es del**
atentado those responsible for the
attack.

autorice [auto'riθe] *etc vb V* **autorizar**.

autoridad [autori'ðað] *nf* authority; ~ **local**
local authority.

autoritario, a [autori'tarjo, a] *adj*
authoritarian.

autorización [autoriθa'θjon] *nf*
authorization.

autorizado, a [autori'θaðo, a] *adj*
authorized; (*aprobado*) approved.

autorizar [autori'θar] *vt* to authorize; to
approve.

autorretrato [autorre'trato] *nm* self-
portrait.

autoservicio [autoser'βiθjo] *nm* self-
service shop *o* store; (*restaurante*) self-
service restaurant.

autostop [auto'stop] *nm* hitch-hiking;
hacer ~ to hitch-hike.

autostopista [autosto'pista] *nm/f* hitch-
hiker.

autosuficiencia [autosufi'θjenθja] *nf* self-
sufficiency.

autosuficiente [autosufi'θjente] *adj* self-
sufficient; (*pey*) smug.

autosugestión [autosuxes'tjon] *nf*
autosuggestion.

autovía [auto'βia] *nf* ≈ dual carriageway
(*BRIT*), separated highway (*US*).

auxiliar [auksi'ljar] *vt* to help ♦ *nm/f*
assistant.

auxilio [auk'siljo] *nm* assistance, help;
primeros ~s first aid *sg*.

Av *abr* (= *Avenida*) Av(e).

a/v *abr* (*COM*: = *a vista*) at sight.

aval [a'βal] *nm* guarantee; (*persona*)
guarantor.

avalancha [aβa'lantʃa] *nf* avalanche.

avalar [aβa'lar] *vt* (*COM etc*) to underwrite;
(*fig*) to endorse.

avalista [aβa'lista] *nm* (*COM*) endorser.

avance [a'βanθe] *etc vb V* **avanzar** ♦ *nm*
advance; (*pago*) advance payment;
(*CINE*) trailer.

avanzado, a [aβan'θaðo, a] *adj* advanced;
de edad avanzada, ~ **de edad** elderly.

avanzar [aβan'θar] *vt, vi* to advance.

avaricia [aβa'riθja] *nf* avarice, greed.

avaricioso, a [aβari'θjoso, a] *adj* avaricious, greedy.

avaro, a [a'βaro, a] *adj* miserly, mean ♦ *nm/f* miser.

avasallar [aβasa'ʎar] *vt* to subdue, subjugate.

avatar [aβa'tar] *nm* change; **~es** ups and downs.

Avda *abr* (= *Avenida*) Av(e).

AVE ['aβe] *nm abr* (= *Alta Velocidad Española*) ≈ Bullet train.

ave ['aβe] *nf* bird; **~ de rapiña** bird of prey.

avecinarse [aβeθi'narse] *vr* (*tormenta, fig*) to approach, be on the way.

avejentar [aβexen'tar] *vt, vi,* **~se** *vr* to age.

avellana [aβe'ʎana] *nf* hazelnut.

avellano [aβe'ʎano] *nm* hazel tree.

avemaría [aβema'ria] *nm* Hail Mary, Ave Maria.

avena [a'βena] *nf* oats *pl.*

avendré [aβen'dre] *etc,* **avenga** [a'βenga] *etc vb V* **avenir.**

avenida [aβe'niða] *nf* (*calle*) avenue.

avenir [aβe'nir] *vt* to reconcile; **~se** *vr* to come to an agreement, reach a compromise.

aventado, a [aβen'taðo, a] *adj* (*AM*) daring.

aventajado, a [aβenta'xaðo, a] *adj* outstanding.

aventajar [aβenta'xar] *vt* (*sobrepasar*) to surpass, outstrip.

aventar [aβen'tar] *vt* to fan, blow; (*grano*) to winnow; (*AM fam: echar*) to chuck out.

aventón [aβen'ton] *nm* (*AM*) push; **pedir ~** to hitch a lift.

aventura [aβen'tura] *nf* adventure; **~ sentimental** love affair.

aventurado, a [aβentu'raðo, a] *adj* risky.

aventurar [aβentu'rar] *vt* to risk; **~se** *vr* to dare; **~se a hacer algo** to venture to do sth.

aventurero, a [aβentu'rero, a] *adj* adventurous.

avergoncé [aβerɣon'θe], **avergoncemos** [aβerɣon'θemos] *etc vb V* **avergonzar.**

avergonzar [aβerɣon'θar] *vt* to shame; (*desconcertar*) to embarrass; **~se** *vr* to be ashamed; to be embarrassed.

avergüence [aβer'ɣwenθe] *etc vb V* **avergonzar.**

avería [aβe'ria] *nf* (*TEC*) breakdown, fault.

averiado, a [aβe'rjaðo, a] *adj* broken-down.

averiar [aβe'rjar] *vt* to break; **~se** *vr* to break down.

averiguación [aβeriɣwa'θjon] *nf* investigation; (*determinación*) ascertainment.

averiguar [aβeri'ɣwar] *vt* to investigate; (*descubrir*) to find out, ascertain.

averigüe [aβe'riɣwe] *etc vb V* **averiguar.**

aversión [aβer'sjon] *nf* aversion, dislike; **cobrar ~ a** to take a strong dislike to.

avestruz [aβes'truθ] *nm* ostrich.

aviación [aβja'θjon] *nf* aviation; (*fuerzas aéreas*) air force.

aviado, a [a'βjaðo, a] *adj:* **estar ~** to be in a mess.

aviador, a [aβja'ðor, a] *nm/f* aviator, airman/woman.

aviar [a'βjar] *vt* to prepare, get ready.

avícola [a'βikola] *adj* poultry *cpd.*

avicultura [aβikul'tura] *nf* poultry farming.

avidez [aβi'ðeθ] *nf* avidity, eagerness.

ávido, a ['aβiðo, a] *adj* avid, eager.

aviente [a'βjente] *etc vb V* **aventar.**

avieso, a [a'βjeso, a] *adj* (*torcido*) distorted; (*perverso*) wicked.

avinagrado, a [aβina'ɣraðo, a] *adj* sour, acid.

avinagrarse [aβina'ɣrarse] *vr* to go o turn sour.

avine [a'βine] *etc vb V* **avenir.**

Aviñón [aβi'ɲon] *nm* Avignon.

avío [a'βio] *nm* preparation; **~s** *nmpl* gear *sg*, kit *sg.*

avión [a'βjon] *nm* aeroplane; (*ave*) martin; **~ de reacción** jet (plane); **por ~** (*CORREOS*) by air mail.

avioneta [aβjo'neta] *nf* light aircraft.

avisar [aβi'sar] *vt* (*advertir*) to warn, notify; (*informar*) to tell; (*aconsejar*) to advise, counsel.

aviso [a'βiso] *nm* warning; (*noticia*) notice; (*COM*) demand note; (*INFORM*) prompt; **~ escrito** notice in writing; **sin previo ~** without warning; **estar sobre ~** to be on the look-out.

avispa [a'βispa] *nf* wasp.

avispado, a [aβis'paðo, a] *adj* sharp, clever.

avispero [aβis'pero] *nm* wasp's nest.

avispón [aβis'pon] *nm* hornet.

avistar [aβis'tar] *vt* to sight, spot.

avitaminosis [aβitami'nosis] *nf inv* vitamin deficiency.

avituallar [aβitwa'ʎar] *vt* to supply with food.

avivar [aβi'βar] *vt* to strengthen, intensify; **~se** *vr* to revive, acquire new life.

avizor [aβi'θor] *adj:* **estar ojo ~** to be on the alert.

avizorar [aβiθo'rar] *vt* to spy on.

axila [ak'sila] *nf* armpit.

axioma [ak'sjoma] *nm* axiom.

ay [ai] *excl* (*dolor*) ow!, ouch!; (*aflicción*)

oh!, oh dear!; ¡~ **de mi!** poor me!

aya ['aja] *nf* governess; (*niñera*) nanny.

ayer [a'jer] *adv, nm* yesterday; **antes de ~** the day before yesterday; **~ por la tarde** yesterday afternoon/evening.

aymara, aymará [ai'mara, aima'ra] *adj, nm/f* Aymara.

ayo ['ajo] *nm* tutor.

ayote [a'jote] *nm* (*AM*) pumpkin.

Ayto. *abr* = **Ayuntamiento.**

ayuda [a'juða] *nf* help, assistance; (*MED*) enema ♦ *nm* page; **~ humanitaria** humanitarian aid.

ayudante, a [aju'ðante, a] *nm/f* assistant, helper; (*ESCOL*) assistant; (*MIL*) adjutant.

ayudar [aju'ðar] *vt* to help, assist.

ayunar [aju'nar] *vi* to fast.

ayunas [a'junas] *nfpl*: **estar en ~** (*no haber comido*) to be fasting; (*ignorar*) to be in the dark.

ayuno [a'juno] *nm* fasting.

ayuntamiento [ajunta'mjento] *nm* (*consejo*) town/city council; (*edificio*) town/city hall; (*cópula*) sexual intercourse.

azabache [aθa'ßatʃe] *nm* jet.

azada [a'θaða] *nf* hoe.

azafata [aθa'fata] *nf* air hostess (*BRIT*) o stewardess.

azafate [asa'fate] *nm* (*AM*) tray.

azafrán [aθa'fran] *nm* saffron.

azahar [aθa'ar] *nm* orange/lemon blossom.

azalea [aθa'lea] *nf* azalea.

azar [a'θar] *nm* (*casualidad*) chance, fate; (*desgracia*) misfortune, accident; **por ~** by chance; **al ~** at random.

azaroso, a [aθa'roso, a] *adj* (*arriesgado*) risky; (*vida*) eventful.

Azerbaiyán [aθerba'jan] *nm* Azerbaijan.

azerbaiyano, a [aθerba'jano, a], **azerí** [aθe'ri] *adj, nm/f* Azerbaijani, Azeri.

azogue [a'θoɣe] *nm* mercury.

azor [a'θor] *nm* goshawk.

azoramiento [aθora'mjento] *nm* alarm; (*confusión*) confusion.

azorar [aθo'rar] *vt* to alarm; **~se** *vr* to get alarmed.

Azores [a'θores] *nfpl*: **las (Islas) ~** the Azores.

azotaina [aθo'taina] *nf* beating.

azotar [aθo'tar] *vt* to whip, beat; (*pegar*) to spank.

azote [a'θote] *nm* (*látigo*) whip; (*latigazo*) lash, stroke; (*en las nalgas*) spank; (*calamidad*) calamity.

azotea [aθo'tea] *nf* (*flat*) roof.

azteca [aθ'teka] *adj, nm/f* Aztec.

azúcar [a'θukar] *nm* sugar.

azucarado, a [aθuka'raðo, a] *adj* sugary, sweet.

azucarero, a [aθuka'rero, a] *adj* sugar *cpd* ♦ *nm* sugar bowl.

azuce [a'θuθe] *etc vb V* **azuzar.**

azucena [aθu'θena] *nf* white lily.

azufre [a'θufre] *nm* sulphur.

azul [a'θul] *adj, nm* blue; **~ celeste/marino** sky/navy blue.

azulejo [aθu'lexo] *nm* tile.

azulgrana [aθul'ɣrana] *adj inv* of Barcelona Football Club ♦ *nm*: **los A~** the Barcelona F.C. players o team.

azuzar [aθu'θar] *vt* to incite, egg on.

B b

B, b [(*ESP*) be, (*AM*) be'larɣa] *nf* (*letra*) B, b; **B de Barcelona** B for Benjamin (*BRIT*) o Baker (*US*).

baba ['baßa] *nf* spittle, saliva; **se le caía la ~** (*fig*) he was thrilled to bits.

babear [baße'ar] *vi* (*echar saliva*) to slobber; (*niño*) to dribble; (*fig*) to drool, slaver.

babel [ba'ßel] *nm o f* bedlam.

babero [ba'ßero] *nm* bib.

Babia ['baßja] *nf*: **estar en ~** to be daydreaming.

bable ['baßle] *nm* Asturian (dialect).

babor [ba'ßor] *nm* port (side); **a ~** to port.

babosada [baßo'saða] *nf*: **decir ~s** (*AM fam*) to talk rubbish.

baboso, a [ba'ßoso, a] *adj* slobbering; (*ZOOL*) slimy; (*AM*) silly ♦ *nm/f* (*AM*) fool.

babucha [ba'ßutʃa] *nf* slipper.

baca ['baka] *nf* (*AUTO*) luggage o roof rack.

bacalao [baka'lao] *nm* cod(fish).

bache ['batʃe] *nm* pothole, rut; (*fig*) bad patch.

bachillerato [batʃiʎe'rato] *nm 2 year secondary school course*; *V tb* **sistema educativo.**

bacilo [ba'θilo] *nm* bacillus, germ.

bacinica [baθi'nika] *nf*, **bacinilla** [baθi'niʎa] *nf* chamber pot.

bacteria [bak'terja] *nf* bacterium, germ.

bacteriológico, a [bakterjo'loxico, a] *adj* bacteriological; **guerra ~a** germ warfare.

báculo ['bakulo] *nm* stick, staff; (*fig*) support.
badajo [ba'ðaxo] *nm* clapper (*of a bell*).
bádminton ['baðminton] *nm* badminton.
baf(f)le ['baf(f)le] *nm* (*ELEC*) speaker.
bagaje [ba'ɣaxe] *nm* baggage; (*fig*) background.
bagatela [baɣa'tela] *nf* trinket, trifle.
Bahama [ba'ama]: **las (Islas) ~, las ~s** *nfpl* the Bahamas.
bahía [ba'ia] *nf* bay.
bailar [bai'lar] *vt*, *vi* to dance.
bailarín, ina [baila'rin, ina] *nm/f* dancer; (*de ballet*) ballet dancer.
baile ['baile] *nm* dance; (*formal*) ball.
baja ['baxa] *nf* drop, fall; (*ECON*) slump; (*MIL*) casualty; (*paro*) redundancy; **dar de ~** (*soldado*) to discharge; (*empleado*) to dismiss, sack; **darse de ~** (*retirarse*) to drop out; (*MED*) to go sick; (*dimitir*) to resign; **estar de ~** (*enfermo*) to be off sick; (*BOLSA*) to be dropping *o* falling; **jugar a la ~** (*ECON*) to speculate on a fall in prices; *V tb* **bajo**.
bajada [ba'xaða] *nf* descent; (*camino*) slope; (*de aguas*) ebb.
bajamar [baxa'mar] *nf* low tide.
bajar [ba'xar] *vi* to go *o* come down; (*temperatura, precios*) to drop, fall ♦ *vt* (*cabeza*) to bow; (*escalera*) to go *o* come down; (*radio etc*) to turn down; (*precio, voz*) to lower; (*llevar abajo*) to take down; **~se** *vr* (*de vehículo*) to get out; (*de autobús*) to get off; **~ de** (*coche*) to get out of; (*autobús*) to get off; **~le los humos a algn** (*fig*) to cut sb down to size.
bajeza [ba'xeθa] *nf* baseness; (*una ~*) vile deed.
bajío [ba'xio] *nm* shoal, sandbank; (*AM*) lowlands *pl*.
bajista [ba'xista] *nm/f* (*MUS*) bassist ♦ *adj* (*BOLSA*) bear *cpd*.
bajo, a ['baxo, a] *adj* (*terreno*) low(-lying); (*mueble, número, precio*) low; (*piso*) ground *cpd*; (*de estatura*) small, short; (*color*) pale; (*sonido*) faint, soft, low; (*voz, tono*) deep; (*metal*) base ♦ *adv* (*hablar*) softly, quietly; (*volar*) low ♦ *prep* under, below, underneath ♦ *nm* (*MUS*) bass; **hablar en voz baja** to whisper; **~ la lluvia** in the rain.
bajón [ba'xon] *nm* fall, drop.
bajura [ba'xura] *nf*: **pesca de ~** coastal fishing.
bakalao [baka'lao] *nm* (*MUS*) rave music.
bala ['bala] *nf* bullet; **~ de goma** plastic bullet.
balacera [bala'sera] *nf* (*AM*) shoot-out.

balada [ba'laða] *nf* ballad.
baladí [bala'ði] *adj* trivial.
baladronada [balaðro'naða] *nf* (*dicho*) boast, brag; (*hecho*) piece of bravado.
balance [ba'lanθe] *nm* (*COM*) balance; (: *libro*) balance sheet; (: *cuenta general*) stocktaking; **~ de comprobación** trial balance; **~ consolidado** consolidated balance sheet; **hacer ~** to take stock.
balancear [balanθe'ar] *vt* to balance ♦ *vi*, **~se** *vr* to swing (to and fro); (*vacilar*) to hesitate.
balanceo [balan'θeo] *nm* swinging.
balandro [ba'landro] *nm* yacht.
balanza [ba'lanθa] *nf* scales *pl*, balance; **~ comercial** balance of trade; **~ de pagos/de poder(es)** balance of payments/of power; (*ASTRO*): **B~** Libra.
balar [ba'lar] *vi* to bleat.
balaustrada [balaus'traða] *nf* balustrade; (*pasamanos*) banister.
balazo [ba'laθo] *nm* (*tiro*) shot; (*herida*) bullet wound.
balboa [bal'ßoa] *nf* Panamanian currency unit.
balbucear [balßuθe'ar] *vi*, *vt* to stammer, stutter.
balbuceo [balßu'θeo] *nm* stammering, stuttering.
balbucir [balßu'θir] *vi*, *vt* to stammer, stutter.
balbuzca [bal'ßuθka] *etc vb V* **balbucir**.
Balcanes [bal'kanes] *nmpl*: **los (Montes) ~** the Balkans, the Balkan Mountains; **la Península de los ~** the Balkan Peninsula.
balcánico, a [bal'kaniko, a] *adj* Balkan.
balcón [bal'kon] *nm* balcony.
balda ['balda] *nf* (*estante*) shelf.
baldar [bal'dar] *vt* to cripple; (*agotar*) to exhaust.
balde ['balde] *nm* (*esp AM*) bucket, pail; **de ~** *adv* (for) free, for nothing; **en ~** *adv* in vain.
baldío, a [bal'dio, a] *adj* uncultivated; (*terreno*) waste; (*inútil*) vain ♦ *nm* wasteland.
baldosa [bal'dosa] *nf* (*azulejo*) floor tile; (*grande*) flagstone.
baldosín [baldo'sin] *nm* wall tile.
balear [bale'ar] *adj* Balearic, of the Balearic Islands ♦ *nm/f* native *o* inhabitant of the Balearic Islands ♦ *vt* (*AM*) to shoot (at).
Baleares [bale'ares] *nfpl*: **las (Islas) ~** the Balearics, the Balearic Islands.
balido [ba'liðo] *nm* bleat, bleating.
balín [ba'lin] *nm* pellet; **balines** *nmpl*

buckshot _sg_.

balística [ba'listika] _nf_ ballistics _pl_.

baliza [ba'liθa] _nf_ (_AVIAT_) beacon; (_NAUT_) buoy.

ballena [ba'ʎena] _nf_ whale.

ballenero, a [baʎe'nero, a] _adj_: **industria ballenera** whaling industry ♦ _nm_ (_pescador_) whaler; (_barco_) whaling ship.

ballesta [ba'ʎesta] _nf_ crossbow; (_AUTO_) spring.

ballet, _pl_ **ballets** [ba'le, ba'les] _nm_ ballet.

balneario, a [balne'arjo, a] _adj_: **estación balnearia** (bathing) resort ♦ _nm_ spa, health resort.

balompié [balom'pje] _nm_ football.

balón [ba'lon] _nm_ ball.

baloncesto [balon'θesto] _nm_ basketball.

balonmano [balon'mano] _nm_ handball.

balonvolea [balombo'lea] _nm_ volleyball.

balsa ['balsa] _nf_ raft; (_BOT_) balsa wood.

bálsamo ['balsamo] _nm_ balsam, balm.

balsón [bal'son] _nm_ (_AM_) swamp, bog.

báltico, a ['baltiko, a] _adj_ Baltic; **el (Mar) B~** the Baltic (Sea).

baluarte [ba'lwarte] _nm_ bastion, bulwark.

bambolearse [bambole'arse] _vr_ to swing, sway; (_silla_) to wobble.

bamboleo [bambo'leo] _nm_ swinging, swaying; wobbling.

bambú [bam'bu] _nm_ bamboo.

banal [ba'nal] _adj_ banal, trivial.

banana [ba'nana] _nf_ (_AM_) banana.

bananal [bana'nal] _nm_ (_AM_) banana plantation.

banano [ba'nano] _nm_ (_AM_) banana tree.

banasta [ba'nasta] _nf_ large basket, hamper.

banca ['banka] _nf_ (_asiento_) bench; (_COM_) banking.

bancario, a [ban'karjo, a] _adj_ banking _cpd_, bank _cpd_; **giro ~** bank draft.

bancarrota [banka'rrota] _nf_ bankruptcy; **declararse en** _o_ **hacer ~** to go bankrupt.

banco ['banko] _nm_ bench; (_ESCOL_) desk; (_COM_) bank; (_GEO_) stratum; **~ comercial** _o_ **mercantil** commercial bank; **~ por acciones** joint-stock bank; **~ de crédito/ de ahorros** credit/savings bank; **~ de arena** sandbank; **~ de datos** (_INFORM_) data bank; **~ de hielo** iceberg.

banda ['banda] _nf_ band; (_cinta_) ribbon; (_pandilla_) gang; (_MUS_) brass band; (_NAUT_) side, edge; **la B~ Oriental** Uruguay; **~ sonora** soundtrack; **~ transportadora** conveyor belt.

bandada [ban'daða] _nf_ (_de pájaros_) flock;

(_de peces_) shoal.

bandazo [ban'daθo] _nm_: **dar ~s** (_coche_) to veer from side to side.

bandeja [ban'dexa] _nf_ tray; **~ de entrada/ salida** in-tray/out-tray.

bandera [ban'dera] _nf_ (_de tela_) flag; (_estandarte_) banner; (_INFORM_) marker, flag; **izar la ~** to hoist the flag.

banderilla [bande'riʎa] _nf_ banderilla; (_tapa_) _savoury appetizer_ (_served on a cocktail stick_).

banderín [bande'rin] _nm_ pennant, small flag.

banderola [bande'rola] _nf_ (_MIL_) pennant.

bandido [ban'diðo] _nm_ bandit.

bando ['bando] _nm_ (_edicto_) edict, proclamation; (_facción_) faction; **pasar al otro ~** to change sides; **los ~s** (_REL_) the banns.

bandolera [bando'lera] _nf_: **bolsa de ~** shoulder bag.

bandolero [bando'lero] _nm_ bandit, brigand.

bandoneón [bandone'on] _nm_ (_AM_) large accordion.

BANESTO [ba'nesto] _nm_ _abr_ = **Banco Español de Crédito**.

banquero [ban'kero] _nm_ banker.

banqueta [ban'keta] _nf_ stool; (_AM: acera_) pavement (_BRIT_), sidewalk (_US_).

banquete [ban'kete] _nm_ banquet; (_para convidados_) formal dinner; **~ de boda** wedding breakfast.

banquillo [ban'kiʎo] _nm_ (_JUR_) dock, prisoner's bench; (_banco_) bench; (_para los pies_) footstool.

bañadera [baɲa'ðera] _nf_ (_AM_) bath(tub).

bañado [baɲa'ðo] _nm_ (_AM_) swamp.

bañador [baɲa'ðor] _nm_ swimming costume (_BRIT_), bathing suit (_US_).

bañar [ba'ɲar] _vt_ (_niño_) to bath, bathe; (_objeto_) to dip; (_de barniz_) to coat; **~se** _vr_ (_en el mar_) to bathe, swim; (_en la bañera_) to have a bath.

bañero, a [ba'ɲero, a] _nm_ lifeguard ♦ _nf_ bath(tub).

bañista [ba'ɲista] _nm/f_ bather.

baño ['baɲo] _nm_ (_en bañera_) bath; (_en río, mar_) dip, swim; (_cuarto_) bathroom; (_bañera_) bath(tub); (_capa_) coating; **ir a tomar los ~s** to take the waters.

baptista [bap'tista] _nm/f_ Baptist.

baqueano, a, baquiano, a [bake'ano, a, baki'ano, a] _nm/f_ (_AM_) guide.

baqueta [ba'keta] _nf_ (_MUS_) drumstick.

bar [bar] _nm_ bar.

barahúnda [bara'unda] _nf_ uproar, hubbub.

baraja [ba'raxa] _nf_ pack (of cards).

> The **baraja española** is the traditional Spanish deck of cards and differs from a standard poker deck. The four **palos** (suits) are **oros** (golden coins), **copas** (goblets), **espadas** (swords), and **bastos** ("clubs", but not like the clubs in a poker pack). Every suit has 9 numbered cards, although for certain games only 7 are used, and 3 face cards: **sota** (Jack), **caballo** (≈ queen) and **rey** (king).

barajar [bara'xar] vt (naipes) to shuffle; (fig) to jumble up.

baranda [ba'randa], **barandilla** [baran'diʎa] nf rail, railing.

baratija [bara'tixa] nf trinket; (fig) trifle; ~s nfpl (COM) cheap goods.

baratillo [bara'tiʎo] nm (tienda) junkshop; (subasta) bargain sale; (conjunto de cosas) second-hand goods pl.

barato, a [ba'rato, a] adj cheap ♦ adv cheap, cheaply.

baratura [bara'tura] nf cheapness.

baraúnda [bara'unda] nf = **barahúnda**.

barba ['barβa] nf (mentón) chin; (pelo) beard; **tener** ~ to be unshaven; **hacer algo en las** ~**s de algn** to do sth under sb's very nose; **reírse en las** ~**s de algn** to laugh in sb's face.

barbacoa [barβa'koa] nf (parrilla) barbecue; (carne) barbecued meat.

barbaridad [barβari'ðað] nf barbarity; (acto) barbarism; (atrocidad) outrage; **una** ~ **de** (fam) loads of; **¡qué** ~! (fam) how awful!; **cuesta una** ~ (fam) it costs a fortune.

barbarie [bar'βarje] nf, **barbarismo** [barβa'rismo] nm barbarism; (crueldad) barbarity.

bárbaro, a ['barβaro, a] adj barbarous, cruel; (grosero) rough, uncouth ♦ nm/f barbarian ♦ adv: **lo pasamos** ~ (fam) we had a great time; **¡qué** ~! (fam) how marvellous!; **un éxito** ~ (fam) a terrific success; **es un tipo** ~ (fam) he's a great bloke.

barbecho [bar'βetʃo] nm fallow land.

barbero [bar'βero] nm barber, hairdresser.

barbilampiño [barβilam'piɲo] adj smooth-faced; (fig) inexperienced.

barbilla [bar'βiʎa] nf chin, tip of the chin.

barbitúrico [barβi'turiko] nm barbiturate.

barbo ['barβo] nm: ~ **de mar** red mullet.

barbotar [barβo'tar], **barbotear** [barβote'ar] vt, vi to mutter, mumble.

barbudo, a [bar'βuðo, a] adj bearded.

barbullar [barβu'ʎar] vi to jabber away.

barca ['barka] nf (small) boat; ~ **pesquera** fishing boat; ~ **de pasaje** ferry.

barcaza [bar'kaθa] nf barge; ~ **de desembarco** landing craft.

Barcelona [barθe'lona] nf Barcelona.

barcelonés, esa [barθelo'nes, esa] adj of o from Barcelona ♦ nm/f native o inhabitant of Barcelona.

barco ['barko] nm boat; (buque) ship; (COM etc) vessel; ~ **de carga** cargo boat; ~ **de guerra** warship; ~ **de vela** sailing ship; **ir en** ~ to go by boat.

baremo [ba'remo] nm scale; (tabla de cuentas) ready reckoner.

barítono [ba'ritono] nm baritone.

barman ['barman] nm barman.

Barna. abr = **Barcelona**.

barnice [bar'niθe] etc vb V **barnizar**.

barniz [bar'niθ] nm varnish; (en la loza) glaze; (fig) veneer.

barnizar [barni'θar] vt to varnish; (loza) to glaze.

barómetro [ba'rometro] nm barometer.

barón [ba'ron] nm baron.

baronesa [baro'nesa] nf baroness.

barquero [bar'kero] nm boatman.

barquilla [bar'kiʎa] nf (NAUT) log.

barquillo [bar'kiʎo] nm cone, cornet.

barra ['barra] nf bar, rod; (JUR) rail; (: banquillo) dock; (de un bar, café) bar; (de pan) French loaf; (palanca) lever; ~ **de carmín** o **de labios** lipstick; ~ **de espaciado** (INFORM) space bar; ~ **inversa** backslash; ~ **libre** free bar; **no pararse en** ~**s** to stick o stop at nothing.

barrabasada [barraβa'saða] nf (piece of) mischief.

barraca [ba'rraka] nf hut, cabin; (en Valencia) thatched farmhouse; (en feria) booth.

barracón [barra'kon] nm (caseta) big hut.

barragana [barra'vana] nf concubine.

barranca [ba'rranka] nf ravine, gully.

barranco [ba'rranko] nm ravine; (fig) difficulty.

barrena [ba'rrena] nf drill.

barrenar [barre'nar] vt to drill (through), bore.

barrendero, a [barren'dero, a] nm/f street-sweeper.

barreno [ba'rreno] nm large drill.

barreño [ba'rreɲo] nm washing-up bowl.

barrer [ba'rrer] vt to sweep; (quitar) to sweep away; (MIL, NAUT) to sweep, rake (with gunfire) ♦ vi to sweep up.

barrera [ba'rrera] nf barrier; (MIL) barricade; (FERRO) crossing gate; **poner** ~**s a** to hinder; ~ **arancelaria** (COM) tariff barrier; ~ **comercial** (*COM*) trade barrier.

barriada [ba'rrjaða] *nf* quarter, district.

barricada [barri'kaða] *nf* barricade.

barrida [ba'rriða] *nf*, **barrido** [ba'rriðo] *nm* sweep, sweeping.

barriga [ba'rriɣa] *nf* belly; (*panza*) paunch; (*vientre*) guts *pl*; **echar** ~ to get middle-age spread.

barrigón, ona [barri'ɣon, ona], **barrigudo, a** [barri'ɣuðo, a] *adj* potbellied.

barril [ba'rril] *nm* barrel, cask; **cerveza de** ~ draught beer.

barrio ['barrjo] *nm* (*vecindad*) area, neighborhood (*US*); (*en las afueras*) suburb; ~**s bajos** poor quarter *sg*; ~ **chino** red-light district.

barriobajero, a [barrjobßa'xero, a] *adj* (*vulgar*) common.

barro ['barro] *nm* (*lodo*) mud; (*objetos*) earthenware; (*MED*) pimple.

barroco, a [ba'rroko, a] *adj* Baroque; (*fig*) elaborate ♦ *nm* Baroque.

barrote [ba'rrote] *nm* (*de ventana etc*) bar.

barruntar [barrun'tar] *vt* (*conjeturar*) to guess; (*presentir*) to suspect.

barrunto [ba'rrunto] *nm* guess; suspicion.

bartola [bar'tola]: **a la** ~ *adv*: **tirarse a la** ~ to take it easy, be lazy.

bártulos ['bartulos] *nmpl* things, belongings.

barullo [ba'ruʎo] *nm* row, uproar.

basa ['basa] *nf* (*ARQ*) base.

basamento [basa'mento] *nm* base, plinth.

basar [ba'sar] *vt* to base; ~**se** *vr*: ~**se en** to be based on.

basca ['baska] *nf* nausea.

báscula ['baskula] *nf* (*platform*) scales *pl*; ~ **biestable** (*INFORM*) flip-flop, toggle.

bascular [basku'lar] *vt* (*INFORM*) to toggle.

base ['base] *nf* base; **a** ~ **de** on the basis of, based on; (*mediante*) by means of; **a** ~ **de bien** in abundance; ~ **de conocimiento** knowledge base; ~ **de datos** database.

básico, a ['basiko, a] *adj* basic.

Basilea [basi'lea] *nf* Basle.

basílica [ba'silika] *nf* basilica.

basilisco [basi'lisko] *nm* (*AM*) iguana; **estar hecho un** ~ to be hopping mad.

basket, básquet ['basket] *nm* basketball.

══════════ *PALABRA CLAVE*

bastante [bas'tante] *adj* **1** (*suficiente*) enough; ~ **dinero** enough *o* sufficient money; ~**s libros** enough books
2 (*valor intensivo*): ~ **gente** quite a lot of people; **tener** ~ **calor** to be rather hot;

hace ~ **tiempo que ocurrió** it happened quite *o* rather a long time ago
♦ *adv*: ~ **bueno/malo** quite good/rather bad; ~ **rico** pretty rich; **(lo)** ~ **inteligente (como) para hacer algo** clever enough *o* sufficiently clever to do sth; **voy a tardar** ~ I'm going to be a while *o* quite some time.

bastar [bas'tar] *vi* to be enough *o* sufficient; ~**se** *vr* to be self-sufficient; ~ **para** to be enough to; **¡basta!** (that's) enough!

bastardilla [bastar'ðiʎa] *nf* italics *pl*.

bastardo, a [bas'tarðo, a] *adj*, *nm/f* bastard.

bastidor [basti'ðor] *nm* frame; (*de coche*) chassis; (*ARTE*) stretcher; (*TEAT*) wing; **entre** ~**es** behind the scenes.

basto, a ['basto, a] *adj* coarse, rough ♦ *nmpl*: ~**s** (*NAIPES*) one of the suits in the Spanish card deck; V tb **Baraja Española**.

bastón [bas'ton] *nm* stick, staff; (*para pasear*) walking stick; ~ **de mando** baton.

bastonazo [basto'naθo] *nm* blow with a stick.

bastoncillo [baston'θiʎo] *nm* (*tb*: ~ **de algodón**) cotton bud.

basura [ba'sura] *nf* rubbish, refuse (*BRIT*), garbage (*US*).

basurero [basu'rero] *nm* (*hombre*) dustman (*BRIT*), garbage collector *o* man (*US*); (*lugar*) rubbish dump; (*cubo*) (rubbish) bin (*BRIT*), trash can (*US*).

bata ['bata] *nf* (*gen*) dressing gown; (*cubretodo*) smock, overall; (*MED, TEC etc*) lab(oratory) coat.

batacazo [bata'kaθo] *nm* bump.

batalla [ba'taʎa] *nf* battle; **de** ~ for everyday use.

batallar [bata'ʎar] *vi* to fight.

batallón [bata'ʎon] *nm* battalion.

batata [ba'tata] *nf* (*AM: CULIN*) sweet potato.

bate ['bate] *nm* (*DEPORTE*) bat.

batea [ba'tea] *nf* (*AM*) washing trough.

bateador [batea'ðor] *nm* (*DEPORTE*) batter, batsman.

batería [bate'ria] *nf* battery; (*MUS*) drums *pl*; (*TEAT*) footlights *pl*; ~ **de cocina** kitchen utensils *pl*.

batiburrillo [batißu'rriʎo] *nm* hotchpotch.

batido, a [ba'tiðo, a] *adj* (*camino*) beaten, well-trodden ♦ *nm* (*CULIN*) batter; ~ (**de leche**) milk shake ♦ *nf* (*AM*) (police) raid.

batidora [bati'ðora] *nf* beater, mixer; ~ **eléctrica** food mixer, blender.

batir [ba'tir] *vt* to beat, strike; (*vencer*) to beat, defeat; (*revolver*) to beat, mix; (*pelo*) to back-comb; **~se** *vr* to fight; **~ palmas** to clap, applaud.

baturro, a [ba'turro, a] *nm/f* Aragonese peasant.

batuta [ba'tuta] *nf* baton; **llevar la ~** (*fig*) to be the boss.

baudio ['bauðjo] *nm* (*INFORM*) baud.

baúl [ba'ul] *nm* trunk; (*AM AUTO*) boot (*BRIT*), trunk (*US*).

bautice [bau'tiθe] *etc vb* V **bautizar**.

bautismo [bau'tismo] *nm* baptism, christening.

bautista [bau'tista] *adj, nm/f* Baptist.

bautizar [bauti'θar] *vt* to baptize, christen; (*fam: diluir*) to water down; (*dar apodo*) to dub.

bautizo [bau'tiθo] *nm* baptism, christening.

bávaro, a ['baβaro, a] *adj, nm/f* Bavarian.

Baviera [ba'βjera] *nf* Bavaria.

baya ['baja] *nf* berry; V *tb* **bayo**.

bayeta [ba'jeta] *nf* (*trapo*) floorcloth; (*AM: pañal*) nappy (*BRIT*), diaper (*US*).

bayo, a ['bajo, a] *adj* bay.

bayoneta [bajo'neta] *nf* bayonet.

baza ['baθa] *nf* trick; **meter ~** to butt in.

bazar [ba'θar] *nm* bazaar.

bazo ['baθo] *nm* spleen.

bazofia [ba'θofja] *nf* pigswill (*BRIT*), hogwash (*US*); (*libro etc*) trash.

beatificar [beatifi'kar] *vt* to beatify.

beato, a [be'ato, a] *adj* blessed; (*piadoso*) pious.

bebe (*AM*), *pl* **bebes, bebé**, *pl* **bebés** ['beβe, 'beβes, be'βe, be'βes] *nm* baby.

bebedero, a [beβe'ðero, a] *nm* (*para animales*) drinking trough.

bebedizo, a [beβe'ðiθo, a] *adj* drinkable ♦ *nm* potion.

bebedor, a [beβe'ðor, a] *adj* hard-drinking.

bebé-probeta [be'βe-pro'βeta], *pl* **bebés-probeta** *nm/f* test-tube baby.

beber [be'βer] *vt, vi* to drink; **~ a sorbos/ tragos** to sip/gulp; **se lo bebió todo** he drank it all up.

bebido, a [be'βiðo, a] *adj* drunk ♦ *nf* drink.

beca ['beka] *nf* grant, scholarship.

becado, a [be'kaðo, a] *nm/f*, **becario, a** [be'karjo, a] *nm/f* scholarship holder.

becerro [be'θerro] *nm* yearling calf.

bechamel [betʃa'mel] *nf* = **besamel**.

becuadro [be'kwaðro] *nm* (*MUS*) natural sign.

bedel [be'ðel] *nm* porter, janitor.

beduino, a [be'ðwino, a] *adj, nm/f* Bedouin.

befarse [be'farse] *vr*: **~ de algo** to scoff at sth.

beige ['beix], **beis** ['beis] *adj, nm* beige.

béisbol ['beisβol] *nm* baseball.

bejuco [be'xuko] *nm* (*AM*) reed, liana.

beldad [bel'dað] *nf* beauty.

Belén [be'len] *nm* Bethlehem; **b~** (*de Navidad*) nativity scene, crib.

belga ['belɣa] *adj, nm/f* Belgian.

Bélgica ['belxika] *nf* Belgium.

Belgrado [bel'ɣraðo] *nm* Belgrade.

Belice [be'liθe] *nm* Belize.

bélico, a ['beliko, a] *adj* (*actitud*) warlike.

belicoso, a [beli'koso, a] *adj* (*guerrero*) warlike; (*agresivo*) aggressive, bellicose.

beligerante [belixe'rante] *adj* belligerent.

bellaco, a [be'ʎako, a] *adj* sly, cunning ♦ *nm* villain, rogue.

belladona [beʎa'ðona] *nf* deadly nightshade.

bellaquería [beʎake'ria] *nf* (*acción*) dirty trick; (*calidad*) wickedness.

belleza [be'ʎeθa] *nf* beauty.

bello, a [be'ʎo, a] *adj* beautiful, lovely; **Bellas Artes** Fine Art *sg*.

bellota [be'ʎota] *nf* acorn.

bemol [be'mol] *nm* (*MUS*) flat; **esto tiene ~es** (*fam*) this is a tough one.

bencina [ben'sina] *nf* (*AM*) petrol (*BRIT*), gas (*US*).

bendecir [bende'θir] *vt* to bless; **~ la mesa** to say grace.

bendición [bendi'θjon] *nf* blessing.

bendiga [ben'diɣa] *etc*, **bendije** [ben'dixe] *etc vb* V **bendecir**.

bendito, a [ben'dito, a] *pp de* **bendecir** ♦ *adj* (*santo*) blessed; (*agua*) holy; (*afortunado*) lucky; (*feliz*) happy; (*sencillo*) simple ♦ *nm/f* simple soul; **¡~ sea Dios!** thank goodness!; **es un ~** he's sweet; **dormir como un ~** to sleep like a log.

benedictino, a [beneðik'tino, a] *adj, nm* Benedictine.

benefactor, a [benefak'tor, a] *nm/f* benefactor/benefactress.

beneficencia [benefi'θenθja] *nf* charity.

beneficiar [benefi'θjar] *vt* to benefit, be of benefit to; **~se** *vr* to benefit, profit.

beneficiario, a [benefi'θjarjo, a] *nm/f* beneficiary; (*de cheque*) payee.

beneficio [bene'fiθjo] *nm* (*bien*) benefit, advantage; (*COM*) profit, gain; **a ~ de** for the benefit of; **en ~ propio** to one's own advantage; **~ bruto/neto** gross/net profit; **~ por acción** earnings *pl* per share.

beneficioso, a [benefi'θjoso, a] *adj* beneficial.

benéfico, a [be'nefiko, a] *adj* charitable;

sociedad ~a charity (organization).
benemérito, a [bene'merito, a] *adj*
meritorious ♦ *nf*: **la Benemérita** (*ESP*) the
Civil Guard; *V tb* **Guardia Civil.**
beneplácito [bene'plaθito] *nm* approval,
consent.
benevolencia [beneßo'lenθja] *nf*
benevolence, kindness.
benévolo, a [be'neßolo, a] *adj* benevolent,
kind.
Bengala [ben'gala] *nf* Bengal; **el Golfo de**
~ the Bay of Bengal.
bengala [ben'gala] *nf* (*MIL*) flare; (*fuego*)
Bengal light; (*materia*) rattan.
bengalí [benga'li] *adj*, *nm/f* Bengali.
benignidad [beniɣni'ðað] *nf* (*afabilidad*)
kindness; (*suavidad*) mildness.
benigno, a [be'niɣno, a] *adj* kind; (*suave*)
mild; (*MED*: *tumor*) benign, non-
malignant.
benjamín [benxa'min] *nm* youngest child.
beodo, a [be'oðo, a] *adj* drunk ♦ *nm/f*
drunkard.
berberecho [berße'retʃo] *nm* cockle.
berenjena [beren'xena] *nf* aubergine
(*BRIT*), eggplant (*US*).
berenjenal [berenxe'nal] *nm* (*AGR*)
aubergine bed; (*fig*) mess; **en buen** ~
nos hemos metido we've got ourselves
into a fine mess.
bergantín [berɣan'tin] *nm* brig(antine).
Berlín [ber'lin] *nm* Berlin.
berlinés, esa [berli'nes, esa] *adj* of *o* from
Berlin ♦ *nm/f* Berliner.
bermejo, a [ber'mexo, a] *adj* red.
bermellón [berme'ʎon] *nm* vermilion.
bermudas [ber'muðas] *nfpl* Bermuda
shorts.
berrear [berre'ar] *vi* to bellow, low.
berrido [be'rriðo] *nm* bellow(ing).
berrinche [be'rrintʃe] *nm* (*fam*) temper,
tantrum.
berro ['berro] *nm* watercress.
berza ['berθa] *nf* cabbage; ~ **lombarda** red
cabbage.
besamel [besa'mel], **besamela**
[besa'mela] *nf* (*CULIN*) white sauce,
bechamel sauce.
besar [be'sar] *vt* to kiss; (*fig*: *tocar*) to
graze; ~**se** *vr* to kiss (one another).
beso ['beso] *nm* kiss.
bestia ['bestja] *nf* beast, animal; (*fig*) idiot;
~ **de carga** beast of burden; ¡~! you
idiot!; ¡**no seas** ~! (*bruto*) don't be such a
brute!; (*idiota*) don't be such an idiot!
bestial [bes'tjal] *adj* bestial; (*fam*) terrific.
bestialidad [bestjali'ðað] *nf* bestiality;
(*fam*) stupidity.

besugo [be'suɣo] *nm* sea bream; (*fam*)
idiot.
besuguera [besu'ɣera] *nf* (*CULIN*) fish pan.
besuquear [besuke'ar] *vt* to cover with
kisses; ~**se** *vr* to kiss and cuddle.
bético, a ['betiko, a] *adj* Andalusian.
betún [be'tun] *nm* shoe polish; (*QUÍMICA*)
bitumen, asphalt.
Bib. *abr* = **Biblioteca.**
biberón [biße'ron] *nm* feeding bottle.
Biblia ['bißlja] *nf* Bible.
bíblico, a ['bißliko, a] *adj* biblical.
bibliografía [bißljoɣra'fia] *nf* bibliography.
biblioteca [bißljo'teka] *nf* library;
(*estantes*) bookcase, bookshelves *pl*; ~ **de**
consulta reference library.
bibliotecario, a [bißljote'karjo, a] *nm/f*
librarian.
B.I.C. [bik] *nf abr* (= *Brigada de Investigación*
Criminal) ≈ CID (*BRIT*), FBI (*US*).
bicarbonato [bikarßo'nato] *nm*
bicarbonate.
bíceps ['biθeps] *nm inv* biceps.
bicho ['bitʃo] *nm* (*animal*) small animal;
(*sabandija*) bug, insect; (*TAUR*) bull; ~
raro (*fam*) queer fish.
bici ['biθi] *nf* (*fam*) bike.
bicicleta [biθi'kleta] *nf* bicycle, cycle; ~
estática/de montaña exercise/mountain
bike.
bicoca [bi'koka] *nf* (*ESP fam*) cushy job.
BID *n abbr* (= *Banco Interamericano de*
Desarrollo) IDB.
bidé [bi'ðe] *nm* bidet.
bidireccional [biðirekθjo'nal] *adj*
bidirectional.
bidón [bi'ðon] *nm* (*grande*) drum;
(*pequeño*) can.
Bielorrusia [bjelo'rrusja] *nf* Belarus,
Byelorussia.
bielorruso, a [bjelo'rruso, a] *adj*, *nm/f*
Belarussian, Belorussian ♦ *nm* (*LING*)
Belarussian, Belorussian.

===== *PALABRA CLAVE*

bien [bjen] *nm* **1** (*bienestar*) good; **te lo digo**
por tu ~ I'm telling you for your own
good; **el** ~ **y el mal** good and evil
2 (*posesión*): ~**es** goods; ~**es de**
consumo/equipo consumer/capital
goods; ~**es inmuebles** *o* **raíces/**~**es**
muebles real estate *sg*/personal
property *sg*
♦ *adv* **1** (*de manera satisfactoria, correcta*
etc) well; **trabaja/come** ~ she works/eats
well; **contestó** ~ he answered correctly;
oler ~ to smell nice *o* good; **me siento** ~
I feel fine; **no me siento** ~ I don't feel

very well; **se está ~ aquí** it's nice here
2 (*frases*): **hiciste ~ en llamarme** you
were right to call me
3 (*valor intensivo*) very; **un cuarto ~
caliente** a nice warm room; **~ de veces**
lots of times; **~ se ve que ...** it's quite
clear that ...
4: **estar ~**: **estoy muy ~ aquí** I feel very
happy here; **¿te encuentras ~?** are you
all right?; **te está ~ la falda** (*ser la talla*)
the skirt fits you; (*sentar*) the skirt suits
you; **el libro está muy ~** the book is
really good; **está ~ que vengan** it's all
right for them to come; **¡está ~! lo haré**
oh all right, I'll do it; **ya está ~ de quejas**
that's quite enough complaining
5 (*de buena gana*): **yo ~ que iría pero ...**
I'd gladly go but ...
♦ *excl*: **¡~!** (*aprobación*) O.K!; **¡muy ~!**
well done!; **¡qué ~!** great!; **~, gracias, ¿y
usted?** fine thanks, and you?
♦ *adj inv*: **niño ~** rich kid; **gente ~** posh
people
♦ *conj* **1**: **~ ... ~**: **~ en coche ~ en tren**
either by car or by train
2: **no ~** (*esp AM*): **no ~ llegue te llamaré**
as soon as I arrive I'll call you
3: **si ~** even though; *V tb* **más.**

bienal [bje'nal] *adj* biennial.
bienaventurado, a [bjenaßentu'raðo, a]
adj (*feliz*) happy; (*afortunado*) fortunate;
(*REL*) blessed.
bienestar [bjenes'tar] *nm* well-being;
estado de ~ welfare state.
bienhechor, a [bjene'tʃor, a] *adj*
beneficent ♦ *nm/f* benefactor/
benefactress.
bienio ['bjenjo] *nm* two-year period.
bienvenido, a [bjembe'niðo, a] *adj*
welcome ♦ *excl* welcome! ♦ *nf* welcome;
dar la bienvenida a algn to welcome sb.
bies ['bjes] *nm*: **falda al ~** bias-cut skirt;
cortar al ~ to cut on the bias.
bifásico, a [bi'fasiko, a] *adj* (*ELEC*) two-
phase.
bife ['bife] *nm* (*AM*) steak.
bifocal [bifo'kal] *adj* bifocal.
bifurcación [bifurka'θjon] *nf* fork; (*FERRO,
INFORM*) branch.
bifurcarse [bifur'karse] *vr* to fork.
bigamia [bi'ɣamja] *nf* bigamy.
bígamo, a ['biɣamo, a] *adj* bigamous ♦ *nm/f*
bigamist.
bígaro ['biɣaro] *nm* winkle.
bigote [bi'ɣote] *nm* (*tb*: **~s**) moustache.
bigotudo, a [biɣo'tuðo, a] *adj* with a big
moustache.

bigudí [biɣu'ði] *nm* (hair-)curler.
bikini [bi'kini] *nm* bikini; (*CULIN*) toasted
cheese and ham sandwich.
bilateral [bilate'ral] *adj* bilateral.
bilbaíno, a [bilßa'ino, a] *adj* of o from
Bilbao ♦ *nm/f* native o inhabitant of
Bilbao.
bilingüe [bi'lingwe] *adj* bilingual.
bilis ['bilis] *nf inv* bile.
billar [bi'ʎar] *nm* billiards *sg*; (*lugar*)
billiard hall; (*galería de atracciones*)
amusement arcade; **~ americano** pool.
billete [bi'ʎete] *nm* ticket; (*de banco*)
banknote (*BRIT*), bill (*US*); (*carta*) note; **~
sencillo, ~ de ida solamente/~ de ida y
vuelta** single (*BRIT*) o one-way (*US*)
ticket/return (*BRIT*) o round-trip (*US*)
ticket; **sacar (un) ~** to get a ticket; **un ~
de 5 libras** a five-pound note.
billetera [biʎe'tera] *nf*, **billetero** [biʎe'tero]
nm wallet.
billón [bi'ʎon] *nm* billion.
bimensual [bimen'swal] *adj* twice
monthly.
bimestral [bimes'tral] *adj* bimonthly.
bimestre [bi'mestre] *nm* two-month
period.
bimotor [bimo'tor] *adj* twin-engined ♦ *nm*
twin-engined plane.
binario, a [bi'narjo, a] *adj* (*INFORM*) binary.
bingo ['bingo] *nm* (*juego*) bingo; (*sala*)
bingo hall.
binóculo [bi'nokulo] *nm* pince-nez.
binomio [bi'nomjo] *nm* (*MAT*) binomial.
biodegradable [bioðeɣra'ðaßle] *adj*
biodegradable.
biodiversidad [bioðißersi'ðað] *nf*
biodiversity.
biografía [bjoɣra'fia] *nf* biography.
biográfico, a [bio'ɣrafiko, a] *adj*
biographical.
biógrafo, a [bi'oɣrafo, a] *nm/f* biographer.
biología [biolo'xia] *nf* biology.
biológico, a [bio'loxiko, a] *adj* biological;
guerra biológica biological warfare.
biólogo, a [bi'oloɣo, a] *nm/f* biologist.
biombo ['bjombo] *nm* (folding) screen.
biopsia [bi'opsja] *nf* biopsy.
bioquímico, a [bio'kimiko, a] *adj*
biochemical ♦ *nm/f* biochemist ♦ *nf*
biochemistry.
biosfera [bios'fera] *nf* biosphere.
bióxido [bi'oksiðo] *nm* dioxide.
bipartidismo [biparti'ðismo] *nm* (*POL*)
two-party system.
biquini [bi'kini] *nm* = **bikini**.
birlar [bir'lar] *vt* (*fam*) to pinch.
birlibirloque [birlißir'loke] *nm*: **por arte de**

~ (as if) by magic.
Birmania [bir'manja] *nf* Burma.
birmano, a [bir'mano, a] *adj nm/f* Burmese.
birrete [bi'rrete] *nm* (*JUR*) judge's cap.
birria ['birrja] *nf* (*fam*): **ser una** ~ to be
rubbish; **ir hecho una** ~ to be *o* look a
sight.
bis [bis] *excl* encore! ♦ *nm* encore ♦ *adv* (*dos
veces*) twice; **viven en el 27** ~ they live
at 27a.
bisabuelo, a [bisa'ßwelo, a] *nm/f* great-
grandfather/mother; **~s** *nmpl* great-
grandparents.
bisagra [bi'saɤra] *nf* hinge.
bisbisar [bisßi'sar], **bisbisear** [bisßise'ar] *vt*
to mutter, mumble.
bisbiseo [bisßi'seo] *nm* muttering.
biselar [bise'lar] *vt* to bevel.
bisexual [bisek'swal] *adj, nm/f* bisexual.
bisiesto [bi'sjesto] *adj*: **año** ~ leap year.
bisnieto, a [bis'njeto, a] *nm/f* great-
grandson/daughter; **~s** *nmpl* great-
grandchildren.
bisonte [bi'sonte] *nm* bison.　　　　　•
bisoñé [biso'ɲe] *nm* toupee.
bisoño, a [bi'soɲo, a] *adj* green,
inexperienced.
bistec [bis'tek], **bisté** [bis'te] *nm* steak.
bisturí [bistu'ri] *nm* scalpel.
bisutería [bisute'ria] *nf* imitation *o*
costume jewellery.
bit [bit] *nm* (*INFORM*) bit; ~ **de parada** stop
bit; ~ **de paridad** parity bit.
bitácora [bi'takora] *nf*: **cuaderno de** ~
logbook, ship's log.
bitio ['bitjo] *nm* (*INFORM*) bit.
bizantino, a [biθan'tino, a] *adj* Byzantine;
(*fig*) pointless.
bizarría [biθa'rria] *nf* (*valor*) bravery;
(*generosidad*) generosity.
bizarro, a [bi'θarro, a] *adj* brave; generous.
bizco, a ['biθko, a] *adj* cross-eyed.
bizcocho [biθ'kotʃo] *nm* (*CULIN*) sponge
cake.
biznieto, a [biθ'njeto, a] *nm/f* = **bisnieto**.
bizquear [biθke'ar] *vi* to squint.
blanco, a ['blanko, a] *adj* white ♦ *nm/f* white
man/woman, white ♦ *nm* (*color*) white;
(*en texto*) blank; (*MIL, fig*) target ♦ *nf*
(*MUS*) minim; **en** ~ blank; **cheque en** ~
blank cheque; **votar en** ~ to spoil one's
vote; **quedarse en** ~ to be disappointed;
noche en ~ sleepless night; **estar sin** ~
to be broke; **ser el** ~ **de las burlas** to be
the butt of jokes.
blancura [blan'kura] *nf* whiteness.
blandengue [blan'denge] *adj* (*fam*) soft,
weak.

blandir [blan'dir] *vt* to brandish.
blando, a ['blando, a] *adj* soft; (*tierno*)
tender, gentle; (*carácter*) mild; (*fam*)
cowardly ♦ *nm/f* (*POL etc*) soft-liner.
blandura [blan'dura] *nf* softness;
tenderness; mildness.
blanquear [blanke'ar] *vt* to whiten;
(*fachada*) to whitewash; (*paño*) to bleach;
(*dinero*) to launder ♦ *vi* to turn white.
blanquecino, a [blanke'θino, a] *adj*
whitish.
blanqueo [blan'keo] *nm* (*de pared*)
whitewashing; (*de dinero*) laundering.
blasfemar [blasfe'mar] *vi* to blaspheme;
(*fig*) to curse.
blasfemia [blas'femja] *nf* blasphemy.
blasfemo, a [blas'femo, a] *adj*
blasphemous ♦ *nm/f* blasphemer.
blasón [bla'son] *nm* coat of arms; (*fig*)
honour.
blasonar [blaso'nar] *vt* to emblazon ♦ *vi* to
boast, brag.
bledo ['bleðo] *nm*: **(no) me importa un** ~ I
couldn't care less.
blindado, a [blin'daðo, a] *adj* (*MIL*)
armour-plated; (*antibalas*) bulletproof;
coche *o* (*AM*) **carro** ~ armoured car;
puertas blindadas security doors.
blindaje [blin'daxe] *nm* armour, armour-
plating.
bloc, *pl* **blocs** [blok, blos] *nm* writing pad;
(*ESCOL*) jotter; ~ **de dibujos** sketch pad.
bloque ['bloke] *nm* (*tb INFORM*) block; (*POL*)
bloc; ~ **de cilindros** cylinder block.
bloquear [bloke'ar] *vt* (*NAUT etc*) to
blockade; (*aislar*) to cut off; (*COM, ECON*)
to freeze; **fondos bloqueados** frozen
assets.
bloqueo [blo'keo] *nm* blockade; (*COM*)
freezing, blocking.
bluejean [blu'jin] *nm* (*AM*) jeans *pl*, denims
pl.
blusa ['blusa] *nf* blouse.
B.º *abr* (*FINANZAS*: = *banco*) bank; (*COM*:
= *beneficiario*) beneficiary.
boa ['boa] *nf* boa.
boato [bo'ato] *nm* show, ostentation.
bobada [bo'ßaða] *nf* foolish action (*o*
statement); **decir ~s** to talk nonsense.
bobalicón, ona [boßali'kon, ona] *adj*
utterly stupid.
bobería [boße'ria] *nf* = **bobada**.
bobina [bo'ßina] *nf* (*TEC*) bobbin; (*FOTO*)
spool; (*ELEC*) coil, winding.
bobo, a ['boßo, a] *adj* (*tonto*) daft, silly;
(*cándido*) naïve ♦ *nm/f* fool, idiot ♦ *nm*
(*TEAT*) clown, funny man.
boca ['boka] *nf* mouth; (*de crustáceo*)

pincer; (*de cañón*) muzzle; (*entrada*) mouth, entrance; (*INFORM*) slot; **~s** *nfpl* (*de río*) mouth *sg*; ~ **abajo/arriba** face down/up; **a** ~ **jarro** point-blank; **se me hace la** ~ **agua** my mouth is watering; **todo salió a pedir de** ~ it all turned out perfectly; **en** ~ **de** (*esp AM*) according to; **la cosa anda de** ~ **en** ~ the story is going the rounds; **¡cállate la** ~**!** (*fam*) shut up!; **quedarse con la** ~ **abierta** to be dumbfounded; **no abrir la** ~ to keep quiet; ~ **del estómago** pit of the stomach; ~ **de metro** tube (*BRIT*) o subway (*US*) entrance.

bocacalle [boka'kaʎe] *nf* (entrance to a) street; **la primera** ~ the first turning o street.

bocadillo [boka'ðiʎo] *nm* sandwich.

bocado [bo'kaðo] *nm* mouthful, bite; (*de caballo*) bridle; ~ **de Adán** Adam's apple.

bocajarro [boka'xarro]: **a** ~ *adv* (*MIL*) at point-blank range; **decir algo a** ~ to say sth bluntly.

bocanada [boka'naða] *nf* (*de vino*) mouthful, swallow; (*de aire*) gust, puff.

bocata [bo'kata] *nm* (*fam*) sandwich.

bocazas [bo'kaθas] *nm/f inv* (*fam*) bigmouth.

boceto [bo'θeto] *nm* sketch, outline.

bocha ['botʃa] *nf* bowl; **~s** *nfpl* bowls *sg*.

bochinche [bo'tʃintʃe] *nm* (*fam*) uproar.

bochorno [bo'tʃorno] *nm* (*vergüenza*) embarrassment; (*calor*): **hace** ~ it's very muggy.

bochornoso, a [botʃor'noso, a] *adj* muggy; embarrassing.

bocina [bo'θina] *nf* (*MUS*) trumpet; (*AUTO*) horn; (*para hablar*) megaphone; **tocar la** ~ (*AUTO*) to sound o blow one's horn.

bocinazo [boθi'naθo] *nm* (*AUTO*) toot, blast (of the horn).

bocio ['boθjo] *nm* (*MED*) goitre.

boda ['boða] *nf* (*tb:* ~**s**) wedding, marriage; (*fiesta*) wedding reception; **~s de plata/de oro** silver/golden wedding *sg*.

bodega [bo'ðeɣa] *nf* (*de vino*) (wine) cellar; (*bar*) bar; (*restaurante*) restaurant; (*depósito*) storeroom; (*de barco*) hold.

bodegón [boðe'ɣon] *nm* (*ARTE*) still life.

bodrio [bo'ðrio] *nm*: **el libro es un** ~ the book is awful o rubbish.

B.O.E. ['boe] *nm abr* = **Boletín Oficial del Estado**.

bofe ['bofe] *nm* (*tb:* ~**s**: *de res*) lights *pl*; **echar los** ~**s** to slave (away).

bofetada [bofe'taða] *nf* slap (in the face); **dar de** ~**s a algn** to punch sb.

bofetón [bofe'ton] *nm* = **bofetada**.

boga ['boɣa] *nf*: **en** ~ in vogue.

bogar [bo'ɣar] *vi* (*remar*) to row; (*navegar*) to sail.

bogavante [boɣa'ßante] *nm* (*NAUT*) stroke, first rower; (*ZOOL*) lobster.

Bogotá [boɣo'ta] *n* Bogota.

bogotano, a [boɣo'tano, a] *adj* of o from Bogota ♦ *nm/f* native o inhabitant of Bogota.

bogue ['boɣe] *etc vb* **V bogar**.

bohemio, a [bo'emjo, a] *adj, nm/f* Bohemian.

boicot, *pl* boicots [boi'ko(t)] *nm* boycott.

boicotear [boikote'ar] *vt* to boycott.

boicoteo [boiko'teo] *nm* boycott.

boina ['boina] *nf* beret.

bola ['bola] *nf* ball; (*canica*) marble; (*NAIPES*) (grand) slam; (*betún*) shoe polish; (*mentira*) tale, story; **~s** *nfpl* (*AM*) bolas; ~ **de billar** billiard ball; ~ **de nieve** snowball.

bolado [bo'laðo] *nm* (*AM*) deal.

bolchevique [boltʃe'ßike] *adj, nm/f* Bolshevik.

boleadoras [bolea'ðoras] *nfpl* (*AM*) bolas *sg*.

bolera [bo'lera] *nf* skittle o bowling alley.

bolero [bo'lero] *nm* bolero.

boleta [bo'leta] *nf* (*AM: permiso*) pass, permit; (*: para votar*) ballot.

boletería [bolete'ria] *nf* (*AM*) ticket office.

boletero, a [bole'tero, a] *nm/f* (*AM*) ticket seller.

boletín [bole'tin] *nm* bulletin; (*periódico*) journal, review; ~ **escolar** (*ESP*) school report; ~ **de noticias** news bulletin; ~ **de pedido** application form; ~ **de precios** price list; ~ **de prensa** press release.

The **Boletín Oficial del Estado**, *abbreviated to* **BOE**, *is the official government record of all laws and resolutions passed by* **las Cortes** (*Spanish Parliament*). *It is widely consulted, mainly because it also publishes the announcements for the* **oposiciones** (*public competitive examinations*).

---

boleto [bo'leto] *nm* (*esp AM*) ticket; ~ **de apuestas** betting slip.

boli ['boli] *nm* Biro ®.

boliche [bo'litʃe] *nm* (*bola*) jack; (*juego*) bowls *sg*; (*lugar*) bowling alley; (*AM: tienda*) small grocery store.

bólido ['boliðo] *nm* meteorite; (*AUTO*) racing car.

bolígrafo [bo'liɣrafo] *nm* ball-point pen, biro ®.

bolillo [bo'liʎo] *nm* (*COSTURA*) bobbin (for lacemaking).

bolívar [bo'lißar] *nm monetary unit of Venezuela.*

Bolivia [bo'lißja] *nf* Bolivia.

boliviano, a [boli'ßjano, a] *adj, nm/f* Bolivian.

bollo ['boʎo] *nm (pan)* roll; *(dulce)* scone; *(bulto)* bump, lump; *(abolladura)* dent; **~s** *nmpl (AM)* troubles.

bolo ['bolo] *nm* skittle; *(píldora)* (large) pill; **(juego de) ~s** skittles *sg.*

Bolonia [bo'lonja] *nf* Bologna.

bolsa ['bolsa] *nf (cartera)* purse; *(saco)* bag; *(AM)* pocket; *(ANAT)* cavity, sac; *(COM)* stock exchange; *(MINERÍA)* pocket; **~ de agua caliente** hot water bottle; **~ de aire** air pocket; **~ de (la) basura** bin-liner; **~ de dormir** *(AM)* sleeping bag; **~ de papel** paper bag; **~ de plástico** plastic *(o* carrier) bag; **"B~ de la propiedad"** "Property Mart"; **~ de trabajo** employment bureau; **jugar a la ~** to play the market.

bolsillo [bol'siʎo] *nm* pocket; *(cartera)* purse; **de ~** pocket *cpd;* **meterse a algn en el ~** to get sb eating out of one's hand.

bolsista [bol'sista] *nm/f* stockbroker.

bolso ['bolso] *nm (bolsa)* bag; *(de mujer)* handbag.

boludo, a [bo'luðo, a] *(AM fam!)* adj stupid ♦ *nm/f* prat (!)

bomba ['bomba] *nf (MIL)* bomb; *(TEC)* pump; *(AM: borrachera)* drunkenness ♦ *adj (fam)*: **noticia ~** bombshell ♦ *adv (fam)*: **pasarlo ~** to have a great time; **~ atómica/de humo/de retardo** atomic/ smoke/time bomb; **~ de gasolina** petrol pump; **~ de incendios** fire engine.

bombacho, a [bom'batʃo, a] *adj* baggy.

bombardear [bombarðe'ar] *vt* to bombard; *(MIL)* to bomb.

bombardeo [bombar'ðeo] *nm* bombardment; bombing.

bombardero [bombar'ðero] *nm* bomber.

bombear [bombe'ar] *vt (agua)* to pump (out *o* up); *(MIL)* to bomb; *(FÚTBOL)* to lob; **~se** *vr* to warp.

bombero [bom'bero] *nm* fireman; **(cuerpo de) ~s** fire brigade.

bombilla [bom'biʎa] *nf (ESP)*, **bombillo** [bom'biʎo] *nm (AM)* (light) bulb.

bombín [bom'bin] *nm* bowler hat.

bombo ['bombo] *nm (MUS)* bass drum; *(TEC)* drum; *(fam)* exaggerated praise; **hacer algo a ~ y platillo** to make a great song and dance about sth; **tengo la cabeza hecha un ~** I've got a splitting headache.

bombón [bom'bon] *nm* chocolate; *(belleza)* gem.

bombona [bom'bona] *nf*: **~ de butano** gas cylinder.

bombonería [bombone'ria] *nf* sweetshop.

bonachón, ona [bona'tʃon, ona] *adj* good-natured.

bonaerense [bonae'rense] *adj* of *o* from Buenos Aires ♦ *nm/f* native *o* inhabitant of Buenos Aires.

bonancible [bonan'θißle] *adj (tiempo)* fair, calm.

bonanza [bo'nanθa] *nf (NAUT)* fair weather; *(fig)* bonanza; *(MINERÍA)* rich pocket *o* vein.

bondad [bon'dað] *nf* goodness, kindness; **tenga la ~ de** (please) be good enough to.

bondadoso, a [bonda'ðoso, a] *adj* good, kind.

bongo ['bonɣo] *nm* large canoe.

boniato [bo'njato] *nm* sweet potato, yam.

bonificación [bonifika'θjon] *nf (COM)* allowance, discount; *(pago)* bonus; *(DEPORTE)* extra points *pl.*

bonito, a [bo'nito, a] *adj (lindo)* pretty; *(agradable)* nice ♦ *adv (AM fam)* well ♦ *nm (atún)* tuna (fish).

bono ['bono] *nm* voucher; *(FIN)* bond; **~ de billetes de metro** booklet of metro tickets; **~ del Tesoro** treasury bill.

bonobús [bono'ßus] *nm (ESP)* bus pass.

Bono Loto, bonoloto [bono'loto] *nm o f (ESP)* state-run weekly lottery; *V tb* **lotería.**

boom, *pl* **booms** ['bum, 'bums] *nm* boom.

boquear [boke'ar] *vi* to gasp.

boquerón [boke'ron] *nm (pez)* (kind of) anchovy; *(agujero)* large hole.

boquete [bo'kete] *nm* gap, hole.

boquiabierto, a [bokia'ßjerto, a] *adj* open-mouthed (in astonishment); **quedar ~** to be left aghast.

boquilla [bo'kiʎa] *nf (para riego)* nozzle; *(para cigarro)* cigarette holder; *(MUS)* mouthpiece.

borbollar [borßo'ʎar], **borbollear** [borßoʎe'ar] *vi* to bubble.

borbollón [borßo'ʎon] *nm* bubbling; **hablar a borbollones** to gabble; **salir a borbollones** *(agua)* to gush out.

borbotar [borßo'tar] *vi* = **borbollar.**

borbotón [borßo'ton] *nm*: **salir a borbotones** to gush out.

borda ['borða] *nf (NAUT)* gunwale; **echar *o* tirar algo por la ~** to throw sth overboard.

bordado [bor'ðaðo] *nm* embroidery.

bordar [bor'ðar] *vt* to embroider.
borde ['borðe] *nm* edge, border; (*de camino etc*) side; (*en la costura*) hem; **al ~ de** (*fig*) on the verge *o* brink of; **ser ~** (*ESP fam*) to be a pain in the neck.
bordear [borðe'ar] *vt* to border.
bordillo [bor'ðiʎo] *nm* kerb (*BRIT*), curb (*US*).
bordo ['borðo] *nm* (*NAUT*) side; **a ~** on board.
Borgoña [bor'ɣoɲa] *nf* Burgundy.
borgoña [bor'ɣoɲa] *nm* burgundy.
boricua [bo'rikwa], **borinqueño, a** [borin'keɲo, a] *adj, nm/f* Puerto Rican.
borla ['borla] *nf* (*gen*) tassel; (*de gorro*) pompon.
borra ['borra] *nf* (*pelusa*) fluff; (*sedimento*) sediment.
borrachera [borra't ʃera] *nf* (*ebriedad*) drunkenness; (*orgía*) spree, binge.
borracho, a [bo'rratʃo, a] *adj* drunk ♦ *nm/f* (*que bebe mucho*) drunkard, drunk; (*temporalmente*) drunk, drunk man/ woman ♦ *nm* (*CULIN*) *cake soaked in liqueur or spirit*.
borrador [borra'ðor] *nm* (*escritura*) first draft, rough sketch; (*cuaderno*) scribbling pad; (*goma*) rubber (*BRIT*), eraser; (*COM*) daybook; (*para pizarra*) duster; **hacer un nuevo ~ de** (*COM*) to redraft.
borrar [bo'rrar] *vt* to erase, rub out; (*tachar*) to delete; (*cinta*) to wipe out; (*INFORM: archivo*) to delete, erase; (*POL etc: eliminar*) to deal with.
borrasca [bo'rraska] *nf* (*METEOROLOGÍA*) storm.
borrascoso, a [borras'koso, a] *adj* stormy.
borrego, a [bo'rreɣo, a] *nm/f* lamb; (*oveja*) sheep; (*fig*) simpleton.
borricada [borri'kaða] *nf* foolish action/ statement.
borrico, a [bo'rriko, a] *nm* donkey; (*fig*) stupid man ♦ *nf* she-donkey; (*fig*) stupid woman.
borrón [bo'rron] *nm* (*mancha*) stain; **~ y cuenta nueva** let bygones be bygones.
borroso, a [bo'rroso, a] *adj* vague, unclear; (*escritura*) illegible; (*escrito*) smudgy; (*FOTO*) blurred.
Bósforo ['bosforo] *nm*: **el (Estrecho del) ~** the Bosp(h)orus.
Bosnia ['bosnja] *nf* Bosnia.
bosnio, a ['bosnjo, a] *adj, nm/f* Bosnian.
bosque ['boske] *nm* wood; (*grande*) forest.
bosquejar [boske'xar] *vt* to sketch.
bosquejo [bos'kexo] *nm* sketch.
bosta ['bosta] *nf* dung, manure.

bostece [bos'teθe] *etc vb V* **bostezar**.
bostezar [boste'θar] *vi* to yawn.
bostezo [bos'teθo] *nm* yawn.
bota ['bota] *nf* (*calzado*) boot; (*saco*) leather wine bottle; **ponerse las ~s** (*fam*) to strike it rich.
botadura [bota'ðura] *nf* launching.
botanas [bo'tanas] *nfpl* (*AM*) hors d'œuvres.
botánico, a [bo'taniko, a] *adj* botanical ♦ *nm/f* botanist ♦ *nf* botany.
botar [bo'tar] *vt* to throw, hurl; (*NAUT*) to launch; (*esp AM fam*) to throw out ♦ *vi* to bounce.
botarate [bota'rate] *nm* (*imbécil*) idiot.
bote ['bote] *nm* (*salto*) bounce; (*golpe*) thrust; (*vasija*) tin, can; (*embarcación*) boat; **de ~ en ~** packed, jammed full; **~ salvavidas** lifeboat; **dar un ~** to jump; **dar ~s** (*AUTO etc*) to bump; **~ de la basura** (*AM*) dustbin (*BRIT*), trashcan (*US*).
botella [bo'teʎa] *nf* bottle; **~ de vino** (*contenido*) bottle of wine; (*recipiente*) wine bottle.
botellero [bote'ʎero] *nm* wine rack.
botellín [bote'ʎin] *nm* small bottle.
botica [bo'tika] *nf* chemist's (shop) (*BRIT*), pharmacy.
boticario, a [boti'karjo, a] *nm/f* chemist (*BRIT*), pharmacist.
botijo [bo'tixo] *nm* (earthenware) jug; (*tren*) excursion train.
botín [bo'tin] *nm* (*calzado*) half boot; (*polaina*) spat; (*MIL*) booty; (*de ladrón*) loot.
botiquín [boti'kin] *nm* (*armario*) medicine chest; (*portátil*) first-aid kit.
botón [bo'ton] *nm* button; (*BOT*) bud; (*de florete*) tip; **~ de arranque** (*AUTO etc*) starter; **~ de oro** buttercup; **pulsar el ~** to press the button.
botones [bo'tones] *nm inv* bellboy, bellhop (*US*).
botulismo [botu'lismo] *nm* botulism, food poisoning.
bóveda ['boβeða] *nf* (*ARQ*) vault.
bovino, a [bo'βino, a] *adj* bovine; (*AGR*): **ganado ~** cattle.
box ['boks] *nm* (*AM*) boxing.
boxeador [boksea'ðor] *nm* boxer.
boxear [bokse'ar] *vi* to box.
boxeo [bok'seo] *nm* boxing.
boya ['boja] *nf* (*NAUT*) buoy; (*flotador*) float.
boyante [bo'jante] *adj* (*NAUT*) buoyant; (*feliz*) buoyant; (*próspero*) prosperous.
bozal [bo'θal] *nm* (*de caballo*) halter; (*de perro*) muzzle.

bozo ['boθo] *nm* (*pelusa*) fuzz; (*boca*) mouth.

bracear [braθe'ar] *vi* (*agitar los brazos*) to wave one's arms.

bracero [bra'θero] *nm* labourer; (*en el campo*) farmhand.

braga ['braɤa] *nf* (*cuerda*) sling, rope; (*de bebé*) nappy, diaper (*US*); ~**s** *nfpl* (*de mujer*) panties.

braguero [bra'ɤero] *nm* (*MED*) truss.

bragueta [bra'ɤeta] *nf* fly (*BRIT*), flies *pl* (*BRIT*), zipper (*US*).

braguetazo [braɤe'taθo] *nm* marriage of convenience.

braille [breil] *nm* braille.

bramante [bra'mante] *nm* twine, string.

bramar [bra'mar] *vi* to bellow, roar.

bramido [bra'miðo] *nm* bellow, roar.

branquias ['brankjas] *nfpl* gills.

brasa ['brasa] *nf* live *o* hot coal; **carne a la ~** grilled meat.

brasero [bra'sero] *nm* brazier; (*AM: chimenea*) fireplace.

Brasil [bra'sil] *nm:* (**el**) ~ Brazil.

brasileño, a [brasi'leɲo, a] *adj, nm/f* Brazilian.

bravata [bra'βata] *nf* boast.

braveza [bra'βeθa] *nf* (*valor*) bravery; (*ferocidad*) ferocity.

bravío, a [bra'βio, a] *adj* wild; (*feroz*) fierce.

bravo, a ['braβo, a] *adj* (*valiente*) brave; (*bueno*) fine, splendid; (*feroz*) ferocious; (*salvaje*) wild; (*mar etc*) rough, stormy; (*CULIN*) hot, spicy ♦ *excl* bravo!

bravucón, ona [braβu'kon, ona] *adj* swaggering ♦ *nm/f* braggart.

bravura [bra'βura] *nf* bravery; ferocity; (*pey*) boast.

braza ['braθa] *nf* fathom; **nadar a la ~** to swim (the) breast-stroke.

brazada [bra'θaða] *nf* stroke.

brazalete [braθa'lete] *nm* (*pulsera*) bracelet; (*banda*) armband.

brazo ['braθo] *nm* arm; (*ZOOL*) foreleg; (*BOT*) limb, branch; ~**s** *nmpl* (*braceros*) hands, workers; ~ **derecho** (*fig*) right-hand man; **a ~ partido** hand-to-hand; **cogidos** *etc* **del** ~ arm in arm; **no dar su ~ a torcer** not to give way easily; **huelga de ~s caídos** sit-down strike.

brea ['brea] *nf* pitch, tar.

brebaje [bre'βaxe] *nm* potion.

brecha ['bretʃa] *nf* breach; (*hoyo vacío*) gap, opening.

brécol ['brekol] *nm* broccoli.

brega ['breɤa] *nf* (*lucha*) struggle; (*trabajo*) hard work.

bregar [bre'ɤar] *vi* (*luchar*) to struggle;

(*trabajar mucho*) to slog away.

bregue ['breɤe] *etc vb V* **bregar**.

breña ['breɲa] *nf* rough ground.

Bretaña [bre'taɲa] *nf* Brittany.

brete ['brete] *nm* (*cepo*) shackles *pl*; (*fig*) predicament; **estar en un ~** to be in a jam.

breteles [bre'teles] *nmpl* (*AM*) straps.

bretón, ona [bre'ton, ona] *adj, nm/f* Breton.

breva ['breβa] *nf* (*BOT*) early fig; (*puro*) flat cigar; **¡no caerá esa ~**! no such luck!

breve ['breβe] *adj* short, brief; **en ~** (*pronto*) shortly; (*en pocas palabras*) in short ♦ *nf* (*MUS*) breve.

brevedad [breβe'ðað] *nf* brevity, shortness; **con** *o* **a la major ~** as soon as possible.

breviario [bre'βjarjo] *nm* (*REL*) breviary.

brezal [bre'θal] *nm* moor(land), heath.

brezo ['breθo] *nm* heather.

bribón, ona [bri'βon, ona] *adj* idle, lazy ♦ *nm/f* (*vagabundo*) vagabond; (*pícaro*) rascal, rogue.

bricolaje [briko'laxe] *nm* do-it-yourself, DIY.

brida ['briða] *nf* bridle, rein; (*TEC*) clamp; **a toda ~** at top speed.

bridge [britʃ] *nm* (*NAIPES*) bridge.

brigada [bri'ɤaða] *nf* (*unidad*) brigade; (*trabajadores*) squad, gang ♦ *nm* warrant officer.

brigadier [briɤa'ðjer] *nm* brigadier (-general).

brillante [bri'ʎante] *adj* brilliant; (*color*) bright; (*joya*) sparkling ♦ *nm* diamond.

brillantez [briʎan'teθ] *nf* (*color etc*) brightness; (*fig*) brilliance.

brillar [bri'ʎar] *vi* (*tb fig*) to shine; (*joyas*) to sparkle; ~ **por su ausencia** to be conspicuous by one's absence.

brillo ['briʎo] *nm* shine; (*brillantez*) brilliance; (*fig*) splendour; **sacar ~ a** to polish.

brilloso, a [bri'ʎoso, a] *adj* (*AM*) = **brillante**.

brincar [brin'kar] *vi* to skip about, hop about, jump about; **está que brinca** he's hopping mad.

brinco ['brinko] *nm* jump, leap; **a ~s** by fits and starts; **de un ~** at one bound.

brindar [brin'dar] *vi:* ~ **a** *o* **por** to drink (a toast) to ♦ *vt* to offer, present; **le brinda la ocasión de** it offers *o* affords him the opportunity to; ~**se** *vr:* ~**se a hacer algo** to offer to do sth.

brindis ['brindis] *nm inv* toast; (*TAUR*) (ceremony of) dedication.

brinque ['brinke] *etc vb V* **brincar**.

brío ['brio] *nm* spirit, dash.

brioso, a [bri'oso, a] *adj* spirited, dashing.
brisa ['brisa] *nf* breeze.
británico, a [bri'taniko, a] *adj* British ♦ *nm/f* Briton, British person; **los ~s** the British.
brizna ['briθna] *nf* (*hebra*) strand, thread; (*de hierba*) blade; (*trozo*) piece.
broca ['broka] *nf* (*COSTURA*) bobbin; (*TEC*) drill bit; (*clavo*) tack.
brocado [bro'kaðo] *nm* brocade.
brocal [bro'kal] *nm* rim.
brocha ['brotʃa] *nf* (large) paintbrush; **~ de afeitar** shaving brush; **pintor de ~ gorda** painter and decorator; (*fig*) poor painter.
brochazo [bro'tʃaθo] *nm* brush-stroke; **a grandes ~s** (*fig*) in general terms.
broche ['brotʃe] *nm* brooch.
broma ['broma] *nf* joke; (*inocentada*) practical joke; **en ~** in fun, as a joke; **gastar una ~ a algn** to play a joke on sb; **tomar algo a ~** to take sth as a joke.
bromear [brome'ar] *vi* to joke.
bromista [bro'mista] *adj* fond of joking ♦ *nm/f* joker, wag.
bromuro [bro'muro] *nm* bromide.
bronca ['bronka] *nf* row; (*regañada*) ticking-off; **armar una ~** to kick up a fuss; **echar una ~ a algn** to tell sb off.
bronce ['bronθe] *nm* bronze; (*latón*) brass.
bronceado, a [bronθe'aðo, a] *adj* bronze *cpd*; (*por el sol*) tanned ♦ *nm* (sun)tan; (*TEC*) bronzing.
bronceador [bronθea'ðor] *nm* suntan lotion.
broncearse [bronθe'arse] *vr* to get a suntan.
bronco, a ['bronko, a] *adj* (*manera*) rude, surly; (*voz*) harsh.
bronquios ['bronkjos] *nmpl* bronchial tubes.
bronquitis [bron'kitis] *nf inv* bronchitis.
brotar [bro'tar] *vt* (*tierra*) to produce ♦ *vi* (*BOT*) to sprout; (*aguas*) to gush (forth); (*lágrimas*) to well up; (*MED*) to break out.
brote ['brote] *nm* (*BOT*) shoot; (*MED, fig*) outbreak.
broza ['broθa] *nf* (*BOT*) dead leaves *pl*; (*fig*) rubbish.
bruces ['bruθes]: **de ~** *adv*: **caer o dar de ~** to fall headlong, fall flat.
bruja ['bruxa] *nf* witch.
Brujas ['bruxas] *nf* Bruges.
brujería [bruxe'ria] *nf* witchcraft.
brujo ['bruxo] *nm* wizard, magician.
brújula ['bruxula] *nf* compass.
bruma ['bruma] *nf* mist.
brumoso, a [bru'moso, a] *adj* misty.

bruñendo [bru'ɲendo] *etc vb V* **bruñir**.
bruñido [bru'ɲiðo] *nm* polish.
bruñir [bru'ɲir] *vt* to polish.
brusco, a ['brusko, a] *adj* (*súbito*) sudden; (*áspero*) brusque.
Bruselas [bru'selas] *nf* Brussels.
brusquedad [bruske'ðað] *nf* suddenness; brusqueness.
brutal [bru'tal] *adj* brutal.
brutalidad [brutali'ðað] *nf* brutality.
bruto, a ['bruto, a] *adj* (*idiota*) stupid; (*bestial*) brutish; (*peso*) gross ♦ *nm* brute; **a la bruta, a lo ~** roughly; **en ~** raw, unworked.
Bs. *abr* = **bolívares**.
Bs.As. *abr* = **Buenos Aires**.
bucal [bu'kal] *adj* oral; **por vía ~** orally.
bucanero [buka'nero] *nm* buccaneer.
bucear [buθe'ar] *vi* to dive ♦ *vt* to explore.
buceo [bu'θeo] *nm* diving; (*fig*) investigation.
buche ['butʃe] *nm* (*de ave*) crop; (*ZOOL*) maw; (*fam*) belly.
bucle ['bukle] *nm* curl; (*INFORM*) loop.
budín [bu'ðin] *nm* pudding.
budismo [bu'ðismo] *nm* Buddhism.
budista [bu'ðista] *adj, nm/f* Buddhist.
buen [bwen] *adj V* **bueno**.
buenamente [bwena'mente] *adv* (*fácilmente*) easily; (*voluntariamente*) willingly.
buenaventura [bwenaßen'tura] *nf* (*suerte*) good luck; (*adivinación*) fortune; **decir o echar la ~ a algn** to tell sb's fortune.

═══════════════════════ PALABRA CLAVE

bueno, a ['bweno, a] (*antes de nmsg*: **buen**) *adj* **1** (*excelente etc*) good; (*MED*) well; **es un libro ~, es un buen libro** it's a good book; **hace ~, hace buen tiempo** the weather is fine, it is fine; **es ~a persona** he's a good sort; **el ~ de Paco** good old Paco; **fue muy ~ conmigo** he was very nice *o* kind to me; **ya está ~** he's fine now
2 (*apropiado*): **ser ~ para** to be good for; **creo que vamos por buen camino** I think we're on the right track
3 (*irónico*): **le di un buen rapapolvo** I gave him a good *o* real ticking off; **¡buen conductor estás hecho!** some driver *o* a fine driver you are!; **¡estaría ~ que ...!** a fine thing it would be if ...!
4 (*atractivo, sabroso*): **está ~ este bizcocho** this sponge is delicious; **Julio está muy ~** (*fam*) Julio is a bit of alright
5 (*grande*) good, big; **un buen número de ...** a good number of ...; **un buen trozo**

de ... a nice big piece of ...
6 (*saludos*): **¡buen día!** (*AM*), **¡~s días!** (good) morning!; **¡buenas (tardes)!** good afternoon!; (*más tarde*) good evening!; **¡buenas noches!** good night!
7 (*otras locuciones*): **estar de buenas** to be in a good mood; **por las buenas o por las malas** by hook or by crook; **de buenas a primeras** all of a sudden
♦ *excl*: **¡~!** all right!; **~, ¿y qué?** well, so what?; **~, lo que pasa es que ...** well, the thing is ...; **pero ¡~!** well, I like that!; **~, pues ...** right, (then) ...

Buenos Aires [bweno'saires] *nm* Buenos Aires.
buey [bwei] *nm* ox.
búfalo ['bufalo] *nm* buffalo.
bufanda [bu'fanda] *nf* scarf.
bufar [bu'far] *vi* to snort.
bufete [bu'fete] *nm* (*despacho de abogado*) lawyer's office; **establecer su ~** to set up in legal practice.
buffer ['bufer] *nm* (*INFORM*) buffer.
bufón [bu'fon] *nm* clown.
bufonada [bufo'naða] *nf* (*dicho*) jest; (*hecho*) piece of buffoonery; (*TEAT*) farce.
buhardilla [buar'ðiʎa] *nf* attic.
búho ['buo] *nm* owl; (*fig*) hermit, recluse.
buhonero [buo'nero] *nm* pedlar.
buitre ['bwitre] *nm* vulture.
bujía [bu'xia] *nf* (*vela*) candle; (*ELEC*) candle (power); (*AUTO*) spark plug.
bula ['bula] *nf* (*papal*) bull.
bulbo ['bulßo] *nm* (*BOT*) bulb.
bulevar [bule'ßar] *nm* boulevard.
Bulgaria [bul'xarja] *nf* Bulgaria.
búlgaro, a ['bulxaro, a] *adj, nm/f* Bulgarian.
bulimia [bu'limja] *nf* bulimia.
bulla ['buʎa] *nf* (*ruido*) uproar; (*de gente*) crowd; **armar o meter ~** to kick up a row.
bullendo [bu'ʎendo] *etc vb V* **bullir**.
bullicio [bu'ʎiθjo] *nm* (*ruido*) uproar; (*movimiento*) bustle.
bullicioso, a [buʎi'θjoso, a] *adj* (*ruidoso*) noisy, (*calle etc*) busy; (*situación*) turbulent.
bullir [bu'ʎir] *vi* (*hervir*) to boil; (*burbujear*) to bubble; (*mover*) to move, stir; (*insectos*) to swarm; **~ de** (*fig*) to teem o seethe with.
bulo ['bulo] *nm* false rumour.
bulto ['bulto] *nm* (*paquete*) package; (*fardo*) bundle; (*tamaño*) size, bulkiness; (*MED*) swelling, lump; (*silueta*) vague shape; (*estatua*) bust, statue; **hacer ~** to take up

space; **escurrir el ~** to make o.s. scarce; (*fig*) to dodge the issue.
buñuelo [bu'ɲwelo] *nm* ≈ doughnut, donut (*US*).
BUP [bup] *nm abr* (*ESP ESCOL*: = *Bachillerato Unificado y Polivalente*) *secondary education for 14-17 age group*; *V tb* **sistema educativo**.
buque ['buke] *nm* ship, vessel; **~ de guerra** warship; **~ mercante** merchant ship; **~ de vela** sailing ship.
burbuja [bur'ßuxa] *nf* bubble; **hacer ~s** to bubble; (*gaseosa*) to fizz.
burbujear [burßuxe'ar] *vi* to bubble.
burdel [bur'ðel] *nm* brothel.
Burdeos [bur'ðeos] *nm* Bordeaux.
burdo, a ['burðo, a] *adj* coarse, rough.
burgalés, esa [burxa'les, esa] *adj* of o from Burgos ♦ *nm/f* native o inhabitant of Burgos.
burgués, esa [bur'xes, esa] *adj* middle-class, bourgeois; **pequeño ~** lower middle-class; (*POL, pey*) petty bourgeois.
burguesía [burxe'sia] *nf* middle class, bourgeoisie.
burla ['burla] *nf* (*mofa*) gibe; (*broma*) joke; (*engaño*) trick; **hacer ~ de** to make fun of.
burladero [burla'ðero] *nm* (bullfighter's) refuge.
burlador, a [burla'ðor, a] *adj* mocking ♦ *nm/f* mocker; (*bromista*) joker ♦ *nm* (*libertino*) seducer.
burlar [bur'lar] *vt* (*engañar*) to deceive; (*seducir*) to seduce ♦ *vi*, **~se** *vr* to joke; **~se de** to make fun of.
burlesco, a [bur'lesko, a] *adj* burlesque.
burlón, ona [bur'lon, ona] *adj* mocking.
buró [bu'ro] *nm* bureau.
burocracia [buro'kraθja] *nf* bureaucracy.
burócrata [bu'rokrata] *nm/f* bureaucrat.
buromática [buro'matika] *nf* office automation.
burrada [bu'rraða] *nf* stupid act; **decir ~s** to talk nonsense.
burro, a ['burro, a] *nm/f* (*ZOOL*) donkey; (*fig*) ass, idiot ♦ *adj* stupid; **caerse del ~** to realise one's mistake; **no ver tres en un ~** to be as blind as a bat.
bursátil [bur'satil] *adj* stock-exchange *cpd*.
bus [bus] *nm* bus.
busca ['buska] *nf* search, hunt ♦ *nm* bleeper, pager; **en ~ de** in search of.
buscador, a [buska'ðor, a] *nm/f* searcher.
buscapiés [buska'pjes] *nm inv* jumping jack (*BRIT*), firecracker (*US*).
buscapleitos [buska'pleitos] *nm/f inv* troublemaker.

buscar [bus'kar] vt to look for; (objeto perdido) to have a look for; (beneficio) to seek; (enemigo) to seek out; (traer) to bring, fetch; (provocar) to provoke; (INFORM) to search ♦ vi to look, search, seek; **ven a ~me a la oficina** come and pick me up at the office; **~le 3 o 4 pies al gato** to split hairs; **"~ y reemplazar"** (INFORM) "search and replace"; **se busca secretaria** secretary wanted; **se la buscó** he asked for it.

buscavidas [buska'βiðas] nmf inv snooper; (persona ambiciosa) go-getter.

buscona [bus'kona] nf whore.

busilis [bu'silis] nm inv (fam) snag.

busque [buske] etc vb V **buscar.**

búsqueda ['buskeða] nf = **busca.**

busto ['busto] nm (ANAT, ARTE) bust.

butaca [bu'taka] nf armchair; (de cine, teatro) stall, seat.

butano [bu'tano] nm butane (gas); **bombona de ~** gas cylinder.

butifarra [buti'farra] nf Catalan sausage.

buzo ['buθo] nm diver; (AM: chandal) tracksuit.

buzón [bu'θon] nm (gen) letter box; (en la calle) pillar box (BRIT); (TELEC) mailbox; **echar al ~** to post.

buzonear [buθone'ar] vt to leaflet.

byte [bait] nm (INFORM) byte.

Cc

C, c [θe, se (esp AM)] nf (letra) C, c; **C de Carmen** C for Charlie.

C. abr (= centígrado) C.; (= compañía) Co.

c. abr (= capítulo) ch.

C/ abr (= calle) St, Rd.

c/ abr (COM: = cuenta) a/c.

ca [ka] excl not a bit of it!

c.a. abr (= corriente alterna) A.C.

cabal [ka'βal] adj (exacto) exact; (correcto) right, proper; (acabado) finished, complete; **~es** nmpl: **estar en sus ~es** to be in one's right mind.

cábala ['kaβala] nf (REL) cab(b)ala; (fig) cabal, intrigue; **~s** nfpl guess sg, supposition sg.

cabalgadura [kaβalɣa'ðura] nf mount, horse.

cabalgar [kaβal'ɣar] vt, vi to ride.

cabalgata [kaβal'ɣata] nf procession; V tb **Reyes Magos.**

cabalgue [ka'βalɣe] etc vb V **cabalgar.**

cabalístico, a [kaβa'listiko, a] adj (fig) mysterious.

caballa [ka'βaʎa] nf mackerel.

caballeresco, a [kaβaʎe'resko, a] adj noble, chivalrous.

caballería [kaβaʎe'ria] nf mount; (MIL) cavalry.

caballeriza [kaβaʎe'riθa] nf stable.

caballerizo [kaβaʎe'riθo] nm groom, stableman.

caballero [kaβa'ʎero] nm gentleman; (de la orden de caballería) knight; (trato directo) sir; **"C~s"** "Gents".

caballerosidad [kaβaʎerosi'ðað] nf chivalry.

caballete [kaβa'ʎete] nm (AGR) ridge; (ARTE) easel.

caballito [kaβa'ʎito] nm (caballo pequeño) small horse, pony; (juguete) rocking horse; **~s** nmpl merry-go-round sg; **~ de mar** seahorse; **~ del diablo** dragonfly.

caballo [ka'βaʎo] nm horse; (AJEDREZ) knight; (NAIPES) ≈ queen; **~ de vapor** o **de fuerza** horsepower; **es su ~ de batalla** it's his hobby-horse; **~ blanco** (COM) backer; V tb **Baraja Española.**

cabaña [ka'βaɲa] nf (casita) hut, cabin.

cabaré, cabaret, pl **cabarets** [kaβa're, kaβa'res] nm cabaret.

cabecear [kaβeθe'ar] vi to nod.

cabecera [kaβe'θera] nf (gen) head; (de distrito) chief town; (de cama) headboard; (IMPRENTA) headline.

cabecilla [kaβe'θiʎa] nm ringleader.

cabellera [kaβe'ʎera] nf (head of) hair; (de cometa) tail.

cabello [ka'βeʎo] nm (tb: ~s) hair sg.

cabelludo [kaβe'ʎuðo] adj V **cuero.**

caber [ka'βer] vi (entrar) to fit, go; **caben 3 más** there's room for 3 more; **cabe preguntar si...** one might ask whether...; **cabe que venga más tarde** he may come later.

cabestrillo [kaβes'triʎo] nm sling.

cabestro [ka'βestro] nm halter.

cabeza [ka'βeθa] nf head; (POL) chief, leader ♦ nm/f: **~ rapada** skinhead; **caer de ~** to fall head first; **sentar la ~** to settle down; **~ de lectura/escritura** read/write head; **~ impresora** o **de impresión** printhead.

cabezada [kaβe'θaða] nf (golpe) butt; **dar una ~** to nod off.

cabezal [kaβe'θal] nm: **~ impresor** print head.

cabezazo [kaße'θaθo] *nm* (*golpe*) headbutt; (*FÚTBOL*) header.

cabezón, ona [kaße'θon, ona] *adj* with a big head; (*vino*) heady; (*obstinado*) obstinate, stubborn.

cabezota [kaße'θota] *adj inv* obstinate, stubborn.

cabezudo, a [kaße'θuðo, a] *adj* with a big head; (*obstinado*) obstinate, stubborn.

cabida [ka'ßiða] *nf* space; **dar ~ a** to make room for; **tener ~ para** to have room for.

cabildo [ka'ßildo] *nm* (*de iglesia*) chapter; (*POL*) town council.

cabina [ka'ßina] *nf* (*de camión*) cabin; **~ telefónica** (tele)phone box (*BRIT*) *o* booth.

cabizbajo, a [kaßiθ'ßaxo, a] *adj* crestfallen, dejected.

cable ['kaßle] *nm* cable; (*de aparato*) lead; **~ aéreo** (*ELEC*) overhead cable; **conectar con ~** (*INFORM*) to hardwire.

cabo ['kaßo] *nm* (*de objeto*) end, extremity; (*MIL*) corporal; (*NAUT*) rope, cable; (*GEO*) cape; (*TEC*) thread; **al ~ de 3 días** after 3 days; **de ~ a rabo** *o* **~** from beginning to end; (*libro: leer*) from cover to cover; **llevar a ~** to carry out; **atar ~s** to tie up the loose ends; **C~ de Buena Esperanza** Cape of Good Hope; **C~ de Hornos** Cape Horn; **las Islas de C~ Verde** the Cape Verde Islands.

cabra ['kaßra] *nf* goat; **estar como una ~** (*fam*) to be nuts.

cabré [ka'ßre] *etc vb V* **caber**.

cabrear [kaßre'ar] *vt* to annoy; **~se** *vr* to fly off the handle.

cabrío, a [ka'ßrio, a] *adj* goatish; **macho ~** (he-)goat, billy goat.

cabriola [ka'ßrjola] *nf* caper.

cabritilla [kaßri'tiʎa] *nf* kid, kidskin.

cabrito [ka'ßrito] *nm* kid.

cabrón [ka'ßron] *nm* (*fig: fam!*) bastard (!).

cabronada [kaßro'naða] *nf* (*fam!*): **hacer una ~ a algn** to be a bastard to sb.

caca ['kaka] *nf* (*palabra de niños*) pooh ♦ *excl:* **no toques, ¡~!** don't touch, it's dirty!

cacahuete [kaka'wete] *nm* (*ESP*) peanut.

cacao [ka'kao] *nm* cocoa; (*BOT*) cacao.

cacarear [kakare'ar] *vi* (*persona*) to boast; (*gallina*) to cackle.

cacatúa [kaka'tua] *nf* cockatoo.

cacereño, a [kaθe'reɲo, a] *adj* of *o* from Cáceres ♦ *nm/f* native *o* inhabitant of Cáceres.

cacería [kaθe'ria] *nf* hunt.

cacerola [kaθe'rola] *nf* pan, saucepan.

cacha ['katʃa] *nf* (*mango*) handle; (*nalga*) buttock.

cachalote [katʃa'lote] *nm* sperm whale.

cacharro [ka'tʃarro] *nm* (*vasija*) (earthenware) pot; (*cerámica*) piece of pottery; (*fam*) useless object; **~s** *nmpl* pots and pans.

cachear [katʃe'ar] *vt* to search, frisk.

cachemir [katʃe'mir] *nm* cashmere.

cacheo [ka'tʃeo] *nm* searching, frisking.

cachete [ka'tʃete] *nm* (*ANAT*) cheek; (*bofetada*) slap (in the face).

cachimba [ka'tʃimba] *nf*, **cachimbo** [ka'tʃimbo] *nm* (*AM*) pipe.

cachiporra [katʃi'porra] *nf* truncheon.

cachivache [katʃi'ßatʃe] *nm* piece of junk; **~s** *nmpl* trash *sg*, junk *sg*.

cacho, a ['katʃo, a] *nm* (small) bit; (*AM: cuerno*) horn.

cachondearse [katʃonde'arse] *vr*: **~ de algn** to tease sb.

cachondeo [katʃon'deo] *nm* (*fam*) farce, joke; (*guasa*) laugh.

cachondo, a [ka'tʃondo, a] *adj* (*ZOOL*) on heat; (*persona*) randy, sexy; (*gracioso*) funny.

cachorro, a [ka'tʃorro, a] *nm/f* (*perro*) pup, puppy; (*león*) cub.

cacique [ka'θike] *nm* chief, local ruler; (*POL*) local party boss; (*fig*) despot.

caco ['kako] *nm* pickpocket.

cacofonía [kakofo'nia] *nf* cacophony.

cacto ['kakto] *nm*, **cactus** ['kaktus] *nm inv* cactus.

cada ['kaða] *adj inv* each; (*antes de número*) every; **~ día** each day, every day; **~ dos días** every other day; **~ uno/a** each one, every one; **~ vez más/menos** more and more/less and less; **uno de ~ diez** one out of every ten; **¿~ cuánto?** how often?

cadalso [ka'ðalso] *nm* scaffold.

cadáver [ka'ðaßer] *nm* (dead) body, corpse.

cadavérico, a [kaða'ßeriko, a] *adj* cadaverous; (*pálido*) deathly pale.

cadena [ka'ðena] *nf* chain; (*TV*) channel; **reacción en ~** chain reaction; **trabajo en ~** assembly line work; **~ midi/mini** (*MUS*) midi/mini system; **~ perpetua** (*JUR*) life imprisonment; **~ de caracteres** (*INFORM*) character string.

cadencia [ka'ðenθja] *nf* cadence, rhythm.

cadera [ka'ðera] *nf* hip.

cadete [ka'ðete] *nm* cadet.

Cádiz ['kaðiθ] *nm* Cadiz.

caducar [kaðu'kar] *vi* to expire.

caducidad [kaðuθi'ðað] *nf*: **fecha de ~** expiry date; (*de comida*) sell-by date.

caduco, a [ka'ðuko, a] *adj* (*idea etc*) outdated, outmoded; **de hoja caduca**

deciduous.

caduque [ka'ðuke] *etc vb* V **caducar**.

C.A.E. *abr* (= *cóbrese al entregar*) COD.

caer [ka'er] *vi* to fall; (*premio*) to go; (*sitio*) to be, lie; (*pago*) to fall due; **~se** *vr* to fall (down); **dejar ~** to drop; **estar al ~** to be due to happen; (*persona*) to be about to arrive; **me cae bien/mal** I like/don't like him; **~ en la cuenta** to catch on; **su cumpleaños cae en viernes** her birthday falls on a Friday; **se me ha caído el guante** I've dropped my glove.

café, *pl* **cafés** [ka'fe, ka'fes] *nm* (*bebida, planta*) coffee; (*lugar*) café ♦ *adj* (*color*) brown; **~ con leche** white coffee; **~ solo, ~ negro** (*AM*) (small) black coffee.

cafeína [kafe'ina] *nf* caffein(e).

cafetal [kafe'tal] *nm* coffee plantation.

cafetera [kafe'tera] *nf* V **cafetero**.

cafetería [kafete'ria] *nf* cafe.

cafetero, a [kafe'tero, a] *adj* coffee *cpd* ♦ *nf* coffee pot; **ser muy ~** to be a coffee addict.

cafre ['kafre] *nm/f*: **como ~s** (*fig*) like savages.

cagalera [kaɣa'lera] *nf* (*fam!*): **tener ~** to have the runs.

cagar [ka'ɣar] (*fam!*) *vt* to shit (*!*); (*fig*) to bungle, mess up ♦ *vi* to have a shit (*!*); **~se** *vr*: **¡me cago en diez** (*etc*)! Christ! (*!*).

cague ['kaɣe] *etc vb* V **cagar**.

caído, a [ka'iðo, a] *adj* fallen; (*INFORM*) down ♦ *nf* fall; (*declive*) slope; (*disminución*) fall, drop; **~ del cielo** out of the blue; **a la caída del sol** at sunset; **sufrir una caída** to have a fall.

caiga ['kaiɣa] *etc vb* V **caer**.

caimán [kai'man] *nm* alligator.

Cairo ['kairo] *nm*: **el ~** Cairo.

caja ['kaxa] *nf* box; (*ataúd*) coffin, casket (*US*); (*para reloj*) case; (*de ascensor*) shaft; (*COM*) cashbox; (*ECON*) fund; (*donde se hacen los pagos*) cashdesk; (*en supermercado*) checkout, till; (*TIP*) case; **~ de ahorros** savings bank; **~ de cambios** gearbox; **~ fuerte, ~ de caudales** safe, strongbox; **ingresar en ~** to be paid in.

cajero, a [ka'xero, a] *nm/f* cashier; (*en banco*) (bank) teller ♦ *nm*: **~ automático** cash dispenser, automatic telling machine, A.T.M.

cajetilla [kaxe'tiʎa] *nf* (*de cigarrillos*) packet.

cajista [ka'xista] *nm/f* typesetter.

cajón [ka'xon] *nm* big box; (*de mueble*) drawer.

cal [kal] *nf* lime; **cerrar algo a ~ y canto** to

shut sth firmly.

cala ['kala] *nf* (*GEO*) cove, inlet; (*de barco*) hold.

calabacín [kalaβa'θin] *nm* (*BOT*) baby marrow, courgette, zucchini (*US*).

calabaza [kala'βaθa] *nf* (*BOT*) pumpkin; **dar ~s a** (*candidato*) to fail.

calabozo [kala'βoθo] *nm* (*cárcel*) prison; (*celda*) cell.

calado, a [ka'laðo, a] *adj* (*prenda*) lace *cpd* ♦ *nm* (*TEC*) fretwork; (*NAUT*) draught ♦ *nf* (*de cigarrillo*) puff; **estar ~ (hasta los huesos)** to be soaked (to the skin).

calamar [kala'mar] *nm* squid.

calambre [ka'lambre] *nm* (*tb:* **~s**) cramp.

calamidad [kalami'ðað] *nf* calamity, disaster; (*persona*): **es una ~** he's a dead loss.

calamina [kala'mina] *nf* calamine.

cálamo ['kalamo] *nm* (*BOT*) stem; (*MUS*) reed.

calaña [ka'laɲa] *nf* model, pattern; (*fig*) nature, stamp.

calar [ka'lar] *vt* to soak, drench; (*penetrar*) to pierce, penetrate; (*comprender*) to see through; (*vela, red*) to lower; **~se** *vr* (*AUTO*) to stall; **~se las gafas** to stick one's glasses on.

calavera [kala'βera] *nf* skull.

calcañal [kalka'ɲal], **calcañar** [kalka'ɲar] *nm* heel.

calcar [kal'kar] *vt* (*reproducir*) to trace; (*imitar*) to copy.

calce ['kalθe] *etc vb* V **calzar**.

calceta [kal'θeta] *nf* (knee-length) stocking; **hacer ~** to knit.

calcetín [kalθe'tin] *nm* sock.

calcinar [kalθi'nar] *vt* to burn, blacken.

calcio ['kalθjo] *nm* calcium.

calco ['kalko] *nm* tracing.

calcomanía [kalkoma'nia] *nf* transfer.

calculador, a [kalkula'ðor, a] *adj* calculating ♦ *nf* calculator.

calcular [kalku'lar] *vt* (*MAT*) to calculate, compute; **~ que ...** to reckon that ....

cálculo ['kalkulo] *nm* calculation; (*MED*) (gall)stone; (*MAT*) calculus; **~ de costo** costing; **~ diferencial** differential calculus; **obrar con mucho ~** to act cautiously.

caldear [kalde'ar] *vt* to warm (up), heat (up); (*metales*) to weld.

caldera [kal'dera] *nf* boiler.

calderero [kalde'rero] *nm* boilermaker.

calderilla [kalde'riʎa] *nf* (*moneda*) small change.

caldero [kal'dero] *nm* small boiler.

caldo ['kaldo] *nm* stock; (*consomé*)

consommé; ~ **de cultivo** (*BIO*) culture medium; **poner a** ~ **a algn** to tear sb off a strip; **los** ~**s jerezanos** sherries.

caldoso, a [kal'doso, a] *adj* (*guisado*) juicy; (*sopa*) thin.

calé [ka'le] *adj* gipsy *cpd*.

calefacción [kalefak'θjon] *nf* heating; ~ **central** central heating.

caleidoscopio [kaleiðos'kopjo] *nm* kaleidoscope.

calendario [kalen'darjo] *nm* calendar.

calentador [kalenta'ðor] *nm* heater.

calentamiento [kalenta'mjento] *nm* (*DEPORTE*) warm-up.

calentar [kalen'tar] *vt* to heat (up); (*fam: excitar*) to turn on; (*AM: enfurecer*) to anger; ~**se** *vr* to heat up, warm up; (*fig: discusión etc*) to get heated.

calentura [kalen'tura] *nf* (*MED*) fever, (high) temperature; (*de boca*) mouth sore.

calenturiento, a [kalentu'rjento, a] *adj* (*mente*) overactive.

calibrar [kali'βrar] *vt* to gauge, measure.

calibre [ka'liβre] *nm* (*de cañón*) calibre, bore; (*diámetro*) diameter; (*fig*) calibre.

calidad [kali'ðað] *nf* quality; **de** ~ quality *cpd*; ~ **de borrador** (*INFORM*) draft quality; ~ **de carta** *o* **de correspondencia** (*INFORM*) letter quality; ~ **texto** (*INFORM*) text quality; ~ **de vida** quality of life; **en** ~ **de** in the capacity of.

cálido, a ['kaliðo, a] *adj* hot; (*fig*) warm.

caliente [ka'ljente] *etc vb V* **calentar** ♦ *adj* hot; (*fig*) fiery; (*disputa*) heated; (*fam: cachondo*) randy.

califa [ka'lifa] *nm* caliph.

calificación [kalifika'θjon] *nf* qualification; (*de alumno*) grade, mark; ~ **de sobresaliente** first-class mark.

calificar [kalifi'kar] *vt* to qualify; (*alumno*) to grade, mark; ~ **de** to describe as.

calificativo, a [kalifika'tiβo, a] *adj* qualifying ♦ *nm* qualifier, epithet.

califique [kali'fike] *etc vb V* **calificar**.

californiano, a [kalifor'njano, a] *adj*, *nm/f* Californian.

caligrafía [kaliɣra'fia] *nf* calligraphy.

calima [ka'lima] *nf* mist.

calina [ka'lina] *nf* haze.

cáliz ['kaliθ] *nm* (*BOT*) calyx; (*REL*) chalice.

caliza [ka'liθa] *nf* limestone.

callado, a [ka'ʎaðo, a] *adj* quiet, silent.

callar [ka'ʎar] *vt* (*asunto delicado*) to keep quiet about, say nothing about; (*omitir*) to pass over in silence; (*persona, oposición*) to silence ♦ *vi*, ~**se** *vr* to keep quiet, be silent; (*dejar de hablar*) to stop

talking; **¡calla!**, be quiet!; **¡cállate!**, **¡cállese!** shut up!; **¡cállate la boca!** shut your mouth!

calle ['kaʎe] *nf* street; (*DEPORTE*) lane; ~ **arriba/abajo** up/down the street; ~ **de sentido único** one-way street; **poner a algn (de patitas) en la** ~ to kick sb out.

calleja [ka'ʎexa] *nf* alley, narrow street.

callejear [kaʎexe'ar] *vi* to wander (about) the streets.

callejero, a [kaʎe'xero, a] *adj* street *cpd* ♦ *nm* street map.

callejón [kaʎe'xon] *nm* alley, passage; (*GEO*) narrow pass; ~ **sin salida** cul-de-sac; (*fig*) blind alley.

callejuela [kaʎe'xwela] *nf* side-street, alley.

callista [ka'ʎista] *nm/f* chiropodist.

callo ['kaʎo] *nm* callus; (*en el pie*) corn; ~**s** *nmpl* (*CULIN*) tripe *sg*.

callosidad [kaʎosi'ðað] *nf* (*de pie*) corn; (*de mano*) callus.

calloso, a [ka'ʎoso, a] *adj* horny, rough.

calma ['kalma] *nf* calm; (*pachorra*) slowness; (*COM, ECON*) calm, lull; ~ **chicha** dead calm; **¡**~**!**, **¡con** ~**!** take it easy!

calmante [kal'mante] *adj* soothing ♦ *nm* sedative, tranquillizer.

calmar [kal'mar] *vt* to calm, calm down; (*dolor*) to relieve ♦ *vi*, ~**se** *vr* (*tempestad*) to abate; (*mente etc*) to become calm.

calmoso, a [kal'moso, a] *adj* calm, quiet.

caló [ka'lo] *nm* (*de gitanos*) gipsy language, Romany; (*argot*) slang.

calor [ka'lor] *nm* heat; (~ *agradable*) warmth; **entrar en** ~ to get warm; **tener** ~ to be *o* feel hot.

caloría [kalo'ria] *nf* calorie.

calorífero, a [kalo'rifero, a] *adj* heat-producing, heat-giving ♦ *nm* heating system.

calque ['kalke] *etc vb V* **calcar**.

calumnia [ka'lumnja] *nf* slander; (*por escrito*) libel.

calumniar [kalum'njar] *vt* to slander; to libel.

calumnioso, a [kalum'njoso, a] *a* slanderous; libellous.

caluroso, a [kalu'roso, a] *adj* hot; (*sin exceso*) warm; (*fig*) enthusiastic.

calva ['kalβa] *nf* bald patch; (*en bosque*) clearing.

calvario [kal'βarjo] *nm* stations *pl* of the cross; (*fig*) cross, heavy burden.

calvicie [kal'βiθje] *nf* baldness.

calvo, a ['kalβo, a] *adj* bald; (*terreno*) bare, barren; (*tejido*) threadbare ♦ *nm* bald man.

calza ['kalθa] nf wedge, chock.

calzado, a [kal'θaðo, a] adj shod ♦ nm footwear ♦ nf roadway, highway.

calzador [kalθa'ðor] nm shoehorn.

calzar [kal'θar] vt (zapatos etc) to wear; (un mueble) to put a wedge under; (TEC: rueda etc) to scotch; ~se vr: ~se los zapatos to put on one's shoes; ¿qué (número) calza? what size do you take?

calzón [kal'θon] nm (tb: **calzones**) shorts pl; (AM: de hombre) pants pl; (: de mujer) panties pl.

calzonazos [kalθo'naθos] nm inv henpecked husband.

calzoncillos [kalθon'θiʎos] nmpl underpants.

cama ['kama] nf bed; (GEO) stratum; ~ **individual/de matrimonio** single/double bed; **guardar** ~ to be ill in bed.

camada [ka'maða] nf litter; (de personas) gang, band.

camafeo [kama'feo] nm cameo.

camaleón [kamale'on] nm chameleon.

cámara ['kamara] nf (POL etc) chamber; (habitación) room; (sala) hall; (CINE) cine camera; (fotográfica) camera; ~ **de aire** inner tube; ~ **alta/baja** upper/lower house; ~ **de comercio** chamber of commerce; ~ **de gas** gas chamber; ~ **de video** video camera; **a** ~ **lenta** in slow motion.

camarada [kama'raða] nm comrade, companion.

camaradería [kamaraðe'ria] nf comradeship.

camarero, a [kama'rero, a] nm waiter ♦ nf (en restaurante) waitress; (en casa, hotel) maid.

camarilla [kama'riʎa] nf (clan) clique; (POL) lobby.

camarín [kama'rin] nm (TEAT) dressing room.

camarón [kama'ron] nm shrimp.

camarote [kama'rote] nm (NAUT) cabin.

cambiable [kam'bjaβle] adj (variable) changeable, variable; (intercambiable) interchangeable.

cambiante [kam'bjante] adj variable.

cambiar [kam'bjar] vt to change; (trocar) to exchange ♦ vi to change; ~se vr (mudarse) to move; (de ropa) to change; ~(se) de ... to change one's ...; ~ **de idea/de ropa** to change one's mind/clothes.

cambiazo [kam'bjaθo] nm: **dar el** ~ **a algn** to swindle sb.

cambio ['kambjo] nm change; (trueque)

exchange; (COM) rate of exchange; (oficina) bureau de change; (dinero menudo) small change; **en** ~ on the other hand; (en lugar de eso) instead; ~ **de divisas** (COM) foreign exchange; ~ **de línea** (INFORM) line feed; ~ **de página** (INFORM) form feed; ~ **a término** (COM) forward exchange; ~ **de velocidades** gear lever; ~ **de vía** points pl.

cambista [kam'bista] nm (COM) exchange broker.

Camboya [kam'boja] nf Cambodia, Kampuchea.

camboyano, a [kambo'jano, a] a, nm/f Cambodian, Kampuchean.

camelar [kame'lar] vt (con mujer) to flirt with; (persuadir) to cajole.

camelia [ka'melia] nf camellia.

camello [ka'meʎo] nm camel; (fam: traficante) pusher.

camelo [ka'melo] nm: **me huele a** ~ it smells fishy.

camerino [kame'rino] nm (TEAT) dressing room.

camilla [ka'miʎa] nf (MED) stretcher.

caminante [kami'nante] nm/f traveller.

caminar [kami'nar] vi (marchar) to walk, go; (viajar) to travel, journey ♦ vt (recorrer) to cover, travel.

caminata [kami'nata] nf long walk.

camino [ka'mino] nm way, road; (sendero) track; **a medio** ~ halfway (there); **en el** ~ on the way, en route; ~ **de** on the way to; ~ **particular** private road; ~ **vecinal** country road; **C~s, Canales y Puertos** (UNIV) Civil Engineering; **ir por buen** ~ (fig) to be on the right track.

The **Camino de Santiago** *is a medieval pilgrim route stretching from the Pyrenees to Santiago de Compostela in north-west Spain, where tradition has it the body of the Apostle James is buried. Nowadays it is a popular tourist route as well as a religious one. The* **concha** *(cockleshell) is a symbol of the* **Camino de Santiago**, *because it is said that when St James' body was found it was covered in shells.*

---

camión [ka'mjon] nm lorry, truck (US); (AM: autobús) bus; ~ **de bomberos** fire engine.

camionero [kamjo'nero] nm lorry o truck (US) driver, trucker (esp US).

camioneta [kamjo'neta] nf van, transit ®, light truck.

camisa [ka'misa] nf shirt; (BOT) skin; ~ **de dormir** nightdress; ~ **de fuerza**

straitjacket.
camisería [kamise'ria] *nf* outfitter's (shop).
camiseta [kami'seta] *nf* tee-shirt; (*ropa interior*) vest; (*de deportista*) top.
camisón [kami'son] *nm* nightdress, nightgown.
camomila [kamo'mila] *nf* camomile.
camorra [ka'morra] *nf*: **armar** ~ to kick up a row; **buscar** ~ to look for trouble.
camorrista [kamo'rrista] *nm/f* thug.
camote [ka'mote] *nm* (*AM*) sweet potato.
campal [kam'pal] *adj*: **batalla** ~ pitched battle.
campamento [kampa'mento] *nm* camp.
campana [kam'pana] *nf* bell.
campanada [kampa'naða] *nf* peal.
campanario [kampa'narjo] *nm* belfry.
campanilla [kampa'niʎa] *nf* (*campana*) small bell.
campante [kam'pante] *adj*: **siguió tan** ~ he went on as if nothing had happened.
campaña [kam'paɲa] *nf* (*MIL, POL*) campaign; **hacer** ~ (**en pro de/contra**) to campaign (for/against); ~ **de venta** sales campaign.
campechano, a [kampe'tʃano, a] *adj* open.
campeón, ona [kampe'on, ona] *nm/f* champion.
campeonato [kampeo'nato] *nm* championship.
campesino, a [kampe'sino, a] *adj* country *cpd*, rural; (*gente*) peasant *cpd* ♦ *nm/f* countryman/woman; (*agricultor*) farmer.
campestre [kam'pestre] *adj* country *cpd*, rural.
camping ['kampin] *nm* camping; (*lugar*) campsite; **ir de** *o* **hacer** ~ to go camping.
campiña [kam'piɲa] *nf* countryside.
campista [kam'pista] *nm/f* camper.
campo ['kampo] *nm* (*fuera de la ciudad*) country, countryside; (*AGR, ELEC, INFORM*) field; (*de fútbol*) pitch; (*de golf*) course; (*MIL*) camp; ~ **de batalla** battlefield; ~ **de minas** minefield; ~ **petrolífero** oilfield; ~ **visual** field of vision; ~ **de concentración/de internación/de trabajo** concentration/internment/labour camp.
camposanto [kampo'santo] *nm* cemetery.
CAMPSA ['kampsa] *nf abr* (*ESP COM*) = *Compañía Arrendataria del Monopolio de Petróleos, S.A.*
campus ['kampus] *nm inv* (*UNIV*) campus.
camuflaje [kamu'flaxe] *nm* camouflage.
camuflar [kamu'flar] *vt* to camouflage.
can [kan] *nm* dog, mutt (*fam*).
cana ['kana] *nf* V **cano**.
Canadá [kana'ða] *nm* Canada.

canadiense [kana'ðjense] *adj, nm/f* Canadian ♦ *nf* fur-lined jacket.
canal [ka'nal] *nm* canal; (*GEO*) channel, strait; (*de televisión*) channel; (*de tejado*) gutter; **C**~ **de la Mancha** English Channel; **C**~ **de Panamá** Panama Canal.
canalice [kana'liθe] *etc vb* V **canalizar**.
canalizar [kanali'θar] *vt* to channel.
canalla [ka'naʎa] *nf* rabble, mob ♦ *nm* swine.
canallada [kana'ʎaða] *nf* (*hecho*) dirty trick.
canalón [kana'lon] *nm* (*conducto vertical*) drainpipe; (*del tejado*) gutter; **canalones** *nmpl* (*CULIN*) cannelloni.
canapé, *pl* **canapés** [kana'pe, kana'pes] *nm* sofa, settee; (*CULIN*) canapé.
Canarias [ka'narjas] *nfpl*: **las (Islas)** ~ the Canaries, the Canary Isles.
canario, a [ka'narjo, a] *adj* of *o* from the Canary Isles ♦ *nm/f* native *o* inhabitant of the Canary Isles ♦ *nm* (*ZOOL*) canary.
canasta [ka'nasta] *nf* (round) basket.
canastilla [kanas'tiʎa] *nf* small basket; (*de niño*) layette.
canasto [ka'nasto] *nm* large basket.
cancela [kan'θela] *nf* (wrought-iron) gate.
cancelación [kanθela'θjon] *nf* cancellation.
cancelar [kanθe'lar] *vt* to cancel; (*una deuda*) to write off.
cáncer ['kanθer] *nm* (*MED*) cancer; **C**~ (*ASTRO*) Cancer.
cancerígeno, a [kanθe'rixeno, a] *adj* carcinogenic.
cancha ['kantʃa] *nf* (*de baloncesto, tenis etc*) court; (*AM: de fútbol etc*) pitch.
canciller [kanθi'ʎer] *nm* chancellor; **C**~ (*AM*) Foreign Minister, ≈ Foreign Secretary (*BRIT*).
Cancillería [kansiʎe'ria] *nf* (*AM*) Foreign Ministry, ≈ Foreign Office (*BRIT*).
canción [kan'θjon] *nf* song; ~ **de cuna** lullaby.
cancionero [kanθjo'nero] *nm* song book.
candado [kan'daðo] *nm* padlock.
candela [kan'dela] *nf* candle.
candelabro [kande'laβro] *nm* candelabra.
candelero [kande'lero] *nm* (*para vela*) candlestick; (*de aceite*) oil lamp.
candente [kan'dente] *adj* red-hot; (*tema*) burning.
candidato, a [kandi'ðato, a] *nm/f* candidate; (*para puesto*) applicant.
candidatura [kandiða'tura] *nf* candidature.
candidez [kandi'ðeθ] *nf* (*sencillez*) simplicity; (*simpleza*) naiveté.
cándido, a ['kandiðo, a] *adj* simple; naive.
candil [kan'dil] *nm* oil lamp.

candilejas [kandi'lexas] *nfpl* (*TEAT*) footlights.
candor [kan'dor] *nm* (*sinceridad*) frankness; (*inocencia*) innocence.
canela [ka'nela] *nf* cinnamon.
canelo [ka'nelo] *nm*: **hacer el** ~ to act the fool.
canelones [kane'lones] *nmpl* cannelloni.
cangrejo [kan'grexo] *nm* crab.
canguro [kan'guro] *nm* (*ZOOL*) kangaroo; (*de niños*) baby-sitter; **hacer de** ~ to baby-sit.
caníbal [ka'niβal] *adj, nm/f* cannibal.
canica [ka'nika] *nf* marble.
caniche [ka'nitʃe] *nm* poodle.
canícula [ka'nikula] *nf* midsummer heat.
canijo, a [ka'nixo, a] *adj* frail, sickly.
canilla [ka'niʎa] *nf* (*TEC*) bobbin.
canino, a [ka'nino, a] *adj* canine ♦ *nm* canine (tooth).
canje [kan'xe] *nm* exchange; (*trueque*) swap.
canjear [kanxe'ar] *vt* to exchange; (*trocar*) to swap.
cano, a ['kano, a] *adj* grey-haired, white-haired ♦ *nf* (*tb*: **canas**) white *o* grey hair; **tener canas** to be going grey.
canoa [ka'noa] *nf* canoe.
canon ['kanon] *nm* canon; (*pensión*) rent; (*COM*) tax.
canonice [kano'niθe] *etc vb V* **canonizar**.
canónico, a [ka'noniko, a] *adj*: **derecho** ~ canon law.
canónigo [ka'noniɣo] *nm* canon.
canonizar [kanoni'θar] *vt* to canonize.
canoro, a [ka'noro, a] *adj* melodious.
canoso, a [ka'noso, a] *adj* (*pelo*) grey (*BRIT*), gray (*US*); (*persona*) grey-haired.
cansado, a [kan'saðo, a] *adj* tired, weary; (*tedioso*) tedious, boring; **estoy** ~ **de hacerlo** I'm sick of doing it.
cansancio [kan'sanθjo] *nm* tiredness, fatigue.
cansar [kan'sar] *vt* (*fatigar*) to tire, tire out; (*aburrir*) to bore; (*fastidiar*) to bother; ~**se** *vr* to tire, get tired; (*aburrirse*) to get bored.
cantábrico, a [kan'taβriko, a] *adj* Cantabrian; **Mar C**~ Bay of Biscay; **(Montes) C**~**s, Cordillera Cantábrica** Cantabrian Mountains.
cántabro, a ['kantaβro, a] *adj, nm/f* Cantabrian.
cantante [kan'tante] *adj* singing ♦ *nm/f* singer.
cantaor, a [kanta'or, a] *nm/f* Flamenco singer.
cantar [kan'tar] *vt* to sing ♦ *vi* to sing;

(*insecto*) to chirp; (*rechinar*) to squeak; (*fam: criminal*) to squeal ♦ *nm* (*acción*) singing; (*canción*) song; (*poema*) poem; ~ **a algn las cuarenta** to tell sb a few home truths; ~ **a dos voces** to sing a duet.
cántara ['kantara] *nf* large pitcher.
cántaro ['kantaro] *nm* pitcher, jug.
cantautor, a [kantau'tor, a] *nm/f* singer-songwriter.
cante ['kante] *nm*: ~ **jondo** flamenco singing.
cantera [kan'tera] *nf* quarry.
cántico ['kantiko] *nm* (*REL*) canticle; (*fig*) song.
cantidad [kanti'ðað] *nf* quantity, amount; (*ECON*) sum ♦ *adv* (*fam*) a lot; ~ **alzada** lump sum; ~ **de** lots of.
cantilena [kanti'lena] *nf* = **cantinela**.
cantimplora [kantim'plora] *nf* (*frasco*) water bottle, canteen.
cantina [kan'tina] *nf* canteen; (*de estación*) buffet; (*esp AM*) bar.
cantinela [kanti'nela] *nf* ballad, song.
canto ['kanto] *nm* singing; (*canción*) song; (*borde*) edge, rim; (*de un cuchillo*) back; ~ **rodado** boulder.
cantón [kan'ton] *nm* canton.
cantor, a [kan'tor, a] *nm/f* singer.
canturrear [kanturre'ar] *vi* to sing softly.
canutas [ka'nutas] *nfpl*: **pasarlas** ~ (*fam*) to have a rough time (of it).
canuto [ka'nuto] *nm* (*tubo*) small tube; (*fam: droga*) joint.
caña ['kaɲa] *nf* (*BOT: tallo*) stem, stalk; (*carrizo*) reed; (*vaso*) tumbler; (*de cerveza*) glass of beer; (*ANAT*) shinbone; (*AM: aguardiente*) cane liquor; ~ **de azúcar** sugar cane; ~ **de pescar** fishing rod.
cañada [ka'ɲaða] *nf* (*entre dos montañas*) gully, ravine; (*camino*) cattle track.
cáñamo ['kaɲamo] *nm* (*BOT*) hemp.
cañaveral [kaɲaβe'ral] *nm* (*BOT*) reedbed; (*AGR*) sugar-cane field.
cañería [kaɲe'ria] *nf* piping; (*tubo*) pipe.
caño ['kaɲo] *nm* (*tubo*) tube, pipe; (*de aguas servidas*) sewer; (*MUS*) pipe; (*NAUT*) navigation channel; (*de fuente*) jet.
cañón [ka'ɲon] *nm* (*MIL*) cannon; (*de fusil*) barrel; (*GEO*) canyon, gorge.
cañonazo [kaɲo'naθo] *nm* (*MIL*) gunshot.
cañonera [kaɲo'nera] *nf* (*tb*: **lancha** ~) gunboat.
caoba [ka'oβa] *nf* mahogany.
caos ['kaos] *nm* chaos.
caótico, a [ka'otiko, a] *adj* chaotic.
C.A.P. *nm abr* (= *Certificado de Aptitud*

Pedagógica) teaching certificate.
cap. *abr* (= *capítulo*) ch.
capa ['kapa] *nf* cloak, cape; (*CULIN*)
coating; (*GEO*) layer, stratum; (*de
pintura*) coat; **de ~ y espada** cloak-and-
dagger; **so ~ de** under the pretext of; **~
de ozono** ozone layer; **~s sociales** social
groups.
capacho [ka'patʃo] *nm* wicker basket.
capacidad [kapaθi'ðað] *nf* (*medida*)
capacity; (*aptitud*) capacity, ability; **una
sala con ~ para 900** a hall seating 900;
~ adquisitiva purchasing power.
capacitación [kapaθita'θjon] *nf* training.
capacitar [kapaθi'tar] *vt*: **~ a algn para
algo** to qualify sb for sth; (*TEC*) to train
sb for sth.
capar [ka'par] *vt* to castrate, geld.
caparazón [kapara'θon] *nm* (*ZOOL*) shell.
capataz [kapa'taθ] *nm* foreman,
chargehand.
capaz [ka'paθ] *adj* able, capable; (*amplio*)
capacious, roomy; **es ~ que venga
mañana** (*AM*) he'll probably come
tomorrow.
capcioso, a [kap'θjoso, a] *adj* wily,
deceitful; **pregunta capciosa** trick
question.
capea [ka'pea] *nf* (*TAUR*) bullfight with
young bulls.
capear [kape'ar] *vt* (*dificultades*) to dodge;
~ el temporal to weather the storm.
capellán [kape'ʎan] *nm* chaplain;
(*sacerdote*) priest.
caperuza [kape'ruθa] *nf* hood; (*de bolígrafo*)
cap.
capi ['kapi] *nf* (*esp AM fam*) capital (city).
capicúa [kapi'kua] *nf* reversible number,
e.g. 1441.
capilar [kapi'lar] *adj* hair *cpd.*
capilla [ka'piʎa] *nf* chapel.
capital [kapi'tal] *adj* capital ♦ *nm* (*COM*)
capital ♦ *nf* (*de nación*) capital (city); (*tb:
~ de provincia*) provincial capital, ≈
county town; **~ activo/en acciones**
working/share *o* equity capital; **~
arriesgado** venture capital; **~ autorizado**
o **social** authorised capital; **~ emitido**
issued capital; **~ improductivo** idle
money; **~ invertido** *o* **utilizado** capital
employed; **~ pagado** paid-up capital; **~
de riesgo** risk capital; **~ social** equity *o*
share capital; **inversión de ~es** capital
investment; *V tb* **provincia.**
capitalice [kapita'liθe] *etc vb V* **capitalizar.**
capitalino, a [kapita'lino, a] *adj* (*AM*) of *o*
from the capital ♦ *nm/f* native *o*
inhabitant of the capital.

capitalismo [kapita'lismo] *nm* capitalism.
capitalista [kapita'lista] *adj, nm/f* capitalist.
capitalizar [kapitali'θar] *vt* to capitalize.
capitán [kapi'tan] *nm* captain; (*fig*) leader.
capitana [kapi'tana] *nf* flagship.
capitanear [kapitane'ar] *vt* to captain.
capitanía [kapita'nia] *nf* captaincy.
capitel [kapi'tel] *nm* (*ARQ*) capital.
capitolio [kapi'toljo] *nm* capitol.
capitulación [kapitula'θjon] *nf* (*rendición*)
capitulation, surrender; (*acuerdo*)
agreement, pact; **capitulaciones
matrimoniales** marriage contract *sg.*
capitular [kapitu'lar] *vi* to come to terms,
make an agreement; (*MIL*) to surrender.
capítulo [ka'pitulo] *nm* chapter.
capo [ka'po] *nm* drugs baron.
capó [ka'po] *nm* (*AUTO*) bonnet (*BRIT*), hood
(*US*).
capón [ka'pon] *nm* capon.
caporal [kapo'ral] *nm* chief, leader.
capota [ka'pota] *nf* (*de mujer*) bonnet;
(*AUTO*) hood (*BRIT*), top (*US*).
capote [ka'pote] *nm* (*abrigo: de militar*)
greatcoat; (*de torero*) cloak.
capricho [ka'pritʃo] *nm* whim, caprice.
caprichoso, a [kapri'tʃoso, a] *adj*
capricious.
Capricornio [kapri'kornjo] *nm* Capricorn.
cápsula ['kapsula] *nf* capsule; **~ espacial**
space capsule.
captar [kap'tar] *vt* (*comprender*) to
understand; (*RADIO*) to pick up; (*atención,
apoyo*) to attract.
captura [kap'tura] *nf* capture; (*JUR*) arrest.
capturar [kaptu'rar] *vt* to capture; (*JUR*) to
arrest; (*datos*) to input.
capucha [ka'putʃa] *nf* hood, cowl.
capullo [ka'puʎo] *nm* (*ZOOL*) cocoon; (*BOT*)
bud; (*fam!*) berk (*BRIT*), jerk (*US*).
caqui ['kaki] *nm* khaki.
cara ['kara] *nf* (*ANAT, de moneda*) face;
(*aspecto*) appearance; (*de disco*) side;
(*fig*) boldness; (*descara*) cheek, nerve
♦ *prep*: **~ a** facing; **de ~ a** opposite,
facing; **dar la ~** to face the
consequences; **echar algo en ~ a algn** to
reproach sb for sth; **¿~ o cruz?** heads or
tails?; **¡qué ~ más dura!** what a nerve!;
de una ~ (*disquete*) single-sided.
carabina [kara'βina] *nf* carbine, rifle;
(*persona*) chaperone.
carabinero [karaβi'nero] *nm* (*de aduana*)
customs officer; (*AM*) gendarme.
Caracas [ka'rakas] *nm* Caracas.
caracol [kara'kol] *nm* (*ZOOL*) snail; (*concha*)
(sea)shell; **escalera de ~** spiral
staircase.

caracolear [karakole'ar] *vi* (*caballo*) to prance about.

carácter, *pl* **caracteres** [ka'rakter, karak'teres] *nm* character; ~ **de cambio de página** (*INFORM*) form feed character; **caracteres de imprenta** (*TIP*) type(face) *sg*; ~ **libre** (*INFORM*) wildcard character; **tener buen/mal** ~ to be good-natured/ bad tempered.

caracterice [karakte'riθe] *etc vb V* **caracterizar.**

característico, a [karakte'ristiko, a] *adj* characteristic ♦ *nf* characteristic.

caracterizar [karakteri'θar] *vt* (*distinguir*) to characterize, typify; (*honrar*) to confer (a) distinction on.

caradura [kara'ðura] *nm/f* cheeky person; **es un** ~ he's got a nerve.

carajilla [kara'xiʎo] *nm black coffee with brandy.*

carajo [ka'raxo] *nm* (*esp AM fam!*): ¡~! shit!(*!*); ¡**qué** ~! what the hell!; **me importa un** ~ I don't give a damn.

caramba [ka'ramba] *excl* well!, good gracious!

carámbano [ka'rambano] *nm* icicle.

carambola [karam'bola] *nf*: **por** ~ by a fluke.

caramelo [kara'melo] *nm* (*dulce*) sweet; (*azúcar fundido*) caramel.

carantoñas [karan'toɲas] *nfpl*: **hacer** ~ **a algn** to (try to) butter sb up.

caraqueño, a [kara'keɲo, a] *adj* of *o* from Caracas ♦ *nm/f* native *o* inhabitant of Caracas.

carátula [ka'ratula] *nf* (*máscara*) mask; (*TEAT*): **la** ~ the stage.

caravana [kara'βana] *nf* caravan; (*fig*) group; (*de autos*) tailback.

carbón [kar'βon] *nm* coal; ~ **de leña** charcoal; **papel** ~ carbon paper.

carbonatado, a [karßono'taðo, a] *adj* carbonated.

carbonato [karßo'nato] *nm* carbonate; ~ **sódico** sodium carbonate.

carboncillo [karßon'θiʎo] *nm* (*ARTE*) charcoal.

carbonice [karßo'niθe] *etc vb V* **carbonizar.**

carbonilla [karßo'niʎa] *nf* coal dust.

carbonizar [karßoni'θar] *vt* to carbonize; (*quemar*) to char; **quedar carbonizado** (*ELEC*) to be electrocuted.

carbono [kar'βono] *nm* carbon.

carburador [karßura'ðor] *nm* carburettor.

carburante [karßu'rante] *nm* fuel.

carca ['karka] *adj, nm/f inv* reactionary.

carcajada [karka'xaða] *nf* (loud) laugh, guffaw.

carcajearse [karkaxe'arse] *vr* to roar with laughter.

cárcel ['karθel] *nf* prison, jail; (*TEC*) clamp.

carcelero, a [karθe'lero, a] *adj* prison *cpd* ♦ *nm/f* warder.

carcoma [kar'koma] *nf* woodworm.

carcomer [karko'mer] *vt* to bore into, eat into; (*fig*) to undermine; ~**se** *vr* to become worm-eaten; (*fig*) to decay.

carcomido, a [karko'miðo, a] *adj* worm-eaten; (*fig*) rotten.

cardar [kar'ðar] *vt* (*TEC*) to card, comb.

cardenal [karðe'nal] *nm* (*REL*) cardinal; (*MED*) bruise.

cárdeno, a ['karðeno, a] *adj* purple; (*lívido*) livid.

cardiaco, a [kar'ðjako, a], **cardíaco, a** [kar'ðiako, a] *adj* cardiac; (*ataque*) heart *cpd.*

cardinal [karði'nal] *adj* cardinal.

cardiólogo, a [karðj'oloɣo, a] *nm/f* cardiologist.

cardo ['karðo] *nm* thistle.

carear [kare'ar] *vt* to bring face to face; (*comparar*) to compare; ~**se** *vr* to come face to face, meet.

carecer [kare'θer] *vi*: ~ **de** to lack, be in need of.

carencia [ka'renθja] *nf* lack; (*escasez*) shortage; (*MED*) deficiency.

carente [ka'rente] *adj*: ~ **de** lacking in, devoid of.

carestía [kares'tia] *nf* (*escasez*) scarcity, shortage; (*COM*) high cost; **época de** ~ period of shortage.

careta [ka'reta] *nf* mask.

carey [ka'rei] *nm* (*tortuga*) turtle; (*concha*) tortoiseshell.

carezca [ka'reθka] *etc vb V* **carecer.**

carga ['karɣa] *nf* (*peso, ELEC*) load; (*de barco*) cargo, freight; (*FINANZAS*) tax, duty; (*MIL*) charge; (*INFORM*) loading; (*obligación, responsabilidad*) duty, obligation; ~ **aérea** (*COM*) air cargo; ~ **útil** (*COM*) payload; **la** ~ **fiscal** the tax burden.

cargadero [karɣa'ðero] *nm* goods platform, loading bay.

cargado, a [kar'ɣaðo, a] *adj* loaded; (*ELEC*) live; (*café, té*) strong; (*cielo*) overcast.

cargador, a [karɣa'ðor, a] *nm/f* loader; (*NAUT*) docker ♦ *nm* (*INFORM*): ~ **de discos** disk pack.

cargamento [karɣa'mento] *nm* (*acción*) loading; (*mercancías*) load, cargo.

cargante [kar'ɣante] *adj* (*persona*) trying.

cargar [kar'ɣar] *vt* (*barco, arma*) to load; (*ELEC*) to charge; (*impuesto*) to impose;

(*COM: algo en cuenta*) to charge, debit; (*MIL: enemigo*) to charge ♦ *vi* (*AUTO*) to load (up); (*inclinarse*) to lean; (*INFORM*) to load, feed in; ~ **con** to pick up, carry away; **~se** *vr* (*fam: estropear*) to break; (*: matar*) to bump off; (*ELEC*) to become charged.

cargo ['karɣo] *nm* (*COM etc*) charge, debit; (*puesto*) post, office; (*responsabilidad*) duty, obligation; (*fig*) weight, burden; (*JUR*) charge; **altos ~s** high-ranking officials; **una cantidad en ~ a algn** a sum chargeable to sb; **hacerse ~ de** to take charge of *o* responsibility for.

cargue ['karɣe] *etc vb* V **cargar**.

carguero [kar'ɣero] *nm* freighter, cargo boat; (*avión*) freight plane.

Caribe [ka'riße] *nm*: **el ~** the Caribbean.

caribeño, a [kari'ßeɲo, a] *adj* Caribbean.

caricatura [karika'tura] *nf* caricature.

caricia [ka'riθja] *nf* caress; (*a animal*) pat, stroke.

caridad [kari'ðað] *nf* charity.

caries ['karjes] *nf inv* (*MED*) tooth decay.

carilla [ka'riʎa] *nf* (*TIP*) page.

cariño [ka'riɲo] *nm* affection, love; (*caricia*) caress; (*en carta*) love ....

cariñoso, a [kari'ɲoso, a] *adj* affectionate.

carioca [ka'rjoka] *adj* (*AM*) of *o* from Rio de Janeiro ♦ *nm/f* native *o* inhabitant of Rio de Janeiro.

carisma [ka'risma] *nm* charisma.

carismático, a [karis'matiko, a] *adj* charismatic.

caritativo, a [karita'tißo, a] *adj* charitable.

cariz [ka'riθ] *nm*: **tener** *o* **tomar buen/mal ~** to look good/bad.

carmesí [karme'si] *adj, nm* crimson.

carmín [kar'min] *nm* (*color*) carmine; **~ (de labios)** lipstick.

carnal [kar'nal] *adj* carnal; **primo ~** first cousin.

carnaval [karna'ßal] *nm* carnival.

The 3 days before **miércoles de ceniza** (*Ash Wednesday*), *when fasting traditionally starts, are the time for* **carnaval**, *an exuberant celebration which dates back to pre-Christian times. Although in decline during the Franco years, the carnaval has grown in popularity recently in Spain, Cádiz and Tenerife being particularly well-known for their celebrations.* **El martes de carnaval** (*Shrove Tuesday*) *is the biggest day, with colourful street parades, fancy dress, fireworks and a general party atmosphere.*

---

carne ['karne] *nf* flesh; (*CULIN*) meat; ~ **de cañón** cannon fodder; ~ **de cerdo/de cordero/de ternera/de vaca** pork/lamb/veal/beef; ~ **picada** mince; ~ **de gallina** (*fig*) gooseflesh.

carné [kar'ne] *nm* = **carnet**.

carnero [kar'nero] *nm* sheep, ram; (*carne*) mutton.

carnet, *pl* **carnets** [kar'ne, kar'nes] *nm*: ~ **de conducir** driving licence; ~ **de identidad** identity card; V *tb* **Documento Nacional de Identidad**.

carnicería [karniθe'ria] *nf* butcher's (shop); (*fig: matanza*) carnage, slaughter.

carnicero, a [karni'θero, a] *adj* carnivorous ♦ *nm/f* (*tb fig*) butcher ♦ *nm* carnivore.

carnívoro, a [kar'nißoro, a] *adj* carnivorous ♦ *nm* carnivore.

carnoso, a [kar'noso, a] *adj* beefy, fat.

caro, a ['karo, a] *adj* dear; (*COM*) dear, expensive ♦ *adv* dear, dearly; **vender ~** to sell at a high price.

carpa ['karpa] *nf* (*pez*) carp; (*de circo*) big top; (*AM: de camping*) tent.

carpeta [kar'peta] *nf* folder, file.

carpetazo [karpe'taθo] *nm*: **dar ~ a** to shelve.

carpintería [karpinte'ria] *nf* carpentry.

carpintero [karpin'tero] *nm* carpenter; **pajaro ~** woodpecker.

carraca [ka'rraka] *nf* (*DEPORTE*) rattle.

carraspear [karraspe'ar] *vi* (*aclararse*) to clear one's throat.

carraspera [karras'pera] *nf* hoarseness.

carrera [ka'rrera] *nf* (*acción*) run(ning); (*espacio recorrido*) run; (*certamen*) race; (*trayecto*) course; (*profesión*) career; (*ESCOL, UNIV*) course; (*de taxi*) ride; (*en medias*) ladder; **a la ~** at (full) speed; **caballo de ~(s)** racehorse; ~ **de armamentos** arms race.

carrerilla [karre'riʎa] *nf*: **decir algo de ~** to reel sth off; **tomar ~** to get up speed.

carreta [ka'rreta] *nf* wagon, cart.

carrete [ka'rrete] *nm* reel, spool; (*TEC*) coil.

carretera [karre'tera] *nf* (*main*) road, highway; ~ **nacional** ≈ A road (*BRIT*), state highway (*US*); ~ **de circunvalación** ring road.

carretilla [karre'tiʎa] *nf* trolley; (*AGR*) (wheel)barrow.

carril [ka'rril] *nm* furrow; (*de autopista*) lane; (*FERRO*) rail.

carrillo [ka'rriʎo] *nm* (*ANAT*) cheek; (*TEC*) pulley.

carro ['karro] *nm* cart, wagon; (*MIL*) tank; (*AM: coche*) car; (*TIP*) carriage; ~ **blindado** armoured car.

carrocería [karroθe'ria] *nf* body, bodywork *no pl* (*BRIT*).

carroña [ka'rroɲa] *nf* carrion *no pl.*

carroza [ka'rroθa] *nf* (*vehículo*) coach ♦ *nm/f* (*fam*) old fogey.

carruaje [ka'rrwaxe] *nm* carriage.

carrusel [karru'sel] *nm* merry-go-round, roundabout (*BRIT*).

carta ['karta] *nf* letter; (*CULIN*) menu; (*naipe*) card; (*mapa*) map; (*JUR*) document; ~ **de crédito** credit card; ~ **de crédito documentaria** (*COM*) documentary letter of credit; ~ **de crédito irrevocable** (*COM*) irrevocable letter of credit; ~ **certificada/urgente** registered/special delivery letter; ~ **marítima** chart; ~ **de pedido** (*COM*) order; ~ **verde** (*AUTO*) green card; ~ **de vinos** wine list; **echar una** ~ **al correo** to post a letter; **echar las** ~**s a algn** to tell sb's fortune.

cartabón [karta'ßon] *nm* set square.

cartearse [karte'arse] *vr* to correspond.

cartel [kar'tel] *nm* (*anuncio*) poster, placard; (*ESCOL*) wall chart; (*COM*) cartel.

cartelera [karte'lera] *nf* hoarding, billboard; (*en periódico etc*) listings *pl*, entertainments guide; "**en ~**" "showing".

cartera [kar'tera] *nf* (*de bolsillo*) wallet; (*de colegial, cobrador*) satchel; (*AM: de señora*) handbag (*BRIT*), purse (*US*); (*para documentos*) briefcase; **ministro sin ~** (*POL*) minister without portfolio; **ocupa la** ~ **de Agricultura** he is Minister of Agriculture; ~ **de pedidos** (*COM*) order book; **efectos en** ~ (*ECON*) holdings.

carterista [karte'rista] *nm/f* pickpocket.

cartero [kar'tero] *nm* postman.

cartílago [kar'tilaxo] *nm* cartilage.

cartilla [kar'tiʎa] *nf* (*ESCOL*) primer, first reading book; ~ **de ahorros** bank book.

cartografía [kartoɣra'fia] *nf* cartography.

cartón [kar'ton] *nm* cardboard.

cartucho [kar'tutʃo] *nm* (*MIL*) cartridge; (*bolsita*) paper cone; ~ **de datos** (*INFORM*) data cartridge.

cartulina [kartu'lina] *nf* fine cardboard, card.

CASA ['kasa] *nf abr* (*ESP AVIAT*) = *Construcciones Aeronáuticas S.A.*

casa ['kasa] *nf* house; (*hogar*) home; (*edificio*) building; (*COM*) firm, company; ~ **consistorial** town hall; ~ **de huéspedes** ≈ guest house; ~ **de socorro** first aid post; ~ **de citas** (*fam*) brothel; **ir a** ~ to go home; **salir de** ~ to go out; (*para siempre*) to leave home; **echar la** ~ **por la ventana** (*gastar*) to spare no expense; *V tb* **hotel**.

casadero, a [kasa'ðero, a] *adj* marriageable.

casado, a [ka'saðo, a] *a* married ♦ *nm/f* married man/woman.

casamiento [kasa'mjento] *nm* marriage, wedding.

casar [ka'sar] *vt* to marry; (*JUR*) to quash, annul; ~**se** *vr* to marry, get married; ~**se por lo civil** to have a civil wedding, get married in a registry office (*BRIT*) .

cascabel [kaska'ßel] *nm* (small) bell; (*ZOOL*) rattlesnake.

cascada [kas'kaða] *nf* waterfall.

cascajo [kas'kaxo] *nm* gravel, stone chippings *pl*.

cascanueces [kaska'nweθes] *nm inv*: **un** ~ a pair of nutcrackers.

cascar [kas'kar] *vt* to split; (*nuez*) to crack ♦ *vi* to chatter; ~**se** *vr* to crack, split, break (open).

cáscara ['kaskara] *nf* (*de huevo, fruta seca*) shell; (*de fruta*) skin; (*de limón*) peel.

cascarón [kaska'ron] *nm* (broken) eggshell.

cascarrabias [kaska'rraßjas] *nm/f inv* (*fam*) hothead.

casco ['kasko] *nm* (*de bombero, soldado*) helmet; (*cráneo*) skull; (*NAUT: de barco*) hull; (*ZOOL: de caballo*) hoof; (*botella*) empty bottle; (*de ciudad*): **el** ~ **antiguo** the old part; **el** ~ **urbano** the town centre; **los** ~**s azules** the UN peace-keeping force, the blue berets.

cascote [kas'kote] *nm* piece of rubble; ~**s** *nmpl* rubble *sg*.

caserío [kase'rio] *nm* hamlet, group of houses; (*casa*) country house.

casero, a [ka'sero, a] *adj*: **ser muy** ~ (*persona*) to be homeloving; "**comida casera**" "home cooking" ♦ *nm/f* (*propietario*) landlord/lady; (*COM*) house agent.

caserón [kase'ron] *nm* large (ramshackle) house.

caseta [ka'seta] *nf* hut; (*para bañista*) cubicle; (*de feria*) stall.

casete [ka'sete] *nm o f* cassette: ~ **digital** digital audio tape, DAT.

casi ['kasi] *adv* almost; ~ **nunca** hardly ever, almost never; ~ **nada** next to nothing; ~ **te caes** you almost *o* nearly fell.

casilla [ka'siʎa] *nf* (*casita*) hut, cabin; (*TEAT*) box office; (*para cartas*) pigeonhole; (*AJEDREZ*) square; **C~ postal**

o **de Correo(s)** (*AM*) P.O. Box; **sacar a algn de sus ~ s** to drive sb round the bend (*fam*), make sb lose his temper.
casillero [kasi'ʎero] *nm* (set of) pigeonholes.
casino [ka'sino] *nm* club; (*de juego*) casino.
caso ['kaso] *nm* case; (*suceso*) event; **en ~ de ...** in case of ...; **el ~ es que** the fact is that; **en el mejor de los ~s** at best; **en ese ~** in that case; **en todo ~** in any case; **en último ~** as a last resort; **hacer ~ a** to pay attention to; **hacer ~ omiso de** to fail to mention, pass over; **hacer o venir al ~** to be relevant.
caspa ['kaspa] *nf* dandruff.
Caspio ['kaspjo] *adj*: **Mar ~** Caspian Sea.
casque ['kaske] *etc vb V* **cascar**.
casquillo [kas'kiʎo] *nm* (*de bombilla*) fitting; (*de bala*) cartridge case.
cassette [ka'set] *nf o m* = **casete**.
casta ['kasta] *nf* caste; (*raza*) breed; (*linaje*) lineage.
castaña [kas'taɲa] *nf V* **castaño**.
castañetear [kastaɲete'ar] *vi* (*dientes*) to chatter.
castaño, a [kas'taɲo, a] *adj* chestnut (-coloured), brown ♦ *nm* chestnut tree ♦ *nf* chestnut; (*fam: golpe*) punch; **~ de Indias** horse chestnut tree.
castañuelas [kasta'ɲwelas] *nfpl* castanets.
castellano, a [kaste'ʎano, a] *adj* Castilian; (*fam*) Spanish ♦ *nm/f* Castilian; (*fam*) Spaniard ♦ *nm* (*LING*) Castilian, Spanish.

The term **castellano** *is now the most widely used term in Spain and Spanish America to refer to the Spanish language, since* **español** *is too closely associated with Spain as a nation. Of course some people maintain that* **castellano** *should only refer to the type of Spanish spoken in* **Castilla**.

---

castellonense [kasteʎo'nense] *adj* of *o* from Castellón de la Plana ♦ *nm/f* native *o* inhabitant of Castellón de la Plana.
castidad [kasti'ðað] *nf* chastity, purity.
castigar [kasti'var] *vt* to punish; (*DEPORTE*) to penalize; (*afligir*) to afflict.
castigo [kas'tiyo] *nm* punishment; (*DEPORTE*) penalty.
castigue [kas'tiye] *etc vb V* **castigar**.
Castilla [kas'tiʎa] *nf* Castile.
castillo [kas'tiʎo] *nm* castle.
castizo, a [kas'tiθo, a] *adj* (*LING*) pure; (*de buena casta*) purebred, pedigree; (*auténtico*) genuine.
casto, a ['kasto, a] *adj* chaste, pure.
castor [kas'tor] *nm* beaver.

castrar [kas'trar] *vt* to castrate; (*gato*) to doctor; (*BOT*) to prune.
castrense [kas'trense] *adj* army *cpd*, military.
casual [ka'swal] *adj* chance, accidental.
casualidad [kaswali'ðað] *nf* chance, accident; (*combinación de circunstancias*) coincidence; **¡qué ~!** what a coincidence!
casualmente [kaswal'mente] *adv* by chance.
cataclismo [kata'klismo] *nm* cataclysm.
catador [kata'ðor] *nm* taster.
catadura [kata'ðura] *nf* (*aspecto*) looks *pl*.
catalán, ana [kata'lan, ana] *adj, nm/f* Catalan ♦ *nm* (*LING*) Catalan; *V tb* **lenguas cooficiales**.
catalejo [kata'lexo] *nm* telescope.
catalizador [kataliθa'ðor] *nm* catalyst; (*AUTO*) catalytic converter.
catalogar [katalo'var] *vt* to catalogue; **~ (de)** (*fig*) to classify (as).
catálogo [ka'taloyo] *nm* catalogue.
catalogue [kata'loye] *etc vb V* **catalogar**.
Cataluña [kata'luɲa] *nf* Catalonia.
cataplasma [kata'plasma] *nf* (*MED*) poultice.
catapulta [kata'pulta] *nf* catapult.
catar [ka'tar] *vt* to taste, sample.
catarata [kata'rata] *nf* (*GEO*) (water)fall; (*MED*) cataract.
catarro [ka'tarro] *nm* catarrh; (*constipado*) cold.
catarsis [ka'tarsis] *nf* catharsis.
catastro [ka'tastro] *nm* property register.
catástrofe [ka'tastrofe] *nf* catastrophe.
catear [kate'ar] *vt* (*fam*) to flunk.
catecismo [kate'θismo] *nm* catechism.
cátedra ['kateðra] *nf* (*UNIV*) chair, professorship; (*ESCOL*) principal teacher's post; **sentar ~ sobre un argumento** to take one's stand on an argument.
catedral [kate'ðral] *nf* cathedral.
catedrático, a [kate'ðratiko, a] *nm/f* professor; (*ESCOL*) principal teacher.
categoría [kateyo'ria] *nf* category; (*rango*) rank, standing; (*calidad*) quality; **de ~** (*hotel*) top-class; **de baja ~** (*oficial*) low-ranking; **de segunda ~** second-rate; **no tiene ~** he has no standing.
categórico, a [kate'voriko, a] *adj* categorical.
catequesis [kate'kesis] *nf* catechism lessons.
caterva [ka'terßa] *nf* throng, crowd.
cateto, a [ka'teto, a] *nm/f* yokel.
cátodo ['katoðo] *nm* cathode.

catolicismo [katoli'θismo] nm Catholicism.
católico, a [ka'toliko, a] adj, nm/f Catholic.
catorce [ka'torθe] num fourteen.
catre ['katre] nm camp bed (BRIT), cot (US); (fam) pit.
Cáucaso ['kaukaso] nm Caucasus.
cauce ['kauθe] nm (de río) riverbed; (fig) channel.
caucho ['kautʃo] nm rubber; (AM: llanta) tyre.
caución [kau'θjon] nf bail.
caucionar [kauθjo'nar] vt (JUR) to bail (out), go bail for.
caudal [kau'ðal] nm (de río) volume, flow; (fortuna) wealth; (abundancia) abundance.
caudaloso, a [kauða'loso, a] adj (río) large; (persona) wealthy, rich.
caudillaje [kauði'ʎaxe] nm leadership.
caudillo [kau'ðiʎo] nm leader, chief.
causa ['kausa] nf cause; (razón) reason; (JUR) lawsuit, case; **a o por ~ de** because of, on account of.
causar [kau'sar] vt to cause.
cáustico, a ['kaustiko, a] adj caustic.
cautela [kau'tela] nf caution, cautiousness.
cauteloso, a [kaute'loso, a] adj cautious, wary.
cautivar [kauti'ßar] vt to capture; (fig) to captivate.
cautiverio [kauti'ßerjo] nm, **cautividad** [kautißi'ðað] nf captivity.
cautivo, a [kau'tißo, a] adj, nm/f captive.
cauto, a ['kauto, a] adj cautious, careful.
cava ['kaßa] nf (bodega) (wine) cellar ♦ nm (vino) champagne-type wine.
cavar [ka'ßar] vt to dig; (AGR) to dig over.
caverna [ka'ßerna] nf cave, cavern.
cavernoso, a [kaßer'noso, a] adj cavernous; (voz) resounding.
caviar [ka'ßjar] nm caviar(e).
cavidad [kaßi'ðað] nf cavity.
cavilación [kaßila'θjon] nf deep thought.
cavilar [kaßi'lar] vt to ponder.
cayado [ka'jaðo] nm (de pastor) crook; (de obispo) crozier.
cayendo [ka'jendo] etc vb V caer.
caza ['kaθa] nf (acción: gen) hunting; (: con fusil) shooting; (una ~) hunt, chase; (animales) game; **coto de ~** hunting estate ♦ nm (AVIAT) fighter.
cazabe [ka'saße] nm (AM) cassava bread o flour.
cazador, a [kaθa'ðor, a] nm/f hunter/huntress ♦ nf jacket.
cazaejecutivos [kaθaexeku'tißos] nm inv (COM) headhunter.
cazar [ka'θar] vt to hunt; (perseguir) to

chase; (prender) to catch; **~las al vuelo** to be pretty sharp.
cazasubmarinos [kaθasußma'rinos] nm inv (NAUT) destroyer; (AVIAT) anti-submarine craft.
cazo ['kaθo] nm saucepan.
cazuela [ka'θwela] nf (vasija) pan; (guisado) casserole.
cazurro, a [ka'θurro, a] adj surly.
CC nm abr (POL: = Comité Central) Central Committee.
c/c. abr (COM: = cuenta corriente) current account.
CC.AA. abr (ESP) = **Comunidades Autónomas**.
CCI nf abr (COM: = Cámara de Comercio Internacional) ICC.
CC.OO. nfpl abr = **Comisiones Obreras**.
CD nm abr (= compact disc) CD ♦ abr (POL: = Cuerpo Diplomático) CD.
c/d abr (= en casa de) c/o; (= con descuento) with discount.
CDN nm abr (= Centro Dramático Nacional) ≈ RADA (BRIT).
CDS nm abr (= Centro Democrático y Social) political party.
CE nm abr (= Consejo de Europa) Council of Europe ♦ nf abr (= Comunidad Europea) EC.
cebada [θe'ßaða] nf barley.
cebar [θe'ßar] vt (animal) to fatten (up); (anzuelo) to bait; (MIL, TEC) to prime; **~se** vr: **~se en** to vent one's fury on, take it out on.
cebo ['θeßo] nm (para animales) feed, food; (para peces, fig) bait; (de arma) charge.
cebolla [θe'ßoʎa] nf onion.
cebolleta [θeßo'ʎeta] nf spring onion.
cebollino [θeßo'ʎino] nm spring onion.
cebón, ona [θe'ßon, ona] adj fat, fattened.
cebra ['θeßra] nf zebra; **paso de ~** zebra crossing.
CECA ['θeka] nf abr (= Comunidad Europea del Carbón y del Acero) ECSC.
ceca ['θeka] nf: **andar o ir de la ~ a la Meca** to chase about all over the place.
cecear [θeθe'ar] vi to lisp.
ceceo [θe'θeo] nm lisp.
cecina [θe'θina] nf cured o smoked meat.
cedazo [θe'ðaθo] nm sieve.
ceder [θe'ðer] vt (entregar) to hand over; (renunciar a) to give up, part with ♦ vi (renunciar) to give in, yield; (disminuir) to diminish, decline; (romperse) to give way; (viento) to drop; (fiebre etc) to abate; **"ceda el paso"** (AUTO) "give way".
cedro ['θeðro] nm cedar.
cédula ['θeðula] nf certificate, document;

~ **de identidad** (*AM*) identity card; ~ **en blanco** blank cheque; *V tb* **Documento Nacional de Identidad.**

CEE *nf abr* (= *Comunidad Económica Europea*) EEC.

cegar [θe'ɣar] *vt* to blind; (*tubería etc*) to block up, stop up ♦ *vi* to go blind; ~**se** *vr* to be blinded (*de* by).

cegué [θe'ɣe] *etc vb V* **cegar.**

ceguemos [θe'ɣemos] *etc vb V* **cegar.**

ceguera [θe'ɣera] *nf* blindness.

CEI *nf abr* (= *Comunidad de Estados Independientes*) CIS.

Ceilán [θei'lan] *nm* Ceylon, Sri Lanka.

ceja ['θexa] *nf* eyebrow; ~**s pobladas** bushy eyebrows; **arquear las** ~**s** to raise one's eyebrows; **fruncir las** ~**s** to frown.

cejar [θe'xar] *vi* (*fig*) to back down; **no** ~ **to keep it up, stick at it.**

cejijunto, a [θexi'xunto, a] *adj* with bushy eyebrows; (*fig*) scowling.

celada [θe'laða] *nf* ambush, trap.

celador, a [θela'ðor, a] *nm/f* (*de edificio*) watchman; (*de museo etc*) attendant; (*de cárcel*) warder.

celda ['θelda] *nf* cell.

celebérrimo, a [θele'ßerrimo, a] *adj superlativo de* **célebre.**

celebración [θeleßra'θjon] *nf* celebration.

celebrar [θele'ßrar] *vt* to celebrate; (*alabar*) to praise ♦ *vi* to be glad; ~**se** *vr* to occur, take place.

célebre ['θeleßre] *adj* celebrated, renowned.

celebridad [θeleßri'ðað] *nf* fame; (*persona*) celebrity.

celeridad [θeleri'ðað] *nf*: **con** ~ promptly.

celeste [θe'leste] *adj* sky-blue; (*cuerpo etc*) heavenly ♦ *nm* sky blue.

celestial [θeles'tjal] *adj* celestial, heavenly.

celibato [θeli'ßato] *nm* celibacy.

célibe ['θeliße] *adj*, *nm/f* celibate.

celo ['θelo] *nm* zeal; (*REL*) fervour; (*pey*) envy; ~**s** *nmpl* jealousy *sg*; **dar** ~**s a algn** to make sb jealous; **tener** ~**s de algn** to be jealous of sb; **en** ~ (*animales*) on heat.

celofán [θelo'fan] *nm* Cellophane ®.

celosía [θelo'sia] *nf* lattice (window).

celoso, a [θe'loso, a] *adj* (*envidioso*) jealous; (*trabajador*) zealous; (*desconfiado*) suspicious.

celta ['θelta] *adj* Celtic ♦ *nm/f* Celt.

célula ['θelula] *nf* cell.

celular [θelu'lar] *adj*: **tejido** ~ cell tissue.

celulitis [θelu'litis] *nf* (*enfermedad*) cellulitis; (*grasa*) cellulite.

celuloide [θelu'loiðe] *nm* celluloid.

celulosa [θelu'losa] *nf* cellulose.

cementerio [θemen'terjo] *nm* cemetery, graveyard; ~ **de coches** scrapyard.

cemento [θe'mento] *nm* cement; (*hormigón*) concrete; (*AM*: *cola*) glue.

CEN *nm abr* (*ESP*) = *Consejo de Economía Nacional.*

cena ['θena] *nf* evening meal, dinner.

cenagal [θena'ɣal] *nm* bog, quagmire.

cenar [θe'nar] *vt* to have for dinner, dine on ♦ *vi* to have dinner, dine.

cencerro [θen'θerro] *nm* cowbell; **estar como un** ~ (*fam*) to be round the bend.

cenicero [θeni'θero] *nm* ashtray.

ceniciento, a [θeni'θjento, a] *adj* ash-coloured, ashen.

cenit [θe'nit] *nm* zenith.

ceniza [θe'niθa] *nf* ash, ashes *pl*.

censar [θen'sar] *vt* to take a census of.

censo ['θenso] *nm* census; ~ **electoral** electoral roll.

censor [θen'sor] *nm* censor; ~ **de cuentas** (*COM*) auditor; ~ **jurado de cuentas** chartered (*BRIT*) *ou* certified public (*US*) accountant.

censura [θen'sura] *nf* (*POL*) censorship; (*moral*) censure, criticism.

censurable [θensu'raßle] *adj* reprehensible.

censurar [θensu'rar] *vt* (*idea*) to censure; (*cortar*: *película*) to censor.

centavo [θen'taßo] *nm* hundredth (part); (*AM*) cent.

centella [θen'teʎa] *nf* spark.

centellear [θenteʎe'ar] *vi* (*metal*) to gleam; (*estrella*) to twinkle; (*fig*) to sparkle.

centelleo [θente'ʎeo] *nm* gleam(ing); twinkling; sparkling.

centena [θen'tena] *nf* hundred.

centenar [θente'nar] *nm* hundred.

centenario, a [θente'narjo, a] *adj* one hundred years old ♦ *nm* centenary.

centeno [θen'teno] *nm* rye.

centésimo, a [θen'tesimo, a] *adj*, *nm* hundredth.

centígrado [θen'tiɣraðo] *adj* centigrade.

centigramo [θenti'ɣramo] *nm* centigramme.

centilitro [θenti'litro] *nm* centilitre (*BRIT*), centiliter (*US*).

centímetro [θen'timetro] *nm* centimetre (*BRIT*), centimeter (*US*).

céntimo, a ['θentimo, a] *adj* hundredth ♦ *nm* cent.

centinela [θenti'nela] *nm* sentry, guard.

centollo, a [θen'toʎo, a] *nm/f* large (*o* spider) crab.

central [θen'tral] *adj* central ♦ *nf* head

office; (*TEC*) plant; (*TELEC*) exchange; ~ **nuclear** nuclear power station.

centralice [θentra'liθe] *etc vb V* **centralizar**.

centralita [θentra'lita] *nf* (*TELEC*) switchboard.

centralización [θentraliθa'θjon] *nf* centralization.

centralizar [θentrali'θar] *vt* to centralize.

centrar [θen'trar] *vt* to centre.

céntrico, a ['θentriko, a] *adj* central.

centrifugar [θentrifu'var] *vt* (*ropa*) to spin-dry.

centrífugo, a [θent'rifuvo, a] *adj* centrifugal.

centrifugue [θentri'fuve] *etc vb V* **centrifugar**.

centrista [θen'trista] *adj* centre *cpd*.

centro ['θentro] *nm* centre; **ser del ~** (*POL*) to be a moderate; **~ de acogida (para niños)** children's home; **~ de beneficios** (*COM*) profit centre; **~ cívico** community centre; **~ comercial** shopping centre; **~ de computatión** computer centre; **~ (de determinación) de costos** (*COM*) cost centre; **~ delantero** (*DEPORTE*) centre forward; **~ docente** teaching institution; **~ juvenil** youth club; **~ social** community centre.

centroafricano, a [θentroafri'kano, a] *adj*: **la República Centroafricana** the Central African Republic.

centroamericano, a [θentroameri'kano, a] *adj, nm/f* Central American.

centrocampista [θentrokam'pista] *nm/f* (*DEPORTE*) midfielder.

ceñido, a [θe'ɲiðo, a] *adj* tight.

ceñir [θe'ɲir] *vt* (*rodear*) to encircle, surround; (*ajustar*) to fit (tightly); (*apretar*) to tighten; **~se** *vr*: **~se algo** to put sth on; **~se al asunto** to stick to the matter in hand.

ceño ['θeɲo] *nm* frown, scowl; **fruncir el ~** to frown, knit one's brow.

CEOE *nf abr* (= *Confederación Española de Organizaciones Empresariales*) ≈ CBI (*BRIT*).

cepa ['θepa] *nf* (*de vid, fig*) stock; (*BIO*) strain.

CEPAL [θe'pal] *nf abr* (= *Comisión Económica de las Naciones Unidas para la América Latina*) ECLA.

cepillar [θepi'ʎar] *vt* to brush; (*madera*) to plane (down).

cepillo [θe'piʎo] *nm* brush; (*para madera*) plane; (*REL*) poorbox, alms box.

cepo ['θepo] *nm* (*caza*) trap.

CEPSA ['θepsa] *nf abr* (*COM*) = *Compañía Española de Petróleos, S.A.*

CEPYME *nf abr* = *Confederación Española de la Pequeña y Mediana Empresa.*

cera ['θera] *nf* wax; **~ de abejas** beeswax.

cerámica [θe'ramika] *nf* pottery; (*arte*) ceramics *sg*.

ceramista [θera'mista] *nm/f* potter.

cerbatana [θerβa'tana] *nf* blowpipe.

cerca ['θerka] *nf* fence ♦ *adv* near, nearby, close; **por aquí ~** nearby ♦ *prep*: **~ de** (*cantidad*) nearly, about; (*distancia*) near, close to ♦ *nmpl*: **~s** foreground *sg*.

cercado [θer'kaðo] *nm* enclosure.

cercanía [θerka'nia] *nf* nearness, closeness; **~s** *nfpl* outskirts, suburbs; **tren de ~s** commuter *o* local train.

cercano, a [θer'kano, a] *adj* close, near; (*pueblo etc*) nearby; **C~ Oriente** Near East.

cercar [θer'kar] *vt* to fence in; (*rodear*) to surround.

cerciorar [θerθjo'rar] *vt* (*asegurar*) to assure; **~se** *vr* (*descubrir*) to find out (de about); (*asegurarse*) to make sure (*de* of).

cerco ['θerko] *nm* (*AGR*) enclosure; (*AM*) fence; (*MIL*) siege.

cerda ['θerða] *nf* (*de cepillo*) bristle; (*ZOOL*) sow.

cerdada [θer'ðaða] *nf* (*fam*): **hacer una ~ a algn** to play a dirty trick on sb.

Cerdeña [θer'ðeɲa] *nf* Sardinia.

cerdo ['θerðo] *nm* pig; **carne de ~** pork.

cereal [θere'al] *nm* cereal; **~es** *nmpl* cereals, grain *sg*.

cerebral [θere'ßral] *adj* (*tb fig*) cerebral; (*tumor*) brain *cpd*.

cerebro [θe'reßro] *nm* brain; (*fig*) brains *pl*; **ser un ~** (*fig*) to be brilliant.

ceremonia [θere'monja] *nf* ceremony; **reunión de ~** formal meeting; **hablar sin ~** to speak plainly.

ceremonial [θeremo'njal] *adj, nm* ceremonial.

ceremonioso, a [θeremo'njoso, a] *adj* ceremonious; (*cumplido*) formal.

cereza [θe'reθa] *nf* cherry.

cerezo [θe'reθo] *nm* cherry tree.

cerilla [θe'riʎa] *nf*, **cerillo** [se'riʎo] *nm* (*AM*) match.

cerner [θer'ner] *vt* to sift, sieve; **~se** *vr* to hover.

cero ['θero] *nm* nothing, zero; (*DEPORTE*) nil; **8 grados bajo ~** 8 degrees below zero; **a partir de ~** from scratch.

cerque ['θerke] *etc vb V* **cercar**.

cerrado, a [θe'rraðo, a] *adj* closed, shut; (*con llave*) locked; (*tiempo*) cloudy, overcast; (*curva*) sharp; (*acento*) thick, broad; **a puerta cerrada** (*JUR*) in camera.

cerradura [θerra'ðura] *nf (acción)* closing; *(mecanismo)* lock.

cerrajería [θerraxe'ria] *nf* locksmith's craft; *(tienda)* locksmith's (shop).

cerrajero, a [θerra'xero, a] *nm/f* locksmith.

cerrar [θe'rrar] *vt* to close, shut; *(paso, carretera)* to close; *(grifo)* to turn off; *(trato, cuenta, negocio)* to close ♦ *vi* to close, shut; *(la noche)* to come down; ~ **con llave** to lock; ~ **el sistema** *(INFORM)* to close *o* shut down the system; ~ **un trato** to strike a bargain; ~**se** *vr* to close, shut; *(herida)* to heal.

cerro ['θerro] *nm* hill; **andar por las** ~**s de Úbeda** to wander from the point, digress.

cerrojo [θe'rroxo] *nm (herramienta)* bolt; *(de puerta)* latch.

certamen [θer'tamen] *nm* competition, contest.

certero, a [θer'tero, a] *adj (gen)* accurate.

certeza [θer'teθa], **certidumbre** [θerti'ðumbre] *nf* certainty.

certificación [θertifika'θjon] *nf* certification; *(JUR)* affidavit.

certificado, a [θertifi'kaðo, a] *adj* certified; *(CORREOS)* registered ♦ *nm* certificate.

certificar [θertifi'kar] *vt (asegurar, atestar)* to certify.

certifique [θerti'fike] *etc vb V* **certificar.**

cervatillo [θerßa'tiʎo] *nm* fawn.

cervecería [θerßeθe'ria] *nf (fábrica)* brewery; *(taberna)* public house.

cerveza [θer'ßeθa] *nf* beer; ~ **de barril** draught beer.

cervical [θerßi'kal] *adj* cervical.

cerviz [θer'ßiθ] *nf* nape of the neck.

cesación [θesa'θjon] *nf* cessation, suspension.

cesante [θe'sante] *adj* redundant; *(AM)* unemployed; *(ministro)* outgoing; *(diplomático)* recalled ♦ *nm/f* redundant worker.

cesar [θe'sar] *vi* to cease, stop; *(de un trabajo)* to leave ♦ *vt (en el trabajo)* to dismiss; *(alto cargo)* to remove from office.

cesárea [θe'sarea] *nf* Caesarean (section).

cese ['θese] *nm (de trabajo)* dismissal; *(de pago)* suspension.

Cesid [θe'sið] *nm abr (ESP: = Centro Superior de Investigación de la Defensa Nacional)* military intelligence service.

cesión [θe'sjon] *nf:* ~ **de bienes** surrender of property.

césped ['θespeð] *nm* grass, lawn.

cesta ['θesta] *nf* basket.

cesto ['θesto] *nm* (large) basket, hamper.

cetrería [θetre'ria] *nf* falconry.

cetrino, a [θe'trino, a] *adj (tez)* sallow.

cetro ['θetro] *nm* sceptre.

Ceuta [θe'uta] *nf* Ceuta.

ceutí [θeu'ti] *adj* of *o* from Ceuta ♦ *nm/f* native *o* inhabitant of Ceuta.

C.F. *nm abr (= Club de Fútbol)* F.C.

CFC *nm abr (= clorofluorocarbono)* CFC.

cfr. *abr (= confróntese, compárese)* cf.

cg. *abr (= centígramo)* cg.

CGPJ *nm abr (= Consejo General del Poder Judicial)* governing body of Spanish legal system.

CGS *nf abr (Guatemala, El Salvador)* = Confederación General de Sindicatos.

CGT *nf abr (Colombia, México, Nicaragua, ESP)* = Confederación General de Trabajadores; *(Argentina)* = Confederación General del Trabajo.

Ch, ch [tʃe] *nf former letter in the Spanish alphabet.*

chabacano, a [tʃaßa'kano, a] *adj* vulgar, coarse.

chabola [tʃa'ßola] *nf* shack; ~**s** *nfpl* shanty town *sg.*

chabolismo [tʃaßo'lismo] *nm:* **el problema del** ~ the problem of substandard housing, the shanty town problem.

chacal [tʃa'kal] *nm* jackal.

chacarero [tʃaka'rero] *nm (AM)* small farmer.

chacha ['tʃatʃa] *nf (fam)* maid.

cháchara ['tʃatʃara] *nf* chatter; **estar de** ~ to chatter away.

chacra ['tʃakra] *nf (AM)* smallholding.

chafar [tʃa'far] *vt (aplastar)* to crush, flatten; *(arruinar)* to ruin.

chaflán [tʃa'flan] *nm (TEC)* bevel.

chal [tʃal] *nm* shawl.

chalado, a [tʃa'laðo, a] *adj (fam)* crazy.

chalé, *pl* **chalés** [tʃa'le, tʃa'les] *nm* = **chalet.**

chaleco [tʃa'leko] *nm* waistcoat, vest *(US)*; ~ **antibala** bulletproof vest; ~ **salvavidas** life jacket.

chalet, *pl* **chalets** [tʃa'le, tʃa'les] *nm* villa, ≈ detached house; ~ **adosado** semi-detached house.

chalupa [tʃa'lupa] *nf* launch, boat.

chamaco, a [tʃa'mako, a] *nm/f (AM)* boy/ girl.

chamarra [tʃa'marra] *nf* sheepskin jacket; *(AM: poncho)* blanket.

champán [tʃam'pan] *nm,* **champaña** [tʃam'paɲa] *nm* champagne.

champiñón [tʃampi'ɲon] *nm* mushroom.

champú [tʃam'pu] *(pl* **champúes,**

champús) *nm* shampoo.

chamuscar [tʃamus'kar] *vt* to scorch, sear, singe.

chamusque [tʃa'muske] *etc vb* V **chamuscar**.

chamusquina [tʃamus'kina] *nf* singeing.

chance ['tʃanθe] *nm* (*a veces nf*) (*AM*) chance, opportunity.

chanchada [tʃan'tʃaða] *nf* (*AM fam*) dirty trick.

chancho, a ['tʃantʃo, a] *nm/f* (*AM*) pig.

chanchullo [tʃan'tʃuʎo] *nm* (*fam*) fiddle, wangle.

chancla ['tʃankla] *nf*, **chancleta** [tʃan'kleta] *nf* flip-flop; (*zapato viejo*) old shoe.

chandal [tʃan'dal] *nm* tracksuit; ~ **(de tactel)** shellsuit.

chantaje [tʃan'taxe] *nm* blackmail; **hacer ~ a uno** to blackmail sb.

chanza ['tʃanθa] *nf* joke.

chao [tʃao] *excl* (*fam*) cheerio.

chapa ['tʃapa] *nf* (*de metal*) plate, sheet; (*de madera*) board, panel; (*de botella*) bottle top; (*insignia*) (lapel) badge; (*AM: AUTO*): ~ **de matrícula** number (*BRIT*) *o* license (*US*) plate; (*AM cerradura*) lock; **de 3 ~s** (*madera*) 3-ply.

chapado, a [tʃa'paðo, a] *adj* (*metal*) plated; (*muebles etc*) finished.

chaparro, a [tʃa'parro, a] *adj* squat; (*AM: bajito*) short.

chaparrón [tʃapa'rron] *nm* downpour, cloudburst.

chapotear [tʃapote'ar] *vt* to sponge down ♦ *vi* (*fam*) to splash about.

chapucero, a [tʃapu'θero, a] *adj* rough, crude ♦ *nm/f* bungler.

chapurr(e)ar [tʃapurr(e)'ar] *vt* (*idioma*) to speak badly.

chapuza [tʃa'puθa] *nf* botched job.

chapuzón [tʃapu'θon] *nm*: **darse un ~** to go for a dip.

chaqué [tʃa'ke] *nm* morning coat.

chaqueta [tʃa'keta] *nf* jacket; **cambiar la ~** (*fig*) to change sides.

chaquetón [tʃake'ton] *nm* three-quarter-length coat.

charca ['tʃarka] *nf* pond, pool.

charco ['tʃarko] *nm* pool, puddle.

charcutería [tʃarkute'ria] *nf* (*tienda*) shop selling chiefly pork meat products; (*productos*) cooked pork meats *pl*.

charla ['tʃarla] *nf* talk, chat; (*conferencia*) lecture.

charlar [tʃar'lar] *vi* to talk, chat.

charlatán, ana [tʃarla'tan, ana] *nm/f* chatterbox; (*estafador*) trickster.

charol¹ [tʃa'rol] *nm* varnish; (*cuero*) patent leather.

charol² [tʃa'rol] *nm* (*AM*), **charola** [tʃa'rola] *nf* (*AM*) tray.

charqui ['tʃarki] *nm* (*AM*) dried beef, jerky (*US*).

charro, a ['tʃarro, a] *adj* Salamancan; (*AM*) Mexican; (*ropa*) loud, gaudy; (*AM: costumbres*) traditional ♦ *nm/f* Salamancan; Mexican.

chárter ['tʃarter] *adj inv*: **vuelo ~** charter flight.

chascarrillo [tʃaska'rriʎo] *nm* (*fam*) funny story.

chasco ['tʃasko] *nm* (*broma*) trick, joke; (*desengaño*) disappointment.

chasis ['tʃasis] *nm inv* (*AUTO*) chassis; (*FOTO*) plateholder.

chasquear [tʃaske'ar] *vt* (*látigo*) to crack; (*lengua*) to click.

chasquido [tʃas'kiðo] *nm* (*de lengua*) click; (*de látigo*) crack.

chatarra [tʃa'tarra] *nf* scrap (metal).

chato, a ['tʃato, a] *adj* flat; (*nariz*) snub ♦ *nm* wine tumbler; **beber unos ~s** to have a few drinks.

chau [tʃau], **chaucito** [tʃau'sito] *excl* (*fam*) cheerio.

chauvinismo [tʃoßi'nismo] *nm* chauvinism.

chauvinista [tʃoßi'nista] *adj*, *nm/f* chauvinist.

chaval, a [tʃa'ßal, a] *nm/f* kid (*fam*), lad/ lass.

chavo ['tʃaßo] *nm* (*AM: fam*) bloke (*BRIT*), guy.

checo, a ['tʃeko, a] *adj*, *nm/f* Czech ♦ *nm* (*LING*) Czech.

checo(e)slovaco, a [tʃeko(e)slo'ßako, a] *adj*, *nm/f* Czech, Czechoslovak.

Checo(e)slovaquia [tʃeko(e)slo'ßakja] *nf* Czechoslovakia.

chepa ['tʃepa] *nf* hump.

cheque ['tʃeke] *nm* cheque (*BRIT*), check (*US*); ~ **abierto/en blanco/cruzado** open/ blank/crossed cheque; ~ **al portador** cheque payable to bearer; ~ **caducado** stale cheque; ~ **de viajero** traveller's cheque.

chequeo [tʃe'keo] *nm* (*MED*) check-up; (*AUTO*) service.

chequera [tʃe'kera] *nf* (*AM*) chequebook (*BRIT*), checkbook (*US*).

chévere ['tʃeßere] *adj* (*AM*) great, fabulous (*fam*).

chicano, a [tʃi'kano, a] *adj*, *nm/f* chicano, Mexican-American.

chicha ['tʃitʃa] *nf* (*AM*) maize liquor.

chícharo ['tʃitʃaro] *nm* (*AM*) pea.
chicharra [tʃi'tʃarra] *nf* harvest bug, cicada.
chicharrón [tʃitʃa'rron] *nm* (pork) crackling.
chichón [tʃi'tʃon] *nm* bump, lump.
chicle ['tʃikle] *nm* chewing gum.
chico, a ['tʃiko, a] *adj* small, little ♦ *nm/f* child; (*muchacho*) boy; (*muchacha*) girl.
chicote [tʃi'kote] *nm* (*AM*) whip.
chiflado, a [tʃi'flaðo, a] *adj* (*fam*) crazy, round the bend ♦ *nm/f* nutcase.
chiflar [tʃi'flar] *vt* to hiss, boo ♦ *vi* (*esp AM*) to whistle.
Chile ['tʃile] *nm* Chile.
chile ['tʃile] *nm* chilli, pepper.
chileno, a [tʃi'leno, a] *adj, nm/f* Chilean.
chillar [tʃi'ʎar] *vi* (*persona*) to yell, scream; (*animal salvaje*) to howl; (*cerdo*) to squeal; (*puerta*) to creak.
chillido [tʃi'ʎiðo] *nm* (*de persona*) yell, scream; (*de animal*) howl; (*de frenos*) screech(ing).
chillón, ona [tʃi'ʎon, ona] *adj* (*niño*) noisy; (*color*) loud, gaudy.
chimenea [tʃime'nea] *nf* chimney; (*hogar*) fireplace.
chimpancé, *pl* **chimpancés** [tʃimpan'θe, tʃimpan'θes] *nm* chimpanzee.
China ['tʃina] *nf*: (**la**) ~ China.
china ['tʃina] *nf* pebble.
chinchar [tʃin'tʃar] (*fam*) *vt* to pester, annoy; ~**se** *vr* to get cross; ¡**chínchate!** tough!
chinche ['tʃintʃe] *nf* bug; (*TEC*) drawing pin (*BRIT*), thumbtack (*US*) ♦ *nm/f* nuisance, pest.
chincheta [tʃin'tʃeta] *nf* drawing pin (*BRIT*), thumbtack (*US*).
chinchorro [tʃin'tʃorro] *nm* (*AM*) hammock.
chingado, a [tʃin'gaðo, a] *adj* (*esp AM fam!*) lousy, bloody (!); **hijo de la** ~**a** bastard (!), son of a bitch (*US!*).
chingar [tʃin'gar] *vt* (*AM: fam!*) to fuck (up) (!), screw (up) (!); ~**se** *vr* (*AM: emborracharse*) to get pissed (*BRIT*), get plastered; (: *fracasar*) to fail.
chingue ['tʃinge] *etc vb V* **chingar**.
chino, a ['tʃino, a] *adj, nm/f* Chinese ♦ *nm* (*LING*) Chinese; (*CULIN*) chinois, conical strainer.
chip [tʃip] *nm* (*INFORM*) chip.
chipirón [tʃipi'ron] *nm* squid.
Chipre ['tʃipre] *nf* Cyprus.
chipriota [tʃi'prjota], **chipriote** [tʃi'prjote] *adj* Cypriot, Cyprian ♦ *nm/f* Cypriot.
chiquillada [tʃiki'ʎada] *nf* childish prank;

(*AM: chiquillos*) kids *pl*.
chiquillo, a [tʃi'kiʎo, a] *nm/f* kid (*fam*), youngster, child.
chiquito, a [tʃi'kito, a] *adj* very small, tiny ♦ *nm/f* kid (*fam*).
chirigota [tʃiri'yota] *nf* joke.
chirimbolo [tʃirim'bolo] *nm* thingummyjig (*fam*).
chirimoya [tʃiri'moja] *nf* custard apple.
chiringuito [tʃirin'gito] *nm* refreshment stall *o* stand.
chiripa [tʃi'ripa] *nf* fluke; **por** ~ by chance.
chirona [tʃi'rona], (*AM*) **chirola** [tʃi'rola] *nf* (*fam*) clink, jail.
chirriar [tʃi'rrjar] *vi* (*goznes*) to creak, squeak; (*pájaros*) to chirp, sing.
chirrido [tʃi'rriðo] *nm* creak(ing), squeak(ing); (*de pájaro*) chirp(ing).
chis [tʃis] *excl* sh!
chisme ['tʃisme] *nm* (*habladurías*) piece of gossip; (*fam: objeto*) thingummyjig.
chismoso, a [tʃis'moso, a] *adj* gossiping ♦ *nm/f* gossip.
chispa ['tʃispa] *nf* spark; (*fig*) sparkle; (*ingenio*) wit; (*fam*) drunkenness.
chispeante [tʃispe'ante] *adj* (*tb fig*) sparkling.
chispear [tʃispe'ar] *vi* to spark; (*lloviznar*) to drizzle.
chisporrotear [tʃisporrote'ar] *vi* (*fuego*) to throw out sparks; (*leña*) to crackle; (*aceite*) to hiss, splutter.
chistar [tʃistar] *vi*: **no** ~ not to say a word.
chiste ['tʃiste] *nm* joke, funny story; ~ **verde** blue joke.
chistera [tʃis'tera] *nf* top hat.
chistoso, a [tʃis'toso, a] *adj* (*gracioso*) funny, amusing; (*bromista*) witty.
chistu ['tʃistu] *nm* = **txistu**.
chivarse [tʃi'βarse] *vr* (*fam*) to grass.
chivatazo [tʃiβa'taθo] *nm* (*fam*) tip-off; **dar** ~ to inform.
chivo, a ['tʃiβo, a] *nm/f* (billy/nanny-)goat; ~ **expiatorio** scapegoat.
chocante [tʃo'kante] *adj* startling; (*extraño*) odd; (*ofensivo*) shocking.
chocar [tʃo'kar] *vi* (*coches etc*) to collide, crash; (*MIL, fig*) to clash ♦ *vt* to shock; (*sorprender*) to startle; ~ **con** to collide with; (*fig*) to run into, run up against; ¡**chócala!** (*fam*) put it there!
chochear [tʃotʃe'ar] *vi* to dodder, be senile.
chocho, a ['tʃotʃo, a] *adj* doddering, senile; (*fig*) soft, doting.
chocolate [tʃoko'late] *adj* chocolate ♦ *nm* chocolate; (*fam*) dope, marijuana.
chocolatería [tʃokolate'ria] *nf* chocolate

factory (o shop).

chófer ['tʃofer], **chofer** [tʃo'fer] (*esp AM*) *nm* driver.

chollo ['tʃoʎo] *nm* (*fam*) bargain, snip.

chomba ['tʃomba], **chompa** ['tʃompa] *nf* (*AM*) jumper, sweater.

chopo ['tʃopo] *nm* black poplar.

choque ['tʃoke] *etc vb V* **chocar** ♦ *nm* (*impacto*) impact; (*golpe*) jolt; (*AUTO*) crash; (*fig*) conflict.

chorizo [tʃo'riθo] *nm* hard pork sausage, (*type of*) salami; (*ladrón*) crook.

chorra ['tʃorra] *nf* luck.

chorrada [tʃo'rraða] *nf* (*fam*): ¡es una ~! that's crap! (*!*); **decir ~s** to talk crap (*!*).

chorrear [tʃorre'ar] *vt* to pour ♦ *vi* to gush (out), spout (out); (*gotear*) to drip, trickle.

chorreras [tʃo'rreras] *nfpl* (*COSTURA*) frill *sg*.

chorro ['tʃorro] *nm* jet; (*caudalito*) dribble, trickle; (*fig*) stream; **salir a ~s** to gush forth; **con propulsión a ~** jet-propelled.

chotearse [tʃote'arse] *vr* to joke.

choteo [tʃo'teo] *nm* kidding.

choto ['tʃoto] *nm* (*cabrito*) kid.

chovinismo [tʃoβi'nismo] *nm* = **chauvinismo**.

chovinista [tʃoβi'nista] *adj, nm/f* = **chauvinista**.

choza ['tʃoθa] *nf* hut, shack.

chubasco [tʃu'βasko] *nm* squall.

chubasquero [tʃuβas'kero] *nm* oilskins *pl*.

chuchería [tʃutʃe'ria] *nf* trinket.

chucho ['tʃutʃo] *nm* (*ZOOL*) mongrel.

chufa ['tʃufa] *nf* chufa, earth almond, tiger nut; **horchata de ~s** *drink made from chufas*.

chuleta [tʃu'leta] *nf* chop, cutlet; (*ESCOL etc: fam*) crib.

chulo, a ['tʃulo, a] *adj* (*encantador*) charming; (*aire*) proud; (*pey*) fresh; (*fam: estupendo*) great, fantastic ♦ *nm* (*pícaro*) rascal; (*madrileño*) working-class Madrilenian; (*rufián: tb:* ~ **de putas**) pimp.

chumbera [tʃum'bera] *nf* prickly pear.

chungo, a ['tʃungo, a] (*fam*) *adj* lousy ♦ *nf*: **estar de chunga** to be in a merry mood.

chupa ['tʃupa] *nf* (*fam*) jacket.

chupado, a [tʃu'paðo, a] *adj* (*delgado*) skinny, gaunt; **está ~** (*fam*) it's simple, it's dead easy.

chupar [tʃu'par] *vt* to suck; (*absorber*) to absorb; **~se** *vr* to grow thin; **para ~se los dedos** mouthwatering.

chupatintas [tʃupa'tintas] *nm inv* penpusher.

chupe ['tʃupe] *nm* (*AM*) stew.

chupete [tʃu'pete] *nm* dummy (*BRIT*), pacifier (*US*).

chupetón [tʃupe'ton] *nm* suck.

churrasco [tʃu'rrasko] *nm* (*AM*) barbecue, barbecued meat.

churrería [tʃurre'ria] *nf* stall or shop which sells "*churros*".

churrete [tʃu'rrete] *nm* grease spot.

churretón [tʃurre'ton] *nm* stain.

churrigueresco, a [tʃurrige'resko, a] *adj* (*ARQ*) baroque; (*fig*) excessively ornate.

churro, a ['tʃurro, a] *adj* coarse ♦ *nm* (*CULIN*) (type of) fritter; (*chapuza*) botch, mess.

Churros, *long fritters made with flour and water, are very popular in much of Spain and are often eaten with thick hot chocolate, either for breakfast or as a snack. In Madrid, they eat a thicker variety of* **churro** *called* **porra.**

---

churruscar [tʃurrus'kar] *vt* to fry crisp.

churrusque [tʃu'rruske] *etc vb V* **churruscar.**

churumbel [tʃurum'bel] *nm* (*fam*) kid.

chus [tʃus] *excl*: **no decir ni ~ ni mus** not to say a word.

chusco, a ['tʃusko, a] *adj* funny.

chusma ['tʃusma] *nf* rabble, mob.

chutar [tʃu'tar] *vi* (*DEPORTE*) to shoot (at goal); **esto va que chuta** it's going fine.

chuzo ['tʃuθo] *nm*: **llueve a ~s, llueven ~s de punta** it's raining cats and dogs.

C.I. *nm abr* = **coeficiente intelectual** *o* **de inteligencia.**

Cía *abr* (= **compañía**) Co.

cianuro [θja'nuro] *nm* cyanide.

ciática ['θjatika] *nf* sciatica.

cibernética [θiβer'netika] *nf* cybernetics *sg*.

cicatrice [θika'triθe] *etc vb V* **cicatrizar.**

cicatriz [θika'triθ] *nf* scar.

cicatrizar [θikatri'θar] *vt* to heal; **~se** *vr* to heal (up), form a scar.

cíclico, a ['θikliko, a] *adj* cyclical.

ciclismo [θi'klismo] *nm* cycling.

ciclista [θi'klista] *nm/f* cyclist.

ciclo ['θiklo] *nm* cycle.

ciclomotor [θiklomo'tor] *nm* moped.

ciclón [θi'klon] *nm* cyclone.

cicloturismo [θiklotu'rismo] *nm* touring by bicycle.

cicuta [θi'kuta] *nf* hemlock.

ciego, a ['θjeɣo, a] *etc vb V* **cegar** ♦ *adj* blind ♦ *nm/f* blind man/woman; **a ciegas** blindly; **me puse ~a mariscos** (*fam*) I stuffed myself with seafood.

ciegue ['θjeɣe] *etc vb* V **cegar**.
cielo ['θjelo] *nm* sky; (*REL*) heaven; (*ARQ: tb*: ~ **raso**) ceiling; ¡~s! good heavens!; **ver el** ~ **abierto** to see one's chance.
ciempiés [θjem'pjes] *nm inv* centipede.
cien [θjen] *num* V **ciento**.
ciénaga ['θjenaɣa] *nf* marsh, swamp.
ciencia ['θjenθja] *nf* science; ~**s** *nfpl* science *sg*; **saber algo a** ~ **cierta** to know sth for certain.
ciencia-ficción ['θjenθjafik'θjon] *nf* science fiction.
cieno ['θjeno] *nm* mud, mire.
científico, a [θjen'tifiko, a] *adj* scientific ♦ *nm/f* scientist.
ciento ['θjento], **cien** *num* hundred; **pagar al 10 por ciento** to pay at 10 per cent.
cierne ['θjerne] *etc vb* V **cerner** ♦ *nm*: **en** ~ in blossom; **en** ~(**s**) (*fig*) in its infancy.
cierre ['θjerre] *etc vb* V **cerrar** ♦ *nm* closing, shutting; (*con llave*) locking; (*RADIO, TV*) close-down; ~ **de cremallera** zip (fastener); **precios de** ~ (*BOLSA*) closing prices; ~ **del sistema** (*INFORM*) system shutdown.
cierto, a ['θjerto, a] *adj* sure, certain; (*un tal*) a certain; (*correcto*) right, correct; ~ **hombre** a certain man; **ciertas personas** certain *o* some people; **sí, es** ~ yes, that's correct; **por** ~ by the way; **lo** ~ **es que** ... the fact is that ...; **estar en lo** ~ to be right.
ciervo ['θjerßo] *nm* (*ZOOL*) deer; (: *macho*) stag.
cierzo ['θjerθo] *nm* north wind.
CIES *nm abr* = *Consejo Interamericano Económico y Social*.
cifra ['θifra] *nf* number, figure; (*cantidad*) number, quantity; (*secreta*) code; ~ **global** lump sum; ~ **de negocios** (*COM*) turnover; **en** ~**s redondas** in round figures; ~ **de referencia** (*COM*) bench mark; ~ **de ventas** (*COM*) sales figures.
cifrado, a [θi'fraðo, a] *adj* in code.
cifrar [θi'frar] *vt* to code, write in code; (*resumir*) to abridge; (*calcular*) to reckon.
cigala [θi'ɣala] *nf* Norway lobster.
cigarra [θi'ɣarra] *nf* cicada.
cigarrera [θiɣa'rrera] *nf* cigar case.
cigarrillo [θiɣa'rriʎo] *nm* cigarette.
cigarro [θi'ɣarro] *nm* cigarette; (*puro*) cigar.
cigüeña [θi'ɣweɲa] *nf* stork.
cilíndrico, a [θi'lindriko, a] *adj* cylindrical.
cilindro [θi'lindro] *nm* cylinder.
cima ['θima] *nf* (*de montaña*) top, peak; (*de árbol*) top; (*fig*) height.
címbalo ['θimbalo] *nm* cymbal.

cimbrear [θimbre'ar] *vt* to brandish; ~**se** *vr* to sway.
cimentar [θimen'tar] *vt* to lay the foundations of; (*fig: reforzar*) to strengthen; (: *fundar*) to found.
cimiento [θi'mjento] *etc vb* V **cimentar** ♦ *nm* foundation.
cinc [θink] *nm* zinc.
cincel [θin'θel] *nm* chisel.
cincelar [θinθe'lar] *vt* to chisel.
cincha ['θintʃa] *nf* girth, saddle strap.
cincho ['θintʃo] *nm* sash, belt.
cinco ['θinko] *num* five; (*fecha*) fifth; **las** ~ five o'clock; **no estar en sus** ~ (*fam*) to be off one's rocker.
cincuenta [θin'kwenta] *num* fifty.
cincuentón, ona [θinkwen'ton, ona] *adj, nm/f* fifty-year-old.
cine ['θine] *nm* cinema; **el** ~ **mudo** silent films *pl*; **hacer** ~ to make films.
cineasta [θine'asta] *nm/f* (*director de cine*) film-maker *o* director.
cine-club ['θine'klub] *nm* film club.
cinéfilo, a [θi'nefilo, a] *nm/f* film buff.
cinematográfico, a [θinemato'ɣrafiko, a] *adj* cine-, film *cpd*.
cínico, a ['θiniko, a] *adj* cynical; (*descarado*) shameless ♦ *nm/f* cynic.
cinismo [θi'nismo] *nm* cynicism.
cinta ['θinta] *nf* band, strip; (*de tela*) ribbon; (*película*) reel; (*de máquina de escribir*) ribbon; (*métrica*) tape measure; (*magnetofónica*) tape; ~ **adhesiva** sticky tape; ~ **aislante** insulating tape; ~ **de carbón** carbon ribbon; ~ **magnética** (*INFORM*) magnetic tape; ~ **métrica** tape measure; ~ **de múltiples impactos** (*en impresora*) multistrike ribbon; ~ **de tela** (*para máquina de escribir*) fabric ribbon; ~ **transportadora** conveyor belt.
cinto ['θinto] *nm* belt, girdle.
cintura [θin'tura] *nf* waist; (*medida*) waistline.
cinturón [θintu'ron] *nm* belt; (*fig*) belt, zone; ~ **salvavidas** lifebelt; ~ **de seguridad** safety belt.
ciña ['θiɲa] *etc*, **ciñendo** [θi'ɲendo] *etc vb* V **ceñir**.
CIP [θip] *nm abr* = *Club Internacional de Prensa* (*Madrid*).
ciprés [θi'pres] *nm* cypress (tree).
circo ['θirko] *nm* circus.
circuito [θir'kwito] *nm* circuit; (*DEPORTE*) lap; **TV por** ~ **cerrado** closed-circuit TV; ~ **experimental** (*INFORM*) breadboard; ~ **impreso** printed circuit; ~ **lógico** (*INFORM*) logical circuit.
circulación [θirkula'θjon] *nf* circulation;

(*AUTO*) traffic; "**cerrado a la ~ rodada**" "closed to vehicles".

circular [θirku'lar] *adj, nf* circular ♦ *vt* to circulate ♦ *vi* to circulate; (*dinero*) to be in circulation; (*AUTO*) to drive; (*autobús*) to run.

círculo ['θirkulo] *nm* circle; (*centro*) clubhouse; (*POL*) political group.

circuncidar [θirkunθi'dar] *vt* to circumcise.

circunciso, a [θirkun'θiso, a] *pp de* **circuncidar**.

circundante [θirkun'dante] *adj* surrounding.

circundar [θirkun'dar] *vt* to surround.

circunferencia [θirkunfe'renθja] *nf* circumference.

circunloquio [θirkun'lokjo] *nm* circumlocution.

circunscribir [θirkunskri'ßir] *vt* to circumscribe; ~**se** *vr* to be limited.

circunscripción [θirkunskrip'θjon] *nf* division; (*POL*) constituency.

circunscrito [θirkuns'krito] *pp de* **circunscribir**.

circunspección [θirkunspek'θjon] *nf* circumspection, caution.

circunspecto, a [θirkuns'pekto, a] *adj* circumspect, cautious.

circunstancia [θirkuns'tanθja] *nf* circumstance; ~**s agravantes/ extenuantes** aggravating/extenuating circumstances; **estar a la altura de las** ~**s** to rise to the occasion.

circunvalación [θirkumbala'θjon] *nf*: **carretera de** ~ ring road.

cirio ['θirjo] *nm* (wax) candle.

cirrosis [θi'rrosis] *nf* cirrhosis (of the liver).

ciruela [θi'rwela] *nf* plum; ~ **pasa** prune.

ciruelo [θi'rwelo] *nm* plum tree.

cirugía [θiru'xia] *nf* surgery; ~ **estética** *o* **plástica** plastic surgery.

cirujano [θiru'xano] *nm* surgeon.

cisco ['θisko] *nm*: **armar un** ~ to kick up a row; **estar hecho** ~ to be a wreck.

cisma ['θisma] *nm* schism; (*POL etc*) split.

cisne ['θisne] *nm* swan; **canto de** ~ swan song.

cisterna [θis'terna] *nf* cistern, tank.

cistitis [θis'titis] *nf* cystitis.

cita ['θita] *nf* appointment, meeting; (*de novios*) date; (*referencia*) quotation; **acudir/faltar a una** ~ to turn up for/miss an appointment

citación [θita'θjon] *nf* (*JUR*) summons *sg*.

citadino, a [sita'ðino, a] (*AM*) *adj* urban ♦ *nm/f* urban *o* city dweller.

citar [θi'tar] *vt* to make an appointment with, arrange to meet; (*JUR*) to summons; (*un autor, texto*) to quote; ~**se** *vr*: ~**se con algn** to arrange to meet sb; **se citaron en el cine** they arranged to meet at the cinema.

cítara ['θitara] *nf* zither.

citología [θitolo'xia] *nf* smear test.

cítrico, a ['θitriko, a] *adj* citric ♦ *nm*: ~**s** citrus fruits.

CiU *nm abr* (*POL*) = **Convergència i Unió**.

ciudad [θju'ðað] *nf* town; (*capital de país etc*) city; ~ **universitaria** university campus; **C~ del Cabo** Cape Town; **la C~ Condal** Barcelona.

ciudadanía [θjuðaða'nia] *nf* citizenship.

ciudadano, a [θjuða'ðano, a] *adj* civic ♦ *nm/f* citizen.

ciudadrealeño, a [θjuðaðrea'leɲo, a] *adj* of *o* from Ciudad Real ♦ *nm/f* native *o* inhabitant of Ciudad Real.

cívico, a ['θißiko, a] *adj* civic; (*fig*) public-spirited.

civil [θi'ßil] *adj* civil ♦ *nm* (*guardia*) policeman.

civilice [θißi'liθe] *etc vb V* **civilizar**.

civilización [θißiliθa'θjon] *nf* civilization.

civilizar [θißili'θar] *vt* to civilize.

civismo [θi'ßismo] *nm* public spirit.

cizaña [θi'θaɲa] *nf* (*fig*) discord; **sembrar** ~ to sow discord.

cl. *abr* (= *centilitro*) cl.

clamar [kla'mar] *vt* to clamour for, cry out for ♦ *vi* to cry out, clamour.

clamor [kla'mor] *nm* (*grito*) cry, shout; (*fig*) clamour, protest.

clamoroso, a [klamo'roso, a] *adj* (*éxito etc*) resounding.

clan ['klan] *nm* clan; (*de gángsters*) gang.

clandestinidad [klandestini'ðað] *nf* secrecy.

clandestino, a [klandes'tino, a] *adj* clandestine; (*POL*) underground.

clara ['klara] *nf* (*de huevo*) eggwhite.

claraboya [klara'ßoja] *nf* skylight.

clarear [klare'ar] *vi* (*el día*) to dawn; (*el cielo*) to clear up, brighten up; ~**se** *vr* to be transparent.

clarete [kla'rete] *nm* rosé (wine).

claridad [klari'ðað] *nf* (*del día*) brightness; (*de estilo*) clarity.

clarificar [klarifi'kar] *vt* to clarify.

clarifique [klari'fike] *etc vb V* **clarificar**.

clarín [kla'rin] *nm* bugle.

clarinete [klari'nete] *nm* clarinet.

clarividencia [klarißi'ðenθja] *nf* clairvoyance; (*fig*) far-sightedness.

claro, a ['klaro, a] *adj* clear; (*luminoso*) bright; (*color*) light; (*evidente*) clear, evident; (*poco espeso*) thin ♦ *nm* (*en bosque*) clearing ♦ *adv* clearly ♦ *excl* of course!; **hablar** ~ (*fig*) to speak plainly; **a las claras** openly; **no sacamos nada en** ~ we couldn't get anything definite.

clase ['klase] *nf* class; (*tipo*) kind, sort; (*ESCOL etc*) class; (: *aula*) classroom; ~ **alta/media/obrera** upper/middle/ working class; **dar** ~s to teach.

clásico, a ['klasiko, a] *adj* classical; (*fig*) classic.

clasificable [klasifi'kaβle] *adj* classifiable.

clasificación [klasifika'θjon] *nf* classification; (*DEPORTE*) league (table); (*COM*) ratings *pl*.

clasificador [klasifika'ðor] *nm* filing cabinet.

clasificar [klasifi'kar] *vt* to classify; (*INFORM*) to sort; ~**se** *vr* (*DEPORTE*: *torneo*) to qualify.

clasifique [klasi'fike] *etc vb V* **clasificar**.

clasista [kla'sista] *adj* (*fam*: *actitud*) snobbish.

claudia ['klauðja] *nf* greengage.

claudicar [klauði'kar] *vi* (*fig*) to back down.

claudique [klau'ðike] *etc vb V* **claudicar**.

claustro ['klaustro] *nm* cloister; (*UNIV*) staff; (*junta*) senate.

claustrofobia [klaustro'foβja] *nf* claustrophobia.

cláusula ['klausula] *nf* clause; ~ **de exclusión** (*COM*) exclusion clause.

clausura [klau'sura] *nf* closing, closure.

clausurar [klausu'rar] *vt* (*congreso etc*) to close, bring to a close; (*POL etc*) to adjourn; (*cerrar*) to close (down).

clavado, a [kla'βaðo, a] *adj* nailed ♦ *excl* exactly!, precisely!

clavar [kla'βar] *vt* (*tablas etc*) to nail (together); (*con alfiler*) to pin; (*clavo*) to hammer in; (*cuchillo*) to stick, thrust; (*mirada*) to fix; (*fam*: *estafar*) to cheat.

clave ['klaβe] *nf* key; (*MUS*) clef ♦ *adj inv* key *cpd*; ~ **de búsqueda** (*INFORM*) search key; ~ **de clasificación** (*INFORM*) sort key.

clavel [kla'βel] *nm* carnation.

clavicémbalo [klaβi'θembalo] *nm* harpsichord.

clavicordio [klaβikor'ðjo] *nm* clavicord.

clavícula [kla'βikula] *nf* collar bone.

clavija [kla'βixa] *nf* peg, pin; (*MUS*) peg; (*ELEC*) plug.

clavo ['klaβo] *nm* (*de metal*) nail; (*BOT*) clove; **dar en el** ~ (*fig*) to hit the nail on the head.

claxon ['klakson], *pl* **claxons** *nm* horn; **tocar el** ~ to sound one's horn.

clemencia [kle'menθja] *nf* mercy, clemency.

clemente [kle'mente] *adj* merciful, clement.

cleptómano, a [klep'tomano, a] *nm/f* kleptomaniac.

clerical [kleri'kal] *adj* clerical.

clérigo ['kleriɣo] *nm* priest, clergyman.

clero ['klero] *nm* clergy.

cliché [kli'tʃe] *nm* cliché; (*TIP*) stencil; (*FOTO*) negative.

cliente, a ['kljente, a] *nm/f* client, customer.

clientela [kljen'tela] *nf* clientele, customers *pl*; (*COM*) goodwill; (*MED*) patients *pl*.

clima ['klima] *nm* climate.

climatizado, a [klimati'θaðo, a] *adj* air-conditioned.

clímax ['klimaks] *nm inv* climax.

clínico, a ['kliniko, a] *adj* clinical ♦ *nf* clinic; (*particular*) private hospital.

clip, *pl* **clips** [klip, klis] *nm* paper clip.

clítoris ['klitoris] *nm inv* clitoris.

cloaca [klo'aka] *nf* sewer, drain.

clonación [klona'θjon] *nf* cloning.

clorhídrico, a [klo'riðriko, a] *adj* hydrochloric.

cloro ['kloro] *nm* chlorine.

clorofila [kloro'fila] *nf* chlorophyl(l).

cloroformo [kloro'formo] *nm* chloroform.

cloruro [klo'ruro] *nm* chloride; ~ **sódico** sodium chloride.

club, *pl* **clubs** *o* **clubes** [klub, klus, 'kluβes] *nm* club; ~ **de jóvenes** youth club.

cm *abr* (= *centímetro*) cm.

C.N.T. *nf abr* (*ESP*: *Confederación Nacional de Trabajo*) Anarchist Union Confederation; (*AM*) = *Confederación Nacional de Trabajadores*.

coacción [koak'θjon] *nf* coercion, compulsion.

coaccionar [koakθjo'nar] *vt* to coerce, compel.

coagular [koaɣu'lar] *vt*, ~**se** *vr* (*sangre*) to clot; (*leche*) to curdle.

coágulo [ko'aɣulo] *nm* clot.

coalición [koali'θjon] *nf* coalition.

coartada [koar'taða] *nf* alibi.

coartar [koar'tar] *vt* to limit, restrict.

coba [ko'βa] *nf*: **dar** ~ **a algn** to soft-soap sb.

cobarde [ko'βarðe] *adj* cowardly ♦ *nm/f* coward.

cobardía [koβar'ðia] *nf* cowardice.

cobaya [ko'βaja] *nf* guinea pig.

cobertizo [koβer'tiθo] *nm* shelter.

cobertor [koβer'tor] *nm* bedspread.

cobertura [koβer'tura] *nf* cover; (*COM*)

coverage; ~ **de dividendo** (*COM*)
dividend cover.
cobija [ko'βixa] *nf* (*AM*) blanket.
cobijar [koβi'xar] *vt* (*cubrir*) to cover;
(*abrigar*) to shelter; ~**se** *vr* to take
shelter.
cobijo [ko'βixo] *nm* shelter.
cobra ['koβra] *nf* cobra.
cobrador, a [koβra'ðor, a] *nm/f* (*de autobús*)
conductor/conductress; (*de impuestos,
gas*) collector.
cobrar [ko'βrar] *vt* (*cheque*) to cash;
(*sueldo*) to collect, draw; (*objeto*) to
recover; (*precio*) to charge; (*deuda*) to
collect ♦ *vi* to draw one's pay; ~**se** *vr* to
recover, get on well; **cóbrese al entregar**
cash on delivery (COD) (*BRIT*), collect on
delivery (COD) (*US*); **a ~** (*COM*)
receivable; **cantidades por ~** sums due.
cobre ['koβre] *nm* copper; (*AM fam*) cent;
~**s** *nmpl* brass instruments.
cobrizo, a [ko'βriθo, a] *adj* coppery.
cobro ['koβro] *nm* (*de cheque*) cashing;
(*pago*) payment; **presentar al ~** to cash;
V tb **llamada**.
coca ['koka] *nf* coca; (*droga*) coke.
Coca-Cola ® ['koka'kola] *nf* Coca-Cola ®.
cocaína [koka'ina] *nf* cocaine.
cocainómano, a [kokai'nomano, a] *nm/f*
cocaine addict.
cocción [kok'θjon] *nf* (*CULIN*) cooking; (*el
hervir*) boiling.
cocear [koθe'ar] *vi* to kick.
cocer [ko'θer] *vt, vi* to cook; (*en agua*) to
boil; (*en horno*) to bake.
coche ['kotʃe] *nm* (*AUTO*) car, automobile
(*US*); (*de tren, de caballos*) coach, carriage; (*para niños*) pram (*BRIT*), baby
carriage (*US*); ~ **de bomberos** fire
engine; ~ **celular** Black Maria, prison
van; ~ (**comedor**) (*FERRO*) (dining) car; ~
fúnebre hearse.
coche-bomba ['kotʃe'βomba], *pl* **coches-
bomba** *nm* car bomb.
coche-cama ['kotʃe'kama], *pl* **coches-
cama** *nm* (*FERRO*) sleeping car, sleeper.
cochera [ko'tʃera] *nf* garage; (*de autobuses,
trenes*) depot.
coche-restaurante, *pl* **coches-
restaurante** ['kotʃerestau'rante] *nm*
(*FERRO*) dining-car, diner.
cochinada [kotʃi'naða] *nf* dirty trick.
cochinillo [kotʃi'niʎo] *nm* piglet, suckling
pig.
cochino, a [ko'tʃino, a] *adj* filthy, dirty
♦ *nm/f* pig.
cocido, a [ko'θiðo, a] *adj* boiled; (*fam*)
plastered ♦ *nm* stew.

cociente [ko'θjente] *nm* quotient.
cocina [ko'θina] *nf* kitchen; (*aparato*)
cooker, stove; (*acto*) cookery; ~ **casera**
home cooking; ~ **eléctrica** electric
cooker; ~ **francesa** French cuisine; ~ **de
gas** gas cooker.
cocinar [koθi'nar] *vt, vi* to cook.
cocinero, a [koθi'nero, a] *nm/f* cook.
coco ['koko] *nm* coconut; (*fantasma*)
bogeyman; (*fam: cabeza*) nut; **comer el ~
a algn** (*fam*) to brainwash sb.
cocodrilo [koko'ðrilo] *nm* crocodile.
cocotero [koko'tero] *nm* coconut palm.
cóctel ['koktel] *nm* (*bebida*) cocktail;
(*reunión*) cocktail party; ~ **Molotov**
Molotov cocktail, petrol bomb.
coctelera [kokte'lera] *nf* cocktail shaker.
cod. *abr* (= *código*) code.
codazo [ko'ðaθo] *nm*: **dar un ~ a algn** to
nudge sb.
codear [koðe'ar] *vi* to elbow, jostle; ~**se** *vr*:
~**se con** to rub shoulders with.
códice ['koðiθe] *nm* manuscript, codex.
codicia [ko'ðiθja] *nf* greed; (*fig*) lust.
codiciar [koði'θjar] *vt* to covet.
codicioso, a [koði'θjoso, a] *adj* covetous.
codificador [koðifika'ðor] *nm* (*INFORM*)
encoder; ~ **digital** digitizer.
codificar [koðifi'kar] *vt* (*mensaje*) to
(en)code; (*leyes*) to codify.
código ['koðiɣo] *nm* code; ~ **de barras**
(*COM*) bar code; ~ **binario** binary code;
~ **de caracteres** (*INFORM*) character
code; ~ **de (la) circulación** highway code;
~ **civil** common law; ~ **de control**
(*INFORM*) control code; ~ **máquina**
(*INFORM*) machine code; ~ **militar**
military law; ~ **de operación** (*INFORM*)
operational *o* machine code; ~ **penal**
penal code; ~ **de práctica** code of
practice.
codillo [ko'ðiʎo] *nm* (*ZOOL*) knee; (*TEC*)
elbow (joint).
codo ['koðo] *nm* (*ANAT, de tubo*) elbow;
(*ZOOL*) knee; **hablar por los** ~**s** to talk
nineteen to the dozen.
codorniz [koðor'niθ] *nf* quail.
coeficiente [koefi'θjente] *nm* (*MAT*)
coefficient; (*ECON etc*) rate; ~ **intelectual**
o **de inteligencia** I.Q.
coerción [koer'θjon] *nf* coercion.
coercitivo, a [koerθi'tiβo, a] *adj* coercive.
coetáneo, a [koe'taneo, a] *nm/f*: ~**s**
contemporaries.
coexistencia [koeksis'tenθja] *nf*
coexistence.
coexistir [koeksis'tir] *vi* to coexist.
cofia ['kofja] *nf* (*de enfermera*) (white) cap.

80 *ESPAÑOL–INGLÉS*

cofradía [kofra'ðia] nf brotherhood,
fraternity; V tb **Semana Santa**.
cofre ['kofre] nm (baúl) trunk; (de joyas)
box; (AM AUTO) bonnet (BRIT), hood (US).
cogedor [koxe'ðor] nm dustpan.
coger [ko'xer] vt (ESP) to take (hold of);
(objeto caído) to pick up; (frutas) to pick,
harvest; (resfriado, ladrón, pelota) to
catch; (AM fam!) to lay (!) ♦ vi: ~ **por el
buen camino** to take the right road; **~se**
vr (el dedo) to catch; ~ **a algn
desprevenido** to take sb unawares; **~se
a algo** to get hold of sth.
cogida [ko'xiða] nf gathering, harvesting;
(de peces) catch; (TAUR) goring.
cogollo [ko'ɣoʎo] nm (de lechuga) heart;
(fig) core, nucleus.
cogorza [ko'ɣorθa] nf (fam): **agarrar una** ~
to get smashed.
cogote [ko'ɣote] nm back o nape of the
neck.
cohabitar [koaßi'tar] vi to live together,
cohabit.
cohecho [ko'etʃo] nm (acción) bribery;
(soborno) bribe.
coherencia [koe'renθja] nf coherence.
coherente [koe'rente] adj coherent.
cohesión [koe'sjon] nm cohesion.
cohete [ko'ete] nm rocket.
cohibido, a [koi'ßiðo, a] adj (PSICO)
inhibited; (tímido) shy; **sentirse** ~ to feel
embarrassed.
cohibir [koi'ßir] vt to restrain, restrict;
~se vr to feel inhibited.
COI nm abr (= Comité Olímpico Internacional)
IOC.
coima ['koima] nf (AM fam) bribe.
coincidencia [koinθi'ðenθja] nf
coincidence.
coincidir [koinθi'ðir] vi (en idea) to
coincide, agree; (en lugar) to coincide.
coito ['koito] nm intercourse, coitus.
cojear [koxe'ar] vi (persona) to limp,
hobble; (mueble) to wobble, rock.
cojera [ko'xera] nf lameness; (andar cojo)
limp.
cojín [ko'xin] nm cushion.
cojinete [koxi'nete] nm small cushion, pad;
(TEC) (ball) bearing.
cojo, a ['koxo, a] etc vb V **coger** ♦ adj (que
no puede andar) lame, crippled; (mueble)
wobbly ♦ nm/f lame person, cripple.
cojón [ko'xon] nm (fam!) ball (!), testicle;
¡cojones! shit! (!).
cojonudo, a [koxo'nuðo, a] adj (ESP fam)
great, fantastic.
col [kol] nf cabbage; **~es de Bruselas**
Brussels sprouts.

col., col.ª abr (= columna) col.
cola ['kola] nf tail; (de gente) queue; (lugar)
end, last place; (para pegar) glue, gum;
(de vestido) train; **hacer** ~ to queue (up).
colaboración [kolaßora'θjon] nf (gen)
collaboration; (en periódico)
contribution.
colaborador, a [kolaßora'ðor, a] nm/f
collaborator; contributor.
colaborar [kolaßo'rar] vi to collaborate.
colación [kola'θjon] nf: **sacar a** ~ to bring
up.
colado, a [ko'laðo, a] adj (metal) cast ♦ nf:
hacer la colada to do the washing.
colador [kola'ðor] nm (de té) strainer; (para
verduras etc) colander.
colapsar [kolap'sar] vt (tráfico etc) to bring
to a standstill.
colapso [ko'lapso] nm collapse; ~ **nervioso**
nervous breakdown.
colar [ko'lar] vt (líquido) to strain off;
(metal) to cast ♦ vi to ooze, seep
(through); **~se** vr to jump the queue; (en
mitin) to sneak in; (equivocarse) to slip
up; **~se en** to get into without paying;
(en una fiesta) to gatecrash.
colateral [kolate'ral] nm collateral.
colcha ['koltʃa] nf bedspread.
colchón [kol'tʃon] nm mattress; ~ **inflable**
inflatable mattress.
colchoneta [koltʃo'neta] nf (en gimnasio)
mattress; ~ **hinchable** airbed.
colear [kole'ar] vi (perro) to wag its tail.
colección [kolek'θjon] nf collection.
coleccionar [kolekθjo'nar] vt to collect.
coleccionista [kolekθjo'nista] nm/f
collector.
colecta [ko'lekta] nf collection.
colectivo, a [kolek'tißo, a] adj collective,
joint ♦ nm (AM: autobús) (small) bus;
(: taxi) collective taxi.
colector [kolek'tor] nm collector;
(sumidero) sewer.
colega [ko'leɣa] nm/f colleague.
colegiado, a [kole'xjaðo, a] adj
(profesional) registered ♦ nm/f referee.
colegial, a [kole'xjal, a] adj (ESCOL etc)
school cpd, college cpd ♦ nm/f schoolboy/
girl.
colegio [ko'lexjo] nm college; (escuela)
school; (de abogados etc) association; ~
de internos boarding school; **ir al** ~ to go
to school.

---

*A **colegio** is normally a private primary or
secondary school. In the state system it
means a primary school although these are
also called **escuela**. State secondary*

schools are called **institutos.**
Extracurricular subjects, such as
computing or foreign languages, are offered
in private schools called **academias.**

colegir [kole'xir] *vt (juntar)* to collect,
gather; *(deducir)* to infer, conclude.

cólera ['kolera] *nf (ira)* anger; **montar en ~**
to get angry ♦ *nm (MED)* cholera.

colérico, a [ko'leriko, a] *adj* angry, furious.

colesterol [koleste'rol] *nm* cholesterol.

coleta [ko'leta] *nf* pigtail.

coletazo [kole'taθo] *nm*: **dar un ~** *(animal)*
to flap its tail; **los últimos ~s** death
throes.

coletilla [kole'tiʎa] *nf (en carta)* postscript;
(en conversación) filler phrase.

colgado, a [kol'ɣaðo, a] *pp de* **colgar** ♦ *adj*
hanging; *(ahorcado)* hanged; **dejar ~ a**
algn to let sb down.

colgajo [kol'ɣaxo] *nm* tatter.

colgante [kol'ɣante] *adj* hanging; *V* **puente**
♦ *nm (joya)* pendant.

colgar [kol'ɣar] *vt* to hang (up); *(tender:*
ropa) to hang out ♦ *vi* to hang; *(teléfono)*
to hang up.

colgué [kol'ɣe], **colguemos** [kol'ɣemos]
etc vb V **colgar.**

colibrí [koli'βri] *nm* hummingbird.

cólico ['koliko] *nm* colic.

coliflor [koli'flor] *nf* cauliflower.

coligiendo [koli'xjenðo] *etc vb V* **colegir.**

colija [ko'lixa] *etc vb V* **colegir.**

colilla [ko'liʎa] *nf* cigarette end, butt.

colina [ko'lina] *nf* hill.

colindante [kolin'dante] *adj* adjacent,
neighbouring.

colindar [kolin'dar] *vi* to adjoin, be
adjacent.

colisión [koli'sjon] *nf* collision; **~ de frente**
head-on crash.

colitis [ko'litis] *nf inv*: **tener ~** to have
diarrhoea.

collar [ko'ʎar] *nm* necklace; *(de perro)*
collar.

colmado, a [kol'maðo, a] *adj* full ♦ *nm*
grocer's (shop) *(BRIT)*, grocery store
(US).

colmar [kol'mar] *vt* to fill to the brim; *(fig)*
to fulfil, realize.

colmena [kol'mena] *nf* beehive.

colmillo [kol'miʎo] *nm (diente)* eye tooth;
(de elefante) tusk; *(de perro)* fang.

colmo ['kolmo] *nm* height, summit; **para ~**
de desgracias to cap it all; **¡eso es ya el**
~! that's beyond a joke!

colocación [koloka'θjon] *nf (acto)* placing;
(empleo) job, position; *(situación)* place,

position; *(COM)* placement.

colocar [kolo'kar] *vt* to place, put, position;
(poner en empleo) to find a job for; **~**
dinero to invest money; **~se** *vr* to place
o.s.; *(conseguir trabajo)* to find a job.

colofón [kolo'fon] *nm*: **como ~ de las**
conversaciones as a sequel to *o*
following the talks.

Colombia [ko'lombja] *nf* Colombia.

colombiano, a [kolom'bjano, a] *adj, nm/f*
Colombian.

colon ['kolon] *nm* colon.

colón [ko'lon] *nm (AM)* monetary unit of
Costa Rica and El Salvador.

Colonia [ko'lonja] *nf* Cologne.

colonia [ko'lonja] *nf* colony; *(de casas)*
housing estate; *(agua de ~)* cologne; **~**
escolar summer camp (for
schoolchildren).

colonice [kolo'niθe] *etc vb V* **colonizar.**

colonización [koloniθa'θjon] *nf*
colonization.

colonizador, a [koloniθa'ðor, a] *adj*
colonizing ♦ *nm/f* colonist, settler.

colonizar [koloni'θar] *vt* to colonize.

colono [ko'lono] *nm (POL)* colonist, settler;
(AGR) tenant farmer.

coloque [ko'loke] *etc vb V* **colocar.**

coloquial [kolo'kjal] *adj* colloquial.

coloquio [ko'lokjo] *nm* conversation;
(congreso) conference; *(INFORM)*
handshake.

color [ko'lor] *nm* colour; **a todo ~** in full
colour; **verlo todo ~ de rosa** to see
everything through rose-coloured
spectacles; **le salieron los ~es** she
blushed.

colorado, a [kolo'raðo, a] *adj (rojo)* red;
(AM: chiste) rude, blue; **ponerse ~** to
blush.

colorante [kolo'rante] *nm* colouring
(matter).

colorar [kolo'rar] *vt* to colour; *(teñir)* to
dye.

colorear [kolore'ar] *vt* to colour.

colorete [kolo'rete] *nm* blusher.

colorido [kolo'riðo] *nm* colour(ing).

coloso [ko'loso] *nm* colossus.

columbrar [kolum'brar] *vt* to glimpse, spy.

columna [ko'lumna] *nf* column; *(pilar)*
pillar; *(apoyo)* support; **~ blindada** *(MIL)*
armoured column; **~ vertebral** spine,
spinal column.

columpiar [kolum'pjar] *vt*, **~se** *vr* to swing.

columpio [ko'lumpjo] *nm* swing.

colza ['kolθa] *nf* rape; **aceite de ~** rapeseed
oil.

coma ['koma] *nf* comma ♦ *nm (MED)* coma.

comadre [ko'maðre] *nf* (*madrina*) godmother; (*vecina*) neighbour; (*chismosa*) gossip.
comadrear [komaðre'ar] *vi* (*esp AM*) to gossip.
comadreja [koma'ðrexa] *nf* weasel.
comadrona [koma'ðrona] *nf* midwife.
comandancia [koman'danθja] *nf* command.
comandante [koman'dante] *nm* commandant; (*grado*) major.
comandar [koman'dar] *vt* to command.
comando [ko'mando] *nm* (*MIL*: *mando*) command; (: *grupo*) commando unit; (*INFORM*) command; ~ **de búsqueda** search command.
comarca [ko'marka] *nf* region; *V tb* **provincia**.
comarcal [komar'kal] *adj* local.
comba ['komba] *nf* (*curva*) curve; (*en viga*) warp; (*cuerda*) skipping rope; **saltar a la** ~ to skip.
combar [kom'bar] *vt* to bend, curve.
combate [kom'bate] *nm* fight; (*fig*) battle; **fuera de** ~ out of action.
combatiente [komba'tjente] *nm* combatant.
combatir [komba'tir] *vt* to fight, combat.
combatividad [kombatiβi'ðað] *nf* (*actitud*) fighting spirit; (*agresividad*) aggressiveness.
combativo, a [komba'tiβo, a] *adj* full of fight.
combi ['kombi] *nm* fridge-freezer.
combinación [kombina'θjon] *nf* combination; (*QUÍMICA*) compound; (*bebida*) cocktail; (*plan*) scheme, setup; (*prenda*) slip.
combinado, a [kombi'naðo, a] *adj*: **plato** ~ main course served with vegetables.
combinar [kombi'nar] *vt* to combine; (*colores*) to match.
combustible [kombus'tiβle] *nm* fuel.
combustión [kombus'tjon] *nf* combustion.
comedia [ko'meðja] *nf* comedy; (*TEAT*) play, drama; (*fig*) farce.
comediante [kome'ðjante] *nm/f* (comic) actor/actress.
comedido, a [kome'ðiðo, a] *adj* moderate.
comedirse [kome'ðirse] *vr* to behave moderately; (*ser cortés*) to be courteous.
comedor, a [kome'ðor, a] *nm/f* (*persona*) glutton ♦ *nm* (*habitación*) dining room; (*restaurante*) restaurant; (*cantina*) canteen.
comencé [komen'θe], **comencemos** [komen'θemos] *etc vb V* **comenzar**.
comensal [komen'sal] *nm/f* fellow guest/

diner.
comentar [komen'tar] *vt* to comment on; (*fam*) to discuss; **comentó que...** he made the comment that....
comentario [komen'tarjo] *nm* comment, remark; (*LIT*) commentary; ~**s** *nmpl* gossip *sg*; **dar lugar a** ~**s** to cause gossip.
comentarista [komenta'rista] *nm/f* commentator.
comenzar [komen'θar] *vt, vi* to begin, start, commence; ~ **a hacer algo** to begin *o* start doing *o* to do sth.
comer [ko'mer] *vt* to eat; (*DAMAS, AJEDREZ*) to take, capture; (*párrafo etc*) to skip ♦ *vi* to eat; (*almorzar*) to have lunch; ~**se** *vr* to eat up; ~ **el coco a** (*fam*) to brainwash; **¡a** ~! food's ready!
comercial [komer'θjal] *adj* commercial; (*relativo al negocio*) business *cpd*.
comerciante [komer'θjante] *nm/f* trader, merchant; (*tendero*) shopkeeper; ~ **exclusivo** (*COM*) sole trader.
comerciar [komer'θjar] *vi* to trade, do business.
comercio [ko'merθjo] *nm* commerce, trade; (*negocio*) business; (*grandes empresas*) big business; (*fig*) dealings *pl*; ~ **autorizado** (*COM*) licensed trade; ~ **exterior** foreign trade.
comestible [komes'tiβle] *adj* eatable, edible ♦ *nm*: ~**s** food *sg*, foodstuffs; (*COM*) groceries.
cometa [ko'meta] *nm* comet ♦ *nf* kite.
cometer [kome'ter] *vt* to commit.
cometido [kome'tiðo] *nm* (*misión*) task, assignment; (*deber*) commitment.
comezón [kome'θon] *nf* itch, itching.
cómic, *pl* **cómics** ['komik, 'komiks] *nm* comic.
comicios [ko'miθjos] *nmpl* elections; (*voto*) voting *sg*.
cómico, a ['komiko, a] *adj* comic(al) ♦ *nm/f* comedian; (*de teatro*) (comic) actor/actress.
comida [ko'miða] *etc vb V* **comedirse** ♦ *nf* (*alimento*) food; (*almuerzo, cena*) meal; (*de mediodía*) lunch; (*AM*) dinner.
comidilla [komi'ðiʎa] *nf*: **ser la** ~ **de la ciudad** to be the talk of the town.
comience [ko'mjenθe] *etc vb V* **comenzar**.
comienzo [ko'mjenθo] *etc vb V* **comenzar** ♦ *nm* beginning, start; **dar** ~ **a un acto** to begin a ceremony; ~ **del archivo** (*INFORM*) top-of-file.
comillas [ko'miʎas] *nfpl* quotation marks.
comilón, ona [komi'lon, ona] *adj* greedy ♦ *nf* (*fam*) blow-out.
comino [ko'mino] *nm* cumin (seed); **no me**

importa un ~ I don't give a damn.
comisaría [komisa'ria] *nf* police station,
precinct (*US*); (*MIL*) commissariat.
comisario [komi'sarjo] *nm* (*MIL etc*)
commissary; (*POL*) commissar.
comisión [komi'sjon] *nf* (*COM: pago*)
commission, rake-off (*fam*); (: *junta*)
board; (*encargo*) assignment; ~ **mixta/**
permanente joint/standing committee;
Comisiones Obreras (*ESP*) *formerly*
Communist Union Confederation.
comisura [komi'sura] *nf*: ~ **de los labios**
corner of the mouth.
comité, *pl* **comités** *nm* [komi'te, komi'tes]
committee; ~ **de empresa** works
council.
comitiva [komi'tißa] *nf* suite, retinue.
como ['komo] *adv* as; (*tal* ~) like;
(*aproximadamente*) about, approximately
♦ *conj* (*ya que, puesto que*) as, since; (*en*
seguida que) as soon as; (*si*: +*subjun*) if;
¡~ no! of course!; ~ **no lo haga hoy**
unless he does it today; ~ **si** as if; **es tan**
alto ~ **ancho** it is as high as it is wide.
cómo ['komo] *adv* how?, why? ♦ *excl* what?,
I beg your pardon? ♦ *nm*: **el** ~ **y el porqué**
the whys and wherefores; ¿~ **está Ud?**
how are you?; ¿~ **no?** why not?; ¡~ **no!**
(*esp AM*) of course!; ¿~ **son?** what are
they like?
cómoda ['komoða] *nf* chest of drawers.
comodidad [komoði'ðað] *nf* comfort;
venga a su ~ come at your convenience.
comodín [komo'ðin] *nm* joker; (*INFORM*)
wild card; **símbolo** ~ wild-card
character.
cómodo, a ['komoðo, a] *adj* comfortable;
(*práctico, de fácil uso*) convenient.
comodón, ona [komo'ðon, ona] *adj*
comfort-loving ♦ *nm/f*: **ser un(a)** ~ to like
one's home comforts.
comoquiera [como'kjera] *conj*: ~ **que**
(+ *subjun*) in whatever way; ~ **que sea**
eso however that may be.
comp. *abr* (= *compárese*) cp.
compacto, a [kom'pakto, a] *adj* compact.
compadecer [kompaðe'θer] *vt* to pity, be
sorry for; ~**se** *vr*: ~**se de** to pity, be
sorry for.
compadezca [kompa'ðeθka] *etc vb V*
compadecer.
compadre [kom'paðre] *nm* (*padrino*)
godfather; (*esp AM*: *amigo*) friend, pal.
compaginar [kompaxi'nar] *vt*: ~ **A con B** to
bring A into line with B; ~**se** *vr*: ~**se con**
to tally with, square with.
compañerismo [kompaɲe'rismo] *nm*
comradeship.

compañero, a [kompa'ɲero, a] *nm/f*
companion; (*novio*) boyfriend/girlfriend;
~ **de clase** classmate.
compañía [kompa'ɲia] *nf* company; ~
afiliada associated company; ~
concesionadora franchiser; ~ **(no)**
cotizable (un)listed company; ~
inversionista investment trust; **hacer** ~ **a**
algn to keep sb company.
comparación [kompara'θjon] *nf*
comparison; **en** ~ **con** in comparison
with.
comparar [kompa'rar] *vt* to compare.
comparativo, a [kompara'tißo, a] *adj*
comparative.
comparecencia [kompare'θenθja] *nf* (*JUR*)
appearance (in court); **orden de** ~
summons *sg*.
comparecer [kompare'θer] *vi* to appear (in
court).
comparezca [kompa'reθka] *etc vb V*
comparecer.
comparsa [kom'parsa] *nm/f* extra.
compartimento [komparti'mento],
compartimiento [komparti'mjento] *nm*
(*FERRO*) compartment; (*de mueble, cajón*)
section; ~ **estanco** (*fig*) watertight
compartment.
compartir [kompar'tir] *vt* to divide (up),
share (out).
compás [kom'pas] *nm* (*MUS*) beat, rhythm;
(*MAT*) compasses *pl*; (*NAUT etc*) compass;
al ~ in time.
compasión [kompa'sjon] *nf* compassion,
pity.
compasivo, a [kompa'sißo, a] *adj*
compassionate.
compatibilidad [kompatißili'ðað] *nf* (*tb*
INFORM) compatibility.
compatible [kompa'tißle] *adj* compatible.
compatriota [kompa'trjota] *nm/f*
compatriot, fellow countryman/woman.
compendiar [kompen'djar] *vt* to
summarize; (*libro*) to abridge.
compendio [kom'pendjo] *nm* summary;
abridgement.
compenetración [kompenetra'θjon] *nf* (*fig*)
mutual understanding.
compenetrarse [kompene'trarse] *vr* (*fig*):
~ **(muy) bien** to get on (very) well
together.
compensación [kompensa'θjon] *nf*
compensation; (*JUR*) damages *pl*; (*COM*)
clearing.
compensar [kompen'sar] *vt* to
compensate; (*pérdida*) to make up for.
competencia [kompe'tenθja] *nf*
(*incumbencia*) domain, field; (*COM*)

receipt; (*JUR, habilidad*) competence; (*rivalidad*) competition.

competente [kompe'tente] *adj* (*JUR, persona*) competent; (*conveniente*) suitable.

competer [kompe'ter] *vi:* ~ **a** to be the responsibility of, fall to.

competición [kompeti'θjon] *nf* competition.

competidor, a [kompeti'ðor, a] *nm/f* competitor.

competir [kompe'tir] *vi* to compete.

competitivo, a [kompeti'tiβo, a] *adj* competitive.

compilación [kompila'θjon] *nf* compilation; **tiempo de** ~ (*INFORM*) compile time.

compilador [kompila'ðor] *nm* compiler.

compilar [kompi'lar] *vt* to compile.

compinche [kom'pintʃe] *nm/f* (*fam*) crony.

compita [kom'pita] *etc vb V* **competir.**

complacencia [kompla'θenθja] *nf* (*placer*) pleasure; (*satisfacción*) satisfaction; (*buena voluntad*) willingness.

complacer [kompla'θer] *vt* to please; ~**se** *vr* to be pleased.

complaciente [kompla'θjente] *adj* kind, obliging, helpful.

complazca [kom'plaθka] *etc vb V* **complacer.**

complejo, a [kom'plexo, a] *adj, nm* complex.

complementario, a [komplemen'tarjo, a] *adj* complementary.

complemento [komple'mento] *nm* (*de moda, diseño*) accessory; (*LING*) complement.

completar [komple'tar] *vt* to complete.

completo, a [kom'pleto, a] *adj* complete; (*perfecto*) perfect; (*lleno*) full ♦ *nm* full complement.

complexión [komple'ksjon] *nf* constitution.

complicación [komplika'θjon] *nf* complication.

complicado, a [kompli'kaðo, a] *adj* complicated; **estar** ~ **en** to be involved in.

complicar [kompli'kar] *vt* to complicate.

cómplice ['kompliθe] *nm/f* accomplice.

complique [kom'plike] *etc vb V* **complicar.**

complot, *pl* **complots** [kom'plo(t), kom'plos] *nm* plot; (*conspiración*) conspiracy.

compondré [kompon'dre] *etc vb V* **componer.**

componenda [kompo'nenda] *nf* compromise; (*pey*) shady deal.

componente [kompo'nente] *adj, nm* component.

componer [kompo'ner] *vt* to make up, put together; (*MUS, LIT, IMPRENTA*) to compose; (*algo roto*) to mend, repair; (*adornar*) to adorn; (*arreglar*) to arrange; (*reconciliar*) to reconcile; ~**se** *vr:* ~**se de** to consist of; **componérselas para hacer algo** to manage to do sth.

componga [kom'ponga] *etc vb V* **componer.**

comportamiento [komporta'mjento] *nm* behaviour, conduct.

comportarse [kompor'tarse] *vr* to behave.

composición [komposi'θjon] *nf* composition.

compositor, a [komposi'tor, a] *nm/f* composer.

compostelano, a [komposte'lano, a] *adj* of *o* from Santiago de Compostela ♦ *nm/f* native *o* inhabitant of Santiago de Compostela.

compostura [kompos'tura] *nf* (*reparación*) mending, repair; (*composición*) composition; (*acuerdo*) agreement; (*actitud*) composure.

compota [kom'pota] *nf* compote, preserve.

compra ['kompra] *nf* purchase; ~**s** *nfpl* purchases, shopping *sg*; **hacer la** ~/**ir de** ~**s** to do the/go shopping; ~ **a granel** (*COM*) bulk buying; ~ **proteccionista** (*COM*) support buying.

comprador, a [kompra'ðor, a] *nm/f* buyer, purchaser.

comprar [kom'prar] *vt* to buy, purchase; ~ **deudas** (*COM*) to factor.

compraventa [kompra'βenta] *nf* (*JUR*) contract of sale.

comprender [kompren'der] *vt* to understand; (*incluir*) to comprise, include.

comprensible [kompren'siβle] *adj* understandable.

comprensión [kompren'sjon] *nf* understanding; (*totalidad*) comprehensiveness.

comprensivo, a [kompren'siβo, a] *adj* comprehensive; (*actitud*) understanding.

compresa [kom'presa] *nf* compress; ~ **higiénica** sanitary towel (*BRIT*) *o* napkin (*US*).

compresión [kompre'sjon] *nf* compression.

comprimido, a [kompri'miðo] *adj* compressed ♦ *nm* (*MED*) pill, tablet; **en caracteres** ~**s** (*TIP*) condensed.

comprimir [kompri'mir] *vt* to compress;

(*fig*) to control; (*INFORM*) to pack.
comprobación [komproßa'θjon] *nf*: ~
   general de cuentas (*COM*) general audit.
comprobante [kompro'ßante] *nm* proof;
   (*COM*) voucher; ~ **(de pago)** receipt.
comprobar [kompro'ßar] *vt* to check;
   (*probar*) to prove; (*TEC*) to check, test.
comprometedor, a [kompromete'ðor, a]
   adj compromising.
comprometer [komprome'ter] *vt* to
   compromise; (*exponer*) to endanger; ~**se**
   vr to compromise o.s.; (*involucrarse*) to
   get involved.
comprometido, a [komprome'tiðo, a] *a*
   (*situación*) awkward; (*escritor etc*)
   committed.
compromiso [kompro'miso] *nm*
   (*obligación*) obligation; (*cita*)
   engagement, date; (*cometido*)
   commitment; (*convenio*) agreement;
   (*dificultad*) awkward situation; **libre de** ~
   (*COM*) without obligation.
comprueba [kom'prweßa] *etc vb V*
   comprobar.
compuerta [kom'pwerta] *nf* (*en canal*)
   sluice, floodgate; (*INFORM*) gate.
compuesto, a [kom'pwesto, a] *pp de*
   componer ♦ *adj*: ~ **de** composed of, made
   up of ♦ *nm* compound; (*MED*)
   preparation.
compulsar [kompul'sar] *vt* (*cotejar*) to
   collate, compare; (*JUR*) to make an
   attested copy of.
compulsivo, a [kompul'sißo, a] *adj*
   compulsive.
compungido, a [kompun'xiðo, a] *adj*
   remorseful.
compuse [com'puse] *etc vb V* **componer**.
computador [komputa'ðor] *nm*,
   computadora [komputa'ðora] *nf*
   computer; ~ **central** mainframe
   computer; ~ **especializado** dedicated
   computer; ~ **personal** personal
   computer.
computar [kompu'tar] *vt* to calculate,
   compute.
cómputo ['komputo] *nm* calculation,
   computation.
comulgar [komul'ɣar] *vi* to receive
   communion.
comulgue [ko'mulɣe] *etc vb V* **comulgar**.
común [ko'mun] *adj* (*gen*) common;
   (*corriente*) ordinary; **por lo** ~ generally
   ♦ *nm*: **el** ~ the community.
comuna [ko'muna] *nf* commune; (*AM*)
   district.
comunicación [komunika'θjon] *nf*
   communication; (*informe*) report.

comunicado [komuni'kaðo] *nm*
   announcement; ~ **de prensa** press
   release.
comunicar [komuni'kar] *vt* to
   communicate; (*ARQ*) to connect ♦ *vi* to
   communicate; to send a report; ~**se** *vr* to
   communicate; **está comunicando** (*TELEC*)
   the line's engaged (*BRIT*) o busy (*US*).
comunicativo, a [komunika'tißo, a] *adj*
   communicative.
comunidad [komuni'ðað] *nf* community; ~
   autónoma autonomous region; ~ **de
   vecinos** residents' association; **C~
   Económica Europea (CEE)** European
   Economic Community (EEC).

---

*The 1978 Constitution provides for a degree
of self-government for the 19 regions, called
comunidades autónomas or **autonomías**.
Some, such as Catalonia and the Basque
Country, with their own language, history
and culture, have long felt separate from
the rest of Spain. This explains why some
of the **autonomías** have more devolved
powers than others, in all matters except
foreign affairs and national defence. The
regions are: **Andalucía, Aragón, Asturias,
Islas Baleares, Canarias, Cantabria, Castilla y
León, Castilla-La Mancha, Cataluña,
Extremadura, Galicia, Madrid, Murcia,
Navarra, País Vasco, La Rioja, Comunidad
Valenciana, Ceuta, Melilla.**

---

comunión [komu'njon] *nf* communion.
comunique [komu'nike] *etc vb V*
   comunicar.
comunismo [komu'nismo] *nm*
   communism.
comunista [komu'nista] *adj, nm/f*
   communist.
comunitario, a [komuni'tarjo, a] *adj* (*de la
   CE*) Community *cpd*, EC *cpd*.

═══════════════════ *PALABRA CLAVE*

con [kon] *prep* **1** (*medio, compañía, modo*)
   with; **comer** ~ **cuchara** to eat with a
   spoon; **café** ~ **leche** white coffee; **estoy**
   ~ **un catarro** I've got a cold; **pasear** ~
   algn to go for a walk with sb; ~
   habilidad skilfully
   2 (*a pesar de*): ~ **todo, merece nuestros
   respetos** all the same o even so, he
   deserves our respect
   3 (*para* ~): **es muy bueno para** ~ **los
   niños** he's very good with (the) children
   4 (+*infin*): ~ **llegar tan tarde se quedó
   sin comer** by arriving o because he
   arrived so late he missed out on eating;

~ **estudiar un poco apruebas** with a bit
of studying you should pass
5 (*queja*): **¡~ las ganas que tenía de ir!**
and I really wanted to go (too)!
♦ *conj*: ~ **que: será suficiente ~ que le
escribas** it will be enough if you write to
her.

conato [ko'nato] *nm* attempt; ~ **de robo**
attempted robbery.
cóncavo, a ['konkaβo, a] *adj* concave.
concebir [konθe'βir] *vt* to conceive;
(*imaginar*) to imagine ♦ *vi* to conceive.
conceder [konθe'ðer] *vt* to concede.
concejal, a [konθe'xal, a] *nm/f* town
councillor.
concejo [kon'θexo] *nm* council.
concentración [konθentra'θjon] *nf*
concentration.
concentrar [konθen'trar] *vt*, ~**se** *vr* to
concentrate.
concéntrico, a [kon'θentriko, a] *adj*
concentric.
concepción [konθep'θjon] *nf* conception.
concepto [kon'θepto] *nm* concept; **por ~
de** as, by way of; **tener buen ~ de algn** to
think highly of sb; **bajo ningún ~** under
no circumstances.
conceptuar [konθep'twar] *vt* to judge.
concernir [konθer'nir] *vi*: **en lo que
concierne a** concerning.
concertar [konθer'tar] *vt* (*MUS*) to
harmonize; (*acordar: precio*) to agree;
(: *tratado*) to conclude; (*trato*) to arrange,
fix up; (*combinar: esfuerzos*) to
coordinate; (*reconciliar: personas*) to
reconcile ♦ *vi* to harmonize, be in tune.
concesión [konθe'sjon] *nf* concession;
(*COM: fabricación*) licence.
concesionario, a [konθesjo'narjo, a] *nm/f*
(*COM*) (licensed) dealer, agent,
concessionaire; (: *de venta*) franchisee;
(: *de transportes etc*) contractor.
concha ['kontʃa] *nf* shell; (*AM fam!*) cunt
(!)
conchabarse [kontʃa'βarse] *vr*: ~ **contra** to
gang up on.
conciencia [kon'θjenθja] *nf* (*moral*)
conscience; (*conocimiento*) awareness;
libertad de ~ freedom of worship;
tener/tomar ~ de to be/become aware
of; **tener la ~ limpia o tranquila** to have a
clear conscience; **tener plena ~ de** to be
fully aware of.
concienciar [konθjen'θjar] *vt* to make
aware; ~**se** *vr* to become aware.
concienzudo, a [konθjen'θuðo, a] *adj*
conscientious.

concierne [kon'θjerne] *etc vb* V **concernir**.
concierto [kon'θjerto] *etc vb* V **concertar**
♦ *nm* concert; (*obra*) concerto.
conciliación [konθilja'θjon] *nf* conciliation.
conciliar [konθi'ljar] *vt* to reconcile ♦ *adj*
(*REL*) of a council; ~ **el sueño** to get to
sleep.
concilio [kon'θiljo] *nm* council.
concisión [konθi'sjon] *nf* conciseness.
conciso, a [kon'θiso, a] *adj* concise.
conciudadano, a [konθjuða'ðano, a] *nm/f*
fellow citizen.
concluir [konklu'ir] *vt* (*acabar*) to conclude;
(*inferir*) to infer, deduce ♦ *vi*, ~**se** *vr* to
conclude; **todo ha concluido** it's all over.
conclusión [konklu'sjon] *nf* conclusion;
llegar a la ~ de que ... to come to the
conclusion that ....
concluya [kon'kluja] *etc vb* V **concluir**.
concluyente [konklu'jente] *adj* (*prueba,
información*) conclusive.
concordancia [konkor'ðanθja] *nf*
agreement.
concordar [konkor'ðar] *vt* to reconcile ♦ *vi*
to agree, tally.
concordia [kon'korðja] *nf* harmony.
concretamente [konkreta'mente] *adv*
specifically, to be exact.
concretar [konkre'tar] *vt* to make
concrete, make more specific;
(*problema*) to pinpoint; ~**se** *vr* to become
more definite.
concreto, a [kon'kreto, a] *adj, nm* (*AM*)
concrete; **en ~** (*en resumen*) to sum up;
(*específicamente*) specifically; **no hay
nada en ~** there's nothing definite.
concubina [konku'βina] *nf* concubine.
concuerde [kon'kwerðe] *etc vb* V
concordar.
concupiscencia [konkupis'θenθja] *nf*
(*avancia*) greed; (*lujuria*) lustfulness.
concurrencia [konku'rrenθja] *nf* turnout.
concurrido, a [konku'rriðo, a] *a* (*calle*)
busy; (*local, reunión*) crowded.
concurrir [konku'rrir] *vi* (*juntarse: ríos*) to
meet, come together; (: *personas*) to
gather, meet.
concursante [konkur'sante] *nm*
competitor.
concursar [konkur'sar] *vi* to compete.
concurso [kon'kurso] *nm* (*de público*)
crowd; (*ESCOL, DEPORTE, competencia*)
competition; (*COM*) invitation to tender;
(*examen*) open competition; (*TV etc*) quiz;
(*ayuda*) help, cooperation.
condado [kon'daðo] *nm* county.
condal [kon'dal] *adj*: **la ciudad ~**
Barcelona.

conde ['konde] *nm* count.
condecoración [kondekora'θjon] *nf* (*MIL*) medal, decoration.
condecorar [kondeko'rar] *vt* to decorate.
condena [kon'dena] *nf* sentence; **cumplir una ~** to serve a sentence.
condenación [kondena'θjon] *nf* condemnation; (*REL*) damnation.
condenado, a [konde'naðo, a] *adj* (*JUR*) condemned; (*fam*: *maldito*) damned ♦ *nm/f* (*JUR*) convicted person.
condenar [konde'nar] *vt* to condemn; (*JUR*) to convict; **~se** *vr* (*JUR*) to confess (one's guilt); (*REL*) to be damned.
condensar [konden'sar] *vt* to condense.
condesa [kon'desa] *nf* countess.
condescendencia [kondesθen'denθja] *nf* condescension; **aceptar algo por ~** to accept sth so as not to hurt feelings.
condescender [kondesθen'der] *vi* to acquiesce, comply.
condescienda [kondes'θjenda] *etc vb V* **condescender**.
condición [kondi'θjon] *nf* (*gen*) condition; (*rango*) social class; **condiciones** *nfpl* (*cualidades*) qualities; (*estado*) condition; **a ~ de que ...** on condition that ...; **las condiciones del contrato** the terms of the contract; **condiciones de trabajo** working conditions; **condiciones de venta** conditions of sale.
condicional [kondiθjo'nal] *adj* conditional.
condicionamiento [kondiθjona'mjento] *nm* conditioning.
condicionar [kondiθjo'nar] *vt* (*acondicionar*) to condition; **~ algo a algo** to make sth conditional *o* dependent on sth.
condimento [kondi'mento] *nm* seasoning.
condiscípulo, a [kondis'θipulo, a] *nm/f* fellow student.
condolerse [kondo'lerse] *vr* to sympathize.
condominio [kondo'minjo] *nm* (*COM*) joint ownership; (*AM*) condominium, apartment.
condón [kon'don] *nm* condom.
condonar [kondo'nar] *vt* (*JUR*: *reo*) to reprieve; (*COM*: *deuda*) to cancel.
cóndor ['kondor] *nm* condor.
conducente [kondu'θente] *adj*: **~ a** conducive to, leading to.
conducir [kondu'θir] *vt* to take, convey; (*ELEC etc*) to carry; (*AUTO*) to drive; (*negocio*) to manage ♦ *vi* to drive; (*fig*) to lead; **~se** *vr* to behave.
conducta [kon'dukta] *nf* conduct, behaviour.
conducto [kon'dukto] *nm* pipe, tube; (*fig*)

channel; (*ELEC*) lead; **por ~ de** through.
conductor, a [konduk'tor, a] *adj* leading, guiding ♦ *nm* (*FÍSICA*) conductor; (*de vehículo*) driver.
conduela [kon'dwela] *etc vb V* **condolerse**.
conduje [kon'duxe] *etc vb V* **conducir**.
conduzca [kon'duθka] *etc vb V* **conducir**.
conectado, a [konek'taðo, a] *a* (*ELEC*) connected, plugged in; (*INFORM*) on-line.
conectar [konek'tar] *vt* to connect (up), plug in; (*INFORM*) to toggle on; **~se** *vr* (*INFORM*) to log in (on).
conejillo [kone'xiʎo] *nm*: **~ de Indias** guinea pig.
conejo [ko'nexo] *nm* rabbit.
conexión [konek'sjon] *nf* connection; (*INFORM*) logging in (on).
confabularse [konfaßu'larse] *vr*: **~ (para hacer algo)** to plot, conspire (to do sth).
confección [konfek'θjon] *nf* (*preparación*) preparation, making-up; (*industria*) clothing industry; (*producto*) article; **de ~** (*ropa*) off-the-peg.
confeccionar [konfe(k)θjo'nar] *vt* to make (up).
confederación [konfeðera'θjon] *nf* confederation.
conferencia [konfe'renθja] *nf* conference; (*lección*) lecture; (*TELEC*) call; **~ de cobro revertido** (*TELEC*) reversed-charge (*BRIT*) *o* collect (*US*) call; **~ cumbre** summit (conference).
conferenciante [konferen'θjante] *nm/f* lecturer.
conferir [konfe'rir] *vt* to award.
confesar [konfe'sar] *vt* (*admitir*) to confess, admit; (*error*) to acknowledge; (*crimen*) to own up to.
confesión [konfe'sjon] *nf* confession.
confesionario [konfesjo'narjo] *nm* confessional.
confeso, a [kon'feso, a] *adj* (*JUR etc*) self-confessed.
confeti [kon'feti] *nm* confetti.
confiado, a [kon'fjaðo, a] *adj* (*crédulo*) trusting; (*seguro*) confident; (*presumido*) conceited, vain.
confianza [kon'fjanθa] *nf* trust; (*aliento, confidencia*) confidence; (*familiaridad*) intimacy, familiarity; (*pey*) vanity, conceit; **margen de ~** credibility gap; **tener ~ con algn** to be on close terms with sb.
confiar [kon'fjar] *vt* to entrust ♦ *vi* (*fiarse*) to trust; (*contar con*) to rely; **~se** *vr* to put one's trust.
confidencia [konfi'ðenθja] *nf* confidence.
confidencial [konfiðen'θjal] *adj*

confidential.

confidente [konfi'ðente] *nm/f* confidant/e; (*policial*) informer.

confiera [kon'fjera] *etc vb V* **conferir.**

confiese [kon'fjese] *etc vb V* **confesar.**

configuración [konfiɣura'θjon] *nf* (*tb* *INFORM*) configuration; **la ~ del terreno** the lie of the land; **~ de bits** (*INFORM*) bit pattern.

configurar [konfiɣu'rar] *vt* to shape, form.

confín [kon'fin] *nm* limit; **confines** *nmpl* confines, limits.

confinar [konfi'nar] *vi* to confine; (*desterrar*) to banish.

confiriendo [konfi'rjendo] *etc vb V* **conferir.**

confirmación [konfirma'θjon] *nf* confirmation; (*REL*) Confirmation.

confirmar [konfir'mar] *vt* to confirm; (*JUR etc*) to corroborate; **la excepción confirma la regla** the exception proves the rule.

confiscar [konfis'kar] *vt* to confiscate.

confisque [kon'fiske] *etc vb V* **confiscar.**

confitado, a [konfi'taðo, a] *adj*: **fruta confitada** crystallized fruit.

confite [kon'fite] *nm* sweet (*BRIT*), candy (*US*).

confitería [konfite'ria] *nf* confectionery; (*tienda*) confectioner's (shop).

confitura [konfi'tura] *nf* jam.

conflagración [konflaɣra'θjon] *nf* conflagration.

conflictivo, a [konflik'tiβo, a] *adj* (*asunto, propuesta*) controversial; (*país, situación*) troubled.

conflicto [kon'flikto] *nm* conflict; (*fig*) clash; (: *dificultad*): **estar en un ~** to be in a jam; **~ laboral** labour dispute.

confluir [konflu'ir] *vi* (*ríos etc*) to meet; (*gente*) to gather.

confluya [kon'fluja] *etc vb V* **confluir.**

conformar [konfor'mar] *vt* to shape, fashion ♦ *vi* to agree; **~se** *vr* to conform; (*resignarse*) to resign o.s.

conforme [kon'forme] *adj* alike, similar; (*de acuerdo*) agreed, in agreement; (*satisfecho*) satisfied ♦ *adv* as ♦ *excl* agreed! ♦ *nm* agreement ♦ *prep*: **~ a** in accordance with.

conformidad [konformi'ðað] *nf* (*semejanza*) similarity; (*acuerdo*) agreement; (*resignación*) resignation; **de/en ~ con** in accordance with; **dar su ~** to consent.

conformismo [konfor'mismo] *nm* conformism.

conformista [konfor'mista] *nm/f* conformist.

confort, ** *pl* **conforts [kon'for, kon'for(t)s] *nm* comfort.

confortable [konfor'taßle] *adj* comfortable.

confortar [konfor'tar] *vt* to comfort.

confraternidad [konfraterni'ðað] *nf* brotherhood; **espíritu de ~** feeling of unity.

confraternizar [konfraterni'θar] *vi* to fraternize.

confrontación [konfronta'θjon] *nf* confrontation.

confrontar [konfron'tar] *vt* to confront; (*dos personas*) to bring face to face; (*cotejar*) to compare ♦ *vi* to border.

confundir [konfun'dir] *vt* (*borrar*) to blur; (*equivocar*) to mistake, confuse; (*mezclar*) to mix; (*turbar*) to confuse; **~se** *vr* (*hacerse borroso*) to become blurred; (*turbarse*) to get confused; (*equivocarse*) to make a mistake; (*mezclarse*) to mix.

confusión [konfu'sjon] *nf* confusion.

confusionismo [konfusjo'nismo] *nm* confusion, uncertainty.

confuso, a [kon'fuso, a] *adj* (*gen*) confused; (*recuerdo*) hazy; (*estilo*) obscure.

congelación [konxela'θjon] *nf* freezing; **~ de créditos** credit freeze.

congelado, a [konxe'laðo, a] *adj* frozen ♦ *nmpl*: **~s** frozen food *sg o* foods.

congelador [konxela'ðor] *nm* freezer, deep freeze.

congelar [konxe'lar] *vt* to freeze; **~se** *vr* (*sangre, grasa*) to congeal.

congénere [kon'xenere] *nm/f*: **sus ~s** his peers.

congeniar [konxe'njar] *vi* to get on (*BRIT*) *o* along (*US*) (well).

congénito, a [kon'xenito, a] *adj* congenital.

congestión [konxes'tjon] *nf* congestion.

congestionado, a [konxestjo'naðo, a] *adj* congested.

congestionar [konxestjo'nar] *vt* to congest; **~se** *vr* to become congested; **se le congestionó la cara** his face became flushed.

conglomerado [konglome'raðo] *nm* conglomerate.

Congo ['kongo] *nm*: **el ~** the Congo.

congoja [kon'goxa] *nf* distress, grief.

congraciarse [kongra'θjarse] *vr* to ingratiate o.s.

congratular [kongratu'lar] *vt* to congratulate.

congregación [kongreɣa'θjon] *nf* congregation.

congregar [kongre'ɣar] *vt,* **~se** *vr* to gather together.

congregue [kon'greɣe] *etc vb V* **congregar.**

congresista [kongre'sista] *nm/f* delegate, congressman/woman.

congreso [kon'greso] *nm* congress; **C~ de los Diputados** (*ESP POL*) ≈ House of Commons (*BRIT*), House of Representatives (*US*); *V tb* **Las Cortes (españolas).**

congrio ['kongrjo] *nm* conger (eel).

congruente [kon'grwente] *adj* congruent, congruous.

conífera [ko'nifera] *nf* conifer.

conjetura [konxe'tura] *nf* guess; (*COM*) guesstimate.

conjeturar [konxetu'rar] *vt* to guess.

conjugación [konxuɣa'θjon] *nf* conjugation.

conjugar [konxu'ɣar] *vt* to combine, fit together; (*LING*) to conjugate.

conjugue [kon'xuɣe] *etc vb V* **conjugar.**

conjunción [konxun'θjon] *nf* conjunction.

conjunctivitis [konxunti'ßitis] *nf* conjunctivitis.

conjunto, a [kon'xunto, a] *adj* joint, united ♦ *nm* whole; (*MUS*) band; (*vestido*) ensemble; (*INFORM*) set; **en ~** as a whole; **~ integrado de programas** (*INFORM*) integrated software suite.

conjura [kon'xura] *nf* plot, conspiracy.

conjurar [konxu'rar] *vt* (*REL*) to exorcise; (*peligro*) to ward off ♦ *vi* to plot.

conjuro [kon'xuro] *nm* spell.

conllevar [konʎe'ßar] *vt* to bear; (*implicar*) to imply, involve.

conmemoración [konmemora'θjon] *nf* commemoration.

conmemorar [konmemo'rar] *vt* to commemorate.

conmigo [kon'miɣo] *pron* with me.

conminar [konmi'nar] *vt* to threaten.

conmiseración [konmisera'θjon] *nf* pity, commiseration.

conmoción [konmo'θjon] *nf* shock; (*POL*) disturbance; (*fig*) upheaval; **~ cerebral** (*MED*) concussion.

conmovedor, a [konmoße'ðor, a] *adj* touching, moving; (*emocionante*) exciting.

conmover [konmo'ßer] *vt* to shake, disturb; (*fig*) to move; **~se** *vr* (*fig*) to be moved.

conmueva [kon'mweßa] *etc vb V* **conmover.**

conmutación [konmuta'θjon] *nf* (*INFORM*) switching; **~ de mensajes** message switching; **~ por paquetes** packet switching.

conmutador [konmuta'ðor] *nm* switch; (*AM TELEC*) switchboard.

conmutar [konmu'tar] *vt* (*JUR*) to commute.

connivencia [konni'ßenθja] *nf*: **estar en ~ con** to be in collusion with.

connotación [konnota'θjon] *nf* connotation.

cono ['kono] *nm* cone; **C~ Sur** Southern Cone.

conocedor, a [konoθe'ðor, a] *adj* expert, knowledgeable ♦ *nm/f* expert, connoisseur.

conocer [kono'θer] *vt* to know; (*por primera vez*) to meet, get to know; (*entender*) to know about; (*reconocer*) to recognize; **~se** *vr* (*una persona*) to know o.s.; (*dos personas*) to (get to) know each other; **darse a ~** (*presentarse*) to make o.s. known; **se conoce que ...** (*parece*) apparently ....

conocido, a [kono'θiðo, a] *adj* (well-)known ♦ *nm/f* acquaintance.

conocimiento [konoθi'mjento] *nm* knowledge; (*MED*) consciousness; (*NAUT: tb:* **~ de embarque**) bill of lading; **~s** *nmpl* (*personas*) acquaintances; (*saber*) knowledge *sg*; **hablar con ~ de causa** to speak from experience; **~ (de embarque) aéreo** (*COM*) air waybill.

conozca [ko'noθka] *etc vb V* **conocer.**

conque ['konke] *conj* and so, so then.

conquense [kon'kense] *adj* of *o* from Cuenca ♦ *nm/f* native *o* inhabitant of Cuenca.

conquista [kon'kista] *nf* conquest.

conquistador, a [konkista'ðor, a] *adj* conquering ♦ *nm* conqueror.

conquistar [konkis'tar] *vt* (*MIL*) to conquer; (*puesto, simpatía*) to win; (*enamorar*) to win the heart of.

consabido, a [konsa'ßiðo, a] *adj* (*frase etc*) old; (*pey*): **las consabidas excusas** the same old excuses.

consagrado, a [konsa'ɣraðo, a] *adj* (*REL*) consecrated; (*actor*) established.

consagrar [konsa'ɣrar] *vt* (*REL*) to consecrate; (*fig*) to devote.

consciente [kons'θjente] *adj* conscious; **ser** *o* **estar ~ de** to be aware of.

consecución [konseku'θjon] *nf* acquisition; (*de fin*) attainment.

consecuencia [konse'kwenθja] *nf* consequence, outcome; (*firmeza*) consistency; **de ~** of importance.

consecuente [konse'kwente] *adj* consistent.

consecutivo, a [konseku'tiβo, a] *adj* consecutive.

conseguir [konse'ɣir] *vt* to get, obtain; (*sus fines*) to attain.

consejería [konsexe'ria] *nf* (*POL*) ministry (*in a regional government*).

consejero, a [konse'xero, a] *nm/f* adviser, consultant; (*POL*) minister (*in a regional government*); (*COM*) director; (*en comisión*) member.

consejo [kon'sexo] *nm* advice; (*POL*) council; (*COM*) board; **un ~** a piece of advice; **~ de administración** board of directors; **~ de guerra** court-martial; **C~ de Europa** Council of Europe.

consenso [kon'senso] *nm* consensus.

consentido, a [konsen'tiðo, a] *adj* (*mimado*) spoiled.

consentimiento [konsenti'mjento] *nm* consent.

consentir [konsen'tir] *vt* (*permitir, tolerar*) to consent to; (*mimar*) to pamper, spoil ♦ *vi* to agree, consent; **~ que algn haga algo** to allow sb to do sth.

conserje [kon'serxe] *nm* caretaker; (*portero*) porter.

conserva [kon'serβa] *nf*: **en ~** (*alimentos*) tinned (*BRIT*), canned; **~s** tinned *o* canned foods.

conservación [konserβa'θjon] *nf* conservation; (*de alimentos, vida*) preservation.

conservador, a [konserβa'ðor, a] *adj* (*POL*) conservative ♦ *nm/f* conservative.

conservadurismo [konserβaðu'rismo] *nm* (*POL etc*) conservatism.

conservante [konser'βante] *nm* preservative.

conservar [konser'βar] *vt* (*gen*) to preserve; (*recursos*) to conserve, keep; (*alimentos, vida*) to preserve; **~se** *vr* to survive.

conservas [kon'serβas] *nfpl*: **~ (alimenticias)** tinned (*BRIT*) *o* canned goods.

conservatorio [konserβa'torjo] *nm* (*MUS*) conservatoire; (*AM*) greenhouse.

considerable [konsiðe'raβle] *adj* considerable.

consideración [konsiðera'θjon] *nf* consideration; (*estimación*) respect; **de ~** important; **De mi *o* nuestra (mayor) ~** (*AM*) Dear Sir(s) *o* Madam; **tomar en ~** to take into account.

considerado, a [konsiðe'raðo, a] *adj* (*atento*) considerate; (*respetado*) respected.

considerar [konsiðe'rar] *vt* (*gen*) to

consider; (*meditar*) to think about; (*tener en cuenta*) to take into account.

consienta [kon'sjenta] *etc vb V* **consentir**.

consigna [kon'siɣna] *nf* (*orden*) order, instruction; (*para equipajes*) left-luggage office (*BRIT*), checkroom (*US*).

consignación [konsiɣna'θjon] *nf* consignment; **~ de créditos** allocation of credits.

consignador [konsiɣna'ðor] *nm* (*COM*) consignor.

consignar [konsiɣ'nar] *vt* (*COM*) to send; (*créditos*) to allocate.

consignatario, a [konsiɣna'tarjo, a] *nm/f* (*COM*) consignee.

consigo [kon'siɣo] *etc vb V* **conseguir** ♦ *pron* (*m*) with him; (*f*) with her; (*usted*) with you; (*reflexivo*) with o.s.

consiguiendo [konsi'ɣjendo] *etc vb V* **conseguir**.

consiguiente [konsi'ɣjente] *adj* consequent; **por ~** and so, therefore, consequently.

consintiendo [konsin'tjendo] *etc vb V* **consentir**.

consistente [konsis'tente] *adj* consistent; (*sólido*) solid, firm; (*válido*) sound; **~ en** consisting of.

consistir [konsis'tir] *vi*: **~ en** (*componerse de*) to consist of; (*ser resultado de*) to be due to.

consola [kon'sola] *nf* console, control panel; (*mueble*) console table; **~ de juegos** games console; **~ de mando** (*INFORM*) control console; **~ de visualización** visual display console.

consolación [konsola'θjon] *nf* consolation.

consolar [konso'lar] *vt* to console.

consolidar [konsoli'ðar] *vt* to consolidate.

consomé [konso'me], *pl* **consomés** [konso'me, konso'mes] *nm* consommé, clear soup.

consonancia [konso'nanθja] *nf* harmony; **en ~ con** in accordance with.

consonante [konso'nante] *adj* consonant, harmonious ♦ *nf* consonant.

consorcio [kon'sorθjo] *nm* (*COM*) consortium, syndicate.

consorte [kon'sorte] *nm/f* consort.

conspicuo, a [kons'pikwo, a] *adj* conspicuous.

conspiración [konspira'θjon] *nf* conspiracy.

conspirador, a [konspira'ðor, a] *nm/f* conspirator.

conspirar [konspi'rar] *vi* to conspire.

constancia [kons'tanθja] *nf* (*gen*) constancy; (*certeza*) certainly; **dejar ~ de algo** to put sth on record.

constante [kons'tante] *adj, nf* constant.

constar [kons'tar] *vi* (*evidenciarse*) to be clear *o* evident; ~ **(en)** to appear (in); ~ **de** to consist of; **hacer** ~ to put on record; **me consta que** ... I have evidence that ...; **que conste que lo hice por ti** believe me, I did it for your own good.

constatar [konsta'tar] *vt* (*controlar*) to check; (*observar*) to note.

constelación [konstela'θjon] *nf* constellation.

consternación [konsterna'θjon] *nf* consternation.

constipado, a [konsti'paðo, a] *adj*: **estar** ~ to have a cold ♦ *nm* cold.

constiparse [konsti'parse] *vr* to catch a cold.

constitución [konstitu'θjon] *nf* constitution; **Día de la C~** (*ESP*) Constitution Day (*6th December*).

constitucional [konstituθjo'nal] *adj* constitutional.

constituir [konstitu'ir] *vt* (*formar, componer*) to constitute, make up; (*fundar, erigir, ordenar*) to establish, (*ser*) to be; **~se** *vr* (*POL etc: cuerpo*) to be composed; (: *fundarse*) to be established.

constitutivo, a [konstitu'tißo, a] *adj* constitutive, constituent.

constituya [konsti'tuja] *etc vb V* **constituir**.

constituyente [konstitu'jente] *adj* constituent.

constreñir [konstre'ɲir] *vt* (*obligar*) to compel, oblige; (*restringir*) to restrict.

constriño [kons'triɲo] *etc*, **constriñendo** [konstri'ɲendo] *etc vb V* **constreñir**.

construcción [konstruk'θjon] *nf* construction, building.

constructivo, a [konstruk'tißo, a] *adj* constructive.

constructor, a [konstruk'tor, a] *nm/f* builder.

construir [konstru'ir] *vt* to build, construct.

construyendo [konstru'jendo] *etc vb V* **construir**.

consuelo [kon'swelo] *etc vb V* **consolar** ♦ *nm* consolation, solace.

consuetudinario, a [konswetuði'narjo, a] *adj* customary; **derecho** ~ common law.

cónsul ['konsul] *nm* consul.

consulado [konsu'laðo] *nm* (*sede*) consulate; (*cargo*) consulship.

consulta [kon'sulta] *nf* consultation; (*MED: consultorio*) consulting room; (*INFORM*) enquiry; **horas de** ~ surgery hours; **obra de** ~ reference book.

consultar [konsul'tar] *vt* to consult; ~ **un archivo** (*INFORM*) to interrogate a file.

consultor, a [konsul'tor, a] *nm*: ~ **en dirección de empresas** management consultant.

consultorio [konsul'torjo] *nm* (*MED*) surgery.

consumado, a [konsu'maðo, a] *adj* perfect; (*bribón*) out-and-out.

consumar [konsu'mar] *vt* to complete, carry out; (*crimen*) to commit; (*sentencia*) to carry out.

consumición [konsumi'θjon] *nf* consumption; (*bebida*) drink; (*comida*) food; ~ **mínima** cover charge.

consumido, a [konsu'miðo, a] *adj* (*flaco*) skinny.

consumidor, a [konsumi'ðor, a] *nm/f* consumer.

consumir [konsu'mir] *vt* to consume; **~se** *vr* to be consumed; (*persona*) to waste away.

consumismo [konsu'mismo] *nm* (*COM*) consumerism.

consumo [kon'sumo] *nm* consumption; **bienes de** ~ consumer goods.

contabilice [kontaßi'liθe] *etc vb V* **contabilizar**.

contabilidad [kontaßili'ðað] *nf* accounting, book-keeping; (*profesión*) accountancy; (*COM*): ~ **analítica** variable costing; ~ **de costos** cost accounting; ~ **de doble partida** double-entry book-keeping; ~ **de gestión** management accounting; ~ **por partida simple** single-entry book-keeping.

contabilizar [kontaßili'ðar] *vt* to enter in the accounts.

contable [kon'taßle] *nm/f* bookkeeper; (*licenciado*) accountant; ~ **de costos** (*COM*) cost accountant.

contactar [kontak'tar] *vi*: ~ **con algn** to contact sb.

contacto [kon'takto] *nm* contact; **lentes de** ~ contact lenses; **estar en** ~ **con** to be in touch with.

contado, a [kon'taðo, a] *adj*: **~s** (*escasos*) numbered, scarce, few ♦ *nm*: **al** ~ for cash; **pagar al** ~ to pay (in) cash; **precio al** ~ cash price.

contador [konta'ðor] *nm* (*aparato*) meter; (*AM: contable*) accountant.

contaduría [kontaðu'ria] *nf* accountant's office.

contagiar [konta'xjar] *vt* (*enfermedad*) to pass on, transmit; (*persona*) to infect; **~se** *vr* to become infected.

contagio [kon'taxjo] *nm* infection.
contagioso, a [konta'xjoso, a] *adj* infectious; (*fig*) catching.
contaminación [kontamina'θjon] *nf* (*gen*) contamination; (*del ambiente etc*) pollution.
contaminar [kontami'nar] *vt* (*gen*) to contaminate; (*aire, agua*) to pollute; (*fig*) to taint.
contante [kon'tante] *adj*: **dinero ~ (y sonante)** hard cash.
contar [kon'tar] *vt* (*páginas, dinero*) to count; (*anécdota etc*) to tell ♦ *vi* to count; **~se** *vr* to be counted, figure; **~ con** to rely on, count on; **sin ~** not to mention; **le cuento entre mis amigos** I reckon him among my friends.
contemplación [kontempla'θjon] *nf* contemplation; **no andarse con contemplaciones** not to stand on ceremony.
contemplar [kontem'plar] *vt* to contemplate; (*mirar*) to look at.
contemporáneo, a [kontempo'raneo, a] *adj, nm/f* contemporary.
contemporizar [kontempori'θar] *vi*: **~ con** to keep in with.
contención [konten'θjon] *nf* (*JUR*) suit; **muro de ~** retaining wall.
contencioso, a [konten'θjoso, a] *adj* (*JUR etc*) contentious ♦ *nm* (*POL*) conflict, dispute.
contender [konten'der] *vi* to contend; (*en un concurso*) to compete.
contendiente [konten'djente] *nm/f* contestant.
contendrá [konten'dra] *etc vb* V **contener**.
contenedor [kontene'ðor] *nm* container; (*de escombros*) skip; **~ de (la) basura** wheelie-bin (*BRIT*); **~ de vidrio** bottle bank.
contener [konte'ner] *vt* to contain, hold; (*risa etc*) to hold back, contain; **~se** *vr* to control *o* restrain o.s.
contenga [kon'tenga] *etc vb* V **contener**.
contenido, a [konte'niðo, a] *adj* (*moderado*) restrained; (*risa etc*) suppressed ♦ *nm* contents *pl*, content.
contentar [konten'tar] *vt* (*satisfacer*) to satisfy; (*complacer*) to please; (*COM*) to endorse; **~se** *vr* to be satisfied.
contento, a [kon'tento, a] *adj* contented, content; (*alegre*) pleased; (*feliz*) happy.
contestación [kontesta'θjon] *nf* answer, reply; **~ a la demanda** (*JUR*) defence plea.
contestador [kontesta'ðor] *nm*: **~ automático** answering machine.

contestar [kontes'tar] *vt* to answer (back), reply; (*JUR*) to corroborate, confirm.
contestario, a [kontes'tarjo, a] *adj* anti-establishment, nonconformist.
contexto [kon'teksto] *nm* context.
contienda [kon'tjenda] *nf* contest, struggle.
contiene [kon'tjene] *etc vb* V **contener**.
contigo [kon'tiɣo] *pron* with you.
contiguo, a [kon'tiɣwo, a] *adj* (*de al lado*) next; (*vecino*) adjacent, adjoining.
continental [kontinen'tal] *adj* continental.
continente [konti'nente] *adj, nm* continent.
contingencia [kontin'xenθja] *nf* contingency; (*riesgo*) risk; (*posibilidad*) eventuality.
contingente [kontin'xente] *adj* contingent ♦ *nm* contingent; (*COM*) quota.
continuación [kontinwa'θjon] *nf* continuation; **a ~** then, next.
continuamente [kon'tinwamente] *adv* (*sin interrupción*) continuously; (*a todas horas*) constantly.
continuar [konti'nwar] *vt* to continue, go on with; (*reanudar*) to resume ♦ *vi* to continue, go on; **~ hablando** to continue talking *o* to talk.
continuidad [kontinwi'ðað] *nf* continuity.
continuo, a [kon'tinwo, a] *adj* (*sin interrupción*) continuous; (*acción perseverante*) continual.
contonearse [kontone'arse] *vr* (*hombre*) to swagger; (*mujer*) to swing her hips.
contorno [kon'torno] *nm* outline; (*GEO*) contour; **~s** *nmpl* neighbourhood *sg*, surrounding area *sg*.
contorsión [kontor'sjon] *nf* contortion.
contra ['kontra] *prep* against; (*COM: giro*) on ♦ *adv* against ♦ *adj, nm/f* (*POL fam*) counter-revolutionary ♦ *nm con* ♦ *nf*: **la C~ (nicaragüense)** the Contras *pl*.
contraalmirante [kontraalmi'rante] *nm* rear admiral.
contraataque [kontraa'take] *nm* counterattack.
contrabajo [kontra'βaxo] *nm* double bass.
contrabandista [kontraβan'dista] *nm/f* smuggler.
contrabando [kontra'βando] *nm* (*acción*) smuggling; (*mercancías*) contraband; **~ de armas** gun-running.
contracción [kontrak'θjon] *nf* contraction.
contrachapado [kontratʃa'paðo] *nm* plywood.
contracorriente [kontrako'rrjente] *nf* cross-current.
contradecir [kontraðe'θir] *vt* to contradict.
contradicción [kontraðik'θjon] *nf*

contradiction; **espíritu de** ~
contrariness.
contradicho [kontra'ðitʃo] pp de
contradecir.
contradiciendo [kontraði'θjendo] etc vb V
contradecir.
contradictorio, a [kontraðik'torjo, a] adj
contradictory.
contradiga [kontra'ðiɣa] etc, **contradije**
[kontra'ðixe], **contradirá** [kontraði'ra] etc
vb V **contradecir.**
contraer [kontra'er] vt to contract; (hábito)
to acquire; (limitar) to restrict; ~se vr to
contract; (limitarse) to limit o.s.
contraespionage [kontraespjo'naxe] nm
counter-espionage.
contrafuerte [kontra'fwerte] nm (ARQ)
buttress.
contragolpe [kontra'ɣolpe] nm backlash.
contrahaga [kontra'aɣa] etc, **contraharé**
[kontraa're] etc vb V **contrahacer.**
contrahecho, a [kontra'etʃo, a] pp de
contrahacer ♦ adj fake; (ANAT)
hunchbacked.
contrahice [kontra'iθe] etc vb V
contrahacer.
contraiga [kon'traiɣa] etc vb V **contraer.**
contraindicaciones [kontraindika'θjones]
nfpl (MED) contraindications.
contraje [kon'traxe] etc vb V **contraer.**
contralor [kontra'lor] nm (AM) government
accounting inspector.
contraluz [kontra'luθ] nf (FOTO etc) back
lighting; **a** ~ against the light.
contramaestre [kontrama'estre] nm
foreman.
contraofensiva [kontraofen'siβa] nf
counteroffensive.
contraorden [kontra'orðen] nf counter-
order, countermand.
contrapartida [kontrapar'tiða] nf (COM)
balancing entry; **como** ~ **(de)** in return
(for), as o in compensation (for).
contrapelo [kontra'pelo]: **a** ~ adv the
wrong way.
contrapesar [kontrape'sar] vt to
counterbalance; (fig) to offset.
contrapeso [kontra'peso] nm
counterweight; (fig) counterbalance;
(COM) makeweight.
contrapondré [kontrapon'dre] etc vb V
contraponer.
contraponer [kontrapo'ner] vt (cotejar) to
compare; (oponer) to oppose.
contraponga [kontra'ponga] etc vb V
contraponer.
contraportada [kontrapor'taða] nf (de
revista) back page.

contraproducente [kontraproðu'θente] adj
counterproductive.
contrapuesto [kontra'pwesto] pp de
contraponer.
contrapunto [kontra'punto] nm
counterpoint.
contrapuse [kontra'puse] etc vb V
contraponer.
contrariar [kontra'rjar] vt (oponerse) to
oppose; (poner obstáculo) to impede;
(enfadar) to vex.
contrariedad [kontrarje'ðað] nf (oposición)
opposition; (obstáculo) obstacle, setback;
(disgusto) vexation, annoyance.
contrario, a [kon'trarjo, a] adj contrary;
(persona) opposed; (sentido, lado)
opposite ♦ nm/f enemy, adversary;
(DEPORTE) opponent; **al** ~, **por el** ~ on the
contrary; **de lo** ~ otherwise.
Contrarreforma [kontrarre'forma] nf
Counter-Reformation.
contrarreloj [kontrarre'lo(x)] nf (tb: **prueba**
~) time trial.
contrarrestar [kontrarres'tar] vt to
counteract.
contrarrevolución [kontrarreβolu'θjon] nf
counter-revolution.
contrasentido [kontrasen'tiðo] nm
contradiction; **es un** ~ **que él** ... it
doesn't make sense for him to ... .
contraseña [kontra'seɲa] nf countersign;
(frase) password.
contrastar [kontras'tar] vt to resist ♦ vi to
contrast.
contraste [kon'traste] nm contrast.
contrata [kon'trata] nf (JUR) written
contract; (empleo) hiring.
contratar [kontra'tar] vt (firmar un acuerdo
para) to contract for; (empleados,
obreros) to hire, engage; (DEPORTE) to
sign up; ~se vr to sign on.
contratiempo [kontra'tjempo] nm (revés)
setback; (accidente) mishap; **a** ~ (MUS)
off-beat.
contratista [kontra'tista] nm/f contractor.
contrato [kon'trato] nm contract; ~ **de
compraventa** contract of sale; ~ **a precio
fijo** fixed-price contract; ~ **a término**
forward contract; ~ **de trabajo** contract
of employment o service.
contravalor [kontraβa'lor] nm exchange
value.
contravención [kontraβen'θjon] nf
contravention, violation.
contravendré [kontraβen'dre] etc,
contravenga [kontra'βenga] etc vb V
contravenir.
contravenir [kontraβe'nir] vi: ~ **a** to

contravene, violate.

contraventana [kontraβen'tana] *nf* shutter.

contraviene [kontra'βjene] *etc*, **contraviniendo** [kontraβi'njendo] *etc vb* V **contravenir**.

contrayendo [kontra'jendo] *vb* V **contraer**.

contribución [kontriβu'θjon] *nf* (*municipal etc*) tax; (*ayuda*) contribution; **exento de contribuciones** tax-free.

contribuir [kontriβu'ir] *vt, vi* to contribute; (*COM*) to pay (in taxes).

contribuyendo [kontriβu'jendo] *etc vb* V **contribuir**.

contribuyente [kontriβu'jente] *nm/f* (*COM*) taxpayer; (*que ayuda*) contributor.

contrincante [kontrin'kante] *nm* opponent, rival.

control [kon'trol] *nm* control; (*inspección*) inspection, check; (*COM*): ~ **de calidad** quality control; ~ **de cambios** exchange control; ~ **de costos** cost control; ~ **de créditos** credit control; ~ **de existencias** stock control; ~ **de precios** price control.

controlador, a [kontrola'ðor, a] *nm/f* controller; ~ **aéreo** air-traffic controller.

controlar [kontro'lar] *vt* to control; to inspect, check; (*COM*) to audit.

controversia [kontro'βersja] *nf* controversy.

contubernio [kontu'βernjo] *nm* ring, conspiracy.

contumaz [kontu'maθ] *adj* obstinate, stubbornly disobedient.

contundente [kontun'dente] *adj* (*prueba*) conclusive; (*fig: argumento*) convincing; **instrumento** ~ blunt instrument.

contusión [kontu'sjon] *nf* bruise.

contuve [kon'tuβe] *etc vb* V **contener**.

convalecencia [kombale'θenθja] *nf* convalescence.

convalecer [kombale'θer] *vi* to convalesce, get better.

convaleciente [kombale'θjente] *adj, nm/f* convalescent.

convalezca [komba'leθka] *etc vb* V **convalecer**.

convalidar [kombali'ðar] *vt* (*título*) to recognize.

convencer [komben'θer] *vt* to convince; (*persuadir*) to persuade.

convencimiento [kombenθi'mjento] *nm* (*acción*) convincing; (*persuasión*) persuasion; (*certidumbre*) conviction; **tener el** ~ **de que** ... to be convinced that ... .

convención [komben'θjon] *nf* convention.

convencional [kombenθjo'nal] *adj* conventional.

convendré [komben'dre] *etc*, **convenga** [kom'benga] *etc vb* V **convenir**.

conveniencia [kombe'njenθja] *nf* suitability; (*conformidad*) agreement; (*utilidad, provecho*) usefulness; ~**s** *nfpl* conventions; (*COM*) property *sg*; **ser de la** ~ **de algn** to suit sb.

conveniente [kombe'njente] *adj* suitable; (*útil*) useful; (*correcto*) fit, proper; (*aconsejable*) advisable.

convenio [kom'benjo] *nm* agreement, treaty; ~ **de nivel crítico** threshold agreement.

convenir [kombe'nir] *vi* (*estar de acuerdo*) to agree; (*ser conveniente*) to suit, be suitable; **"sueldo a** ~**"** "salary to be agreed"; **conviene recordar que** ... it should be remembered that ....

convento [kom'bento] *nm* monastery; (*de monjas*) convent.

convenza [kom'benθa] *etc vb* V **convencer**.

convergencia [komber'xenθja] *nf* convergence.

converger [komber'xer], **convergir** [komber'xir] *vi* to converge; **sus esfuerzos convergen a un fin común** their efforts are directed towards the same objective.

converja [kom'berxa] *etc vb* V **converger**, **convergir**.

conversación [kombersa'θjon] *nf* conversation.

conversar [komber'sar] *vi* to talk, converse.

conversión [komber'sjon] *nf* conversion.

converso, a [kom'berso, a] *nm/f* convert.

convertir [komber'tir] *vt* to convert; (*transformar*) to transform, turn; (*COM*) to (ex)change; ~**se** *vr* (*REL*) to convert.

convexo, a [kom'bekso, a] *adj* convex.

convicción [kombik'θjon] *nf* conviction.

convicto , a [kom'bikto, a] *adj* convicted; (*condenado*) condemned.

convidado, a [kombi'ðaðo, a] *nm/f* guest.

convidar [kombi'ðar] *vt* to invite.

conviene [kom'bjene] *etc vb* V **convenir**.

convierta [kom'bjerta] *etc vb* V **convertir**.

convincente [kombin'θente] *adj* convincing.

conviniendo [kombi'njendo] *etc vb* V **convenir**.

convirtiendo [kombir'tjendo] *etc vb* V **convertir**.

convite [kom'bite] *nm* invitation; (*banquete*) banquet.

convivencia [kombi'ßenθja] *nf* coexistence, living together.
convivir [kombi'ßir] *vi* to live together; (*POL*) to coexist.
convocar [kombo'kar] *vt* to summon, call (together).
convocatoria [komboka'torja] *nf* summons *sg*; (*anuncio*) notice of meeting; (*ESCOL*) examination session.
convoque [kom'boke] *etc vb V* **convocar**.
convoy [kom'boj] *nm* (*FERRO*) train.
convulsión [kombul'sjon] *nf* convulsion; (*POL etc*) upheaval.
conyugal [konju'ʁal] *adj* conjugal; **vida ~** married life.
cónyuge [ˈkonyuxe] *nm/f* spouse, partner.
coña [ˈkoɲa] *nf*: **tomar algo a ~** (*fam!*) to take sth as a joke.
coñac, *pl* **coñacs** [ˈkoɲa(k), ˈkoɲas] *nm* cognac, brandy.
coñazo [koˈɲaθo] *nm* (*fam*) pain; **dar el ~** to be a real pain.
coño [ˈkoɲo] (*fam!*) *nm* cunt (*!*); (*AM pey*) Spaniard ♦ *excl* (*enfado*) shit (*!*); (*sorpresa*) bloody hell (*!*); **¡qué ~!** what a pain in the arse (*!*).
cooperación [koopera'θjon] *nf* cooperation.
cooperar [koope'rar] *vi* to cooperate.
cooperativo, a [koopera'tißo, a] *adj* cooperative ♦ *nf* cooperative.
coordenada [koorðe'naða] *nf* (*MAT*) coordinate; (*fig*): **~s** *nfpl* guidelines, framework *sg*.
coordinación [koorðina'θjon] *nf* coordination.
coordinador, a [koorðina'ðor, a] *nm/f* coordinator ♦ *nf* coordinating committee.
coordinar [koorði'nar] *vt* to coordinate.
copa [ˈkopa] *nf* (*tb DEPORTE*) cup; (*vaso*) glass; (*de árbol*) top; (*de sombrero*) crown; **~s** *nfpl* (*NAIPES*) *one of the suits in the Spanish card deck*; (**tomar una**) **~** (to have a) drink; **ir de ~s** to go out for a drink; *V tb* **Baraja Española**.
copar [ko'par] *vt* (*puestos*) to monopolize.
coparticipación [kopartiθipa'θjon] *nf* (*COM*) co-ownership.
COPE *nf abr* (= *Cadena de Ondas Populares Españolas*) *Spanish radio network*.
Copenhague [kope'naʁe] Copenhagen.
copete [ko'pete] *nm* tuft (of hair); **de alto ~** aristocratic, upper-crust (*fam*).
copia [ˈkopja] *nf* copy; (*ARTE*) replica; (*COM etc*) duplicate; (*INFORM*): **~ impresa** hard copy; **~ de respaldo** *o* **de seguridad** backup copy; **hacer ~ de seguridad** to

back up; **~ de trabajo** working copy; **~ vaciada** dump.
copiadora [kopja'ðora] *nf* photocopier; **~ al alcohol** spirit duplicator.
copiar [ko'pjar] *vt* to copy; **~ al pie de la letra** to copy word for word.
copiloto [kopi'loto] *nm* (*AVIAT*) co-pilot; (*AUTO*) co-driver.
copioso, a [ko'pjoso, a] *adj* copious, plentiful.
copita [ko'pita] *nf* (small) glass; (*GOLF*) tee.
copla [ˈkopla] *nf* verse; (*canción*) (popular) song.
copo [ˈkopo] *nm*: **~s de maíz** cornflakes; **~ de nieve** snowflake.
coprocesador [koproθesa'ðor] *nm* (*INFORM*) co-processor.
coproducción [koproðuk'θjon] *nf* (*CINE etc*) joint production.
copropietarios [kopropje'tarjos] *nmpl* (*COM*) joint owners.
cópula [ˈkopula] *nf* copulation.
copular [kopu'lar] *vi* to copulate.
coqueta [ko'keta] *adj* flirtatious, coquettish ♦ *nf* (*mujer*) flirt.
coquetear [kokete'ar] *vi* to flirt.
coraje [ko'raxe] *nm* courage; (*ánimo*) spirit; (*ira*) anger.
coral [ko'ral] *adj* choral ♦ *nf* choir ♦ *nm* (*ZOOL*) coral.
Corán [ko'ran] *nm*: **el ~** the Koran.
coraza [ko'raθa] *nf* (*armadura*) armour; (*blindaje*) armour-plating.
corazón [kora'θon] *nm* heart; (*BOT*) core; **corazones** *nmpl* (*NAIPES*) hearts; **de buen ~** kind-hearted; **de todo ~** wholeheartedly; **estar mal del ~** to have heart trouble.
corazonada [koraθo'naða] *nf* impulse; (*presentimiento*) presentiment, hunch.
corbata [kor'ßata] *nf* tie.
corbeta [kor'ßeta] *nf* corvette.
Córcega [ˈkorθeʁa] *nf* Corsica.
corcel [kor'θel] *nm* steed.
corchea [kor'tʃea] *nf* quaver.
corchete [kor'tʃete] *nm* catch, clasp; **~s** *nmpl* (*TIP*) square brackets.
corcho [ˈkortʃo] *nm* cork; (*PESCA*) float.
corcovado, a [korko'ßaðo, a] *adj* hunchbacked ♦ *nm/f* hunchback.
cordel [kor'ðel] *nm* cord, line.
cordero [kor'ðero] *nm* lamb; (*piel*) lambskin.
cordial [kor'ðjal] *adj* cordial ♦ *nm* cordial, tonic.
cordialidad [korðjali'ðað] *nf* warmth, cordiality.

cordillera [korði'ʎera] *nf* range (of mountains).

Córdoba ['korðoßa] *nf* Cordova.

cordobés, esa [korðo'ßes, esa] *adj, nm/f* Cordovan.

cordón [kor'ðon] *nm* (*cuerda*) cord, string; (*de zapatos*) lace; (*ELEC*) flex, wire (*US*); (*MIL etc*) cordon.

cordura [kor'ðura] *nf* (*MED*) sanity; (*fig*) good sense.

Corea [ko'rea] *nf* Korea; ~ **del Norte/Sur** North/South Korea.

coreano, a [kore'ano, a] *adj, nm/f* Korean.

corear [kore'ar] *vt* to chorus.

coreografía [koreoɣra'fia] *nf* choreography.

corista [ko'rista] *nf* (*TEAT etc*) chorus girl.

cornada [kor'naða] *nf* (*TAUR etc*) butt, goring.

córner, pl córners ['korner, 'korners] *nm* corner (kick).

corneta [kor'neta] *nf* bugle.

cornisa [kor'nisa] *nf* cornice.

Cornualles [kor'nwaʎes] *nm* Cornwall.

cornudo, a [kor'nuðo, a] *adj* (*ZOOL*) horned; (*marido*) cuckolded.

coro ['koro] *nm* chorus; (*conjunto de cantores*) choir.

corolario [koro'larjo] *nm* corollary.

corona [ko'rona] *nf* crown; (*de flores*) garland.

coronación [korona'θjon] *nf* coronation.

coronar [koro'nar] *vt* to crown.

coronel [koro'nel] *nm* colonel.

coronilla [koro'niʎa] *nf* (*ANAT*) crown (of the head); **estar hasta la ~ (de)** to be utterly fed up (with).

corpiño [korpiɲo] *nm* bodice; (*AM: sostén*) bra.

corporación [korpora'θjon] *nf* corporation.

corporal [korpo'ral] *adj* corporal, bodily.

corporativo, a [korpora'tißo, a] *adj* corporate.

corpulento, a [korpu'lento, a] *adj* (*persona*) well-built.

corral [ko'rral] *nm* (*patio*) farmyard; (*AGR: de aves*) poultry yard; (*redil*) pen.

correa [ko'rrea] *nf* strap; (*cinturón*) belt; (*de perro*) lead, leash; ~ **transportadora** conveyor belt.

correaje [korre'axe] *nm* (*AGR*) harness.

corrección [korrek'θjon] *nf* correction; (*reprensión*) rebuke; (*cortesía*) good manners; (*INFORM*): ~ **por líneas** line editing; ~ **en pantalla** screen editing; ~ **(de pruebas)** (*TIP*) proofreading.

correccional [korrekθjo'nal] *nm* reformatory.

correcto, a [ko'rrekto, a] *adj* correct; (*persona*) well-mannered.

corrector, a [korrek'tor, a] *nm/f*: ~ **de pruebas** proofreader.

corredera [korre'ðera] *nf*: **puerta de ~** sliding door.

corredizo, a [korre'ðiθo, a] *adj* (*puerta etc*) sliding; (*nudo*) running.

corredor, a [korre'ðor, a] *adj* running; (*rápido*) fast ♦ *nm/f* (*DEPORTE*) runner ♦ *nm* (*pasillo*) corridor; (*balcón corrido*) gallery; (*COM*) agent, broker; (*pasillo*) corridor, passage; ~ **de bienes raíces** real-estate broker; ~ **de bolsa** stockbroker; ~ **de seguros** insurance broker.

corregir [korre'xir] *vt* (*error*) to correct; (*amonestar, reprender*) to rebuke, reprimand; ~**se** *vr* to reform.

correo [ko'rreo] *nm* post, mail; (*persona*) courier; **C~s** *nmpl* Post Office *sg*; ~ **aéreo** airmail; ~ **certificado** registered mail; ~ **electrónico** E-mail, electronic mail; ~ **urgente** special delivery; **a vuelta de ~** by return (of post).

correr [ko'rrer] *vt* to run; (*viajar*) to cover, travel; (*riesgo*) to run; (*aventura*) to have; (*cortinas*) to draw; (*cerrojo*) to shoot ♦ *vi* to run; (*líquido*) to run, flow; (*rumor*) to go round; ~**se** *vr* to slide, move; (*colores*) to run; (*fam: tener orgasmo*) to come; **echar a ~** to break into a run; ~ **con los gastos** to pay the expenses; **eso corre de mi cuenta** I'll take care of that.

correspondencia [korrespon'denθja] *nf* correspondence; (*FERRO*) connection; (*reciprocidad*) return; ~ **directa** (*COM*) direct mail.

corresponder [korrespon'der] *vi* to correspond; (*convenir*) to be suitable; (*pertenecer*) to belong; (*tocar*) to concern; (*favor*) to repay; ~**se** *vr* (*por escrito*) to correspond; (*amarse*) to love one another; **"a quien corresponda"** "to whom it may concern".

correspondiente [korrespon'djente] *adj* corresponding; (*respectivo*) respective.

corresponsal [korrespon'sal] *nm/f* (newspaper) correspondent; (*COM*) agent.

corretaje [korre'taxe] *nm* (*COM*) brokerage.

corretear [korrete'ar] *vi* to loiter.

corrido, a [ko'rriðo, a] *adj* (*avergonzado*) abashed; (*fluido*) fluent ♦ *nf* run, dash; (*de toros*) bullfight; **de ~** fluently; **3 noches corridas** 3 nights running; **un kilo ~** a good kilo.

corriente [ko'rrjente] *adj* (*agua*) running;

(fig) flowing; *(dinero, cuenta etc)* current; *(común)* ordinary, normal ♦ *nf* current; *(fig: tendencia)* course ♦ *nm* current month; ~ *f* **de aire** draught; ~ **eléctrica** electric current; **las ~s modernas del arte** modern trends in art; **estar al** ~ **de** to be informed about.

corrigiendo [korri'xjendo] *etc vb V* **corregir.**

corrija [ko'rrixa] *etc vb V* **corregir.**

corrillo [ko'rriʎo] *nm* ring, circle (of people); *(fig)* clique.

corro ['korro] *nm* ring, circle (of people); *(baile)* ring-a-ring-a-roses; **la gente hizo** ~ the people formed a ring.

corroborar [korroßo'rar] *vt* to corroborate.

corroer [korro'er] *vt (tb fig)* to corrode, eat away; *(GEO)* to erode.

corromper [korrom'per] *vt (madera)* to rot; *(fig)* to corrupt.

corrompido, a [korrom'piðo, a] *adj* corrupt.

corrosivo, a [korro'sißo, a] *adj* corrosive.

corroyendo [korro'jendo] *etc vb V* **corroer.**

corrupción [korrup'θjon] *nf* rot, decay; *(fig)* corruption.

corrupto, a [ko'rrupto, a] *adj* corrupt.

corsario [kor'sarjo] *nm* privateer, corsair.

corsé [kor'se] *nm* corset.

corso, a ['korso, a] *adj, nm/f* Corsican.

cortacésped [korta'θespeð] *nm* lawn mower.

cortado, a [kor'taðo, a] *adj (con cuchillo)* cut; *(leche)* sour; *(confuso)* confused; *(desconcertado)* embarrassed; *(tímido)* shy ♦ *nm* white coffee (with a little milk).

cortadora [korta'ðora] *nf* cutter, slicer.

cortadura [korta'ðura] *nf* cut.

cortante [kor'tante] *adj (viento)* biting; *(frío)* bitter.

cortapisa [korta'pisa] *nf (restricción)* restriction; *(traba)* snag.

cortar [kor'tar] *vt* to cut; *(suministro)* to cut off; *(un pasaje)* to cut out; *(comunicación, teléfono)* to cut off ♦ *vi* to cut; *(AM TELEC)* to hang up; **~se** *vr (turbarse)* to become embarrassed; *(leche)* to turn, curdle; ~ **por lo sano** to settle things once and for all; **~se el pelo** to have one's hair cut; **se cortó la línea** *o* **el teléfono** I got cut off.

cortauñas [korta'uɲas] *nm inv* nail clippers *pl.*

corte ['korte] *nm* cut, cutting; *(filo)* edge; *(de tela)* piece, length; *(COSTURA)* tailoring ♦ *nf (real)* (royal) court; ~ **y confección** dressmaking; ~ **de corriente** *o* **luz** power cut; **me da** ~ **pedírselo** I'm

embarrassed to ask him for it; **¡qué** ~ **le di!** I left him with no comeback!; **C~ Internacional de Justicia** International Court of Justice; **las C~s** the Spanish Parliament *sg*; **hacer la** ~ **a** to woo, court.

The Spanish Parliament, **Las Cortes (Españolas),** *has a Lower and an Upper Chamber, the* **Congreso de los Diputados** *and the* **Senado** *respectively. Members of Parliament are called* **diputados** *and are elected in national elections by proportional representation. Some Senate members,* **senadores,** *are chosen by being voted in during national elections and others are appointed by the regional parliaments.*

---

cortedad [korte'ðað] *nf* shortness; *(fig)* bashfulness, timidity.

cortejar [korte'xar] *vt* to court.

cortejo [kor'texo] *nm* entourage; ~ **fúnebre** funeral procession, cortège.

cortés [kor'tes] *adj* courteous, polite.

cortesano, a [korte'sano, a] *adj* courtly.

cortesía [korte'sia] *nf* courtesy.

corteza [kor'teθa] *nf (de árbol)* bark; *(de pan)* crust; *(de fruta)* peel, skin; *(de queso)* rind.

cortijo [kor'tixo] *nm* farmhouse.

cortina [kor'tina] *nf* curtain; ~ **de humo** smoke screen.

corto, a ['korto, a] *adj (breve)* short; *(tímido)* bashful; ~ **de luces** not very bright; ~ **de oído** hard of hearing; ~ **de vista** short-sighted; **estar** ~ **de fondos** to be short of funds.

cortocircuito [kortoθir'kwito] *nm* short-circuit.

cortometraje [kortome'traxe] *nm (CINE)* short.

Coruña [ko'ruɲa] *nf:* **La** ~ Corunna.

coruñés, esa [koru'ɲes, esa] *adj* of *o* from Corunna ♦ *nm/f* native *o* inhabitant of Corunna.

corvo, a ['korßo, a] *adj* curved; *(nariz)* hooked ♦ *nf* back of knee.

cosa ['kosa] *nf* thing; *(asunto)* affair; ~ **de** about; **eso es** ~ **mía** that's my business; **es poca** ~ it's not important; **¡qué** ~ **más rara!** how strange; **en** ~ **de 10 minutos** in about 10 minutes.

cosaco, a [ko'sako, a] *adj, nm/f* Cossack.

coscorrón [kosko'rron] *nm* bump on the head.

cosecha [ko'setʃa] *nf (AGR)* harvest; *(acto)* harvesting; *(de vino)* vintage; *(producción)* yield.

cosechadora [kosetʃa'ðora] *nf* combine harvester.

cosechar [kose'tʃar] *vt* to harvest, gather (in).

coser [ko'ser] *vt* to sew; (*MED*) to stitch (up).

cosido [ko'siðo] *nm* sewing.

cosmético, a [kos'metiko, a] *adj, nm* cosmetic ♦ *nf* cosmetics *pl*.

cosmopolita [kosmopo'lita] *adj* cosmopolitan.

cosmos ['kosmos] *nm* cosmos.

coso ['koso] *nm* bullring.

cosquillas [kos'kiʎas] *nfpl*: **hacer** ~ to tickle; **tener** ~ to be ticklish.

cosquilleo [koski'ʎeo] *nm* tickling (sensation).

costa ['kosta] *nf* (*GEO*) coast; **C~ Brava** Costa Brava; **C~ Cantábrica** Cantabrian Coast; **C~ de Marfil** Ivory Coast; **C~ del Sol** Costa del Sol; **a** ~ (*COM*) at cost; **a** ~ **de** at the expense of; **a toda** ~ at any price.

costado [kos'taðo] *nm* side; **de** ~ (*dormir*) on one's side; **español por los 4 ~s** Spanish through and through.

costal [kos'tal] *nm* sack.

costalada [kosta'laða] *nf* bad fall.

costanera [kosta'nera] *nf* (*AM*) (seaside) promenade.

costar [kos'tar] *vt* (*valer*) to cost; **me cuesta hablarle** I find it hard to talk to him; **¿cuánto cuesta?** how much does it cost?

Costa Rica [kosta'rika] *nf* Costa Rica.

costarricense [kostarri'θense], **costarriqueño, a** [kostarri'keɲo, a] *adj, nm/f* Costa Rican.

coste ['koste] *nm* (*COM*): ~ **promedio** average cost; ~**s fijos** fixed costs; *V tb* **costo.**

costear [koste'ar] *vt* to pay for; (*COM etc*) to finance; (*NAUT*) to sail along the coast of; ~**se** *vr* (*negocio*) to pay for itself, cover its costs.

costeño, a [kos'teɲo, a] *adj* coastal.

costero, a [kos'tero, a] *adj* coastal, coast *cpd*.

costilla [kos'tiʎa] *nf* rib; (*CULIN*) cutlet.

costo ['kosto] *nm* cost, price; ~ **directo** direct cost; ~ **de expedición** shipping charges; ~ **de sustitución** replacement cost; ~ **unitario** unit cost; ~ **de la vida** cost of living.

costoso, a [kos'toso, a] *adj* costly, expensive.

costra ['kostra] *nf* (*corteza*) crust; (*MED*) scab.

costumbre [kos'tumbre] *nf* custom, habit;

como de ~ as usual.

costura [kos'tura] *nf* sewing, needlework; (*confección*) dressmaking; (*zurcido*) seam.

costurera [kostu'rera] *nf* dressmaker.

costurero [kostu'rero] *nm* sewing box *o* case.

cota ['kota] *nf* (*GEO*) height above sea level; (*fig*) height.

cotarro [ko'tarro] *nm*: **dirigir el** ~ (*fam*) to rule the roost.

cotejar [kote'xar] *vt* to compare.

cotejo [ko'texo] *nm* comparison.

cotice [ko'tiθe] *etc vb V* **cotizar.**

cotidiano, a [koti'ðjano, a] *adj* daily, day to day.

cotilla [ko'tiʎa] *nf* busybody, gossip.

cotillear [kotiʎe'ar] *vi* to gossip.

cotilleo [koti'ʎeo] *nm* gossip(ing).

cotización [kotiθa'θjon] *nf* (*COM*) quotation, price; (*de club*) dues *pl*.

cotizado, a [koti'θaðo, a] *adj* (*fig*) highly-prized.

cotizar [koti'θar] *vt* (*COM*) to quote, price; ~**se** *vr* (*fig*) to be highly prized; ~**se a** to sell at, fetch; (*BOLSA*) to stand at, be quoted at.

coto ['koto] *nm* (*terreno cercado*) enclosure; (*de caza*) reserve; (*COM*) price-fixing agreement; **poner** ~ **a** to put a stop to.

cotorra [ko'torra] *nf* (*ZOOL: loro*) parrot; (*fam: persona*) windbag.

COU [kou] *nm abr* (*ESP.* = *Curso de Orientación Universitario*) *one year course leading to final school leaving certificate and university entrance examinations*; *V tb* **sistema educativo.**

coyote [ko'jote] *nm* coyote, prairie wolf.

coyuntura [kojun'tura] *nf* (*ANAT*) joint; (*fig*) juncture, occasion; **esperar una** ~ **favorable** to await a favourable moment.

coz [koθ] *nf* kick.

CP *nm abr* (= *computador personal*) PC.

C.P. *abr* (*ESP*) = *Caja Postal*.

C.P.A. *nf abr* (= *Caja Postal de Ahorros*) Post Office Savings Bank.

CP/M *nm abr* (= *Programa de control para microprocesadores*) CP/M.

CPN *nm abr* (*ESP*) = *Cuerpo de la Policía Nacional*.

cps *abr* (= *caracteres por segundo*) c.p.s.

crac [krak] *nm* (*ECON*) crash.

cráneo ['kraneo] *nm* skull, cranium.

crápula ['krapula] *nf* drunkenness.

cráter ['krater] *nm* crater.

creación [krea'θjon] *nf* creation.

creador, a [krea'ðor, a] *adj* creative ♦ *nm/f* creator.

crear [kre'ar] vt to create, make; (originar) to originate; (INFORM: archivo) to create; ~**se** vr (comité etc) to be set up.
creativo, a [krea'tiβo, a] adj creative.
crecer [kre'θer] vi to grow; (precio) to rise; ~**se** vr (engreírse) to get cocky.
creces ['kreθes]: **con** ~ adv amply, fully.
crecido, a [kre'θiðo, a] adj (persona, planta) full-grown; (cantidad) large ♦ nf (de río) spate, flood.
creciente [kre'θjente] adj growing; (cantidad) increasing; (luna) crescent ♦ nm crescent.
crecimiento [kreθi'mjento] nm growth; (aumento) increase; (COM) rise.
credenciales [kreðen'θjales] nfpl credentials.
crédito ['kreðito] nm credit; **a** ~ on credit; **dar** ~ **a** to believe (in); ~ **al consumidor** consumer credit; ~ **rotativo** o **renovable** revolving credit.
credo ['kreðo] nm creed.
crédulo, a ['kreðulo, a] adj credulous.
creencia [kre'enθja] nf belief.
creer [kre'er] vt, vi to think, believe; (considerar) to think, consider; ~**se** vr to believe o.s. (to be); ~ **en** to believe in; **¡ya lo creo!** I should think so!
creíble [kre'iβle] adj credible, believable.
creído, a [kre'iðo, a] adj (engreído) conceited.
crema ['krema] adj inv cream (coloured) ♦ nf cream; (natillas) custard; **la** ~ **de la sociedad** the cream of society.
cremallera [krema'ʎera] nf zip (fastener) (BRIT), zipper (US).
crematorio [krema'torjo] nm crematorium (BRIT), crematory (US).
cremoso, a [kre'moso, a] adj creamy.
crepitar [krepi'tar] vi (fuego) to crackle.
crepúsculo [kre'puskulo] nm twilight, dusk.
crespo, a ['krespo, a] adj (pelo) curly.
crespón [kres'pon] nm crêpe.
cresta ['kresta] nf (GEO, ZOOL) crest.
Creta ['kreta] nf Crete.
cretino, a [kre'tino, a] adj cretinous ♦ nm/f cretin.
creyendo [kre'jendo] etc vb V **creer**.
creyente [kre'jente] nm/f believer.
crezca ['kreθka] etc vb V **crecer**.
cría ['kria] etc vb V **criar** ♦ nf V **crío, a**.
criada [kri'aða] nf V **criado, a**.
criadero [kria'ðero] nm nursery; (ZOOL) breeding place.
criadillas [kria'ðiʎas] nfpl (CULIN) bull's (o sheep's) testicles.
criado, a [kri'aðo, a] nm servant ♦ nf servant, maid.
criador [kria'ðor] nm breeder.
crianza [kri'anθa] nf rearing, breeding; (fig) breeding; (MED) lactation.
criar [kri'ar] vt (amamantar) to suckle, feed; (educar) to bring up; (producir) to grow, produce; (animales) to breed; ~**se** vr to grow (up); ~ **cuervos** to nourish a viper in one's bosom; **Dios los cría y ellos se juntan** birds of a feather flock together.
criatura [kria'tura] nf creature; (niño) baby, (small) child.
criba ['kriβa] nf sieve.
cribar [kri'βar] vt to sieve.
crimen ['krimen] nm crime; ~ **pasional** crime of passion.
criminal [krimi'nal] adj, nm/f criminal.
crin [krin] nf (tb: ~**es**) mane.
crío, a ['krio, a] nm/f (fam: chico) kid ♦ nf (de animales) rearing, breeding; (animal) young.
criollo, a [kri'oʎo, a] adj (gen) Creole; (AM) native (to America), national ♦ nm/f (gen) Creole; (AM) native American.
cripta ['kripta] nf crypt.
crisis ['krisis] nf inv crisis; ~ **nerviosa** nervous breakdown.
crisma ['krisma] nf: **romperle la** ~ **a algn** (fam) to knock sb's block off.
crisol [kri'sol] nm (TEC) crucible; (fig) melting pot.
crispación [krispa'θjon] nf tension.
crispar [kris'par] vt (músculo) to cause to contract; (nervios) to set on edge.
cristal [kris'tal] nm crystal; (de ventana) glass, pane; (lente) lens; **de** ~ glass cpd; ~ **ahumado/tallado** smoked/cut glass.
cristalería [kristale'ria] nf (tienda) glassware shop; (objetos) glassware.
cristalice [krista'liθe] etc vb V **cristalizar**.
cristalino, a [krista'lino, a] adj crystalline; (fig) clear ♦ nm lens of the eye.
cristalizar [kristali'θar] vt, vi to crystallize.
cristiandad [kristjan'daθ] nf,
cristianismo [kristja'nismo] nm Christianity.
cristiano, a [kris'tjano, a] adj, nm/f Christian; **hablar en** ~ to speak proper Spanish; (fig) to speak clearly.
Cristo ['kristo] nm (dios) Christ; (crucifijo) crucifix.
Cristóbal [kris'toβal] nm: ~ **Colón** Christopher Columbus.
criterio [kri'terjo] nm criterion; (juicio) judgement; (enfoque) attitude, approach; (punto de vista) view, opinion; ~ **de clasificación** (INFORM) sort criterion.
criticar [kriti'kar] vt to criticize.

crítico, a ['kritiko, a] *adj* critical ♦ *nm* critic ♦ *nf* criticism; (*TEAT etc*) review, notice; **la crítica** the critics *pl*.

critique [kri'tike] *etc vb V* **criticar**.

Croacia [kro'aθja] *nf* Croatia.

croar [kro'ar] *vi* to croak.

croata [kro'ata] *adj, nm/f* Croat(ian) ♦ *nm* (*LING*) Croat(ian).

croissan(t) [krwa'san] *nm* croissant.

crol ['krol] *nm* crawl.

cromado [kro'maðo] *nm* chromium plating, chrome.

cromo ['kromo] *nm* chrome; (*TIP*) coloured print.

cromosoma [kromo'soma] *nm* chromosome.

crónico, a ['kroniko, a] *adj* chronic ♦ *nf* chronicle, account; (*de periódico*) feature, article.

cronología [kronolo'xia] *nf* chronology.

cronológico, a [krono'loxiko, a] *adj* chronological.

cronometraje [kronome'traxe] *nm* timing.

cronometrar [kronome'trar] *vt* to time.

cronómetro [kro'nometro] *nm* (*DEPORTE*) stopwatch; (*TEC etc*) chronometer.

croqueta [kro'keta] *nf* croquette, rissole.

croquis ['krokis] *nm inv* sketch.

cruce ['kruθe] *etc vb V* **cruzar** ♦ *nm* crossing; (*de carreteras*) crossroads; (*AUTO etc*) junction, intersection; (*BIO: proceso*) crossbreeding; **luces de** ~ dipped headlights.

crucero [kru'θero] *nm* (*NAUT: barco*) cruise ship; (: *viaje*) cruise.

crucial [kru'θjal] *adj* crucial.

crucificar [kruθifi'kar] *vt* to crucify; (*fig*) to torment.

crucifijo [kruθi'fixo] *nm* crucifix.

crucifique [kruθi'fike] *etc vb V* **crucificar**.

crucigrama [kruθi'γrama] *nm* crossword (puzzle).

crudeza [kru'ðeθa] *nf* (*rigor*) harshness; (*aspereza*) crudeness.

crudo, a [' kruðo, a] *adj* raw; (*no maduro*) unripe; (*petróleo*) crude; (*rudo, cruel*) cruel; (*agua*) hard; (*clima etc*) harsh ♦ *nm* crude (oil).

cruel [krwel] *adj* cruel.

crueldad [krwel'ðað] *nf* cruelty.

cruento, a ['krwento, a] *adj* bloody.

crujido [kru'xiðo] *nm* (*de madera etc*) creak.

crujiente [kru'xjente] *adj* (*galleta etc*) crunchy.

crujir [kru'xir] *vi* (*madera etc*) to creak; (*dedos*) to crack; (*dientes*) to grind; (*nieve, arena*) to crunch.

cruz [kruθ] *nf* cross; (*de moneda*) tails *sg*; (*fig*) burden; ~ **gamada** swastika; **C~ Roja** Red Cross.

cruzado, a [kru'θaðo, a] *adj* crossed ♦ *nm* crusader ♦ *nf* crusade.

cruzar [kru'θar] *vt* to cross; (*palabras*) to exchange; ~**se** *vr* (*líneas etc*) to cross, intersect; (*personas*) to pass each other; ~**se de brazos** to fold one's arms; (*fig*) not to lift a finger to help; ~**se con algn en la calle** to pass sb in the street.

c.s.f. *abr* (= *costo, seguro y flete*) c.i.f.

CSIC [θe'sik] *nm abr* (*ESP ESCOL*) = *Consejo Superior de Investigaciones Científicas.*

cta, c.ta *nf abr* (= *cuenta*) a/c.

cta. cto. *abr* (= *carta de crédito*) L.C.

cte. *abr* (= *corriente, de los corrientes*) inst.

CTNE *nf abr* (*TELEC*) = *Compañía Telefónica Nacional de España.*

c/u *abr* (= *cada uno*) ea.

cuaco ['kwako] *nm* (*AM*) nag.

cuaderno [kwa'ðerno] *nm* notebook; (*de escuela*) exercise book; (*NAUT*) logbook.

cuadra ['kwaðra] *nf* (*caballeriza*) stable; (*AM*) (city) block.

cuadrado, a [kwa'ðraðo, a] *adj* square ♦ *nm* (*MAT*) square.

cuadragésimo, a [kwaðra'xesimo, a] *num* fortieth.

cuadrángulo [kwa'ðrangulo, a] *nm* quadrangle.

cuadrante [kwa'ðrante] *nm* quadrant.

cuadrar [kwa'ðrar] *vt* to square; (*TIP*) to justify ♦ *vi*: ~ **con** (*cuenta*) to square with, tally with; ~**se** *vr* (*soldado*) to stand to attention; ~ **por la derecha/izquierda** to right-/left-justify.

cuadrícula [kwa'ðrikula] *nf* (*TIP etc*) grid, ruled squares.

cuadriculado, a [kwaðriku'laðo, a] *adj*: **papel** ~ squared *o* graph paper.

cuadrilátero [kwaðri'latero] *nm* (*DEPORTE*) boxing ring; (*GEOM*) quadrilateral.

cuadrilla [kwa'ðriʎa] *nf* (*amigos*) party, group; (*pandilla*) gang; (*obreros*) team.

cuadro ['kwaðro] *nm* square; (*PINTURA*) painting; (*TEAT*) scene; (*diagrama: tb:* ~ **sinóptico**) chart, table, diagram; (*DEPORTE, MED*) team; (*POL*) executive; ~ **de mandos** control panel; **a** ~**s** check *cpd*.

cuadruplicarse [kwaðrupli'karse] *vr* to quadruple.

cuádruplo, a ['kwaðruplo, a], **cuádruple** ['kwaðruple] *adj* quadruple.

cuajado, a [kwa'xaðo, a] *adj*: ~ **de** (*fig*) full of ♦ *nf* (*de leche*) curd.

cuajar [kwa'xar] *vt* to thicken; (*leche*) to curdle; (*sangre*) to congeal; (*adornar*) to adorn; (*CULIN*) to set ♦ *vi* (*nieve*) to lie; (*fig*) to become set, become established; (*idea*) to be received, be acceptable; **~se** *vr* to curdle; to congeal; (*llenarse*) to fill up.

cuajo ['kwaxo] *nm*: **arrancar algo de ~** to tear sth out by its roots.

cual [kwal] *adv* like, as ♦ *pron*: **el ~** *etc* which; (*persona: sujeto*) who; (: *objeto*) whom; **lo ~** (*relativo*) which; **allá cada ~** every man to his own taste; **son a ~ más gandul** each is as idle as the other; **cada ~ each one** ♦ *adj* such as; **tal ~** just as it is.

cuál [kwal] *pron interrogativo* which (one), what.

cualesquier(a) [kwales'kjer(a)] *pl de* **cualquier(a).**

cualidad [kwali'ðað] *nf* quality.

cualificado, a [kwalifi'kaðo, a] *adj* (*obrero*) skilled, qualified.

cualquiera [kwal'kjera], **cualquier** [kwal'kjer], *pl* **cualesquier(a)** *adj* any ♦ *pron* anybody, anyone; (*quienquiera*) whoever; **en cualquier momento** any time; **en cualquier parte** anywhere; **cualquiera que sea** whichever it is; (*persona*) whoever it is.

cuán [kwan] *adv* how.

cuando ['kwando] *adv* when; (*aún si*) if, even if ♦ *conj* (*puesto que*) since ♦ *prep*: **yo, ~ niño** ... when I was a child *o* as a child I ...; **~ no sea así** even if it is not so; **~ más** at (the) most; **~ menos** at least; **~ no** if not, otherwise; **de ~ en ~** from time to time; **ven ~ quieras** come when(ever) you like.

cuándo ['kwando] *adv* when; **¿desde ~?**, **¿de ~ acá?** since when?

cuantía [kwan'tia] *nf* (*alcance*) extent; (*importancia*) importance.

cuantioso, a [kwan'tjoso, a] *adj* substantial.

===================== *PALABRA CLAVE*

cuanto, a ['kwanto, a] *adj* **1** (*todo*): **tiene todo ~ desea** he's got everything he wants; **le daremos ~s ejemplares necesite** we'll give him as many copies as *o* all the copies he needs; **~s hombres la ven** all the men who see her
2: **unos ~s**: **había unos ~s periodistas** there were (quite) a few journalists
3 (+*más*): **~ más vino bebas peor te sentirás** the more wine you drink the worse you'll feel; **~s más, mejor** the more the merrier
♦ *pron*: **tiene ~ desea** he has everything

he wants; **tome ~/~s quiera** take as much/many as you want
♦ *adv*: **en ~**: **en ~ profesor** as a teacher; **en ~ a mí** as for me; *V tb* **antes**
♦ *conj* **1**: **~ más gana menos gasta** the more he earns the less he spends; **~ más joven se es más se es confiado** the younger you are the more trusting you are
2: **en ~**: **en ~ llegue/llegué** as soon as I arrive/arrived.

cuánto, a ['kwanto, a] *adj* (*exclamación*) what a lot of; (*interrogativo: sg*) how much?; (: *pl*) how many? ♦ *pron, adv* how; (*interrogativo: sg*) how much?; (: *pl*) how many? ♦ *excl*: **¡~ me alegro!** I'm so glad!; **¡cuánta gente!** what a lot of people!; **¿~ tiempo?** how long?; **¿~ cuesta?** how much does it cost?; **¿a ~s estamos?** what's the date?; **¿~ hay de aquí a Bilbao?** how far is it from here to Bilbao?; **Señor no sé ~s** Mr. So-and-So.

cuarenta [kwa'renta] *num* forty.

cuarentena [kwaren'tena] *nf* (*MED etc*) quarantine; (*conjunto*) forty(-odd).

cuarentón, ona [kwaren'ton, ona] *adj* forty-year-old, fortyish ♦ *nm/f* person of about forty.

cuaresma [kwa'resma] *nf* Lent.

cuarta ['kwarta] *nf V* **cuarto.**

cuartear [kwarte'ar] *vt* to quarter; (*dividir*) to divide up; **~se** *vr* to crack, split.

cuartel [kwar'tel] *nm* (*de ciudad*) quarter, district; (*MIL*) barracks *pl*; **~ general** headquarters *pl*.

cuartelazo [kwarte'laθo] *nm* coup, military uprising.

cuarteto [kwar'teto] *nm* quartet.

cuartilla [kwar'tiʎa] *nf* (*hoja*) sheet (of paper); **~s** *nfpl* (*TIP*) copy *sg*.

cuarto, a ['kwarto, a] *adj* fourth ♦ *nm* (*MAT*) quarter, fourth; (*habitación*) room ♦ *nf* (*MAT*) quarter, fourth; (*palmo*) span; **~ de baño** bathroom; **~ de estar** living room; **~ de hora** quarter (of an) hour; **~ de kilo** quarter kilo; **no tener un ~** to be broke (*fam*).

cuarzo ['kwarθo] *nm* quartz.

cuatrero [kwa'trero] *nm* (*AM*) rustler, stock thief.

cuatrimestre [kwatri'mestre] *nm* four-month period.

cuatro ['kwatro] *num* four; **las ~** four o'clock; **el ~ de octubre** (on) the fourth of October; *V tb* **seis.**

cuatrocientos, as [kwatro'θjentos, as] *num* four hundred; *V tb* **seiscientos.**

Cuba ['kuβa] _nf_ Cuba.

cuba ['kuβa] _nf_ cask, barrel; **estar como una ~** (_fam_) to be sloshed.

cubalibre [kuβa'liβre] _nm_ (white) rum and coke ®.

cubano, a [ku'βano, a] _adj, nm/f_ Cuban.

cubata [ku'βata] _nm_ = **cubalibre**.

cubertería [kuβerte'ria] _nf_ cutlery.

cúbico, a ['kuβiko, a] _adj_ cubic.

cubierto, a [ku'βjerto, a] _pp de_ **cubrir** ♦ _adj_ covered; (_cielo_) overcast ♦ _nm_ cover; (_en la mesa_) place ♦ _nf_ cover, covering; (_neumático_) tyre; (_NAUT_) deck; **~s** _nmpl_ cutlery _sg_; **a ~ de** covered with _o_ in; **precio del ~** cover charge.

cubil [ku'βil] _nm_ den.

cubilete [kuβi'lete] _nm_ (_en juegos_) cup.

cubito [ku'βito] _nm_: **~ de (la) basura** dustbin; **~ de hielo** ice cube.

cubo ['kuβo] _nm_ cube; (_balde_) bucket, tub; (_TEC_) drum.

cubrecama [kuβre'kama] _nm_ bedspread.

cubrir [ku'βrir] _vt_ to cover; (_vacante_) to fill; (_BIO_) to mate with; (_gastos_) to meet; **~se** _vr_ (_cielo_) to become overcast; (_COM: gastos_) to be met _o_ paid; (: _deuda_) to be covered; **~ las formas** to keep up appearances; **lo cubrieron las aguas** the waters closed over it; **el agua casi me cubría** I was almost out of my depth.

cucaracha [kuka'ratʃa] _nf_ cockroach.

cuchara [ku'tʃara] _nf_ spoon; (_TEC_) scoop.

cucharada [kutʃa'raða] _nf_ spoonful; **~ colmada** heaped spoonful.

cucharadita [kutʃara'ðita] _nf_ teaspoonful.

cucharilla [kutʃa'riʎa] _nf_ teaspoon.

cucharita [kutʃa'rita] _nf_ teaspoon.

cucharón [kutʃa'ron] _nm_ ladle.

cuchichear [kutʃitʃe'ar] _vi_ to whisper.

cuchicheo [kutʃi'tʃeo] _nm_ whispering.

cuchilla [ku'tʃiʎa] _nf_ (large) knife; (_de arma blanca_) blade; **~ de afeitar** razor blade; **pasar a ~** to put to the sword.

cuchillada [kutʃi'ʎaða] _nf_ (_golpe_) stab; (_herida_) knife _o_ stab wound.

cuchillo [ku'tʃiʎo] _nm_ knife.

cuchitril [kutʃi'tril] _nm_ hovel; (_habitación etc_) pigsty.

cuclillas [ku'kliʎas] _nfpl_: **en ~** squatting.

cuco, a ['kuko, a] _adj_ pretty; (_astuto_) sharp ♦ _nm_ cuckoo.

cucurucho [kuku'rutʃo] _nm_ paper cone, cornet.

cuece ['kweθe] _etc vb V_ **cocer**.

cuele ['kwele] _etc vb V_ **colar**.

cuelgue ['kwelγe] _etc vb V_ **colgar**.

cuello ['kweʎo] _nm_ (_ANAT_) neck; (_de vestido, camisa_) collar.

cuenca ['kwenka] _nf_ (_ANAT_) eye socket; (_GEO: valle_) bowl, deep valley; (: _fluvial_) basin.

cuenco ['kwenko] _nm_ (earthenware) bowl.

cuenta ['kwenta] _etc vb V_ **contar** ♦ _nf_ (_cálculo_) count, counting; (_en café, restaurante_) bill; (_COM_) account; (_de collar_) bead; (_fig_) account; **a fin de ~s** in the end; **en resumidas ~s** in short; **caer en la ~** to catch on; **dar ~ a algn de sus actos** to account to sb for one's actions; **darse ~ de** to realize; **tener en ~** to bear in mind; **echar ~s** to take stock; **~ de atrás** countdown; **~ corriente/de ahorros/a plazo (fijo)** current/savings/ deposit account; **~ de asignación** appropriation account; **~ de caja** cash account; **~ de capital** capital account; **~ por cobrar** account receivable; **~ de crédito** credit _o_ loan account; **~ de gastos e ingresos** income and expenditure account; **~ por pagar** account payable; **abonar una cantidad en ~ a algn** to credit a sum to sb's account; **ajustar _o_ liquidar una ~** to settle an account; **pasar la ~** to send the bill.

cuentagotas [kwenta'γotas] _nm inv_ (_MED_) dropper; **a _o_ con ~** (_fam, fig_) drop by drop, bit by bit.

cuentakilómetros [kwentaki'lometros] _nm inv_ (_de distancias_) ≈ milometer, clock; (_velocímetro_) speedometer.

cuentista [kwen'tista] _nm/f_ gossip; (_LIT_) short-story writer.

cuento ['kwento] _etc vb V_ **contar** ♦ _nm_ story; (_LIT_) short story; **~ de hadas** fairy story; **es el ~ de nunca acabar** it's an endless business; **eso no viene a ~** that's irrelevant.

cuerda ['kwerða] _nf_ rope; (_hilo_) string; (_de reloj_) spring; (_MUS: de violín etc_) string; (_MAT_) chord; (_ANAT_) cord; **~ floja** tightrope; **~s vocales** vocal cords; **dar ~ a un reloj** to wind up a clock.

cuerdo, a ['kwerðo, a] _adj_ sane; (_prudente_) wise, sensible.

cuerear [kwere'ar] _vt_ (_AM_) to skin.

cuerno ['kwerno] _nm_ (_ZOOL: gen_) horn; (: _de ciervo_) antler; **poner los ~s a** (_fam_) to cuckold; **saber a ~ quemado** to leave a nasty taste.

cuero ['kwero] _nm_ (_ZOOL_) skin, hide; (_TEC_) leather; **en ~s** stark naked; **~ cabelludo** scalp.

cuerpo ['kwerpo] _nm_ body; (_cadáver_) corpse; (_fig_) main part; **~ de bomberos** fire brigade; **~ diplomático** diplomatic

corps; **luchar** ~ **a** ~ to fight hand-to-hand; **tomar** ~ (*plan etc*) to take shape.
cuervo ['kwerßo] *nm* (*ZOOL*) raven, crow; *V* **criar.**
cuesta ['kwesta] *etc vb V* **costar** ♦ *nf* slope; (*en camino etc*) hill; ~ **arriba/abajo** uphill/downhill; **a** ~**s** on one's back.
cuestión [kwes'tjon] *nf* matter, question, issue; (*riña*) quarrel, dispute; **eso es otra** ~ that's another matter.
cuestionar [kwestjo'nar] *vt* to question.
cuestionario [kwestjo'narjo] *nm* questionnaire.
cueva ['kweßa] *nf* cave.
cueza ['kweθa] *etc vb V* **cocer.**
cuidado [kwi'ðaðo] *nm* care, carefulness; (*preocupación*) care, worry ♦ *excl* careful!, look out!; **eso me tiene sin** ~ I'm not worried about that.
cuidadoso, a [kwiða'ðoso, a] *adj* careful; (*preocupado*) anxious.
cuidar [kwi'ðar] *vt* (*MED*) to care for; (*ocuparse de*) to take care of, look after; (*detalles*) to pay attention to ♦ *vi*: ~ **de** to take care of, look after; ~**se** *vr* to look after o.s.; ~**se de hacer algo** to take care to do something.
cuita ['kwita] *nf* (*preocupación*) worry, trouble; (*pena*) grief.
culata [ku'lata] *nf* (*de fusil*) butt.
culatazo [kula'taθo] *nm* kick, recoil.
culebra [ku'leßra] *nf* snake; ~ **de cascabel** rattlesnake.
culebrear [kuleßre'ar] *vi* to wriggle along; (*río*) to meander.
culebrón [kule'ßron] *nm* (*fam*) soap (opera).
culinario, a [kuli'narjo, a] *adj* culinary, cooking *cpd*.
culminación [kulmina'θjon] *nf* culmination.
culminante [kulmi'nante] *adj*: **momento** ~ climax, highlight, highspot.
culminar [kulmi'nar] *vi* to culminate.
culo ['kulo] *nm* (*fam: asentaderas*) bottom, backside, bum (*BRIT*); (: *ano*) arse(hole) (*BRIT!*), ass(hole) (*US!*); (*de vaso*) bottom.
culpa ['kulpa] *nf* fault; (*JUR*) guilt; ~**s** *nfpl* sins; **por** ~ **de** through, because of; **tener la** ~ (**de**) to be to blame (for).
culpabilidad [kulpaßili'ðað] *nf* guilt.
culpable [kul'paßle] *adj* guilty ♦ *nm/f* culprit; **confesarse** ~ to plead guilty; **declarar** ~ **a algn** to find sb guilty.
culpar [kul'par] *vt* to blame; (*acusar*) to accuse.
cultivadora [kultißa'ðora] *nf* cultivator.
cultivar [kulti'ßar] *vt* to cultivate; (*cosecha*)

to raise; (*talento*) to develop.
cultivo [kul'tißo] *nm* (*acto*) cultivation; (*plantas*) crop; (*BIO*) culture.
culto, a ['kulto, a] *adj* (*cultivado*) cultivated; (*que tiene cultura*) cultured, educated ♦ *nm* (*homenaje*) worship; (*religión*) cult; (*POL etc*) cult.
cultura [kul'tura] *nf* culture.
cultural [kultu'ral] *adj* cultural.
culturismo [kultu'rismo] *nm* body-building.
cumbre ['kumbre] *nf* summit, top; (*fig*) top, height; **conferencia (en la)** ~ summit (conference).
cumpleaños [kumple'aɲos] *nm inv* birthday.
cumplido, a [kum'pliðo, a] *adj* complete, perfect; (*abundante*) plentiful; (*cortés*) courteous ♦ *nm* compliment; **visita de** ~ courtesy call.
cumplidor, a [kumpli'ðor, a] *adj* reliable.
cumplimentar [kumplimen'tar] *vt* to congratulate; (*órdenes*) to carry out.
cumplimiento [kumpli'mjento] *nm* (*de un deber*) fulfilment, execution, performance; (*acabamiento*) completion; (*COM*) expiry, end.
cumplir [kum'plir] *vt* (*orden*) to carry out, obey; (*promesa*) to carry out, fulfil; (*condena*) to serve; (*años*) to reach, attain ♦ *vi* (*pago*) to fall due; (*plazo*) to expire; ~**se** *vr* (*plazo*) to expire; (*plan etc*) to be fulfilled; (*vaticinio*) to come true; **hoy cumple dieciocho años** he is eighteen today; ~ **con** (*deberes*) to carry out, fulfil.
cúmulo ['kumulo] *nm* (*montón*) heap; (*nube*) cumulus.
cuna ['kuna] *nf* cradle, cot; **canción de** ~ lullaby.
cundir [kun'dir] *vi* (*noticia, rumor, pánico*) to spread; (*rendir*) to go a long way.
cuneta [ku'neta] *nf* ditch.
cuña ['kuɲa] *nf* (*TEC*) wedge; (*COM*) advertising spot; (*MED*) bedpan; **tener** ~**s** to have influence.
cuñado, a [ku'ɲaðo, a] *nm/f* brother/sister-in-law.
cuño ['kuɲo] *nm* (*TEC*) die-stamp; (*fig*) stamp.
cuota ['kwota] *nf* (*parte proporcional*) share; (*cotización*) fee, dues *pl*; ~ **inicial** (*COM*) down payment.
cupo ['kupo] *etc vb V* **caber** ♦ *nm* quota, share; (*COM*): ~ **de importación** import quota; ~ **de ventas** sales quota.
cupón [ku'pon] *nm* coupon; ~ **de la ONCE** *o* **de los ciegos** ONCE lottery ticket; *V tb*

lotería.

cúpula ['kupula] *nf* (*ARQ*) dome.

cura ['kura] *nf* (*curación*) cure; (*método curativo*) treatment ♦ *nm* priest; ~ **de emergencia** emergency treatment.

curación [kura'θjon] *nf* cure; (*acción*) curing.

curado, a [ku'raðo, a] *adj* (*CULIN*) cured; (*pieles*) tanned.

curandero, a [kuran'dero, a] *nm/f* healer.

curar [ku'rar] *vt* (*MED: herida*) to treat, dress; (: *enfermo*) to cure; (*CULIN*) to cure, salt; (*cuero*) to tan ♦ *vi*, ~**se** *vr* to get well, recover.

curda ['kurða] (*fam*) *nm* drunk ♦ *nf*: **agarrar una/estar** ~ to get/be sloshed.

curiosear [kurjose'ar] *vt* to glance at, look over ♦ *vi* to look round, wander round; (*explorar*) to poke about.

curiosidad [kurjosi'ðað] *nf* curiosity.

curioso, a [ku'rjoso, a] *adj* curious; (*aseado*) neat ♦ *nm/f* bystander, onlooker; ¡qué ~! how odd!

curita [ku'rita] *nf* (*AM*) sticking plaster.

currante [ku'rrante] *nm/f* (*fam*) worker.

currar [ku'rrar] *vi* (*fam*), **currelar** [kurre'lar] *vi* (*fam*) to work.

currículo [ku'rrikulo] *nm*, **currículum** [ku'rrikulum] *nm* curriculum vitae.

curro ['kurro] *nm* (*fam*) work, job.

cursar [kur'sar] *vt* (*ESCOL*) to study.

cursi ['kursi] *adj* (*fam*) pretentious; (: *amanerado*) affected.

cursilada [kursi'laða] *nf*: ¡qué ~! how tacky!

cursilería [kursile'ria] *nf* (*vulgaridad*) bad taste; (*amaneramiento*) affectation.

cursillo [kur'siʎo] *nm* short course.

cursiva [kur'sißa] *nf* italics *pl*.

curso ['kurso] *nm* (*dirección*) course; (*fig*) progress; (*ESCOL*) school year; (*UNIV*) academic year; **en** ~ (*año*) current; (*proceso*) going on, under way; **moneda de** ~ **legal** legal tender.

cursor [kur'sor] *nm* (*INFORM*) cursor; (*TEC*) slide.

curtido, a [kur'tiðo, a] *adj* (*cara etc*) weather-beaten; (*fig: persona*) experienced.

curtir [kur'tir] *vt* (*piel*) to tan; (*fig*) to harden.

curvo, a ['kurßo, a] *adj* (*gen*) curved; (*torcido*) bent ♦ *nf* (*gen*) curve, bend; **curva de rentabilidad** (*COM*) break-even chart.

cúspide ['kuspiðe] *nf* (*GEO*) summit, peak; (*fig*) top, pinnacle.

custodia [kus'toðja] *nf* (*cuidado*) safekeeping; (*JUR*) custody.

custodiar [kusto'ðjar] *vt* (*conservar*) to keep, take care of; (*vigilar*) to guard.

custodio [kus'toðjo] *nm* guardian, keeper.

cutáneo, a [ku'taneo, a] *adj* skin *cpd*.

cutícula [ku'tikula] *nf* cuticle.

cutis ['kutis] *nm inv* skin, complexion.

cutre ['kutre] *adj* (*fam: lugar*) grotty; (: *persona*) naff.

cuyo, a ['kujo, a] *pron* (*de quien*) whose; (*de que*) whose, of which; **la señora en cuya casa me hospedé** the lady in whose house I stayed; **el asunto cuyos detalles conoces** the affair the details of which you know; **por** ~ **motivo** for which reason.

C.V. *abr* (= *caballos de vapor*) H.P.

C y F *abr* (= *costo y flete*) C & F.

D d

D, d [de] *nf* (*letre*) D, d; **D de Dolores** D for David (*BRIT*), D for Dog (*US*).

D. *abr* = **Don.**

D.ª *abr* = **Doña.**

dactilar [dakti'lar] *adj*: **huellas** ~**es** fingerprints.

dactilógrafo, a [dakti'loɣrafo, a] *nm/f* typist.

dádiva ['daðißa] *nf* (*donación*) donation; (*regalo*) gift.

dadivoso, a [daði'ßoso, a] *adj* generous.

dado, a ['daðo, a] *pp* **de dar** ♦ *nm* die; ~**s** *nmpl* dice ♦ *adj*: **en un momento** ~ at a certain point; **ser** ~ **a** (*hacer algo*) to be very fond of (doing sth); ~ **que** *conj* given that.

daga ['daɣa] *nf* dagger.

daltónico, a [dal'toniko, a] *adj* colour-blind.

daltonismo [dalto'nismo] *nm* colour blindness.

dama ['dama] *nf* (*gen*) lady; (*AJEDREZ*) queen; ~**s** *nfpl* draughts; **primera** ~ (*TEAT*) leading lady; (*POL*) president's wife, first lady (*US*); ~ **de honor** (*de reina*) lady-in-waiting; (*de novia*) bridesmaid.

damasco [da'masko] *nm* (*tela*) damask; (*AM: árbol*) apricot tree; (: *fruta*) apricot.

damnificado, a [damnifi'kaðo, a] *nm/f*: **los**

~s the victims.

damnificar [damnifi'kar] *vt* to harm; (*persona*) to injure.

damnifique [damni'fike] *etc vb V* **damnificar**.

dance ['danθe] *etc vb V* **danzar**.

danés, esa [da'nes, esa] *adj* Danish ♦ *nm/f* Dane ♦ *nm* (*LING*) Danish.

Danubio [da'nuβjo] *nm* Danube.

danza ['danθa] *nf* (*gen*) dancing; (*una* ~) dance.

danzar [dan'θar] *vt, vi* to dance.

danzarín, ina [danθa'rin, ina] *nm/f* dancer.

dañar [da'ɲar] *vt* (*objeto*) to damage; (*persona*) to hurt; (*estropear*) to spoil; ~**se** *vr* (*objeto*) to get damaged.

dañino, a [da'ɲino, a] *adj* harmful.

daño ['daɲo] *nm* (*a un objeto*) damage; (*a una persona*) harm, injury; ~**s y perjuicios** (*JUR*) damages; **hacer** ~ **a** to damage; (*persona*) to hurt, injure; **hacerse** ~ to hurt o.s.

DAO *abr* (=*Diseño Asistido por Ordenador*) CAD.

═══════════════ PALABRA CLAVE

dar [dar] *vt* **1** (*gen*) to give; (*obra de teatro*) to put on; (*film*) to show; (*fiesta*) to have; ~ **algo a algn** to give sb sth *o* sth to sb; ~ **una patada a algn/algo** to kick sb/sth, give sb/sth a kick; ~ **un susto a algn** to give sb a fright; ~ **de beber a algn** to give sb a drink

2 (*producir: intereses*) to yield; (*fruta*) to produce

3 (*locuciones* + *n*): **da gusto escucharle** it's a pleasure to listen to him; **me da pena/asco** it frightens/sickens me; *V tb* **paseo** *y otros sustantivos*

4 (*considerar*): ~ **algo por descontado/ entendido** to take sth for granted/as read; ~ **algo por concluido** to consider sth finished; **le dieron por desaparecido** they gave him up as lost

5 (*hora*): **el reloj dio las 6** the clock struck 6 (o'clock)

6: me da lo mismo it's all the same to me; *V tb* **igual, más**

7: ¡y dale! (¡otra vez!) not again!; **estar/ seguir dale que dale** *o* **dale que te pego** *o* (*AM*) **dale y dale** to go/keep on and on

♦ *vi* **1**: ~ **a** (*habitación*) to overlook, look on to; (*accionar: botón etc*) to press, hit

2: ~ **con: dimos con él dos horas más tarde** we came across him two hours later; **al final di con la solución** I eventually came up with the answer

3: ~ **en** (*blanco, suelo*) to hit; **el sol me da**

en la cara the sun is shining (right) in my face

4: ~ **de sí** (*zapatos etc*) to stretch, give

5: ~ **para** to be enough for; **nuestro presupuesto no da para más** our budget's really tight

6: ~ **por: le ha dado por estudiar música** now he's into studying music

7: ~ **que hablar** to set people talking; **una película que da que pensar** a thought-provoking film

♦ ~**se** *vr* **1**: ~**se un baño** to have a bath; ~**se un golpe** to hit o.s.

2: ~**se por vencido** to give up; **con eso me doy por satisfecho** I'd settle for that

3 (*ocurrir*): **se han dado muchos casos** there have been a lot of cases

4: ~**se a: se ha dado a la bebida** he's taken to drinking

5: **se me dan bien/mal las ciencias** I'm good/bad at science

6: **dárselas de: se las da de experto** he fancies himself *o* poses as an expert.

dardo ['darðo] *nm* dart.

dársena ['darsena] *nf* (*NAUT*) dock.

datar [da'tar] *vi*: ~ **de** to date from.

dátil ['datil] *nm* date.

dativo [da'tiβo] *nm* (*LING*) dative.

dato ['dato] *nm* fact, piece of information; (*MAT*) datum; ~**s** *nmpl* (*INFORM*) data; ~**s de entrada/salida** input/output data; ~**s personales** personal particulars.

dcha. *abr* (= *derecha*) r.h.

d. de J. C. *abr* (= *después de Jesucristo*) A.D.

═══════════════ PALABRA CLAVE

de [de] *prep* (*de*+*el* = *del*) **1** (*posesión, pertenencia*) of; **la casa** ~ **Isabel/mis padres** Isabel's/my parents' house; **es** ~ **ellos/ella** it's theirs/hers; **un libro** ~ **Unamuno** a book by Unamuno

2 (*origen, distancia, con números*) from; **soy** ~ **Gijón** I'm from Gijón; ~ **8 a 20** from 8 to 20; **5 metros** ~ **largo** 5 metres long; **salir del cine** to go out of *o* leave the cinema; ~ **... en ...** from ... to ...; ~ **2 en 2** 2 by 2, 2 at a time; **9** ~ **cada 10** 9 out of every 10

3 (*valor descriptivo*): **una copa** ~ **vino** a glass of wine; **una silla** ~ **madera** a wooden chair; **la mesa** ~ **la cocina** the kitchen table; **un viaje** ~ **dos días** a two-day journey; **un billete** ~ **1000 pesetas** a 1000 peseta note; **un niño** ~ **tres años** a three-year-old (child); **una máquina** ~ **coser** a sewing machine; **la ciudad** ~

Madrid the city of Madrid; **el tonto** ~ **Juan** that idiot Juan; **ir vestido** ~ **gris** to be dressed in grey; **la niña del vestido azul** the girl in the blue dress; **la chica del pelo largo** the girl with long hair; **trabaja** ~ **profesora** she works as a teacher; ~ **lado** sideways; ~ **atrás/delante** rear/front
4 (*hora, tiempo*): **a las 8** ~ **la mañana** at 8 o'clock in the morning; ~ **día/noche** by day/night; ~ **hoy en ocho días** a week from now; ~ **niño era gordo** as a child he was fat
5 (*comparaciones*): **más/menos** ~ **cien personas** more/less than a hundred people; **el más caro** ~ **la tienda** the most expensive in the shop; **menos/más** ~ **lo pensado** less/more than expected
6 (*causa*): **del calor** from the heat; ~ **puro tonto** out of sheer stupidity
7 (*tema*) about; **clases** ~ **inglés** English classes; **¿sabes algo** ~ **él?** do you know anything about him?; **un libro** ~ **física** a physics book
8 (*adj + de + infin*): **fácil** ~ **entender** easy to understand
9 (*oraciones pasivas*): **fue respetado** ~ **todos** he was loved by all
10 (*condicional + infin*) if; ~ **ser posible** if possible; ~ **no terminarlo hoy** if I *etc* don't finish it today.

dé [de] *vb V* **dar**.
deambular [deambu'lar] *vi* to stroll, wander.
debajo [de'βaxo] *adv* underneath; ~ **de** below, under; **por** ~ **de** beneath.
debate [de'βate] *nm* debate.
debatir [deβa'tir] *vt* to debate; ~**se** *vr* to struggle.
debe ['deβe] *nm* (*en cuenta*) debit side; ~ **y haber** debit and credit.
deber [de'βer] *nm* duty ♦ *vt* to owe ♦ *vi*: **debe (de)** it must, it should; ~**se** *vr*: ~**se a** to be owing *o* due to; ~**es** *nmpl* (*ESCOL*) homework *sg*; **debo hacerlo** I must do it; **debe de ir** he should go; **¿qué** *o* **cuánto le debo?** how much is it?
debidamente [deβiða'mente] *adv* properly; (*rellenar: documento, solicitud*) duly.
debido, a [de'βiðo, a] *adj* proper, due; ~ **a** due to, because of; **en debida forma** duly.
débil ['deβil] *adj* weak; (*persona: físicamente*) feeble; (*salud*) poor; (*voz, ruido*) faint; (*luz*) dim.
debilidad [deβili'ðað] *nf* weakness; feebleness; dimness; **tener** ~ **por algn** to

have a soft spot for sb.
debilitar [deβili'tar] *vt* to weaken; ~**se** *vr* to grow weak.
débito ['deβito] *nm* debit; (*deuda*) debt.
debutante [deβu'tante] *nm/f* beginner.
debutar [deβu'tar] *vi* to make one's debut.
década ['dekaða] *nf* decade.
decadencia [deka'ðenθja] *nf* (*estado*) decadence; (*proceso*) decline, decay.
decadente [deka'ðente] *adj* decadent.
decaer [deka'er] *vi* (*declinar*) to decline; (*debilitarse*) to weaken; (*salud*) to fail; (*negocio*) to fall off.
decaído, a [deka'iðo, a] *adj*: **estar** ~ (*persona*) to be down.
decaiga [de'kaiɣa] *etc vb V* **decaer**.
decaimiento [dekai'mjento] *nm* (*declinación*) decline; (*desaliento*) discouragement; (*MED: depresión*) depression.
decanato [deka'nato] *nm* (*cargo*) deanship; (*despacho*) dean's office.
decano, a [de'kano, a] *nm/f* (*UNIV etc*) dean; (*de grupo*) senior member.
decantar [dekan'tar] *vt* (*vino*) to decant.
decapitar [dekapi'tar] *vt* to behead.
decayendo [deka'jendo] *etc vb V* **decaer**.
decena [de'θena] *nf*: **una** ~ ten (or so).
decencia [de'θenθja] *nf* (*modestia*) modesty; (*honestidad*) respectability.
decenio [de'θenjo] *nm* decade.
decente [de'θente] *adj* (*correcto*) proper; (*honesto*) respectable.
decepción [deθep'θjon] *nf* disappointment.
decepcionante [deθepθjo'nante] *adj* disappointing.
decepcionar [deθepθjo'nar] *vt* to disappoint.
decibelio [deθi'βeljo] *nm* decibel.
decidido, a [deθi'ðiðo, a] *a* decided; (*resuelto*) resolute.
decidir [deθi'ðir] *vt* (*persuadir*) to convince, persuade; (*resolver*) to decide ♦ *vi* to decide; ~**se** *vr*: ~**se a** to make up one's mind to; ~**se por** to decide *o* settle on, choose.
decimal [deθi'mal] *adj, nm* decimal.
décimo, a ['deθimo, a] *num* tenth ♦ *nf* (*MAT*) tenth; **tiene unas** ~**as de fiebre** he has a slight temperature.
decimoctavo, a [deθimok'taβo, a] *num* eighteenth; *V tb* **sexto**.
decimocuarto, a [deθimo'kwarto, a] *num* fourteenth; *V tb* **sexto**.
decimonoveno, a [deθimono'βeno, a] *num* nineteenth; *V tb* **sexto**.
decimoquinto, a [deθimo'kinto, a] *num* fifteenth; *V tb* **sexto**.

decimoséptimo, a [deθimo'septimo, a] *num* seventeenth; *V tb* **sexto.**

decimosexto, a [deθimo'seksto, a] *num* sixteenth; *V tb* **sexto.**

decimotercero, a [deθimoter'θero, a] *num* thirteenth; *V tb* **sexto.**

decir [de'θir] *vt* (*expresar*) to say; (*contar*) to tell; (*hablar*) to speak; (*indicar*) to show; (*revelar*) to reveal; (*fam: nombrar*) to call ♦ *nm* saying; ~**se** *vr*: **se dice** it is said, they say; (*se cuenta*) the story goes; **¿cómo se dice en inglés "cursi"?** what's the English for "cursi"?; ~ **para** *o* **entre sí** to say to o.s.; ~ **por** ~ to talk for talking's sake; **dar que** ~ **(a la gente)** to make people talk; **querer** ~ to mean; **es** ~ that is to say, namely; **ni que** ~ **tiene que ...** it goes without saying that ...; **como quien dice** so to speak; **¡quién lo diría!** would you believe it!; **el qué dirán** gossip; **¡diga!, ¡dígame!** (*en tienda etc*) can I help you?; (*TELEC*) hello?; **le dije que fuera más tarde** I told her to go later; **es un** ~ it's just a phrase.

decisión [deθi'sjon] *nf* decision; (*firmeza*) decisiveness; (*voluntad*) determination.

decisivo, a [deθi'siβo, a] *adj* decisive.

declamar [dekla'mar] *vt, vi* to declaim; (*versos etc*) to recite.

declaración [deklara'θjon] *nf* (*manifestación*) statement; (*explicación*) explanation; (*JUR*: *testimonio*) evidence; ~ **de derechos** (*POL*) bill of rights; ~ **de impuestos** (*COM*) tax return; ~ **de ingresos** *o* **de la renta** income tax return; ~ **jurada** affidavit; **falsa** ~ (*JUR*) misrepresentation.

declarar [dekla'rar] *vt* to declare ♦ *vi* to declare; (*JUR*) to testify; ~**se** *vr* (*opinión*) to make one's opinion known; (*a una chica*) to propose; (*guerra, incendio*) to break out; ~ **culpable/inocente a algn** to find sb guilty/not guilty; ~**se culpable/ inocente** to plead guilty/not guilty.

declinación [deklina'θjon] *nf* (*decaimiento*) decline; (*LING*) declension.

declinar [dekli'nar] *vt* (*gen*, *LING*) to decline; (*JUR*) to reject ♦ *vi* (*el día*) to draw to a close.

declive [de'kliβe] *nm* (*cuesta*) slope; (*inclinación*) incline; (*fig*) decline; (*COM*: *tb*: ~ **económico**) slump.

decodificador [dekoðifika'ðor] *nm* (*INFORM*) decoder.

decolorarse [dekolo'rarse] *vr* to become discoloured.

decomisar [dekomi'sar] *vt* to seize, confiscate.

decomiso [deko'miso] *nm* seizure.

decoración [dekora'θjon] *nf* decoration; (*TEAT*) scenery, set; ~ **de escaparates** window dressing.

decorado [deko'raðo] *nm* (*CINE*, *TEAT*) scenery, set.

decorador, a [dekora'ðor, a] *nm/f* (*de interiores*) (interior) decorator; (*TEAT*) stage *o* set designer.

decorar [deko'rar] *vt* to decorate.

decorativo, a [dekora'tiβo, a] *adj* ornamental, decorative.

decoro [de'koro] *nm* (*respeto*) respect; (*dignidad*) decency; (*recato*) propriety.

decoroso, a [deko'roso, a] *adj* (*decente*) decent; (*modesto*) modest; (*digno*) proper.

decrecer [dekre'θer] *vi* to decrease, diminish; (*nivel de agua*) to go down; (*días*) to draw in.

decrépito, a [de'krepito, a] *adj* decrepit.

decretar [dekre'tar] *vt* to decree.

decreto [de'kreto] *nm* decree; (*POL*) act.

decreto-ley [dekreto'lei], *pl* **decretos-leyes** *nm* decree.

decrezca [de'kreθka] *etc vb V* **decrecer.**

decúbito [de'kuβito] *nm* (*MED*): ~ **prono/ supino** prone/supine position.

dedal [de'ðal] *nm* thimble.

dedalera [deða'lera] *nf* foxglove.

dédalo ['deðalo] *nm* (*laberinto*) labyrinth; (*fig*) tangle, mess.

dedicación [deðika'θjon] *nf* dedication; **con** ~ **exclusiva** *o* **plena** full-time.

dedicar [deði'kar] *vt* (*libro*) to dedicate; (*tiempo, dinero*) to devote; ~**se** *vr*: ~**se a** to devote o.s. to (*hacer algo* doing sth); (*carrera, estudio*) to go in for, take up; **¿a qué se dedica usted?** what do you do (for a living)?

dedicatoria [deðika'torja] *nf* (*de libro*) dedication.

dedillo [de'ðiʎo] *nm*: **saber algo al** ~ **to** have sth at one's fingertips.

dedique [de'ðike] *etc vb V* **dedicar.**

dedo ['deðo] *nm* finger; (*de vino etc*) drop; ~ **(del pie)** toe; ~ **pulgar** thumb; ~ **índice** index finger; ~ **mayor** *o* **cordial** middle finger; ~ **anular** ring finger; ~ **meñique** little finger; **contar con los** ~**s** to count on one's fingers; **comerse los** ~**s** to get very impatient; **entrar a** ~ to get a job by pulling strings; **hacer** ~ (*fam*) to hitch (a lift); **poner el** ~ **en la llaga** to put one's finger on it; **no tiene dos** ~**s de frente** he's pretty dim.

deducción [deðuk'θjon] *nf* deduction.

deducir [deðu'θir] *vt* (*concluir*) to deduce,

infer; (*COM*) to deduct.

deduje [de'ðuxe] *etc*, **dedujera**
[deðu'xera] *etc*, **deduzca** [de'ðuθka] *etc*
vb V **deducir**.

defección [defek'θjon] *nf* defection,
desertion.

defecto [de'fekto] *nm* defect, flaw; (*de
cara*) imperfection; ~ **de pronunciación**
speech defect; **por ~** (*INFORM*) default; ~
latente (*COM*) latent defect.

defectuoso, a [defek'twoso, a] *adj*
defective, faulty.

defender [defen'der] *vt* to defend; (*ideas*)
to uphold; (*causa*) to champion; (*amigos*)
to stand up for; **~se** *vr* to defend o.s.;
~se bien to give a good account of o.s.;
me defiendo en inglés (*fig*) I can get by
in English.

defendible [defen'diβle] *adj* defensible.

defensa [de'fensa] *nf* defence; (*NAUT*)
fender ♦ *nm* (*DEPORTE*) back; **en ~ propia**
in self-defence.

defensivo, a [defen'siβo, a] *adj* defensive
♦ *nf*: **a la defensiva** on the defensive.

defensor, a [defen'sor, a] *adj* defending
♦ *nmf* (*abogado* ~) defending counsel;
(*protector*) protector; ~ **del pueblo** (*ESP*)
≈ ombudsman.

deferente [defe'rente] *adj* deferential.

deferir [defe'rir] *vt* (*JUR*) to refer, delegate
♦ *vi*: ~ **a** to defer to.

deficiencia [defi'θjenθja] *nf* deficiency.

deficiente [defi'θjente] *adj* (*defectuoso*)
defective; ~ **en** lacking *o* deficient in
♦ *nmf*: **ser un ~ mental** to be mentally
handicapped.

déficit, ~s ['defiθit] *nm* (*COM*) deficit; (*fig*)
lack, shortage; ~ **presupuestario** budget
deficit.

deficitario, a [defiθi'tarjo, a] *adj* (*COM*) in
deficit; (*empresa*) loss-making.

defienda [de'fjenda] *etc vb V* **defender**.

defiera [de'fjera] *etc vb V* **deferir**.

definición [defini'θjon] *nf* definition;
(*INFORM: de pantalla*) resolution.

definido, a [defi'niðo, a] *adj* (*tb LING*)
definite; **bien ~** well *o* clearly defined; ~
por el usuario (*INFORM*) user-defined.

definir [defi'nir] *vt* (*determinar*) to
determine, establish; (*decidir, INFORM*) to
define; (*aclarar*) to clarify.

definitivo, a [defini'tiβo, a] *adj* (*edición,
texto*) definitive; (*fecha*) definite; **en
definitiva** definitively; (*en conclusión*)
finally; (*en resumen*) in short.

defiriendo [defi'rjendo] *etc vb V* **deferir**.

deflacionario, a [deflaθjo'narjo, a],
deflacionista [deflaθjo'nista] *adj*

deflationary.

deflector [deflek'tor] *nm* (*TEC*) baffle.

deforestación [deforesta'θjon] *nf*
deforestation.

deformación [deforma'θjon] *nf* (*alteración*)
deformation; (*RADIO etc*) distortion.

deformar [defor'mar] *vt* (*gen*) to deform;
~se *vr* to become deformed.

deforme [de'forme] *adj* (*informe*)
deformed; (*feo*) ugly; (*mal hecho*)
misshapen.

deformidad [deformi'ðað] *nf* (*forma
anormal*) deformity; (*fig: defecto*) (moral)
shortcoming.

defraudar [defrau'ðar] *vt* (*decepcionar*) to
disappoint; (*estafar*) to cheat; to defraud;
~ **impuestos** to evade tax.

defunción [defun'θjon] *nf* decease,
demise.

degeneración [dexenera'θjon] *nf* (*de las
células*) degeneration; (*moral*)
degeneracy.

degenerar [dexene'rar] *vi* to degenerate;
(*empeorar*) to get worse.

deglutir [deɣlu'tir] *vt*, *vi* to swallow.

degolladero [deɣoʎa'ðero] *nm* (*ANAT*)
throat; (*cadalso*) scaffold; (*matadero*)
slaughterhouse.

degollar [deɣo'ʎar] *vt* to slaughter.

degradar [deɣra'ðar] *vt* to debase,
degrade; (*INFORM: datos*) to corrupt; **~se**
vr to demean o.s.

degüelle [de'ɣweʎe] *etc vb V* **degollar**.

degustación [deɣusta'θjon] *nf* sampling,
tasting.

deificar [deifi'kar] *vt* (*persona*) to deify.

deifique [dei'fike] *etc vb V* **deificar**.

dejadez [dexa'ðeθ] *nf* (*negligencia*) neglect;
(*descuido*) untidiness, carelessness.

dejado, a [de'xaðo, a] *adj* (*desaliñado*)
slovenly; (*negligente*) careless;
(*indolente*) lazy.

dejar [de'xar] *vt* (*gen*) to leave; (*permitir*) to
allow, let; (*abandonar*) to abandon,
forsake; (*actividad, empleo*) to give up;
(*beneficios*) to produce, yield ♦ *vi*: ~ **de**
(*parar*) to stop; **~se** *vr* (*abandonarse*) to let
o.s. go; **no puedo ~ de fumar** I can't give
up smoking; **no dejes de visitarles** don't
fail to visit them; **no dejes de comprar
un billete** make sure you buy a ticket; ~
a un lado to leave *o* set aside; ~ **caer** to
drop; ~ **entrar/salir** to let in/out; ~ **pasar**
to let through; **¡déjalo!** (*no te preocupes*)
don't worry about it; **te dejo en tu casa**
I'll drop you off at your place; **deja
mucho que desear** it leaves a lot to be
desired; **~se persuadir** to allow o.s. to *o*

let o.s. be persuaded; **¡déjate de tonterías!** stop messing about!

deje ['dexe] *nm* (trace of) accent.

dejo ['dexo] *nm* (*LING*) accent.

del [del] = **de + el**; *V* **de**.

del. *abr* (*ADMIN*: = *Delegación*) district office.

delantal [delan'tal] *nm* apron.

delante [de'lante] *adv* in front; (*enfrente*) opposite; (*adelante*) ahead ♦ *prep*: ~ **de** in front of, before; **la parte de** ~ the front part; **estando otros** ~ with others present.

delantero, a [delan'tero, a] *adj* front; (*patas de animal*) fore ♦ *nm* (*DEPORTE*) forward ♦ *nf* (*de vestido, casa etc*) front part; (*TEAT*) front row; (*DEPORTE*) forward line; **llevar la delantera (a algn)** to be ahead (of sb).

delatar [dela'tar] *vt* to inform on *o* against, betray; **los delató a la policía** he reported them to the police.

delator, a [dela'tor, a] *nm/f* informer.

delegación [deleɣa'θjon] *nf* (*acción, delegados*) delegation; (*COM: oficina, district office, branch*); ~ **de poderes** (*POL*) devolution; ~ **de policía** police station.

delegado, a [dele'ɣaðo, a] *nm/f* delegate; (*COM*) agent.

delegar [dele'ɣar] *vt* to delegate.

delegue [de'leɣe] *etc vb V* **delegar**.

deleitar [delei'tar] *vt* to delight; ~**se** *vr*: ~**se con** *o* **en** to delight in, take pleasure in.

deleite [de'leite] *nm* delight, pleasure.

deletrear [deletre'ar] *vt* (*tb fig*) to spell (out).

deletreo [dele'treo] *nm* spelling; (*fig*) interpretation, decipherment.

deleznable [deleθ'naßle] *adj* (*frágil*) fragile; (*fig: malo*) poor; (*excusa*) feeble.

delfín [del'fin] *nm* dolphin.

delgadez [delɣa'ðeθ] *nf* thinness, slimness.

delgado, a [del'ɣaðo, a] *adj* thin; (*persona*) slim, thin; (*tierra*) poor; (*tela etc*) light, delicate ♦ *adv*: **hilar (muy)** ~ (*fig*) to split hairs.

deliberación [delißera'θjon] *nf* deliberation.

deliberar [deliße'rar] *vt* to debate, discuss ♦ *vi* to deliberate.

delicadeza [delika'ðeθa] *nf* delicacy; (*refinamiento, sutileza*) refinement.

delicado, a [deli'kaðo, a] *adj* delicate; (*sensible*) sensitive; (*rasgos*) dainty; (*gusto*) refined; (*situación: difícil*) tricky; (: *violento*) embarrassing; (*punto, tema*) sore; (*persona: difícil de contentar*) hard to

please; (: *sensible*) touchy, hypersensitive; (: *atento*) considerate.

delicia [de'liθja] *nf* delight.

delicioso, a [deli'θjoso, a] *adj* (*gracioso*) delightful; (*exquisito*) delicious.

delictivo, a [delik'tißo, a] *adj* criminal *cpd*.

delimitar [delimi'tar] *vt* to delimit.

delincuencia [delin'kwenθja] *nf*: ~ **juvenil** juvenile delinquency; **cifras de la** ~ crime rate.

delincuente [delin'kwente] *nm/f* delinquent; (*criminal*) criminal; ~ **sin antecedentes** first offender; ~ **habitual** hardened criminal.

delineante [deline'ante] *nm/f* draughtsman.

delinear [deline'ar] *vt* to delineate; (*dibujo*) to draw; (*contornos, fig*) to outline; ~ **un proyecto** to outline a project.

delinquir [delin'kir] *vi* to commit an offence.

delirante [deli'rante] *adj* delirious.

delirar [deli'rar] *vi* to be delirious, rave; (*fig: desatinar*) to talk nonsense.

delirio [de'lirjo] *nm* (*MED*) delirium; (*palabras insensatas*) ravings *pl*; ~ **de grandeza** megalomania; ~ **de persecución** persecution mania; **con** ~ (*fam*) madly; **¡fue el** ~**!** (*fam*) it was great!

delito [de'lito] *nm* (*gen*) crime; (*infracción*) offence.

delta ['delta] *nm* delta.

demacrado, a [dema'kraðo, a] *adj* emaciated.

demagogia [dema'ɣoxja] *nf* demagogy, demagoguery.

demagogo [dema'ɣoɣo] *nm* demagogue.

demanda [de'manda] *nf* (*pedido, COM*) demand; (*petición*) request; (*pregunta*) inquiry; (*reivindicación*) claim; (*JUR*) action, lawsuit; (*TEAT*) call; (*ELEC*) load; ~ **de pago** demand for payment; **escribir en** ~ **de ayuda** to write asking for help; **entablar** ~ (*JUR*) to sue; **presentar** ~ **de divorcio** to sue for divorce; ~ **final** final demand; ~ **indirecta** derived demand; ~ **de mercado** market demand.

demandado, a [deman'daðo, a] *nm/f* defendant; (*en divorcio*) respondent.

demandante [deman'dante] *nm/f* claimant; (*JUR*) plaintiff.

demandar [deman'dar] *vt* (*gen*) to demand; (*JUR*) to sue, file a lawsuit against, start proceedings against; ~ **a algn por calumnia/daños y perjuicios** to sue sb for libel/damages.

demarcación [demarka'θjon] *nf* (*de terreno*) demarcation.

demás [de'mas] *adj:* **los ~ niños** the other children, the remaining children ♦ *pron:* **los/las ~** the others, the rest (of them); **lo ~** the rest (of it); **por ~** moreover; (*en vano*) in vain; **y ~** etcetera.

demasía [dema'sia] *nf* (*exceso*) excess, surplus; **comer en ~** to eat to excess.

demasiado, a [dema'sjaðo, a] *adj:* **~ vino** too much wine ♦ *adv* (*antes de adj, adv*) too; **~s libros** too many books; **¡es ~!** it's too much!; **es ~ pesado para levantar** it is too heavy to lift; **~ lo sé** I know it only too well; **hace ~ calor** it's too hot.

demencia [de'menθja] *nf* (*locura*) madness.

demencial [demen'θjal] *adj* crazy.

demente [de'mente] *adj* mad, insane ♦ *nm/f* lunatic.

democracia [demo'kraθja] *nf* democracy.

demócrata [de'mokrata] *nm/f* democrat.

democratacristiano, a [demokrata kris'tjano, a], **democristiano, a** [demokris'tjano, a] *adj, nm/f* Christian Democrat.

democrático, a [demo'kratiko, a] *adj* democratic.

demográfico, a [demo'ɣrafiko, a] *adj* demographic, population *cpd*; **la explosión demográfica** the population explosion.

demoledor, a [demole'ðor, a] *adj* (*fig: argumento*) overwhelming; (: *ataque*) shattering.

demoler [demo'ler] *vt* to demolish; (*edificio*) to pull down.

demolición [demoli'θjon] *nf* demolition.

demonio [de'monjo] *nm* devil, demon; **¡~s!** hell!; **¿cómo ~s?** how the hell?; **¿qué ~s será?** what the devil can it be?; **¿dónde ~ lo habré dejado?** where the devil can I have left it?; **tener el ~ en el cuerpo** (*no parar*) to be always on the go.

demora [de'mora] *nf* delay.

demorar [demo'rar] *vt* (*retardar*) to delay, hold back; (*dilatar*) to hold up ♦ *vi* to linger, stay on; **~se** *vr* to linger, stay on; (*retrasarse*) to take a long time; **~se en hacer algo** (*esp AM*) to take time doing sth.

demos ['demos] *vb V* dar.

demostración [demostra'θjon] *nf* (*gen, MAT*) demonstration; (*de cariño, fuerza*) show; (*de teorema*) proof; (*de amistad*) gesture; (*de cólera, gimnasia*) display; **~ comercial** commercial exhibition.

demostrar [demos'trar] *vt* (*probar*) to prove; (*mostrar*) to show; (*manifestar*) to demonstrate.

demostrativo, a [demostra'tiβo, a] *adj* demonstrative.

demudado, a [demu'ðaðo, a] *adj* (*rostro*) pale; (*fig*) upset; **tener el rostro ~** to look pale.

demudar [demu'ðar] *vt* to change, alter; **~se** *vr* (*expresión*) to alter; (*perder color*) to change colour.

demuela [de'mwela] *etc vb V* demoler.

demuestre [de'mwestre] *etc vb V* demostrar.

den [den] *vb V* dar.

denegación [deneɣa'θjon] *nf* refusal, denial.

denegar [dene'ɣar] *vt* (*rechazar*) to refuse; (*negar*) to deny; (*JUR*) to reject.

denegué [dene'ɣe], **deneguemos** [dene'ɣemos] *etc*, **deniego** [de'njeɣo] *etc*, **deniegue** [de'njeɣe] *etc vb V* denegar.

dengue ['denɣe] *nm* dengue *o* breakbone fever.

denigrante [deni'ɣrante] *adj* (*injurioso*) insulting; (*deshonroso*) degrading.

denigrar [deni'ɣrar] *vt* (*desacreditar*) to denigrate; (*injuriar*) to insult.

denodado, a [deno'ðaðo, a] *adj* bold, brave.

denominación [denomina'θjon] *nf* (*acto*) naming; (*clase*) denomination.

> The **denominación de origen**, *often abbreviated to* **D.O.**, *is a prestigious product classification given to designated regions by the awarding body, the* **Consejo Regulador de la Denominación de Origen**, *when their produce meets the required quality and production standards. It is often associated with* **manchego** *cheeses and many of the wines from the* **Rioja** *and* **Ribera de Duero** *regions.*

denominador [denomina'ðor] *nm:* **~ común** common denominator.

denostar [denos'tar] *vt* to insult.

denotar [deno'tar] *vt* (*indicar*) to indicate, denote.

densidad [densi'ðað] *nf* (*FÍSICA*) density; (*fig*) thickness; **~ de caracteres** (*INFORM*) pitch.

denso, a ['denso, a] *adj* (*apretado*) solid; (*espeso, pastoso*) thick; (*fig*) heavy.

dentado, a [den'taðo, a] *adj* (*rueda*) cogged; (*filo*) jagged; (*sello*) perforated; (*BOT*) dentate.

dentadura [denta'ðura] *nf* (set of) teeth *pl*; **~ postiza** false teeth *pl*.

dental [den'tal] *adj* dental.

dentellada [dente'ʎaða] *nf* (*mordisco*) bite, nip; (*señal*) tooth mark; **partir algo a ~s**

to sever sth with one's teeth.

dentera [den'tera] *nf* (*sensación desagradable*) the shivers *pl*.

dentición [denti'θjon] *nf* (*acto*) teething; (*ANAT*) dentition; **estar con la ~** to be teething.

dentífrico, a [den'tifriko, a] *adj* dental, tooth *cpd* ♦ *nm* toothpaste; **pasta dentífrica** toothpaste.

dentista [den'tista] *nm/f* dentist.

dentro ['dentro] *adv* inside ♦ *prep*: **~ de** in, inside, within; **allí ~** in there; **mirar por ~** to look inside; **~ de lo posible** as far as possible; **~ de todo** all in all; **~ de tres meses** within three months.

denuedo [de'nweðo] *nm* boldness, daring.

denuesto [de'nwesto] *nm* insult.

denuncia [de'nunθja] *nf* (*delación*) denunciation; (*acusación*) accusation; (*de accidente*) report; **hacer** *o* **poner una ~** to report an incident to the police.

denunciable [denun'θjaβle] *adj* indictable, punishable.

denunciante [denun'θjante] *nm/f* accuser; (*delator*) informer.

denunciar [denun'θjar] *vt* to report; (*delatar*) to inform on *o* against.

Dep. *abr* (= *Departamento*) Dept.; (= *Depósito*) dep.

deparar [depa'rar] *vt* (*brindar*) to provide *o* furnish with; (*suj: futuro, destino*) to have in store for; **los placeres que el viaje nos deparó** the pleasures which the trip afforded us.

departamento [departa'mento] *nm* (*sección administrativa*) department, section; (*AM: piso*) flat (*BRIT*), apartment (*US*); (*distrito*) department, province; **~ de envíos** (*COM*) dispatch department; **~ de máquinas** (*NAUT*) engine room.

departir [depar'tir] *vi* to talk, converse.

dependencia [depen'denθja] *nf* dependence; (*POL*) dependency; (*COM*) office, section; (*sucursal*) branch office; (*ARQ: cuarto*) room; **~s** *nfpl* outbuildings.

depender [depen'der] *vi*: **~ de** to depend on; (*contar con*) to rely on; (*de autoridad*) to be under, be answerable to; **depende** it (all) depends; **no depende de mí** it's not up to me.

dependienta [depen'djenta] *nf* saleswoman, shop assistant.

dependiente [depen'djente] *adj* dependent ♦ *nm* salesman, shop assistant.

depilación [depila'θjon] *nf* hair removal.

depilar [depi'lar] *vt* (*con cera: piernas*) to wax; (*cejas*) to pluck.

depilatorio, a [depila'torjo, a] *adj* depilatory ♦ *nm* hair remover.

deplorable [deplo'raβle] *adj* deplorable.

deplorar [deplo'rar] *vt* to deplore.

depondré [depon'dre] *etc vb V* **deponer**.

deponer [depo'ner] *vt* (*armas*) to lay down; (*rey*) to depose; (*gobernante*) to oust; (*ministro*) to remove from office ♦ *vi* (*JUR*) to give evidence; (*declarar*) to make a statement.

deponga [de'ponga] *etc vb V* **deponer**.

deportación [deporta'θjon] *nf* deportation.

deportar [depor'tar] *vt* to deport.

deporte [de'porte] *nm* sport.

deportista [depor'tista] *adj* sports *cpd* ♦ *nm/f* sportsman/woman.

deportivo, a [depor'tiβo, a] *adj* (*club, periódico*) sports *cpd* ♦ *nm* sports car.

deposición [deposi'θjon] *nf* (*de funcionario etc*) removal from office; (*JUR: testimonio*) evidence.

depositante [deposi'tante] *nm/f* depositor.

depositar [deposi'tar] *vt* (*dinero*) to deposit; (*mercaderías*) to put away, store; **~se** *vr* to settle; **~ la confianza en algn** to place one's trust in sb.

depositario, a [deposi'tarjo, a] *nm/f* trustee; **~ judicial** official receiver.

depósito [de'posito] *nm* (*gen*) deposit; (*de mercaderías*) warehouse, store; (*de animales, coches*) pound; (*de agua, gasolina etc*) tank; (*en retrete*) cistern; **~ afianzado** bonded warehouse; **~ bancario** bank deposit; **~ de cadáveres** mortuary; **~ de maderas** timber yard; **~ de suministro** feeder bin.

depravar [depra'βar] *vt* to deprave, corrupt; **~se** *vr* to become depraved.

depreciación [depreθja'θjon] *nf* depreciation.

depreciar [depre'θjar] *vt* to depreciate, reduce the value of; **~se** *vr* to depreciate, lose value.

depredador, a [depreða'ðor, a] (*ZOOL*) *adj* predatory ♦ *nm* predator.

depredar [depre'ðar] *vt* to pillage.

depresión [depre'sjon] *nf* (*gen, MED*) depression; (*hueco*) hollow; (*en horizonte, camino*) dip; (*merma*) drop; (*ECON*) slump, recession; **~ nerviosa** nervous breakdown.

deprimente [depri'mente] *adj* depressing.

deprimido, a [depri'miðo, a] *adj* depressed.

deprimir [depri'mir] *vt* to depress; **~se** *vr* (*persona*) to become depressed.

deprisa [de'prisa] *adv V* **prisa**.

depuesto [de'pwesto] *pp de* **deponer**.

depuración [depura'θjon] *nf* purification; (*POL*) purge; (*INFORM*) debugging.
depurador [depura'ðor] *nm* purifier.
depuradora [depura'ðora] *nf* (*de agua*) water-treatment plant; (*tb*: ~ **de aguas residuales**) sewage farm.
depurar [depu'rar] *vt* to purify; (*purgar*) to purge; (*INFORM*) to debug.
depuse [de'puse] *etc vb V* **deponer**.
der., der.º *abr* (= *derecho*) r.
derecha [de'retʃa] *nf V* **derecho, a**.
derechazo [dere'tʃaθo] *nm* (*BOXEO*) right; (*TENIS*) forehand drive; (*TAUR*) *a pass with the cape*.
derechista [dere'tʃista] (*POL*) *adj* right-wing ♦ *nm/f* right-winger.
derecho, a [de'retʃo, a] *adj* right, right-hand ♦ *nm* (*privilegio*) right; (*título*) claim, title; (*lado*) right(-hand) side; (*leyes*) law ♦ *nf* right(-hand) side ♦ *adv* straight, directly; ~**s** *nmpl* dues; (*profesionales*) fees; (*impuestos*) taxes; (*de autor*) royalties; **la(s) derecha(s)** (*pl*) (*POL*) the Right; ~**s civiles** civil rights; ~**s de muelle** (*COM*) dock dues; ~**s de patente** patent rights; ~**s portuarios** (*COM*) harbour dues; ~ **de propiedad literaria** copyright; ~ **de retención** (*COM*) lien; ~ **de timbre** (*COM*) stamp duty; ~ **de votar** right to vote; ~ **a voto** voting right; **Facultad de D**~ Faculty of Law; **a derechas** rightly, correctly; **de derechas** (*POL*) right-wing; "**reservados todos los** ~**s**" "all rights reserved"; **¡no hay** ~**!** it's not fair!; **tener** ~ **a** to have a right to; **a la derecha** on the right; (*dirección*) to the right.
deriva [de'riβa] *nf*: **ir** *o* **estar a la** ~ to drift, be adrift.
derivación [deriβa'θjon] *nf* derivation.
derivado, a [deri'βaðo, a] *adj* derived ♦ *nm* (*LING*) derivative; (*INDUSTRIA, QUÍMICA*) by-product.
derivar [deri'βar] *vt* to derive; (*desviar*) to direct ♦ *vi*, ~**se** *vr* to derive, be derived; ~**(se) de** (*consecuencia*) to spring from.
dermatólogo, a [derma'toloɣo, a] *nm/f* dermatologist.
dérmico, a ['dermiko, a] *adj* skin *cpd*.
dermoprotector, a [dermoprotek'tor, a] *adj* protective.
derogación [deroɣa'θjon] *nf* repeal.
derogar [dero'ɣar] *vt* (*ley*) to repeal; (*contrato*) to revoke.
derogue [de'roɣe] *etc vb V* **derogar**.
derramamiento [derrama'mjento] *nm* (*dispersión*) spilling; (*fig*) squandering; ~ **de sangre** bloodshed.
derramar [derra'mar] *vt* to spill; (*verter*) to

pour out; (*esparcir*) to scatter; ~**se** *vr* to pour out; ~ **lágrimas** to weep.
derrame [de'rrame] *nm* (*de líquido*) spilling; (*de sangre*) shedding; (*de tubo etc*) overflow; (*perdida*) leakage; (*MED*) discharge; (*declive*) slope; ~ **cerebral** brain haemorrhage; ~ **sinovial** water on the knee.
derrapar [derra'par] *vi* to skid.
derredor [derre'ðor] *adv*: **al** *o* **en** ~ **de** around, about.
derrengado, a [derren'gaðo, a] *adj* (*torcido*) bent; (*cojo*) crippled; **estar** ~ (*fig*) to ache all over; **dejar** ~ **a algn** (*fig*) to wear sb out.
derretido, a [derre'tiðo, a] *adj* melted; (*metal*) molten; **estar** ~ **por algn** (*fig*) to be crazy about sb.
derretir [derre'tir] *vt* (*gen*) to melt; (*nieve*) to thaw; (*fig*) to squander; ~**se** *vr* to melt.
derribar [derri'βar] *vt* to knock down; (*construcción*) to demolish; (*persona, gobierno, político*) to bring down.
derribo [de'rriβo] *nm* (*de edificio*) demolition; (*LUCHA*) throw; (*AVIAT*) shooting down; (*POL*) overthrow; ~**s** *nmpl* rubble *sg*, debris *sg*.
derrita [de'rrita] *etc vb V* **derretir**.
derrocar [derro'kar] *vt* (*gobierno*) to bring down, overthrow; (*ministro*) to oust.
derrochador, a [derrotʃa'ðor, a] *adj, nm/f* spendthrift.
derrochar [derro'tʃar] *vt* (*dinero, recursos*) to squander; (*energía, salud*) to be bursting with *o* full of.
derroche [de'rrotʃe] *nm* (*despilfarro*) waste, squandering; (*exceso*) extravagance; **con un** ~ **de buen gusto** with a fine display of good taste.
derroque [de'rroke] *etc vb V* **derrocar**.
derrota [de'rrota] *nf* (*NAUT*) course; (*MIL*) defeat, rout; **sufrir una grave** ~ (*fig*) to suffer a grave setback.
derrotar [derro'tar] *vt* (*gen*) to defeat.
derrotero [derro'tero] *nm* (*rumbo*) course; **tomar otro** ~ (*fig*) to adopt a different course.
derrotista [derro'tista] *adj, nm/f* defeatist.
derruir [derru'ir] *vt* to demolish, tear down.
derrumbamiento [derrumba'mjento] *nm* (*caída*) plunge; (*demolición*) demolition; (*desplome*) collapse; ~ **de tierra** landslide.
derrumbar [derrum'bar] *vt* to throw down; (*despeñar*) to fling *o* hurl down; (*volcar*) to upset; ~**se** *vr* (*hundirse*) to collapse; (: *techo*) to fall in, cave in; (*fig: esperanzas*)

to collapse.

derrumbe [de'rrumbe] *nm*
= **derrumbamiento**.

derruyendo [derru'jendo] *etc vb V* **derruir**.

des [des] *vb V* **dar**.

desabastecido, a [desaßaste'θiðo, a] *adj*:
estar ~ de algo to be short of *o* out of
sth.

desabotonar [desaßoto'nar] *vt* to
unbutton, undo ♦ *vi* (*flores*) to blossom;
~**se** *vr* to come undone.

desabrido, a [desa'ßriðo, a] *adj* (*comida*)
insipid, tasteless; (*persona: soso*) dull;
(: *antipático*) rude, surly; (*respuesta*)
sharp; (*tiempo*) unpleasant.

desabrigado, a [desaßri'yaðo, a] *adj* (*sin
abrigo*) not sufficiently protected; (*fig*)
exposed.

desabrigar [desaßri'yar] *vt* (*quitar ropa a*) to
remove the clothing of; (*descubrir*) to
uncover; (*fig*) to deprive of protection;
~**se** *vr*: **me desabrigué en la cama** the
bedclothes came off.

desabrigue [desa'ßriye] *etc vb V*
desabrigar.

desabrochar [desaßro'tʃar] *vt* (*botones,
broches*) to undo, unfasten; ~**se** *vr* (*ropa
etc*) to come undone.

desacatar [desaka'tar] *vt* (*ley*) to disobey.

desacato [desa'kato] *nm* (*falta de respeto*)
disrespect; (*JUR*) contempt.

desacertado, a [desaθer'taðo, a] *adj*
(*equivocado*) mistaken; (*inoportuno*)
unwise.

desacierto [desa'θjerto] *nm* (*error*)
mistake, error; (*dicho*) unfortunate
remark.

desaconsejable [desakonse'xaßle] *adj*
inadvisable.

desaconsejado, a [desakonse'xaðo, a] *adj*
ill-advised.

desaconsejar [desakonse'xar] *vt*: ~ **algo a
algn** to advise sb against sth.

desacoplar [desako'plar] *vt* (*ELEC*) to
disconnect; (*TEC*) to take apart.

desacorde [desa'korðe] *adj* (*MUS*)
discordant; (*fig: opiniones*) conflicting;
estar ~ con algo to disagree with sth.

desacreditar [desakreði'tar] *vt*
(*desprestigiar*) to discredit, bring into
disrepute; (*denigrar*) to run down.

desactivar [desakti'ßar] *vt* to deactivate;
(*bomba*) to defuse.

desacuerdo [desa'kwerðo] *nm* (*conflicto*)
disagreement, discord; (*error*) error,
blunder; **en ~** out of keeping.

desafiante [desa'fjante] *adj* (*insolente*)
defiant; (*retador*) challenging ♦ *nm/f*

challenger.

desafiar [desa'fjar] *vt* (*retar*) to challenge;
(*enfrentarse a*) to defy.

desafilado, a [desafi'laðo, a] *adj* blunt.

desafinado, a [desafi'naðo, a] *adj*: **estar ~**
to be out of tune.

desafinar [desafi'nar] *vi* to be out of tune;
~**se** *vr* to go out of tune.

desafío [desa'fio] *nm* (*reto*) challenge;
(*combate*) duel; (*resistencia*) defiance.

desaforadamente [desaforaða'mente] *adv*:
gritar ~ to shout one's head off.

desaforado, a [desafo'raðo, a] *adj* (*grito*)
ear-splitting; (*comportamiento*)
outrageous.

desafortunadamente [desafortunaða
'mente] *adv* unfortunately.

desafortunado, a [desafortu'naðo, a] *adj*
(*desgraciado*) unfortunate, unlucky.

desagradable [desaɣra'ðaßle] *adj*
(*fastidioso, enojoso*) unpleasant; (*irritante*)
disagreeable; **ser ~ con algn** to be rude
to sb.

desagradar [desaɣra'ðar] *vi* (*disgustar*) to
displease; (*molestar*) to bother.

desagradecido, a [desaɣraðe'θiðo, a] *adj*
ungrateful.

desagrado [desa'ɣraðo] *nm* (*disgusto*)
displeasure; (*contrariedad*)
dissatisfaction; **con ~** unwillingly.

desagraviar [desaɣra'ßjar] *vt* to make
amends to.

desagravio [desa'ɣraßjo] *nm* (*satisfacción*)
amends; (*compensación*) compensation.

desaguadero [desaɣwa'ðero] *nm* drain.

desagüe [de'saɣwe] *nm* (*de un líquido*)
drainage; (*cañería: tb*: **tubo de ~**)
drainpipe; (*salida*) outlet, drain.

desaguisado, a [desaɣi'saðo, a] *adj* illegal
♦ *nm* outrage.

desahogado, a [desao'xaðo, a] *adj*
(*holgado*) comfortable; (*espacioso*)
roomy.

desahogar [desao'ɣar] *vt* (*aliviar*) to ease,
relieve; (*ira*) to vent; ~**se** *vr* (*distenderse*)
to relax; (*desfogarse*) to let off steam
(*fam*); (*confesarse*) to confess, get sth off
one's chest (*fam*).

desahogo [desa'oɣo] *nm* (*alivio*) relief;
(*comodidad*) comfort, ease; **vivir con ~** to
be comfortably off.

desahogue [desa'oɣe] *etc vb V* **desahogar**.

desahuciado, a [desau'θjaðo, a] *adj*
hopeless.

desahuciar [desau'θjar] *vt* (*enfermo*) to
give up hope for; (*inquilino*) to evict.

desahucio [de'sauθjo] *nm* eviction.

desairado, a [desai'raðo, a] *adj*

(*menospreciado*) disregarded;
(*desgarbado*) shabby; (*sin éxito*)
unsuccessful; **quedar** ~ to come off
badly.

desairar [desai'rar] *vt* (*menospreciar*) to
slight, snub; (*cosa*) to disregard; (*COM*)
to default on.

desaire [des'aire] *nm* (*menosprecio*) slight;
(*falta de garbo*) unattractiveness; **dar** *o*
hacer un ~ **a algn** to offend sb; ¿**me va**
usted a hacer ese ~? I won't take no for
an answer!

desajustar [desaxus'tar] *vt* (*desarreglar*) to
disarrange; (*desconcertar*) to throw off
balance; (*fig: planes*) to upset; ~**se** *vr* to
get out of order; (*aflojarse*) to loosen.

desajuste [desa'xuste] *nm* (*de máquina*)
disorder; (*avería*) breakdown; (*situación*)
imbalance; (*desacuerdo*) disagreement.

desalentador, a [desalenta'ðor, a] *adj*
discouraging.

desalentar [desalen'tar] *vt* (*desanimar*) to
discourage; ~**se** *vr* to get discouraged.

desaliento [desa'ljento] *etc vb V*
desalentar ♦ *nm* discouragement;
(*abatimiento*) depression.

desaliñado, a [desali'ɲaðo, a] *adj*
(*descuidado*) slovenly; (*raído*) shabby;
(*desordenado*) untidy; (*negligente*)
careless.

desaliño [desa'liɲo] *nm* (*descuido*)
slovenliness; (*negligencia*) carelessness.

desalmado, a [desal'maðo, a] *adj* (*cruel*)
cruel, heartless.

desalojar [desalo'xar] *vt* (*gen*) to remove,
expel; (*expulsar, echar*) to eject;
(*abandonar*) to move out of ♦ *vi* to move
out; **la policía desalojó el local** the police
cleared people out of the place.

desalquilar [desalki'lar] *vt* to vacate, move
out; ~**se** *vr* to become vacant.

desamarrar [desama'rrar] *vt* to untie;
(*NAUT*) to cast off.

desamor [desa'mor] *nm* (*frialdad*)
indifference; (*odio*) dislike.

desamparado, a [desampa'raðo, a] *adj*
(*persona*) helpless; (*lugar: expuesto*)
exposed; (: *desierto*) deserted.

desamparar [desampa'rar] *vt* (*abandonar*)
to desert, abandon; (*JUR*) to leave
defenceless; (*barco*) to abandon.

desamparo [desam'paro] *nm* (*acto*)
desertion; (*estado*) helplessness.

desamueblado, a [desamwe'ßlaðo, a] *adj*
unfurnished.

desandar [desan'dar] *vt:* ~ **lo andado** *o* **el**
camino to retrace one's steps.

desanduve [desan'duße] *etc,*

desanduviera [desandu'ßjera] *etc vb V*
desandar.

desangelado, a [desanxe'laðo, a] *adj*
(*habitación, edificio*) lifeless.

desangrar [desan'grar] *vt* to bleed; (*fig:*
persona) to bleed dry; (*lago*) to drain;
~**se** *vr* to lose a lot of blood; (*morir*) to
bleed to death.

desanimado, a [desani'maðo, a] *adj*
(*persona*) downhearted; (*espectáculo,*
fiesta) dull.

desanimar [desani'mar] *vt* (*desalentar*) to
discourage; (*deprimir*) to depress; ~**se** *vr*
to lose heart.

desánimo [de'sanimo] *nm* despondency;
(*abatimiento*) dejection; (*falta de*
animación) dullness.

desanudar [desanu'ðar] *vt* to untie; (*fig*) to
clear up.

desapacible [desapa'θißle] *adj* unpleasant.

desaparecer [desapare'θer] *vi* to
disappear; (*el sol, la luz*) to vanish; (~ *de*
vista) to drop out of sight; (*efectos,*
señales) to wear off ♦ *vt* (*esp AM POL*) to
cause to disappear; (: *eufemismo*) to
murder.

desaparecido, a [desapare'θiðo, a] *adj*
missing; (*especie*) extinct ♦ *nm/f* (*AM POL*)
kidnapped *o* missing person.

desaparezca [desapa'reθka] *etc vb V*
desaparecer.

desaparición [desapari'θjon] *nf*
disappearance; (*de especie etc*)
extinction.

desapasionado, a [desapasjo'naðo, a] *adj*
dispassionate, impartial.

desapego [desa'peɣo] *nm* (*frialdad*)
coolness; (*distancia*) detachment.

desapercibido, a [desaperθi'ßiðo, a] *adj*
unnoticed; (*desprevenido*) unprepared;
pasar ~ to go unnoticed.

desaplicado, a [desapli'kaðo, a] *adj* slack,
lazy.

desaprensivo, a [desapren'sißo, a] *adj*
unscrupulous.

desaprobar [desapro'ßar] *vt* (*reprobar*) to
disapprove of; (*condenar*) to condemn;
(*no consentir*) to reject.

desaprovechado, a [desaproße'tʃaðo, a]
adj (*oportunidad, tiempo*) wasted;
(*estudiante*) slack.

desaprovechar [desaproße'tʃar] *vt* to
waste; (*talento*) not to use to the full ♦ *vi*
(*perder terreno*) to lose ground.

desapruebe [desa'prweße] *etc vb V*
desaprobar.

desarmar [desar'mar] *vt* (*MIL, fig*) to
disarm; (*TEC*) to take apart, dismantle.

desarme [de'sarme] *nm* disarmament.
desarraigado, a [desarrai'ɣaðo, a] *adj*
(*persona*) without roots, rootless.
desarraigar [desarrai'ɣar] *vt* to uproot; (*fig:
costumbre*) to root out; (: *persona*) to
banish.
desarraigo [desa'rraiɣo] *nm* uprooting.
desarraigue [desa'rraiɣe] *etc vb V*
desarraigar.
desarreglado, a [desarre'ɣlaðo, a] *adj*
(*desordenado*) disorderly, untidy;
(*hábitos*) irregular.
desarreglar [desarre'ɣlar] *vt* to mess up;
(*desordenar*) to disarrange; (*trastocar*) to
upset, disturb.
desarreglo [desa'rreɣlo] *nm* (*de casa,
persona*) untidiness; (*desorden*)
disorder; (*TEC*) trouble; (*MED*) upset;
viven en el mayor ~ they live in
complete chaos.
desarrollado, a [desarro'ʎaðo, a] *adj*
developed.
desarrollar [desarro'ʎar] *vt* (*gen*) to
develop; (*extender*) to unfold; (*teoría*) to
explain; ~**se** *vr* to develop; (*extenderse*)
to open (out); (*film*) to develop; (*fig*) to
grow; (*tener lugar*) to take place; **aquí
desarrollan un trabajo muy importante**
they carry on *o* out very important
work here; **la acción se desarrolla en
Roma** (*CINE etc*) the scene is set in Rome.
desarrollo [desa'rroʎo] *nm* development;
(*de acontecimientos*) unfolding; (*de
industria, mercado*) expansion, growth;
país en vías de ~ developing country; **la
industria está en pleno** ~ industry is
expanding steadily.
desarrugar [desarru'ɣar] *vt* (*alisar*) to
smooth (out); (*ropa*) to remove the
creases from.
desarrugue [desa'rruɣe] *etc vb V*
desarrugar.
desarticulado, a [desartiku'laðo, a] *adj*
disjointed.
desarticular [desartiku'lar] *vt* (*huesos*) to
dislocate, put out of joint; (*objeto*) to
take apart; (*grupo terrorista etc*) to break
up.
desaseado, a [desase'aðo, a] *adj* (*sucio*)
dirty; (*desaliñado*) untidy.
desaseo [desa'seo] *nm* (*suciedad*) dirtiness;
(*desarreglo*) untidiness.
desasga [de'sasɣa] *etc vb V* **desasir**.
desasir [desa'sir] *vt* to loosen; ~**se** *vr* to
extricate o.s.; ~**se de** to let go, give up.
desasosegar [desasose'ɣar] *vt* (*inquietar*)
to disturb, make uneasy; ~**se** *vr* to
become uneasy.

desasosegué [desasose'ɣe],
desasoseguemos [desasose'ɣemos] *etc
vb V* **desasosegar**.
desasosiego [desaso'sjeɣo] *etc vb V*
desasosegar ♦ *nm* (*intranquilidad*)
uneasiness, restlessness; (*ansiedad*)
anxiety; (*POL etc*) unrest.
desasosiegue [desaso'sjeɣue] *etc vb V*
desasosegar.
desastrado, a [desas'traðo, a] *adj*
(*desaliñado*) shabby; (*sucio*) dirty.
desastre [de'sastre] *nm* disaster; ¡un ~!
how awful!; **la función fue un** ~ the show
was a shambles.
desastroso, a [desas'troso, a] *adj*
disastrous.
desatado, a [desa'taðo, a] *adj* (*desligado*)
untied; (*violento*) violent, wild.
desatar [desa'tar] *vt* (*nudo*) to untie;
(*paquete*) to undo; (*perro, odio*) to
unleash; (*misterio*) to solve; (*separar*) to
detach; ~**se** *vr* (*zapatos*) to come untied;
(*tormenta*) to break; (*perder control de sí*)
to lose self-control; ~**se en injurias** to
pour out a stream of insults.
desatascar [desatas'kar] *vt* (*cañería*) to
unblock, clear; (*carro*) to pull out of the
mud; ~ **a algn** (*fig*) to get sb out of a
jam.
desatasque [desa'taske] *etc vb V*
desatascar.
desatención [desaten'θjon] *nf* (*descuido*)
inattention; (*distracción*) absent-
mindedness.
desatender [desaten'der] *vt* (*no prestar
atención a*) to disregard; (*abandonar*) to
neglect.
desatento, a [desa'tento, a] *adj* (*distraído*)
inattentive; (*descortés*) discourteous.
desatienda [desa'tjenda] *etc vb V*
desatender.
desatinado, a [desati'naðo, a] *adj* foolish,
silly.
desatino [desa'tino] *nm* (*idiotez*)
foolishness, folly; (*error*) blunder; ~**s**
nmpl nonsense *sg*; ¡qué ~! how silly!,
what rubbish!
desatornillar [desatorni'ʎar] *vt* to
unscrew.
desatrancar [desatran'kar] *vt* (*puerta*) to
unbolt; (*cañería*) to unblock.
desatranque [desa'tranke] *etc vb V*
desatrancar.
desautorice [desauto'riθe] *etc vb V*
desautorizar.
desautorizado, a [desautori'θaðo, a] *adj*
unauthorized.
desautorizar [desautori'θar] *vt* (*oficial*) to

deprive of authority; (*informe*) to deny.

desavendré [desaßen'dre] *etc vb V*
desavenir.

desavenencia [desaße'nenθja] *nf*
(*desacuerdo*) disagreement;
(*discrepancia*) quarrel.

desavenga [desa'ßenga] *etc vb V*
desavenir.

desavenido, a [desaße'niðo, a] *adj*
(*opuesto*) contrary; (*reñidos*) in
disagreement; **ellos están ~s** they
are at odds.

desavenir [desaße'nir] *vt* (*enemistar*) to
make trouble between; **~se** *vr* to fall out.

desaventajado, a [desaßenta'xaðo, a] *adj*
(*inferior*) inferior; (*poco ventajoso*)
disadvantageous.

desaviene [desa'ßjene] *etc,*
desaviniendo [desaßi'njendo] *etc vb V*
desavenir.

desayunar [desaju'nar] *vi,* **~se** *vr* to have
breakfast ♦ *vt* to have for breakfast; **~**
con café to have coffee for breakfast; **~**
con algo (*fig*) to get the first news of sth.

desayuno [desa'juno] *nm* breakfast.

desazón [desa'θon] *nf* (*angustia*) anxiety;
(*MED*) discomfort; (*fig*) annoyance.

desazonar [desaθo'nar] *vt* (*fig*) to annoy,
upset; **~se** *vr* (*enojarse*) to be annoyed;
(*preocuparse*) to worry, be anxious.

desbancar [desßan'kar] *vt* (*quitar el puesto
a*) to oust; (*suplantar*) to supplant (in sb's
affections).

desbandada [desßan'daða] *nf* rush; **~**
general mass exodus; **a la ~** in disorder.

desbandarse [desßan'darse] *vr* (*MIL*) to
disband; (*fig*) to flee in disorder.

desbanque [des'ßanke] *etc vb V* **desbancar**.

desbarajuste [desßara'xuste] *nm*
confusion, disorder; **¡qué ~!** what a
mess!

desbaratar [desßara'tar] *vt* (*gen*) to mess
up; (*plan*) to spoil; (*deshacer, destruir*) to
ruin ♦ *vi* to talk nonsense; **~se** *vr*
(*máquina*) to break down; (*persona:
irritarse*) to fly off the handle (*fam*).

desbarrar [desßa'rrar] *vi* to talk nonsense.

desbloquear [desßloke'ar] *vt*
(*negociaciones, tráfico*) to get going
again; (*COM: cuenta*) to unfreeze.

desbocado, a [desßo'kaðo, a] *adj* (*caballo*)
runaway; (*herramienta*) worn.

desbocar [desßo'kar] *vt* (*vasija*) to break
the rim of; **~se** *vr* (*caballo*) to bolt;
(*persona: soltar injurias*) to let out a
stream of insults.

desboque [des'ßoke] *etc vb V* **desbocar**.

desbordamiento [desßorða'mjento] *nm*

(*de río*) overflowing; (*INFORM*) overflow;
(*de cólera*) outburst; (*de entusiasmo*)
upsurge.

desbordar [desßor'ðar] *vt* (*sobrepasar*) to
go beyond; (*exceder*) to exceed ♦ *vi,* **~se**
vr (*líquido, río*) to overflow; (*entusiasmo*)
to erupt; (*persona: exaltarse*) to get
carried away.

desbravar [desßra'ßar] *vt* (*caballo*) to break
in; (*animal*) to tame.

descabalgar [deskaßal'xar] *vi* to dismount.

descabalgue [deska'ßalɣe] *etc vb V*
descabalgar.

descabellado, a [deskaße'ʎaðo, a] *adj*
(*disparatado*) wild, crazy; (*insensato*)
preposterous.

descabellar [deskaße'ʎar] *vt* to ruffle;
(*TAUR: toro*) to give the coup de grace to.

descabezado, a [deskaße'θaðo, a] *adj* (*sin
cabeza*) headless; (*insensato*) wild.

descafeinado, a [deskafei'naðo, a] *adj*
decaffeinated ♦ *nm* decaffeinated
coffee, de-caff.

descalabrar [deskala'ßrar] *vt* to smash;
(*persona*) to hit; (: *en la cabeza*) to hit on
the head; (*NAUT*) to cripple; (*dañar*) to
harm, damage; **~se** *vr* to hurt one's
head.

descalabro [deska'laßro] *nm* blow;
(*desgracia*) misfortune.

descalce [des'kalθe] *etc vb V* **descalzar**.

descalificación [deskalifika'θjon] *nf*
disqualification; **descalificaciones** *nfpl*
discrediting *sg*.

descalificar [deskalifi'kar] *vt* to disqualify;
(*desacreditar*) to discredit.

descalifique [deskali'fike] *etc vb V*
descalificar.

descalzar [deskal'θar] *vt* (*zapato*) to take
off.

descalzo, a [des'kalθo, a] *adj* barefoot(ed);
(*fig*) destitute; **estar (con los pies) ~(s)** to
be barefooted.

descambiar [deskam'bjar] *vt* to exchange.

descaminado, a [deskami'naðo, a] *adj*
(*equivocado*) on the wrong road; (*fig*)
misguided; **en eso no anda usted muy ~**
you're not far wrong there.

descamisado, a [deskami'saðo, a] *adj*
bare-chested.

descampado [deskam'paðo] *nm* open
space, piece of empty ground; **comer al**
~ to eat in the open air.

descansado, a [deskan'saðo, a] *adj* (*gen*)
rested; (*que tranquiliza*) restful.

descansar [deskan'sar] *vt* (*gen*) to rest;
(*apoyar*): **~ (sobre)** to lean (on) ♦ *vi* to
rest, have a rest; (*echarse*) to lie down;

(*cadáver, restos*) to lie; ¡**que usted descanse!** sleep well!; ~ **en** (*argumento*) to be based on.

descansillo [deskan'siʎo] *nm* (*de escalera*) landing.

descanso [des'kanso] *nm* (*reposo*) rest; (*alivio*) relief; (*pausa*) break; (DEPORTE) interval, half time; **día de** ~ day off; ~ **de enfermedad/maternidad** sick/maternity leave; **tomarse unos días de** ~ to take a few days' leave *o* rest.

descapitalizado, a [deskapitali'θaðo, a] *adj* undercapitalized.

descapotable [deskapo'taβle] *nm* (*tb:* **coche** ~) convertible.

descarado, a [deska'raðo, a] *adj* (*sin vergüenza*) shameless; (*insolente*) cheeky.

descarga [des'karγa] *nf* (ARQ, ELEC, MIL) discharge; (NAUT) unloading.

descargador [deskarγa'ðor] *nm* (*de barcos*) docker.

descargar [deskar'γar] *vt* to unload; (*golpe*) to let fly; (*arma*) to fire; (ELEC) to discharge; (*pila*) to run down; (*conciencia*) to relieve; (COM) to take up; (*persona: de una obligación*) to release; (: *de una deuda*) to free; (JUR) to clear ♦ *vi* (*río*): ~ **(en)** to flow (into); ~**se** *vr* to unburden o.s.; ~**se de algo** to get rid of sth.

descargo [des'karγo] *nm* (*de obligación*) release; (COM: *recibo*) receipt; (: *de deuda*) discharge; (JUR) evidence; ~ **de una acusación** acquittal on a charge.

descargue [des'karγe] *etc vb V* **descargar**.

descarnado, a [deskar'naðo, a] *adj* scrawny; (*fig*) bare; (*estilo*) straightforward.

descaro [des'karo] *nm* nerve.

descarriar [deska'rrjar] *vt* (*descaminar*) to misdirect; (*fig*) to lead astray; ~**se** *vr* (*perderse*) to lose one's way; (*separarse*) to stray; (*pervertirse*) to err, go astray.

descarrilamiento [deskarrila'mjento] *nm* (*de tren*) derailment.

descarrilar [deskarri'lar] *vi* to be derailed.

descartable [deskar'taβle] *adj* (INFORM) temporary.

descartar [deskar'tar] *vt* (*rechazar*) to reject; (*eliminar*) to rule out; ~**se** *vr* (NAIPES) to discard; ~**se de** to shirk.

descascarar [deskaska'rar] *vt* (*naranja, limón*) to peel; (*nueces, huevo duro*) to shell; ~**se** *vr* to peel (off).

descascarillado, a [deskaskari'ʎaðo, a] *adj* (*paredes*) peeling.

descendencia [desθen'denθja] *nf* (*origen*) origin, descent; (*hijos*) offspring; **morir**

sin dejar ~ to die without issue.

descendente [desθen'dente] *adj* (*cantidad*) diminishing; (INFORM) top-down.

descender [desθen'der] *vt* (*bajar: escalera*) to go down ♦ *vi* to descend; (*temperatura, nivel*) to fall, drop; (*líquido*) to run; (*cortina etc*) to hang; (*fuerzas, persona*) to fail, get weak; ~ **de** to be descended from.

descendiente [desθen'djente] *nm/f* descendant.

descenso [des'θenso] *nm* descent; (*de temperatura*) drop; (*de producción*) downturn; (*de calidad*) decline; (MINERÍA) collapse; (*bajada*) slope; (*fig: decadencia*) decline; (*de empleado etc*) demotion.

descentrado, a [desθen'traðo, a] *adj* (*pieza de una máquina*) off-centre; (*rueda*) out of true; (*persona*) bewildered; (*desequilibrado*) unbalanced; (*problema*) out of focus; **todavía está algo** ~ he is still somewhat out of touch.

descentralice [desθentra'liθe] *etc vb V* **descentralizar**.

descentralizar [desθentrali'θar] *vt* to decentralize.

descerrajar [desθerra'xar] *vt* (*puerta*) to break open.

descienda [des'θjenda] *etc vb V* **descender**.

descifrable [desθi'fraβle] *adj* (*gen*) decipherable; (*letra*) legible.

descifrar [desθi'frar] *vt* (*escritura*) to decipher; (*mensaje*) to decode; (*problema*) to puzzle out; (*misterio*) to solve.

descocado, a [desko'kaðo, a] *adj* (*descarado*) cheeky; (*desvergonzado*) brazen.

descoco [des'koko] *nm* (*descaro*) cheek; (*atrevimiento*) brazenness.

descodificador [deskoðifika'ðor] *nm* decoder.

descodificar [deskoðifi'kar] *vt* to decode.

descolgar [deskol'γar] *vt* (*bajar*) to take down; (*desde una posición alta*) to lower; (*de una pared etc*) to unhook; (*teléfono*) to pick up; ~**se** *vr* to let o.s. down; ~**se por** (*bajar escurriéndose*) to slip down; (*pared*) to climb down; **dejó el teléfono descolgado** he left the phone off the hook.

descolgué [deskol'ɣe], **descolguemos** [deskol'ɣemos] *etc vb V* **descolgar**.

descollar [desko'ʎar] *vi* (*sobresalir*) to stand out; (*montaña etc*) to rise; **la obra que más descuella de las suyas** his most outstanding work.

descolocado, a [deskolo'kaðo, a] *adj:* **estar**

~ (*cosa*) to be out of place; (*criada*) to be unemployed.

descolorido, a [deskolo'riðo, a] *adj* (*color, tela*) faded; (*pálido*) pale; (*fig: estilo*) colourless.

descompaginar [deskompaxi'nar] *vt* (*desordenar*) to disarrange, mess up.

descompasado, a [deskompa'saðo, a] *adj* (*sin proporción*) out of all proportion; (*excesivo*) excessive; (*hora*) unearthly.

descompensar [deskompen'sar] *vt* to unbalance.

descompondré [deskompon'dre] *etc vb V* **descomponer**.

descomponer [deskompo'ner] *vt* (*gen, LING, MAT*) to break down; (*desordenar*) to disarrange, disturb; (*materia orgánica*) to rot, decompose; (*TEC*) to put out of order; (*facciones*) to distort; (*estómago etc*) to upset; (*planes*) to mess up; (*persona: molestar*) to upset; (: *irritar*) to annoy; ~**se** *vr* (*corromperse*) to rot, decompose; (*estómago*) to get upset; (*el tiempo*) to change (for the worse); (*TEC*) to break down.

descomponga [deskom'ponga] *etc vb V* **descomponer**.

descomposición [deskomposi'θjon] *nf* (*gen*) breakdown; (*de fruta etc*) decomposition; (*putrefacción*) rotting; (*de cara*) distortion; ~ **de vientre** (*MED*) stomach upset, diarrhoea.

descompostura [deskompos'tura] *nf* (*TEC*) breakdown; (*desorganización*) disorganization; (*desorden*) untidiness.

descompuesto, a [deskom'pwesto, a] *pp de* **descomponer** ♦ *adj* (*corrompido*) decomposed; (*roto*) broken (down).

descompuse [deskom'puse] *etc vb V* **descomponer**.

descomunal [deskomu'nal] *adj* (*enorme*) huge; (*fam: excelente*) fantastic.

desconcertado, a [deskonθer'taðo, a] *adj* disconcerted, bewildered.

desconcertar [deskonθer'tar] *vt* (*confundir*) to baffle; (*incomodar*) to upset, put out; (*orden*) to disturb; ~**se** *vr* (*turbarse*) to be upset; (*confundirse*) to be bewildered.

desconchado, a [deskon't∫aðo, a] *adj* (*pintura*) peeling.

desconchar [deskon't∫ar] *vt* (*pared*) to strip off; (*loza*) to chip off.

desconcierto [deskon'θjerto] *etc vb V* **desconcertar** ♦ *nm* (*gen*) disorder; (*desorientación*) uncertainty; (*inquietud*) uneasiness; (*confusión*) bewilderment.

desconectado, a [deskonek'taðo, a] *adj* (*ELEC*) disconnected, switched off;

(*INFORM*) offline; **estar** ~ **de** (*fig*) to have no contact with.

desconectar [deskonek'tar] *vt* to disconnect; (*desenchufar*) to unplug; (*radio, televisión*) to switch off; (*INFORM*) to toggle off.

desconfiado, a [deskon'fjaðo, a] *adj* suspicious.

desconfianza [deskon'fjanθa] *nf* distrust.

desconfiar [deskon'fjar] *vi* to be distrustful; ~ **de** (*sospechar*) to mistrust, suspect; (*no tener confianza en*) to have no faith in confidence in; **desconfío de ello** I doubt it; **desconfíe de las imitaciones** (*COM*) beware of imitations.

desconforme [deskon'forme] *adj* = **disconforme**.

descongelar [deskonxe'lar] *vt* (*nevera*) to defrost; (*comida*) to thaw; (*AUTO*) to de-ice; (*COM, POL*) to unfreeze.

descongestionar [desconxestjo'nar] *vt* (*cabeza, tráfico*) to clear; (*calle, ciudad*) to relieve congestion in; (*fig: despejar*) to clear.

desconocer [deskono'θer] *vt* (*ignorar*) not to know, be ignorant of; (*no aceptar*) to deny; (*repudiar*) to disown.

desconocido, a [deskono'θiðo, a] *adj* unknown; (*que no se conoce*) unfamiliar; (*no reconocido*) unrecognized ♦ *nm/f* stranger; (*recién llegado*) newcomer; **está** ~ he is hardly recognizable.

desconocimiento [deskonoθi'mjento] *nm* (*falta de conocimientos*) ignorance; (*repudio*) disregard.

desconozca [desko'noθka] *etc vb V* **desconocer**.

desconsiderado, a [deskonsiðe'raðo, a] *adj* inconsiderate; (*insensible*) thoughtless.

desconsolado, a [deskonso'laðo, a] *adj* (*afligido*) disconsolate; (*cara*) sad; (*desanimado*) dejected.

desconsolar [deskonso'lar] *vt* to distress; ~**se** *vr* to despair.

desconsuelo [deskon'swelo] *etc vb V* **desconsolar** ♦ *nm* (*tristeza*) distress; (*desesperación*) despair.

descontado, a [deskon'taðo, a] *adj:* **por** ~ of course; **dar por** ~ (**que**) to take it for granted (that).

descontar [deskon'tar] *vt* (*deducir*) to take away, deduct; (*rebajar*) to discount.

descontento, a [deskon'tento, a] *adj* dissatisfied ♦ *nm* dissatisfaction, discontent.

descontrol [deskon'trol] *nm* (*fam*) lack of control.

descontrolado, a [deskontro'laðo, a] *adj* uncontrolled.

descontrolarse [deskontro'larse] *vr* (*persona*) to lose control.

desconvenir [deskombe'nir] *vi* (*personas*) to disagree; (*no corresponder*) not to fit; (*no convenir*) to be inconvenient.

desconvocar [deskombo'kar] *vt* to call off.

descorazonar [deskoraθo'nar] *vt* to discourage, dishearten; ~se *vr* to get discouraged, lose heart.

descorchador [deskortʃa'ðor] *nm* corkscrew.

descorchar [deskor'tʃar] *vt* to uncork, open.

descorrer [desko'rrer] *vt* (*cortina, cerrojo*) to draw back; (*velo*) to remove.

descortés [deskor'tes] *adj* (*mal educado*) discourteous; (*grosero*) rude.

descortesía [deskorte'sia] *nf* discourtesy; (*grosería*) rudeness.

descoser [desko'ser] *vt* to unstitch; ~se *vr* to come apart (at the seams); (*fam: descubrir un secreto*) to blurt out a secret; ~se de risa to split one's sides laughing.

descosido, a [desko'siðo, a] *adj* (*costura*) unstitched; (*desordenado*) disjointed ♦ *nm*: como un ~ (*obrar*) wildly; (*beber, comer*) to excess; (*estudiar*) like mad.

descoyuntar [deskojun'tar] *vt* (ANAT) to dislocate; (*hechos*) to twist; ~se *vr*: ~se un hueso (ANAT) to put a bone out of joint; ~se de risa (*fam*) to split one's sides laughing; estar descoyuntado (*persona*) to be double-jointed.

descrédito [des'kreðito] *nm* discredit; caer en ~ to fall into disrepute; ir en ~ de to be to the discredit of.

descreído, a [deskre'iðo, a] *adj* (*incrédulo*) incredulous; (*falto de fe*) unbelieving.

descremado, a [deskre'maðo, a] *adj* skimmed.

descremar [deskre'mar] *vt* (*leche*) to skim.

describir [deskri'ßir] *vt* to describe.

descripción [deskrip'θjon] *nf* description.

descrito [des'krito] *pp de* **describir**.

descuajar [deskwa'xar] *vt* (*disolver*) to melt; (*planta*) to pull out by the roots; (*extirpar*) to eradicate, wipe out; (*desanimar*) to dishearten.

descuajaringarse [deskwaxarin'garse] *vr* to fall to bits.

descuajaringue [deskwaxa'ringe] *etc vb V* **descuajaringarse**.

descuartice [deskwar'tiθe] *etc vb V*

descuartizar.

descuartizar [deskwarti'θar] *vt* (*animal*) to carve up, cut up; (*fig: hacer pedazos*) to tear apart.

descubierto, a [desku'ßjerto, a] *pp de* **descubrir** ♦ *adj* uncovered, bare; (*persona*) bare-headed; (*cielo*) clear; (*coche*) open; (*campo*) treeless ♦ *nm* (*lugar*) open space; (COM: en el presupuesto) shortage; (: *bancario*) overdraft; al ~ in the open; poner al ~ to lay bare; quedar al ~ to be exposed; estar en ~ to be overdrawn.

descubridor, a [desku'ßri'ðor, a] *nm/f* discoverer.

descubrimiento [deskußri'mjento] *nm* (*hallazgo*) discovery; (*de criminal, fraude*) detection; (*revelación*) revelation; (*de secreto etc*) disclosure; (*de estatua etc*) unveiling.

descubrir [desku'ßrir] *vt* to discover, find; (*petróleo*) to strike; (*inaugurar*) to unveil; (*vislumbrar*) to detect; (*sacar a luz: crimen*) to bring to light; (*revelar*) to reveal, show; (*poner al descubierto*) to expose to view; (*naipes*) to lay down; (*quitar la tapa de*) to uncover; (*cacerola*) to take the lid off; (*enterarse de: causa, solución*) to find out; (*divisar*) to see, make out; (*delatar*) to give away, betray; ~se *vr* to reveal o.s.; (*quitarse sombrero*) to take off one's hat; (*confesar*) to confess; (*fig: salir a luz*) to come out o to light.

descuelga [des'kwelɣa] *etc*, **descuelgue** [des'kwelɣe] *etc vb V* **descolgar**.

descuelle [des'kweʎe] *etc vb V* **descollar**.

descuento [des'kwento] *etc vb V* **descontar** ♦ *nm* discount; ~ del 3% 3% off; con ~ at a discount; ~ por pago al contado (COM) cash discount; ~ por volumen de compras (COM) volume discount.

descuidado, a [deskwi'ðaðo, a] *adj* (*sin cuidado*) careless; (*desordenado*) untidy; (*olvidadizo*) forgetful; (*dejado*) neglected; (*desprevenido*) unprepared.

descuidar [deskwi'ðar] *vt* (*dejar*) to neglect; (*olvidar*) to overlook ♦ *vi*, ~se *vr* (*distraerse*) to be careless; (*estar desaliñado*) to let o.s. go; (*desprevenirse*) to drop one's guard; ¡descuida! don't worry!

descuido [des'kwiðo] *nm* (*dejadez*) carelessness; (*olvido*) negligence; (*un ~*) oversight; al ~ casually; (*sin cuidado*) carelessly; al menor ~ if my *etc* attention wanders for a minute; con ~ thoughtlessly; por ~ by an oversight.

desentonar [desento'nar] *vi* (*MUS*) to sing
(*o* play) out of tune; (*no encajar*) to be out
of place; (*color*) to clash.
desentorpecer [desentorpe'θer] *vt*
(*miembro*) to stretch; (*fam: persona*) to
polish up.
desentorpezca [desentor'peθka] *etc vb V*
desentorpecer.
desentrañar [desentra'ɲar] *vt* (*misterio*) to
unravel.
desentrenado, a [desentre'naðo, a] *adj* out
of training.
desentumecer [desentume'θer] *vt* (*pierna
etc*) to stretch; (*DEPORTE*) to loosen up.
desentumezca [desentu'meθka] *etc vb V*
desentumecer.
desenvainar [desembai'nar] *vt* (*espada*) to
draw, unsheathe.
desenvoltura [desembol'tura] *nf* (*libertad,
gracia*) ease; (*descaro*) free and easy
manner; (*al hablar*) fluency.
desenvolver [desembol'ßer] *vt* (*paquete*) to
unwrap; (*fig*) to develop; ~**se** *vr*
(*desarrollarse*) to unfold, develop;
(*suceder*) to go off; (*prosperar*) to
prosper; (*arreglárselas*) to cope.
desenvolvimiento [desembolßi'mjento]
nm (*desarrollo*) development; (*de idea*)
exposition.
desenvuelto, a [desem'bwelto, a] *pp de*
desenvolver ♦ *adj* (*suelto*) easy;
(*desenfadado*) confident; (*al hablar*) fluent;
(*pey*) forward.
desenvuelva [desem'buelßa] *etc vb V*
desenvolver.
deseo [de'seo] *nm* desire, wish; ~ **de saber**
thirst for knowledge; **buen** ~ good
intentions *pl*; **arder en** ~**s de algo** to
yearn for sth.
deseoso, a [dese'oso, a] *adj*: **estar** ~ **de
hacer** to be anxious to do.
deseque [de'seke] *etc vb V* **desecar**.
desequilibrado, a [desekili'ßraðo, a] *adj*
unbalanced ♦ *nm/f* unbalanced person; ~
mental mentally disturbed person.
desequilibrar [desekili'ßrar] *vt* (*mente*) to
unbalance; (*objeto*) to throw out of
balance; (*persona*) to throw off balance.
desequilibrio [deseki'lißrio] *nm* (*de mente*)
unbalance; (*entre cantidades*) imbalance;
(*MED*) unbalanced mental condition.
desertar [deser'tar] *vt* (*JUR: derecho de
apelación*) to forfeit ♦ *vi* to desert; ~ **de
sus deberes** to neglect one's duties.
desértico, a [de'sertiko, a] *adj* desert *cpd*;
(*vacío*) deserted.
desertor, a [deser'tor, a] *nm/f* deserter.
desesperación [desespera'θjon] *nf*

desperation, despair; (*irritación*) fury; **es
una** ~ it's maddening; **es una** ~ **tener
que** ... it's infuriating to have to ....
desesperado, a [desespe'raðo, a] *adj*
(*persona: sin esperanza*) desperate; (*caso,
situación*) hopeless; (*esfuerzo*) furious
♦ *nm*: **como un** ~ like mad ♦ *nf*: **hacer
algo a la desesperada** to do sth as a last
resort *o* in desperation.
desesperance [desespe'ranθe] *etc vb V*
desesperanzar.
desesperante [desespe'rante] *adj* (*exaspe-
rante*) infuriating; (*persona*) hopeless.
desesperanzar [desesperan'θar] *vt* to drive
to despair; ~**se** *vr* to lose hope, despair.
desesperar [desespe'rar] *vt* to drive to
despair; (*exasperar*) to drive to
distraction ♦ *vi*: ~ **de** to despair of; ~**se**
vr to despair, lose hope.
desespero [deses'pero] *nm* (*AM*) despair.
desestabilice [desestaßi'liθe] *etc vb V*
desestabilizar.
desestabilizar [desestaßili'θar] *vt* to
destabilize.
desestimar [desesti'mar] *vt* (*menospreciar*)
to have a low opinion of; (*rechazar*) to
reject.
desfachatez [desfatʃa'teθ] *nf* (*insolencia*)
impudence; (*descaro*) rudeness.
desfalco [des'falko] *nm* embezzlement.
desfallecer [desfaʎe'θer] *vi* (*perder las
fuerzas*) to become weak; (*desvanecerse*)
to faint.
desfallecido, a [desfaʎe'θiðo, a] *adj* (*débil*)
weak.
desfallezca [desfa'ʎeθka] *etc vb V*
desfallecer.
desfasado, a [desfa'saðo, a] *adj* (*anticuado*)
old-fashioned; (*TEC*) out of phase.
desfasar [desfa'sar] *vt* to phase out.
desfase [des'fase] *nm* (*diferencia*) gap.
desfavorable [desfaßo'raßle] *adj*
unfavourable.
desfavorecer [desfaßore'θer] *vt* (*sentar
mal*) not to suit.
desfavorezca [desfaßo'reθka] *etc vb V*
desfavorecer.
desfiguración [desfiɣura'θjon] *nf*,
desfiguramiento [desfiɣura'mjento] *nm*
(*de persona*) disfigurement; (*de
monumento*) defacement; (*FOTO*)
blurring.
desfigurar [desfiɣu'rar] *vt* (*cara*) to
disfigure; (*cuerpo*) to deform; (*cuadro,
monumento*) to deface; (*FOTO*) to blur;
(*sentido*) to twist; (*suceso*) to
misrepresent.
desfiladero [desfila'ðero] *nm* gorge, defile.

desfilar [desfi'lar] *vi* to parade; **desfilaron ante el general** they marched past the general.

desfile [des'file] *nm* procession; (*MIL*) parade; ~ **de modelos** fashion show.

desflorar [desflo'rar] *vt* (*mujer*) to deflower; (*arruinar*) to tarnish; (*asunto*) to touch on.

desfogar [desfo'xar] *vt* (*fig*) to vent ♦ *vi* (*NAUT: tormenta*) to burst; ~**se** *vr* (*fig*) to let off steam.

desfogue [des'foxe] *etc vb V* **desfogar**.

desgajar [desxa'xar] *vt* (*arrancar*) to tear off; (*romper*) to break off; (*naranja*) to split into segments; ~**se** *vr* to come off.

desgana [des'xana] *nf* (*falta de apetito*) loss of appetite; (*renuencia*) unwillingness; **hacer algo a** ~ to do sth unwillingly.

desganado, a [desxa'naðo, a] *adj*: **estar** ~ (*sin apetito*) to have no appetite; (*sin entusiasmo*) to have lost interest.

desgañitarse [desxaɲi'tarse] *vr* to shout o.s. hoarse.

desgarbado, a [desxar'ßaðo, a] *adj* (*sin gracia*) clumsy, ungainly.

desgarrador, a [desxarra'ðor, a] *adj* heartrending.

desgarrar [desxa'rrar] *vt* to tear (up); (*fig*) to shatter.

desgarro [des'xarro] *nm* (*en tela*) tear; (*aflicción*) grief; (*descaro*) impudence.

desgastar [desxas'tar] *vt* (*deteriorar*) to wear away o down; (*estropear*) to spoil; ~**se** *vr* to get worn out.

desgaste [des'xaste] *nm* wear (and tear); (*de roca*) erosion; (*de cuerda*) fraying; (*de metal*) corrosion; ~ **económico** drain on one's resources.

desglosar [desxlo'sar] *vt* to detach.

desgobierno [desxo'ßjerno] *etc vb V* **desgobernar** ♦ *nm* (*POL*) misgovernment, misrule.

desgracia [des'xraθja] *nf* misfortune; (*accidente*) accident; (*vergüenza*) disgrace; (*contratiempo*) setback; **por** ~ unfortunately; **en el accidente no hay que lamentar** ~**s personales** there were no casualties in the accident; **caer en** ~ to fall from grace; **tener la** ~ **de** to be unlucky enough to.

desgraciadamente [desxraθjaða'mente] *adv* unfortunately.

desgraciado, a [desxra'θjaðo, a] *adj* (*sin suerte*) unlucky, unfortunate; (*miserable*) wretched; (*infeliz*) miserable ♦ *nm/f* (*malo*) swine; (*infeliz*) poor creature; **¡esa radio desgraciada!** (*esp AM*) that lousy radio!

desgraciar [desxra'θjar] *vt* (*estropear*) to spoil; (*ofender*) to displease.

desgranar [desxra'nar] *vt* (*trigo*) to thresh; (*guisantes*) to shell; ~ **un racimo** to pick the grapes from a bunch; ~ **mentiras** to come out with a string of lies.

desgravación [desxraßa'θjon] *nf* (*COM*): ~ **de impuestos** tax relief; ~ **personal** personal allowance.

desgravar [desxra'ßar] *vt* (*producto*) to reduce the tax o duty on.

desgreñado, a [desxre'ɲaðo, a] *adj* dishevelled.

desguace [des'xwaθe] *nm* (*de coches*) scrapping; (*lugar*) scrapyard.

desguazar [desxwa'θar] *vt* (*coche*) to scrap.

deshabitado, a [desaßi'taðo, a] *adj* uninhabited.

deshabitar [desaßi'tar] *vt* (*casa*) to leave empty; (*despoblar*) to depopulate.

deshacer [desa'θer] *vt* (*lo hecho*) to undo, unmake; (*proyectos: arruinar*) to spoil; (*casa*) to break up; (*TEC*) to take apart; (*enemigo*) to defeat; (*diluir*) to melt; (*contrato*) to break; (*intriga*) to solve; (*cama*) to strip; (*maleta*) to unpack; (*paquete*) to unwrap; (*nudo*) to untie; (*costura*) to unpick; ~**se** *vr* (*desatarse*) to come undone; (*estropearse*) to be spoiled; (*descomponerse*) to fall to pieces; (*disolverse*) to melt; (*despedazarse*) to come apart o undone; ~**se de** to get rid of; (*COM*) to dump, unload; ~**se en** (*cumplidos, elogios*) to be lavish with; ~**se en lágrimas** to burst into tears; ~**se por algo** to be crazy about sth.

deshaga [de'saxa] *etc*, **desharé** [desa're] *etc vb V* **deshacer**.

des(h)arrapado, a [desarra'paðo, a] *adj* ragged; (*de aspecto*) ~ shabby.

deshecho, a [de'setʃo, a] *pp de* **deshacer** ♦ *adj* (*lazo, nudo*) undone; (*roto*) smashed; (*despedazado*) in pieces; (*cama*) unmade; (*MED: persona*) weak, emaciated; (: *salud*) broken; **estoy** ~ I'm shattered.

deshelar [dese'lar] *vt* (*cañería*) to thaw; (*heladera*) to defrost.

desheredar [desere'ðar] *vt* to disinherit.

deshice [de'siθe] *etc vb V* **deshacer**.

deshidratación [desiðrata'θjon] *nf* dehydration.

deshidratar [desiðra'tar] *vt* to dehydrate.

deshielo [des'jelo] *etc vb V* **deshelar** ♦ *nm* thaw.

deshilachar [desila'tʃar] *vt*, **deshilacharse** *vr* to fray.

deshilar [desi'lar] *vt* (*tela*) to unravel.

deshilvanado, a [desilßa'naðo, a] *adj* (*fig*) disjointed, incoherent.

deshinchar [desin'tʃar] *vt* (*neumático*) to let down; (*herida etc*) to reduce (the swelling of); ~**se** *vr* (*neumático*) to go flat; (*hinchazón*) to go down.

deshojar [deso'xar] *vt* (*árbol*) to strip the leaves off; (*flor*) to pull the petals off; ~**se** *vr* to lose its leaves *etc*.

deshollinar [desoʎi'nar] *vt* (*chimenea*) to sweep.

deshonesto, a [deso'nesto, a] *adj* (*no honrado*) dishonest; (*indecente*) indecent.

deshonor [deso'nor] *nm* dishonour, disgrace; (*un* ~) insult, affront.

deshonra [de'sonra] *nf* (*deshonor*) dishonour; (*vergüenza*) shame.

deshonrar [deson'rar] *vt* to dishonour.

deshonroso, a [deson'roso, a] *adj* dishonourable, disgraceful.

deshora [de'sora]: **a** ~ *adv* at the wrong time; (*llegar*) unexpectedly; (*acostarse*) at some unearthly hour.

deshuesar [deswe'sar] *vt* (*carne*) to bone; (*fruta*) to stone.

desidia [de'siðja] *nf* (*pereza*) idleness.

desierto, a [de'sjerto, a] *adj* (*casa, calle, negocio*) deserted; (*paisaje*) bleak ♦ *nm* desert.

designación [desixna'θjon] *nf* (*para un cargo*) appointment; (*nombre*) designation.

designar [desix'nar] *vt* (*nombrar*) to designate; (*indicar*) to fix.

designio [de'sixnjo] *nm* plan; **con el** ~ **de** with the intention of.

desigual [desi'ɣwal] *adj* (*lucha*) unequal; (*diferente*) different; (*terreno*) uneven; (*tratamiento*) unfair; (*cambiadizo: tiempo*) changeable; (: *carácter*) unpredictable.

desigualdad [desixwal'ðað] *nf* (*ECON, POL*) inequality; (*de carácter, tiempo*) unpredictability; (*de escritura*) unevenness; (*de terreno*) roughness.

desilusión [desilu'sjon] *nf* disillusionment; (*decepción*) disappointment.

desilusionar [desilusjo'nar] *vt* to disillusion; (*decepcionar*) to disappoint; ~**se** *vr* to become disillusioned.

desinencia [desi'nenθja] *nf* (*LING*) ending.

desinfectar [desinfek'tar] *vt* to disinfect.

desinfestar [desinfes'tar] *vt* to decontaminate.

desinflación [desinfla'θjon] *nf* (*COM*) disinflation.

desinflar [desin'flar] *vt* to deflate; ~**se** *vr* (*neumático*) to go down *o* flat.

desintegración [desinteɣra'θjon] *nf*

disintegration; ~ **nuclear** nuclear fission.

desintegrar [desinte'ɣrar] *vt* (*gen*) to disintegrate; (*átomo*) to split; (*grupo*) to break up; ~**se** *vr* to disintegrate; to split; to break up.

desinterés [desinte'res] *nm* (*objetividad*) disinterestedness; (*altruismo*) unselfishness.

desinteresado, a [desintere'saðo, a] *adj* (*imparcial*) disinterested; (*altruista*) unselfish.

desintoxicar [desintoksi'kar] *vt* to detoxify; ~**se** *vr* (*drogadicto*) to undergo treatment for drug addiction; ~**se de** (*rutina, trabajo*) to get away from.

desintoxique [desintok'sike] *etc vb V* **desintoxicar**.

desistir [desis'tir] *vi* (*renunciar*) to stop, desist; ~ **de** (*empresa*) to give up; (*derecho*) to waive.

deslavazado, a [deslaßa'θaðo, a] *adj* (*lacio*) limp; (*desteñido*) faded; (*insípido*) colourless; (*incoherente*) disjointed.

desleal [desle'al] *adj* (*infiel*) disloyal; (*COM: competencia*) unfair.

deslealtad [desleal'tað] *nf* disloyalty.

desleído, a [desle'iðo, a] *adj* weak, woolly.

desleír [desle'ir] *vt* (*líquido*) to dilute; (*sólido*) to dissolve.

deslenguado, a [deslen'gwaðo, a] *adj* (*grosero*) foul-mouthed.

deslía [des'lia] *etc vb V* **desleír**.

desliar [des'ljar] *vt* (*desatar*) to untie; (*paquete*) to open; ~**se** *vr* to come undone.

deslice [des'liθe] *etc vb V* **deslizar**.

desliendo [desli'endo] *etc vb V* **desleír**.

desligar [desli'ɣar] *vt* (*desatar*) to untie, undo; (*separar*) to separate; ~**se** *vr* (*de un compromiso*) to extricate o.s.

desligue [des'liɣe] *etc vb V* **desligar**.

deslindar [deslin'dar] *vt* (*señalar las lindes de*) to mark out, fix the boundaries of; (*fig*) to define.

desliz [des'liθ] *nm* (*fig*) lapse; ~ **de lengua** slip of the tongue; **cometer un** ~ to slip up.

deslizar [desli'θar] *vt* to slip, slide; ~**se** *vr* (*escurrirse: persona*) to slip, slide; (: *coche*) to skid; (*aguas mansas*) to flow gently; (*error*) to creep in; (*tiempo*) to pass; (*persona: irse*) to slip away; ~**se en un cuarto** to slip into a room.

deslomar [deslo'mar] *vt* (*romper el lomo de*) to break the back of; (*fig*) to wear out; ~**se** *vr* (*fig fam*) to work one's guts out.

deslucido, a [deslu'θiðo, a] *adj* dull; (*torpe*)

awkward, graceless; (*deslustrado*)
tarnished; (*fracasado*) unsuccessful;
quedar ~ to make a poor impression.
deslucir [deslu'θir] *vt* (*deslustrar*) to
tarnish; (*estropear*) to spoil, ruin;
(*persona*) to discredit; **la lluvia deslució
el acto** the rain ruined the ceremony.
deslumbrar [deslum'brar] *vt* (*con la luz*) to
dazzle; (*cegar*) to blind; (*impresionar*) to
dazzle; (*dejar perplejo a*) to puzzle,
confuse.
deslustrar [deslus'trar] *vt* (*vidrio*) to frost;
(*quitar lustre a*) to dull; (*reputación*) to
sully.
desluzca [des'luθka] *etc vb V* **deslucir**.
desmadrarse [desma'ðrarse] *vr* (*fam*) to
run wild.
desmadre [des'maðre] *nm* (*fam*:
desorganización) chaos; (: *jaleo*)
commotion.
desmán [des'man] *nm* (*exceso*) outrage;
(*abuso de poder*) abuse.
desmandarse [desman'darse] *vr* (*portarse
mal*) to behave badly; (*excederse*) to get
out of hand; (*caballo*) to bolt.
desmano [des'mano]: **a** ~ *adv*: **me coge** *o*
pilla a ~ it's out of my way.
desmantelar [desmante'lar] *vt* (*deshacer*)
to dismantle; (*casa*) to strip;
(*organización*) to disband; (*MIL*) to raze;
(*andamio*) to take down; (*NAUT*) to unrig.
desmaquillador [desmakiʎa'ðor] *nm*
make-up remover.
desmaquillarse [desmaki'ʎarse] *vr* to take
off one's make up.
desmarcarse [desmar'karse] *vr*: ~ **de**
(*DEPORTE*) to get clear of; (*fig*) to
distance o.s. from.
desmayado, a [desma'jaðo, a] *adj* (*sin
sentido*) unconscious; (*carácter*) dull;
(*débil*) faint, weak; (*color*) pale.
desmayar [desma'jar] *vi* to lose heart; ~**se**
vr (*MED*) to faint.
desmayo [des'majo] *nm* (*MED*: *acto*) faint;
(*estado*) unconsciousness; (*depresión*)
dejection; (*de voz*) faltering; **sufrir un** ~
to have a fainting fit.
desmedido, a [desme'ðiðo, a] *adj*
excessive; (*ambición*) boundless.
desmejorado, a [desmexo'raðo, a] *adj*:
está muy desmejorada (*MED*) she's not
looking too well.
desmejorar [desmexo'rar] *vt* (*dañar*) to
impair, spoil; (*MED*) to weaken.
desmembración [desmembra'θjon] *nf*
dismemberment; (*fig*) break-up.
desmembrar [desmem'brar] *vt* (*MED*) to
dismember; (*fig*) to separate.

desmemoriado, a [desmemo'rjaðo, a] *adj*
forgetful, absent-minded.
desmentir [desmen'tir] *vt* (*contradecir*) to
contradict; (*refutar*) to deny; (*rumor*) to
scotch ♦ *vi*: ~ **de** to refute; ~**se** *vr* to
contradict o.s.
desmenuce [desme'nuθe] *etc vb V*
desmenuzar.
desmenuzar [desmenu'θar] *vt* (*deshacer*) to
crumble; (*carne*) to chop; (*examinar*) to
examine closely.
desmerecer [desmere'θer] *vt* to be
unworthy of ♦ *vi* (*deteriorarse*) to
deteriorate.
desmerezca [desme're∫ka] *etc vb V*
desmerecer.
desmesurado, a [desmesu'raðo, a] *adj*
(*desmedido*) disproportionate; (*enorme*)
enormous; (*ambición*) boundless;
(*descarado*) insolent.
desmiembre [des'mjembre] *etc vb V*
desmembrar.
desmienta [des'mjenta] *etc vb V*
desmentir.
desmigajar [desmiɣa'xar], **desmigar**
[desmi'ɣar] *vt* to crumble.
desmigue [des'miɣe] *etc vb V* **desmigar**.
desmilitarice [desmilita'riθe] *etc vb V*
desmilitarizar.
desmilitarizar [desmilitari'θar] *vt* to
demilitarize.
desmintiendo [desmin'tjendo] *etc vb V*
desmentir.
desmochar [desmo't∫ar] *vt* (*árbol*) to lop;
(*texto*) to cut, hack about.
desmontable [desmon'taßle] *adj* (*que se
quita*) detachable; (*en compartimientos*)
sectional; (*que se puede plegar etc*)
collapsible.
desmontar [desmon'tar] *vt* (*deshacer*) to
dismantle; (*motor*) to strip down;
(*máquina*) to take apart; (*escopeta*) to
uncock; (*tienda de campaña*) to take
down; (*tierra*) to level; (*quitar los árboles
a*) to clear; (*jinete*) to throw ♦ *vi* to
dismount.
desmonte [des'monte] *nm* (*de tierra*)
levelling; (*de árboles*) clearing; (*terreno*)
levelled ground; (*FERRO*) cutting.
desmoralice [desmora'liθe] *etc vb V*
desmoralizar.
desmoralizador, a [desmoraliθa'ðor, a] *adj*
demoralizing.
desmoralizar [desmorali'θar] *vt* to
demoralize.
desmoronado, a [desmoro'naðo, a] *adj*
(*casa, edificio*) dilapidated.
desmoronamiento [desmorona'mjento]

nm (*tb fig*) crumbling.

desmoronar [desmoro'nar] *vt* to wear away, erode; ~**se** *vr* (*edificio, dique*) to fall into disrepair; (*economía*) to decline.

desmovilice [desmoßi'liθe] *etc vb V* **desmovilizar**.

desmovilizar [desmoßili'θar] *vt* to demobilize.

desnacionalización [desnaθjonaliθa'θjon] *nf* denationalization.

desnacionalizado, a [desnaθjonali'θaðo, a] *adj* (*industria*) denationalized; (*persona*) stateless.

desnatado, a [desna'taðo, a] *adj* skimmed; (*yogur*) low fat.

desnatar [desna'tar] *vt* (*leche*) to skim; **leche sin** ~ whole milk.

desnaturalice [desnatura'liθe] *etc vb V* **desnaturalizar**.

desnaturalizado, a [desnaturali'θaðo, a] *adj* (*persona*) unnatural; **alcohol** ~ methylated spirits.

desnaturalizar [desnaturali'θar] *vt* (*QUÍMICA*) to denature; (*corromper*) to pervert; (*sentido de algo*) to distort; ~**se** *vr* (*perder la nacionalidad*) to give up one's nationality.

desnivel [desni'ßel] *nm* (*de terreno*) unevenness; (*POL*) inequality; (*diferencia*) difference.

desnivelar [desniße'lar] *vt* (*terreno*) to make uneven; (*fig: desequilibrar*) to unbalance; (*balanza*) to tip.

desnuclearizado, a [desnukleari'θaðo, a] *adj*: **región desnuclearizada** nuclear-free zone.

desnudar [desnu'ðar] *vt* (*desvestir*) to undress; (*despojar*) to strip; ~**se** *vr* (*desvestirse*) to get undressed.

desnudez [desnu'ðeθ] *nf* (*de persona*) nudity; (*fig*) bareness.

desnudo, a [des'nuðo, a] *adj* (*cuerpo*) naked; (*árbol, brazo*) bare; (*paisaje*) flat; (*estilo*) unadorned; (*verdad*) plain ♦ *nm/f* nude; ~ **de** devoid *o* bereft of; **la retrató al** ~ he painted her in the nude; **poner al** ~ to lay bare.

desnutrición [desnutri'θjon] *nf* malnutrition.

desnutrido, a [desnu'triðo, a] *adj* undernourished.

desobedecer [desoßeðe'θer] *vt, vi* to disobey.

desobedezca [desoße'ðeθka] *etc vb V* **desobedecer**.

desobediencia [desoße'ðjenθja] *nf* disobedience.

desocupación [desokupa'θjon] *nf* (*AM*) unemployment.

desocupado, a [desoku'paðo, a] *adj* at leisure; (*desempleado*) unemployed; (*deshabitado*) empty, vacant.

desocupar [desoku'par] *vt* to vacate; ~**se** *vr* (*quedar libre*) to be free; **se ha desocupado aquella mesa** that table's free now.

desodorante [desoðo'rante] *nm* deodorant.

desoiga [de'soiɣa] *etc vb V* **desoír**.

desoír [deso'ir] *vt* to ignore, disregard.

desolación [desola'θjon] *nf* (*de lugar*) desolation; (*fig*) grief.

desolar [deso'lar] *vt* to ruin, lay waste.

desollar [deso'ʎar] *vt* (*quitar la piel a*) to skin; (*criticar*): ~ **vivo a** to criticize unmercifully.

desorbitado, a [desorßi'taðo, a] *adj* (*excesivo*) excessive; (*precio*) exorbitant; **con los ojos** ~**s** pop-eyed.

desorbitar [desorßi'tar] *vt* (*exagerar*) to exaggerate; (*interpretar mal*) to misinterpret; ~**se** *vr* (*persona*) to lose one's sense of proportion; (*asunto*) to get out of hand.

desorden [de'sorðen] *nm* confusion; (*de casa, cuarto*) mess; (*político*) disorder; **desórdenes** *nmpl* (*alborotos*) disturbances; (*excesos*) excesses; **en** ~ (*gente*) in confusion.

desordenado, a [desorðe'naðo, a] *adj* (*habitación, persona*) untidy; (*objetos: revueltos*) in a mess, jumbled; (*conducta*) disorderly.

desordenar [desorðe'nar] *vt* (*gen*) to disarrange; (*pelo*) to mess up; (*cuarto*) to make a mess in; (*causar confusión a*) to throw into confusion.

desorganice [desorɣa'niθe] *etc vb V* **desorganizar**.

desorganizar [desorɣani'θar] *vt* to disorganize.

desorientar [desorjen'tar] *vt* (*extraviar*) to mislead; (*confundir, desconcertar*) to confuse; ~**se** *vr* (*perderse*) to lose one's way.

desovar [deso'ßar] *vi* (*peces*) to spawn; (*insectos*) to lay eggs.

desoyendo [deso'jendo] *etc vb V* **desoír**.

despabilado, a [despaßi'laðo, a] *adj* (*despierto*) wide-awake; (*fig*) alert, sharp.

despabilar [despaßi'lar] *vt* (*despertar*) to wake up; (*fig: persona*) to liven up; (*trabajo*) to get through quickly ♦ *vi*, ~**se** *vr* to wake up; (*fig*) to get a move on.

despachar [despa'tʃar] *vt* (*negocio*) to do, complete; (*resolver: problema*) to settle; (*correspondencia*) to deal with; (*fam:*

comida) to polish off; (: *bebida*) to knock back; (*enviar*) to send, dispatch; (*vender*) to sell, deal in; (*COM: cliente*) to attend to; (*billete*) to issue; (*mandar ir*) to send away ♦ *vi* (*decidirse*) to get things settled; (*apresurarse*) to hurry up; ~**se** *vr* to finish off; (*apresurarse*) to hurry up; ~**se de algo** to get rid of sth; ~**se a su gusto con algn** to give sb a piece of one's mind; **¿quién despacha?** is anybody serving?

despacho [des'patʃo] *nm* (*oficina*) office; (: *en una casa*) study; (*de paquetes*) dispatch; (*COM: venta*) sale (of goods); (*comunicación*) message; ~ **de billetes** *o* **boletos** (*AM*) booking office; ~ **de localidades** box office; **géneros sin** ~ unsaleable goods; **tener buen** ~ to find a ready sale.

despachurrar [despatʃu'rrar] *vt* (*aplastar*) to crush; (*persona*) to flatten.

despacio [des'paθjo] *adv* (*lentamente*) slowly; (*esp AM: en voz baja*) softly; ¡~! take it easy!

despacito [despa'θito] *adv* (*fam*) slowly; (*suavemente*) softly.

despampanante [despampa'nante] *adj* (*fam: chica*) stunning.

desparejado, a [despare'xaðo, a] *adj* odd.

desparpajo [despar'paxo] *nm* (*desenvoltura*) self-confidence; (*pey*) nerve.

desparramar [desparra'mar] *vt* (*esparcir*) to scatter; (*líquido*) to spill.

despatarrarse [despata'rrarse] *vr* (*abrir las piernas*) to open one's legs wide; (*caerse*) to tumble; (*fig*) to be flabbergasted.

despavorido, a [despaβo'riðo, a] *adj* terrified.

despecho [des'petʃo] *nm* spite; **a** ~ **de** in spite of; **por** ~ out of (sheer) spite.

despectivo, a [despek'tiβo, a] *adj* (*despreciativo*) derogatory; (*LING*) pejorative.

despedace [despe'ðaθe] *etc vb V* **despedazar**.

despedazar [despeða'θar] *vt* to tear to pieces.

despedida [despe'ðiða] *nf* (*adiós*) goodbye, farewell; (*antes de viaje*) send-off; (*en carta*) closing formula; (*de obrero*) sacking; (*INFORM*) logout; **cena/función de** ~ farewell dinner/performance; **regalo de** ~ parting gift; ~ **de soltero/ soltera** stag/hen party.

despedir [despe'ðir] *vt* (*visita*) to see off, show out; (*empleado*) to dismiss; (*inquilino*) to evict; (*objeto*) to hurl; (*olor etc*) to give out *o* off; ~**se** *vr* (*dejar un*

empleo) to give up one's job; (*INFORM*) to log out *o* off; ~**se de** to say goodbye to; **se despidieron** they said goodbye to each other.

despegado, a [despe'ɣaðo, a] *adj* (*separado*) detached; (*persona: poco afectuoso*) cold, indifferent ♦ *nm/f*: **es un** ~ he has cut himself off from his family.

despegar [despe'ɣar] *vt* to unstick; (*sobre*) to open ♦ *vi* (*avión*) to take off; (*cohete*) to blast off; ~**se** *vr* to come loose, come unstuck; **sin** ~ **los labios** without uttering a word.

despego [des'peɣo] *nm* detachment.

despegue [des'peɣe] *etc vb V* **despegar** ♦ *nm* takeoff; (*de cohete*) blastoff.

despeinado, a [despei'naðo, a] *adj* dishevelled, unkempt.

despeinar [despei'nar] *vt* (*pelo*) to ruffle; **¡me has despeinado todo!** you've completely ruined my hairdo!

despejado, a [despe'xaðo, a] *adj* (*lugar*) clear, free; (*cielo*) clear; (*persona*) wide-awake, bright.

despejar [despe'xar] *vt* (*gen*) to clear; (*misterio*) to clarify, clear up; (*MAT: incógnita*) to find ♦ *vi* (*el tiempo*) to clear; ~**se** *vr* (*tiempo, cielo*) to clear (up); (*misterio*) to become clearer; (*cabeza*) to clear; **¡despejen!** (*moverse*) move along!; (*salirse*) everybody out!

despeje [des'pexe] *nm* (*DEPORTE*) clearance.

despellejar [despeʎe'xar] *vt* (*animal*) to skin; (*criticar*) to criticize unmercifully; (*fam: arruinar*) to fleece.

despelotarse [despelo'tarse] *vr* (*fam*) to strip off; (*fig*) to let one's hair down.

despelote [despe'lote] (*fam*) *nm* (*AM: lío*) mess; **¡qué** *o* **vaya** ~! what a riot *o* laugh!

despenalizar [despenali'θar] *vt* to decriminalize.

despensa [des'pensa] *nf* (*armario*) larder; (*NAUT*) storeroom; (*provisión de comestibles*) stock of food.

despeñadero [despeɲa'ðero] *nm* (*GEO*) cliff, precipice.

despeñar [despe'ɲar] *vt* (*arrojar*) to fling down; ~**se** *vr* to fling o.s. down; (*caer*) to fall headlong.

desperdiciar [desperði'θjar] *vt* (*comida, tiempo*) to waste; (*oportunidad*) to throw away.

desperdicio [desper'ðiθjo] *nm* (*despilfarro*) squandering; (*residuo*) waste; ~**s** *nmpl* (*basura*) rubbish *sg*, refuse *sg*, garbage *sg*

(*US*); (*residuos*) waste *sg*; ~**s de cocina** kitchen scraps; **el libro no tiene** ~ the book is excellent from beginning to end.

desperdigar [desperði'yar] *vt* (*esparcir*) to scatter; (*energía*) to dissipate; ~**se** *vr* to scatter.

desperdigue [desper'ðiye] *etc vb V* **desperdigar.**

desperece [despe'reθe] *etc vb V* **desperezarse.**

desperezarse [despere'θarse] *vr* to stretch.

desperfecto [desper'fekto] *nm* (*deterioro*) slight damage; (*defecto*) flaw, imperfection.

despertador [desperta'ðor] *nm* alarm clock; ~ **de viaje** travelling clock.

despertar [desper'tar] *vt* (*persona*) to wake up; (*recuerdos*) to revive; (*esperanzas*) to raise; (*sentimiento*) to arouse ♦ *vi*, ~**se** *vr* to awaken, wake up ♦ *nm* awakening; ~**se a la realidad** to wake up to reality.

despiadado a [despja'ðaðo, a] *adj* (*ataque*) merciless; (*persona*) heartless.

despido [des'piðo] *etc vb V* **despedir** ♦ *nm* dismissal, sacking; ~ **improcedente** *o* **injustificado** wrongful dismissal; ~ **injusto** unfair dismissal; ~ **libre** right to hire and fire; ~ **voluntario** voluntary redundancy.

despierto, a [des'pjerto, a] *etc vb V* **despertar** ♦ *adj* awake; (*fig*) sharp, alert.

despilfarrar [despilfa'rrar] *vt* (*gen*) to waste; (*dinero*) to squander.

despilfarro [despil'farro] *nm* (*derroche*) squandering; (*lujo desmedido*) extravagance.

despintar [despin'tar] *vt* (*quitar pintura a*) to take the paint off; (*hechos*) to distort ♦ *vi*: **A no despinta a B** A is in no way inferior to B; ~**se** *vr* (*desteñir*) to fade.

despiojar [despjo'xar] *vt* to delouse.

despistado, a [despis'taðo, a] *adj* (*distraído*) vague, absent-minded; (*poco práctico*) unpractical; (*confuso*) confused; (*desorientado*) off the track ♦ *nm/f* (*tipo: distraído*) scatterbrain, absent-minded person.

despistar [despis'tar] *vt* to throw off the track *o* scent; (*fig*) to mislead, confuse; ~**se** *vr* to take the wrong road; (*fig*) to become confused.

despiste [des'piste] *nm* (*AUTO etc*) swerve; (*error*) slip; (*distracción*) absent-mindedness; **tiene un terrible** ~ he's terribly absent-minded.

desplace [des'plaθe] *etc vb V* **desplazar.**

desplante [des'plante] *nm*: **hacer un** ~ **a algn** to be rude to sb.

desplazado, a [despla'θaðo, a] *adj* (*pieza*) wrongly placed ♦ *nm/f* (*inadaptado*) misfit; **sentirse un poco** ~ to feel rather out of place.

desplazamiento [desplaθa'mjento] *nm* displacement; (*viaje*) journey; (*de opinión, votos*) shift, swing; (*INFORM*) scrolling; ~ **hacia arriba/abajo** (*INFORM*) scroll up/down.

desplazar [despla'θar] *vt* (*gen*) to move; (*FÍSICA, NAUT, TEC*) to displace; (*tropas*) to transfer; (*suplantar*) to take the place of; (*INFORM*) to scroll; ~**se** *vr* (*persona, vehículo*) to travel, go; (*objeto*) to move, shift; (*votos, opinión*) to shift, swing.

desplegar [desple'yar] *vt* (*tela, papel*) to unfold, open out; (*bandera*) to unfurl; (*alas*) to spread; (*MIL*) to deploy; (*manifestar*) to display.

desplegué [desple'ye], **despleguemos** [desple'yemos] *etc vb V* **desplegar.**

despliegue [des'pljeye] *etc vb V* **desplegar** ♦ *nm* unfolding, opening; deployment, display.

desplomarse [desplo'marse] *vr* (*edificio, gobierno, persona*) to collapse; (*derrumbarse*) to topple over; (*precios*) to slump; **se ha desplomado el techo** the ceiling has fallen in.

desplumar [desplu'mar] *vt* (*ave*) to pluck; (*fam: estafar*) to fleece.

despoblado, a [despo'ßlaðo, a] *adj* (*sin habitantes*) uninhabited; (*con pocos habitantes*) depopulated; (*con insuficientes habitantes*) underpopulated ♦ *nm* deserted spot.

despojar [despo'xar] *vt* (*alguien: de sus bienes*) to divest of, deprive of; (*casa*) to strip, leave bare; (*de su cargo*) to strip of; ~**se** *vr* (*desnudarse*) to undress; ~**se de** (*ropa, hojas*) to shed; (*poderes*) to relinquish.

despojo [des'poxo] *nm* (*acto*) plundering; (*objetos*) plunder, loot; ~**s** *nmpl* (*de ave, res*) offal *sg*.

desposado, a [despo'saðo, a] *adj, nm/f* newly-wed.

desposar [despo'sar] *vt* (*suj: sacerdote: pareja*) to marry; ~**se** *vr* (*casarse*) to marry, get married.

desposeer [despose'er] *vt* (*despojar*) to dispossess; ~ **a algn de su autoridad** to strip sb of his authority.

desposeído, a [despose'iðo, a] *nm/f*: **los** ~**s** the have-nots.

desposeyendo [despose'jendo] *etc vb V* **desposeer.**

desposorios [despo'sorjos] *nmpl*

(*esponsales*) betrothal *sg*; (*boda*) marriage ceremony *sg*.

déspota ['despota] *nm/f* despot.

despotismo [despo'tismo] *nm* despotism.

despotricar [despotri'kar] *vi*: ~ **contra** to moan *o* complain about.

despotrique [despo'trike] *etc vb* V **despotricar**.

despreciable [despre'θjaßle] *adj* (*moralmente*) despicable; (*objeto*) worthless; (*cantidad*) negligible.

despreciar [despre'θjar] *vt* (*desdeñar*) to despise, scorn; (*afrentar*) to slight.

despreciativo, a [despreθja'tißo, a] *adj* (*observación, tono*) scornful, contemptuous; (*comentario*) derogatory.

desprecio [des'preθjo] *nm* scorn, contempt; slight.

desprender [despren'der] *vt* (*soltar*) to loosen; (*separar*) to separate; (*desatar*) to unfasten; (*olor*) to give off; ~**se** *vr* (*botón: caerse*) to fall off; (: *abrirse*) to unfasten; (*olor, perfume*) to be given off; ~**se de** to follow from; ~**se de algo** (*ceder*) to give sth up; (*desembarazarse*) to get rid of sth; **se desprende que** it transpires that.

desprendido, a [despren'dido, a] *adj* (*pieza*) loose; (*sin abrochar*) unfastened; (*desinteresado*) disinterested; (*generoso*) generous.

desprendimiento [desprendi'mjento] *nm* (*gen*) loosening; (*generosidad*) disinterestedness; (*indiferencia*) detachment; (*de gas*) leak; (*de tierra, rocas*) landslide.

despreocupado, a [despreoku'paðo, a] *adj* (*sin preocupación*) unworried, unconcerned; (*tranquilo*) nonchalant; (*en el vestir*) casual; (*negligente*) careless.

despreocuparse [despreoku'parse] *vr* to be carefree; (*dejar de inquietarse*) to stop worrying; (*ser indiferente*) to be unconcerned; ~ **de** to have no interest in.

desprestigiar [despresti'xjar] *vt* (*criticar*) to run down, disparage; (*desacreditar*) to discredit.

desprestigio [despres'tixjo] *nm* (*denigración*) disparagement; (*impopularidad*) unpopularity.

desprevenido, a [despreße'niðo, a] *adj* (*no preparado*) unprepared, unready; **coger** (*ESP*) *o* **agarrar** (*AM*) **a algn** ~ to catch sb unawares.

desproporción [despropor'θjon] *nf* disproportion, lack of proportion.

desproporcionado, a [desproporθjo'naðo, a] *adj* disproportionate, out of proportion.

despropósito [despro'posito] *nm* (*salida de tono*) irrelevant remark; (*disparate*) piece of nonsense.

desprovisto, a [despro'ßisto, a] *adj*: ~ **de** devoid of; **estar** ~ **de** to lack.

después [des'pwes] *adv* afterwards, later; (*desde entonces*) since (then); (*próximo paso*) next; **poco** ~ soon after; **un año** ~ a year later; ~ **se debatió el tema** next the matter was discussed ♦ *prep*: ~ **de** (*tiempo*) after, since; (*orden*) next (to); ~ **de comer** after lunch; ~ **de corregido el texto** after the text had been corrected; ~ **de esa fecha** (*pasado*) since that date; (*futuro*) from *o* after that date; ~ **de todo** after all; ~ **de verlo** after seeing it, after I *etc* saw it; **mi nombre está** ~ **del tuyo** my name comes next to yours ♦ *conj*: ~ (**de**) **que** after; ~ (**de**) **que lo escribí** after *o* since I wrote it, after writing it.

despuntar [despun'tar] *vt* (*lápiz*) to blunt ♦ *vi* (*BOT: plantas*) to sprout; (: *flores*) to bud; (*alba*) to break; (*día*) to dawn; (*persona: descollar*) to stand out.

desquiciar [deski'θjar] *vt* (*puerta*) to take off its hinges; (*descomponer*) to upset; (*persona: turbar*) to disturb; (: *volver loco a*) to unhinge.

desquitarse [deski'tarse] *vr* to obtain satisfaction; (*COM*) to recover a debt; (*fig: vengarse de*) to get one's own back; ~ **de una pérdida** to make up for a loss.

desquite [des'kite] *nm* (*satisfacción*) satisfaction; (*venganza*) revenge.

Dest. *abr* = **destinatario**.

destacado, a [desta'kaðo, a] *adj* outstanding.

destacamento [destaka'mento] *nm* (*MIL*) detachment.

destacar [desta'kar] *vt* (*ARTE: hacer resaltar*) to make stand out; (*subrayar*) to emphasize, point up; (*MIL*) to detach, detail; (*INFORM*) to highlight ♦ *vi*, ~**se** *vr* (*resaltarse*) to stand out; (*persona*) to be outstanding *o* exceptional; **quiero** ~ **que...** I wish to emphasize that...; ~(**se**) **contra** *o* **en** *o* **sobre** to stand out *o* be outlined against.

destajo [des'taxo] *nm*: **a** ~ (*por pieza*) by the job; (*con afán*) eagerly; **trabajar a** ~ to do piecework; (*fig*) to work one's fingers to the bone.

destapar [desta'par] *vt* (*botella*) to open; (*cacerola*) to take the lid off; (*descubrir*) to uncover; ~**se** *vr* (*descubrirse*) to get uncovered; (*revelarse*) to reveal one's true character.

arrest; (*cuidado*) care; ~ **de juego**
(*DEPORTE*) stoppage of play; ~ **ilegal**
unlawful detention.
detendré [deten'dre] *etc vb V* **detener**.
detener [dete'ner] *vt* (*gen*) to stop; (*JUR:
arrestar*) to arrest; (: *encarcelar*) to detain;
(*objeto*) to keep; (*retrasar*) to hold up,
delay; (*aliento*) to hold; ~**se** *vr* to stop;
~**se en** (*demorarse*) to delay over, linger
over.
detenga [de'tenga] *etc vb V* **detener**.
detenidamente [deteniða'mente] *adv*
(*minuciosamente*) carefully;
(*extensamente*) at great length.
detenido, a [dete'niðo, a] *adj* (*arrestado*)
under arrest; (*minucioso*) detailed;
(*examen*) thorough; (*tímido*) timid ♦ *nm/f*
person under arrest, prisoner.
detenimiento [deteni'mjento] *nm* care;
con ~ thoroughly.
detentar [deten'tar] *vt* to hold; (*sin derecho:
título*) to hold unlawfully; (: *puesto*) to
occupy unlawfully.
detergente [deter'xente] *adj, nm*
detergent.
deteriorado, a [deterjo'raðo, a] *adj*
(*estropeado*) damaged; (*desgastado*)
worn.
deteriorar [deterjo'rar] *vt* to spoil,
damage; ~**se** *vr* to deteriorate.
deterioro [dete'rjoro] *nm* deterioration.
determinación [determina'θjon] *nf*
(*empeño*) determination; (*decisión*)
decision; (*de fecha, precio*) settling,
fixing.
determinado, a [determi'naðo, a] *adj*
(*preciso*) fixed, set; (*LING: artículo*)
definite; (*persona: resuelto*) determined;
un día ~ on a certain day; **no hay ningún
tema** ~ there is no particular theme.
determinar [determi'nar] *vt* (*plazo*) to fix;
(*precio*) to settle; (*daños, impuestos*) to
assess; (*pleito*) to decide; (*causar*) to
cause; ~**se** *vr* to decide; **el reglamento
determina que** ... the rule lays it down *o*
states that ...; **aquello determinó la caída
del gobierno** that brought about the fall
of the government; **esto le determinó**
this decided him.
detestable [detes'taßle] *adj* (*persona*)
hateful; (*acto*) detestable.
detestar [detes'tar] *vt* to detest.
detonación [detona'θjon] *nf* detonation;
(*sonido*) explosion.
detonante [deto'nante] *nm* (*fig*) trigger.
detonar [deto'nar] *vi* to detonate.
detractor, a [detrak'tor, a] *adj* disparaging
♦ *nm/f* detractor.

detrás [de'tras] *adv* behind; (*atrás*) at the
back ♦ *prep*: ~ **de** behind; **por** ~ **de algn**
(*fig*) behind sb's back; **salir de** ~ to come
out from behind; **por** ~ behind.
detrasito [detra'sito] *adv* (*AM fam*)
behind.
detrimento [detri'mento] *nm*: **en** ~ **de** to
the detriment of.
detuve [de'tuße] *etc vb V* **detener**.
deuda [de'uða] *nf* (*condición*) indebtedness,
debt; (*cantidad*) debt; ~ **a largo plazo**
long-term debt; ~ **exterior/pública**
foreign/national debt; ~ **incobrable** *o*
morosa bad debt; ~**s activas/pasivas**
assets/liabilities; **contraer** ~**s** to get
into debt.
deudor, a [deu'ðor, a] *nm/f* debtor; ~
hipotecario mortgager; ~ **moroso** slow
payer.
devaluación [deßalwa'θjon] *nf*
devaluation.
devaluar [deßalu'ar] *vt* to devalue.
devanar [deßa'nar] *vt* (*hilo*) to wind; ~**se** *vr*:
~**se los sesos** to rack one's brains.
devaneo [deßa'neo] *nm* (*MED*) delirium;
(*desatino*) nonsense; (*fruslería*) idle
pursuit; (*amorío*) flirtation.
devastar [deßas'tar] *vt* (*destruir*) to
devastate.
devendré [deßen'dre] *etc*, **devenga**
[de'ßenga] *etc vb V* **devenir**.
devengar [deßen'gar] *vt* (*salario: ganar*) to
earn; (: *tener que cobrar*) to be due;
(*intereses*) to bring in, accrue, earn.
devengue [de'ßenge] *etc vb V* **devengar**.
devenir [deße'nir] *vi*: ~ **en** to become, turn
into ♦ *nm* (*movimiento progresivo*) process
of development; (*transformación*)
transformation.
deviene [de'ßjene] *etc*, **deviniendo**
[deßi'njendo] *etc vb V* **devenir**.
devoción [deßo'θjon] *nf* devotion; (*afición*)
strong attachment.
devolución [deßolu'θjon] *nf* (*reenvío*)
return, sending back; (*reembolso*)
repayment; (*JUR*) devolution.
devolver [deßol'ßer] *vt* (*lo extraviado,
prestado*) to give back; (*a su sitio*) to put
back; (*carta al correo*) to send back;
(*COM*) to repay, refund; (*visita, la palabra*)
to return; (*salud, vista*) to restore; (*fam:
vomitar*) to throw up ♦ *vi* (*fam*) to be sick;
~**se** *vr* (*AM*) to return; ~ **mal por bien** to
return ill for good; ~ **la pelota a algn** to
give sb tit for tat.
devorar [deßo'rar] *vt* to devour; (*comer
ávidamente*) to gobble up; (*fig: fortuna*) to
run through; **todo lo devoró el fuego** the

fire consumed everything; **le devoran los celos** he is consumed with jealousy.

devoto, a [de'ßoto, a] adj (REL: persona) devout; (: obra) devotional; (amigo): ~ **(de algn)** devoted (to sb) ♦ nm/f admirer; **los ~s** (REL) the faithful; **su muy ~** your devoted servant.

devuelto [de'ßwelto], **devuelva** [de'ßwelßa] etc vb V **devolver**.

D.F. abr (México) = Distrito Federal.

dg. abr (= decigramo) dg.

D.G. abr = Dirección General; (= Director General) D.G.

DGT nf abr = Dirección General de Tráfico; = Dirección General de Turismo.

di [di] vb V **dar; decir**.

día ['dia] nm day; **~ de asueto** day off; **~ feriado** (AM) o **festivo** (public) holiday; **~ hábil/inhábil** working/non-working day; **~ domingo, ~ lunes** (AM) Sunday, Monday; **~ lectivo** teaching day; **~ libre** day off; **D~ de Reyes** Epiphany (6 January); **¿qué ~ es?** what's the date?; **estar/poner al ~** to be/keep up to date; **el ~ de hoy/de mañana** today/tomorrow; **el ~ menos pensado** when you least expect it; **al ~ siguiente** on the following day; **todos los ~s** every day; **un ~ sí y otro no** every other day; **vivir al ~** to live from hand to mouth; **de ~** during the day, by day; **es de ~** it's daylight; **del ~** (estilos) fashionable; (menú) today's; **de un ~ para otro** any day now; **en pleno ~** in full daylight; **en su ~** in due time; **¡hasta otro ~!** so long!

diabetes [dja'ßetes] nf diabetes sg.

diabético, a [dja'ßetiko, a] adj, nm/f diabetic.

diablo ['djaßlo] nm (tb fig) devil; **pobre ~** poor devil; **hace un frío de todos los ~s** it's hellishly cold.

diablura [dja'ßlura] nf prank; (travesura) mischief.

diabólico, a [dja'ßoliko, a] adj diabolical.

diadema [dja'ðema] nf (para el pelo) Alice band, headband; (joya) tiara.

diáfano, a ['djafano, a] adj (tela) diaphanous; (agua) crystal-clear.

diafragma [dja'fraɣma] nm diaphragm.

diagnosis [djaɣ'nosis] nf inv, **diagnóstico** [djaɣ'nostiko] nm diagnosis.

diagnosticar [djaɣnosti'kar] vt to diagnose.

diagonal [djaɣo'nal] adj diagonal ♦ nf (GEOM) diagonal; **en ~** diagonally.

diagrama [dja'ɣrama] nm diagram; **~ de barras** (COM) bar chart; **~ de dispersión** (COM) scatter diagram; **~ de flujo**

(INFORM) flowchart.

dial [di'al] nm dial.

dialecto [dja'lekto] nm dialect.

dialogar [djalo'ɣar] vt to write in dialogue form ♦ vi (conversar) to have a conversation; **~ con** (POL) to hold talks with.

diálogo ['djaloɣo] nm dialogue.

dialogue [dja'loɣe] etc vb V **dialogar**.

diamante [dja'mante] nm diamond.

diametralmente [djametral'mente] adv diametrically; **~ opuesto a** diametrically opposed to.

diámetro [di'ametro] nm diameter; **~ de giro** (AUTO) turning circle; **faros de gran ~** wide-angle headlights.

diana ['djana] nf (MIL) reveille; (de blanco) centre, bull's-eye.

diantre ['djantre] nm: **¡~!** (fam) oh hell!

diapasón [djapa'son] nm (instrumento) tuning fork; (de violín etc) fingerboard; (de voz) tone.

diapositiva [djaposi'tißa] nf (FOTO) slide, transparency.

diario, a ['djarjo, a] adj daily ♦ nm newspaper; (libro diario) diary; (: COM) daybook; (COM: gastos) daily expenses; **~ de navegación** (NAUT) logbook; **~ hablado** (RADIO) news (bulletin); **~ de sesiones** parliamentary report; **a ~** daily; **de o para ~** everyday.

diarrea [dja'rrea] nf diarrhoea.

diatriba [dja'trißa] nf diatribe, tirade.

dibujante [dißu'xante] nm/f (de bosquejos) sketcher; (de dibujos animados) cartoonist; (de moda) designer; **~ de publicidad** commercial artist.

dibujar [dißu'xar] vt to draw, sketch; **~se** vr (emoción) to show; **~se contra** to be outlined against.

dibujo [di'ßuxo] nm drawing; (TEC) design; (en papel, tela) pattern; (en periódico) cartoon; (fig) description; **~s animados** cartoons; **~ del natural** drawing from life.

dic., dic.ᵉ abr (= diciembre) Dec.

diccionario [dikθjo'narjo] nm dictionary.

dicharachero, a [ditʃara'tʃero, a] adj talkative ♦ nm/f (ingenioso) wit; (parlanchín) chatterbox.

dicho, a ['ditʃo, a] pp de **decir** ♦ adj (susodicho) aforementioned ♦ nm saying; (proverbio) proverb; (ocurrencia) bright remark ♦ nf (buena suerte) good luck; **mejor ~** rather; **~ y hecho** no sooner said than done.

dichoso, a [di'tʃoso, a] adj (feliz) happy; (afortunado) lucky; **¡aquel ~ coche!** (fam) that blessed car!

diciembre [di'θjembre] *nm* December.

diciendo [di'θjendo] *etc vb V* **decir**.

dictado [dik'taðo] *nm* dictation; **escribir al** ~ to take dictation; **los ~s de la conciencia** (*fig*) the dictates of conscience.

dictador [dikta'ðor] *nm* dictator.

dictadura [dikta'ðura] *nf* dictatorship.

dictáfono ® [dik'tafono] *nm* Dictaphone ®.

dictamen [dik'tamen] *nm* (*opinión*) opinion; (*informe*) report; ~ **contable** auditor's report; ~ **facultativo** (*MED*) medical report.

dictar [dik'tar] *vt* (*carta*) to dictate; (*JUR: sentencia*) to pass; (*decreto*) to issue; (*AM: clase*) to give; (: *conferencia*) to deliver.

didáctico, a [di'ðaktiko, a] *adj* didactic; (*material*) teaching *cpd*; (*juguete*) educational.

diecinueve [djeθinu'eße] *num* nineteen; (*fecha*) nineteenth; *V tb* **seis**.

dieciochesco, a [djeθio'tʃesko, a] *adj* eighteenth-century.

dieciocho [djeθi'otʃo] *num* eighteen; (*fecha*) eighteenth; *V tb* **seis**.

dieciséis [djeθi'seis] *num* sixteen; (*fecha*) sixteenth; *V tb* **seis**.

diecisiete [djeθi'sjete] *num* seventeen; (*fecha*) seventeenth; *V tb* **seis**.

diente ['djente] *nm* (*ANAT, TEC*) tooth; (*ZOOL*) fang; (: *de elefante*) tusk; (*de ajo*) clove; ~ **de león** dandelion; **~s postizos** false teeth; **enseñar los ~s** (*fig*) to show one's claws; **hablar entre ~s** to mutter, mumble; **hincar el ~ en** (*comida*) to bite into.

diera ['djera] *etc vb V* **dar**.

diéresis [di'eresis] *nf* diaeresis.

dieron ['djeron] *vb V* **dar**.

diesel ['disel] *adj:* **motor** ~ diesel engine.

diestro, a ['djestro, a] *adj* (*derecho*) right; (*hábil*) skilful; (: *con las manos*) handy ♦ *nm* (*TAUR*) matador ♦ *nf* right hand; **a ~ y siniestro** (*sin método*) wildly.

dieta ['djeta] *nf* diet; **~s** *nfpl* expenses; **estar a ~** to be on a diet.

dietético, a [dje'tetiko, a] *adj* dietetic ♦ *nm/f* dietician ♦ *nf* dietetics *sg*.

dietista [dje'tista] *nm/f* dietician.

diez [djeθ] *num* ten; (*fecha*) tenth; **hacer las ~ de últimas** (*NAIPES*) to sweep the board; *V tb* **seis**.

diezmar [djeθ'mar] *vt* to decimate.

difamación [difama'θjon] *nf* slander; libel.

difamar [difa'mar] *vt* (*JUR: hablando*) to slander; (: *por escrito*) to libel.

difamatorio, a [difama'torjo, a] *adj*

slanderous; libellous.

diferencia [dife'renθja] *nf* difference; **a ~ de** unlike; **hacer ~ entre** to make a distinction between; ~ **salarial** (*COM*) wage differential.

diferencial [diferen'θjal] *nm* (*AUTO*) differential.

diferenciar [diferen'θjar] *vt* to differentiate between ♦ *vi* to differ; **~se** *vr* to differ, be different; (*distinguirse*) to distinguish o.s.

diferente [dife'rente] *adj* different.

diferido [dife'riðo] *nm:* **en** ~ (*TV etc*) recorded.

diferir [dife'rir] *vt* to defer.

difícil [di'fiθil] *adj* difficult; (*tiempos, vida*) hard; (*situación*) delicate; **es un hombre** ~ he's a difficult man to get on with.

difícilmente [di'fiθilmente] *adv* (*con dificultad*) with difficulty; (*apenas*) hardly.

dificultad [difikul'tað] *nf* difficulty; (*problema*) trouble; (*objeción*) objection.

dificultar [difikul'tar] *vt* (*complicar*) to complicate, make difficult; (*estorbar*) to obstruct; **las restricciones dificultan el comercio** the restrictions hinder trade.

dificultoso, a [difikul'toso, a] *adj* (*difícil*) difficult, hard; (*fam: cara*) odd, ugly; (*persona: exigente*) fussy.

difiera [di'fjera] *etc,* **difiriendo** [difi'rjendo] *etc vb V* **diferir**.

difuminar [difumi'nar] *vt* to blur.

difundir [difun'dir] *vt* (*calor, luz*) to diffuse; (*RADIO*) to broadcast; **~se** *vr* to spread (out); ~ **una noticia** to spread a piece of news.

difunto, a [di'funto, a] *adj* dead, deceased ♦ *nm/f:* **el** ~ the deceased.

difusión [difu'sjon] *nf* (*de calor, luz*) diffusion; (*de noticia, teoría*) dissemination; (*de programa*) broadcasting; (*programa*) broadcast.

difuso, a [di'fuso, a] *adj* (*luz*) diffused; (*conocimientos*) widespread; (*estilo, explicación*) wordy.

diga ['diɣa] *etc vb V* **decir**.

digerir [dixe'rir] *vt* to digest; (*fig*) to absorb; (*reflexionar sobre*) to think over.

digestión [dixes'tjon] *nf* digestion; **corte de** ~ indigestion.

digestivo, a [dixes'tißo, a] *adj* digestive ♦ *nm* (*bebida*) liqueur, digestif.

digiera [di'xjera] *etc,* **digiriendo** [dixi'rjendo] *etc vb V* **digerir**.

digital [dixi'tal] *adj* (*INFORM*) digital; (*dactilar*) finger *cpd* ♦ *nf* (*BOT*) foxglove; (*droga*) digitalis.

digitalizador [dixitaliθa'ðor] *nm* (*INFORM*) digitizer.
dignarse [diɣ'narse] *vr* to deign to.
dignidad [diɣni'ðað] *nf* dignity; (*honra*) honour; (*rango*) rank; (*persona*) dignitary; **herir la ~ de algn** to hurt sb's pride.
dignificar [diɣnifi'kar] *vt* to dignify.
dignifique [diɣni'fike] *etc vb V* **dignificar**.
digno, a ['diɣno, a] *adj* worthy; (*persona: honesto*) honourable; **~ de elogio** praiseworthy; **~ de mención** worth mentioning; **es ~ de verse** it is worth seeing; **poco ~** unworthy.
digresión [diɣre'sjon] *nf* digression.
dije ['dixe] *etc*, **dijera** [di'xera] *etc vb V* **decir**.
dilación [dila'θjon] *nf* delay; **sin ~** without delay, immediately.
dilapidar [dilapi'ðar] *vt* to squander, waste.
dilatación [dilata'θjon] *nf* (*expansión*) dilation.
dilatado, a [dila'taðo, a] *adj* dilated; (*período*) long drawn-out; (*extenso*) extensive.
dilatar [dila'tar] *vt* (*gen*) to dilate; (*prolongar*) to prolong; (*aplazar*) to delay; **~se** *vr* (*pupila etc*) to dilate; (*agua*) to expand.
dilema [di'lema] *nm* dilemma.
diligencia [dili'xenθja] *nf* diligence; (*rapidez*) speed; (*ocupación*) errand, job; (*carruaje*) stagecoach; **~s** *nfpl* (*JUR*) formalities; **~s judiciales** judicial proceedings; **~s previas** inquest *sg*.
diligente [dili'xente] *adj* diligent; **poco ~** slack.
dilucidar [diluθi'ðar] *vt* (*aclarar*) to elucidate, clarify; (*misterio*) to clear up.
diluir [dilu'ir] *vt* to dilute; (*aguar, fig*) to water down.
diluviar [dilu'ßjar] *vi* to pour with rain.
diluvio [di'lußjo] *nm* deluge, flood; **un ~ de cartas** (*fig*) a flood of letters.
diluyendo [dilu'jendo] *etc vb V* **diluir**.
dimanar [dima'nar] *vi*: **~ de** to arise *o* spring from.
dimensión [dimen'sjon] *nf* dimension; **dimensiones** *nfpl* size *sg*; **tomar las dimensiones de** to take the measurements of.
dimes ['dimes] *nmpl*: **andar en ~ y diretes con algn** to bicker *o* squabble with sb.
diminutivo [diminu'tißo] *nm* diminutive.
diminuto, a [dimi'nuto, a] *adj* tiny, diminutive.
dimisión [dimi'sjon] *nf* resignation.

dimitir [dimi'tir] *vt* (*cargo*) to give up; (*despedir*) to sack ♦ *vi* to resign.
dimos ['dimos] *vb V* **dar**.
Dinamarca [dina'marka] *nf* Denmark.
dinamarqués, esa [dinamar'kes, esa] *adj* Danish ♦ *nm/f* Dane ♦ *nm* (*LING*) Danish.
dinámico, a [di'namiko, a] *adj* dynamic ♦ *nf* dynamics *sg*.
dinamita [dina'mita] *nf* dynamite.
dinamitar [dinami'tar] *vt* to dynamite.
dinamo [di'namo], **dínamo** ['dinamo] *nf* (*nm en AM*) dynamo.
dinastía [dinas'tia] *nf* dynasty.
dineral [dine'ral] *nm* fortune.
dinero [di'nero] *nm* money; (**~ en circulación**) currency; **~ caro** (*COM*) dear money; **~ contante (y sonante)** hard cash; **~ de curso legal** legal tender; **~ efectivo** cash, ready cash; **es hombre de ~** he is a man of means; **andar mal de ~** to be short of money; **ganar ~ a espuertas** to make money hand over fist.
dinosaurio [dino'saurjo] *nm* dinosaur.
dintel [din'tel] *nm* lintel; (*umbral*) threshold.
diñar [di'ɲar] *vt* (*fam*) to give; **~la** to kick the bucket.
dio [djo] *vb V* **dar**.
diócesis ['djoθesis] *nf inv* diocese.
Dios [djos] *nm* God; **~ mediante** God willing; **a ~ gracias** thank heaven; **a la buena de ~** any old how; **una de ~ es Cristo** an almighty row; **~ los cría y ellos se juntan** birds of a feather flock together; **como ~ manda** as is proper; **¡~ mío!** (oh,) my God!; **¡por ~!** for God's sake!; **¡válgame ~!** bless my soul!
dios [djos] *nm* god.
diosa ['djosa] *nf* goddess.
Dip. *abr* (= *Diputación*) ≈ CC.
diploma [di'ploma] *nm* diploma.
diplomacia [diplo'maθja] *nf* diplomacy; (*fig*) tact.
diplomado, a [diplo'maðo, a] *adj* qualified ♦ *nm/f* holder of a diploma; (*UNIV*) graduate; *V tb* **licenciado**.
diplomático, a [diplo'matiko, a] *adj* (*cuerpo*) diplomatic; (*que tiene tacto*) tactful ♦ *nm/f* diplomat.
diptongo [dip'tongo] *nm* diphthong.
diputación [diputa'θjon] *nf* deputation; **~ permanente** (*POL*) standing committee; **~ provincial** ≈ county council.
diputado, a [dipu'taðo, a] *nm/f* delegate; (*POL*) ≈ member of parliament (*BRIT*), ≈ representative (*US*); *V tb* **Las Cortes (españolas)**.
dique ['dike] *nm* dyke; (*rompeolas*)

breakwater; ~ **de contención**
dam.

Dir. *abr* = **dirección**; (= *director*) dir.

diré [di're] *etc vb V* **decir.**

dirección [direk'θjon] *nf* direction; (*fig:*
tendencia) trend; (*señas, tb INFORM*)
address; (*AUTO*) steering; (*gerencia*)
management; (*de periódico*) editorship;
(*en escuela*) headship; (*POL*) leadership;
(*junta*) board of directors; (*despacho*)
director's/manager's/headmaster's/
editor's office; ~ **absoluta** (*INFORM*)
absolute address; ~ **administrativa**
office management; ~ **asistida** power-
assisted steering; **D~ General de**
Seguridad/Turismo State Security/
Tourist Office; ~ **relativa** (*INFORM*)
relative address; ~ **única** *o* **prohibida**
one-way; **tomar la** ~ **de una empresa** to
take over the running of a company.

direccionamiento [direkθjona'mjento] *nm*
(*INFORM*) addressing.

directivo, a [direk'tiβo, a] *adj* (*junta*)
managing; (*función*) administrative
♦ *nm/f* (*COM*) manager ♦ *nf* (*norma*)
directive; (*tb: junta directiva*) board of
directors.

directo, a [di'rekto, a] *adj* direct; (*línea*)
straight; (*inmediato*) immediate; (*tren*)
through; (*TV*) live; **en** ~ (*INFORM*) on line;
transmitir en ~ to broadcast live.

director, a [direk'tor, a] *adj* leading ♦ *nm/f*
director; (*ESCOL*) head (teacher) (*BRIT*),
principal (*US*); (*gerente*) manager(ess);
(*de compañía*) president; (*jefe*) head;
(*PRENSA*) editor; (*de prisión*) governor;
(*MUS*) conductor; ~ **adjunto** assistant
manager; ~ **de cine** film director; ~
comercial marketing manager; ~
ejecutivo executive director; ~ **de**
empresa company director; ~ **general**
general manager; ~ **gerente** managing
director; ~ **de sucursal** branch manager.

directorio [direk'torjo] *nm* (*INFORM*)
directory.

directrices [direk'triθes] *nfpl* guidelines.

dirigente [diri'xente] *adj* leading ♦ *nm/f*
(*POL*) leader; **los ~s del partido** the party
leaders.

dirigible [diri'xiβle] *adj* (*AVIAT, NAUT*)
steerable ♦ *nm* airship.

dirigir [diri'xir] *vt* to direct; (*acusación*) to
level; (*carta*) to address; (*obra de teatro,*
film) to produce, direct; (*MUS*) to
conduct; (*comercio*) to manage;
(*expedición*) to lead; (*sublevación*) to
head; (*periódico*) to edit; (*guiar*) to guide;
~**se** *vr:* ~**se a** to go towards, make one's

way towards; (*hablar con*) to speak to;
~**se a algn solicitando algo** to apply to
sb for sth; "**diríjase a ...**" "apply to ...".

dirigismo [diri'xismo] *nm* management,
control; ~ **estatal** state control.

dirija [di'rixa] *etc vb V* **dirigir.**

dirimir [diri'mir] *vt* (*contrato, matrimonio*) to
dissolve.

discado [dis'kaðo] *nm:* ~ **automático**
autodial.

discernir [disθer'nir] *vt* to discern ♦ *vi* to
distinguish.

discierna [dis'θjerna] *etc vb V* **discernir.**

disciplina [disθi'plina] *nf* discipline.

disciplinar [disθipli'nar] *vt* to discipline;
(*enseñar*) to school; (*MIL*) to drill; (*azotar*)
to whip.

discípulo, a [dis'θipulo, a] *nm/f* disciple;
(*seguidor*) follower; (*ESCOL*) pupil.

disco ['disko] *nm* disc (*BRIT*), disk (*US*);
(*DEPORTE*) discus; (*TELEC*) dial; (*AUTO:*
semáforo) light; (*MUS*) record; (*INFORM*)
disk; ~ **de arranque** boot disk; ~
compacto compact disc; ~ **de densidad**
sencilla/doble single/double density
disk; ~ **de larga duración** long-playing
record (LP); ~ **flexible** *o* **floppy** floppy
disk; ~ **de freno** brake disc; ~ **maestro**
master disk; ~ **de reserva** backup disk;
~ **rígido** hard disk; ~ **de una cara/dos**
caras single-/double-sided disk; ~ **virtual**
ramdisk.

discóbolo [dis'koβolo] *nm* discus thrower.

discográfico, a [disko'ɤrafiko, a] *adj*
record *cpd*; **casa discográfica** record
company; **sello** ~ label.

díscolo, a ['diskolo, a] *adj* (*rebelde*) unruly.

disconforme [diskon'forme] *adj* differing;
estar ~ (**con**) to be in disagreement
(with).

discontinuo, a [diskon'tinwo, a] *adj*
discontinuous; (*AUTO: línea*) broken.

discordar [diskor'ðar] *vi* (*MUS*) to be out of
tune; (*estar en desacuerdo*) to disagree;
(*colores, opiniones*) to clash.

discorde [dis'korðe] *adj* (*sonido*)
discordant; (*opiniones*) clashing.

discordia [dis'korðja] *nf* discord.

discoteca [disko'teka] *nf* disco(theque).

discreción [diskre'θjon] *nf* discretion;
(*reserva*) prudence; **¡a ~!** (*MIL*) stand
easy!; **añadir azúcar a** ~ (*CULIN*) add
sugar to taste; **comer a** ~ to eat as much
as one wishes.

discrecional [diskreθjo'nal] *adj* (*facultativo*)
discretionary; **parada** ~ request stop.

discrepancia [diskre'panθja] *nf* (*diferencia*)
discrepancy; (*desacuerdo*) disagreement.

discrepante [diskre'pante] *adj* divergent;
hubo varias voces ~s there were some
dissenting voices.

discrepar [diskre'par] *vi* to disagree.

discreto, a [dis'kreto, a] *adj* (*diplomático*)
discreet; (*sensato*) sensible; (*reservado*)
quiet; (*sobrio*) sober; (*mediano*) fair,
fairly good; **le daremos un plazo ~** we'll
allow him a reasonable time.

discriminación [diskrimina'θjon] *nf*
discrimination.

discriminar [diskrimi'nar] *vt* to
discriminate against; (*diferenciar*) to
discriminate between.

discuerde [dis'kwerðe] *etc vb* V **discordar**.

disculpa [dis'kulpa] *nf* excuse; (*pedir
perdón*) apology; **pedir ~s a/por** to
apologize to/for.

disculpar [diskul'par] *vt* to excuse, pardon;
~se *vr* to excuse o.s.; to apologize.

discurrir [disku'rrir] *vt* to contrive, think
up ♦ *vi* (*pensar, reflexionar*) to think,
meditate; (*recorrer*) to roam, wander;
(*río*) to flow; (*el tiempo*) to pass, flow by.

discurso [dis'kurso] *nm* speech; **~ de
clausura** closing speech; **pronunciar un
~** to make a speech; **en el ~ del tiempo**
with the passage of time.

discusión [disku'sjon] *nf* (*diálogo*)
discussion; (*riña*) argument; **tener una ~**
to have an argument.

discutible [disku'tißle] *adj* debatable; **de
mérito ~** of dubious worth.

discutido, a [disku'tiðo, a] *adj*
controversial.

discutir [disku'tir] *vt* (*debatir*) to discuss;
(*pelear*) to argue about; (*contradecir*) to
argue against ♦ *vi* to discuss; (*disputar*)
to argue; **~ de política** to argue about
politics; **¡no discutas!** don't argue!

disecar [dise'kar] *vt* (*para conservar: animal*)
to stuff; (: *planta*) to dry.

diseminar [disemi'nar] *vt* to disseminate,
spread.

disentir [disen'tir] *vi* to dissent, disagree.

diseñador, a [diseɲa'dor, a] *nm/f* designer.

diseñar [dise'ɲar] *vt* to design.

diseño [di'seɲo] *nm* (*TEC*) design; (*ARTE*)
drawing; (*COSTURA*) pattern; **de ~
italiano** Italian-designed; **~ asistido por
ordenador** computer-assisted design,
CAD.

diseque [di'seke] *etc vb* V **disecar**.

disertar [diser'tar] *vi* to speak.

disfrace [dis'fraθe] *etc vb* V **disfrazar**.

disfraz [dis'fraθ] *nm* (*máscara*) disguise;
(*traje*) fancy dress; (*excusa*) pretext; **bajo
el ~ de** under the cloak of.

disfrazado, a [disfra'θaðo, a] *adj*
disguised; **ir ~ de** to masquerade as.

disfrazar [disfra'θar] *vt* to disguise; **~se** *vr*
to dress (o.s.) up; **~se de** to disguise o.s.
as.

disfrutar [disfru'tar] *vt* to enjoy ♦ *vi* to
enjoy o.s.; **¡que disfrutes!** have a good
time; **~ de** to enjoy, possess; **~ de buena
salud** to enjoy good health.

disfrute [dis'frute] *nm* (*goce*) enjoyment;
(*aprovechamiento*) use.

disgregar [disɣre'ɣar] *vt* (*desintegrar*) to
disintegrate; (*manifestantes*) to disperse;
~se *vr* to disintegrate, break up.

disgregue [dis'ɣreɣe] *etc vb* V **disgregar**.

disgustar [disɣus'tar] *vt* (*no gustar*) to
displease; (*contrariar, enojar*) to annoy; to
upset; **~se** *vr* to be annoyed; (*dos
personas*) to fall out; **estaba muy
disgustado con el asunto** he was very
upset about the affair.

disgusto [dis'ɣusto] *nm* (*repugnancia*)
disgust; (*contrariedad*) annoyance;
(*desagrado*) displeasure; (*tristeza*) grief;
(*riña*) quarrel; (*avería*) misfortune; **hacer
algo a ~** to do sth unwillingly; **matar a
algn a ~s** to drive sb to distraction.

disidente [disi'ðente] *nm* dissident.

disienta [di'sjenta] *etc vb* V **disentir**.

disimulado, a [disimu'laðo, a] *adj*
(*solapado*) furtive, underhand; (*oculto*)
covert; **hacerse el ~** to pretend not to
notice.

disimular [disimu'lar] *vt* (*ocultar*) to hide,
conceal ♦ *vi* to dissemble.

disimulo [disi'mulo] *nm* (*fingimiento*)
dissimulation; **con ~** cunningly.

disipar [disi'par] *vt* (*duda, temor*) to dispel;
(*esperanza*) to destroy; (*fortuna*) to
squander; **~se** *vr* (*nubes*) to vanish;
(*dudas*) to be dispelled; (*indisciplinarse*)
to dissipate.

diskette [dis'ket] *nm* (*INFORM*) diskette,
floppy disk.

dislate [dis'late] *nm* (*absurdo*) absurdity;
~s *nmpl* nonsense *sg*.

dislexia [dis'leksja] *nf* dyslexia.

dislocar [dislo'kar] *vt* (*gen*) to dislocate;
(*tobillo*) to sprain.

disloque [dis'loke] *etc vb* V **dislocar** ♦ *nm*:
es el ~ (*fam*) it's the last straw.

disminución [disminu'θjon] *nf* diminution.

disminuido, a [disminu'iðo, a] *nm/f*: **~
mental/físico** mentally/physically-
handicapped person.

disminuir [disminu'ir] *vt* to decrease,
diminish; (*estrechar*) to lessen;
(*temperatura*) to lower; (*gastos, raciones*)

to cut down; (*dolor*) to relieve; (*autoridad, prestigio*) to weaken; (*entusiasmo*) to damp ♦ *vi* (*días*) to grow shorter; (*precios, temperatura*) to drop, fall; (*velocidad*) to slacken; (*población*) to decrease; (*beneficios, número*) to fall off; (*memoria, vista*) to fail.

disminuyendo [disminu'jendo] *etc vb V* **disminuir.**

disociar [diso'θjar] *vt* to disassociate; ~**se** *vr* to disassociate o.s.

disoluble [diso'luβle] *adj* soluble.

disolución [disolu'θjon] *nf* (*acto*) dissolution; (*QUÍMICA*) solution; (*COM*) liquidation; (*moral*) dissoluteness.

disoluto, a [diso'luto, a] *adj* dissolute.

disolvente [disol'βente] *nm* (*solvent*) thinner.

disolver [disol'βer] *vt* (*gen*) to dissolve; (*manifestación*) to break up; ~**se** *vr* to dissolve; (*COM*) to go into liquidation.

dispar [dis'par] *adj* (*distinto*) different; (*irregular*) uneven.

disparado, a [dispa'raðo, a] *adj*: **entrar** ~ to shoot in; **salir** ~ to shoot out; **ir** ~ to go like mad.

disparador [dispara'ðor] *nm* (*de arma*) trigger; (*FOTO, TEC*) release; ~ **atómico** aerosol; ~ **de bombas** bomb release.

disparar [dispa'rar] *vt, vi* to shoot, fire; ~**se** *vr* (*arma de fuego*) to go off; (*persona: marcharse*) to rush off; (*caballo*) to bolt; (*enojarse*) to lose control.

disparatado, a [dispara'taðo, a] *adj* crazy.

disparate [dispa'rate] *nm* (*tontería*) foolish remark; (*error*) blunder; **decir** ~**s** to talk nonsense; **¡qué** ~**!** how absurd!; **costar un** ~ to cost a hell of a lot.

disparo [dis'paro] *nm* shot; (*acto*) firing; ~**s** *nmpl* shooting *sg*, (exchange of) shots (*sg*); ~ **inicial** (*de cohete*) blastoff.

dispendio [dis'pendjo] *nm* waste.

dispensar [dispen'sar] *vt* to dispense; (*ayuda*) to give; (*honores*) to grant; (*disculpar*) to excuse; **¡usted dispense!** I beg your pardon!; ~ **a algn de hacer algo** to excuse sb from doing sth.

dispensario [dispen'sarjo] *nm* (*clínica*) community clinic; (*de hospital*) outpatients' department.

dispersar [disper'sar] *vt* to disperse; (*manifestación*) to break up; ~**se** *vr* to scatter.

disperso, a [dis'perso, a] *adj* scattered.

displicencia [displi'θenθja] *nf* (*mal humor*) peevishness; (*desgana*) lack of enthusiasm.

displicente [displi'θente] *adj*

(*malhumorado*) peevish; (*poco entusiasta*) unenthusiastic.

dispondré [dispon'dre] *etc vb V* **disponer.**

disponer [dispo'ner] *vt* (*arreglar*) to arrange; (*ordenar*) to put in order; (*preparar*) to prepare, get ready ♦ *vi*: ~ **de** to have, own; ~**se** *vr*: ~**se para** to prepare to, prepare for; **la ley dispone que ...** the law provides that ...; **no puede** ~ **de esos bienes** she cannot dispose of those properties.

disponga [dis'ponga] *etc vb V* **disponer.**

disponibilidad [disponiβili'ðað] *nf* availability; ~**es** *nfpl* (*COM*) resources, financial assets.

disponible [dispo'niβle] *adj* available; (*tiempo*) spare; (*dinero*) on hand.

disposición [disposi'θjon] *nf* arrangement, disposition; (*de casa, INFORM*) layout; (*ley*) order; (*cláusula*) provision; (*aptitud*) aptitude; ~ **de ánimo** attitude of mind; **última** ~ last will and testament; **a la** ~ **de** at the disposal of; **a su** ~ at your service.

dispositivo [disposi'tiβo] *nm* device, mechanism; ~ **de alimentación** hopper; ~ **de almacenaje** storage device; ~ **periférico** peripheral (device); ~ **de seguridad** safety catch; (*fig*) security measure.

dispuesto, a [dis'pwesto, a] *pp de* **disponer** ♦ *adj* (*arreglado*) arranged; (*preparado*) disposed; (*persona: dinámico*) bright; **estar** ~**/poco** ~ **a hacer algo** to be inclined/reluctant to do sth.

dispuse [dis'puse] *etc vb V* **disponer.**

disputa [dis'puta] *nf* (*discusión*) dispute, argument; (*controversia*) controversy.

disputar [dispu'tar] *vt* (*discutir*) to dispute, question; (*contender*) to contend for ♦ *vi* to argue.

disquete [dis'kete] *nm* (*INFORM*) diskette, floppy disk.

disquetera [diske'tera] *nf* disk drive.

Dist. *abr* (= *distancia, Distrito*) dist.

distancia [dis'tanθja] *nf* distance; (*de tiempo*) interval; ~ **de parada** braking distance; ~ **del suelo** (*AUTO etc*) height off the ground; **a gran** *o* **a larga** ~ long-distance; **mantenerse a** ~ to keep one's distance; (*fig*) to remain aloof; **guardar las** ~**s** to keep one's distance.

distanciado, a [distan'θjaðo, a] *adj* (*remoto*) remote; (*fig: alejado*) far apart; **estamos** ~**s en ideas** our ideas are poles apart.

distanciamiento [distanθja'mjento] *nm* (*acto*) spacing out; (*estado*) remoteness;

(*fig*) distance.
distanciar [distan'θjar] *vt* to space out;
~**se** *vr* to become estranged.
distante [dis'tante] *adj* distant.
distar [dis'tar] *vi*: **dista 5 kms de aquí** it is 5
kms from here; **¿dista mucho?** is it far?;
dista mucho de la verdad it's very far
from the truth.
diste ['diste], **disteis** ['disteis] *vb V* dar.
distensión [disten'sjon] *nf* distension;
(*POL*) détente; ~ **muscular** (*MED*)
muscular strain.
distinción [distin'θjon] *nf* distinction;
(*elegancia*) elegance; (*honor*) honour; **a** ~
de unlike; **sin** ~ indiscriminately; **sin** ~
de edades irrespective of age.
distinga [dis'tinga] *etc vb V* **distinguir**.
distinguido, a [distin'giðo, a] *adj*
distinguished; (*famoso*) prominent,
well-known; (*elegante*) elegant.
distinguir [distin'gir] *vt* to distinguish;
(*divisar*) to make out; (*escoger*) to single
out; (*caracterizar*) to mark out; ~**se** *vr* to
be distinguished; (*destacarse*) to
distinguish o.s.; **a lo lejos no se distingue**
it's not visible from a distance.
distintivo, a [distin'tiβo, a] *adj* distinctive;
(*signo*) distinguishing ♦ *nm* (*de policía etc*)
badge; (*fig*) characteristic.
distinto, a [dis'tinto, a] *adj* different;
(*claro*) clear; ~**s** several, various.
distorsión [distor'sjon] *nf* (*ANAT*) twisting;
(*RADIO etc*) distortion.
distorsionar [distorsjo'nar] *vt, vi* to distort.
distracción [distrak'θjon] *nf* distraction;
(*pasatiempo*) hobby, pastime; (*olvido*)
absent-mindedness, distraction.
distraer [distra'er] *vt* (*atención*) to distract;
(*divertir*) to amuse; (*fondos*) to embezzle
♦ *vi* to be relaxing; ~**se** *vr* (*entretenerse*)
to amuse o.s.; (*perder la concentración*) to
allow one's attention to wander; ~ **a**
algn de su pensamiento to divert sb
from his train of thought; **el pescar**
distrae fishing is a relaxation.
distraído, a [distra'iðo, a] *adj* (*gen*)
absent-minded; (*desatento*) inattentive;
(*entretenido*) amusing ♦ *nm*: **hacerse el** ~
to pretend not to notice; **con aire** ~ idly;
me miró distraída she gave me a casual
glance.
distraiga [dis'traixa] *etc*, **distraje**
[dis'traxe] *etc*, **distrajera** [distra'xera]
etc, **distrayendo** [distra'jendo] *vb V*
distraer.
distribución [distriβu'θjon] *nf* distribution;
(*entrega*) delivery; (*en estadística*)
distribution, incidence; (*ARQ*) layout; ~

de premios prize giving; **la** ~ **de los**
impuestos the incidence of taxes.
distribuidor, a [distriβui'ðor, a] *nm/f*
(*persona: gen*) distributor; (: *CORREOS*)
sorter; (: *COM*) dealer; **su** ~ **habitual**
your regular dealer.
distribuir [distriβu'ir] *vt* to distribute;
(*prospectos*) to hand out; (*cartas*) to
deliver; (*trabajo*) to allocate; (*premios*) to
award; (*dividendos*) to pay; (*peso*) to
distribute; (*ARQ*) to plan.
distribuyendo [distriβu'jendo] *etc vb V*
distribuir.
distrito [dis'trito] *nm* (*sector, territorio*)
region; (*barrio*) district; ~ **electoral**
constituency; ~ **postal** postal district.
disturbio [dis'turβjo] *nm* disturbance;
(*desorden*) riot; **los** ~**s** the troubles.
disuadir [diswa'ðir] *vt* to dissuade.
disuasión [diswa'sjon] *nf* dissuasion; (*MIL*)
deterrent; ~ **nuclear** nuclear deterrent.
disuasivo, a [diswa'siβo, a] *adj* dissuasive;
arma disuasiva deterrent.
disuasorio, a [diswa'sorjo, a] *adj*
= **disuasivo**.
disuelto [di'swelto] *pp de* **disolver**.
disuelva [di'swelβa] *etc vb V* **disolver**.
disuene [di'swene] *etc vb V* **disonar**.
disyuntiva [disjun'tiβa] *nf* (*dilema*)
dilemma.
DIU ['diu] *nm abr* (= *dispositivo intrauterino*)
I.U.D.
diurno, a ['djurno, a] *adj* day *cpd*, diurnal.
diva ['diβa] *nf* prima donna.
divagar [diβa'xar] *vi* (*desviarse*) to digress.
divague [di'βaxe] *etc vb V* **divagar**.
diván [di'βan] *nm* divan.
divergencia [diβer'xenθja] *nf* divergence.
divergir [diβer'xir] *vi* (*líneas*) to diverge;
(*opiniones*) to differ; (*personas*) to
disagree.
diverja [di'βerxa] *etc vb V* **divergir**.
diversidad [diβersi'ðað] *nf* diversity,
variety.
diversificación [diβersifika'θjon] *nf* (*COM*)
diversification.
diversificar [diβersifi'kar] *vt* to diversify.
diversifique [diβersi'fike] *etc vb V*
diversificar.
diversión [diβer'sjon] *nf* (*gen*)
entertainment; (*actividad*) hobby,
pastime.
diverso, a [di'βerso, a] *adj* diverse;
(*diferente*) different ♦ *nm*: ~**s** (*COM*)
sundries; ~**s libros** several books.
divertido, a [diβer'tiðo, a] *adj* (*chiste*)
amusing, funny; (*fiesta etc*) enjoyable;
(*película, libro*) entertaining; **está** ~

(*irónico*) this is going to be fun.

divertir [diβer'tir] *vt* (*entretener, recrear*) to amuse, entertain; ~**se** *vr* (*pasarlo bien*) to have a good time; (*distraerse*) to amuse o.s.

dividendo [diβi'ðendo] *nm* (*COM*): ~**s** *nmpl* dividends; ~**s por acción** earnings per share; ~ **definitivo** final dividend.

dividir [diβi'ðir] *vt* (*gen*) to divide; (*separar*) to separate; (*distribuir*) to distribute, share out.

divierta [di'βjerta] *etc vb V* **divertir**.

divinidad [diβini'ðað] *nf* (*esencia divina*) divinity; **la D**~ God.

divino, a [di'βino, a] *adj* divine; (*fig*) lovely.

divirtiendo [diβir'tjendo] *etc vb V* **divertir**.

divisa [di'βisa] *nf* (*emblema, moneda*) emblem, badge; ~**s** *nfpl* currency *sg*; (*COM*) foreign exchange *sg*; **control de** ~**s** exchange control; ~ **de reserva** reserve currency.

divisar [diβi'sar] *vt* to make out, distinguish.

división [diβi'sjon] *nf* division; (*de partido*) split; (*de país*) partition.

divisorio, a [diβi'sorjo, a] *adj* (*línea*) dividing; **línea divisoria de las aguas** watershed.

divorciado, a [diβor'θjaðo, a] *adj* divorced; (*opinion*) split ♦ *nm/f* divorcé(e).

divorciar [diβor'θjar] *vt* to divorce; ~**se** *vr* to get divorced.

divorcio [di'βorθjo] *nm* divorce; (*fig*) split.

divulgación [diβulɣa'θjon] *nf* (*difusión*) spreading; (*popularización*) popularization.

divulgar [diβul'ɣar] *vt* (*desparramar*) to spread; (*popularizar*) to popularize; (*hacer circular*) to divulge, circulate; ~**se** *vr* (*secreto*) to leak out; (*rumor*) to get about.

divulgue [di'βulɣe] *etc vb V* **divulgar**.

dizque ['diske] *adv* (*AM fam*) apparently.

Dls., dls *abr* (*AM*) = **dólares**.

DM *abr* = **decimal**.

dm. *abr* (= *decímetro*) dm.

DNI *nm abr* (*ESP*) = **Documento Nacional de Identidad**.

Dña. *abr* = **Doña**.

do [do] *nm* (*MUS*) C.

D.O. *abr* = **Denominación de Origen**.

dobladillo [doβla'ðiʎo] *nm* (*de vestido*) hem; (*de pantalón: vuelta*) turn-up (*BRIT*), cuff (*US*).

doblaje [do'βlaxe] *nm* (*CINE*) dubbing.

doblar [do'βlar] *vt* to double; (*papel*) to fold; (*caño*) to bend; (*la esquina*) to turn,

go round; (*film*) to dub ♦ *vi* to turn; (*campana*) to toll; ~**se** *vr* (*plegarse*) to fold (up), crease; (*encorvarse*) to bend.

doble ['doβle] *adj* (*gen*) double; (*de dos aspectos*) dual; (*cuerda*) thick; (*fig*) two-faced ♦ *nm* double ♦ *nm/f* (*TEAT*) double, stand-in; ~**s** *nmpl* (*DEPORTE*) doubles *sg*; ~ **o nada** double or quits; ~ **página** double-page spread; **con** ~ **sentido** with a double meaning; **el** ~ twice the quantity *o* as much; **su sueldo es el** ~ **del mío** his salary is twice (as much as) mine; (*INFORM*): ~ **cara** double-sided; ~ **densidad** double density; ~ **espacio** double spacing.

doblegar [doβle'ɣar] *vt* to fold, crease; ~**se** *vr* to yield.

doblegue [do'βleɣe] *etc vb V* **doblegar**.

doblez [do'βleθ] *nm* (*pliegue*) fold, hem ♦ *nf* (*falsedad*) duplicity.

doc. *abr* (= *docena*) doz.; (= *documento*) doc.

doce ['doθe] *num* twelve; (*fecha*) twelfth; **las** ~ twelve o'clock; *V tb* **seis**.

docena [do'θena] *nf* dozen; **por** ~**s** by the dozen.

docente [do'θente] *adj*: **centro/personal** ~ teaching institution/staff.

dócil ['doθil] *adj* (*pasivo*) docile; (*manso*) gentle; (*obediente*) obedient.

docto, a ['dokto, a] *adj* learned, erudite ♦ *nm/f* scholar.

doctor, a [dok'tor, a] *nm/f* doctor; ~ **en filosofía** Doctor of Philosophy.

doctorado [dokto'raðo] *nm* doctorate.

doctorarse [dokto'rarse] *vr* to get a doctorate.

doctrina [dok'trina] *nf* doctrine, teaching.

documentación [dokumenta'θjon] *nf* documentation; (*de identidad etc*) papers *pl*.

documental [dokumen'tal] *adj, nm* documentary.

documentar [dokumen'tar] *vt* to document; ~**se** *vr* to gather information.

documento [doku'mento] *nm* (*certificado*) document; (*JUR*) exhibit; ~**s** *nmpl* papers; ~ **justificativo** voucher; **D**~ **Nacional de Identidad** national identity card.

A laminated plastic ID card with the holder's personal details and photograph, the **Documento Nacional de Identidad** *is renewed every 10 years. People are required to carry it at all times and to produce it on request for the police. In Spain it is commonly known as the* **DNI** *or* **carnet de identidad**. *In Spanish America a* similar card is called the **cédula (de identidad).**

dogma ['doɣma] nm dogma.
dogmático, a [doɣ'matiko, a] adj dogmatic.
dogo ['doɣo] nm bulldog.
dólar ['dolar] nm dollar.
dolencia [do'lenθja] nf (achaque) ailment; (dolor) ache.
doler [do'ler] vt, vi to hurt; (fig) to grieve; ~**se** vr (de su situación) to grieve, feel sorry; (de las desgracias ajenas) to sympathize; (quejarse) to complain; **me duele el brazo** my arm hurts; **no me duele el dinero** I don't mind about the money; **¡ahí le duele!** you've put your finger on it!
doliente [do'ljente] adj (enfermo) sick; (dolorido) aching; (triste) sorrowful; **la familia** ~ the bereaved family.
dolor [do'lor] nm pain; (fig) grief, sorrow; ~ **de cabeza** headache; ~ **de estómago** stomach ache; ~ **de oídos** earache; ~ **sordo** dull ache.
dolorido, a [dolo'riðo, a] adj (MED) sore; **la parte dolorida** the part which hurts.
doloroso, a [dolo'roso, a] adj (MED) painful; (fig) distressing.
domar [do'mar] vt to tame.
domesticado, a [domesti'kaðo, a] adj (amansado) tame.
domesticar [domesti'kar] vt to tame.
doméstico, a [do'mestiko, a] adj domestic ♦ nm/f servant; **economía doméstica** home economy; **gastos** ~**s** household expenses.
domestique [domes'tike] etc vb V **domesticar.**
domiciliación [domiθilja'θjon] nf: ~ **de pagos** (COM) standing order, direct debit.
domiciliar [domiθi'ljar] vt to domicile; ~**se** vr to take up (one's) residence.
domiciliario, a [domiθi'ljarjo, a] adj: **arresto** ~ house arrest.
domicilio [domi'θiljo] nm home; ~ **particular** private residence; ~ **social** (COM) head office, registered office; **servicio a** ~ delivery service; **sin** ~ **fijo** of no fixed abode.
dominante [domi'nante] adj dominant; (person) domineering.
dominar [domi'nar] vt (gen) to dominate; (países) to rule over; (adversario) to overpower; (caballo, nervios, emoción) to control; (incendio, epidemia) to bring under control; (idiomas) to be fluent in

♦ vi to dominate, prevail; ~**se** vr to control o.s.
domingo [do'mingo] nm Sunday; **D**~ **de Ramos** Palm Sunday; **D**~ **de Resurrección** Easter Sunday; V tb **sábado; Semana Santa.**
dominguero, a [domin'gero, a] adj Sunday cpd.
dominical [domini'kal] adj Sunday cpd; **periódico** ~ Sunday newspaper.
dominicano, a [domini'kano, a] adj, nm/f Dominican.
dominio [do'minjo] nm (tierras) domain; (POL) dominion; (autoridad) power, authority; (supremacía) supremacy; (de las pasiones) grip, hold; (de idioma) command; **ser del** ~ **público** to be widely known.
dominó [domi'no] nm (pieza) domino; (juego) dominoes.
dom.º abr (= domingo) Sun.
don [don] nm (talento) gift; **D**~ **Juan Gómez** Mr Juan Gomez, Juan Gomez Esq.; **tener** ~ **de gentes** to known how to handle people; ~ **de lenguas** gift for languages; ~ **de mando** (qualities of) leadership; ~ **de palabra** gift of the gab.

Don or **doña** is a term used before someone's first name – eg Don Diego, Doña Inés – when showing respect or being polite to someone of a superior social standing or to an older person. It is becoming somewhat rare, but it does however continue to be used with names and surnames in official documents and in correspondence: eg Sr. D. Pedro Rodríguez Hernández, Sra. Dña Inés Rodríguez Hernández.

---

donación [dona'θjon] nf donation.
donaire [do'naire] nm charm.
donante [do'nante] nm/f donor; ~ **de sangre** blood donor.
donar [do'nar] vt to donate.
donativo [dona'tiβo] nm donation.
doncella [don'θeʎa] nf (criada) maid.
donde ['donde] adv where ♦ prep: **el coche está allí** ~ **el farol** the car is over there by the lamppost o where the lamppost is; **por** ~ through which; **a** ~ to where, to which; **en** ~ where, in which; **es a** ~ **vamos nosotros** that's where we're going.
dónde ['donde] adv interrogativo where?; **¿a** ~ **vas?** where are you going (to)?; **¿de** ~ **vienes?** where have you come from?; **¿en** ~**?** where?; **¿por** ~**?** where?,

whereabouts?; **¿por ~ se va al estadio?** how do you get to the stadium?

dondequiera [donde'kjera] *adv* anywhere ♦ *conj*: **~ que** wherever; **por ~** everywhere, all over the place.

donostiarra [donos'tjarra] *adj* of *o* from San Sebastián ♦ *nm/f* native *o* inhabitant of San Sebastián.

doña ['doɲa] *nf*: **D~ Carmen Gómez** Mrs Carmen Gómez; *V tb* **don**.

dopar [do'par] *vt* to dope, drug.

doping ['dopin] *nm* doping, drugging.

doquier [do'kjer] *adv*: **por ~** all over, everywhere.

dorado, a [do'raðo, a] *adj* (*color*) golden; (*TEC*) gilt.

dorar [do'rar] *vt* (*TEC*) to gild; (*CULIN*) to brown, cook lightly; **~ la píldora** to sweeten the pill.

dormilón, ona [dormi'lon, ona] *adj* fond of sleeping ♦ *nm/f* sleepyhead.

dormir [dor'mir] *vt*: **~ la siesta por la tarde** to have an afternoon nap ♦ *vi* to sleep; **~se** *vr* (*persona, brazo, pierna*) to fall asleep; **~la** (*fam*) to sleep it off; **~ la mona** (*fam*) to sleep off a hangover; **~ como un lirón** *o* **tronco** to sleep like a log; **~ a pierna suelta** to sleep soundly.

dormitar [dormi'tar] *vi* to doze.

dormitorio [dormi'torjo] *nm* bedroom; **~ común** dormitory.

dorsal [dor'sal] *adj* dorsal ♦ *nm* (*DEPORTE*) number.

dorso ['dorso] *nm* back; **escribir algo al ~** to write sth on the back; **"vease al ~"** "see other side", "please turn over".

DOS *nm abr* (= *sistema operativo de disco*) DOS.

dos [dos] *num* two; (*fecha*) second; **los ~** the two of them, both of them; **cada ~ por tres** every five minutes; **de ~ en ~** in twos; **estamos a ~** (*TENIS*) the score is deuce; *V tb* **seis**.

doscientos, as [dos'θjentos, as] *num* two hundred.

dosel [do'sel] *nm* canopy.

dosificar [dosifi'kar] *vt* (*CULIN, MED, QUÍMICA*) to measure out; (*no derrochar*) to be sparing with.

dosifique [dosi'fike] *etc vb V* **dosificar**.

dosis ['dosis] *nf inv* dose, dosage.

dossier [do'sjer] *nm* dossier, file.

dotación [dota'θjon] *nf* (*acto, dinero*) endowment; (*plantilla*) staff; (*NAUT*) crew; **la ~ es insuficiente** we are under staffed.

dotado, a [do'taðo, a] *adj* gifted; **~ de** (*persona*) endowed with; (*máquina*) equipped with.

dotar [do'tar] *vt* to endow; (*TEC*) to fit; (*barco*) to man; (*oficina*) to staff.

dote ['dote] *nf* (*de novia*) dowry; **~s** *nfpl* (*talentos*) gifts.

doy [doj] *vb V* **dar**.

Dpto. *abr* (= *Departamento*) dept.

Dr(a). *abr* (= *Doctor, Doctora*) Dr.

draga ['draɣa] *nf* dredge.

dragado [dra'ɣaðo] *nm* dredging.

dragar [dra'ɣar] *vt* to dredge; (*minas*) to sweep.

dragón [dra'ɣon] *nm* dragon.

drague ['draɣe] *etc vb V* **dragar**.

drama ['drama] *nm* drama; (*obra*) play.

dramático, a [dra'matiko, a] *adj* dramatic ♦ *nm/f* dramatist; (*actor*) actor; **obra dramática** play.

dramaturgo, a [drama'turɣo, a] *nm/f* dramatist, playwright.

dramón [dra'mon] *nm* (*TEAT*) melodrama; **¡qué ~!** what a scene!

drástico, a ['drastiko, a] *adj* drastic.

drenaje [dre'naxe] *nm* drainage.

drenar [dre'nar] *vt* to drain.

droga ['droɣa] *nf* drug; (*DEPORTE*) dope; **el problema de la ~** the drug problem.

drogadicto, a [droɣa'ðikto, a] *nm/f* drug addict.

drogar [dro'ɣar] *vt* to drug; (*DEPORTE*) to dope; **~se** *vr* to take drugs.

drogodependencia [droɣoðepen'denθja] *nf* drug addiction.

drogue ['droɣe] *etc vb V* **drogar**.

droguería [droɣe'ria] *nf* ≈ hardware shop (*BRIT*) *o* store (*US*).

dromedario [drome'ðarjo] *nm* dromedary.

Dto., D.to *abr* = **descuento**.

Dtor(a). *abr* (= *Director, Directora*) Dir.

ducado [du'kaðo] *nm* duchy, dukedom.

ducha ['dutʃa] *nf* (*baño*) shower; (*MED*) douche.

ducharse [du'tʃarse] *vr* to take a shower.

ducho, a ['dutʃo, a] *adj*: **~ en** (*experimentado*) experienced in; (*hábil*) skilled at.

dúctil ['duktil] *adj* (*metal*) ductile; (*persona*) easily influenced.

duda ['duða] *nf* doubt; **sin ~** no doubt, doubtless; **¡sin ~!** of course!; **no cabe ~** there is no doubt about it; **no le quepa ~** make no mistake about it; **no quiero poner en ~ su conducta** I don't want to call his behaviour into question; **sacar a algn de la ~** to settle sb's doubts; **tengo una ~** I have a query.

dudar [du'ðar] *vt* to doubt ♦ *vi* to doubt, have doubts; **~ acerca de algo** to be uncertain about sth; **dudó en comprarlo** he hesitated to buy it; **dudan que sea verdad** they doubt whether *o* if it's true.

dudoso, a [du'ðoso, a] *adj* (*incierto*) hesitant; (*sospechoso*) doubtful; (*conducta*) dubious.

duelo ['dwelo] *etc vb V* **doler** ♦ *nm* (*combate*) duel; (*luto*) mourning; **batirse en** ~ to fight a duel.

duende ['dwende] *nm* imp, goblin; **tiene** ~ he's got real soul.

dueño, a ['dweɲo, a] *nm/f* (*propietario*) owner; (*de pensión, taberna*) landlord/lady; (*de casa, perro*) master/mistress; (*empresario*) employer; **ser** ~ **de sí mismo** to have self-control; (*libre*) to be one's own boss; **eres** ~ **de hacer como te parezca** you're free to do as you think fit; **hacerse** ~ **de una situación** to take command of a situation.

duerma ['dwerma] *etc vb V* **dormir**.

duermevela [dwerme'ßela] *nf* (*fam*) nap, snooze.

Duero ['dwero] *nm* Douro.

dulce ['dulθe] *adj* sweet; (*carácter, clima*) gentle, mild ♦ *adv* gently, softly ♦ *nm* sweet.

dulcificar [dulθifi'kar] *vt* (*fig*) to soften.

dulcifique [dulθi'fike] *etc vb V* **dulcificar**.

dulzón, ona [dul'θon, ona] *adj* (*alimento*) sickly-sweet, too sweet; (*canción etc*) gooey.

dulzura [dul'θura] *nf* sweetness; (*ternura*) gentleness.

duna ['duna] *nf* dune.

Dunquerque [dun'kerke] *nm* Dunkirk.

dúo ['duo] *nm* duet, duo.

duodécimo, a [duo'deθimo, a] *adj* twelfth; *V tb* **sexto, a**.

dup., dup.do *abr* (= *duplicado*) duplicated.

dúplex ['dupleks] *nm inv* (*piso*) flat on two floors; (*TELEC*) link-up; (*INFORM*): ~ **integral** full duplex.

duplicar [dupli'kar] *vt* (*hacer el doble de*) to duplicate; (*cantidad*) to double; ~**se** *vr* to double.

duplique [du'plike] *etc vb V* **duplicar**.

duque ['duke] *nm* duke.

duquesa [du'kesa] *nf* duchess.

duración [dura'θjon] *nf* duration, length; (*de máquina*) life; ~ **media de la vida** average life expectancy; **de larga** ~ (*enfermedad*) lengthy; (*pila*) long-life; (*disco*) long-playing; **de poca** ~ short.

duradero, a [dura'ðero, a] *adj* (*tela*) hard-wearing; (*fe, paz*) lasting.

durante [du'rante] *adv* during; ~ **toda la noche** all night long; **habló** ~ **una hora** he spoke for an hour.

durar [du'rar] *vi* (*permanecer*) to last; (*recuerdo*) to remain; (*ropa*) to wear (well).

durazno [du'rasno] *nm* (*AM: fruta*) peach; (: *árbol*) peach tree.

durex ['dureks] *nm* (*AM: tira adhesiva*) Sellotape ® (*BRIT*), Scotch tape ® (*US*).

dureza [du'reθa] *nf* (*cualidad*) hardness; (*de carácter*) toughness.

durmiendo [dur'mjendo] *etc vb V* **dormir**.

durmiente [dur'mjente] *adj* sleeping ♦ *nm/f* sleeper.

duro, a ['duro, a] *adj* hard; (*carácter*) tough; (*pan*) stale; (*cuello, puerta*) stiff; (*clima, luz*) harsh ♦ *adv* hard ♦ *nm* (*moneda*) five peseta coin; **el sector** ~ **del partido** the hardliners *pl* in the party; **ser** ~ **con algn** to be tough with *o* hard on sb; ~ **de mollera** (*torpe*) dense; ~ **de oído** hard of hearing; **trabajar** ~ to work hard; **estar sin un** ~ to be broke.

E e

E, e [e] *nf* (*letra*) E, e; **E de Enrique** E for Edward (*BRIT*) *o* Easy (*US*).

E *abr* (= *este*) E.

e [e] *conj* (*delante de* i- *e* hi-, *pero no* **hie**-) and; *V tb* **y**.

e/ *abr* (*COM*: = *envío*) shpt.

ebanista [eßa'nista] *nm/f* cabinetmaker.

ébano ['eßano] *nm* ebony.

ebrio, a ['eßrjo, a] *adj* drunk.

Ebro ['eßro] *nm* Ebro.

ebullición [eßuʎi'θjon] *nf* boiling; **punto de** ~ boiling point.

eccema [ek'θema] *nm* (*MED*) eczema.

echar [e'tʃar] *vt* to throw; (*agua, vino*) to pour (out); (*CULIN*) to put in, add; (*dientes*) to cut; (*discurso*) to give; (*empleado: despedir*) to fire, sack; (*hojas*) to sprout; (*cartas*) to post; (*humo*) to emit, give out; (*reprimenda*) to deal out; (*cuenta*) to make up; (*freno*) to put on ♦ *vi*: ~ **a correr/llorar** to break into a run/burst into tears; ~ **a reír** to burst out laughing; ~**se** *vr* to lie down; ~ **abajo** (*gobierno*) to overthrow; (*edificio*) to demolish; ~ **la buenaventura a algn** to tell sb's fortune; ~ **la culpa a** to lay the blame on; ~ **de menos** to miss; ~**se atrás** to throw o.s. back(wards); (*fig*) to go back on what one has said; ~**se una novia** to get o.s. a girlfriend; ~**se una siestecita** to have a nap.

echarpe [e't∫arpe] *nm* (woman's) stole.

eclesiástico, a [ekle'sjastiko, a] *adj* ecclesiastical; (*autoridades etc*) church *cpd* ♦ *nm* clergyman.

eclipsar [eklip'sar] *vt* to eclipse; (*fig*) to outshine, overshadow.

eclipse [e'klipse] *nm* eclipse.

eco ['eko] *nm* echo; **encontrar un ~ en** to produce a response from; **hacerse ~ de una opinión** to echo an opinion; **tener ~** to catch on.

ecografía [ekoɣra'fia] *nf* ultrasound.

ecología [ekolo'xia] *nf* ecology.

ecológico, a [eko'loxiko, a] *adj* ecological; (*producto, método*) environmentally-friendly; (*agricultura*) organic.

ecologista [ekolo'xista] *adj* environmental, conservation *cpd* ♦ *nm/f* environmentalist.

economato [ekono'mato] *nm* cooperative store.

economía [ekono'mia] *nf* (*sistema*) economy; (*cualidad*) thrift; ~ **dirigida** planned economy; ~ **doméstica** housekeeping; ~ **de mercado** market economy; ~ **mixta** mixed economy; ~ **sumergida** black economy; **hacer ~s** to economize; ~**s de escala** economies of scale.

economice [ekono'miθe] *etc vb V* **economizar.**

económico, a [eko'nomiko, a] *adj* (*barato*) cheap, economical; (*persona*) thrifty; (*COM: año etc*) financial; (: *situación*) economic.

economista [ekono'mista] *nm/f* economist.

economizar [ekonomi'θar] *vt* to economize on ♦ *vi* (*ahorrar*) to save up; (*pey*) to be miserly.

ecosistema [ekosis'tema] *nm* ecosystem.

ecu ['eku] *nm* ecu.

ecuación [ekwa'θjon] *nf* equation.

ecuador [ekwa'ðor] *nm* equator; (**el**) **E~** Ecuador.

ecuánime [e'kwanime] *adj* (*carácter*) level-headed; (*estado*) calm.

ecuatorial [ekwato'rjal] *adj* equatorial.

ecuatoriano, a [ekwato'rjano, a] *adj, nm/f* Ecuador(i)an.

ecuestre [e'kwestre] *adj* equestrian.

eczema [ek'θema] *nm* = **eccema.**

ed. *abr* (= *edición*) ed.

edad [e'ðað] *nf* age; **¿qué ~ tienes?** how

old are you?; **tiene ocho años de ~** he is eight (years old); **de ~ corta** young; **ser de ~ mediana/avanzada** to be middle-aged/getting on; **ser mayor de ~** to be of age; **llegar a mayor ~** to come of age; **ser menor de ~** to be under age; **la E~ Media** the Middle Ages; **la E~ de Oro** the Golden Age.

Edén [e'ðen] *nm* Eden.

edición [eði'θjon] *nf* (*acto*) publication; (*ejemplar*) edition; "**al cerrar la ~**" (*TIP*) "stop press".

edicto [e'ðikto] *nm* edict, proclamation.

edificante [eðifi'kante] *adj* edifying.

edificar [eðifi'kar] *vt* (*ARQ*) to build.

edificio [eði'fiθjo] *nm* building; (*fig*) edifice, structure.

edifique [eði'fike] *etc vb V* **edificar.**

Edimburgo [eðim'burxo] *nm* Edinburgh.

editar [eði'tar] *vt* (*publicar*) to publish; (*preparar textos, tb INFORM*) to edit.

editor, a [eði'tor, a] *nm/f* (*que publica*) publisher; (*redactor*) editor ♦ *adj*: **casa ~a** publishing company.

editorial [eðito'rjal] *adj* editorial ♦ *nm* leading article, editorial ♦ *nf* (*tb*: **casa ~**) publishers.

editorialista [eðitorja'lista] *nm/f* leader-writer.

Edo. *abr* (*AM*) = **Estado.**

edredón [eðre'ðon] *nm* eiderdown, quilt; ~ **nórdico** continental quilt, duvet.

educación [eðuka'θjon] *nf* education; (*crianza*) upbringing; (*modales*) (good) manners *pl*; (*formación*) training; **sin ~** ill-mannered; **¡qué falta de ~!** how rude!

educado, a [eðu'kaðo, a] *adj* well-mannered; **mal ~** ill-mannered.

educar [eðu'kar] *vt* to educate; (*criar*) to bring up; (*voz*) to train.

educativo, a [eðuka'tiβo, a] *adj* educational; (*política*) education *cpd*.

eduque [e'ðuke] *etc vb V* **educar.**

EE.UU. *nmpl abr* (= *Estados Unidos*) USA.

efectista [efek'tista] *adj* sensationalist.

efectivamente [efektiβa'mente] *adv* (*como respuesta*) exactly, precisely; (*verdaderamente*) really; (*de hecho*) in fact.

efectivo, a [efek'tiβo, a] *adj* effective; (*real*) actual, real ♦ *nm*: **pagar en ~** to pay (in) cash; **hacer ~ un cheque** to cash a cheque.

efecto [e'fekto] *nm* effect, result; (*objetivo*) purpose, end; ~**s** *nmpl* (*personales*) effects; (*bienes*) goods; (*COM*) assets; (*ECON*) bills, securities; ~ **invernadero** greenhouse effect; ~**s de consumo** consumer goods; ~**s a cobrar** bills

receivable; ~s **especiales** special
effects; ~s **personales** personal effects;
~ **secundarios** (*COM*) spin-off effects; ~s
sonoros sound effects; **hacer** *o* **surtir** ~
to have the desired effect; **hacer** ~
(*impresionar*) to make an impression;
llevar algo a ~ to carry sth out; **en** ~ in
fact; (*respuesta*) exactly, indeed.
efectuar [efek'twar] *vt* to carry out; (*viaje*)
to make.
efervescente [eferßes'θente] *adj* (*bebida*)
fizzy, bubbly.
eficacia [efi'kaθja] *nf* (*de persona*)
efficiency; (*de medicamento etc*)
effectiveness.
eficaz [efi'kaθ] *adj* (*persona*) efficient;
(*acción*) effective.
eficiencia [efi'θjenθja] *nf* efficiency.
eficiente [efi'θjente] *adj* efficient.
efigie [e'fixje] *nf* effigy.
efímero, a [e'fimero, a] *adj* ephemeral.
efusión [efu'sjon] *nf* outpouring; (*en el
trato*) warmth; **con** ~ effusively.
efusivo, a [efu'sißo, a] *adj* effusive; **mis
más efusivas gracias** my warmest
thanks.
EGB *nf abr* (*ESP ESCOL*: = *Educación General
Básica*) primary education *for* 6-14 year
olds; *V tb* **sistema educativo**.
Egeo [e'xeo] *nm*: **(Mar)** ~ Aegean (Sea).
egipcio, a [e'xipθjo, a] *adj, nm/f* Egyptian.
Egipto [e'xipto] *nm* Egypt.
egocéntrico, a [eɣo'θentriko, a] *adj* self-
centred.
egoísmo [eɣo'ismo] *nm* egoism.
egoísta [eɣo'ista] *adj* egoistical, selfish
♦ *nm/f* egoist.
ególatra [e'ɣolatra] *adj* big-headed.
egregio, a [e'ɣrexjo, a] *adj* eminent,
distinguished.
egresado, a [eɣre'saðo, a] *nm/f* (*AM*)
graduate.
egresar [eɣre'sar] *vi* (*AM*) to graduate.
eh [e] *excl* hey!, hi!
Eire ['eire] *nm* Eire.
ej. *abr* (= *ejemplo*) ex.
eje ['exe] *nm* (*GEO, MAT*) axis; (*POL, fig*)
axis, main line; (*de rueda*) axle; (*de
máquina*) shaft, spindle.
ejecución [exeku'θjon] *nf* execution;
(*cumplimiento*) fulfilment; (*actuación*)
performance; (*JUR: embargo de deudor*)
attachment.
ejecutar [exeku'tar] *vt* to execute, carry
out; (*matar*) to execute; (*cumplir*) to fulfil;
(*MUS*) to perform; (*JUR: embargar*) to
attach, distrain; (*deseos*) to fulfil;
(*INFORM*) to run.

ejecutivo, a [exeku'tißo, a] *adj, nm/f* executive; **el (poder)** ~ the Executive (Power).
ejecutor [exeku'tor] *nm* (*tb*: ~
testamentario) executor.
ejecutoria [exeku'torja] *nf* (*JUR*) final
judgment.
ejemplar [exem'plar] *adj* exemplary ♦ *nm*
example; (*ZOOL*) specimen; (*de libro*)
copy; (*de periódico*) number, issue; ~ **de
regalo** complimentary copy; **sin** ~
unprecedented.
ejemplificar [exemplifi'kar] *vt* to
exemplify, illustrate.
ejemplifique [exempli'fike] *etc vb V*
ejemplificar.
ejemplo [e'xemplo] *nm* example; (*caso*)
instance; **por** ~ for example; **dar** ~ to
set an example.
ejercer [exer'θer] *vt* to exercise; (*funciones*)
to perform; (*negocio*) to manage;
(*influencia*) to exert; (*un oficio*) to
practise; (*poder*) to wield ♦ *vi*: ~ **de** to
practise as.
ejercicio [exer'θiθjo] *nm* exercise; (*MIL*)
drill; (*COM*) fiscal *o* financial year;
(*período*) tenure; ~ **acrobático** (*AVIAT*)
stunt; ~ **comercial** business year; ~s
espirituales (*REL*) retreat *sg*; **hacer** ~ to
take exercise.
ejercitar [exerθi'tar] *vt* to exercise; (*MIL*) to
drill.
ejército [e'xerθito] *nm* army; **E~ del Aire/
de Tierra** Air Force/Army; ~ **de
ocupación** army of occupation; ~
permanente standing army; **entrar en el**
~ to join the army, join up.
ejerza [e'xerθa] *etc vb V* **ejercer.**
ejote [e'xote] *nm* (*AM*) green bean.

═══════════════════════ *PALABRA CLAVE*

el [el] (*f* **la**, *pl* **los, las,** *neutro* **lo**) *art def* **1** the;
**el libro/la mesa/los estudiantes/las
flores** the book/table/students/flowers;
me gusta el fútbol I like football; **está en
la cama** she's in bed
2 (*con n abstracto o propio: no se traduce*):
el amor/la juventud love/youth; ~ **Conde
Drácula** Count Dracula
3 (*posesión: se traduce a menudo por adj
posesivo*): **romperse el brazo** to break
one's arm; **levantó la mano** he put his
hand up; **se puso el sombrero** she put
her hat on
4 (*valor descriptivo*): **tener la boca
grande/los ojos azules** to have a big
mouth/blue eyes
5 (*con días*) on; **me iré el viernes** I'll
leave on Friday; **los domingos suelo ir a**

nadar on Sundays I generally go swimming
6 (lo + adj): **lo difícil/caro** what is difficult/expensive; (= cuán): **no se da cuenta de lo pesado que es** he doesn't realise how boring he is
♦ pron demos **1: mi libro y el de usted** my book and yours; **las de Pepe son mejores** Pepe's are better; **no la(s) blanca(s) sino la(s) gris(es)** not the white one(s) but the grey one(s)
2: lo de: lo de ayer what happened yesterday; **lo de las facturas** that business about the invoices
♦ pron relativo: **el que** etc **1** (indef): **el (los) que quiera(n) que se vaya(n)** anyone who wants to can leave; **llévese el/la que más le guste** take the one you like best
2 (def): **el que compré ayer** the one I bought yesterday; **los que se van** those who leave
3: lo que: lo que pienso yo/más me gusta what I think/like most
♦ conj: **el que: el que lo diga** the fact that he says so; **el que sea tan vago me molesta** his being so lazy bothers me
♦ excl: **¡el susto que me diste!** what a fright you gave me!
♦ pron personal **1** (persona: m) him; (: f) her; (: pl) them; **lo/las veo** I can see him/them
2 (animal, cosa: sg) it; (: pl) them; **lo** (o **la**) **veo** I can see it; **los** (o **las**) **veo** I can see them
3: lo (como sustituto de frase): **no lo sabía** I didn't know; **ya lo entiendo** I understand now.

él [el] pron (persona) he; (cosa) it; (después de prep: persona) him; (: cosa) it; **mis libros y los de** ~ my books and his.
elaboración [elaβora'θjon] nf (producción) manufacture; ~ **de presupuestos** (COM) budgeting.
elaborar [elaβo'rar] vt (producto) to make, manufacture; (preparar) to prepare; (madera, metal etc) to work; (proyecto etc) to work on o out.
elasticidad [elastiθi'ðað] nf elasticity.
elástico, a [e'lastiko, a] adj elastic; (flexible) flexible ♦ nm elastic; (gomita) elastic band.
elección [elek'θjon] nf election; (selección) choice, selection; **elecciones parciales** by-election sg; **elecciones generales** general election sg.
electo, a [e'lekto, a] adj elect; **el presidente** ~ the president-elect.
electorado [elekto'raðo] nm electorate,

voters pl.
electoral [elekto'ral] adj electoral.
electrice [elek'triθe] etc vb V **electrizar**.
electricidad [elektriθi'ðað] nf electricity.
electricista [elektri'θista] nm/f electrician.
eléctrico, a [e'lektriko, a] adj electric.
electrificar [elektrifi'kar] vt to electrify.
electrizar [elektri'θar] vt (FERRO, fig) to electrify.
electro... [elektro] pref electro....
electrocardiograma [elektrokarðjo'ɣrama] nm electrocardiogram.
electrocución [elektroku'θjon] nf electrocution.
electrocutar [elektroku'tar] vt to electrocute.
electrodo [elek'troðo] nm electrode.
electrodomésticos [elektroðo'mestikos] nmpl (electrical) household appliances; (COM) white goods.
electroimán [electroi'man] nm electromagnet.
electromagnético, a [elektromaɣ'netiko, a] adj electromagnetic.
electrón [elek'tron] nm electron.
electrónico, a [elek'troniko, a] adj electronic ♦ nf electronics sg; **proceso** ~ **de datos** (INFORM) electronic data processing.
electrotecnia [elektro'teknja] nf electrical engineering.
electrotécnico, a [elektro'tekniko, a] nm/f electrical engineer.
elefante [ele'fante] nm elephant.
elegancia [ele'ɣanθja] nf elegance, grace; (estilo) stylishness.
elegante [ele'ɣante] adj elegant, graceful; (traje etc) smart, fashionable; (decoración) tasteful.
elegía [ele'xia] nf elegy.
elegir [ele'xir] vt (escoger) to choose, select; (optar) to opt for; (presidente) to elect.
elemental [elemen'tal] adj (claro, obvio) elementary; (fundamental) elemental, fundamental.
elemento [ele'mento] nm element; (fig) ingredient; (AM) person, individual; (tipo raro) odd person; (de pila) cell; ~**s** elements, rudiments; **estar en su** ~ to be in one's element; **vino a verle un** ~ someone came to see you.
elenco [e'lenko] nm catalogue, list; (TEAT) cast; (AM: equipo) team.
elepé [ele'pe] nm LP.
elevación [eleβa'θjon] nf elevation; (acto) raising, lifting; (de precios) rise; (GEO

E~ Your Eminence.
eminente [emi'nente] *adj* eminent, distinguished; (*elevado*) high.
emisario [emi'sarjo] *nm* emissary.
emisión [emi'sjon] *nf* (*acto*) emission; (*COM etc*) issue; (*RADIO, TV: acto*) broadcasting; (: *programa*) broadcast, programme, program (*US*); ~ **de acciones** (*COM*) share issue; ~ **gratuita de acciones** (*COM*) rights issue; ~ **de valores** (*COM*) flotation.
emisor, a [emi'sor, a] *nm* transmitter ♦ *nf* radio *o* broadcasting station.
emitir [emi'tir] *vt* (*olor etc*) to emit, give off; (*moneda etc*) to issue; (*opinión*) to express; (*voto*) to cast; (*señal*) to send out; (*RADIO*) to broadcast; ~ **una señal sonora** to beep.
emoción [emo'θjon] *nf* emotion; (*excitación*) excitement; (*sentimiento*) feeling; ¡**qué** ~! how exciting!; (*irónico*) what a thrill!
emocionado, a [emoθjo'naðo, a] *adj* deeply moved, stirred.
emocionante [emoθjo'nante] *adj* (*excitante*) exciting, thrilling.
emocionar [emoθjo'nar] *vt* (*excitar*) to excite, thrill; (*conmover*) to move, touch; (*impresionar*) to impress; ~**se** *vr* to get excited.
emotivo, a [emo'tiβo, a] *adj* emotional.
empacar [empa'kar] *vt* (*gen*) to pack; (*en caja*) to bale, crate.
empacharse [empa'tʃarse] *vr* (*MED*) to get indigestion.
empacho [em'patʃo] *nm* (*MED*) indigestion; (*fig*) embarrassment.
empadronamiento [empaðrona'mjento] *nm* census; (*de electores*) electoral register.
empadronarse [empaðro'narse] *vr* (*POL: como elector*) to register.
empalagar [empala'xar] *vt* (*suj: comida*) to cloy; (*hartar*) to pall on ♦ *vi* to pall.
empalagoso, a [empala'xoso, a] *adj* cloying; (*fig*) tiresome.
empalague [empa'laxe] *etc vb V* **empalagar**.
empalizada [empali'θaða] *nf* fence; (*MIL*) palisade.
empalmar [empal'mar] *vt* to join, connect ♦ *vi* (*dos caminos*) to meet, join.
empalme [em'palme] *nm* joint, connection; (*de vías*) junction; (*de trenes*) connection.
empanada [empa'naða] *nf* pie, pasty.
empanar [empa'nar] *vt* (*CULIN*) to cook *o* roll in breadcrumbs *o* pastry.
empantanarse [empanta'narse] *vr* to get

swamped; (*fig*) to get bogged down.
empañarse [empa'ɲarse] *vr* (*nublarse*) to get misty, steam up.
empapar [empa'par] *vt* (*mojar*) to soak, saturate; (*absorber*) to soak up, absorb; ~**se** *vr*: ~**se de** to soak up.
empapelar [empape'lar] *vt* (*paredes*) to paper.
empaque [em'pake] *etc vb V* **empacar**.
empaquetar [empake'tar] *vt* to pack, parcel up; (*COM*) to package.
emparedado [empare'ðaðo] *nm* sandwich.
emparejar [empare'xar] *vt* to pair ♦ *vi* to catch up.
emparentar [emparen'tar] *vi*: ~ **con** to marry into.
empariente [empa'rjente] *etc vb V* **emparentar**.
empastar [empas'tar] *vt* (*embadurnar*) to paste; (*diente*) to fill.
empaste [em'paste] *nm* (*de diente*) filling.
empatar [empa'tar] *vi* to draw, tie.
empate [em'pate] *nm* draw, tie; **un** ~ **a cero** a no-score draw.
empecé [empe'θe], **empecemos** [empe'θemos] *etc vb V* **empezar**.
empecinado, a [empeθi'naðo, a] *adj* stubborn.
empedernido, a [empeðer'niðo, a] *adj* hard, heartless; (*fijado*) hardened, inveterate; **un fumador** ~ a heavy smoker.
empedrado, a [empe'ðraðo, a] *adj* paved ♦ *nm* paving.
empedrar [empe'ðrar] *vt* to pave.
empeine [em'peine] *nm* (*de pie, zapato*) instep.
empellón [empe'ʎon] *nm* push, shove; **abrirse paso a empellones** to push *o* shove one's way past *o* through.
empeñado, a [empe'ɲaðo, a] *adj* (*persona*) determined; (*objeto*) pawned.
empeñar [empe'ɲar] *vt* (*objeto*) to pawn, pledge; (*persona*) to compel; ~**se** *vr* (*obligarse*) to bind o.s., pledge o.s.; (*endeudarse*) to get into debt; ~**se en hacer** to be set on doing, be determined to do.
empeño [em'peɲo] *nm* (*determinación*) determination; (*cosa prendada*) pledge; **casa de** ~**s** pawnshop; **con** ~ insistently; (*con celo*) eagerly; **tener** ~ **en hacer algo** to be bent on doing sth.
empeoramiento [empeora'mjento] *nm* worsening.
empeorar [empeo'rar] *vt* to make worse, worsen ♦ *vi* to get worse, deteriorate.
empequeñecer [empekeɲe'θer] *vt* to

dwarf; (*fig*) to belittle.

empequeñezca [empeke'neθka] *etc vb V* **empequeñecer**.

emperador [empera'ðor] *nm* emperor.

emperatriz [empera'triθ] *nf* empress.

emperrarse [empe'rrarse] *vr* to get stubborn; ~ **en algo** to persist in sth.

empezar [empe'θar] *vt, vi* to begin, start; **empezó a llover** it started to rain; **bueno, para** ~ well, to start with.

empiece [em'pjeθe] *etc vb V* **empezar**.

empiedre [em'pjeðre] *etc vb V* **empedrar**.

empiezo [em'pjeθo] *etc vb V* **empezar**.

empinado, a [empi'naðo, a] *adj* steep.

empinar [empi'nar] *vt* to raise; (*botella*) to tip up; ~**se** *vr* (*persona*) to stand on tiptoe; (*animal*) to rear up; (*camino*) to climb steeply; ~ **el codo** to booze (*fam*).

empingorotado, a [empingoro'taðo, a] *adj* (*fam*) stuck-up.

empírico, a [em'piriko, a] *adj* empirical.

emplace [em'plaθe] *etc vb V* **emplazar**.

emplaste [em'plaste], **emplasto** [em'plasto] *nm* (*MED*) plaster.

emplazamiento [emplaθa'mjento] *nm* site, location; (*JUR*) summons *sg*.

emplazar [empla'θar] *vt* (*ubicar*) to site, place, locate; (*JUR*) to summons; (*convocar*) to summon.

empleado, a [emple'aðo, a] *nm/f* (*gen*) employee; (*de banco etc*) clerk; ~ **público** civil servant.

emplear [emple'ar] *vt* (*usar*) to use, employ; (*dar trabajo a*) to employ; ~**se** *vr* (*conseguir trabajo*) to be employed; (*ocuparse*) to occupy o.s.; ~ **mal el tiempo** to waste time; **¡te está bien empleado!** it serves you right!

empleo [em'pleo] *nm* (*puesto*) job; (*puestos: colectivamente*) employment; (*uso*) use, employment; "**modo de** ~" "instructions for use".

emplumar [emplu'mar] *vt* (*estafar*) to swindle.

empobrecer [empoβre'θer] *vt* to impoverish; ~**se** *vr* to become poor *o* impoverished.

empobrecimiento [empoβreθi'mjento] *nm* impoverishment.

empobrezca [empo'βreθka] *etc vb V* **empobrecer**.

empollar [empo'ʎar] *vt* to incubate; (*ESCOL fam*) to swot (up) ♦ *vi* (*gallina*) to brood; (*ESCOL fam*) to swot.

empollón, ona [empo'ʎon, ona] *nm/f* (*ESCOL fam*) swot.

empolvar [empol'βar] *vt* (*cara*) to powder; ~**se** *vr* to powder one's face; (*superficie*)

to get dusty.

emponzoñar [emponθo'nar] *vt* (*esp fig*) to poison.

emporio [em'porjo] *nm* emporium, trading centre; (*AM: gran almacén*) department store.

empotrado, a [empo'traðo, a] *adj* (*armario etc*) built-in.

empotrar [empo'trar] *vt* to embed; (*armario etc*) to build in.

emprendedor, a [emprende'ðor, a] *adj* enterprising.

emprender [empren'der] *vt* to undertake; (*empezar*) to begin, embark on; (*acometer*) to tackle, take on; ~ **marcha a** to set out for.

empresa [em'presa] *nf* enterprise; (*COM: sociedad*) firm, company; (: *negocio*) business; (*esp TEAT*) management; ~ **filial** (*COM*) affiliated company; ~ **matriz** (*COM*) parent company.

empresario, a [empre'sarjo, a] *nm/f* (*COM*) businessman/woman, entrepreneur; (*TEC*) manager; (*MUS: de ópera etc*) impresario; ~ **de pompas fúnebres** undertaker (*BRIT*), mortician (*US*).

empréstito [em'prestito] *nm* (public) loan; (*COM*) loan capital.

empujar [empu'xar] *vt* to push, shove.

empuje [em'puxe] *nm* thrust; (*presión*) pressure; (*fig*) vigour, drive.

empujón [empu'xon] *nm* push, shove; **abrirse paso a empujones** to shove one's way through.

empuñadura [empuɲa'ðura] *nf* (*de espada*) hilt; (*de herramienta etc*) handle.

empuñar [empu'ɲar] *vt* (*asir*) to grasp, take (firm) hold of; ~ **las armas** (*fig*) to take up arms.

emulación [emula'θjon] *nf* emulation.

emular [emu'lar] *vt* to emulate; (*rivalizar*) to rival.

émulo, a ['emulo, a] *nm/f* rival, competitor.

emulsión [emul'sjon] *nf* emulsion.

<hr>

PALABRA CLAVE

en [en] *prep* **1** (*posición*) in; (: *sobre*) on; **está** ~ **el cajón** it's in the drawer; ~ **Argentina/La Paz** in Argentina/La Paz; ~ **el colegio/la oficina** at school/the office; ~ **casa** at home; **está** ~ **el suelo/quinto piso** it's on the floor/the fifth floor; ~ **el periódico** in the paper
2 (*dirección*) into; **entró** ~ **el aula** she went into the classroom; **meter algo** ~ **el bolso** to put sth into one's bag; **ir de puerta** ~ **puerta** to go from door to door

3 (*tiempo*) in; on; ~ **1605/3 semanas/ invierno** in 1605/3 weeks/winter; ~ **(el mes de) enero** in (the month of) January; ~ **aquella ocasión/época** on that occasion/at that time
4 (*precio*) for; **lo vendió ~ 20 dólares** he sold it for 20 dollars
5 (*diferencia*) by; **reducir/aumentar ~ una tercera parte/un 20 por ciento** to reduce/increase by a third/20 per cent
6 (*manera, forma*): ~ **avión/autobús** by plane/bus; **escrito ~ inglés** written in English; ~ **serio** seriously; ~ **espiral/ círculo** in a spiral/circle
7 (*después de vb que indica gastar etc*) on; **han cobrado demasiado ~ dietas** they've charged too much to expenses; **se le va la mitad del sueldo ~ comida** half his salary goes on food
8 (*tema, ocupación*): **experto ~ la materia** expert on the subject; **trabaja ~ la construcción** he works in the building industry
9 (*adj + ~ + infin*): **lento ~ reaccionar** slow to react.

enagua(s) [enaɣwa(s)] *nf(pl)* (*esp AM*) petticoat.

enajenación [enaxena'θjon] *nf*, **enajenamiento** [enaxena'mjento] *nm* alienation; (*fig: distracción*) absent-mindedness; (: *embelesamiento*) rapture, trance; ~ **mental** mental derangement.

enajenar [enaxe'nar] *vt* to alienate; (*fig*) to carry away.

enamorado, a [enamo'raðo, a] *adj* in love ♦ *nm/f* lover; **estar ~ (de)** to be in love (with).

enamorar [enamo'rar] *vt* to win the love of; ~**se** *vr*: ~**se (de)** to fall in love (with).

enano, a [e'nano, a] *adj* tiny, dwarf ♦ *nm/f* dwarf; (*pey*) runt.

enarbolar [enarβo'lar] *vt* (*bandera etc*) to hoist; (*espada etc*) to brandish.

enardecer [enarðe'θer] *vt* (*pasiones*) to fire, inflame; (*persona*) to fill with enthusiasm; ~**se** *vr* to get excited; ~**se por** to get enthusiastic about.

enardezca [enar'deθka] *etc vb V* **enardecer**.

encabece [enka'βeθe] *etc vb V* **encabezar**.

encabezado [enkaβe'θaðo] *nm* (*COM*) header.

encabezamiento [enkaβeθa'mjento] *nm* (*de carta*) heading; (*COM*) billhead, letterhead; (*de periódico*) headline; (*preámbulo*) foreword, preface; ~ **normal** (*TIP etc*) running head.

encabezar [enkaβe'θar] *vt* (*movimiento,*

revolución) to lead, head; (*lista*) to head; (*carta*) to put a heading to; (*libro*) to entitle.

encadenar [enkaðe'nar] *vt* to chain (together); (*poner grilletes a*) to shackle.

encajar [enka'xar] *vt* (*ajustar*): ~ **en** to fit (into); (*meter a la fuerza*) to push in; (*máquina etc*) to house; (*partes*) to join; (*fam: golpe*) to give, deal; (*entrometer*) to insert ♦ *vi* to fit (well); (*fig: corresponder a*) to match; ~**se** *vr*: ~**se en un sillón** to squeeze into a chair.

encaje [en'kaxe] *nm* (*labor*) lace.

encajonar [enkaxo'nar] *vt* to box (up), put in a box.

encalar [enka'lar] *vt* (*pared*) to whitewash.

encallar [enka'ʎar] *vi* (*NAUT*) to run aground.

encaminado, a [enkami'naðo, a] *adj*: **medidas encaminadas a ...** measures designed to *o* aimed at ....

encaminar [enkami'nar] *vt* to direct, send; ~**se** *vr*: ~**se a** to set out for; ~ **por** (*expedición etc*) to route via.

encandilar [enkandi'lar] *vt* to dazzle; (*persona*) to daze, bewilder.

encanecer [enkane'θer] *vi*, **encanecerse** *vr* (*pelo*) to go grey.

encanezca [enka'neθka] *etc vb V* **encanecer**.

encantado, a [enkan'taðo, a] *adj* delighted; ¡~! how do you do!, pleased to meet you.

encantador, a [enkanta'ðor, a] *adj* charming, lovely ♦ *nm/f* magician, enchanter/enchantress.

encantar [enkan'tar] *vt* to charm, delight; (*cautivar*) to fascinate; (*hechizar*) to bewitch, cast a spell on.

encanto [en'kanto] *nm* (*magia*) spell, charm; (*fig*) charm, delight; (*expresión de ternura*) sweetheart; **como por ~** as if by magic.

encapotado, a [enkapo'taðo, a] *adj* (*cielo*) overcast.

encapricharse [enkapri'tʃarse] *vr*: **se ha encaprichado con ir** he's taken it into his head to go; **se ha encaprichado** he's digging his heels in.

encaramar [enkara'mar] *vt* (*subir*) to raise, lift up; ~**se** *vr* (*subir*) to perch; ~**se a** (*árbol etc*) to climb.

encararse [enka'rarse] *vr*: ~ **a** *o* **con** to confront, come face to face with.

encarcelar [enkarθe'lar] *vt* to imprison, jail.

encarecer [enkare'θer] *vt* to put up the price of ♦ *vi*, ~**se** *vr* to get dearer.

encarecidamente [enkareθiða'mente] *adv* earnestly.

encarecimiento [enkareθi'mjento] *nm* price increase.

encarezca [enka're θka] *etc vb V* **encarecer**.

encargado, a [enkar'ɣaðo, a] *adj* in charge ♦ *nm/f* agent, representative; (*responsable*) person in charge.

encargar [enkar'ɣar] *vt* to entrust; (*COM*) to order; (*recomendar*) to urge, recommend; ~**se** *vr*: ~**se de** to look after, take charge of; ~ **algo a algn** to put sb in charge of sth.

encargo [en'karɣo] *nm* (*pedido*) assignment, job; (*responsabilidad*) responsibility; (*recomendación*) recommendation; (*COM*) order.

encargue [en'karɣe] *etc vb V* **encargar**.

encariñarse [enkari'ɲarse] *vr*: ~ **con** to grow fond of, get attached to.

encarnación [enkarna'θjon] *nf* incarnation, embodiment.

encarnado, a [enkar'naðo, a] *adj* (*color*) red; **ponerse** ~ to blush.

encarnar [enkar'nar] *vt* to personify; (*TEAT*: *papel*) to play ♦ *vi* (*REL etc*) to become incarnate.

encarnizado, a [enkarni'θaðo, a] *adj* (*lucha*) bloody, fierce.

encarrilar [enkarri'lar] *vt* (*tren*) to put back on the rails; (*fig*) to correct, put on the right track.

encasillar [enkasi'ʎar] *vt* (*TEAT*) to typecast; (*clasificar*: *pey*) to pigeonhole.

encasquetar [enkaske'tar] *vt* (*sombrero*) to pull down *o* on; ~**se** *vr*: ~**se el sombrero** to pull one's hat down *o* on; ~ **algo a algn** to offload sth onto sb.

encauce [en'kauθe] *etc vb V* **encauzar**.

encausar [enkau'sar] *vt* to prosecute, sue.

encauzar [enkau'θar] *vt* to channel; (*fig*) to direct.

encendedor [enθende'ðor] *nm* lighter.

encender [enθen'der] *vt* (*con fuego*) to light; (*incendiar*) to set fire to; (*luz, radio*) to put on, switch on; (*INFORM*) to toggle on, switch on; (*avivar*: *pasiones etc*) to inflame; (*despertar*: *entusiasmo*) to arouse; (*odio*) to awaken; ~**se** *vr* to catch fire; (*excitarse*) to get excited; (*de cólera*) to flare up; (*el rostro*) to blush.

encendidamente [enθendiða'mente] *adv* passionately.

encendido, a [enθen'diðo, a] *adj* alight; (*aparato*) (switched) on; (*mejillas*) glowing; (*cara*: *por el vino etc*) flushed; (*mirada*) passionate ♦ *nm* (*AUTO*) ignition; (*de faroles*) lighting.

encerado, a [enθe'raðo, a] *adj* (*suelo*) waxed, polished ♦ *nm* (*ESCOL*) blackboard; (*hule*) oilcloth.

encerar [enθe'rar] *vt* (*suelo*) to wax, polish.

encerrar [enθe'rrar] *vt* (*confinar*) to shut in *o* up; (*con llave*) to lock in *o* up; (*comprender, incluir*) to include, contain; ~**se** *vr* to shut *o* lock o.s. up *o* in.

encerrona [enθe'rrona] *nf* trap.

encestar [enθes'tar] *vi* to score a basket.

encharcar [entʃar'kar] *vt* to swamp, flood; ~**se** *vr* to become flooded.

encharque [en'tʃarke] *etc vb V* **encharcar**.

enchufar [entʃu'far] *vt* (*ELEC*) to plug in; (*TEC*) to connect, fit together; (*COM*) to merge.

enchufe [en'tʃufe] *nm* (*ELEC*: *clavija*) plug; (: *toma*) socket; (*de dos tubos*) joint, connection; (*fam*: *influencia*) contact, connection; (: *puesto*) cushy job; ~ **de clavija** jack plug; **tiene un** ~ **en el ministerio** he can pull strings in the ministry.

encía [en'θia] *nf* (*ANAT*) gum.

enciclopedia [enθiklo'peðja] *nf* encyclopaedia.

encienda [en'θjenda] *etc vb V* **encender**.

encierro [en'θjerro] *etc vb V* **encerrar** ♦ *nm* shutting in *o* up; (*calabozo*) prison; (*AGR*) pen; (*TAUR*) penning.

encima [en'θima] *adv* (*sobre*) above, over; (*además*) besides; ~ **de** (*en*) on, on top of; (*sobre*) above, over; (*además de*) besides, on top of; **por** ~ **de** over; **¿llevas dinero** ~**?** have you (got) any money on you?; **se me vino** ~ it took me by surprise.

encina [en'θina] *nf* (*holm*) oak.

encinta [en'θinta] *adj f* pregnant.

enclave [en'klaβe] *nm* enclave.

enclenque [en'klenke] *adj* weak, sickly.

encoger [enko'xer] *vt* (*gen*) to shrink, contract; (*fig*: *asustar*) to scare; (: *desanimar*) to discourage; ~**se** *vr* to shrink, contract; (*fig*) to cringe; ~**se de hombros** to shrug one's shoulders.

encoja [en'koxa] *etc vb V* **encoger**.

encolar [enko'lar] *vt* (*engomar*) to glue, paste; (*pegar*) to stick down.

encolerice [enkole'riθe] *etc vb V* **encolerizar**.

encolerizar [enkoleri'θar] *vt* to anger, provoke; ~**se** *vr* to get angry.

encomendar [enkomen'dar] *vt* to entrust, commend; ~**se** *vr*: ~**se a** to put one's trust in.

encomiar [enko'mjar] *vt* to praise, pay tribute to.

encomienda [enko'mjenda] *etc vb V*

encomendar ♦ *nf* (*encargo*) charge, commission; (*elogio*) tribute; (*AM*) parcel, package; ~ **postal** (*AM*) parcel post.

encomio [en'komjo] *nm* praise, tribute.

encono [en'kono] *nm* (*rencor*) rancour, spite.

encontrado, a [enkon'trado, a] *adj* (*contrario*) contrary, conflicting; (*hostil*) hostile.

encontrar [enkon'trar] *vt* (*hallar*) to find; (*inesperadamente*) to meet, run into; ~**se** *vr* to meet (each other); (*situarse*) to be (situated); (*persona*) to find o.s., be; (*entrar en conflicto*) to crash, collide; ~**se con** to meet; ~**se bien (de salud)** to feel well; **no se encuentra aquí en este momento** he's not in at the moment.

encontronazo [enkontro'naθo] *nm* collision, crash.

encorvar [enkor'ßar] *vt* to curve; (*inclinar*) to bend (down); ~**se** *vr* to bend down, bend over.

encrespado, a [enkres'paðo, a] *adj* (*pelo*) curly; (*mar*) rough.

encrespar [enkres'par] *vt* (*cabellos*) to curl; (*fig*) to anger, irritate; ~**se** *vr* (*el mar*) to get rough; (*fig*) to get cross o irritated.

encrucijada [enkruθi'xaða] *nf* crossroads *sg*; (*empalme*) junction.

encuadernación [enkwaðerna'θjon] *nf* binding; (*taller*) binder's.

encuadernador, a [enkwaðerna'ðor, a] *nm/f* bookbinder.

encuadrar [enkwa'ðrar] *vt* (*retrato*) to frame; (*ajustar*) to fit, insert; (*encerrar*) to contain.

encubierto [enku'ßjerto] *pp de* **encubrir**.

encubrir [enku'ßrir] *vt* (*ocultar*) to hide, conceal; (*criminal*) to harbour, shelter; (*ayudar*) to be an accomplice in.

encuentro [en'kwentro] *etc vb V* **encontrar** ♦ *nm* (*de personas*) meeting; (*AUTO etc*) collision, crash; (*DEPORTE*) match, game; (*MIL*) encounter.

encuesta [en'kwesta] *nf* inquiry, investigation; (*sondeo*) public opinion poll; ~ **judicial** post mortem.

encumbrado, a [enkum'braðo, a] *adj* eminent, distinguished.

encumbrar [enkum'brar] *vt* (*persona*) to exalt; ~**se** *vr* (*fig*) to become conceited.

endeble [en'deßle] *adj* (*argumento, excusa, persona*) weak.

endémico, a [en'demiko, a] *adj* endemic.

endemoniado, a [endemo'njaðo, a] *adj* possessed (of the devil); (*travieso*) devilish.

enderece [ende'reθe] *etc vb V* **enderezar**.

enderezar [endere'θar] *vt* (*poner derecho*) to straighten (out); (: *verticalmente*) to set upright; (*fig*) to straighten o sort out; (*dirigir*) to direct; ~**se** *vr* (*persona sentada*) to sit up straight.

endeudarse [endeu'ðarse] *vr* to get into debt.

endiablado, a [endja'ßlaðo, a] *adj* devilish, diabolical; (*hum*) mischievous.

endibia [en'dißja] *nf* endive.

endilgar [endil'γar] *vt* (*fam*): ~ **algo a algn** to lumber sb with sth; ~ **un sermón a algn** to give sb a lecture.

endilgue [en'dilγe] *etc vb V* **endilgar**.

endiñar [endi'ɲar] *vt*: ~ **algo a algn** to land sth on sb.

endomingarse [endomin'garse] *vr* to dress up, put on one's best clothes.

endomingue [endo'minge] *etc vb V* **endomingarse**.

endosar [endo'sar] *vt* (*cheque etc*) to endorse.

endulce [en'dulθe] *etc vb V* **endulzar**.

endulzar [endul'θar] *vt* to sweeten; (*suavizar*) to soften.

endurecer [endure'θer] *vt* to harden; ~**se** *vr* to harden, grow hard.

endurecido, a [endure'θiðo, a] *adj* (*duro*) hard; (*fig*) hardy, tough; **estar ~ a algo** to be hardened o used to sth.

endurezca [endu're θka] *etc vb V* **endurecer**.

ene. *abr* (= *enero*) Jan.

enemigo, a [ene'miγo, a] *adj* enemy, hostile ♦ *nm/f* enemy ♦ *nf* enmity, hostility; **ser ~ de** (*persona*) to dislike; (*suj: tendencia*) to be inimical to.

enemistad [enemis'tað] *nf* enmity.

enemistar [enemis'tar] *vt* to make enemies of, cause a rift between; ~**se** *vr* to become enemies; (*amigos*) to fall out.

energético, a [ener'xetiko, a] *adj*: **política energética** energy policy.

energía [ener'xia] *nf* (*vigor*) energy, drive; (*TEC, ELEC*) energy, power; ~ **atómica/ eléctrica/eólica** atomic/electric/wind power.

enérgico, a [e'nerxiko, a] *adj* (*gen*) energetic; (*ataque*) vigorous; (*ejercicio*) strenuous; (*medida*) bold; (*voz, modales*) forceful.

energúmeno, a [ener'γumeno, a] *nm/f* madman/woman; **ponerse como un ~ con algn** to get furious with sb.

enero [e'nero] *nm* January.

enervar [ener'ßar] *vt* (*poner nervioso a*) to get on sb's nerves.

enésimo, a [e'nesimo, a] *adj* (*MAT*) nth; **por enésima vez** (*fig*) for the umpteenth time.

enfadado, a [enfa'ðaðo, a] _adj_ angry, annoyed.

enfadar [enfa'ðar] _vt_ to anger, annoy; ~**se** _vr_ to get angry o annoyed.

enfado [en'faðo] _nm_ (_enojo_) anger, annoyance; (_disgusto_) trouble, bother.

énfasis ['enfasis] _nm_ emphasis, stress; **poner ~ en** to stress.

enfático, a [en'fatiko, a] _adj_ emphatic.

enfatizado, a [enfati'θaðo, a] _adj_: **en caracteres ~s** (_INFORM_) emphasized.

enfermar [enfer'mar] _vt_ to make ill ♦ _vi_ to fall ill, be taken ill; **su actitud me enferma** his attitude makes me sick; ~ **del corazón** to develop heart trouble.

enfermedad [enferme'ðað] _nf_ illness; ~ **venérea** venereal disease.

enfermera [enfer'mera] _nf_ V **enfermero**.

enfermería [enferme'ria] _nf_ infirmary; (_de colegio etc_) sick bay.

enfermero, a [enfer'mero, a] _nm_ (male) nurse ♦ _nf_ nurse; **enfermera jefa** matron.

enfermizo, a [enfer'miθo, a] _adj_ (_persona_) sickly, unhealthy; (_fig_) unhealthy.

enfermo, a [en'fermo, a] _adj_ ill, sick ♦ _nm/f_ invalid, sick person; (_en hospital_) patient.

enfilar [enfi'lar] _vt_ (_aguja_) to thread; (_calle_) to go down.

enflaquecer [enflake'θer] _vt_ (_adelgazar_) to make thin; (_debilitar_) to weaken.

enflaquezca [enfla'keθka] _etc vb_ V **enflaquecer**.

enfocar [enfo'kar] _vt_ (_foto etc_) to focus; (_problema etc_) to consider, look at.

enfoque [en'foke] _etc vb_ V **enfocar** ♦ _nm_ focus; (_acto_) focusing; (_óptica_) approach.

enfrascado, a [enfras'kaðo, a] _adj_: **estar ~ en algo** (_fig_) to be wrapped up in sth.

enfrascarse [enfras'karse] _vr_: ~ **en un libro** to bury o.s. in a book.

enfrasque [en'fraske] _etc vb_ V **enfrascar**.

enfrentamiento [enfrenta'mjento] _nm_ confrontation.

enfrentar [enfren'tar] _vt_ (_peligro_) to face (up to), confront; (_oponer_) to bring face to face; ~**se** _vr_ (_dos personas_) to face o confront each other; (_DEPORTE: dos equipos_) to meet; ~**se a** o **con** to face up to, confront.

enfrente [en'frente] _adv_ opposite; ~ **de** _prep_ opposite, facing; **la casa de ~** the house opposite, the house across the street.

enfriamiento [enfria'mjento] _nm_ chilling, refrigeration; (_MED_) cold, chill.

enfriar [enfri'ar] _vt_ (_alimentos_) to cool, chill; (_algo caliente_) to cool down;

(_habitación_) to air, freshen; (_entusiasmo_) to dampen; ~**se** _vr_ to cool down; (_MED_) to catch a chill; (_amistad_) to cool.

enfurecer [enfure'θer] _vt_ to enrage, madden; ~**se** _vr_ to become furious, fly into a rage; (_mar_) to get rough.

enfurezca [enfu're θka] _etc vb_ V **enfurecer**.

engalanar [engala'nar] _vt_ (_adornar_) to adorn; (_ciudad_) to decorate; ~**se** _vr_ to get dressed up.

enganchar [engan't ʃar] _vt_ to hook; (_ropa_) to hang up; (_dos vagones_) to hitch up; (_TEC_) to couple, connect; (_MIL_) to recruit; (_fam: atraer: persona_) to rope into; ~**se** _vr_ (_MIL_) to enlist, join up; ~**se (a)** (_drogas_) to get hooked (on).

enganche [en'gant ʃe] _nm_ hook; (_TEC_) coupling, connection; (_acto_) hooking (up); (_MIL_) recruitment, enlistment; (_AM: depósito_) deposit.

engañar [enga'ɲar] _vt_ to deceive; (_estafar_) to cheat, swindle ♦ _vi_: **las apariencias engañan** appearances are deceptive; ~**se** _vr_ (_equivocarse_) to be wrong; (_asímismo_) to deceive o kid o.s.; **engaña a su mujer** he's unfaithful to o cheats on his wife.

engaño [en'gaɲo] _nm_ deceit; (_estafa_) trick, swindle; (_error_) mistake, misunderstanding; (_ilusión_) delusion.

engañoso, a [enga'ɲoso, a] _adj_ (_tramposo_) crooked; (_mentiroso_) dishonest, deceitful; (_aspecto_) deceptive; (_consejo_) misleading.

engarce [en'garθe] _etc vb_ V **engarzar**.

engarzar [engar'θar] _vt_ (_joya_) to set, mount; (_fig_) to link, connect.

engatusar [engatu'sar] _vt_ (_fam_) to coax.

engendrar [enxen'drar] _vt_ to breed; (_procrear_) to beget; (_fig_) to cause, produce.

engendro [en'xendro] _nm_ (_BIO_) foetus; (_fig_) monstrosity; (_idea_) brainchild.

englobar [englo'βar] _vt_ (_comprender_) to include, comprise; (_incluir_) to lump together.

engomar [engo'mar] _vt_ to glue, stick.

engordar [engor'ðar] _vt_ to fatten ♦ _vi_ to get fat, put on weight.

engorro [en'gorro] _nm_ bother, nuisance.

engorroso, a [engo'rroso, a] _adj_ bothersome, trying.

engranaje [engra'naxe] _nm_ (_AUTO_) gear; (_juego_) gears _pl_.

engrandecer [engrande'θer] _vt_ to enlarge, magnify; (_alabar_) to praise, speak highly of; (_exagerar_) to exaggerate.

engrandezca [engran'deθka] _etc vb_ V

engrandecer.

engrasar [engra'sar] *vt* (*TEC: poner grasa*) to grease; (: *lubricar*) to lubricate, oil; (*manchar*) to make greasy.

engrase [en'grase] *nm* greasing, lubrication.

engreído, a [engre'iðo, a] *adj* vain, conceited.

engrosar [engro'sar] *vt* (*ensanchar*) to enlarge; (*aumentar*) to increase; (*hinchar*) to swell.

engrudo [en'gruðo] *nm* paste.

engruese [en'grwese] *etc vb V* **engrosar.**

engullir [engu'ʎir] *vt* to gobble, gulp (down).

enhebrar [ene'ßrar] *vt* to thread.

enhiesto, a [e'njesto, a] *adj* (*derecho*) erect; (*bandera*) raised; (*edificio*) lofty.

enhorabuena [enora'ßwena] *excl* congratulations.

enigma [e'niɣma] *nm* enigma; (*problema*) puzzle; (*misterio*) mystery.

enigmático, a [eniɣ'matiko, a] *adj* enigmatic.

enjabonar [enxaßo'nar] *vt* to soap; (*barba*) to lather; (*fam: adular*) to soft-soap; (: *regañar*) to tick off.

enjalbegar [enxalße'ɣar] *vt* (*pared*) to whitewash.

enjalbegue [enxal'ßeɣe] *etc vb V* **enjalbegar.**

enjambre [en'xamßre] *nm* swarm.

enjaular [enxau'lar] *vt* (*put in a*) cage; (*fam*) to jail, lock up.

enjuagar [enxwa'ɣar] *vt* (*ropa*) to rinse (out).

enjuague [en'xwaɣe] *etc vb V* **enjuagar** ♦ *nm* (*MED*) mouthwash; (*de ropa*) rinse, rinsing.

enjugar [enxu'ɣar] *vt* to wipe (off); (*lágrimas*) to dry; (*déficit*) to wipe out.

enjugue [en'xuɣe] *etc vb V* **enjugar.**

enjuiciar [enxwi'θjar] *vt* (*JUR: procesar*) to prosecute, try; (*fig*) to judge.

enjuto, a [en'xuto, a] *adj* dry, dried up; (*fig*) lean, skinny.

enlace [en'laθe] *etc vb V* **enlazar** ♦ *nm* link, connection; (*relación*) relationship; (*tb:* ~ **matrimonial**) marriage; (*de trenes*) connection; ~ **de datos** data link; ~ **sindical** shop steward; ~ **telefónico** telephone link-up.

enlazar [enla'θar] *vt* (*unir con lazos*) to bind together; (*atar*) to tie; (*conectar*) to link, connect; (*AM*) to lasso.

enlodar [enlo'ðar] *vt* to cover in mud; (*fig: manchar*) to stain; (: *rebajar*) to debase.

enloquecer [enloke'θer] *vt* to drive mad

♦ *vi,* ~**se** *vr* to go mad.

enloquezca [enlo'keθka] *etc vb V* **enloquecer.**

enlutado, a [enlu'taðo, a] *adj* (*persona*) in mourning.

enlutar [enlu'tar] *vt* to dress in mourning; ~**se** *vr* to go into mourning.

enmarañar [enmara'ɲar] *vt* (*enredar*) to tangle up, entangle; (*complicar*) to complicate; (*confundir*) to confuse; ~**se** *vr* (*enredarse*) to become entangled; (*confundirse*) to get confused.

enmarcar [enmar'kar] *vt* (*cuadro*) to frame; (*fig*) to provide a setting for.

enmarque [en'marke] *etc vb V* **enmarcar.**

enmascarar [enmaska'rar] *vt* to mask; (*intenciones*) to disguise; ~**se** *vr* to put on a mask.

enmendar [enmen'dar] *vt* to emend, correct; (*constitución etc*) to amend; (*comportamiento*) to reform; ~**se** *vr* to reform, mend one's ways.

enmienda [en'mjenda] *etc vb V* **enmendar** ♦ *nf* correction; amendment; reform.

enmohecerse [enmoe'θerse] *vr* (*metal*) to rust, go rusty; (*muro, plantas*) to go mouldy.

enmohezca [enmo'eθka] *etc vb V* **enmohecerse.**

enmudecer [enmuðe'θer] *vt* to silence ♦ *vi,* ~**se** *vr* (*perder el habla*) to fall silent; (*guardar silencio*) to remain silent; (*por miedo*) to be struck dumb.

enmudezca [enmu'ðeθka] *etc vb V* **enmudecer.**

ennegrecer [enneɣre'θer] *vt* (*poner negro*) to blacken; (*oscurecer*) to darken; ~**se** *vr* to turn black; (*oscurecerse*) to get dark, darken.

ennegrezca [enne'ɣreθka] *etc vb V* **ennegrecer.**

ennoblecer [ennoßle'θer] *vt* to ennoble.

ennoblezca [enno'ßleθka] *etc vb V* **ennoblecer.**

en.º *abr* (= *enero*) Jan.

enojadizo, a [enoxa'ðiθo, a] *adj* irritable, short-tempered.

enojar [eno'xar] (*esp AM*) *vt* (*encolerizar*) to anger; (*disgustar*) to annoy, upset; ~**se** *vr* to get angry; to get annoyed.

enojo [e'noxo] (*esp AM*) *nm* (*cólera*) anger; (*irritación*) annoyance; ~**s** *nmpl* trials, problems.

enojoso, a [eno'xoso, a] *adj* annoying.

enorgullecerse [enorɣuʎe'θerse] *vr* to be proud; ~ **de** to pride o.s. on, be proud of.

enorgullezca [enorɣu'ʎeθka] *etc vb V* **enorgullecerse.**

enorme [e'norme] *adj* enormous, huge; (*fig*) monstrous.

enormidad [enormi'ðað] *nf* hugeness, immensity.

enraice [en'raiθe] *etc vb V* **enraizar.**

enraizar [enrai'θar] *vi* to take root.

enrarecido, a [enrare'θiðo, a] *adj* rarefied.

enredadera [enreða'ðera] *nf* (*BOT*) creeper, climbing plant.

enredar [enre'ðar] *vt* (*cables, hilos etc*) to tangle (up), entangle; (*situación*) to complicate, confuse; (*meter cizaña*) to sow discord among *o* between; (*implicar*) to embroil, implicate; ~**se** *vr* to get entangled, get tangled (up); (*situación*) to get complicated; (*persona*) to get embroiled.

enredo [en'reðo] *nm* (*maraña*) tangle; (*confusión*) mix-up, confusion; (*intriga*) intrigue; (*apuro*) jam; (*amorío*) love affair.

enrejado [enre'xaðo] *nm* grating; (*de ventana*) lattice; (*en jardín*) trellis.

enrevesado, a [enreße'saðo, a] *adj* (*asunto*) complicated, involved.

enriquecer [enrike'θer] *vt* to make rich; (*fig*) to enrich; ~**se** *vr* to get rich.

enriquezca [enri'keθka] *etc vb V* **enriquecer.**

enrojecer [enroxe'θer] *vt* to redden ♦ *vi*, ~**se** *vr* (*persona*) to blush.

enrojezca [enro'xeθka] *etc vb V* **enrojecer.**

enrolar [enro'lar] *vt* (*MIL*) to enlist; (*reclutar*) to recruit; ~**se** *vr* (*MIL*) to join up; (*afiliarse*) to enrol, sign on.

enrollar [enro'ʎar] *vt* to roll (up), wind (up); ~**se** *vr*: ~**se con algn** to get involved with sb.

enroque [en'roke] *nm* (*AJEDREZ*) castling.

enroscar [enros'kar] *vt* (*torcer, doblar*) to twist; (*arrollar*) to coil (round), wind; (*tornillo, rosca*) to screw in; ~**se** *vr* to coil, wind.

enrosque [en'roske] *etc vb V* **enroscar.**

ensalada [ensa'laða] *nf* salad; (*lío*) mix-up.

ensaladilla [ensala'ðiʎa] *nf* (*tb*: ~ **rusa**) ≈ Russian salad.

ensalce [en'salθe] *etc vb V* **ensalzar.**

ensalzar [ensal'θar] *vt* (*alabar*) to praise, extol; (*exaltar*) to exalt.

ensamblador [ensambla'ðor] *nm* (*INFORM*) assembler.

ensambladura [ensambla'ðura] *nf*, **ensamblaje** [ensam'blaxe] *nm* assembly; (*TEC*) joint.

ensamblar [ensam'blar] *vt* (*montar*) to assemble; (*madera etc*) to join.

ensanchar [ensan't ʃar] *vt* (*hacer más*

ancho*) to widen; (*agrandar*) to enlarge, expand; (*COSTURA*) to let out; ~**se** *vr* to get wider, expand; (*pey*) to give o.s. airs.

ensanche [en'sant ʃe] *nm* (*de calle*) widening; (*de negocio*) expansion.

ensangrentado, a [ensangren'taðo, a] *adj* bloodstained, covered with blood.

ensangrentar [ensangren'tar] *vt* to stain with blood.

ensangriente [ensan'grjente] *etc vb V* **ensangrentar.**

ensañarse [ensa'ɲarse] *vr*: ~ **con** to treat brutally.

ensartar [ensar'tar] *vt* (*gen*) to string (together); (*carne*) to spit, skewer.

ensayar [ensa'jar] *vt* to test, try (out); (*TEAT*) to rehearse.

ensayista [ensa'jista] *nm/f* essayist.

ensayo [en'sajo] *nm* test, trial; (*QUÍMICA*) experiment; (*TEAT*) rehearsal; (*DEPORTE*) try; (*ESCOL, LITERATURA*) essay; **pedido de** ~ (*COM*) trial order; ~ **general** (*TEAT*) dress rehearsal; (*MUS*) full rehearsal.

enseguida [ense'ɣuiða] *adv* at once, right away; ~ **termino** I've nearly finished, I shan't be long now.

ensenada [ense'naða] *nf* inlet, cove.

enseña [en'seɲa] *nf* ensign, standard.

enseñante [ense'ɲante] *nm/f* teacher.

enseñanza [ense'ɲanθa] *nf* (*educación*) education; (*acción*) teaching; (*doctrina*) teaching, doctrine; ~ **primaria/ secundaria/superior** primary/ secondary/higher education.

enseñar [ense'ɲar] *vt* (*educar*) to teach; (*instruir*) to teach, instruct; (*mostrar, señalar*) to show.

enseres [en'seres] *nmpl* belongings.

ENSIDESA [ensi'ðesa] *abr* (*ESP COM*) = *Empresa Nacional Siderúrgica, S. A.*

ensillar [ensi'ʎar] *vt* to saddle (up).

ensimismarse [ensimis'marse] *vr* (*abstraerse*) to become lost in thought; (*estar absorto*) to be lost in thought; (*AM*) to become conceited.

ensopar [enso'par] *vt* (*AM*) to soak.

ensordecer [ensorðe'θer] *vt* to deafen ♦ *vi* to go deaf.

ensordezca [ensor'ðeθka] *etc vb V* **ensordecer.**

ensortijado, a [ensorti'xaðo, a] *adj* (*pelo*) curly.

ensuciar [ensu'θjar] *vt* (*manchar*) to dirty, soil; (*fig*) to defile; ~**se** *vr* (*mancharse*) to get dirty; (*niño*) to dirty (*o* wet) o.s.

ensueño [en'sweɲo] *nm* (*sueño*) dream, fantasy; (*ilusión*) illusion; (*soñando despierto*) daydream; **de** ~ dream-like.

entablado [enta'ßlaðo] *nm* (*piso*)
floorboards *pl*; (*armazón*) boarding.

entablar [enta'ßlar] *vt* (*recubrir*) to board
(up); (*AJEDREZ, DAMAS*) to set up;
(*conversación*) to strike up; (*JUR*) to file
♦ *vi* to draw.

entablillar [entaßli'ʎar] *vt* (*MED*) to (put in
a) splint.

entallado, a [enta'ʎaðo, a] *adj* waisted.

entallar [enta'ʎar] *vt* (*traje*) to tailor ♦ *vi*: **el
traje entalla bien** the suit fits well.

ente ['ente] *nm* (*organización*) body,
organization; (*compañía*) company; (*fam:
persona*) odd character; (*ser*) being; ~
público (*ESP*) state(-owned) body.

entender [enten'der] *vt* (*comprender*) to
understand; (*darse cuenta*) to realize;
(*querer decir*) to mean ♦ *vi* to understand;
(*creer*) to think, believe ♦ *nm*: **a mi** ~ in
my opinion; ~ **de** to know all about; ~
algo de to know a little about; ~ **en** to
deal with, have to do with; ~**se** *vr*
(*comprenderse*) to be understood; (*2
personas*) to get on together; (*ponerse de
acuerdo*) to agree, reach an agreement;
dar a ~ **que** ... to lead to believe that ...;
~**se mal** to get on badly; **¿entiendes?** (do
you) understand?

entendido, a [enten'diðo, a] *adj*
(*comprendido*) understood; (*hábil*)
skilled; (*inteligente*) knowledgeable
♦ *nm/f* (*experto*) expert ♦ *excl* agreed!

entendimiento [entendi'mjento] *nm*
(*comprensión*) understanding;
(*inteligencia*) mind, intellect; (*juicio*)
judgement.

enterado, a [ente'raðo, a] *adj* well-
informed; **estar** ~ **de** to know about, be
aware of; **no darse por** ~ to pretend not
to understand.

enteramente [entera'mente] *adv* entirely,
completely.

enterarse [ente'rarse] *vr*: ~ (**de**) to find out
(about); **para que te enteres** ... (*fam*) for
your information ....

entereza [ente'reθa] *nf* (*totalidad*) entirety;
(*fig: carácter*) strength of mind; (*honradez*)
integrity.

enternecedor, a [enterneθe'ðor, a] *adj*
touching.

enternecer [enterne'θer] *vt* (*ablandar*) to
soften; (*apiadar*) to touch, move; ~**se** *vr*
to be touched, be moved.

enternezca [enter'neθka] *etc vb V*
enternecer.

entero, a [en'tero, a] *adj* (*total*) whole,
entire; (*fig: recto*) honest; (: *firme*) firm,
resolute ♦ *nm* (*MAT*) integer; (*COM: punto*)

point; (*AM: pago*) payment; **las acciones
han subido dos** ~**s** the shares have gone
up two points.

enterrador [enterra'ðor] *nm* gravedigger.

enterrar [ente'rrar] *vt* to bury; (*fig*) to
forget.

entibiar [enti'ßjar] *vt* (*enfriar*) to cool;
(*calentar*) to warm; ~**se** *vr* (*fig*) to
cool.

entidad [enti'ðað] *nf* (*empresa*) firm,
company; (*organismo*) body; (*sociedad*)
society; (*FILOSOFÍA*) entity.

entienda [en'tjenda] *etc vb V* **entender**.

entierro [en'tjerro] *etc vb V* **enterrar** ♦ *nm*
(*acción*) burial; (*funeral*) funeral.

entomología [entomolo'xia] *nf*
entomology.

entomólogo, a [ento'moloɣo, a] *nm/f*
entomologist.

entonación [entona'θjon] *nf* (*LING*)
intonation; (*fig*) conceit.

entonar [ento'nar] *vt* (*canción*) to intone;
(*colores*) to tone; (*MED*) to tone up ♦ *vi* to
be in tune; ~**se** *vr* (*engreírse*) to give o.s.
airs.

entonces [en'tonθes] *adv* then, at that
time; **desde** ~ since then; **en aquel** ~ at
that time; (**pues**) ~ and so; **el** ~
embajador de España the then Spanish
ambassador.

entornar [entor'nar] *vt* (*puerta, ventana*) to
half close, leave ajar; (*los ojos*) to screw
up.

entorno [en'torno] *nm* setting,
environment; ~ **de redes** (*INFORM*)
network environment.

entorpecer [entorpe'θer] *vt* (*entendimiento*)
to dull; (*impedir*) to obstruct, hinder;
(: *tránsito*) to slow down, delay.

entorpezca [entor'peθka] *etc vb V*
entorpecer.

entrado, a [en'traðo, a] *adj*: ~ **en años**
elderly; (**una vez**) ~ **el verano** in the
summer(time), when summer comes
♦ *nf* (*acción*) entry, access; (*sitio*)
entrance, way in; (*principio*) beginning;
(*COM*) receipts *pl*, takings *pl*; (*CULIN*)
entrée; (*DEPORTE*) innings *sg*; (*TEAT*)
house, audience; (*para el cine etc*) ticket;
(*INFORM*) input; (*ECON*): **entradas** *nfpl*
income *sg*; **entradas brutas** gross
receipts; **entradas y salidas** (*COM*)
income and expenditure; **entrada de aire**
(*TEC*) air intake *o* inlet; **de entrada** right
away; "**entrada gratis**" "admission
free"; **entrada de datos vocal** (*INFORM*)
voice input; **tiene entradas** he's losing
his hair.

entrante [en'trante] *adj* next, coming;
(*POL*) incoming ♦ *nm* inlet; (*CULIN*)
starter; **mes/año** ~ next month/year.

entraña [en'traɲa] *nf* (*fig: centro*) heart,
core; (*raíz*) root; ~**s** *nfpl* (*ANAT*) entrails;
(*fig*) heart *sg*.

entrañable [entra'ɲaßle] *adj* (*persona,
lugar*) dear; (*relación*) close; (*acto*)
intimate.

entrañar [entra'ɲar] *vt* to entail.

entrar [en'trar] *vt* (*introducir*) to bring in;
(*persona*) to show in; (*INFORM*) to input
♦ *vi* (*meterse*) to go *o* come in, enter;
(*comenzar*): ~ **diciendo** to begin by
saying; **entré en** *o* **a** (*AM*) **la casa** I went
into the house; **le entraron ganas de reír**
he felt a sudden urge to laugh; **no me
entra** I can't get the hang of it.

entre ['entre] *prep* (*dos*) between; (*en medio
de*) among(st); (*por*): **se abrieron paso** ~
la multitud they forced their way
through the crowd; ~ **una cosa y otra**
what with one thing and another; ~ **más
estudia más aprende** (*AM*) the more he
studies the more he learns.

entreabierto [entrea'ßjerto] *pp de*
entreabrir.

entreabrir [entrea'ßrir] *vt* to half-open,
open halfway.

entreacto [entre'akto] *nm* interval.

entrecano, a [entre'kano, a] *a* greying; **ser**
~ (*persona*) to be going grey.

entrecejo [entre'θexo] *nm*: **fruncir el** ~ to
frown.

entrechocar [entretʃo'kar] *vi* (*dientes*) to
chatter.

entrechoque [entre'tʃoke] *etc vb V*
entrechocar.

entrecomillado, a [entrekomi'ʎaðo, a] *adj*
in inverted commas.

entrecortado, a [entrekor'taðo, a] *adj*
(*respiración*) laboured, difficult; (*habla*)
faltering.

entrecot [entre'ko(t)] *nm* (*CULIN*) sirloin
steak.

entrecruce [entre'kruθe] *etc vb V*
entrecruzarse.

entrecruzarse [entrekru'θarse] *vr* (*BIO*) to
interbreed.

entredicho [entre'ðitʃo] *nm* (*JUR*)
injunction; **poner en** ~ to cast doubt on;
estar en ~ to be in doubt.

entrega [en'treɣa] *nf* (*de mercancías*)
delivery; (*de premios*) presentation; (*de
novela etc*) instalment; "~ **a domicilio**"
"door-to-door delivery service".

entregar [entre'ɣar] *vt* (*dar*) to hand
(over), deliver; (*ejercicios*) to hand in;

~**se** *vr* (*rendirse*) to surrender, give in,
submit; ~**se a** (*dedicarse*) to devote o.s.
to; **a** ~ (*COM*) to be supplied.

entregue [en'treɣe] *etc vb V* **entregar**.

entrelace [entre'laθe] *etc vb V* **entrelazar**.

entrelazar [entrela'θar] *vt* to entwine.

entremedias [entre'meðjas] *adv* (*en medio*)
in between, halfway.

entremeses [entre'meses] *nmpl* hors
d'œuvres.

entremeter [entreme'ter] *vt* to insert, put
in; ~**se** *vr* to meddle, interfere.

entremetido, a [entreme'tiðo, a] *adj*
meddling, interfering.

entremezclar [entremeθ'klar] *vt*, ~**se** *vr* to
intermingle.

entrenador, a [entrena'ðor, a] *nm/f* trainer,
coach.

entrenamiento [entrena'mjento] *nm*
training.

entrenar [entre'nar] *vt* (*DEPORTE*) to train;
(*caballo*) to exercise ♦ *vi*, ~**se** *vr* to train.

entrepierna [entre'pjerna] *nf* (*tb*: ~**s**)
crotch, crutch.

entresacar [entresa'kar] *vt* to pick out,
select.

entresaque [entre'sake] *etc vb V*
entresacar.

entresuelo [entre'swelo] *nm* mezzanine,
entresol; (*TEAT*) dress *o* first circle.

entretanto [entre'tanto] *adv* meanwhile,
meantime.

entretejer [entrete'xer] *vt* to interweave.

entretela [entre'tela] *nf* (*de ropa*)
interlining; ~**s** *nfpl* heart-strings.

entretención [entreten'sjon] *nf* (*AM*)
entertainment.

entretendré [entreten'dre] *etc vb V*
entretener.

entretener [entrete'ner] *vt* (*divertir*) to
entertain, amuse; (*detener*) to hold up,
delay; (*mantener*) to maintain; ~**se** *vr*
(*divertirse*) to amuse o.s.; (*retrasarse*) to
delay, linger; **no le entretengo más** I
won't keep you any longer.

entretenga [entre'tenga] *etc vb V*
entretener.

entretenido, a [entrete'niðo, a] *adj*
entertaining, amusing.

entretenimiento [entreteni'mjento] *nm*
entertainment, amusement;
(*mantenimiento*) upkeep, maintenance.

entretiempo [entre'tjempo] *nm*: **ropa de** ~
clothes for spring and autumn.

entretiene [entre'tjene] *etc*, **entretuve**
[entre'tuße] *etc vb V* **entretener**.

entreveía [entreße'ia] *etc vb V* **entrever**.

entrever [entre'ßer] *vt* to glimpse, catch a

glimpse of.

entrevista [entre'βista] *nf* interview.

entrevistar [entreβis'tar] *vt* to interview; ~**se** *vr*: ~**se con** to have an interview with, see; **el ministro se entrevistó con el Rey ayer** the minister had an audience with the King yesterday.

entrevisto [entre'βisto] *pp de* **entrever**.

entristecer [entriste'θer] *vt* to sadden, grieve; ~**se** *vr* to grow sad.

entristezca [entris'teθka] *etc vb V* **entristecer**.

entrometerse [entrome'terse] *vr*: ~ **(en)** to interfere (in *o* with).

entrometido, a [entrome'tiðo, a] *adj* interfering, meddlesome.

entroncar [entron'kar] *vi* to be connected *o* related.

entronque [en'tronke] *etc vb V* **entroncar**.

entuerto [en'twerto] *nm* wrong, injustice; ~**s** *nmpl* (*MED*) afterpains.

entumecer [entume'θer] *vt* to numb, benumb; ~**se** *vr* (*por el frío*) to go *o* become numb.

entumecido, a [entume'θiðo, a] *adj* numb, stiff.

entumezca [entu'meθka] *etc vb V* **entumecer**.

enturbiar [entur'βjar] *vt* (*el agua*) to make cloudy; (*fig*) to confuse; ~**se** *vr* (*oscurecerse*) to become cloudy; (*fig*) to get confused, become obscure.

entusiasmar [entusjas'mar] *vt* to excite, fill with enthusiasm; (*gustar mucho*) to delight; ~**se** *vr*: ~**se con** *o* **por** to get enthusiastic *o* excited about.

entusiasmo [entu'sjasmo] *nm* enthusiasm; (*excitación*) excitement.

entusiasta [entu'sjasta] *adj* enthusiastic ♦ *nm/f* enthusiast.

enumerar [enume'rar] *vt* to enumerate.

enunciación [enunθja'θjon] *nf*, **enunciado** [enun'θjaðo] *nm* enunciation; (*declaración*) declaration, statement.

enunciar [enun'θjar] *vt* to enunciate; to declare, state.

envainar [embai'nar] *vt* to sheathe.

envalentonar [embalento'nar] *vt* to give courage to; ~**se** *vr* (*pey: jactarse*) to boast, brag.

envanecer [embane'θer] *vt* to make conceited; ~**se** *vr* to grow conceited.

envanezca [emba'neθka] *etc vb V* **envanecer**.

envasar [emba'sar] *vt* (*empaquetar*) to pack, wrap; (*enfrascar*) to bottle; (*enlatar*) to can; (*embolsar*) to pocket.

envase [em'base] *nm* packing, wrapping;

bottling; canning; pocketing; (*recipiente*) container; (*paquete*) package; (*botella*) bottle; (*lata*) tin (*BRIT*), can.

envejecer [embexe'θer] *vt* to make old, age ♦ *vi*, ~**se** *vr* (*volverse viejo*) to grow old; (*parecer viejo*) to age.

envejecido, a [embexe'θiðo, a] *adj* old, aged; (*de aspecto*) old-looking.

envejezca [embe'xeθka] *etc vb V* **envejecer**.

envenenar [embene'nar] *vt* to poison; (*fig*) to embitter.

envergadura [emberɣa'ðura] *nf* (*expansión*) expanse; (*NAUT*) breadth; (*fig*) scope; **un programa de gran** ~ a wide-ranging programme.

envés [em'bes] *nm* (*de tela*) back, wrong side.

enviado, a [em'bjaðo, a] *nm/f* (*POL*) envoy; ~ **especial** (*de periódico, TV*) special correspondent.

enviar [em'bjar] *vt* to send.

enviciar [embi'θjar] *vt* to corrupt ♦ *vi* (*trabajo etc*) to be addictive; ~**se** *vr*: ~**se (con** *o* **en)** to get addicted (to).

envidia [em'biðja] *nf* envy; **tener** ~ **a** to envy, be jealous of.

envidiar [embi'ðjar] *vt* (*desear*) to envy; (*tener celos de*) to be jealous of.

envidioso, a [embi'ðjoso, a] *adj* envious, jealous.

envío [em'bio] *nm* (*acción*) sending; (*de mercancías*) consignment; (*de dinero*) remittance; (*en barco*) shipment; **gastos de** ~ postage and packing; ~ **contra reembolso** COD shipment.

enviudar [embju'ðar] *vi* to be widowed.

envoltura [embol'tura] *nf* (*cobertura*) cover; (*embalaje*) wrapper, wrapping.

envolver [embol'βer] *vt* to wrap (up); (*cubrir*) to cover; (*enemigo*) to surround; (*implicar*) to involve, implicate.

envuelto [em'bwelto], **envuelva** [em'bwelβa] *etc vb V* **envolver**.

enyesar [enje'sar] *vt* (*pared*) to plaster; (*MED*) to put in plaster.

enzarzarse [enθar'θarse] *vr*: ~ **en algo** to get mixed up in sth.

epa ['epa], **épale** ['epale] (*AM*) *excl* hey!, wow!

E.P.D. *abr* (= *en paz descanse*) R.I.P.

epicentro [epi'θentro] *nm* epicentre.

épico, a ['epiko, a] *adj* epic ♦ *nf* epic (poetry).

epidemia [epi'ðemja] *nf* epidemic.

epidémico, a [epi'ðemiko, a] *adj* epidemic.

epidermis [epi'ðermis] *nf* epidermis.

epifanía [epifa'nia] *nf* Epiphany.

epilepsia [epi'lepsja] *nf* epilepsy.

epiléptico, a [epi'leptiko, a] *adj, nm/f* epileptic.

epílogo [e'piloɣo] *nm* epilogue.

episcopado [episko'paðo] *nm* (*cargo*) bishopric; (*obispos*) bishops *pl* (*collectively*).

episodio [epi'soðjo] *nm* episode; (*suceso*) incident.

epístola [e'pistola] *nf* epistle.

epitafio [epi'tafjo] *nm* epitaph.

epíteto [e'piteto] *nm* epithet.

época ['epoka] *nf* period, time; (*temporada*) season; (*HISTORIA*) age, epoch; **hacer** ~ to be epoch-making.

equidad [eki'ðað] *nf* equity, fairness.

equilibrar [ekili'ßrar] *vt* to balance.

equilibrio [eki'lißrjo] *nm* balance, equilibrium; ~ **político** balance of power.

equilibrista [ekili'ßrista] *nmlf* (*funámbulo*) tightrope walker; (*acróbata*) acrobat.

equinoccio [eki'nokθjo] *nm* equinox.

equipaje [eki'paxe] *nm* luggage (*BRIT*), baggage (*US*); (*avíos*) equipment, kit; ~ **de mano** hand luggage; **hacer el** ~ to pack.

equipar [eki'par] *vt* (*proveer*) to equip.

equiparar [ekipa'rar] *vt* (*igualar*) to put on the same level; (*comparar*) to compare (*con* with); ~**se** *vr*: ~**se con** to be on a level with.

equipo [e'kipo] *nm* (*conjunto de cosas*) equipment; (*DEPORTE, grupo*) team; (*de obreros*) shift; (*de máquinas*) plant; (*turbinas etc*) set; ~ **de caza** hunting gear; ~ **físico** (*INFORM*) hardware; ~ **médico** medical team; ~ **de música** music centre.

equis ['ekis] *nf* (the letter) X.

equitación [ekita'θjon] *nf* (*acto*) riding; (*arte*) horsemanship.

equitativo, a [ekita'tißo, a] *adj* equitable, fair.

equivaldré [ekißal'dre] *etc vb V* **equivaler**.

equivalencia [ekißa'lenθja] *nf* equivalence.

equivalente [ekißa'lente] *adj, nm* equivalent.

equivaler [ekißa'ler] *vi*: ~ **a** to be equivalent *o* equal to; (*en rango*) to rank as.

equivalga [eki'ßalɣa] *etc vb V* **equivaler**.

equivocación [ekißoka'θjon] *nf* mistake, error; (*malentendido*) misunderstanding.

equivocado, a [ekißo'kaðo, a] *adj* wrong, mistaken.

equivocarse [ekißo'karse] *vr* to be wrong, make a mistake; ~ **de camino** to take the wrong road.

equívoco, a [e'kißoko, a] *adj* (*dudoso*) suspect; (*ambiguo*) ambiguous ♦ *nm* ambiguity; (*malentendido*) misunderstanding.

equivoque [eki'ßoke] *etc vb V* **equivocar**.

era ['era] *vb V* **ser** ♦ *nf* era, age; (*AGR*) threshing floor.

erais ['erais], **éramos** ['eramos], **eran** ['eran] *vb V* **ser**.

erario [e'rarjo] *nm* exchequer, treasury.

eras ['eras], **eres** ['eres] *vb V* **ser**.

erección [erek'θjon] *nf* erection.

ergonomía [erɣono'mia] *nf* ergonomics *sg*, human engineering.

erguir [er'ɣir] *vt* to raise, lift; (*poner derecho*) to straighten; ~**se** *vr* to straighten up.

erice [e'riθe] *etc vb V* **erizarse**.

erigir [eri'xir] *vt* to erect, build; ~**se** *vr*: ~**se en** to set o.s. up as.

erija [e'rixa] *etc vb V* **erigir**.

erizado, a [eri'θaðo, a] *adj* bristly.

erizarse [eri'θarse] *vr* (*pelo: de perro*) to bristle; (: *de persona*) to stand on end.

erizo [e'riθo] *nm* hedgehog; ~ **de mar** sea urchin.

ermita [er'mita] *nf* hermitage.

ermitaño, a [ermi'taɲo, a] *nm/f* hermit.

erosión [ero'sjon] *nf* erosion.

erosionar [erosjo'nar] *vt* to erode.

erótico, a [e'rotiko, a] *adj* erotic.

erotismo [ero'tismo] *nm* eroticism.

erradicar [erraði'kar] *vt* to eradicate.

erradique [erra'ðike] *etc vb V* **erradicar**.

errado, a [e'rraðo, a] *adj* mistaken, wrong.

errante [e'rrante] *adj* wandering, errant.

errar [e'rrar] *vi* (*vagar*) to wander, roam; (*equivocarse*) to be mistaken ♦ *vt*: ~ **el camino** to take the wrong road; ~ **el tiro** to miss.

errata [e'rrata] *nf* misprint.

erre ['erre] *nf* (the letter) R; ~ **que** ~ stubbornly.

erróneo, a [e'rroneo, a] *adj* (*equivocado*) wrong, mistaken; (*falso*) false, untrue.

error [e'rror] *nm* error, mistake; (*INFORM*) bug; ~ **de imprenta** misprint; ~ **de lectura/escritura** (*INFORM*) read/write error; ~ **sintáctico** syntax error; ~ **judicial** miscarriage of justice.

Ertzaintza [er'tʃantʃa] *nf* Basque police; *V tb* **policía**.

eructar [eruk'tar] *vt* to belch, burp.

eructo [e'rukto] *nm* belch.

erudición [eruði'θjon] *nf* erudition, learning.

erudito, a [eru'ðito, a] *adj* erudite, learned ♦ *nm/f* scholar; **los** ~**s en esta materia** the

experts in this field.
erupción [erup'θjon] *nf* eruption; (*MED*)
rash; (*de violencia*) outbreak; (*de ira*)
outburst.
es [es] *vb V* **ser.**
E/S *abr* (*INFORM: entrada/salida*) I/O.
esa ['esa], **esas** ['esas] *adj demostrativo V* **ese.**
ésa ['esa], **ésas** ['esas] *pron V* **ése.**
esbelto, a [es'ßelto, a] *adj* slim, slender.
esbirro [es'ßirro] *nm* henchman.
esbozar [esßo'θar] *vt* to sketch, outline.
esbozo [es'ßoθo] *nm* sketch, outline.
escabeche [eska'ßetʃe] *nm* brine; (*de
aceitunas etc*) pickle; **en ~** pickled.
escabechina [eskaße'tʃina] *nf* (*batalla*)
massacre; **hacer una ~** (*ESCOL*) to fail a
lot of students.
escabroso, a [eska'ßroso, a] *adj*
(*accidentado*) rough, uneven; (*fig*) tough,
difficult; (: *atrevido*) risqué.
escabullirse [eskaßu'ʎirse] *vr* to slip away;
(*largarse*) to clear out.
escacharrar [eskatʃa'rrar] *vt* (*fam*) to
break; **~se** *vr* to get broken.
escafandra [eska'fandra] *nf* (*buzo*) diving
suit; (**~** *espacial*) spacesuit.
escala [es'kala] *nf* (*proporción, MUS*) scale;
(*de mano*) ladder; (*AVIAT*) stopover; (*de
colores etc*) range; **~ de tiempo** time
scale; **~ de sueldos** salary scale; **una
investigación a ~ nacional** a nationwide
inquiry; **reproducir según ~** to
reproduce to scale; **hacer ~ en** to stop
off *o* over at.
escalada [eska'laða] *nf* (*de montaña*) climb;
(*de pared*) scaling.
escalafón [eskala'fon] *nm* (*escala de
salarios*) salary scale, wage scale.
escalar [eska'lar] *vt* to climb, scale ♦ *vi*
(*MIL, POL*) to escalate.
escaldar [eskal'dar] *vt* (*quemar*) to scald;
(*escarmentar*) to teach a lesson.
escalera [eska'lera] *nf* stairs *pl*, staircase;
(*escala*) ladder; (*NAIPES*) run; (*de camión*)
tailboard; **~ mecánica** escalator; **~ de
caracol** spiral staircase; **~ de incendios**
fire escape.
escalerilla [eskale'riʎa] *nf* (*de avión*) steps
pl.
escalfar [eskal'far] *vt* (*huevos*) to poach.
escalinata [eskali'nata] *nf* staircase.
escalofriante [eskalo'frjante] *adj* chilling.
escalofrío [eskalo'frio] *nm* (*MED*) chill; **~s**
nmpl (*fig*) shivers.
escalón [eska'lon] *nm* step, stair; (*de
escalera*) rung; (*fig: paso*) step; (*al éxito*)
ladder.
escalonar [eskalo'nar] *vt* to spread out;

(*tierra*) to terrace; (*horas de trabajo*) to
stagger.
escalope [eska'lope] *nm* (*CULIN*) escalope.
escama [es'kama] *nf* (*de pez, serpiente*)
scale; (*de jabón*) flake; (*fig*) resentment.
escamar [eska'mar] *vt* (*pez*) to scale;
(*producir recelo*) to make wary.
escamotear [eskamote'ar] *vt* (*fam: robar*)
to lift, swipe; (*hacer desaparecer*) to make
disappear.
escampar [eskam'par] *vb impersonal* to stop
raining.
escanciar [eskan'θjar] *vt* (*vino*) to pour (out).
escandalice [eskanda'liθe] *etc vb V*
escandalizar.
escandalizar [eskandali'θar] *vt* to
scandalize, shock; **~se** *vr* to be shocked;
(*ofenderse*) to be offended.
escándalo [es'kandalo] *nm* scandal;
(*alboroto, tumulto*) row, uproar; **armar un
~** to make a scene; **¡es un ~!** it's
outrageous!
escandaloso, a [eskanda'loso, a] *adj*
scandalous, shocking; (*risa*) hearty;
(*niño*) noisy.
Escandinavia [eskandi'naßja] *nf*
Scandinavia.
escandinavo, a [eskandi'naßo, a] *adj, nm/f*
Scandinavian.
escáner [es'kaner] *nm* scanner.
escaño [es'kaɲo] *nm* bench; (*POL*) seat.
escapada [eska'paða] *nf* (*huida*) escape,
flight; (*deportes*) breakaway; (*viaje*)
quick trip.
escapar [eska'par] *vi* (*gen*) to escape, run
away; (*DEPORTE*) to break away; **~se** *vr* to
escape, get away; (*agua, gas, noticias*) to
leak (out); **se me escapa su nombre** his
name escapes me.
escaparate [eskapa'rate] *nm* shop window;
(*COM*) showcase.
escapatoria [eskapa'torja] *nf*: **no tener ~**
(*fig*) to have no way out.
escape [es'kape] *nm* (*huida*) escape; (*de
agua, gas*) leak; (*de motor*) exhaust; **salir
a ~** to rush out.
escapismo [eska'pismo] *nm* escapism.
escaquearse [eskake'arse] *vr* (*fam*) to duck
out.
escarabajo [eskara'ßaxo] *nm* beetle.
escaramuza [eskara'muθa] *nf* skirmish;
(*fig*) brush.
escarbar [eskar'ßar] *vt* (*gallina*) to scratch;
(*fig*) to inquire into, investigate.
escarceos [eskar'θeos] *nmpl*: **en sus ~ con
la política** in his occasional forays into
politics; **~ amorosos** flirtations.
escarcha [es'kartʃa] *nf* frost.

escarlata [eskar'lata] *adj inv* scarlet.
escarlatina [eskarla'tina] *nf* scarlet fever.
escarmentar [eskarmen'tar] *vt* to punish severely ♦ *vi* to learn one's lesson; **¡para que escarmientes!** that'll teach you!
escarmiento [eskar'mjento] *etc vb* V
escarmentar ♦ *nm (ejemplo)* lesson; *(castigo)* punishment.
escarnio [es'karnjo] *nm* mockery; *(injuria)* insult.
escarola [eska'rola] *nf (BOT)* endive.
escarpado, a [eskar'paðo, a] *adj (pendiente)* sheer, steep; *(rocas)* craggy.
escasamente [eskasa'mente] *adv (insuficientemente)* scantily; *(apenas)* scarcely.
escasear [eskase'ar] *vi* to be scarce.
escasez [eska'seθ] *nf (falta)* shortage, scarcity; *(pobreza)* poverty; **vivir con ~** to live on the breadline.
escaso, a [es'kaso, a] *adj (poco)* scarce; *(raro)* rare; *(ralo)* thin, sparse; *(limitado)* limited; *(recursos)* scanty; *(público)* sparse; *(posibilidad)* slim; *(visibilidad)* poor.
escatimar [eskati'mar] *vt (limitar)* to skimp (on), be sparing with; **no ~ esfuerzos (para)** to spare no effort (to).
escayola [eska'jola] *nf* plaster.
escayolar [eskajo'lar] *vt* to put in plaster.
escena [es'θena] *nf* scene; *(decorado)* scenery; *(escenario)* stage; **poner en ~** to put on.
escenario [esθe'narjo] *nm (TEAT)* stage; *(CINE)* set; *(fig)* scene; **el ~ del crimen** the scene of the crime; **el ~ político** the political scene.
escenografía [esθenoɣra'fia] *nf* set o stage design.
escepticismo [esθepti'θismo] *nm* scepticism.
escéptico, a [es'θeptiko, a] *adj* sceptical ♦ *nm/f* sceptic.
escindir [esθin'dir] *vt* to split; **~se** *vr (facción)* to split off; **~se en** to split into.
escisión [esθi'sjon] *nf (MED)* excision; *(fig, POL)* split; **~ nuclear** nuclear fission.
esclarecer [esklare'θer] *vt (iluminar)* to light up, illuminate; *(misterio, problema)* to shed light on.
esclarezca [eskla're θka] *etc vb* V
esclarecer.
esclavice [eskla'ßiθe] *etc vb* V **esclavizar.**
esclavitud [esklaßi'tuð] *nf* slavery.
esclavizar [esklaßi'θar] *vt* to enslave.
esclavo, a [es'klaßo, a] *nm/f* slave.
esclusa [es'klusa] *nf (de canal)* lock; *(compuerta)* floodgate.

escoba [es'koßa] *nf* broom; **pasar la ~** to sweep up.
escobazo [esko'ßaθo] *nm (golpe)* blow with a broom; **echar a algn a ~s** to kick sb out.
escobilla [esko'ßiʎa] *nf* brush.
escocer [esko'θer] *vi* to burn, sting; **~se** *vr* to chafe, get chafed.
escocés, esa [esko'θes, esa] *adj* Scottish; *(whisky)* Scotch ♦ *nm/f* Scotsman/woman, Scot ♦ *nm (LING)* Scots *sg*; **tela escocesa** tartan.
Escocia [es'koθja] *nf* Scotland.
escoger [esko'xer] *vt* to choose, pick, select.
escogido, a [esko'xiðo, a] *adj* chosen, selected; *(calidad)* choice, select; *(persona)*: **ser muy ~** to be very fussy.
escoja [es'koxa] *etc vb* V **escoger.**
escolar [esko'lar] *adj* school *cpd* ♦ *nm/f* schoolboy/girl, pupil.
escolaridad [eskolari'ðað] *nf* schooling; **libro de ~** school record.
escolarización [eskolariθa'θjon] *nf*: **~ obligatoria** compulsory education.
escolarizado, a [eskolari'θaðo, a] *adj, nm/f*: **los ~s** those in o attending school.
escollo [es'koʎo] *nm (arrecife)* reef, rock; *(fig)* pitfall.
escolta [es'kolta] *nf* escort.
escoltar [eskol'tar] *vt* to escort; *(proteger)* to guard.
escombros [es'kombros] *nmpl (basura)* rubbish *sg*; *(restos)* debris *sg.*
esconder [eskon'der] *vt* to hide, conceal; **~se** *vr* to hide.
escondidas [eskon'diðas] *nfpl (AM)* hide-and-seek *sg*; **a ~** secretly; **hacer algo a ~ de algn** to do sth behind sb's back.
escondite [eskon'dite] *nm* hiding place; *(juego)* hide-and-seek.
escondrijo [eskon'drixo] *nm* hiding place, hideout.
escopeta [esko'peta] *nf* shotgun; **~ de aire comprimido** air gun.
escoria [es'korja] *nf (desecho mineral)* slag; *(fig)* scum, dregs *pl.*
Escorpio [es'korpjo] *nm (ASTRO)* Scorpio.
escorpión [eskor'pjon] *nm* scorpion.
escotado, a [esko'taðo, a] *adj* low-cut.
escotar [esko'tar] *vt (vestido: ajustar)* to cut to fit; *(cuello)* to cut low.
escote [es'kote] *nm (de vestido)* low neck; **pagar a ~** to share the expenses.
escotilla [esko'tiʎa] *nf (NAUT)* hatchway.
escotillón [eskoti'ʎon] *nm* trapdoor.
escozor [esko'θor] *nm (dolor)* sting(ing).
escribano, a [eskri'ßano, a], **escribiente**

[eskri'ßjente] nm/f clerk; (secretario judicial) court o lawyer's clerk.

escribir [eskri'ßir] vt, vi to write; ~ a máquina to type; ¿cómo se escribe? how do you spell it?

escrito, a [es'krito, a] pp de **escribir** ♦ adj written, in writing; (examen) written ♦ nm (documento) document; (manuscrito) text, manuscript; por ~ in writing.

escritor, a [eskri'tor, a] nm/f writer.

escritorio [eskri'torjo] nm desk; (oficina) office.

escritura [eskri'tura] nf (acción) writing; (caligrafía) (hand)writing; (JUR: documento) deed; (COM) indenture; ~ de propiedad title deed; **Sagrada E~** (Holy) Scripture; ~ **social** articles pl of association.

escroto [es'kroto] nm scrotum.

escrúpulo [es'krupulo] nm scruple; (minuciosidad) scrupulousness.

escrupuloso, a [eskrupu'loso, a] adj scrupulous.

escrutar [eskru'tar] vt to scrutinize, examine; (votos) to count.

escrutinio [eskru'tinjo] nm (examen atento) scrutiny; (POL: recuento de votos) count(ing).

escuadra [es'kwaðra] nf (TEC) square; (MIL etc) squad; (NAUT) squadron; (de coches etc) fleet.

escuadrilla [eskwa'ðriʎa] nf (de aviones) squadron.

escuadrón [eskwa'ðron] nm squadron.

escuálido, a [es'kwaliðo, a] adj skinny, scraggy; (sucio) squalid.

escucha [es'kutʃa] nf (acción) listening ♦ nm (TELEC: sistema) monitor; (oyente) listener; **estar a la** ~ to listen in; **estar de** ~ to spy; ~**s telefónicas** (phone) tapping sg.

escuchar [esku'tʃar] vt to listen to; (consejo) to heed; (esp AM: oír) to hear ♦ vi to listen; ~**se** vr: **se escucha muy mal** (TELEC) it's a very bad line.

escudarse [esku'ðarse] vr: ~ **en** (fig) to hide behind.

escudería [eskuðe'ria] nf: **la** ~ **Ferrari** the Ferrari team.

escudero [esku'ðero] nm squire.

escudilla [esku'ðiʎa] nf bowl, basin.

escudo [es'kuðo] nm shield; ~ **de armas** coat of arms.

escudriñar [eskuðri'ɲar] vt (examinar) to investigate, scrutinize; (mirar de lejos) to scan.

escuece [es'kweθe] etc vb V **escocer**.

escuela [es'kwela] nf (tb fig) school; ~ **normal** teacher training college; ~

técnica superior university offering 5-year courses in engineering and technical subjects; ~ **universitaria** university offering 3-year diploma courses; ~ **de párvulos** kindergarten; V tb **colegio**.

escueto, a [es'kweto, a] adj plain; (estilo) simple; (explicación) concise.

escueza [es'kweθa] etc vb V **escocer**.

escuincle [es'kwinkle] nm (AM fam) kid.

esculpir [eskul'pir] vt to sculpt; (grabar) to engrave; (tallar) to carve.

escultor, a [eskul'tor, a] nm/f sculptor.

escultura [eskul'tura] nf sculpture.

escupidera [eskupi'ðera] nf spittoon.

escupir [esku'pir] vt to spit (out) ♦ vi to spit.

escupitajo [eskupi'taxo] nm (fam) gob of spit.

escurreplatos [eskurre'platos] nm inv plate rack.

escurridizo, a [eskurri'ðiθo, a] adj slippery.

escurrir [esku'rrir] vt (ropa) to wring out; (verduras, platos) to drain ♦ vi (los líquidos) to drip; ~**se** vr (secarse) to drain; (resbalarse) to slip, slide; (escaparse) to slip away.

ese¹ ['ese] nf (the letter) S; **hacer** ~**s** (carretera) to zigzag; (borracho) to reel about.

ese² ['ese], **esa** ['esa], **esos** ['esos], **esas** ['esas] adj demostrativo (sg) that; (pl) those.

ése ['ese], **ésa** ['esa], **ésos** ['esos], **ésas** ['esas] pron (sg) that (one); (pl) those (ones); **ése** ... **éste** ... the former ... the latter ...; **¡no me vengas con ésas!** don't give me any more of that nonsense!

esencia [e'senθja] nf essence.

esencial [esen'θjal] adj essential; (principal) chief; **lo** ~ the main thing.

esfera [es'fera] nf sphere; (de reloj) face; ~ **de acción** scope; ~ **terrestre** globe.

esférico, a [es'feriko, a] adj spherical.

esfinge [es'finxe] nf sphinx.

esforcé [esfor'θe], **esforcemos** [esfor'θemos] etc vb V **esforzar**.

esforzado, a [esfor'θaðo, a] adj (enérgico) energetic, vigorous.

esforzarse [esfor'θarse] vr to exert o.s., make an effort.

esfuerce [es'fwerθe] etc vb V **esforzar**.

esfuerzo [es'fwerθo] etc vb V **esforzar** ♦ nm effort; **sin** ~ effortlessly.

esfumarse [esfu'marse] vr (apoyo, esperanzas) to fade away; (persona) to vanish.

esgrima [es'ɣrima] nf fencing.

esgrimidor [esɣrimi'ðor] *nm* fencer.
esgrimir [esɣri'mir] *vt* (*arma*) to brandish;
(*argumento*) to use ♦ *vi* to fence.
esguince [es'ɣinθe] *nm* (*MED*) sprain.
eslabón [esla'ßon] *nm* link; ~ **perdido** (*BIO*,
fig) missing link.
eslabonar [eslaßo'nar] *vt* to link, connect.
eslálom [es'lalom] *nm* slalom.
eslavo, a [es'laßo, a] *adj* Slav, Slavonic
♦ *nm/f* Slav ♦ *nm* (*LING*) Slavonic.
eslogan [es'loɣan] *nm, pl* **eslogans**
= **slogan**.
eslora [es'lora] *nf* (*NAUT*) length.
eslovaco, a [eslo'ßako, a] *adj, nm/f* Slovak,
Slovakian ♦ *nm* (*LING*) Slovak, Slovakian.
Eslovaquia [eslo'ßakja] *nf* Slovakia.
Eslovenia [eslo'ßenja] *nf* Slovenia.
esloveno, a [eslo'ßeno, a] *adj, nm/f* Slovene,
Slovenian ♦ *nm* (*LING*) Slovene,
Slovenian.
esmaltar [esmal'tar] *vt* to enamel.
esmalte [es'malte] *nm* enamel; ~ **de uñas**
nail varnish *o* polish.
esmerado, a [esme'raðo, a] *adj* careful,
neat.
esmeralda [esme'ralda] *nf* emerald.
esmerarse [esme'rarse] *vr* (*aplicarse*) to
take great pains, exercise great care;
(*afanarse*) to work hard; (*hacer lo mejor*)
to do one's best.
esmero [es'mero] *nm* (great) care.
esmirriado, a [esmi'rrjaðo, a] *adj* puny.
esmoquin [es'mokin] *nm* dinner jacket
(*BRIT*), tuxedo (*US*).
esnob [es'nob] *adj inv* (*persona*) snobbish;
(*coche etc*) posh ♦ *nm/f* snob.
esnobismo [esno'ßismo] *nm* snobbery.
eso ['eso] *pron* that, that thing *o* matter; ~
de su coche that business about his car;
~ **de ir al cine** all that about going to the
cinema; **a** ~ **de las cinco** at about five
o'clock; **en** ~ thereupon, at that point;
por ~ therefore; ~ **es** that's it; **nada de**
~ far from it; **¡** ~ **sí que es vida!** now this
is really living!; **por** ~ **te lo dije** that's
why I told you; **y** ~ **que llovía** in spite of
the fact it was raining.
esófago [e'sofaɣo] *nm* (*ANAT*) oesophagus.
esos ['esos] *adj demostrativo V* **ese**.
ésos ['esos] *pron V* **ése**.
esotérico, a [eso'teriko, a] *adj* esoteric.
esp. *abr* (= *español*) Sp., Span.
espabilado, a [espaßi'laðo, a] *adj* quick-
witted.
espabilar [espaßi'lar] *vt*, **espabilarse** *vr*
= **despabilar(se)**.
espachurrar [espatʃu'rrar] *vt* to squash;
~**se** *vr* to get squashed.

espaciado [espa'θjaðo] *nm* (*INFORM*)
spacing.
espacial [espa'θjal] *adj* (*del espacio*) space
cpd.
espaciar [espa'θjar] *vt* to space (out).
espacio [es'paθjo] *nm* space; (*MUS*)
interval; (*RADIO, TV*) programme,
program (*US*); **el** ~ space; **ocupar mucho**
~ to take up a lot of room; **a dos** ~**s, a**
doble ~ (*TIP*) double-spaced; **por** ~ **de**
during, for.
espacioso, a [espa'θjoso, a] *adj* spacious,
roomy.
espada [es'paða] *nf* sword ♦ *nm*
swordsman; (*TAUR*) matador; ~**s** *nfpl*
(*NAIPES*) one of the suits in the Spanish
card deck; **estar entre la** ~ **y la pared** to
be between the devil and the deep blue
sea; *V tb* **baraja española**.
espadachín [espaða'tʃin] *nm* (*esgrimidor*)
skilled swordsman.
espaguetis [espa'ɣetis] *nmpl* spaghetti *sg*.
espalda [es'palda] *nf* (*gen*) back;
(*NATACIÓN*) backstroke; ~**s** *nfpl* (*hombros*)
shoulders; **a** ~**s de algn** behind sb's
back; **estar de** ~**s** to have one's back
turned; **tenderse de** ~**s** to lie (down) on
one's back; **volver la** ~ **a algn** to cold-
shoulder sb.
espaldarazo [espalda'raθo] *nm* (*tb fig*) slap
on the back.
espaldilla [espal'ðiʎa] *nf* shoulder blade.
espantadizo, a [espanta'ðiθo, a] *adj* timid,
easily frightened.
espantajo [espan'taxo] *nm*,
espantapájaros [espanta'paxaros] *nm inv*
scarecrow.
espantar [espan'tar] *vt* (*asustar*) to
frighten, scare; (*ahuyentar*) to frighten
off; (*asombrar*) to horrify, appal; ~**se** *vr*
to get frightened *o* scared; to be
appalled.
espanto [es'panto] *nm* (*susto*) fright;
(*terror*) terror; (*asombro*) astonishment;
¡qué ~**!** how awful!
espantoso, a [espan'toso, a] *adj*
frightening, terrifying; (*ruido*) dreadful.
España [es'paɲa] *nf* Spain; **la** ~ **de**
pandereta touristy Spain.
español, a [espa'ɲol, a] *adj* Spanish ♦ *nm/f*
Spaniard ♦ *nm* (*LING*) Spanish; *V tb*
castellano.
españolice [espaɲo'liθe] *etc vb V*
españolizar.
españolizar [espaɲoli'θar] *vt* to make
Spanish, Hispanicize; ~**se** *vr* to adopt
Spanish ways.
esparadrapo [espara'ðrapo] *nm* (sticking)

plaster, Band-Aid ® (US).

esparcido, a [espar'θiðo, a] *adj* scattered.

esparcimiento [esparθi'mjento] *nm*
(*dispersión*) spreading; (*derramamiento*)
scattering; (*fig*) cheerfulness.

esparcir [espar'θir] *vt* to spread; (*derramar*)
to scatter; ~**se** *vr* to spread (out); to
scatter; (*divertirse*) to enjoy o.s.

espárrago [es'parraɣo] *nm* (*tb*: ~**s**)
asparagus; **estar hecho un** ~ to be as
thin as a rake; **¡vete a freír** ~**s!** (*fam*) go
to hell!

esparto [es'parto] *nm* esparto (grass).

esparza [es'parθa] *etc vb V* **esparcir**.

espasmo [es'pasmo] *nm* spasm.

espátula [es'patula] *nf* (*MED*) spatula;
(*ARTE*) palette knife; (*CULIN*) fish slice.

especia [es'peθja] *nf* spice.

especial [espe'θjal] *adj* special.

especialidad [espeθjali'ðað] *nf* speciality,
specialty (*US*); (*ESCOL: ramo*) specialism.

especialista [espeθja'lista] *nm/f* specialist;
(*CINE*) stuntman/woman.

especializado, a [espeθjali'θaðo, a] *adj*
specialized; (*obrero*) skilled.

especialmente [espeθjal'mente] *adv*
particularly, especially.

especie [es'peθje] *nf* (*BIO*) species; (*clase*)
kind, sort; **pagar en** ~ to pay in kind.

especificar [espeθifi'kar] *vt* to specify.

específico, a [espe'θifiko, a] *adj* specific.

especifique [espeθi'fike] *etc vb V*
especificar.

espécimen [es'peθimen], *pl* **especímenes**
nm specimen.

espectáculo [espek'takulo] *nm* (*gen*)
spectacle; (*TEAT etc*) show; (*función*)
performance; **dar un** ~ to make a scene.

espectador, a [espekta'ðor, a] *nm/f*
spectator; (*de incidente*) onlooker; **los**
~**es** (*TEAT*) the audience *sg*.

espectro [es'pektro] *nm* ghost; (*fig*)
spectre.

especulación [espekula'θjon] *nf*
speculation; ~ **bursátil** speculation on
the Stock Market.

especular [espeku'lar] *vt, vi* to speculate.

especulativo, a [espekula'tiβo, a] *adj*
speculative.

espejismo [espe'xismo] *nm* mirage.

espejo [es'pexo] *nm* mirror; (*fig*) model; ~
retrovisor rear-view mirror; **mirarse al**
~ to look at (o.s.) in the mirror.

espeleología [espeleolo'xia] *nf* potholing.

espeluznante [espeluθ'nante] *adj*
horrifying, hair-raising.

espera [es'pera] *nf* (*pausa, intervalo*) wait;
(*JUR: plazo*) respite; **en** ~ **de** waiting for;

(*con expectativa*) expecting; **en** ~ **de su**
contestación awaiting your reply.

esperance [espe'ranθe] *etc vb V*
esperanzar.

esperanza [espe'ranθa] *nf* (*confianza*) hope;
(*expectativa*) expectation; **hay pocas** ~**s**
de que venga there is little prospect of
his coming.

esperanzador, a [esperanθa'ðor, a] *adj*
hopeful, encouraging.

esperanzar [esperan'θar] *vt* to give hope
to.

esperar [espe'rar] *vt* (*aguardar*) to wait for;
(*tener expectativa de*) to expect; (*desear*)
to hope for ♦ *vi* to wait; to expect; to
hope; ~**se** *vr*: **como podía** ~**se** as was to
be expected; **hacer** ~ **a uno** to keep sb
waiting; **ir a** ~ **a uno** to go and meet sb;
~ **un bebé** to be expecting (a baby).

esperma [es'perma] *nf* sperm.

espermatozoide [espermato'θoiðe] *nm*
spermatozoid.

esperpento [esper'pento] *nm* (*persona*)
sight (*fam*); (*disparate*) (piece of)
nonsense.

espesar [espe'sar] *vt* to thicken; ~**se** *vr* to
thicken, get thicker.

espeso, a [es'peso, a] *adj* thick; (*bosque*)
dense; (*nieve*) deep; (*sucio*) dirty.

espesor [espe'sor] *nm* thickness; (*de nieve*)
depth.

espesura [espe'sura] *nf* (*bosque*) thicket.

espetar [espe'tar] *vt* (*reto, sermón*) to give.

espía [es'pia] *nm/f* spy.

espiar [espi'ar] *vt* (*observar*) to spy on ♦ *vi*:
~ **para** to spy for.

espiga [es'piɣa] *nf* (*BOT: de trigo etc*) ear;
(: *de flores*) spike.

espigado, a [espi'ɣaðo, a] *adj* (*BOT*) ripe;
(*fig*) tall, slender.

espigón [espi'ɣon] *nm* (*BOT*) ear; (*NAUT*)
breakwater.

espina [es'pina] *nf* thorn; (*de pez*) bone; ~
dorsal (*ANAT*) spine; **me da mala** ~ I
don't like the look of it.

espinaca [espi'naka] *nf* (*tb*: ~**s**) spinach.

espinar [espi'nar] *nm* (*matorral*) thicket.

espinazo [espi'naθo] *nm* spine, backbone.

espinilla [espi'niʎa] *nf* (*ANAT: tibia*)
shin(bone); (: *en la piel*) blackhead.

espino [es'pino] *nm* hawthorn.

espinoso, a [espi'noso, a] *adj* (*planta*)
thorny, prickly; (*fig*) bony; (*problema*)
knotty.

espionaje [espjo'naxe] *nm* spying,
espionage.

espiral [espi'ral] *adj*, *nf* spiral; **la** ~
inflacionista the inflationary spiral.

to be ill; **está muy elegante** he's looking very smart; ~ **lejos** to be far (away); **¿cómo estás?** how are you keeping?

3 (+*gerundio*) to be; **estoy leyendo** I'm reading

4 (*uso pasivo*): **está condenado a muerte** he's been condemned to death; **está envasado en ...** it's packed in ...

5: ~ **a: ¿a cuántos estamos?** what's the date today?; **estamos a 5 de mayo** it's the 5th of May; **las manzanas están a 200 ptas** apples are (selling at) 200 pesetas; **estamos a 25 grados** it's 25 degrees today

6 (*locuciones*): **¿estamos?** (*¿de acuerdo?*) okay?; (*¿listo?*) ready?; **¡ya está bien!** that's enough!; **¿está la comida?** is dinner ready?; **¡ya está!**, (*AM*) **¡ya estuvo!** that's it!

7: ~ **con: está con gripe** he's got (the) flu

8: ~ **de:** ~ **de vacaciones/viaje** to be on holiday/away *o* on a trip; **está de camarero** he's working as a waiter

9: ~ **para: está para salir** he's about to leave; **no estoy para bromas** I'm not in the mood for jokes

10: ~ **por** (*propuesta etc*) to be in favour of; (*persona etc*) to support, side with; **está por limpiar** it still has to be cleaned; **¡estoy por dejarlo!** I think I'm going to leave this!

11 (+*que*): **está que rabia** (*fam*) he's hopping mad (*fam*); **estoy que me caigo de sueño** I'm terribly sleepy, I can't keep my eyes open

12: ~ **sin:** ~ **sin dinero** to have no money; **está sin terminar** it isn't finished yet

♦ ~**se** *vr*: **se estuvo en la cama toda la tarde** he stayed in bed all afternoon; **¡estáte quieto!** stop fidgeting!

estárter [es'tarter] *nm* (*AUTO*) choke.
estas ['estas] *adj demostrativo V* **este**.
éstas ['estas] *pron V* **éste**.
estás [es'tas] *vb V* **estar**.
estatal [esta'tal] *adj* state *cpd*.
estático, a [es'tatiko, a] *adj* static.
estatua [es'tatwa] *nf* statue.
estatura [esta'tura] *nf* stature, height.
estatus [es'tatus] *nm inv* status.
estatutario, a [estatu'tarjo, a] *adj* statutory.
estatuto [esta'tuto] *nm* (*JUR*) statute; (*de ciudad*) bye-law; (*de comité*) rule; ~**s sociales** (*COM*) articles of association.
este¹ ['este] *adj* (*lado*) east; (*dirección*) easterly ♦ *nm* east; **en la parte del** ~ in

the eastern part.
este² ['este], **esta** ['esta], **estos** ['estos], **estas** ['estas] *adj demostrativo* (*sg*) this; (*pl*) these; (*AM: como muletilla*) er, um.
éste ['este], **ésta** ['esta], **éstos** ['estos], **éstas** ['estas] *pron* (*sg*) this (one); (*pl*) these (ones); **ése ... éste ...** the former ... the latter ....
esté [es'te] *vb V* **estar**.
estela [es'tela] *nf* wake, wash; (*fig*) trail.
estelar [este'lar] *adj* (*ASTRO*) stellar; (*TEAT*) star *cpd*.
estén [es'ten] *vb V* **estar**.
estenografía [estenoɣra'fia] *nf* shorthand.
estentóreo, a [esten'toreo, a] *adj* (*sonido*) strident; (*voz*) booming.
estepa [es'tepa] *nf* (*GEO*) steppe.
estera [es'tera] *nf* (*alfombra*) mat; (*tejido*) matting.
estercolero [esterko'lero] *nm* manure heap, dunghill.
estéreo [es'tereo] *adj inv, nm* stereo.
estereofónico, a [estereo'foniko, a] *adj* stereophonic.
estereotipar [estereoti'par] *vt* to stereotype.
estereotipo [estereo'tipo] *nm* stereotype.
estéril [es'teril] *adj* sterile, barren; (*fig*) vain, futile.
esterilice [esteri'liθe] *etc vb V* **esterilizar**.
esterilizar [esterili'θar] *vt* to sterilize.
esterilla [este'riʎa] *nf* (*alfombrilla*) small mat.
esterlina [ester'lina] *adj*: **libra** ~ pound sterling.
esternón [ester'non] *nm* breastbone.
estero [es'tero] *nm* (*AM*) swamp.
estertor [ester'tor] *nm* death rattle.
estés [es'tes] *vb V* **estar**.
esteta [es'teta] *nm/f* aesthete.
esteticienne [esteti'θjen] *nf* beautician.
estético, a [es'tetiko, a] *adj* aesthetic ♦ *nf* aesthetics *sg*.
estetoscopio [estetos'kopjo] *nm* stethoscope.
estibador [estiβa'ðor] *nm* stevedore.
estibar [esti'ßar] *vt* (*NAUT*) to stow.
estiércol [es'tjerkol] *nm* dung, manure.
estigma [es'tiɣma] *nm* stigma.
estigmatice [estiɣma'tiθe] *etc vb V* **estigmatizar**.
estigmatizar [estiɣmati'θar] *vt* to stigmatize.
estilarse [esti'larse] *vr* (*estar de moda*) to be in fashion; (*usarse*) to be used.
estilice [esti'liθe] *etc vb V* **estilizar**.
estilizar [estili'θar] *vt* to stylize; (*TEC*) to design.

estilo [es'tilo] *nm* style; (*TEC*) stylus; (*NATACIÓN*) stroke; ~ **de vida** lifestyle; **al** ~ **de** in the style of; **algo por el** ~ something along those lines.

estilográfica [estilo'ɣrafika] *nf* fountain pen.

estima [es'tima] *nf* esteem, respect.

estimación [estima'θjon] *nf* (*evaluación*) estimation; (*aprecio, afecto*) esteem, regard.

estimado, a [esti'maðo, a] *adj* esteemed; "**E**~ **Señor**" "Dear Sir".

estimar [esti'mar] *vt* (*evaluar*) to estimate; (*valorar*) to value; (*apreciar*) to esteem, respect; (*pensar, considerar*) to think, reckon.

estimulante [estimu'lante] *adj* stimulating ♦ *nm* stimulant.

estimular [estimu'lar] *vt* to stimulate; (*excitar*) to excite; (*animar*) to encourage.

estímulo [es'timulo] *nm* stimulus; (*ánimo*) encouragement; (*INFORM*) prompt.

estío [es'tio] *nm* summer.

estipendio [esti'pendjo] *nm* salary; (*COM*) stipend.

estipulación [estipula'θjon] *nf* stipulation, condition.

estipular [estipu'lar] *vt* to stipulate.

estirado, a [esti'raðo, a] *adj* (*tenso*) (stretched *o* drawn) tight; (*fig: persona*) stiff, pompous; (*engreído*) stuck-up.

estirar [esti'rar] *vt* to stretch; (*dinero, suma etc*) to stretch out; (*cuello*) to crane; (*dinero*) to eke out; (*discurso*) to spin out; ~ **la pata** (*fam*) to kick the bucket; ~**se** *vr* to stretch.

estirón [esti'ron] *nm* pull, tug; (*crecimiento*) spurt, sudden growth; **dar un** ~ (*niño*) to shoot up.

estirpe [es'tirpe] *nf* stock, lineage.

estival [esti'ßal] *adj* summer *cpd*.

esto ['esto] *pron* this, this thing *o* matter; (*como muletilla*) er, um; ~ **de la boda** this business about the wedding; **en** ~ at this *o* that point; **por** ~ for this reason.

estocada [esto'kaða] *nf* (*acción*) stab; (*TAUR*) death blow.

Estocolmo [esto'kolmo] *nm* Stockholm.

estofa [es'tofa] *nf*: **de baja** ~ poor-quality.

estofado [esto'faðo] *nm* stew.

estofar [esto'far] *vt* (*bordar*) to quilt; (*CULIN*) to stew.

estoico, a [es'toiko, a] *adj* (*FILOSOFÍA*) stoic(al); (*fig*) cold, indifferent.

estomacal [estoma'kal] *adj* stomach *cpd*; **trastorno** ~ stomach upset.

estómago [es'tomaɣo] *nm* stomach; **tener** ~ to be thick-skinned.

Estonia [es'tonja] *nf* Estonia.

estonio, a [es'tonjo, a] *adj, nm/f* Estonian ♦ *nm* (*LING*) Estonian.

estoque [es'toke] *nm* rapier, sword.

estorbar [estor'ßar] *vt* to hinder, obstruct; (*fig*) to bother, disturb ♦ *vi* to be in the way.

estorbo [es'torßo] *nm* (*molestia*) bother, nuisance; (*obstáculo*) hindrance, obstacle.

estornino [estor'nino] *nm* starling.

estornudar [estornu'ðar] *vi* to sneeze.

estornudo [estor'nuðo] *nm* sneeze.

estos ['estos] *adj demostrativo V* **este**.

éstos ['estos] *pron V* **éste**.

estoy [es'toi] *vb V* **estar**.

estrabismo [estra'ßismo] *nm* squint.

estrado [es'traðo] *nm* (*tarima*) platform; (*MUS*) bandstand; ~**s** *nmpl* law courts.

estrafalario, a [estrafa'larjo, a] *adj* odd, eccentric; (*desarreglado*) slovenly, sloppy.

estrago [es'traɣo] *nm* ruin, destruction; **hacer** ~**s en** to wreak havoc among.

estragón [estra'ɣon] *nm* (*CULIN*) tarragon.

estrambótico, a [estram'botiko, a] *adj* odd, eccentric.

estrangulación [estrangula'θjon] *nf* strangulation.

estrangulador, a [estrangula'ðor, a] *nm/f* strangler ♦ *nm* (*TEC*) throttle; (*AUTO*) choke.

estrangulamiento [estrangula'mjento] *nm* (*AUTO*) bottleneck.

estrangular [estrangu'lar] *vt* (*persona*) to strangle; (*MED*) to strangulate.

estraperlista [estraper'lista] *nm/f* black marketeer.

estraperlo [estra'perlo] *nm* black market.

estratagema [estrata'xema] *nf* (*MIL*) stratagem; (*astucia*) cunning.

estratega [estra'teɣa] *nm/f* strategist.

estrategia [estra'texja] *nf* strategy.

estratégico, a [estra'texiko, a] *adj* strategic.

estratificar [estratifi'kar] *vt* to stratify.

estratifique [estrati'fike] *etc vb V* **estratificar**.

estrato [es'trato] *nm* stratum, layer.

estratosfera [estratos'fera] *nf* stratosphere.

estrechar [estre'tʃar] *vt* (*reducir*) to narrow; (*vestido*) to take in; (*persona*) to hug, embrace; ~**se** *vr* (*reducirse*) to narrow, grow narrow; (*2 personas*) to embrace; ~ **la mano** to shake hands.

estrechez [estre'tʃeθ] *nf* narrowness; (*de ropa*) tightness; (*intimidad*) intimacy;

(*COM*) want *o* shortage of money;
estrecheces *nfpl* financial difficulties.
estrecho, a [es'tretʃo, a] *adj* narrow;
(*apretado*) tight; (*íntimo*) close, intimate;
(*miserable*) mean ♦ *nm* strait; ~ **de miras**
narrow-minded; **E~ de Gibraltar** Straits
of Gibraltar.
estrella [es'treʎa] *nf* star; ~ **fugaz** shooting
star; ~ **de mar** starfish; **tener (buena)/
mala** ~ to be lucky/unlucky.
estrellado, a [estre'ʎaðo, a] *adj* (*forma*)
star-shaped; (*cielo*) starry; (*huevos*)
fried.
estrellar [estre'ʎar] *vt* (*hacer añicos*) to
smash (to pieces); (*huevos*) to fry; ~**se** *vr*
to smash; (*chocarse*) to crash; (*fracasar*)
to fail.
estrellato [estre'ʎato] *nm* stardom.
estremecer [estreme'θer] *vt* to shake; ~**se**
vr to shake, tremble; ~ **de** (*horror*) to
shudder with; (*frío*) to shiver with.
estremecimiento [estremeθi'mjento] *nm*
(*temblor*) trembling, shaking.
estremezca [estre'meθka] *etc vb V*
estremecer.
estrenar [estre'nar] *vt* (*vestido*) to wear for
the first time; (*casa*) to move into;
(*película, obra de teatro*) to present for the
first time; ~**se** *vr* (*persona*) to make one's
début; (*película*) to have its premiere;
(*TEAT*) to open.
estreno [es'treno] *nm* (*primer uso*) first use;
(*CINE etc*) premiere.
estreñido, a [estre'ɲiðo, a] *adj*
constipated.
estreñimiento [estreɲi'mjento] *nm*
constipation.
estreñir [estre'ɲir] *vt* to constipate.
estrépito [es'trepito] *nm* noise, racket;
(*fig*) fuss.
estrepitoso, a [estrepi'toso, a] *adj* noisy;
(*fiesta*) rowdy.
estrés [es'tres] *nm* stress.
estresante [estre'sante] *adj* stressful.
estría [es'tria] *nf* groove; ~**s (en el cutis)**
stretchmarks.
estribación [estriβa'θjon] *nf* (*GEO*) spur;
estribaciones *nfpl* foothills.
estribar [estri'βar] *vi*: ~ **en** to rest on, be
supported by; **la dificultad estriba en el
texto** the difficulty lies in the text.
estribillo [estri'βiʎo] *nm* (*LITERATURA*)
refrain; (*MUS*) chorus.
estribo [es'triβo] *nm* (*de jinete*) stirrup; (*de
coche, tren*) step; (*de puente*) support;
(*GEO*) spur; **perder los** ~**s** to fly off the
handle.
estribor [estri'βor] *nm* (*NAUT*) starboard.

estricnina [estrik'nina] *nf* strychnine.
estricto, a [es'trikto, a] *adj* (*riguroso*)
strict; (*severo*) severe.
estridente [estri'ðente] *adj* (*color*) loud;
(*voz*) raucous.
estro ['estro] *nm* inspiration.
estrofa [es'trofa] *nf* verse.
estropajo [estro'paxo] *nm* scourer.
estropeado, a [estrope'aðo, a] *adj*: **está** ~
it's not working.
estropear [estrope'ar] *vt* (*arruinar*) to spoil;
(*dañar*) to damage; (: *máquina*) to break;
~**se** *vr* (*objeto*) to get damaged; (*coche*) to
break down; (*la piel etc*) to be ruined.
estropicio [estro'piθjo] *nm* (*rotura*)
breakage; (*efectos*) harmful effects *pl*.
estructura [estruk'tura] *nf* structure.
estruendo [es'trwendo] *nm* (*ruido*) racket,
din; (*fig: alboroto*) uproar, turmoil.
estrujar [estru'xar] *vt* (*apretar*) to squeeze;
(*aplastar*) to crush; (*fig*) to drain, bleed.
estuario [es'twarjo] *nm* estuary.
estuche [es'tutʃe] *nm* box, case.
estudiante [estu'ðjante] *nmlf* student.
estudiantil [estuðjan'til] *adj inv* student *cpd*.
estudiantina [estuðjan'tina] *nf* student
music group.
estudiar [estu'ðjar] *vt* to study; (*propuesta*)
to think about *o* over; ~ **para abogado** to
study to become a lawyer.
estudio [es'tuðjo] *nm* study; (*encuesta*)
research; (*proyecto*) plan; (*piso*) studio
flat; (*CINE, ARTE, RADIO*) studio; ~**s** *nmpl*
studies; (*erudición*) learning *sg*; **cursar** *o*
hacer ~**s** to study; ~ **de casos prácticos**
case study; ~ **de desplazamientos y
tiempos** (*COM*) time and motion study;
~**s de motivación** motivational research
sg; ~ **del trabajo** (*COM*) work study; ~ **de
viabilidad** (*COM*) feasibility study.
estudioso, a [estu'ðjoso, a] *adj* studious.
estufa [es'tufa] *nf* heater, fire.
estulticia [estul'tiθja] *nf* foolishness.
estupefaciente [estupefa'θjente] *adj, nm*
narcotic.
estupefacto, a [estupe'fakto, a] *adj*
speechless, thunderstruck.
estupendamente [estupenda'mente] *adv*
(*fam*): **estoy** ~ I feel great; **le salió** ~ he
did it very well.
estupendo, a [estu'pendo, a] *adj*
wonderful, terrific; (*fam*) great; ¡~!
that's great!, fantastic!
estupidez [estupi'ðeθ] *nf* (*torpeza*)
stupidity; (*acto*) stupid thing (to do); **fue
una** ~ **mía** that was a silly thing for me
to do *o* say.
estúpido, a [es'tupiðo, a] *adj* stupid, silly.

estupor [estu'por] *nm* stupor; (*fig*) astonishment, amazement.

estupro [es'tupro] *nm* rape.

estuve [es'tuße] *etc*, **estuviera** [estu'ßjera] *etc vb V* **estar**.

esvástica [es'ßastika] *nf* swastika.

ET *abr* = *Ejército de Tierra*.

ETA ['eta] *nf abr* (*POL*: = *Euskadi Ta Askatasuna*) ETA.

etapa [e'tapa] *nf* (*de viaje*) stage; (*DEPORTE*) leg; (*parada*) stopping place; (*fig*) stage, phase; **por ~s** gradually *o* in stages.

etarra [e'tarra] *adj* ETA *cpd* ♦ *nm/f* member of ETA.

etc. *abr* (= *etcétera*) etc.

etcétera [et'θetera] *adv* etcetera.

etéreo, a [e'tereo, a] *adj* ethereal.

eternice [eter'niθe] *etc vb V* **eternizar**.

eternidad [eterni'ðað] *nf* eternity.

eternizarse [eterni'θarse] *vr*: **~ en hacer algo** to take ages to do sth.

eterno, a [e'terno, a] *adj* eternal, everlasting; (*despectivo*) never-ending.

ético, a ['etiko, a] *adj* ethical ♦ *nf* ethics.

etimología [etimolo'xia] *nf* etymology.

etiqueta [eti'keta] *nf* (*modales*) etiquette; (*rótulo*) label, tag; **de ~** formal.

etnia ['etnja] *nf* ethnic group.

étnico, a ['etniko, a] *adj* ethnic.

EU(A) *abr* (*esp AM*) = **Estados Unidos (de América)**.

eucalipto [euka'lipto] *nm* eucalyptus.

Eucaristía [eukaris'tia] *nf* Eucharist.

eufemismo [eufe'mismo] *nm* euphemism.

euforia [eu'forja] *nf* euphoria.

eufórico, a [eu'foriko, a] *adj* euphoric.

eunuco [eu'nuko] *nm* eunuch.

eurodiputado, a [euroðipu'taðo, a] *nm/f* Euro MP, MEP.

Europa [eu'ropa] *nf* Europe.

europeice [euro'peiθe] *etc vb V* **europeizar**.

europeizar [europei'θar] *vt* to Europeanize; **~se** *vr* to become Europeanized.

europeo, a [euro'peo, a] *adj, nm/f* European.

Euskadi [eus'kaði] *nm* the Basque Provinces *pl*.

euskera, eusquera [eus'kera] *nm* (*LING*) Basque; *V tb* **lenguas cooficiales**.

eutanasia [euta'nasja] *nf* euthanasia.

evacuación [eßakwa'θjon] *nf* evacuation.

evacuar [eßa'kwar] *vt* to evacuate.

evadir [eßa'ðir] *vt* to evade, avoid; **~se** *vr* to escape.

evaluación [eßalwa'θjon] *nf* evaluation, assessment.

evaluar [eßa'lwar] *vt* to evaluate, assess.

evangélico, a [eßan'xeliko, a] *adj* evangelical.

evangelio [eßan'xeljo] *nm* gospel.

evaporación [eßapora'θjon] *nf* evaporation.

evaporar [eßapo'rar] *vt* to evaporate; **~se** *vr* to vanish.

evasión [eßa'sjon] *nf* escape, flight; (*fig*) evasion; **~ fiscal** *o* **tributaria** tax evasion.

evasivo, a [eßa'sißo, a] *adj* evasive, non-committal ♦ *nf* (*pretexto*) excuse; **contestar con evasivas** to avoid giving a straight answer.

evento [e'ßento] *nm* event; (*eventualidad*) eventuality.

eventual [eßen'twal] *adj* possible, conditional (upon circumstances); (*trabajador*) casual, temporary.

Everest [eße'rest] *nm*: **el (Monte) ~** (Mount) Everest.

evidencia [eßi'ðenθja] *nf* evidence, proof; **poner en ~** to make clear; **ponerse en ~** (*persona*) to show o.s. up.

evidenciar [eßiðen'θjar] *vt* (*hacer patente*) to make evident; (*probar*) to prove, show; **~se** *vr* to be evident.

evidente [eßi'ðente] *adj* obvious, clear, evident.

evitar [eßi'tar] *vt* (*evadir*) to avoid; (*impedir*) to prevent; (*peligro*) to escape; (*molestia*) to save; (*tentación*) to shun; **si puedo ~lo** if I can help it.

evocador, a [eßoka'ðor, a] *adj* (*sugestivo*) evocative.

evocar [eßo'kar] *vt* to evoke, call forth.

evolución [eßolu'θjon] *nf* (*desarrollo*) evolution, development; (*cambio*) change; (*MIL*) manoeuvre.

evolucionar [eßoluθjo'nar] *vi* to evolve; (*MIL, AVIAT*) to manoeuvre.

evoque [e'ßoke] *etc vb V* **evocar**.

ex [eks] *adj* ex-; **el ~ ministro** the former minister, the ex-minister.

exabrupto [eksa'ßrupto] *nm* interjection.

exacción [eksak'θjon] *nf* (*acto*) exaction; (*de impuestos*) demand.

exacerbar [eksaθer'ßar] *vt* to irritate, annoy.

exactamente [eksakta'mente] *adv* exactly.

exactitud [eksakti'tuð] *nf* exactness; (*precisión*) accuracy; (*puntualidad*) punctuality.

exacto, a [ek'sakto, a] *adj* exact; accurate; punctual; **¡~!** exactly!; **eso no es del todo ~** that's not quite right; **para ser ~** to be precise.

exageración [eksaxera'θjon] *nf* exaggeration.

exagerado, a [eksaxe'raðo, a] *adj* (*relato*) exaggerated; (*precio*) excessive; (*persona*) over-demonstrative; (*gesto*) theatrical.

exagerar [eksaxe'rar] *vt* to exaggerate; (*exceder*) to overdo.

exaltado, a [eksal'taðo, a] *adj* (*apasionado*) over-excited, worked up; (*exagerado*) extreme; (*fanático*) hot-headed; (*discurso*) impassioned ♦ *nm/f* (*fanático*) hothead; (*POL*) extremist.

exaltar [eksal'tar] *vt* to exalt, glorify; ~se *vr* (*excitarse*) to get excited o worked up.

examen [ek'samen] *nm* examination; (*de problema*) consideration; ~ **de** (*encuesta*) inquiry into; ~ **de ingreso** entrance examination; ~ **de conducir** driving test; ~ **eliminatorio** qualifying examination.

examinar [eksami'nar] *vt* to examine; (*poner a prueba*) to test; (*inspeccionar*) to inspect; ~se *vr* to be examined, take an examination.

exánime [ek'sanime] *adj* lifeless; (*fig*) exhausted.

exasperar [eksaspe'rar] *vt* to exasperate; ~se *vr* to get exasperated, lose patience.

Exc.ª *abr* = **Excelencia**.

excarcelar [ekskarθe'lar] *vt* to release (from prison).

excavador, a [ekskaßa'ðor, a] *nm/f* (*persona*) excavator ♦ *nf* (*TEC*) digger.

excavar [ekska'ßar] *vt* to excavate, dig (out).

excedencia [eksθe'ðenθja] *nf* (*MIL*) leave; (*ESCOL*) sabbatical.

excedente [eksθe'ðente] *adj, nm* excess, surplus.

exceder [eksθe'ðer] *vt* to exceed, surpass; ~se *vr* (*extralimitarse*) to go too far; (*sobrepasarse*) to excel o.s.

excelencia [eksθe'lenθja] *nf* excellence; E~ Excellency; **por** ~ par excellence.

excelente [eksθe'lente] *adj* excellent.

excelso, a [eks'θelso, a] *adj* lofty, sublime.

excentricidad [eksθentriθi'ðað] *nf* eccentricity.

excéntrico, a [eks'θentriko, a] *adj, nm/f* eccentric.

excepción [eksθep'θjon] *nf* exception; **la** ~ **confirma la regla** the exception proves the rule.

excepcional [eksθepθjo'nal] *adj* exceptional.

excepto [eks'θepto] *adv* excepting, except (for).

exceptuar [eksθep'twar] *vt* to except, exclude.

excesivo, a [eksθe'sißo, a] *adj* excessive.

exceso [eks'θeso] *nm* excess; (*COM*) surplus; ~ **de equipaje/peso** excess luggage/weight; ~ **de velocidad** speeding; **en** o **por** ~ excessively.

excitación [eksθita'θjon] *nf* (*sensación*) excitement; (*acción*) excitation.

excitado, a [eksθi'taðo, a] *adj* excited; (*emociones*) aroused.

excitante [eksθi'tante] *adj* exciting; (*MED*) stimulating ♦ *nm* stimulant.

excitar [eksθi'tar] *vt* to excite; (*incitar*) to urge; (*emoción*) to stir up; (*esperanzas*) to raise; (*pasión*) to arouse; ~se *vr* to get excited.

exclamación [eksklama'θjon] *nf* exclamation.

exclamar [ekskla'mar] *vi* to exclaim; ~se *vr*: ~se (**contra**) to complain (about).

excluir [eksklu'ir] *vt* to exclude; (*dejar fuera*) to shut out; (*solución*) to reject; (*posibilidad*) to rule out.

exclusión [eksklu'sjon] *nf* exclusion.

exclusiva [eksklu'sißa] *nf* V **exclusivo**.

exclusive [eksklu'siße] *prep* exclusive of, not counting.

exclusivo, a [eksklu'sißo, a] *adj* exclusive ♦ *nf* (*PRENSA*) exclusive, scoop; (*COM*) sole right o agency; **derecho** ~ sole o exclusive right.

excluyendo [eksklu'jendo] *etc vb* V **excluir**.

Excma., Excmo. *abr* (= *Excelentísima, Excelentísimo*) *courtesy title*.

excombatiente [ekskomba't jente] *nm* exserviceman, war veteran (*US*).

excomulgar [ekskomul'ɣar] *vt* (*REL*) to excommunicate.

excomulgue [eksko'mulɣe] *etc vb* V **excomulgar**.

excomunión [ekskomu'njon] *nf* excommunication.

excoriar [eksko'rjar] *vt* to flay, skin.

excremento [ekskre'mento] *nm* excrement.

exculpar [ekskul'par] *vt* to exonerate; (*JUR*) to acquit; ~se *vr* to exonerate o.s.

excursión [ekskur'sjon] *nf* excursion, outing; **ir de** ~ to go (off) on a trip.

excursionista [ekskursjo'nista] *nm/f* (*turista*) sightseer.

excusa [eks'kusa] *nf* excuse; (*disculpa*) apology; **presentar sus** ~s to excuse o.s.

excusado, a [eksku'saðo, a] *adj* unnecessary; (*disculpado*) excused, forgiven.

excusar [eksku'sar] *vt* to excuse; (*evitar*) to avoid, prevent; ~se *vr* (*disculparse*) to apologize.

execrable [ekse'kraßle] *adj* appalling.

exención [eksen'θjon] *nf* exemption.

exento, a [ek'sento, a] *pp de* eximir ♦ *adj* exempt.

exequias [ek'sekjas] *nfpl* funeral rites.

exfoliar [eksfo'ljar] *vt* to exfoliate.

exhalación [eksala'θjon] *nf (del aire)* exhalation; (*vapor*) fumes *pl*, vapour; (*rayo*) shooting star; **salir como una ~** to shoot out.

exhalar [eksa'lar] *vt* to exhale, breathe out; (*olor etc*) to give off; (*suspiro*) to breathe, heave.

exhaustivo, a [eksaus'tiβo, a] *adj* exhaustive.

exhausto, a [ek'sausto, a] *adj* exhausted, worn-out.

exhibición [eksiβi'θjon] *nf* exhibition; (*demostración*) display, show; (*de película*) showing; (*de equipo*) performance.

exhibicionista [eksiβiθjo'nista] *adj, nmf* exhibitionist.

exhibir [eksi'βir] *vt* to exhibit; to display, show; (*cuadros*) to exhibit; (*artículos*) to display; (*pasaporte*) to show; (*película*) to screen; (*mostrar con orgullo*) to show; **~se** *vr* (*mostrarse en público*) to show o.s. off; (*fam: indecentemente*) to expose o.s.

exhortación [eksorta'θjon] *nf* exhortation.

exhortar [eksor'tar] *vt:* **~ a** to exhort to.

exhumar [eksu'mar] *vt* to exhume.

exigencia [eksi'xenθja] *nf* demand, requirement.

exigente [eksi'xente] *adj* demanding; (*profesor*) strict; **ser ~ con algn** to be hard on sb.

exigir [eksi'xir] *vt* (*gen*) to demand, require; (*impuestos*) to exact, levy; **~ el pago** to demand payment.

exiguo, a [ek'siɣwo, a] *adj* (*cantidad*) meagre; (*objeto*) tiny.

exija [e'ksixa] *etc vb V* exigir.

exiliado, a [eksi'ljaðo, a] *adj* exiled, in exile ♦ *nmf* exile.

exiliar [eksi'ljar] *vt* to exile; **~se** *vr* to go into exile.

exilio [ek'siljo] *nm* exile.

eximio, a [ek'simjo, a] *adj* (*eminente*) distinguished, eminent.

eximir [eksi'mir] *vt* to exempt.

existencia [eksis'tenθja] *nf* existence; **~s** *nfpl* stock *sg*; **~ de mercancías** (*COM*) stock-in-trade; **tener en ~** to have in stock; **amargar la ~ a algn** to make sb's life a misery.

existir [eksis'tir] *vi* to exist, be.

éxito ['eksito] *nm* (*resultado*) result, outcome; (*triunfo*) success; (*MUS, TEAT*) hit; **~ editorial** bestseller; **~ rotundo**

smash hit; **tener ~** to be successful.

exitoso, a [eksi'toso, a] *adj* (*esp AM*) successful.

éxodo ['eksoðo] *nm* exodus; **el ~ rural** the drift from the land.

ex oficio [ekso'fiθjo] *adj, adv* ex officio.

exonerar [eksone'rar] *vt* to exonerate; **~ de una obligación** to free from an obligation.

exorcice [eksor'θiθe] *etc vb V* exorcizar.

exorcismo [eksor'θismo] *nm* exorcism.

exorcizar [eksorθi'θar] *vt* to exorcize.

exótico, a [ek'sotiko, a] *adj* exotic.

expandido, a [ekspan'diðo, a] *adj:* **en caracteres ~s** (*INFORM*) double width.

expandir [ekspan'dir] *vt* to expand; (*COM*) to expand, enlarge; **~se** *vr* to expand, spread.

expansión [ekspan'sjon] *nf* expansion; (*recreo*) relaxation; **la ~ económica** economic growth; **economía en ~** expanding economy.

expansionarse [ekspansjo'narse] *vr* (*dilatarse*) to expand; (*recrearse*) to relax.

expansivo, a [ekspan'siβo, a] *adj* expansive; (*efusivo*) communicative.

expatriado, a [ekspa'trjaðo, a] *nmf* (*emigrado*) expatriate; (*exiliado*) exile.

expatriarse [ekspa'trjarse] *vr* to emigrate; (*POL*) to go into exile.

expectación [ekspekta'θjon] *nf* (*esperanza*) expectation; (*ilusión*) excitement.

expectativa [ekspekta'tiβa] *nf* (*espera*) expectation; (*perspectiva*) prospect; **~ de vida** life expectancy; **estar a la ~** to wait and see (what will happen).

expedición [ekspeði'θjon] *nf* (*excursión*) expedition; **gastos de ~** shipping charges.

expedientar [ekspeðjen'tar] *vt* to open a file on; (*funcionario*) to discipline, start disciplinary proceedings against.

expediente [ekspe'ðjente] *nm* expedient; (*JUR: procedimento*) action, proceedings *pl;* (*: papeles*) dossier, file, record; **~ judicial** court proceedings *pl;* **~ académico** (student's) record.

expedir [ekspe'ðir] *vt* (*despachar*) to send, forward; (*pasaporte*) to issue; (*cheque*) to make out.

expedito, a [ekspe'ðito, a] *adj* (*libre*) clear, free.

expeler [ekspe'ler] *vt* to expel, eject.

expendedor, a [ekspende'ðor, a] *nmf* (*vendedor*) dealer; (*TEAT*) ticket agent ♦ *nm* (*aparato*) (vending) machine; **~ de cigarrillos** cigarette machine.

expendeduría [ekspendedu'ria] *nf* (*estanco*)

extraviar [ekstra'βjar] *vt* to mislead,
misdirect; (*perder*) to lose, misplace;
~**se** *vr* to lose one's way, get lost; (*objeto*)
to go missing, be mislaid.

extravío [ekstra'βio] *nm* loss; (*fig*)
misconduct.

extrayendo [ekstra'jendo] *vb* V **extraer**.

extremado, a [ekstre'maðo, a] *adj*
extreme, excessive.

Extremadura [ekstrema'ðura] *nf*
Estremadura.

extremar [ekstre'mar] *vt* to carry to
extremes; ~**se** *vr* to do one's utmost,
make every effort.

extremaunción [ekstremaun'θjon] *nf*
extreme unction, last rites *pl*.

extremidad [ekstremi'ðað] *nf* (*punta*)
extremity; (*fila*) edge; ~**es** *nfpl* (*ANAT*)
extremities.

extremista [ekstre'mista] *adj, nm/f*
extremist.

extremo, a [eks'tremo, a] *adj* extreme;
(*más alejado*) furthest; (*último*) last ♦ *nm*
end; (*situación*) extreme; **E~ Oriente** Far
East; **en último** ~ as a last resort; **pasar
de un** ~ **a otro** (*fig*) to go from one
extreme to the other; **con** ~ in the
extreme; **la extrema derecha** (*POL*) the
far right; ~ **derecho/izquierdo** (*DEPORTE*)
outside right/left.

extrínseco, a [eks'trinseko, a] *adj*
extrinsic.

extrovertido, a [ekstroβer'tiðo, a] *adj*
extrovert, outgoing ♦ *nm/f* extrovert.

exuberancia [eksuβe'ranθja] *nf*
exuberance.

exuberante [eksuβe'rante] *adj* exuberant;
(*fig*) luxuriant, lush.

exudar [eksu'ðar] *vt, vi* to exude.

exultar [eksul'tar] *vi*: ~ (**en**) to exult (in);
(*pey*) to gloat (over).

exvoto [eks'βoto] *nm* votive offering.

eyaculación [ejakula'θjon] *nf* ejaculation.

eyacular [ejaku'lar] *vt, vi* ejaculate.

F, f ['efe] *nf* (*letra*) F, f; **F de Francia** F for
Frederick (*BRIT*), F for Fox (*US*).

fa [fa] *nm* (*MUS*) F.

f.ª *abr* (*COM*: = *factura*) Inv.

f.a.b. *abr* (= *franco a bordo*) f.o.b.

fabada [fa'βaða] *nf* bean and sausage
stew.

fábrica ['faβrika] *nf* factory; ~ **de moneda**
mint; **marca de** ~ trademark; **precio de**
~ factory price.

fabricación [faβrika'θjon] *nf* (*manufactura*)
manufacture; (*producción*) production;
de ~ **casera** home-made; **de** ~ **nacional**
home produced; ~ **en serie** mass
production.

fabricante [faβri'kante] *nm/f*
manufacturer.

fabricar [faβri'kar] *vt* (*manufacturar*) to
manufacture, make; (*construir*) to build;
(*cuento*) to fabricate, devise; ~ **en serie**
to mass-produce.

fabril [fa'βril] *adj*: **industria** ~
manufacturing industry.

fabrique [fa'βrike] *etc vb* V **fabricar**.

fábula ['faβula] *nf* (*cuento*) fable; (*chisme*)
rumour; (*mentira*) fib.

fabuloso, a [faβu'loso, a] *adj* fabulous,
fantastic.

FACA ['faka] *nm abr* (*ESP AVIAT*) = *Futuro
Avión de Combate y Ataque*.

facción [fak'θjon] *nf* (*POL*) faction;
facciones *nfpl* (*del rostro*) features.

faceta [fa'θeta] *nf* facet.

facha ['fatʃa] (*fam*) *nm/f* fascist, right-wing
extremist ♦ *nf* (*aspecto*) look; (*cara*) face;
¡qué ~ **tienes!** you look a sight!

fachada [fa'tʃaða] *nf* (*ARQ*) façade, front;
(*TIP*) title page; (*fig*) façade, outward
show.

facial [fa'θjal] *adj* facial.

fácil ['faθil] *adj* (*simple*) easy; (*sencillo*)
simple, straightforward; (*probable*)
likely; (*respuesta*) facile; ~ **de usar**
(*INFORM*) user-friendly.

facilidad [faθili'ðað] *nf* (*capacidad*) ease;
(*sencillez*) simplicity; (*de palabra*)
fluency; ~**es** *nfpl* facilities; "~**es de
pago**" (*COM*) "credit facilities",

facilitar – falto

"payment terms".

facilitar [faθili'tar] *vt* (*hacer fácil*) to make easy; (*proporcionar*) to provide; (*documento*) to issue; **le agradecería me facilitara** ... I would be grateful if you could let me have ....

fácilmente ['faθilmente] *adv* easily.

facsímil [fak'simil] *nm* (*documento*) facsimile; **enviar por** ~ to fax.

factible [fak'tiβle] *adj* feasible.

factor [fak'tor] *nm* factor; (*COM*) agent; (*FERRO*) freight clerk.

factoría [fakto'ria] *nf* (*COM: agencia*) agency; (: *fábrica*) factory.

factura [fak'tura] *nf* (*cuenta*) bill; (*nota de pago*) invoice; (*hechura*) manufacture; **presentar** ~ **a** to invoice.

facturación [faktura'θjon] *nf* (*COM*) invoicing; (: *ventas*) turnover; ~ **de equipajes** luggage check-in.

facturar [faktu'rar] *vt* (*COM*) to invoice, charge for; (*AVIAT*) to check in; (*equipaje*) to register, check (*US*).

facultad [fakul'taθ] *nf* (*aptitud, ESCOL etc*) faculty; (*poder*) power.

facultativo, a [fakulta'tiβo, a] *adj* optional; (*de un oficio*) professional; **prescripción facultativa** medical prescription.

FAD *nm abr* (*ESP*) = *Fondo de Ayuda y Desarrollo*.

faena [fa'ena] *nf* (*trabajo*) work; (*quehacer*) task, job; ~**s domésticas** housework *sg*.

faenar [fae'nar] *vi* to fish.

fagot [fa'γot] *nm* (*MUS*) bassoon.

faisán [fai'san] *nm* pheasant.

faja ['faxa] *nf* (*para la cintura*) sash; (*de mujer*) corset; (*de tierra*) strip.

fajo ['faxo] *nm* (*de papeles*) bundle; (*de billetes*) role, wad.

falange [fa'lanxe] *nf*: **la F**~ (*POL*) the Falange.

falda ['falda] *nf* (*prenda de vestir*) skirt; (*GEO*) foothill; ~ **escocesa** kilt.

fálico, a ['faliko, a] *adj* phallic.

falla ['faʎa] *nf* (*defecto*) fault, flaw.

fallar [fa'ʎar] *vt* (*JUR*) to pronounce sentence on; (*NAIPES*) to trump ♦ *vi* (*memoria*) to fail; (*plan*) to go wrong; (*motor*) to miss; ~ **a algn** to let sb down.

*In the week of the 19th of March (the feast of St Joseph, **San José**), Valencia honours its patron saint with a spectacular fiesta called **las Fallas**. The **Fallas** are huge sculptures, made of wood, cardboard, paper and cloth, depicting famous politicians and other targets for ridicule, which are set alight and burned by the*

falleros, *members of the competing local groups who have just spent months preparing them.*

fallecer [faʎe'θer] *vi* to pass away, die.

fallecido, a [faʎe'θiðo, a] *adj* late ♦ *nm/f* deceased.

fallecimiento [faʎeθi'mjento] *nm* decease, demise.

fallero, a [fa'ʎero, a] *nm/f* maker of "Fallas".

fallezca [fa'ʎeθka] *etc vb* V **fallecer**.

fallido, a [fa'ʎiðo, a] *adj* vain; (*intento*) frustrated, unsuccessful; (*esperanza*) disappointed.

fallo ['faʎo] *nm* (*JUR*) verdict, ruling; (*decisión*) decision; (*de jurado*) findings; (*fracaso*) failure; (*DEPORTE*) miss; (*INFORM*) bug.

falo ['falo] *nm* phallus.

falsear [false'ar] *vt* to falsify; (*firma etc*) to forge ♦ *vi* (*MUS*) to be out of tune.

falsedad [false'ðað] *nf* falseness; (*hipocresía*) hypocrisy; (*mentira*) falsehood.

falsificación [falsifika'θjon] *nf* (*acto*) falsification; (*objeto*) forgery.

falsificar [falsifi'kar] *vt* (*firma etc*) to forge; (*voto etc*) to rig; (*moneda*) to counterfeit.

falsifique [falsi'fike] *etc vb* V **falsificar**.

falso, a ['falso, a] *adj* false; (*erróneo*) wrong, mistaken; (*firma, documento*) forged; (*documento, moneda etc*) fake; **en** ~ falsely; **dar un paso en** ~ to trip; (*fig*) to take a false step.

falta ['falta] *nf* (*defecto*) fault, flaw; (*privación*) lack, want; (*ausencia*) absence; (*carencia*) shortage; (*equivocación*) mistake; (*JUR*) default; (*DEPORTE*) foul; (*TENIS*) fault; ~ **de ortografía** spelling mistake; ~ **de respeto** disrespect; **echar en** ~ to miss; **hacer** ~ **hacer algo** to be necessary to do sth; **me hace** ~ **una pluma** I need a pen; **sin** ~ without fail; **por** ~ **de** through *o* for lack of.

faltar [fal'tar] *vi* (*escasear*) to be lacking, be wanting; (*ausentarse*) to be absent, be missing; **¿falta algo?** is anything missing?; **falta mucho todavía** there's plenty of time yet; **¿falta mucho?** is there long to go?; **faltan 2 horas para llegar** there are 2 hours to go till arrival; ~ **(al respeto) a algn** to be disrespectful to sb; ~ **a una cita** to miss an appointment; ~ **a la verdad** to lie; **¡no faltaba más!** that's the last straw!

falto, a ['falto, a] *adj* (*desposeído*) deficient,

lacking; (*necesitado*) poor, wretched; **estar ~ de** to be short of.

fama ['fama] *nf* (*renombre*) fame; (*reputación*) reputation.

famélico, a [fa'meliko, a] *adj* starving.

familia [fa'milja] *nf* family; **~ política** in-laws *pl*.

familiar [fami'ljar] *adj* (*relativo a la familia*) family *cpd*; (*conocido, informal*) familiar; (*estilo*) informal; (*LING*) colloquial ♦ *nm/f* relative, relation.

familiarice [familja'riθe] *etc vb* V **familiarizarse**.

familiaridad [familjari'ðað] *nf* familiarity; (*informalidad*) homeliness.

familiarizarse [familjari'θarse] *vr*: **~ con** to familiarize o.s. with.

famoso, a [fa'moso, a] *adj* (*renombrado*) famous.

fan, *pl* **fans** [fan, fans] *nm* fan.

fanático, a [fa'natiko, a] *adj* fanatical ♦ *nm/f* fanatic; (*CINE, DEPORTE etc*) fan.

fanatismo [fana'tismo] *nm* fanaticism.

fanfarrón, ona [fanfa'rron, ona] *adj* boastful; (*pey*) showy.

fanfarronear [fanfarrone'ar] *vi* to boast.

fango ['fango] *nm* mud.

fangoso, a [fan'goso, a] *adj* muddy.

fantasear [fantase'ar] *vi* to fantasize; **~ con una idea** to toy with an idea.

fantasía [fanta'sia] *nf* fantasy, imagination; (*MUS*) fantasia; (*capricho*) whim; **joyas de ~** imitation jewellery *sg*.

fantasma [fan'tasma] *nm* (*espectro*) ghost, apparition; (*presumido*) show-off.

fantástico, a [fan'tastiko, a] *adj* (*irreal, fam*) fantastic.

fanzine [fan'θine] *nm* fanzine.

FAO ['fao] *nf abr* (= *Organización de las Naciones Unidas para la Agricultura y la Alimentación*) FAO.

faquir [fa'kir] *nm* fakir.

faraón [fara'on] *nm* Pharaoh.

faraónico, a [fara'oniko, a] *adj* Pharaonic; (*fig*) grandiose.

fardar [far'ðar] *vi* to show off; **~ de** to boast about.

fardo ['farðo] *nm* bundle; (*fig*) burden.

faringe [fa'rinxe] *nf* pharynx.

faringitis [farin'xitis] *nf* pharyngitis.

farmacéutico, a [farma'θeutiko, a] *adj* pharmaceutical ♦ *nm/f* chemist (*BRIT*), pharmacist.

farmacia [far'maθja] *nf* (*ciencia*) pharmacy; (*tienda*) chemist's (shop) (*BRIT*), pharmacy, drugstore (*US*); **~ de turno** duty chemist.

fármaco ['farmako] *nm* medicine, drug.

faro ['faro] *nm* (*NAUT: torre*) lighthouse; (*señal*) beacon; (*AUTO*) headlamp; **~s antiniebla** fog lamps; **~s delanteros/traseros** headlights/rear lights.

farol [fa'rol] *nm* (*luz*) lantern, lamp; (*FERRO*) headlamp; (*poste*) lamppost; **echarse un ~** (*fam*) to show off.

farola [fa'rola] *nf* street lamp (*BRIT*) o light (*US*), lamppost.

farruco, a [fa'rruko, a] *adj* (*fam*): **estar** o **ponerse ~** to get aggressive.

farsa ['farsa] *nf* (*gen*) farce.

farsante [far'sante] *nm/f* fraud, fake.

FASA ['fasa] *nf abr* (*ESP AUTO*) = *Fábrica de Automóviles, S.A.*

fascículo [fas'θikulo] *nm* (*gen*) part, instalment (*BRIT*), installment (*US*).

fascinante [fasθi'nante] *adj* fascinating.

fascinar [fasθi'nar] *vt* to fascinate; (*encantar*) to captivate.

fascismo [fas'θismo] *nm* fascism.

fascista [fas'θista] *adj, nm/f* fascist.

fase ['fase] *nf* phase.

fastidiar [fasti'ðjar] *vt* (*disgustar*) to annoy, bother; (*estropear*) to spoil; **~se** *vr* (*disgustarse*) to get annoyed o cross; **¡no fastidies!** you're joking!; **¡que se fastidie!** (*fam*) he'll just have to put up with it!

fastidio [fas'tiðjo] *nm* (*disgusto*) annoyance.

fastidioso, a [fasti'ðjoso, a] *adj* (*molesto*) annoying.

fastuoso, a [fas'twoso, a] *adj* (*espléndido*) magnificent; (*banquete etc*) lavish.

fatal [fa'tal] *adj* (*gen*) fatal; (*desgraciado*) ill-fated; (*fam: malo, pésimo*) awful ♦ *adv* terribly; **lo pasó ~** he had a terrible time (of it).

fatalidad [fatali'ðað] *nf* (*destino*) fate; (*mala suerte*) misfortune.

fatídico, a [fa'tiðiko, a] *adj* fateful.

fatiga [fa'tiɣa] *nf* (*cansancio*) fatigue, weariness; **~s** *nfpl* hardships.

fatigar [fati'ɣar] *vt* to tire, weary; **~se** *vr* to get tired.

fatigoso, a [fati'ɣoso, a] *adj* (*cansador*) tiring.

fatigue [fa'tiɣe] *etc vb* V **fatigar**.

fatuo, a ['fatwo, a] *adj* (*vano*) fatuous; (*presuntuoso*) conceited.

fauces ['fauθes] *nfpl* (*ANAT*) gullet *sg*; (*fam*) jaws.

fauna ['fauna] *nf* fauna.

favor [fa'βor] *nm* favour (*BRIT*), favor (*US*); **haga el ~ de ...** would you be so good as to ..., kindly ...; **por ~** please; **a ~** in favo(u)r; **a ~ de** to be in favo(u)r of;

(*COM*) to the order of.
favorable [faβo'raβle] *adj* favourable
(*BRIT*), favorable (*US*); (*condiciones etc*)
advantageous.
favorecer [faβore'θer] *vt* to favour (*BRIT*),
favor (*US*); (*amparar*) to help; (*vestido etc*)
to become, flatter; **este peinado le
favorece** this hairstyle suits him.
favorezca [faβo'reθka] *etc vb V* **favorecer**.
favorito, a [faβo'rito, a] *adj, nm/f* favourite
(*BRIT*), favorite (*US*).
fax [faks] *nm inv* fax; **mandar por** ~ to fax.
faz [faθ] *nf* face; **la** ~ **de la tierra** the face
of the earth.
F.C., f.c. *abr* = **ferrocarril**.
FE *nf abr* = *Falange Española*.
fe [fe] *nf* (*REL*) faith; (*confianza*) belief;
(*documento*) certificate; **de buena** ~
(*JUR*) bona fide; **prestar** ~ **a** to believe,
credit; **actuar con buena/mala** ~ to act
in good/bad faith; **dar** ~ **de** to bear
witness to; ~ **de erratas** errata.
fealdad [feal'daθ] *nf* ugliness.
feb., feb.° *abr* (= *febrero*) Feb.
febrero [fe'βrero] *nm* February.
febril [fe'βril] *adj* feverish; (*movido*) hectic.
fecha ['fetʃa] *nf* date; ~ **límite** *o* **tope**
closing *o* last date; ~ **límite de venta** (*de
alimentos*) sell-by date; ~ **de caducidad**
(*de alimentos*) sell-by date; (*de contrato*)
expiry date; **en** ~ **próxima** soon; **hasta la**
~ to date, so far; ~ **de vencimiento**
(*COM*) due date; ~ **de vigencia** (*COM*)
effective date.
fechar [fe'tʃar] *vt* to date.
fechoría [fetʃo'ria] *nf* misdeed.
fécula ['fekula] *nf* starch.
fecundación [fekunda'θjon] *nf*
fertilization; ~ **in vitro** in vitro
fertilization, I.V.F.
fecundar [fekun'dar] *vt* (*generar*) to
fertilize, make fertile.
fecundidad [fekundi'ðaθ] *nf* fertility; (*fig*)
productiveness.
fecundo, a [fe'kundo, a] *adj* (*fértil*) fertile;
(*fig*) prolific; (*productivo*) productive.
FED *nm abr* (= *Fondo Europeo de Desarrollo*)
EDF.
FEDER *nm abr* (= *Fondo Europeo de
Desarrollo Regional*) ERDF.
federación [feðera'θjon] *nf* federation.
federal [feðe'ral] *adj* federal.
federalismo [feðera'lismo] *nm* federalism.
FEF [fef] *nf abr* = *Federación Española de
Fútbol*.
felicidad [feliθi'ðaθ] *nf* (*satisfacción,
contento*) happiness; ~**es** *nfpl* best
wishes, congratulations.

felicitación [feliθita'θjon] *nf* (*tarjeta*)
greetings card; **felicitaciones** *nfpl*
(*enhorabuena*) congratulations; ~
navideña *o* **de Navidad** Christmas
Greetings.
felicitar [feliθi'tar] *vt* to congratulate.
feligrés, esa [feli'ɣres, esa] *nm/f*
parishioner.
felino, a [fe'lino, a] *adj* cat-like; (*ZOOL*)
feline ♦ *nm* feline.
feliz [fe'liθ] *adj* (*contento*) happy;
(*afortunado*) lucky.
felonía [felo'nia] *nf* felony, crime.
felpa ['felpa] *nf* (*terciopelo*) plush; (*toalla*)
towelling.
felpudo [fel'puðo] *nm* doormat.
femenino, a [feme'nino, a] *adj* feminine;
(*ZOOL etc*) female ♦ *nm* (*LING*) feminine.
feminismo [femi'nismo] *nm* feminism.
feminista [femi'nista] *adj, nm/f* feminist.
fenomenal [fenome'nal] *adj* phenomenal;
(*fam*) great, terrific.
fenómeno [fe'nomeno] *nm* phenomenon;
(*fig*) freak, accident ♦ *adv:* **lo pasamos** ~
we had a great time ♦ *excl* great!,
marvellous!
feo, a ['feo, a] *adj* (*gen*) ugly; (*desagradable*)
bad, nasty ♦ *nm* insult; **hacer un** ~ **a
algn** to offend sb; **más** ~ **que Picio** as
ugly as sin.
féretro ['feretro] *nm* (*ataúd*) coffin;
(*sarcófago*) bier.
feria ['ferja] *nf* (*gen*) fair; (*AM: mercado*)
market; (*descanso*) holiday, rest day;
(*AM: cambio*) small change; ~ **comercial**
trade fair; ~ **de muestras** trade show.
feriado, a [fe'rjaðo, a] (*AM*) *adj:* **día** ~
(public) holiday ♦ *nm* (public) holiday.
fermentar [fermen'tar] *vi* to ferment.
fermento [fer'mento] *nm* leaven,
leavening.
ferocidad [feroθi'ðaθ] *nf* fierceness,
ferocity.
ferocísimo, a [fero'θisimo, a] *adj superlativo
de* **feroz**.
feroz [fe'roθ] *adj* (*cruel*) cruel; (*salvaje*)
fierce.
férreo, a ['ferreo, a] *adj* iron *cpd*; (*TEC*)
ferrous; (*fig*) (of) iron.
ferretería [ferrete'ria] *nf* (*tienda*)
ironmonger's (shop) (*BRIT*), hardware
store.
ferrocarril [ferroka'rril] *nm* railway,
railroad (*US*); ~ **de vía estrecha/única**
narrow-gauge/single-track railway *o*
line.
ferroviario, a [ferrovja'rjo, a] *adj* rail *cpd*,
railway *cpd* (*BRIT*), railroad *cpd* (*US*) ♦ *nm:*

~s railway (*BRIT*) *o* railroad (*US*) workers.

fértil ['fertil] *adj* (*productivo*) fertile; (*rico*) rich.

fertilice [ferti'liθe] *etc vb V* **fertilizar.**

fertilidad [fertili'ðað] *nf* (*gen*) fertility; (*productividad*) fruitfulness.

fertilizante [fertili'θante] *nm* fertilizer.

fertilizar [fertili'θar] *vt* to fertilize.

ferviente [fer'ßjente] *adj* fervent.

fervor [fer'ßor] *nm* fervour (*BRIT*), fervor (*US*).

fervoroso, a [ferßo'roso, a] *adj* fervent.

festejar [feste'xar] *vt* (*agasajar*) to wine and dine, fête; (*galantear*) to court; (*celebrar*) to celebrate.

festejo [fes'texo] *nm* (*diversión*) entertainment; (*galanteo*) courtship; (*fiesta*) celebration.

festín [fes'tin] *nm* feast, banquet.

festival [festi'ßal] *nm* festival.

festividad [festißi'ðað] *nf* festivity.

festivo, a [fes'tißo, a] *adj* (*de fiesta*) festive; (*fig*) witty; (*CINE, LIT*) humorous; **día ~** holiday.

fetiche [fe'titʃe] *nm* fetish.

fetichista [feti'tʃista] *adj* fetishistic ♦ *nm/f* fetishist.

fétido, a ['fetiðo, a] *adj* (*hediondo*) foul-smelling.

feto ['feto] *nm* foetus; (*fam*) monster.

F.E.V.E. *nf abr* (= *Ferrocarriles Españoles de Vía Estrecha*) *Spanish narrow-gauge railways.*

FF.AA. *nfpl abr* (*MIL*) = **Fuerzas Armadas.**

FF.CC. *nmpl abr* = **Ferrocarriles.**

fiable [fi'aßle] *adj* (*persona*) trustworthy; (*máquina*) reliable.

fiado [fi'aðo] *nm:* **comprar al ~** to buy on credit; **en ~** on bail.

fiador, a [fia'ðor, a] *nm/f* (*JUR*) surety, guarantor; (*COM*) backer; **salir ~ por algn** to stand bail for sb.

fiambre ['fjambre] *adj* (*CULIN*) (served) cold ♦ *nm* (*CULIN*) cold meat (*BRIT*), cold cut (*US*); (*fam*) corpse, stiff.

fiambrera [fjam'brera] *nf* ≈ lunch box, dinner pail (*US*).

fianza ['fjanθa] *nf* surety; (*JUR*): **libertad bajo ~** release on bail.

fiar [fi'ar] *vt* (*salir garante de*) to guarantee; (*JUR*) to stand bail *o* bond (*US*) for; (*vender a crédito*) to sell on credit; (*secreto*) to confide ♦ *vi:* **~ (de)** to trust (in); **ser de ~** to be trustworthy; **~se** *vr:* **~ de** to trust (in), rely on.

fiasco ['fjasko] *nm* fiasco.

fibra ['fißra] *nf* fibre (*BRIT*), fiber (*US*); (*fig*)

vigour (*BRIT*), vigor (*US*); **~ óptica** (*INFORM*) optical fibre (*BRIT*) *o* fiber (*US*).

ficción [fik'θjon] *nf* fiction.

ficha ['fitʃa] *nf* (*TELEC*) token; (*en juegos*) counter, marker; (*en casino*) chip; (*COM, ECON*) tally, check (*US*); (*INFORM*) file; (*tarjeta*) index card; (*ELEC*) plug; (*en hotel*) registration form; **~ policíaca** police dossier.

fichaje [fi'tʃaxe] *nm* signing(-up).

fichar [fi'tʃar] *vt* (*archivar*) to file, index; (*DEPORTE*) to sign (up) ♦ *vi* (*deportista*) to sign (up); (*obrero*) to clock in *o* on; **estar fichado** to have a record.

fichero [fi'tʃero] *nm* card index; (*archivo*) filing cabinet; (*COM*) box file; (*INFORM*) file, archive; (*de policía*) criminal records; **~ activo** (*INFORM*) active file; **~ archivado** (*INFORM*) archived file; **~ indexado** (*INFORM*) index file; **~ de reserva** (*INFORM*) backup file; **~ de tarjetas** card index; **nombre de ~** filename.

ficticio, a [fik'tiθjo, a] *adj* (*imaginario*) fictitious; (*falso*) fabricated.

ficus ['fikus] *nm inv* (*BOT*) rubber plant.

fidedigno, a [fiðe'ðixno, a] *adj* reliable.

fideicomiso [fiðeiko'miso] *nm* (*COM*) trust.

fidelidad [fiðeli'ðað] *nf* (*lealtad*) fidelity, loyalty; (*exactitud: de dato etc*) accuracy; **alta ~** high fidelity, hi-fi.

fidelísimo, a [fiðe'lisimo, a] *adj superlativo de* **fiel.**

fideos [fi'ðeos] *nmpl* noodles.

fiduciario, a [fiðu'θjarjo, a] *nm/f* fiduciary.

fiebre ['fjeßre] *nf* (*MED*) fever; (*fig*) fever, excitement; **~ amarilla/del heno** yellow/hay fever; **~ palúdica** malaria; **tener ~** to have a temperature.

fiel [fjel] *adj* (*leal*) faithful, loyal; (*fiable*) reliable; (*exacto*) accurate ♦ *nm* (*aguja*) needle, pointer; **los ~es** the faithful.

fieltro ['fjeltro] *nm* felt.

fiera ['fjera] *nf V* **fiero.**

fiereza [fje'reθa] *nf* (*ZOOL*) wildness; (*bravura*) fierceness.

fiero, a ['fjero, a] *adj* (*cruel*) cruel; (*feroz*) fierce; (*duro*) harsh ♦ *nm/f* (*fig*) fiend ♦ *nf* (*animal feroz*) wild animal *o* beast; (*fig*) dragon.

fierro ['fjerro] *nm* (*AM*) iron.

fiesta ['fjesta] *nf* party; (*de pueblo*) festival; **la ~ nacional** bullfighting; (**día de**) **~** (public) holiday; **mañana es ~** it's a holiday tomorrow; **~ de guardar** (*REL*) day of obligation.

Fiestas *can be official public holidays (such as the* **Día de la Constitución**)*, or special holidays for each* **comunidad autónoma***, many of which are religious feast days. All over Spain there are also special local* **fiestas** *for a patron saint or the Virgin Mary. These often last several days and can include religious processions, carnival parades, bullfights, dancing and feasts of typical local produce.*

FIFA *nf abr* (= *Federación Internacional de Fútbol Asociación*) FIFA.

figura [fi'ɣura] *nf* (*gen*) figure; (*forma, imagen*) shape, form; (*NAIPES*) face card.

figurado, a [fiɣu'raðo, a] *adj* figurative.

figurante [fiɣu'rante] *nm/f* (*TEAT*) walk-on part; (*CINE*) extra.

figurar [fiɣu'rar] *vt* (*representar*) to represent; (*fingir*) to feign ♦ *vi* to figure; **~se** *vr* (*imaginarse*) to imagine; (*suponer*) to suppose; **ya me lo figuraba** I thought as much.

fijador [fixa'ðor] *nm* (*FOTO etc*) fixative; (*de pelo*) gel.

fijar [fi'xar] *vt* (*gen*) to fix; (*cartel*) to post, put up; (*estampilla*) to affix, stick (on); (*pelo*) to set; (*fig*) to settle (on), decide; **~se** *vr*: **~se en** to notice; **¡fíjate!** just imagine!; **¿te fijas?** see what I mean?

fijo, a ['fixo, a] *adj* (*gen*) fixed; (*firme*) firm; (*permanente*) permanent; (*trabajo*) steady; (*color*) fast ♦ *adv*: **mirar ~** to stare.

fila ['fila] *nf* row; (*MIL*) rank; (*cadena*) line; (*MIL*) rank; (*en marcha*) file; **~ india** single file; **ponerse en ~** to line up, get into line; **primera ~** front row.

filántropo, a [fi'lantropo, a] *nm/f* philanthropist.

filarmónico, a [filar'moniko, a] *adj, nf* philharmonic.

filatelia [fila'telja] *nf* philately, stamp collecting.

filatelista [filate'lista] *nm/f* philatelist, stamp collector.

filete [fi'lete] *nm* (*carne*) fillet steak; (*de cerdo*) tenderloin; (*pescado*) fillet; (*MEC: rosca*) thread.

filiación [filja'θjon] *nf* (*POL etc*) affiliation; (*señas*) particulars *pl*; (*MIL, POLICÍA*) records *pl*.

filial [fi'ljal] *adj* filial ♦ *nf* subsidiary; (*sucursal*) branch.

filibustero [filiβus'tero] *nm* pirate.

Filipinas [fili'pinas] *nfpl*: **las (Islas) ~** the Philippines.

filipino, a [fili'pino, a] *adj, nm/f* Philippine.

film [film], *pl* **films** *nm* = **filme.**

filmación [filma'θjon] *nf* filming, shooting.

filmar [fil'mar] *vt* to film, shoot.

filme ['filme] *nm* film, movie (*US*).

filmoteca [filmo'teka] *nf* film library.

filo ['filo] *nm* (*gen*) edge; **sacar ~ a** to sharpen; **al ~ del medio día** at about midday; **de doble ~** double-edged.

filología [filolo'xia] *nf* philology.

filólogo, a [fi'loloɣo, a] *nm/f* philologist.

filón [fi'lon] *nm* (*MINERÍA*) vein, lode; (*fig*) gold mine.

filoso, a [fi'loso, a] *adj* (*AM*) sharp.

filosofía [filoso'fia] *nf* philosophy.

filosófico, a [filo'sofiko, a] *adj* philosophic(al).

filósofo, a [fi'losofo, a] *nm/f* philosopher.

filtración [filtra'θjon] *nf* (*TEC*) filtration; (*INFORM*) sorting; (*fig: de fondos*) misappropriation; (*de datos*) leak.

filtrar [fil'trar] *vt, vi* to filter, strain; (*información*) to leak; **~se** *vr* to filter; (*fig: dinero*) to dwindle.

filtro ['filtro] *nm* (*TEC, utensilio*) filter.

filudo, a [fi'luðo, a] *adj* (*AM*) sharp.

fin [fin] *nm* end; (*objetivo*) aim, purpose; **a ~ de cuentas** at the end of the day; **al ~ y al cabo** when all's said and done; **a ~ de** in order to; **por ~** finally; **en ~** (*resumiendo*) in short; **¡en ~!** (*resignación*) oh, well!; **~ de archivo** (*INFORM*) end-of-file; **~ de semana** weekend; **sin ~** endless(ly).

final [fi'nal] *adj* final ♦ *nm* end, conclusion ♦ *nf* (*DEPORTE*) final.

finalice [fina'liθe] *etc vb V* **finalizar.**

finalidad [finali'ðað] *nf* finality; (*propósito*) purpose, aim.

finalista [fina'lista] *nm/f* finalist.

finalizar [finali'θar] *vt* to end, finish ♦ *vi* to end, come to an end; **~ la sesión** (*INFORM*) to log out *o* off.

financiación [finanθja'θjon] *nf* financing.

financiar [finan'θjar] *vt* to finance.

financiero, a [finan'θjero, a] *adj* financial ♦ *nm/f* financier.

financista [finan'sista] *nm/f* (*AM*) financier.

finanzas [fi'nanθas] *nfpl* finances.

finca ['finka] *nf* country estate.

fineza [fi'neθa] *nf* (*cualidad*) fineness; (*modales*) refinement.

fingir [fin'xir] *vt* (*simular*) to simulate, feign; (*pretextar*) to sham, fake ♦ *vi* (*aparentar*) to pretend; **~se** *vr*: **~se dormido** to pretend to be asleep.

finiquitar [finiki'tar] *vt* (*ECON: cuenta*) to settle and close.

Finisterre [finis'terre] *nm*: **el cabo de ~**

footing ['futin] *nm* jogging; **hacer** ~ to jog.
F.O.P. [fop] *nfpl abr* (*ESP*) = **Fuerzas del Orden Público.**
forajido [fora'xiðo] *nm* outlaw.
foráneo, a [fo'raneo, a] *adj* foreign ♦ *nm/f* outsider.
forastero, a [foras'tero, a] *nm/f* stranger.
forcé [for'θe] *vb* V **forzar.**
forcejear [forθexe'ar] *vi* (*luchar*) to struggle.
forcemos [for'θemos] *etc vb* V **forzar.**
fórceps ['forθeps] *nm inv* forceps.
forense [fo'rense] *adj* forensic ♦ *nm/f* pathologist.
forestal [fores'tal] *adj* forest *cpd*.
forjar [for'xar] *vt* to forge; (*formar*) to form.
forma ['forma] *nf* (*figura*) form, shape; (*molde*) mould, pattern; (*MED*) fitness; (*método*) way, means; **estar en** ~ to be fit; ~ **de pago** (*COM*) method of payment; **las** ~**s** the conventions; **de** ~ **que** ... so that ...; **de todas** ~**s** in any case.
formación [forma'θjon] *nf* (*gen*) formation; (*enseñanza*) training; ~ **profesional** vocational training; ~ **fuera del trabajo** off-the-job training; ~ **en el trabajo** *o* **sobre la práctica** on-the-job training.
formal [for'mal] *adj* (*gen*) formal; (*fig: persona*) serious; (: *de fiar*) reliable; (*conducta*) steady.
formalice [forma'liθe] *etc vb* V **formalizar.**
formalidad [formali'ðað] *nf* formality; seriousness; reliability; steadiness.
formalizar [formali'θar] *vt* (*JUR*) to formalize; (*plan*) to draw up; (*situación*) to put in order, regularize; ~**se** *vr* (*situación*) to be put in order, be regularized.
formar [for'mar] *vt* (*componer*) to form, shape; (*constituir*) to make up, constitute; (*ESCOL*) to train, educate ♦ *vi* (*MIL*) to fall in; (*DEPORTE*) to line up; ~**se** *vr* (*ESCOL*) to be trained (*o* educated); (*cobrar forma*) to form, take form; (*desarrollarse*) to develop.
formatear [formate'ar] *vt* (*INFORM*) to format.
formateo [forma'teo] *nm* (*INFORM*) formatting.
formato [for'mato] *nm* (*INFORM*): **sin** ~ (*disco, texto*) unformatted; ~ **de registro** record format.
formica ® [for'mika] *nf* Formica ®.
formidable [formi'ðaßle] *adj* (*temible*) formidable; (*asombroso*) tremendous.
fórmula ['formula] *nf* formula.
formular [formu'lar] *vt* (*queja*) to lodge; (*petición*) to draw up; (*pregunta*) to pose,

formulate; (*idea*) to formulate.
formulario [formu'larjo] *nm* form; ~ **de solicitud/de pedido** (*COM*) application/ order form; **llenar un** ~ to fill in a form; ~ **contínuo desplegable** (*INFORM*) fanfold paper.
fornicar [forni'kar] *vi* to fornicate.
fornido, a [for'niðo, a] *adj* well-built.
fornique [for'nike] *etc vb* V **fornicar.**
foro ['foro] *nm* (*gen*) forum; (*JUR*) court.
forofo, a [fo'rofo, a] *nm/f* fan.
FORPPA ['forpa] *nm abr* (*ESP*) = *Fondo de Ordenación y Regulación de Productos y Precios Agrarios.*
FORPRONU [for'pronu] *nf abr* (= *Fuerza de Protección de las Naciones Unidas*) UNPROFOR.
forrado, a [fo'rraðo, a] *adj* (*ropa*) lined; (*fam*) well-heeled.
forrar [fo'rrar] *vt* (*abrigo*) to line; (*libro*) to cover; (*coche*) to upholster; ~**se** *vr* (*fam*) to line one's pockets.
forro ['forro] *nm* (*de cuaderno*) cover; (*costura*) lining; (*de sillón*) upholstery.
fortalecer [fortale'θer] *vt* to strengthen; ~**se** *vr* to fortify o.s.; (*opinión etc*) to become stronger.
fortaleza [forta'leθa] *nf* (*MIL*) fortress, stronghold; (*fuerza*) strength; (*determinación*) resolution.
fortalezca [forta'leθka] *etc vb* V **fortalecer.**
fortificar [fortifi'kar] *vt* to fortify; (*fig*) to strengthen.
fortifique [forti'fike] *etc vb* V **fortificar.**
fortísimo, a [for'tisimo, a] *adj superlativo de* **fuerte.**
fortuito, a [for'twito, a] *adj* accidental, chance *cpd*.
fortuna [for'tuna] *nf* (*suerte*) fortune, (good) luck; (*riqueza*) fortune, wealth.
forzar [for'θar] *vt* (*puerta*) to force (open); (*compeler*) to compel; (*violar*) to rape; (*ojos etc*) to strain.
forzoso, a [for'θoso, a] *adj* necessary; (*inevitable*) inescapable; (*obligatorio*) compulsory.
forzudo, a [for'θuðo, a] *adj* burly.
fosa ['fosa] *nf* (*sepultura*) grave; (*en tierra*) pit; (*MED*) cavity; ~**s nasales** nostrils.
fosfato [fos'fato] *nm* phosphate.
fosforescente [fosfores'θente] *adj* phosphorescent.
fósforo ['fosforo] *nm* (*QUÍMICA*) phosphorus; (*esp AM: cerilla*) match.
fósil ['fosil] *adj* fossil, fossilized ♦ *nm* fossil.
foso ['foso] *nm* ditch; (*TEAT*) pit; (*AUTO*): ~ **de reconocimiento** inspection pit.

foto ['foto] *nf* photo, snap(shot); **sacar una** ~ to take a photo *o* picture.

fotocopia [foto'kopja] *nf* photocopy.

fotocopiadora [fotokopja'ðora] *nf* photocopier.

fotocopiar [fotoko'pjar] *vt* to photocopy.

fotogénico, a [foto'xeniko, a] *adj* photogenic.

fotografía [fotoɣra'fia] *nf* (*arte*) photography; (*una* ~) photograph.

fotografiar [fotoɣra'fjar] *vt* to photograph.

fotógrafo, a [fo'toɣrafo, a] *nmf* photographer.

fotomatón [fotoma'ton] *nm* (*cabina*) photo booth.

fotómetro [fo'tometro] *nm* (*FOTO*) light meter.

fotonovela [fotono'ßela] *nf* photo-story.

foulard [fu'lar] *nm* (head)scarf.

FP *nf abr* (*ESP. ESCOL*, *COM*) = *Formación Profesional* ♦ *nm abr* (*POL*) = *Frente Popular*.

FPLP *nm abr* (*POL*: = *Frente Popular para la Liberación de Palestina*) PFLP.

Fr. *abr* (= *Fray, franco*) Fr.

frac [frak], *pl* **fracs** *o* **fraques** ['frakes] *nm* dress coat, tails.

fracasar [fraka'sar] *vi* (*gen*) to fail; (*plan etc*) to fall through.

fracaso [fra'kaso] *nm* (*desgracia, revés*) failure; (*de negociaciones etc*) collapse, breakdown.

fracción [frak'θjon] *nf* fraction; (*POL*) faction, splinter group.

fraccionamiento [fraksjona'mjento] *nm* (*AM*) housing estate.

fractura [frak'tura] *nf* fracture, break.

fragancia [fra'ɣanθja] *nf* (*olor*) fragrance, perfume.

fragante [fra'ɣante] *adj* fragrant, scented.

fraganti [fra'ɣanti]: **in** ~ *adv*: **coger a algn in** ~ to catch sb red-handed.

fragata [fra'ɣata] *nf* frigate.

frágil ['fraxil] *adj* (*débil*) fragile; (*COM*) breakable; (*fig*) frail, delicate.

fragilidad [fraxili'ðað] *nf* fragility; (*de persona*) frailty.

fragmento [fraɣ'mento] *nm* fragment; (*pedazo*) piece; (*de discurso*) excerpt; (*de canción*) snatch.

fragor [fra'ɣor] *nm* (*ruido intenso*) din.

fragua ['fraɣwa] *nf* forge.

fraguar [fra'ɣwar] *vt* to forge; (*fig*) to concoct ♦ *vi* to harden.

fragüe ['fraɣwe] *etc vb V* **fraguar**.

fraile ['fraile] *nm* (*REL*) friar; (: *monje*) monk.

frambuesa [fram'bwesa] *nf* raspberry.

francés, esa [fran'θes, esa] *adj* French

♦ *nm/f* Frenchman/woman ♦ *nm* (*LING*) French.

Francia ['franθja] *nf* France.

franco, a ['franko, a] *adj* (*cándido*) frank, open; (*COM: exento*) free ♦ *nm* (*moneda*) franc; ~ **de derechos** duty-free; ~ **al costado del buque** (*COM*) free alongside ship; ~ **puesto sobre vagón** (*COM*) free on rail; ~ **a bordo** free on board.

francotirador, a [frankotira'ðor, a] *nm/f* sniper.

franela [fra'nela] *nf* flannel.

franja ['franxa] *nf* fringe; (*de uniforme*) stripe; (*de tierra etc*) strip.

franquear [franke'ar] *vt* (*camino*) to clear; (*carta, paquete postal*) to frank, stamp; (*obstáculo*) to overcome; (*COM etc*) to free, exempt.

franqueo [fran'keo] *nm* postage.

franqueza [fran'keθa] *nf* (*candor*) frankness.

franquicia [fran'kiθja] *nf* exemption; ~ **aduanera** exemption from customs duties.

franquismo [fran'kismo] *nm*: **el** ~ (*sistema*) the Franco system; (*período*) the Franco years.

> Tł e political reign and style of government of Francisco Franco (from the end of the Spanish Civil War in 1939 until his death in 1975) are commonly called **franquismo**. He was a powerful, authoritarian, right-wing dictator, who promoted a traditional, Catholic and self-sufficient country. From the 1960s Spain gradually opened its doors to the international community, coinciding with a rise in economic growth and internal political opposition. On his death Spain became a democratic constitutional monarchy.

franquista [fran'kista] *adj* pro-Franco ♦ *nm/f* supporter of Franco.

frasco ['frasko] *nm* bottle, flask; ~ **al vacío** (vacuum) flask.

frase ['frase] *nf* sentence; (*locución*) phrase, expression; ~ **hecha** set phrase; (*despectivo*) cliché.

fraternal [frater'nal] *adj* brotherly, fraternal.

fraude ['frauðe] *nm* (*cualidad*) dishonesty; (*acto*) fraud, swindle.

fraudulento, a [frauðu'lento, a] *adj* fraudulent.

frazada [fra'saða] *nf* (*AM*) blanket.

frecuencia [fre'kwenθja] *nf* frequency; **con** ~ frequently, often; ~ **de red** (*INFORM*) mains frequency; ~ **del reloj** (*INFORM*) clock speed; ~ **telefónica** voice frequency.

frecuentar [frekwen'tar] *vt* (*lugar*) to frequent; (*persona*) to see frequently *o* often; ~ **la buena sociedad** to mix in high society.

frecuente [fre'kwente] *adj* frequent; (*costumbre*) common; (*vicio*) rife.

fregadero [freɣa'ðero] *nm* (kitchen) sink.

fregado, a [fre'gaðo, a] *adj* (*AM fam!*) damn, bloody (*!*).

fregar [fre'ɣar] *vt* (*frotar*) to scrub; (*platos*) to wash (up); (*AM*) to annoy.

fregón, ona [fre'ɣon, ona] *adj* = **fregado** ♦ *nf* (*utensilio*) mop; (*pey: sirvienta*) skivvy.

fregué [fre'ɣe], **freguemos** [fre'ɣemos] *etc vb V* **fregar**.

freidora [frei'ðora] *nf* deep-fat fryer.

freír [fre'ir] *vt* to fry.

fréjol ['frexol] *nm* = **fríjol**.

frenar [fre'nar] *vt* to brake; (*fig*) to check.

frenazo [fre'naθo] *nm*: **dar un** ~ to brake sharply.

frenesí [frene'si] *nm* frenzy.

frenético, a [fre'netiko, a] *adj* frantic; **ponerse** ~ to lose one's head.

freno ['freno] *nm* (*TEC, AUTO*) brake; (*de cabalgadura*) bit; (*fig*) check.

frente ['frente] *nm* (*ARQ, MIL, POL*) front; (*de objeto*) front part ♦ *nf* forehead, brow; ~ **de batalla** battle front; **hacer** ~ **común con algn** to make common cause with sb; ~ **a** in front of; (*en situación opuesta de*) opposite; **chocar de** ~ to crash head-on; **hacer** ~ **a** to face up to.

fresa ['fresa] *nf* (*ESP: fruta*) strawberry; (*de dentista*) drill.

fresco, a ['fresko, a] *adj* (*nuevo*) fresh; (*huevo*) newly-laid; (*frío*) cool; (*descarado*) cheeky, bad-mannered ♦ *nm* (*aire*) fresh air; (*ARTE*) fresco; (*AM: bebida*) fruit juice *o* drink ♦ *nmf* (*fam*) shameless person; (*persona insolente*) impudent person; **tomar el** ~ to get some fresh air; **¡qué** ~! what a cheek!

frescor [fres'kor] *nm* freshness.

frescura [fres'kura] *nf* freshness; (*descaro*) cheek, nerve; (*calma*) calmness.

fresno ['fresno] *nm* ash (tree).

fresón [fre'son] *nm* strawberry.

frialdad [frjal'dað] *nf* (*gen*) coldness; (*indiferencia*) indifference.

fricción [frik'θjon] *nf* (*gen*) friction; (*acto*) rub(bing); (*MED*) massage; (*POL, fig etc*) friction, trouble.

friega ['frjeɣa] *etc*, **friegue** ['frjeɣe] *etc vb V* **fregar**.

friendo [fri'endo] *etc vb V* **freír**.

frigidez [frixi'ðeθ] *nf* frigidity.

frígido, a ['frixiðo, a] *adj* frigid.

frigorífico, a [frixo'rifiko, a] *adj* refrigerating ♦ *nm* refrigerator; (*camión*) freezer lorry *o* truck (*US*); **instalación frigorífica** cold-storage plant.

frijol [fri'xol], **fríjol** ['frixol] *nm* kidney bean.

frió [fri'o] *vb V* **freír**.

frío, a ['frio, a] *etc vb V* **freír** ♦ *adj* cold; (*fig: indiferente*) unmoved, indifferent; (*poco entusiasta*) chilly ♦ *nm* cold(ness); indifference; **¡que** ~! how cold it is!

friolento, a [frjo'lento, a] (*AM*), **friolero, a** [frjo'lero, a] *adj* sensitive to cold.

frito, a ['frito, a] *pp de* **freír** ♦ *adj* fried ♦ *nm* fry; **me trae** ~ **ese hombre** I'm sick and tired of that man; ~**s variados** mixed grill.

frívolo, a ['friβolo, a] *adj* frivolous.

frondoso, a [fron'doso, a] *adj* leafy.

frontal [fron'tal] *nm*: **choque** ~ head-on collision.

frontera [fron'tera] *nf* frontier; (*línea divisoria*) border; (*zona*) frontier area.

fronterizo, a [fronte'riθo, a] *adj* frontier *cpd*; (*contiguo*) bordering.

frontón [fron'ton] *nm* (*DEPORTE: cancha*) pelota court; (: *juego*) pelota.

frotar [fro'tar] *vt* to rub; (*fósforo*) to strike; ~**se** *vr*: ~**se las manos** to rub one's hands.

frs. *abr* (= *francos*) fr.

fructífero, a [fruk'tifero, a] *adj* productive, fruitful.

frugal [fru'ɣal] *adj* frugal.

fruncir [frun'θir] *vt* (*COSTURA*) to gather; (*ceño*) to frown; (*labios*) to purse.

frunza ['frunθa] *etc vb V* **fruncir**.

frustración [frustra'θjon] *nf* frustration.

frustrar [frus'trar] *vt* to frustrate; ~**se** *vr* to be frustrated; (*plan etc*) to fail.

fruta ['fruta] *nf* fruit.

frutal [fru'tal] *adj* fruit-bearing, fruit *cpd* ♦ *nm*: (**árbol**) ~ fruit tree.

frutería [frute'ria] *nf* fruit shop.

frutero, a [fru'tero, a] *adj* fruit *cpd* ♦ *nm/f* fruiterer ♦ *nm* fruit dish *o* bowl.

frutilla [fru'tiʎa] *nf* (*AM*) strawberry.

fruto ['fruto] *nm* (*BOT*) fruit; (*fig: resultado*) result, outcome; ~**s secos** ≈ nuts and raisins.

FSLN *nm abr* (*POL: Nicaragua*) = *Frente Sandinista de Liberación Nacional*.

fue [fwe] *vb V* **ser**, **ir**.

fuego ['fweɣo] *nm* (*gen*) fire; (*CULIN*: *gas*)
burner, ring; (*MIL*) fire; (*fig*: *pasión*) fire,
passion; ~s **artificiales** *o* **de artificio**
fireworks; **prender** ~ **a** to set fire to; **a** ~
lento on a low flame *o* gas; ¡**alto el** ~!
cease fire!; **estar entre dos** ~s to be in
the crossfire; **¿tienes** ~? have you (got)
a light?

fuelle ['fweʎe] *nm* bellows *pl*.

fuel-oil [fuel'oil] *nm* paraffin (*BRIT*),
kerosene (*US*).

fuente ['fwente] *nf* fountain; (*manantial*,
fig) spring; (*origen*) source; (*plato*) large
dish; ~ **de alimentación** (*INFORM*) power
supply; **de** ~ **desconocida/fidedigna**
from an unknown/reliable source.

fuera ['fwera] *etc vb* **ser, ir** ♦ *adv* out(side);
(*en otra parte*) away; (*excepto*, *salvo*)
except, save ♦ *prep*: ~ **de** outside; (*fig*)
besides; ~ **de alcance** out of reach; ~ **de
combate** out of action; (*boxeo*) knocked
out; ~ **de sí** beside o.s.; **por** ~ (on the)
outside; **los de** ~ strangers, newcomers;
estar ~ (*en el extranjero*) to be abroad.

fuera-borda [fwera'βorða] *nm inv* outboard
engine *o* motor.

fuerce ['fwerθe] *etc vb* V **forzar**.

fuereño, a [fwe'reɲo, a] *nm/f* (*AM*)
outsider.

fuero ['fwero] *nm* (*carta municipal*)
municipal charter; (*leyes locales*) local *o*
regional law code; (*privilegio*) privilege;
(*autoridad*) jurisdiction; (*fig*): **en mi** *etc* ~
interno in my *etc* heart of hearts ...,
deep down ....

fuerte ['fwerte] *adj* strong; (*golpe*) hard;
(*ruido*) loud; (*comida*) rich; (*lluvia*) heavy;
(*dolor*) intense ♦ *adv* strongly; hard;
loud(ly) ♦ *nm* (*MIL*) fort, strongpoint;
(*fig*): **el canto no es mi** ~ singing is not
my strong point.

fuerza ['fwerθa] *etc vb* V **forzar** ♦ *nf*
(*fortaleza*) strength; (*TEC, ELEC*) power;
(*coacción*) force; (*violencia*) violence;
(*MIL*: *tb*: ~s) forces *pl*; ~ **de arrastre** (*TEC*)
pulling power; ~ **de brazos** manpower;
~ **mayor** force majeure; ~ **bruta** brute
force; ~s **armadas** (**FF.AA.**) armed
forces; ~ **de Orden Público** (**F.O.P.**)
police (forces); ~ **vital** vitality; **a** ~ **de**
by (dint of); **cobrar** ~s to recover one's
strength; **tener** ~s **para** to have the
strength to; **hacer algo a la** ~ to be
forced to do sth; **con** ~ **legal** (*COM*)
legally binding; **a la** ~, **por** ~ of
necessity; ~ **de voluntad** willpower.

fuete ['fwete] *nm* (*AM*) whip.

fuga ['fuɣa] *nf* (*huida*) flight, escape; (*de*
enamorados) elopement; (*de gas etc*) leak;
~ **de cerebros** (*fig*) brain drain.

fugarse [fu'ɣarse] *vr* to flee, escape.

fugaz [fu'ɣaθ] *adj* fleeting.

fugitivo, a [fuxi'tiβo, a] *adj* fugitive,
fleeing ♦ *nm/f* fugitive.

fugue ['fuɣe] *etc vb* V **fugarse**.

fui [fwi] *etc vb* V **ser, ir**.

fulano, a [fu'lano, a] *nm/f* so-and-so,
what's-his-name.

fulgor [ful'ɣor] *nm* brilliance.

fulminante [fulmi'nante] *adj* (*pólvora*)
fulminating; (*fig*: *mirada*) withering;
(*MED*) fulminant; (*fam*) terrific,
tremendous.

fulminar [fulmi'nar] *vt*: **caer fulminado por
un rayo** to be struck down by lightning;
~ **a algn con la mirada** to look daggers
at sb.

fumador, a [fuma'ðor, a] *nm/f* smoker; **no**
~ non-smoker.

fumar [fu'mar] *vt*, *vi* to smoke; ~**se** *vr*
(*disipar*) to squander; ~ **en pipa** to smoke
a pipe.

fumigar [fumi'ɣar] *vt* to fumigate.

funámbulo, a [fu'nambulo, a],
funambulista [funambu'lista] *nm/f*
tightrope walker.

función [fun'θjon] *nf* function; (*de puesto*)
duties *pl*; (*TEAT etc*) show; **entrar en
funciones** to take up one's duties; ~ **de
tarde/de noche** matinée/evening
performance.

funcional [funθjo'nal] *adj* functional.

funcionamiento [funθjona'mjento] *nm*
functioning; (*TEC*) working; **en** ~ (*COM*)
on stream; **entrar en** ~ to come into
operation.

funcionar [funθjo'nar] *vi* (*gen*) to function;
(*máquina*) to work; "**no funciona**" "out of
order".

funcionario, a [funθjo'narjo, a] *nm/f*
official; (*público*) civil servant.

funda ['funda] *nf* (*gen*) cover; (*de
almohada*) pillowcase; ~ **protectora del
disco** (*INFORM*) disk-jacket.

fundación [funda'θjon] *nf* foundation.

fundado, a [fun'daðo, a] *adj* (*justificado*)
well-founded.

fundamental [fundamen'tal] *adj*
fundamental, basic.

fundamentalismo [fundamenta'lismo] *nm*
fundamentalism.

fundamentalista [fundamenta'lista] *adj*,
nm/f fundamentalist.

fundamentar [fundamen'tar] *vt* (*poner
base*) to lay the foundations of;
(*establecer*) to found; (*fig*) to base.

fundamento [funda'mento] *nm* (*base*) foundation; (*razón*) grounds; **eso carece de** ~ that is groundless.

fundar [fun'dar] *vt* to found; (*crear*) to set up; (*fig: basar*): ~ **(en)** to base *o* found (on); ~**se** *vr*: ~**se en** to be founded on.

fundición [fundi'θjon] *nf* (*acción*) smelting; (*fábrica*) foundry; (*TIP*) fount (*BRIT*), font.

fundir [fun'dir] *vt* (*gen*) to fuse; (*metal*) to smelt, melt down; (*COM*) to merge; (*estatua*) to cast; ~**se** *vr* (*colores etc*) to merge, blend; (*unirse*) to fuse together; (*ELEC: fusible, lámpara etc*) to blow; (*nieve etc*) to melt.

fúnebre ['funeßre] *adj* funeral *cpd*, funereal.

funeral [fune'ral] *nm* funeral.

funeraria [fune'rarja] *nf* undertaker's (*BRIT*), mortician's (*US*).

funesto, a [fu'nesto, a] *adj* ill-fated; (*desastroso*) fatal.

fungir [fun'xir] *vi*: ~ **de** (*AM*) to act as.

furgón [fur'ɣon] *nm* wagon.

furgoneta [furɣo'neta] *nf* (*AUTO, COM*) (transit) van (*BRIT*), pickup (truck) (*US*).

furia ['furja] *nf* (*ira*) fury; (*violencia*) violence.

furibundo, a [furi'ßundo, a] *adj* furious.

furioso, a [fu'rjoso, a] *adj* (*iracundo*) furious; (*violento*) violent.

furor [fu'ror] *nm* (*cólera*) rage; (*pasión*) frenzy, passion; **hacer** ~ to be a sensation.

furtivo, a [fur'tißo, a] *adj* furtive ♦ *nm* poacher.

furúnculo [fu'runkulo] *nm* (*MED*) boil.

fuselaje [fuse'laxe] *nm* fuselage.

fusible [fu'sißle] *nm* fuse.

fusil [fu'sil] *nm* rifle.

fusilamiento [fusila'mjento] *nm* (*JUR*) execution by firing squad.

fusilar [fusi'lar] *vt* to shoot.

fusión [fu'sjon] *nf* (*gen*) melting; (*unión*) fusion; (*COM*) merger, amalgamation.

fusionar [fusjo'nar] *vt* to fuse (together); (*COM*) to merge; ~**se** *vr* (*COM*) to merge, amalgamate.

fusta ['fusta] *nf* (*látigo*) riding crop.

fútbol ['futßol] *nm* football.

futbolín [futßo'lin] *nm* table football.

futbolista [futßo'lista] *nm/f* footballer.

fútil ['futil] *adj* trifling.

futilidad [futili'ðað] *nf*, **futileza** [futi'leθa] *nf* triviality.

futón [fu'ton] *nm* futon.

futuro, a [fu'turo, a] *adj* future ♦ *nm* future; (*LING*) future tense; ~**s** *nmpl* (*COM*) futures.

G g

G, g [xe] *nf* (*letra*) G, g; **G de Gerona** G for George.

g/ *abr* = **giro**.

gabacho, a [ga'ßatʃo, a] *adj* Pyrenean; (*fam*) Frenchified ♦ *nm/f* Pyrenean villager; (*fam*) Frenchy.

gabán [ga'ßan] *nm* overcoat.

gabardina [gaßar'ðina] *nf* (*tela*) gabardine; (*prenda*) raincoat.

gabinete [gaßi'nete] *nm* (*POL*) cabinet; (*estudio*) study; (*de abogados etc*) office; ~ **de consulta/de lectura** consulting/reading room.

gacela [ga'θela] *nf* gazelle.

gaceta [ga'θeta] *nf* gazette.

gacetilla [gaθe'tiʎa] *nf* (*en periódico*) news in brief; (*de personalidades*) gossip column.

gachas ['gatʃas] *nfpl* porridge *sg*.

gacho, a ['gatʃo, a] *adj* (*encorvado*) bent down; (*orejas*) drooping.

gaditano, a [gaði'tano, a] *adj* of *o* from Cadiz ♦ *nm/f* native *o* inhabitant of Cadiz.

GAE *nm abr* (*ESP MIL*) = *Grupo Aéreo Embarcado.*

gaélico, a [ga'eliko, a] *adj* Gaelic ♦ *nm/f* Gael ♦ *nm* (*LING*) Gaelic.

gafar [ga'far] *vt* (*fam: traer mala suerte*) to put a jinx on.

gafas ['gafas] *nfpl* glasses; ~ **oscuras** dark glasses; ~ **de sol** sunglasses.

gafe ['gafe] *adj*: **ser** ~ to be jinxed ♦ *nm* (*fam*) jinx.

gaita ['gaita] *nf* flute; (~ *gallega*) bagpipes *pl*; (*dificultad*) bother; (*cosa engorrosa*) tough job.

gajes ['gaxes] *nmpl* (*salario*) pay *sg*; **los** ~ **del oficio** occupational hazards; ~ **y emolumentos** perquisites.

gajo ['gaxo] *nm* (*gen*) bunch; (*de árbol*) bough; (*de naranja*) segment.

gala ['gala] *nf* full dress; (*fig: lo mejor*) cream, flower; ~**s** *nfpl* finery *sg*; **estar de** ~ to be in one's best clothes; **hacer** ~ **de** to display, show off; **tener algo a** ~ to be proud of sth.

galaico, a [ga'laiko, a] *adj* Galician.

galán [ga'lan] *nm* lover, gallant; (*hombre*

atractivo) ladies' man; (*TEAT*): **primer** ~ leading man.

galante [ga'lante] *adj* gallant; (*atento*) charming; (*cortés*) polite.

galantear [galante'ar] *vt* (*hacer la corte a*) to court, woo.

galanteo [galan'teo] *nm* (*coqueteo*) flirting; (*de pretendiente*) wooing.

galantería [galante'ria] *nf* (*caballerosidad*) gallantry; (*cumplido*) politeness; (*piropo*) compliment.

galápago [ga'lapaɣo] *nm* (*ZOOL*) freshwater tortoise.

galardón [galar'ðon] *nm* award, prize.

galardonar [galarðo'nar] *vt* (*premiar*) to reward; (*una obra*) to award a prize for.

galaxia [ga'laksja] *nf* galaxy.

galbana [gal'ßana] *nf* (*pereza*) sloth, laziness.

galeote [gale'ote] *nm* galley slave.

galera [ga'lera] *nf* (*nave*) galley; (*carro*) wagon; (*MED*) hospital ward; (*TIP*) galley.

galería [gale'ria] *nf* (*gen*) gallery; (*balcón*) veranda(h); (*de casa*) corridor; (*fam: público*) audience; ~ **secreta** secret passage.

Gales ['gales] *nm*: (**el País de**) ~ Wales.

galés, esa [ga'les, esa] *adj* Welsh ♦ *nmf* Welshman/woman ♦ *nm* (*LING*) Welsh.

galgo, a ['galɣo, a] *nmf* greyhound.

Galia ['galja] *nf* Gaul.

Galicia [ga'liθja] *nf* Galicia.

galicismo [gali'θismo] *nm* gallicism.

Galilea [gali'lea] *nf* Galilee.

galimatías [galima'tias] *nm inv* (*asunto*) rigmarole; (*lenguaje*) gibberish, nonsense.

gallardía [gaʎar'ðia] *nf* (*galantería*) dash; (*gracia*) gracefulness; (*valor*) bravery; (*elegancia*) elegance; (*nobleza*) nobleness.

gallego, a [ga'ʎeɣo, a] *adj* Galician; (*AM pey*) Spanish ♦ *nmf* Galician; (*AM pey*) Spaniard ♦ *nm* (*LING*) Galician; *V tb* **lenguas cooficiales.**

galleta [ga'ʎeta] *nf* biscuit; (*fam: bofetada*) whack, slap.

gallina [ga'ʎina] *nf* hen ♦ *nm* (*fam*) coward; ~ **ciega** blind man's buff; ~ **llueca** broody hen.

gallinazo [gaʎi'naso] *nm* (*AM*) turkey buzzard.

gallinero [gaʎi'nero] *nm* (*criadero*) henhouse; (*TEAT*) gods *sg*, top gallery; (*voces*) hubbub.

gallo ['gaʎo] *nm* cock, rooster; (*MUS*) false *o* wrong note; (*cambio de voz*) break in the voice; **en menos que canta un** ~ in an instant.

galo, a ['galo, a] *adj* Gallic; (= *francés*) French ♦ *nmf* Gaul.

galón [ga'lon] *nm* (*COSTURA*) braid; (*MIL*) stripe; (*medida*) gallon.

galopante [galo'pante] *adj* galloping.

galopar [galo'par] *vi* to gallop.

galope [ga'lope] *nm* gallop; **al** ~ (*fig*) in great haste; **a** ~ **tendido** at full gallop.

galvanice [galßa'niθe] *etc vb V* **galvanizar.**

galvanizar [galßani'θar] *vt* to galvanize.

gama ['gama] *nf* (*MUS*) scale; (*fig*) range; (*ZOOL*) doe.

gamba ['gamba] *nf* prawn.

gamberrada [gambe'rraða] *nf* act of hooliganism.

gamberro, a [gam'berro, a] *nmf* hooligan, lout.

gamo ['gamo] *nm* (*ZOOL*) buck.

gamuza [ga'muθa] *nf* chamois; (*bayeta*) duster; (*AM: piel*) suede.

gana ['gana] *nf* (*deseo*) desire, wish; (*apetito*) appetite; (*voluntad*) will; (*añoranza*) longing; **de buena** ~ willingly; **de mala** ~ reluctantly; **me dan** ~**s de** I feel like, I want to; **tener** ~**s de** to feel like; **no me da la (real)** ~ I don't (damned well) want to; **son** ~**s de molestar** they're just trying to be awkward.

ganadería [ganaðe'ria] *nf* (*ganado*) livestock; (*ganado vacuno*) cattle *pl*; (*cría, comercio*) cattle raising.

ganadero, a [gana'ðero, a] *adj* stock *cpd* ♦ *nm* stockman.

ganado [ga'naðo] *nm* livestock; ~ **caballar/cabrío** horses *pl*/goats *pl*; ~ **lanar** *u* **ovejuno** sheep *pl*; ~ **porcino/vacuno** pigs *pl*/cattle *pl*.

ganador, a [gana'ðor, a] *adj* winning ♦ *nmf* winner; (*ECON*) earner.

ganancia [ga'nanθja] *nf* (*lo ganado*) gain; (*aumento*) increase; (*beneficio*) profit; ~**s** *nfpl* (*ingresos*) earnings; (*beneficios*) profit *sg*, winnings; ~**s y pérdidas** profit and loss; ~ **bruta/líquida** gross/net profit; ~**s de capital** capital gains; **sacar** ~ **de** to draw profit from.

ganapán [gana'pan] *nm* (*obrero casual*) odd-job man; (*individuo tosco*) lout.

ganar [ga'nar] *vt* (*obtener*) to get, obtain; (*sacar ventaja*) to gain; (*COM*) to earn; (*DEPORTE, premio*) to win; (*derrotar*) to beat; (*alcanzar*) to reach; (*MIL: objetivo*) to take; (*apoyo*) to gain, win ♦ *vi* (*DEPORTE*) to win; ~**se** *vr*: ~**se la vida** to earn one's living; **se lo ha ganado** he deserves it; ~ **tiempo** to gain time.

ganchillo [gan'tʃiʎo] *nm* (*para croché*)

genuino, a [xe'nwino, a] adj genuine.
GEO ['xeo] nmpl abr (ESP. = Grupos
Especiales de Operaciones) Special Police
Units used in anti-terrorist operations
etc.
geografía [xeoɤra'fia] nf geography.
geográfico, a [xeo'ɤrafiko, a] adj
geographic(al).
geología [xeolo'xia] nf geology.
geólogo, a [xe'oloɤo, a] nm/f geologist.
geometría [xeome'tria] nf geometry.
geométrico, a [xeo'metriko, a] adj
geometric(al).
Georgia [xe'orxja] nf Georgia.
georgiano, a [xeor'xjano, a] adj, nm/f
Georgian ♦ nm (LING) Georgian.
geranio [xe'ranjo] nm (BOT) geranium.
gerencia [xe'renθja] nf management;
(cargo) post of manager; (oficina)
manager's office.
gerente [xe'rente] nm/f (supervisor)
manager; (jefe) director.
geriatría [xerja'tria] nf (MED) geriatrics sg.
geriátrico, a [xer'jatriko, a] adj geriatric.
germano, a [xer'mano, a] adj German,
Germanic ♦ nm/f German.
germen ['xermen] nm germ.
germinar [xermi'nar] vi to germinate;
(brotar) to sprout.
gerundense [xerun'dense] adj of o from
Gerona ♦ nm/f native o inhabitant of
Gerona.
gerundio [xe'rundjo] nm (LING) gerund.
gestación [xesta'θjon] nf gestation.
gesticulación [xestikula'θjon] nf (ademán)
gesticulation; (mueca) grimace.
gesticular [xestiku'lar] vi (con ademanes)
to gesture; (con muecas) to make faces.
gestión [xes'tjon] nf management;
(diligencia, acción) negotiation; **hacer las
gestiones preliminares** to do the
groundwork; ~ **de cartera** (COM)
portfolio management; ~ **financiera**
(COM) financial management; ~ **interna**
(INFORM) housekeeping; ~ **de personal**
personnel management; ~ **de riesgos**
(COM) risk management.
gestionar [xestjo'nar] vt (lograr) to try to
arrange; (llevar) to manage.
gesto ['xesto] nm (mueca) grimace;
(ademán) gesture; **hacer ~s** to make
faces.
gestor, a [xes'tor, a] adj managing ♦ nm/f
manager; (promotor) promoter; (agente)
business agent.
gestoría [xesto'ria] nf agency undertaking
business with government departments,
insurance companies etc.

Gibraltar [xiβral'tar] nm Gibraltar.
gibraltareño, a [xiβralta'reɲo, a] adj of o
from Gibraltar ♦ nm/f native o inhabitant
of Gibraltar.
gigante [xi'ɣante] adj, nm/f giant.
gijonés [xixo'nes, esa] adj of o from Gijón
♦ nm/f native o inhabitant of Gijón.
gilipollas [xili'poʎas] (fam) adj inv daft
♦ nm/f berk.
gilipollez [xilipo'ʎez] nf (fam): **es una** ~
that's a load of crap (!); **decir gilipolleces**
to talk crap (!).
gima ['xima] etc vb V **gemir**.
gimnasia [xim'nasja] nf gymnastics pl;
confundir la ~ **con la magnesia** to get
things mixed up.
gimnasio [xim'nasjo] nm gym(nasium).
gimnasta [xim'nasta] nm/f gymnast.
gimotear [ximote'ar] vi to whine,
whimper; (lloriquear) to snivel.
Ginebra [xi'neβra] n Geneva.
ginebra [xi'neβra] nf gin.
ginecología [xinekolo'xia] nf
gyn(a)ecology.
ginecológico, a [xineko'loxiko, a] adj
gyn(a)ecological.
ginecólogo, a [xine'koloɤo, a] nm/f
gyn(a)ecologist.
gira ['xira] nf tour, trip.
girar [xi'rar] vt (dar la vuelta) to turn
(around); (: rápidamente) to spin; (COM:
giro postal) to draw; (comerciar: letra de
cambio) to issue ♦ vi to turn (round); (dar
vueltas) to rotate; (rápido) to spin; **la
conversación giraba en torno a las
elecciones** the conversation centred on
the election; ~ **en descubierto** to
overdraw.
giratorio, a [xira'torjo, a] adj (gen)
revolving; (puente) swing cpd; (silla)
swivel cpd.
giro ['xiro] nm (movimiento) turn,
revolution; (LING) expression; (COM)
draft; (de sucesos) trend, course; ~
bancario money order, bank giro; ~ **de
existencias** (COM) stock turnover; ~
postal postal order; ~ **a la vista** (COM)
sight draft.
gis [xis] nm (AM) chalk.
gitano, a [xi'tano, a] adj, nm/f gypsy.
glacial [gla'θjal] adj icy, freezing.
glaciar [gla'θjar] nm glacier.
glándula ['glandula] nf (ANAT, BOT) gland.
glicerina [gliθe'rina] nf (TEC) glycerin(e).
global [glo'βal] adj (en conjunto) global;
(completo) total; (investigación) full;
(suma) lump cpd.
globo ['gloβo] nm (esfera) globe, sphere;

(*aeróstato, juguete*) balloon.

glóbulo ['gloßulo] *nm* globule; (*ANAT*)
corpuscle; ~ **blanco/rojo** white/red
corpuscle.

gloria ['glorja] *nf* glory; (*fig*) delight;
(*delicia*) bliss.

glorieta [glo'rjeta] *nf* (*de jardín*) bower,
arbour, (*US*) arbor; (*AUTO*) roundabout
(*BRIT*), traffic circle (*US*); (*plaza redonda*)
circus; (*cruce*) junction.

glorificar [glorifi'kar] *vt* (*enaltecer*) to
glorify, praise.

glorifique [glori'fike] *etc vb V* **glorificar**.

glorioso, a [glo'rjoso, a] *adj* glorious.

glosa ['glosa] *nf* comment; (*explicación*)
gloss.

glosar [glo'sar] *vt* (*comentar*) to comment
on.

glosario [glo'sarjo] *nm* glossary.

glotón, ona [glo'ton, ona] *adj* gluttonous,
greedy ♦ *nm/f* glutton.

glotonería [glotone'ria] *nf* gluttony, greed.

glúteo ['gluteo] *nm* (*fam: nalga*) buttock.

gnomo ['nomo] *nm* gnome.

gobernación [goßerna'θjon] *nf*
government, governing; (*POL*)
Provincial Governor's office; **Ministro
de la G~** Minister of the Interior, Home
Secretary (*BRIT*).

gobernador, a [goßerna'ðor, a] *adj*
governing ♦ *nm/f* governor.

gobernanta [goßer'nanta] *nf* (*esp AM*:
niñera) governess.

gobernante [goßer'nante] *adj* governing
♦ *nm* ruler, governor ♦ *nf* (*en hotel etc*)
housekeeper.

gobernar [goßer'nar] *vt* (*dirigir*) to guide,
direct; (*POL*) to rule, govern ♦ *vi* to
govern; (*NAUT*) to steer; ~ **mal** to
misgovern.

gobierno [go'ßjerno] *etc vb V* **gobernar**
♦ *nm* (*POL*) government; (*gestión*)
management; (*dirección*) guidance,
direction; (*NAUT*) steering; (*puesto*)
governorship.

goce ['goθe] *etc vb V* **gozar** ♦ *nm*
enjoyment.

godo, a ['goðo, a] *nm/f* Goth; (*AM pey*)
Spaniard.

gol [gol] *nm* goal.

golear [gole'ar] *vt* (*marcar*) to score a goal
against.

golf [golf] *nm* golf.

golfo, a ['golfo, a] *nm/f* (*pilluelo*) street
urchin; (*vago*) tramp; (*gorrón*) loafer;
(*gamberro*) lout ♦ *nm* (*GEO*) gulf ♦ *nf* (*fam*:
prostituta) slut, whore, hooker (*US*).

golondrina [golon'drina] *nf* swallow.

golosina [golo'sina] *nf* titbit; (*dulce*) sweet.

goloso, a [go'loso, a] *adj* sweet-toothed;
(*fam: glotón*) greedy.

golpe ['golpe] *nm* blow; (*de puño*) punch;
(*de mano*) smack; (*de remo*) stroke;
(*FÚTBOL*) kick; (*TENIS etc*) hit, shot; (*mala
suerte*) misfortune; (*fam: atraco*) job,
heist (*US*); (*fig: choque*) clash; **no dar** ~ to
be bone idle; **de un** ~ with one blow; **de**
~ **suddenly**; ~ **(de estado)** coup (d'état);
~ **de gracia** coup de grâce (*tb fig*); ~ **de
fortuna/maestro** stroke of luck/genius;
cerrar una puerta de ~ to slam a door.

golpear [golpe'ar] *vt, vi* to strike, knock;
(*asestar*) to beat; (*de puño*) to punch;
(*golpetear*) to tap; (*mesa*) to bang.

golpista [gol'pista] *adj*: **intentona** ~ coup
attempt ♦ *nm/f* participant in a coup
(d'état).

golpiza [gol'pisa] *nf*: **dar una** ~ **a algn** (*AM*)
to beat sb up.

goma ['goma] *nf* (*caucho*) rubber; (*elástico*)
elastic; (*tira*) rubber *o* elastic (*BRIT*)
band; (*fam: preservativo*) condom; (*droga*)
hashish; (*explosivo*) plastic explosive; ~
(de borrar) eraser, rubber (*BRIT*); ~ **de
mascar** chewing gum; ~ **de pegar** gum,
glue.

goma-espuma [gomaes'puma] *nf* foam
rubber.

gomina [go'mina] *nf* hair gel.

gomita [go'mita] *nf* rubber *o* elastic (*BRIT*)
band.

góndola ['gondola] *nf* (*barco*) gondola; (*de
tren*) goods wagon.

gordo, a ['gorðo, a] *adj* (*gen*) fat; (*persona*)
plump; (*agua*) hard; (*fam*) enormous
♦ *nm/f* fat man *o* woman; **el (premio)** ~
(*en lotería*) first prize; ¡~! (*fam*) fatty!

gordura [gor'ðura] *nf* fat; (*corpulencia*)
fatness, stoutness.

gorgojo [gor'ɣoxo] *nm* (*insecto*) grub.

gorgorito [gorɣo'rito] *nm* (*gorjeo*) trill,
warble.

gorila [go'rila] *nm* gorilla; (*fam*) tough,
thug; (*guardaespaldas*) bodyguard.

gorjear [gorxe'ar] *vi* to twitter, chirp.

gorjeo [gor'xeo] *nm* twittering, chirping.

gorra ['gorra] *nf* (*gen*) cap; (*de niño*)
bonnet; (*militar*) bearskin; ~ **de montar/
de paño/de punto/de visera** riding/
cloth/knitted/peaked cap; **andar** *o* **ir** *o*
vivir de ~ to sponge, scrounge; **entrar de**
~ (*fam*) to gatecrash.

gorrión [go'rrjon] *nm* sparrow.

gorro ['gorro] *nm* cap; (*de niño, mujer*)
bonnet; **estoy hasta el** ~ I am fed up.

gorrón, ona [go'rron, ona] *nm* pebble;

(*TEC*) pivot ♦ *nm/f* scrounger.

gorronear [gorrone'ar] *vi* (*fam*) to sponge, scrounge.

gota ['gota] *nf* (*gen*) drop; (*de pintura*) blob; (*de sudor*) bead; (*MED*) gout; ~ **a** ~ drop by drop; **caer a** ~**s** to drip.

gotear [gote'ar] *vi* to drip; (*escurrir*) to trickle; (*salirse*) to leak; (*cirio*) to gutter; (*lloviznar*) to drizzle.

gotera [go'tera] *nf* leak.

gótico, a ['gotiko, a] *adj* Gothic.

gozar [go'θar] *vi* to enjoy o.s.; ~ **de** (*disfrutar*) to enjoy; (*poseer*) to possess; ~ **de buena salud** to enjoy good health.

gozne ['goθne] *nm* hinge.

gozo ['goθo] *nm* (*alegría*) joy; (*placer*) pleasure; ¡**mi** ~ **en el pozo!** that's torn it!, just my luck!

g.p. *nm abr* (= *giro postal*) m.o.

gr. *abr* (= *gramo(s)*) g.

grabación [graβa'θjon] *nf* recording.

grabado, a [gra'βaðo, a] *adj* (*MUS*) recorded; (*en cinta*) taped, on tape ♦ *nm* print, engraving; ~ **al agua fuerte** etching; ~ **al aguatinta** aquatint; ~ **en cobre** copperplate; ~ **en madera** woodcut; ~ **rupestre** rock carving.

grabador, a [graβa'ðor, a] *nm/f* engraver ♦ *nf* tape-recorder; ~**a de cassettes** cassette recorder.

grabar [gra'βar] *vt* to engrave; (*discos, cintas*) to record; (*impresionar*) to impress.

gracejo [gra'θexo] *nm* (*humor*) wit, humour; (*elegancia*) grace.

gracia ['graθja] *nf* (*encanto*) grace, gracefulness; (*REL*) grace; (*chiste*) joke; (*humor*) humour, wit; ¡**muchas** ~**s!** thanks very much!; ~**s a** thanks to; **tener** ~ (*chiste etc*) to be funny; ¡**qué** ~! how funny!; (*irónico*) what a nerve!; **no me hace** ~ (*broma*) it's not funny; (*plan*) I am not too keen; **con** ~**s anticipadas/ repetidas** thanking you in advance/ again; **dar las** ~**s a algn por algo** to thank sb for sth.

grácil ['graθil] *adj* (*sutil*) graceful; (*delgado*) slender; (*delicado*) delicate.

gracioso, a [gra'θjoso, a] *adj* (*garboso*) graceful; (*chistoso*) funny; (*cómico*) comical; (*agudo*) witty; (*título*) gracious ♦ *nm/f* (*TEAT*) comic character, fool; **su graciosa Majestad** His/Her Gracious Majesty.

grada ['graða] *nf* (*de escalera*) step; (*de anfiteatro*) tier, row; ~**s** *nfpl* (*de estadio*) terraces.

gradación [graða'θjon] *nf* gradation; (*serie*) graded series.

gradería [graðe'ria] *nf* (*gradas*) (flight of) steps *pl*; (*de anfiteatro*) tiers *pl*, rows *pl*; ~ **cubierta** covered stand.

grado ['graðo] *nm* degree; (*etapa*) stage, step; (*nivel*) rate; (*de parentesco*) order of lineage; (*de aceite, vino*) grade; (*grada*) step; (*ESCOL*) class, year, grade (*US*); (*UNIV*) degree; (*LING*) degree of comparison; (*MIL*) rank; **de buen** ~ willingly; **en sumo** ~, **en** ~ **superlativo** in the highest degree.

graduación [graðwa'θjon] *nf* (*acto*) gradation; (*clasificación*) rating; (*del alcohol*) proof, strength; (*ESCOL*) graduation; (*MIL*) rank; **de alta** ~ high-ranking.

gradual [gra'ðwal] *adj* gradual.

graduar [gra'ðwar] *vt* (*gen*) to graduate; (*medir*) to gauge; (*TEC*) to calibrate; (*UNIV*) to confer a degree on; (*MIL*) to commission; ~**se** *vr* to graduate; ~**se la vista** to have one's eyes tested.

grafía [gra'fia] *nf* (*escritura*) writing; (*ortografía*) spelling.

gráfico, a ['grafiko, a] *adj* graphic; (*fig: vívido*) vivid, lively ♦ *nm* diagram ♦ *nf* graph; ~ **de barras** (*COM*) bar chart; ~ **de sectores** o **de tarta** (*COM*) pie chart; ~**s** *nmpl* (*tb INFORM*) graphics; ~**s empresariales** (*COM*) business graphics.

grafito [gra'fito] *nm* (*TEC*) graphite, black lead.

grafología [grafolo'xia] *nf* graphology.

gragea [gra'xea] *nf* (*MED*) pill; (*caramelo*) dragée.

grajo ['graxo] *nm* rook.

Gral. *abr* (*MIL*: = *General*) Gen.

gramático, a [gra'matiko, a] *nm/f* (*persona*) grammarian ♦ *nf* grammar.

gramo ['gramo] *nm* gramme (*BRIT*), gram (*US*).

gran [gran] *adj* V **grande.**

grana ['grana] *nf* (*BOT*) seedling; (*color*) scarlet; **ponerse como la** ~ to go as red as a beetroot.

granada [gra'naða] *nf* pomegranate; (*MIL*) grenade; ~ **de mano** hand grenade; ~ **de metralla** shrapnel shell.

granadilla [grana'ðiʎa] *nf* (*AM*) passion fruit.

granadino, a [grana'ðino, a] *adj* of o from Granada ♦ *nm/f* native o inhabitant of Granada ♦ *nf* grenadine.

granar [gra'nar] *vi* to seed.

granate [gra'nate] *adj inv* maroon ♦ *nm* garnet; (*color*) maroon.

Gran Bretaña [grambre'taɲa] *nf* Great

Britain.

Gran Canaria [granka'narja] nf Grand Canary.

grancanario, a [granka'narjo, a] adj of o from Grand Canary ♦ nm/f native o inhabitant of Grand Canary.

grande ['grande], **gran** adj (de tamaño) big, large; (alto) tall; (distinguido) great; (impresionante) grand ♦ nm grandee; ¿cómo es de ~? how big is it?, what size is it?; **pasarlo en** ~ to have a tremendous time.

grandeza [gran'deθa] nf greatness; (tamaño) bigness; (esplendidez) grandness; (nobleza) nobility.

grandioso, a [gran'djoso, a] adj magnificent, grand.

grandullón, ona [granðu'ʎon, ona] adj oversized.

granel [gra'nel] nm (montón) heap; **a** ~ (COM) in bulk.

granero [gra'nero] nm granary, barn.

granice [gra'niθe] etc vb V **granizar**.

granito [gra'nito] nm (AGR) small grain; (roca) granite.

granizada [grani'θaða] nf hailstorm; (fig) hail; **una** ~ **de balas** a hail of bullets.

granizado [grani'θaðo] nm iced drink; ~ **de café** iced coffee.

granizar [grani'θar] vi to hail.

granizo [gra'niθo] nm hail.

granja ['granxa] nf (gen) farm; ~ **avícola** chicken o poultry farm.

granjear [granxe'ar] vt (cobrar) to earn; (ganar) to win; (avanzar) to gain; ~**se** vr (amistad etc) to gain for o.s.

granjero, a [gran'xero, a] nm/f farmer.

grano ['grano] nm grain; (semilla) seed; (baya) berry; (MED) pimple, spot; (partícula) particle; (punto) speck; ~**s** nmpl cereals; ~ **de café** coffee bean; **ir al** ~ to get to the point.

granuja [gra'nuxa] nm rogue; (golfillo) urchin.

grapa ['grapa] nf staple; (TEC) clamp; (sujetador) clip, fastener; (ARQ) cramp.

grapadora [grapa'ðora] nf stapler.

GRAPO ['grapo] nm abr (ESP POL) = Grupo de Resistencia Antifascista Primero de Octubre.

grasa ['grasa] nf V **graso**.

grasiento, a [gra'sjento, a] adj greasy; (de aceite) oily; (mugriento) filthy.

graso, a ['graso, a] adj fatty; (aceitoso) greasy, oily ♦ nf (gen) grease; (de cocina) fat, lard; (sebo) suet; (mugre) filth; (AUTO) oil; (lubricante) grease; ~ **de ballena** blubber; ~ **de pescado** fish oil.

grasoso, a [gra'soso, a] adj (AM) greasy, sticky.

gratificación [gratifika'θjon] nf (propina) tip; (aguinaldo) gratuity; (bono) bonus; (recompensa) reward.

gratificar [gratifi'kar] vt (dar propina) to tip; (premiar) to reward; **"se gratificará"** "a reward is offered".

gratifique [grati'fike] etc vb V **gratificar**.

gratinar [grati'nar] vt to cook au gratin.

gratis ['gratis] adv free, for nothing.

gratitud [grati'tuð] nf gratitude.

grato, a ['grato, a] adj (agradable) pleasant, agreeable; (bienvenido) welcome; **nos es** ~ **informarle que** ... we are pleased to inform you that ....

gratuito, a [gra'twito, a] adj (gratis) free; (sin razón) gratuitous; (acusación) unfounded.

grava ['graβa] nf (guijos) gravel; (piedra molida) crushed stone; (en carreteras) road metal.

gravamen [gra'βamen] nm (carga) burden; (impuesto) tax; **libre de** ~ (ECON) free from encumbrances.

gravar [gra'βar] vt to burden; (COM) to tax; (ECON) to assess for tax; ~ **con impuestos** to burden with taxes.

grave ['graβe] adj heavy; (fig, MED) grave, serious; (importante) important; (herida) severe; (MUS) low, deep; (LING: acento) grave; **estar** ~ to be seriously ill.

gravedad [graβe'ðað] nf gravity; (fig) seriousness; (grandeza) importance; (dignidad) dignity; (MUS) depth.

grávido, a ['graβiðo, a] adj (preñada) pregnant.

gravilla [gra'βiʎa] nf gravel.

gravitación [graβita'θjon] nf gravitation.

gravitar [graβi'tar] vi to gravitate; ~ **sobre** to rest on.

gravoso, a [gra'βoso, a] adj (pesado) burdensome; (costoso) costly.

graznar [graθ'nar] vi (cuervo) to squawk; (pato) to quack; (hablar ronco) to croak.

graznido [graθ'niðo] nm squawk; croak.

Grecia ['greθja] nf Greece.

gregario, a [gre'ɣarjo, a] adj gregarious; **instinto** ~ herd instinct.

gremio ['gremjo] nm (asociación) professional association, guild.

greña ['greɲa] nf (cabellos) shock of hair; (maraña) tangle; **andar a la** ~ to bicker, squabble.

greñudo, a [gre'ɲuðo, a] adj (persona) dishevelled; (hair) tangled.

gresca ['greska] nf uproar; (trifulca) row.

griego, a ['grjeɣo, a] adj Greek, Grecian

♦ *nm/f* Greek ♦ *nm* (*LING*) Greek.

grieta ['grjeta] *nf* crack; (*hendidura*) chink; (*quiebra*) crevice; (*MED*) chap; (*POL*) rift.

grifa ['grifa] *nf* (*fam: droga*) marijuana.

grifo ['grifo] *nm* tap (*BRIT*), faucet (*US*); (*AM*) petrol (*BRIT*) *o* gas (*US*) station.

grilletes [gri'ʎetes] *nmpl* fetters, shackles.

grillo ['griʎo] *nm* (*ZOOL*) cricket; (*BOT*) shoot; ~s *nmpl* shackles, irons.

grima ['grima] *nf* (*horror*) loathing; (*desagrado*) reluctance; (*desazón*) uneasiness; **me da ~** it makes me sick.

gringo, a ['gringo, a] *adj* (*pey: extranjero*) foreign; (: *norteamericano*) Yankee; (*idioma*) foreign ♦ *nm/f* foreigner; Yank.

gripa ['gripa] *nf* (*AM*) flu, influenza.

gripe ['gripe] *nf* flu, influenza.

gris [gris] *adj* grey.

grisáceo, a [gri'saθeo, a] *adj* greyish.

grisoso, a [gri'soso, a] *adj* (*AM*) greyish, grayish (*esp US*).

gritar [gri'tar] *vt, vi* to shout, yell; ¡no grites! stop shouting!

grito ['grito] *nm* shout, yell; (*de horror*) scream; **a ~ pelado** at the top of one's voice; **poner el ~ en el cielo** to scream blue murder; **es el último ~** (*de moda*) it's all the rage.

groenlandés, esa [groenlan'des, esa] *adj* Greenland *cpd* ♦ *nm/f* Greenlander.

Groenlandia [groen'landja] *nf* Greenland.

grosella [gro'seʎa] *nf* (red)currant; **~ negra** blackcurrant.

grosería [grose'ria] *nf* (*actitud*) rudeness; (*comentario*) vulgar comment; (*palabrota*) swearword.

grosero, a [gro'sero, a] *adj* (*poco cortés*) rude, bad-mannered; (*ordinario*) vulgar, crude.

grosor [gro'sor] *nm* thickness.

grotesco, a [gro'tesko, a] *adj* grotesque; (*absurdo*) bizarre.

grúa ['grua] *nf* (*TEC*) crane; (*de petróleo*) derrick; **~ corrediza** *o* **móvil/de pescante/puente/de torre** travelling/jib/ overhead/tower crane.

grueso, a ['grweso, a] *adj* thick; (*persona*) stout; (*calidad*) coarse ♦ *nm* bulk; (*espesor*) thickness; (*densidad*) density; (*de gente*) main body, mass; **el ~ de** the bulk of.

grulla ['gruʎa] *nf* (*ZOOL*) crane.

grumete [gru'mete] *nm* (*NAUT*) cabin *o* ship's boy.

grumo ['grumo] *nm* (*coágulo*) clot, lump; (*masa*) dollop.

gruñido [gru'ɲiðo] *nm* grunt, growl; (*fig*) grumble.

gruñir [gru'ɲir] *vi* (*animal*) to grunt, growl; (*fam*) to grumble.

gruñón, ona [gru'ɲon, ona] *adj* grumpy ♦ *nm/f* grumbler.

grupa ['grupa] *nf* (*ZOOL*) rump.

grupo ['grupo] *nm* group; (*TEC*) unit, set; (*de árboles*) cluster; **~ sanguíneo** blood group.

gruta ['gruta] *nf* grotto.

Gta. *abr* (*AUTO*) = **Glorieta.**

guaca ['gwaka] *nf* Indian tomb.

guacamole [gwaka'mole] *nm* (*AM*) avocado salad.

guachimán [gwatʃi'man] *nm* (*AM*) night watchman.

guadalajareño, a [gwaðalaxa'reɲo, a] *adj* of *o* from Guadalajara ♦ *nm/f* native *o* inhabitant of Guadalajara.

Guadalquivir [gwaðalki'ßir] *nm*: **el (Río) ~** the Guadalquivir.

guadaña [gwa'ðaɲa] *nf* scythe.

guadañar [gwaða'ɲar] *vt* to scythe, mow.

Guadiana [gwa'ðjana] *nm*: **el (Río) ~** the Guadiana.

guagua ['gwaɣwa] *nf* (*AM, Canarias*) bus; (*AM: criatura*) baby.

guajolote [gwaxo'lote] *nm* (*AM*) turkey.

guano ['gwano] *nm* guano.

guantada [gwan'taða] *nf*, **guantazo** [gwan'taθo] *nm* slap.

guante ['gwante] *nm* glove; **se ajusta como un ~** it fits like a glove; **echar el ~ a algn** to catch hold of sb; (*fig: policía*) to catch sb.

guapo, a ['gwapo, a] *adj* good-looking; (*mujer*) pretty, attractive; (*hombre*) handsome; (*elegante*) smart ♦ *nm* lover, gallant; (*AM fam*) tough guy, bully.

guaraní [gwara'ni] *adj, nm/f* Guarani ♦ *nm* (*moneda*) monetary unit of Paraguay.

guarapo [gwa'rapo] *nm* (*AM*) fermented cane juice.

guarda ['gwarða] *nm/f* (*persona*) warden, keeper ♦ *nf* (*acto*) guarding; (*custodia*) custody; (*TIP*) flyleaf, endpaper; **~ forestal** game warden.

guarda(a)gujas [gwarda'ɣuxas] *nm inv* (*FERRO*) switchman.

guardabarros [gwarða'ßarros] *nm inv* mudguard (*BRIT*), fender (*US*).

guardabosques [gwarda'ßoskes] *nm inv* gamekeeper.

guardacoches [gwarða'kotʃes] *nm/f inv* (*celador*) parking attendant.

guardacostas [gwarda'kostas] *nm inv* coastguard vessel.

guardador, a [gwarða'ðor, a] *adj* protective; (*tacaño*) mean, stingy ♦ *nm/f*

guardian, protector.
guardaespaldas [gwardaes'paldas] *nm/f inv*
bodyguard.
guardameta [gwarða'meta] *nm*
goalkeeper.
guardapolvo [gwarda'polßo] *nm* dust
cover; (*prenda de vestir*) overalls *pl*.
guardar [gwar'ðar] *vt* (*gen*) to keep;
(*vigilar*) to guard, watch over; (*conservar*)
to put away; (*dinero: ahorrar*) to save;
(*promesa etc*) to keep; (*ley*) to observe;
(*rencor*) to bear, harbour; (*INFORM:*
archivo) to save; **~se** *vr* (*preservarse*) to
protect o.s.; **~se de algo** (*evitar*) to avoid
sth; (*abstenerse*) to refrain from sth; **~se**
de hacer algo to be careful not to do sth;
guardársela a algn to have it in for sb.
guardarropa [gwarða'rropa] *nm* (*armario*)
wardrobe; (*en establecimiento público*)
cloakroom.
guardería [gwarðe'ria] *nf* nursery.
guardia ['gwarðja] *nf* (*MIL*) guard;
(*cuidado*) care, custody ♦ *nm/f* guard;
(*policía*) policeman/woman; **estar de ~** to
be on guard; **montar ~** to mount guard;
la G~ Civil the Civil Guard; **~ municipal**
o **urbana** municipal police; **un ~ civil** a
Civil Guard(sman); **un(a) ~ nacional** a
policeman/woman; **~ urbano** traffic
policeman.

> The **Guardia Civil** *is a branch of the* **Ejército**
> **de Tierra** (*Army*) *run along military lines,*
> *which fulfils a policing role outside large*
> *urban communities and is under the joint*
> *control of the Spanish Ministry of Defence*
> *and the Ministry of the Interior. It is also*
> *known as* **La Benemérita.**

guardián, ana [gwar'ðjan, ana] *nm/f* (*gen*)
guardian, keeper.
guarecer [gware'θer] *vt* (*proteger*) to
protect; (*abrigar*) to shelter; **~se** *vr* to
take refuge.
guarezca [gwa'reθka] *etc vb V* **guarecer.**
guarida [gwa'riða] *nf* (*de animal*) den, lair;
(*de persona*) haunt, hideout; (*refugio*)
refuge.
guarnecer [gwarne'θer] *vt* (*equipar*) to
provide; (*adornar*) to adorn; (*TEC*) to
reinforce.
guarnezca [gwar'neθka] *etc vb V*
guarnecer.
guarnición [gwarni'θjon] *nf* (*de vestimenta*)
trimming; (*de piedra*) mount; (*CULIN*)
garnish; (*arneses*) harness; (*MIL*)
garrison.
guarrada [gwa'rraða] (*fam*) *nf* (*cosa sucia*)

dirty mess; (*acto o dicho obsceno*)
obscenity; **hacer una ~ a algn** to do the
dirty on sb.
guarrería [gwarre'ria] *nf* = **guarrada.**
guarro, a ['gwarro, a] *nm/f* (*fam*) pig; (*fig*)
dirty *o* slovenly person.
guasa ['gwasa] *nf* joke; **con** *o* **de ~**
jokingly, in fun.
guasón, ona [gwa'son, ona] *adj* witty;
(*bromista*) joking ♦ *nm/f* wit; joker.
Guatemala [gwate'mala] *nf* Guatemala.
guatemalteco, a [gwatemal'teko, a] *adj*,
nm/f Guatemalan.
guateque [gwa'teke] *nm* (*fiesta*) party,
binge.
guay [gwai] *adj* (*fam*) super, great.
guayaba [gwa'jaßa] *nf* (*BOT*) guava.
Guayana [gwa'jana] *nf* Guyana, Guiana.
gubernamental [gußernamen'tal],
gubernativo, a [gußerna'tißo, a] *adj*
governmental.
guedeja [ge'ðexa] *nf* long hair.
guerra ['gerra] *nf* war; (*arte*) warfare;
(*pelea*) struggle; **~ atómica/**
bacteriológica/nuclear/de guerrillas
atomic/germ/nuclear/guerrilla warfare;
Primera/Segunda G~ Mundial First/
Second World War; **~ de precios** (*COM*)
price war; **~ civil/fría** civil/cold war; **~ a**
muerte fight to the death; **de ~** military,
war *cpd*; **estar en ~** to be at war; **dar ~** to
be annoying.
guerrear [gerre'ar] *vi* to wage war.
guerrero, a [ge'rrero, a] *adj* fighting;
(*carácter*) warlike ♦ *nm/f* warrior.
guerrilla [ge'rriʎa] *nf* guerrilla warfare;
(*tropas*) guerrilla band *o* group.
guerrillero, a [gerri'ʎero, a] *nm/f* guerrilla
(fighter); (*contra invasor*) partisan.
gueto ['geto] *nm* ghetto.
guía ['gia] *etc vb V* **guiar** ♦ *nm/f* (*persona*)
guide ♦ *nf* (*libro*) guidebook; (*manual*)
handbook; (*INFORM*) prompt; **~ de**
ferrocarriles railway timetable; **~**
telefónica telephone directory; **~ del**
turista/del viajero tourist/traveller's
guide.
guiar [gi'ar] *vt* to guide, direct; (*dirigir*) to
lead; (*orientar*) to advise; (*AUTO*) to steer;
~se *vr*: **~se por** to be guided by.
guijarro [gi'xarro] *nm* pebble.
guillotina [giʎo'tina] *nf* guillotine.
guinda ['ginda] *nf* morello cherry; (*licor*)
cherry liqueur.
guindar [gin'dar] *vt* to hoist; (*fam: robar*) to
nick.
guindilla [gin'diʎa] *nf* chil(l)i pepper.
Guinea [gi'nea] *nf* Guinea.

guineo, a [gi'neo, a] *adj* Guinea *cpd*, Guinean ♦ *nm/f* Guinean.

guiñapo [gi'ɲapo] *nm* (*harapo*) rag; (*persona*) rogue.

guiñar [gi'ɲar] *vi* to wink.

guiño ['giɲo] *nm* (*parpadeo*) wink; (*muecas*) grimace; **hacer ~s a** (*enamorados*) to make eyes at.

guiñol [gi'ɲol] *nm* (*TEAT*) puppet theatre.

guión [gi'on] *nm* (*LING*) hyphen, dash; (*esquema*) summary, outline; (*CINE*) script.

guionista [gjo'nista] *nm/f* scriptwriter.

guipuzcoano, a [gipuθko'ano, a] *adj* of *o* from Guipúzcoa ♦ *nm/f* native *o* inhabitant of Guipúzcoa.

guiri ['giri] *nm/f* (*fam, pey*) foreigner.

guirigay [giri'gai] *nm* (*griterío*) uproar; (*confusión*) chaos.

guirnalda [gir'nalda] *nf* garland.

guisa ['gisa] *nf*: **a ~ de** as, like.

guisado [gi'saðo] *nm* stew.

guisante [gi'sante] *nm* pea.

guisar [gi'sar] *vt, vi* to cook; (*fig*) to arrange.

guiso ['giso] *nm* cooked dish.

guita ['gita] *nf* twine; (*fam: dinero*) dough.

guitarra [gi'tarra] *nf* guitar.

guitarrista [gita'rrista] *nm/f* guitarist.

gula ['gula] *nf* gluttony, greed.

gusano [gu'sano] *nm* maggot, worm; (*de mariposa, polilla*) caterpillar; (*fig*) worm; (*ser despreciable*) creep; **~ de seda** silkworm.

gustar [gus'tar] *vt* to taste, sample ♦ *vi* to please, be pleasing; **~ de algo** to like *o* enjoy sth; **me gustan las uvas** I like grapes; **le gusta nadar** she likes *o* enjoys swimming; **¿gusta Ud?** would you like some?; **como Ud guste** as you wish.

gusto ['gusto] *nm* (*sentido, sabor*) taste; (*agrado*) liking; (*placer*) pleasure; **tiene un ~ amargo** it has a bitter taste; **tener buen ~** to have good taste; **sobre ~s no hay nada escrito** there's no accounting for tastes; **de buen/mal ~** in good/bad taste; **sentirse a ~** to feel at ease; **¡mucho *o* tanto ~ (en conocerle)!** how do you do?, pleased to meet you; **el ~ es mío** the pleasure is mine; **tomar ~ a** to take a liking to; **con ~** willingly, gladly.

gustoso, a [gus'toso, a] *adj* (*sabroso*) tasty; (*agradable*) pleasant; (*con voluntad*) willing, glad; **lo hizo ~** he did it gladly.

gutural [gutu'ral] *adj* guttural.

guyanés, esa [gwaja'nes, esa] *adj, nm/f* Guyanese.

H h

H, h ['atʃe] *nf* (*letra*) H, h; **H de Historia** H for Harry (*BRIT*) *o* How (*US*).

H. *abr* (*QUÍMICA*: = Hidrógeno) H; (= Hectárea(s)) ha.; (*COM*: = Haber) cr.

h. *abr* (= hora(s)) h., hr(s).; (= hacia) c. ♦ *nmpl abr* (= habitantes) pop.

ha [a] *vb V* **haber.**

Ha. *abr* (= Hectárea(s)) ha.

haba ['aβa] *nf* bean; **son ~s contadas** it goes without saying; **en todas partes cuecen ~s** it's the same (story) the whole world over.

Habana [a'βana] *nf*: **la ~** Havana.

habanero, a [aβa'nero, a] *adj* of *o* from Havana ♦ *nm/f* native *o* inhabitant of Havana ♦ *nf* (*MUS*) habanera.

habano [a'βano] *nm* Havana cigar.

habeas corpus [a'βeas'korpus] *nm* (*LAW*) habeas corpus.

════════ PALABRA CLAVE

haber [a'βer] *vb aux* **1** (*tiempos compuestos*) to have; **había comido** I have/had eaten; **antes/después de ~lo visto** before seeing/after seeing *o* having seen it; **si lo hubiera sabido habría ido** if I had known I would have gone

2: **¡~lo dicho antes!** you should have said so before!; **¿habráse visto (cosa igual)?** have you ever seen anything like it?

3: **~ de**: **he de hacerlo** I must do it; **ha de llegar mañana** it should arrive tomorrow

♦ *vb impers* **1** (*existencia: sg*) there is; (: *pl*) there are; **hay un hermano/dos hermanos** there is one brother/there are two brothers; **¿cuánto hay de aquí a Sucre?** how far is it from here to Sucre?; **habrá unos 4 grados** it must be about 4 degrees; **no hay quien te entienda** there's no understanding you

2 (*obligación*): **hay que hacer algo** something must be done; **hay que apuntarlo para acordarse** you have to write it down to remember

3: **¡hay que ver!** well I never!

4: **¡no hay de *o* por (AM) qué!** don't

mention it!, not at all!
5: **¿qué hay?** (*¿qué pasa?*) what's up?,
what's the matter?; (*¿qué tal?*) how's it
going?
♦ **~se** *vr*: **habérselas con algn** to have it
out with sb
♦ *vt*: **he aquí unas sugerencias** here are
some suggestions; **todos los inventos
habidos y por ~** all inventions present
and future; **en el encuentro habido ayer**
in yesterday's game
♦ *nm* (*en cuenta*) credit side; **~es** *nmpl*
assets; **¿cuánto tengo en el ~?** how
much do I have in my account?; **tiene
varias novelas en su ~** he has several
novels to his credit.

habichuela [aβi't∫wela] *nf* kidney bean.
hábil ['aβil] *adj* (*listo*) clever, smart; (*capaz*)
fit, capable; (*experto*) expert; **día ~**
working day.
habilidad [aβili'ðað] *nf* (*gen*) skill, ability;
(*inteligencia*) cleverness; (*destreza*)
expertness, expertise; (*JUR*)
competence; **~ (para)** fitness (for); **tener
~ manual** to be clever with one's hands.
habilitación [aβilita'θjon] *nf* qualification;
(*colocación de muebles*) fitting out;
(*financiamiento*) financing; (*oficina*)
paymaster's office.
habilitado [aβili'taðo] *nm* paymaster.
habilitar [aβili'tar] *vt* to qualify; (*autorizar*)
to authorize; (*capacitar*) to enable; (*dar
instrumentos*) to equip; (*financiar*) to
finance.
hábilmente [aβil'mente] *adv* skilfully,
expertly.
habitable [aβi'taβle] *adj* inhabitable.
habitación [aβita'θjon] *nf* (*cuarto*) room;
(*casa*) dwelling, abode; (*BIO: morada*)
habitat; **~ sencilla** *o* **individual** single
room; **~ doble** *o* **de matrimonio** double
room.
habitante [aβi'tante] *nmlf* inhabitant.
habitar [aβi'tar] *vt* (*residir en*) to inhabit;
(*ocupar*) to occupy ♦ *vi* to live.
hábitat, *pl* **hábitats** ['aβitat, 'aβitats] *nm*
habitat.
hábito ['aβito] *nm* habit; **tener el ~ de
hacer algo** to be in the habit of doing
sth.
habitual [aβi'twal] *adj* habitual.
habituar [aβi'twar] *vt* to accustom; **~se** *vr*:
~se a to get used to.
habla ['aβla] *nf* (*capacidad de hablar*)
speech; (*idioma*) language; (*dialecto*)
dialect; **perder el ~** to become
speechless; **de ~ francesa** French-

speaking; **estar al ~** to be in contact;
(*TELEC*) to be on the line; **¡González al ~!**
(*TELEC*) Gonzalez speaking!
hablador, a [aβla'ðor, a] *adj* talkative
♦ *nmlf* chatterbox.
habladuría [aβlaðu'ria] *nf* rumour; **~s** *nfpl*
gossip *sg*.
hablante [a'βlante] *adj* speaking ♦ *nmlf*
speaker.
hablar [a'βlar] *vt* to speak, talk ♦ *vi* to
speak; **~se** *vr* to speak to each other; **~
con** to speak to; **¡hable!, ¡puede ~!**
(*TELEC*) you're through!; **de eso ni ~** no
way, that's not on; **~ alto/bajo/claro** to
speak loudly/quietly/plainly *o* bluntly; **~
de** to speak of *o* about; **"se habla inglés"**
"English spoken here"; **no se hablan**
they are not on speaking terms.
habré [a'βre] *etc vb* V **haber**.
hacedor, a [aθe'ðor, a] *nmlf* maker.
hacendado, a [aθen'daðo, a] *adj* property-
owning ♦ *nm* (*terrateniente*) large
landowner.
hacendoso, a [aθen'doso, a] *adj*
industrious, hard-working.

===================== *PALABRA CLAVE*

hacer [a'θer] *vt* **1** (*fabricar, producir,
conseguir*) to make; (*construir*) to build; **~
una película/un ruido** to make a film/
noise; **el guisado lo hice yo** I made *o*
cooked the stew; **~ amigos** to make
friends

2 (*ejecutar: trabajo etc*) to do; **~ la colada**
to do the washing; **~ la comida** to do the
cooking; **¿qué haces?** what are you
doing?; **¡eso está hecho!** you've got it!;
~ el tonto/indio to act the fool/clown; **~
el malo** *o* **el papel del malo** (*TEAT*) to play
the villain

3 (*estudios, algunos deportes*) to do; **~
español/económicas** to do *o* study
Spanish/economics; **~ yoga/gimnasia** to
do yoga/go to gym

4 (*transformar, incidir en*): **esto lo hará
más difícil** this will make it more
difficult; **salir te hará sentir mejor** going
out will make you feel better; **te hace
más joven** it makes you look younger

5 (*cálculo*): **2 y 2 hacen 4** 2 and 2 make 4;
éste hace 100 this one makes 100

6 (*+ sub*): **esto hará que ganemos** this
will make us win; **harás que no quiera
venir** you'll stop him wanting to come

7 (*como sustituto de vb*) to do; **él bebió y
yo hice lo mismo** he drank and I did
likewise

8: **no hace más que criticar** all he does is

criticize
♦ *vb semi-aux:* ~ +*infin* **1** (*directo*): **les hice
venir** I made *o* had them come; ~
trabajar a los demás to get others to
work
2 (*por intermedio de otros*): ~ **reparar
algo** to get sth repaired
♦ *vi* **1**: **haz como que no lo sabes** act as if
you don't know; **hiciste bien en
decírmelo** you were right to tell me
2 (*ser apropiado*): **si os hace** if it's alright
with you
3: ~ **de**: ~ **de madre para uno** to be like a
mother to sb; (*TEAT*): ~ **de Otelo** to play
Othello; **la tabla hace de mesa** the board
does as a table
♦ *vb impers* **1**: **hace calor/frío** it's hot/cold;
V tb **bueno; sol; tiempo**
2 (*tiempo*): **hace 3 años** 3 years ago;
hace un mes que voy/no voy I've been
going/I haven't been for a month; **no le
veo desde hace mucho** I haven't seen
him for a long time
3: **¿cómo has hecho para llegar tan
rápido?** how did you manage to get here
so quickly?
♦ ~**se** *vr* **1** (*volverse*) to become; **se
hicieron amigos** they became friends;
~**se viejo** to get *o* grow old; **se hace
tarde** it's getting late
2: ~**se algo**: **me hice un traje** I got a suit
made
3 (*acostumbrarse*): ~**se a** to get used to;
~**se a la idea** to get used to the idea
4: **se hace con huevos y leche** it's made
out of eggs and milk; **eso no se hace**
that's not done
5 (*obtener*): ~**se de** *o* **con algo** to get
hold of sth
6 (*fingirse*): ~**se el sordo/sueco** to turn a
deaf ear/pretend not to notice.

hacha ['atʃa] *nf* axe; (*antorcha*) torch.
hachazo [a'tʃaθo] *nm* axe blow.
hache ['atʃe] *nf* (the letter) H; **llámele
usted** ~ call it what you will.
hachís [a'tʃis] *nm* hashish.
hacia ['aθja] *prep* (*en dirección de, actitud*)
towards; (*cerca de*) near; ~ **arriba/abajo**
up(wards)/down(wards); ~ **mediodía**
about noon.
hacienda [a'θjenda] *nf* (*propiedad*)
property; (*finca*) farm; (*AM*) ranch; ~
pública public finance; **(Ministerio de)
H~** Exchequer (*BRIT*), Treasury
Department (*US*).
hacinar [aθi'nar] *vt* to pile (up); (*AGR*) to
stack; (*fig*) to overcrowd.

hada ['aða] *nf* fairy; ~ **madrina** fairy
godmother.
hado ['aðo] *nm* fate, destiny.
haga ['aɣa] *etc vb V* **hacer.**
Haití [ai'ti] *nm* Haiti.
haitiano, a [ai'tjano, a] *adj, nm/f* Haitian.
hala ['ala] *excl* (*vamos*) come on!; (*anda*)
get on with it!
halagar [ala'ɣar] *vt* (*lisonjear*) to flatter.
halago [a'laɣo] *nm* (*adulación*) flattery.
halague [a'laɣe] *etc vb V* **halagar.**
halagüeño, a [ala'ɣweɲo, a] *adj* flattering.
halcón [al'kon] *nm* falcon, hawk.
hálito ['alito] *nm* breath.
halitosis [ali'tosis] *nf* halitosis, bad breath.
hallar [a'ʎar] *vt* (*gen*) to find; (*descubrir*) to
discover; (*toparse con*) to run into; ~**se** *vr*
to be (situated); (*encontrarse*) to find o.s.;
se halla fuera he is away; **no se halla** he
feels out of place.
hallazgo [a'ʎaθɣo] *nm* discovery; (*cosa*)
find.
halo ['alo] *nm* halo.
halógeno, a [a'loxeno, a] *adj*: **faro** ~
halogen lamp.
halterofilia [altero'filja] *nf* weightlifting.
hamaca [a'maka] *nf* hammock.
hambre ['ambre] *nf* hunger; (*carencia*)
famine; (*inanición*) starvation; (*fig*)
longing; **tener** ~ to be hungry.
hambriento, a [am'brjento, a] *adj* hungry,
starving ♦ *nm/f* starving person; **los** ~**s**
the hungry; ~ **de** hungry *o* longing for.
hambruna [am'bruna] *nf* famine.
Hamburgo [am'burɣo] *nm* Hamburg.
hamburguesa [ambur'ɣesa] *nf*
hamburger, burger.
hampa ['ampa] *nf* underworld.
hampón [am'pon] *nm* thug.
han [an] *vb V* **haber.**
haragán, ana [ara'ɣan, ana] *adj, nm/f* good-
for-nothing.
haraganear [araɣane'ar] *vi* to idle, loaf
about.
harapiento, a [ara'pjento, a] *adj* tattered,
in rags.
harapo [a'rapo] *nm* rag.
hardware ['xardwer] *nm* (*INFORM*)
hardware.
haré [a're] *etc vb V* **hacer.**
harén [a'ren] *nm* harem.
harina [a'rina] *nf* flour; **eso es** ~ **de otro
costal** that's another kettle of fish.
harinero, a [ari'nero, a] *nm/f* flour
merchant.
harinoso, a [ari'noso, a] *adj* floury.
hartar [ar'tar] *vt* to satiate, glut; (*fig*) to
tire, sicken; ~**se** *vr* (*de comida*) to fill o.s.,

gorge o.s.; (*cansarse*) to get fed up (*de with*).

hartazgo [ar'taθɣo] *nm* surfeit, glut.

harto, a ['arto, a] *adj* (*lleno*) full; (*cansado*) fed up ♦ *adv* (*bastante*) enough; (*muy*) very; **estar** ~ **de** to be fed up with; ¡**estoy** ~ **de decírtelo!** I'm sick and tired of telling you (so)!

hartura [ar'tura] *nf* (*exceso*) surfeit; (*abundancia*) abundance; (*satisfacción*) satisfaction.

has [as] *vb V* **haber.**

Has. *abr* (= *Hectáreas*) ha.

hasta ['asta] *adv* even ♦ *prep* (*alcanzando a*) as far as, up/down to; (*de tiempo: a tal hora*) till, until; (: *antes de*) before ♦ *conj*: ~ **que** until; ~ **luego** *o* **ahora** (*fam*)/**el sábado** see you soon/on Saturday; ~ **la fecha** (up) to date; ~ **nueva orden** until further notice; ~ **en Valencia hiela a veces** even in Valencia it freezes sometimes.

hastiar [as'tjar] *vt* (*gen*) to weary; (*aburrir*) to bore; ~**se** *vr*: ~**se de** to get fed up with.

hastío [as'tio] *nm* weariness; boredom.

hatajo [a'taxo] *nm*: **un** ~ **de gamberros** a bunch of hooligans.

hatillo [a'tiʎo] *nm* belongings *pl*, kit; (*montón*) bundle, heap.

Hawai [a'wai] *nm* (*tb*: **las Islas** ~) Hawaii.

hawaianas [awa'janas] *nfpl* (*esp AM*) flip-flops (*BRIT*), thongs.

hawaiano, a [awa'jano, a] *adj, nm/f* Hawaiian.

hay [ai] *vb V* **haber.**

Haya ['aja] *nf*: **la** ~ The Hague.

haya ['aja] *etc vb V* **haber** ♦ *nf* beech tree.

hayal [a'jal] *nm* beech grove.

haz [aθ] *vb V* **hacer** ♦ *nm* bundle, bunch; (*rayo: de luz*) beam ♦ *nf*: ~ **de la tierra** face of the earth.

hazaña [a'θaɲa] *nf* feat, exploit; **sería una** ~ it would be a great achievement.

hazmerreír [aθmerre'ir] *nm inv* laughing stock.

HB *abr* (= *Herri Batasuna*) *Basque political party.*

he [e] *vb V* **haber** ♦ *adv*: ~ **aquí** here is, here are; ~ **aquí por qué** ... that is why ....

hebilla [e'βiʎa] *nf* buckle, clasp.

hebra ['eβra] *nf* thread; (*BOT: fibra*) fibre, grain.

hebreo, a [e'βreo, a] *adj, nm/f* Hebrew ♦ *nm* (*LING*) Hebrew.

Hébridas ['eβriðas] *nfpl*: **las** ~ the Hebrides.

hechice [e'tʃiθe] *etc vb V* **hechizar.**

hechicero, a [etʃi'θero, a] *nm/f* sorcerer/sorceress.

hechizar [etʃi'θar] *vt* to cast a spell on, bewitch.

hechizo [e'tʃiθo] *nm* witchcraft, magic; (*acto de magia*) spell, charm.

hecho, a ['etʃo, a] *pp de* **hacer** ♦ *adj* complete; (*maduro*) mature; (*COSTURA*) ready-to-wear ♦ *nm* deed, act; (*dato*) fact; (*cuestión*) matter; (*suceso*) event ♦ *excl* agreed!, done!; ¡**bien** ~! well done!; **de** ~ in fact, as a matter of fact; (*POL etc*: *adj, adv*) de facto; **de** ~ **y de derecho** de facto and de jure; ~ **a la medida** made-to-measure; **a lo** ~, **pecho** it's no use crying over spilt milk.

hechura [e'tʃura] *nf* making, creation; (*producto*) product; (*forma*) form, shape; (*de persona*) build; (*TEC*) craftsmanship.

hectárea [ek'tarea] *nf* hectare.

heder [e'ðer] *vi* to stink, smell; (*fig*) to be unbearable.

hediondez [eðjon'deθ] *nf* stench, stink; (*cosa*) stinking thing.

hediondo, a [e'ðjondo, a] *adj* stinking.

hedor [e'ðor] *nm* stench.

hegemonía [exemo'nia] *nf* hegemony.

helada [e'laða] *nf* frost.

heladera [ela'ðera] *nf* (*AM*: *refrigerador*) refrigerator.

heladería [elaðe'ria] *nf* ice-cream stall (*o* parlour).

helado, a [e'laðo, a] *adj* frozen; (*glacial*) icy; (*fig*) chilly, cold ♦ *nm* ice-cream; **dejar** ~ **a algn** to dumbfound sb.

helador, a [ela'ðor, a] *adj* (*viento etc*) icy, freezing.

helar [e'lar] *vt* to freeze, ice (up); (*dejar atónito*) to amaze; (*desalentar*) to discourage ♦ *vi*, ~**se** *vr* to freeze; (*AVIAT, FERRO etc*) to ice (up), freeze up; (*líquido*) to set.

helecho [e'letʃo] *nm* bracken, fern.

helénico, a [e'leniko, a] *adj* Hellenic, Greek.

heleno, a [e'leno, a] *nm/f* Hellene, Greek.

hélice ['eliθe] *nf* spiral; (*TEC*) propeller; (*MAT*) helix.

helicóptero [eli'koptero] *nm* helicopter.

helio ['eljo] *nm* helium.

helmántico, a [el'mantiko, a] *adj* of *o* from Salamanca.

helvético, a [el'βetiko, a] *adj, nm/f* Swiss.

hematoma [ema'toma] *nm* bruise.

hembra ['embra] *nf* (*BOT, ZOOL*) female; (*mujer*) woman; (*TEC*) nut; **un elefante** ~ a she-elephant.

hemeroteca [emero'teka] *nf* newspaper

library.
hemiciclo [emi'θiklo] *nm*: **el** ~ (*POL*) the floor.
hemisferio [emis'ferjo] *nm* hemisphere.
hemofilia [emo'filja] *nf* haemophilia (*BRIT*), hemophilia (*US*).
hemorragia [emo'rraxja] *nf* haemorrhage (*BRIT*), hemorrhage (*US*).
hemorroides [emo'rroiðes] *nfpl* haemorrhoids (*BRIT*), hemorrhoids (*US*).
hemos ['emos] *vb* V **haber**.
henar [e'nar] *nm* meadow, hayfield.
henchir [en'tʃir] *vt* to fill, stuff; **~se** *vr* (*llenarse de comida*) to stuff o.s. (with food); (*inflarse*) to swell (up).
Hendaya [en'daja] *nf* Hendaye.
hender [en'der] *vt* to cleave, split.
hendidura [endi'ðura] *nf* crack, split; (*GEO*) fissure.
henequén [ene'ken] *nm* (*AM*) henequen.
heno ['eno] *nm* hay.
hepatitis [epa'titis] *nf inv* hepatitis.
herbario, a [er'ßarjo, a] *adj* herbal ♦ *nm* (*colección*) herbarium; (*especialista*) herbalist; (*botánico*) botanist.
herbicida [erßi'θiða] *nm* weedkiller.
herbívoro, a [er'ßißoro, a] *adj* herbivorous.
herboristería [erßoriste'ria] *nf* herbalist's shop.
heredad [ere'ðað] *nf* landed property; (*granja*) farm.
heredar [ere'ðar] *vt* to inherit.
heredero, a [ere'ðero, a] *nm/f* heir(ess); ~ **del trono** heir to the throne.
hereditario, a [ereði'tarjo, a] *adj* hereditary.
hereje [e'rexe] *nm/f* heretic.
herejía [ere'xia] *nf* heresy.
herencia [e'renθja] *nf* inheritance; (*fig*) heritage; (*BIO*) heredity.
herético, a [e'retiko, a] *adj* heretical.
herido, a [e'riðo, a] *adj* injured, wounded; (*fig*) offended ♦ *nm/f* casualty ♦ *nf* wound, injury.
herir [e'rir] *vt* to wound, injure; (*fig*) to offend; (*conmover*) to touch, move.
hermana [er'mana] *nf* V **hermano**.
hermanar [erma'nar] *vt* to match; (*unir*) to join; (*ciudades*) to twin.
hermanastro, a [erma'nastro, a] *nm/f* stepbrother/sister.
hermandad [erman'dað] *nf* brotherhood; (*de mujeres*) sisterhood; (*sindicato etc*) association.
hermano, a [er'mano, a] *adj* similar ♦ *nm* brother ♦ *nf* sister; ~ **gemelo** twin brother; ~ **político** brother-in-law; ~ **primo** first cousin; **mis ~s** my brothers,

my brothers and sisters; **hermana política** sister-in-law.
hermético, a [er'metiko, a] *adj* hermetic; (*fig*) watertight.
hermoso, a [er'moso, a] *adj* beautiful, lovely; (*estupendo*) splendid; (*guapo*) handsome.
hermosura [ermo'sura] *nf* beauty; (*de hombre*) handsomeness.
hernia ['ernja] *nf* hernia, rupture; ~ **discal** slipped disc.
herniarse [er'njarse] *vr* to rupture o.s.; (*fig*) to break one's back.
héroe ['eroe] *nm* hero.
heroicidad [eroiθi'ðað] *nf* heroism; (*una* ~) heroic deed.
heroico, a [e'roiko, a] *adj* heroic.
heroína [ero'ina] *nf* (*mujer*) heroine; (*droga*) heroin.
heroinómano, a [eroi'nomano, a] *nm/f* heroin addict.
heroísmo [ero'ismo] *nm* heroism.
herpes ['erpes] *nmpl o nfpl* (*MED: gen*) herpes *sg*; (: *de la piel*) shingles *sg*.
herradura [erra'ðura] *nf* horseshoe.
herraje [e'rraxe] *nm* (*trabajos*) ironwork.
herramienta [erra'mjenta] *nf* tool.
herrería [erre'ria] *nf* smithy; (*TEC*) forge.
herrero [e'rrero] *nm* blacksmith.
herrumbre [e'rrumbre] *nf* rust.
herrumbroso, a [errum'broso, a] *adj* rusty.
hervidero [erßi'ðero] *nm* (*fig*) swarm; (*POL etc*) hotbed.
hervir [er'ßir] *vi* to boil; (*burbujear*) to bubble; (*fig*): ~ **de** to teem with; ~ **a fuego lento** to simmer.
hervor [er'ßor] *nm* boiling; (*fig*) ardour, fervour.
heterogéneo, a [etero'xeneo, a] *adj* heterogeneous.
heterosexual [eterosek'swal] *adj, nm/f* heterosexual.
hez [eθ] *nf* (*tb*: **heces** *pl*) dregs.
hibernar [ißer'nar] *vi* to hibernate.
híbrido, a ['ißriðo, a] *adj* hybrid.
hice ['iθe] *etc vb* V **hacer**.
hidalgo, a [i'ðalɣo, a] *adj* noble; (*honrado*) honourable (*BRIT*), honorable (*US*) ♦ *nm/f* noble(man/woman).
hidratante [iðra'tante] *adj*: **crema** ~ moisturizing cream, moisturizer.
hidratar [iðra'tar] *vt* to moisturize.
hidrato [i'ðrato] *nm* hydrate; ~ **de carbono** carbohydrate.
hidráulico, a [i'ðrauliko, a] *adj* hydraulic ♦ *nf* hydraulics *sg*.
hidro... [iðro] *pref* hydro..., water-....
hidroavión [iðroa'ßjon] *nm* seaplane.

hidroeléctrico, a [iðroe'lektriko, a] *adj* hydroelectric.

hidrófilo, a [i'ðrofilo, a] *adj* absorbent; **algodón ~** cotton wool (*BRIT*), absorbent cotton (*US*).

hidrofobia [iðro'foßja] *nf* hydrophobia, rabies.

hidrófugo, a [i'ðrofuɣo, a] *adj* damp-proof.

hidrógeno [i'ðroxeno] *nm* hydrogen.

hieda ['jeða] *etc vb V* **heder**.

hiedra ['jeðra] *nf* ivy.

hiel [jel] *nf* gall, bile; (*fig*) bitterness.

hielo ['jelo] *etc vb V* **helar** ♦ *nm* (*gen*) ice; (*escarcha*) frost; (*fig*) coldness, reserve; **romper el ~** (*fig*) to break the ice.

hiena ['jena] *nf* (*ZOOL*) hyena.

hiera ['jera] *etc vb V* **herir**.

hierba ['jerßa] *nf* (*pasto*) grass; (*CULIN, MED: planta*) herb; **mala ~** weed; (*fig*) evil influence.

hierbabuena [jerßa'ßwena] *nf* mint.

hierro ['jerro] *nm* (*metal*) iron; (*objeto*) iron object; **~ acanalado** corrugated iron; **~ colado** *o* **fundido** cast iron; **de ~** iron *cpd*.

hierva ['jerßa] *etc vb V* **hervir**.

hígado ['iɣaðo] *nm* liver; **~s** *nmpl* (*fig*) guts; **echar los ~s** to wear o.s. out.

higiene [i'xjene] *nf* hygiene.

higiénico, a [i'xjeniko, a] *adj* hygienic.

higo ['iɣo] *nm* fig; **~ seco** dried fig; **~ chumbo** prickly pear; **de ~s a brevas** once in a blue moon.

higuera [i'ɣera] *nf* fig tree.

hijastro, a [i'xastro, a] *nm/f* stepson/ daughter.

hijo, a ['ixo, a] *nm/f* son/daughter, child; (*uso vocativo*) dear; **~s** *nmpl* children, sons and daughters; **sin ~s** childless; **~/hija político/a** son-/daughter-in-law; **~ pródigo** prodigal son; **~ de papá/mamá** daddy's/mummy's boy; **~ de puta** (*fam!*) bastard (*!*), son of a bitch (*!*); **cada ~ de vecino** any Tom, Dick or Harry.

hilacha [i'latʃa] *nf* ravelled thread; **~ de acero** steel wool.

hilado, a [i'laðo, a] *adj* spun.

hilandero, a [ilan'dero, a] *nm/f* spinner.

hilar [i'lar] *vt* to spin; (*fig*) to reason, infer; **~ delgado** to split hairs.

hilera [i'lera] *nf* row, file.

hilo ['ilo] *nm* thread; (*BOT*) fibre; (*tela*) linen; (*metal*) wire; (*de agua*) trickle, thin stream; (*de luz*) beam, ray; (*de conversación*) thread, theme; (*de pensamientos*) train; **~ dental** dental floss; **colgar de un ~** (*fig*) to hang by a thread; **traje de ~** linen suit.

hilvanar [ilßa'nar] *vt* (*COSTURA*) to tack

(*BRIT*), baste (*US*); (*fig*) to do hurriedly.

Himalaya [ima'laja] *nm*: **el ~, los Montes ~** the Himalayas.

himno ['imno] *nm* hymn; **~ nacional** national anthem.

hincapié [inka'pje] *nm*: **hacer ~ en** to emphasize, stress.

hincar [in'kar] *vt* to drive (in), thrust (in); (*diente*) to sink; **~se** *vr*: **~se de rodillas** (*esp AM*) to kneel down.

hincha ['intʃa] *nm/f* (*fam: DEPORTE*) fan.

hinchado, a [in'tʃaðo, a] *adj* (*gen*) swollen; (*persona*) pompous ♦ *nf* (group of) supporters *o* fans.

hinchar [in'tʃar] *vt* (*gen*) to swell; (*inflar*) to blow up, inflate; (*fig*) to exaggerate; **~se** *vr* (*inflarse*) to swell up; (*fam: llenarse*) to stuff o.s.; (*fig*) to get conceited; **~se de reír** to have a good laugh.

hinchazón [intʃa'θon] *nf* (*MED*) swelling; (*protuberancia*) bump, lump; (*altivez*) arrogance.

hindú [in'du] *adj, nm/f* Hindu.

hinojo [i'noxo] *nm* fennel.

hinque ['inke] *etc vb V* **hincar**.

hipar [i'par] *vi* to hiccup.

hiper... [iper] *pref* hyper....

hiperactivo, a [iperak'tißo, a] *adj* hyperactive.

hipermercado [ipermer'kaðo] *nm* hypermarket, superstore.

hipersensible [ipersen'sißle] *adj* hypersensitive.

hipertensión [iperten'sjon] *nf* high blood pressure, hypertension.

hípico, a ['ipiko, a] *adj* horse *cpd*, equine; **club ~** riding club.

hipnosis [ip'nosis] *nf inv* hypnosis.

hipnotice [ipno'tiθe] *etc vb V* **hipnotizar**.

hipnotismo [ipno'tismo] *nm* hypnotism.

hipnotizar [ipnoti'θar] *vt* to hypnotize.

hipo ['ipo] *nm* hiccups *pl*; **quitar el ~ a algn** to cure sb's hiccups.

hipocondría [ipokon'dria] *nf* hypochondria.

hipocondríaco, a [ipokon'driako, a] *adj, nm/f* hypochondriac.

hipocresía [ipokre'sia] *nf* hypocrisy.

hipócrita [i'pokrita] *adj* hypocritical ♦ *nm/f* hypocrite.

hipodérmico, a [ipo'ðermiko, a] *adj*: **aguja hipodérmica** hypodermic needle.

hipódromo [i'poðromo] *nm* racetrack.

hipopótamo [ipo'potamo] *nm* hippopotamus.

hipoteca [ipo'teka] *nf* mortgage; **redimir una ~** to pay off a mortgage.

hipotecar [ipote'kar] *vt* to mortgage; (*fig*)

to jeopardize.

hipotecario, a [ipote'karjo, a] *adj* mortgage *cpd*.

hipótesis [i'potesis] *nf inv* hypothesis; **es una ~ (nada más)** that's just a theory.

hipotético, a [ipo'tetiko, a] *adj* hypothetic(al).

hiriendo [i'rjendo] *etc vb V* herir.

hiriente [i'rjente] *adj* offensive, wounding.

hirsuto, a [ir'suto, a] *adj* hairy.

hirviendo [ir'ßjendo] *etc vb V* hervir.

hisopo [i'sopo] *nm (REL)* sprinkler; *(BOT)* hyssop; *(de algodón)* swab.

hispánico, a [is'paniko, a] *adj* Hispanic, Spanish.

hispanidad [ispani'ðað] *nf (cualidad)* Spanishness; *(POL)* Spanish *o* Hispanic world.

hispanista [ispa'nista] *nmf (UNIV etc)* Hispan(ic)ist.

hispano, a [is'pano, a] *adj* Hispanic, Spanish, Hispano- ♦ *nm/f* Spaniard.

Hispanoamérica [ispanoa'merika] *nf* Spanish *o* Latin America.

hispanoamericano, a [ispanoameri'kano, a] *adj, nm/f* Spanish *o* Latin American.

hispanohablante [ispanoa'ßlante], **hispanoparlante** [ispanopar'lante] *adj* Spanish-speaking.

histeria [is'terja] *nf* hysteria.

histérico, a [is'teriko, a] *adj* hysterical.

histerismo [iste'rismo] *nm (MED)* hysteria; *(fig)* hysterics.

histograma [isto'xrama] *nm* histogram.

historia [is'torja] *nf* history; *(cuento)* story, tale; **~s** *nfpl (chismes)* gossip *sg*; **dejarse de ~s** to come to the point; **pasar a la ~** to go down in history.

historiador, a [istorja'ðor, a] *nm/f* historian.

historial [isto'rjal] *nm* record; *(profesional)* curriculum vitae, c.v., résumé *(US)*; *(MED)* case history.

histórico, a [is'toriko, a] *adj* historical; *(fig)* historic.

historieta [isto'rjeta] *nf* tale, anecdote; *(dibujos)* comic strip.

histrionismo [istrjo'nismo] *nm (TEAT)* acting; *(fig)* histrionics *pl*.

hito ['ito] *nm (fig)* landmark; *(objetivo)* goal, target; *(fig)* milestone.

hizo ['iθo] *vb V* hacer.

Hna(s). *abr* (= *Hermana(s)*) Sr(s).

Hno(s). *abr* (= *Hermano(s)*) Bro(s).

hocico [o'θiko] *nm* snout; *(fig)* grimace.

hockey ['xoki] *nm* hockey; **~ sobre hielo** ice hockey.

hogar [o'xar] *nm* fireplace, hearth; *(casa)*

home; *(vida familiar)* home life.

hogareño, a [oxa'reɲo, a] *adj* home *cpd*; *(persona)* home-loving.

hogaza [o'xaθa] *nf (pan)* large loaf.

hoguera [o'xera] *nf (gen)* bonfire; *(para herejes)* stake.

hoja ['oxa] *nf (gen)* leaf; *(de flor)* petal; *(de hierba)* blade; *(de papel)* sheet; *(página)* page; *(formulario)* form; *(de puerta)* leaf; **~ de afeitar** razor blade; **~ de cálculo electrónico** spreadsheet; **~ de trabajo** *(INFORM)* worksheet; **de ~ ancha** broad-leaved; **de ~ caduca/perenne** deciduous/evergreen.

hojalata [oxa'lata] *nf* tin(plate).

hojaldre [o'xaldre] *nm (CULIN)* puff pastry.

hojarasca [oxa'raska] *nf (hojas)* dead *o* fallen leaves *pl*; *(fig)* rubbish.

hojear [oxe'ar] *vt* to leaf through, turn the pages of.

hola ['ola] *excl* hello!

Holanda [o'landa] *nf* Holland.

holandés, esa [olan'des, esa] *adj* Dutch ♦ *nm/f* Dutchman/woman; **los holandeses** the Dutch ♦ *nm (LING)* Dutch.

holgado, a [ol'xaðo, a] *adj* loose, baggy; *(rico)* well-to-do.

holgar [ol'xar] *vi (descansar)* to rest; *(sobrar)* to be superfluous; **huelga decir que** it goes without saying that.

holgazán, ana [olxa'θan, ana] *adj* idle, lazy ♦ *nm/f* loafer.

holgazanear [olxaθane'ar] *vi* to laze *o* loaf around.

holgura [ol'xura] *nf* looseness, bagginess; *(TEC)* play, free movement; *(vida)* comfortable living, luxury.

hollar [o'ʎar] *vt* to tread (on), trample.

hollín [o'ʎin] *nm* soot.

hombre ['ombre] *nm* man; *(raza humana)*: **el ~** man(kind) ♦ *excl*: **¡sí ~!** *(claro)* of course!; *(para énfasis)* man, old chap; **~ de negocios** businessman; **~-rana** frogman; **~ de bien** *o* **pro** honest man; **~ de confianza** right-hand man; **~ de estado** statesman; **el ~ medio** the average man.

hombrera [om'brera] *nf* shoulder strap.

hombro ['ombro] *nm* shoulder; **arrimar el ~** to lend a hand; **encogerse de ~s** to shrug one's shoulders.

hombruno, a [om'bruno, a] *adj* mannish.

homenaje [ome'naxe] *nm (gen)* homage; *(tributo)* tribute; **un partido ~** a benefit match.

homeopatía [omeopa'tia] *nf* hom(o)eopathy.

homeopático, a [omeo'patiko, a] *adj*

hom(o)eopathic.

homicida [omi'θiða] *adj* homicidal ♦ *nm/f* murderer.

homicidio [omi'θiðjo] *nm* murder, homicide; (*involuntario*) manslaughter.

homologación [omoloɣa'θjon] *nf* (*de sueldo, condiciones*) parity.

homologar [omolo'ɣar] *vt* (*COM*) to standardize; (*ESCOL*) to officially approve; (*DEPORTE*) to officially recognize; (*sueldos*) to equalize.

homólogo, a [o'moloɣo, a] *nm/f* counterpart, opposite number.

homónimo [o'monimo] *nm* (*tocayo*) namesake.

homosexual [omosek'swal] *adj*, *nm/f* homosexual.

hondo, a ['ondo, a] *adj* deep; **lo** ~ the depth(s) (*pl*), the bottom; **con** ~ **pesar** with deep regret.

hondonada [ondo'naða] *nf* hollow, depression; (*cañón*) ravine; (*GEO*) lowland.

hondura [on'dura] *nf* depth, profundity.

Honduras [on'duras] *nf* Honduras.

hondureño, a [ondu'reɲo, a] *adj*, *nm/f* Honduran.

honestidad [onesti'ðað] *nf* purity, chastity; (*decencia*) decency.

honesto, a [o'nesto, a] *adj* chaste; decent, honest; (*justo*) just.

hongo ['ongo] *nm* (*BOT: gen*) fungus; (: *comestible*) mushroom; (: *venenoso*) toadstool; (*sombrero*) bowler (hat) (*BRIT*), derby (*US*); ~**s del pie** footrot *sg*, athlete's foot *sg*.

honor [o'nor] *nm* (*gen*) honour (*BRIT*), honor (*US*); (*gloria*) glory; ~ **profesional** professional etiquette; **en** ~ **a la verdad** to be fair.

honorable [ono'raßle] *adj* honourable (*BRIT*), honorable (*US*).

honorario, a [ono'rarjo, a] *adj* honorary ♦ *nm*: ~**s** fees.

honorífico, a [ono'rifiko, a] *adj* honourable (*BRIT*), honorable (*US*); **mención honorífica** hono(u)rable mention.

honra ['onra] *nf* (*gen*) honour; (*renombre*) good name; ~**s fúnebres** funeral rites; **tener algo a mucha** ~ to be proud of sth.

honradez [onra'ðeθ] *nf* honesty; (*de persona*) integrity.

honrado, a [on'raðo, a] *adj* honest, upright.

honrar [on'rar] *vt* to honour; ~**se** *vr*: ~**se con algo/de hacer algo** to be honoured by sth/to do sth.

honroso, a [on'roso, a] *adj* (*honrado*)

honourable; (*respetado*) respectable.

hora ['ora] *nf* hour; (*tiempo*) time; **¿qué ~ es?** what time is it?; **¿a qué ~?** at what time?; **media** ~ half an hour; **a la ~ de comer/de recreo** at lunchtime/at playtime; **a primera** ~ first thing (in the morning); **a última** ~ at the last moment; **"última ~"** "stop press"; **noticias de última** ~ last-minute news; **a altas ~s** in the small hours; **a la ~ en punto** on the dot; **¡a buena ~!** about time, too!; **en mala** ~ unluckily; **dar la** ~ to strike the hour; **poner el reloj en** ~ to set one's watch; ~**s de oficina/de trabajo** office/working hours; ~**s de visita** visiting times; ~**s extras** o **extraordinarias** overtime *sg*; ~**s punta** rush hours; **no ver la** ~ **de** to look forward to; **¡ya era** ~**!** and about time too!

horadar [ora'ðar] *vt* to drill, bore.

horario, a [o'rarjo, a] *adj* hourly, hour *cpd* ♦ *nm* timetable; ~ **comercial** business hours.

horca ['orka] *nf* gallows *sg*; (*AGR*) pitchfork.

horcajadas [orka'xaðas]: **a** ~ *adv* astride.

horchata [or'tʃata] *nf* cold drink made from tiger nuts and water, tiger nut milk.

horda ['orða] *nf* horde.

horizontal [oriθon'tal] *adj* horizontal.

horizonte [ori'θonte] *nm* horizon.

horma ['orma] *nf* mould; ~ (**de calzado**) last; ~ **de sombrero** hat block.

hormiga [or'miɣa] *nf* ant; ~**s** *nfpl* (*MED*) pins and needles.

hormigón [ormi'ɣon] *nm* concrete; ~ **armado/pretensado** reinforced/ prestressed concrete.

hormigueo [ormi'ɣeo] *nm* (*comezón*) itch; (*fig*) uneasiness.

hormiguero [ormi'ɣero] *nm* (*ZOOL*) ant's nest; **era un** ~ it was swarming with people.

hormona [or'mona] *nf* hormone.

hornada [or'naða] *nf* batch of loaves (*etc*).

hornillo [or'niʎo] *nm* (*cocina*) portable stove.

horno ['orno] *nm* (*CULIN*) oven; (*TEC*) furnace; (*para cerámica*) kiln; ~ **microondas** microwave (oven); **alto** ~ blast furnace; ~ **crematorio** crematorium.

horóscopo [o'roskopo] *nm* horoscope.

horquilla [or'kiʎa] *nf* hairpin; (*AGR*) pitchfork.

horrendo, a [o'rrendo, a] *adj* horrendous,

frightful.

horrible [o'rriβle] *adj* horrible, dreadful.

horripilante [orripi'lante] *adj* hair-raising, horrifying.

horripilar [orripi'lar] *vt*: ~ **a algn** to horrify sb; **~se** *vr* to be horrified.

horror [o'rror] *nm* horror, dread; (*atrocidad*) atrocity; ¡**qué** ~! (*fam*) how awful!; **estudia horrores** he studies a hell of a lot.

horrorice [orro'riθe] *etc vb V* **horrorizar.**

horrorizar [orrori'θar] *vt* to horrify, frighten; **~se** *vr* to be horrified.

horroroso, a [orro'roso, a] *adj* horrifying, ghastly.

hortaliza [orta'liθa] *nf* vegetable.

hortelano, a [orte'lano, a] *nm/f* (market) gardener.

hortera [or'tera] *adj* (*fam*) vulgar, naff.

horterada [orte'raða] *nf* (*fam*): **es una** ~ it's really naff.

hortícola [or'tikola] *adj* horticultural.

horticultura [ortikul'tura] *nf* horticulture.

hortofrutícola [ortofru'tikola] *adj* fruit and vegetable *cpd*.

hosco, a ['osko, a] *adj* dark; (*persona*) sullen, gloomy.

hospedaje [ospe'ðaxe] *nm* (cost of) board and lodging.

hospedar [ospe'ðar] *vt* to put up; **~se** *vr*: **~se (con/en)** to stay *o* lodge (with/at).

hospedería [ospeðe'ria] *nf* (*edificio*) inn; (*habitación*) guest room.

hospicio [os'piθjo] *nm* (*para niños*) orphanage.

hospital [ospi'tal] *nm* hospital.

hospitalario, a [ospita'larjo, a] *adj* (*acogedor*) hospitable.

hospitalice [ospita'liθe] *etc vb V* **hospitalizar.**

hospitalidad [ospitali'ðað] *nf* hospitality.

hospitalizar [ospitali'θar] *vt* to send *o* take to hospital, hospitalize.

hosquedad [oske'ðað] *nf* sullenness.

hostal [os'tal] *nm* small hotel; *V tb* **hotel.**

hostelería [ostele'ria] *nf* hotel business *o* trade.

hostia ['ostja] *nf* (*REL*) host, consecrated wafer; (*fam: golpe*) whack, punch ♦ *excl*: ¡**~(s)!** (*fam!*) damn!

hostigar [osti'ɣar] *vt* to whip; (*fig*) to harass, pester.

hostigue [os'tiɣe] *etc vb V* **hostigar.**

hostil [os'til] *adj* hostile.

hostilidad [ostili'ðað] *nf* hostility.

hotel [o'tel] *nm* hotel.

In Spain you can choose from the following categories of accommodation, in descending order of quality and price: **hotel** (*from 5 stars to 1*), **hostal, pensión, casa de huéspedes, fonda**. Quality can vary widely even within these categories. The State also runs luxury hotels called **paradores**, which are usually sited in places of particular historical interest and are often historic buildings themselves.

---

hotelero, a [ote'lero, a] *adj* hotel *cpd* ♦ *nm/f* hotelier.

hoy [oi] *adv* (*este día*) today; (*en la actualidad*) now(adays) ♦ *nm* present time; ~ (**en**) **día** now(adays); **el día de** ~, ~ **día** (*AM*) this very day; ~ **por** ~ right now; **de** ~ **en ocho días** a week today; **de** ~ **en adelante** from now on.

hoya ['oja] *nf* pit; (*sepulcro*) grave; (*GEO*) valley.

hoyo ['ojo] *nm* hole, pit; (*tumba*) grave; (*GOLF*) hole; (*MED*) pockmark.

hoyuelo [oj'welo] *nm* dimple.

hoz [oθ] *nf* sickle.

hube ['uβe] *etc vb V* **haber.**

hucha ['utʃa] *nf* money box.

hueco, a ['weko, a] *adj* (*vacío*) hollow, empty; (*resonante*) booming; (*sonido*) resonant; (*persona*) conceited; (*estilo*) pompous ♦ *nm* hollow, cavity; (*agujero*) hole; (*de escalera*) well; (*de ascensor*) shaft; (*vacante*) vacancy; ~ **de la mano** hollow of the hand.

huela ['wela] *etc vb V* **oler.**

huelga ['welɣa] *etc vb V* **holgar** ♦ *nf* strike; **declararse en** ~ to go on strike, come out on strike; ~ **general** general strike; ~ **de hambre** hunger strike; ~ **oficial** official strike.

huelgue ['welɣe] *etc vb V* **holgar.**

huelguista [wel'ɣista] *nm/f* striker.

huella ['weʎa] *nf* (*acto de pisar, pisada*) tread(ing); (*marca del paso*) footprint, footstep; (: *de animal, máquina*) track; ~ **digital** fingerprint; **sin dejar** ~ without leaving a trace.

huérfano, a ['werfano, a] *adj* orphan(ed); (*fig*) unprotected ♦ *nm/f* orphan.

huerta ['werta] *nf* market garden (*BRIT*), truck farm (*US*); (*Murcia, Valencia*) irrigated region.

huerto ['werto] *nm* kitchen garden; (*de árboles frutales*) orchard.

hueso ['weso] *nm* (*ANAT*) bone; (*de fruta*) stone, pit (*US*); **sin** ~ (*carne*) boned; **estar en los ~s** to be nothing but skin and bone; **ser un** ~ (*profesor*) to be terribly strict; **un** ~ **duro de roer** a hard nut to crack.

huesoso, a [we'soso, a] *adj* (*esp AM*) bony.

huésped, a ['wespeð, a] *nm/f* (*invitado*) guest; (*habitante*) resident; (*anfitrión*) host(ess).

huesudo, a [we'suðo, a] *adj* bony, bigboned.

huevas ['weßas] *nfpl* eggs, roe *sg*; (*AM: fam!*) balls (*!*).

huevera [we'ßera] *nf* eggcup.

huevo ['weßo] *nm* egg; (*fam!*) ball (*!*), testicle; ~ **duro/escalfado/estrellado** *o* **frito/pasado por agua** hard-boiled/poached/fried/soft-boiled egg; ~**s revueltos** scrambled eggs; **me costó un** ~ (*fam!*) it was hard work; **tener** ~**s** (*fam!*) to have guts.

huevón, ona [we'ßon, ona] *nm/f* (*AM fam!*) stupid bastard (*!*), stupid idiot.

huida [u'iða] *nf* escape, flight; ~ **de capitales** (*COM*) flight of capital.

huidizo, a [ui'ðiθo, a] *adj* (*tímido*) shy; (*pasajero*) fleeting.

huir [u'ir] *vt* (*escapar*) to flee, escape; (*evadir*) to avoid ♦ *vi* to flee, run away; ~**se** *vr* (*escaparse*) to escape.

hule ['ule] *nm* (*encerado*) oilskin; (*esp AM*) rubber.

hulla ['uʎa] *nf* bituminous coal.

humanice [uma'niθe] *etc vb V* **humanizar.**

humanidad [umani'ðað] *nf* (*género humano*) man(kind); (*cualidad*) humanity; (*fam: gordura*) corpulence.

humanitario, a [umani'tarjo, a] *adj* humanitarian; (*benévolo*) humane.

humanizar [umani'θar] *vt* to humanize; ~**se** *vr* to become more human.

humano, a [u'mano, a] *adj* (*gen*) human; (*humanitario*) humane ♦ *nm* human; **ser** ~ human being.

humareda [uma'reða] *nf* cloud of smoke.

humeante [ume'ante] *adj* smoking, smoky.

humedad [ume'ðað] *nf* (*del clima*) humidity; (*de pared etc*) dampness; **a prueba de** ~ damp-proof.

humedecer [umeðe'θer] *vt* to moisten, wet; ~**se** *vr* to get wet.

humedezca [ume'ðeθka] *etc vb V* **humedecer.**

húmedo, a ['umeðo, a] *adj* (*mojado*) damp, wet; (*tiempo etc*) humid.

humildad [umil'dað] *nf* humility, humbleness.

humilde [u'milde] *adj* humble, modest; (*clase etc*) low, modest.

humillación [umiʎa'θjon] *nf* humiliation.

humillante [umi'ʎante] *adj* humiliating.

humillar [umi'ʎar] *vt* to humiliate; ~**se** *vr* to humble o.s., grovel.

humo ['umo] *nm* (*de fuego*) smoke; (*gas nocivo*) fumes *pl*; (*vapor*) steam, vapour; ~**s** *nmpl* (*fig*) conceit *sg*; **irse todo en** ~ (*fig*) to vanish without trace; **bajar los** ~**s a algn** to take sb down a peg or two.

humor [u'mor] *nm* (*disposición*) mood, temper; (*lo que divierte*) humour; **de buen/mal** ~ in a good/bad mood.

humorismo [umo'rismo] *nm* humour.

humorista [umo'rista] *nm/f* comic.

humorístico, a [umo'ristiko, a] *adj* funny, humorous.

hundimiento [undi'mjento] *nm* (*gen*) sinking; (*colapso*) collapse.

hundir [un'dir] *vt* to sink; (*edificio, plan*) to ruin, destroy; ~**se** *vr* to sink, collapse; (*fig: arruinarse*) to be ruined; (*desaparecer*) to disappear; **se hundió la economía** the economy collapsed; **se hundieron los precios** prices slumped.

húngaro, a ['ungaro, a] *adj, nm/f* Hungarian ♦ *nm* (*LING*) Hungarian, Magyar.

Hungría [un'gria] *nf* Hungary.

huracán [ura'kan] *nm* hurricane.

huraño, a [u'rano, a] *adj* shy; (*antisocial*) unsociable.

hurgar [ur'ɣar] *vt* to poke, jab; (*remover*) to stir (up); ~**se** *vr*: ~**se (las narices)** to pick one's nose.

hurgonear [urɣone'ar] *vt* to poke.

hurgue ['urɣe] *etc vb V* **hurgar.**

hurón [u'ron] *nm* (*ZOOL*) ferret.

hurra ['urra] *excl* hurray!, hurrah!

hurtadillas [urta'ðiʎas]: **a** ~ *adv* stealthily, on the sly.

hurtar [ur'tar] *vt* to steal; ~**se** *vr* to hide, keep out of the way.

hurto ['urto] *nm* theft, stealing; (*lo robado*) (piece of) stolen property, loot.

husmear [usme'ar] *vt* (*oler*) to sniff out, scent; (*fam*) to pry into ♦ *vi* to smell bad.

huso ['uso] *nm* (*TEC*) spindle; (*de torno*) drum.

huy ['ui] *excl* (*dolor*) ow!, ouch!; (*sorpresa*) well!; (*alivio*) phew!; ¡~, **perdona!** oops, sorry!

huyendo [u'jendo] *etc vb V* **huir.**

I i

I, i [i] nf (letra) I, i; **I de Inés** I for Isaac (BRIT) o Item (US).

I.A. abr = **inteligencia artificial**.

iba ['iβa] etc vb V **ir**.

Iberia [i'βerja] nf Iberia.

ibérico, a [i'βeriko, a] adj Iberian; **la Península ibérica** the Iberian Peninsula.

ibero, a [i'βero, a], **íbero, a** ['iβero, a] adj, nm/f Iberian.

iberoamericano, a [iβeroameri'kano, a] adj, nm/f Latin American.

íbice ['iβiθe] nm ibex.

ibicenco, a [iβi'θenko, a] adj of o from Ibiza ♦ nm/f native o inhabitant of Ibiza.

Ibiza [i'βiθa] nf Ibiza.

ice ['iθe] etc vb V **izar**.

iceberg [iθe'ber] nm iceberg.

ICONA [i'kona] nm abr (ESP) = Instituto Nacional para la Conservación de la Naturaleza.

icono [i'kono] nm (tb INFORM) icon.

iconoclasta [ikono'klasta] adj iconoclastic ♦ nm/f iconoclast.

ictericia [ikte'riθja] nf jaundice.

íd. abr = **ídem**.

I+D abr (= Investigación y Desarrollo) R&D.

ida ['iða] nf going, departure; ~ **y vuelta** round trip, return; ~**s y venidas** comings and goings.

IDE [iðe] nf abr (= Iniciativa de Defensa Estratégica) SDI.

idea [i'ðea] nf idea; (impresión) opinion; (propósito) intention; ~ **genial** brilliant idea; **a mala** ~ out of spite; **no tengo la menor** ~ I haven't a clue.

ideal [iðe'al] adj, nm ideal.

idealice [iðea'liθe] etc vb V **idealizar**.

idealista [iðea'lista] adj idealistic ♦ nm/f idealist.

idealizar [iðeali'θar] vt to idealize.

idear [iðe'ar] vt to think up; (aparato) to invent; (viaje) to plan.

ídem ['iðem] pron ditto.

idéntico, a [i'ðentiko, a] adj identical.

identidad [iðenti'ðað] nf identity; ~ **corporativa** corporate identity o image.

identificación [iðentifika'θjon] nf identification.

identificar [iðentifi'kar] vt to identify; ~**se** vr: ~**se con** to identify with.

identifique [iðenti'fike] etc vb V **identificar**.

ideología [iðeolo'xia] nf ideology.

ideológico, a [iðeo'loxiko, a] adj ideological.

idílico, a [i'ðiliko, a] adj idyllic.

idilio [i'ðiljo] nm love affair.

idioma [i'ðjoma] nm language.

idiomático, a [iðjo'matiko, a] adj idiomatic.

idiota [i'ðjota] adj idiotic ♦ nm/f idiot.

idiotez [iðjo'teθ] nf idiocy.

idolatrar [iðola'trar] vt (fig) to idolize.

ídolo ['iðolo] nm (tb fig) idol.

idoneidad [iðonei'ðað] nf suitability; (capacidad) aptitude.

idóneo, a [i'ðoneo, a] adj suitable.

iglesia [i'ɣlesja] nf church; ~ **parroquial** parish church; ¡**con la** ~ **hemos topado!** now we're really up against it!

iglú [i'ɣlu] nm igloo; (contenedor) bottle bank.

ignición [iɣni'θjon] nf ignition.

ignominia [iɣno'minja] nf ignominy.

ignominioso, a [iɣnomi'njoso, a] adj ignominious.

ignorado, a [iɣno'raðo, a] adj unknown; (dato) obscure.

ignorancia [iɣno'ranθja] nf ignorance; **por** ~ through ignorance.

ignorante [iɣno'rante] adj ignorant, uninformed ♦ nm/f ignoramus.

ignorar [iɣno'rar] vt not to know, be ignorant of; (no hacer caso a) to ignore; **ignoramos su paradero** we don't know his whereabouts.

ignoto, a [iɣ'noto, a] adj unknown.

igual [i'ɣwal] adj equal; (similar) like, similar; (mismo) (the) same; (constante) constant; (temperatura) even ♦ nm/f equal; **al** ~ **que** prep, conj like, just like; ~ **que** the same as; **sin** ~ peerless; **me da** o **es** ~ I don't care, it makes no difference; **no tener** ~ to be unrivalled; **son** ~**es** they're the same.

iguala [i'ɣwala] nf equalization; (COM) agreement.

igualada [iɣwa'laða] nf equalizer.

igualar [iɣwa'lar] vt (gen) to equalize, make equal; (terreno) to make even; (COM) to agree upon; ~**se** vr (platos de balanza) to balance out; ~**se (a)** (equivaler) to be equal (to).

igualdad [iɣwal'dað] nf equality; (similaridad) sameness; (uniformidad) uniformity; **en** ~ **de condiciones** on an equal basis.

igualmente [iɣwal'mente] adv equally; (también) also, likewise ♦ excl the same to you!

iguana [i'ɣwana] nf iguana.

ikurriña [iku'rriɲa] nf Basque flag.

ilegal [ile'ɣal] adj illegal.

ilegitimidad [ilexitimi'ðað] nf illegitimacy.

ilegítimo, a [ile'xitimo, a] adj illegitimate.

ileso, a [i'leso, a] adj unhurt, unharmed.

ilícito, a [i'liθito, a] adj illicit.

ilimitado, a [ilimi'taðo, a] adj unlimited.

Ilma., Ilmo. abr (= Ilustrísima, Ilustrísimo) courtesy title.

ilógico, a [i'loxiko, a] adj illogical.

iluminación [ilumina'θjon] nf illumination; (alumbrado) lighting; (fig) enlightenment.

iluminar [ilumi'nar] vt to illuminate, light (up); (fig) to enlighten.

ilusión [ilu'sjon] nf illusion; (quimera) delusion; (esperanza) hope; (emoción) excitement, thrill; **hacerse ilusiones** to build up one's hopes; **no te hagas ilusiones** don't build up your hopes o get too excited.

ilusionado, a [ilusjo'naðo, a] adj excited.

ilusionar [ilusjo'nar] vt: ~ **a algn** (falsamente) to build up sb's hopes; **~se** vr (falsamente) to build up one's hopes; (entusiasmarse) to get excited; **me ilusiona mucho el viaje** I'm really excited about the trip.

ilusionista [ilusjo'nista] nmf conjurer.

iluso, a [i'luso, a] adj gullible, easily deceived ♦ nmf dreamer, visionary.

ilusorio, a [ilu'sorjo, a] adj (de ilusión) illusory, deceptive; (esperanza) vain.

ilustración [ilustra'θjon] nf illustration; (saber) learning, erudition; **la I~** the Enlightenment.

ilustrado, a [ilus'traðo, a] adj illustrated; learned.

ilustrar [ilus'trar] vt to illustrate; (instruir) to instruct; (explicar) to explain, make clear; **~se** vr to acquire knowledge.

ilustre [i'lustre] adj famous, illustrious.

imagen [i'maxen] nf (gen) image; (dibujo, TV) picture; (REL) statue; **ser la viva ~ de** to be the spitting o living image of; **a su ~** in one's own image.

imaginación [imaxina'θjon] nf imagination; (fig) fancy; **ni por ~** on no account; **no se me pasó por la ~ que ...** it never even occurred to me that ....

imaginar [imaxi'nar] vt (gen) to imagine; (idear) to think up; (suponer) to suppose; **~se** vr to imagine; **¡imagínate!** just imagine!, just fancy!; **imagínese que ...**

suppose that ...; **me imagino que sí** I should think so.

imaginario, a [imaxi'narjo, a] adj imaginary.

imaginativo, a [imaxina'tiβo, a] adj imaginative ♦ nf imagination.

imán [i'man] nm magnet.

iman(t)ar [ima'n(t)ar] vt to magnetize.

imbécil [im'beθil] nmf imbecile, idiot.

imbecilidad [imbeθili'ðað] nf imbecility, stupidity.

imberbe [im'berβe] adj beardless.

imborrable [imbo'rraβle] adj indelible; (inolvidable) unforgettable.

imbuir [imbu'ir] vt to imbue.

imbuyendo [imbu'jendo] etc vb V imbuir.

imitación [imita'θjon] nf imitation; (parodia) mimicry; **a ~ de** in imitation of; **desconfíe de las imitaciones** (COM) beware of copies o imitations.

imitador, a [imita'ðor, a] adj imitative ♦ nmf imitator; (TEAT) mimic.

imitar [imi'tar] vt to imitate; (parodiar, remedar) to mimic, ape; (copiar) to follow.

impaciencia [impa'θjenθja] nf impatience.

impacientar [impaθjen'tar] vt to make impatient; (enfadar) to irritate; **~se** vr to get impatient; (inquietarse) to fret.

impaciente [impa'θjente] adj impatient; (nervioso) anxious.

impacto [im'pakto] nm impact; (esp AM: fig) shock.

impagado, a [impa'ɣaðo, a] adj unpaid, still to be paid.

impar [im'par] adj odd ♦ nm odd number.

imparable [impa'raβle] adj unstoppable.

imparcial [impar'θjal] adj impartial, fair.

imparcialidad [imparθjali'ðað] nf impartiality, fairness.

impartir [impar'tir] vt to impart, give.

impasible [impa'siβle] adj impassive.

impávido, a [im'paβiðo, a] adj fearless, intrepid.

IMPE ['impe] nm abr (ESP COM) = Instituto de la Mediana y Pequeña Empresa.

impecable [impe'kaβle] adj impeccable.

impedido, a [impe'ðiðo, a] adj: **estar ~ to** be an invalid ♦ nmf: **ser un ~ físico** to be an invalid.

impedimento [impeði'mento] nm impediment, obstacle.

impedir [impe'ðir] vt (obstruir) to impede, obstruct; (estorbar) to prevent; **~ el tráfico** to block the traffic.

impeler [impe'ler] vt to drive, propel; (fig) to impel.

impenetrabilidad [impenetraβili'ðað] nf

(*imprudencia*) indiscretion; (*irreflexión*)
tactlessness; (*acto*) gaffe, faux pas; ..., **si
no es** ~ ..., if I may say so.
indiscreto, a [indis'kreto, a] *adj* indiscreet.
indiscriminado, a [indiskrimi'naðo, a] *adj*
indiscriminate.
indiscutible [indisku'tiβle] *adj*
indisputable, unquestionable.
indispensable [indispen'saβle] *adj*
indispensable.
indispondré [indispon'dre] *etc vb V*
indisponer.
indisponer [indispo'ner] *vt* to spoil, upset;
(*salud*) to make ill; ~**se** *vr* to fall ill; ~**se
con algn** to fall out with sb.
indisponga [indis'ponga] *etc vb V*
indisponer.
indisposición [indisposi'θjon] *nf*
indisposition; (*desgana*) unwillingness.
indispuesto, a [indis'pwesto, a] *pp de*
indisponer ♦ *adj* indisposed; **sentirse** ~ to
feel unwell *o* indisposed.
indispuse [indis'puse] *etc vb V* **indisponer.**
indistinto, a [indis'tinto, a] *adj* indistinct;
(*vago*) vague.
individual [indiβi'ðwal] *adj* individual;
(*habitación*) single ♦ *nm* (*DEPORTE*) singles
sg.
individuo, a [indi'βiðwo, a] *adj* individual
♦ *nm* individual.
Indochina [indo'tʃina] *nf* Indochina.
indocumentado, a [indokumen'taðo, a]
adj without identity papers.
indoeuropeo, a [indoeuro'peo, a] *adj, nm/f*
Indo-European.
índole ['indole] *nf* (*naturaleza*) nature;
(*clase*) sort, kind.
indolencia [indo'lenθja] *nf* indolence,
laziness.
indoloro, a [in'doloro, a] *adj* painless.
indomable [indo'maβle] *adj* (*animal*)
untameable; (*espíritu*) indomitable.
indómito, a [in'domito, a] *adj* indomitable.
Indonesia [indo'nesja] *nf* Indonesia.
indonesio, a [indo'nesjo, a] *adj, nm/f*
Indonesian.
inducción [induk'θjon] *nf* (*FILOSOFÍA, ELEC*)
induction; **por** ~ by induction.
inducir [indu'θir] *vt* to induce; (*inferir*) to
infer; (*persuadir*) to persuade; ~ **a algn
en el error** to mislead sb.
indudable [indu'ðaβle] *adj* undoubted;
(*incuestionable*) unquestionable; **es** ~ **que**
... there is no doubt that ....
indulgencia [indul'xenθja] *nf* indulgence;
(*JUR etc*) leniency; **proceder sin** ~ **contra**
to proceed ruthlessly against.
indultar [indul'tar] *vt* (*perdonar*) to pardon,

reprieve; (*librar de pago*) to exempt.
indulto [in'dulto] *nm* pardon; exemption.
indumentaria [indumen'tarja] *nf* (*ropa*)
clothing, dress.
industria [in'dustrja] *nf* industry;
(*habilidad*) skill; ~ **agropecuaria** farming
and fishing; ~ **pesada** heavy industry; ~
petrolífera oil industry.
industrial [indus'trjal] *adj* industrial ♦ *nm*
industrialist.
industrializar [industrjali'θar] *vt* to
industrialize; ~**se** *vr* to become
industrialized.
INE ['ine] *nm abr* (*ESP*) = *Instituto Nacional
de Estadística.*
inédito, a [i'neðito, a] *adj* (*libro*)
unpublished; (*nuevo*) unheard-of.
inefable [ine'faβle] *adj* ineffable,
indescribable.
ineficacia [inefi'kaθja] *nf* (*de medida*)
ineffectiveness; (*de proceso*)
inefficiency.
ineficaz [inefi'kaθ] *adj* (*inútil*) ineffective;
(*ineficiente*) inefficient.
ineludible [inelu'ðiβle] *adj* inescapable,
unavoidable.
INEM, Inem [i'nem] *nm abr* (*ESP*. = *Instituto
Nacional de Empleo*) ≈ Department of
Employment (*BRIT*).
INEN ['inen] *nm abr* (*México*) = *Instituto
Nacional de Energía Nuclear.*
inenarrable [inena'rraβle] *adj*
inexpressible.
ineptitud [inepti'tuð] *nf* ineptitude,
incompetence.
inepto, a [i'nepto, a] *adj* inept,
incompetent.
inequívoco, a [ine'kiβoko, a] *adj*
unequivocal; (*inconfundible*)
unmistakable.
inercia [i'nerθja] *nf* inertia; (*pasividad*)
passivity.
inerme [i'nerme] *adj* (*sin armas*) unarmed;
(*indefenso*) defenceless.
inerte [i'nerte] *adj* inert; (*inmóvil*)
motionless.
inescrutable [ineskru'taβle] *adj*
inscrutable.
inesperado, a [inespe'raðo, a] *adj*
unexpected, unforeseen.
inestable [ines'taβle] *adj* unstable.
inestimable [inesti'maβle] *adj* inestimable;
de valor ~ invaluable.
inevitable [ineβi'taβle] *adj* inevitable.
inexactitud [ineksakti'tuð] *nf* inaccuracy.
inexacto, a [inek'sakto, a] *adj* inaccurate;
(*falso*) untrue.
inexistente [ineksis'tente] *adj* non-

existent.
inexorable [inekso'raβle] *adj* inexorable.
inexperiencia [inekspe'rjenθja] *nf*
inexperience, lack of experience.
inexperto, a [ineks'perto, a] *adj* (*novato*)
inexperienced.
inexplicable [inekspli'kaβle] *adj*
inexplicable.
inexpresable [inekspre'saβle] *adj*
inexpressible.
inexpresivo, a [inekspre'siβo, a] *adj*
inexpressive; (*ojos*) dull; (*cara*) wooden.
inexpugnable [inekspuɣ'naβle] *adj* (*MIL*)
impregnable; (*fig*) firm.
infalible [infa'liβle] *adj* infallible;
(*indefectible*) certain, sure; (*plan*)
foolproof.
infame [in'fame] *adj* infamous.
infamia [in'famja] *nf* infamy; (*deshonra*)
disgrace.
infancia [in'fanθja] *nf* infancy, childhood;
jardín de la ~ nursery school.
infanta [in'fanta] *nf* (*hija del rey*) infanta,
princess.
infante [in'fante] *nm* (*hijo del rey*) infante,
prince.
infantería [infante'ria] *nf* infantry.
infantil [infan'til] *adj* child's, children's;
(*pueril, aniñado*) infantile; (*cándido*)
childlike.
infarto [in'farto] *nm* (*tb:* ~ **de miocardio**)
heart attack.
infatigable [infati'ɣaβle] *adj* tireless,
untiring.
infección [infek'θjon] *nf* infection.
infeccioso, a [infek'θjoso, a] *adj*
infectious.
infectar [infek'tar] *vt* to infect; ~**se** *vr:* ~**se**
(**de**) (*tb fig*) to become infected (with).
infecundidad [infekundi'ðað] *nf* (*de tierra*)
infertility, barrenness; (*de mujer*)
sterility.
infecundo, a [infe'kundo, a] *adj* infertile,
barren; sterile.
infeliz [infe'liθ] *adj* (*desgraciado*) unhappy,
wretched; (*inocente*) gullible ♦ *nm/f*
(*desgraciado*) wretch; (*inocentón*)
simpleton.
inferior [infe'rjor] *adj* inferior; (*situación,*
MAT) lower ♦ *nm/f* inferior, subordinate;
cualquier número ~ **a 9** any number less
than *o* under *o* below 9; **una cantidad** ~ a
lesser quantity.
inferioridad [inferjori'ðað] *nf* inferiority;
estar en ~ **de condiciones** to be at a
disadvantage.
inferir [infe'rir] *vt* (*deducir*) to infer,
deduce; (*causar*) to cause.

infernal [infer'nal] *adj* infernal.
infértil [in'fertil] *adj* infertile.
infestar [infes'tar] *vt* to infest.
infidelidad [infiðeli'ðað] *nf* (*gen*) infidelity,
unfaithfulness.
infiel [in'fjel] *adj* unfaithful, disloyal;
(*falso*) inaccurate ♦ *nm/f* infidel,
unbeliever.
infiera [in'fjera] *etc vb* V **inferir**.
infierno [in'fjerno] *nm* hell; **¡vete al** ~**!** go
to hell; **está en el quinto** ~ it's at the
back of beyond.
infiltrar [infil'trar] *vt* to infiltrate; ~**se** *vr* to
infiltrate, filter; (*líquidos*) to percolate.
ínfimo, a ['infimo, a] *adj* (*vil*) vile, mean;
(*más bajo*) lowest; (*peor*) worst;
(*miserable*) wretched.
infinidad [infini'ðað] *nf* infinity;
(*abundancia*) great quantity; ~ **de** vast
numbers of; ~ **de veces** countless times.
infinitivo [infini'tiβo] *nm* infinitive.
infinito, a [infi'nito, a] *adj* infinite; (*fig*)
boundless ♦ *adv* infinitely ♦ *nm* infinite;
(*MAT*) infinity; **hasta lo** ~ ad infinitum.
infiriendo [infi'rjendo] *etc vb* V **inferir**.
inflación [infla'θjon] *nf* (*hinchazón*)
swelling; (*monetaria*) inflation; (*fig*)
conceit.
inflacionario, a [inflaθjo'narjo, a] *adj*
inflationary.
inflacionismo [inflaθjo'nismo] *nm* (*ECON*)
inflation.
inflacionista [inflaθjo'nista] *adj*
inflationary.
inflamar [infla'mar] *vt* to set on fire; (*MED,*
fig) to inflame; ~**se** *vr* to catch fire; to
become inflamed.
inflar [in'flar] *vt* (*hinchar*) to inflate, blow
up; (*fig*) to exaggerate; ~**se** *vr* to swell
(up); (*fig*) to get conceited.
inflexible [inflek'siβle] *adj* inflexible; (*fig*)
unbending.
infligir [infli'xir] *vt* to inflict.
inflija [in'flixa] *etc vb* V **infligir**.
influencia [in'flwenθja] *nf* influence.
influenciar [inflwen'θjar] *vt* to influence.
influir [influ'ir] *vt* to influence ♦ *vi* to have
influence, carry weight; ~ **en** *o* **sobre** to
influence, affect; (*contribuir a*) to have a
hand in.
influjo [in'fluxo] *nm* influence; ~ **de**
capitales (*ECON etc*) capital influx.
influyendo [influ'jendo] *etc vb* V **influir**.
influyente [influ'jente] *adj* influential.
información [informa'θjon] *nf*
information; (*noticias*) news *sg*; (*informe*)
report; (*INFORM: datos*) data; (*JUR*)
inquiry; **I**~ (*oficina*) Information; (*TELEC*)

Directory Enquiries (*BRIT*), Directory Assistance (*US*); (*mostrador*) Information Desk; **una** ~ a piece of information; **abrir una** ~ (*JUR*) to begin proceedings; ~ **deportiva** (*en periódico*) sports section.

informal [infor'mal] *adj* (*gen*) informal.

informante [infor'mante] *nm/f* informant.

informar [infor'mar] *vt* (*gen*) to inform; (*revelar*) to reveal, make known ♦ *vi* (*JUR*) to plead; (*denunciar*) to inform; (*dar cuenta de*) to report on; ~**se** *vr* to find out; ~**se de** to inquire into.

informática [infor'matika] *nf* V **informático**.

informatice [informa'tiθe] *etc vb* V **informatizar**.

informático, a [infor'matiko, a] *adj* computer *cpd* ♦ *nf* (*TEC*) information technology; computing; (*ESCOL*) computer science *o* studies; ~ **de gestión** commercial computing.

informativo, a [informa'tiβo, a] *adj* (*libro*) informative; (*folleto*) information *cpd*; (*RADIO, TV*) news *cpd* ♦ *nm* (*RADIO, TV*) news programme.

informatización [informatiθa'θjon] *nf* computerization.

informatizar [informati'θar] *vt* to computerize.

informe [in'forme] *adj* shapeless ♦ *nm* report; (*dictamen*) statement; (*MIL*) briefing; (*JUR*) plea; ~**s** *nmpl* information *sg*; (*datos*) data; ~ **anual** annual report; ~ **del juez** summing-up.

infortunio [infor'tunjo] *nm* misfortune.

infracción [infrak'θjon] *nf* infraction, infringement; (*AUTO*) offence.

infraestructura [infraestruk'tura] *nf* infrastructure.

in fraganti [infra'ɣanti] *adv*: **pillar a algn** ~ to catch sb red-handed.

infranqueable [infranke'aβle] *adj* impassable; (*fig*) insurmountable.

infrarrojo, a [infra'rroxo, a] *adj* infrared.

infravalorar [infraβalo'rar] *vt* to undervalue; (*FIN*) to underestimate.

infringir [infrin'xir] *vt* to infringe, contravene.

infrinja [in'frinxa] *etc vb* V **infringir**.

infructuoso, a [infruk'twoso, a] *adj* fruitless, unsuccessful.

infundado, a [infun'daðo, a] *adj* groundless, unfounded.

infundir [infun'dir] *vt* to infuse, instil; ~ **ánimo a algn** to encourage sb; ~ **miedo a algn** to intimidate sb.

infusión [infu'sjon] *nf* infusion; ~ **de manzanilla** camomile tea.

Ing. *abr* = **Ingeniero**.

ingeniar [inxe'njar] *vt* to think up, devise; ~**se** *vr* to manage; ~**se para** to manage to.

ingeniería [inxenje'ria] *nf* engineering; ~ **genética** genetic engineering; ~ **de sistemas** (*INFORM*) systems engineering.

ingeniero, a [inxe'njero, a] *nm/f* engineer; ~ **de sonido** sound engineer; ~ **de caminos** civil engineer.

ingenio [in'xenjo] *nm* (*talento*) talent; (*agudeza*) wit; (*habilidad*) ingenuity, inventiveness; (*TEC*): ~ **azucarero** sugar refinery.

ingenioso, a [inxe'njoso, a] *adj* ingenious, clever; (*divertido*) witty.

ingente [in'xente] *adj* huge, enormous.

ingenuidad [inxenwi'ðað] *nf* ingenuousness; (*sencillez*) simplicity.

ingenuo, a [in'xenwo, a] *adj* ingenuous.

ingerir [inxe'rir] *vt* to ingest; (*tragar*) to swallow; (*consumir*) to consume.

ingiera [in'xjera] *etc*, **ingiriendo** [inxi'rjenðo] *etc vb* V **ingerir**.

Inglaterra [ingla'terra] *nf* England.

ingle ['ingle] *nf* groin.

inglés, esa [in'gles, esa] *adj* English ♦ *nm/f* Englishman/woman ♦ *nm* (*LING*) English; **los ingleses** the English.

ingratitud [ingrati'tuð] *nf* ingratitude.

ingrato, a [in'grato, a] *adj* ungrateful; (*tarea*) thankless.

ingravidez [ingraβi'ðeθ] *nf* weightlessness.

ingrediente [ingre'ðjente] *nm* ingredient; ~**s** *nmpl* (*AM: tapas*) titbits.

ingresar [ingre'sar] *vt* (*dinero*) to deposit ♦ *vi* to come *o* go in; ~ **a** (*esp AM*) to enter; ~ **en** (*club*) to join; (*MIL, ESCOL*) to enrol in; ~ **en el hospital** to go into hospital.

ingreso [in'greso] *nm* (*entrada*) entry; (: *en hospital etc*) admission; (*MIL, ESCOL*) enrolment; ~**s** *nmpl* (*dinero*) income *sg*; (: *COM*) takings *pl*; ~ **gravable** taxable income *sg*; ~**s accesorios** fringe benefits; ~**s brutos** gross receipts; ~**s devengados** earned income *sg*; ~**s exentos de impuestos** non-taxable income *sg*; ~**s personales disponibles** disposable personal income *sg*.

íngrimo, a ['ingrimo, a] *adj* (*AM*: tb ~ **y solo**) all alone.

inhábil [i'naβil] *adj* unskilful, clumsy.

inhabilitar [inaβili'tar] *vt* (*POL, MED*): ~ **a algn (para hacer algo)** to disqualify sb (from doing sth).

inhabitable [inaβi'taβle] *adj* uninhabitable.

inhabituado, a [inaβi'twaðo, a] *adj* unaccustomed.

inhalador [inala'ðor] *nm* (*MED*) inhaler.
inhalar [ina'lar] *vt* to inhale.
inherente [ine'rente] *adj* inherent.
inhibición [iniβi'θjon] *nf* inhibition.
inhibir [ini'βir] *vt* to inhibit; (*REL*) to restrain; ~**se** *vr* to keep out.
inhospitalario, a [inospita'larjo, a], **inhóspito, a** [i'nospito, a] *adj* inhospitable.
inhumación [inuma'θjon] *nf* burial, interment.
inhumano, a [inu'mano, a] *adj* inhuman.
INI ['ini] *nm abr* = **Instituto Nacional de Industria.**
inicial [ini'θjal] *adj, nf* initial.
inicialice [iniθja'liθe] *etc vb V* **inicializar.**
inicializar [iniθjali'θar] *vt* (*INFORM*) to initialize.
iniciar [ini'θjar] *vt* (*persona*) to initiate; (*empezar*) to begin, commence; (*conversación*) to start up; ~ **a algn en un secreto** to let sb into a secret; ~ **la sesión** (*INFORM*) to log in *o* on.
iniciativa [iniθja'tiβa] *nf* initiative; (*liderazgo*) leadership; **la ~ privada** private enterprise.
inicio [i'niθjo] *nm* start, beginning.
inicuo, a [i'nikwo, a] *adj* iniquitous.
inigualado, a [iniɣwa'laðo, a] *adj* unequalled.
ininteligible [ininteli'xiβle] *adj* unintelligible.
ininterrumpido, a [ininterrum'piðo, a] *adj* uninterrupted; (*proceso*) continuous; (*progreso*) steady.
injerencia [inxe'renθja] *nf* interference.
injertar [inxer'tar] *vt* to graft.
injerto [in'xerto] *nm* graft; ~ **de piel** skin graft.
injuria [in'xurja] *nf* (*agravio, ofensa*) offence; (*insulto*) insult; ~**s** *nfpl* abuse *sg*.
injuriar [inxu'rjar] *vt* to insult.
injurioso, a [inxu'rjoso, a] *adj* offensive; insulting.
injusticia [inxus'tiθja] *nf* injustice, unfairness; **con ~** unjustly.
injusto, a [in'xusto, a] *adj* unjust, unfair.
inmaculado, a [inmaku'laðo, a] *adj* immaculate, spotless.
inmadurez [inmaðu'reθ] *nf* immaturity.
inmaduro, a [inma'ðuro, a] *adj* immature; (*fruta*) unripe.
inmediaciones [inmeðja'θjones] *nfpl* neighbourhood *sg*, environs.
inmediatez [inmeðja'teθ] *nf* immediacy.
inmediato, a [inme'ðjato, a] *adj* immediate; (*contiguo*) adjoining; (*rápido*) prompt; (*próximo*) neighbouring, next;

de ~ (*esp AM*) immediately.
inmejorable [inmexo'raβle] *adj* unsurpassable; (*precio*) unbeatable.
inmemorable [inmemo'raβle], **inmemorial** [inmemo'rjal] *adj* immemorial.
inmenso, a [in'menso, a] *adj* immense, huge.
inmerecido, a [inmere'θiðo, a] *adj* undeserved.
inmersión [inmer'sjon] *nf* immersion; (*buzo*) dive.
inmigración [inmiɣra'θjon] *nf* immigration.
inmigrante [inmi'ɣrante] *adj, nm/f* immigrant.
inminente [inmi'nente] *adj* imminent, impending.
inmiscuirse [inmisku'irse] *vr* to interfere, meddle.
inmiscuyendo [inmisku'jendo] *etc vb V* **inmiscuirse.**
inmobiliario, a [inmoβi'ljarjo, a] *adj* real-estate *cpd*, property *cpd* ♦ *nf* estate agency.
inmolar [inmo'lar] *vt* to immolate, sacrifice.
inmoral [inmo'ral] *adj* immoral.
inmortal [inmor'tal] *adj* immortal.
inmortalice [inmorta'liθe] *etc vb V* **inmortalizar.**
inmortalizar [inmortali'θar] *vt* to immortalize.
inmotivado, a [inmoti'βaðo, a] *adj* motiveless; (*sospecha*) groundless.
inmóvil [in'moβil] *adj* immobile.
inmovilizar [inmoβili'θar] *vt* to immobilize; (*paralizar*) to paralyse; ~**se** *vr*: **se le ha inmovilizado la pierna** her leg was paralysed.
inmueble [in'mweβle] *adj*: **bienes ~s** real estate *sg*, landed property *sg* ♦ *nm* property.
inmundicia [inmun'diθja] *nf* filth.
inmundo, a [in'mundo, a] *adj* filthy.
inmune [in'mune] *adj* (*MED*) immune.
inmunidad [inmuni'ðað] *nf* immunity; (*fisco*) exemption; ~ **diplomática/ parlamentaria** diplomatic/parliamentary immunity.
inmunitario, a [inmuni'tarjo, a] *adj*: **sistema ~** immune system.
inmunización [inmuniθa'θjon] *nf* immunization.
inmunizar [inmuni'θar] *vt* to immunize.
inmutable [inmu'taβle] *adj* immutable; **permaneció ~** he didn't flinch.
inmutarse [inmu'tarse] *vr*: **siguió sin ~** he

carried on unperturbed.
innato, a [in'nato, a] *adj* innate.
innecesario, a [inneθe'sarjo, a] *adj* unnecessary.
innegable [inne'ɣaßle] *adj* undeniable.
innoble [in'noßle] *adj* ignoble.
innovación [innoßa'θjon] *nf* innovation.
innovador, a [innoßa'ðor, a] *adj* innovatory, innovative ♦ *nm/f* innovator.
innovar [inno'ßar] *vt* to introduce.
innumerable [innume'raßle] *adj* countless.
inocencia [ino'θenθja] *nf* innocence.
inocentada [inoθen'taða] *nf* practical joke.
inocente [ino'θente] *adj* (*ingenuo*) naive, innocent; (*inculpable*) innocent; (*sin malicia*) harmless ♦ *nm/f* simpleton; **día de los (Santos) I~s** ≈ April Fool's Day.

The 28th December, **el día de los (Santos) Inocentes,** *is when the Church commemorates the story of Herod's slaughter of the innocent children of Judea in the time of Christ. On this day Spaniards play* **inocentadas** *(practical jokes) on each other, much like our April Fools' Day pranks, eg typically sticking a* **monigote** *(cut-out paper figure) on someone's back, or broadcasting unlikely news stories.*

---

inocuidad [inokwi'ðað] *nf* harmlessness.
inocular [inoku'lar] *vt* to inoculate.
inocuo, a [i'nokwo, a] *adj* (*sustancia*) harmless.
inodoro, a [ino'ðoro, a] *adj* odourless ♦ *nm* toilet (*BRIT*), lavatory (*BRIT*), washroom (*US*).
inofensivo, a [inofen'sißo, a] *adj* inoffensive.
inolvidable [inolßi'ðaßle] *adj* unforgettable.
inoperante [inope'rante] *adj* ineffective.
inopinado, a [inopi'naðo, a] *adj* ineffective.
inoportuno, a [inopor'tuno, a] *adj* untimely; (*molesto*) inconvenient; (*inapropiado*) inappropriate.
inoxidable [inoksi'ðaßle] *adj* stainless; **acero ~** stainless steel.
inquebrantable [inkeßran'taßle] *adj* unbreakable; (*fig*) unshakeable.
inquiera [in'kjera] *etc vb V* **inquirir**.
inquietante [inkje'tante] *adj* worrying.
inquietar [inkje'tar] *vt* to worry, trouble; **~se** *vr* to worry, get upset.
inquieto, a [in'kjeto, a] *adj* anxious, worried; **estar ~ por** to be worried about.
inquietud [inkje'tuð] *nf* anxiety, worry.

inquilino, a [inki'lino, a] *nm/f* tenant; (*COM*) lessee.
inquina [in'kina] *nf* (*aversión*) dislike; (*rencor*) ill will; **tener ~ a algn** to have a grudge against sb.
inquiriendo [inki'rjendo] *etc vb V* **inquirir**.
inquirir [inki'rir] *vt* to enquire into, investigate.
insaciable [insa'θjaßle] *adj* insatiable.
insalubre [insa'lußre] *adj* unhealthy; (*condiciones*) insanitary.
INSALUD [insa'luð] *nm abr* (*ESP*) = *Instituto Nacional de la Salud.*
insano, a [in'sano, a] *adj* (*loco*) insane; (*malsano*) unhealthy.
insatisfacción [insatisfak'θjon] *nf* dissatisfaction.
insatisfecho, a [insatis'fetʃo, a] *adj* (*condición*) unsatisfied; (*estado de ánimo*) dissatisfied.
inscribir [inskri'ßir] *vt* to inscribe; (*en lista*) to put; (*en censo*) to register; **~se** *vr* to register; (*ESCOL etc*) to enrol.
inscripción [inskrip'θjon] *nf* inscription; (*ESCOL etc*) enrolment; (*en censo*) registration.
inscrito [ins'krito] *pp de* **inscribir**.
insecticida [insekti'θiða] *nm* insecticide.
insecto [in'sekto] *nm* insect.
inseguridad [inseɣuri'ðað] *nf* insecurity.
inseguro, a [inse'ɣuro, a] *adj* insecure; (*inconstante*) unsteady; (*incierto*) uncertain.
inseminación [insemina'θjon] *nf:* **~ artificial** artificial insemination (A.I.).
inseminar [insemi'nar] *vt* to inseminate, fertilize.
insensato, a [insen'sato, a] *adj* foolish, stupid.
insensibilice [insensißi'liθe] *etc vb V* **insensibilizar**.
insensibilidad [insensißili'ðað] *nf* (*gen*) insensitivity; (*dureza de corazón*) callousness.
insensibilizar [insensißili'θar] *vt* to desensitize; (*MED*) to anaesthetize (*BRIT*), anesthetize (*US*); (*eufemismo*) to knock out *o* unconscious.
insensible [insen'sißle] *adj* (*gen*) insensitive; (*movimiento*) imperceptible; (*sin sentido*) numb.
inseparable [insepa'raßle] *adj* inseparable.
INSERSO [in'serso] *nm abr* (= *Instituto Nacional de Servicios Sociales*) *branch of social services.*
insertar [inser'tar] *vt* to insert.
inservible [inser'ßißle] *adj* useless.
insidioso, a [insi'ðjoso, a] *adj* insidious.

insigne [in'siɣne] *adj* distinguished;
(*famoso*) notable.
insignia [in'siɣnja] *nf* (*señal distintivo*)
badge; (*estandarte*) flag.
insignificante [insiɣnifi'kante] *adj*
insignificant.
insinuar [insi'nwar] *vt* to insinuate, imply;
~**se** *vr*: ~**se con algn** to ingratiate o.s.
with sb.
insípido, a [in'sipiðo, a] *adj* insipid.
insistencia [insis'tenθja] *nf* insistence.
insistir [insis'tir] *vi* to insist; ~ **en algo** to
insist on sth; (*enfatizar*) to stress sth.
in situ [in'situ] *adv* on the spot, in situ.
insobornable [insoβor'naβle] *adj*
incorruptible.
insociable [inso'θjaβle] *adj* unsociable.
insolación [insola'θjon] *nf* (*MED*)
sunstroke.
insolencia [inso'lenθja] *nf* insolence.
insolente [inso'lente] *adj* insolent.
insólito, a [in'solito, a] *adj* unusual.
insoluble [inso'luβle] *adj* insoluble.
insolvencia [insol'βenθja] *nf* insolvency.
insomne [in'somne] *adj* sleepless ♦ *nm/f*
insomniac.
insomnio [in'somnjo] *nm* insomnia.
insondable [inson'daβle] *adj* bottomless.
insonorización [insonoriθa'θjon] *nf*
soundproofing.
insonorizado, a [insonori'θaðo, a] *adj*
(*cuarto etc*) soundproof.
insoportable [insopor'taβle] *adj*
unbearable.
insoslayable [insosla'jaβle] *adj*
unavoidable.
insospechado, a [insospe'tʃaðo, a] *adj*
(*inesperado*) unexpected.
insostenible [insoste'niβle] *adj* untenable.
inspección [inspek'θjon] *nf* inspection,
check; I~ inspectorate; ~ **técnica (de**
vehículos) ≈ MOT (test) (*BRIT*).
inspeccionar [inspekθjo'nar] *vt* (*examinar*)
to inspect, examine; (*controlar*) to check;
(*INFORM*) to peek.
inspector, a [inspek'tor, a] *nm/f* inspector.
inspectorado [inspekto'raðo] *nm*
inspectorate.
inspiración [inspira'θjon] *nf* inspiration.
inspirador, a [inspira'ðor, a] *adj* inspiring.
inspirar [inspi'rar] *vt* to inspire; (*MED*) to
inhale; ~**se** *vr*: ~**se en** to be inspired by.
instalación [instala'θjon] *nf* (*equipo*)
fittings *pl*, equipment; ~ **eléctrica** wiring.
instalar [insta'lar] *vt* (*establecer*) to instal;
(*erguir*) to set up, erect; ~**se** *vr* to
establish o.s.; (*en una vivienda*) to move
into.

instancia [ins'tanθja] *nf* (*solicitud*)
application; (*ruego*) request; (*JUR*)
petition; **a** ~ **de** at the request of; **en**
última ~ in the last resort.
instantáneo, a [instan'taneo, a] *adj*
instantaneous ♦ *nf* snap(shot); **café** ~
instant coffee.
instante [ins'tante] *nm* instant, moment;
en un ~ in a flash.
instar [ins'tar] *vt* to press, urge.
instaurar [instau'rar] *vt* (*establecer*) to
establish, set up.
instigador, a [instiɣa'ðor, a] *nm/f*
instigator; ~ **de un delito** (*JUR*)
accessory before the fact.
instigar [insti'ɣar] *vt* to instigate.
instigue [ins'tiɣe] *etc vb V* **instigar**.
instintivo, a [instin'tiβo, a] *adj* instinctive.
instinto [ins'tinto] *nm* instinct; **por** ~
instinctively.
institución [institu'θjon] *nf* institution,
establishment; ~ **benéfica** charitable
foundation.
instituir [institu'ir] *vt* to establish; (*fundar*)
to found.
instituto [insti'tuto] *nm* (*gen*) institute; I~
Nacional de Enseñanza (*ESP*) ≈ comprehensive (*BRIT*) o high (*US*) school; I~
Nacional de Industria (INI) (*ESP COM*)
≈ National Enterprise Board (*BRIT*) .
institutriz [institu'triθ] *nf* governess.
instituyendo [institu'jendo] *etc vb V*
instituir.
instrucción [instruk'θjon] *nf* instruction;
(*enseñanza*) education, teaching; (*JUR*)
proceedings *pl*; (*MIL*) training; (*DEPORTE*)
coaching; (*conocimientos*) knowledge;
(*INFORM*) statement; **instrucciones para**
el uso directions for use; **instrucciones**
de funcionamiento operating
instructions.
instructivo, a [instruk'tiβo, a] *adj*
instructive.
instruir [instru'ir] *vt* (*gen*) to instruct;
(*enseñar*) to teach, educate; (*JUR:*
proceso) to prepare, draw up; ~**se** *vr* to
learn, teach o.s.
instrumento [instru'mento] *nm* (*gen*, *MUS*)
instrument; (*herramienta*) tool,
implement; (*COM*) indenture; (*JUR*) legal
document; ~ **de percusión/cuerda/**
viento percussion/string(ed)/wind
instrument.
instruyendo [instru'jendo] *etc vb V*
instruir.
insubordinarse [insuβorði'narse] *vr* to
rebel.
insuficiencia [insufi'θjenθja] *nf* (*carencia*)

car!; (*desprecio*) that's a terrible car!;
¡**vaya!** (*regular*) so so; (*desagrado*) come
on!; ¡**vamos!** come on!; ¡**que le vaya
bien!** (*adiós*) take care!
**8: no vaya a ser: tienes que correr, no
vaya a ser que pierdas el tren** you'll have
to run so as not to miss the train
9: no me *etc* **va ni me viene** I *etc* don't
care
♦ *vb aux* **1:** ~ **a: voy/iba a hacerlo hoy** I
am/was going to do it today
2 (+*gerundio*): **iba anocheciendo** it was
getting dark; **todo se me iba aclarando**
everything was gradually becoming
clearer to me
3 (+*pp = pasivo*): **van vendidos 300
ejemplares** 300 copies have been sold so
far
♦ ~**se** *vr* **1:** ¿**por dónde se va al
zoológico?** which is the way to the zoo?
2 (*marcharse*) to leave; **ya se habrán ido**
they must already have left *o* gone;
¡**vámonos!**, (*AM*) ¡**nos fuimos!** let's go!;
¡**vete!** go away!; ¡**vete a saber!** your
guess is as good as mine!, who knows!

ira ['ira] *nf* anger, rage.
iracundo, a [ira'kundo, a] *adj* irascible.
Irak [i'rak] *nm* = **Iraq**.
Irán [i'ran] *nm* Iran.
iraní [ira'ni] *adj*, *nm/f* Iranian.
Iraq [i'rak] *nm* Iraq.
iraquí [ira'ki] *adj*, *nm/f* Iraqui.
irascible [iras'θiβle] *adj* irascible.
irguiendo [ir'xjendo] *etc vb V* **erguir**.
iris ['iris] *nm inv* (*arco* ~) rainbow; (*ANAT*)
iris.
Irlanda [ir'landa] *nf* Ireland; ~ **del Norte**
Northern Ireland, Ulster.
irlandés, esa [irlan'des, esa] *adj* Irish
♦ *nm/f* Irishman/woman ♦ *nm* (*LING*)
Gaelic, Irish; **los irlandeses** *npl* the Irish.
ironía [iro'nia] *nf* irony.
irónico, a [i'roniko, a] *adj* ironic(al).
IRPF *nm abr* (*ESP*) = **impuesto sobre la renta
de las personas físicas**.
irracional [irraθjo'nal] *adj* irrational.
irrazonable [irraθo'naβle] *adj*
unreasonable.
irreal [irre'al] *adj* unreal.
irrealizable [irreali'θaβle] *adj* (*gen*)
unrealizable; (*meta*) unrealistic.
irrebatible [irreβa'tiβle] *adj* irrefutable.
irreconocible [irrekono'θiβle] *adj*
unrecognizable.
irrecuperable [irrekupe'raβle] *adj*
irrecoverable, irretrievable.
irreembolsable [irreembol'saβle] *adj* (*COM*)

non-returnable.
irreflexión [irreflek'sjon] *nf*
thoughtlessness; (*ímpetu*) rashness.
irregular [irreɣu'lar] *adj* irregular;
(*situación*) abnormal, anomalous; **margen
izquierdo/derecho** ~ (*texto*) ragged left/
right (margin).
irregularidad [irreɣulari'ðað] *nf*
irregularity.
irremediable [irreme'ðjaβle] *adj*
irremediable; (*vicio*) incurable.
irreprochable [irrepro'tʃaβle] *adj*
irreproachable.
irresistible [irresis'tiβle] *adj* irresistible.
irresoluto, a [irreso'luto, a] *adj* irresolute,
hesitant; (*sin resolver*) unresolved.
irrespetuoso, a [irrespe'twoso, a] *adj*
disrespectful.
irresponsable [irrespon'saβle] *adj*
irresponsible.
irreverente [irreβe'rente] *adj*
disrespectful.
irreversible [irreβer'siβle] *adj* irreversible.
irrevocable [irreβo'kaβle] *adj* irrevocable.
irrigar [irri'ɣar] *vt* to irrigate.
irrigue [i'rriɣe] *etc vb V* **irrigar**.
irrisorio, a [irri'sorjo, a] *adj* derisory,
ridiculous; (*precio*) bargain *cpd*.
irritación [irrita'θjon] *nf* irritation.
irritar [irri'tar] *vt* to irritate, annoy; ~**se** *vr*
to get angry, lose one's temper.
irrompible [irrom'piβle] *adj* unbreakable.
irrumpir [irrum'pir] *vi:* ~ **en** to burst *o* rush
into.
irrupción [irrup'θjon] *nf* irruption;
(*invasión*) invasion.
IRTP *nm abr* (*ESP*) = **impuesto sobre el
rendimiento del trabajo personal**) ≈ PAYE.
isla ['isla] *nf* (*GEO*) island; **I~s Británicas**
British Isles; **I~s Filipinas/Malvinas/
Canarias** Philippines/Falklands/
Canaries.
Islam [is'lam] *nm* Islam.
islámico, a [is'lamiko, a] *adj* Islamic.
islandés, esa [islan'des, esa] *adj* Icelandic
♦ *nm/f* Icelander ♦ *nm* (*LING*) Icelandic.
Islandia [is'landja] *nf* Iceland.
isleño, a [is'leɲo, a] *adj* island *cpd* ♦ *nm/f*
islander.
islote [is'lote] *nm* small island.
isotónico, a [iso'toniko, a] *adj* isotonic.
isótopo [i'sotopo] *nm* isotope.
Israel [isra'el] *nm* Israel.
israelí [israe'li] *adj*, *nm/f* Israeli.
istmo ['istmo] *nm* isthmus; **el I~ de
Panamá** the Isthmus of Panama.
Italia [i'talja] *nf* Italy.
italiano, a [ita'ljano, a] *adj*, *nm/f* Italian

♦ *nm* (*LING*) Italian.
itinerante [itine'rante] *adj* travelling; (*embajador*) roving.
itinerario [itine'rarjo] *nm* itinerary, route.
ITV *nf abr* (= *Inspección Técnica de Vehículos*) ≈ MOT (test) (*BRIT*).
IVA ['iβa] *nm abr* (*ESP COM*: = *Impuesto sobre el Valor Añadido*) VAT.
IVP *nm abr* = *Instituto Venezolano de Petroquímica*.
izada [i'saða] *nf* (*AM*) lifting, raising.
izar [i'θar] *vt* to hoist.
izda, izq.ᵃ *abr* = **izquierda**.
izdo, izq, izq.º *abr* = **izquierdo**.
izquierda [iθ'kjerða] *nf* V **izquierdo**.
izquierdista [iθkjer'ðista] *adj* leftist, left-wing ♦ *nm/f* left-winger, leftist.
izquierdo, a [iθ'kjerðo, a] *adj* left ♦ *nf* left; (*POL*) left (wing); **a la ~** on the left; **es un cero a la ~** (*fam*) he is a nonentity; **conducción por la ~** left-hand drive.

J j

J, j ['xota] *nf* (*letra*) J, j; **J de José** J for Jack (*BRIT*) *o* Jig (*US*).
jabalí [xaβa'li] *nm* wild boar.
jabalina [xaβa'lina] *nf* javelin.
jabato, a [xa'βato, a] *adj* brave, bold ♦ *nm* young wild boar.
jabón [xa'βon] *nm* soap; (*fam: adulación*) flattery; **~ de afeitar** shaving soap; **~ de tocador** toilet soap; **dar ~ a algn** to soft-soap sb.
jabonar [xaβo'nar] *vt* to soap.
jaca ['xaka] *nf* pony.
jacinto [xa'θinto] *nm* hyacinth.
jactancia [xak'tanθja] *nf* boasting, boastfulness.
jactarse [xak'tarse] *vr*: **~ (de)** to boast *o* brag (about *o* of).
jadear [xaðe'ar] *vi* to pant, gasp for breath.
jadeo [xa'ðeo] *nm* panting, gasping.
jaguar [xa'ɣwar] *nm* jaguar.
jalar [xa'lar] *vt* (*AM*) to pull.
jalbegue [xal'βeɣe] *nm* (*pintura*) whitewash.
jalea [xa'lea] *nf* jelly.
jaleo [xa'leo] *nm* racket, uproar; **armar un ~** to kick up a racket.

jalón [xa'lon] *nm* (*AM*) tug.
jalonar [xalo'nar] *vt* to stake out; (*fig*) to mark.
Jamaica [xa'maika] *nf* Jamaica.
jamaicano, a [xamai'kano, a] *adj, nm/f* Jamaican.
jamás [xa'mas] *adv* never, not ... ever; (*interrogativo*) ever; **¿~ se vio tal cosa?** did you ever see such a thing?
jamón [xa'mon] *nm* ham; **~ dulce/serrano** boiled/cured ham.
Japón [xa'pon] *nm*: **el ~** Japan.
japonés, esa [xapo'nes, esa] *adj, nm/f* Japanese ♦ *nm* (*LING*) Japanese.
jaque ['xake] *nm*: **~ mate** checkmate.
jaqueca [xa'keka] *nf* (very bad) headache, migraine.
jarabe [xa'raβe] *nm* syrup; **~ para la tos** cough syrup *o* mixture.
jarana [xa'rana] *nf* (*juerga*) spree (*fam*); **andar/ir de ~** to be/go on a spree.
jarcia ['xarθja] *nf* (*NAUT*) ropes *pl*, rigging.
jardín [xar'ðin] *nm* garden; **~ botánico** botanical garden; **~ de (la) infancia** (*ESP*) *o* **de niños** (*AM*) *o* **infantil** (*AM*) kindergarten, nursery school.
jardinería [xarðine'ria] *nf* gardening.
jardinero, a [xarði'nero, a] *nm/f* gardener.
jarra ['xarra] *nf* jar; (*jarro*) jug; (*de leche*) churn; (*de cerveza*) mug; **de *o* en ~s** with arms akimbo.
jarro ['xarro] *nm* jug.
jarrón [xa'rron] *nm* vase; (*ARQUEOLOGÍA*) urn.
jaspeado, a [xaspe'aðo, a] *adj* mottled, speckled.
jaula ['xaula] *nf* cage; (*embalaje*) crate.
jauría [xau'ria] *nf* pack of hounds.
jazmín [xaθ'min] *nm* jasmine.
J. C. *abr* = **Jesucristo**.
jeep [jip] *pl* **jeeps** ® [jip, jips] *nm* jeep ®.
jefa ['xefa] *nf* V **jefe**.
jefatura [xefa'tura] *nf* (*liderato*) leadership; (*sede*) central office; **J~ de la aviación civil** ≈ Civil Aviation Authority; **~ de policía** police headquarters *sg*.
jefazo [xe'faθo] *nm* bigwig.
jefe, a ['xefe, a] *nm/f* (*gen*) chief, head; (*patrón*) boss; (*POL*) leader; (*COM*) manager(ess); **~ de camareros** head waiter; **~ de cocina** chef; **~ ejecutivo** (*COM*) chief executive; **~ de estación** stationmaster; **~ de estado** head of state; **~ de oficina** (*COM*) office manager; **~ de producción** (*COM*) production manager; **~ supremo** commander-in-chief; **ser el ~** (*fig*) to be the boss.
JEN [xen] *nf abr* (*ESP*) = *Junta de Energía*

Nuclear.

jengibre [xen'xiβre] *nm* ginger.

jeque ['xeke] *nm* sheik(h).

jerarquía [xerar'kia] *nf (orden)* hierarchy; *(rango)* rank.

jerárquico, a [xe'rarkiko, a] *adj* hierarchic(al).

jerez [xe'reθ] *nm* sherry; **J~ de la Frontera** Jerez.

jerezano, a [xere'θano, a] *adj* of *o* from Jerez ♦ *nm/f* native *o* inhabitant of Jerez.

jerga ['xerɣa] *nf (tela)* coarse cloth; *(lenguaje)* jargon; **~ informática** computer jargon.

jerigonza [xeri'ɣonθa] *nf (jerga)* jargon, slang; *(galimatías)* nonsense, gibberish.

jeringa [xe'ringa] *nf* syringe; *(AM)* annoyance, bother; **~ de engrase** grease gun.

jeringar [xerin'gar] *vt* to annoy, bother.

jeringue [xe'ringe] *etc vb* V **jeringar**.

jeringuilla [xerin'guiʎa] *nf* hypodermic (syringe).

jeroglífico [xero'ɣlifiko] *nm* hieroglyphic.

jersey [xer'sei], *pl* **jerseys** *nm* jersey, pullover, jumper.

Jerusalén [xerusa'len] *n* Jerusalem.

Jesucristo [xesu'kristo] *nm* Jesus Christ.

jesuita [xe'swita] *adj, nm* Jesuit.

Jesús [xe'sus] *nm* Jesus; ¡~! good heavens!; *(al estornudar)* bless you!

jet, *pl* **jets** [jet, jet] *nm* jet (plane) ♦ *nf*: **la ~** the jet set.

jeta ['xeta] *nf (ZOOL)* snout; *(fam: cara)* mug; ¡**que ~ tienes!** *(fam: insolencia)* you've got a nerve!

jíbaro, a ['xiβaro, a] *adj, nm/f* Jíbaro (Indian).

jícara ['xikara] *nf* small cup.

jiennense [xjen'nense] *adj* of *o* from Jaén ♦ *nm/f* native *o* inhabitant of Jaén.

jilguero [xil'ɣero] *nm* goldfinch.

jinete, a [xi'nete, a] *nm/f* horseman/woman.

jipijapa [xipi'xapa] *nm (AM)* straw hat.

jira ['xira] *nf (de tela)* strip; *(excursión)* picnic.

jirafa [xi'rafa] *nf* giraffe.

jirón [xi'ron] *nm* rag, shred.

JJ.OO. *nmpl abr* = **Juegos Olímpicos**.

jocosidad [xokosi'ðað] *nf* humour; *(chiste)* joke.

jocoso, a [xo'koso, a] *adj* humorous, jocular.

joder [xo'ðer] *(fam!)* *vt* to fuck *(!)*, screw *(!)*; *(fig: fastidiar)* to piss off *(!)*, bug; **~se** *vr (fracasar)* to fail; ¡~! damn it!; **se jodió todo** everything was ruined.

jodido, a [xo'ðiðo, a] *adj (fam!: difícil)*

awkward; **estoy ~** I'm knackered *o* buggered *(!)*.

jofaina [xo'faina] *nf* washbasin.

jojoba [xo'xoβa] *nf* jojoba.

jolgorio [xol'ɣorjo] *nm (juerga)* fun, revelry.

jonrón [xon'ron] *nm* home run.

Jordania [xor'ðanja] *nf* Jordan.

jornada [xor'naða] *nf (viaje de un día)* day's journey; *(camino o viaje entero)* journey; *(día de trabajo)* working day; **~ de 8 horas** 8-hour day; **(trabajar a) ~ partida** (to work a) split shift.

jornal [xor'nal] *nm* (day's) wage.

jornalero, a [xorna'lero, a] *nm/f* (day) labourer.

joroba [xo'roβa] *nf* hump.

jorobado, a [xoro'βaðo, a] *adj* hunchbacked ♦ *nm/f* hunchback.

jorobar [xoro'βar] *vt* to annoy, pester, bother; **~se** *vr* to get cross; ¡**hay que ~se!** to hell with it!; **esto me joroba** I'm fed up with this!

jota ['xota] *nf* letter J; *(danza)* Aragonese dance; *(fam)* jot, iota; **no saber ~** to have no idea.

joven ['xoβen] *adj* young ♦ *nm* young man, youth ♦ *nf* young woman, girl.

jovencito, a [xoβen'θito, a] *nm/f* youngster.

jovial [xo'βjal] *adj* cheerful, jolly.

jovialidad [xoβjali'ðað] *nf* cheerfulness, jolliness.

joya ['xoja] *nf* jewel, gem; *(fig: persona)* gem; **~s de fantasía** imitation jewellery *sg*.

joyería [xoje'ria] *nf (joyas)* jewellery; *(tienda)* jeweller's (shop).

joyero [xo'jero] *nm (persona)* jeweller; *(caja)* jewel case.

The **Noche de San Juan** *(evening of the Feast of Saint John) on the 24th June is a* **fiesta** *coinciding with the summer solstice, and which has taken the place of other ancient pagan festivals. Traditionally fire plays a major part in these festivities, which can last for days in certain areas. Celebrations and dancing take place around* **hogueras** *(bonfires) in towns and villages across the country.*

---

juanete [xwa'nete] *nm (del pie)* bunion.

jubilación [xuβila'θjon] *nf (retiro)* retirement.

jubilado, a [xuβi'lado, a] *adj* retired ♦ *nm/f* retired person, pensioner *(BRIT)*, senior citizen.

jubilar [xuβi'lar] *vt* to pension off, retire;

(*fam*) to discard; ~**se** *vr* to retire.
jubileo [xuβi'leo] *nm* jubilee.
júbilo ['xuβilo] *nm* joy, rejoicing.
jubiloso, a [xuβi'loso, a] *adj* jubilant.
judaísmo [xuða'ismo] *nm* Judaism.
judía [xu'ðia] *nf V* **judío**.
judicatura [xuðika'tura] *nf* (*cargo de juez*) office of judge; (*cuerpo de jueces*) judiciary.
judicial [xuði'θjal] *adj* judicial.
judío, a [xu'ðio, a] *adj* Jewish ♦ *nm* Jew ♦ *nf* Jewess, Jewish woman; (*CULIN*) bean; **judía blanca** haricot bean; **judía verde** French *o* string bean.
juego ['xweɣo] *etc vb V* **jugar** ♦ *nm* (*gen*) play; (*pasatiempo, partido*) game; (*en casino*) gambling; (*deporte*) sport; (*conjunto*) set; (*herramientas*) kit; ~ **de azar** game of chance; ~ **de café** coffee set; ~ **de caracteres** (*INFORM*) font; ~ **limpio/sucio** fair/foul *o* dirty play; **J~s Olímpicos** Olympic Games; ~ **de programas** (*INFORM*) suite of programs; **fuera de** ~ (*DEPORTE: persona*) offside; (: *pelota*) out of play; **por** ~ in fun, for fun.
juegue ['xweɣe] *etc vb V* **jugar**.
juerga ['xwerɣa] *nf* binge; (*fiesta*) party; **ir de** ~ to go out on a binge.
juerguista [xwer'ɣista] *nm/f* reveller.
jueves ['xweβes] *nm inv* Thursday.
juez [xweθ] *nm/f* (*f tb:* **jueza**) judge; (*TENIS*) umpire; ~ **de línea** linesman; ~ **de paz** justice of the peace; ~ **de salida** starter.
jugada [xu'ɣaða] *nf* play; **buena** ~ good move (*o* shot *o* stroke) *etc*.
jugador, a [xuɣa'ðor, a] *nm/f* player; (*en casino*) gambler.
jugar [xu'ɣar] *vt* to play; (*en casino*) to gamble; (*apostar*) to bet ♦ *vi* to play; to gamble; (*COM*) to speculate; ~**se** *vr* to gamble (away); ~**se el todo por el todo** to stake one's all, to go for bust; **¿quién juega?** whose move is it?; **¡me la han jugado!** (*fam*) I've been had!
jugarreta [xuɣa'rreta] *nf* (*mala jugada*) bad move; (*trampa*) dirty trick; **hacer una** ~ **a algn** to play a dirty trick on sb.
juglar [xu'ɣlar] *nm* minstrel.
jugo ['xuɣo] *nm* (*BOT, de fruta*) juice; (*fig*) essence, substance; ~ **de naranja** (*esp AM*) orange juice.
jugoso, a [xu'ɣoso, a] *adj* juicy; (*fig*) substantial, important.
jugué [xu'ɣe], **juguemos** [xu'ɣemos] *etc vb V* **jugar**.
juguete [xu'ɣete] *nm* toy.
juguetear [xuɣete'ar] *vi* to play.
juguetería [xuɣete'ria] *nf* toyshop.

juguetón, ona [xuɣe'ton, ona] *adj* playful.
juicio ['xwiθjo] *nm* judgement; (*sana razón*) sanity, reason; (*opinión*) opinion; (*JUR: proceso*) trial; **estar fuera de** ~ to be out of one's mind; **a mi** ~ in my opinion.
juicioso, a [xwi'θjoso, a] *adj* wise, sensible.
JUJEM [xu'xem] *nf abr* (*ESP MIL*) = *Junta de Jefes del Estado Mayor*.
jul. *abr* (= *julio*) Jul.
julio ['xuljo] *nm* July.
jumento, a [xu'mento, a] *nm/f* donkey.
jun. *abr* (= *junio*) Jun.
junco ['xunko] *nm* rush, reed.
jungla ['xungla] *nf* jungle.
junio ['xunjo] *nm* June.
junta ['xunta] *nf V* **junto**.
juntar [xun'tar] *vt* to join, unite; (*maquinaria*) to assemble, put together; (*dinero*) to collect; ~**se** *vr* to join, meet; (*reunirse: personas*) to meet, assemble; (*arrimarse*) to approach, draw closer; ~**se con algn** to join sb.
junto, a ['xunto, a] *adj* joined; (*unido*) united; (*anexo*) near, close; (*contiguo, próximo*) next, adjacent ♦ *nf* (*asamblea*) meeting, assembly; (*comité, consejo*) board, council, committee; (*MIL, POL*) junta; (*articulación*) joint ♦ *adv*: **todo** ~ all at once ♦ *prep*: ~ **a** near (to), next to; ~**s** together; **junta constitutiva** (*COM*) statutory meeting; **junta directiva** (*COM*) board of management; **junta general extraordinaria** (*COM*) extraordinary general meeting.
juntura [xun'tura] *nf* (*punto de unión*) join, junction; (*articulación*) joint.
jura ['xura] *nf* oath, pledge; ~ **de bandera** (ceremony of taking the) oath of allegiance.
jurado [xu'raðo] *nm* (*JUR: individuo*) juror; (: *grupo*) jury; (*de concurso: grupo*) panel (of judges); (: *individuo*) member of a panel.
juramentar [xuramen'tar] *vt* to swear in, administer the oath to; ~**se** *vr* to be sworn in, take the oath.
juramento [xura'mento] *nm* oath; (*maldición*) oath, curse; **bajo** ~ on oath; **prestar** ~ to take the oath; **tomar** ~ **a** to swear in, administer the oath to.
jurar [xu'rar] *vt, vi* to swear; ~ **en falso** to commit perjury; **jurárselas a algn** to have it in for sb.
jurídico, a [xu'riðiko, a] *adj* legal, juridical.
jurisdicción [xurisðik'θjon] *nf* (*poder, autoridad*) jurisdiction; (*territorio*)

district.

jurisprudencia [xurispru'ðenθja] _nf_ jurisprudence.

jurista [xu'rista] _nm/f_ jurist.

justamente [xusta'mente] _adv_ justly, fairly; (_precisamente_) just, exactly.

justicia [xus'tiθja] _nf_ justice; (_equidad_) fairness, justice; **de** ~ deservedly.

justiciero, a [xusti'θjero, a] _adj_ just, righteous.

justificable [xustifi'kaßle] _adj_ justifiable.

justificación [xustifika'θjon] _nf_ justification; ~ **automática** (_INFORM_) automatic justification.

justificado, a [xustifi'kaðo, a] _adj_ (_TIP_): **(no)** ~ (un)justified.

justificante [xustifi'kante] _nm_ voucher; ~ **médico** sick note.

justificar [xustifi'kar] _vt_ (_tb TIP_) to justify; (_probar_) to verify.

justifique [xusti'fike] _etc vb_ V **justificar**.

justo, a ['xusto, a] _adj_ (_equitativo_) just, fair, right; (_preciso_) exact, correct; (_ajustado_) tight ♦ _adv_ (_precisamente_) exactly, precisely; (_apenas a tiempo_) just in time; ¡~! that's it!, correct!; **llegaste muy** ~ you just made it; **vivir muy** ~ to be hard up.

juvenil [xuße'nil] _adj_ youthful.

juventud [xußen'tuð] _nf_ (_adolescencia_) youth; (_jóvenes_) young people _pl._

juzgado [xuθ'ɣaðo] _nm_ tribunal; (_JUR_) court.

juzgar [xuθ'ɣar] _vt_ to judge; **a** ~ **por** ... to judge by ..., judging by ...; ~ **mal** to misjudge; **júzguelo usted mismo** see for yourself.

Kenia ['kenja] _nf_ Kenya.

keniata [ke'njata] _adj, nm/f_ Kenyan.

kepí, kepis [ke'pi, 'kepis] _nm_ (_esp AM_) kepi, military hat.

kerosene [kero'sene] _nm_ kerosene.

kg. _abr_ (= _kilogramo(s)_) kg.

kilate [ki'late] _nm_ = **quilate**.

kilo ['kilo] _nm_ kilo.

kilobyte ['kiloßait] _nm_ (_INFORM_) kilobyte.

kilogramo [kilo'ɣramo] _nm_ kilogramme (_BRIT_), kilogram (_US_).

kilolitro [kilo'litro] _nm_ kilolitre (_BRIT_), kiloliter (_US_).

kilometraje [kilome'traxe] _nm_ distance in kilometres, ≈ mileage.

kilométrico, a [kilo'metriko, a] _adj_ kilometric; (_fam_) very long; **(billete)** ~ (_FERRO_) mileage ticket.

kilómetro [ki'lometro] _nm_ kilometre (_BRIT_), kilometer (_US_).

kiloocteto [kilook'teto] _nm_ (_INFORM_) kilobyte.

kilovatio [kilo'ßatjo] _nm_ kilowatt.

kiosco ['kjosko] _nm_ = **quiosco**.

Kirguizistán [kirɣiθis'tan] _nm_ Kirghizia.

kiwi ['kiwi] _nm_ kiwi (fruit).

km _abr_ (= _kilómetro(s)_) km.

km/h _abr_ (= _kilómetros por hora_) km/h.

knock-out ['nokau], **K.O.** ['kao] _nm_ knockout; (_golpe_) knockout blow; **dejar** o **poner a algn** ~ to knock sb out.

k.p.h. _abr_ (= _kilómetros por hora_) km/h.

k.p.l. _abr_ (= _kilómetros por litro_) ≈ m.p.g.

kurdo, a ['kurðo, a] _adj_ Kurdish ♦ _nm/f_ Kurd ♦ _nm_ (_LING_) Kurdish.

kuwaití [kußai'ti] _adj, nm/f_ Kuwaiti.

kv _abr_ (= _kilovatio_) kw.

kv/h _abr_ (= _kilovatios-hora_) kw-h.

_Kk_

K, k [ka] _nf_ (_letra_) K, k; **K de Kilo** K for King.

K _abr_ (= _1.000_) K; (_INFORM_: = _1.024_) K.

Kampuchea [kampu'tʃea] _nf_ Kampuchea.

karaoke [kara'oke] _nm_ karaoke.

karate [ka'rate] _nm_ karate.

KAS _nf abr_ (= _Koordinadora Abertzale Sozialista_) _Basque nationalist umbrella group._

Kazajstán [kaθaxs'tan] _nm_ Kazakhstan.

k/c. _abr_ (= _kilociclos_) kc.

_Ll_

L, l ['ele] _nf_ (_letra_) L, l; **L de Lorenzo** L for Lucy (_BRIT_) o Love (_US_).

l. _abr_ (= _litro(s)_) l.; (_JUR_) = **ley**; (_LITERATURA_: = _libro_) bk.

L/ _abr_ (_COM_) = **letra**.

la [la] _artículo definido fsg_ the ♦ _pron_ her; (_usted_) you; (_cosa_) it ♦ _nm_ (_MUS_) A; **está en** ~ **cárcel** he's in jail; ~ **del sombrero rojo** the woman/girl/one in the red hat.

laberinto [laße'rinto] *nm* labyrinth.
labia ['laßja] *nf* fluency; (*pey*) glibness;
tener mucha ~ to have the gift of the
gab.
labial [la'ßjal] *adj* labial.
labio ['laßjo] *nm* lip; (*de vasija etc*) edge,
rim; ~ **inferior/superior** lower/upper lip.
labor [la'ßor] *nf* labour; (*AGR*) farm work;
(*tarea*) job, task; (*COSTURA*) needlework,
sewing; (*punto*) knitting; ~ **de equipo**
teamwork; ~ **de ganchillo** crochet.
laborable [laßo'raßle] *adj* (*AGR*) workable;
día ~ working day.
laboral [laßo'ral] *adj* (*accidente,
conflictividad*) industrial; (*jornada*)
working; (*derecho, relaciones*) labour *cpd*.
laboralista [laßora'lista] *adj*: **abogado** ~
labour lawyer.
laborar [laßo'rar] *vi* to work.
laboratorio [laßora'torjo] *nm* laboratory.
laborioso, a [laßo'rjoso, a] *a* (*persona*)
hard-working; (*trabajo*) tough.
laborista [laßo'rista] (*BRIT POL*) *adj*: **Partido
L~** Labour Party ♦ *nm/f* Labour Party
member *o* supporter.
labrado, a [la'ßraðo, a] *adj* worked;
(*madera*) carved; (*metal*) wrought ♦ *nm*
(*AGR*) cultivated field.
Labrador [laßra'ðor] *nm* Labrador.
labrador, a [laßra'ðor, a] *nm/f* farmer.
labranza [la'ßranθa] *nf* (*AGR*) cultivation.
labrar [la'ßrar] *vt* (*gen*) to work; (*madera
etc*) to carve; (*fig*) to cause, bring about.
labriego, a [la'ßrjeγo, a] *nm/f* peasant.
laca ['laka] *nf* lacquer; (*de pelo*) hairspray;
~ **de uñas** nail varnish.
lacayo [la'kajo] *nm* lackey.
lacerar [laθe'rar] *vt* to lacerate.
lacio, a [a 'laθjo, a] *adj* (*pelo*) lank, straight.
lacón [la'kon] *nm* shoulder of pork.
lacónico, a [la'koniko, a] *adj* laconic.
lacra ['lakra] *nf* (*defecto*) blemish; ~ **social**
social disgrace.
lacrar [la'krar] *vt* (*cerrar*) to seal (with
sealing wax).
lacre ['lakre] *nm* sealing wax.
lacrimógeno, a [lakri'moxeno, a] *adj* (*fig*)
sentimental; **gas** ~ tear gas.
lacrimoso, a [lakri'moso, a] *adj* tearful.
lactancia [lak'tanθja] *nf* breast-feeding.
lactar [lak'tar] *vt, vi* to suckle, breast-feed.
lácteo, a ['lakteo, a] *adj*: **productos** ~**s**
dairy products.
ladear [laðe'ar] *vt* to tip, tilt ♦ *vi* to tilt; ~**se**
vr to lean; (*DEPORTE*) to swerve; (*AVIAT*)
to bank, turn.
ladera [la'ðera] *nf* slope.
ladino, a [la'ðino, a] *adj* cunning.

lado ['laðo] *nm* (*gen*) side; (*fig*) protection;
(*MIL*) flank; ~ **izquierdo** left(-hand) side;
~ **a** ~ side by side; **al** ~ **de** next to,
beside; **hacerse a un** ~ to stand aside;
poner de ~ to put on its side; **poner a un**
~ to put aside; **me da de** ~ I don't care;
por un ~ ..., **por otro** ~ ... on the one
hand ..., on the other (hand), ...; **por
todos** ~**s** on all sides, all round (*BRIT*).
ladrar [la'ðrar] *vi* to bark.
ladrido [la'ðriðo] *nm* bark, barking.
ladrillo [la'ðriλo] *nm* (*gen*) brick; (*azulejo*)
tile.
ladrón, ona [la'ðron, ona] *nm/f* thief.
lagar [la'γar] *nm* (wine/oil) press.
lagartija [laγar'tixa] *nf* (small) lizard, wall
lizard.
lagarto [la'γarto] *nm* (*ZOOL*) lizard; (*AM*)
alligator.
lago ['laγo] *nm* lake.
Lagos ['laγos] *nm* Lagos.
lágrima ['laγrima] *nf* tear.
lagrimal [laγri'mal] *nm* (inner) corner of
the eye.
lagrimear [laγrime'ar] *vi* to weep; (*ojos*) to
water.
laguna [la'γuna] *nf* (*lago*) lagoon; (*en
escrito, conocimientos*) gap.
laico, a ['laiko, a] *adj* lay ♦ *nm/f* layman/
woman.
laja ['laxa] *nf* rock.
lamber [lam'ber] *vt* (*AM*) to lick.
lambiscón, ona [lambis'kon, ona] *adj*
flattering ♦ *nm/f* flatterer.
lameculos [lame'kulos] *nm/f inv* (*fam*)
arselicker (!), crawler.
lamentable [lamen'taßle] *adj* lamentable,
regrettable; (*miserable*) pitiful.
lamentación [lamenta'θjon] *nf*
lamentation; **ahora no sirven
lamentaciones** it's no good crying over
spilt milk.
lamentar [lamen'tar] *vt* (*sentir*) to regret;
(*deplorar*) to lament; ~**se** *vr* to lament; **lo
lamento mucho** I'm very sorry.
lamento [la'mento] *nm* lament.
lamer [la'mer] *vt* to lick.
lámina ['lamina] *nf* (*plancha delgada*) sheet;
(*para estampar, estampa*) plate; (*grabado*)
engraving.
laminar [lami'nar] *vt* (*en libro*) to laminate;
(*TEC*) to roll.
lámpara ['lampara] *nf* lamp; ~ **de alcohol/
gas** spirit/gas lamp; ~ **de pie** standard
lamp.
lamparilla [lampa'riλa] *nf* nightlight.
lamparón [lampa'ron] *nm* (*MED*) scrofula;
(*mancha*) (large) grease spot.

lampiño, a [lam'piɲo, a] *adj* (*sin pelo*) hairless.

lana ['lana] *nf* wool; (*tela*) woollen (*BRIT*) *o* woolen (*US*) cloth; (*AM fam: dinero*) dough; **(hecho) de** ~ wool *cpd*.

lance ['lanθe] *etc vb V* **lanzar** ♦ *nm* (*golpe*) stroke; (*suceso*) event, incident.

lanceta [lan'seta] *nf* (*AM*) sting.

lancha ['lantʃa] *nf* launch; ~ **motora** motorboat; ~ **de pesca** fishing boat; ~ **salvavidas/torpedera** lifeboat/torpedo boat; ~ **neumática** rubber dinghy.

lanero, a [la'nero, a] *adj* wool *cpd*.

langosta [lan'gosta] *nf* (*insecto*) locust; (*crustáceo*) lobster (: *de río*) crayfish.

langostino [langos'tino] *nm* prawn; (*de agua dulce*) crayfish.

languidecer [langiðe'θer] *vi* to languish.

languidez [langi'ðeθ] *nf* languor.

languidezca [langi'ðeθka] *etc vb V* **languidecer.**

lánguido, a ['langiðo, a] *adj* (*gen*) languid; (*sin energía*) listless.

lanilla [la'niʎa] *nf* nap; (*tela*) thin flannel cloth.

lanolina [lano'lina] *nf* lanolin(e).

lanudo, a [la'nuðo, a] *adj* woolly, fleecy.

lanza ['lanθa] *nf* (*arma*) lance, spear; **medir** ~**s** to cross swords.

lanzacohetes [lanθako'etes] *nm inv* rocket launcher.

lanzadera [lanθa'ðera] *nf* shuttle.

lanzado, a [lan'θaðo, a] *adj* (*atrevido*) forward; (*decidido*) determined; **ir** ~ (*rápido*) to fly along.

lanzallamas [lanθa'ʎamas] *nm inv* flamethrower.

lanzamiento [lanθa'mjento] *nm* (*gen*) throwing; (*NAUT, COM*) launch, launching; ~ **de pesos** putting the shot.

lanzar [lan'θar] *vt* (*gen*) to throw; (*con violencia*) to fling; (*DEPORTE: pelota*) to bowl; (: *US*) to pitch; (*NAUT, COM*) to launch; (*JUR*) to evict; (*grito*) to give, utter; ~**se** *vr* to throw o.s.; (*fig*) to take the plunge; ~**se a** (*fig*) to embark upon.

Lanzarote [lanθa'rote] *nm* Lanzarote.

lanzatorpedos [lanθator'peðos] *nm inv* torpedo tube.

lapa ['lapa] *nf* limpet.

La Paz *nf* La Paz.

lapicero [lapi'θero] *nm* pencil; (*AM*) propelling (*BRIT*) *o* mechanical (*US*) pencil; (: *bolígrafo*) Biro ®.

lápida ['lapiða] *nf* stone; ~ **conmemorativa** memorial stone; ~ **mortuoria** headstone.

lapidar [lapi'ðar] *vt* to stone; (*TEC*) to

polish, lap.

lapidario, a [lapi'ðarjo, a] *adj, nm* lapidary.

lápiz ['lapiθ] *nm* pencil; ~ **de color** coloured pencil; ~ **de labios** lipstick; ~ **óptico** *o* **luminoso** light pen.

lapón, ona [la'pon, ona] *adj* Lapp ♦ *nm/f* Laplander, Lapp ♦ *nm* (*LING*) Lapp.

Laponia [la'ponja] *nf* Lapland.

lapso ['lapso] *nm* lapse; (*error*) error; ~ **de tiempo** interval of time.

lapsus ['lapsus] *nm inv* error, mistake.

LAR [lar] *nf abr* (*ESP JUR*) = *Ley de Arrendamientos Rústicos.*

largamente [larɣa'mente] *adv* for a long time; (*relatar*) at length.

largar [lar'ɣar] *vt* (*soltar*) to release; (*aflojar*) to loosen; (*lanzar*) to launch; (*fam*) to let fly; (*velas*) to unfurl; (*AM*) to throw; ~**se** *vr* (*fam*) to beat it; ~**se a** (*AM*) to start to.

largo, a ['larɣo, a] *adj* (*longitud*) long; (*tiempo*) lengthy; (*persona: alta*) tall; (: *fig*) generous ♦ *nm* length; (*MUS*) largo; **dos años** ~**s** two long years; **a** ~ **plazo** in the long term; **tiene 9 metros de** ~ it is 9 metres long; **a lo** ~ (*posición*) lengthways; **a lo** ~ **de** along; (*tiempo*) all through, throughout; **a la larga** in the long run; **me dio largas con una promesa** she put me off with a promise; ¡~ **de aquí!** (*fam*) clear off!

largometraje [larɣome'traxe] *nm* full-length *o* feature film.

largue ['larɣe] *etc vb V* **largar.**

larguero [lar'ɣero] *nm* (*ARQ*) main beam, chief support; (*de puerta*) jamb; (*DEPORTE*) crossbar; (*en cama*) bolster.

largueza [lar'ɣeθa] *nf* generosity.

larguirucho, a [larɣi'rutʃo, a] *adj* lanky, gangling.

larguísimo, a [lar'ɣisimo, a] *adj superlativo de* **largo.**

largura [lar'ɣura] *nf* length.

laringe [la'rinxe] *nf* larynx.

laringitis [larin'xitis] *nf* laryngitis.

larva ['larβa] *nf* larva.

las [las] *artículo definido fpl* the ♦ *pron* them; ~ **que cantan** the ones/women/girls who sing.

lasaña [la'saɲa] *nf* lasagne, lasagna.

lasca ['laska] *nf* chip of stone.

lascivia [las'θiβja] *nf* lewdness; (*lujuria*) lust; (*fig*) playfulness.

lascivo, a [las'θiβo, a] *adj* lewd.

láser ['laser] *nm* laser.

Las Palmas *nf* Las Palmas.

lástima ['lastima] *nf* (*pena*) pity; **dar** ~ **to** be pitiful; **es una** ~ **que** it's a pity that;

¡qué ~! what a pity!; **estar hecho una** ~ to be a sorry sight.

lastimar [lasti'mar] vt (herir) to wound; (ofender) to offend; **~se** vr to hurt o.s.

lastimero, a [lasti'mero, a] adj pitiful, pathetic.

lastre ['lastre] nm (TEC, NAUT) ballast; (fig) dead weight.

lata ['lata] nf (metal) tin; (envase) tin, can; (fam) nuisance; **en** ~ tinned; **dar (la)** ~ to be a nuisance.

latente [la'tente] adj latent.

lateral [late'ral] adj side, lateral ♦ nm (TEAT) wings pl.

latido [la'tiðo] nm (del corazón) beat; (de herida) throb(bing).

latifundio [lati'fundjo] nm large estate.

latifundista [latifun'dista] nm/f owner of a large estate.

latigazo [lati'ɣaθo] nm (golpe) lash; (sonido) crack; (fig: regaño) dressing-down.

látigo ['latiɣo] nm whip.

latiguillo [lati'ɣiʎo] nm (TEAT) hamming.

latín [la'tin] nm Latin; **saber (mucho)** ~ (fam) to be pretty sharp.

latinajo [lati'naxo] nm dog Latin; **echar ~s** to come out with Latin words.

latino, a [la'tino, a] adj Latin.

Latinoamérica [latinoa'merika] nf Latin America.

latinoamericano, a [latinoameri'kano, a] adj, nm/f Latin American.

latir [la'tir] vi (corazón, pulso) to beat.

latitud [lati'tuð] nf (GEO) latitude; (fig) breadth, extent.

lato, a ['lato, a] adj broad.

latón [la'ton] nm brass.

latoso, a [la'toso, a] adj (molesto) annoying; (aburrido) boring.

latrocinio [latro'θinjo] nm robbery.

LAU nf abr (ESP JUR) = Ley de Arrendamientos Urbanos.

laúd [la'uð] nm lute.

laudatorio, a [lauða'torjo, a] adj laudatory.

laudo ['lauðo] nm (JUR) decision, finding.

laurear [laure'ar] vt to honour, reward.

laurel [lau'rel] nm (BOT) laurel; (CULIN) bay.

Lausana [lau'sana] nf Lausanne.

lava ['laβa] nf lava.

lavable [la'βaβle] adj washable.

lavabo [la'βaβo] nm (jofaina) washbasin; (retrete) lavatory (BRIT), toilet (BRIT), washroom (US).

lavadero [laβa'ðero] nm laundry.

lavado [la'βaðo] nm washing; (de ropa) wash, laundry; (ARTE) wash; ~ **de**

cerebro brainwashing.

lavadora [laβa'ðora] nf washing machine.

lavanda [la'βanda] nf lavender.

lavandería [laβande'ria] nf laundry; ~ **automática** launderette.

lavaparabrisas [laβapara'βrisas] nm inv windscreen washer.

lavaplatos [laβa'platos] nm inv dishwasher.

lavar [la'βar] vt to wash; (borrar) to wipe away; **~se** vr to wash o.s.; **~se las manos** to wash one's hands; (fig) to wash one's hands of it; ~ **y marcar** (pelo) to shampoo and set; ~ **en seco** to dry-clean.

lavativa [laβa'tiβa] nf (MED) enema.

lavavajillas [laβaβa'xiʎas] nm inv dishwasher.

laxante [lak'sante] nm laxative.

laxitud [laksi'tuð] nf laxity, slackness.

lazada [la'θaða] nf bow.

lazarillo [laθa'riʎo] nm: **perro de** ~ guide dog.

lazo ['laθo] nm knot; (lazada) bow; (para animales) lasso; (trampa) snare; (vínculo) tie; ~ **corredizo** slipknot.

LBE nf abr (ESP JUR) = Ley Básica de Empleo.

lb(s) abr = **libra(s)**.

L/C abr (= Letra de Crédito) B/E.

Lda., Ldo. abr = **Licenciado, a**.

le [le] pron (directo) him (o her); (: usted) you; (indirecto) to him (o her o it); (: usted) to you.

leal [le'al] adj loyal.

lealtad [leal'tað] nf loyalty.

lebrel [le'βrel] nm greyhound.

lección [lek'θjon] nf lesson; ~ **práctica** object lesson; **dar lecciones** to teach, give lessons; **dar una** ~ **a algn** (fig) to teach sb a lesson.

leche ['letʃe] nf milk; (fam!) semen, spunk (!); **dar una** ~ **a algn** (fam) to belt sb; **estar de mala** ~ (fam) to be in a foul mood; **tener mala** ~ (fam) to be a nasty piece of work; ~ **condensada/en polvo** condensed/powdered milk; ~ **desnatada** skimmed milk; ~ **de magnesia** milk of magnesia; ¡~! hell!

lechera [le'tʃera] nf V **lechero**.

lechería [letʃe'ria] nf dairy.

lechero, a [le'tʃero, a] adj milk cpd ♦ nm milkman ♦ nf (vendedora) milkmaid; (recipiente) milk pan; (para servir) milk churn.

lecho ['letʃo] nm (cama, de río) bed; (GEO) layer; ~ **mortuorio** deathbed.

lechón [le'tʃon] nm sucking (BRIT) o suckling (US) pig.

lechoso, a [le'tʃoso, a] adj milky.

lechuga [le'tʃuɣa] *nf* lettuce.
lechuza [le'tʃuθa] *nf* (barn) owl.
lectivo, a [lek'tiβo, a] *adj* (*horas*) teaching *cpd*; **año** *o* **curso** ~ (*ESCOL*) school year; (*UNIV*) academic year.
lector, a [lek'tor, a] *nm/f* reader; (*ESCOL, UNIV*) (conversation) assistant ♦ *nm*: ~ **óptico de caracteres** (*INFORM*) optical character reader ♦ *nf*: ~**a de fichas** (*INFORM*) card reader.
lectura [lek'tura] *nf* reading; ~ **de marcas sensibles** (*INFORM*) mark sensing.
leer [le'er] *vt* to read; ~ **entre líneas** to read between the lines.
legación [leɣa'θjon] *nf* legation.
legado [le'ɣaðo] *nm* (*don*) bequest; (*herencia*) legacy; (*enviado*) legate.
legajo [le'ɣaxo] *nm* file, bundle (of papers).
legal [le'ɣal] *adj* legal, lawful; (*persona*) trustworthy.
legalice [leɣa'liθe] *etc vb* V **legalizar**.
legalidad [leɣali'ðað] *nf* legality.
legalizar [leɣali'θar] *vt* to legalize; (*documento*) to authenticate.
legaña [le'ɣaɲa] *nf* sleep (*in eyes*).
legar [le'ɣar] *vt* to bequeath, leave.
legatario, a [leɣa'tarjo, a] *nm/f* legatee.
legendario, a [lexen'darjo, a] *adj* legendary.
legible [le'xiβle] *adj* legible; ~ **por máquina** (*INFORM*) machine-readable.
legión [le'xjon] *nf* legion.
legionario, a [lexjo'narjo, a] *adj* legionary ♦ *nm* legionnaire.
legislación [lexisla'θjon] *nf* legislation; (*leyes*) laws *pl*; ~ **antimonopolio** (*COM*) anti-trust legislation.
legislar [lexis'lar] *vt* to legislate.
legislativo, a [lexisla'tiβo, a] *adj*: (**elecciones**) **legislativas** ≈ general election.
legislatura [lexisla'tura] *nf* (*POL*) period of office.
legitimar [lexiti'mar] *vt* to legitimize.
legítimo, a [le'xitimo, a] *adj* (*genuino*) authentic; (*legal*) legitimate, rightful.
lego, a ['leɣo, a] *adj* (*REL*) secular; (*ignorante*) ignorant ♦ *nm* layman.
legua ['leɣwa] *nf* league; **se ve** (*o* **nota**) **a la** ~ you can tell a mile off.
legue ['leɣe] *etc vb* V **legar**.
leguleyo [leɣu'lejo] *nm* (*pey*) petty *o* shyster (*US*) lawyer.
legumbres [le'ɣumbres] *nfpl* pulses.
leído, a [le'iðo, a] *adj* well-read.
lejanía [lexa'nia] *nf* distance.
lejano, a [le'xano, a] *adj* far-off; (*en el tiempo*) distant; (*fig*) remote; **L~ Oriente** Far East.
lejía [le'xia] *nf* bleach.
lejísimos [le'xisimos] *adv* a long, long way.
lejos ['lexos] *adv* far, far away; **a lo** ~ in the distance; **de** *o* **desde** ~ from a distance; **está muy** ~ it's a long way (away); **¿está** ~**?** is it far?; ~ **de** *prep* far from.
lelo, a ['lelo, a] *adj* silly ♦ *nm/f* idiot.
lema ['lema] *nm* motto; (*POL*) slogan.
lencería [lenθe'ria] *nf* (*telas*) linen, drapery; (*ropa interior*) lingerie.
lendakari [lenda'kari] *nm* head of the Basque Autonomous Government.
lengua ['lengwa] *nf* tongue; ~ **materna** mother tongue; ~ **de tierra** (*GEO*) spit *o* tongue of land; **dar a la** ~ to chatter; **morderse la** ~ to hold one's tongue; **sacar la** ~ **a algn** (*fig*) to cock a snook at sb.

Under the Spanish constitution **lenguas cooficiales** *or* **oficiales** *enjoy the same status as* **castellano** *in those regions which have retained their own distinct language, ie in Galicia,* **gallego***; in the Basque Country,* **euskera***; in Catalonia and the Balearic Islands,* **catalán***. The regional governments actively promote their own language through the media and the education system. Of the three regions with their own language, Catalonia has the highest number of people who speak the* **lengua cooficial***.

---

lenguado [len'gwaðo] *nm* sole.
lenguaje [len'gwaxe] *nm* language; (*forma de hablar*) (mode of) speech; ~ **comercial** business language; ~ **ensamblador** *o* **de alto nivel** (*INFORM*) high-level language; ~ **máquina** (*INFORM*) machine language; ~ **original** source language; ~ **periodístico** journalese; ~ **de programación** (*INFORM*) programming language; **en** ~ **llano** ≈ in plain English.
lenguaraz [lengwa'raθ] *adj* talkative; (*pey*) foul-mouthed.
lengüeta [len'gweta] *nf* (*ANAT*) epiglottis; (*de zapatos, MUS*) tongue.
lenidad [leni'ðað] *nf* lenience.
Leningrado [lenin'graðo] *nm* Leningrad.
lente ['lente] *nm o nf* lens; (*lupa*) magnifying glass; ~**s** *pl* glasses; ~**s de contacto** contact lenses.
lenteja [len'texa] *nf* lentil.
lentejuela [lente'xwela] *nf* sequin.
lentilla [len'tiʎa] *nf* contact lens.
lentitud [lenti'tuð] *nf* slowness; **con** ~

slowly.
lento, a ['lento, a] *adj* slow.
leña ['leɲa] *nf* firewood; **dar** ~ **a** to thrash;
 echar ~ **al fuego** to add fuel to the
 flames.
leñador, a [leɲa'ðor, a] *nm/f* woodcutter.
leño ['leɲo] *nm* (*trozo de árbol*) log;
 (*madera*) timber; (*fig*) blockhead.
Leo ['leo] *nm* (*ASTRO*) Leo.
león [le'on] *nm* lion; ~ **marino** sea lion.
leonera [leo'nera] *nf* (*jaula*) lion's cage;
 parece una ~ it's shockingly dirty.
leonés, esa [leo'nes, esa] *adj*, *nm/f* Leonese
 ♦ *nm* (*LING*) Leonese.
leonino, a [leo'nino, a] *adj* leonine.
leopardo [leo'parðo] *nm* leopard.
leotardos [leo'tarðos] *nmpl* tights.
lepra ['lepra] *nf* leprosy.
leprosería [leprose'ria] *nf* leper colony.
leproso, a [le'proso, a] *nm/f* leper.
lerdo, a ['lerðo, a] *adj* (*lento*) slow; (*patoso*)
 clumsy.
leridano, a [leri'ðano, a] *adj* of *o* from
 Lérida ♦ *nm/f* native *o* inhabitant of
 Lérida.
les [les] *pron* (*directo*) them; (: *ustedes*) you;
 (*indirecto*) to them; (: *ustedes*) to you.
lesbiana [les'βjana] *nf* lesbian.
lesión [le'sjon] *nf* wound, lesion; (*DEPORTE*)
 injury.
lesionado, a [lesjo'naðo, a] *adj* injured
 ♦ *nm/f* injured person.
lesionar [lesjo'nar] *vt* (*dañar*) to hurt;
 (*herir*) to wound; ~**se** *vr* to get hurt.
letal [le'tal] *adj* lethal.
letanía [leta'nia] *nf* litany; (*retahíla*) long
 list.
letárgico, a [le'tarxiko, a] *adj* lethargic.
letargo [le'tarɣo] *nm* lethargy.
letón, ona [le'ton, ona] *adj*, *nm/f* Latvian
 ♦ *nm* (*LING*) Latvian.
Letonia [le'tonja] *nf* Latvia.
letra ['letra] *nf* letter; (*escritura*)
 handwriting; (*COM*) letter, bill, draft;
 (*MUS*) lyrics *pl*; ~**s** *nfpl* (*UNIV*) arts; ~
 bastardilla/negrilla italics *pl*/bold type; ~
 de cambio bill of exchange; ~ **de**
 imprenta print; ~ **inicial/mayúscula/**
 minúscula initial/capital/small letter; **lo**
 tomó al pie de la ~ he took it literally; ~
 bancaria (*COM*) bank draft; ~ **de patente**
 (*COM*) letters patent *pl*; **escribir 4** ~**s a**
 algn to drop a line to sb.
letrado, a [le'traðo, a] *adj* learned; (*fam*)
 pedantic ♦ *nm/f* lawyer.
letrero [le'trero] *nm* (*cartel*) sign; (*etiqueta*)
 label.
letrina [le'trina] *nf* latrine.

leucemia [leu'θemja] *nf* leukaemia.
leucocito [leuko'θito] *nm* white blood cell,
 leucocyte.
leva ['leβa] *nf* (*NAUT*) weighing anchor;
 (*MIL*) levy; (*TEC*) lever.
levadizo, a [leβa'ðiθo, a] *adj*: **puente** ~
 drawbridge.
levadura [leβa'ðura] *nf* yeast, leaven; ~ **de**
 cerveza brewer's yeast.
levantamiento [leβanta'mjento] *nm*
 raising, lifting; (*rebelión*) revolt, rising;
 (*GEO*) survey; ~ **de pesos** weightlifting.
levantar [leβan'tar] *vt* (*gen*) to raise; (*del*
 suelo) to pick up; (*hacia arriba*) to lift
 (up); (*plan*) to make, draw up; (*mesa*) to
 clear; (*campamento*) to strike; (*fig*) to
 cheer up, hearten; ~**se** *vr* to get up;
 (*enderezarse*) to straighten up; (*rebelarse*)
 to rebel; (*sesión*) to be adjourned;
 (*niebla*) to lift; (*viento*) to rise; ~**se (de la**
 cama) to get up, get out of bed; ~ **el**
 ánimo to cheer up.
levante [le'βante] *nm* east; (*viento*) east
 wind; **el L**~ region of Spain extending
 from Castellón to Murcia.
levantino, a [leβan'tino, a] *adj* of *o* from
 the *Levante* ♦ *nm/f*: **los** ~**s** the people of
 the *Levante*.
levar [le'βar] *vi* to weigh anchor.
leve ['leβe] *adj* light; (*fig*) trivial; (*mínimo*)
 slight.
levedad [leβe'ðað] *nf* lightness; (*fig*) levity.
levita [le'βita] *nf* frock coat.
léxico, a ['leksiko, a] *adj* lexical ♦ *nm*
 (*vocabulario*) vocabulary; (*LING*) lexicon.
ley [lei] *nf* (*gen*) law; (*metal*) standard;
 decreto-~ decree law; **de buena** ~ (*fig*)
 genuine; **según la** ~ in accordance with
 the law, by law, in law.
leyenda [le'jenda] *nf* legend; (*TIP*)
 inscription.
leyendo [le'jendo] *etc vb V* **leer**.
liar [li'ar] *vt* to tie (up); (*unir*) to bind;
 (*envolver*) to wrap (up); (*cigarrillo*) to
 confuse; (*cigarrillo*) to roll; ~**se** *vr* (*fam*) to
 get involved; (*confundirse*) to get mixed
 up; ~**se a palos** to get involved in a
 fight.
lib. *abr* (= *libro*) bk.
libanés, esa [liβa'nes, esa] *adj*, *nm/f*
 Lebanese.
Líbano ['liβano] *nm*: **el** ~ the Lebanon.
libar [li'βar] *vt* to suck.
libelo [li'βelo] *nm* satire, lampoon; (*JUR*)
 petition.
libélula [li'βelula] *nf* dragonfly.
liberación [liβera'θjon] *nf* liberation; (*de la*
 cárcel) release.

liberado, a [liße'raðo, a] *adj* liberated; (*COM*) paid-up, paid-in (*US*).

liberal [liße'ral] *adj*, *nmf* liberal.

liberalidad [lißerali'ðað] *nf* liberality, generosity.

liberar [liße'rar] *vt* to liberate.

libertad [lißer'tað] *nf* liberty, freedom; ~ de asociación/de culto/de prensa/de comercio/de palabra freedom of association/of worship/of the press/of trade/of speech; ~ **condicional** probation; ~ **bajo palabra** parole; ~ **bajo fianza** bail; **estar en** ~ to be free; **poner a algn en** ~ to set sb free.

libertador, a [lißerta'ðor, a] *adj* liberating ♦ *nmf* liberator; **El L**~ (*AM*) The Liberator.

libertar [lißer'tar] *vt* (*preso*) to set free; (*de una obligación*) to release; (*eximir*) to exempt.

libertinaje [lißerti'naxe] *nm* licentiousness.

libertino, a [lißer'tino, a] *adj* permissive ♦ *nmf* permissive person.

Libia ['lißja] *nf* Libya.

libidinoso, a [lißiði'noso, a] *adj* lustful; (*viejo*) lecherous.

libido [li'ßiðo] *nf* libido.

libio, a ['lißjo, a] *adj*, *nmf* Libyan.

libra ['lißra] *nf* pound; **L**~ (*ASTRO*) Libra; ~ **esterlina** pound sterling.

librador, a [lißra'ðor, a] *nmf* drawer.

libramiento [lißra'mjento] *nm* rescue; (*COM*) delivery.

libranza [li'ßranθa] *nf* (*COM*) draft; (*letra de cambio*) bill of exchange.

librar [li'ßrar] *vt* (*de peligro*) to save; (*batalla*) to wage, fight; (*de impuestos*) to exempt; (*cheque*) to make out; (*JUR*) to exempt; ~**se** *vr*: ~**se de** to escape from, free o.s. from; **de buena nos hemos librado** we're well out of that.

libre ['lißre] *adj* (*gen*) free; (*lugar*) unoccupied; (*tiempo*) spare; (*asiento*) vacant; (*COM*): ~ **a bordo** free on board; ~ **de franqueo** post-free; ~ **de impuestos** free of tax; **tiro** ~ free kick; **los 100 metros** ~ the 100 metres freestyle (race); **al aire** ~ in the open air; **¿estás** ~? are you free?

librecambio [lißre'kambjo] *nm* free trade.

librecambista [lißrekam'bista] *adj* free-trade *cpd* ♦ *nm* free-trader.

librería [lißre'ria] *nf* (*tienda*) bookshop; (*estante*) bookcase; ~ **de ocasión** secondhand bookshop.

librero, a [li'ßrero, a] *nmf* bookseller.

libreta [li'ßreta] *nf* notebook; (*pan*) one-pound loaf; ~ **de ahorros** savings book.

libro ['lißro] *nm* book; ~ **de actas** minute book; ~ **de bolsillo** paperback; ~ **de cabecera** bedside book; ~ **de caja** (*COM*) cashbook; ~ **de caja auxiliar** (*COM*) petty cash book; ~ **de cocina** cookery book (*BRIT*), cookbook (*US*); ~ **de consulta** reference book; ~ **de cuentas** account book; ~ **de cuentos** storybook; ~ **de cheques** cheque (*BRIT*) *o* check (*US*) book; ~ **diario** journal; ~ **de entradas y salidas** (*COM*) daybook; ~ **de honor** visitors' book; ~ **mayor** (*COM*) general ledger; ~ **de reclamaciones** complaints book; ~ **de texto** textbook.

Lic. *abr* = **Licenciado, a.**

licencia [li'θenθja] *nf* (*gen*) licence; (*permiso*) permission; ~ **por enfermedad/con goce de sueldo** sick/paid leave; ~ **de armas/de caza** gun/game licence; ~ **de exportación** (*COM*) export licence; ~ **poética** poetic licence.

licenciado, a [liθen'θjaðo, a] *adj* licensed ♦ *nmf* graduate; **L**~ **en Filosofía y Letras** ≈ Bachelor of Arts.

> *When students finish University after an average of five years they receive the degree of* **licenciado**. *If the course is only three years such as Nursing, or if they choose not to do the optional two-year specialization, they are awarded the degree of* **diplomado**. **Cursos de posgrado**, *postgraduate courses, are becoming increasingly popular, especially one-year specialist courses called* **masters**.

licenciar [liθen'θjar] *vt* (*empleado*) to dismiss; (*permitir*) to permit, allow; (*soldado*) to discharge; (*estudiante*) to confer a degree upon; ~**se** *vr*: ~**se en letras** to get an arts degree.

licenciatura [liθenθja'tura] *nf* (*título*) degree; (*estudios*) degree course.

licencioso, a [liθen'θjoso, a] *adj* licentious.

liceo [li'θeo] *nm* (*esp AM*) (high) school.

licitación [liθita'θjon] *nf* bidding; (*oferta*) tender, offer.

licitador [liθita'ðor] *nm* bidder.

licitar [liθi'tar] *vt* to bid for ♦ *vi* to bid.

lícito, a ['liθito, a] *adj* (*legal*) lawful; (*justo*) fair, just; (*permisible*) permissible.

licor [li'kor] *nm* spirits *pl* (*BRIT*), liquor (*US*); (*con hierbas etc*) liqueur.

licra ® ['likra] *nf* Lycra ®.

licuadora [likwa'ðora] *nf* blender.

licuar [li'kwar] *vt* to liquidize.

lid [lið] *nf* combat; (*fig*) controversy.

líder ['liðer] *nmf* leader.

liderato [liðe'rato] *nm* = **liderazgo**.
liderazgo [liðe'raθɣo] *nm* leadership.
lidia ['liðja] *nf* bullfighting; (*una ~*) bullfight; **toros de** ~ fighting bulls.
lidiar [li'ðjar] *vt, vi* to fight.
liebre ['ljeßre] *nf* hare; **dar gato por** ~ to con.
Lieja ['ljexa] *nf* Liège.
lienzo ['ljenθo] *nm* linen; (*ARTE*) canvas; (*ARQ*) wall.
lifting ['liftin] *nm* facelift.
liga ['liɣa] *nf* (*de medias*) garter, suspender; (*confederación*) league; (*AM: gomita*) rubber band.
ligadura [liɣa'ðura] *nf* bond, tie; (*MED, MUS*) ligature.
ligamento [liɣa'mento] *nm* (*ANAT*) ligament; (*atadura*) tie; (*unión*) bond.
ligar [li'ɣar] *vt* (*atar*) to tie; (*unir*) to join; (*MED*) to bind up; (*MUS*) to slur; (*fam*) to get off with, pick up ♦ *vi* to mix, blend; (*fam*) to get off with sb; (*2 personas*) to get off with one another; ~**se** *vr* (*fig*) to commit o.s.; ~ **con** (*fam*) to get off with, pick up; ~**se a algn** to get off with o pick up sb.
ligereza [lixe'reθa] *nf* lightness; (*rapidez*) swiftness; (*agilidad*) agility; (*superficialidad*) flippancy.
ligero, a [li'xero, a] *adj* (*de peso*) light; (*tela*) thin; (*rápido*) swift, quick; (*ágil*) agile, nimble; (*de importancia*) slight; (*de carácter*) flippant, superficial ♦ *adv* quickly, swiftly; **a la ligera** superficially; **juzgar a la ligera** to jump to conclusions.
light ['lait] *adj inv* (*cigarrillo*) low-tar; (*comida*) diet *cpd*.
ligón [li'ɣon] *nm* (*fam*) Romeo.
ligue ['liɣe] *etc vb V* **ligar** ♦ *nm/f* boyfriend/girlfriend ♦ *nm* (*persona*) pick-up.
liguero [li'ɣero] *nm* suspender (*BRIT*) o garter (*US*) belt.
lija ['lixa] *nf* (*ZOOL*) dogfish; (**papel de**) ~ sandpaper.
lijar [li'xar] *vt* to sand.
lila ['lila] *adj inv, nf* lilac ♦ *nm* (*fam*) twit.
lima ['lima] *nf* file; (*BOT*) lime; ~ **de uñas** nail file; **comer como una** ~ to eat like a horse.
limar [li'mar] *vt* to file; (*alisar*) to smooth over; (*fig*) to polish up.
limbo ['limbo] *nm* (*REL*) limbo; **estar en el** ~ to be on another planet.
limitación [limita'θjon] *nf* limitation, limit; ~ **de velocidad** speed limit.
limitado, a [limi'taðo, a] *adj* limited; **sociedad limitada** (*COM*) limited company.

limitar [limi'tar] *vt* to limit; (*reducir*) to reduce, cut down ♦ *vi*: ~ **con** to border on; ~**se** *vr*: ~**se a** to limit o confine o.s. to.
límite ['limite] *nm* (*gen*) limit; (*fin*) end; (*frontera*) border; **como** ~ at (the) most; (*fecha*) at the latest; **no tener** ~**s** to know no bounds; ~ **de crédito** (*COM*) credit limit; ~ **de página** (*INFORM*) page break; ~ **de velocidad** speed limit.
limítrofe [li'mitrofe] *adj* bordering, neighbouring.
limón [li'mon] *nm* lemon ♦ *adj*: **amarillo** ~ lemon-yellow.
limonada [limo'naða] *nf* lemonade.
limonero [limo'nero] *nm* lemon tree.
limosna [li'mosna] *nf* alms *pl*; **pedir** ~ to beg; **vivir de** ~ to live on charity.
limpiabotas [limpja'ßotas] *nm/f inv* bootblack (*BRIT*), shoeshine boy/girl.
limpiacristales [limpjakris'tales] *nm inv* (*detergente*) window cleaner.
limpiador, a [limpja'ðor, a] *adj* cleaning, cleansing ♦ *nm/f* cleaner.
limpiaparabrisas [limpjapara'ßrisas] *nm inv* windscreen (*BRIT*) o windshield (*US*) wiper.
limpiar [lim'pjar] *vt* to clean; (*con trapo*) to wipe; (*quitar*) to wipe away; (*zapatos*) to shine, polish; (*casa*) to tidy up; (*fig*) to clean up; (: *purificar*) to cleanse, purify; (*MIL*) to mop up; ~ **en seco** to dry-clean.
limpieza [lim'pjeθa] *nf* (*estado*) cleanliness; (*acto*) cleaning; (: *de las calles*) cleansing; (: *de zapatos*) polishing; (*habilidad*) skill; (*fig: POLICÍA*) clean-up; (*pureza*) purity; (*MIL*): **operación de** ~ mopping-up operation; ~ **étnica** ethnic cleansing; ~ **en seco** dry cleaning.
limpio, a ['limpjo, a] *adj* clean; (*moralmente*) pure; (*ordenado*) tidy; (*despejado*) clear; (*COM*) clear, net; (*fam*) honest ♦ *adv*: **jugar** ~ to play fair; **pasar a** ~ to make a fair copy; **sacar algo en** ~ to get benefit from sth; ~ **de** free from.
linaje [li'naxe] *nm* lineage, family.
linaza [li'naθa] *nf* linseed; **aceite de** ~ linseed oil.
lince ['linθe] *nm* lynx; **ser un** ~ (*fig: observador*) to be very observant; (: *astuto*) to be shrewd.
linchar [lin'tʃar] *vt* to lynch.
lindante [lin'dante] *adj* adjoining; ~ **con** bordering on.
lindar [lin'dar] *vi* to adjoin; ~ **con** to border on; (*ARQ*) to abut on.
linde ['linde] *nm o nf* boundary.
lindero, a [lin'dero, a] *adj* adjoining ♦ *nm*

boundary.

lindo, a ['lindo, a] *adj* pretty, lovely ♦ *adv*
(*esp AM: fam*) nicely, very well; **canta**
muy ~ (*AM*) he sings beautifully; **se**
divertían de lo ~ they enjoyed
themselves enormously.

línea ['linea] *nf* (*gen, moral, POL etc*) line;
(*talle*) figure; (*INFORM*): **en** ~ on line;
fuera de ~ off line; ~ **de estado** status
line; ~ **de formato** format line; ~ **aérea**
airline; ~ **de alto el fuego** ceasefire line;
~ **de fuego** firing line; ~ **de meta** goal
line; (*de carrera*) finishing line; ~ **de**
montaje assembly line; ~ **dura** (*POL*)
hard line; ~ **recta** straight line; **la** ~ **de**
1995 (*moda*) the 1995 look.

lineal [line'al] *adj* linear; (*INFORM*) on-line.

lingote [lin'gote] *nm* ingot.

lingüista [lin'gwista] *nm/f* linguist.

lingüística [lin'gwistika] *nf* linguistics *sg*.

linimento [lini'mento] *nm* liniment.

lino ['lino] *nm* linen; (*BOT*) flax.

linóleo [li'noleo] *nm* lino, linoleum.

linterna [lin'terna] *nf* lantern, lamp; ~
eléctrica *o* **a pilas** torch (*BRIT*), flashlight
(*US*).

lío ['lio] *nm* bundle; (*desorden*) muddle,
mess; (*fam: follón*) fuss; (: *relación*
amorosa) affair; **armar un** ~ to make a
fuss; **meterse en un** ~ to get into a jam;
tener un ~ **con algn** to be having an
affair with sb.

lipotimia [lipo'timja] *nf* blackout.

liquen ['liken] *nm* lichen.

liquidación [likiða'θjon] *nf* liquidation;
(*cuenta*) settlement; **venta de** ~
clearance sale.

liquidar [liki'ðar] *vt* (*QUÍMICA*) to liquefy;
(*COM*) to liquidate; (*deudas*) to pay off;
(*empresa*) to wind up; ~ **a algn** to bump
sb off, rub sb out (*fam*).

liquidez [liki'ðeθ] *nf* liquidity.

líquido, a ['likiðo, a] *adj* liquid; (*ganancia*)
net ♦ *nm* liquid; (*COM: efectivo*) ready
cash *o* money; (: *ganancia*) net amount *o*
profit; ~ **imponible** net taxable income.

lira ['lira] *nf* (*MUS*) lyre; (*moneda*) lira.

lírico, a ['liriko, a] *adj* lyrical.

lirio ['lirjo] *nm* (*BOT*) iris.

lirismo [li'rismo] *nm* lyricism;
(*sentimentalismo*) sentimentality.

lirón [li'ron] *nm* (*ZOOL*) dormouse; (*fig*)
sleepyhead.

Lisboa [lis'βoa] *nf* Lisbon.

lisboeta [lisβo'eta] *adj* of *o* from Lisbon
♦ *nm/f* native *o* inhabitant of Lisbon.

lisiado, a [li'sjaðo, a] *adj* injured ♦ *nm/f*
cripple.

lisiar [li'sjar] *vt* to maim; ~**se** *vr* to injure
o.s.

liso, a ['liso, a] *adj* (*terreno*) flat; (*cabello*)
straight; (*superficie*) even; (*tela*) plain;
lisa y llanamente in plain language,
plainly.

lisonja [li'sonxa] *nf* flattery.

lisonjear [lisonxe'ar] *vt* to flatter; (*fig*) to
please.

lisonjero, a [lison'xero, a] *adj* flattering;
(*agradable*) gratifying, pleasing ♦ *nm/f*
flatterer.

lista ['lista] *nf* list; (*de alumnos*) school
register; (*de libros*) catalogue; (*de*
correos) poste restante; (*de platos*) menu;
(*de precios*) price list; **pasar** ~ to call the
roll; (*ESCOL*) to call the register; ~ **de**
correos poste restante; ~ **de direcciones**
mailing list; ~ **electoral** electoral roll; ~
de espera waiting list; **tela a** ~**s** striped
material.

listado, a [lis'taðo, a] *adj* striped ♦ *nm*
(*COM, INFORM*) listing; ~ **paginado**
(*INFORM*) paged listing.

listar [lis'tar] *vt* (*INFORM*) to list.

listo, a ['listo, a] *adj* (*perspicaz*) smart,
clever; (*preparado*) ready; ~ **para usar**
ready-to-use; **¿estás** ~**?** are you ready?;
pasarse de ~ to be too clever by half.

listón [lis'ton] *nm* (*tela*) ribbon; (*de madera,*
metal) strip.

litera [li'tera] *nf* (*en barco, tren*) berth; (*en*
dormitorio) bunk, bunk bed.

literal [lite'ral] *adj* literal.

literario, a [lite'rarjo, a] *adj* literary.

literato, a [lite'rato, a] *nm/f* writer.

literatura [litera'tura] *nf* literature.

litigante [liti'γante] *nm/f* litigant, claimant.

litigar [liti'γar] *vt* to fight ♦ *vi* (*JUR*) to go to
law; (*fig*) to dispute, argue.

litigio [li'tixjo] *nm* (*JUR*) lawsuit; (*fig*): **en** ~
con in dispute with.

litigue [li'tiγe] *etc vb V* **litigar**.

litografía [litoγra'fia] *nf* lithography; (*una*
~) lithograph.

litoral [lito'ral] *adj* coastal ♦ *nm* coast,
seaboard.

litro ['litro] *nm* litre, liter (*US*).

Lituania [li'twanja] *nf* Lithuania.

lituano, a [li'twano, a] *adj, nm/f* Lithuanian
♦ *nm* (*LING*) Lithuanian.

liturgia [li'turxja] *nf* liturgy.

liviano, a [li'βjano, a] *adj* (*persona*) fickle;
(*cosa, objeto*) trivial; (*AM*) light.

lívido, a ['liβiðo, a] *adj* livid.

living ['liβin], *pl* **livings** *nm* (*esp AM*) sitting
room.

Ll, ll ['eʎe] *nf former letter in the Spanish*

alphabet.

llaga ['ʎaɣa] *nf* wound.

llagar [ʎa'ɣar] *vt* to make sore; (*herir*) to wound.

llague ['ʎaɣe] *etc vb* V **llagar.**

llama ['ʎama] *nf* flame; (*fig*) passion; (*ZOOL*) llama; **en ~s** burning, ablaze.

llamada [ʎa'maða] *nf* call; (*a la puerta*) knock; (: *timbre*) ring; **~ a cobro revertido** reverse-charge call; **~ al orden** call to order; **~ a pie de página** reference note; **~ a procedimiento** (*INFORM*) procedure call; **~ interurbana** trunk call.

llamado [ʎa'maðo] *nm* (*AM*) (telephone) call; (*llamamiento*) appeal, call.

llamamiento [ʎama'mjento] *nm* call; **hacer un ~ a algn para que haga algo** to appeal to sb to do sth.

llamar [ʎa'mar] *vt* to call; (*convocar*) to summon; (*invocar*) to invoke; (*atraer con gesto*) to beckon; (*atención*) to attract; (*TELEC: tb*: **~ por teléfono**) to call, ring up, telephone; (*MIL*) to call up ♦ *vi* (*por teléfono*) to phone; (*a la puerta*) to knock (*o* ring); (*por señas*) to beckon; **~se** *vr* to be called, be named; **¿cómo se llama usted?** what's your name?; **¿quién llama?** (*TELEC*) who's calling?, who's that?; **no me llama la atención** (*fam*) I don't fancy it.

llamarada [ʎama'raða] *nf* (*llamas*) blaze; (*rubor*) flush; (*fig*) flare-up.

llamativo, a [ʎama'tiβo, a] *adj* showy; (*color*) loud.

llamear [ʎame'ar] *vi* to blaze.

llanamente [ʎana'mente] *adv* (*lisamente*) smoothly; (*sin ostentaciones*) plainly; (*sinceramente*) frankly; V *tb* **liso.**

llaneza [ʎa'neθa] *nf* (*gen*) simplicity; (*honestidad*) straightforwardness, frankness.

llano, a ['ʎano, a] *adj* (*superficie*) flat; (*persona*) straightforward; (*estilo*) clear ♦ *nm* plain, flat ground.

llanta ['ʎanta] *nf* (wheel) rim; (*AM: neumático*) tyre; (: *cámara*) (inner) tube.

llanto ['ʎanto] *nm* weeping; (*fig*) lamentation; (*canción*) dirge, lament.

llanura [ʎa'nura] *nf* (*lisura*) flatness, smoothness; (*GEO*) plain.

llave ['ʎaβe] *nf* key; (*de gas, agua*) tap (*BRIT*), faucet (*US*); (*MECÁNICA*) spanner; (*de la luz*) switch; (*MUS*) key; **~ inglesa** monkey wrench; **~ maestra** master key; **~ de contacto** (*AUTO*) ignition key; **~ de paso** stopcock; **echar ~ a** to lock up.

llavero [ʎa'βero] *nm* keyring.

llavín [ʎa'βin] *nm* latchkey.

llegada [ʎe'ɣaða] *nf* arrival.

llegar [ʎe'ɣar] *vt* to bring up, bring over ♦ *vi* to arrive; (*bastar*) to be enough; **~se** *vr*: **~se a** to approach; **~ a** (*alcanzar*) to reach; to manage to, succeed in; **~ a saber** to find out; **~ a ser famoso/el jefe** to become famous/the boss; **~ a las manos** to come to blows; **~ a las manos de** to come into the hands of; **no llegues tarde** don't be late; **esta cuerda no llega** this rope isn't long enough.

llegue ['ʎeɣe] *etc vb* V **llegar.**

llenar [ʎe'nar] *vt* to fill; (*superficie*) to cover; (*espacio, tiempo*) to fill, take up; (*formulario*) to fill in *o* out; (*deber*) to fulfil; (*fig*) to heap; **~se** *vr* to fill (up); **~se de** (*fam*) to stuff o.s. with.

lleno, a ['ʎeno, a] *adj* full, filled; (*repleto*) full up ♦ *nm* (*abundancia*) abundance; (*TEAT*) full house; **dar de ~ contra un muro** to hit a wall head-on.

llevadero, a [ʎeβa'ðero, a] *adj* bearable, tolerable.

llevar [ʎe'βar] *vt* to take; (*ropa*) to wear; (*cargar*) to carry; (*quitar*) to take away; (*en coche*) to drive; (*transportar*) to transport; (*ruta*) to follow, keep to; (*traer: dinero*) to carry; (*suj: camino etc*): **~ a** to lead to; (*MAT*) to carry; (*aguantar*) to bear; (*negocio*) to conduct, direct; to manage; **~se** *vr* to carry off, take away; **llevamos dos días aquí** we have been here for two days; **él me lleva 2 años** he's 2 years older than me; **~ adelante** (*fig*) to carry forward; **~ por delante a uno** (*en coche etc*) to run sb over; (*fig*) to ride roughshod over sb; **~ la ventaja** to be winning *o* in the lead; **~ los libros** (*COM*) to keep the books; **llevo las de perder** I'm likely to lose; **no las lleva todas consigo** he's not all there; **nos llevó a cenar fuera** she took us out for a meal; **~se a uno por delante** (*atropellar*) to run sb over; **~se bien** to get on well (together).

llorar [ʎo'rar] *vt* to cry, weep ♦ *vi* to cry, weep; (*ojos*) to water; **~ a moco tendido** to sob one's heart out; **~ de risa** to cry with laughter.

lloriquear [ʎorike'ar] *vi* to snivel, whimper.

lloro ['ʎoro] *nm* crying, weeping.

llorón, ona [ʎo'ron, ona] *adj* tearful ♦ *nm/f* cry-baby.

lloroso, a [ʎo'roso, a] *adj* (*gen*) weeping, tearful; (*triste*) sad, sorrowful.

llover – lonja

llover [ʎoˈβer] *vi* to rain; ~ **a cántaros** *o* **a cubos** *o* **a mares** to rain cats and dogs, pour (down); **ser una cosa llovida del cielo** to be a godsend; **llueve sobre mojado** it never rains but it pours.

llovizna [ʎoˈβiθna] *nf* drizzle.

lloviznar [ʎoβiθˈnar] *vi* to drizzle.

llueve [ˈʎweβe] *etc vb V* **llover**.

lluvia [ˈʎuβja] *nf* rain; (*cantidad*) rainfall; (*fig: balas etc*) hail, shower; ~ **radioactiva** radioactive fallout; **día de** ~ rainy day; **una** ~ **de regalos** a shower of gifts.

lluvioso, a [ʎuˈβjoso, a] *adj* rainy.

lo [lo] *artículo definido neutro*: ~ **bueno** the good ♦ *pron* (*persona*) him; (*cosa*) it; ~ **mío** what is mine; ~ **difícil es que** ... the difficult thing about it is that ...; **no saben** ~ **aburrido que es** they don't know how boring it is; **viste a** ~ **americano** he dresses in the American style; ~ **de** that matter of; ~ **que** what, that which; **toma** ~ **que quieras** take what(ever) you want; ~ **que sea** whatever; ¡**toma** ~ **que he dicho!** I stand by what I said!

loa [ˈloa] *nf* praise.

loable [loˈaβle] *adj* praiseworthy.

LOAPA [loˈapa] *nf abr* (*ESP JUR*) = *Ley Orgánica de Armonización del Proceso Autónomo*.

loar [loˈar] *vt* to praise.

lobato [loˈβato] *nm* (*ZOOL*) wolf cub.

lobo [ˈloβo] *nm* wolf; ~ **de mar** (*fig*) sea dog; ~ **marino** seal.

lóbrego, a [ˈloβreɣo, a] *adj* dark; (*fig*) gloomy.

lóbulo [ˈloβulo] *nm* lobe.

LOC *nm abr* (= *lector óptico de caracteres*) OCR.

local [loˈkal] *adj* local ♦ *nm* place, site; (*oficinas*) premises *pl*.

localice [lokaˈliθe] *etc vb V* **localizar**.

localidad [lokaliˈðað] *nf* (*barrio*) locality; (*lugar*) location; (*TEAT*) seat, ticket.

localizar [lokaliˈθar] *vt* (*ubicar*) to locate, find; (*encontrar*) to find, track down; (*restringir*) to localize; (*situar*) to place.

loción [loˈθjon] *nf* lotion, wash.

loco, a [ˈloko, a] *adj* mad; (*fig*) wild, mad ♦ *nm/f* lunatic, madman/woman; ~ **de atar**, ~ **de remate**, ~ **rematado** raving mad; **a lo** ~ without rhyme or reason; **ando** ~ **con el examen** the exam is driving me crazy; **estar** ~ **de alegría** to be overjoyed *o* over the moon.

locomoción [lokomoˈθjon] *nf* locomotion.

locomotora [lokomoˈtora] *nf* engine, locomotive.

locuaz [loˈkwaθ] *adj* loquacious, talkative.

locución [lokuˈθjon] *nf* expression.

locura [loˈkura] *nf* madness; (*acto*) crazy act.

locutor, a [lokuˈtor, a] *nm/f* (*RADIO*) announcer; (*comentarista*) commentator; (*TV*) newscaster, newsreader.

locutorio [lokuˈtorjo] *nm* (*TELEC*) telephone box *o* booth.

lodo [ˈlodo] *nm* mud.

logia [ˈloxja] *nf* (*MIL, de masones*) lodge; (*ARQ*) loggia.

lógico, a [ˈloxiko, a] *adj* logical; (*correcto*) natural; (*razonable*) reasonable ♦ *nm* logician ♦ *nf* logic; **es** ~ **que** ... it stands to reason that ...; **ser de una lógica aplastante** to be as clear as day.

logístico, a [loˈxistiko, a] *adj* logistical ♦ *nf* logistics *pl*.

logotipo [loɣoˈtipo] *nm* logo.

logrado, a [loˈɣrado, a] *adj* accomplished.

lograr [loˈɣrar] *vt* (*obtener*) to get, obtain; (*conseguir*) to achieve, attain; ~ **hacer** to manage to do; ~ **que algn venga** to manage to get sb to come; ~ **acceso a** (*INFORM*) to access.

logro [ˈloɣro] *nm* achievement, success; (*COM*) profit.

logroñés, esa [loɣroˈɲes, esa] *adj* of *o* from Logroño ♦ *nm/f* native *o* inhabitant of Logroño.

LOGSE *nf abr* (= *Ley Orgánica de Ordenación General del Sistema Educativo*) educational reform act.

Loira [ˈloira] *nm* Loire.

loma [ˈloma] *nf* hillock, low ridge.

Lombardía [lombarˈðia] *nf* Lombardy.

lombriz [lomˈbriθ] *nf* (*earth*)worm.

lomo [ˈlomo] *nm* (*de animal*) back; (*CULIN: de cerdo*) pork loin; (: *de vaca*) rib steak; (*de libro*) spine.

lona [ˈlona] *nf* canvas.

loncha [ˈlontʃa] *nf* = **lonja**.

lonche [ˈlontʃe] *nm* (*AM*) lunch.

lonchería [lontʃeˈria] *nf* (*AM*) snack bar, diner (*US*).

londinense [londiˈnense] *adj* London *cpd*, of *o* from London ♦ *nm/f* Londoner.

Londres [ˈlondres] *nm* London.

longaniza [longaˈniθa] *nf* pork sausage.

longevidad [lonxeβiˈðað] *nf* longevity.

longitud [lonxiˈtuð] *nf* length; (*GEO*) longitude; **tener 3 metros de** ~ to be 3 metres long; ~ **de onda** wavelength; **salto de** ~ long jump.

longitudinal [lonxituðiˈnal] *adj* longitudinal.

lonja [ˈlonxa] *nf* slice; (*de tocino*) rasher; (*COM*) market, exchange; ~ **de pescado**

fish market.
lontananza [lonta'nanθa] *nf* background;
  en ~ far away, in the distance.
loor [lo'or] *nm* praise.
Lorena [lo'rena] *nf* Lorraine.
loro ['loro] *nm* parrot.
los [los] *artículo definido mpl* the ♦ *pron* them;
  (*ustedes*) you; **mis libros y ~ de usted** my
  books and yours.
losa ['losa] *nf* stone; **~ sepulcral**
  gravestone.
lote ['lote] *nm* portion, share; (*COM*) lot;
  (*INFORM*) batch.
lotería [lote'ria] *nf* lottery; (*juego*) lotto; **le
  tocó la ~** he won a big prize in the
  lottery; (*fig*) he struck lucky; **~ nacional**
  national lottery; **~ primitiva** (*ESP*) *type
  of state-run lottery.*

*Millions of pounds are spent every year on
loterías, lotteries. There is the weekly
Lotería Nacional which is very popular
especially at Christmas. Other weekly
lotteries are the **Bono Loto** and the (**Lotería)
Primitiva**. One of the most famous lotteries
is run by the wealthy and influential
society for the blind, **la ONCE**, and the form
is called the **cupón de la ONCE** or **el cupón de
los ciegos**.*

lotero, a [lo'tero, a] *nm/f* seller of lottery
  tickets.
Lovaina [lo'βaina] *nf* Louvain.
loza ['loθa] *nf* crockery; **~ fina** china.
lozanía [loθa'nia] *nf* (*lujo*) luxuriance.
lozano, a [lo'θano, a] *adj* luxuriant;
  (*animado*) lively.
lubina [lu'βina] *nf* (*ZOOL*) sea bass.
lubricante [luβri'kante] *adj*, *nm* lubricant.
lubricar [luβri'kar], **lubrificar** [luβrifi'kar]
  vt to lubricate.
lubrifique [luβri'fike] *etc vb V* **lubrificar.**
lubrique [lu'βrike] *etc vb V* **lubricar.**
lucense [lu'θense] *adj* of *o* from Lugo ♦ *nm/f*
  native *o* inhabitant of Lugo.
Lucerna [lu'θerna] *nf* Lucerne.
lucero [lu'θero] *nm* (*ASTRO*) bright star;
  (*fig*) brilliance; **~ del alba/de la tarde**
  morning/evening star.
luces ['luθes] *nfpl de* **luz.**
lucha ['lutʃa] *nf* fight, struggle; **~ de clases**
  class struggle; **~ libre** wrestling.
luchar [lu'tʃar] *vi* to fight.
lucidez [luθi'ðeθ] *nf* lucidity.
lucido, a [lu'θiðo, a] *adj* (*espléndido*)
  splendid, brilliant; (*elegante*) elegant;
  (*exitoso*) successful.
lúcido, a ['luθiðo, a] *adj* lucid.

luciérnaga [lu'θjernaɣa] *nf* glow-worm.
lucimiento [luθi'mjento] *nm* (*brillo*)
  brilliance; (*éxito*) success.
lucio ['luθjo] *nm* (*ZOOL*) pike.
lucir [lu'θir] *vt* to illuminate, light (up);
  (*ostentar*) to show off ♦ *vi* (*brillar*) to
  shine; (*AM*: *parecer*) to look, seem; **~se** *vr*
  (*irónico*) to make a fool of o.s.;
  (*ostentarse*) to show off; **la casa luce
  limpia** the house looks clean.
lucrativo, a [lukra'tiβo, a] *adj* lucrative,
  profitable; **institución no lucrativa** non
  profit-making institution.
lucro ['lukro] *nm* profit, gain; **~s y daños**
  (*COM*) profit and loss *sg*.
luctuoso, a [luk'twoso, a] *adj* mournful.
lúdico, a ['luðiko, a] *adj* playful; (*actividad*)
  recreational.
ludopatía [luðopa'tia] *nf* addiction to
  gambling (*o* videogames).
luego ['lweɣo] *adv* (*después*) next; (*más
  tarde*) later, afterwards; (*AM fam*: **en
  seguida**) at once, immediately; **desde ~**
  of course; **¡hasta ~!** see you later!, so
  long!; **¿y ~?** what next?
lugar [lu'ɣar] *nm* place; (*sitio*) spot; (*pueblo*)
  village, town; **en ~ de** instead of; **en
  primer ~** in the first place, firstly; **dar ~
  a** to give rise to; **hacer ~** to make room;
  fuera de ~ out of place; **tener ~** to take
  place; **~ común** commonplace; **yo en su
  ~** if I were him; **no hay ~ para
  preocupaciones** there is no cause for
  concern.
lugareño, a [luɣa'reɲo, a] *adj* village *cpd*
  ♦ *nm/f* villager.
lugarteniente [luɣarte'njente] *nm* deputy.
lúgubre ['luɣuβre] *adj* mournful.
lujo ['luxo] *nm* luxury; (*fig*) profusion,
  abundance; **de ~** luxury *cpd*, de luxe.
lujoso, a [lu'xoso, a] *adj* luxurious.
lujuria [lu'xurja] *nf* lust.
lumbago [lum'baɣo] *nm* lumbago.
lumbre ['lumbre] *nf* (*luz*) light; (*fuego*) fire;
  cerca de la ~ near the fire, at the
  fireside; **¿tienes ~?** (*para cigarro*) have
  you got a light?
lumbrera [lum'brera] *nf* luminary; (*fig*)
  leading light.
luminoso, a [lumi'noso, a] *adj* luminous,
  shining; (*idea*) bright, brilliant.
luna ['luna] *nf* moon; (*vidrio*: *escaparate*)
  plate glass; (: *de un espejo*) glass; (: *de
  gafas*) lens; (*fig*) crescent; **~ creciente/
  llena/menguante/nueva** crescent/full/
  waning/new moon; **~ de miel**
  honeymoon; **estar en la ~** to have one's
  head in the clouds.

lunar [lu'nar] adj lunar ♦ nm (ANAT) mole;
tela a ~es spotted material.
lunes ['lunes] nm inv Monday.
luneta [lu'neta] nf lens.
lupa ['lupa] nf magnifying glass.
lusitano, a [lusi'tano, a], **luso, a** ['luso, a]
adj, nm/f Portuguese.
lustrador [lustra'ðor] nm (AM) bootblack.
lustrar [lus'trar] vt (esp AM) (mueble) to
polish; (zapatos) to shine.
lustre ['lustre] nm polish; (fig) lustre; **dar ~
a** to polish.
lustro ['lustro] nm period of five years.
lustroso, a [lus'troso, a] adj shining.
luterano, a [lute'rano, a] adj Lutheran.
luto ['luto] nm mourning; (congoja) grief,
sorrow; **llevar el o vestirse de ~** to be in
mourning.
luxación [luksa'θjon] nf (MED) dislocation;
tener una ~ de tobillo to have a
dislocated ankle.
Luxemburgo [luksem'burɣo] nm
Luxembourg.
luz [luθ], pl **luces** nf (tb fig) light; (fam)
electricity; **dar a ~ un niño** to give birth
to a child; **sacar a la ~** to bring to light;
dar la ~ to switch on the light; **encender**
(ESP) o **prender** (AM)/**apagar la ~** to
switch the light on/off; **les cortaron la ~**
their (electricity) supply was cut off; **a
la ~ de** in the light of; **a todas luces** by
any reckoning; **hacer la ~ sobre** to shed
light on; **tener pocas luces** to be dim o
stupid; **~ de la luna/del sol o solar**
moonlight/sunlight; **~ eléctrica** electric
light; **~ roja/verde** red/green light; **~ de
cruce** (AUTO) dipped headlight; **~ de
freno** brake light; **~ intermitente/trasera**
flashing/rear light; **luces de tráfico**
traffic lights; **el Siglo de las Luces** the
Age of Enlightenment; **traje de luces**
bullfighter's costume.

M m

M, m ['eme] nf (letra) M, m; **M de Madrid** M
for Mike.
M. abr (FERRO) = **Metro.**
m. abr (= metro(s)) m; (= minuto(s)) min.,
m; (= masculino) m., masc.
M.ª abr = **María.**
macabro, a [ma'kaβro, a] adj macabre.
macaco [ma'kako] nm (ZOOL) rhesus
monkey; (fam) runt, squirt.
macana [ma'kana] nf (AM: porra) club;
(: mentira) lie, fib; (: tontería) piece of
nonsense.
macanudo, a [maka'nuðo, a] adj (AM fam)
great.
macarra [ma'karra] nm (fam) thug.
macarrones [maka'rrones] nmpl macaroni
sg.
Macedonia [maθe'ðonja] nf Macedonia.
macedonia [maθe'ðonja] nf: **~ de frutas**
fruit salad.
macedonio [maθe'ðonjo] adj, nm/f
Macedonian ♦ nm (LING) Macedonian.
macerar [maθe'rar] vt (CULIN) to soak,
macerate; **~se** vr to soak, soften.
maceta [ma'θeta] nf (de flores) pot of
flowers; (para plantas) flowerpot.
macetero [maθe'tero] nm flowerpot stand
o holder.
machacar [matʃa'kar] vt to crush, pound;
(moler) to grind (up); (aplastar) to mash
♦ vi (insistir) to go on, keep on.
machacón, ona [matʃa'kon, ona] adj
(pesado) tiresome; (insistente) insistent;
(monótono) monotonous.
machamartillo [matʃamar'tiʎo]: **a ~** adv:
creer a ~ (firmemente) to believe
firmly.
machaque [ma'tʃake] etc vb V **machacar.**
machete [ma'tʃete] nm machete, (large)
knife.
machismo [ma'tʃismo] nm sexism; male
chauvinism.
machista [ma'tʃista] adj, nm sexist; male
chauvinist.
macho ['matʃo] adj male; (fig) virile ♦ nm
male; (fig) he-man, tough guy (US); (TEC:
perno) pin, peg; (ELEC) pin, plug;
(COSTURA) hook.

macilento, a [maθi'lento, a] *adj* (*pálido*)
pale; (*ojeroso*) haggard.
macizo, a [ma'θiθo, a] *adj* (*grande*)
massive; (*fuerte, sólido*) solid ♦ *nm* mass,
chunk; (*GEO*) massif.
macramé [makra'me] *nm* macramé.
macrobiótico, a [makro'ßjotiko, a] *adj*
macrobiotic.
macro-comando [makroko'mando] *nm*
(*INFORM*) macro (command).
macroeconomía [makroekono'mia] *nf*
(*COM*) macroeconomics *sg*.
mácula ['makula] *nf* stain, blemish.
macuto [ma'kuto] *nm* (*MIL*) knapsack.
Madagascar [maðaɣas'kar] *nm*
Madagascar.
madeja [ma'ðexa] *nf* (*de lana*) skein, hank.
madera [ma'ðera] *nf* wood; (*fig*) nature,
character; (: *aptitud*) aptitude; **una ~ a**
piece of wood; **~ contrachapada *o***
laminada plywood; **tiene buena ~** he's
made of solid stuff; **tiene ~ de futbolista**
he's got the makings of a footballer.
maderaje [maðe'raxe], **maderamen**
[maðe'ramen] *nm* timber; (*trabajo*)
woodwork, timbering.
maderero [maðe'rero] *nm* timber
merchant.
madero [ma'ðero] *nm* beam; (*fig*) ship.
madrastra [ma'ðrastra] *nf* stepmother.
madre ['maðre] *adj* mother *cpd*; (*AM*)
tremendous ♦ *nf* mother; (*de vino etc*)
dregs *pl*; **~ adoptiva/política/soltera**
foster mother/mother-in-law/unmarried
mother; **la M~ Patria** the Mother
Country; **sin ~** motherless; **¡~ mía!** oh
dear!; **¡tu ~!** (*fam!*) fuck off! (*!*); **salirse**
de ~ (*río*) to burst its banks; (*persona*) to
lose all self-control.
madreperla [maðre'perla] *nf* mother-of-
pearl.
madreselva [maðre'selßa] *nf* honeysuckle.
Madrid [ma'ðrið] *n* Madrid.
madriguera [maðri'ɣera] *nf* burrow.
madrileño, a [maðri'leɲo, a] *adj* of *o* from
Madrid ♦ *nm/f* native *o* inhabitant of
Madrid.
Madriles [ma'ðriles] *nmpl*: **Los ~** (*fam*)
Madrid *sg*.
madrina [ma'ðrina] *nf* godmother; (*ARQ*)
prop, shore; (*TEC*) brace; **~ de boda**
bridesmaid.
madroño [ma'ðroɲo] *nm* (*BOT*) strawberry
tree, arbutus.
madrugada [maðru'ɣaða] *nf* early
morning, small hours; (*alba*) dawn,
daybreak; **a las 4 de la ~** at 4 o'clock in
the morning.

madrugador, a [maðruɣa'ðor, a] *adj*
early-rising.
madrugar [maðru'ɣar] *vi* to get up early;
(*fig*) to get a head start.
madrugue [ma'ðruɣe] *etc vb* V **madrugar**.
madurar [maðu'rar] *vt, vi* (*fruta*) to ripen;
(*fig*) to mature.
madurez [maðu'reθ] *nf* ripeness; (*fig*)
maturity.
maduro, a [ma'ðuro, a] *adj* ripe; (*fig*)
mature; **poco ~** unripe.
MAE *nm abr* (*ESP POL*) = **Ministerio de**
Asuntos Exteriores.
maestra [ma'estra] *nf* V **maestro**.
maestría [maes'tria] *nf* mastery; (*habilidad*)
skill, expertise; (*AM*) Master's Degree.
maestro, a [ma'estro, a] *adj* masterly;
(*perito*) skilled, expert; (*principal*) main;
(*educado*) trained ♦ *nm/f* master/mistress;
(*profesor*) teacher ♦ *nm* (*autoridad*)
authority; (*MUS*) maestro; (*obrero*)
skilled workman; **~ albañil** master
mason; **~ de obras** foreman.
mafia ['mafja] *nf* mafia; **la M~** the Mafia.
mafioso [ma'fjoso] *nm* gangster.
Magallanes [maɣa'ʎanes] *nm*: **Estrecho de**
~ Strait of Magellan.
magia ['maxja] *nf* magic.
mágico, a ['maxiko, a] *adj* magic(al) ♦ *nm/f*
magician.
magisterio [maxis'terjo] *nm* (*enseñanza*)
teaching; (*profesión*) teaching
profession; (*maestros*) teachers *pl*.
magistrado [maxis'traðo] *nm* magistrate;
Primer M~ (*AM*) President, Prime
Minister.
magistral [maxis'tral] *adj* magisterial; (*fig*)
masterly.
magistratura [maxistra'tura] *nf*
magistracy; **M~ del Trabajo** (*ESP*)
≈ Industrial Tribunal.
magnánimo, a [maɣ'nanimo, a] *adj*
magnanimous.
magnate [maɣ'nate] *nm* magnate, tycoon;
~ de la prensa press baron.
magnesio [maɣ'nesjo] *nm* (*QUÍMICA*)
magnesium.
magnetice [maɣne'tiθe] *etc vb* V
magnetizar.
magnético, a [maɣ'netiko, a] *adj*
magnetic.
magnetismo [maɣne'tismo] *nm*
magnetism.
magnetizar [maɣneti'θar] *vt* to magnetize.
magnetofón [maɣneto'fon],
magnetófono [maɣne'tofono] *nm* tape
recorder.
magnetofónico, a [maɣneto'foniko, a] *adj*:

cinta magnetofónica recording tape.

magnicidio [maɣni'θiðjo] *nm* assassination (*of an important person*).

magnífico, a [maɣ'nifiko, a] *adj* splendid, magnificent.

magnitud [maɣni'tuð] *nf* magnitude.

mago, a ['maɣo, a] *nm/f* magician, wizard; **los Reyes M~s** the Magi, the Three Wise Men; *V tb* **Reyes Magos**.

magrear [maɣre'ar] *vt* (*fam*) to touch up.

magro, a ['maɣro, a] *adj* (*persona*) thin, lean; (*carne*) lean.

maguey [ma'ɣei] *nm* (*BOT*) agave.

magulladura [maɣuʎa'ðura] *nf* bruise.

magullar [maɣu'ʎar] *vt* (*amoratar*) to bruise; (*dañar*) to damage; (*fam: golpear*) to bash, beat.

Maguncia [ma'ɣunθja] *nf* Mainz.

mahometano, a [maome'tano, a] *adj* Mohammedan.

mahonesa [mao'nesa] *nf* = **mayonesa**.

maicena [mai'θena] *nf* cornflour, corn starch (*US*).

maillot [ma'jot] *nm* swimming costume; (*DEPORTE*) vest.

maître ['metre] *nm* head waiter.

maíz [ma'iθ] *nm* maize (*BRIT*), corn (*US*); sweet corn.

maizal [mai'θal] *nm* maize field, cornfield.

majadero, a [maxa'ðero, a] *adj* silly, stupid.

majar [ma'xar] *vt* to crush, grind.

majareta [maxa'reta] *adj* (*fam*) cracked, potty.

majestad [maxes'tað] *nf* majesty; **Su M~** His/Her Majesty; **(Vuestra) M~** Your Majesty.

majestuoso, a [maxes'twoso, a] *adj* majestic.

majo, a ['maxo, a] *adj* nice; (*guapo*) attractive, good-looking; (*elegante*) smart.

mal [mal] *adv* badly; (*equivocadamente*) wrongly; (*con dificultad*) with difficulty ♦ *adj* = **malo, a** ♦ *nm* evil; (*desgracia*) misfortune; (*daño*) harm, damage; (*MED*) illness ♦ *conj*: ~ **que le pese** whether he likes it or not; **me entendió** ~ he misunderstood me; **hablar** ~ **de algn** to speak ill of sb; **huele** ~ it smells bad; **ir de** ~ **en peor** to go from bad to worse; **oigo/veo** ~ I can't hear/see very well; **si** ~ **no recuerdo** if my memory serves me right; **¡menos** ~! just as well!; ~ **que bien** rightly or wrongly; **no hay** ~ **que por bien no venga** every cloud has a silver lining; ~ **de ojo** evil eye.

malabarismo [malaβa'rismo] *nm* juggling.

malabarista [malaβa'rista] *nm/f* juggler.

malaconsejado, a [malakonse'xaðo, a] *adj* ill-advised.

malacostumbrado, a [malakostum'braðo, a] *adj* (*consentido*) spoiled.

malacostumbrar [malakostum'brar] *vt*: ~ **a algn** to get sb into bad habits.

malagueño, a [mala'ɣeɲo, a] *adj* of *o* from Málaga ♦ native *o* inhabitant of Málaga.

Malaisia [ma'laisja] *nf* Malaysia.

malaria [ma'larja] *nf* malaria.

Malasia [ma'lasja] *nf* Malaysia.

malavenido, a [malaβe'niðo, a] *adj* incompatible.

malayo, a [ma'lajo, a] *adj* Malay(an) ♦ *nm/f* Malay ♦ *nm* (*LING*) Malay.

Malaysia [ma'laisia] *nf* Malaysia.

malcarado, a [malka'raðo, a] *adj* ugly, grim-faced.

malcriado, a [mal'krjaðo, a] *adj* (*consentido*) spoiled.

malcriar [mal'krjar] *vt* to spoil, pamper.

maldad [mal'dað] *nf* evil, wickedness.

maldecir [malde'θir] *vt* to curse ♦ *vi*: ~ **de** to speak ill of.

maldiciendo [maldi'θjendo] *etc vb V* **maldecir**.

maldición [maldi'θjon] *nf* curse; **¡~!** curse it!, damn!

maldiga [mal'diɣa] *etc*, **maldije** [mal'dixe] *etc vb V* **maldecir**.

maldito, a [mal'dito, a] *adj* (*condenado*) damned; (*perverso*) wicked ♦ *nm*: **el** ~ **the devil**; **¡~ sea!** damn it!; **no le hace** ~ **(el) caso** he doesn't take a blind bit of notice.

maleable [male'aβle] *adj* malleable.

maleante [male'ante] *adj* wicked ♦ *nm/f* criminal, crook.

malecón [male'kon] *nm* pier, jetty.

maledicencia [maleði'θenθja] *nf* slander, scandal.

maleducado, a [maleðu'kaðo, a] *adj* bad-mannered, rude.

maleficio [male'fiθjo] *nm* curse, spell.

malentendido [malenten'diðo] *nm* misunderstanding.

malestar [males'tar] *nm* (*gen*) discomfort; (*enfermedad*) indisposition; (*fig: inquietud*) uneasiness; (*POL*) unrest; **siento un** ~ **en el estómago** my stomach is upset.

maleta [ma'leta] *nf* case, suitcase; (*AUTO*) boot (*BRIT*), trunk (*US*); **hacer la** ~ to pack.

maletera [male'tera] *nf* (*AM AUTO*) boot (*BRIT*), trunk (*US*).

maletero [male'tero] *nm* (*AUTO*) boot

(*BRIT*), trunk (*US*); (*persona*) porter.
maletín [male'tin] *nm* small case, bag;
(*portafolio*) briefcase.
malevolencia [maleßo'lenθja] *nf* malice,
spite.
malévolo, a [ma'leßolo, a] *adj* malicious,
spiteful.
maleza [ma'leθa] *nf* (*hierbas malas*) weeds
pl; (*arbustos*) thicket.
malgache [mal'ɣatʃe] *adj* of *o* from
Madagascar ♦ *nm/f* native *o* inhabitant of
Madagascar.
malgastar [malɣas'tar] *vt* (*tiempo, dinero*)
to waste; (*recursos*) to squander; (*salud*)
to ruin.
malhaya [ma'laja] *excl* (*esp AM*: *fam!*) damn
(it)! (*!*); ¡~ **sea/sean!** damn it/them! (*!*).
malhechor, a [male'tʃor, a] *nm/f*
delinquent; (*criminal*) criminal.
malherido, a [male'riðo, a] *adj* badly
injured.
malhumorado, a [malumo'raðo, a] *adj*
bad-tempered.
malicia [ma'liθja] *nf* (*maldad*) wickedness;
(*astucia*) slyness, guile; (*mala intención*)
malice, spite; (*carácter travieso*)
mischievousness.
malicioso, a [mali'θjoso, a] *adj* wicked,
evil; sly, crafty; malicious, spiteful;
mischievous.
malignidad [maliɣni'ðað] *nf* (*MED*)
malignancy; (*malicia*) malice.
maligno, a [ma'liɣno, a] *adj* evil; (*dañino*)
pernicious, harmful; (*malévolo*)
malicious; (*MED*) malignant ♦ *nm*: **el ~**
the devil.
malintencionado, a [malintenθjo'naðo, a]
adj (*comentario*) hostile; (*persona*)
malicious.
malla ['maʎa] *nf* (*de una red*) mesh; (*red*)
network; (*AM*: *de baño*) swimsuit; (*de
ballet, gimnasia*) leotard; ~**s** *nfpl* tights; ~
de alambre wire mesh.
Mallorca [ma'ʎorka] *nf* Majorca.
mallorquín, ina [maʎor'kin, ina] *adj, nm/f*
Majorcan ♦ *nm* (*LING*) Majorcan.
malnutrido, a [malnu'triðo, a] *adj*
undernourished.
malo, a ['malo, a] *adj* (**mal** *before nmsg*)
bad; (*calidad*) poor; (*falso*) false;
(*espantoso*) dreadful; (*niño*) naughty
♦ *nm/f* villain ♦ *nm* (*CINE fam*) bad guy
♦ *nf* spell of bad luck; **estar ~** to be ill;
andar a malas con algn to be on bad
terms with sb; **estar de malas** (*mal
humor*) to be in a bad mood; **lo ~ es
que ...** the trouble is that ....
malograr [malo'ɣrar] *vt* to spoil; (*plan*) to

upset; (*ocasión*) to waste; ~**se** *vr* (*plan etc*)
to fail, come to grief; (*persona*) to die
before one's time.
maloliente [malo'ljente] *adj* stinking,
smelly.
malparado, a [malpa'raðo, a] *adj*: **salir ~** to
come off badly.
malpensado, a [malpen'saðo, a] *adj* evil-
minded.
malquerencia [malke'renθja] *nf* dislike.
malquistar [malkis'tar] *vt*: ~ **a dos
personas** to cause a rift between two
people; ~**se** *vr* to fall out.
malsano, a [mal'sano, a] *adj* unhealthy.
malsonante [malso'nante] *adj* (*palabra*)
nasty, rude.
Malta ['malta] *nf* Malta.
malta ['malta] *nf* malt.
malteada [malte'aða] *nf* (*AM*) milk shake.
maltés, esa [mal'tes, esa] *adj, nm/f* Maltese.
maltraer [maltra'er] *vt* (*abusar*) to insult,
abuse; (*maltratar*) to ill-treat.
maltratar [maltra'tar] *vt* to ill-treat,
mistreat.
maltrecho, a [mal'tretʃo, a] *adj* battered,
damaged.
malva ['malßa] *nf* mallow; ~ **loca**
hollyhock; (**de color de**) ~ mauve.
malvado, a [mal'ßaðo, a] *adj* evil,
villainous.
malvavisco [malßa'ßisko] *nm*
marshmallow.
malvender [malßen'der] *vt* to sell off
cheap *o* at a loss.
malversación [malßersa'θjon] *nf*
embezzlement, misappropriation.
malversar [malßer'sar] *vt* to embezzle,
misappropriate.
Malvinas [mal'ßinas] *nfpl*: **Islas ~** Falkland
Islands.
mama ['mama] *pl* **mamás** *nf* (*de animal*)
teat; (*de mujer*) breast.
mamá [ma'ma] *nf* (*fam*) mum, mummy.
mamacita [mama'sita] *nf* (*AM fam*) mum,
mummy.
mamadera [mama'dera] *nf* (*AM*) baby's
bottle.
mamagrande [mama'grande] *nf* (*AM*)
grandmother.
mamar [ma'mar] *vt* (*pecho*) to suck; (*fig*) to
absorb, assimilate ♦ *vi* to suck; **dar de ~**
to (breast-)feed; (*animal*) to suckle.
mamarracho [mama'rratʃo] *nm* sight,
mess.
mambo ['mambo] *nf* (*MUS*) mambo.
mamífero, a [ma'mifero, a] *adj*
mammalian, mammal *cpd* ♦ *nm* mammal.
mamón, ona [ma'mon, ona] *adj* small,

baby *cpd* ♦ *nm/f* small baby; (*fam!*)
wanker (*!*).

mamotreto [mamo'treto] *nm* hefty
volume; (*fam*) whacking great thing.

mampara [mam'para] *nf* (*entre
habitaciones*) partition; (*biombo*) screen.

mamporro [mam'porro] *nm* (*fam*): **dar un ~
a** to clout.

mampostería [mamposte'ria] *nf* masonry.

mamut [ma'mut] *nm* mammoth.

maná [ma'na] *nm* manna.

manada [ma'naθa] *nf* (*ZOOL*) herd; (: *de
leones*) pride; (: *de lobos*) pack; **llegaron
en ~s** (*fam*) they came in droves.

Managua [ma'naɣwa] *n* Managua.

manantial [manan'tjal] *nm* spring; (*fuente*)
fountain; (*fig*) source.

manar [ma'nar] *vt* to run with, flow with
♦ *vi* to run, flow; (*abundar*) to abound.

manaza [ma'naθa] *nf* big hand ♦ *adj, nm/f inv*:
~s: ser un ~s to be clumsy.

mancebo [man'θeβo] *nm* (*joven*) young
man.

mancha ['mantʃa] *nf* stain, mark; (*de tinta*)
blot; (*de vegetación*) patch; (*imperfección*)
stain, blemish, blot; (*boceto*) sketch,
outline; **la M~** La Mancha.

manchado, a [man'tʃaðo, a] *adj* (*sucio*)
dirty; (*animal*) spotted; (*ave*) speckled;
(*tinta*) smudged.

manchar [man'tʃar] *vt* to stain, mark;
(*ZOOL*) to patch; (*ensuciar*) to soil, dirty;
~se *vr* to get dirty; (*fig*) to dirty one's
hands.

manchego, a [man'tʃeɣo, a] *adj* of *o* from
La Mancha ♦ *nm/f* native *o* inhabitant of
La Mancha.

mancilla [man'θiʎa] *nf* stain, blemish.

mancillar [manθi'ʎar] *vt* to stain, sully.

manco, a ['manko, a] *adj* one-armed; one-
handed; (*fig*) defective, faulty; **no ser ~**
to be useful *o* active.

mancomunar [mankomu'nar] *vt* to unite,
bring together; (*recursos*) to pool; (*JUR*)
to make jointly responsible.

mancomunidad [mankomuni'ðað] *nf*
union, association; (*comunidad*)
community; (*JUR*) joint responsibility.

mandado [man'daðo] *nm* (*orden*) order;
(*recado*) commission, errand.

mandamás [manda'mas] *adj, nm/f inv* boss;
ser un ~ to be very bossy.

mandamiento [manda'mjento] *nm* (*orden*)
order, command; (*REL*) commandment;
~ judicial warrant.

mandar [man'dar] *vt* (*ordenar*) to order;
(*dirigir*) to lead, command; (*país*) to rule
over; (*enviar*) to send; (*pedir*) to order,

ask for ♦ *vi* to be in charge; (*pey*) to be
bossy; **~se** *vr*: **~se mudar** (*AM fam*) to go
away, clear off; **¿mande?** pardon?,
excuse me? (*US*); **¿manda usted algo
más?** is there anything else?; **~ a algn a
paseo *o* a la porra** to tell sb to go to hell;
se lo mandaremos por correo we'll post
it to you; **~ hacer un traje** to have a suit
made.

mandarín [manda'rin] *nm* petty
bureaucrat.

mandarina [manda'rina] *nf* (*fruta*)
tangerine, mandarin (orange).

mandatario, a [manda'tarjo, a] *nm/f*
(*representante*) agent; **primer ~** (*esp AM*)
head of state.

mandato [man'dato] *nm* (*orden*) order;
(*POL: período*) term of office; (: *territorio*)
mandate; (*INFORM*) command; **~ judicial**
(search) warrant.

mandíbula [man'diβula] *nf* jaw.

mandil [man'dil] *nm* (*delantal*) apron.

Mandinga [man'dinɣa] *nm* (*AM*) Devil.

mandioca [man'djoka] *nf* cassava.

mando ['mando] *nm* (*MIL*) command; (*de
país*) rule; (*el primer lugar*) lead; (*POL*)
term of office; (*TEC*) control; **~ a la
izquierda** left-hand drive; **los altos ~s**
the high command *sg*; **~ por botón**
push-button control; **al ~ de** in charge
of; **tomar el ~** to take the lead.

mandolina [mando'lina] *nf* mandolin(e).

mandón, ona [man'don, ona] *adj* bossy,
domineering.

manecilla [mane'θiʎa] *nf* (*TEC*) pointer; (*de
reloj*) hand.

manejable [mane'xaβle] *adj* manageable;
(*fácil de usar*) handy.

manejar [mane'xar] *vt* to manage;
(*máquina*) to work, operate; (*caballo etc*)
to handle; (*casa*) to run, manage; (*AM
AUTO*) to drive ♦ *vi* (*AM AUTO*) to drive;
~se *vr* (*comportarse*) to act, behave;
(*arreglárselas*) to manage; "**~ con
cuidado**" "handle with care".

manejo [ma'nexo] *nm* management;
handling; running; driving; (*facilidad de
trato*) ease, confidence; (*de idioma*)
command; **~s** *nmpl* intrigues; **tengo ~
del francés** I have a good command of
French.

manera [ma'nera] *nf* way, manner,
fashion; (*ARTE, LITERATURA etc: estilo*)
manner, style; **~s** *nfpl* (*modales*)
manners; **su ~ de ser** the way he is;
(*aire*) his manner; **de mala ~** (*fam*) badly,
unwillingly; **de ninguna ~** no way, by no
means; **de otra ~** otherwise; **de todas ~s**

at any rate; **en gran** ~ to a large extent; **sobre** ~ exceedingly; **a mi** ~ **de ver** in my view; **no hay** ~ **de persuadirle** there's no way of convincing him.

manga ['manga] *nf* (*de camisa*) sleeve; (*de riego*) hose; **de** ~ **corta/larga** short-/long-sleeved; **andar** ~ **por hombro** (*desorden*) to be topsy-turvy; **tener** ~ **ancha** to be easy-going.

mangante [man'gante] *adj* (*descarado*) brazen ♦ *nm* (*mendigo*) beggar.

mangar [man'gar] *vt* (*unir*) to plug in; (*fam: birlar*) to pinch, nick, swipe; (*mendigar*) to beg.

mango ['mango] *nm* handle; (*BOT*) mango; ~ **de escoba** broomstick.

mangonear [mangone'ar] *vt* to boss about ♦ *vi* to be bossy.

mangue ['mange] *etc vb V* **mangar**.

manguera [man'gera] *nf* (*de riego*) hose; (*tubo*) pipe; ~ **de incendios** fire hose.

manía [ma'nia] *nf* (*MED*) mania; (*fig: moda*) rage, craze; (*disgusto*) dislike; (*malicia*) spite; **tiene** ~**s** she's a bit fussy; **tener** ~ **a algn** to dislike sb.

maníaco, a [ma'niako, a] *adj* maniac(al) ♦ *nm/f* maniac.

maniatar [manja'tar] *vt* to tie the hands of.

maniático, a [ma'njatiko, a] *adj* maniac(al); (*loco*) crazy; (*tiquismiquis*) fussy ♦ *nm/f* maniac.

manicomio [mani'komjo] *nm* mental hospital (*BRIT*), insane asylum (*US*).

manicuro, a [mani'kuro, a] *nm/f* manicurist ♦ *nf* manicure.

manido, a [ma'niðo, a] *adj* (*tema etc*) trite, stale.

manifestación [manifesta'θjon] *nf* (*declaración*) statement, declaration; (*demostración*) show, display; (*POL*) demonstration.

manifestante [manifes'tante] *nm/f* demonstrator.

manifestar [manifes'tar] *vt* to show, manifest; (*declarar*) to state, declare; ~**se** *vr* to show, become apparent; (*POL: desfilar*) to demonstrate; (: *reunirse*) to hold a mass meeting.

manifiesto, a [mani'fjesto, a] *etc vb V* **manifestar** ♦ *adj* clear, manifest ♦ *nm* manifesto; (*ANAT, NAUT*) manifest; **poner algo de** ~ (*aclarar*) to make sth clear; (*revelar*) to reveal sth; **quedar** ~ to be plain *o* clear.

manija [ma'nixa] *nf* handle.

manilla [ma'niʎa] *nf* (*de reloj*) hand; (*AM*) handle, lever; ~**s (de hierro)** *nfpl* handcuffs.

manillar [mani'ʎar] *nm* handlebars *pl.*

maniobra [ma'njoßra] *nf* manœuvring; (*maneja*) handling; (*fig: movimiento*) manœuvre, move; (: *estratagema*) trick, stratagem; ~**s** *nfpl* manœuvres.

maniobrar [manio'ßrar] *vt* to manœuvre; (*manejar*) to handle ♦ *vi* to manœuvre.

manipulación [manipula'θjon] *nf* manipulation; (*COM*) handling.

manipular [manipu'lar] *vt* to manipulate; (*manejar*) to handle.

maniquí [mani'ki] *nm/f* model ♦ *nm* dummy.

manirroto, a [mani'rroto, a] *adj* lavish, extravagant ♦ *nm/f* spendthrift.

maní(s) [ma'ni] *nm, pl* **maníes** *o* **manises** (*AM: cacahuete*) peanut; (: *planta*) groundnut plant.

manita [ma'nita] *nf* little hand; ~**s de plata** artistic hands.

manitas [ma'nitas] *adj inv* good with one's hands ♦ *nm/f inv*: **ser un** ~ to be very good with one's hands.

manito [ma'nito] *nm* (*AM: en conversación*) mate (*fam*), chum.

manivela [mani'ßela] *nf* crank.

manjar [man'xar] *nm* (tasty) dish.

mano¹ ['mano] *nf* hand; (*ZOOL*) foot, paw; (*de pintura*) coat; (*serie*) lot, series; **a** ~ by hand; **a** ~ **derecha/izquierda** on (*o* to) the right(-hand side)/left(-hand side); **hecho a** ~ handmade; **a** ~**s llenas** lavishly, generously; **de primera** ~ (at) first hand; **de segunda** ~ (at) second hand; **robo a** ~ **armada** armed robbery; **Pedro es mi** ~ **derecha** Pedro is my right-hand man; ~ **de obra** labour, manpower; ~ **de santo** sure remedy; **darse la(s)** ~**(s)** to shake hands; **echar una** ~ to lend a hand; **echar una** ~ **a** to lay hands on; **echar** ~ **de** to make use of; **estrechar la** ~ **a algn** to shake sb's hand; **traer** *o* **llevar algo entre** ~**s** to deal *o* be busy with sth; **está en tus** ~**s** it's up to you; **se le fue la** ~ ~ his hand slipped; (*fig*) he went too far; ¡~**s a la obra!** to work!

mano² ['mano] *nm* (*AM fam*) friend, mate.

manojo [ma'noxo] *nm* handful, bunch; ~ **de llaves** bunch of keys.

manómetro [ma'nometro] *nm* (pressure) gauge.

manopla [ma'nopla] *nf* (*paño*) flannel; ~**s** *nfpl* mittens.

manoseado, a [manose'aðo, a] *adj* well-worn.

manosear [manose'ar] *vt* (*tocar*) to handle, touch; (*desordenar*) to mess up, rumple; (*insistir en*) to overwork; (*acariciar*) to caress, fondle; (*pey: persona*) to feel *o* touch up.

manotazo [mano'taθo] *nm* slap, smack.

mansalva [man'salβa]: **a ~** *adv*
indiscriminately.

mansedumbre [manse'ðumbre] *nf*
gentleness, meekness; (*de animal*)
tameness.

mansión [man'sjon] *nf* mansion.

manso, a ['manso, a] *adj* gentle, mild;
(*animal*) tame.

manta ['manta] *nf* blanket; (*AM*) poncho.

manteca [man'teka] *nf* fat; (*AM*) butter; **~
de cacahuete/cacao** peanut/cocoa
butter; **~ de cerdo** lard.

mantecado [mante'kaðo] *nm* ice cream.

mantecoso, a [mante'koso, a] *adj* fat,
greasy; **queso ~** soft cheese.

mantel [man'tel] *nm* tablecloth.

mantelería [mantele'ria] *nf* table linen.

mantendré [manten'dre] *etc vb* V
mantener.

mantener [mante'ner] *vt* to support,
maintain; (*alimentar*) to sustain;
(*conservar*) to keep; (*TEC*) to maintain,
service; **~se** *vr* (*seguir de pie*) to be still
standing; (*no ceder*) to hold one's
ground; (*subsistir*) to sustain o.s., keep
going; **~ algo en equilibrio** to keep sth
balanced; **~se a distancia** to keep one's
distance; **~se firme** to hold one's
ground.

mantenga [man'tenga] *etc vb* V **mantener.**

mantenimiento [manteni'mjento] *nm*
maintenance; sustenance; (*sustento*)
support.

mantequería [manteke'ria] *nf*
(*ultramarinos*) grocer's (shop).

mantequilla [mante'kiʎa] *nf* butter.

mantilla [man'tiʎa] *nf* mantilla; **~s** *nfpl*
baby clothes; **estar en ~s** (*persona*) to be
terribly innocent; (*proyecto*) to be in its
infancy.

manto ['manto] *nm* (*capa*) cloak; (*de
ceremonia*) robe, gown.

mantón [man'ton] *nm* shawl.

mantuve [man'tuβe] *etc vb* V **mantener.**

manual [ma'nwal] *adj* manual ♦ *nm*
manual, handbook; **habilidad ~** manual
skill.

manubrio [ma'nuβrio] *nm* (*AM AUTO*)
steering wheel.

manufactura [manufak'tura] *nf*
manufacture; (*fábrica*) factory.

manufacturado, a [manufaktu'raðo, a] *adj*
manufactured.

manuscrito, a [manus'krito, a] *adj*
handwritten ♦ *nm* manuscript.

manutención [manuten'θjon] *nf*

maintenance; (*sustento*) support.

manzana [man'θana] *nf* apple; (*ARQ*) block;
~ de la discordia (*fig*) bone of
contention.

manzanal [manθa'nal] *nm* apple orchard.

manzanilla [manθa'niʎa] *nf* (*planta*)
camomile; (*infusión*) camomile tea;
(*vino*) manzanilla.

manzano [man'θano] *nm* apple tree.

maña ['maɲa] *nf* (*gen*) skill, dexterity;
(*pey*) guile; (*costumbre*) habit; (*una ~*)
trick, knack; **con ~** craftily.

mañana [ma'ɲana] *adv* tomorrow ♦ *nm*
future ♦ *nf* morning; **de o por la ~** in the
morning; **¡hasta ~!** see you tomorrow!;
pasado ~ the day after tomorrow; **~ por
la ~** tomorrow morning.

mañanero, a [maɲa'nero, a] *adj* early-
rising.

maño, a ['maɲo, a] *adj* Aragonese ♦ *nm/f*
native *o* inhabitant of Aragon.

mañoso, a [ma'ɲoso, a] *adj* (*hábil*) skilful;
(*astuto*) smart, clever.

mapa ['mapa] *nm* map.

mapuche, a [ma'putʃe, a] *adj*, *nm/f*
Mapuche, Araucanian.

maqueta [ma'keta] *nf* (scale) model.

maquiavélico, a [makja'βeliko, a] *adj*
Machiavellian.

maquillador, a [makiʎa'ðor, a] *nm/f* (*TEAT
etc*) make-up artist.

maquillaje [maki'ʎaxe] *nm* make-up; (*acto*)
making up.

maquillar [maki'ʎar] *vt* to make up; **~se** *vr*
to put on (some) make-up.

máquina ['makina] *nf* machine; (*de tren*)
locomotive, engine; (*FOTO*) camera; (*AM:
coche*) car; (*fig*) machinery; (: *proyecto*)
plan, project; **a toda ~** at full speed;
escrito a ~ typewritten; **~ de escribir**
typewriter; **~ de coser/lavar** sewing/
washing machine; **~ de facsímil**
facsimile (machine), fax; **~ de franqueo**
franking machine; **~ tragaperras** fruit
machine; (*COM*) slot machine.

maquinación [makina'θjon] *nf*
machination, plot.

maquinal [maki'nal] *adj* (*fig*) mechanical,
automatic.

maquinar [maki'nar] *vt, vi* to plot.

maquinaria [maki'narja] *nf* (*máquinas*)
machinery; (*mecanismo*) mechanism,
works *pl*.

maquinilla [maki'niʎa] *nf* small machine;
(*torno*) winch; **~ de afeitar** razor; **~
eléctrica** electric razor.

maquinista [maki'nista] *nm* (*FERRO*) engine
driver (*BRIT*), engineer (*US*); (*TEC*)

operator; (*NAUT*) engineer.

mar [mar] *nm* sea; ~ **de fondo**
groundswell; ~ **llena** high tide; ~
adentro *o* **afuera** out at sea; **en alta** ~ on
the high seas; **por** ~ by sea *o* boat;
hacerse a la ~ to put to sea; **a** ~**es** in
abundance; **un** ~ **de** lots of; **es la** ~ **de
guapa** she is ever so pretty; **el M**~
Negro/Báltico the Black/Baltic Sea; **el
M**~ **Muerto/Rojo** the Dead/Red Sea; **el
M**~ **del Norte** the North Sea.

mar. *abr* (= *marzo*) Mar.

maraca [maˈraka] *nf* maraca.

maraña [maˈraɲa] *nf* (*maleza*) thicket;
(*confusión*) tangle.

maravilla [maraˈβiʎa] *nf* marvel, wonder;
(*BOT*) marigold; **hacer** ~**s** to work
wonders; **a (las mil)** ~**s** wonderfully
well.

maravillar [maraβiˈʎar] *vt* to astonish,
amaze; ~**se** *vr* to be astonished, be
amazed.

maravilloso, a [maraβiˈʎoso, a] *adj*
wonderful, marvellous.

marbellí [marβeˈʎi] *adj* of *o* from Marbella
♦ *nm/f* native *o* inhabitant of Marbella.

marca [ˈmarka] *nf* mark; (*sello*) stamp;
(*COM*) make, brand; (*de ganado*) brand;
(: *acto*) branding; (*NAUT*) seamark;
(: *boya*) marker; (*DEPORTE*) record; **de** ~
excellent, outstanding; ~ **de fábrica**
trademark; ~ **propia** own brand; ~
registrada registered trademark.

marcación [markaˈθjon] *nf* (*TELEC*): ~
automática autodial.

marcado, a [marˈkaðo, a] *adj* marked,
strong.

marcador [markaˈðor] *nm* marker;
(*rotulador*) marker (pen); (*de libro*)
bookmark; (*DEPORTE*) scoreboard;
(: *persona*) scorer.

marcapasos [markaˈpasos] *nm inv*
pacemaker.

marcar [marˈkar] *vt* to mark; (*número de
teléfono*) to dial; (*gol*) to score; (*números*)
to record, keep a tally of; (*el pelo*) to set;
(*ganado*) to brand; (*suj: termómetro*) to
read, register; (: *reloj*) to show; (*tarea*) to
assign; (*COM*) to put a price on ♦ *vi*
(*DEPORTE*) to score; (*TELEC*) to dial; **mi
reloj marca las 2** it's 2 o'clock by my
watch; ~ **el compás** (*MUS*) to keep time;
~ **el paso** (*MIL*) to mark time.

marcha [ˈmartʃa] *nf* march; (*DEPORTE*)
walk; (*TEC*) running, working; (*AUTO*)
gear; (*velocidad*) speed; (*fig*) progress;
(*dirección*) course; **dar** ~ **atrás** to
reverse, put into reverse; **estar en** ~ to

be under way, be in motion; **hacer algo
sobre la** ~ to do sth as you *etc* go along;
poner en ~ to put into gear; **ponerse en**
~ to start, get going; **a** ~**s forzadas** (*fig*)
with all speed; **¡en** ~! (*MIL*) forward
march!; (*fig*) let's go!; "~ **moderada**"
(*AUTO*) "drive slowly"; **que tiene** *o* **de
mucha** ~ (*fam*) very lively.

marchante, a [marˈtʃante, a] *nm/f* dealer,
merchant.

marchar [marˈtʃar] *vi* (*ir*) to go; (*funcionar*)
to work, go; (*fig*) to go, proceed; ~**se** *vr*
to go (away), leave; **todo marcha bien**
everything is going well.

marchitar [martʃiˈtar] *vt* to wither, dry up;
~**se** *vr* (*BOT*) to wither; (*fig*) to fade away.

marchito, a [marˈtʃito, a] *adj* withered,
faded; (*fig*) in decline.

marchoso, a [marˈtʃoso, a] *adj* (*fam:
animado*) lively; (: *moderno*) modern.

marcial [marˈθjal] *adj* martial, military.

marciano, a [marˈθjano, a] *adj* Martian, of
o from Mars.

marco [ˈmarko] *nm* frame; (*DEPORTE*)
goalposts *pl*; (*moneda*) mark; (*fig*)
setting; (*contexto*) framework; ~ **de
chimenea** mantelpiece.

marea [maˈrea] *nf* tide; (*llovizna*) drizzle; ~
alta/baja high/low tide; ~ **negra** oil slick.

mareado, a [mareˈaðo, a] *adj*: **estar** ~ (*con
náuseas*) to feel sick; (*aturdido*) to feel
dizzy.

marear [mareˈar] *vt* (*fig: irritar*) to annoy,
upset; (*MED*): ~ **a algn** to make sb feel
sick; ~**se** *vr* (*tener náuseas*) to feel sick;
(*desvanecerse*) to feel faint; (*aturdirse*) to
feel dizzy; (*fam: emborracharse*) to get
tipsy.

marejada [mareˈxaða] *nf* (*NAUT*) swell,
heavy sea.

maremágnum [mareˈmaɣnum] *nm* (*fig*)
ocean, abundance.

maremoto [mareˈmoto] *nm* tidal wave.

mareo [maˈreo] *nm* (*náusea*) sick feeling;
(*aturdimiento*) dizziness; (*fam: lata*)
nuisance.

marfil [marˈfil] *nm* ivory.

margarina [marɣaˈrina] *nf* margarine.

margarita [marɣaˈrita] *nf* (*BOT*) daisy;
(**rueda**) ~ (*en máquina impresora*) daisy
wheel.

margen [ˈmarxen] *nm* (*borde*) edge,
border; (*fig*) margin, space ♦ *nf* (*de río
etc*) bank; ~ **de beneficio** *o* **de ganancia**
profit margin; ~ **comercial** mark-up; ~
de confianza credibility gap; **dar** ~ **para**
to give an opportunity for; **dejar a algn
al** ~ to leave sb out (in the cold);

materialmente [materjal'mente] *adv* materially; (*fig*) absolutely.

maternal [mater'nal] *adj* motherly, maternal.

maternidad [materni'ðað] *nf* motherhood, maternity.

materno, a [ma'terno, a] *adj* maternal; (*lengua*) mother *cpd*.

matice [ma'tiθe] *etc vb V* **matizar**.

matinal [mati'nal] *adj* morning *cpd*.

matiz [ma'tiθ] *nm* shade; (*de sentido*) shade, nuance; (*ironía etc*) touch.

matizar [mati'θar] *vt* (*variar*) to vary; (*ARTE*) to blend; ~ **de** to tinge with.

matón [ma'ton] *nm* bully.

matorral [mato'rral] *nm* thicket.

matraca [ma'traka] *nf* rattle; (*fam*) nuisance.

matraz [ma'traθ] *nm* (*QUÍMICA*) flask.

matriarcado [matrjar'kaðo] *nm* matriarchy.

matrícula [ma'trikula] *nf* (*registro*) register; (*ESCOL: inscripción*) registration; (*AUTO*) registration number; (: *placa*) number plate.

matricular [matriku'lar] *vt* to register, enrol.

matrimonial [matrimo'njal] *adj* matrimonial.

matrimonio [matri'monjo] *nm* (*pareja*) (married) couple; (*acto*) marriage; ~ **civil/clandestino** civil/secret marriage; **contraer** ~ (**con**) to marry.

matriz [ma'triθ] *nf* (*ANAT*) womb; (*TEC*) mould; (*MAT*) matrix; **casa** ~ (*COM*) head office.

matrona [ma'trona] *nf* (*persona de edad*) matron.

matutino, a [matu'tino, a] *adj* morning *cpd*.

maula ['maula] *adj* (*persona*) good-for-nothing ♦ *nm/f* (*vago*) idler, slacker ♦ *nf* (*persona*) dead loss (*fam*).

maullar [mau'ʎar] *vi* to mew, miaow.

maullido [mau'ʎiðo] *nm* mew(ing), miaow(ing).

Mauricio [mau'riθjo] *nm* Mauritius.

Mauritania [mauri'tanja] *nf* Mauritania.

mausoleo [mauso'leo] *nm* mausoleum.

maxilar [maksi'lar] *nm* jaw(bone).

máxima ['maksima] *nf V* **máximo**.

máxime ['maksime] *adv* especially.

máximo, a ['maksimo, a] *adj* maximum; (*más alto*) highest; (*más grande*) greatest ♦ *nm* maximum ♦ *nf* maxim; ~ **jefe** *o* **líder** (*AM*) President, leader; **como** ~ at most; **al** ~ to the utmost.

maxisingle [maksi'singel] *nm* twelve-inch (single).

maya ['maja] *adj* Mayan ♦ *nm/f* Maya(n).

mayo ['majo] *nm* May.

mayonesa [majo'nesa] *nf* mayonnaise.

mayor [ma'jor] *adj* main, chief; (*adulto*) grown-up, adult; (*JUR*) of age; (*de edad avanzada*) elderly; (*MUS*) major; (*comparativo: de tamaño*) bigger; (: *de edad*) older; (*superlativo: de tamaño*) biggest; (*tb: fig*) greatest; (: *de edad*) oldest ♦ *nm* chief, boss; (*adulto*) adult; **al por** ~ wholesale; ~ **de edad** adult; *V tb* **mayores**.

mayoral [majo'ral] *nm* foreman.

mayordomo [major'ðomo] *nm* butler.

mayoreo [majo'reo] *nm* (*AM*) wholesale (trade).

mayores [ma'jores] *nmpl* grown-ups; **llegar a** ~**es** to get out of hand.

mayoría [majo'ria] *nf* majority, greater part; **en la** ~ **de los casos** in most cases; **en su** ~ on the whole.

mayorista [majo'rista] *nm/f* wholesaler.

mayoritario, a [majori'tarjo, a] *adj* majority *cpd*; **gobierno** ~ majority government.

mayúsculo, a [ma'juskulo, a] *adj* (*fig*) big, tremendous ♦ *nf* capital (letter); **mayúsculas** *nfpl* capitals; (*TIP*) upper case *sg*.

maza ['maθa] *nf* (*arma*) mace; (*DEPORTE*) bat; (*POLO*) stick.

mazacote [maθa'kote] *nm* hard mass; (*CULIN*) dry doughy food; (*ARTE, LITERATURA etc*) mess, hotchpotch.

mazapán [maθa'pan] *nm* marzipan.

mazmorra [maθ'morra] *nf* dungeon.

mazo ['maθo] *nm* (*martillo*) mallet; (*de mortero*) pestle; (*de flores*) bunch; (*DEPORTE*) bat.

mazorca [ma'θorka] *nf* (*BOT*) spike; (*de maíz*) cob, ear.

MCAC *nm abr* = *Mercado Común de la América Central*.

MCI *nm abr* = *Mercado Común Iberoamericano*.

me [me] *pron* (*directo*) me; (*indirecto*) (to) me; (*reflexivo*) (to) myself; **¡dámelo!** give it to me!; ~ **lo compró** (*de mí*) he bought it from me; (*para mí*) he bought it for me.

meandro [me'andro] *nm* meander.

mear [me'ar] (*fam*) *vt* to piss on (*!*) ♦ *vi* to pee, piss (*!*), have a piss (*!*); ~**se** *vr* to wet o.s.

Meca ['meka] *nf*: **La** ~ Mecca.

mecánica [me'kanika] *nf V* **mecánico**.

mecanice [meka'niθe] *etc vb V* **mecanizar**.

mecánico, a [me'kaniko, a] *adj*

mechanical; (*repetitivo*) repetitive ♦ *nm/f*
mechanic ♦ *nf* (*estudio*) mechanics *sg*;
(*mecanismo*) mechanism.
mecanismo [meka'nismo] *nm* mechanism;
(*engranaje*) gear.
mecanizar [mekani'θar] *vt* to mechanize.
mecanografía [mekanoɣra'fia] *nf*
typewriting.
mecanografiado, a [mekanoɣra'fjaðo, a]
adj typewritten ♦ *nm* typescript.
mecanógrafo, a [meka'noɣrafo, a] *nm/f*
(*copy*) typist.
mecate [me'kate] *nm* (*AM*) rope.
mecedor [mese'ðor] *nm* (*AM*), **mecedora**
[meθe'ðora] *nf* rocking chair.
mecenas [me'θenas] *nm inv* patron.
mecenazgo [meθe'naθɣo] *nm* patronage.
mecer [me'θer] *vt* (*cuna*) to rock; ~**se** *vr* to
rock; (*rama*) to sway.
mecha ['metʃa] *nf* (*de vela*) wick; (*de
bomba*) fuse; **a toda** ~ at full speed;
ponerse ~**s** to streak one's hair.
mechero [me'tʃero] *nm* (cigarette) lighter.
mechón [me'tʃon] *nm* (*gen*) tuft; (*manojo*)
bundle; (*de pelo*) lock.
medalla [me'ðaʎa] *nf* medal.
media ['meðja] *nf* V **medio**.
mediación [meða'θjon] *nf* mediation; **por**
~ **de** through.
mediado, a [me'ðjaðo, a] *adj* half-full;
(*trabajo*) half-completed; **a** ~**s de** in the
middle of, halfway through.
medianamente [meðjana'mente] *adv*
(*moderadamente*) moderately, fairly;
(*regularmente*) moderately well.
mediano, a [me'ðjano, a] *adj* (*regular*)
medium, average; (*mediocre*) mediocre
♦ *nf* (*AUT*) central reservation, median
(*US*); (**de tamaño**) ~ medium-sized.
medianoche [meðja'notʃe] *nf* midnight.
mediante [me'ðjante] *adv* by (means of),
through.
mediar [me'ðjar] *vi* (*tiempo*) to elapse;
(*interceder*) to mediate, intervene;
(*existir*) to exist; **media el hecho de que**
... there is the fact that ....
medicación [meðika'θjon] *nf* medication,
treatment.
medicamento [meðika'mento] *nm*
medicine, drug.
medicina [meði'θina] *nf* medicine.
medicinal [meðiθi'nal] *adj* medicinal.
medición [meði'θjon] *nf* measurement.
médico, a ['meðiko, a] *adj* medical ♦ *nm/f*
doctor; ~ **de cabecera** family doctor; ~
pediatra paediatrician; ~ **residente**
house physician, intern (*US*).
medida [me'ðiða] *nf* measure; (*medición*)

measurement; (*de camisa, zapato etc*)
size, fitting; (*prudencia*) moderation,
prudence; **en cierta/gran** ~ up to a
point/to a great extent; **un traje a la** ~
made-to-measure suit; ~ **de cuello** collar
size; **a** ~ **de** in proportion to; (*de acuerdo
con*) in keeping with; **con** ~ with
restraint; **sin** ~ immoderately; **a** ~ **que**
... (at the same time) as ...; **tomar** ~**s** to
take steps.
medieval [meðje'ßal] *adj* medieval.
medio, a ['meðjo, a] *adj* half (a); (*punto*)
mid, middle; (*promedio*) average ♦ *adv*
half-; (*esp AM*: *un tanto*) rather, quite
♦ *nm* (*centro*) middle, centre; (*promedio*)
average; (*método*) means, way;
(*ambiente*) environment ♦ *nf* (*prenda de
vestir*) stocking, (*AM*) sock; (*promedio*)
average; ~**s** *nfpl* tights; **media hora** half
an hour; ~ **litro** half a litre; **las tres y
media** half past three; **M~ Oriente**
Middle East; **a** ~ **camino** halfway
(there); ~ **dormido** half asleep; ~
enojado (*esp AM*) rather annoyed; **lo dejó
a** ~**s** he left it half-done; **ir a** ~**s** to go
fifty-fifty; **a** ~ **terminar** half finished; **en**
~ in the middle; (*entre*) in between; **por**
~ **de** by (means of), through; **en los** ~**s
financieros** in financial circles;
encontrarse en su ~ to be in one's
element; ~ **circulante** (*COM*) money
supply; *V tb* **medios**.
medioambiental [meðjoambjen'tal] *adj*
environmental.
mediocre [me'ðjokre] *adj* middling,
average; (*pey*) mediocre.
mediocridad [meðjokri'ðað] *nf* middling
quality; (*pey*) mediocrity.
mediodía [meðjo'ðia] *nm* midday, noon.
mediopensionista [meðjopensjo'nista]
nm/f day boy/girl.
medios ['meðjos] *nmpl* means, resources;
los ~ **de comunicación** the media.
medir [me'ðir] *vt* (*gen*) to measure ♦ *vi* to
measure; ~**se** *vr* (*moderarse*) to be
moderate, act with restraint; **¿cuánto
mides? — mido 1.50 m** how tall are you?
— I am 1.50 m tall.
meditabundo, a [meðita'ßundo, a] *adj*
pensive.
meditar [meði'tar] *vt* to ponder, think
over, meditate on; (*planear*) to think out
♦ *vi* to ponder, think, meditate.
mediterráneo, a [meðite'rraneo, a] *adj*
Mediterranean ♦ *nm*: **el (mar) M~** the
Mediterranean (Sea).
medrar [me'ðrar] *vi* to increase, grow;
(*mejorar*) to improve; (*prosperar*) to

prosper, thrive; (*animal, planta etc*) to grow.

medroso, a [me'ðroso, a] *adj* fearful, timid.

médula ['meðula] *nf* (*ANAT*) marrow; (*BOT*) pith; ~ **espinal** spinal cord; **hasta la** ~ (*fig*) to the core.

medusa [me'ðusa] *nf* (*ESP*) jellyfish.

megabyte ['meɣaβait] *nm* (*INFORM*) megabyte.

megafonía [meɣafo'nia] *nf* PA *o* public address system.

megáfono [me'ɣafono] *nm* public address system.

megalomanía [meɣaloma'nia] *nf* megalomania.

megalómano, a [meɣa'lomano, a] *nm/f* megalomaniac.

megaocteto [meɣaok'teto] *nm* (*INFORM*) megabyte.

mejicano, a [mexi'kano, a] *adj, nm/f* Mexican.

Méjico ['mexiko] *nm* Mexico.

mejilla [me'xiʎa] *nf* cheek.

mejillón [mexi'ʎon] *nm* mussel.

mejor [me'xor] *adj, adv* (*comparativo*) better; (*superlativo*) best; **lo** ~ the best thing; **lo** ~ **de la vida** the prime of life; **a lo** ~ probably; (*quizá*) maybe; ~ **dicho** rather; **tanto** ~ so much the better; **es el** ~ **de todos** he's the best of all.

mejora [me'xora] *nf*, **mejoramiento** [mexora'mjento] *nm* improvement.

mejorar [mexo'rar] *vt* to improve, make better ♦ *vi*, ~**se** *vr* to improve, get better; (*COM*) to do well, prosper; ~ **a** to be better than; **los negocios mejoran** business is picking up.

mejoría [mexo'ria] *nf* improvement; (*restablecimiento*) recovery.

mejunje [me'xunxe] *nm* (*pey*) concoction.

melancolía [melanko'lia] *nf* melancholy.

melancólico, a [melan'koliko, a] *adj* (*triste*) sad, melancholy; (*soñador*) dreamy.

melena [me'lena] *nf* (*de persona*) long hair; (*ZOOL*) mane.

melillense [meli'ʎense] *adj* of *o* from Melilla ♦ *nm/f* native *o* inhabitant of Melilla.

mella ['meʎa] *nf* (*rotura*) notch, nick; **hacer** ~ (*fig*) to make an impression.

mellizo, a [me'ʎiθo, a] *adj, nm/f* twin.

melocotón [meloko'ton] *nm* (*ESP*) peach.

melodía [melo'ðia] *nf* melody; (*aire*) tune.

melodrama [melo'ðrama] *nm* melodrama.

melodramático, a [meloðra'matiko, a] *adj* melodramatic.

melón [me'lon] *nm* melon.

melopea [melo'pea] *nf* (*fam*): **tener una** ~ to be sloshed.

meloso, a [me'loso, a] *adj* honeyed, sweet; (*empalagoso*) sickly, cloying; (*voz*) sweet; (*zalamero*) smooth.

membrana [mem'brana] *nf* membrane.

membrete [mem'brete] *nm* letterhead; **papel con** ~ headed notepaper.

membrillo [mem'briʎo] *nm* quince; **carne de** ~ quince jelly.

memo, a ['memo, a] *adj* silly, stupid ♦ *nm/f* idiot.

memorable [memo'raβle] *adj* memorable.

memorándum [memo'randum] *nm* (*libro*) notebook; (*comunicación*) memorandum.

memoria [me'morja] *nf* (*gen*) memory; (*artículo*) (learned) paper; ~**s** *nfpl* (*de autor*) memoirs; ~ **anual** annual report; **aprender algo de** ~ to learn sth by heart; **si tengo buena** ~ if my memory serves me right; **venir a la** ~ to come to mind; (*INFORM*): ~ **de acceso aleatorio** random access memory, RAM; ~ **auxiliar** backing storage; ~ **fija** read-only memory, ROM; ~ **fija programable** programmable memory; ~ **del teclado** keyboard memory.

memorice [memo'riθe] *etc vb V* **memorizar**.

memorizar [memori'θar] *vt* to memorize.

menaje [me'naxe] *nm* (*muebles*) furniture; (*utensilios domésticos*) household equipment; ~ **de cocina** kitchenware.

mención [men'θjon] *nf* mention; **digno de** ~ noteworthy; **hacer** ~ **de** to mention.

mencionar [menθjo'nar] *vt* to mention; (*nombrar*) to name; **sin** ~ ... let alone ....

mendicidad [mendiθi'ðað] *nf* begging.

mendigar [mendi'ɣar] *vt* to beg (for).

mendigo, a [men'diɣo, a] *nm/f* beggar.

mendigue [men'diɣe] *etc vb V* **mendigar**.

mendrugo [men'druɣo] *nm* crust.

menear [mene'ar] *vt* to move; (*cola*) to wag; (*cadera*) to swing; (*fig*) to handle; ~**se** *vr* to shake; (*balancearse*) to sway; (*moverse*) to move; (*fig*) to get a move on.

menester [menes'ter] *nm* (*necesidad*) necessity; ~**es** *nmpl* (*deberes*) duties; **es** ~ **hacer algo** it is necessary to do sth, sth must be done.

menestra [me'nestra] *nf*: ~ **de verduras** vegetable stew.

mengano, a [men'gano, a] *nm/f* Mr (*o* Mrs *o* Miss) So-and-so.

mengua ['mengwa] *nf* (*disminución*) decrease; (*falta*) lack; (*pobreza*) poverty; (*fig*) discredit; **en** ~ **de** to the detriment of.

menguante – menudear

menguante [men'gwante] *adj* decreasing, diminishing; (*luna*) waning; (*marea*) ebb *cpd*.

menguar [men'gwar] *vt* to lessen, diminish; (*fig*) to discredit ♦ *vi* to diminish, decrease; (*fig*) to decline.

mengüe ['mengwe] *etc vb* V **menguar**.

menopausia [meno'pausja] *nf* menopause.

menor [me'nor] *adj* (*más pequeño: comparativo*) smaller; (*número*) less, lesser; (: *superlativo*) smallest; (*número*) least; (*más joven: comparativo*) younger; (: *superlativo*) youngest; (*MUS*) minor ♦ *nm/f* (*joven*) young person, juvenile; **Juanito es ~ que Pepe** Juanito is younger than Pepe; **ella es la ~ de todas** she is the youngest of all; **no tengo la ~ idea** I haven't the faintest idea; **al por ~** retail; **~ de edad** under age.

Menorca [me'norka] *nf* Minorca.

menorquín, ina [menor'kin, ina] *adj, nm/f* Minorcan.

═══════════════ *PALABRA CLAVE*

menos [menos] *adj* **1**: **~ (que, de)** (*compar: cantidad*) less (than); (: *número*) fewer (than); **con ~ entusiasmo** with less enthusiasm; **~ gente** fewer people; *V tb* **cada**
2 (*superl*): **es el que ~ culpa tiene** he is the least to blame; **donde ~ problemas hay** where there are fewest problems
♦ *adv* **1** (*compar*): **~ (que, de)** less (than); **me gusta ~ que el otro** I like it less than the other one; **~ de 5** less than 5; **~ de lo que piensas** less than you think
2 (*superl*): **es el ~ listo (de su clase)** he's the least bright (in his class); **de todas ellas es la que ~ me agrada** out of all of them she's the one I like least; **(por) lo ~** at (the very) least; **es lo ~ que puedo hacer** it's the least I can do; **lo ~ posible** as little as possible
3 (*locuciones*): **no quiero verle y ~ visitarle** I don't want to see him let alone visit him; **tenemos 7 (de) ~** we're 7 short; **eso es lo de ~** that's the least of it; **¡todo ~ eso!** anything but that!; **al/ por lo ~** at (the very) least; **si al ~** if only
♦ *prep* except; (*cifras*) minus; **todos ~ él** everyone except (for) him; **5 ~ 2 5** minus 2; **las 7 ~ 20** (*hora*) 20 to 7
♦ *conj*: **a ~ que: a ~ que venga mañana** unless he comes tomorrow.

menoscabar [menoska'βar] *vt* (*estropear*) to damage, harm; (*fig*) to discredit.

menospreciar [menospre'θjar] *vt* to underrate, undervalue; (*despreciar*) to scorn, despise.

menosprecio [menos'preθjo] *nm* underrating, undervaluation; scorn, contempt.

mensaje [men'saxe] *nm* message; **~ de error** (*INFORM*) error message.

mensajero, a [mensa'xero, a] *nm/f* messenger.

menstruación [menstrwa'θjon] *nf* menstruation.

menstruar [mens'trwar] *vi* to menstruate.

mensual [men'swal] *adj* monthly; **100 ptas ~es** 100 ptas. a month.

mensualidad [menswali'ðað] *nf* (*salario*) monthly salary; (*COM*) monthly payment *o* instalment.

menta ['menta] *nf* mint.

mentado, a [men'taðo, a] *adj* (*mencionado*) aforementioned; (*famoso*) well-known ♦ *nf*: **hacerle una mentada a algn** (*AM fam*) to (seriously) insult sb.

mental [men'tal] *adj* mental.

mentalidad [mentali'ðað] *nf* mentality, way of thinking.

mentalizar [mentali'θar] *vt* (*sensibilizar*) to make aware; (*convencer*) to convince; (*preparar mentalmente*) to psych up; **~se** *vr* (*concienciarse*) to become aware; (*prepararse mentalmente*) to get psyched up; **~se de que ...** (*convencerse*) to get it into one's head that ...

mentar [men'tar] *vt* to mention, name; **~ la madre a algn** to swear at sb.

mente ['mente] *nf* mind; (*inteligencia*) intelligence; **no tengo en ~ hacer eso** it is not my intention to do that.

mentecato, a [mente'kato, a] *adj* silly, stupid ♦ *nm/f* fool, idiot.

mentir [men'tir] *vi* to lie; **¡miento!** sorry, I'm wrong!

mentira [men'tira] *nf* (*una ~*) lie; (*acto*) lying; (*invención*) fiction; **~ piadosa** white lie; **una ~ como una casa** a whopping great lie (*fam*); **parece ~ que ...** it seems incredible that ..., I can't believe that ....

mentiroso, a [menti'roso, a] *adj* lying; (*falso*) deceptive ♦ *nm/f* liar.

mentís [men'tis] *nm inv* denial; **dar el ~ a** to deny.

mentón [men'ton] *nm* chin.

menú [me'nu] *nm* (*tb INFORM*) menu; (*en restaurante*) set meal; **guiado por ~** (*INFORM*) menu-driven.

menudear [menuðe'ar] *vt* (*repetir*) to repeat frequently ♦ *vi* (*ser frecuente*) to be frequent; (_detallar_) to go into great detail.

menudencia [menu'ðenθja] _nf_ (_bagatela_) trifle; ~**s** _nfpl_ odds and ends.

menudeo [menu'ðeo] _nm_ retail sales _pl_.

menudillos [menu'ðiʎos] _nmpl_ giblets.

menudo, a [me'nuðo, a] _adj_ (_pequeño_) small, tiny; (_sin importancia_) petty, insignificant; ¡~ **negocio!** (_fam_) some deal!; **a** ~ often, frequently.

meñique [me'ɲike] _nm_ little finger.

meollo [me'oʎo] _nm_ (_fig_) essence, core.

mequetrefe [meke'trefe] _nm_ good-for-nothing, whippersnapper.

mercader [merka'ðer] _nm_ merchant.

mercadería [merkaðe'ria] _nf_ commodity; ~**s** _nfpl_ goods, merchandise _sg_.

mercado [mer'kaðo] _nm_ market; ~ **en baja** falling market; **M~ Común** Common Market; ~ **de demanda/de oferta** seller's/buyer's market; ~ **laboral** labour market; ~ **objetivo** target market; ~ **de productos básicos** commodity market; ~ **de valores** stock market; ~ **exterior/interior** _o_ **nacional/ libre** overseas/home/free market.

mercancía [merkan'θia] _nf_ commodity; ~**s** _nfpl_ goods, merchandise _sg_; ~**s en depósito** bonded goods; ~**s perecederas** perishable goods.

mercancías [merkan'θias] _nm inv_ goods train, freight train (_US_).

mercantil [merkan'til] _adj_ mercantile, commercial.

mercenario, a [merθe'narjo, a] _adj, nm_ mercenary.

mercería [merθe'ria] _nf_ (_artículos_) haberdashery (_BRIT_), notions _pl_ (_US_); (_tienda_) haberdasher's shop (_BRIT_), drapery (_BRIT_), notions store (_US_).

Mercosur [merko'sur] _nm abr_ = _Mercado Común del Sur_.

mercurio [mer'kurjo] _nm_ mercury.

merecedor, a [mereθe'ðor, a] _adj_ deserving; ~ **de confianza** trustworthy.

merecer [mere'θer] _vt_ to deserve, merit ♦ _vi_ to be deserving, be worthy; **merece la pena** it's worthwhile.

merecido, a [mere'θiðo, a] _adj_ (well) deserved; **llevarse su** ~ to get one's deserts.

merendar [meren'dar] _vt_ to have for tea ♦ _vi_ to have tea; (_en el campo_) to have a picnic.

merendero [meren'dero] _nm_ (_café_) tearoom; (_en el campo_) picnic spot.

merengue [me'renge] _nm_ meringue.

merezca [me'reθka] _etc vb V_ **merecer**.

meridiano [meri'ðjano] _nm_ (_ASTRO, GEO_) meridian; **la explicación es de una claridad meridiana** the explanation is as clear as day.

meridional [meriðjo'nal] _adj_ Southern ♦ _nm/f_ Southerner.

merienda [me'rjenda] _etc vb V_ **merendar** ♦ _nf_ (light) tea, afternoon snack; (_de campo_) picnic; ~ **de negros** free-for-all.

mérito ['merito] _nm_ merit; (_valor_) worth, value; **hacer** ~**s** to make a good impression; **restar** ~ **a** to detract from.

meritorio, a [meri'torjo, a] _adj_ deserving.

merluza [mer'luθa] _nf_ hake; **coger una** ~ (_fam_) to get sozzled.

merma ['merma] _nf_ decrease; (_pérdida_) wastage.

mermar [mer'mar] _vt_ to reduce, lessen ♦ _vi_ to decrease, dwindle.

mermelada [merme'laða] _nf_ jam; ~ **de naranja** marmalade.

mero, a ['mero, a] _adj_ mere, simple; (_AM fam_) real ♦ _adv_ (_AM_) just, right ♦ _nm_ (_ZOOL_) grouper; **el** ~ ~ (_AM fam_) the boss.

merodear [meroðe'ar] _vi_ (_MIL_) to maraud; (_de noche_) to prowl (about); (_curiosear_) to snoop around.

mes [mes] _nm_ month; (_salario_) month's pay; **el** ~ **corriente** this _o_ the current month.

mesa ['mesa] _nf_ table; (_de trabajo_) desk; (_COM_) counter; (_en mitin_) platform; (_GEO_) plateau; (_ARQ_) landing; ~ **de noche/de tijera/de operaciones** _u_ **operatoria** bedside/folding/operating table; ~ **redonda** (_reunión_) round table; ~ **digitalizadora** (_INFORM_) graph pad; ~ **directiva** board; ~ **y cama** bed and board; **poner/quitar la** ~ to lay/clear the table.

mesarse [me'sarse] _vr_: ~ **el pelo** _o_ **los cabellos** to tear one's hair.

mesera [me'sera] _nf_ (_AM_) waitress.

mesero [me'sero] _nm_ (_AM_) waiter.

meseta [me'seta] _nf_ (_GEO_) meseta, tableland; (_ARQ_) landing.

mesilla [me'siʎa], **mesita** [me'sita] _nf_: ~ **de noche** bedside table.

mesón [me'son] _nm_ inn.

mestizo, a [mes'tiθo, a] _adj_ half-caste, of mixed race; (_ZOOL_) crossbred ♦ _nm/f_ half-caste.

mesura [me'sura] _nf_ (_calma_) calm; (_moderación_) moderation, restraint; (_cortesía_) courtesy.

mesurar [mesu'rar] _vt_ (_contener_) to restrain; ~**se** _vr_ to restrain o.s.

meta ['meta] nf goal; (de carrera) finish;
(fig) goal, aim, objective.
metabolismo [metaßo'lismo] nm
metabolism.
metafísico, a [meta'fisiko, a] adj
metaphysical ♦ nf metaphysics sg.
metáfora [me'tafora] nf metaphor.
metafórico, a [meta'foriko, a] adj
metaphorical.
metal [me'tal] nm (materia) metal; (MUS)
brass.
metálico, a [me'taliko, a] adj metallic; (de
metal) metal ♦ nm (dinero contante) cash.
metalurgia [meta'lurxja] nf metallurgy.
metalúrgico, a [meta'lurxiko, a] adj
metallurgic(al); **industria ~a**
engineering industry.
metamorfosear [metamorfose'ar] vt: ~
(en) to metamorphose o transform
(into).
metamorfosis [metamor'fosis] nf inv
metamorphosis, transformation.
metedura [mete'ðura] nf: ~ de pata (fam)
blunder.
meteorito [meteo'rito] nm meteorite.
meteoro [mete'oro] nm meteor.
meteorología [meteorolo'xia] nf
meteorology.
meteorólogo, a [meteo'roloɣo, a] nm/f
meteorologist; (RADIO, TV) weather
reporter.
meter [me'ter] vt (colocar) to put, place;
(introducir) to put in, insert; (involucrar)
to involve; (causar) to make, cause; ~**se**
vr: ~**se en** to go into, enter; (fig) to
interfere in, meddle in; ~**se a** to start;
~**se a escritor** to become a writer; ~**se
con algn** to provoke sb, pick a quarrel
with sb; ~ **prisa a algn** to hurry sb up.
meticuloso, a [metiku'loso, a] adj
meticulous, thorough.
metido, a [me'tiðo, a] adj: **estar muy ~ en
un asunto** to be deeply involved in a
matter; ~ **en años** elderly; ~ **en carne**
plump.
metódico, a [me'toðiko, a] adj methodical.
metodismo [meto'ðismo] nm Methodism.
método ['metoðo] nm method.
metodología [metoðolo'xia] nf
methodology.
metomentodo [metomen'toðo] nm inv
meddler, busybody.
metraje [me'traxe] nm (CINE) length; **cinta
de largo/corto** ~ full-length film/short.
metralla [me'traʎa] nf shrapnel.
metralleta [metra'ʎeta] nf sub-machine-
gun.
métrico, a ['metriko, a] adj metric ♦ nf

metrics pl; **cinta métrica** tape measure.
metro ['metro] nm metre; (tren: tb:
metropolitano) underground (BRIT),
subway (US); (instrumento) rule; ~
cuadrado/cúbico square/cubic metre.
metrópoli [me'tropoli], **metrópolis**
[me'tropolis] nf (ciudad) metropolis;
(colonial) mother country.
mexicano, a [mexi'kano, a] adj, nm/f (AM)
Mexican.
México ['mexiko] nm (AM) Mexico; **Ciudad
de** ~ Mexico City.
mezcla ['meθkla] nf mixture; (fig) blend.
mezclar [meθ'klar] vt to mix (up);
(armonizar) to blend; (combinar) to
merge; ~**se** vr to mix, mingle; ~ **en** to
get mixed up in, get involved in.
mezcolanza [meθko'lanθa] nf hotchpotch,
jumble.
mezquindad [meθkin'dað] nf (cicatería)
meanness; (miras estrechas) pettiness;
(acto) mean action.
mezquino, a [meθ'kino, a] adj (cicatero)
mean ♦ nm/f (avaro) mean person;
(miserable) petty individual.
mezquita [meθ'kita] nf mosque.
MF abr (= Modulación de Frecuencia) FM.
mg. abr (= miligramo(s)) mg.
mi [mi] adj posesivo my ♦ nm (MUS) E.
mí [mi] pron me, myself; ¿y a ~ qué? so
what?
miaja ['mjaxa] nf crumb; **ni una** ~ (fig) not
the least little bit.
miau [mjau] nm miaow.
michelín [mitʃe'lin] nm (fam) spare tyre.
mico ['miko] nm monkey.
micro ['mikro] nm (RADIO) mike,
microphone; (AM: pequeño) minibus.
(: grande) coach, bus.
microbio [mi'kroßjo] nm microbe.
microbús [mikro'ßus] nm minibus.
microchip [mikro'tʃip] nm microchip.
microcomputador [mikrokomputa'ðor]
nm, **microcomputadora**
[mikrokomputa'ðora] nf micro(computer).
microeconomía [mikroekono'mia] nf
microeconomics sg.
microficha [mikro'fitʃa] nf microfiche.
microfilm [mikro'film, pl **microfilms** [mikro'film,
mikro'films] nm microfilm.
micrófono [mi'krofono] nm microphone.
microinformática [mikroinfor'matika] nf
microcomputing.
micrómetro [mi'krometro] nm
micrometer.
microonda [mikro'onda] nf microwave;
(horno) ~**s** microwave (oven).
microordenador [mikroordena'ðor] nm

microcomputer.

micropastilla [mikropas'tiʎa], **microplaqueta** [mikropla'keta] *nf* (*INFORM*) chip, wafer.

microplaquita [mikropla'kita] *nf*: ~ **de silicio** silicon chip.

microprocesador [mikroprocesa'ðor] *nm* microprocessor.

microprograma [mikropro'ɣrama] *nm* (*INFORM*) firmware.

microscópico, a [mikros'kopiko, a] *adj* microscopic.

microscopio [mikros'kopjo] *nm* microscope.

midiendo [mi'ðjendo] *etc vb V* **medir**.

miedo ['mjeðo] *nm* fear; (*nerviosismo*) apprehension, nervousness; **meter** ~ **a** to scare, frighten; **tener** ~ to be afraid; **de** ~ wonderful, marvellous; ¡**qué** ~! (*fam*) how awful!; **me da** ~ it scares me; **hace un frío de** ~ (*fam*) it's terribly cold.

miedoso, a [mje'ðoso, a] *adj* fearful, timid.

miel [mjel] *nf* honey; **no hay** ~ **sin hiel** there's no rose without a thorn.

miembro ['mjembro] *nm* limb; (*socio*) member; (*de institución*) fellow; ~ **viril** penis.

mientes ['mjentes] *etc vb V* **mentar**; **mentir** ♦ *nfpl*: **no parar** ~ **en** to pay no attention to; **traer a las** ~ to recall.

mientras ['mjentras] *conj* while; (*duración*) as long as ♦ *adv* meanwhile; ~ (**que**) whereas; ~ **tanto** meanwhile; ~ **más tiene, más quiere** the more he has, the more he wants.

miérc. *abr* (= *miércoles*) Wed.

miércoles ['mjerkoles] *nm inv* Wednesday; ~ **de ceniza** Ash Wednesday; *V tb* **Carnaval**.

mierda ['mjerða] *nf* (*fam!*) shit (*!*), crap (*!*); (*fig*) filth, dirt; ¡**vete a la** ~! go to hell!

mies [mjes] *nf* (ripe) corn, wheat, grain.

miga ['miɣa] *nf* crumb; (*fig: meollo*) essence; **hacer buenas** ~**s** (*fam*) to get on well; **esto tiene su** ~ there's more to this than meets the eye.

migaja [mi'ɣaxa] *nf*: **una** ~ **de** (*un poquito*) a little; ~**s** *nfpl* crumbs; (*pey*) left-overs.

migración [miɣra'θjon] *nf* migration.

migratorio, a [miɣra'torjo, a] *adj* migratory.

mil [mil] *num* thousand; **dos** ~ **libras** two thousand pounds.

milagro [mi'laɣro] *nm* miracle; **hacer** ~**s** (*fig*) to work wonders.

milagroso, a [mila'ɣroso, a] *adj* miraculous.

Milán [mi'lan] *nm* Milan.

milenario, a [mile'narjo, a] *adj* millennial; (*fig*) very ancient.

milenio [mi'lenjo] *nm* millennium.

milésimo, a [mi'lesimo, a] *num* thousandth.

mili ['mili] *nf*: **hacer la** ~ (*fam*) to do one's military service.

La **mili**, *military service, is compulsory in Spain although the number of months' service has been reduced and recruits are now posted close to their home town. There continues to be strong opposition from* **objetores de conciencia**, *conscientious objectors, who are obliged to do* **Prestación Social Sustitutoria** *in place of military service; this usually involves doing community service and lasts longer. Those who refuse to do either of these,* **los insumisos**, *can be sent to prison.*

milicia [mi'liθja] *nf* (*MIL*) militia; (*servicio militar*) military service.

miligramo [mili'ɣramo] *nm* milligram.

milímetro [mi'limetro] *nm* millimetre (*BRIT*), millimeter (*US*).

militante [mili'tante] *adj* militant.

militar [mili'tar] *adj* military ♦ *nm/f* soldier ♦ *vi* to serve in the army; (*fig*) to militate, fight.

militarismo [milita'rismo] *nm* militarism.

milla ['miʎa] *nf* mile; ~ **marina** nautical mile.

millar [mi'ʎar] *num* thousand; **a** ~**es** in thousands.

millón [mi'ʎon] *num* million.

millonario, a [miʎo'narjo, a] *nm/f* millionaire.

millonésimo, a [miʎo'nesimo, a] *num* millionth.

mimado, a [mi'maðo, a] *adj* spoiled.

mimar [mi'mar] *vt* to spoil, pamper.

mimbre ['mimbre] *nm* wicker; **de** ~ wicker *cpd*, wickerwork.

mimetismo [mime'tismo] *nm* mimicry.

mímica ['mimika] *nf* (*para comunicarse*) sign language; (*imitación*) mimicry.

mimo ['mimo] *nm* (*caricia*) caress; (*de niño*) spoiling; (*TEAT*) mime; (: *actor*) mime artist.

mina ['mina] *nf* mine; (*pozo*) shaft; (*de lápiz*) lead refill; **hullera** *o* ~ **de carbón** coalmine.

minar [mi'nar] *vt* to mine; (*fig*) to undermine.

mineral [mine'ral] *adj* mineral ♦ *nm* (*GEO*) mineral; (*mena*) ore.

minería [mine'ria] *nf* mining.

minero - miserable

minero, a [mi'nero, a] *adj* mining *cpd* ♦ *nm/f* miner.

miniatura [minja'tura] *adj inv, nf* miniature.

minicadena [minika'ðena] *nf* (*MUS*) mini hi-fi.

minicomputador [minikomputa'ðor] *nm* minicomputer.

minidisco [mini'ðisko] *nm* diskette.

minifalda [mini'falda] *nf* miniskirt.

minifundio [mini'fundjo] *nm* smallholding, small farm.

minimizar [minimi'θar] *vt* to minimize.

mínimo, a ['minimo, a] *adj* minimum; (*insignificante*) minimal ♦ *nm* minimum; **precio/salario** ~ minimum price/wage; **lo** ~ **que pueden hacer** the least they can do.

minino, a [mi'nino, a] *nm/f* (*fam*) puss, pussy.

ministerio [minis'terjo] *nm* ministry (*BRIT*), department (*US*); **M~ de Asuntos Exteriores** Foreign Office (*BRIT*), State Department (*US*); **M~ del Comercio e Industria** Department of Trade and Industry; **M~ de (la) Gobernación** *o* **del Interior** ≈ Home Office (*BRIT*), Ministry of the Interior; **M~ de Hacienda** Treasury (*BRIT*), Treasury Department (*US*).

ministro, a [mi'nistro, a] *nm/f* minister, secretary (*esp US*); **M~ de Hacienda** Chancellor of the Exchequer, Secretary of the Treasury (*US*); **M~ de (la) Gobernación** *o* **del Interior** ≈ Home Secretary (*BRIT*), Secretary of the Interior (*US*).

minoría [mino'ria] *nf* minority.

minorista [mino'rista] *nm* retailer.

mintiendo [min'tjendo] *etc vb* V **mentir**.

minucia [mi'nuθja] *nf* (*detalle insignificante*) trifle; (*bagatela*) mere nothing.

minuciosidad [minuθjosi'ðað] *nf* (*meticulosidad*) thoroughness, meticulousness.

minucioso, a [minu'θjoso, a] *adj* thorough, meticulous; (*prolijo*) very detailed.

minúsculo, a [mi'nuskulo, a] *adj* tiny, minute ♦ *nf* small letter; **minúsculas** *nfpl* (*TIP*) lower case *sg*.

minusvalía [minusβa'lia] *nf* physical handicap; (*COM*) depreciation, capital loss.

minusválido, a [minus'βaliðo, a] *adj* (physically) handicapped *o* disabled ♦ *nm/f* disabled person.

minuta [mi'nuta] *nf* (*de comida*) menu; (*de abogado etc*) fee.

minutero [minu'tero] *nm* minute hand.

minuto [mi'nuto] *nm* minute.

Miño ['miɲo] *nm*: **el (río)** ~ the Miño.

mío, a ['mio, a] *adj, pron*: **el** ~ mine; **un amigo** ~ a friend of mine; **lo** ~ what is mine; **los** ~**s** my people, my relations.

miope ['mjope] *adj* short-sighted.

miopía [mjo'pia] *nf* near- *o* short-sightedness.

MIR [mir] *nm abr* (*POL*) = *Movimiento de Izquierda Revolucionaria*; (*ESP MED*) = *Médico Interno y Residente*.

mira ['mira] *nf* (*de arma*) sight(s) (*pl*); (*fig*) aim, intention; **de amplias/estrechas** ~**s** broad-/narrow-minded.

mirada [mi'raða] *nf* look, glance; (*expresión*) look, expression; ~ **de soslayo** sidelong glance; ~ **fija** stare, gaze; ~ **perdida** distant look; **echar una** ~ **a** to glance at; **levantar/bajar la** ~ to look up/down; **resistir la** ~ **de algn** to stare sb out.

mirado, a [mi'raðo, a] *adj* (*sensato*) sensible; (*considerado*) considerate; **bien/mal** ~ well/not well thought of.

mirador [mira'ðor] *nm* viewpoint, vantage point.

miramiento [mira'mjento] *nm* (*consideración*) considerateness; **tratar sin** ~**s a algn** to ride roughshod over sb.

mirar [mi'rar] *vt* to look at; (*observar*) to watch; (*considerar*) to consider, think over; (*vigilar, cuidar*) to watch, look after ♦ *vi* to look; (*ARQ*) to face; ~**se** *vr* (*dos personas*) to look at each other; ~ **algo/a algn de reojo** *o* **de través** to look askance at sth/sb; ~ **algo/a algn por encima del hombro** to look down on sth/sb; ~ **bien/mal** to think highly of/have a poor opinion of; ~ **fijamente** to stare *o* gaze at; ~ **por** (*fig*) to look after; ~ **por la ventana** to look out of the window; ~**se al espejo** to look at o.s. in the mirror; ~**se a los ojos** to look into each other's eyes.

mirilla [mi'riʎa] *nf* (*agujero*) spyhole, peephole.

mirlo ['mirlo] *nm* blackbird.

misa ['misa] *nf* mass; ~ **del gallo** midnight mass (*on Christmas Eve*); ~ **de difuntos** requiem mass; **como en** ~ in dead silence; **estos datos van a** ~ (*fig*) these facts are utterly trustworthy.

misántropo [mi'santropo] *nm* misanthrope, misanthropist.

miscelánea [misθe'lanea] *nf* miscellany.

miserable [mise'raβle] *adj* (*avaro*) mean, stingy; (*nimio*) miserable, paltry; (*lugar*) squalid; (*fam*) vile, despicable ♦ *nm/f* (*malvado*) rogue.

miseria [mi'serja] *nf* misery; (*pobreza*) poverty; (*tacañería*) meanness, stinginess; (*condiciones*) squalor; **una ~** a pittance.

misericordia [miseri'korðja] *nf* (*compasión*) compassion, pity; (*perdón*) forgiveness, mercy.

misil [mi'sil] *nm* missile.

misión [mi'sjon] *nf* mission; (*tarea*) job, duty; (*POL*) assignment; **misiones** *nfpl* (*REL*) overseas missions.

misionero, a [misjo'nero, a] *nm/f* missionary.

mismamente [misma'mente] *adv* (*fam*: *sólo*) only, just.

mismísimo, a [mis'misimo, a] *adj superlativo* selfsame, very (same).

mismo, a ['mismo, a] *adj* (*semejante*) same; (*después de pronombre*) -self; (*para énfasis*) very ♦ *adv*: **aquí/ayer/hoy ~** right here/only yesterday/this very day; **ahora ~** right now ♦ *conj*: **lo ~ que** just like, just as; **por lo ~** for the same reason; **el ~ traje** the same suit; **en ese ~ momento** at that very moment; **vino el ~ Ministro** the Minister himself came; **yo ~ lo vi** I saw it myself; **lo hizo por sí ~** he did it by himself; **lo ~ the** same (thing); **da lo ~** it's all the same; **quedamos en las mismas** we're no further forward.

misógino [mi'soxino] *nm* misogynist.

miss [mis] *nf* beauty queen.

misterio [mis'terjo] *nm* mystery; (*lo secreto*) secrecy.

misterioso, a [miste'rjoso, a] *adj* mysterious; (*inexplicable*) puzzling.

misticismo [misti'θismo] *nm* mysticism.

místico, a ['mistiko, a] *adj* mystic(al) ♦ *nm/f* mystic ♦ *nf* mysticism.

mitad [mi'tað] *nf* (*medio*) half; (*centro*) middle; **~ (y) ~** half-and-half; (*fig*) yes and no; **a ~ de precio** (at) half-price; **en** *o* **a ~ del camino** halfway along the road; **cortar por la ~** to cut through the middle.

mítico, a ['mitiko, a] *adj* mythical.

mitigar [miti'ɣar] *vt* to mitigate; (*dolor*) to relieve; (*sed*) to quench; (*ira*) to appease; (*preocupación*) to allay; (*soledad*) to alleviate.

mitigue [mi'tiɣe] *etc vb V* **mitigar**.

mitin ['mitin] *nm* (*esp POL*) meeting.

mito ['mito] *nm* myth.

mitología [mitolo'xia] *nf* mythology.

mitológico, a [mito'loxiko, a] *adj* mythological.

mixto, a ['miksto, a] *adj* mixed; (*comité*) joint.

ml. *abr* (= *mililitro*) ml.

mm. *abr* (= *milímetro*) mm.

m/n *abr* (*ECON*) = **moneda nacional.**

M.º *abr* (*POL*: = *Ministerio*) Min.

m/o *abr* (*COM*) = **mi orden.**

mobiliario [moßi'ljarjo] *nm* furniture.

MOC *nm abr* = **Movimiento de Objeción de Conciencia.**

mocasín [moka'sin] *nm* moccasin.

mocedad [moθe'ðað] *nf* youth.

mochila [mo't ʃila] *nf* rucksack (*BRIT*), backpack.

moción [mo'θjon] *nf* motion; **~ compuesta** (*POL*) composite motion.

moco ['moko] *nm* mucus; **limpiarse los ~s** to blow one's nose; **no es ~ de pavo** it's no trifle.

mocoso, a [mo'koso, a] *adj* snivelling; (*fig*) ill-bred ♦ *nm/f* (*fam*) brat.

moda ['moða] *nf* fashion; (*estilo*) style; **de** *o* **a la ~** in fashion, fashionable; **pasado de ~** out of fashion; **vestido a la última ~** trendily dressed.

modal [mo'ðal] *adj* modal ♦ *nm*: **~es** *nmpl* manners.

modalidad [moðali'ðað] *nf* (*clase*) kind, variety; (*manera*) way; (*INFORM*) mode; **~ de texto** (*INFORM*) text mode.

modelar [moðe'lar] *vt* to model.

modelo [mo'ðelo] *adj inv* model ♦ *nm/f* model ♦ *nm* (*patrón*) pattern; (*norma*) standard.

módem ['moðem] *nm* (*INFORM*) modem.

moderado, a [moðe'raðo, a] *adj* moderate.

moderar [moðe'rar] *vt* to moderate; (*violencia*) to restrain, control; (*velocidad*) to reduce; **~se** *vr* to restrain o.s., control o.s.

modernice [moðer'niθe] *etc vb V* **modernizar.**

modernizar [moðerni'θar] *vt* to modernize; (*INFORM*) to upgrade.

moderno, a [mo'ðerno, a] *adj* modern; (*actual*) present-day; (*equipo etc*) up-to-date.

modestia [mo'ðestja] *nf* modesty.

modesto, a [mo'ðesto, a] *adj* modest.

módico, a ['moðiko, a] *adj* moderate, reasonable.

modificar [moðifi'kar] *vt* to modify.

modifique [moði'fike] *etc vb V* **modificar.**

modismo [mo'ðismo] *nm* idiom.

modisto, a [mo'ðisto, a] *nm/f* dressmaker.

modo ['moðo] *nm* (*manera, forma*) way, manner; (*INFORM, MUS*) mode; (*LING*) mood; **~s** *nmpl* manners; **"~ de empleo"** "instructions for use"; **~ de gobierno**

form of government; **a ~ de** like; **de
este ~** in this way; **de ningún ~** in no
way; **de todos ~s** at any rate; **de un ~ u
otro** (in) one way or another.
modorra [mo'ðorra] *nf* drowsiness.
modoso, a [mo'ðoso, a] *adj* (*educado*)
quiet, well-mannered.
modulación [moðula'θjon] *nf* modulation;
~ de frecuencia (*RADIO*) frequency
modulation, FM.
módulo ['moðulo] *nm* module; (*de mueble*)
unit.
mofarse [mo'farse] *vr*: **~ de** to mock, scoff
at.
moflete [mo'flete] *nm* fat cheek, chubby
cheek.
mogollón [moɣo'ʎon] (*fam*) *nm*: **~ de
discos** *etc* loads of records *etc* ♦ *adv*: **un
~** a hell of a lot.
mohín [mo'in] *nm* (*mueca*) (wry) face;
(*pucheros*) pout.
mohíno, a [mo'ino, a] *adj* (*triste*) gloomy,
depressed; (*enojado*) sulky.
moho ['moo] *nm* (*BOT*) mould, mildew; (*en
metal*) rust.
mohoso, a [mo'oso, a] *adj* mouldy; rusty.
mojado, a [mo'xaðo, a] *adj* wet; (*húmedo*)
damp; (*empapado*) drenched.
mojar [mo'xar] *vt* to wet; (*humedecer*) to
damp(en), moisten; (*calar*) to soak; **~se**
vr to get wet; **~ el pan en el café** to dip *o*
dunk one's bread in one's coffee.
mojigato, a [moxi'ɣato, a] *adj* (*hipócrita*)
hypocritical; (*santurrón*) sanctimonious;
(*gazmoño*) prudish ♦ *nm/f* hypocrite;
sanctimonious person; prude.
mojón [mo'xon] *nm* (*hito*) landmark; (*en un
camino*) signpost; (*~ kilométrico*)
milestone.
mol. *abr* (= *molécula*) mol.
molar [mo'lar] *nm* molar ♦ *vt* (*fam*): **lo que
más me mola es ...** what I'm really into
is ...; **¿te mola un pitillo?** do you fancy a
smoke?
Moldavia [mol'ðaβja], **Moldova**
[mol'ðoβa] *nf* Moldavia, Moldova.
moldavo, a [mol'ðaβo, a] *adj, nm/f*
Moldavian, Moldovan.
molde ['molde] *nm* mould; (*vaciado*) cast;
(*de costura*) pattern; (*fig*) model.
moldear [molde'ar] *vt* to mould; (*en yeso
etc*) to cast.
mole ['mole] *nf* mass, bulk; (*edificio*) pile.
molécula [mo'lekula] *nf* molecule.
moler [mo'ler] *vt* to grind, crush;
(*pulverizar*) to pound; (*trigo etc*) to mill;
(*cansar*) to tire out, exhaust; **~ a algn a
palos** to give sb a beating.

molestar [moles'tar] *vt* to bother; (*fastidiar*)
to annoy; (*incomodar*) to inconvenience,
put out; (*perturbar*) to trouble, upset ♦ *vi*
to be a nuisance; **~se** *vr* to bother;
(*incomodarse*) to go to a lot of trouble;
(*ofenderse*) to take offence; **¿le molesta
el ruido?** do you mind the noise?; **siento
~le** I'm sorry to trouble you.
molestia [mo'lestja] *nf* bother, trouble;
(*incomodidad*) inconvenience; (*MED*)
discomfort; **no es ninguna ~** it's no
trouble at all.
molesto, a [mo'lesto, a] *adj* (*que fastidia*)
annoying; (*incómodo*) inconvenient;
(*inquieto*) uncomfortable, ill at ease;
(*enfadado*) annoyed; **estar ~** (*MED*) to be
in some discomfort; **estar ~ con algn**
(*fig*) to be cross with sb; **me sentí ~** I
felt embarrassed.
molido, a [mo'liðo, a] *adj* (*machacado*)
ground; (*pulverizado*) powdered; **estar ~**
(*fig*) to be exhausted *o* dead beat.
molinero [moli'nero] *nm* miller.
molinillo [moli'niʎo] *nm* hand mill; **~ de
carne/café** mincer/coffee grinder.
molino [mo'lino] *nm* (*edificio*) mill;
(*máquina*) grinder.
mollera [mo'ʎera] *nf* (*ANAT*) crown of the
head; (*fam: seso*) brains *pl*; **duro de ~**
(*estúpido*) thick.
Molucas [mo'lukas] *nfpl*: **las (Islas) ~** the
Moluccas, the Molucca Islands.
molusco [mo'lusko] *nm* mollusc.
momentáneo, a [momen'taneo, a] *adj*
momentary.
momento [mo'mento] *nm* (*gen*) moment;
(*TEC*) momentum; **de ~** at the moment,
for the moment; **en ese ~** at that
moment, just then; **por el ~** for the time
being.
momia ['momja] *nf* mummy.
mona ['mona] *nf* V **mono**.
Mónaco ['monako] *nm* Monaco.
monada [mo'naða] *nf* (*de niño*) charming
habit; (*cosa primorosa*) lovely thing;
(*chica*) pretty girl; **¡qué ~!** isn't it cute?
monaguillo [mona'ɣiʎo] *nm* altar boy.
monarca [mo'narka] *nm/f* monarch, ruler.
monarquía [monar'kia] *nf* monarchy.
monárquico, a [mo'narkiko, a] *nm/f*
royalist, monarchist.
monasterio [monas'terjo] *nm* monastery.
Moncloa [mon'kloa] *nf*: **la ~** *official
residence of the Spanish Prime
Minister*.
monda ['monda] *nf* (*poda*) pruning; (: *de
árbol*) lopping; (: *de fruta*) peeling;
(*cáscara*) skin; **¡es la ~!** (*fam: fantástico*)

it's great!; (: *el colmo*) it's the limit!;
(: *persona: gracioso*) he's a knockout!
mondadientes [monda'ðjentes] *nm inv*
toothpick.
mondar [mon'dar] *vt* (*limpiar*) to clean;
(*pelar*) to peel; ~**se** *vr*: ~**se de risa** (*fam*)
to split one's sides laughing.
moneda [mo'neða] *nf* (*tipo de dinero*)
currency, money; (*pieza*) coin; **una** ~ **de
5 pesetas** a 5 peseta coin; ~ **de curso
legal** tender; ~ **extranjera** foreign
exchange; ~ **única** single currency; **es** ~
corriente (*fig*) it's common knowledge.
monedero [mone'ðero] *nm* purse.
monegasco, a [mone'yasko, a] *adj* of *o*
from Monaco, Monegasque ♦ *nm/f*
Monegasque.
monetario, a [mone'tarjo, a] *adj*
monetary, financial.
monetarista [moneta'rista] *adj, nm/f*
monetarist.
mongólico, a [mon'goliko, a] *adj, nm/f*
Mongol.
monigote [moni'yote] *nm* (*dibujo*) doodle;
(*de papel*) cut-out figure; (*pey*) wimp; *V tb*
Día de los (Santos) Inocentes.
monitor [moni'tor] *nm* (*INFORM*) monitor;
~ **en color** colour monitor; ~ **fósfor
verde** green screen.
monja ['monxa] *nf* nun.
monje ['monxe] *nm* monk.
mono, a ['mono, a] *adj* (*bonito*) lovely,
pretty; (*gracioso*) nice, charming ♦ *nm/f*
monkey, ape ♦ *nm* dungarees *pl*; (*overo-
les*) overalls *pl*; (*fam: de droges*) cold
turkey; **una chica muy mona** a very
pretty girl; **dormir la** ~ to sleep it off.
monóculo [mo'nokulo] *nm* monocle.
monografía [monoyra'fia] *nf* monograph.
monolingüe [mono'lingwe] *adj*
monolingual.
monólogo [mo'noloyo] *nm* monologue.
monomando [mono'mando] *nm* (*tb:* **grifo**
~) mixer tap.
monoparental [monoparen'tal] *adj:* **familia**
~ single-parent family.
monopatín [monopa'tin] *nm* skateboard.
monopolice [monopo'liθe] *etc vb V*
monopolizar.
monopolio [mono'poljo] *nm* monopoly; ~
total absolute monopoly.
monopolista [monopo'lista] *adj, nm/f*
monopolist.
monopolizar [monopoli'θar] *vt* to
monopolize.
monosílabo, a [mono'silaβo, a] *adj*
monosyllabic ♦ *nm* monosyllable.
monotonía [monoto'nia] *nf* (*sonido*)

monotone; (*fig*) monotony.
monótono, a [mo'notono, a] *adj*
monotonous.
mono-usuario, a [monou'swarjo, a] *adj*
(*INFORM*) single-user.
monóxido [mo'noksiðo] *nm* monoxide; ~
de carbono carbon monoxide.
Mons. *abr* (*REL*) = **Monseñor.**
monseñor [monse'ɲor] *nm* monsignor.
monserga [mon'serɣa] *nf* (*lenguaje
confuso*) gibberish; (*tonterías*) drivel.
monstruo ['monstrwo] *nm* monster ♦ *adj
inv* fantastic.
monstruoso, a [mons'trwoso, a] *adj*
monstrous.
monta ['monta] *nf* total, sum; **de poca** ~
unimportant, of little account.
montacargas [monta'karɣas] *nm inv*
service lift (*BRIT*), freight elevator (*US*).
montador [monta'ðor] *nm* (*para montar*)
mounting block; (*profesión*) fitter; (*CINE*)
film editor.
montaje [mon'taxe] *nm* assembly;
(*organización*) fitting up; (*TEAT*) décor;
(*CINE*) montage.
montante [mon'tante] *nm* (*poste*) upright;
(*soporte*) stanchion; (*ARQ: de puerta*)
transom; (: *de ventana*) mullion; (*suma*)
amount, total.
montaña [mon'taɲa] *nf* (*monte*) mountain;
(*sierra*) mountains *pl*, mountainous area;
(*AM: selva*) forest; ~ **rusa** roller coaster.
montañero, a [monta'ɲero, a] *adj*
mountain *cpd* ♦ *nm/f* mountaineer,
climber.
montañés, esa [monta'ɲes, esa] *adj*
mountain *cpd*; (*de Santander*) of *o* from
the Santander region ♦ *nm/f* highlander;
native *o* inhabitant of the Santander
region.
montañismo [monta'ɲismo] *nm*
mountaineering, climbing.
montañoso, a [monta'ɲoso, a] *adj*
mountainous.
montar [mon'tar] *vt* (*subir a*) to mount, get
on; (*caballo etc*) to ride; (*TEC*) to
assemble, put together; (*negocio*) to set
up; (*colocar*) to lift on to; (*CINE: película*)
to edit; (*TEAT: obra*) to stage, put on;
(*CULIN: batir*) to whip, beat
♦ *vi* to mount, get on; (*sobresalir*) to
overlap; ~ **en cólera** to get angry; ~ **un
número** *o* **numerito** to make a scene;
tanto monta it makes no odds.
montaraz [monta'raθ] *adj* mountain *cpd*,
highland *cpd*; (*pey*) uncivilized.
monte ['monte] *nm* (*montaña*) mountain;
(*bosque*) woodland; (*área sin cultivar*) wild

perdiz [per'ðiθ] *nf* partridge.
perdón [per'ðon] *nm* (*disculpa*) pardon,
forgiveness; (*clemencia*) mercy; ¡~!
sorry!, I beg your pardon!; **con** ~ if I
may, if you don't mind.
perdonar [perðo'nar] *vt* to pardon, forgive;
(*la vida*) to spare; (*excusar*) to exempt,
excuse ♦ *vi* to pardon, forgive; ¡**perdone
(usted)**! sorry!, I beg your pardon!;
perdone, pero me parece que ... excuse
me, but I think ...
perdurable [perðu'raßle] *adj* lasting;
(*eterno*) everlasting.
perdurar [perðu'rar] *vi* (*resistir*) to last,
endure; (*seguir existiendo*) to stand, still
exist.
perecedero, a [pereθe'ðero, a] *adj*
perishable.
perecer [pere'θer] *vi* to perish, die.
peregrinación [pereɣrina'θjon] *nf* (*REL*)
pilgrimage.
peregrino, a [pere'ɣrino] *adj* (*extraño*)
strange; (*singular*) rare ♦ *nm/f* pilgrim.
perejil [pere'xil] *nm* parsley.
perenne [pe'renne] *adj* everlasting,
perennial.
perentorio, a [peren'torjo, a] *adj* (*urgente*)
urgent; (*terminante*) peremptory; (*fijo*)
set, fixed.
pereza [pe'reθa] *nf* (*flojera*) laziness;
(*lentitud*) sloth, slowness.
perezca [pe'reθka] *etc vb V* **perecer**.
perezoso, a [pere'θoso, a] *adj* lazy; slow,
sluggish.
perfección [perfek'θjon] *nf* perfection; **a la**
~ to perfection.
perfeccionar [perfekθjo'nar] *vt* to perfect;
(*acabar*) to complete, finish.
perfecto, a [per'fekto, a] *adj* perfect ♦ *nm*
(*LING*) perfect (tense).
perfidia [per'fiðja] *nf* perfidy, treachery.
pérfido, a ['perfiðo, a] *adj* perfidious,
treacherous.
perfil [per'fil] *nm* (*parte lateral*) profile;
(*silueta*) silhouette, outline; (*TEC*) (cross)
section; ~**es** *nmpl* features; (*fig*) social
graces; ~ **del cliente** (*COM*) customer
profile; **en** ~ from the side, in profile.
perfilado, a [perfi'laðo, a] *adj* (*bien
formado*) well-shaped; (*largo: cara*) long.
perfilar [perfi'lar] *vt* (*trazar*) to outline; (*dar
carácter a*) to give character to;
~**se** *vr* to be silhouetted (*en* against); **el
proyecto se va perfilando** the project is
taking shape.
perforación [perfora'θjon] *nf* perforation;
(*con taladro*) drilling.
perforadora [perfora'ðora] *nf* drill; ~ **de**

fichas card-punch.
perforar [perfo'rar] *vt* to perforate;
(*agujero*) to drill, bore; (*papel*) to punch a
hole in ♦ *vi* to drill, bore.
perfumado, a [perfu'maðo, a] *adj* scented,
perfumed.
perfumar [perfu'mar] *vt* to scent, perfume.
perfume [per'fume] *nm* perfume, scent.
pergamino [perɣa'mino] *nm* parchment.
pericia [pe'riθja] *nf* skill, expertise.
periferia [peri'ferja] *nf* periphery; (*de
ciudad*) outskirts *pl.*
periférico, a [peri'feriko, a] *adj* peripheral
♦ *nm* (*INFORM*) peripheral; (*AM: AUTO*)
ring road; **barrio** ~ outlying district.
perilla [pe'riʎa] *nf* goatee.
perímetro [pe'rimetro] *nm* perimeter.
periódico, a [pe'rjoðiko, a] *adj* periodic(al)
♦ *nm* (news)paper; ~ **dominical** Sunday
(news)paper.
periodismo [perjo'ðismo] *nm* journalism.
periodista [perjo'ðista] *nm/f* journalist.
periodístico, a [perjo'ðistiko, a] *adj*
journalistic.
periodo [pe'rjoðo], **período** [pe'rioðo] *nm*
period; ~ **contable** (*COM*) accounting
period.
peripecias [peri'peθjas] *nfpl* adventures.
peripuesto, a [peri'pwesto, a] *adj* dressed
up; **tan** ~ all dressed up (to the nines).
perito, a [pe'rito, a] *adj* (*experto*) expert;
(*diestro*) skilled, skilful ♦ *nm/f* expert;
skilled worker; (*técnico*) technician.
perjudicar [perxuði'kar] *vt* (*gen*) to
damage, harm; (*fig*) to prejudice.
perjudicial [perxuði'θjal] *adj* damaging,
harmful; (*en detrimento*) detrimental.
perjudique [perxu'ðike] *etc vb V*
perjudicar.
perjuicio [per'xwiθjo] *nm* damage, harm;
en/sin ~ **de** to the detriment of/without
prejudice to.
perjurar [perxu'rar] *vi* to commit perjury.
perla ['perla] *nf* pearl; **me viene de** ~**s** it
suits me fine.
permanecer [permane'θer] *vi* (*quedarse*) to
stay, remain; (*seguir*) to continue to be.
permanencia [perma'nenθja] *nf* (*duración*)
permanence; (*estancia*) stay.
permanente [perma'nente] *adj* (*que queda*)
permanent; (*constante*) constant;
(*comisión etc*) standing ♦ *nf* perm;
hacerse una ~ to have one's hair
permed.
permanezca [perma'neθka] *etc vb V*
permanecer.
permisible [permi'sißle] *adj* permissible,
allowable.

this kid's too much for me
7: él me puede (*fam*) he's stronger than
me
♦ *nm* power; **el** ~ the Government; ~
adquisitivo purchasing power; **detentar**
u **ocupar** *o* **estar en el** ~ to be in power *o*
office; **estar** *u* **obrar en** ~ **de** to be in the
hands *o* possession of; **por** ~**(es)** by
proxy.

poderío [poðe'rio] *nm* power; (*autoridad*)
authority.
poderoso, a [poðe'roso, a] *adj* powerful.
podio ['poðjo] *nm* podium.
podólogo, a [po'ðoloɣo, a] *nm/f*
chiropodist (*BRIT*), podiatrist (*US*).
podré [po'ðre] *etc vb V* **poder.**
podrido, a [po'ðriðo, a] *adj* rotten, bad;
(*fig*) rotten, corrupt.
podrir [po'ðrir] = **pudrir.**
poema [po'ema] *nm* poem.
poesía [poe'sia] *nf* poetry.
poeta [po'eta] *nm* poet.
poético, a [po'etiko, a] *adj* poetic(al).
poetisa [poe'tisa] *nf* (woman) poet.
póker ['poker] *nm* poker.
polaco, a [po'lako, a] *adj* Polish ♦ *nm/f* Pole
♦ *nm* (*LING*) Polish.
polar [po'lar] *adj* polar.
polarice [pola'riθe] *etc vb V* **polarizar.**
polaridad [polari'ðað] *nf* polarity.
polarizar [polari'θar] *vt* to polarize.
polea [po'lea] *nf* pulley.
polémica [po'lemika] *nf* polemics *sg*; (*una*
~) controversy.
polemice [pole'miθe] *etc vb V* **polemizar.**
polémico, a [po'lemiko, a] *adj* polemic(al).
polemizar [polemi'θar] *vi* to indulge in a
polemic, argue.
polen ['polen] *nm* pollen.
poleo [po'leo] *nm* pennyroyal.
poli ['poli] *nm* (*fam*) cop (*fam*) ♦ *nf*: **la** ~ the
cops *pl* (*fam*).
policía [poli'θia] *nm/f* policeman/woman
♦ *nf* police.

*There are two branches of the police, both
armed: the* **policía nacional,** *in charge of
national security and public order in
general, and the* **policía municipal,** *with
duties of regulating traffic and policing the
local community. Catalonia and the
Basque Country have their own police
forces, the* **Mossos d'Esquadra** *and the*
Ertzaintza *respectively.*

policíaco, a [poli'θiako, a] *adj* police *cpd*;
novela policíaca detective story.

polideportivo [poliðepor'tiβo] *nm* sports
centre.
poliéster [poli'ester] *nm* polyester.
polietileno [polieti'leno] *nm* polythene
(*BRIT*), polyethylene (*US*).
polifacético, a [polifa'θetiko, a] *adj*
(*persona, talento*) many-sided, versatile.
poligamia [poli'ɣamja] *nf* polygamy.
polígamo, a [po'liɣamo, a] *adj* polygamous
♦ *nm* polygamist.
polígono [po'liɣono] *nm* (*MAT*) polygon;
(*solar*) building lot; (*zona*) area; (*unidad
vecina*) housing estate; ~ **industrial**
industrial estate.
polígrafo [po'liɣrafo] *nm* polygraph.
polilla [po'liʎa] *nf* moth.
Polinesia [poli'nesja] *nf* Polynesia.
polinesio, a [poli'nesjo, a] *adj, nm/f*
Polynesian.
polio ['poljo] *nf* polio.
Polisario [poli'sarjo] *nm abr* (*POL: tb:* **Frente**
~) = *Frente Político de Liberación del
Sáhara y Río de Oro.*
politécnico [poli'tekniko] *nm* polytechnic.
politicastro [politi'kastro] *nm* (*pey*)
politician, politico.
político, a [po'litiko, a] *adj* political;
(*discreto*) tactful; (*pariente*) in-law ♦ *nm/f*
politician ♦ *nf* politics *sg*; (*económica,
agraria*) policy; **padre** ~ father-in-law;
política exterior/de ingresos y precios
foreign/prices and incomes policy.
póliza ['poliθa] *nf* certificate, voucher;
(*impuesto*) tax *o* fiscal stamp; ~ **de
seguro(s)** insurance policy.
polizón [poli'θon] *nm* (*AVIAT, NAUT*)
stowaway.
pollera [po'ʎera] *nf* (*criadero*) hencoop;
(*AM*) skirt, overskirt.
pollería [poʎe'ria] *nf* poulterer's (shop).
pollo ['poʎo] *nm* chicken; (*joven*) young
man; (*señorito*) playboy; ~ **asado** roast
chicken.
polo ['polo] *nm* (*GEO, ELEC*) pole; (*helado*)
ice lolly; (*DEPORTE*) polo; (*suéter*) polo-
neck; **P**~ **Norte/Sur** North/South Pole;
esto es el ~ **opuesto de lo que dijo antes**
this is the exact opposite of what he
said before.
Polonia [po'lonja] *nf* Poland.
poltrona [pol'trona] *nf* reclining chair,
easy chair.
polución [polu'θjon] *nf* pollution; ~
ambiental environmental pollution.
polvera [pol'βera] *nf* powder compact.
polvo ['polβo] *nm* dust; (*QUÍMICA, CULIN,
MED*) powder; (*fam!*) screw(!); **en** ~
powdered; ~ **de talco** talcum powder;

estar hecho ~ to be worn out o exhausted; **hacer algo** ~ to smash sth; **hacer** ~ **a algn** to shatter sb; V tb **polvos.**

pólvora ['polßora] nf gunpowder; (fuegos artificiales) fireworks pl; **propagarse como la** ~ (noticia) to spread like wildfire.

polvoriento, a [polßo'rjento, a] adj (superficie) dusty; (sustancia) powdery.

polvorín [polßo'rin] nm (fig) powder keg.

polvorosa [polßo'rosa] adj (fam): **poner pies en** ~ to beat it.

polvos ['polßos] nmpl powder sg.

polvoso, a [pol'ßoso, a] adj (AM) dusty.

pomada [po'maða] nf pomade.

pomelo [po'melo] nm grapefruit.

pómez ['pomeθ] nf: **piedra** ~ pumice stone.

pomo ['pomo] nm handle.

pompa ['pompa] nf (burbuja) bubble; (bomba) pump; (esplendor) pomp, splendour; ~**s funebres** funeral sg.

pomposo, a [pom'poso, a] adj splendid, magnificent; (pey) pompous.

pómulo ['pomulo] nm cheekbone.

ponche ['pontʃe] nm punch.

poncho ['pontʃo] nm (AM) poncho, cape.

ponderar [ponde'rar] vt (considerar) to weigh up, consider; (elogiar) to praise highly, speak in praise of.

pondré [pon'dre] etc vb V **poner.**

ponencia [po'nenθja] nf (exposición) (learned) paper, communication; (informe) report.

=========== PALABRA CLAVE ===========

poner [po'ner] vt **1** to put; (colocar) to place, set; (ropa) to put on; (problema, la mesa) to set; (interés) to show; (telegrama) to send; (obra de teatro) to put on; (película) to show; **ponlo más alto** turn it up; **¿qué ponen en el Excelsior?** what's on at the Excelsior?; ~ **algo a secar** to put sth (out) to dry; **¡no pongas esa cara!** don't look at me like that!
2 (tienda) to open; (instalar: gas etc) to put in; (radio, TV) to switch o turn on
3 (suponer): **pongamos que** ... let's suppose that ...
4 (contribuir): **el gobierno ha puesto otro millón** the government has contributed another million
5 (TELEC): **póngame con el Sr. López** can you put me through to Mr. López?
6 (estar escrito): **¿qué pone aquí?** what does it say here?
7: ~ **de: le han puesto de director general** they've appointed him general manager

8 (+adj) to make; **me estás poniendo nerviosa** you're making me nervous
9 (dar nombre): **al hijo le pusieron Diego** they called their son Diego
♦ vi (gallina) to lay
♦ ~**se** vr **1** (colocarse): **se puso a mi lado** he came and stood beside me; **tú ponte en esa silla** you go and sit on that chair
2 (vestido, cosméticos) to put on; **¿por qué no te pones el vestido nuevo?** why don't you put on o wear your new dress?
3 (sol) to set
4 (+adj) to get, become; to turn; ~**se enfermo/gordo/triste** to get ill/fat/sad; **se puso muy serio** he got very serious; **después de lavarla la tela se puso azul** after washing it the material turned blue; **¡no te pongas así!** don't be like that!; ~**se cómodo** to make o.s. comfortable
5: ~ **se a: se puso a llorar** he started to cry; **tienes que** ~**te a estudiar** you must get down to studying
6: ~**se a bien con algn** to make it up with sb; ~**se a mal con algn** to get on the wrong side of sb
7 (AM): **se me pone que** ... it seems to me that ..., I think that ....

ponga ['ponga] etc vb V **poner.**

poniente [po'njente] nm west.

pontevedrés, esa [ponteße'ðres, esa] adj of o from Pontevedra ♦ nm/f native o inhabitant of Pontevedra.

pontificado [pontifi'kaðo] nm papacy, pontificate.

pontífice [pon'tifiθe] nm pope, pontiff; **el Sumo P**~ His Holiness the Pope.

pontón [pon'ton] nm pontoon.

ponzoña [pon'θoɲa] nf poison, venom.

ponzoñoso, a [ponθo'ɲoso, a] adj poisonous, venomous.

pop [pop] adj inv, nm (MUS) pop.

popa ['popa] nf stern; **a** ~ astern, abaft; **de** ~ **a proa** fore and aft.

popular [popu'lar] adj popular; (del pueblo) of the people.

popularice [popula'riθe] etc vb V **popularizarse.**

popularidad [populari'ðað] nf popularity.

popularizarse [populari'θarse] vr to become popular.

poquísimo, a [po'kisimo, a] adj (superlativo de poco) very little; (pl) very few; (casi nada) hardly any.

poquito [po'kito] nm: **un** ~ a little bit ♦ adv a little, a bit; **a** ~**s** bit by bit.

═══════════════ PALABRA CLAVE

por [por] prep **1** (objetivo) for; **luchar ~ la patria** to fight for one's country; **hazlo ~ mí** do it for my sake
2 (+infin): **~ no llegar tarde** so as not to arrive late; **~ citar unos ejemplos** to give a few examples
3 (causa) out of, because of; **no es ~ eso** that's not the reason; **~ escasez de fondos** through o for lack of funds
4 (tiempo): **~ la mañana/noche** in the morning/at night; **se queda ~ una semana** she's staying (for) a week
5 (lugar): **pasar ~ Madrid** to pass through Madrid; **ir a Guayaquil ~ Quito** to go to Guayaquil via Quito; **caminar ~ la calle** to walk along the street; **~ allí** over there; **se va ~ ahí** we have to go that way; **¿~ dónde?** which way?; **~ el norte** it's somewhere in the north; **~ todo el país** throughout the country
6 (cambio, precio): **te doy uno nuevo ~ el que tienes** I'll give you a new one (in return) for the one you've got; **lo vendí ~ 15 dólares** I sold it for 15 dollars
7 (valor distributivo): **550 pesetas ~ hora/cabeza** 550 pesetas an o per hour/a o per head; **10 ~ ciento** 10 per cent; **80 (kms) ~ hora** 80 (km) an o per hour
8 (modo, medio) by; **~ correo/avión** by post/air; **día ~ día** day by day; **~ orden** in order; **entrar ~ la entrada principal** to go in through the main entrance
9 (agente) by; **hecho ~ él** done by him; **"dirigido ~"** "directed by"
10: **10 ~ 10 son 100** 10 by 10 is 100
11 (en lugar de): **vino él ~ su jefe** he came instead of his boss
12: **~ mí que revienten** as far as I'm concerned they can drop dead
13 (evidencia): **~ lo que dicen** judging by o from what they say
14: **estar/quedar ~ hacer** to be still o remain to be done
15: **~ (muy) difícil que sea** however hard it is o may be; **~ más que lo intente** no matter how o however hard I try
16: **~ qué** why; **¿~ qué?** why?; **¿~?** (fam) why (do you ask)?

porcelana [porθe'lana] nf porcelain; (china) china.
porcentaje [porθen'taxe] nm percentage; **~ de actividad** (INFORM) hit rate.
porche ['portʃe] nm (de una plaza) arcade; (de casa) porch.
porción [por'θjon] nf (parte) portion, share;

(cantidad) quantity, amount.
pordiosero, a [porðjo'sero, a] nm/f beggar.
porfía [por'fia] nf persistence; (terquedad) obstinacy.
porfiado, a [por'fjaðo, a] adj persistent; obstinate.
porfiar [por'fjar] vi to persist, insist; (disputar) to argue stubbornly.
pormenor [porme'nor] nm detail, particular.
pormenorice [pormeno'riθe] etc vb V **pormenorizar**.
pormenorizar [pormenori'θar] vt to (set out in) detail ♦ vi to go into detail.
porno ['porno] adj inv porno ♦ nm porn.
pornografía [pornoɣra'fia] nf pornography.
poro ['poro] nm pore.
poroso, a [po'roso, a] adj porous.
poroto [po'roto] nm (AM) kidney bean.
porque ['porke] conj (a causa de) because; (ya que) since; **~ sí** because I feel like it.
porqué [por'ke] nm reason, cause.
porquería [porke'ria] nf (suciedad) filth, muck, dirt; (acción) dirty trick; (objeto) small thing, trifle; (fig) rubbish.
porqueriza [porke'riθa] nf pigsty.
porra ['porra] nf (arma) stick, club; (cachiporra) truncheon; **¡~s!** oh heck!; **¡vete a la ~!** go to heck!
porrazo [po'rraθo] nm (golpe) blow; (caída) bump; **de un ~** in one go.
porro ['porro] nm joint.
porrón [po'rron] nm glass wine jar with a long spout.
port [por(t)] nm (INFORM) port.
portaaviones [porta(a)'βjones] nm inv aircraft carrier.
portada [por'taða] nf (TIP) title page; (: de revista) cover.
portador, a [porta'ðor, a] nm/f carrier, bearer; (COM) bearer, payee; (MED) carrier; **ser ~ del virus del sida** to be HIV-positive.
portaequipajes [portaeki'paxes] nm inv boot (BRIT), trunk (US); (baca) luggage rack.
portafolio(s) [porta'foljo(s)] nm (AM) briefcase; **~ de inversiones** (COM) investment portfolio.
portal [por'tal] nm (entrada) vestibule, hall; (pórtico) porch, doorway; (puerta de entrada) main door; (DEPORTE) goal; **~es** nmpl arcade sg.
portaligas [porta'liɣas] nm inv (AM) suspender belt.
portamaletas [portama'letas] nm inv roof rack.

portamonedas [portamo'neðas] *nm inv* purse.

portar [por'tar] *vt* to carry, bear; **~se** *vr* to behave, conduct o.s.; **~se mal** to misbehave; **se portó muy bien conmigo** he treated me very well.

portátil [por'tatil] *adj* portable.

portaviones [porta'βjones] *nm inv* aircraft carrier.

portavoz [porta'βoθ] *nm/f* spokesman/woman.

portazo [por'taθo] *nm:* **dar un ~** to slam the door.

porte ['porte] *nm (COM)* transport; *(precio)* transport charges *pl*; *(CORREOS)* postage; **~ debido** *(COM)* carriage forward; **~ pagado** *(COM)* carriage paid, post-paid.

portento [por'tento] *nm* marvel, wonder.

portentoso, a [porten'toso, a] *adj* marvellous, extraordinary.

porteño, a [por'teɲo, a] *adj* of o from Buenos Aires ♦ *nm/f* native o inhabitant of Buenos Aires.

portería [porte'ria] *nf (oficina)* porter's office; *(gol)* goal.

portero, a [por'tero, a] *nm/f* porter; *(conserje)* caretaker; *(DEPORTE)* goalkeeper.

pórtico ['portiko] *nm (porche)* portico, porch; *(fig)* gateway; *(arcada)* arcade.

portilla [por'tiʎa] *nf,* **portillo** [por'tiʎo] *nm* gate.

portón [pro'ton] *nm* proton.

portorriqueño, a [portorri'keɲo, a] *adj, nm/f* Puerto Rican.

portuario, a [por'twarjo] *adj (del puerto)* port *cpd,* harbour *cpd;* *(del muelle)* dock *cpd;* **trabajador ~** docker.

Portugal [portu'ɣal] *nm* Portugal.

portugués, esa [portu'ɣes, esa] *adj, nm/f* Portuguese ♦ *nm (LING)* Portuguese.

porvenir [porβe'nir] *nm* future.

pos [pos]: **en ~ de:** *prep* after, in pursuit of.

posada [po'saða] *nf (refugio)* shelter, lodging; *(mesón)* guest house; **dar ~ a** to give shelter to, take in.

posaderas [posa'ðeras] *nfpl* backside *sg,* buttocks.

posar [po'sar] *vt (en el suelo)* to lay down, put down; *(la mano)* to place, put gently ♦ *vi* to sit, pose; **~se** *vr* to settle; *(pájaro)* to perch; *(avión)* to land, come down.

posdata [pos'ðata] *nf* postscript.

pose ['pose] *nf (ARTE, afectación)* pose.

poseedor, a [posee'ðor, a] *nm/f* owner, possessor; *(de récord, puesto)* holder.

poseer [pose'er] *vt* to have, possess, own; *(ventaja)* to enjoy; *(récord, puesto)* to hold.

poseído, a [pose'iðo, a] *adj* possessed; **estar muy ~ de** to be very vain about.

posesión [pose'sjon] *nf* possession; **tomar ~ (de)** to take over.

posesionarse [posesjo'narse] *vr:* **~ de** to take possession of, take over.

posesivo, a [pose'siβo, a] *adj* possessive.

poseyendo [pose'jendo] *etc vb V* **poseer.**

posgrado [pos'ɣraðo] *nm* = **postgrado.**

posgraduado, a [posɣra'ðwaðo, a] *adj, nm/f* = **postgraduado.**

posibilidad [posiβili'ðað] *nf* possibility; *(oportunidad)* chance.

posibilitar [posiβili'tar] *vt* to make possible, permit; *(hacer factible)* to make feasible.

posible [po'siβle] *adj* possible; *(factible)* feasible ♦ *nm:* **~s** means; *(bienes)* funds, assets; **de ser ~** if possible; **en o dentro de lo ~** as far as possible; **lo antes ~** as quickly as possible.

posición [posi'θjon] *nf (gen)* position; *(rango social)* status.

positivo, a [posi'tiβo, a] *adj* positive ♦ *nf (FOTO)* print.

poso ['poso] *nm* sediment.

posoperatorio, a [posopera'torjo, a] *adj, nm* = **postoperatorio.**

posponer [pospo'ner] *vt* to put behind o below; *(aplazar)* to postpone.

posponga [pos'ponga] *etc,* **pospuesto** [pos'pwesto], **pospuse** [pos'puse] *etc vb V* **posponer.**

posta ['posta] *nf (de caballos)* relay, team; **a ~** on purpose, deliberately.

postal [pos'tal] *adj* postal ♦ *nf* postcard.

poste ['poste] *nm (de telégrafos)* post, pole; *(columna)* pillar.

póster ['poster], *pl* **posters** ['posters] *nm* poster.

postergar [poster'ɣar] *vt (esp AM)* to put off, postpone, delay.

postergue [pos'terɣe] *etc vb V* **postergar.**

posteridad [posteri'ðað] *nf* posterity.

posterior [poste'rjor] *adj* back, rear; *(siguiente)* following, subsequent; *(más tarde)* later; **ser ~ a** to be later than.

posterioridad [posterjori'ðað] *nf:* **con ~** later, subsequently.

postgrado [post'ɣraðo] *nm:* **curso de ~** postgraduate course.

postgraduado, a [postɣra'ðwaðo, a] *adj, nm/f* postgraduate.

pos(t)guerra [pos(t)'ɣerra] *nf* postwar period; **en la ~** after the war.

postigo [pos'tiɣo] *nm (portillo)* postern;

postín – preciar

(*contraventana*) shutter.
postín [pos'tin] *nm* (*fam*) elegance; **de ~**
posh; **darse ~** to show off.
postizo, a [pos'tiθo, a] *adj* false, artificial;
(*sonrisa*) false, phoney ♦ *nm* hairpiece.
postoperatorio, a [postopera'torjo, a] *adj*
postoperative ♦ *nm* postoperative
period.
postor, a [pos'tor, a] *nm/f* bidder; **mejor ~**
highest bidder.
postrado, a [pos'traðo, a] *adj* prostrate.
postrar [pos'trar] *vt* (*derribar*) to cast
down, overthrow; (*humillar*) to humble;
(*MED*) to weaken, exhaust; **~se** *vr* to
prostrate o.s.
postre ['postre] *nm* sweet, dessert ♦ *nf*: **a la**
~ in the end, when all is said and done;
para ~ (*fam*) to crown it all; **llegar a los**
~s (*fig*) to come too late.
postrero, a [pos'trero, a] *adj* (*delante de*
nmsg: **postrer**: *último*) last; (: *que viene*
detrás) rear.
postrimerías [postrime'rias] *nfpl* final
stages.
postulado [postu'laðo] *nm* postulate.
postulante [postu'lante] *nm/f* petitioner;
(*REL*) postulant.
póstumo, a ['postumo, a] *adj* posthumous.
postura [pos'tura] *nf* (*del cuerpo*) posture,
position; (*fig*) attitude, position.
post-venta [pos'ßenta] *adj* (*COM*) after-
sales.
potable [po'taßle] *adj* drinkable.
potaje [po'taxe] *nm* thick vegetable soup.
pote ['pote] *nm* pot, jar.
potencia [po'tenθja] *nf* power; (*capacidad*)
capacity; **~ (en caballos)** horsepower; **en**
~ potential, in the making; **las grandes**
~s the great powers.
potencial [poten'θjal] *adj, nm* potential.
potenciar [poten'θjar] *vt* (*promover*) to
promote; (*fortalecer*) to boost.
potente [po'tente] *adj* powerful.
potestad [potes'taθ] *nf* authority; **patria ~**
paternal authority.
potosí [poto'si] *nm* fortune; **cuesta un ~** it
costs the earth.
potra ['potra] *nf* (*ZOOL*) filly; **tener ~** to be
lucky.
potro ['potro] *nm* (*ZOOL*) colt; (*DEPORTE*)
vaulting horse.
pozo ['poθo] *nm* well; (*de río*) deep pool;
(*de mina*) shaft; **~ negro** cesspool; **ser un**
~ de ciencia (*fig*) to be deeply learned.
PP *abr* (= *por poderes*) pp; (= *porte pagado*)
carriage paid.
p.p.m. *abr* (= *palabras por minuto*) wpm.
práctica ['praktika] *nf* V **práctico**.

practicable [prakti'kaßle] *adj* practicable;
(*camino*) passable, usable.
prácticamente ['praktikamente] *adv*
practically.
practicante [prakti'kante] *nm/f* (*MED*:
ayudante de doctor) medical assistant;
(: *enfermero*) nurse; (*quien practica algo*)
practitioner ♦ *adj* practising.
practicar [prakti'kar] *vt* to practise;
(*deporte*) to go in for, play; (*ejecutar*) to
carry out, perform.
práctico, a ['praktiko, a] *adj* (*gen*)
practical; (*conveniente*) handy; (*instruído*:
persona) skilled, expert ♦ *nf* practice;
(*método*) method; (*arte, capacidad*) skill;
en la práctica in practice.
practique [prak'tike] *etc vb* V **practicar**.
pradera [pra'ðera] *nf* meadow; (*de Canadá*)
prairie.
prado ['praðo] *nm* (*campo*) meadow, field;
(*pastizal*) pasture; (*AM*) lawn.
Praga ['praɣa] *nf* Prague.
pragmático, a [praɣ'matiko, a] *adj*
pragmatic.
preámbulo [pre'ambulo] *nm* preamble,
introduction; **decir algo sin ~s** to say sth
without beating about the bush.
precalentamiento [prekalenta'mjento] *nm*
(*DEPORTE*) warm-up.
precalentar [prekalen'tar] *vt* to preheat.
precaliente [preka'ljente] *etc vb* V
precalentar.
precario, a [pre'karjo, a] *adj* precarious.
precaución [prekau'θjon] *nf* (*medida*
preventiva) preventive measure,
precaution; (*prudencia*) caution,
wariness.
precaver [preka'ßer] *vt* to guard against;
(*impedir*) to forestall; **~se** *vr*: **~se de** *o*
contra algo to (be on one's) guard
against sth.
precavido, a [preka'ßiðo, a] *adj* cautious,
wary.
precedencia [preθe'ðenθja] *nf* precedence;
(*prioridad*) priority; (*superioridad*)
greater importance, superiority.
precedente [preθe'ðente] *adj* preceding;
(*anterior*) former ♦ *nm* precedent; **sin**
~(s) unprecedented; **establecer** *o* **sentar**
un ~ to establish *o* set a precedent.
preceder [preθe'ðer] *vt, vi* to precede, go/
come before.
precepto [pre'θepto] *nm* precept.
preceptor [preθep'tor] *nm* (*maestro*)
teacher; (: *particular*) tutor.
preciado, a [pre'θjaðo, a] *adj* (*estimado*)
esteemed, valuable.
preciar [pre'θjar] *vt* to esteem, value; **~se**

vr to boast; **~se de** to pride o.s. on.
precintar [preθin'tar] *vt* (*local*) to seal off;
(*producto*) to seal.
precinto [pre'θinto] *nm* (*COM*: *tb*: **~ de
garantía**) seal.
precio ['preθjo] *nm* (*de mercado*) price;
(*costo*) cost; (*valor*) value, worth; (*de
viaje*) fare; **~ de coste** *o* **de cobertura**
cost price; **~ al contado** cash price; **~ al
detalle** *o* **al por menor** retail price; **~ al
detallista** trade price; **~ de entrega
inmediata** spot price; **~ de oferta** offer
price; **~ de oportunidad** bargain price;
~ de salida upset price; **~ tope** top
price; **~ unitario** unit price; **no tener ~**
(*fig*) to be priceless; **"no importa ~"**
"cost no object".
preciosidad [preθjosi'ðað] *nf* (*valor*) (high)
value, (great) worth; (*encanto*) charm;
(*cosa bonita*) beautiful thing; **es una ~**
it's lovely, it's really beautiful.
precioso, a [pre'θjoso, a] *adj* precious; (*de
mucho valor*) valuable; (*fam*) lovely,
beautiful.
precipicio [preθi'piθjo] *nm* cliff, precipice;
(*fig*) abyss.
precipitación [preθipita'θjon] *nf* (*prisa*)
haste; (*lluvia*) rainfall; (*QUÍMICA*)
precipitation.
precipitado, a [preθipi'taðo, a] *adj* hasty,
rash; (*salida*) hasty, sudden ♦ *nm*
(*QUÍMICA*) precipitate.
precipitar [preθipi'tar] *vt* (*arrojar*) to hurl,
throw; (*apresurar*) to hasten; (*acelerar*) to
speed up, accelerate; (*QUÍMICA*) to
precipitate; **~se** *vr* to throw o.s.;
(*apresurarse*) to rush; (*actuar sin pensar*)
to act rashly; **~se hacia** to rush towards.
precisado, a [preθi'saðo, a] *adj*: **verse ~ a
hacer algo** to be obliged to do sth.
precisamente [preθisa'mente] *adv*
precisely; (*justo*) precisely, exactly,
just; **~ por eso** for that very reason; **~
fue él quien lo dijo** as a matter of fact he
said it; **no es eso ~** it's not really that.
precisar [preθi'sar] *vt* (*necesitar*) to need,
require; (*fijar*) to determine exactly, fix;
(*especificar*) to specify; (*señalar*) to
pinpoint.
precisión [preθi'sjon] *nf* (*exactitud*)
precision.
preciso, a [pre'θiso, a] *adj* (*exacto*) precise;
(*necesario*) necessary, essential; (*estilo,
lenguaje*) concise; **es ~ que lo hagas** you
must do it.
precocidad [prekoθi'ðað] *nf*
precociousness, precocity.
preconcebido, a [prekonθe'βiðo, a] *adj*
preconceived.
preconice [preko'niθe] *etc vb V* **preconizar**.
preconizar [prekoni'θar] *vt* (*aconsejar*) to
advise; (*prever*) to foresee.
precoz [pre'koθ] *adj* (*persona*) precocious;
(*calvicie*) premature.
precursor, a [prekur'sor, a] *nm/f*
precursor.
predecesor, a [preðeθe'sor, a] *nm/f*
predecessor.
predecir [preðe'θir] *vt* to predict, foretell,
forecast.
predestinado, a [preðesti'naðo, a] *adj*
predestined.
predeterminar [preðetermi'nar] *vt* to
predetermine.
predicado [preði'kaðo] *nm* predicate.
predicador, a [preðika'ðor, a] *nm/f*
preacher.
predicar [preði'kar] *vt, vi* to preach.
predicción [preðik'θjon] *nf* prediction;
(*pronóstico*) forecast; **~ del tiempo**
weather forecast(ing).
predicho [pre'ðitʃo], **prediga** [pre'ðiɣa]
etc, **predije** [pre'ðixe] *etc vb V* **predecir**.
predilecto, a [preði'lekto, a] *adj* favourite.
predique [pre'ðike] *etc vb V* **predicar**.
prediré [preði're] *etc vb V* **predecir**.
predispondré [preðispon'dre] *etc vb V*
predisponer.
predisponer [preðispo'ner] *vt* to
predispose; (*pey*) to prejudice.
predisponga [preðis'ponga] *etc vb V*
predisponer.
predisposición [preðisposi'θjon] *nf*
predisposition, inclination; prejudice,
bias; (*MED*) tendency.
predispuesto, a [preðis'pwesto, a],
predispuse [preðis'puse] *etc vb V*
predisponer.
predominante [preðomi'nante] *adj*
predominant; (*preponderante*) prevailing;
(*interés*) controlling.
predominar [preðomi'nar] *vt* to dominate
♦ *vi* to predominate; (*prevalecer*) to
prevail.
predominio [preðo'minjo] *nm*
predominance; prevalence.
preescolar [preesko'lar] *adj* preschool.
preestreno [prees'treno] *nm* preview,
press view.
prefabricado, a [prefaβri'kaðo, a] *adj*
prefabricated.
prefacio [pre'faθjo] *nm* preface.
preferencia [prefe'renθja] *nf* preference;
de ~ preferably, for preference;
localidad de ~ reserved seat.
preferible [prefe'riβle] *adj* preferable.

preferir [prefe'rir] *vt* to prefer.
prefiera [pre'fjera] *etc vb V* **preferir**.
prefijo [pre'fixo] *nm* prefix.
prefiriendo [prefi'rjendo] *etc vb V* **preferir**.
pregón [pre'ɤon] *nm* proclamation, announcement.
pregonar [preɤo'nar] *vt* to proclaim, announce; (*mercancía*) to hawk.
pregonero [preɤo'nero] *nm* town crier.
pregunta [pre'ɤunta] *nf* question; ~ **capciosa** catch question; **hacer una** ~ to ask a question.
preguntar [preɤun'tar] *vt* to ask; (*cuestionar*) to question ♦ *vi* to ask; ~**se** *vr* to wonder; ~ **por algn** to ask for sb; ~ **por la salud de algn** to ask after sb's health.
preguntón, ona [preɤun'ton, ona] *adj* inquisitive.
prehistórico, a [preis'toriko, a] *adj* prehistoric.
prejuicio [pre'xwiθjo] *nm* prejudgement; (*preconcepción*) preconception; (*pey*) prejudice, bias.
prejuzgar [prexuθ'ɤar] *vt* (*predisponer*) to prejudge.
prejuzgue [pre'xuθɤe] *etc vb V* **prejuzgar**.
preliminar [prelimi'nar] *adj*, *nm* preliminary.
preludio [pre'luðjo] *nm* (*MUS*, *fig*) prelude.
premamá [prema'ma] *adj*: **vestido** ~ maternity dress.
prematrimonial [prematrimo'njal] *adj*: **relaciones** ~**es** premarital sex.
prematuro, a [prema'turo, a] *adj* premature.
premeditación [premeðita'θjon] *nf* premeditation.
premeditado, a [premeði'taðo, a] *adj* premeditated, deliberate; (*intencionado*) wilful.
premeditar [premeði'tar] *vt* to premeditate.
premiar [pre'mjar] *vt* to reward; (*en un concurso*) to give a prize to.
premio ['premjo] *nm* reward; prize; (*COM*) premium; ~ **gordo** first prize.
premisa [pre'misa] *nf* premise.
premonición [premoni'θjon] *nf* premonition.
premura [pre'mura] *nf* (*prisa*) haste, urgency.
prenatal [prena'tal] *adj* antenatal, prenatal.
prenda ['prenda] *nf* (*ropa*) garment, article of clothing; (*garantía*) pledge; (*fam*) darling!; ~**s** *nfpl* talents, gifts; **dejar algo en** ~ to pawn sth; **no soltar** ~ to give

nothing away; (*fig*) not to say a word.
prendar [pren'dar] *vt* to captivate, enchant; ~**se de algo** to fall in love with sth.
prendedor [prende'ðor] *nm* brooch.
prender [pren'der] *vt* (*captar*) to catch, capture; (*detener*) to arrest; (*coser*) to pin, attach; (*sujetar*) to fasten; (*AM*) to switch on ♦ *vi* to catch; (*arraigar*) to take root; ~**se** *vr* (*encenderse*) to catch fire.
prendido, a [pren'diðo, a] *adj* (*AM*: *luz etc*) on.
prensa ['prensa] *nf* press; **la P**~ the press; **tener mala** ~ to have *o* get a bad press; **la** ~ **nacional** the national press.
prensar [pren'sar] *vt* to press.
preñado, a [pre'naðo, a] *adj* (*mujer*) pregnant; ~ **de** pregnant with, full of.
preocupación [preokupa'θjon] *nf* worry, concern; (*ansiedad*) anxiety.
preocupado, a [preoku'paðo, a] *adj* worried, concerned; anxious.
preocupar [preoku'par] *vt* to worry; ~**se** *vr* to worry; ~**se de algo** (*hacerse cargo*) to take care of sth; ~**se por algo** to worry about sth.
preparación [prepara'θjon] *nf* (*acto*) preparation; (*estado*) preparedness, readiness; (*entrenamiento*) training.
preparado, a [prepa'raðo, a] *adj* (*dispuesto*) prepared; (*CULIN*) ready (to serve) ♦ *nm* (*MED*) preparation; ¡~**s, listos, ya!** ready, steady, go!
preparar [prepa'rar] *vt* (*disponer*) to prepare, get ready; (*TEC*: *tratar*) to prepare, process, treat; (*entrenar*) to teach, train; ~**se** *vr*: ~**se a** *o* **para hacer algo** to prepare *o* get ready to do sth.
preparativo, a [prepara'tiβo] *adj* preparatory, preliminary ♦ *nm*: ~**s** *nmpl* preparations.
preparatoria [prepara'torja] *nf* (*AM*) sixth form college (*BRIT*), senior high school (*US*).
preposición [preposi'θjon] *nf* preposition.
prepotencia [prepo'tenθja] *nf* abuse of power; (*POL*) high-handedness; (*soberbia*) arrogance.
prepotente [prepo'tente] *adj* (*POL*) high-handed; (*soberbio*) arrogant.
prerrogativa [prerroɤa'tiβa] *nf* prerogative, privilege.
presa ['presa] *nf* (*cosa apresada*) catch; (*víctima*) victim; (*de animal*) prey; (*de agua*) dam; **hacer** ~ **en** to clutch (on to), seize; **ser** ~ **de** (*fig*) to be a prey to.
presagiar [presa'xjar] *vt* to threaten.
presagio [pre'saxjo] *nm* omen.

presbítero [pres'ßitero] *nm* priest.
prescindir [presθin'dir] *vi*: ~ **de** (*privarse de*) to do without, go without; (*descartar*) to dispense with; **no podemos** ~ **de él** we can't manage without him.
prescribir [preskri'ßir] *vt* to prescribe.
prescripción [preskrip'θjon] *nf* prescription; ~ **facultativa** medical prescription.
prescrito [pres'krito] *pp de* **prescribir**.
preseleccionar [preselekθjo'nar] *vt* (*DEPORTE*) to seed.
presencia [pre'senθja] *nf* presence; **en** ~ **de** in the presence of.
presencial [presen'θjal] *adj*: **testigo** ~ eyewitness.
presenciar [presen'θjar] *vt* to be present at; (*asistir a*) to attend; (*ver*) to see, witness.
presentación [presenta'θjon] *nf* presentation; (*introducción*) introduction.
presentador, a [presenta'ðor, a] *nm/f* compère.
presentar [presen'tar] *vt* to present; (*ofrecer*) to offer; (*mostrar*) to show, display; (*renuncia*) to tender; (*moción*) to propose; (*a una persona*) to introduce; ~**se** *vr* (*llegar inesperadamente*) to appear, turn up; (*ofrecerse: como candidato*) to run, stand; (*aparecer*) to show, appear; (*solicitar empleo*) to apply; ~ **al cobro** (*COM*) to present for payment; ~**se a la policía** to report to the police.
presente [pre'sente] *adj* present ♦ *nm* present; (*LING*) present (tense); (*regalo*) gift; **los** ~**s** those present; **hacer** ~ **to** state, declare; **tener** ~ to remember, bear in mind; **la carta** ~, **la** ~ this letter.
presentimiento [presenti'mjento] *nm* premonition, presentiment.
presentir [presen'tir] *vt* to have a premonition of.
preservación [preserßa'θjon] *nf* protection, preservation.
preservar [preser'ßar] *vt* to protect, preserve.
preservativo [preserßa'tißo] *nm* sheath, condom.
presidencia [presi'ðenθja] *nf* presidency; (*de comité*) chairmanship; **ocupar la** ~ to preside, be in *o* take the chair.
presidente [presi'ðente] *nm/f* president; chairman/woman; (*en parlamento*) speaker; (*JUR*) presiding magistrate.
presidiario [presi'ðjarjo] *nm* convict.
presidio [pre'siðjo] *nm* prison, penitentiary.
presidir [presi'ðir] *vt* (*dirigir*) to preside at,

preside over; (: *comité*) to take the chair at; (*dominar*) to dominate, rule ♦ *vi* to preside; to take the chair.
presienta [pre'sjenta] *etc*, **presintiendo** [presin'tjendo] *etc vb V* **presentir**.
presión [pre'sjon] *nf* pressure; ~ **arterial** *o* **sanguínea** blood pressure; **a** ~ under pressure.
presionar [presjo'nar] *vt* to press; (*botón*) to push, press; (*fig*) to press, put pressure on ♦ *vi*: ~ **para** *o* **por** to press for.
preso, a ['preso, a] *adj*: **estar** ~ **de terror** *o* **pánico** to be panic-stricken ♦ *nm/f* prisoner; **tomar** *o* **llevar** ~ **a algn** to arrest sb, take sb prisoner.
prestación [presta'θjon] *nf* (*aportación*) lending; (*INFORM*) capability; (*servicio*) service; (*subsidio*) benefit; **prestaciones** *nfpl* (*AUTO*) performance features; ~ **de juramento** oath-taking; ~ **personal** obligatory service; **P**~ **Social Sustitutoria** community service for conscientious objectors; *V tb* **mili**.
prestado, a [pres'taðo, a] *adj* on loan; **dar algo** ~ to lend sth; **pedir** ~ to borrow.
prestamista [presta'mista] *nm/f* moneylender.
préstamo [pres'tamo] *nm* loan; ~ **con garantía** loan against collateral; ~ **hipotecario** mortgage.
prestar [pres'tar] *vt* to lend, loan; (*atención*) to pay; (*ayuda*) to give; (*servicio*) to do, render; (*juramento*) to take, swear; ~**se** *vr* (*ofrecerse*) to offer *o* volunteer.
prestatario, a [presta'tarjo, a] *nm/f* borrower.
presteza [pres'teθa] *nf* speed, promptness.
prestidigitador [prestiðixita'ðor] *nm* conjurer.
prestigio [pres'tixjo] *nm* prestige; (*reputación*) face; (*renombre*) good name.
prestigioso, a [presti'xjoso, a] *adj* (*honorable*) prestigious; (*famoso, renombrado*) renowned, famous.
presto, a ['presto, a] *adj* (*rápido*) quick, prompt; (*dispuesto*) ready ♦ *adv* at once, right away.
presumido, a [presu'miðo, a] *adj* conceited.
presumir [presu'mir] *vt* to presume ♦ *vi* (*tener aires*) to be conceited; **según cabe** ~ as may be presumed, presumably; ~ **de listo** to think o.s. very smart.
presunción [presun'θjon] *nf* presumption; (*sospecha*) suspicion; (*vanidad*) conceit.
presunto, a [pre'sunto, a] *adj* (*supuesto*)

_AM_) national hero.

procesado, a [proθe'saðo, a] _nm/f_ accused (person).

procesador [proθesa'ðor] _nm_: ~ **de textos** (_INFORM_) word processor.

procesamiento [proθesa'mjento] _nm_ (_INFORM_) processing; ~ **de datos** data processing; ~ **por lotes** batch processing; ~ **solapado** multiprogramming; ~ **de textos** word processing.

procesar [proθe'sar] _vt_ to try, put on trial; (_INFORM_) to process.

procesión [proθe'sjon] _nf_ procession; **la** ~ **va por dentro** he keeps his troubles to himself.

proceso [pro'θeso] _nm_ process; (_JUR_) trial; (_lapso_) course (of time); (_INFORM_): ~ **(automático) de datos** (automatic) data processing; ~ **no prioritario** background process; ~ **por pasadas** batch processing; ~ **en tiempo real** real-time programming.

proclama [pro'klama] _nf_ (_acto_) proclamation; (_cartel_) poster.

proclamar [prokla'mar] _vt_ to proclaim.

proclive [pro'kliβe] _adj_: ~ **(a)** inclined _o_ prone (to).

procreación [prokrea'θjon] _nf_ procreation.

procrear [prokre'ar] _vt, vi_ to procreate.

procurador, a [prokura'ðor, a] _nm/f_ attorney, solicitor.

procurar [proku'rar] _vt_ (_intentar_) to try, endeavour; (_conseguir_) to get, obtain; (_asegurar_) to secure; (_producir_) to produce.

prodigar [proði'ɣar] _vt_ to lavish; ~**se** _vr_: ~**se en** to be lavish with.

prodigio [pro'ðixjo] _nm_ prodigy; (_milagro_) wonder, marvel; **niño** ~ child prodigy.

prodigioso, a [proði'xjoso, a] _adj_ prodigious, marvellous.

pródigo, a ['proðixo, a] _adj_ (_rico_) rich, productive; **hijo** ~ prodigal son.

producción [proðuk'θjon] _nf_ production; (_suma de productos_) output; (_producto_) product; ~ **en serie** mass production.

producir [proðu'θir] _vt_ to produce; (_generar_) to cause, bring about; (_impresión_) to give; (_COM: interés_) to bear; ~**se** _vr_ (_gen_) to come about, happen; (_hacerse_) to be produced, be made; (_estallar_) to break out; (_accidente_) to take place.

productividad [proðuktiβi'ðað] _nf_ productivity.

productivo, a [proðuk'tiβo, a] _adj_ productive; (_provechoso_) profitable.

producto [pro'ðukto] _nm_ (_resultado_)

product; _producción_) production; ~ **alimenticio** foodstuff; ~ **(nacional) bruto** gross (national) product; ~ **interno bruto** gross domestic product.

productor, a [pro'ðuk'tor, a] _adj_ productive, producing ♦ _nm/f_ producer.

produje [pro'ðuxe], **produjera** [proðu'xera], **produzca** [pro'ðuθka] _etc vb_ V **producir**.

proeza [pro'eθa] _nf_ exploit, feat.

profanar [profa'nar] _vt_ to desecrate, profane.

profano, a [pro'fano, a] _adj_ profane ♦ _nm/f_ (_inexperto_) layman/woman; **soy** ~ **en música** I don't know anything about music.

profecía [profe'θia] _nf_ prophecy.

proferir [profe'rir] _vt_ (_palabra, sonido_) to utter; (_injuria_) to hurl, let fly.

profesar [profe'sar] _vt_ (_declarar_) to profess; (_practicar_) to practise.

profesión [profe'sjon] _nf_ profession; (_confesión_) avowal; **abogado de** ~, **de** ~ **abogado** a lawyer by profession.

profesional [profesjo'nal] _adj_ professional.

profesor, a [profe'sor, a] _nm/f_ teacher; (_instructor_) instructor; (~ **de universidad**) lecturer; ~ **adjunto** assistant lecturer, associate professor (_US_).

profesorado [profeso'raðo] _nm_ (_profesión_) teaching profession; (_cuerpo_) teaching staff, faculty (_US_); (_cargo_) professorship.

profeta [pro'feta] _nm/f_ prophet.

profetice [profe'tiθe] _etc vb_ V **profetizar**.

profetizar [profeti'θar] _vt, vi_ to prophesy.

profiera [pro'fjera] _etc_, **profiriendo** [profi'rjendo] _etc vb_ V **proferir**.

profilaxis [profi'laksis] _nf inv_ prevention.

prófugo, a ['profuɣo, a] _nm/f_ fugitive; (_desertor_) deserter.

profundice [profun'diθe] _etc vb_ V **profundizar**.

profundidad [profundi'ðað] _nf_ depth; **tener una** ~ **de 30 cm** to be 30 cm deep.

profundizar [profundi'θar] _vt_ (_fig_) to go deeply into, study in depth.

profundo, a [pro'fundo, a] _adj_ deep; (_misterio, pensador_) profound; **poco** ~ shallow.

profusión [profu'sjon] _nf_ (_abundancia_) profusion; (_prodigalidad_) wealth.

progenie [pro'xenje] _nf_ offspring.

progenitor [proxeni'tor] _nm_ ancestor; ~**es** _nmpl_ (_fam_) parents.

programa [pro'ɣrama] _nm_ programme; (_INFORM_) program; ~ **de estudios** curriculum, syllabus; ~ **verificador de**

ortografía (*INFORM*) spelling checker.
programación [proɣrama'θjon] *nf*
(*INFORM*) programming; ~ **estructurada**
structured programming.
programador, a [proɣrama'ðor, a] *nm/f*
(computer) programmer; ~ **de**
aplicaciones applications programmer.
programar [proɣra'mar] *vt* (*INFORM*) to
programme.
programería [proɣrame'ria] *nf* (*INFORM*): ~
fija firmware.
progre ['proɣre] *adj* (*fam*) liberal.
progresar [proɣre'sar] *vi* to progress,
make progress.
progresión [proɣres'jon] *nf*: ~
geométrica/aritmética geometric/
arithmetic progression.
progresista [proɣre'sista] *adj, nm/f*
progressive.
progresivo, a [proɣre'siβo, a] *adj*
progressive; (*gradual*) gradual;
(*continuo*) continuous.
progreso [pro'ɣreso] *nm* (*tb*: ~**s**) progress;
hacer ~**s** to progress, advance.
prohibición [proiβi'θjon] *nf* prohibition,
ban; **levantar la** ~ **de** to remove the ban
on.
prohibir [proi'βir] *vt* to prohibit, ban,
forbid; **se prohíbe fumar** no smoking.
prohibitivo, a [proiβi'tiβo, a] *adj*
prohibitive.
prójimo, a ['proximo, a] *nm* fellow man
♦ *nm/f* (*vecino*) neighbour.
prole ['prole] *nf* (*descendencia*) offspring.
proletariado [proleta'rjaðo] *nm*
proletariat.
proletario, a [prole'tarjo, a] *adj, nm/f*
proletarian.
proliferación [prolifera'θjon] *nf*
proliferation; ~ **de armas nucleares**
spread of nuclear arms.
proliferar [prolife'rar] *vi* to proliferate.
prolífico, a [pro'lifiko, a] *adj* prolific.
prolijo, a [pro'lixo, a] *adj* long-winded,
tedious; (*AM*) neat.
prólogo ['proloɣo] *nm* prologue;
(*preámbulo*) preface, introduction.
prolongación [prolonga'θjon] *nf*
extension.
prolongado, a [prolon'gaðo, a] *adj* (*largo*)
long; (*alargado*) lengthy.
prolongar [prolon'gar] *vt* (*gen*) to extend;
(*en el tiempo*) to prolong; (*calle, tubo*) to
make longer, extend; ~**se** *vr* (*alargarse*)
to extend, go on.
prolongue [pro'longe] *etc vb V* **prolongar**.
prom. *abr* (= *promedio*) av.
promedio [pro'meðjo] *nm* average; (*de*

distancia) middle, mid-point.
promesa [pro'mesa] *nf* promise ♦ *adj*:
jugador ~ promising player; **faltar a una**
~ to break a promise.
prometer [prome'ter] *vt* to promise ♦ *vi* to
show promise; ~**se** *vr* (*dos personas*) to
get engaged.
prometido, a [prome'tiðo, a] *adj* promised;
engaged ♦ *nm/f* fiancé/fiancée.
prominente [promi'nente] *adj* prominent.
promiscuidad [promiskwi'ðað] *nf*
promiscuity.
promiscuo, a [pro'miskwo, a] *adj*
promiscuous.
promoción [promo'θjon] *nf* promotion;
(*año*) class, year; ~ **por correspondencia**
directa (*COM*) direct mailshot; ~ **de**
ventas sales promotion *o* drive.
promocionar [promoθjo'nar] *vt* (*COM*: *dar*
publicidad) to promote.
promontorio [promon'torjo] *nm*
promontory.
promotor [promo'tor] *nm* promoter;
(*instigador*) instigator.
promover [promo'βer] *vt* to promote;
(*causar*) to cause; (*juicio*) to bring;
(*motín*) to instigate, stir up.
promueva [pro'mweβa] *etc vb V* **promover**.
promulgar [promul'ɣar] *vt* to promulgate;
(*fig*) to proclaim.
promulgue [pro'mulɣe] *etc vb V*
promulgar.
pronombre [pro'nombre] *nm* pronoun.
pronosticar [pronosti'kar] *vt* to predict,
foretell, forecast.
pronóstico [pro'nostiko] *nm* prediction,
forecast; (*profecía*) omen; (*MED*:
diagnóstico) prognosis; **de** ~ **leve** slight,
not serious; ~ **del tiempo** weather
forecast.
pronostique [pronos'tike] *etc vb V*
pronosticar.
prontitud [pronti'tuð] *nf* speed, quickness.
pronto, a ['pronto, a] *adj* (*rápido*) prompt,
quick; (*preparado*) ready ♦ *adv* quickly,
promptly; (*en seguida*) at once, right
away; (*dentro de poco*) soon; (*temprano*)
early ♦ *nm* urge, sudden feeling; **tener**
~**s de enojo** to be quick-tempered; **al** ~
at first; **de** ~ suddenly; **¡hasta** ~**!** see
you soon!; **lo más** ~ **posible** as soon as
possible; **por lo** ~ meanwhile, for the
present; **tan** ~ **como** as soon as.
pronunciación [pronunθja'θjon] *nf*
pronunciation.
pronunciado, a [pronun'θjaðo, a] *adj*
(*marcado*) pronounced; (*curva etc*) sharp;
(*facciones*) marked.

pronunciamiento [pronunθja'mjento] *nm* (*rebelión*) insurrection.

pronunciar [pronun'θjar] *vt* to pronounce; (*discurso*) to make, deliver; (*JUR: sentencia*) to pass, pronounce; ~**se** *vr* to revolt, rise, rebel; (*declararse*) to declare o.s.; ~**se sobre** to pronounce on.

propagación [propaɣa'θjon] *nf* propagation; (*difusión*) spread(ing).

propaganda [propa'ɣanda] *nf* (*política*) propaganda; (*comercial*) advertising; **hacer ~ de** (*COM*) to advertise.

propagar [propa'ɣar] *vt* to propagate; (*difundir*) to spread, disseminate; ~**se** *vr* (*BIO*) to propagate; (*fig*) to spread.

propague [pro'paɣe] *etc vb V* **propagar**.

propalar [propa'lar] *vt* (*divulgar*) to divulge; (*publicar*) to publish an account of.

propano [pro'pano] *nm* propane.

propasarse [propa'sarse] *vr* (*excederse*) to go too far; (*sexualmente*) to take liberties.

propensión [propen'sjon] *nf* inclination, propensity.

propenso, a [pro'penso, a] *adj*: ~ **a** prone *o* inclined to; **ser ~ a hacer algo** to be inclined *o* have a tendency to do sth.

propiamente [propja'mente] *adv* properly; (*realmente*) really, exactly; ~ **dicho** real, true.

propicio, a [pro'piθjo, a] *adj* favourable, propitious.

propiedad [propje'ðað] *nf* property; (*posesión*) possession, ownership; (*conveniencia*) suitability; (*exactitud*) accuracy; ~ **particular** private property; ~ **pública** (*COM*) public ownership; **ceder algo a algn en ~** to transfer to sb the full rights over sth.

propietario, a [propje'tarjo, a] *nm/f* owner, proprietor.

propina [pro'pina] *nf* tip; **dar algo de ~** to give something extra.

propinar [propi'nar] *vt* (*golpe*) to strike; (*azotes*) to give.

propio, a ['propjo, a] *adj* own, of one's own; (*característico*) characteristic, typical; (*conveniente*) proper; (*mismo*) selfsame, very; **el ~ ministro** the minister himself; **¿tienes casa propia?** have you a house of your own?; **eso es muy ~ de él** that's just like him; **tiene un olor muy ~** it has a smell of its own.

propondré [propon'dre] *etc vb V* **proponer**.

proponente [propo'nente] *nm* proposer, mover.

proponer [propo'ner] *vt* to propose, put

forward; (*candidato*) to propose, nominate; (*problema*) to pose; ~**se** *vr* to propose, plan, intend.

proponga [pro'ponga] *etc vb V* **proponer**.

proporción [propor'θjon] *nf* proportion; (*MAT*) ratio; (*razón, porcentaje*) rate; **proporciones** *nfpl* dimensions; (*fig*) size *sg*; **en ~ con** in proportion to.

proporcionado, a [proporθjo'naðo, a] *adj* proportionate; (*regular*) medium, middling; (*justo*) just right; **bien ~** well-proportioned.

proporcional [proporθjo'nal] *adj* proportional; ~ **a** proportional to.

proporcionar [proporθjo'nar] *vt* (*dar*) to give, supply, provide; **esto le proporciona una renta anual de ...** this brings him in a yearly income of ....

proposición [proposi'θjon] *nf* proposition; (*propuesta*) proposal.

propósito [pro'posito] *nm* (*intención*) purpose; (*intento*) aim, intention ♦ *adv*: **a ~** by the way, incidentally; **a ~ de** about, with regard to.

propuesto, a [pro'pwesto, a] *pp de* **proponer** ♦ *nf* proposal.

propugnar [propuɣ'nar] *vt* to uphold.

propulsar [propul'sar] *vt* to drive, propel; (*fig*) to promote, encourage.

propulsión [propul'sjon] *nf* propulsion; ~ **a chorro** *o* **por reacción** jet propulsion.

propuse [pro'puse] *etc vb V* **proponer**.

prorrata [pro'rrata] *nf* (*porción*) share, quota, prorate (*US*) ♦ *adv* (*COM*) pro rata.

prorratear [prorrate'ar] *vt* (*dividir*) to share out, prorate (*US*).

prórroga ['prorroɣa] *nf* (*gen*) extension; (*JUR*) stay; (*COM*) deferment.

prorrogable [prorro'ɣaßle] *adj* which can be extended.

prorrogar [prorro'ɣar] *vt* (*período*) to extend; (*decisión*) to defer, postpone.

prorrogue [pro'rroɣe] *etc vb V* **prorrogar**.

prorrumpir [prorrum'pir] *vi* to burst forth, break out; ~ **en gritos** to start shouting; ~ **en lágrimas** to burst into tears.

prosa ['prosa] *nf* prose.

prosaico, a [pro'saiko, a] *adj* prosaic, dull.

proscribir [proskri'ßir] *vt* to prohibit, ban; (*desterrar*) to exile, banish; (*partido*) to proscribe.

proscripción [proskrip'θjon] *nf* prohibition, ban; banishment; proscription.

proscrito, a [pros'krito, a] *pp de* **proscribir** ♦ *adj* (*prohibido*) banned; (*desterrado*) outlawed ♦ *nm/f* (*exilado*) exile; (*bandido*) outlaw.

prosecución [proseku'θjon] *nf*
continuation; (*persecución*) pursuit.
proseguir [prose'ɣir] *vt* to continue, carry
on, proceed with; (*investigación, estudio*)
to pursue ♦ *vi* to continue, go on.
prosiga [pro'siɣa] *etc*, **prosiguiendo**
[prosi'ɣjenðo] *etc vb V* **proseguir**.
prosista [pro'sista] *nm/f* (*escritor*) prose
writer.
prospección [prospek'θjon] *nf* exploration;
(*del petróleo, del oro*) prospecting.
prospecto [pros'pekto] *nm* prospectus;
(*folleto*) leaflet, sheet of instructions.
prosperar [prospe'rar] *vi* to prosper,
thrive, flourish.
prosperidad [prosperi'ðað] *nf* prosperity;
(*éxito*) success.
próspero, a ['prospero, a] *adj* prosperous,
thriving, flourishing; (*que tiene éxito*)
successful.
prostíbulo [pros'tiβulo] *nm* brothel.
prostitución [prostitu'θjon] *nf*
prostitution.
prostituir [prosti'twir] *vt* to prostitute; ~**se**
vr to prostitute o.s., become a prostitute.
prostituta [prosti'tuta] *nf* prostitute.
prostituyendo [prostitu'jendo] *etc vb V*
prostituir.
protagonice [protaɣo'niθe] *etc vb V*
protagonizar.
protagonista [protaɣo'nista] *nm/f*
protagonist; (*LIT: personaje*) main
character, hero(ine).
protagonizar [protaɣoni'θar] *vt* to head,
take the chief role in.
protección [protek'θjon] *nf* protection.
proteccionismo [protekθjo'nismo] *nm*
(*COM*) protectionism.
protector, a [protek'tor, a] *adj* protective,
protecting; (*tono*) patronizing ♦ *nm/f*
protector; (*bienhechor*) patron; (*de la
tradición*) guardian.
proteger [prote'xer] *vt* to protect; ~ **contra
grabación o contra escritura** (*INFORM*) to
write-protect.
protegido, a [prote'xiðo, a] *nm/f* protégé/
protégée.
proteína [prote'ina] *nf* protein.
proteja [pro'texa] *etc vb V* **proteger**.
prótesis ['protesis] *nf* (*MED*) prosthesis.
protesta [pro'testa] *nf* protest;
(*declaración*) protestation.
protestante [protes'tante] *adj* Protestant.
protestar [protes'tar] *vt* to protest,
declare; (*fe*) to protest ♦ *vi* to protest;
(*objetar*) to object; **cheque protestado
por falta de fondos** cheque referred to
drawer.

protocolo [proto'kolo] *nm* protocol; **sin ~s**
(*formalismo*) informal(ly), without
formalities.
protón [pro'ton] *nm* proton.
prototipo [proto'tipo] *nm* prototype; (*ideal*)
model.
protuberancia [protuβe'ranθja] *nf*
protuberance.
prov. *abr* (= *provincia*) prov.
provecho [pro'βetʃo] *nm* advantage,
benefit; (*FINANZAS*) profit; **¡buen ~!** bon
appétit!; **en ~ de** to the benefit of; **sacar
~ de** to benefit from, profit by.
provechoso, a [proβe'tʃoso, a] *adj*
(*ventajoso*) advantageous; (*beneficioso*)
beneficial, useful; (*FINANZAS: lucrativo*)
profitable.
proveedor, a [proβee'ðor, a] *nm/f*
(*abastecedor*) supplier; (*distribuidor*)
dealer.
proveer [proβe'er] *vt* to provide, supply;
(*preparar*) to provide, get ready;
(*vacante*) to fill; (*negocio*) to transact,
dispatch ♦ *vi*: ~ **a** to provide for; ~**se** *vr*:
~**se de** to provide o.s. with.
provendré [proβen'dre] *etc*, **provenga**
[pro'βenga] *etc vb V* **provenir**.
provenir [proβe'nir] *vi*: ~ **de** to come from,
stem from.
Provenza [pro'βenθa] *nf* Provence.
proverbial [proβer'βjal] *adj* proverbial;
(*fig*) notorious.
proverbio [pro'βerβjo] *nm* proverb.
proveyendo [proβe'jendo] *etc vb V*
proveer.
providencia [proβi'ðenθja] *nf* providence;
(*previsión*) foresight; ~**s** *nfpl* measures,
steps.
provincia [pro'βinθja] *nf* province; (*ESP:
ADMIN*) ≈ county, ≈ region (*Scot*); **un
pueblo de ~(s)** a country town.

---

*Spain is divided up into 55 administrative
provincias, including the islands, and
territories in North Africa. Each one has a
capital de provincia, which generally bears
the same name. **Provincias** are grouped by
geography, history and culture into
comunidades autónomas. It should be
noted that the term **comarca** normally has
a purely geographical function in Spanish,
but in Catalonia it designates
administrative boundaries.*

---

provinciano, a [proβin'θjano, a] *adj*
provincial; (*del campo*) country *cpd*.
proviniendo [proβi'njendo] *etc vb V*
provenir.

provisión [proßi'sjon] _nf_ provision; (_abastecimiento_) provision, supply; (_medida_) measure, step.

provisional [proßisjo'nal] _adj_ provisional.

provisorio, a [proßi'sorjo, a] _adj_ (_esp AM_) provisional.

provisto, a [pro'ßisto, a] _adj_: ~ **de** provided _o_ supplied with; (_que tiene_) having, possessing.

provocación [proßoka'θjon] _nf_ provocation.

provocador, a [proßoka'ðor, a] _adj_ provocative, provoking.

provocar [proßo'kar] _vt_ to provoke; (_alentar_) to tempt, invite; (_causar_) to bring about, lead to; (_promover_) to promote; (_estimular_) to rouse, stir, stimulate; (_protesta, explosión_) to cause, spark off; (_AM_): ¿**te provoca un café?** would you like a coffee?

provocativo, a [proßoka'tißo, a] _adj_ provocative.

provoque [pro'ßoke] _etc vb_ V **provocar**.

proxeneta [prokse'neta] _nm/f_ go-between; (_de prostitutas_) pimp/procuress.

próximamente [proksima'mente] _adv_ shortly, soon.

proximidad [proksimi'ðað] _nf_ closeness, proximity.

próximo, a ['proksimo, a] _adj_ near, close; (_vecino_) neighbouring; (_el que viene_) next; **en fecha próxima** at an early date; **el mes** ~ next month.

proyección [projek'θjon] _nf_ projection; (_CINE_) showing; (_diapositiva_) slide, transparency; (_influencia_) influence; **el tiempo de** ~ **es de 35 minutos** the film runs for 35 minutes.

proyectar [projek'tar] _vt_ (_objeto_) to hurl, throw; (_luz_) to cast, shed; (_CINE_) to screen, show; (_planear_) to plan.

proyectil [projek'til] _nm_ projectile, missile; ~ (**tele**)**dirigido** guided missile.

proyecto [pro'jekto] _nm_ plan; (_idea_) project; (_estimación de costo_) detailed estimate; **tener algo en** ~ to be planning sth; ~ **de ley** (_POL_) bill.

proyector [projek'tor] _nm_ (_CINE_) projector.

prudencia [pru'ðenθja] _nf_ (_sabiduría_) wisdom, prudence; (_cautela_) care.

prudente [pru'ðente] _adj_ sensible, wise, prudent; (_cauteloso_) careful.

prueba ['prweßa] _etc vb_ V **probar** ♦ _nf_ proof; (_ensayo_) test, trial; (_cantidad_) taste, sample; (_saboreo_) testing, sampling; (_de ropa_) fitting; (_DEPORTE_) event; **a** ~ on trial; (_COM_) on approval; **a** ~ **de** proof against; **a** ~ **de agua/fuego** waterproof/

fireproof; ~ **de capacitación** (_COM_) proficiency test; ~ **de fuego** (_fig_) acid test; ~ **de vallas** hurdles; **someter a** ~ to put to the test; ¿**tiene usted** ~ **de ello?** can you prove it?, do you have proof?

prurito [pru'rito] _nm_ itch; (_de bebé_) nappy rash; (_anhelo_) urge.

psico... [siko] _pref_ psycho...

psicoanálisis [sikoa'nalisis] _nm_ psychoanalysis.

psicoanalista [sikoana'lista] _nm/f_ psychoanalyst.

psicología [sikolo'xia] _nf_ psychology.

psicológico, a [siko'loxiko, a] _adj_ psychological.

psicólogo, a [si'koloɣo, a] _nm/f_ psychologist.

psicópata [si'kopata] _nm/f_ psychopath.

psicosis [si'kosis] _nf inv_ psychosis.

psicosomático, a [sikoso'matiko, a] _adj_ psychosomatic.

psicoterapia [sikote'rapja] _nf_ psychotherapy.

psiquiatra [si'kjatra] _nm/f_ psychiatrist.

psiquiátrico, a [si'kjatriko, a] _adj_ psychiatric ♦ _nm_ mental hospital.

psíquico, a ['sikiko, a] _adj_ psychic(al).

PSOE [pe'soe] _nm abr_ = _Partido Socialista Obrero Español_.

PSS _nf abr_ (= _Prestación Social Sustitutoria_) community service for conscientious objectors.

Pta. _abr_ (_GEO_: = _Punta_) Pt.

pta(s). _abr_ = **peseta(s)**.

ptmo. _abr_ (_COM_) = **préstamo**.

pts. _abr_ = **pesetas**.

púa ['pua] _nf_ sharp point; (_para guitarra_) plectrum; **alambre de** ~**s** barbed wire.

pub [puß/paß/paf] _nm_ bar.

púber, a ['pußer, a] _adj, nm/f_ adolescent.

pubertad [pußer'tað] _nf_ puberty.

publicación [pußlika'θjon] _nf_ publication.

publicar [pußli'kar] _vt_ (_editar_) to publish; (_hacer público_) to publicize; (_divulgar_) to make public, divulge.

publicidad [pußliθi'ðað] _nf_ publicity; (_COM_) advertising; **dar** ~ **a** to publicize, give publicity to; ~ **gráfica** display advertising; ~ **en el punto de venta** point-of-sale advertising.

publicitar [pußliθi'tar] _vt_ to publicize.

publicitario, a [pußliθi'tarjo, a] _adj_ publicity _cpd_; advertising _cpd_.

público, a ['pußliko, a] _adj_ public ♦ _nm_ public; (_TEAT etc_) audience; (_DEPORTE_) spectators _pl_, crowd; (_restaurantes etc_) clients _pl_; **el gran** ~ the general public; **hacer** ~ to publish; (_difundir_) to disclose;

~ **objetivo** (*COM*) target audience.
publique [pu'βlike] *etc vb* V **publicar**.
pucherazo [putʃe'raθo] *nm* (*fraude*)
electoral fiddle; **dar** ~ to rig an election.
puchero [pu'tʃero] *nm* (*CULIN*: *olla*) cooking
pot; (: *guiso*) stew; **hacer** ~**s** to pout.
pudibundo, a [puði'βundo, a] *adj* bashful.
púdico, a ['puðiko, a] *adj* modest;
(*pudibundo*) bashful.
pudiendo [pu'ðjendo] *etc vb* V **poder**.
pudiente [pu'ðjente] *adj* (*opulento*)
wealthy; (*poderoso*) powerful.
pudín [pu'ðin] *nm* pudding.
pudor [pu'ðor] *nm* modesty; (*vergüenza*)
(sense of) shame.
pudoroso, a [puðo'roso, a] *adj* (*modesto*)
modest; (*casto*) chaste.
pudrir [pu'ðrir] *vt* to rot; (*fam*) to upset,
annoy; ~**se** *vr* to rot, decay; (*fig*) to rot,
languish.
pueblerino, a [pweβle'rino, a] *adj*
(*lugareño*) small-town *cpd*; (*persona*)
rustic, provincial ♦ *nm/f* (*aldeano*)
country person.
pueblo ['pweβlo] *etc vb* V **poblar** ♦ *nm*
people; (*nación*) nation; (*aldea*) village;
(*plebe*) common people; (*población
pequeña*) small town, country town.
pueda ['pweða] *etc vb* V **poder**.
puente ['pwente] *nm* (*gen*) bridge; (*NAUT*:
tb: ~ **de mando**) bridge; (: *cubierta*) deck;
~ **aéreo** airlift; ~ **colgante** suspension
bridge; ~ **levadizo** drawbridge; **hacer
(el)** ~ (*fam*) to take a long weekend.
puenting ['pwentin] *nm* bungee jumping.
puerco, a ['pwerko, a] *adj* (*sucio*) dirty,
filthy; (*obsceno*) disgusting ♦ *nm/f* pig/
sow.
pueril [pwe'ril] *adj* childish.
puerro ['pwerro] *nm* leek.
puerta ['pwerta] *nf* door; (*de jardín*) gate;
(*portal*) doorway; (*fig*) gateway; (*gol*)
goal; (*INFORM*) port; **a la** ~ at the door; **a**
~ **cerrada** behind closed doors; ~
corredera/giratoria sliding/swing *o*
revolving door; ~ **principal/trasera** *o* **de
servicio** front/back door; ~ **(de
transmisión en) paralelo/serie** (*INFORM*)
parallel/serial port; **tomar la** ~ (*fam*) to
leave.
puerto ['pwerto] *nm* (*tb INFORM*) port; (*de
mar*) seaport; (*paso*) pass; (*fig*) haven,
refuge; **llegar a** ~ (*fig*) to get over a
difficulty.
Puerto Rico [pwerto'riko] *nm* Puerto Rico.
puertorriqueño, a [pwertorri'keɲo, a] *adj*,
nm/f Puerto Rican.
pues [pwes] *adv* (*entonces*) then;

(¡*entonces!*) well, well then; (*así que*) so
♦ *conj* (*porque*) since; ~ ... **no sé** well ... I
don't know.
puesto, a ['pwesto, a] *pp de* **poner** ♦ *adj*
dressed ♦ *nm* (*lugar, posición*) place;
(*trabajo*) post, job; (*MIL*) post; (*COM*) stall;
(*quiosco*) kiosk ♦ *conj*: ~ **que** since, as ♦ *nf*
(*apuesta*) bet, stake; ~ **de mercado**
market stall; ~ **de policía** police station;
~ **de socorro** first aid post; **puesta en
escena** staging; **puesta en marcha**
starting; **puesta del sol** sunset; **puesta a
cero** (*INFORM*) reset.
pugna ['puɣna] *nf* battle, conflict.
pugnar [puɣ'nar] *vi* (*luchar*) to struggle,
fight; (*pelear*) to fight.
puja ['puxa] *nf* (*esfuerzo*) attempt; (*en una
subasta*) bid.
pujante [pu'xante] *adj* strong, vigorous.
pujar [pu'xar] *vt* (*precio*) to raise, push up
♦ *vi* (*en licitación*) to bid, bid up; (*fig*:
esforzarse) to struggle, strain.
pulcro, a ['pulkro, a] *adj* neat, tidy.
pulga ['pulɣa] *nf* flea; **tener malas** ~**s** to be
short-tempered.
pulgada [pul'ɣaða] *nf* inch.
pulgar [pul'ɣar] *nm* thumb.
pulgón [pul'ɣon] *nm* plant louse, greenfly.
pulir [pu'lir] *vt* to polish; (*alisar*) to smooth;
(*fig*) to polish up, touch up.
pulla ['puʎa] *nf* cutting remark.
pulmón [pul'mon] *nm* lung; **a pleno** ~
(*respirar*) deeply; (*gritar*) at the top of
one's voice; ~ **de acero** iron lung.
pulmonía [pulmo'nia] *nf* pneumonia.
pulpa ['pulpa] *nf* pulp; (*de fruta*) flesh, soft
part.
pulpería [pulpe'ria] *nf* (*AM*) small grocery
store.
púlpito ['pulpito] *nm* pulpit.
pulpo ['pulpo] *nm* octopus.
pulsación [pulsa'θjon] *nf* beat, pulsation;
(*ANAT*) throb(bing); (*en máquina de
escribir*) tap; (*de pianista, mecanógrafo*)
touch; (*de una tecla*) (*INFORM*)
keystroke; ~ **doble** (*INFORM*) strikeover.
pulsador [pulsa'ðor] *nm* button, push
button.
pulsar [pul'sar] *vt* (*tecla*) to touch, tap;
(*MUS*) to play; (*botón*) to press, push ♦ *vi*
to pulsate; (*latir*) to beat, throb.
pulsera [pul'sera] *nf* bracelet; **reloj de** ~
wristwatch.
pulso ['pulso] *nm* (*MED*) pulse; **hacer algo a**
~ to do sth unaided *o* by one's own
efforts.
pulular [pulu'lar] *vi* (*estar plagado*): ~ **(de)**
to swarm (with).

pulverice [pulße'riθe] *etc vb V* **pulverizar**.
pulverizador [pulßeriθa'ðor] *nm* spray, spray gun.
pulverizar [pulßeri'θar] *vt* to pulverize; (*líquido*) to spray.
puna ['puna] *nf* (*AM MED*) mountain sickness.
punce ['punθe] *etc vb V* **punzar**.
punción [pun'θjon] *nf* (*MED*) puncture.
pundonor [pundo'nor] *nm* (*dignidad*) self-respect.
punición [puni'θjon] *nf* punishment.
punitivo, a [puni'tißo, a] *adj* punitive.
punki ['punki] *adj, nm/f* punk.
punta ['punta] *nf* point, tip; (*extremidad*) end; (*promontorio*) headland; (*COSTURA*) corner; (*TEC*) small nail; (*fig*) touch, trace; **horas ~s** peak hours, rush hours; **sacar ~ a** to sharpen; **de ~** on end; **de ~ a ~** from one end to the other; **estar de ~** to be edgy; **ir de ~ en blanco** to be all dressed up to the nines; **tener algo en la ~ de la lengua** to have sth on the tip of one's tongue; **se le pusieron los pelos de ~** her hair stood on end.
puntada [pun'taða] *nf* (*COSTURA*) stitch.
puntal [pun'tal] *nm* prop, support.
puntapié [punta'pje], *pl* **puntapiés** *nm* kick; **echar a algn a ~s** to kick sb out.
punteado, a [punte'aðo, a] *adj* (*moteado*) dotted; (*diseño*) of dots ♦ *nm* (*MUS*) twang.
puntear [punte'ar] *vt* to tick, mark; (*MUS*) to pluck.
puntería [punte'ria] *nf* (*de arma*) aim, aiming; (*destreza*) marksmanship.
puntero, a [pun'tero, a] *adj* leading ♦ *nm* (*señal, INFORM*) pointer; (*dirigente*) leader.
puntiagudo, a [puntja'ɣuðo, a] *adj* sharp, pointed.
puntilla [pun'tiʎa] *nf* (*TEC*) tack, braid; (*COSTURA*) lace edging; (**andar**) **de ~s** (to walk) on tiptoe.
puntilloso, a [punti'ʎoso, a] *adj* (*pundonoroso*) punctilious; (*susceptible*) touchy.
punto ['punto] *nm* (*gen*) point; (*señal diminuta*) spot, dot; (*lugar*) spot, place; (*momento*) point, moment; (*en un examen*) mark; (*tema*) item; (*COSTURA*) stitch; (*INFORM: impresora*) pitch; (: *pantalla*) pixel; **a ~** ready; **estar a ~ de** to be on the point of *o* about to; **llegar a ~** to come just at the right moment; **al ~** at once; **en ~** on the dot; **estar en su ~** (*CULIN*) to be done to a turn; **hasta cierto ~** to some extent; **hacer ~** to knit; **poner**

un motor en ~ to tune an engine; **~ de partida/de congelación/de fusión** starting/freezing/melting point; **~ de vista** point of view, viewpoint; **~ muerto** dead centre; (*AUTO*) neutral (gear); **~s a tratar** matters to be discussed, agenda *sg*; **~ final** full stop; **dos ~s** colon; **~ y coma** semicolon; **~ acápite** (*AM*) full stop, new paragraph; **~ de interrogación** question mark; **~s suspensivos** suspension points; **~ de equilibrio/de pedido** (*COM*) breakeven/reorder point; **~ inicial** *o* **de partida** (*INFORM*) home; **~ de referencia/de venta** (*COM*) benchmark point/point-of-sale.
puntuación [puntwa'θjon] *nf* punctuation; (*puntos: en examen*) mark(s) (*pl*); (: *DEPORTE*) score.
puntual [pun'twal] *adj* (*a tiempo*) punctual; (*cálculo*) exact, accurate; (*informe*) reliable.
puntualice [puntwa'liθe] *etc vb V* **puntualizar**.
puntualidad [puntwali'ðað] *nf* punctuality; exactness, accuracy; reliability.
puntualizar [puntwali'θar] *vt* to fix, specify.
puntuar [pun'twar] *vt* (*LING, TIP*) to punctuate; (*examen*) to mark ♦ *vi* (*DEPORTE*) to score, count.
punzada [pun'θaða] *nf* (*puntura*) prick; (*MED*) stitch; (*dolor*) twinge (of pain).
punzante [pun'θante] *adj* (*dolor*) shooting, sharp; (*herramienta*) sharp; (*comentario*) biting.
punzar [pun'θar] *vt* to prick, pierce ♦ *vi* to shoot, stab.
punzón [pun'θon] *nm* (*TEC*) punch.
puñado [pu'ɲaðo] *nm* handful (*tb fig*); **a ~s** by handfuls.
puñal [pu'ɲal] *nm* dagger.
puñalada [puɲa'laða] *nf* stab.
puñeta [pu'ɲeta] *nf*: **¡~!, ¡qué ~(s)!** (*fam!*) hell!; **mandar a algn a hacer ~s** (*fam*) to tell sb to go to hell.
puñetazo [puɲe'taθo] *nm* punch.
puño ['puɲo] *nm* (*ANAT*) fist; (*cantidad*) fistful, handful; (*COSTURA*) cuff; (*de herramienta*) handle; **como un ~** (*verdad*) obvious; (*palpable*) tangible, visible; **de ~ y letra del poeta** in the poet's own handwriting.
pupila [pu'pila] *nf* (*ANAT*) pupil.
pupitre [pu'pitre] *nm* desk.
puré [pu're], *pl* **purés** *nm* puree; (*sopa*) (thick) soup; **~ de patatas** mashed potatoes; **estar hecho ~** (*fig*) to be knackered.

pureza [pu'reθa] *nf* purity.
purga ['purɣa] *nf* purge.
purgante [pur'ɣante] *adj, nm* purgative.
purgar [pur'ɣar] *vt* to purge; (*POL: depurar*)
  to purge, liquidate; ~**se** *vr* (*MED*) to take
  a purge.
purgatorio [purɣa'torjo] *nm* purgatory.
purgue ['purɣe] *etc vb V* **purgar**.
purificar [purifi'kar] *vt* to purify; (*refinar*)
  to refine.
purifique [puri'fike] *etc vb V* **purificar**.
puritano, a [puri'tano, a] *adj* (*actitud*)
  puritanical; (*iglesia, tradición*) puritan
  ♦ *nm/f* puritan.
puro, a ['puro, a] *adj* pure; (*depurado*)
  unadulterated; (*oro*) solid; (*cielo*) clear;
  (*verdad*) simple, plain ♦ *adv*: **de ~
  cansado** out of sheer tiredness ♦ *nm*
  cigar; **por pura casualidad** by sheer
  chance.
púrpura ['purpura] *nf* purple.
purpúreo, a [pur'pureo, a] *adj* purple.
pus [pus] *nm* pus.
puse ['puse] *etc vb V* **poner**.
pústula ['pustula] *nf* pimple, sore.
puta ['puta] *nf* whore, prostitute.
putada [pu'taða] *nf* (*fam!*): **hacer una ~ a
  algn** to play a dirty trick on sb; **¡qué ~!**
  what a pain in the arse!(*!*).
putería [pute'ria] *nf* (*prostitución*)
  prostitution; (*prostíbulo*) brothel.
putrefacción [putrefak'θjon] *nf* rotting,
  putrefaction.
pútrido, a ['putriðo, a] *adj* rotten.
puzzle ['puθle] *nm* puzzle.
PVP *abr* (*ESP*: = *Precio Venta al Público*)
  ≈ RRP.
PYME *nf abr* (= *Pequeña y Mediana
  Empresa*) SME.

Q q

Q, q [ku] *nf* (*letra*) Q, q; **Q de Querido** Q for
  Queen.
q.e.g.e. *abr* (= *que en gloria esté*) R.I.P.
q.e.p.d. *abr* (= *que en paz descanse*)
  R.I.P.
q.e.s.m. *abr* (= *que estrecha su mano*)
  courtesy formula.
qm. *abr* = **quintal(es) métrico(s)**.
qts. *abr* = **quilates**.

PALABRA CLAVE

que [ke] *conj* **1** (*con oración subordinada*:
  muchas veces no se traduce) that; **dijo ~
  vendría** he said (that) he would come;
  espero ~ lo encuentres I hope (that) you
  find it; **dile ~ me llame** ask him to call
  me; *V tb* **el**
  2 (*en oración independiente*): **¡~ entre!**
  send him in; **¡que se mejore tu padre!** I
  hope your father gets better; **¡~ lo haga
  él!** he can do it!; (*orden*) get him to do it!
  3 (*enfático*): **¿me quieres? – ¡~ sí!** do you
  love me? – of course!; **te digo ~ sí** I'm
  telling you
  4 (*consecutivo*: *muchas veces no se
  traduce*) that; **es tan grande ~ no lo
  puedo levantar** it's so big (that) I can't
  lift it
  5 (*comparaciones*) than; **yo ~ tú/él** if I
  were you/him; *V tb* **más; menos**
  6 (*valor disyuntivo*): **~ le guste o no**
  whether he likes it or not; **~ venga o ~
  no venga** whether he comes or not
  7 (*porque*): **no puedo, ~ tengo ~
  quedarme en casa** I can't, I've got to
  stay in
  8: **siguió toca ~ toca** he kept on playing
  ♦ *pron* **1** (*cosa*) that, which; (+*prep*)
  which; **el sombrero ~ te compraste** the
  hat (that *o* which) you bought; **la cama
  en ~ dormí** the bed (that *o* which) I
  slept in; **el día (en) ~ ella nació** the day
  (when) she was born
  2 (*persona*: *suj*) that, who; (: *objeto*) that,
  whom; **el amigo ~ me acompañó al
  museo** the friend that *o* who went to the
  museum with me: **la chica ~ invité** the
  girl (that *o* whom) I invited.

qué [ke] *adj* what?, which? ♦ *pron* what?; **¡~
  divertido/asco!** how funny/revolting!; **¡~
  día más espléndido!** what a glorious
  day!; **¿~ edad tienes?** how old are you?;
  ¿de ~ me hablas? what are you saying
  to me?; **¿~ tal?** how are you?, how are
  things?; **¿~ hay (de nuevo)?** what's
  new?; **¿~ más?** anything else?
quebrada [ke'βraða] *nf V* **quebrado**.
quebradero [keβra'ðero] *nm*: **~ de cabeza**
  headache, worry.
quebradizo, a [keβra'ðiθo, a] *adj* fragile;
  (*persona*) frail.
quebrado, a [ke'βraðo, a] *adj* (*roto*)
  broken; (*terreno*) rough, uneven ♦ *nm/f*
  bankrupt ♦ *nm* (*MAT*) fraction ♦ *nf* ravine;
  ~ rehabilitado discharged bankrupt.
quebradura [keβra'ðura] *nf* (*fisura*) fissure;

(*MED*) rupture.

quebrantamiento [keßranta'mjento] *nm* (*acto*) breaking; (*de ley*) violation; (*estado*) exhaustion.

quebrantar [keßran'tar] *vt* (*infringir*) to violate, transgress; ~**se** *vr* (*persona*) to fail in health.

quebranto [ke'ßranto] *nm* damage, harm; (*decaimiento*) exhaustion; (*dolor*) grief, pain.

quebrar [ke'ßrar] *vt* to break, smash ♦ *vi* to go bankrupt; ~**se** *vr* to break, get broken; (*MED*) to be ruptured.

quechua ['ketʃua] *adj*, *nm/f* Quechua.

queda ['keða] *nf:* (**toque de**) ~ curfew.

quedar [ke'ðar] *vi* to stay, remain; (*encontrarse*) to be; (*restar*) to remain, be left; ~**se** *vr* to remain, stay (behind); ~ **en** (*acordar*) to agree on/to; (*acabar siendo*) to end up as; ~ **por hacer** to be still to be done; ~ **ciego/mudo** to be left blind/dumb; **no te queda bien ese vestido** that dress doesn't suit you; **quedamos a las seis** we agreed to meet at six; **eso queda muy lejos** that's a long way (away); **nos quedan 12 kms para llegar al pueblo** there are still 12 kms before we get to the village; **no queda otra** there's no alternative; ~**se con algn** (*fam*) to keep sth; ~**se con algn** (*fam*) to swindle sb; ~**se en nada** to come to nothing *o* nought; ~**se sin** to run out of.

quedo, a ['keðo, a] *adj* still ♦ *adv* softly, gently.

quehacer [kea'θer] *nm* task, job; ~**es** (**domésticos**) household chores.

queja ['kexa] *nf* complaint.

quejarse [ke'xarse] *vr* (*enfermo*) to moan, groan; (*protestar*) to complain; ~ **de que** ... to complain (about the fact) that ....

quejica [ke'xika] *adj* grumpy, complaining ♦ *nm/f* grumbler, whinger.

quejido [ke'xiðo] *nm* moan.

quejoso, a [ke'xoso, a] *adj* complaining.

quema ['kema] *nf* fire; (*combustión*) burning.

quemado, a [ke'maðo, a] *adj* burnt; (*irritado*) annoyed.

quemadura [kema'ðura] *nf* burn, scald; (*de sol*) sunburn; (*de fusible*) blow-out.

quemar [ke'mar] *vt* to burn; (*fig: malgastar*) to burn up, squander; (*COM: precios*) to slash, cut; (*fastidiar*) to annoy, bug ♦ *vi* to be burning hot; ~**se** *vr* (*consumirse*) to burn (up); (*del sol*) to get sunburnt.

quemarropa [kema'rropa]: **a** ~ *adv* point-blank.

quemazón [kema'θon] *nf* burn; (*calor*)

intense heat; (*sensación*) itch.

quena ['kena] *nf* (*AM*) Indian flute.

quepo ['kepo] *etc vb V* **caber.**

querella [ke'reʎa] *nf* (*JUR*) charge; (*disputa*) dispute.

querellarse [kere'ʎarse] *vr* to file a complaint.

querencia [ke'renθja] *nf* (*ZOOL*) homing instinct; (*fig*) homesickness.

══════════════ PALABRA CLAVE

querer [ke'rer] *vt* **1** (*desear*) to want; **quiero más dinero** I want more money; **quisiera** *o* **querría un té** I'd like a tea; **quiero ayudar/que vayas** I want to help/you to go; **como Vd quiera** as you wish, as you please; **ven cuando quieras** come when you like; **lo hizo sin** ~ he didn't mean to do it; **no quiero** I don't want to; **le pedí que me dejara ir pero no quiso** I asked him to let me go but he refused

2 (*preguntas: para pedir u ofrecer algo*): **¿quiere abrir la ventana?** could you open the window?; **¿quieres echarme una mano?** can you give me a hand?; **¿quiere un café?** would you like some coffee?

3 (*amar*) to love; (*tener cariño a*) to be fond of; **quiere mucho a sus hijos** he's very fond of his children

4 (*requerir*): **esta planta quiere más luz** this plant needs more light

5: ~ **decir** to mean; **¿qué quieres decir?** what do you mean?

querido, a [ke'riðo, a] *adj* dear ♦ *nm/f* darling; (*amante*) lover; **nuestra querida patria** our beloved country.

querosén [kero'sen], **querosene** [kero'sene] *nm* (*AM*) kerosene, paraffin.

querré [ke'rre] *etc vb V* **querer.**

quesería [kese'ria] *nf* dairy; (*fábrica*) cheese factory.

quesero, a [ke'sero, a] *adj:* **la industria quesera** the cheese industry ♦ *nm/f* cheesemaker ♦ *nf* cheese dish.

queso ['keso] *nm* cheese; ~ **rallado** grated cheese; ~ **crema** cream cheese; **dárselas con** ~ **a algn** (*fam*) to take sb in.

quetzal [ket'sal] *nm* monetary unit of Guatemala.

quicio ['kiθjo] *nm* hinge; **estar fuera de** ~ to be beside o.s.; **sacar a algn de** ~ to drive sb up the wall.

quid [kið] *nm* gist, crux; **dar en el** ~ to hit the nail on the head.

quiebra ['kjeßra] *nf* break, split; (*COM*) bankruptcy; (*ECON*) slump.

quiebro ['kjeßro] *etc vb V* **quebrar** ♦ *nm* (*del*

cuerpo) swerve.

quien [kjen] *pron relativo (suj)* who; *(complemento)* whom; *(indefinido)*: ~ **dice eso es tonto** whoever says that is a fool; **hay** ~ **piensa que** there are those who think that; **no hay** ~ **lo haga** no-one will do it; ~ **más,** ~ **menos tiene sus problemas** everybody has problems.

quién [kjen] *pron interrogativo* who; *(complemento)* whom; *¿*~ **es?** who is it?, who's there?; *(TELEC)* who's calling?

quienquiera [kjen'kjera] *(pl* **quienesquiera)** *pron* whoever.

quiera ['kjera] *etc vb V* **querer**.

quieto, a ['kjeto, a] *adj* still; *(carácter)* placid; **¡estáte** ~**!** keep still!

quietud [kje'tuð] *nf* stillness.

quijada [ki'xaða] *nf* jaw, jawbone.

quijote [ki'xote] *nm* dreamer; **Don Q**~ Don Quixote.

quil. *abr* = **quilates**.

quilate [ki'late] *nm* carat.

quilla ['kiʎa] *nf* keel.

quilo... ['kilo] = **kilo...**

quimera [ki'mera] *nf (sueño)* pipe dream.

quimérico, a [ki'meriko, a] *adj* fantastic.

químico, a ['kimiko, a] *adj* chemical ♦ *nm/f* chemist ♦ *nf* chemistry.

quimioterapia [kimiote'rapia] *nf* chemotherapy.

quina ['kina] *nf* quinine.

quincallería [kinkaʎe'ria] *nf* ironmonger's (shop), hardware store *(US)*.

quince ['kinθe] *num* fifteen; ~ **días** a fortnight.

quinceañero, a [kinθea'ɲero, a] *adj* fifteen-year-old; *(adolescente)* teenage ♦ *nm/f* fifteen-year-old; *(adolescente)* teenager.

quincena [kin'θena] *nf* fortnight; *(pago)* fortnightly pay.

quincenal [kinθe'nal] *adj* fortnightly.

quincuagésimo, a [kinkwa'xesimo, a] *num* fiftieth.

quiniela [ki'njela] *nf* football pools *pl*; ~**s** *nfpl* pools coupon *sg*.

quinientos, as [ki'njentos, as] *num* five hundred.

quinina [ki'nina] *nf* quinine.

quinqué [kin'ke] *nm* oil lamp.

quinquenal [kinke'nal] *adj* five-year *cpd*.

quinqui ['kinki] *nm* delinquent.

quinta ['kinta] *nf V* **quinto**.

quintaesencia [kintae'senθja] *nf* quintessence.

quintal [kin'tal] *nm (Castilla: peso)* = *46kg*; ~ **métrico** = *100kg*.

quinteto [kin'teto] *nm* quintet.

quinto, a ['kinto, a] *adj* fifth ♦ *nm (MIL)* conscript, draftee ♦ *nf* country house; *(MIL)* call-up, draft.

quintuplo, a [kin'tuplo, a] *adj* quintuple, five-fold.

quiosco ['kjosko] *nm (de música)* bandstand; *(de periódicos)* news stand *(also selling sweets, cigarettes etc)*.

quirófano [ki'rofano] *nm* operating theatre.

quiromancia [kiro'manθja] *nf* palmistry.

quirúrgico, a [ki'rurxiko, a] *adj* surgical.

quise ['kise] *etc vb V* **querer**.

quisque ['kiske] *pron (fam)*: **cada** *o* **todo** ~ (absolutely) everyone.

quisquilloso [kiski'ʎoso, a] *adj* *(susceptible)* touchy; *(meticuloso)* pernickety.

quiste ['kiste] *nm* cyst.

quitaesmalte [kitaes'malte] *nm* nail polish remover.

quitamanchas [kita'mantʃas] *nm inv* stain remover.

quitanieves [kita'njeßes] *nm inv* snowplough *(BRIT)*, snowplow *(US)*.

quitar [ki'tar] *vt* to remove, take away; *(ropa)* to take off; *(dolor)* to relieve; *(vida)* to take; *(valor)* to reduce; *(hurtar)* to remove, steal ♦ *vi*: **¡quita de ahí!** get away!; ~**se** *vr* to withdraw; *(mancha)* to come off *o* out; *(ropa)* to take off; **me quita mucho tiempo** it takes up a lot of my time; **el café me quita el sueño** coffee stops me sleeping; ~ **de en medio a algn** to get rid of sb; ~**se algo de encima** to get rid of sth; ~**se del tabaco** to give up smoking; **se quitó el sombrero** he took off his hat.

quitasol [kita'sol] *nm* sunshade *(BRIT)*, parasol.

quite ['kite] *nm (esgrima)* parry; *(evasión)* dodge; **estar al** ~ to be ready to go to sb's aid.

Quito ['kito] *n* Quito.

quizá(s) [ki'θa(s)] *adv* perhaps, maybe.

quórum ['kworum] *pl* **quórums** ['kworum] *nm* quorum.

R r

R, r ['erre] *nf (letra)* R, r; **R de Ramón** R for Robert (*BRIT*) o Roger (*US*).
R. *abr* = **Remite, Remitente.**
rabadilla [raßa'ðiʎa] *nf* base of the spine.
rábano ['raßano] *nm* radish; **me importa un ~** I don't give a damn.
rabia ['raßja] *nf (MED)* rabies *sg*; (*fig: ira*) fury, rage; ¡**qué ~!** isn't it infuriating!; **me da ~** it maddens me; **tener ~ a algn** to have a grudge against sb.
rabiar [ra'ßjar] *vi* to have rabies; to rage, be furious; **~ por algo** to long for sth.
rabieta [ra'ßjeta] *nf* tantrum, fit of temper.
rabino [ra'ßino] *nm* rabbi.
rabioso, a [ra'ßjoso, a] *adj* rabid; (*fig*) furious.
rabo ['raßo] *nm* tail.
racanear [rakane'ar] *vi (fam)* to skive.
rácano ['rakano] *nm (fam)* slacker, skiver.
RACE *nm abr* (= *Real Automóvil Club de España*) ≈ RAC.
racha ['ratʃa] *nf* gust of wind; (*serie*) string, series; **buena/mala ~** spell of good/bad luck.
racial [ra'θjal] *adj* racial, race *cpd*.
racimo [ra'θimo] *nm* bunch.
raciocinio [raθjo'θinjo] *nm* reason; (*razonamiento*) reasoning.
ración [ra'θjon] *nf* portion; **raciones** *nfpl* rations.
racional [raθjo'nal] *adj (razonable)* reasonable; (*lógico*) rational.
racionalice [raθjona'liθe] *etc vb V* **racionalizar.**
racionalizar [raθjonali'θar] *vt* to rationalize; (*COM*) to streamline.
racionamiento [raθjona'mjento] *nm (COM)* rationing.
racionar [raθjo'nar] *vt* to ration (out).
racismo [ra'θismo] *nm* racialism, racism.
racista [ra'θista] *adj, nm/f* racist.
radar [ra'ðar] *nm* radar.
radiación [raðja'θjon] *nf* radiation; (*TELEC*) broadcasting.
radiactividad [raðjaktißi'ðað] *nf* radioactivity.
radiado, a [ra'ðjaðo, a] *adj* radio *cpd*, broadcast.

radiador [raðja'ðor] *nm* radiator.
radial [ra'ðjal] *adj (AM)* radio *cpd*.
radiante [ra'ðjante] *adj* radiant.
radiar [ra'ðjar] *vt* to radiate; (*TELEC*) to broadcast; (*MED*) to give radiotherapy to.
radical [raði'kal] *adj, nm/f* radical ♦ *nm* (*LING*) root; (*MAT*) square-root sign.
radicar [raði'kar] *vi* to take root; **~ en** to lie o consist in; **~se** *vr* to establish o.s., put down (one's) roots.
radio ['raðjo] *nf* radio; (*aparato*) radio (set) ♦ *nm (MAT)* radius; (*AM*) radio; (*QUÍMICA*) radium; **~ de acción** extent of one's authority, sphere of influence.
radioactivo, a [raðjoak'tißo, a] *adj* radioactive.
radioaficionado, a [raðjoafiθjo'naðo, a] *nm/f* radio ham.
radiocasete [raðjoka'sete] *nm* radiocassette (player).
radiodifusión [raðjodifu'sjon] *nf* broadcasting.
radioemisora [raðjoemi'sora] *nf* transmitter, radio station.
radiofónico, a [raðjo'foniko, a] *adj* radio *cpd*.
radiografía [raðjoɤra'fia] *nf* X-ray.
radiólogo, a [ra'ðjoloɤo, a] *nm/f* radiologist.
radionovela [raðjono'ßela] *nf* radio series.
radiotaxi [raðjo'taksi] *nm* radio taxi.
radioterapia [raðjote'rapja] *nf* radiotherapy.
radioyente [raðjo'jente] *nm/f* listener.
radique [ra'ðike] *etc vb V* **radicar.**
RAE *nf abr* = **Real Academia Española.**
ráfaga ['rafaɤa] *nf* gust; (*de luz*) flash; (*de tiros*) burst.
raído, a [ra'iðo, a] *adj (ropa)* threadbare; (*persona*) shabby.
raigambre [rai'ɤambre] *nf (BOT)* roots *pl*; (*fig*) tradition.
raíz [ra'iθ] (*pl* **raíces**) *nf* root; **~ cuadrada** square root; **a ~ de** as a result of; (*después de*) immediately after.
raja ['raxa] *nf (de melón etc)* slice; (*hendedura*) slit, split; (*grieta*) crack.
rajar [ra'xar] *vt* to split; (*fam*) to slash; **~se** *vr* to split, crack; **~se de** to back out of.
rajatabla [raxa'taßla]: **a ~** *adv* (*estrictamente*) strictly, to the letter.
ralea [ra'lea] *nf (pey)* kind, sort.
ralentí [ra'lenti] *nm (TV etc)* slow motion; (*AUTO*) neutral; **al ~** in slow motion; (*AUTO*) ticking over.
rallador [raʎa'ðor] *nm* grater.
rallar [ra'ʎar] *vt* to grate.

ralo, a ['ralo, a] *adj* thin, sparse.
RAM [ram] *nf abr* (= *random access memory*) RAM.
rama ['rama] *nf* bough, branch; **andarse por las ~s** (*fig*, *fam*) to beat about the bush.
ramaje [ra'maxe] *nm* branches *pl*, foliage.
ramal [ra'mal] *nm* (*de cuerda*) strand; (*FERRO*) branch line; (*AUTO*) branch (road).
rambla ['rambla] *nf* (*avenida*) avenue.
ramera [ra'mera] *nf* whore, hooker (*US*).
ramificación [ramifika'θjon] *nf* ramification.
ramificarse [ramifi'karse] *vr* to branch out.
ramifique [rami'fike] *etc vb V* **ramificarse**.
ramillete [rami'ʎete] *nm* bouquet; (*fig*) select group.
ramo ['ramo] *nm* branch, twig; (*sección*) department, section; (*sector*) field, sector.
rampa ['rampa] *nf* ramp.
ramplón, ona [ram'plon, ona] *adj* uncouth, coarse.
rana ['rana] *nf* frog; **salto de ~** leapfrog; **cuando las ~s críen pelos** when pigs fly.
ranchero [ran'tʃero] *nm* (*AM*) rancher; (*pequeño propietario*) smallholder.
rancho ['rantʃo] *nm* (*MIL*) food; (*AM: grande*) ranch; (: *pequeño*) small farm.
rancio, a ['ranθjo, a] *adj* (*comestibles*) stale, rancid; (*vino*) aged, mellow; (*fig*) ancient.
rango ['rango] *nm* rank; (*prestigio*) standing.
ranura [ra'nura] *nf* groove; (*de teléfono etc*) slot; **~ de expansión** (*INFORM*) expansion slot.
rap [rap] *nm* (*MUS*) rap.
rapacidad [rapaθi'ðað] *nf* rapacity.
rapapolvo [rapa'polβo] *nm:* **echar un ~ a algn** to give sb a ticking off.
rapar [ra'par] *vt* to shave; (*los cabellos*) to crop.
rapaz [ra'paθ] *adj* (*ZOOL*) predatory ♦ *nm/f* (*f:* **rapaza**) young boy/girl.
rape ['rape] *nm* quick shave; (*pez*) angler (fish); **al ~** cropped.
rapé [ra'pe] *nm* snuff.
rapidez [rapi'ðeθ] *nf* speed, rapidity.
rápido, a ['rapiðo, a] *adj* fast, quick ♦ *adv* quickly ♦ *nm* (*FERRO*) express; **~s** *nmpl* rapids.
rapiña [ra'piɲa] *nm* robbery; **ave de ~** bird of prey.
rap(p)el [ra'pel] *nm* (*DEPORTE*) abseiling.
raptar [rap'tar] *vt* to kidnap.
rapto ['rapto] *nm* kidnapping; (*impulso*)

sudden impulse; (*éxtasis*) ecstasy, rapture.
raqueta [ra'keta] *nf* racquet.
raquítico, a [ra'kitiko, a] *adj* stunted; (*fig*) poor, inadequate.
raquitismo [raki'tismo] *nm* rickets *sg*.
rareza [ra'reθa] *nf* rarity; (*fig*) eccentricity.
raro, a ['raro, a] *adj* (*poco común*) rare; (*extraño*) odd, strange; (*excepcional*) remarkable; **¡qué ~!** how (very) odd!; **¡(qué) cosa más rara!** how strange!
ras [ras] *nm:* **a ~ de** level with; **a ~ de tierra** at ground level.
rasar [ra'sar] *vt* to level.
rascacielos [raska'θjelos] *nm inv* skyscraper.
rascar [ras'kar] *vt* (*con las uñas etc*) to scratch; (*raspar*) to scrape; **~se** *vr* to scratch (o.s.).
rasgar [ras'xar] *vt* to tear, rip (up).
rasgo ['rasxo] *nm* (*con pluma*) stroke; **~s** *nmpl* features, characteristics; **a grandes ~s** in outline, broadly.
rasgue ['rasxe] *etc vb V* **rasgar**.
rasguear [rasxe'ar] *vt* (*MUS*) to strum.
rasguñar [rasxu'ɲar] *vt* to scratch; (*bosquejar*) to sketch.
rasguño [ras'xuɲo] *nm* scratch.
raso, a ['raso, a] *adj* (*liso*) flat, level; (*a baja altura*) very low ♦ *nm* satin; (*campo llano*) flat country; **cielo ~** clear sky; **al ~** in the open.
raspado [ras'paðo] *nm* (*MED*) scrape.
raspador [raspa'ðor] *nm* scraper.
raspadura [raspa'ðura] *nf* (*acto*) scrape, scraping; (*marca*) scratch; **~s** *nfpl* scrapings.
raspar [ras'par] *vt* to scrape; (*arañar*) to scratch; (*limar*) to file ♦ *vi* (*manos*) to be rough; (*vino*) to be sharp, have a rough taste.
rasque ['raske] *etc vb V* **rascar**.
rastra ['rastra] *nf:* **a ~s** by dragging; (*fig*) unwillingly.
rastreador [rastrea'ðor] *nm* tracker; **~ de minas** minesweeper.
rastrear [rastre'ar] *vt* (*seguir*) to track; (*minas*) to sweep.
rastrero, a [ras'trero, a] *adj* (*BOT*, *ZOOL*) creeping; (*fig*) despicable, mean.
rastrillar [rastri'ʎar] *vt* to rake.
rastrillo [ras'triʎo] *nm* rake; (*AM*) safety razor.
rastro ['rastro] *nm* (*AGR*) rake; (*pista*) track, trail; (*vestigio*) trace; (*mercado*) fleamarket; **el R~** *the Madrid fleamarket*; **perder el ~** to lose the scent; **desaparecer sin ~** to vanish without

trace.

rastrojo [ras'troxo] nm stubble.

rasurador [rasura'ðor] nm, (AM)
rasuradora [rasura'ðora] nf electric
shaver o razor.

rasurarse [rasu'rarse] vr to shave.

rata ['rata] nf rat.

ratear [rate'ar] vt (robar) to steal.

ratero, a [ra'tero, a] adj light-fingered
♦ nm/f pickpocket; (AM: de casas) burglar.

ratificar [ratifi'kar] vt to ratify.

ratifique [rati'fike] etc vb V ratificar.

rato ['rato] nm while, short time; **a ~s**
from time to time; **al poco ~** shortly
after, soon afterwards; **~s libres** o **de
ocio** leisure sg, spare o free time sg; **hay
para ~** there's still a long way to go;
pasar el ~ to kill time; **pasar un buen/
mal ~** to have a good/rough time.

ratón [ra'ton] nm (tb INFORM) mouse.

ratonera [rato'nera] nf mousetrap.

RAU nf abr (= República Árabe Unida) UAR.

raudal [rau'ðal] nm torrent; **a ~es** in
abundance; **entrar a ~es** to pour in.

raudo, a ['rauðo, a] adj (rápido) swift;
(precipitado) rushing.

raya ['raja] nf line; (marca) scratch; (en
tela) stripe; (TIP) hyphen; (de pelo)
parting; (límite) boundary; (pez) ray; **a
~s** striped; **pasarse de la ~** to overstep
the mark, go too far; **tener a ~** to keep
in check.

rayado, a [ra'jaðo, a] adj (papel) ruled;
(tela, diseño) striped.

rayar [ra'jar] vt to line; to scratch;
(subrayar) to underline ♦ vi: **~ en** o **con** to
border on; **al ~ el alba** at first light.

rayo ['rajo] nm (del sol) ray, beam; (de luz)
shaft; (en una tormenta) (flash of)
lightning; **~ solar** o **de sol** sunbeam; **~s
infrarrojos** infrared rays; **~s X** X-rays;
como un ~ like a shot; **la noticia cayó
como un ~** the news was a bombshell;
pasar como un ~ to flash past.

raza ['raθa] nf race; (de animal) breed; **~
humana** human race; **de pura ~** (caballo)
thoroughbred; (perro etc) pedigree.

razón [ra'θon] nf reason; (justicia) right,
justice; (razonamiento) reasoning;
(motivo) reason, motive; (proporción)
rate; (MAT) ratio; **a ~ de 10 cada día** at
the rate of 10 a day; **"~: ..."** "inquiries
to ..."; **en ~ de** with regard to; **perder la
~** to go out of one's mind; **dar ~ a algn**
to agree that sb is right; **dar ~ de** to
give an account of, report on; **tener/no
tener ~** to be right/wrong; **~ directa/
inversa** direct/inverse proportion; **~ de**

ser raison d'être.

razonable [raθo'naβle] adj reasonable;
(justo, moderado) fair.

razonado, a [raθo'naðo, a] adj (COM: cuenta
etc) itemized.

razonamiento [raθona'mjento] nm (juicio)
judgement; (argumento) reasoning.

razonar [raθo'nar] vt, vi to reason, argue.

RDA nf = República Democrática Alemana.

Rdo. abr (REL: = Reverendo) Rev.

re [re] nm (MUS) D.

reabierto [rea'βjerto] pp de reabrir.

reabrir [rea'βrir] vt, **~se** vr to reopen.

reacción [reak'θjon] nf reaction; **avión a ~**
jet plane; **~ en cadena** chain reaction.

reaccionar [reakθjo'nar] vi to react.

reaccionario, a [reakθjo'narjo, a] adj
reactionary.

reacio, a [re'aθjo, a] adj stubborn; **ser** o
estar ~ a to be opposed to.

reactivar [reakti'βar] vt to reactivate; **~se**
vr (economía) to be on the upturn.

reactor [reak'tor] nm reactor; (avión) jet
plane; **~ nuclear** nuclear reactor.

readaptación [reaðapta'θjon] nf: **~
profesional** industrial retraining.

readmitir [reaðmi'tir] vt to readmit.

reafirmar [reafir'mar] vt to reaffirm.

reagrupar [reaɣru'par] vt to regroup.

reajustar [reaxus'tar] vt (INFORM) to reset.

reajuste [rea'xuste] nm readjustment; **~
salarial** wage increase; **~ de plantilla**
rationalization.

real [re'al] adj real; (del rey, fig) royal;
(espléndido) grand ♦ nm (de feria)
fairground.

The **Real Academia Española (RAE)** is the
regulatory body for the Spanish language in
Spain and was founded in 1713. It produces
dictionaries and grammars bearing its own
name, and is considered the authority on
the language, although it has been critized
for being too conservative. In 1994, along
with the Spanish American academias, it
approved a change to the Spanish
alphabet, no longer treating "ch" and "ll"
as separate letters. "ñ" continues to be
treated separately.

---

realce [re'alθe] etc vb V realzar ♦ nm (TEC)
embossing; (lustre, fig) splendour (BRIT),
splendor (US); (ARTE) highlight; **poner de
~** to emphasize.

real-decreto [re'alde'kreto] (pl **~es-~s**) nm
royal decree.

realeza [rea'leθa] nf royalty.

realice [rea'liθe] etc vb V realizar.

realidad [reali'ðað] *nf* reality; (*verdad*) truth; ~ **virtual** virtual reality; **en** ~ in fact.

realismo [rea'lismo] *nm* realism.

realista [rea'lista] *nmlf* realist.

realización [realiθa'θjon] *nf* fulfilment, realization; (*COM*) selling up (*BRIT*), conversion into money (*US*); ~ **de plusvalías** profit-taking.

realizador, a [realiθa'ðor, a] *nmlf* (*TV etc*) producer.

realizar [reali'θar] *vt* (*objetivo*) to achieve; (*plan*) to carry out; (*viaje*) to make, undertake; (*COM*) to realize; ~**se** *vr* to come about, come true; ~**se como persona** to fulfil one's aims in life.

realmente [real'mente] *adv* really.

realojar [realo'xar] *vt* to rehouse.

realquilar [realki'lar] *vt* (*subarrendar*) to sublet; (*alquilar de nuevo*) to relet.

realzar [real'θar] *vt* (*TEC*) to raise; (*embellecer*) to enhance; (*acentuar*) to highlight.

reanimar [reani'mar] *vt* to revive; (*alentar*) to encourage; ~**se** *vr* to revive.

reanudar [reanu'ðar] *vt* (*renovar*) to renew; (*historia, viaje*) to resume.

reaparición [reapari'θjon] *nf* reappearance; (*vuelta*) return.

reapertura [reaper'tura] *nf* reopening.

rearme [re'arme] *nm* rearmament.

reata [re'ata] *nf* (*AM*) lasso.

reavivar [reaβi'βar] *vt* (*persona*) to revive; (*fig*) to rekindle.

rebaja [re'βaxa] *nf* reduction, lowering; (*COM*) discount; **"grandes ~s"** "big reductions", "sale".

rebajar [reβa'xar] *vt* (*bajar*) to lower; (*reducir*) to reduce; (*precio*) to cut; (*disminuir*) to lessen; (*humillar*) to humble; ~**se** *vr*: ~**se a hacer algo** to stoop to doing sth.

rebanada [reβa'naða] *nf* slice.

rebañar [reβa'ɲar] *vt* to scrape clean.

rebaño [re'βaɲo] *nm* herd; (*de ovejas*) flock.

rebasar [reβa'sar] *vt* (*tb*: ~ **de**) to exceed; (*AUTO*) to overtake.

rebatir [reβa'tir] *vt* to refute; (*rebajar*) to reduce; (*ataque*) to repel.

rebato [re'βato] *nm* alarm; (*ataque*) surprise attack; **llamar** *o* **tocar a** ~ (*fig*) to sound the alarm.

rebeca [re'βeka] *nf* cardigan.

rebelarse [reβe'larse] *vr* to rebel, revolt.

rebelde [re'βelde] *adj* rebellious; (*niño*) unruly ♦ *nmlf* rebel; **ser** ~ **a** to be in revolt against, rebel against.

rebeldía [reβel'dia] *nf* rebelliousness; (*desobediencia*) disobedience; (*JUR*) default.

rebelión [reβe'ljon] *nf* rebellion.

rebenque [re'βenke] *nm* (*AM*) whip.

reblandecer [reβlande'θer] *vt* to soften.

reblandezca [reβlan'deθka] *etc vb V* **reblandecer**.

rebobinar [reβoβi'nar] *vt* to rewind.

reboce [re'βoθe] *etc vb V* **rebozar**.

rebosante [reβo'sante] *adj*: ~ **de** (*fig*) brimming *o* overflowing with.

rebosar [reβo'sar] *vi* to overflow; (*abundar*) to abound, be plentiful; ~ **de salud** to be bursting *o* brimming with health.

rebotar [reβo'tar] *vt* to bounce; (*rechazar*) to repel.

rebote [re'βote] *nm* rebound; **de** ~ on the rebound.

rebozado, a [reβo'θaðo, a] *adj* (*CULIN*) fried in batter *o* breadcrumbs *o* flour.

rebozar [reβo'θar] *vt* to wrap up; (*CULIN*) to fry in batter *etc*.

rebozo [reβo'θo] *nm*: **sin** ~ openly.

rebuscado, a [reβus'kaðo, a] *adj* affected.

rebuscar [reβus'kar] *vi* (*en bolsillo, cajón*) to fish; (*en habitación*) to search high and low.

rebuznar [reβuθ'nar] *vi* to bray.

recabar [reka'βar] *vt* (*obtener*) to manage to get; ~ **fondos** to collect money.

recadero [reka'ðero] *nm* messenger.

recado [re'kaðo] *nm* message; **dejar/tomar un** ~ (*TELEC*) to leave/take a message.

recaer [reka'er] *vi* to relapse; ~ **en** to fall to *o* on; (*criminal etc*) to fall back into, relapse into; (*premio*) to go to.

recaída [reka'iða] *nf* relapse.

recaiga [re'kaiɣa] *etc vb V* **recaer**.

recalcar [rekal'kar] *vt* (*fig*) to stress, emphasize.

recalcitrante [rekalθi'trante] *adj* recalcitrant.

recalentamiento [rekalenta'mjento] *nm*: ~ **global** global warming.

recalentar [rekalen'tar] *vt* (*comida*) to warm up, reheat; (*demasiado*) to overheat; ~**se** *vr* to overheat, get too hot.

recaliente [reka'ljente] *etc vb V* **recalentar**.

recalque [re'kalke] *etc vb V* **recalcar**.

recámara [re'kamara] *nf* side room; (*AM*) bedroom.

recamarera [rekama'rera] *nf* (*AM*) maid.

recambio [re'kambjo] *nm* spare; (*de pluma*) refill; **piezas de** ~ spares.

recapacitar [rekapaθi'tar] *vi* to reflect.

recapitular [rekapitu'lar] *vt* to recap.

recargable [rekar'ɣaβle] *adj* (*batería, pila*)

rechargeable; (*mechero, pluma*) refillable.

recargado, a [rekar'ɣaðo, a] *adj* overloaded; (*exagerado*) over-elaborate.

recargar [rekar'ɣar] *vt* to overload; (*batería*) to recharge; (*mechero, pluma*) to refill.

recargo [re'karɣo] *nm* surcharge; (*aumento*) increase.

recargue [re'karɣe] *etc vb V* recargar.

recatado, a [reka'taðo, a] *adj* (*modesto*) modest, demure; (*prudente*) cautious.

recato [re'kato] *nm* (*modestia*) modesty, demureness; (*cautela*) caution.

recauchutado, a [rekautʃu'taðo, a] *adj* remould *cpd*.

recaudación [rekauða'θjon] *nf* (*acción*) collection; (*cantidad*) takings *pl*; (*en deporte*) gate; (*oficina*) tax office.

recaudador, a [rekauða'ðor, a] *nm/f* tax collector.

recaudar [rekau'ðar] *vt* to collect.

recaudo [re'kauðo] *nm* (*impuestos*) collection; (*JUR*) surety; **estar a buen ~** to be in safekeeping; **poner algo a buen ~** to put sth in a safe place.

recayendo [reka'jendo] *etc vb V* recaer.

rece ['reθe] *etc vb V* rezar.

recelar [reθe'lar] *vt*: **~ que** (*sospechar*) to suspect that; (*temer*) to fear that ♦ *vi*: **~(se) de** to distrust.

recelo [re'θelo] *nm* distrust, suspicion.

receloso, a [reθe'loso, a] *adj* distrustful, suspicious.

recepción [reθep'θjon] *nf* reception; (*acto de recibir*) receipt.

recepcionista [reθepθjo'nista] *nm/f* receptionist.

receptáculo [reθep'takulo] *nm* receptacle.

receptivo, a [reθep'tiβo, a] *adj* receptive.

receptor, a [reθep'tor, a] *nm/f* recipient ♦ *nm* (*TELEC*) receiver; **descolgar el ~** to pick up the receiver.

recesión [reθe'sjon] *nf* (*COM*) recession.

receta [re'θeta] *nf* (*CULIN*) recipe; (*MED*) prescription.

recetar [reθe'tar] *vt* to prescribe.

rechace [re'tʃaθe] *etc vb V* rechazar.

rechazar [retʃa'θar] *vt* to repel, drive back; (*idea*) to reject; (*oferta*) to turn down.

rechazo [re'tʃaθo] *nm* (*de fusil*) recoil; (*rebote*) rebound; (*negación*) rebuff.

rechifla [re'tʃifla] *nf* hissing, booing; (*fig*) derision.

rechinar [retʃi'nar] *vi* to creak; (*dientes*) to grind; (*máquina*) to clank, clatter; (*metal seco*) to grate; (*motor*) to hum.

rechistar [retʃis'tar] *vi*: **sin ~** without complaint.

rechoncho, a [re'tʃontʃo, a] *adj* (*fam*) stocky, thickset (*BRIT*), heavy-set (*US*).

rechupete [retʃu'pete]: **de ~** *adj* (*comida*) delicious.

recibidor [reθiβi'ðor] *nm* entrance hall.

recibimiento [reθiβi'mjento] *nm* reception, welcome.

recibir [reθi'βir] *vt* to receive; (*dar la bienvenida*) to welcome; (*salir al encuentro de*) to go and meet ♦ *vi* to entertain; **~se** *vr*: **~se de** to qualify as.

recibo [re'θiβo] *nm* receipt; **acusar ~ de** to acknowledge receipt of.

reciclaje [reθi'klaxe] *nm* recycling; (*de trabajadores*) retraining; **cursos de ~** refresher courses.

reciclar [reθi'klar] *vt* to recycle; (*trabajador*) to retrain.

recién [re'θjen] *adv* recently, newly; (*AM*) just, recently; **~ casado** newly-wed; **el ~ llegado** the newcomer; **el ~ nacido** the newborn child; **~ a las seis** only at six o'clock.

reciente [re'θjente] *adj* recent; (*fresco*) fresh.

recientemente [reθjente'mente] *adv* recently.

recinto [re'θinto] *nm* enclosure; (*área*) area, place.

recio, a [re'θjo, a] *adj* strong, tough; (*voz*) loud ♦ *adv* hard; loud(ly).

recipiente [reθi'pjente] *nm* (*objeto*) container, receptacle; (*persona*) recipient.

reciprocidad [reθiproθi'ðað] *nf* reciprocity.

recíproco, a [re'θiproco, a] *adj* reciprocal.

recital [reθi'tal] *nm* (*MUS*) recital; (*LIT*) reading.

recitar [reθi'tar] *vt* to recite.

reclamación [reklama'θjon] *nf* claim, demand; (*queja*) complaint; **~ salarial** pay claim.

reclamar [rekla'mar] *vt* to claim, demand ♦ *vi*: **~ contra** to complain about; **~ a algn en justicia** to take sb to court.

reclamo [re'klamo] *nm* (*anuncio*) advertisement; (*tentación*) attraction.

reclinar [rekli'nar] *vt* to recline, lean; **~se** *vr* to lean back.

recluir [reklu'ir] *vt* to intern, confine.

reclusión [reklu'sjon] *nf* (*prisión*) prison; (*refugio*) seclusion; **~ perpetua** life imprisonment.

recluso, a [re'kluso, a] *adj* imprisoned; **población reclusa** prison population ♦ *nm/f* (*solitario*) recluse; (*JUR*) prisoner.

recluta [re'kluta] *nm/f* recruit ♦ *nf*

recruitment.

reclutamiento [rekluta'mjento] *nm*
recruitment.

recluyendo [reklu'jendo] *etc vb V* **recluir.**

recobrar [reko'ßrar] *vt* (*recuperar*) to
recover; (*rescatar*) to get back; (*ciudad*)
to recapture; (*tiempo*) to make up (for);
~**se** *vr* to recover.

recochineo [rekotʃi'neo] *nm* (*fam*)
mickey-taking.

recodo [re'koðo] *nm* (*de río, camino*) bend.

recogedor, a [rekoxe'ðor, a] *nm/f* picker,
harvester.

recoger [reko'xer] *vt* to collect; (*AGR*) to
harvest; (*fruta*) to pick; (*levantar*) to pick
up; (*juntar*) to gather; (*pasar a buscar*) to
come for, get; (*dar asilo*) to give shelter
to; (*faldas*) to gather up; (*mangas*) to roll
up; (*pelo*) to put up; ~**se** *vr* (*retirarse*) to
retire; **me recogieron en la estación** they
picked me up at the station.

recogido, a [reko'xiðo, a] *adj* (*lugar*) quiet,
secluded; (*pequeño*) small ♦ *nf* (*CORREOS*)
collection; (*AGR*) harvest; **recogida de
datos** (*INFORM*) data capture.

recogimiento [rekoxi'mjento] *nm*
collection; (*AGR*) harvesting.

recoja [re'koxa] *etc vb V* **recoger.**

recolección [rekolek'θjon] *nf* (*AGR*)
harvesting; (*colecta*) collection.

recomencé [rekomen'θe],
recomencemos [rekomen'θemos] *etc vb*
V **recomenzar.**

recomendable [rekomen'daßle] *adj*
recommendable; **poco** ~ inadvisable.

recomendación [rekomenda'θjon] *nf*
(*sugerencia*) suggestion,
recommendation; (*referencia*) reference;
carta de ~ **para** letter of introduction to.

recomendar [rekomen'dar] *vt* to suggest,
recommend; (*confiar*) to entrust.

recomenzar [rekomen'θar] *vt*, *vi* to begin
again, recommence.

recomience [reko'mjenθe] *etc vb V*
recomenzar.

recomiende [reko'mjende] *etc vb V*
recomendar.

recomienzo [reko'mjenθo] *etc vb V*
recomenzar.

recompensa [rekom'pensa] *nf* reward,
recompense; (*compensación*): ~ **(de una
pérdida)** compensation (for a loss);
como *o* **en** ~ **por** in return for.

recompensar [rekompen'sar] *vt* to reward,
recompense.

recompondré [rekompon'dre] *etc vb V*
recomponer.

recomponer [rekompo'ner] *vt* to mend;

(*INFORM: texto*) to reformat.

recomponga [rekom'ponga] *etc*,
recompuesto [rekom'pwesto],
recompuse [rekom'puse] *etc vb V*
recomponer.

reconciliación [rekonθilja'θjon] *nf*
reconciliation.

reconciliar [rekonθi'ljar] *vt* to reconcile;
~**se** *vr* to become reconciled.

recóndito, a [re'kondito, a] *adj* (*lugar*)
hidden, secret.

reconfortar [rekonfor'tar] *vt* to comfort.

reconocer [rekono'θer] *vt* to recognize; ~
los hechos to face the facts.

reconocido, a [rekono'θiðo, a] *adj*
recognized; (*agradecido*) grateful.

reconocimiento [rekonoθi'mjento] *nm*
recognition; (*registro*) search;
(*inspección*) examination; (*gratitud*)
gratitude; (*confesión*) admission; ~
óptico de caracteres (*INFORM*) optical
character recognition; ~ **de la voz**
(*INFORM*) speech recognition.

reconozca [reko'noθka] *etc vb V* **reconocer.**

reconquista [rekon'kista] *nf* reconquest.

reconquistar [rekonkis'tar] *vt* (*MIL*) to
reconquer; (*fig*) to recover, win back.

reconstituyente [rekonstitu'jente] *nm*
tonic.

reconstruir [rekonstru'ir] *vt* to reconstruct.

reconstruyendo [rekonstru'jendo] *etc vb V*
reconstruir.

reconversión [rekomber'sjon] *nf*
restructuring, reorganization; (*tb*: ~
industrial) rationalization.

recopilación [rekopila'θjon] *nf* (*resumen*)
summary; (*compilación*) compilation.

recopilar [rekopi'lar] *vt* to compile.

récord ['rekorð] *adj inv* record; **cifras** ~
record figures ♦ *nm*, *pl* **records, récords**
['rekorð] record; **batir el** ~ to break the
record.

recordar [rekor'ðar] *vt* (*acordarse de*) to
remember; (*traer a la memoria*) to recall;
(*acordar a otro*) to remind ♦ *vi* to
remember; **recuérdale que me debe 5
dólares** remind him that he owes me 5
dollars; **que yo recuerde** as far as I can
remember; **creo** ~, **si mal no recuerdo** if
my memory serves me right.

recordatorio [rekorða'torjo] *nm* (*de
fallecimiento*) in memoriam card; (*de
bautizo, comunión*) commemorative card.

recorrer [reko'rrer] *vt* (*país*) to cross,
travel through; (*distancia*) to cover;
(*registrar*) to search; (*repasar*) to look
over.

recorrido [reko'rriðo] *nm* run, journey;

tren de largo ~ main-line o inter-city (*BRIT*) train.

recortado, a [rekor'taðo, a] *adj* uneven, irregular.

recortar [rekor'tar] *vt* (*papel*) to cut out; (*el pelo*) to trim; (*dibujar*) to draw in outline; ~**se** *vr* to stand out, be silhouetted.

recorte [re'korte] *nm* (*acción, de prensa*) cutting; (*de telas, chapas*) trimming; ~ **presupuestario** budget cut; ~ **salarial** wage cut.

recostado, a [rekos'taðo, a] *adj* leaning; **estar** ~ to be lying down.

recostar [rekos'tar] *vt* to lean; ~**se** *vr* to lie down.

recoveco [reko'βeko] *nm* (*de camino, río etc*) bend; (*en casa*) cubbyhole.

recreación [rekrea'θjon] *nf* recreation.

recrear [rekre'ar] *vt* (*entretener*) to entertain; (*volver a crear*) to recreate.

recreativo, a [rekrea'tiβo, a] *adj* recreational.

recreo [re'kreo] *nm* recreation; (*ESCOL*) break, playtime.

recriminar [rekrimi'nar] *vt* to reproach ♦ *vi* to recriminate; ~**se** *vr* to reproach each other.

recrudecer [rekruðe'θer] *vt, vi*, **recrudecerse** *vr* to worsen.

recrudecimiento [rekruðeθi'mjento] *nm* upsurge.

recrudezca [recru'ðeθka] *etc vb V* **recrudecer**.

recta ['rekta] *nf V* **recto**.

rectangular [rektangu'lar] *adj* rectangular.

rectángulo, a [rek'tangulo, a] *adj* rectangular ♦ *nm* rectangle.

rectificable [rektifi'kaβle] *adj* rectifiable; **fácilmente** ~ easily rectified.

rectificación [rektifika'θjon] *nf* correction.

rectificar [rektifi'kar] *vt* to rectify; (*volverse recto*) to straighten ♦ *vi* to correct o.s.

rectifique [rekti'fike] *etc vb V* **rectificar**.

rectitud [rekti'tuð] *nf* straightness; (*fig*) rectitude.

recto, a ['rekto, a] *adj* straight; (*persona*) honest, upright; (*estricto*) strict; (*juez*) fair; (*juicio*) sound ♦ *nm* rectum; (*ATLETISMO*) straight ♦ *nf* straight line; **en el sentido** ~ **de la palabra** in the proper sense of the word; **recta final** o **de llegada** home straight.

rector, a [rek'tor, a] *adj* governing ♦ *nm/f* head, chief; (*ESCOL*) rector, president (*US*).

rectorado [rekto'raðo] *nm* (*cargo*) rectorship, presidency (*US*); (*oficina*) rector's office.

recuadro [re'kwaðro] *nm* box; (*TIP*) inset.

recubrir [reku'βir] *vt* to cover.

recuento [re'kwento] *nm* inventory; **hacer el** ~ **de** to count o reckon up.

recuerdo [re'kwerðo] *etc vb V* **recordar** ♦ *nm* souvenir; ~**s** *nmpl* memories; ¡~**s a tu madre!** give my regards to your mother!; **"R**~ **de Mallorca"** "a present from Majorca"; **contar los** ~**s** to reminisce.

recueste [re'kweste] *etc vb V* **recostar**.

recular [reku'lar] *vi* to back down.

recuperable [rekupe'raβle] *adj* recoverable.

recuperación [rekupera'θjon] *nf* recovery; ~ **de datos** (*INFORM*) data retrieval.

recuperar [rekupe'rar] *vt* to recover; (*tiempo*) to make up; (*INFORM*) to retrieve; ~**se** *vr* to recuperate.

recurrir [reku'rrir] *vi* (*JUR*) to appeal; ~ **a** to resort to; (*persona*) to turn to.

recurso [re'kurso] *nm* resort; (*medio*) means *pl*, resource; (*JUR*) appeal; **como último** ~ as a last resort; ~**s económicos** economic resources; ~**s naturales** natural resources.

recusar [reku'sar] *vt* to reject, refuse.

red [reð] *nf* net, mesh; (*FERRO, INFORM*) network; (*ELEC, de agua*) mains, supply system; (*de tiendas*) chain; (*trampa*) trap; **estar conectado con la** ~ to be connected to the mains; ~ **local** (*INFORM*) local area network; ~ **de transmisión** (*INFORM*) data network.

redacción [reðak'θjon] *nf* (*acción*) writing; (*ESCOL*) essay, composition; (*limpieza de texto*) editing; (*personal*) editorial staff.

redactar [reðak'tar] *vt* to draw up, draft; (*periódico, INFORM*) to edit.

redactor, a [reðak'tor, a] *nm/f* writer; (*en periódico*) editor.

redada [re'ðaða] *nf* (*PESCA*) cast, throw; (*fig*) catch; ~ **policial** police raid, round-up.

redención [reðen'θjon] *nf* redemption.

redentor, a [reðen'tor, a] *adj* redeeming ♦ *nm/f* (*COM*) redeemer.

redescubierto [reðesku'βjerto] *pp de* **redescubrir**.

redescubrir [reðesku'βrir] *vt* to rediscover.

redesignar [reðesiɣ'nar] *vt* (*INFORM*) to rename.

redicho, a [re'ðitʃo, a] *adj* affected.

redil [re'ðil] *nm* sheepfold.

redimir [reði'mir] *vt* to redeem; (*rehén*) to ransom.

redistribución [reðistriβu'θjon] *nf* (*COM*)

redeployment.

rédito ['reðito] *nm* interest, yield.

redoblar [reðo'ßlar] *vt* to redouble ♦ *vi* (*tambor*) to play a roll on the drums.

redoble [re'ðoßle] *nm* (*MUS*) drumroll, drumbeat; (*de trueno*) roll.

redomado, a [reðo'maðo, a] *adj* (*astuto*) sly, crafty; (*perfecto*) utter.

redonda [re'ðonda] *nf V* redondo.

redondear [reðonde'ar] *vt* to round, round off; (*cifra*) to round up.

redondel [reðon'del] *nm* (*círculo*) circle; (*TAUR*) bullring, arena; (*AUTO*) roundabout.

redondo, a [re'ðondo, a] *adj* (*circular*) round; (*completo*) complete ♦ *nf*: **a la redonda** around, round about; **en muchas millas a la redonda** for many miles around; **rehusar en ~ to** give a flat refusal.

reducción [reðuk'θjon] *nf* reduction; **~ del activo** (*COM*) divestment; **~ de precios** (*COM*) price-cutting.

reducido, a [reðu'θiðo, a] *adj* reduced; (*limitado*) limited; (*pequeño*) small; **quedar ~ a** to be reduced to.

reducir [reðu'θir] *vt* to reduce, limit; (*someter*) to bring under control; **~se** *vr* to diminish; (*MAT*): **~ (a)** to reduce (to), convert (into); **~ las millas a kilómetros** to convert miles into kilometres; **~se a** (*fig*) to come *o* boil down to.

reducto [re'ðukto] *nm* redoubt.

reduje [re'ðuxe] *etc vb V* reducir.

redundancia [reðun'danθja] *nf* redundancy.

reduzca [re'ðuθka] *etc vb V* reducir.

reedición [re(e)ði'θjon] *nf* reissue.

reeditar [re(e)ði'tar] *vt* to reissue.

reelección [re(e)lek'θjon] *nf* re-election.

reelegir [re(e)le'xir] *vt* to re-elect.

reembolsable [re(e)mbol'saßle] *adj* (*COM*) redeemable, refundable.

reembolsar [re(e)mbol'sar] *vt* (*persona*) to reimburse; (*dinero*) to repay, pay back; (*depósito*) to refund.

reembolso [re(e)m'bolso] *nm* reimbursement; refund; **enviar algo contra ~** to send sth cash on delivery; **contra ~ del flete** freight forward; **~ fiscal** tax rebate.

reemplace [re(e)m'plaθe] *etc vb V* reemplazar.

reemplazar [re(e)mpla'θar] *vt* to replace.

reemplazo [re(e)m'plaθo] *nm* replacement; **de ~** (*MIL*) reserve.

reencuentro [re(e)n'kwentro] *nm* reunion.

reengancharse [re(e)ngan'tʃarse] *vr* (*MIL*) to re-enlist.

reestreno [re(e)s'treno] *nm* rerun.

reestructurar [re(e)struktu'rar] *vt* to restructure.

reexportación [re(e)ksporta'θjon] *nf* (*COM*) re-export.

reexportar [re(e)kspor'tar] *vt* (*COM*) to re-export.

REF *nm abr* (*ESP ECON*) = *Régimen Económico Fiscal.*

Ref.ª *abr* (= *referencia*) ref.

refacción [refak'θjon] *nf* (*AM*) repair(s); **refacciones** *nfpl* (*piezas de repuesto*) spare parts.

referencia [refe'renθja] *nf* reference; **con ~ a** with reference to; **hacer ~ a** to refer *o* allude to; **~ comercial** (*COM*) trade reference.

referéndum [refe'rendum], *pl* **referéndums** *nm* referendum.

referente [refe'rente] *adj*: **~ a** concerning, relating to.

referir [refe'rir] *vt* (*contar*) to tell, recount; (*relacionar*) to refer, relate; **~se** *vr*: **~se a** to refer to; **~ al lector a un apéndice** to refer the reader to an appendix; **~ a** (*COM*) to convert into; **por lo que se refiere a eso** as for that, as regards that.

refiera [re'fjera] *etc vb V* referir.

refilón [refi'lon]: **de ~** *adv* obliquely; **mirar a algn de ~** to look out of the corner of one's eye at sb.

refinado, a [refi'naðo, a] *adj* refined.

refinamiento [refina'mjento] *nm* refinement; **~ por pasos** (*INFORM*) stepwise refinement.

refinar [refi'nar] *vt* to refine.

refinería [refine'ria] *nf* refinery.

refiriendo [refi'rjendo] *etc vb V* referir.

reflector [reflek'tor] *nm* reflector; (*ELEC*) spotlight; (*AVIAT, MIL*) searchlight.

reflejar [refle'xar] *vt* to reflect; **~se** *vr* to be reflected.

reflejo, a [re'flexo, a] *adj* reflected; (*movimiento*) reflex ♦ *nm* reflection; (*ANAT*) reflex; (*en el pelo*): **~s** *nmpl* highlights; **tiene el pelo castaño con ~s rubios** she has chestnut hair with blond streaks.

reflexión [reflek'sjon] *nf* reflection.

reflexionar [refleksjo'nar] *vt* to reflect on ♦ *vi* to reflect; (*detenerse*) to pause (to think); **¡reflexione!** you think it over!

reflexivo, a [reflek'sißo, a] *adj* thoughtful; (*LING*) reflexive.

refluir [reflu'ir] *vi* to flow back.

reflujo [re'fluxo] *nm* ebb.

refluyendo [reflu'jendo] *etc vb V* refluir.

reforcé [refor'θe], **reforcemos** [refor'θemos] *etc vb* V **reforzar.**

reforma [re'forma] *nf* reform; (*ARQ etc*) repair; ~ **agraria** agrarian reform.

reformar [refor'mar] *vt* to reform; (*modificar*) to change, alter; (*texto*) to revise; (*ARQ*) to repair; ~**se** *vr* to mend one's ways.

reformatear [reformate'ar] *vt* (*INFORM*: *disco*) to reformat.

reformatorio [reforma'torjo] *nm* reformatory; ~ **de menores** remand home.

reformista [refor'mista] *adj*, *nm/f* reformist.

reforzamiento [reforθa'mjento] *nm* reinforcement.

reforzar [refor'θar] *vt* to strengthen; (*ARQ*) to reinforce; (*fig*) to encourage.

refractario, a [refrak'tarjo, a] *adj* (*TEC*) heat-resistant; **ser ~ a una reforma** to resist *o* be opposed to a reform.

refrán [re'fran] *nm* proverb, saying.

refregar [refre'ɣar] *vt* to scrub.

refrenar [refre'nar] *vt* to check, restrain.

refrendar [refren'dar] *vt* (*firma*) to endorse, countersign; (*ley*) to approve.

refrescante [refres'kante] *adj* refreshing, cooling.

refrescar [refres'kar] *vt* to refresh ♦ *vi* to cool down; ~**se** *vr* to get cooler; (*tomar aire fresco*) to go out for a breath of fresh air; (*beber*) to have a drink.

refresco [re'fresko] *nm* soft drink, cool drink; "~**s**" "refreshments".

refresque [re'freske] *etc vb* V **refrescar.**

refriega [re'frjeɣa] *etc vb* V **refregar** ♦ *nf* scuffle, brawl.

refriegue [re'frjeɣe] *etc vb* V **refregar.**

refrigeración [refrixera'θjon] *nf* refrigeration; (*de casa*) air-conditioning.

refrigerado, a [refrixe'raðo, a] *adj* cooled; (*sala*) air-conditioned.

refrigerador [refrixera'ðor] *nm*, (*AM*) **refrigeradora** [refrixera'ðora] *nf* refrigerator, icebox (*US*).

refrigerar [refrixe'rar] *vt* to refrigerate; (*sala*) to air-condition.

refrito [re'frito] *nm* (*CULIN*): **un ~ de cebolla y tomate** sautéed onions and tomatoes; **un ~** (*fig*) a rehash.

refuerce [re'fwerθe] *etc vb* V **reforzar.**

refuerzo [re'fwerθo] *etc vb* V **reforzar** ♦ *nm* reinforcement; (*TEC*) support.

refugiado, a [refu'xjaðo, a] *nm/f* refugee.

refugiarse [refu'xjarse] *vr* to take refuge, shelter.

refugio [re'fuxjo] *nm* refuge; (*protección*) shelter; (*AUTO*) street *o* traffic island; ~

alpino *o* **de montaña** mountain hut; ~ **subterráneo** (*MIL*) underground shelter.

refulgencia [reful'xenθja] *nf* brilliance.

refulgir [reful'xir] *vi* to shine, be dazzling.

refulja [re'fulxa] *etc vb* V **refulgir.**

refundir [refun'dir] *vt* to recast; (*escrito etc*) to adapt, rewrite.

refunfuñar [refunfu'ɲar] *vi* to grunt, growl; (*quejarse*) to grumble.

refunfuñón, ona [refunfu'ɲon, ona] (*fam*) *adj* grumpy ♦ *nm/f* grouch.

refutación [refuta'θjon] *nf* refutation.

refutar [refu'tar] *vt* to refute.

regadera [reɣa'ðera] *nf* watering can; (*AM*) shower; **estar como una ~** (*fam*) to be as mad as a hatter.

regadío [reɣa'ðio] *nm* irrigated land.

regalado, a [reɣa'laðo, a] *adj* comfortable, luxurious; (*gratis*) free, for nothing; **lo tuvo ~** it was handed to him on a plate.

regalar [reɣa'lar] *vt* (*dar*) to give (as a present); (*entregar*) to give away; (*mimar*) to pamper, make a fuss of; ~**se** *vr* to treat *o.s.* to.

regalía [reɣa'lia] *nf* privilege, prerogative; (*COM*) bonus; (*de autor*) royalty.

regaliz [reɣa'liθ] *nm* liquorice.

regalo [re'ɣalo] *nm* (*obsequio*) gift, present; (*gusto*) pleasure; (*comodidad*) comfort.

regañadientes [reɣaɲa'ðjentes]: **a ~** *adv* reluctantly.

regañar [reɣa'ɲar] *vt* to scold ♦ *vi* to grumble; (*dos personas*) to fall out, quarrel.

regañón, ona [reɣa'ɲon, ona] *adj* nagging.

regar [re'ɣar] *vt* to water, irrigate; (*fig*) to scatter, sprinkle.

regata [re'ɣata] *nf* (*NAUT*) race.

regatear [reɣate'ar] *vt* (*COM*) to bargain over; (*escatimar*) to be mean with ♦ *vi* to bargain, haggle; (*DEPORTE*) to dribble; **no ~ esfuerzo** to spare no effort.

regateo [reɣa'teo] *nm* bargaining; (*DEPORTE*) dribbling; (*del cuerpo*) swerve, dodge.

regazo [re'ɣaθo] *nm* lap.

regencia [re'xenθja] *nf* regency.

regeneración [rexenera'θjon] *nf* regeneration.

regenerar [rexene'rar] *vt* to regenerate.

regentar [rexen'tar] *vt* to direct, manage; (*puesto*) to hold in an acting capacity; (*negocio*) to be in charge of.

regente, a [re'xente, a] *adj* (*príncipe*) regent; (*director*) managing ♦ *nm* (*COM*) manager; (*POL*) regent.

régimen ['reximen], *pl* **regímenes**

[re'ximenes] *nm* regime; (*reinado*) rule; (*MED*) diet; (*reglas*) (set of) rules *pl*; (*manera de vivir*) lifestyle; **estar a** ~ to be on a diet.

regimiento [rexi'mjento] *nm* regiment.

regio, a ['rexjo, a] *adj* royal, regal; (*fig: suntuoso*) splendid; (*AM fam*) great, terrific.

región [re'xjon] *nf* region; (*área*) area.

regional [rexjo'nal] *adj* regional.

regir [re'xir] *vt* to govern, rule; (*dirigir*) to manage, run; (*ECON, JUR, LING*) to govern ♦ *vi* to apply, be in force.

registrador [rexistra'ðor] *nm* registrar, recorder.

registrar [rexis'trar] *vt* (*buscar*) to search; (*en cajón*) to look through; (*inspeccionar*) to inspect; (*anotar*) to register, record; (*INFORM, MUS*) to record; ~**se** *vr* to register; (*ocurrir*) to happen.

registro [re'xistro] *nm* (*acto*) registration; (*MUS, libro*) register; (*lista*) list, record; (*INFORM*) record; (*inspección*) inspection, search; ~ **civil** registry office; ~ **electoral** voting register; ~ **de la propiedad** land registry (office).

regla ['rexla] *nf* (*ley*) rule, regulation; (*de medir*) ruler, rule; (*MED: período*) period; (~ *científica*) law, principle; **no hay** ~ **sin excepción** every rule has its exception.

reglamentación [rexlamenta'θjon] *nf* (*acto*) regulation; (*lista*) rules *pl*.

reglamentar [rexlamen'tar] *vt* to regulate.

reglamentario, a [rexlamen'tarjo, a] *adj* statutory; **en la forma reglamentaria** in the properly established way.

reglamento [rexla'mento] *nm* rules *pl*, regulations *pl*; ~ **del tráfico** highway code.

reglar [re'xlar] *vt* (*acciones*) to regulate; ~**se** *vr*: ~**se por** to be guided by.

regocijarse [rexoθi'xarse] *vr*: ~ **de** *o* **por** to rejoice at, be glad about.

regocijo [rexo'θixo] *nm* joy, happiness.

regodearse [rexoðe'arse] *vr* to be glad, be delighted; (*pey*): ~ **con** *o* **en** to gloat over.

regodeo [rexo'ðeo] *nm* delight; (*pey*) perverse pleasure.

regresar [rexre'sar] *vi* to come/go back, return; ~**se** *vr* (*AM*) to return.

regresivo, a [rexre'siβo, a] *adj* backward; (*fig*) regressive.

regreso [re'xreso] *nm* return; **estar de** ~ to be back, be home.

regué [re'xe], **reguemos** [re'xemos] *etc vb V* **regar**.

reguero [re'xero] *nm* (*de sangre*) trickle;

(*de humo*) trail.

regulación [rexula'θjon] *nf* regulation; (*TEC*) adjustment; (*control*) control; ~ **de empleo** redundancies *pl*; ~ **del tráfico** traffic control.

regulador [rexula'ðor] *nm* (*TEC*) regulator; (*de radio etc*) knob, control.

regular [rexu'lar] *adj* regular; (*normal*) normal, usual; (*común*) ordinary; (*organizado*) regular, orderly; (*mediano*) average; (*fam*) not bad, so-so ♦ *adv*: **estar** ~ to be so-so *o* alright ♦ *vt* (*controlar*) to control, regulate; (*TEC*) to adjust; **por lo** ~ as a rule.

regularice [rexula'riθe] *etc vb V* **regularizar**.

regularidad [rexulari'ðað] *nf* regularity; **con** ~ regularly.

regularizar [rexulari'θar] *vt* to regularize.

regusto [re'xusto] *nm* aftertaste.

rehabilitación [reaβilita'θjon] *nf* rehabilitation; (*ARQ*) restoration.

rehabilitar [reaβili'tar] *vt* to rehabilitate; (*ARQ*) to restore; (*reintegrar*) to reinstate.

rehacer [rea'θer] *vt* (*reparar*) to mend, repair; (*volver a hacer*) to redo, repeat; ~**se** *vr* (*MED*) to recover.

rehaga [re'axa] *etc*, **reharé** [rea're] *etc*, **rehaz** [re'aθ], **rehecho** [re'etʃo] *vb V* **rehacer**.

rehén [re'en] *nm/f* hostage.

rehice [re'iθe] *etc*, **rehizo** [re'iθo] *vb V* **rehacer**.

rehogar [reo'xar] *vt* to sauté, toss in oil.

rehuir [reu'ir] *vt* to avoid, shun.

rehusar [reu'sar] *vt, vi* to refuse.

rehuyendo [reu'jendo] *etc vb V* **rehuir**.

reina ['reina] *nf* queen.

reinado [rei'naðo] *nm* reign.

reinante [rei'nante] *adj* (*fig*) prevailing.

reinar [rei'nar] *vi* to reign; (*fig: prevalecer*) to prevail, be general.

reincidir [reinθi'ðir] *vi* to relapse; (*criminal*) to repeat an offence.

reincorporarse [reinkorpo'rarse] *vr*: ~ **a** to rejoin.

reinicializar [reiniθjali'θar] *vt* (*INFORM*) to reset.

reino ['reino] *nm* kingdom; **el R~ Unido** the United Kingdom.

reinserción [reinser'θjon] *nf* rehabilitation.

reinsertar [reinser'tar] *vt* to rehabilitate.

reintegración [reintexra'θjon] *nf* (*COM*) reinstatement.

reintegrar [reinte'xrar] *vt* (*reconstituir*) to reconstruct; (*persona*) to reinstate; (*dinero*) to refund, pay back; ~**se** *vr*: ~**se a** to return to.

reintegro [rein'texro] *nm* refund,

reimbursement; (*en banco*) withdrawal.
reír [re'ir] *vi*, **reírse** *vr* to laugh; ~**se de** to laugh at.
reiterado, a [reite'raðo, a] *adj* repeated.
reiterar [reite'rar] *vt* to reiterate; (*repetir*) to repeat.
reivindicación [reißindika'θjon] *nf* (*demanda*) claim, demand; (*justificación*) vindication.
reivindicar [reißindi'kar] *vt* to claim.
reivindique [reißin'dike] *etc vb V* **reivindicar**.
reja ['rexa] *nf* (*de ventana*) grille, bars *pl*; (*en la calle*) grating.
rejamos [re'xamos] *etc vb V* **regir**.
rejilla [re'xiʎa] *nf* grating, grille; (*muebles*) wickerwork; (*de ventilación*) vent; (*de coche etc*) luggage rack.
rejuvenecer [rexußene'θer] *vt, vi* to rejuvenate.
rejuvenezca [rexuße'neθka] *etc vb V* **rejuvenecer**.
relación [rela'θjon] *nf* relation, relationship; (*MAT*) ratio; (*lista*) list; (*narración*) report; ~ **costo-efectivo** *o* **costo-rendimiento** (*COM*) cost-effectiveness; **relaciones** *nfpl* (*enchufes*) influential friends, connections; **relaciones carnales** sexual relations; **relaciones comerciales** business connections; **relaciones empresariales/ humanas** industrial/human relations; **relaciones laborales/públicas** labour/public relations; **con** ~ **a, en** ~ **con** in relation to; **estar en** *o* **tener buenas relaciones con** to be on good terms with.
relacionar [relaθjo'nar] *vt* to relate, connect; ~**se** *vr* to be connected *o* linked.
relajación [relaxa'θjon] *nf* relaxation.
relajado, a [rela'xaðo, a] *adj* (*disoluto*) loose; (*cómodo*) relaxed; (*MED*) ruptured.
relajante [rela'xante] *adj* relaxing; (*MED*) sedative.
relajar [rela'xar] *vt*, **relajarse** *vr* to relax.
relamerse [rela'merse] *vr* to lick one's lips.
relamido, a [rela'miðo, a] *adj* (*pulcro*) overdressed; (*afectado*) affected.
relámpago [re'lampaɣo] *nm* flash of lightning ♦ *adj* lightning *cpd*; **como un** ~ as quick as lightning, in a flash; **visita/ huelga** ~ lightning visit/strike.
relampaguear [relampaɣe'ar] *vi* to flash.
relanzar [relan'θar] *vt* to relaunch.
relatar [rela'tar] *vt* to tell, relate.
relatividad [relatißi'ðað] *nf* relativity.
relativo, a [rela'tißo, a] *adj* relative; **en lo** ~ **a** concerning.
relato [re'lato] *nm* (*narración*) story, tale.

relax [re'las] *nm* rest; "R~" (*en anuncio*) "Personal services".
relegar [rele'ɣar] *vt* to relegate; ~ **algo al olvido** to banish sth from one's mind.
relegue [re'leɣe] *etc vb V* **relegar**.
relevante [rele'ßante] *adj* eminent, outstanding.
relevar [rele'ßar] *vt* (*sustituir*) to relieve; ~**se** *vr* to relay; ~ **a algn de un cargo** to relieve sb of his post.
relevo [re'leßo] *nm* relief; **carrera de** ~**s** relay race; ~ **con cinta** (*INFORM*) tape relay; **coger** *o* **tomar el** ~ to take over, stand in.
relieve [re'ljeße] *nm* (*ARTE, TEC*) relief; (*fig*) prominence, importance; **bajo** ~ bas-relief; **un personaje de** ~ an important man; **dar** ~ **a** to highlight.
religión [reli'xjon] *nf* religion.
religioso, a [reli'xjoso, a] *adj* religious ♦ *nm/f* monk/nun.
relinchar [relin'tʃar] *vi* to neigh.
relincho [re'lintʃo] *nm* neigh; (*acto*) neighing.
reliquia [re'likja] *nf* relic; ~ **de familia** heirloom.
rellano [re'ʎano] *nm* (*ARQ*) landing.
rellenar [reʎe'nar] *vt* (*llenar*) to fill up; (*CULIN*) to stuff; (*COSTURA*) to pad; (*formulario etc*) to fill in *o* out.
relleno, a [re'ʎeno, a] *adj* full up; (*CULIN*) stuffed ♦ *nm* stuffing; (*de tapicería*) padding.
reloj [re'lo(x)] *nm* clock; ~ **de pie** grandfather clock; ~ **(de pulsera)** wristwatch; ~ **de sol** sundial; ~ **despertador** alarm (clock); **como un** ~ like clockwork; **contra (el)** ~ against the clock.
relojería [reloxe'ria] (*tienda*) watchmaker's (shop); **aparato de** ~ clockwork; **bomba de** ~ time bomb.
relojero, a [relo'xero, a] *nm/f* clockmaker; watchmaker.
reluciente [relu'θjente] *adj* brilliant, shining.
relucir [relu'θir] *vi* to shine; (*fig*) to excel; **sacar algo a** ~ to show sth off.
relumbrante [relum'brante] *adj* dazzling.
relumbrar [relum'brar] *vi* to dazzle, shine brilliantly.
reluzca [re'luθka] *etc vb V* **relucir**.
remachar [rema'tʃar] *vt* to rivet; (*fig*) to hammer home, drive home.
remache [re'matʃe] *nm* rivet.
remanente [rema'nente] *nm* remainder; (*COM*) balance; (*de producto*) surplus.
remangarse [reman'garse] *vr* to roll one's

sleeves up.

remanso [re'manso] *nm* pool.

remar [re'mar] *vi* to row.

rematado, a [rema'taðo, a] *adj* complete, utter; **es un loco** ~ he's a raving lunatic.

rematar [rema'tar] *vt* to finish off; (*animal*) to put out of its misery; (*COM*) to sell off cheap ♦ *vi* to end, finish off; (*DEPORTE*) to shoot.

remate [re'mate] *nm* end, finish; (*punta*) tip; (*DEPORTE*) shot; (*ARQ*) top; (*COM*) auction sale; **de o para** ~ to crown it all (*BRIT*), to top it off.

remediable [reme'ðjaßle] *adj*: **fácilmente** ~ easily remedied.

remediar [reme'ðjar] *vt* (*gen*) to remedy; (*subsanar*) to make good, repair; (*evitar*) to avoid; **sin poder** ~**lo** without being able to prevent it.

remedio [re'meðjo] *nm* remedy; (*JUR*) recourse, remedy; **poner** ~ **a** to correct, stop; **no tener más** ~ to have no alternative; **¡qué** ~**!** there's no other way; **como último** ~ as a last resort; **sin** ~ inevitable; (*MED*) hopeless.

remedo [re'meðo] *nm* imitation; (*pey*) parody.

remendar [remen'dar] *vt* to repair; (*con parche*) to patch; (*fig*) to correct.

remesa [re'mesa] *nf* remittance; (*COM*) shipment.

remiendo [re'mjendo] *etc vb V* **remendar** ♦ *nm* mend; (*con parche*) patch; (*cosido*) darn; (*fig*) correction.

remilgado, a [remil'ɣaðo, a] *adj* prim; (*afectado*) affected.

remilgo [re'milɣo] *nm* primness; (*afectación*) affectation.

reminiscencia [reminis'θenθja] *nf* reminiscence.

remirar [remi'rar] *vt* (*volver a mirar*) to look at again; (*examinar*) to look hard at.

remisión [remi'sjon] *nf* (*acto*) sending, shipment; (*REL*) forgiveness, remission; **sin** ~ hopelessly.

remiso, a [re'miso, a] *adj* remiss.

remite [re'mite] *nm* (*en sobre*) name and address of sender.

remitente [remi'tente] *nm/f* (*CORREOS*) sender.

remitir [remi'tir] *vt* to remit, send ♦ *vi* to slacken.

remo ['remo] *nm* (*de barco*) oar; (*DEPORTE*) rowing; **cruzar un río a** ~ to row across a river.

remoce [re'moθe] *etc vb V* **remozar**.

remodelación [remodela'θjon] *nf* (*POL*): ~ **del gobierno** cabinet reshuffle.

remojar [remo'xar] *vt* to steep, soak; (*galleta etc*) to dip, dunk; (*fam*) to celebrate with a drink.

remojo [re'moxo] *nm* steeping, soaking; (*por la lluvia*) drenching, soaking; **dejar la ropa en** ~ to leave clothes to soak.

remojón [remo'xon] *nm* soaking; **darse un** ~ (*fam*) to go (in) for a dip.

remolacha [remo'latʃa] *nf* beet, beetroot (*BRIT*).

remolcador [remolka'ðor] *nm* (*NAUT*) tug; (*AUTO*) breakdown lorry.

remolcar [remol'kar] *vt* to tow.

remolino [remo'lino] *nm* eddy; (*de agua*) whirlpool; (*de viento*) whirlwind; (*de gente*) crowd.

remolón, ona [remo'lon, ona] *adj* lazy ♦ *nm/f* slacker, shirker.

remolque [re'molke] *etc vb V* **remolcar** ♦ *nm* tow, towing; (*cuerda*) towrope; **llevar a** ~ to tow.

remontar [remon'tar] *vt* to mend; (*obstáculo*) to negotiate, get over; ~**se** *vr* to soar; ~**se a** (*COM*) to amount to; (*en tiempo*) to go back to, date from; ~ **el vuelo** to soar.

rémora ['remora] *nf* hindrance.

remorder [remor'ðer] *vt* to distress, disturb.

remordimiento [remorði'mjento] *nm* remorse.

remotamente [remota'mente] *adv* vaguely.

remoto, a [re'moto, a] *adj* remote.

remover [remo'ßer] *vt* to stir; (*tierra*) to turn over; (*objetos*) to move round.

remozar [remo'θar] *vt* (*ARQ*) to refurbish; (*fig*) to brighten *o* polish up.

remuerda [re'mwerða] *etc vb V* **remorder**.

remueva [re'mweßa] *etc vb V* **remover**.

remuneración [remunera'θjon] *nf* remuneration.

remunerado, a [remune'raðo, a] *adj*: **trabajo bien/mal** ~ well-/badly-paid job.

remunerar [remune'rar] *vt* to remunerate; (*premiar*) to reward.

renacer [rena'θer] *vi* to be reborn; (*fig*) to revive.

renacimiento [renaθi'mjento] *nm* rebirth; **el R**~ the Renaissance.

renacuajo [rena'kwaxo] *nm* (*ZOOL*) tadpole.

renal [re'nal] *adj* renal, kidney *cpd*.

Renania [re'nanja] *nf* Rhineland.

renazca [re'naθka] *etc vb V* **renacer**.

rencilla [ren'θiʎa] *nf* quarrel; ~**s** *nfpl* bickering *sg*.

rencor [ren'kor] *nm* rancour, bitterness; (*resentimiento*) ill feeling, resentment;

guardar ~ **a** to have a grudge against.
rencoroso, a [renko'roso, a] *adj* spiteful.
rendición [rendi'θjon] *nf* surrender.
rendido, a [ren'diðo, a] *adj (sumiso)*
submissive; *(agotado)* worn-out,
exhausted; *(enamorado)* devoted.
rendija [ren'dixa] *nf (hendedura)* crack;
(abertura) aperture; *(fig)* rift, split; *(JUR)*
loophole.
rendimiento [rendi'mjento] *nm*
(producción) output; *(COM)* yield,
profit(s) *(pl)*; *(TEC, COM)* efficiency; ~ **de**
capital *(COM)* return on capital.
rendir [ren'dir] *vt (vencer)* to defeat;
(producir) to produce; *(dar beneficio)* to
yield; *(agotar)* to exhaust ◊ *vi* to pay;
(COM) to yield, produce; ~**se** *vr*
(someterse) to surrender; *(ceder)* to
yield; *(cansarse)* to wear o.s. out; ~
homenaje *o* **culto a** to pay homage to; **el**
negocio no rinde the business doesn't
pay.
renegado, a [rene'xaðo, a] *adj, nm/f*
renegade.
renegar [rene'xar] *vt (negar)* to deny
vigorously ◊ *vi (blasfemar)* to blaspheme;
~ **de** *(renunciar)* to renounce; *(quejarse)*
to complain about.
renegué [rene'xe], **reneguemos**
[rene'xemos] *etc vb V* **renegar**.
RENFE ['renfe] *nf abr ESP.* = *Red Nacional de*
Ferrocarriles Españoles.
renglón [ren'glon] *nm (línea)* line; *(COM)*
item, article; **a** ~ **seguido** immediately
after.
rengo, a ['rengo, a] *adj (AM)* lame.
reniego [re'njexo] *etc*, **reniegue**
[re'njexe] *etc vb V* **renegar**.
reno ['reno] *nm* reindeer.
renombrado, a [renom'braðo, a] *adj*
renowned.
renombre [re'nombre] *nm* renown.
renovable [reno'ßaßle] *adj* renewable.
renovación [renoßa'θjon] *nf (de contrato)*
renewal; *(ARQ)* renovation.
renovar [reno'ßar] *vt* to renew; *(ARQ)* to
renovate; *(sala)* to redecorate.
renquear [renke'ar] *vi* to limp; *(fam)* to get
along, scrape by.
renta ['renta] *nf (ingresos)* income;
(beneficio) profit; *(alquiler)* rent; ~
gravable *o* **imponible** taxable income; ~
nacional (bruta) (gross) national income;
~ **no salarial** unearned income; ~ **sobre**
el terreno *(COM)* ground rent; ~ **vitalicia**
annuity; **política de** ~**s** incomes policy;
vivir de sus ~**s** to live on one's private
income.

rentabilizar [rentaßili'θar] *vt* to make
profitable.
rentable [ren'taßle] *adj* profitable; **no** ~
unprofitable.
rentar [ren'tar] *vt* to produce, yield; *(AM)*
to rent.
rentista [ren'tista] *nm/f (accionista)*
shareholder *(BRIT)*, stockholder *(US)*.
renuencia [re'nwenθja] *nf* reluctance.
renuente [re'nwente] *adj* reluctant.
renueve [re'nweße] *etc vb V* **renovar**.
renuncia [re'nunθja] *nf* resignation.
renunciar [renun'θjar] *vt* to renounce, give
up ◊ *vi* to resign; ~ **a hacer algo** to give
up doing sth.
reñido, a [re'niðo, a] *adj (batalla)* bitter,
hard-fought; **estar** ~ **con algn** to be on
bad terms with sb; **está** ~ **con su familia**
he has fallen out with his family.
reñir [re'nir] *vt (regañar)* to scold ◊ *vi (estar*
peleado) to quarrel, fall out; *(combatir)* to
fight.
reo ['reo] *nm/f* culprit, offender; *(JUR)*
accused.
reojo [re'oxo]: **de** ~ *adv* out of the corner
of one's eye.
reorganice [reorxa'niθe] *etc vb V*
reorganizar.
reorganizar [reorxani'θar] *vt* to
reorganize.
Rep *abr* = **República**.
reparación [repara'θjon] *nf (acto)* mending,
repairing; *(TEC)* repair; *(fig)* amends,
reparation; **"reparaciones en el acto"**
"repairs while you wait".
reparar [repa'rar] *vt* to repair; *(fig)* to make
amends for; *(suerte)* to retrieve;
(observar) to observe ◊ *vi:* ~ **en** *(darse*
cuenta de) to notice; *(poner atención en)* to
pay attention to; **sin** ~ **en los gastos**
regardless of the cost.
reparo [re'paro] *nm (advertencia)*
observation; *(duda)* doubt; *(dificultad)*
difficulty; *(escrúpulo)* scruple, qualm;
poner ~**s (a)** to raise objections (to);
(criticar) to criticize; **no tuvo** ~ **en**
hacerlo he did not hesitate to do it.
repartición [reparti'θjon] *nf* distribution;
(división) division.
repartidor, a [reparti'ðor, a] *nm/f*
distributor; ~ **de leche** milkman.
repartir [repar'tir] *vt* to distribute, share
out; *(COM, CORREOS)* to deliver; *(MIL)* to
partition; *(libros)* to give out; *(comida)* to
serve out; *(NAIPES)* to deal.
reparto [re'parto] *nm* distribution; *(COM,*
CORREOS) delivery; *(TEAT, CINE)* cast;
(AM: urbanización) housing estate *(BRIT)*,

real estate development (*US*); "~ **a domicilio**" "home delivery service".

repasar [repa'sar] *vt* (*ESCOL*) to revise; (*MECÁNICA*) to check, overhaul; (*COSTURA*) to mend.

repaso [re'paso] *nm* revision; (*MECÁNICA*) overhaul, checkup; (*COSTURA*) mending; ~ **general** servicing, general overhaul; **curso de** ~ refresher course.

repatriar [repa'trjar] *vt* to repatriate; ~**se** *vr* to return home.

repelente [repe'lente] *adj* repellent, repulsive.

repeler [repe'ler] *vt* to repel; (*idea, oferta*) to reject.

repensar [repen'sar] *vt* to reconsider.

repente [re'pente] *nm* sudden movement; (*fig*) impulse; **de** ~ suddenly; ~ **de ira** fit of anger.

repentice [repen'tiθe] *etc vb V* **repentizar**.

repentino, a [repen'tino, a] *adj* sudden; (*imprevisto*) unexpected.

repentizar [repenti'θar] *vi* (*MUS*) to sight-read.

repercusión [reperku'sjon] *nf* repercussion; **de amplia** *o* **ancha** ~ far-reaching.

repercutir [reperku'tir] *vi* (*objeto*) to rebound; (*sonido*) to echo; ~ **en** (*fig*) to have repercussions *o* effects on.

repertorio [reper'torjo] *nm* list; (*TEAT*) repertoire.

repesca [re'peska] *nf* (*ESCOL fam*) resit.

repetición [repeti'θjon] *nf* repetition.

repetido, a [repe'tiðo, a] *adj* repeated; **repetidas veces** repeatedly.

repetir [repe'tir] *vt* to repeat; (*plato*) to have a second helping of; (*TEAT*) to give as an encore, sing *etc* again ♦ *vi* to repeat; (*sabor*) to come back; ~**se** *vr* to repeat o.s.; (*suceso*) to recur.

repetitivo, a [repeti'tiβo, a] *adj* repetitive, repetitious.

repicar [repi'kar] *vi* (*campanas*) to ring (out).

repiense [re'pjense] *etc vb V* **repensar**.

repipi [re'pipi] *adj* la-di-da ♦ *nf*: **es una** ~ she's a little madam.

repique [re'pike] *etc vb V* **repicar** ♦ *nm* pealing, ringing.

repiqueteo [repike'teo] *nm* pealing; (*de tambor*) drumming.

repisa [re'pisa] *nf* ledge, shelf; ~ **de chimenea** mantelpiece; ~ **de ventana** windowsill.

repitiendo [repi'tjendo] *etc vb V* **repetir**.

replantear [replante'ar] *vt* (*cuestión pública*) to readdress; (*problema personal*)

to reconsider; (*en reunión*) to raise again; ~**se** *vr*: ~**se algo** to reconsider sth.

replegarse [reple'ɣarse] *vr* to fall back, retreat.

replegué [reple'ɣe], **repleguemos** [reple'ɣemos] *etc vb V* **replegarse**.

repleto, a [re'pleto, a] *adj* replete, full up; ~ **de** filled *o* crammed with.

réplica ['replika] *nf* answer; (*ARTE*) replica; **derecho de** ~ right of *o* to reply.

replicar [repli'kar] *vi* to answer; (*objetar*) to argue, answer back.

repliego [re'pljeɣo] *etc vb V* **replegarse**.

repliegue [re'pljeɣe] *etc vb V* **replegarse** ♦ *nm* (*MIL*) withdrawal.

replique [re'plike] *etc vb V* **replicar**.

repoblación [repoßla'θjon] *nf* repopulation; (*de río*) restocking; ~ **forestal** reafforestation.

repoblar [repo'ßlar] *vt* to repopulate; to restock.

repollo [re'poʎo] *nm* cabbage.

repondré [repon'dre] *etc vb V* **reponer**.

reponer [repo'ner] *vt* to replace, put back; (*máquina*) to re-set; (*TEAT*) to revive; ~**se** *vr* to recover; ~ **que** to reply that.

reponga [re'ponga] *etc vb V* **reponer**.

reportaje [repor'taxe] *nm* report, article; ~ **gráfico** illustrated report.

reportar [repor'tar] *vt* (*traer*) to bring, carry; (*conseguir*) to obtain; (*fig*) to check; ~**se** *vr* (*contenerse*) to control o.s.; (*calmarse*) to calm down; **la cosa no le reportó sino disgustos** the affair brought him nothing but trouble.

reportero, a [repor'tero, a] *nm/f* reporter; ~ **gráfico/a** news photographer.

reposacabezas [reposaka'ßeθas] *nm inv* headrest.

reposado, a [repo'saðo, a] *adj* (*descansado*) restful; (*tranquilo*) calm.

reposar [repo'sar] *vi* to rest, repose; (*muerto*) to lie, rest.

reposición [reposi'θjon] *nf* replacement; (*CINE*) second showing; (*TEAT*) revival.

reposo [re'poso] *nm* rest.

repostar [repos'tar] *vt* to replenish; (*AUTO*) to fill up (with petrol *o* gasoline).

repostería [reposte'ria] *nf* (*arte*) confectionery, pastry-making; (*tienda*) confectioner's (shop).

repostero, a [repos'tero, a] *nm/f* confectioner.

reprender [repren'der] *vt* to reprimand; (*niño*) to scold.

reprensión [repren'sjon] *nf* rebuke, reprimand; (*de niño*) telling-off, scolding.

represa [re'presa] *nf* dam; (*lago artificial*) lake, pool.

represalia [repre'salja] *nf* reprisal; **tomar ~s** to take reprisals, retaliate.

representación [representa'θjon] *nf* representation; (*TEAT*) performance; **en ~ de** representing; **por ~** by proxy; **~ visual** (*INFORM*) display.

representante [represen'tante] *nm/f* (*POL, COM*) representative; (*TEAT*) performer.

representar [represen'tar] *vt* to represent; (*significar*) to mean; (*TEAT*) to perform; (*edad*) to look; **~se** *vr* to imagine; **tal acto representaría la guerra** such an act would mean war.

representativo, a [representa'tißo, a] *adj* representative.

represión [repre'sjon] *nf* repression.

represivo, a [repre'sißo, a] *adj* repressive.

reprimenda [repri'menda] *nf* reprimand, rebuke.

reprimir [repri'mir] *vt* to repress; **~se** *vr*: **~se de hacer algo** to stop o.s. from doing sth.

reprobación [reproßa'θjon] *nf* reproval; (*culpa*) blame.

reprobar [repro'ßar] *vt* to censure, reprove.

réprobo, a ['reproßo, a] *nm/f* reprobate.

reprochar [repro't far] *vt* to reproach; (*censurar*) to condemn, censure.

reproche [re'prot fe] *nm* reproach.

reproducción [reproðuk'θjon] *nf* reproduction.

reproducir [reproðu'θir] *vt* to reproduce; **~se** *vr* to breed; (*situación*) to recur.

reproductor, a [reproðuk'tor, a] *adj* reproductive ♦ *nm*: **~ de discos compactos** CD player.

reproduje [repro'ðuxe], **reprodujera** [reproðu'xera] *etc*, **reproduzca** [repro'ðuθka] *etc vb V* **reproducir**.

repruebe [re'prweße] *etc vb V* **reprobar**.

reptar [rep'tar] *vi* to creep, crawl.

reptil [rep'til] *nm* reptile.

república [re'pußlika] *nf* republic; **R~ Dominicana** Dominican Republic; **R~ Democrática Alemana (RDA)** German Democratic Republic; **R~ Federal Alemana (RFA)** Federal Republic of Germany; **R~ Árabe Unida** United Arab Republic.

republicano, a [repußli'kano, a] *adj, nm/f* republican.

repudiar [repu'ðjar] *vt* to repudiate; (*fe*) to renounce.

repudio [re'puðjo] *nm* repudiation.

repueble [re'pweßle] *etc vb V* **repoblar**.

repuesto [re'pwesto] *pp de* **reponer** ♦ *nm* (*pieza de recambio*) spare (part); (*abastecimiento*) supply; **rueda de ~** spare wheel; **y llevamos otro de ~** and we have another as a spare *o* in reserve.

repugnancia [repuɣ'nanθja] *nf* repugnance.

repugnante [repuɣ'nante] *adj* repugnant, repulsive.

repugnar [repuɣ'nar] *vt* to disgust ♦ *vi*, **~se** *vr* (*contradecirse*) to contradict each other; (*dar asco*) to be disgusting.

repujar [repu'xar] *vt* to emboss.

repulsa [re'pulsa] *nf* rebuff.

repulsión [repul'sjon] *nf* repulsion, aversion.

repulsivo, a [repul'sißo, a] *adj* repulsive.

repuse [re'puse] *etc vb V* **reponer**.

reputación [reputa'θjon] *nf* reputation.

reputar [repu'tar] *vt* to consider, deem.

requemado, a [reke'maðo, a] *adj* (*quemado*) scorched; (*bronceado*) tanned.

requemar [reke'mar] *vt* (*quemar*) to scorch; (*secar*) to parch; (*CULIN*) to overdo, burn; (*la lengua*) to burn, sting.

requerimiento [rekeri'mjento] *nm* request; (*demanda*) demand; (*JUR*) summons.

requerir [reke'rir] *vt* (*pedir*) to ask, request; (*exigir*) to require; (*ordenar*) to call for; (*llamar*) to send for, summon.

requesón [reke'son] *nm* cottage cheese.

requete... [rekete] *pref* extremely.

requiebro [re'kjeßro] *nm* (*piropo*) compliment, flirtatious remark.

réquiem ['rekjem] *nm* requiem.

requiera [re'kjera] *etc*, **requiriendo** [reki'rjendo] *etc vb V* **requerir**.

requisa [re'kisa] *nf* (*inspección*) survey, inspection; (*MIL*) requisition.

requisar [reki'sar] *vt* (*MIL*) to requisition; (*confiscar*) to seize, confiscate.

requisito [reki'sito] *nm* requirement, requisite; **~ previo** prerequisite; **tener los ~s para un cargo** to have the essential qualifications for a post.

res [res] *nf* beast, animal.

resabio [re'saßjo] *nm* (*maña*) vice, bad habit; (*dejo*) (unpleasant) aftertaste.

resaca [re'saka] *nf* (*en el mar*) undertow, undercurrent; (*fig*) backlash; (*fam*) hangover.

resaltar [resal'tar] *vi* to project, stick out; (*fig*) to stand out.

resarcir [resar'θir] *vt* to compensate; (*pagar*) to repay; **~se** *vr* to make up for; **~ a algn de una pérdida** to compensate sb for a loss; **~ a algn de una cantidad** to repay sb a sum.

resarza [re'sarθa] *etc vb V* **resarcir**.

resbalada [resßa'laða] *nf (AM)* slip.

resbaladizo, a [resßala'ðiθo, a] *adj* slippery.

resbalar [resßa'lar] *vi*, **resbalarse** *vr* to slip, slide; (*fig*) to slip (up); **le resbalaban las lágrimas por las mejillas** tears were trickling down his cheeks.

resbalón [resßa'lon] *nm (acción)* slip; (*deslizamiento*) slide; (*fig*) slip.

rescatar [reska'tar] *vt (salvar)* to save, rescue; (*objeto*) to get back, recover; (*cautivos*) to ransom.

rescate [res'kate] *nm* rescue; (*objeto*) recovery; **pagar un** ~ to pay a ransom.

rescindir [resθin'dir] *vt (contrato)* to annul, rescind.

rescisión [resθi'sjon] *nf* cancellation.

rescoldo [res'koldo] *nm* embers *pl*.

resecar [rese'kar] *vt* to dry off, dry thoroughly; (*MED*) to cut out, remove; ~**se** *vr* to dry up.

reseco, a [re'seko, a] *adj* very dry; (*fig*) skinny.

resentido, a [resen'tiðo, a] *adj* resentful; **es un** ~ he's bitter.

resentimiento [resenti'mjento] *nm* resentment, bitterness.

resentirse [resen'tirse] *vr (debilitarse: persona)* to suffer; ~ **con** to resent; ~ **de** (*consecuencias*) to feel the effects of.

reseña [re'seɲa] *nf (cuenta)* account; (*informe*) report; (*LIT*) review.

reseñar [rese'ɲar] *vt* to describe; (*LIT*) to review.

reseque [re'seke] *etc vb V* **resecar**.

reserva [re'serßa] *nf* reserve; (*reservación*) reservation; **a** ~ **de que** ... unless ...; **con toda** ~ in strictest confidence; **de** ~ spare; **tener algo de** ~ to have sth in reserve; ~ **de indios** Indian reservation; (*COM*): ~ **para amortización** depreciation allowance; ~ **de caja** *o* **en efectivo** cash reserves; ~**s del Estado** government stock; ~**s en oro** gold reserves.

reservado, a [reser'ßaðo, a] *adj* reserved; (*retraído*) cold, distant ♦ *nm* private room; (*FERRO*) reserved compartment.

reservar [reser'ßar] *vt (guardar)* to keep; (*FERRO, TEAT etc*) to reserve, book; ~**se** *vr* to save o.s.; (*callar*) to keep to o.s.; ~ **con exceso** to overbook.

resfriado [res'friaðo] *nm* cold.

resfriarse [res'friarse] *vr* to cool off; (*MED*) to catch (a) cold.

resfrío [res'frio] *nm (esp AM)* cold.

resguardar [resɣwar'ðar] *vt* to protect,

shield; ~**se** *vr*: ~**se de** to guard against.

resguardo [res'ɣwarðo] *nm* defence; (*vale*) voucher; (*recibo*) receipt, slip.

residencia [resi'ðenθja] *nf* residence; (*UNIV*) hall of residence; ~ **para ancianos** *o* **jubilados** rest home.

residencial [resiðen'θjal] *adj* residential ♦ *nf (urbanización)* housing estate (*BRIT*), real estate development (*US*).

residente [resi'ðente] *adj, nm/f* resident.

residir [resi'ðir] *vi* to reside, live; ~ **en** to reside *o* lie in; (*consistir en*) to consist of.

residual [resi'ðwal] *adj* residual; **aguas** ~**es** sewage.

residuo [re'siðwo] *nm* residue; ~**s atmosféricos** *o* **radiactivos** fallout *sg*.

resienta [re'sjenta] *etc vb V* **resentir**.

resignación [resiɣna'θjon] *nf* resignation.

resignarse [resiɣ'narse] *vr*: ~ **a** *o* **con** to resign o.s. to, be resigned to.

resina [re'sina] *nf* resin.

resintiendo [resin'tjendo] *etc vb V* **resentir**.

resistencia [resis'tenθja] *nf (dureza)* endurance, strength; (*oposición, ELEC*) resistance; **la R**~ (*MIL*) the Resistance.

resistente [resis'tente] *adj* strong, hardy; (*TEC*) resistant; ~ **al calor** heat-resistant.

resistir [resis'tir] *vt (soportar)* to bear; (*oponerse a*) to resist, oppose; (*aguantar*) to put up with ♦ *vi* to resist; (*aguantar*) to last, endure; ~**se** *vr*: ~**se a** to refuse to, resist; **no puedo** ~ **este frío** I can't bear *o* stand this cold; **me resisto a creerlo** I refuse to believe it; **se le resiste la química** chemistry escapes her.

resol [re'sol] *nm* glare of the sun.

resollar [reso'ʎar] *vi* to breathe noisily, wheeze.

resolución [resolu'θjon] *nf* resolution; (*decisión*) decision; (*moción*) motion; ~ **judicial** legal ruling; **tomar una** ~ to take a decision.

resoluto, a [reso'luto, a] *adj* resolute.

resolver [resol'ßer] *vt* to resolve; (*solucionar*) to solve, resolve; (*decidir*) to decide, settle; ~**se** *vr* to make up one's mind.

resonancia [reso'nanθja] *nf (del sonido)* resonance; (*repercusión*) repercussion; (*fig*) wide effect, impact.

resonante [reso'nante] *adj* resonant, resounding; (*fig*) tremendous.

resonar [reso'nar] *vi* to ring, echo.

resoplar [reso'plar] *vi* to snort; (*por cansancio*) to puff.

resoplido [reso'pliðo] *nm* heavy breathing.

resorte [re'sorte] *nm* spring; (*fig*) lever.

respaldar [respal'dar] *vt* to back (up),

support; (*INFORM*) to back up; ~**se** *vr* to lean back; ~**se con** *o* **en** (*fig*) to take one's stand on.

respaldo [res'paldo] *nm* (*de sillón*) back; (*fig*) support, backing.

respectivo, a [respek'tiβo, a] *adj* respective; **en lo** ~ **a** with regard to.

respecto [res'pekto] *nm*: **al** ~ on this matter; **con** ~ **a,** ~ **de** with regard to, in relation to.

respetable [respe'taβle] *adj* respectable.

respetar [respe'tar] *vt* to respect.

respeto [res'peto] *nm* respect; (*acatamiento*) deference; ~**s** *nmpl* respects; **por** ~ **a** out of consideration for; **presentar sus** ~**s a** to pay one's respects to.

respetuoso, a [respe'twoso, a] *adj* respectful.

respingo [res'pingo] *nm* start, jump.

respiración [respira'θjon] *nf* breathing; (*MED*) respiration; (*ventilación*) ventilation.

respirar [respi'rar] *vt, vi* to breathe; **no dejar** ~ **a algn** to keep on at sb; **estuvo escuchándole sin** ~ he listened to him in complete silence.

respiratorio, a [respira'torjo, a] *adj* respiratory.

respiro [res'piro] *nm* breathing; (*fig: descanso*) respite, rest; (*COM*) period of grace.

resplandecer [resplande'θer] *vi* to shine.

resplandeciente [resplande'θjente] *adj* resplendent, shining.

resplandezca [resplan'deθka] *etc vb V* **resplandecer.**

resplandor [resplan'dor] *nm* brilliance, brightness; (*del fuego*) blaze.

responder [respon'der] *vt* to answer ♦ *vi* to answer; (*fig*) to respond; (*pey*) to answer back; (*corresponder*) to correspond; ~ **a** (*situación etc*) to respond to; ~ **a una pregunta** to answer a question; ~ **a una descripción** to fit a description; ~ **de** *o* **por** to answer for.

respondón, ona [respon'don, ona] *adj* cheeky.

responsabilice [responsaβi'liθe] *etc vb V* **responsabilizarse.**

responsabilidad [responsaβili'ðað] *nf* responsibility; **bajo mi** ~ on my authority; ~ **ilimitada** (*COM*) unlimited liability.

responsabilizarse [responsaβili'θarse] *vr* to make o.s. responsible, take charge.

responsable [respon'sable] *adj* responsible; **la persona** ~ the person in

charge; **hacerse** ~ **de algo** to assume responsibility for sth.

respuesta [res'pwesta] *nf* answer, reply; (*reacción*) response.

resquebrajar [reskeβra'xar] *vt,* **resquebrajarse** *vr* to crack, split.

resquemor [reske'mor] *nm* resentment.

resquicio [res'kiθjo] *nm* chink; (*hendedura*) crack.

resta ['resta] *nf* (*MAT*) remainder.

restablecer [restaβle'θer] *vt* to re-establish, restore; ~**se** *vr* to recover.

restablecimiento [restaβleθi'mjento] *nm* re-establishment; (*restauración*) restoration; (*MED*) recovery.

restablezca [resta'βleθka] *etc vb V* **restablecer.**

restallar [resta'ʎar] *vi* to crack.

restante [res'tante] *adj* remaining; **lo** ~ the remainder; **los** ~**s** the rest, those left (over).

restar [res'tar] *vt* (*MAT*) to subtract; (*descontar*) to deduct; (*fig*) to take away ♦ *vi* to remain, be left.

restauración [restaura'θjon] *nf* restoration.

restaurador, a [restaura'ðor, a] *nm/f* (*persona*) restorer.

restaurante [restau'rante] *nm* restaurant.

restaurar [restau'rar] *vt* to restore.

restitución [restitu'θjon] *nf* return, restitution.

restituir [restitu'ir] *vt* (*devolver*) to return, give back; (*rehabilitar*) to restore.

restituyendo [restitu'jendo] *etc vb V* **restituir.**

resto ['resto] *nm* (*residuo*) rest, remainder; (*apuesta*) stake; ~**s** *nmpl* remains; (*CULIN*) leftovers, scraps; ~**s mortales** mortal remains.

restregar [restre'ɣar] *vt* to scrub, rub.

restregué [restre'ɣe], **restreguemos** [restre'ɣemos] *etc vb V* **restregar.**

restricción [restrik'θjon] *nf* restriction; **sin** ~ without restrictions on *o* as to; **hablar sin restricciones** to talk freely.

restrictivo, a [restrik'tiβo, a] *adj* restrictive.

restriego [res'trjeɣo] *etc*, **restriegue** [res'trjeɣe] *etc vb V* **restregar.**

restringir [restrin'xir] *vt* to restrict, limit.

restrinja [res'trinxa] *etc vb V* **restringir.**

resucitar [resuθi'tar] *vt, vi* to resuscitate, revive.

resuello [re'sweʎo] *etc vb V* **resollar** ♦ *nm* (*aliento*) breath.

resuelto, a [re'swelto, a] *pp de* **resolver** ♦ *adj* resolute, determined; **estar** ~ **a**

algo to be set on sth; **estar ~ a hacer algo** to be determined to do sth.
resuelva [re'swelßa] *etc vb* V **resolver**.
resuene [re'swene] *etc vb* V **resonar**.
resulta [re'sulta] *nf* result; **de ~s de** as a result of.
resultado [resul'taðo] *nm* result; (*conclusión*) outcome; **~s** *nmpl* (*INFORM*) output *sg*; **dar ~** to produce results.
resultante [resul'tante] *adj* resulting, resultant.
resultar [resul'tar] *vi* (*ser*) to be; (*llegar a ser*) to turn out to be; (*salir bien*) to turn out well; (*seguir*) to ensue; **~ a** (*COM*) to amount to; **~ de** to stem from; **~ en** to result in, produce; **resulta que ...** (*por consecuencia*) it follows that ...; (*parece que*) it seems that ...; **el conductor resultó muerto** the driver was killed; **no resultó** it didn't work *o* come off; **me resulta difícil hacerlo** it's difficult for me to do it.
resumen [re'sumen] *nm* summary, résumé; **en ~** in short.
resumir [resu'mir] *vt* to sum up; (*condensar*) to summarize; (*cortar*) to abridge, cut down; (*condensar*) to summarize; **~se** *vr*: **la situación se resume en pocas palabras** the situation can be summed up in a few words.
resurgir [resur'xir] *vi* (*reaparecer*) to reappear.
resurrección [resurrek'θjon] *nf* resurrection.
retablo [re'taßlo] *nm* altarpiece.
retaguardia [reta'ywarðja] *nf* rearguard.
retahíla [reta'ila] *nf* series, string; (*de injurias*) volley, stream.
retal [re'tal] *nm* remnant.
retar [re'tar] *vt* (*gen*) to challenge; (*desafiar*) to defy, dare.
retardar [retar'ðar] *vt* (*demorar*) to delay; (*hacer más lento*) to slow down; (*retener*) to hold back.
retardo [re'tarðo] *nm* delay.
retazo [re'taθo] *nm* snippet (*BRIT*), fragment.
RETD *nf abr* (*ESP TELEC*) = Red Especial de Transmisión de Datos.
rete... ['rete] *pref* very, extremely.
retén [re'ten] *nm* (*AM*) roadblock, checkpoint.
retención [reten'θjon] *nf* retention; (*de pago*) deduction; **~ de llamadas** (*TELEC*) hold facility.
retendré [reten'dre] *etc vb* V **retener**.
retener [rete'ner] *vt* (*guardar*) to retain, keep; (*intereses*) to withhold.

retenga [re'tenga] *etc vb* V **retener**.
reticencia [reti'θenθja] *nf* (*sugerencia*) insinuation, (malevolent) suggestion; (*engaño*) half-truth.
reticente [reti'θente] *adj* (*insinuador*) insinuating; (*engañoso*) deceptive.
retiene [re'tjene] *etc vb* V **retener**.
retina [re'tina] *nf* retina.
retintín [retin'tin] *nm* jangle, jingle; **decir algo con ~** to say sth sarcastically.
retirado, a [reti'raðo, a] *adj* (*lugar*) remote; (*vida*) quiet; (*jubilado*) retired ♦ *nf* (*MIL*) retreat; (*de dinero*) withdrawal; (*de embajador*) recall; (*refugio*) safe place; **batirse en retirada** to retreat.
retirar [reti'rar] *vt* to withdraw; (*la mano*) to draw back; (*quitar*) to remove; (*dinero*) to take out, withdraw; (*jubilar*) to retire, pension off; **~se** *vr* to retreat, withdraw; (*jubilarse*) to retire; (*acostarse*) to retire, go to bed.
retiro [re'tiro] *nm* retreat; (*jubilación, tb DEPORTE*) retirement; (*pago*) pension; (*lugar*) quiet place.
reto ['reto] *nm* dare, challenge.
retocar [reto'kar] *vt* to touch up, retouch.
retoce [re'toθe] *etc vb* V **retozar**.
retoño [re'toɲo] *nm* sprout, shoot; (*fig*) offspring, child.
retoque [re'toke] *etc vb* V **retocar** ♦ *nm* retouching.
retorcer [retor'θer] *vt* to twist; (*argumento*) to turn, twist; (*manos, lavado*) to wring; **~se** *vr* to become twisted; (*persona*) to writhe; **~se de dolor** to writhe in *o* squirm with pain.
retorcido, a [retor'θiðo, a] *adj* (*tb fig*) twisted.
retorcimiento [retorθi'mjento] *nm* twist, twisting; (*fig*) deviousness.
retórico, a [re'toriko, a] *adj* rhetorical; (*pey*) affected, windy ♦ *nf* rhetoric; (*pey*) affectedness.
retornable [retor'naßle] *adj* returnable.
retornar [retor'nar] *vt* to return, give back ♦ *vi* to return, go/come back.
retorno [re'torno] *nm* return; **~ del carro** (*INFORM, TIP*) carriage return; **~ del carro automático** (*INFORM*) wordwrap, word wraparound.
retortero [retor'tero] *nm*: **andar al ~** to bustle about, have heaps of things to do; **andar al ~ por algn** to be madly in love with sb.
retortijón [retorti'xon] *nm* twist, twisting; **~ de tripas** stomach cramp.
retorzamos [retor'θamos] *etc vb* V **retorcer**.

retozar [reto'θar] *vi* (*juguetear*) to frolic, romp; (*saltar*) to gambol.

retozón, ona [reto'θon, ona] *adj* playful.

retracción [retrak'θjon] *nf* retraction.

retractarse [retrak'tarse] *vr* to retract; **me retracto** I take that back.

retraerse [retra'erse] *vr* to retreat, withdraw.

retraído, a [retra'iðo, a] *adj* shy, retiring.

retraiga [re'traiɣa] *etc vb V* **retraerse**.

retraimiento [retrai'mjento] *nm* retirement; (*timidez*) shyness.

retraje [re'traxe] *etc*, **retrajera** [retra'xera] *etc vb V* **retraerse**.

retransmisión [retransmi'sjon] *nf* repeat (broadcast).

retransmitir [retransmi'tir] *vt* (*mensaje*) to relay; (*TV etc*) to repeat, retransmit; (: *en vivo*) to broadcast live.

retrasado, a [retra'saðo, a] *adj* late; (*MED*) mentally retarded; (*país etc*) backward, underdeveloped; **estar ~** (*reloj*) to be slow; (*persona, industria*) to be *o* lag behind.

retrasar [retra'sar] *vt* (*demorar*) to postpone, put off; (*retardar*) to slow down ♦ *vi*, **~se** *vr* (*atrasarse*) to be late; (*reloj*) to be slow; (*producción*) to fall (away); (*quedarse atrás*) to lag behind.

retraso [re'traso] *nm* (*demora*) delay; (*lentitud*) slowness; (*tardanza*) lateness; (*atraso*) backwardness; **~s** *nmpl* (*COM*) arrears; (*deudas*) deficit *sg*, debts; **llegar con ~** to arrive late; **llegar con 25 minutos de ~** to be 25 minutes late; **llevo un ~ de 6 semanas** I'm 6 weeks behind (with my work *etc*); **~ mental** mental deficiency.

retratar [retra'tar] *vt* (*ARTE*) to paint the portrait of; (*fotografiar*) to photograph; (*fig*) to depict, describe; **~se** *vr* to have one's portrait painted; to have one's photograph taken.

retratista [retra'tista] *nmf* (*pintura*) (portrait) painter; (*FOTO*) photographer.

retrato [re'trato] *nm* portrait; (*FOTO*) photograph; (*descripción*) portrayal, depiction; (*fig*) likeness; **ser el vivo ~ de** to be the spitting image of.

retrato-robot [re'tratoro'βo(t)], *pl* **retratos-robot** *nm* identikit picture.

retrayendo [retra'jendo] *etc vb V* **retraerse**.

retreta [re'treta] *nf* retreat.

retrete [re'trete] *nm* toilet.

retribución [retriβu'θjon] *nf* (*recompensa*) reward; (*pago*) pay, payment.

retribuir [retriβu'ir] *vt* (*recompensar*) to reward; (*pagar*) to pay.

retribuyendo [retriβu'jendo] *etc vb V* **retribuir**.

retro... [retro] *pref* retro....

retroactivo, a [retroak'tiβo, a] *adj* retroactive, retrospective; **dar efecto ~ a un pago** to backdate a payment.

retroalimentación [retroalimenta'θjon] *nf* (*INFORM*) feedback.

retroceder [retroθe'ðer] *vi* (*echarse atrás*) to move back(wards); (*fig*) to back down; **no ~** to stand firm; **la policía hizo ~ a la multitud** the police forced the crowd back.

retroceso [retro'θeso] *nm* backward movement; (*MED*) relapse; (*COM*) recession, depression; (*fig*) backing down.

retrógrado, a [re'troɣraðo, a] *adj* retrograde, retrogressive; (*POL*) reactionary.

retropropulsión [retropropul'sjon] *nf* jet propulsion.

retrospectivo, a [retrospek'tiβo, a] *adj* retrospective; **mirada retrospectiva** backward glance.

retrovisor [retroβi'sor] *nm* rear-view mirror.

retuerce [re'twerθe] *etc*, **retuerza** [re'twerθa] *etc vb V* **retorcer**.

retumbante [retum'bante] *adj* resounding.

retumbar [retum'bar] *vi* to echo, resound; (*continuamente*) to reverberate.

retuve [re'tuβe] *etc vb V* **retener**.

reuma ['reuma] *nm* rheumatism.

reumático, a [reu'matiko, a] *adj* rheumatic.

reumatismo [reuma'tismo] *nm* rheumatism.

reunificar [reunifi'kar] *vt* to reunify.

reunifique [reuni'fike] *etc vb V* **reunificar**.

reunión [reu'njon] *nf* (*asamblea*) meeting; (*fiesta*) party; **~ en la cumbre** summit meeting; **~ de ventas** (*COM*) sales meeting.

reunir [reu'nir] *vt* (*juntar*) to reunite, join (together); (*recoger*) to gather (together); (*personas*) to bring *o* get together; (*cualidades*) to combine; **~se** *vr* (*personas: en asamblea*) to meet, gather; **reunió a sus amigos para discutirlo** he got his friends together to talk it over.

reválida [re'βaliða] *nf* (*ESCOL*) final examination.

revalidar [reβali'ðar] *vt* (*ratificar*) to confirm, ratify.

revalorar [reβalo'rar] *vt* to revalue, reassess.

revalor(iz)ación [reβalor(iθ)a'θjon] *nf*

revaluation; (*ECON*) reassessment.

revancha [re'ßantʃa] *nf* revenge; (*DEPORTE*) return match; (*BOXEO*) return fight.

revelación [reßela'θjon] *nf* revelation.

revelado [reße'laðo] *nm* developing.

revelador, a [reßela'ðor, a] *adj* revealing.

revelar [reße'lar] *vt* to reveal; (*secreto*) to disclose; (*mostrar*) to show; (*FOTO*) to develop.

revendedor, a [reßende'ðor, a] *nm/f* retailer; (*pey*) ticket tout.

revendré [reßen'dre] *etc,* **revenga** [re'ßenga] *etc vb V* **revenirse.**

revenirse [reße'nirse] *vr* to shrink; (*comida*) to go bad *o* off; (*vino*) to sour; (*CULIN*) to get tough.

reventa [re'ßenta] *nf* resale; (*especulación*) speculation; (*de entradas*) touting.

reventar [reßen'tar] *vt* to burst, explode; (*molestar*) to annoy, rile ♦ *vi,* ~**se** *vr* (*estallar*) to burst, explode; **me revienta tener que ponérmelo** I hate having to wear it; ~ **de** (*fig*) to be bursting with; ~ **por** to be bursting to.

reventón [reßen'ton] *nm* (*AUTO*) blow-out (*BRIT*), flat (*US*).

reverberación [reßerßera'θjon] *nf* reverberation.

reverberar [reßerße'rar] *vi* (*luz*) to play, be reflected; (*superficie*) to shimmer; (*nieve*) to glare; (*sonido*) to reverberate.

reverbero [reßer'ßero] *nm* play; shimmer, shine; glare; reverberation.

reverencia [reße'renθja] *nf* reverence; (*inclinación*) bow.

reverenciar [reßeren'θjar] *vt* to revere.

reverendo, a [reße'rendo, a] *adj* reverend; (*fam*) big, awful; **un ~ imbécil** an awful idiot.

reverente [reße'rente] *adj* reverent.

reversible [reßer'sißle] *adj* reversible.

reverso [re'ßerso] *nm* back, other side; (*de moneda*) reverse.

revertir [reßer'tir] *vi* to revert; ~ **en beneficio de** to be to the advantage of; ~ **en perjuicio de** to be to the detriment of.

revés [re'ßes] *nm* back, wrong side; (*fig*) reverse, setback; (*DEPORTE*) backhand; **al ~** the wrong way round; (*de arriba abajo*) upside down; (*ropa*) inside out; **y al ~** and vice versa; **volver algo al ~** to turn sth round; (*ropa*) to turn sth inside out; **los reveses de la fortuna** the blows of fate.

revestir [reßes'tir] *vt* (*poner*) to put on; (*cubrir*) to cover, coat; (*cualidad*) to have, possess; ~**se** *vr* (*REL*) to put on one's vestments; (*ponerse*) to put on; ~ **con** *o*

de to arm o.s. with; **el acto revestía gran solemnidad** the ceremony had great dignity.

reviejo, a [re'ßjexo, a] *adj* very old, ancient.

reviene [re'ßjene] *etc vb V* **revenirse.**

reviente [re'ßjente] *etc vb V* **reventar.**

revierta [re'ßjerta] *etc vb V* **revertir.**

reviniendo [reßi'njendo] *etc vb V* **revenirse.**

revirtiendo [reßir'tjendo] *etc vb V* **revertir.**

revisar [reßi'sar] *vt* (*examinar*) to check; (*texto etc*) to revise; (*JUR*) to review.

revisión [reßi'sjon] *nf* revision; ~ **aduanera** customs inspection; ~ **de cuentas** audit.

revisor, a [reßi'sor, a] *nm/f* inspector; (*FERRO*) ticket collector; ~ **de cuentas** auditor.

revista [re'ßista] *etc vb V* **revestir** ♦ *nf* magazine, review; (*sección*) section, page; (*TEAT*) revue; (*inspección*) inspection; ~ **literaria** literary review; ~ **de libros** book reviews (page); **pasar ~ a** to review, inspect.

revivir [reßi'ßir] *vt* (*recordar*) to revive memories of ♦ *vi* to revive.

revocación [reßoka'θjon] *nf* repeal.

revocar [reßo'kar] *vt* (*decisión*) to revoke; (*ARQ*) to plaster.

revolcar [reßol'kar] *vt* to knock down, send flying; ~**se** *vr* to roll about.

revolcón [reßol'kon] *nm* tumble.

revolotear [reßolote'ar] *vi* to flutter.

revoloteo [reßolo'teo] *nm* fluttering.

revolqué [reßol'ke], **revolquemos** [reßol'kemos] *etc vb V* **revolcar.**

revoltijo [reßol'tixo] *nm* mess, jumble.

revoltoso, a [reßol'toso, a] *adj* (*travieso*) naughty, unruly.

revolución [reßolu'θjon] *nf* revolution.

revolucionar [reßoluθjo'nar] *vt* to revolutionize.

revolucionario, a [reßoluθjo'narjo, a] *adj, nm/f* revolutionary.

revolver [reßol'ßer] *vt* (*desordenar*) to disturb, mess up; (*agitar*) to shake; (*líquido*) to stir; (*mover*) to move about; (*POL*) to stir up ♦ *vi*: ~ **en** to go through, rummage (about) in; ~**se** *vr* (*en cama*) to toss and turn; (*METEOROLOGÍA*) to break, turn stormy; ~**se contra** to turn on *o* against; **han revuelto toda la casa** they've turned the whole house upside down.

revólver [re'ßolßer] *nm* revolver.

revoque [re'ßoke] *etc vb V* **revocar.**

revuelco [re'ßwelko] *etc vb V* **revolcar.**

revuelo [re'ßwelo] *nm* fluttering; (*fig*) commotion; **armar** *o* **levantar un gran ~**

to cause a great stir.
revuelque [re'ßwelke] *etc vb V* **revolcar**.
revuelto, a [re'ßwelto, a] *pp de* **revolver**
♦ *adj* (*mezclado*) mixed-up, in disorder;
(*mar*) rough; (*tiempo*) unsettled ♦ *nf*
(*motín*) revolt; (*agitación*) commotion;
todo estaba ~ everything was in
disorder *o* was topsy-turvy.
revuelva [re'ßwelßa] *etc vb V* **revolver**.
revulsivo [reßul'sißo] *nm*: **servir de ~** to
have a salutary effect.
rey [rei] *nm* king; **los R~es** the King and
Queen; *V tb* **Baraja Española**.

---

*The night before the 6th of January (the
Epiphany), which is a holiday in Spain,
children go to bed expecting* **los Reyes
Magos**, *the Three Wise Men who visited the
baby Jesus, to bring them presents. Twelfth
night processions, known as* **cabalgatas**,
*take place that evening, when 3 people
dressed as* **los Reyes Magos** *arrive in the
town by land or sea to the delight of the
children.*

---

reyerta [re'jerta] *nf* quarrel, brawl.
rezagado, a [reθa'ɣaðo, a] *adj*: **quedar ~** to
be left behind; (*estar retrasado*) to be
late, be behind ♦ *nm/f* straggler.
rezagar [reθa'ɣar] *vt* (*dejar atrás*) to leave
behind; (*retrasar*) to delay, postpone; **~se**
vr (*atrasarse*) to fall behind.
rezague [re'θaɣe] *etc vb V* **rezagar**.
rezar [re'θar] *vi* to pray; **~ con** (*fam*) to
concern, have to do with.
rezo [re'θo] *nm* prayer.
rezongar [reθon'gar] *vi* to grumble;
(*murmurar*) to mutter; (*refunfuñar*) to
growl.
rezongue [re'θonge] *etc vb V* **rezongar**.
rezumar [reθu'mar] *vt* to ooze ♦ *vi* to leak;
~se *vr* to leak out.
RFA *nf abr* = **República Federal Alemana**.
ría ['ria] *nf* estuary.
riachuelo [rja'tʃwelo] *nm* stream.
riada [ri'aða] *nf* flood.
ribera [ri'ßera] *nf* (*de río*) bank; (: *área*)
riverside.
ribete [ri'ßete] *nm* (*de vestido*) border; (*fig*)
addition.
ribetear [rißete'ar] *vt* to edge, border.
rice ['riθe] *etc vb V* **rizar**.
ricino [ri'θino] *nm*: **aceite de ~** castor oil.
rico, a ['riko, a] *adj* (*adinerado*) rich,
wealthy; (*lujoso*) luxurious; (*comida*)
delicious; (*niño*) lovely, cute ♦ *nm/f* rich
person; **nuevo ~** nouveau riche.

de amargura bitter smile.
ridiculez [riðiku'leθ] *nf* absurdity.
ridiculice [riðiku'liθe] *etc vb V* **ridiculizar**.
ridiculizar [riðikuli'θar] *vt* to ridicule.
ridículo, a [ri'ðikulo, a] *adj* ridiculous;
hacer el ~ to make a fool of o.s.; **poner a
algn en ~** to make a fool of sb; **ponerse
en ~** to make a fool *o* laughing-stock of
o.s.
riego ['rjeɣo] *etc vb V* **regar** ♦ *nm*
(*aspersión*) watering; (*irrigación*)
irrigation.
riegue ['rjeɣe] *etc vb V* **regar**.
riel [rjel] *nm* rail.
rienda ['rjenda] *nf* rein; (*fig*) restraint,
moderating influence; **dar ~ suelta a** to
give free rein to; **llevar las ~s** to be in
charge.
riendo ['rjendo] *vb V* **reír**.
riesgo ['rjesɣo] *nm* risk; **seguro a *o* contra
todo ~** comprehensive insurance; **~
para la salud** health hazard; **correr el ~
de** to run the risk of.
Rif [rif] *nm* Rif(f).
rifa ['rifa] *nf* (*lotería*) raffle.
rifar [ri'far] *vt* to raffle.
rifeño, a [ri'feɲo, a] *adj* of the Rif(f),
Rif(f)ian ♦ *nm/f* Rif(f)ian, Rif(f).
rifle ['rifle] *nm* rifle.
rigidez [rixi'ðeθ] *nf* rigidity, stiffness; (*fig*)
strictness.
rígido, a ['rixiðo, a] *adj* rigid, stiff;
(*moralmente*) strict, inflexible; (*cara*)
wooden, expressionless.
rigiendo [ri'xjendo] *etc vb V* **regir**.
rigor [ri'ɣor] *nm* strictness, rigour; (*dureza*)
toughness; (*inclemencia*) harshness;
(*meticulosidad*) accuracy; **el ~ del verano**
the hottest part of the summer; **con
todo ~ científico** with scientific
precision; **de ~** de rigueur, essential;
después de los saludos de ~ after the
inevitable greetings.
riguroso, a [riɣu'roso, a] *adj* rigorous;
(*METEOROLOGÍA*) harsh; (*severo*) severe.
rija ['rixa] *etc vb V* **regir** ♦ *nf* quarrel.
rima ['rima] *nf* rhyme; **~s** *nfpl* verse *sg*; **~
imperfecta** assonance; **~ rimando** (*fam*)
merrily.
rimar [ri'mar] *vi* to rhyme.
rimbombante [rimbom'bante] *adj* (*fig*)
pompous.
rímel, rímmel ['rimel] *nm* mascara.
rimero [ri'mero] *nm* stack, pile.
Rin [rin] *nm* Rhine.
rincón [rin'kon] *nm* corner (*inside*).
rindiendo [rin'djendo] *etc vb V* **rendir**.
ring [riŋ] *nm* (*BOXEO*) ring.

rinoceronte [rinoθe'ronte] *nm* rhinoceros.
riña ['riɲa] *nf (disputa)* argument; *(pelea)* brawl.
riñendo [ri'ɲendo] *etc vb V* **reñir.**
riñón [ri'ɲon] *nm* kidney; **me costó un ~** *(fam)* it cost me an arm and a leg; **tener riñones** to have guts.
río ['rio] *etc vb V* **reír** ♦ *nm* river; *(fig)* torrent, stream; **~ abajo/arriba** downstream/upstream; **cuando el ~ suena, agua lleva** there's no smoke without fire.
rió [ri'o] *vb V* **reír.**
Río de Janeiro ['rioðexa'neiro] *nm* Rio de Janeiro.
Río de la Plata ['rioðela'plata] *nm* Rio de la Plata, River Plate.
Rioja [ri'oxa] *nf*: **La ~** La Rioja ♦ *nm*: **r~** rioja wine.
riojano, a [rjo'xano, a] *adj, nm/f* Riojan.
rioplatense [riopla'tense] *adj* of *o* from the River Plate region ♦ *nm/f* native *o* inhabitant of the River Plate region.
riqueza [ri'keθa] *nf* wealth, riches *pl*; *(cualidad)* richness.
risa ['risa] *nf* laughter; *(una ~)* laugh; **¡qué ~!** what a laugh!; **caerse o morirse de ~** to split one's sides laughing, die laughing; **tomar algo a ~** to laugh sth off.
risco ['risko] *nm* crag, cliff.
risible [ri'siβle] *adj* ludicrous, laughable.
risotada [riso'taða] *nf* guffaw, loud laugh.
ristra ['ristra] *nf* string.
ristre ['ristre] *nm*: **en ~** at the ready.
risueño, a [ri'sweɲo, a] *adj (sonriente)* smiling; *(contento)* cheerful.
ritmo ['ritmo] *nm* rhythm; **a ~ lento** slowly; **trabajar a ~ lento** to go slow.
rito ['rito] *nm* rite.
ritual [ri'twal] *adj, nm* ritual.
rival [ri'βal] *adj, nm/f* rival.
rivalice [riβa'liθe] *etc vb V* **rivalizar.**
rivalidad [riβali'ðað] *nf* rivalry, competition.
rivalizar [riβali'θar] *vi*: **~ con** to rival, compete with.
rizado, a [ri'θaðo, a] *adj (pelo)* curly; *(superficie)* ridged; *(terreno)* undulating; *(mar)* choppy ♦ *nm* curls *pl*.
rizar [ri'θar] *vt* to curl; **~se** *vr (el pelo)* to curl; *(agua)* to ripple; *(el mar)* to become choppy.
rizo ['riθo] *nm* curl; *(agua)* ripple.
Rma. *abr (= Reverendísima) courtesy title.*
Rmo. *abr (= Reverendísimo)* Rt. Rev.
RNE *nf abr = Radio Nacional de España.*
R. O. *abr (=Real Orden)* royal order.

robar [ro'βar] *vt* to rob; *(objeto)* to steal; *(casa etc)* to break into; *(NAIPES)* to draw; *(atención)* to steal, capture; *(paciencia)* to exhaust.
roble ['roβle] *nm* oak.
robledal [roβle'ðal]**, robledo** [ro'βleðo] *nm* oakwood.
robo ['roβo] *nm* robbery, theft; *(objeto robado)* stolen article *o* goods *pl*; **¡esto es un ~!** this is daylight robbery!
robot [ro'βo(t)], *pl* **robots** *adj, nm* robot ♦ *nm (tb*: **~ de cocina)** food processor.
robótica [ro'βotika] *nf* robotics *sg.*
robustecer [roβuste'θer] *vt* to strengthen.
robustezca [roβus'teθka] *etc vb V* **robustecer.**
robusto, a [ro'βusto, a] *adj* robust, strong.
ROC *abr (INFORM*: = *reconocimiento óptico de caracteres)* OCR.
roca ['roka] *nf* rock; **la R~** the Rock (of Gibraltar).
roce ['roθe] *etc vb V* **rozar** ♦ *nm* rub, rubbing; *(caricia)* brush; *(TEC)* friction; *(en la piel)* graze; **tener ~ con** to have a brush with.
rociar [ro'θjar] *vt* to sprinkle, spray.
rocín [ro'θin] *nm* nag, hack.
rocío [ro'θio] *nm* dew.
rock [rok] *adj inv, nm (MUS)* rock *(cpd).*
rockero, a [ro'kero, a] *adj* rock *cpd* ♦ *nm/f* rocker.
rocoso, a [ro'koso, a] *adj* rocky.
rodado, a [ro'ðaðo, a] *adj (con ruedas)* wheeled ♦ *nf* rut.
rodaja [ro'ðaxa] *nf (raja)* slice.
rodaje [ro'ðaxe] *nm (CINE)* shooting, filming; *(AUTO)*: **en ~** running in.
rodamiento [roða'mjento] *nm (AUTO)* tread.
Ródano ['roðano] *nm* Rhône.
rodar [ro'ðar] *vt (vehículo)* to wheel (along); *(escalera)* to roll down; *(viajar por)* to travel (over) ♦ *vi* to roll; *(coche)* to go, run; *(CINE)* to shoot, film; *(persona)* to move about (from place to place), drift; **echarlo todo a ~** *(fig)* to mess it all up.
Rodas ['roðas] *nf* Rhodes.
rodear [roðe'ar] *vt* to surround ♦ *vi* to go round; **~se** *vr*: **~se de amigos** to surround o.s. with friends.
rodeo [ro'ðeo] *nm (ruta indirecta)* long way round, roundabout way; *(desvío)* detour; *(evasión)* evasion; *(AM)* rodeo; **dejarse de ~s** to talk straight; **hablar sin ~s** to come to the point, speak plainly.
rodilla [ro'ðiʎa] *nf* knee; **de ~s** kneeling.
rodillo [ro'ðiʎo] *nm* roller; *(CULIN)* rolling-pin; *(en máquina de escribir, impresora)*

platen.

rododendro [roðo'ðendro] *nm* rhododendron.

roedor, a [roe'ðor, a] *adj* gnawing ♦ *nm* rodent.

roer [ro'er] *vt* (*masticar*) to gnaw; (*corroer, fig*) to corrode.

rogar [ro'ɣar] *vt* (*pedir*) to beg, ask for ♦ *vi* (*suplicar*) to beg, plead; **~se** *vr*: **se ruega no fumar** please do not smoke; **~ que** + *subjun* to ask to ...; **ruegue a este señor que nos deje en paz** please ask this gentleman to leave us alone; **no se hace de ~** he doesn't have to be asked twice.

rogué [ro'ɣe], **roguemos** [ro'ɣemos] *etc vb V* **rogar**.

rojizo, a [ro'xiθo, a] *adj* reddish.

rojo, a ['roxo, a] *adj* red ♦ *nm* red (colour); (*POL*) red; **ponerse ~** to turn red, blush; **al ~ vivo** red-hot.

rol [rol] *nm* list, roll; (*esp AM: papel*) role.

rollizo, a [ro'ʎiθo, a] *adj* (*objeto*) cylindrical; (*persona*) plump.

rollo, a ['roʎo, a] *adj* (*fam*) boring, tedious ♦ *nm* roll; (*de cuerda*) coil; (*madera*) log; (*fam*) bore; (*discurso*) boring speech; **¡qué ~!** what a carry-on!; **la conferencia fue un ~** the lecture was a big drag.

ROM [rom] *nf abr* (= *memoria de sólo lectura*) ROM.

Roma ['roma] *nf* Rome; **por todas partes se va a ~** all roads lead to Rome.

romance [ro'manθe] *nm* (*LING*) Romance language; (*LIT*) ballad; **hablar en ~** to speak plainly.

románico, a [ro'maniko, a] *adj, nm* Romanesque.

romano, a [ro'mano, a] *adj* Roman, of Rome ♦ *nm/f* Roman.

romanticismo [romanti'θismo] *nm* romanticism.

romántico, a [ro'mantiko, a] *adj* romantic.

rombo ['rombo] *nm* (*GEOM*) rhombus; (*diseño*) diamond; (*TIP*) lozenge.

romería [rome'ria] *nf* (*REL*) pilgrimage; (*excursión*) trip, outing.

Originally a pilgrimage to a shrine or church to express devotion to Our Lady or a local Saint, the **romería** *has also become a rural fiesta which accompanies the pilgrimage. People come from all over to attend, bringing their own food and drink, and spend the day in celebration.*

romero, a [ro'mero, a] *nm/f* pilgrim ♦ *nm* rosemary.

romo, a ['romo, a] *adj* blunt; (*fig*) dull.

rompecabezas [rompeka'βeθas] *nm inv* riddle, puzzle; (*juego*) jigsaw (puzzle).

rompehielos [rompe'jelos] *nm inv* icebreaker.

rompeolas [rompe'olas] *nm inv* breakwater.

romper [rom'per] *vt* to break; (*hacer pedazos*) to smash; (*papel, tela etc*) to tear, rip; (*relaciones*) to break off ♦ *vi* (*olas*) to break; (*sol, diente*) to break through; **~ un contrato** to break a contract; **~ a** to start (suddenly) to; **~ a llorar** to burst into tears; **~ con algn** to fall out with sb; **ha roto con su novio** she has broken up with her fiancé.

rompimiento [rompi'mjento] *nm* (*acto*) breaking; (*fig*) break; (*quiebra*) crack; **~ de relaciones** breaking off of relations.

ron [ron] *nm* rum.

roncar [ron'kar] *vi* (*al dormir*) to snore; (*animal*) to roar.

roncha ['rontʃa] *nf* (*cardenal*) bruise; (*hinchazón*) swelling.

ronco, a ['ronko, a] *adj* (*afónico*) hoarse; (*áspero*) raucous.

ronda ['ronda] *nf* (*de bebidas etc*) round; (*patrulla*) patrol; (*de naipes*) hand, game; **ir de ~** to do one's round.

rondar [ron'dar] *vt* to patrol; (*a una persona*) to hang round; (*molestar*) to harass; (*a una chica*) to court ♦ *vi* to patrol; (*fig*) to prowl round; (*MUS*) to go serenading.

rondeño, a [ron'deɲo, a] *adj* of o from Ronda ♦ *nm/f* native o inhabitant of Ronda.

ronque ['ronke] *etc vb V* **roncar**.

ronquera [ron'kera] *nf* hoarseness.

ronquido [ron'kiðo] *nm* snore, snoring.

ronronear [ronrone'ar] *vi* to purr.

ronroneo [ronro'neo] *nm* purr.

roña ['roɲa] *nf* (*veterinaria*) mange; (*mugre*) dirt, grime; (*óxido*) rust.

roñica [ro'ɲika] *nm/f* (*fam*) skinflint.

roñoso, a [ro'ɲoso, a] *adj* (*mugriento*) filthy; (*tacaño*) mean.

ropa ['ropa] *nf* clothes *pl*, clothing; **~ blanca** linen; **~ de cama** bed linen; **~ interior** underwear; **~ lavada** o **para lavar** washing; **~ planchada** ironing; **~ sucia** dirty clothes *pl*, washing; **~ usada** secondhand clothes.

ropaje [ro'paxe] *nm* gown, robes *pl*.

ropero [ro'pero] *nm* linen cupboard; (*guardarropa*) wardrobe.

roque ['roke] *nm* (*AJEDREZ*) rook, castle; **estar ~** to be fast asleep.

rosa ['rosa] *adj inv* pink ♦ *nf* rose; (*ANAT*)

red birthmark; ~ **de los vientos** the
compass; **estar como una** ~ to feel as
fresh as a daisy; **(color) de** ~ pink.

rosado, a [ro'saðo, a] *adj* pink ♦ *nm* rosé.

rosal [ro'sal] *nm* rosebush.

rosaleda [rosa'leða] *nf* rose bed *o* garden.

rosario [ro'sarjo] *nm* (*REL*) rosary; (*fig:
serie*) string; **rezar el** ~ to say the rosary.

rosbif [ros'βif] *nm* roast beef.

rosca ['roska] *nf* (*de tornillo*) thread; (*de
humo*) coil, spiral; (*pan, postre*) ring-
shaped roll/pastry; **hacer la** ~ **a algn**
(*fam*) to suck up to sb; **pasarse de** ~ (*fig*)
to go too far.

Rosellón [rose'ʎon] *nm* Roussillon.

rosetón [rose'ton] *nm* rosette; (*ARQ*) rose
window.

rosquilla [ros'kiʎa] *nf small ring-shaped
cake*; (*de humo*) ring.

rosticería [rostise'ria] *nf* (*AM*) *roast
chicken shop*.

rostro ['rostro] *nm* (*cara*) face; (*fig*) cheek.

rotación [rota'θjon] *nf* rotation; ~ **de
cultivos** crop rotation.

rotativo, a [rota'tiβo, a] *adj* rotary ♦ *nm*
newspaper.

roto, a ['roto, a] *pp de* **romper** ♦ *adj* broken;
(*en pedazos*) smashed; (*tela, papel*) torn;
(*vida*) shattered ♦ *nm* (*en vestido*) hole,
tear.

rótula ['rotula] *nf* kneecap; (*TEC*) ball-and-
socket joint.

rotulador [rotula'ðor] *nm* felt-tip pen.

rotular [rotu'lar] *vt* (*carta, documento*) to
head, entitle; (*objeto*) to label.

rótulo ['rotulo] *nm* (*título*) heading, title;
(*etiqueta*) label; (*letrero*) sign.

rotundo, a [ro'tundo, a] *adj* round;
(*enfático*) emphatic.

rotura [ro'tura] *nf* (*rompimiento*) breaking;
(*MED*) fracture.

roturar [rotu'rar] *vt* to plough.

roulote [ru'lote] *nf* caravan (*BRIT*), trailer
(*US*).

rozado, a [ro'θaðo, a] *adj* worn.

rozadura [roθa'ðura] *nf* abrasion, graze.

rozar [ro'θar] *vt* (*frotar*) to rub; (*ensuciar*) to
dirty; (*MED*) to graze; (*tocar ligeramente*)
to shave, skim; (*fig*) to touch *o* border
on; ~**se** *vr* to rub (together); ~ **con** (*fam*)
to rub shoulders with.

Rte. *abr* = **remite, remitente.**

RTVE *nf abr* (*TV*) = *Radiotelevisión Española.*

Ruán [ru'an] *nm* Rouen.

rubéola [ru'βeola] *nf* German measles,
rubella.

rubí [ru'βi] *nm* ruby; (*de reloj*) jewel.

rubio, a ['ruβjo, a] *adj* fair-haired, blond(e)

♦ *nm/f* blond/blonde; **tabaco** ~ Virginia
tobacco; **(cerveza) rubia** lager.

rubor [ru'βor] *nm* (*sonrojo*) blush; (*timidez*)
bashfulness.

ruborice [ruβo'riθe] *etc vb V* **ruborizarse.**

ruborizarse [ruβori'θarse] *vr* to blush.

ruboroso, a [ruβo'roso, a] *adj* blushing.

rúbrica ['ruβrika] *nf* (*título*) title, heading;
(*de la firma*) flourish; **bajo la** ~ **de** under
the heading of.

rubricar [ruβri'kar] *vt* (*firmar*) to sign with
a flourish; (*concluir*) to sign and seal.

rubrique [ru'βrike] *etc vb V* **rubricar.**

rudeza [ru'ðeθa] *nf* (*tosquedad*) coarseness;
(*sencillez*) simplicity.

rudimentario, a [ruðimen'tarjo, a] *adj*
rudimentary, basic.

rudo, a ['ruðo, a] *adj* (*sin pulir*) unpolished;
(*grosero*) coarse; (*violento*) violent;
(*sencillo*) simple.

rueda ['rweða] *nf* wheel; (*círculo*) ring,
circle; (*rodaja*) slice, round; (*en
impresora etc*) sprocket; ~ **delantera/
trasera/de repuesto** front/back/spare
wheel; ~ **impresora** (*INFORM*) print
wheel; ~ **de prensa** press conference.

ruedo ['rweðo] *etc vb V* **rodar** ♦ *nm*
(*contorno*) edge, border; (*de vestido*)
hem; (*círculo*) circle; (*TAUR*) arena,
bullring; (*esterilla*) (round) mat.

ruego ['rweɣo] *etc vb V* **rogar** ♦ *nm* request;
a ~ **de** at the request of; "~**s y
preguntas**" "question and answer
session".

ruegue ['rweɣe] *etc vb V* **rogar.**

rufián [ru'fjan] *nm* scoundrel.

rugby ['ruɣβi] *nm* rugby.

rugido [ru'xiðo] *nm* roar.

rugir [ru'xir] *vi* to roar; (*toro*) to bellow;
(*estómago*) to rumble.

rugoso, a [ru'ɣoso, a] *adj* (*arrugado*)
wrinkled; (*áspero*) rough; (*desigual*)
ridged.

ruibarbo [rwi'βarβo] *nm* rhubarb.

ruido [rwi'ðo] *nm* noise; (*sonido*) sound;
(*alboroto*) racket, row; (*escándalo*)
commotion, rumpus; ~ **de fondo**
background noise; **hacer** *o* **meter** ~ to
cause a stir.

ruidoso, a [rwi'ðoso, a] *adj* noisy, loud;
(*fig*) sensational.

ruin [rwin] *adj* contemptible, mean.

ruina ['rwina] *nf* ruin; (*colapso*) collapse;
(*de persona*) ruin, downfall; **estar hecho
una** ~ to be a wreck; **la empresa le llevó
a la** ~ the venture ruined him
(financially).

ruindad [rwin'dað] *nf* lowness, meanness;

(*acto*) low *o* mean act.
ruinoso, a [rwi'noso, a] *adj* ruinous;
(*destartalado*) dilapidated, tumbledown;
(*COM*) disastrous.
ruiseñor [rwise'ɲor] *nm* nightingale.
ruja ['ruxa] *etc vb V* **rugir**.
ruleta [ru'leta] *nf* roulette.
rulo ['rulo] *nm* (*para el pelo*) curler.
rulot(e) [ru'lot(e)] *nf* caravan (*BRIT*), trailer
(*US*).
Rumania [ru'manja] *nf* Rumania.
rumano, a [ru'mano, a] *adj, nm/f* Rumanian.
rumba ['rumba] *nf* rumba.
rumbo ['rumbo] *nm* (*ruta*) route, direction;
(*ángulo de dirección*) course, bearing;
(*fig*) course of events; **con ~ a** in the
direction of; **ir con ~ a** to be heading
for; (*NAUT*) to be bound for.
rumboso, a [rum'boso, a] *adj* (*generoso*)
generous.
rumiante [ru'mjante] *nm* ruminant.
rumiar [ru'mjar] *vt* to chew; (*fig*) to chew
over ♦ *vi* to chew the cud.
rumor [ru'mor] *nm* (*ruido sordo*) low sound;
(*murmuración*) murmur, buzz.
rumorearse [rumore'arse] *vr*: **se rumorea
que** it is rumoured that.
rumoroso, a [rumo'roso, a] *adj* full of
sounds; (*arroyo*) murmuring.
runrún [run'run] *nm* (*voces*) murmur,
sound of voices; (*fig*) rumour; (*de una
máquina*) whirr.
rupestre [ru'pestre] *adj* rock *cpd*; **pintura ~**
cave painting.
ruptura [rup'tura] *nf* (*gen*) rupture;
(*disputa*) split; (*de contrato*) breach; (*de
relaciones*) breaking-off.
rural [ru'ral] *adj* rural.
Rusia ['rusja] *nf* Russia.
ruso, a ['ruso, a] *adj, nm/f* Russian ♦ *nm*
(*LING*) Russian.
rústico, a ['rustiko, a] *adj* rustic; (*ordinario*)
coarse, uncouth ♦ *nm/f* yokel ♦ *nf*: **libro en
rústica** paperback (book).
ruta ['ruta] *nf* route.
rutina [ru'tina] *nf* routine; **~ diaria** daily
routine; **por ~** as a matter of course.
rutinario, a [ruti'narjo, a] *adj* routine.

S s

S, s ['ese] *nf* S, s; **S de Sábado** S for Sugar.
S *abr* (= *san, santo, a*) St.; (= *sur*) S.
s. *abr* (= *siglo*) c.; (= *siguiente*) foll.
s/ *abr* (*COM*) = **su(s)**.
S.ª *abr* (= *Sierra*) Mts.
S.A. *abr* (= *Sociedad Anónima*) Ltd., Inc.
(*US*); (= *Su Alteza*) H.H.
sáb. *abr* (= *sábado*) Sun.
sábado ['saβaðo] *nm* Saturday; (*de los
judíos*) Sabbath; **del ~ en ocho días** a
week on Saturday; **un ~ sí y otro no,
cada dos ~s** every other Saturday; **S~
Santo** Holy Saturday; *V tb* **Semana
Santa**.
sabana [sa'βana] *nf* savannah.
sábana ['saβana] *nf* sheet; **se le pegan las
~s** he can't get up in the morning.
sabandija [saβan'dixa] *nf* (*bicho*) bug; (*fig*)
louse.
sabañón [saβa'ɲon] *nm* chilblain.
sabático, a [sa'βatiko, a] *adj* (*REL, UNIV*)
sabbatical.
sabelotodo [saβelo'toðo] *nm/f inv* know-all.
saber [sa'βer] *vt* to know; (*llegar a conocer*)
to find out, learn; (*tener capacidad de*) to
know how to ♦ *vi*: **~ a** to taste of, taste
like ♦ *nm* knowledge, learning; **~se** *vr*: **se
sabe que** ... it is known that ...; **no se
sabe** nobody knows; **a ~** namely; **¿sabes
conducir/nadar?** can you drive/swim?;
¿sabes francés? do you *o* can you speak
French?; **~ de memoria** to know by
heart; **lo sé** I know; **hacer ~** to inform,
let know; **que yo sepa** as far as I know;
vete *o* anda a ~ your guess is as good as
mine, who knows!; **¿sabe?** (*fam*) you
know (what I mean)?; **le sabe mal que
otro la saque a bailar** it upsets him that
anybody else should ask her to dance.
sabido, a [sa'βiðo, a] *adj* (*consabido*) well-
known; **como es ~** as we all know.
sabiduría [saβiðu'ria] *nf* (*conocimientos*)
wisdom; (*instrucción*) learning; **~ popular**
folklore.
sabiendas [sa'βjendas]: **a ~** *adv*
knowingly; **a ~ de que** ... knowing full
well that ....
sabihondo, a [sa'βjondo, a] *adj, nm/f*

know-all, know-it-all (US).

sabio, a ['saβjo,a] adj (docto) learned; (prudente) wise, sensible.

sablazo [sa'βlaθo] nm (herida) sword wound; (fam) sponging; **dar un ~ a algn** to tap sb for money.

sable [sa'βle] nm sabre.

sabor [sa'βor] nm taste, flavour; (fig) flavour; **sin ~** flavourless.

saborear [saβore'ar] vt to taste, savour; (fig) to relish.

sabotaje [saβo'taxe] nm sabotage.

saboteador, a [saβotea'ðor, a] nm/f saboteur.

sabotear [saβote'ar] vt to sabotage.

Saboya [sa'βoja] nf Savoy.

sabré [sa'βre] etc vb V **saber**.

sabroso, a [sa'βroso, a] adj tasty; (fig fam) racy, salty.

saca ['saka] nf big sack; **~ de correo(s)** mailbag; (COM) withdrawal.

sacacorchos [saka'kortʃos] nm inv corkscrew.

sacapuntas [saka'puntas] nm inv pencil sharpener.

sacar [sa'kar] vt to take out; (fig: extraer) to get (out); (quitar) to remove, get out; (hacer salir) to bring out; (fondos: de cuenta) to draw out, withdraw; (obtener: legado etc) to get; (demostrar) to show; (conclusión) to draw; (novela etc) to publish, bring out; (ropa) to take off; (obra) to make; (premio) to receive; (entradas) to get; (TENIS) to serve; (FÚTBOL) to put into play; **~ adelante** (niño) to bring up; **~ a algn a bailar** to dance with sb; **~ a algn de sí** to infuriate sb; **~ una foto** to take a photo; **~ la lengua** to stick out one's tongue; **~ buenas/malas notas** to get good/bad marks.

sacarina [saka'rina] nf saccharin(e).

sacerdote [saθer'ðote] nm priest.

saciar [sa'θjar] vt (hartar) to satiate; (fig) to satisfy; **~se** vr (fig) to be satisfied.

saciedad [saθje'ðað] nf satiety; **hasta la ~** (comer) one's fill; (repetir) ad nauseam.

saco ['sako] nm bag; (grande) sack; (su contenido) bagful; (AM: chaqueta) jacket; **~ de dormir** sleeping bag.

sacramento [sakra'mento] nm sacrament.

sacrificar [sakrifi'kar] vt to sacrifice; (animal) to slaughter; (perro etc) to put to sleep; **~se** vr to sacrifice o.s.

sacrificio [sakri'fiθjo] nm sacrifice.

sacrifique [sakri'fike] etc vb V **sacrificar**.

sacrilegio [sakri'lexjo] nm sacrilege.

sacrílego, a [sa'krileɣo, a] adj sacrilegious.

sacristán [sakris'tan] nm verger.

sacristía [sakris'tia] nf sacristy.

sacro, a ['sakro, a] adj sacred.

sacudida [saku'ðiða] nf (agitación) shake, shaking; (sacudimiento) jolt, bump; (fig) violent change; (POL etc) upheaval; **~ eléctrica** electric shock.

sacudir [saku'ðir] vt to shake; (golpear) to hit; (ala) to flap; (alfombra) to beat; **~ a algn** (fam) to belt sb.

sádico, a ['saðiko, a] adj sadistic ♦ nm/f sadist.

sadismo [sa'ðismo] nm sadism.

sadomasoquismo [saðomaso'kismo] nm sadomasochism, S & M.

sadomasoquista [saðomaso'kista] adj sadomasochistic ♦ nm/f sadomasochist.

saeta [sa'eta] nf (flecha) arrow; (MUS) sacred song in flamenco style.

safari [sa'fari] nm safari.

sagacidad [saɣaθi'ðað] nf shrewdness, cleverness.

sagaz [sa'ɣaθ] adj shrewd, clever.

Sagitario [saxi'tarjo] nm (ASTRO) Sagittarius.

sagrado, a [sa'ɣraðo, a] adj sacred, holy.

Sáhara ['saara] nm: **el ~** the Sahara (desert).

saharaui [saxa'rawi] adj Saharan ♦ nm/f native o inhabitant of the Sahara.

sajón, ona [sa'xon, 'xona] adj, nm/f Saxon.

Sajonia [sa'xonja] nf Saxony.

sal [sal] vb ver **salir** ♦ nf salt; (gracia) wit; (encanto) charm; **~es de baño** bath salts; **~ gorda** o **de cocina** kitchen o cooking salt.

sala ['sala] nf (cuarto grande) large room; (~ de estar) living room; (TEAT) house, auditorium; (de hospital) ward; **~ de apelación** court; **~ de conferencias** lecture hall; **~ de espera** waiting room; **~ de embarque** departure lounge; **~ de estar** living room; **~ de fiestas** function room; **~ de juntas** (COM) boardroom.

salado, a [sa'laðo, a] adj salty; (fig) witty, amusing; **agua salada** salt water.

salar [sa'lar] vt to salt, add salt to.

salarial [sala'rjal] adj (aumento, revisión) wage cpd, salary cpd, pay cpd.

salario [sa'larjo] nm wage, pay.

salchicha [sal'tʃitʃa] nf (pork) sausage.

salchichón [saltʃi'tʃon] nm (salami-type) sausage.

saldar [sal'dar] vt to pay; (vender) to sell off; (fig) to settle, resolve.

saldo ['saldo] nm (pago) settlement; (de una cuenta) balance; (lo restante) remnant(s) (pl), remainder; (liquidación) sale; (*COM*): ~ **anterior** balance brought forward; ~ **acreedor/deudor** *o* **pasivo** credit/debit balance; ~ **final** final balance.

saldré [sal'dre] *etc vb V* **salir**.

salero [sa'lero] *nm* salt cellar; (*ingenio*) wit; (*encanto*) charm.

salga ['salɣa] *etc vb V* **salir**.

salida [sa'liða] *nf* (*puerta etc*) exit, way out; (*acto*) leaving, going out; (*de tren*, *AVIAT*) departure; (*COM*, *TEC*) output, production; (*fig*) way out; (*resultado*) outcome; (*COM*: *oportunidad*) opening; (*GEO*, *válvula*) outlet; (*de gas*) escape; (*ocurrencia*) joke; **calle sin ~** cul-de-sac; **a la ~ del teatro** after the theatre; **dar la ~** (*DEPORTE*) to give the starting signal; ~ **de incendios** fire escape; ~ **impresa** (*INFORM*) hard copy; **no hay ~** there's no way out of it; **no tenemos otra ~** we have no option; **tener ~s** to be witty.

salido, a [sa'liðo, a] *adj* (*fam*) randy.

saliente [sa'ljente] *adj* (*ARQ*) projecting; (*sol*) rising; (*fig*) outstanding.

salina [sa'lina] *nf* salt mine; ~**s** *nfpl* saltworks *sg*.

================ *PALABRA CLAVE* ================

salir [sa'lir] *vi* **1** (*persona*) to come *o* go out; (*tren*, *avión*) to leave; **Juan ha salido** Juan has gone out; **salió de la cocina** he came out of the kitchen; **salimos de Madrid a las 8** we left Madrid at 8 (o'clock); **salió corriendo (del cuarto)** he ran out (of the room); ~ **de un apuro** to get out of a jam
2 (*pelo*) to grow; (*diente*) to come through; (*disco*, *libro*) to come out; (*planta*, *número de lotería*) to come up; ~ **a la superficie** to come to the surface; **anoche salió en la tele** she appeared *o* was on TV last night; **salió en todos los periódicos** it was in all the papers; **le salió un trabajo** he got a job
3 (*resultar*): **la muchacha nos salió muy trabajadora** the girl turned out to be a very hard worker; **la comida te ha salido exquisita** the food was delicious; **sale muy caro** it's very expensive; **la entrevista que hice me salió bien/mal** the interview I did turned out *o* went well/badly; **nos salió a 5.000 ptas cada uno** it worked out at 5,000 pesetas each; **no salen las cuentas** it doesn't work out *o* add up; ~ **ganando** to come out on top; ~ **perdiendo** to lose out
4 (*DEPORTE*) to start; (*NAIPES*) to lead
5: ~ **con algn** to go out with sb
6: ~ **adelante: no sé como haré para ~ adelante** I don't know how I'll get by
♦ ~**se** *vr* **1** (*líquido*) to spill; (*animal*) to escape
2 (*desviarse*): ~**se de la carretera** to leave *o* go off the road; ~**se de lo normal** to be unusual; ~**se del tema** to get off the point
3: ~**se con la suya** to get one's own way

saliva [sa'liβa] *nf* saliva.

salivadera [saliβa'ðera] *nf* (*AM*) spittoon.

salmantino, a [salman'tino, a] *adj* of *o* from Salamanca ♦ *nm/f* native *o* inhabitant of Salamanca.

salmo ['salmo] *nm* psalm.

salmón [sal'mon] *nm* salmon.

salmonete [salmo'nete] *nm* red mullet.

salmuera [sal'mwera] *nf* pickle, brine.

salón [sa'lon] *nm* (*de casa*) living-room, lounge; (*muebles*) lounge suite; ~ **de belleza** beauty parlour; ~ **de baile** dance hall; ~ **de sesiones** assembly hall.

salpicadero [salpika'ðero] *nm* (*AUTO*) dashboard.

salpicar [salpi'kar] *vt* (*de barro*, *pintura*) to splash; (*rociar*) to sprinkle, spatter; (*esparcir*) to scatter.

salpicón [salpi'kon] *nm* (*acto*) splashing; (*CULIN*) meat *o* fish salad.

salpimentar [salpimen'tar] *vt* (*CULIN*) to season.

salpique [sal'pike] *etc vb V* **salpicar**.

salsa ['salsa] *nf* sauce; (*con carne asada*) gravy; (*fig*) spice; ~ **mayonesa** mayonnaise; **estar en su ~** (*fam*) to be in one's element.

saltamontes [salta'montes] *nm inv* grasshopper.

saltar [sal'tar] *vt* to jump (over), leap (over); (*dejar de lado*) to skip, miss out
♦ *vi* to jump, leap; (*pelota*) to bounce; (*al aire*) to fly up; (*quebrarse*) to break; (*al agua*) to dive; (*fig*) to explode, blow up; (*botón*) to come off; (*corcho*) to pop out; ~**se** *vr* (*omitir*) to skip, miss; **salta a la vista** it's obvious; ~**se todas las reglas** to break all the rules.

salteado, a [salte'aðo, a] *adj* (*CULIN*) sauté(ed).

salteador [saltea'ðor] *nm* (*tb*: ~ **de caminos**) highwayman.

saltear [salte'ar] *vt* (*robar*) to rob (in a holdup); (*asaltar*) to assault, attack; (*CULIN*) to sauté.

saltimbanqui [saltim'banki] *nm/f* acrobat.

salto ['salto] *nm* jump, leap; (*al agua*) dive; **a ~s** by jumping; ~ **de agua** waterfall; ~ **de altura** high jump; ~ **de cama**

negligee; ~ **mortal** somersault;
(*INFORM*): ~ **de línea** line feed; ~ **de línea
automático** wordwrap; ~ **de página**
formfeed.

saltón, ona [sal'ton, ona] *adj* (*ojos*)
bulging, popping; (*dientes*) protruding.

salubre [sa'luβre] *adj* healthy, salubrious.

salud [sa'luð] *nf* health; **estar bien/mal de
~** to be in good/poor health; **¡(a su) ~!**
cheers!, good health!; **beber a la ~ de** to
drink (to) the health of.

saludable [salu'ðaβle] *adj* (*de buena salud*)
healthy; (*provechoso*) good, beneficial.

saludar [salu'ðar] *vt* to greet; (*MIL*) to
salute; **ir a ~ a algn** to drop in to see sb;
salude de mi parte a X give my regards
to X; **le saluda atentamente** (*en carta*)
yours faithfully.

saludo [sa'luðo] *nm* greeting; **~s** (*en carta*)
best wishes, regards; **un ~ afectuoso** *o*
cordial yours sincerely.

salva ['salβa] *nf* (*MIL*) salvo; **una ~ de
aplausos** thunderous applause.

salvación [salβa'θjon] *nf* salvation;
(*rescate*) rescue.

salvado [sal'βaðo] *nm* bran.

salvador [salβa'ðor] *nm* rescuer, saviour;
el S~ the Saviour; **El S~** El Salvador;
San S~ San Salvador.

salvadoreño, a [salβaðo'reɲo, a] *adj*, *nm/f*
Salvadoran, Salvadorian.

salvaguardar [salβaɣwar'ðar] *vt* to
safeguard; (*INFORM*) to back up, make a
backup copy of.

salvajada [salβa'xaða] *nf* savage deed,
atrocity.

salvaje [sal'βaxe] *adj* wild; (*tribu*) savage.

salvajismo [salβa'xismo] *nm* savagery.

salvamento [salβa'mento] *nm* (*acción*)
rescue; (*de naufragio*) salvage; **~ y
socorrismo** life-saving.

salvar [sal'βar] *vt* (*rescatar*) to save, rescue;
(*resolver*) to overcome, resolve; (*cubrir
distancias*) to cover, travel; (*hacer
excepción*) to except, exclude; (*un barco*)
to salvage; **~se** *vr* to save o.s., escape;
¡sálvese el que pueda! every man for
himself!

salvavidas [salβa'βiðas] *adj inv*: **bote/
chaleco/cinturón ~** lifeboat/lifejacket/
lifebelt.

salvedad [salβe'ðað] *nf* reservation,
qualification; **con la ~ de que ...** with the
proviso that ....

salvia ['salβja] *nf* sage.

salvo, a ['salβo, a] *adj* safe ♦ *prep* except
(for), save; **~ error u omisión** (*COM*)
errors and omissions excepted; **a ~ out**

of danger; **~ que** unless.

salvoconducto [salβokon'dukto] *nm* safe-
conduct.

samba ['samba] *nf* samba.

san [san] *nm* (*apócope de* **santo**) saint; **~
Juan** St. John; *V tb* **Juan.**

sanar [sa'nar] *vt* (*herida*) to heal; (*persona*)
to cure ♦ *vi* (*persona*) to get well,
recover; (*herida*) to heal.

sanatorio [sana'torjo] *nm* sanatorium.

sanción [san'θjon] *nf* sanction.

sancionar [sanθjo'nar] *vt* to sanction.

sancocho [san'kotʃo] *nm* (*AM*) stew.

sandalia [san'dalja] *nf* sandal.

sándalo ['sandalo] *nm* sandal(wood).

sandez [san'deθ] *nf* (*cualidad*) foolishness;
(*acción*) stupid thing; **decir sandeces** to
talk nonsense.

sandía [san'dia] *nf* watermelon.

sandinista [sanði'nista] *adj*, *nm/f*
Sandinist(a).

sandwich ['sandwitʃ], *pl* **sandwichs** *o*
sandwiches *nm* sandwich.

saneamiento [sanea'mjento] *nm*
sanitation.

sanear [sane'ar] *vt* to drain; (*indemnizar*) to
compensate; (*ECON*) to reorganize.

---

*The **Sanfermines** are a week of fiestas in
Pamplona, the capital of Navarre, made
famous by Ernest Hemingway. From the
7th of July, the feast of **San Fermín**, crowds
of mainly young people take to the streets
drinking, singing and dancing. Early in the
morning bulls are released along the
narrow streets leading to the bullring, and
people risk serious injury by running out in
front of them, a custom which is also
typical of many Spanish villages.*

---

sangrante [san'grante] *adj* (*herida*)
bleeding; (*fig*) flagrant.

sangrar [san'grar] *vt*, *vi* to bleed; (*texto*) to
indent.

sangre ['sangre] *nf* blood; **~ fría** sangfroid;
a ~ fría in cold blood.

sangría [san'gria] *nf* (*MED*) bleeding;
(*CULIN*) sangria, sweetened drink of red
wine with fruit, ≈ fruit cup.

sangriento, a [san'grjento, a] *adj* bloody.

sanguijuela [sangi'xwela] *nf* (*ZOOL*, *fig*)
leech.

sanguinario, a [sangi'narjo, a] *adj*
bloodthirsty.

sanguíneo, a [san'gineo, a] *adj* blood *cpd*.

sanguinolento, a [sangino'lento, a] *adj*
(*que echa sangre*) bleeding; (*manchado*)
bloodstained; (*ojos*) bloodshot.

sanidad [sani'ðað] *nf* sanitation; (*calidad de sano*) health, healthiness; ~ **pública** public health (department).

sanitario, a [sani'tarjo, a] *adj* sanitary; (*de la salud*) health *cpd* ♦ *nm*: ~**s** *nmpl* toilets (*BRIT*), restroom *sg* (*US*).

San Marino [sanma'rino] *nm*: (**La República de**) ~ San Marino.

sano, a ['sano, a] *adj* healthy; (*sin daños*) sound; (*comida*) wholesome; (*entero*) whole, intact; ~ **y salvo** safe and sound.

santanderino, a [santande'rino, a] *adj* of *o* from Santander ♦ *nm/f* native *o* inhabitant of Santander.

Santiago [san'tjaɣo] *nm*: ~ (**de Chile**) Santiago.

santiamén [santja'men] *nm*: **en un** ~ in no time at all.

santidad [santi'ðað] *nf* holiness, sanctity.

santificar [santifi'kar] *vt* to sanctify, make holy.

santifique [santi'fike] *etc vb V* **santificar**.

santiguarse [santi'ɣwarse] *vr* to make the sign of the cross.

santigüe [san'tiɣwe] *etc vb V* **santiguarse**.

santo, a ['santo, a] *adj* holy; (*fig*) wonderful, miraculous ♦ *nm/f* saint ♦ *nm* saint's day; **hacer su santa voluntad** to do as one jolly well pleases; **¿a** ~ **de qué ...?** why on earth ...?; **se le fue el** ~ **al cielo** he forgot what he was about to say; ~ **y seña** password.

> As well as celebrating their birthday Spaniards have traditionally celebrated **el santo**, their Saint's day, when the Saint they were called after at birth, eg **San Pedro** or **la Virgen de los Dolores**, is honoured in the Christian calendar. This is a custom which is gradually dying out.

santuario [san'twarjo] *nm* sanctuary, shrine.

saña ['saɲa] *nf* rage, fury.

sapo ['sapo] *nm* toad.

saque ['sake] *etc vb V* **sacar** ♦ *nm* (*TENIS*) service, serve; (*FÚTBOL*) throw-in; ~ **inicial** kick-off; ~ **de esquina** corner (kick); **tener buen** ~ to eat heartily.

saquear [sake'ar] *vt* (*MIL*) to sack; (*robar*) to loot, plunder; (*fig*) to ransack.

saqueo [sa'keo] *nm* sacking; looting, plundering, ransacking.

S.A.R. *abr* (= *Su Alteza Real*) HRH.

sarampión [saram'pjon] *nm* measles *sg*.

sarape [sa'rape] *nm* (*AM*) blanket.

sarcasmo [sar'kasmo] *nm* sarcasm.

sarcástico, a [sar'kastiko, a] *adj* sarcastic.

sarcófago [sar'kofaɣo] *nm* sarcophagus.

sardina [sar'ðina] *nf* sardine.

sardo, a ['sarðo, a] *adj, nm/f* Sardinian.

sardónico, a [sar'ðoniko, a] *adj* sardonic; (*irónico*) ironical, sarcastic.

sargento [sar'xento] *nm* sergeant.

sarmiento [sar'mjento] *nm* vine shoot.

sarna ['sarna] *nf* itch; (*MED*) scabies.

sarpullido [sarpu'ʎiðo] *nm* (*MED*) rash.

sarro ['sarro] *nm* deposit; (*en dientes*) tartar.

sarta ['sarta] *nf* (*fig*): **una** ~ **de mentiras** a pack of lies.

sartén [sar'ten] *nf* frying pan; **tener la** ~ **por el mango** to rule the roost.

sastre ['sastre] *nm* tailor.

sastrería [sastre'ria] *nf* (*arte*) tailoring; (*tienda*) tailor's (shop).

Satanás [sata'nas] *nm* Satan.

satélite [sa'telite] *nm* satellite.

satinado, a [sati'naðo, a] *adj* glossy ♦ *nm* gloss, shine.

sátira ['satira] *nf* satire.

satírico, a [sa'tiriko, a] *adj* satiric(al).

sátiro ['satiro] *nm* (*MITOLOGÍA*) satyr; (*fig*) sex maniac.

satisfacción [satisfak'θjon] *nf* satisfaction.

satisfacer [satisfa'θer] *vt* to satisfy; (*gastos*) to meet; (*deuda*) to pay; (*COM*: *letra de cambio*) to honour (*BRIT*), honor (*US*); (*pérdida*) to make good; ~**se** *vr* to satisfy o.s., be satisfied; (*vengarse*) to take revenge.

satisfaga [satis'faɣa] *etc*, **satisfaré** [satisfa're] *etc vb V* **satisfacer**.

satisfecho, a [satis'fetʃo, a] *pp de* **satisfacer** ♦ *adj* satisfied; (*contento*) content(ed), happy; (*tb*: ~ **de sí mismo**) self-satisfied, smug.

satisfice [satis'fiθe] *etc vb V* **satisfacer**.

saturación [satura'θjon] *nf* saturation; **llegar a la** ~ to reach saturation point.

saturar [satu'rar] *vt* to saturate; ~**se** *vr* (*mercado, aeropuerto*) to reach saturation point; **¡estoy saturado de tanta televisión!** I can't take any more television!

sauce ['sauθe] *nm* willow; ~ **llorón** weeping willow.

saúco [sa'uko] *nm* (*BOT*) elder.

saudí [sau'ði] *adj, nm/f* Saudi.

sauna ['sauna] *nf* sauna.

savia ['saβja] *nf* sap.

saxo ['sakso] *nm* sax.

saxofón [sakso'fon] *nm* saxophone.

saya ['saja] *nf* (*falda*) skirt; (*enagua*) petticoat.

sayo ['sajo] *nm* smock.

sazón [sa'θon] nf (de fruta) ripeness; **a la ~** then, at that time.
sazonado, a [saθo'naðo, a] adj (fruta) ripe; (CULIN) flavoured, seasoned.
sazonar [saθo'nar] vt to ripen; (CULIN) to flavour, season.
s/c abr (COM: = su casa) your firm; (: = su cuenta) your account.
Sdo. abr (COM: = Saldo) bal.
SE abr (= sudeste) SE.

=========== PALABRA CLAVE

se [se] pron **1** (reflexivo: sg: m) himself; (: f) herself; (: pl) themselves; (: cosa) itself; (: de Vd) yourself; (: de Vds) yourselves; (indefinido) oneself; **~ mira en el espejo** he looks at himself in the mirror; **¡siénte~!** sit down!; **~ durmió** he fell asleep; **~ está preparando** she's getting (herself) ready; para usos léxicos del pron ver el vb en cuestión, p.ej. **arrepentirse**
2 (como complemento indirecto) to him; to her; to them; to it; to you; **~ lo dije ayer** (a Vd) I told you yesterday; **~ compró un sombrero** he bought himself a hat; **~ rompió la pierna** he broke his leg; **cortar~ el pelo** to get one's hair cut; (uno mismo) to cut one's hair; **~ comió un pastel** he ate a cake
3 (uso recíproco) each other, one another; **~ miraron (el uno al otro)** they looked at each other o one another
4 (en oraciones pasivas): **se han vendido muchos libros** a lot of books have been sold; **"~ vende coche"** "car for sale"
5 (impers): **~ dice que** people say that, it is said that; **allí ~ come muy bien** the food there is very good, you can eat very well there.

sé [se] vb V **saber, ser.**
sea ['sea] etc vb V **ser.**
SEAT ['seat] nf abr = Sociedad Española de Automóviles de Turismo.
sebo ['seßo] nm fat, grease.
Sec. abr (= Secretario) Sec.
seca ['seka] nf V **seco.**
secado [se'kaðo] nm drying; **~ a mano** blow-dry.
secador [seka'ðor] nm: **~ para el pelo** hairdryer.
secadora [seka'ðora] nf tumble dryer; **~ centrífuga** spin-dryer.
secano [se'kano] nm (AGR: tb: tierra de ~) dry land o region; **cultivo de ~** dry farming.
secante [se'kante] adj (viento) drying ♦ nm blotting paper.

secar [se'kar] vt to dry; (superficie) to wipe dry; (frente, suelo) to mop; (líquido) to mop up; (tinta) to blot; **~se** vr to dry (off); (río, planta) to dry up.
sección [sek'θjon] nf section; (COM) department; **~ deportiva** (en periódico) sports page(s).
seco, a ['seko, a] adj dry; (fruta) dried; (persona: magro) thin, skinny; (carácter) cold; (antipático) disagreeable; (respuesta) sharp, curt ♦ nf dry season; **habrá pan a secas** there will be just bread; **decir algo a secas** to say sth curtly; **parar en ~** to stop dead.
secreción [sekre'θjon] nf secretion.
secretaría [sekreta'ria] nf secretariat; (oficina) secretary's office.
secretariado [sekreta'rjaðo] nm (oficina) secretariat; (cargo) secretaryship; (curso) secretarial course.
secretario, a [sekre'tarjo, a] nm/f secretary; **~ adjunto** (COM) assistant secretary.
secreto, a [se'kreto, a] adj secret; (información) confidential; (persona) secretive ♦ nm secret; (calidad) secrecy.
secta ['sekta] nf sect.
sectario, a [sek'tarjo, a] adj sectarian.
sector [sek'tor] nm sector (tb INFORM); (de opinión) section; (fig: campo) area, field; **~ privado/público** (COM, ECON) private/public sector.
secuela [se'kwela] nf consequence.
secuencia [se'kwenθja] nf sequence.
secuestrar [sekwes'trar] vt to kidnap; (avión) to hijack; (bienes) to seize, confiscate.
secuestro [se'kwestro] nm kidnapping; hijack; seizure, confiscation.
secular [seku'lar] adj secular.
secundar [sekun'dar] vt to second, support.
secundario, a [sekun'darjo, a] adj secondary; (carretera) side cpd; (INFORM) background cpd ♦ nf secondary education; V tb **sistema educativo.**
sed [seð] nf thirst; (fig) thirst, craving; **tener ~** to be thirsty.
seda ['seða] nf silk; **~ dental** dental floss.
sedal [se'ðal] nm fishing line.
sedante [se'ðante] nm sedative.
sede ['seðe] nf (de gobierno) seat; (de compañía) headquarters pl, head office; **Santa S~** Holy See.
sedentario, a [seðen'tarjo, a] adj sedentary.
SEDIC [se'ðik] nf abr = Sociedad Española de

Documentación e Información Científica.

sedición [seði'θjon] *nf* sedition.

sediento, a [se'ðjento, a] *adj* thirsty.

sedimentar [seðimen'tar] *vt* to deposit; ~**se** *vr* to settle.

sedimento [seði'mento] *nm* sediment.

sedoso, a [se'ðoso, a] *adj* silky, silken.

seducción [seðuk'θjon] *nf* seduction.

seducir [seðu'θir] *vt* to seduce; (*sobornar*) to bribe; (*cautivar*) to charm, fascinate; (*atraer*) to attract.

seductor, a [seðuk'tor, a] *adj* seductive; charming, fascinating; attractive; (*engañoso*) deceptive, misleading ♦ *nm/f* seducer.

seduje [se'ðuxe] *etc*, **seduzca** [se'ðuθka] *etc vb V* **seducir**.

sefardí [sefar'ði], **sefardita** [sefar'ðita] *adj* Sephardi(c) ♦ *nm/f* Sephardi.

segador, a [seɣa'ðor, a] *nm/f* (*persona*) harvester ♦ *nf* (*TEC*) mower, reaper.

segadora-trilladora [seɣa'ðoratriʎa'ðora] *nf* combine harvester.

segar [se'ɣar] *vt* (*mies*) to reap, cut; (*hierba*) to mow, cut; (*esperanzas*) to ruin.

seglar [se'ɣlar] *adj* secular, lay.

segoviano, a [seɣo'βjano, a] *adj* of *o* from Segovia ♦ *nm/f* native *o* inhabitant of Segovia.

segregación [seɣreɣa'θjon] *nf* segregation; ~ **racial** racial segregation.

segregar [seɣre'ɣar] *vt* to segregate, separate.

segregue [se'ɣreɣe] *etc vb V* **segregar**.

segué [se'ɣe], **seguemos** [se'ɣemos] *etc vb V* **segar**.

seguidamente [seɣiða'mente] *adv* (*sin parar*) without a break; (*inmediatamente después*) immediately after.

seguido, a [se'ɣiðo, a] *adj* (*continuo*) continuous, unbroken; (*recto*) straight ♦ *adv* (*directo*) straight (on); (*después*) after; (*AM: a menudo*) often ♦ *nf*: **en seguida** at once, right away; **5 días ~s** 5 days running, 5 days in a row; **en seguida termino** I've nearly finished, I shan't be long now.

seguimiento [seɣi'mjento] *nm* chase, pursuit; (*continuación*) continuation.

seguir [se'ɣir] *vt* to follow; (*venir después*) to follow on, come after; (*proseguir*) to continue; (*perseguir*) to chase, pursue; (*indicio*) to follow up; (*mujer*) to court ♦ *vi* (*gen*) to follow; (*continuar*) to continue, carry *o* go on; ~**se** *vr* to follow; **a ~** to be continued; **sigo sin comprender** I still don't understand; **sigue lloviendo** it's

still raining; **sigue** (*en carta*) P.T.O.; (*en libro, TV*) continued; "**hágase ~**" "please forward"; **¡siga!** (*AM: pase*) come in!

según [se'ɣun] *prep* according to ♦ *adv*: ~ (**y conforme**) it all depends ♦ *conj* as; ~ **esté el tiempo** depending on the weather; ~ **me consta** as far as I know; **está ~ lo dejaste** it is just as you left it.

segundo, a [se'ɣundo, a] *adj* second; (*en discurso*) secondly ♦ *nm* (*gen, medida de tiempo*) second; (*piso*) second floor ♦ *nf* (*sentido*) second meaning; ~ (**de a bordo**) (*NAUT*) first mate; **segunda** (**clase**) (*FERRO*) second class; **segunda** (**marcha**) (*AUTO*) second (gear); **de segunda mano** second hand.

seguramente [seɣura'mente] *adv* surely; (*con certeza*) for sure, with certainty; (*probablemente*) probably; **¿lo va a comprar? — ~** is he going to buy it? — I should think so.

seguridad [seɣuri'ðað] *nf* safety; (*del estado, de casa etc*) security; (*certidumbre*) certainty; (*confianza*) confidence; (*estabilidad*) stability; ~ **social** social security; ~ **contra incendios** fire precautions *pl*; ~ **en sí mismo** (self-) confidence.

seguro, a [se'ɣuro, a] *adj* (*cierto*) sure, certain; (*fiel*) trustworthy; (*libre de peligro*) safe; (*bien defendido, firme*) secure; (*datos etc*) reliable; (*fecha*) firm ♦ *adv* for sure, certainly ♦ *nm* (*dispositivo*) safety device; (*de cerradura*) tumbler; (*de arma*) safety catch; (*COM*) insurance; ~ **contra accidentes/incendios** fire/ accident insurance; ~ **contra terceros/a todo riesgo** third party/comprehensive insurance; ~ **dotal con beneficios** with- profits endowment assurance; **S~ de Enfermedad** ≈ National Insurance; ~ **marítimo** marine insurance; ~ **mixto** endowment assurance; ~ **temporal** term insurance; ~ **de vida** life insurance.

seis [seis] *num* six; ~ **mil** six thousand; **tiene ~ años** she is six (years old); **unos ~** about six; **hoy es el ~** today is the sixth.

seiscientos, as [seis'θjentos, as] *num* six hundred.

seísmo [se'ismo] *nm* tremor, earthquake.

selección [selek'θjon] *nf* selection; ~ **múltiple** multiple choice; ~ **nacional** (*DEPORTE*) national team.

seleccionador, a [selekθjona'ðor, a] *nm/f* (*DEPORTE*) selector.

seleccionar [selekθjo'nar] *vt* to pick, choose, select.

selectividad [selektiβi'ðað] *nf* (*UNIV*) entrance examination.

School leavers wishing to go on to University sit the dreaded **selectividad** in June, with resits in September. When student numbers are too high for a particular course only the best students get their choice. Some of the others then wait a year to sit the exam again rather than do a course they don't want.

selecto, a [se'lekto, a] *adj* select, choice; (*escogido*) selected.

sellado, a [se'ʎaðo, a] *adj* (*documento oficial*) sealed; (*pasaporte*) stamped.

sellar [se'ʎar] *vt* (*documento oficial*) to seal; (*pasaporte, visado*) to stamp; (*marcar*) to brand; (*pacto, labios*) to seal.

sello ['seʎo] *nm* stamp; (*precinto*) seal; (*fig: tb:* ~ **distintivo**) hallmark; ~ **fiscal** revenue stamp; ~**s de prima** (*COM*) trading stamps.

selva ['selβa] *nf* (*bosque*) forest, woods *pl*; (*jungla*) jungle; **la S**~ **Negra** the Black Forest.

selvático, a [sel'βatiko, a] *adj* woodland *cpd*; (*BOT*) wild.

semáforo [se'maforo] *nm* (*AUTO*) traffic lights *pl*; (*FERRO*) signal.

semana [se'mana] *nf* week; ~ **inglesa** 5-day (working) week; ~ **laboral** working week; **S**~ **Santa** Holy Week; **entre** ~ during the week.

Semana Santa is a holiday in Spain; all regions take **Viernes Santo**, Good Friday, **Sábado Santo**, Holy Saturday, and **Domingo de Resurrección**, Easter Sunday. Other holidays at this time vary according to each region. There are spectacular **procesiones** all over the country, with members of **cofradías** (brotherhoods) dressing in hooded robes and parading their **pasos** (religious floats or sculptures) through the streets. Seville has the most renowned celebrations, on account of the religious fervour shown by the locals.

semanal [sema'nal] *adj* weekly.

semanario [sema'narjo] *nm* weekly (magazine).

semántica [se'mantika] *nf* semantics *sg*.

semblante [sem'blante] *nm* face; (*fig*) look.

semblanza [sem'blanθa] *nf* biographical sketch, profile.

sembrar [sem'brar] *vt* to sow; (*objetos*) to sprinkle, scatter about; (*noticias etc*) to spread.

semejante [seme'xante] *adj* (*parecido*) similar; (*tal*) such; ~**s** alike, similar ♦ *nm* fellow man, fellow creature; **son muy** ~**s** they are very much alike; **nunca hizo cosa** ~ he never did such a o any such thing.

semejanza [seme'xanθa] *nf* similarity, resemblance; **a** ~ **de** like, as.

semejar [seme'xar] *vi* to seem like, resemble; ~**se** *vr* to look alike, be similar.

semen ['semen] *nm* semen.

semental [semen'tal] *nm* (*macho*) stud.

sementera [semen'tera] *nf* (*acto*) sowing; (*temporada*) seedtime; (*tierra*) sown land.

semestral [semes'tral] *adj* half-yearly, bi-annual.

semestre [se'mestre] *nm* period of six months; (*US UNIV*) semester; (*COM*) half-yearly payment.

semicírculo [semi'θirkulo] *nm* semicircle.

semiconductor [semikonduk'tor] *nm* semiconductor.

semiconsciente [semikons'θjente] *adj* semiconscious.

semidesnatado, a [semiðesna'taðo, a] *adj* semi-skimmed.

semifinal [semifi'nal] *nf* semifinal.

semiinconsciente [semi(i)nkons'θjente] *adj* semiconscious.

semilla [se'miʎa] *nf* seed.

semillero [semi'ʎero] *nm* (*AGR etc*) seedbed; (*fig*) hotbed.

seminario [semi'narjo] *nm* (*REL*) seminary; (*ESCOL*) seminar.

semiseco [semi'seko] *nm* medium-dry.

semita [se'mita] *adj* Semitic ♦ *nm/f* Semite.

sémola ['semola] *nf* semolina.

sempiterno, a [sempi'terno, a] *adj* everlasting.

Sena ['sena] *nm*: **el** ~ the (river) Seine.

senado [se'naðo] *nm* senate; *V tb* **Las Cortes (españolas)**.

senador, a [sena'ðor, a] *nm/f* senator.

sencillez [senθi'ʎeθ] *nf* simplicity; (*de persona*) naturalness.

sencillo, a [sen'θiʎo, a] *adj* simple; (*carácter*) natural, unaffected; (*billete*) single ♦ *nm* (*disco*) single; (*AM*) small change.

senda ['senda] *nf*, **sendero** [sen'dero] *nm* path, track; **Sendero Luminoso** the Shining Path (guerrilla movement).

senderismo [sende'rismo] *nm* trekking.

sendos, as ['sendos, as] *adj pl*: **les dio** ~ **golpes** he hit both of them.

senil [se'nil] *adj* senile.

seno ['seno] *nm* (*ANAT*) bosom, bust; (*fig*)

serigrafía [seriɣra'fia] *nf* silk screen printing.

serio, a ['serjo, a] *adj* serious; reliable, dependable; grave, serious; **poco** ~ (*actitud*) undignified; (*carácter*) unreliable; **en** ~ seriously.

sermón [ser'mon] *nm* (*REL*) sermon.

sermonear [sermone'ar] *vt* (*fam*) to lecture ♦ *vi* to sermonize.

seropositivo, a [seroposi'tiβo, a] *adj* HIV-positive.

serpentear [serpente'ar] *vi* to wriggle; (*camino, río*) to wind, snake.

serpentina [serpen'tina] *nf* streamer.

serpiente [ser'pjente] *nf* snake; ~ **boa** boa constrictor; ~ **de cascabel** rattlesnake.

serranía [serra'nia] *nf* mountainous area.

serrano, a [se'rrano, a] *adj* highland *cpd*, hill *cpd* ♦ *nm/f* highlander.

serrar [se'rrar] *vt* to saw.

serrín [se'rrin] *nm* sawdust.

serrucho [se'rrutʃo] *nm* handsaw.

Servia ['serßja] *nf* Serbia.

servicial [serßi'θjal] *adj* helpful, obliging.

servicio [ser'ßiθjo] *nm* service; (*CULIN etc*) set; ~**s** *nmpl* toilet(s) (*pl*); **estar de** ~ to be on duty; ~ **aduanero** *o* **de aduana** customs service; ~ **a domicilio** home delivery service; ~ **incluido** (*en hotel etc*) service charge included; ~ **militar** military service; ~ **público** (*COM*) public utility.

servidor, a [serßi'ðor, a] *nm/f* servant ♦ *nm* (*INFORM*) server; **su seguro** ~ (**s.s.s.**) yours faithfully; **un** ~ (*el que habla o escribe*) your humble servant.

servidumbre [serßi'ðumbre] *nf* (*sujeción*) servitude; (*criados*) servants *pl*, staff.

servil [ser'ßil] *adj* servile.

servilleta [serßi'ʎeta] *nf* serviette, napkin.

servilletero [serßiʎe'tero] *nm* napkin ring.

servir [ser'ßir] *vt* to serve; (*comida*) to serve out *o* up; (*TENIS etc*) to serve ♦ *vi* to serve; (*camarero*) to serve, wait; (*tener utilidad*) to be of use, be useful; ~**se** *vr* to serve *o* help o.s.; **¿en qué puedo** ~**le?** how can I help you?; ~ **vino a algn** to pour out wine for sb; ~ **de guía** to act *o* serve as a guide; **no sirve para nada** it's no use at all; ~**se de algo** to make use of sth, use sth; **sírvase pasar** please come in.

sesantía [θesan'tia] *nf* (*AM*) unemployment.

sesenta [se'senta] *num* sixty.

sesentón, ona [sesen'ton, ona] *adj, nm/f* sixty-year-old.

sesgado, a [ses'ɣaðo, a] *adj* slanted, slanting.

sesgo ['sesɣo] *nm* slant; (*fig*) slant, twist.

sesión [se'sjon] *nf* (*POL*) session, sitting; (*CINE*) showing; (*TEAT*) performance; **abrir/levantar la** ~ to open/close *o* adjourn the meeting; **la segunda** ~ the second house.

seso ['seso] *nm* brain; (*fig*) intelligence; ~**s** *nmpl* (*CULIN*) brains; **devanarse los** ~**s** to rack one's brains.

sesudo, a [se'suðo, a] *adj* sensible, wise.

set, *pl* **sets** [set, sets] *nm* (*TENIS*) set.

Set. *abr* (= *setiembre*) Sept.

seta ['seta] *nf* mushroom; ~ **venenosa** toadstool.

setecientos, as [sete'θjentos, as] *num* seven hundred.

setenta [se'tenta] *num* seventy.

setiembre [se'tjembre] *nm* = **septiembre**.

seto ['seto] *nm* fence; ~ **vivo** hedge.

seudo... [seuðo] *pref* pseudo....

seudónimo [seu'ðonimo] *nm* pseudonym.

Seúl [se'ul] *nm* Seoul.

s.e.u.o. *abr* (= *salvo error u omisión*) E & O E.

severidad [seßeri'ðað] *nf* severity.

severo, a [se'ßero, a] *adj* severe; (*disciplina*) strict; (*frío*) bitter.

Sevilla [se'ßiʎa] *nf* Seville.

sevillano, a [seßi'ʎano, a] *adj* of *o* from Seville ♦ *nm/f* native *o* inhabitant of Seville.

sexagenario, a [seksaxe'narjo, a] *adj* sixty-year-old ♦ *nm/f* person in his/her sixties.

sexagésimo, a [seksa'xesimo, a] *num* sixtieth.

sexo ['sekso] *nm* sex; **el** ~ **femenino/masculino** the female/male sex.

sexto, a ['seksto, a] *num* sixth; **Juan S**~ John the Sixth.

sexual [sek'swal] *adj* sexual; **vida** ~ sex life.

sexualidad [sekswali'ðað] *nf* sexuality.

s.f. *abr* (= *sin fecha*) no date.

s/f *abr* (*COM*: = *su favor*) your favour.

sgte(s). *abr* (= *siguiente(s)*) foll.

si [si] *conj* if; (*en pregunta indirecta*) if, whether ♦ *nm* (*MUS*) B; ~ ... ~ ... whether ... *o* ...; **me pregunto** ~ ... I wonder if *o* whether ...; ~ **no** if not, otherwise; ¡~ **fuera verdad!** if only it were true!; **por** ~ **viene** in case he comes.

sí [si] *adv* yes ♦ *nm* consent ♦ *pron* (*uso impersonal*) oneself; (*sg: m*) himself; (*: f*) herself; (*: de cosa*) itself; (*: de usted*) yourself; (*pl*) themselves; (*: de ustedes*) yourselves; (*: recíproco*) each other; **él no**

quiere pero yo ~ he doesn't want to but I do; **ella** ~ **vendrá** she will certainly come, she is sure to come; **claro que** ~ of course; **creo que** ~ I think so; **porque** ~ because that's the way it is; (*porque lo digo yo*) because I say so; ¡~ **que lo es!** I'll say it is!; ¡**eso** ~ **que no!** never; **se ríe de** ~ **misma** she laughs at herself; **cambiaron una mirada entre** ~ they gave each other a look; **de por** ~ in itself.

siamés, esa [sja'mes, esa] *adj, nm/f* Siamese.

sibarita [siβa'rita] *adj* sybaritic ♦ *nm/f* sybarite.

sicario [si'karjo] *nm* hired killer.

Sicilia [si'θilja] *nf* Sicily.

siciliano, a [siθi'ljano, a] *adj, nm/f* Sicilian ♦ *nm* (*LING*) Sicilian.

SIDA ['siða] *nm abr* (= *síndrome de inmunodeficiencia adquirida*) AIDS.

sida ['siða] *nm* AIDS.

siderurgia [siðe'rurxja] *nf* iron and steel industry.

siderúrgico, a [siðe'rurxico, a] *adj* iron and steel *cpd*.

sidra ['siðra] *nf* cider.

siega ['sjeɣa] *etc vb V* segar ♦ *nf* (*cosechar*) reaping; (*segar*) mowing; (*época*) harvest (time).

siegue ['sjeɣe] *etc vb V* segar.

siembra ['sjembra] *etc vb V* sembrar ♦ *nf* sowing.

siempre ['sjempre] *adv* always; (*todo el tiempo*) all the time; (*AM: así y todo*) still ♦ *conj:* ~ **que** ... (+ *indic*) whenever ...; (+ *subjun*) provided that ...; **es lo de** ~ it's the same old story; **como** ~ as usual; **para** ~ forever; ~ **me voy mañana** (*AM*) I'm still leaving tomorrow.

sien [sjen] *nf* (*ANAT*) temple.

siento ['sjento] *etc vb V* sentar, sentir.

sierra ['sjerra] *etc vb V* serrar ♦ *nf* (*TEC*) saw; (*GEO*) mountain range; **S**~ **Leona** Sierra Leone.

siervo, a ['sjerβo, a] *nm/f* slave.

siesta ['sjesta] *nf* siesta, nap; **dormir la** *o* **echarse una** *o* **tomar una** ~ to have an afternoon nap *o* a doze.

siete ['sjete] *num* seven ♦ *excl* (*AM fam*): ¡**la gran** ~! wow!, hell!; **hijo de la gran** ~ (*fam!*) bastard(*!*), son of a bitch (*US!*).

sífilis ['sifilis] *nf* syphilis.

sifón [si'fon] *nm* syphon; **whisky con** ~ whisky and soda.

siga ['siɣa] *etc vb V* seguir.

sigilo [si'xilo] *nm* secrecy; (*discreción*) discretion.

sigla ['siɣla] *nf* initial, abbreviation.

siglo ['siɣlo] *nm* century; (*fig*) age; **S**~ **de las Luces** Age of Enlightenment; **S**~ **de Oro** Golden Age.

significación [siɣnifika'θjon] *nf* significance.

significado [siɣnifi'kaðo] *nm* significance; (*de palabra etc*) meaning.

significar [siɣnifi'kar] *vt* to mean, signify; (*notificar*) to make known, express.

significativo, a [siɣnifika'tiβo, a] *adj* significant.

signifique [siɣni'fike] *etc vb V* significar.

signo ['siɣno] *nm* sign; ~ **de admiración** *o* **exclamación** exclamation mark; ~ **igual** equals sign; ~ **de interrogación** question mark; ~ **de más/de menos** plus/minus sign; ~**s de puntuación** punctuation marks.

siguiendo [si'ɣjendo] *etc vb V* seguir.

siguiente [si'ɣjente] *adj* following; (*próximo*) next.

silbar [sil'βar] *vt, vi* to whistle; (*silbato*) to blow; (*TEAT etc*) to hiss.

silbato [sil'βato] *nm* (*instrumento*) whistle.

silbido [sil'βiðo] *nm* whistle, whistling; (*abucheo*) hiss.

silenciador [silenθja'ðor] *nm* silencer.

silenciar [silen'θjar] *vt* (*persona*) to silence; (*escándalo*) to hush up.

silencio [si'lenθjo] *nm* silence, quiet; **en el** ~ **más absoluto** in dead silence; **guardar** ~ to keep silent.

silencioso, a [silen'θjoso, a] *adj* silent, quiet.

sílfide ['silfiðe] *nf* sylph.

silicio [si'liθjo] *nm* silicon.

silla ['siʎa] *nf* (*asiento*) chair; (*tb:* ~ **de montar**) saddle; ~ **de ruedas** wheelchair.

sillería [siʎe'ria] *nf* (*asientos*) chairs *pl*, set of chairs; (*REL*) choir stalls *pl*; (*taller*) chairmaker's workshop.

sillín [si'ʎin] *nm* saddle, seat.

sillón [si'ʎon] *nm* armchair, easy chair.

silueta [si'lweta] *nf* silhouette; (*de edificio*) outline; (*figura*) figure.

silvestre [sil'βestre] *adj* (*BOT*) wild; (*fig*) rustic, rural.

sima ['sima] *nf* abyss, chasm.

simbolice [simbo'liθe] *etc vb V* simbolizar.

simbólico, a [sim'boliko, a] *adj* symbolic(al).

simbolizar [simboli'θar] *vt* to symbolize.

símbolo ['simbolo] *nm* symbol; ~ **gráfico** (*INFORM*) icon.

simetría [sime'tria] *nf* symmetry.

simétrico, a [si'metriko, a] *adj* symmetrical.

simiente [si'mjente] *nf* seed.

similar [simi'lar] *adj* similar.
similitud [simili'tuð] *nf* similarity,
resemblance.
simio ['simjo] *nm* ape.
simpatía [simpa'tia] *nf* liking; (*afecto*)
affection; (*amabilidad*) kindness; (*de
ambiente*) friendliness; (*de persona,
lugar*) charm, attractiveness;
(*solidaridad*) mutual support, solidarity;
tener ~ a to like; **la famosa ~ andaluza**
that well-known Andalusian charm.
simpatice [simpa'tiθe] *etc vb V* **simpatizar**.
simpático, a [sim'patiko, a] *adj* nice,
pleasant; (*bondadoso*) kind; **no le hemos
caído muy ~s** she didn't much take to
us.
simpatiquísimo, a [simpati'kisimo, a] *adj*
(*superl de* **simpático**) ever so nice; ever
so kind.
simpatizante [simpati'θante] *nm/f*
sympathizer.
simpatizar [simpati'θar] *vi*: **~ con** to get on
well with.
simple ['simple] *adj* simple; (*elemental*)
simple, easy; (*mero*) mere; (*puro*) pure,
sheer ♦ *nm/f* simpleton; **un ~ soldado** an
ordinary soldier.
simpleza [sim'pleθa] *nf* simpleness;
(*necedad*) silly thing.
simplicidad [simpliθi'ðað] *nf* simplicity.
simplificar [simplifi'kar] *vt* to simplify.
simplifique [simpli'fike] *etc vb V*
simplificar.
simplón, ona [sim'plon, ona] *adj* simple,
gullible ♦ *nm/f* simple soul.
simposio [sim'posjo] *nm* symposium.
simulacro [simu'lakro] *nm* (*apariencia*)
semblance; (*fingimiento*) sham.
simular [simu'lar] *vt* to simulate; (*fingir*) to
feign, sham.
simultanear [simultane'ar] *vt*: **~ dos cosas**
to do two things simultaneously.
simultáneo, a [simul'taneo, a] *adj*
simultaneous.
sin [sin] *prep* without; (*a no ser por*) but for
♦ *conj*: **~ que** (+ *subjun*) without; **~ decir
nada** without a word; **~ verlo yo** without
my seeing it; **platos ~ lavar** unwashed *o*
dirty dishes; **la ropa está ~ lavar** the
clothes are unwashed; **~ que lo sepa él**
without his knowing; **~ embargo**
however.
sinagoga [sina'ɣoɣa] *nf* synagogue.
Sinaí [sina'i] *nm*: **El ~** Sinai, the Sinai
Peninsula; **el Monte ~** Mount Sinai.
sinceridad [sinθeri'ðað] *nf* sincerity.
sincero, a [sin'θero, a] *adj* sincere;
(*persona*) genuine; (*opinión*) frank;

(*felicitaciones*) heartfelt.
síncope ['sinkope] *nm* (*desmayo*) blackout;
~ cardíaco (*MED*) heart failure.
sincronice [sinkro'niθe] *etc vb V*
sincronizar.
sincronizar [sinkroni'θar] *vt* to
synchronize.
sindical [sindi'kal] *adj* union *cpd*, trade-
union *cpd*.
sindicalista [sindika'lista] *adj* trade-union
cpd ♦ *nm/f* trade unionist.
sindicar [sindi'kar] *vt* (*obreros*) to organize,
unionize; **~se** *vr* (*obrero*) to join a union.
sindicato [sindi'kato] *nm* (*de trabajadores*)
trade(s) *o* labor (*US*) union; (*de
negociantes*) syndicate.
sindique [sin'dike] *etc vb V* **sindicar**.
síndrome ['sindrome] *nm* syndrome; **~ de
abstinencia** withdrawal symptoms.
sine qua non [sine'kwanon] *adj*: **condición
~** sine qua non.
sinfín [sin'fin] *nm*: **un ~ de** a great many,
no end of.
sinfonía [sinfo'nia] *nf* symphony.
sinfónico, a [sin'foniko, a] *adj* (*música*)
symphonic; **orquesta sinfónica**
symphony orchestra.
Singapur [singa'pur] *nm* Singapore.
singular [singu'lar] *adj* singular; (*fig*)
outstanding, exceptional; (*pey*) peculiar,
odd ♦ *nm* (*LING*) singular; **en ~** in the
singular.
singularice [singula'riθe] *etc vb V* **singularizar**.
singularidad [singulari'ðað] *nf* singularity,
peculiarity.
singularizar [singulari'θar] *vt* to single out;
~se *vr* to distinguish o.s., stand out.
siniestro, a [si'njestro, a] *adj* left; (*fig*) sinister ♦ *nm* (*accidente*) accident; (*desastre*)
natural disaster.
sinnúmero [sin'numero] *nm* = **sinfín**.
sino ['sino] *nm* fate, destiny ♦ *conj* (*pero*)
but; (*salvo*) except, save; **no son 8 ~ 9**
there are not 8 but 9; **todos ~ él** all
except him.
sinónimo, a [si'nonimo, a] *adj*
synonymous ♦ *nm* synonym.
sinrazón [sinra'θon] *nf* wrong, injustice.
sinsabor [sinsa'ßor] *nm* (*molestia*) trouble;
(*dolor*) sorrow; (*preocupación*)
uneasiness.
sintaxis [sin'taksis] *nf* syntax.
síntesis ['sintesis] *nf inv* synthesis.
sintetice [sinte'tiθe] *etc vb V* **sintetizar**.
sintético, a [sin'tetiko, a] *adj* synthetic.
sintetizador [sinteti'θa'ðor] *nm*
synthesizer.

sintetizar [sinteti'θar] *vt* to synthesize.
sintiendo [sin'tjendo] *etc vb* V **sentir**.
síntoma ['sintoma] *nm* symptom.
sintomático, a [sinto'matiko, a] *adj*
   symptomatic.
sintonía [sinto'nia] *nf* (RADIO) tuning;
   (*melodía*) signature tune.
sintonice [sinto'niθe] *etc vb* V **sintonizar**.
sintonizador [sintoniθa'ðor] *nm* (RADIO)
   tuner.
sintonizar [sintoni'θar] *vt* (RADIO) to tune
   (in) to, pick up.
sinuoso, a [si'nwoso, a] *adj* (*camino*)
   winding; (*rumbo*) devious.
sinvergüenza [simber'ɣwenθa] *nm/f* rogue,
   scoundrel.
sionismo [sjo'nismo] *nm* Zionism.
siquiera [si'kjera] *conj* even if, even though
   ♦ *adv* (*esp AM*) at least; **ni** ~ not even; ~
   bebe algo at least drink something.
sirena [si'rena] *nf* siren, mermaid; (*bocina*)
   siren, hooter.
Siria ['sirja] *nf* Syria.
sirio, a ['sirjo, a] *adj, nm/f* Syrian.
sirviendo [sir'βjendo] *etc vb* V **servir**.
sirviente, a [sir'βjente, a] *nm/f* servant.
sisa ['sisa] *nf* petty theft; (COSTURA) dart;
   (*sobaquera*) armhole.
sisar [si'sar] *vt* (*robar*) to thieve; (COSTURA)
   to take in.
sisear [sise'ar] *vt, vi* to hiss.
sísmico, a ['sismiko, a] *adj*: **movimiento** ~
   earthquake.
sismógrafo [sis'moɣrafo] *nm* seismograph.
sistema [sis'tema] *nm* system; (*método*)
   method; ~ **impositivo** *o* **tributario**
   taxation, tax system; ~ **pedagógico**
   educational system; ~ **de alerta**
   inmediata early-warning system; ~
   binario (INFORM) binary system; ~
   experto expert system; ~ **de facturación**
   (COM) invoicing system; ~ **de fondo fijo**
   (COM) imprest system; ~ **de lógica**
   compartida (INFORM) shared logic
   system; ~ **métrico** metric system; ~
   operativo (en disco) (INFORM) (disk-
   based) operating system.

The reform of the Spanish **sistema**
educativo (*education system*) *begun in the*
early 90s has replaced the courses **EGB,**
BUP *and* **COU** *with the following:* **Primaria:**
a compulsory 6 years; **Secundaria** *a*
compulsory 4 years; **Bachillerato** *an*
optional 2 year secondary school course,
essential for those wishing to go on to
higher education.

---

sistemático, a [siste'matiko, a] *adj*
   systematic.
sitiar [si'tjar] *vt* to besiege, lay siege to.
sitio ['sitjo] *nm* (*lugar*) place; (*espacio*)
   room, space; (MIL) siege; ¿**hay** ~? is
   there any room?; **hay** ~ **de sobra** there's
   plenty of room.
situación [sitwa'θjon] *nf* situation,
   position; (*estatus*) position, standing.
situado, a [si'twaðo, a] *adj* situated,
   placed; **estar** ~ (COM) to be financially
   secure.
situar [si'twar] *vt* to place, put; (*edificio*) to
   locate, situate.
S.L. *abr* (COM: = *Sociedad Limitada*) Ltd.
slip [es'lip], *pl* **slips** *nm* pants *pl*, briefs *pl*.
slot [es'lot], *pl* **slots** *nm*: ~ **de expansión**
   expansion slot.
S.M. *abr* (= *Su Majestad*) HM.
SME *nm abr* (= *Sistema Monetario Europeo*)
   EMS; **(mecanismo de cambios del)** ~
   ERM.
smoking [(e)'smokin] (*pl* ~**s**) *nm* dinner
   jacket (BRIT), tuxedo (US).
s/n *abr* (= *sin número*) no number.
snob [es'nob] = **esnob**.
SO *abr* (= *suroeste*) SW.
so [so] *excl* whoa!; ¡~ **burro!** you idiot!
   ♦ *prep* under.
s/o *abr* (COM: = *su orden*) your order.
sobaco [so'βako] *nm* armpit.
sobado, a [so'βaðo, a] *adj* (*ropa*) worn;
   (*arrugado*) crumpled; (*libro*) well-
   thumbed; (CULIN: *masa*) short.
sobar [so'βar] *vt* (*tela*) to finger; (*ropa*) to
   rumple, mess up; (*músculos*) to rub,
   massage.
soberanía [soβera'nia] *nf* sovereignty.
soberano, a [soβe'rano, a] *adj* sovereign;
   (*fig*) supreme ♦ *nm/f* sovereign; **los** ~**s**
   the king and queen.
soberbio, a [so'βerβjo, a] *adj* (*orgulloso*)
   proud; (*altivo*) haughty, arrogant; (*fig*)
   magnificent, superb ♦ *nf* pride;
   haughtiness, arrogance; magnificence.
sobornar [soβor'nar] *vt* to bribe.
soborno [so'βorno] *nm* (*un* ~) bribe; (*el* ~)
   bribery.
sobra ['soβra] *nf* excess, surplus; ~**s** *nfpl*
   left-overs, scraps; **de** ~ surplus, extra;
   lo sé de ~ I'm only too aware of it;
   tengo de ~ I've more than
   enough.
sobradamente [soβraða'mente] *adv*
   amply; (*saber*) only too well.
sobrado, a [so'βraðo, a] *adj* (*más que*
   suficiente) more than enough; (*superfluo*)
   excessive ♦ *adv* too, exceedingly;

sobradas veces repeatedly.
sobrante [so'ßrante] *adj* remaining, extra ♦ *nm* surplus, remainder.
sobrar [so'ßrar] *vt* to exceed, surpass ♦ *vi* (*tener de más*) to be more than enough; (*quedar*) to remain, be left (over).
sobrasada [soßra'saða] *nf* ≈ sausage spread.
sobre ['soßre] *prep* (*gen*) on; (*encima*) on (top of); (*por encima de, arriba de*) over, above; (*más que*) more than; (*además*) in addition to, besides; (*alrededor de*) about; (*porcentaje*) in, out of; (*tema*) about, on ♦ *nm* envelope; ~ **todo** above all; **3 ~ 100** 3 in a 100, 3 out of every 100; **un libro ~ Tirso** a book about Tirso; **~ de ventanilla** window envelope.
sobrecama [sóßre'kama] *nf* bedspread.
sobrecapitalíce [soßrekapita'liθe] *etc vb V* **sobrecapitalizar**.
sobrecapitalizar [soßrekapitali'θar] *vi* to overcapitalize.
sobrecargar [soßrekar'ɣar] *vt* (*camión*) to overload; (*COM*) to surcharge.
sobrecargue [soßre'karɣe] *etc vb V* **sobrecargar**.
sobrecoger [soßreko'xer] *vt* (*sobresaltar*) to startle; (*asustar*) to scare; ~**se** *vr* (*sobresaltarse*) to be startled; (*asustarse*) to get scared; (*quedar impresionado*): ~**se (de)** to be overawed (by).
sobrecoja [soßre'koxa] *etc vb V* **sobrecoger**.
sobredosis [soßre'ðosis] *nf inv* overdose.
sobre(e)ntender [soßre(e)nten'der] *vt* to understand; (*adivinar*) to deduce, infer; ~**se** *vr*: **se sobre(e)ntiende que ...** it is implied that ....
sobreescribir [soßreeskri'ßir] *vt* (*INFORM*) to overwrite.
sobre(e)stimar [soßre(e)sti'mar] *vt* to overestimate.
sobregiro [soßre'xiro] *nm* (*COM*) overdraft.
sobrehumano, a [soßreu'mano, a] *adj* superhuman.
sobreimprimir [soßreimpri'mir] *vt* (*COM*) to merge.
sobrellevar [soßreʎe'ßar] *vt* (*fig*) to bear, endure.
sobremesa [soßre'mesa] *nf* (*después de comer*) sitting on after a meal; (*INFORM*) desktop; **conversación de ~** table talk.
sobremodo [soßre'moðo] *adv* very much, enormously.
sobrenatural [soßrenatu'ral] *adj* supernatural.
sobrenombre [soßre'nombre] *nm* nickname.

sobrepasar [soßrepa'sar] *vt* to exceed, surpass.
sobrepondré [soßrepon'dre] *etc vb V* **sobreponer**.
sobreponer [soßrepo'ner] *vt* (*poner encima*) to put on top; (*añadir*) to add; ~**se** *vr*: ~**se a** to overcome.
sobreponga [soßre'ponga] *etc vb V* **sobreponer**.
sobreprima [soßre'prima] *nf* (*COM*) loading.
sobreproducción [soßreproðuk'θjon] *nf* overproduction.
sobrepuesto [soßre'pwesto], **sobrepuse** [soßre'puse] *etc vb V* **sobreponer**.
sobresaldré [soßresal'dre] *etc*, **sobresalga** [soßre'salɣa] *etc vb V* **sobresalir**.
sobresaliente [soßresa'ljente] *adj* projecting; (*fig*) outstanding, excellent; (*UNIV etc*) first class ♦ *nm* (*UNIV etc*) first class (mark), distinction.
sobresalir [soßresa'lir] *vi* to project, jut out; (*fig*) to stand out, excel.
sobresaltar [soßresal'tar] *vt* (*asustar*) to scare, frighten; (*sobrecoger*) to startle.
sobresalto [soßre'salto] *nm* (*movimiento*) start; (*susto*) scare; (*turbación*) sudden shock.
sobreseer [soßrese'er] *vt*: ~ **una causa** (*JUR*) to stop a case.
sobrestadía [soßresta'ðia] *nf* (*COM*) demurrage.
sobretensión [soßreten'sjon] *nf* (*ELEC*): ~ **transitoria** surge.
sobretiempo [soßre'tjempo] *nm* (*AM*) overtime.
sobretodo [soßre'toðo] *nm* overcoat.
sobrevendré [soßreßen'dre] *etc*, **sobrevenga** [soßre'ßenga] *etc vb V* **sobrevenir**.
sobrevenir [soßreße'nir] *vi* (*ocurrir*) to happen (unexpectedly); (*resultar*) to follow, ensue.
sobreviene [soßre'ßjene] *etc*, **sobrevine** [soßre'ßine] *etc vb V* **sobrevenir**.
sobreviviente [soßreßi'ßjente] *adj* surviving ♦ *nmlf* survivor.
sobrevivir [soßreßi'ßir] *vi* to survive; (*persona*) to outlive; (*objeto etc*) to outlast.
sobrevolar [soßreßo'lar] *vt* to fly over.
sobrevuele [soßre'ßwele] *etc vb V* **sobrevolar**.
sobriedad [soßrje'ðað] *nf* sobriety, soberness; (*moderación*) moderation, restraint.
sobrino, a [so'ßrino, a] *nmlf* nephew/niece.

sobrio, a ['soßrjo, a] adj (moderado) moderate, restrained.

socarrón, ona [soka'rron, ona] adj (sarcástico) sarcastic, ironic(al).

socavar [soka'ßar] vt to undermine; (excavar) to dig underneath o below.

socavón [soka'ßon] nm (en mina) gallery; (hueco) hollow; (en la calle) hole.

sociable [so'θjaßle] adj (persona) sociable, friendly; (animal) social.

social [so'θjal] adj social; (COM) company cpd.

socialdemócrata [soθjalde'mokrata] adj social-democratic ♦ nm/f social democrat.

socialice [soθja'liθe] etc vb V **socializar**.

socialista [soθja'lista] adj, nm/f socialist.

socializar [soθjali'θar] vt to socialize.

sociedad [soθje'ðað] nf society; (COM) company; ~ **de ahorro y préstamo** savings and loan society; ~ **anónima (S.A.)** limited company (Ltd) (BRIT), incorporated company (Inc) (US); ~ **de beneficiencia** friendly society (BRIT), benefit association (US); ~ **de cartera** investment trust; ~ **comanditaria** (COM) co-ownership; ~ **conjunta** (COM) joint venture; ~ **inmobiliaria** building society (BRIT), savings and loan (society) (US); ~ **de responsabilidad limitada** (COM) private limited company.

socio, a ['soθjo, a] nm/f (miembro) member; (COM) partner; ~ **activo** active partner; ~ **capitalista** o **comanditario** sleeping o silent (US) partner.

socioeconómico, a [soθjoeko'nomiko, a] adj socio-economic.

sociología [soθjolo'xia] nf sociology.

sociólogo, a [so'θjoloxo, a] nm/f sociologist.

socorrer [soko'rrer] vt to help.

socorrido, a [soko'rriðo, a] adj (tienda) well-stocked; (útil) handy; (persona) helpful.

socorrismo [soko'rrismo] nm life-saving.

socorrista [soko'rrista] nm/f first aider; (en piscina, playa) lifeguard.

socorro [so'korro] nm (ayuda) help, aid; (MIL) relief; ¡~! help!

soda ['soða] nf (sosa) soda; (bebida) soda (water).

sódico, a ['soðiko, a] adj sodium cpd.

soez [so'eθ] adj dirty, obscene.

sofá [so'fa] nm sofa, settee.

sofá-cama [so'fakama] nm studio couch, sofa bed.

Sofia ['sofja] nf Sofia.

sofisticación [sofistika'θjon] nf sophistication.

sofisticado, a [sofisti'kaðo, a] adj sophisticated.

sofocado, a [sofo'kaðo, a] adj: **estar ~** (fig) to be out of breath; (ahogarse) to feel stifled.

sofocar [sofo'kar] vt to suffocate; (apagar) to smother, put out; **~se** vr to suffocate; (fig) to blush, feel embarrassed.

sofoco [so'foko] nm suffocation; (azoro) embarrassment.

sofocón [sofo'kon] nm: **llevarse** o **pasar un ~** to have a sudden shock.

sofreír [sofre'ir] vt to fry lightly.

sofría [so'fria] etc, **sofriendo** [so'frjendo] etc, **sofrito** [so'frito] vb V **sofreír**.

soft(ware) ['sof(wer)] nm (INFORM) software.

soga ['soɣa] nf rope.

sois [sois] vb V **ser**.

soja ['soxa] nf soya.

sojuzgar [soxu0'ɣar] vt to subdue, rule despotically.

sojuzgue [so'xuθɣe] etc vb V **sojuzgar**.

sol [sol] nm sun; (luz) sunshine, sunlight; (MUS) G; ~ **naciente/poniente** rising/ setting sun; **tomar el ~** to sunbathe; **hace ~** it is sunny.

solace [so'laθe] etc vb V **solazar**.

solamente [sola'mente] adv only, just.

solapa [so'lapa] nf (de chaqueta) lapel; (de libro) jacket.

solapado, a [sola'paðo, a] adj sly, underhand.

solar [so'lar] adj solar, sun cpd ♦ nm (terreno) plot (of ground); (local) undeveloped site.

solaz [so'laθ] nm recreation, relaxation.

solazar [sola'θar] vt (divertir) to amuse; **~se** vr to enjoy o.s., relax.

soldada [sol'daða] nf pay.

soldado [sol'daðo] nm soldier; ~ **raso** private.

soldador [solda'ðor] nm soldering iron; (persona) welder.

soldar [sol'dar] vt to solder, weld; (unir) to join, unite.

soleado, a [sole'aðo, a] adj sunny.

soledad [sole'ðað] nf solitude; (estado infeliz) loneliness.

solemne [so'lemne] adj solemn; (tontería) utter; (error) complete.

solemnidad [solemni'ðað] nf solemnity.

soler [so'ler] vi to be in the habit of, be accustomed to; **suele salir a las ocho** she usually goes out at 8 o'clock; **solíamos ir todos los años** we used to go every year.

solera [so'lera] *nf* (*tradición*) tradition; **vino de** ~ vintage wine.

solfeo [sol'feo] *nm* singing of scales; **ir a clases de** ~ to take singing lessons.

solicitar [soliθi'tar] *vt* (*permiso*) to ask for, seek; (*puesto*) to apply for; (*votos*) to canvass for; (*atención*) to attract; (*persona*) to pursue, chase after.

solícito, a [so'liθito, a] *adj* (*diligente*) diligent; (*cuidadoso*) careful.

solicitud [soliθi'tuð] *nf* (*calidad*) great care; (*petición*) request; (*a un puesto*) application.

solidaridad [soliðari'ðað] *nf* solidarity; **por** ~ **con** (*POL etc*) out of *o* in solidarity with.

solidario, a [soli'ðarjo, a] *adj* (*participación*) joint, common; (*compromiso*) mutually binding; **hacerse** ~ **de** to declare one's solidarity with.

solidarizarse [soliðari'θarse] *vr*: ~ **con algn** to support sb, sympathize with sb.

solidez [soli'ðeθ] *nf* solidity.

sólido, a ['soliðo, a] *adj* solid; (*TEC*) solidly made; (*bien construido*) well built.

soliloquio [soli'lokjo] *nm* soliloquy.

solista [so'lista] *nm/f* soloist.

solitario, a [soli'tarjo, a] *adj* (*persona*) lonely, solitary; (*lugar*) lonely, desolate ◆ *nm/f* (*reclusa*) recluse; (*en la sociedad*) loner ◆ *nm* solitaire ◆ *nf* tapeworm.

soliviantar [soliβjan'tar] *vt* to stir up, rouse (to revolt); (*enojar*) to anger; (*sacar de quicio*) to exasperate.

solloce [so'ʎoθe] *etc vb V* **sollozar**.

sollozar [soʎo'θar] *vi* to sob.

sollozo [so'ʎoθo] *nm* sob.

solo, a ['solo, a] *adj* (*único*) single, sole; (*sin compañía*) alone; (*MUS*) solo; (*solitario*) lonely; **hay una sola dificultad** there is just one difficulty; **a solas** alone, by o.s.

sólo ['solo] *adv* only, just; (*exclusivamente*) solely; **tan** ~ only just.

solomillo [solo'miʎo] *nm* sirloin.

solsticio [sols'tiθjo] *nm* solstice.

soltar [sol'tar] *vt* (*dejar ir*) to let go of; (*desprender*) to unfasten, loosen; (*librar*) to release, set free; (*amarras*) to cast off; (*AUTO: freno etc*) to release; (*suspiro*) to heave; (*risa etc*) to let out; ~**se** *vr* (*desanudarse*) to come undone; (*desprenderse*) to come off; (*adquirir destreza*) to become expert; (*en idioma*) to become fluent.

soltero, a [sol'tero, a] *adj* single, unmarried ◆ *nm* bachelor ◆ *nf* single woman, spinster.

solterón [solte'ron] *nm* confirmed bachelor.

solterona [solte'rona] *nf* spinster, maiden lady; (*pey*) old maid.

soltura [sol'tura] *nf* looseness, slackness; (*de los miembros*) agility, ease of movement; (*en el hablar*) fluency, ease.

soluble [so'luβle] *adj* (*QUÍMICA*) soluble; (*problema*) solvable; ~ **en agua** soluble in water.

solución [solu'θjon] *nf* solution; ~ **de continuidad** break in continuity.

solucionar [soluθjo'nar] *vt* (*problema*) to solve; (*asunto*) to settle, resolve.

solvencia [sol'βenθja] *nf* (*COM: estado*) solvency; (: *acción*) settlement, payment.

solventar [solβen'tar] *vt* (*pagar*) to settle, pay; (*resolver*) to resolve.

solvente [sol'βente] *adj* solvent, free of debt.

Somalia [so'malja] *nf* Somalia.

sombra ['sombra] *nf* shadow; (*como protección*) shade; ~**s** *nfpl* darkness *sg*, shadows; **sin** ~ **de duda** without a shadow of doubt; **tener buena/mala** ~ (*suerte*) to be lucky/unlucky; (*carácter*) to be likeable/disagreeable.

sombrero [som'brero] *nm* hat; ~ **hongo** bowler (hat), derby (*US*); ~ **de copa** *o* **de pelo** (*AM*) top hat.

sombrilla [som'briʎa] *nf* parasol, sunshade.

sombrío, a [som'brio, a] *adj* (*oscuro*) shady; (*fig*) sombre, sad; (*persona*) gloomy.

somero, a [so'mero, a] *adj* superficial.

someter [some'ter] *vt* (*país*) to conquer; (*persona*) to subject to one's will; (*informe*) to present, submit; ~**se** *vr* to give in, yield, submit; ~**se a** to submit to; ~**se a una operación** to undergo an operation.

sometimiento [someti'mjento] *nm* (*estado*) submission; (*acción*) presentation.

somier [so'mjer] *pl* **somiers** *nm* spring mattress.

somnífero [som'nifero] *nm* sleeping pill *o* tablet.

somnolencia [somno'lenθja] *nf* sleepiness, drowsiness.

somos ['somos] *vb V* **ser**.

son [son] *vb V* **ser** ◆ *nm* sound; **en** ~ **de broma** as a joke.

sonado, a [so'naðo, a] *adj* (*comentado*) talked-of; (*famoso*) famous; (*COM: pey*) hyped(-up).

sonajero [sona'xero] *nm* (baby's) rattle.

sonambulismo [sonambu'lismo] *nm*

sleepwalking.

sonámbulo, a [so'nambulo, a] *nm/f* sleepwalker.

sonar [so'nar] *vt* (*campana*) to ring; (*trompeta, sirena*) to blow ♦ *vi* to sound; (*hacer ruido*) to make a noise; (*LING*) to be sounded, be pronounced; (*ser conocido*) to sound familiar; (*campana*) to ring; (*reloj*) to strike, chime; **~se** *vr*: **~se (la nariz)** to blow one's nose; **es un nombre que suena** it's a name that's in the news; **me suena ese nombre** that name rings a bell.

sonda ['sonda] *nf* (*NAUT*) sounding; (*TEC*) bore, drill; (*MED*) probe.

sondear [sonde'ar] *vt* to sound; to bore (into), drill; to probe, sound; (*fig*) to sound out.

sondeo [son'deo] *nm* sounding; boring, drilling; (*encuesta*) poll, enquiry; **~ de la opinión pública** public opinion poll.

sónico, a ['soniko, a] *adj* sonic, sound *cpd*.

sonido [so'niðo] *nm* sound.

sonoro, a [so'noro, a] *adj* sonorous; (*resonante*) loud, resonant; (*LING*) voiced; **efectos ~s** sound effects.

sonreír [sonre'ir] *vi*, **sonreírse** *vr* to smile.

sonría [son'ria] *etc*, **sonriendo** [son'rjendo] *etc vb V* **sonreír**.

sonriente [son'rjente] *adj* smiling.

sonrisa [son'risa] *nf* smile.

sonrojar [sonro'xar] *vt*: **~ a algn** to make sb blush; **~se** *vr*: **~se (de)** to blush (at).

sonrojo [son'roxo] *nm* blush.

sonsacar [sonsa'kar] *vt* to wheedle, coax; **~ a algn** to pump sb for information.

sonsaque [son'sake] *etc vb V* **sonsacar**.

sonsonete [sonso'nete] *nm* (*golpecitos*) tap(ping); (*voz monótona*) monotonous delivery, singsong (voice).

soñador, a [sona'ðor, a] *nm/f* dreamer.

soñar [so'ɲar] *vt, vi* to dream; **~ con** to dream about *o* of; **soñé contigo anoche** I dreamed about you last night.

soñoliento, a [sono'ljento, a] *adj* sleepy, drowsy.

sopa ['sopa] *nf* soup; **~ de fideos** noodle soup.

sopero, a [so'pero, a] *adj* (*plato, cuchara*) soup *cpd* ♦ *nm* soup plate ♦ *nf* soup tureen.

sopesar [sope'sar] *vt* to try the weight of; (*fig*) to weigh up.

sopetón [sope'ton] *nm*: **de ~** suddenly, unexpectedly.

soplar [so'plar] *vt* (*polvo*) to blow away, blow off; (*inflar*) to blow up; (*vela*) to blow out; (*ayudar a recordar*) to prompt; (*birlar*) to nick; (*delatar*) to split on ♦ *vi* to

blow; (*delatar*) to squeal; (*beber*) to booze, bend the elbow.

soplete [so'plete] *nm* blowlamp; **~ soldador** welding torch.

soplo ['soplo] *nm* blow, puff; (*de viento*) puff, gust.

soplón, ona [so'plon, ona] *nm/f* (*fam*: *chismoso*) telltale; (: *de policía*) informer, grass.

soponcio [so'ponθjo] *nm* dizzy spell.

sopor [so'por] *nm* drowsiness.

soporífero, a [sopo'rifero, a] *adj* sleep-inducing; (*fig*) soporific ♦ *nm* sleeping pill.

soportable [sopor'taßle] *adj* bearable.

soportal [sopor'tal] *nm* porch; **~es** *nmpl* arcade *sg*.

soportar [sopor'tar] *vt* to bear, carry; (*fig*) to bear, put up with.

soporte [so'porte] *nm* support; (*fig*) pillar, support; (*INFORM*) medium; **~ de entrada/salida** input/output medium.

soprano [so'prano] *nf* soprano.

sor [sor] *nf*: **S~ María** Sister Mary.

sorber [sor'ßer] *vt* (*chupar*) to sip; (*inhalar*) to sniff, inhale; (*absorber*) to soak up, absorb.

sorbete [sor'ßete] *nm* sherbet.

sorbo ['sorßo] *nm* (*trago*) gulp, swallow; (*chupada*) sip; **beber a ~s** to sip.

sordera [sor'ðera] *nf* deafness.

sórdido, a [sor'ðiðo, a] *adj* dirty, squalid.

sordo, a ['sorðo, a] *adj* (*persona*) deaf; (*ruido*) dull; (*LING*) voiceless ♦ *nm/f* deaf person; **quedarse ~** to go deaf.

sordomudo, a [sorðo'muðo, a] *adj* deaf and dumb ♦ *nm/f* deaf-mute.

soriano, a [so'rjano, a] *adj* of *o* from Soria ♦ *nm/f* native *o* inhabitant of Soria.

sorna ['sorna] *nf* (*malicia*) slyness; (*tono burlón*) sarcastic tone.

soroche [so'rotʃe] *nm* (*AM MED*) mountain sickness.

sorprendente [sorpren'dente] *adj* surprising.

sorprender [sorpren'der] *vt* to surprise; (*asombrar*) to amaze; (*sobresaltar*) to startle; (*coger desprevenido*) to catch unawares; **~se** *vr*: **~se (de)** to be surprised *o* amazed (at).

sorpresa [sor'presa] *nf* surprise.

sorpresivo, a [sorpre'sißo, a] *adj* (*AM*) surprising; (*imprevisto*) sudden.

sortear [sorte'ar] *vt* to draw lots for; (*rifar*) to raffle; (*dificultad*) to dodge, avoid.

sorteo [sor'teo] *nm* (*en lotería*) draw; (*rifa*) raffle.

sortija [sor'tixa] *nf* ring; (*rizo*) ringlet, curl.

sortilegio [sorti'lexjo] nm (hechicería) sorcery; (hechizo) spell.

sosegado, a [sose'ɣaðo, a] adj quiet, calm.

sosegar [sose'ɣar] vt to quieten, calm; (el ánimo) to reassure ♦ vi to rest.

sosegué [sose'ɣe], **soseguemos** [sose'ɣemos] etc vb V **sosegar**.

sosiego [so'sjeɣo] etc vb V **sosegar** ♦ nm quiet(ness), calm(ness).

sosiegue [so'sjeɣe] etc vb V **sosegar**.

soslayar [sosla'jar] vt (preguntas) to get round.

soslayo [sos'lajo]: **de** ~ adv obliquely, sideways; **mirar de** ~ to look out of the corner of one's eye (at).

soso, a ['soso, a] adj (CULIN) tasteless; (fig) dull, uninteresting.

sospecha [sos'petʃa] nf suspicion.

sospechar [sospe'tʃar] vt to suspect ♦ vi: ~ **de** to be suspicious of.

sospechoso, a [sospe'tʃoso, a] adj suspicious; (testimonio, opinión) suspect ♦ nm/f suspect.

sostén [sos'ten] nm (apoyo) support; (sujetador) bra; (alimentación) sustenance, food.

sostendré [sosten'dre] etc vb V **sostener**.

sostener [soste'ner] vt to support; (mantener) to keep up, maintain; (alimentar) to sustain, keep going; ~**se** vr to support o.s.; (seguir) to continue, remain.

sostenga [sos'tenga] etc vb V **sostener**.

sostenido, adj [soste'niðo, a] adj continuous, sustained; (prolongado) prolonged; (MUS) sharp ♦ nm (MUS) sharp.

sostuve [sos'tuße] etc vb V **sostener**.

sota ['sota] nf (NAIPES) ≈ jack; V tb **baraja española**.

sotana [so'tana] nf (REL) cassock.

sótano ['sotano] nm basement.

sotavento [sota'ßento] nm (NAUT) lee, leeward.

soterrar [sote'rrar] vt to bury; (esconder) to hide away.

sotierre [so'tjerre] etc vb V **soterrar**.

soviético, a [so'ßjetiko, a] adj, nm/f Soviet; **los** ~**s** the Soviets, the Russians.

soy [soi] vb V **ser**.

soya ['soja] nf (AM) soya (bean).

SP abr (AUTO) = **servicio público**.

SPM nm abr (= síndrome premenstrual) PMS.

spooling [es'pulin] nm (INFORM) spooling.

sport [es'por(t)] nm sport.

spot [es'pot], pl **spot** nm (publicitario) ad.

squash [es'kwas] nm (DEPORTE) squash.

Sr. abr (= Señor) Mr.

Sra. abr (= Señora) Mrs.

S.R.C. abr (= se ruega contestación) R.S.V.P.

Sres., Srs. abr (= Señores) Messrs.

Sri Lanka [sri'lanka] nm Sri Lanka.

Srta. abr = **Señorita**.

SS abr (= Santos, Santas) SS.

ss. abr (= siguientes) foll.

S.S. abr (REL: = Su Santidad) H.H.

SS.MM. abr (= Sus Majestades) Their Royal Highnesses.

Sta. abr (= Santa) St; (= Señorita) Miss.

stand, pl stands [es'tan, es'tan(s)] nm (COM) stand.

stárter [es'tarter] nm (AUTO) self-starter, starting motor.

status ['status, es'tatus] nm inv status.

statu(s) quo [es'tatu(s)'kuo] nm status quo.

Sto. abr (= Santo) St.

stop, pl stops [es'top, es'top(s)] nm (AUTO) stop sign.

su [su] pron (de él) his; (de ella) her; (de una cosa) its; (de ellos, ellas) their; (de usted, ustedes) your.

suave ['swaße] adj gentle; (superficie) smooth; (trabajo) easy; (música, voz) soft, sweet; (clima, carácter) mild.

suavice [swa'ßiθe] etc vb V **suavizar**.

suavidad [swaßi'ðað] nf gentleness; (de superficie) smoothness; (de música) softness, sweetness.

suavizante [swaßi'θante] nm conditioner.

suavizar [swaßi'θar] vt to soften; (quitar la aspereza) to smooth (out); (pendiente) to ease; (colores) to tone down; (carácter) to mellow; (dureza) to temper.

subalimentado, a [sußalimen'taðo, a] adj undernourished.

subalterno, a [sußal'terno, a] adj (importancia) secondary; (personal) minor, auxiliary ♦ nm subordinate.

subarrendar [sußarren'dar] vt (COM) to lease back.

subarriendo [sußa'rrjendo] nm (COM) leaseback.

subasta [su'ßasta] nf auction; **poner en** o **sacar a pública** ~ to put up for public auction; ~ **a la rebaja** Dutch auction.

subastador, a [sußasta'ðor, a] nm/f auctioneer.

subastar [sußas'tar] vt to auction (off).

subcampeón, ona [sußkampe'on, ona] nm/f runner-up.

subconsciente [sußkons'θjente] adj subconscious.

subcontratar [sußkontra'tar] vt (COM) to

subcontract.

subcontrato [suβkon'trato] *nm* (*COM*) subcontract.

subdesarrollado, a [suβðesarro'ʎaðo, a] *adj* underdeveloped.

subdesarrollo [suβðesa'rroʎo] *nm* underdevelopment.

subdirector, a [suβðirek'tor, a] *nm/f* assistant *o* deputy manager.

subdirectorio [suβðirek'torjo] *nm* (*INFORM*) subdirectory.

súbdito, a ['suβðito, a] *nm/f* subject.

subdividir [suβðiβi'ðir] *vt* to subdivide.

subempleo [suβem'pleo] *nm* underemployment.

subestimar [suβesti'mar] *vt* to underestimate, underrate.

subido, a [su'βiðo, a] *adj* (*color*) bright, strong; (*precio*) high ♦ *nf* (*de montaña etc*) ascent, climb; (*de precio*) rise, increase; (*pendiente*) slope, hill.

subíndice [su'βindiθe] *nm* (*INFORM, TIP*) subscript.

subir [su'βir] *vt* (*objeto*) to raise, lift up; (*cuesta, calle*) to go up; (*colina, montaña*) to climb; (*precio*) to raise, put up; (*empleado etc*) to promote ♦ *vi* to go/come up; (*a un coche*) to get in; (*a un autobús, tren*) to get on; (*precio*) to rise, go up; (*en el empleo*) to be promoted; (*río, marea*) to rise; ~**se** *vr* to get up, climb; ~**se a un coche** to get in(to) a car.

súbito, a ['suβito, a] *adj* (*repentino*) sudden; (*imprevisto*) unexpected.

subjetivo, a [suβxe'tiβo, a] *adj* subjective.

subjuntivo [suβxun'tiβo] *nm* subjunctive (mood).

sublevación [suβleβa'θjon] *nf* revolt, rising.

sublevar [suβle'βar] *vt* to rouse to revolt; ~**se** *vr* to revolt, rise.

sublimar [suβli'mar] *vt* (*persona*) to exalt; (*deseos etc*) to sublimate.

sublime [su'βlime] *adj* sublime.

subliminal [suβlimi'nal] *adj* subliminal.

submarinista [suβmari'nista] *nm/f* underwater explorer.

submarino, a [suβma'rino, a] *adj* underwater ♦ *nm* submarine.

subnormal [suβnor'mal] *adj* subnormal ♦ *nm/f* subnormal person.

suboficial [suβofi'θjal] *nm* non-commissioned officer.

subordinado, a [suβorði'naðo, a] *adj, nm/f* subordinate.

subproducto [suβpro'ðukto] *nm* by-product.

subrayado [suβra'jaðo] *nm* underlining.

subrayar [suβra'jar] *vt* to underline; (*recalcar*) to underline, emphasize.

subrepticio, a [suβrep'tiθjo, a] *adj* surreptitious.

subrutina [suβru'tina] *nf* (*INFORM*) subroutine.

subsanar [suβsa'nar] *vt* (*reparar*) to make good; (*perdonar*) to excuse; (*sobreponerse a*) to overcome.

subscribir [suβskri'βir] *vt* = **suscribir**.

subscrito [suβs'krito] *pp de* **subscribir**.

subsecretario, a [suβsekre'tarjo, a] *nm/f* undersecretary, assistant secretary.

subsidiariedad [suβsiðjarie'ðað] *nf* (*POL*) subsidiarity.

subsidiario, a [suβsi'ðjarjo, a] *adj* subsidiary.

subsidio [suβ'siðjo] *nm* (*ayuda*) aid, financial help; (*subvención*) subsidy, grant; (*de enfermedad, paro etc*) benefit, allowance.

subsistencia [suβsis'tenθja] *nf* subsistence.

subsistir [suβsis'tir] *vi* to subsist; (*vivir*) to live; (*sobrevivir*) to survive, endure.

subsuelo [suβ'swelo] *nm* subsoil.

subterfugio [suβter'fuxjo] *nm* subterfuge.

subterráneo, a [suβte'rraneo, a] *adj* underground, subterranean ♦ *nm* underpass, underground passage; (*AM*) underground railway, subway (*US*).

subtítulo [suβ'titulo] *nm* subtitle, subheading.

suburbano, a [suβur'βano, a] *adj* suburban.

suburbio [su'βurβjo] *nm* (*barrio*) slum quarter; (*afueras*) suburbs *pl*.

subvención [suββen'θjon] *nf* subsidy, subvention, grant; ~ **estatal** state subsidy *o* support; ~ **para la inversión** (*COM*) investment grant.

subvencionar [suββenθjo'nar] *vt* to subsidize.

subversión [suββer'sjon] *nf* subversion.

subversivo, a [suββer'siβo, a] *adj* subversive.

subyacente [suβja'θente] *adj* underlying.

subyugar [suβju'ɣar] *vt* (*país*) to subjugate, subdue; (*enemigo*) to overpower; (*voluntad*) to dominate.

subyugue [sub'juxe] *etc vb V* **subyugar**.

succión [suk'θjon] *nf* suction.

succionar [sukθjo'nar] *vt* (*sorber*) to suck; (*TEC*) to absorb, soak up.

sucedáneo, a [suθe'ðaneo, a] *adj* substitute ♦ *nm* substitute (food).

suceder [suθe'ðer] *vi* to happen; ~ **a** (*seguir*) to succeed, follow; **lo que sucede**

es que ... the fact is that ...; ~ **al trono** to succeed to the throne.

sucesión [suθe'sjon] nf succession; (serie) sequence, series; (hijos) issue, offspring.

sucesivamente [suθesißa'mente] adv: **y así** ~ and so on.

sucesivo, a [suθe'sißo, a] adj successive, following; **en lo** ~ in future, from now on.

suceso [su'θeso] nm (hecho) event, happening; (incidente) incident.

sucesor, a [suθe'sor, a] nm/f successor; (heredero) heir/heiress.

suciedad [suθje'ðað] nf (estado) dirtiness; (mugre) dirt, filth.

sucinto, a [su'θinto, a] adj (conciso) succinct, concise.

sucio, a ['suθjo, a] adj dirty; (mugriento) grimy; (manchado) grubby; (borroso) smudged; (conciencia) bad; (conducta) vile; (táctica) dirty, unfair.

Sucre ['sukre] n Sucre.

sucre ['sukre] nm Ecuadorean monetary unit.

suculento, a [suku'lento, a] adj (sabroso) tasty; (jugoso) succulent.

sucumbir [sukum'bir] vi to succumb.

sucursal [sukur'sal] nf branch (office); (filial) subsidiary.

Sudáfrica [su'ðafrika] nf South Africa.

sudafricano, a [suðafri'kano, a] adj, nm/f South African.

Sudamérica [suða'merika] nf South America.

sudamericano, a [suðameri'kano, a] adj, nm/f South American.

sudanés, esa [suða'nes, esa] adj, nm/f Sudanese.

sudar [su'ðar] vt, vi to sweat; (BOT) to ooze, give out o off.

sudeste [su'ðeste] adj south-east(ern); (rumbo, viento) south-easterly ♦ nm south-east; (viento) south-east wind.

sudoeste [suðo'este] adj south-west(ern); (rumbo, viento) south-westerly ♦ nm south-west; (viento) south-west wind.

sudor [su'ðor] nm sweat.

sudoroso, a [suðo'roso, a] adj sweaty, sweating.

Suecia ['sweθja] nf Sweden.

sueco, a ['sweko, a] adj Swedish ♦ nm/f Swede ♦ nm (LING) Swedish; **hacerse el** ~ to pretend not to hear o understand.

suegro, a ['sweɣro, a] nm/f father-/mother-in-law; **los** ~s one's in-laws.

suela ['swela] nf (de zapato, tb pescado) sole.

sueldo ['sweldo] etc vb V **soldar** ♦ nm pay, wage(s) (pl).

suelo ['swelo] etc vb V **soler** ♦ nm (tierra) ground; (de casa) floor.

suelto, a ['swelto, a] etc vb V **soltar** ♦ adj loose; (libre) free; (separado) detached; (ágil) quick, agile; (corriente) fluent, flowing ♦ nm (loose) change, small change; **está muy** ~ **en inglés** he is very good at o fluent in English.

suene ['swene] etc vb V **sonar**.

sueño ['sweɲo] etc vb V **soñar** ♦ nm sleep; (somnolencia) sleepiness, drowsiness; (lo soñado, fig) dream; ~ **pesado** o **profundo** deep o heavy sleep; **tener** ~ to be sleepy.

suero ['swero] nm (MED) serum; (de leche) whey.

suerte ['swerte] nf (fortuna) luck; (azar) chance; (destino) fate, destiny; (condición) lot; (género) sort, kind; **lo echaron a** ~s they drew lots o tossed up for it; **tener** ~ to be lucky; **de otra** ~ otherwise, if not; **de** ~ **que** so that, in such a way that.

suéter ['sweter], pl **suéters** nm sweater.

suficiencia [sufi'θjenθja] nf (cabida) sufficiency; (idoneidad) suitability; (aptitud) adequacy.

suficiente [sufi'θjente] adj enough, sufficient.

sufijo [su'fixo] nm suffix.

sufragar [sufra'ɣar] vt (ayudar) to help; (gastos) to meet; (proyecto) to pay for.

sufragio [su'fraxjo] nm (voto) vote; (derecho de voto) suffrage.

sufrague [su'fraxe] etc vb V **sufragar**.

sufrido, a [su'friðo, a] adj (de carácter fuerte) tough; (paciente) long-suffering; (tela) hard-wearing; (color) that does not show the dirt; (marido) complaisant.

sufrimiento [sufri'mjento] nm suffering.

sufrir [su'frir] vt (padecer) to suffer; (soportar) to bear, stand, put up with; (apoyar) to hold up, support ♦ vi to suffer.

sugerencia [suxe'renθja] nf suggestion.

sugerir [suxe'rir] vt to suggest; (sutilmente) to hint; (idea: incitar) to prompt.

sugestión [suxes'tjon] nf suggestion; (sutil) hint; (poder) hypnotic power.

sugestionar [suxestjo'nar] vt to influence.

sugestivo, a [suxes'tißo, a] adj stimulating; (atractivo) attractive; (fascinante) fascinating.

sugiera [su'xjera] etc, **sugiriendo** [suxi'rjendo] etc vb V **sugerir**.

suicida [sui'θiða] adj suicidal ♦ nm/f

suicidal person; (*muerto*) suicide, person who has committed suicide.

suicidarse [suiθi'ðarse] *vr* to commit suicide, kill o.s.

suicidio [sui'θiðjo] *nm* suicide.

Suiza ['swiθa] *nf* Switzerland.

suizo, a ['swiθo, a] *adj, nm/f* Swiss ♦ *nm* sugared bun.

sujeción [suxe'θjon] *nf* subjection.

sujetador [suxeta'ðor] *nm* fastener, clip; (*prenda femenina*) bra, brassiere.

sujetapapeles [suxetapa'peles] *nm inv* paper clip.

sujetar [suxe'tar] *vt* (*fijar*) to fasten; (*detener*) to hold down; (*fig*) to subject, subjugate; (*pelo etc*) to keep o hold in place; (*papeles*) to fasten together; ~**se** *vr* to subject o.s.

sujeto, a [su'xeto, a] *adj* fastened, secure ♦ *nm* subject; (*individuo*) individual; (*fam: tipo*) fellow, character, type, guy (*US*); ~ **a** subject to.

sulfurar [sulfu'rar] *vt* (*TEC*) to sulphurate; (*sacar de quicio*) to annoy; ~**se** *vr* (*enojarse*) to get riled, see red, blow up.

sulfuro [sul'furo] *nm* sulphide.

suma ['suma] *nf* (*cantidad*) total, sum; (*de dinero*) sum; (*acto*) adding (up), addition; en ~ in short; ~ **y sigue** (*COM*) carry forward.

sumador [suma'ðor] *nm* (*INFORM*) adder.

sumamente [suma'mente] *adv* extremely, exceedingly.

sumar [su'mar] *vt* to add (up); (*reunir*) to collect, gather ♦ *vi* to add up.

sumario, a [su'marjo, a] *adj* brief, concise ♦ *nm* summary.

sumergir [sumer'xir] *vt* to submerge; (*hundir*) to sink; (*bañar*) to immerse, dip; ~**se** *vr* (*hundirse*) to sink beneath the surface.

sumerja [su'merxa] *etc vb V* **sumergir**.

sumidero [sumi'ðero] *nm* drain, sewer; (*TEC*) sump.

suministrador, a [suministra'ðor, a] *nm/f* supplier.

suministrar [suminis'trar] *vt* to supply, provide.

suministro [sumi'nistro] *nm* supply; (*acto*) supplying, providing.

sumir [su'mir] *vt* to sink, submerge; (*fig*) to plunge; ~**se** *vr* (*objeto*) to sink; ~**se en el estudio** to become absorbed in one's studies.

sumisión [sumi'sjon] *nf* (*acto*) submission; (*calidad*) submissiveness, docility.

sumiso, a [su'miso, a] *adj* submissive, docile.

súmmum ['sumum] *nm inv* (*fig*) height.

sumo, a ['sumo, a] *adj* great, extreme; (*mayor*) highest, supreme ♦ *nm* sumo (wrestling); **a lo** ~ at most.

suntuoso, a [sun'twoso, a] *adj* sumptuous, magnificent; (*lujoso*) lavish.

sup. *abr* (= *superior*) sup.

supe ['supe] *etc vb V* **saber**.

supeditar [supeði'tar] *vt* to subordinate; (*sojuzgar*) to subdue; (*oprimir*) to oppress; ~**se** *vr*: ~**se a** to subject o.s. to.

supensivo, a [suspen'siβo, a] *adj*: **puntos** ~**s** dots, suspension points.

super... [super] *pref* super..., over....

súper ['super] *adj* (*fam*) super, great.

superable [supe'raβle] *adj* (*dificultad*) surmountable; (*tarea*) that can be performed.

superación [supera'θjon] *nf* (*tb*: ~ **personal**) self-improvement.

superar [supe'rar] *vt* (*sobreponerse a*) to overcome; (*rebasar*) to surpass, do better than; (*pasar*) to go beyond; (*marca, récord*) to break; (*etapa: dejar atrás*) to get past; ~**se** *vr* to excel o.s.

superávit [supe'raβit], *pl* **superávits** *nm* surplus.

superchería [supertʃe'ria] *nf* fraud, trick, swindle.

superficial [superfi'θjal] *adj* superficial; (*medida*) surface *cpd*.

superficie [super'fiθje] *nf* surface; (*área*) area; **grandes** ~**s** (*COM*) superstores.

superfluo, a [su'perflwo, a] *adj* superfluous.

superíndice [supe'rindiθe] *nm* (*INFORM, TIP*) superscript.

superintendente [superinten'dente] *nm/f* supervisor, superintendent.

superior [supe'rjor] *adj* (*piso, clase*) upper; (*temperatura, número, nivel*) higher; (*mejor: calidad, producto*) superior, better ♦ *nm/f* superior.

superiora [supe'rjora] *nf* (*REL*) mother superior.

superioridad [superjori'ðað] *nf* superiority.

superlativo, a [superla'tiβo, a] *adj, nm* superlative.

supermercado [supermer'kaðo] *nm* supermarket.

superpoblación [superpoβla'θjon] *nf* overpopulation; (*congestionamiento*) overcrowding.

superponer [superpo'ner] *vt* (*INFORM*) to overstrike.

superposición [superposi'θjon] *nf* (*en impresora*) overstrike.

superpotencia [superpo'tenθja] *nf* superpower, great power.
superproducción [superproðuk'θjon] *nf* overproduction.
supersónico, a [super'soniko, a] *adj* supersonic.
superstición [supersti'θjon] *nf* superstition.
supersticioso, a [supersti'θjoso, a] *adj* superstitious.
supervisar [superßi'sar] *vt* to supervise; (*COM*) to superintend.
supervisor, a [superßi'sor, a] *nm/f* supervisor.
supervivencia [superßi'ßenθja] *nf* survival.
superviviente [superßi'ßjente] *adj* surviving ♦ *nm/f* survivor.
suplantar [suplan'tar] *vt* (*persona*) to supplant; (*hacerse pasar por otro*) to take the place of.
suplementario, a [suplemen'tarjo, a] *adj* supplementary.
suplemento [suple'mento] *nm* supplement.
suplencia [su'plenθja] *nf* substitution, replacement; (*etapa*) period during which one deputizes *etc*.
suplente [su'plente] *adj* substitute; (*disponible*) reserve ♦ *nm/f* substitute.
supletorio, a [suple'torjo, a] *adj* supplementary; (*adicional*) extra ♦ *nm* supplement; **mesa supletoria** spare table.
súplica ['suplika] *nf* request; (*REL*) supplication; (*JUR: instancia*) petition; **~s** *nfpl* entreaties.
suplicar [supli'kar] *vt* (*cosa*) to beg (for), plead for; (*persona*) to beg, plead with; (*JUR*) to appeal to, petition.
suplicio [su'pliθjo] *nm* torture; (*tormento*) torment; (*emoción*) anguish; (*experiencia penosa*) ordeal.
suplique [su'plike] *etc vb V* **suplicar.**
suplir [su'plir] *vt* (*compensar*) to make good, make up for; (*reemplazar*) to replace, substitute ♦ *vi*: **~ a** to take the place of, substitute for.
supo ['supo] *etc vb V* **saber.**
supondré [supon'dre] *etc vb V* **suponer.**
suponer [supo'ner] *vt* to suppose; (*significar*) to mean; (*acarrear*) to involve ♦ *vi* to count, have authority; **era de ~ que ...** it was to be expected that ....
suponga [su'ponga] *etc vb V* **suponer.**
suposición [suposi'θjon] *nf* supposition.
supositorio [suposi'torjo] *nm* suppository.
supremacía [suprema'θia] *nf* supremacy.
supremo, a [su'premo, a] *adj* supreme.

supresión [supre'sjon] *nf* suppression; (*de derecho*) abolition; (*de dificultad*) removal; (*de palabra etc*) deletion; (*de restricción*) cancellation, lifting.
suprimir [supri'mir] *vt* to suppress; (*derecho, costumbre*) to abolish; (*dificultad*) to remove; (*palabra etc, INFORM*) to delete; (*restricción*) to cancel, lift.
supuestamente [supwesta'mente] *adv* supposedly.
supuesto, a [su'pwesto, a] *pp de* **suponer** ♦ *adj* (*hipotético*) supposed; (*falso*) false ♦ *nm* assumption, hypothesis ♦ *conj*: **~ que** since; **dar por ~ algo** to take sth for granted; **por ~** of course.
supurar [supu'rar] *vi* to fester, suppurate.
supuse [su'puse] *etc vb V* **suponer.**
sur [sur] *adj* southern; (*rumbo*) southerly ♦ *nm* south; (*viento*) south wind.
Suráfrica [su'rafrika] *etc* = **Sudáfrica** *etc*.
Suramérica [sura'merika] *etc* = **Sudamérica** *etc*.
surcar [sur'kar] *vt* to plough; (*superficie*) to cut, score.
surco ['surko] *nm* (*en metal, disco*) groove; (*AGR*) furrow.
surcoreano, a [surkore'ano, a] *adj, nm/f* South Korean.
sureño, a [su'reɲo, a] *adj* southern ♦ *nm/f* southerner.
sureste [su'reste] = **sudeste.**
surf [surf] *nm* surfing.
surgir [sur'xir] *vi* to arise, emerge; (*dificultad*) to come up, crop up.
surja ['surxa] *etc vb V* **surgir.**
suroeste [suro'este] = **sudoeste.**
surque ['surke] *etc vb V* **surcar.**
surrealismo [surrea'lismo] *nm* surrealism.
surrealista [surrea'lista] *adj, nm/f* surrealist.
surtido, a [sur'tiðo, a] *adj* mixed, assorted ♦ *nm* (*selección*) selection, assortment; (*abastecimiento*) supply, stock.
surtidor [surti'ðor] *nm* (*chorro*) jet, spout; (*fuente*) fountain; **~ de gasolina** petrol (*BRIT*) *o* gas (*US*) pump.
surtir [sur'tir] *vt* to supply, provide; (*efecto*) to have, produce ♦ *vi* to spout, spurt; **~se** *vr*: **~se de** to provide o.s. with.
susceptible [susθep'tißle] *adj* susceptible; (*sensible*) sensitive; **~ de** capable of.
suscitar [susθi'tar] *vt* to cause, provoke; (*discusión*) to start; (*duda, problema*) to raise; (*interés, sospechas*) to arouse.
suscribir [suskri'ßir] *vt* (*firmar*) to sign; (*respaldar*) to subscribe to, endorse; (*COM: acciones*) to take out an option on;

~**se** *vr* to subscribe; ~ **a algn a una
revista** to take out a subscription to a
journal for sb.

suscripción [suskrip'θjon] *nf* subscription.

suscrito, a [sus'krito, a] *pp de* **suscribir**
♦ *adj:* ~ **en exceso** oversubscribed.

susodicho, a [suso'ditʃo, a] *adj* above-
mentioned.

suspender [suspen'der] *vt* (*objeto*) to hang
(up), suspend; (*trabajo*) to stop, suspend;
(*ESCOL*) to fail.

suspense [sus'pense] *nm* suspense.

suspensión [suspen'sjon] *nf* suspension;
(*fig*) stoppage, suspension; (*JUR*) stay; ~
de fuego *o* **de hostilidades** ceasefire,
cessation of hostilities; ~ **de pagos**
suspension of payments.

suspenso, a [sus'penso, a] *adj* hanging,
suspended; (*ESCOL*) failed ♦ *nm* (*ESCOL*)
fail(ure); **quedar** *o* **estar en** ~ to be
pending.

suspicacia [suspi'kaθja] *nf* suspicion,
mistrust.

suspicaz [suspi'kaθ] *adj* suspicious,
distrustful.

suspirar [suspi'rar] *vi* to sigh.

suspiro [sus'piro] *nm* sigh.

sustancia [sus'tanθja] *nf* substance; ~ **gris**
(*ANAT*) grey matter; **sin** ~ lacking in
substance, shallow.

sustancial [sustan'θjal] *adj* substantial.

sustancioso, a [sustan'θjoso, a] *adj*
substantial; (*discurso*) solid.

sustantivo, a [sustan'tiβo, a] *adj*
substantive; (*LING*) substantival, noun
cpd ♦ *nm* noun, substantive.

sustentar [susten'tar] *vt* (*alimentar*) to
sustain, nourish; (*objeto*) to hold up,
support; (*idea, teoría*) to maintain,
uphold; (*fig*) to sustain, keep going.

sustento [sus'tento] *nm* support; (*alimento*)
sustenance, food.

sustituir [sustitu'ir] *vt* to substitute,
replace.

sustituto, a [susti'tuto, a] *nm/f* substitute,
replacement.

sustituyendo [sustitu'jendo] *etc vb V*
sustituir.

susto ['susto] *nm* fright, scare; **dar un** ~ **a
algn** to give sb a fright; **darse** *o* **pegarse
un** ~ (*fam*) to get a fright.

sustraer [sustra'er] *vt* to remove, take
away; (*MAT*) to subtract.

sustraiga [sus'traixa] *etc,* **sustraje**
[sus'traxe] *etc,* **sustrajera** [sustra'xera]
etc vb V **sustraer.**

sustrato [sus'trato] *nm* substratum.

sustrayendo [sustra'jendo] *etc vb V*
sustraer.

susurrar [susu'rrar] *vi* to whisper.

susurro [su'surro] *nm* whisper.

sutil [su'til] *adj* (*aroma*) subtle; (*tenue*) thin;
(*hilo, hebra*) fine; (*olor*) delicate; (*brisa*)
gentle; (*diferencia*) fine, subtle;
(*inteligencia*) sharp, keen.

sutileza [suti'leθa] *nf* subtlety; (*delgadez*)
thinness; (*delicadeza*) delicacy; (*agudeza*)
keenness.

sutura [su'tura] *nf* suture.

suturar [sutu'rar] *vt* to suture; (*juntar con
puntos*) to stitch.

suyo, a ['sujo, a] *adj* (*con artículo o después
del verbo ser: de él*) his; (: *de ella*) hers;
(: *de ellos, ellas*) theirs; (: *de usted,
ustedes*) yours; (*después de un nombre: de
él*) of his; (: *de ella*) of hers; (: *de ellos,
ellas*) of theirs; (: *de usted, ustedes*) of
yours; **lo** ~ (what is) his; (*su parte*) his
share, what he deserves; **los** ~**s** (*familia*)
one's family *o* relations; (*partidarios*)
one's own people *o* supporters; ~
afectísimo (*en carta*) yours faithfully *o*
sincerely; **de** ~ in itself; **eso es muy** ~
that's just like him; **hacer de las suyas** to
get up to one's old tricks; **ir a la suya, ir
a lo** ~ to go one's own way; **salirse con la
suya** to get one's way.

T t

T, t [te] *nf* (*letra*) T, t; **T de Tarragona** T for
Tommy.

t *abr* = **tonelada.**

T. *abr* (= *Telefón, Telégrafo*) tel.; (*COM*)
= **Tarifa; Tasa.**

t. *abr* (= *tomo(s)*) vol(s).

Tabacalera [taβaka'lera] *nf Spanish state
tobacco monopoly.*

tabaco [ta'βako] *nm* tobacco; (*fam*)
cigarettes *pl.*

tábano ['taβano] *nm* horsefly.

tabaquería [tabake'ria] *nf* tobacconist's
(*BRIT*), cigar store (*US*).

tabarra [ta'βarra] *nf* (*fam*) nuisance; **dar la**
~ to be a pain in the neck.

taberna [ta'βerna] *nf* bar.

tabernero, a [taβer'nero, a] *nm/f*
(*encargado*) publican; (*camarero*)
barman/barmaid.

tabique [ta'ßike] nm (*pared*) thin wall; (*para dividir*) partition.

tabla ['taßla] nf (*de madera*) plank; (*estante*) shelf; (*de anuncios*) board; (*lista, catálogo*) list; (*mostrador*) counter; (*de vestido*) pleat; (*ARTE*) panel; ~s nfpl (*TAUR, TEAT*) boards; **hacer** ~s to draw; ~ **de consulta** (*INFORM*) lookup table.

tablado [ta'ßlaðo] nm (*plataforma*) platform; (*suelo*) plank floor; (*TEAT*) stage.

tablao [ta'ßlao] nm (*tb:* ~ **flamenco**) flamenco show.

tablero [ta'ßlero] nm (*de madera*) plank, board; (*pizarra*) blackboard; (*de ajedrez, damas*) board; (*AUTO*) dashboard; ~ **de gráficos** (*INFORM*) graph pad.

tableta [ta'ßleta] nf (*MED*) tablet; (*de chocolate*) bar.

tablilla [ta'ßliʎa] nf small board; (*MED*) splint.

tablón [ta'ßlon] nm (*de suelo*) plank; (*de techo*) beam; (*de anuncios*) notice board.

tabú [ta'ßu] nm taboo.

tabulación [taßula'θjon] nf (*INFORM*) tab(bing).

tabulador [taßula'ðor] nm (*INFORM, TIP*) tab.

tabuladora [taßula'ðora] nf: ~ **eléctrica** electric accounting machine.

tabular [taßu'lar] vt to tabulate; (*INFORM*) to tab.

taburete [taßu'rete] nm stool.

tacaño, a [ta'kaɲo, a] adj (*avaro*) mean; (*astuto*) crafty.

tacha ['tatʃa] nf (*defecto*) flaw, defect; (*TEC*) stud; **poner** ~ **a** to find fault with; **sin** ~ flawless.

tachar [ta'tʃar] vt (*borrar*) to cross out; (*corregir*) to correct; (*criticar*) to criticize; ~ **de** to accuse of.

tacho ['tatʃo] nm (*AM*) bucket, pail.

tachón [ta'tʃon] nm erasure; (*tachadura*) crossing-out; (*TEC*) ornamental stud; (*COSTURA*) trimming.

tachuela [ta'tʃwela] nf (*clavo*) tack.

tácito, a ['taθito, a] adj tacit; (*acuerdo*) unspoken; (*LING*) understood; (*ley*) unwritten.

taciturno, a [taθi'turno, a] adj (*callado*) silent; (*malhumorado*) sullen.

taco ['tako] nm (*BILLAR*) cue; (*libro de billetes*) book; (*manojo de billetes*) wad; (*AM*) heel; (*tarugo*) peg; (*fam: bocado*) snack; (: *palabrota*) swear word; (: *trago de vino*) swig; (*Méjico*) filled tortilla; **armarse o hacerse un** ~ to get into a mess.

tacógrafo [ta'koɣrafo] nm (*COM*) tachograph.

tacón [ta'kon] nm heel; **de** ~ **alto** high-heeled.

taconear [takone'ar] vi (*dar golpecitos*) to tap with one's heels; (*MIL etc*) to click one's heels.

taconeo [tako'neo] nm (heel) tapping o clicking.

táctico, a ['taktiko, a] adj tactical ♦ nf tactics pl.

tacto ['takto] nm touch; (*acción*) touching; (*fig*) tact.

TAE nf abr (= *tasa anual equivalente*) APR.

tafetán [tafe'tan] nm taffeta; **tafetanes** nmpl (*fam*) frills; ~ **adhesivo o inglés** sticking plaster.

tafilete [tafi'lete] nm morocco leather.

tahona [ta'ona] nf (*panadería*) bakery; (*molino*) flourmill.

tahur [ta'ur] nm gambler; (*pey*) cheat.

tailandés, esa [tailan'des, esa] adj, nm/f Thai ♦ nm (*LING*) Thai.

Tailandia [tai'landja] nf Thailand.

taimado, a [tai'maðo, a] adj (*astuto*) sly; (*resentido*) sullen.

taita ['taita] nm dad, daddy.

tajada [ta'xaða] nf slice; (*fam*) rake-off; **sacar** ~ to get one's share.

tajante [ta'xante] adj sharp; (*negativa*) emphatic; **es una persona** ~ he's an emphatic person.

tajar [ta'xar] vt to cut, slice.

Tajo ['taxo] nm Tagus.

tajo ['taxo] nm (*corte*) cut; (*filo*) cutting edge; (*GEO*) cleft.

tal [tal] adj such; **un** ~ **García** a man called García; ~ **vez** perhaps ♦ pron (*persona*) someone, such a one; (*cosa*) something, such a thing; ~ **como** such as; ~ **para cual** tit for tat; (*dos iguales*) two of a kind; **hablábamos de que si** ~ **si cual** we were talking about this, that and the other ♦ adv: ~ **como** (*igual*) just as; ~ **cual** (*como es*) just as it is; ~ **el padre, cual el hijo** like father, like son; **¿qué** ~**?** how are things?; **¿qué** ~ **te gusta?** how do you like it? ♦ conj: **con** ~ **(de) que** provided that.

tala ['tala] nf (*de árboles*) tree felling.

taladradora [talaðra'ðora] nf drill; ~ **neumática** pneumatic drill.

taladrar [tala'ðrar] vt to drill; (*fig: suj: ruido*) to pierce.

taladro [ta'laðro] nm (*gen*) drill; (*hoyo*) drill hole; ~ **neumático** pneumatic drill.

talante [ta'lante] nm (*humor*) mood; (*voluntad*) will, willingness.

talar [ta'lar] vt to fell, cut down; (*fig*) to devastate.

tarro ['tarro] *nm* jar, pot.

tarta ['tarta] *nf (pastel)* cake; *(torta)* tart.

tartajear [tartaxe'ar] *vi* to stammer.

tartamudear [tartamuðe'ar] *vi* to stutter, stammer.

tartamudo, a [tarta'muðo, a] *adj* stuttering, stammering ♦ *nm/f* stutterer, stammerer.

tartárico, a [tar'tariko, a] *adj*: **ácido ~** tartaric acid.

tártaro ['tartaro] *adj, nm* Tartar ♦ *nm (QUIMICA)* tartar.

tarugo, a [ta'ruɣo, a] *adj* stupid ♦ *nm (de madera)* lump.

tarumba [ta'rumba] *adj (confuso)* confused.

tasa ['tasa] *nf (precio)* (fixed) price, rate; *(valoración)* valuation; *(medida, norma)* measure, standard; **~ básica (COM)** basic rate; **~ de cambio** exchange rate; **de ~ cero (COM)** zero-rated; **~ de crecimiento** growth rate; **~ de interés/de nacimiento** rate of interest/birth rate; **~ de rendimiento (COM)** rate of return; **~s universitarias** university fees.

tasación [tasa'θjon] *nf* assessment, valuation; *(fig)* appraisal.

tasador, a [tasa'ðor, a] *nm/f* valuer; *(COM: de impuestos)* assessor.

tasar [ta'sar] *vt (arreglar el precio)* to fix a price for; *(valorar)* to value, assess; *(limitar)* to limit.

tasca ['taska] *nf (fam)* pub.

tata ['tata] *nm (fam)* dad(dy) ♦ *nf (niñera)* nanny, maid.

tatarabuelo, a [tatara'ßwelo, a] *nm/f* great-great-grandfather/mother; **los ~s** one's great-great-grandparents.

tatuaje [ta'twaxe] *nm (dibujo)* tattoo; *(acto)* tattooing.

tatuar [ta'twar] *vt* to tattoo.

taumaturgo [tauma'turɣo] *nm* miracle-worker.

taurino, a [tau'rino, a] *adj* bullfighting *cpd*.

Tauro ['tauro] *nm* Taurus.

tauromaquia [tauro'makja] *nf* (art of) bullfighting.

tautología [tautolo'xia] *nf* tautology.

taxativo, a [taksa'tißo, a] *adj (restringido)* limited; *(sentido)* specific.

taxi ['taksi] *nm* taxi.

taxidermia [taksi'ðermja] *nf* taxidermy.

taxímetro [tak'simetro] *nm* taximeter.

taxista [tak'sista] *nm/f* taxi driver.

Tayikistán [tajikis'tan] *nm* Tajikistan.

taza ['taθa] *nf* cup; *(de retrete)* bowl; **~ para café** coffee cup.

tazón [ta'θon] *nm* mug, large cup;

(escudilla) basin.

TCI *nf abr* (= *tarjeta de circuito impreso*) PCB.

te [te] *pron (complemento de objeto)* you; *(complemento indirecto)* (to) you; *(reflexivo)* (to) yourself; **¿~ duele mucho el brazo?** does your arm hurt a lot?; **~ equivocas** you're wrong; **¡cálma~!** calm yourself!

té [te] *pl* **tés** *nm* tea; *(reunión)* tea party.

tea ['tea] *nf (antorcha)* torch.

teatral [tea'tral] *adj* theatre *cpd*; *(fig)* theatrical.

teatro [te'atro] *nm* theatre; *(LITERATURA)* plays *pl*, drama; **el ~** *(carrera)* the theatre, acting; **~ de aficionados/de variedades** amateur/variety theatre, vaudeville theater *(US)*; **hacer ~** *(fig)* to make a fuss.

tebeo [te'ßeo] *nm* children's comic.

techado [te'tʃaðo] *nm (techo)* roof; **bajo ~** under cover.

techo ['tetʃo] *nm (externo)* roof; *(interno)* ceiling.

techumbre [te'tʃumbre] *nf* roof.

tecla ['tekla] *nf (INFORM, MUS, TIP)* key; *(INFORM)*: **~ de anulación/de borrar** cancel/delete key; **~ de control/de edición** control/edit key; **~ con flecha** arrow key; **~ programable** user-defined key; **~ de retorno/de tabulación** return/tab key; **~ del cursor** cursor key; **~s de control direccional del cursor** cursor control keys.

teclado [te'klaðo] *nm* keyboard *(tb INFORM)*; **~ numérico** *(INFORM)* numeric keypad.

teclear [tekle'ar] *vi* to strum; *(fam)* to drum ♦ *vt (INFORM)* to key (in), type in, keyboard.

tecleo [te'kleo] *nm (MUS: sonido)* strumming; *(: forma de tocar)* fingering; *(fam)* drumming.

tecnicismo [tekni'θismo] *nm (carácter técnico)* technical nature; *(LING)* technical term.

técnico, a ['tekniko, a] *adj* technical ♦ *nm* technician; *(experto)* expert ♦ *nf (procedimientos)* technique; *(arte, oficio)* craft.

tecnicolor [tekniko'lor] *nm* Technicolor ®.

tecnócrata [tek'nokrata] *nm/f* technocrat.

tecnología [teknolo'xia] *nf* technology; **~ de estado sólido** *(INFORM)* solid-state technology; **~ de la información** information technology.

tecnológico, a [tekno'loxiko, a] *adj* technological.

tesis ['tesis] nf inv thesis.
tesón [te'son] nm (firmeza) firmness; (tenacidad) tenacity.
tesorería [tesore'ria] nf treasurership.
tesorero, a [teso'rero, a] nm/f treasurer.
tesoro [te'soro] nm treasure; **T~ público** (POL) Exchequer.
test, pl **tests** [tes(t), tes(t)] nm test.
testaferro [testa'ferro] nm figurehead.
testamentaría [testamenta'ria] nf execution of a will.
testamentario, a [testamen'tarjo, a] adj testamentary ♦ nm/f executor/executrix.
testamento [testa'mento] nm will.
testar [tes'tar] vi to make a will.
testarada [testa'raða] nf, **testarazo** [testa'raθo] nm: **darse un(a) ~** (fam) to bump one's head.
testarudo, a [testa'ruðo, a] adj stubborn.
testículo [tes'tikulo] nm testicle.
testificar [testifi'kar] vt to testify; (fig) to attest ♦ vi to give evidence.
testifique [testi'fike] etc vb V **testificar**.
testigo [tes'tiɣo] nm/f witness; **~ de cargo/descargo** witness for the prosecution/defence; **~ ocular** eye witness; **poner a algn por ~** to cite sb as a witness.
testimonial [testimo'njal] adj (prueba) testimonial; (gesto) token.
testimoniar [testimo'njar] vt to testify to; (fig) to show.
testimonio [testi'monjo] nm testimony; **en ~ de** as a token o mark of; **falso ~** perjured evidence, false witness.
teta ['teta] nf (de biberón) teat; (ANAT) nipple; (fam) breast; (fam!) tit (!).
tétanos ['tetanos] nm tetanus.
tetera [te'tera] nf teapot; **~ eléctrica** (electric) kettle.
tetilla [te'tiʎa] nf (ANAT) nipple; (de biberón) teat.
tétrico, a ['tetriko, a] adj gloomy, dismal.
textil [teks'til] adj textile.
texto ['teksto] nm text.
textual [teks'twal] adj textual; **palabras ~es** exact words.
textura [teks'tura] nf (de tejido) texture; (de mineral) structure.
tez [teθ] nf (cutis) complexion; (color) colouring.
tfno. abr (= teléfono) tel.
ti [ti] pron you; (reflexivo) yourself.
tía ['tia] nf (pariente) aunt; (mujer cualquiera) girl, bird (col); (fam: pej: vieja) old bag; (: prostituta) whore.
Tibet [ti'ßet] nm: **El ~** Tibet.

tibetano, a [tiße'tano, a] adj, nm/f Tibetan ♦ nm (LING) Tibetan.
tibia ['tißja] nf tibia.
tibieza [ti'ßjeθa] nf (temperatura) tepidness; (fig) coolness.
tibio, a ['tißjo, a] adj lukewarm, tepid.
tiburón [tißu'ron] nm shark.
tic [tik] nm (ruido) click; (de reloj) tick; **~ nervioso** (MED) nervous tic.
tico, a ['tiko, a] adj, nm/f (AM fam) Costa Rican.
tictac [tik'tak] nm (de reloj) tick tock.
tiemble ['tjemble] etc vb V **temblar**.
tiempo ['tjempo] nm (gen) time; (época, período) age, period; (METEOROLOGÍA) weather; (LING) tense; (edad) age; (de juego) half; **a ~** in time; **a un o al mismo ~** at the same time; **al poco ~** very soon (after); **andando el ~** in due course; **cada cierto ~** every so often; **con ~** in time; **con el ~** eventually; **de ~ en ~** from time to time; **en mis ~s** in my time; **en los buenos ~s** in the good old days; **hace buen/mal ~** the weather is fine/bad; **estar a ~** to be in time; **hace ~** some time ago; **hacer ~** to while away the time; **¿qué ~ tiene?** how old is he?; **motor de 2 ~s** two-stroke engine; **~ compartido** (INFORM) time sharing; **~ de ejecución** (INFORM) run time; **~ inactivo** (COM) downtime; **~ libre** spare time; **~ de paro** (COM) idle time; **a ~ partido** (trabajar) part-time; **~ preferencial** (COM) prime time; **en ~ real** (INFORM) real time.
tienda ['tjenda] etc vb V **tender** ♦ nf shop; (más grande) store; (NAUT) awning; **~ de campaña** tent.
tiene ['tjene] etc vb V **tener**.
tienta ['tjenta] nf (MED) probe; (fig) tact; **andar a ~s** to grope one's way along.
tiento ['tjento] etc vb V **tentar** ♦ nm (tacto) touch; (precaución) wariness; (pulso) steady hand; (ZOOL) feeler, tentacle.
tierno, a ['tjerno, a] adj (blando, dulce) tender; (fresco) fresh.
tierra ['tjerra] nf earth; (suelo) soil; (mundo) world; (país) country, land; (ELEC) earth, ground (US); **~ adentro** inland; **~ natal** native land; **echar ~ a un asunto** to hush an affair up; **no es de estas ~s** he's not from these parts; **la T~ Santa** the Holy Land.
tieso, a ['tjeso, a] etc vb V **tesar** ♦ adj (rígido) rigid; (duro) stiff; (fig: testarudo) stubborn; (fam: orgulloso) conceited ♦ adv strongly.
tiesto ['tjesto] nm flowerpot; (pedazo)

piece of pottery.

tifoidea [tifoi'ðea] nf typhoid.

tifón [ti'fon] nm (huracán) typhoon; (de mar) tidal wave.

tifus ['tifus] nm typhus; ~ **icteroides** yellow fever.

tigre ['tiɣre] nm tiger; (AM) jaguar.

tijera [ti'xera] nf (una ~) (pair of) scissors pl; (ZOOL) claw; (persona) gossip; **de ~** folding; **~s** nfpl scissors; (para plantas) shears; **unas ~s** a pair of scissors.

tijeretear [tixerete'ar] vt to snip ♦ vi (fig) to meddle.

tila ['tila] nf (BOT) lime tree; (CULIN) lime flower tea.

tildar [til'dar] vt: ~ **de** to brand as.

tilde ['tilde] nf (defecto) defect; (trivialidad) triviality; (TIP) tilde.

tilín [ti'lin] nm tinkle.

tilo ['tilo] nm lime tree.

timador, a [tima'ðor, a] nm/f swindler.

timar [ti'mar] vt (robar) to steal; (estafar) to swindle; (persona) to con; **~se** vr (fam) to make eyes (con algn at sb).

timbal [tim'bal] nm small drum.

timbrar [tim'brar] vt to stamp; (sellar) to seal; (carta) to postmark.

timbrazo [tim'braθo] nm ring; **dar un ~** to ring the bell.

timbre ['timbre] nm (sello) stamp; (campanilla) bell; (tono) timbre; (COM) stamp duty.

timidez [timi'ðeθ] nf shyness.

tímido, a ['timiðo, a] adj shy, timid.

timo ['timo] nm swindle; **dar un ~ a algn** to swindle sb.

timón [ti'mon] nm helm, rudder; (AM) steering wheel; **coger el ~** (fig) to take charge.

timonel [timo'nel] nm helmsman.

timorato, a [timo'rato, a] adj God-fearing; (mojigato) sanctimonious.

tímpano ['timpano] nm (ANAT) eardrum; (MUS) small drum.

tina ['tina] nf tub; (AM: baño) bath(tub).

tinaja [ti'naxa] nf large earthen jar.

tinerfeño, a [tiner'feɲo, a] adj of o from Tenerife ♦ nm/f native o inhabitant of Tenerife.

tinglado [tin'glaðo] nm (cobertizo) shed; (fig: truco) trick; (intriga) intrigue; **armar un ~** to lay a plot.

tinieblas [ti'njeβlas] nfpl darkness sg; (sombras) shadows; **estamos en ~ sobre sus proyectos** (fig) we are in the dark about his plans.

tino ['tino] nm (habilidad) skill; (MIL) marksmanship; (juicio) insight;

(moderación) moderation; **sin ~** immoderately; **coger el ~** to get the feel o hang of it.

tinta ['tinta] nf ink; (TEC) dye; (ARTE) colour; ~ **china** Indian ink; **~s** nfpl (fig) shades; **medias ~s** (fig) half measures; **saber algo de buena ~** to have sth on good authority.

tinte ['tinte] nm (acto) dyeing; (fig) tinge; (barniz) veneer.

tintero [tin'tero] nm inkwell; **se le quedó en el ~** he clean forgot about it.

tintinear [tintine'ar] vt to tinkle.

tinto, a ['tinto, a] adj (teñido) dyed; (manchado) stained ♦ nm red wine.

tintorera [tinto'rera] nf shark.

tintorería [tintore'ria] nf dry cleaner's.

tintorero [tinto'rero] nm dry cleaner('s).

tintura [tin'tura] nf (acto) dyeing; (QUÍMICA) dye; (farmacéutico) tincture.

tiña ['tiɲa] etc vb V **teñir** ♦ nf (MED) ringworm.

tío ['tio] nm (pariente) uncle; (fam: viejo) old fellow; (: individuo) bloke, chap, guy (US).

tiovivo [tio'βiβo] nm roundabout.

típico, a ['tipiko, a] adj typical; (pintoresco) picturesque.

tiple ['tiple] nm soprano (voice) ♦ nf soprano.

tipo ['tipo] nm (clase) type, kind; (norma) norm; (patrón) pattern; (fam: hombre) fellow, bloke, guy (US); (ANAT) build; (: de mujer) figure; (IMPRENTA) type; ~ **bancario/de descuento** bank/discount rate; ~ **de interés** interest rate; ~ **de interés vigente** (COM) standard rate; ~ **de cambio** exchange rate; ~ **base** (COM) base rate; ~ **a término** (COM) forward rate; **dos ~s sospechosos** two suspicious characters; ~ **de letra** (INFORM, TIP) typeface; ~ **de datos** (INFORM) data type.

tipografía [tipoɣra'fia] nf (tipo) printing; (lugar) printing press.

tipográfico, a [tipo'ɣrafiko, a] adj printing.

tipógrafo, a [ti'poɣrafo, a] nm/f printer.

tique(t) ['tike], pl **tique(t)s** ['tikes] nm ticket; (en tienda) cash slip.

tiquismiquis [tikis'mikis] nm fussy person ♦ nmpl (querellas) squabbling sg; (escrúpulos) silly scruples.

tira ['tira] nf strip; (fig) abundance ♦ nm: ~ **y afloja** give and take; (cautela) caution; **la ~ de ...** (fam) lots of ....

tirabuzón [tiraβu'θon] nm corkscrew; (rizo) curl.

tiradero [tira'ðero] nm (AM) rubbish dump.

tirado, a [ti'raðo, a] *adj* (*barato*) dirt-cheap; (*fam: fácil*) very easy ♦ *nf* (*acto*) cast, throw; (*distancia*) distance; (*serie*) series; (*TIP*) printing, edition; **de una tirada** at one go; **está ~** (*fam*) it's a cinch.

tirador, a [tira'ðor, a] *nm/f* (*persona*) shooter ♦ *nm* (*mango*) handle; (*ELEC*) flex; **~ certero** sniper.

tiralíneas [tira'lineas] *nm inv* ruling-pen.

tiranía [tira'nia] *nf* tyranny.

tiránico, a [ti'raniko, a] *adj* tyrannical.

tiranizar [tirani'θar] *vt* (*pueblo, empleado*) to tyrannize.

tirano, a [ti'rano, a] *adj* tyrannical ♦ *nm/f* tyrant.

tirante [ti'rante] *adj* (*cuerda*) tight, taut; (*relaciones*) strained ♦ *nm* (*ARQ*) brace; (*TEC*) stay; (*correa*) shoulder strap; **~s** *nmpl* braces, suspenders (*US*).

tirantez [tiran'teθ] *nf* tightness; (*fig*) tension.

tirar [ti'rar] *vt* to throw; (*volcar*) to upset; (*derribar*) to knock down *o* over; (*tiro*) to fire; (*cohete*) to launch; (*bomba*) to drop; (*edificio*) to pull down; (*desechar*) to throw out *o* away; (*disipar*) to squander; (*imprimir*) to print; (*dar: golpe*) to deal ♦ *vi* (*disparar*) to shoot; (*jalar*) to pull; (*fig*) to draw; (*interesar*) to appeal; (*fam: andar*) to go; (*tender a, buscar realizar*) to tend to; (*DEPORTE*) to shoot; **~se** *vr* to throw o.s.; (*fig*) to demean o.s.; (*fam !*) to screw (*!*); **~ abajo** to bring down, destroy; **tira más a su padre** he takes more after his father; **~ de algo** to pull *o* tug (on) sth; **ir tirando** to manage; **~ a la derecha** to turn *o* go right; **a todo ~** at the most.

tirita [ti'rita] *nf* (sticking) plaster, bandaid (*US*).

tiritar [tiri'tar] *vi* to shiver.

tiritona [tiri'tona] *nf* shivering (fit).

tiro ['tiro] *nm* (*lanzamiento*) throw; (*disparo*) shot; (*tiroteo*) shooting; (*DEPORTE*) shot; (*TENIS, GOLF*) drive; (*alcance*) range; (*de escalera*) flight (of stairs); (*golpe*) blow; (*engaño*) hoax; **~ al blanco** target practice; **caballo de ~** cart-horse; **andar de ~s largos** to be all dressed up; **al ~** (*AM*) at once; **de a ~** (*AM fam*) completely; **se pegó un ~** he shot himself; **le salió el ~ por la culata** it backfired on him.

tiroides [ti'roiðes] *nm inv* thyroid.

Tirol [ti'rol] *nm*: **El ~** the Tyrol.

tirolés, esa [tiro'les, esa] *adj, nm/f* Tyrolean.

tirón [ti'ron] *nm* (*sacudida*) pull, tug; **de un ~** in one go; **dar un ~ a** to pull at, tug at.

tirotear [tirote'ar] *vt* to shoot at; **~se** *vr* to exchange shots.

tiroteo [tiro'teo] *nm* exchange of shots, shooting; (*escaramuza*) skirmish.

tirria ['tirrja] *nf*: **tener una ~ a algn** to have a grudge against sb.

tísico, a ['tisiko, a] *adj, nm/f* consumptive.

tisis ['tisis] *nf* consumption, tuberculosis.

tít. *abr* = **título**.

titánico, a [ti'taniko, a] *adj* titanic.

títere ['titere] *nm* puppet; **no dejar ~ con cabeza** to turn everything upside-down.

titilar [titi'lar] *vi* (*luz, estrella*) to twinkle; (*parpado*) to flutter.

titiritero, a [titiri'tero, a] *nm/f* (*acróbata*) acrobat; (*malabarista*) juggler.

titubeante [tituße'ante] *adj* (*inestable*) shaky, tottering; (*farfullante*) stammering; (*dudoso*) hesitant.

titubear [tituße'ar] *vi* to stagger; (*tartamudear*) to stammer; (*vacilar*) to hesitate.

titubeo [titu'ßeo] *nm* staggering; stammering; hesitation.

titulado, a [titu'laðo, a] *adj* (*libro*) entitled; (*persona*) titled.

titular [titu'lar] *adj* titular ♦ *nm/f* (*de oficina*) occupant; (*de pasaporte*) holder ♦ *nm* headline ♦ *vt* to title; **~se** *vr* to be entitled.

título ['titulo] *nm* (*gen*) title; (*de diario*) headline; (*certificado*) professional qualification; (*universitario*) university degree; (*COM*) bond; (*fig*) right; **~s** *nmpl* qualifications; **a ~ de** by way of; (*en calidad de*) in the capacity of; **a ~ de curiosidad** as a matter of interest; **~ de propiedad** title deed; **~s convertibles de interés fijo** (*COM*) convertible loan stock *sg*.

tiza ['tiθa] *nf* chalk; **una ~** a piece of chalk.

tizna ['tiθna] *nf* grime.

tiznar [tiθ'nar] *vt* to blacken; (*manchar*) to smudge, stain; (*fig*) to tarnish.

tizón [ti'θon], **tizo** ['tiθo] *nm* brand; (*fig*) stain.

TLC *nm abr* (= *Tratado de Libre Comercio*) NAFTA.

Tm. *abr* = **tonelada(s) métrica(s)**.

toalla [to'aʎa] *nf* towel.

tobillo [to'βiʎo] *nm* ankle.

tobogán [toßo'ɣan] *nm* toboggan; (*montaña rusa*) switchback; (*resbaladilla*) chute, slide.

toca ['toka] *nf* headdress.

tocadiscos [toka'ðiskos] *nm inv* record player.

tocado, a [to'kaðo, a] *adj (fruta etc)* rotten; ◊ *nm* headdress; **estar ~ de la cabeza** *(fam)* to be weak in the head.

tocador [toka'ðor] *nm (mueble)* dressing table; *(cuarto)* boudoir; *(neceser)* toilet case; *(fam)* ladies' room.

tocante [to'kante]: **~ a** *prep* with regard to; **en lo ~ a** as for, so far as concerns.

tocar [to'kar] *vt* to touch; *(sentir)* to feel; *(con la mano)* to handle; *(MUS)* to play; *(campana)* to ring; *(tambor)* to beat; *(trompeta)* to blow; *(topar con)* to run into, strike; *(referirse a)* to allude to; *(ser emparentado con)* to be related to ◊ *vi (a la puerta)* to knock (on *o* at the door); *(ser de turno)* to fall to, be the turn of; *(ser hora)* to be due; *(atañer)* to concern; **~se** *vr (cubrirse la cabeza)* to cover one's head; *(tener contacto)* to touch (each other); **~le a algn** to fall to sb's lot; **~ en** *(NAUT)* to call at; **por lo que a mí me toca** as far as I am concerned; **esto toca en la locura** this verges on madness.

tocateja [toka'texa] *(fam)*: **a ~** *adv* in readies.

tocayo, a [to'kajo, a] *nm/f* namesake.

tocino [to'θino] *nm* (bacon) fat; **~ de panceta** bacon.

todavía [toða'ßia] *adv (aun)* even; *(aún)* still, yet; **~ más** yet *o* still more; **~ no** not yet; **~ en 1970** as late as 1970; **está lloviendo ~** it's still raining.

toditito, a [toði'tito, a], **todito, a** [to'ðito, a] *adj (AM fam)* (absolutely) all.

================== *PALABRA CLAVE*

todo, a ['toðo, a] *adj* **1** *(sg)* all; **toda la carne** all the meat; **toda la noche** all night, the whole night; **~ el libro** the whole book; **toda una botella** a whole bottle; **~ lo contrario** quite the opposite; **está toda sucia** she's all dirty; **a toda velocidad** at full speed; **por ~ el país** throughout the whole country; **es ~ un hombre** he's every inch a man; **soy ~ oídos** I'm all ears

2 *(pl)* all; every; **~s los libros** all the books; **todas las noches** every night; **~s los que quieran salir** all those who want to leave; **~s vosotros** all of you

◊ *pron* **1** everything, all; **~s** everyone, everybody; **lo sabemos ~** we know everything; **~s querían más tiempo** everybody *o* everyone wanted more time; **nos marchamos ~s** all of us left; **corriendo y ~, no llegaron a tiempo** even though they ran, they still didn't arrive in time

2 *(con preposición)*: **a pesar de ~** even so, in spite of everything; **con ~ él me sigue gustando** even so I still like him; **le llamaron de todo** they called him all the names under the sun; **no me agrada del ~** I don't entirely like it

◊ *adv* all; **vaya ~ seguido** keep straight on *o* ahead

◊ *nm*: **como un ~** as a whole; **arriba del ~** at the very top.

todopoderoso, a [toðopoðe'roso, a] *adj* all powerful; *(REL)* almighty.

todoterreno [toðote'rreno] *nm (tb: vehículo ~)* four-by-four.

toga ['toɣa] *nf* toga; *(ESCOL)* gown.

Tokio ['tokjo] *n* Tokyo.

toldo ['toldo] *nm (para el sol)* sunshade; *(tienda)* marquee; *(fig)* pride.

tole ['tole] *nm (fam)* commotion.

toledano, a [tole'ðano, a] *adj* of *o* from Toledo ◊ *nm/f* native *o* inhabitant of Toledo.

tolerable [tole'raßle] *adj* tolerable.

tolerancia [tole'ranθja] *nf* tolerance.

tolerante [tole'rante] *adj* tolerant; *(fig)* open-minded.

tolerar [tole'rar] *vt* to tolerate; *(resistir)* to endure.

Tolón [to'lon] *nm* Toulon.

toma ['toma] *nf (gen)* taking; *(MED)* dose; *(ELEC: tb:* **~ de corriente**) socket; *(MEC)* inlet; **~ de posesión** *(por presidente)* taking up office; **~ de tierra** *(AVIAT)* landing.

tomadura [toma'ðura] *nf*: **~ de pelo** hoax.

tomar [to'mar] *vt (gen, CINE, FOTO, TV)* to take; *(actitud)* to adopt; *(aspecto)* to take on; *(notas)* to take down; *(beber)* to drink ◊ *vi* to take; *(AM)* to drink; **~se** *vr* to take; **~se por** to consider o.s. to be; **¡toma!** here you are!; **~ asiento** to sit down; **~ a algn por loco** to think sb mad; **~ a bien/a mal** to take well/badly; **~ en serio** to take seriously; **~ el pelo a algn** to pull sb's leg; **~la con algn** to pick a quarrel with sb; **~ por escrito** to write down; **toma y daca** give and take.

tomate [to'mate] *nm* tomato.

tomatera [toma'tera] *nf* tomato plant.

tomavistas [toma'ßistas] *nm inv* movie camera.

tomillo [to'miʎo] *nm* thyme.

tomo ['tomo] *nm (libro)* volume; *(fig)* importance.

ton [ton] *abr* = **tonelada** ◊ *nm*: **sin ~ ni son** without rhyme or reason.

tonada [to'naða] *nf* tune.

tonalidad [tonali'ðað] *nf* tone.

tonel [to'nel] *nm* barrel.

tonelada [tone'laða] *nf* ton; ~ **métrica** metric ton.

tonelaje [tone'laxe] *nm* tonnage.

tonelero [tone'lero] *nm* cooper.

tongo ['tongo] *nm* (*DEPORTE*) fix.

tónico, a ['toniko, a] *adj* tonic ♦ *nm* (*MED*) tonic ♦ *nf* (*MUS*) tonic; (*fig*) keynote.

tonificador, a [tonifika'ðor, a], **tonificante** [tonifi'kante] *adj* invigorating, stimulating.

tonificar [tonifi'kar] *vt* to tone up.

tonifique [toni'fike] *etc vb V* **tonificar**.

tonillo [to'niʎo] *nm* monotonous voice.

tono ['tono] *nm* (*MUS*) tone; (*altura*) pitch; (*color*) shade; **fuera de** ~ inappropriate; ~ **de marcar** (*TELEC*) dialling tone; **darse** ~ to put on airs.

tontear [tonte'ar] *vi* (*fam*) to fool about; (*enamorados*) to flirt.

tontería [tonte'ria] *nf* (*estupidez*) foolishness; (*una* ~) silly thing; ~**s** *nfpl* rubbish *sg*, nonsense *sg*.

tonto, a ['tonto, a] *adj* stupid; (*ridículo*) silly ♦ *nm/f* fool; (*payaso*) clown; **a tontas y a locas** anyhow; **hacer(se) el** ~ to act the fool.

topacio [to'paθjo] *nm* topaz.

topar [to'par] *vt* (*tropezar*) to bump into; (*encontrar*) to find, come across; (*cabra etc*) to butt ♦ *vi*: ~ **contra** *o* **en** to run into; ~ **con** to run up against; **el problema topa en eso** that's where the problem lies.

tope ['tope] *adj* maximum ♦ *nm* (*fin*) end; (*límite*) limit; (*riña*) quarrel; (*FERRO*) buffer; (*AUTO*) bumper; **al** ~ end to end; **fecha** ~ closing date; **precio** ~ top price; **sueldo** ~ maximum salary; ~ **de tabulación** tab stop.

tópico, a ['topiko, a] *adj* topical; (*MED*) local ♦ *nm* platitude, cliché; **de uso** ~ for external application.

topo ['topo] *nm* (*ZOOL*) mole; (*fig*) blunderer.

topografía [topoɣra'fia] *nf* topography.

topógrafo, a [to'poɣrafo, a] *nm/f* topographer; (*agrimensor*) surveyor.

toponimia [topo'nimja] *nf* place names *pl*; (*estudio*) study of place names.

toque ['toke] *etc vb V* **tocar** ♦ *nm* touch; (*MUS*) beat; (*de campana*) ring, chime; (*MIL*) bugle call; (*fig*) crux; **dar un** ~ **a** to test; **dar el último** ~ **a** to put the final touch to; ~ **de queda** curfew.

toquetear [tokete'ar] *vt* to handle; (*fam!*) to touch up.

toquilla [to'kiʎa] *nf* (*chal*) shawl.

torax ['toraks] *nm inv* thorax.

torbellino [torbe'ʎino] *nm* whirlwind; (*fig*) whirl.

torcedura [torθe'ðura] *nf* twist; (*MED*) sprain.

torcer [tor'θer] *vt* to twist; (*la esquina*) to turn; (*MED*) to sprain; (*cuerda*) to plait; (*ropa, manos*) to wring; (*persona*) to corrupt; (*sentido*) to distort ♦ *vi* (*cambiar de dirección*) to turn; ~**se** *vr* to twist; (*doblar*) to bend; (*desviarse*) to go astray; (*fracasar*) to go wrong; ~ **el gesto** to scowl; ~**se un pie** to twist one's foot; **el coche torció a la derecha** the car turned right.

torcido, a [tor'θiðo, a] *adj* twisted; (*fig*) crooked ♦ *nm* curl.

tordo, a ['torðo, a] *adj* dappled ♦ *nm* thrush.

torear [tore'ar] *vt* (*fig: evadir*) to dodge; (*toro*) to fight ♦ *vi* to fight bulls.

toreo [to'reo] *nm* bullfighting.

torero, a [to'rero, a] *nm/f* bullfighter.

toril [to'ril] *nm* bullpen.

tormenta [tor'menta] *nf* storm; (*fig: confusión*) turmoil.

tormento [tor'mento] *nm* torture; (*fig*) anguish.

tormentoso, a [tormen'toso, a] *adj* stormy.

tornar [tor'nar] *vt* (*devolver*) to return, give back; (*transformar*) to transform ♦ *vi* to go back; ~**se** *vr* (*ponerse*) to become; (*volver*) to return.

tornasol [torna'sol] *nm* (*BOT*) sunflower; **papel de** ~ litmus paper.

tornasolado, a [tornaso'laðo, a] *adj* (*brillante*) iridescent; (*reluciente*) shimmering.

torneo [tor'neo] *nm* tournament.

tornero, a [tor'nero, a] *nm/f* machinist.

tornillo [tor'niʎo] *nm* screw; **apretar los** ~**s a algn** to apply pressure on sb; **le falta un** ~ (*fam*) he's got a screw loose.

torniquete [torni'kete] *nm* (*puerta*) turnstile; (*MED*) tourniquet.

torno ['torno] *nm* (*TEC: grúa*) winch; (*: de carpintero*) lathe; (*tambor*) drum; ~ **de banco** vice, vise (*US*); **en** ~ **(a)** round, about.

toro ['toro] *nm* bull; (*fam*) he-man; **los** ~**s** bullfighting *sg*.

toronja [to'ronxa] *nf* grapefruit.

torpe ['torpe] *adj* (*poco hábil*) clumsy, awkward; (*movimiento*) sluggish; (*necio*) dim; (*lento*) slow; (*indecente*) crude; (*no honrado*) dishonest.

torpedo [tor'peðo] nm torpedo.
torpemente [torpe'mente] adv (sin destreza) clumsily; (lentamente) slowly.
torpeza [tor'peθa] nf (falta de agilidad) clumsiness; (lentitud) slowness; (rigidez) stiffness; (error) mistake; (crudeza) obscenity.
torre ['torre] nf tower; (de petróleo) derrick; (de electricidad) pylon; (AJEDREZ) rook; (AVIAT, MIL, NAUT) turret.
torrefacto, a [torre'fakto, a] adj: **café ~** high roast coffee.
torrencial [torren'θjal] adj torrential.
torrente [to'rrente] nm torrent.
tórrido, a ['torriðo, a] adj torrid.
torrija [to'rrixa] nf fried bread; **~s** French toast sg.
torsión [tor'sjon] nf twisting.
torso ['torso] nm torso.
torta ['torta] nf cake; (fam) slap; **~ de huevos** (AM) omelette; **no entendió ni ~** he didn't understand a word of it.
tortazo [tor'taθo] nm (bofetada) slap; (de coche) crash.
tortícolis [tor'tikolis] nm inv stiff neck.
tortilla [tor'tiʎa] nf omelette; (AM) maize pancake; **~ francesa/española** plain/potato omelette; **cambiar o volver la ~ a algn** to turn the tables on sb.
tortillera [torti'ʎera] nf (fam!) lesbian.
tórtola ['tortola] nf turtledove.
tortuga [tor'tuɣa] nf tortoise; **~ marina** turtle.
tortuoso, a [tor'twoso, a] adj winding.
tortura [tor'tura] nf torture.
torturar [tortu'rar] vt to torture.
torvo, a ['torßo, a] adj grim, fierce.
torzamos [tor'θamos] etc vb V torcer.
tos [tos] nf inv cough; **~ ferina** whooping cough.
Toscana [tos'kana] nf: **La ~** Tuscany.
tosco, a ['tosko, a] adj coarse.
toser [to'ser] vi to cough; **no hay quien le tosa** he's in a class by himself.
tostado, a [tos'taðo, a] adj toasted; (por el sol) dark brown; (piel) tanned ♦ nf tan; (pan) piece of toast; **tostadas** nfpl toast sg.
tostador [tosta'ðor] nm toaster.
tostar [tos'tar] vt to toast; (café) to roast; (al sol) to tan; **~se** vr to get brown.
tostón [tos'ton] nm: **ser un ~** to be a drag.
total [to'tal] adj total ♦ adv in short; (al fin y al cabo) when all is said and done ♦ nm total; **en ~** in all; **~ que** to cut a long story short; **~ de comprobación** (INFORM) hash total; **~ debe/haber** (COM) debit/assets total.
totalidad [totali'ðað] nf whole.

totalitario, a [totali'tarjo, a] adj totalitarian.
totalmente [to'talmente] adv totally.
tóxico, a ['toksiko, a] adj toxic ♦ nm poison.
toxicómano, a [toksi'komano, a] adj addicted to drugs ♦ nm/f drug addict.
toxina [to'ksina] nf toxin.
tozudo, a [to'θuðo, a] adj obstinate.
traba ['traßa] nf bond, tie; (cadena) fetter; **poner ~s a** to restrain.
trabajador, a [traßaxa'ðor, a] nm/f worker ♦ adj hard-working.
trabajar [traßa'xar] vt to work; (arar) to till; (empeñarse en) to work at; (empujar: persona) to push; (convencer) to persuade ♦ vi to work; (esforzarse) to strive; **¡a ~!** let's get to work!; **~ por hacer algo** to strive to do sth.
trabajo [tra'ßaxo] nm work; (tarea) task; (POL) labour; (fig) effort; **tomarse el ~ de** to take the trouble to; **~ por turno/a destajo** shift work/piecework; **~ en proceso** (COM) work-in-progress.
trabajoso, a [traßa'xoso, a] adj hard; (MED) pale.
trabalenguas [traßa'lengwas] nm inv tongue twister.
trabar [tra'ßar] vt (juntar) to join, unite; (atar) to tie down, fetter; (agarrar) to seize; (amistad) to strike up; **~se** vr to become entangled; (reñir) to squabble; **se le traba la lengua** he gets tongue-tied.
trabazón [traßa'θon] nf (TEC) joining, assembly; (fig) bond, link.
trabucar [traßu'kar] vt (confundir) to confuse, mix up; (palabras) to misplace.
trabuque [tra'ßuke] etc vb V trabucar.
tracción [trak'θjon] nf traction; **~ delantera/trasera** front-wheel/rear-wheel drive.
trace ['traθe] etc vb V trazar.
tractor [trak'tor] nm tractor.
trad. abr (= traducido) trans.
tradición [traði'θjon] nf tradition.
tradicional [traðiθjo'nal] adj traditional.
traducción [traðuk'θjon] nf translation; **~ asistida por ordenador** computer-assisted translation.
traducible [traðu'θißle] adj translatable.
traducir [traðu'θir] vt to translate; **~se** vr: **~se en** (fig) to entail, result in.
traductor, a [traðuk'tor, a] nm/f translator.
traduzca [tra'ðuθka] etc vb V traducir.
traer [tra'er] vt to bring; (llevar) to carry; (ropa) to wear; (incluir) to carry; (fig) to cause; **~se** vr: **~se algo** to be up to sth; **~se bien/mal** to dress well/badly; **traérselas** to be annoying; **~ consigo** to involve, entail; **es un problema que se**

las trae it's a difficult problem.
traficante [trafi'kante] *nm/f* trader, dealer.
traficar [trafi'kar] *vi* to trade; ~ **con** (*pey*)
to deal illegally in.
tráfico ['trafiko] *nm* (*COM*) trade; (*AUTO*)
traffic.
trafique [tra'fike] *etc vb* V **traficar**.
tragaderas [traɣa'ðeras] *nfpl* (*garganta*)
throat *sg*, gullet *sg*; (*credulidad*) gullibility
sg.
tragaluz [traɣa'luθ] *nm* skylight.
tragamonedas [traɣamo'neðas] *nm inv*,
tragaperras [traɣa'perras] *nm inv* slot
machine.
tragar [tra'ɣar] *vt* to swallow; (*devorar*) to
devour, bolt down; ~**se** *vr* to swallow;
(*tierra*) to absorb, soak up; **no le puedo** ~
(*persona*) I can't stand him.
tragedia [tra'xeðja] *nf* tragedy.
trágico, a ['traxiko, a] *adj* tragic.
trago ['traɣo] *nm* (*líquido*) drink; (*comido
de golpe*) gulp; (*fam: de bebida*) swig;
(*desgracia*) blow; ~ **amargo** (*fig*) hard
time.
trague ['traɣe] *etc vb* V **tragar**.
traición [trai'θjon] *nf* treachery; (*JUR*)
treason; (*una* ~) act of treachery.
traicionar [traiθjo'nar] *vt* to betray.
traicionero, a [traiθjo'nero, a] = **traidor, a**.
traída [tra'iða] *nf* carrying; ~ **de aguas**
water supply.
traidor, a [trai'ðor, a] *adj* treacherous
♦ *nm/f* traitor.
traiga ['traiɣa] *etc vb* V **traer**.
trailer, *pl* **trailers** ['trailer, 'trailer(s)] *nm*
trailer.
traje ['traxe] *etc vb* V **traer** ♦ *nm* (*gen*)
dress; (*de hombre*) suit; (~ *típico*)
costume; (*fig*) garb; ~ **de baño** swimsuit;
~ **de luces** bullfighter's costume; ~
hecho a la medida made-to-measure
suit.
trajera [tra'xera] *etc vb* V **traer**.
trajín [tra'xin] *nm* haulage; (*fam:
movimiento*) bustle; **trajines** *nmpl* goings-
on.
trajinar [traxi'nar] *vt* (*llevar*) to carry,
transport ♦ *vi* (*moverse*) to bustle about;
(*viajar*) to travel around.
trama ['trama] *nf* (*fig*) link; (: *intriga*) plot;
(*de tejido*) weft.
tramar [tra'mar] *vt* to plot; (*TEC*) to weave;
~**se** *vr* (*fig*): **algo se está tramando**
there's something going on.
tramitar [trami'tar] *vt* (*asunto*) to transact;
(*negociar*) to negotiate; (*manejar*) to handle.
trámite ['tramite] *nm* (*paso*) step; (*JUR*)

transaction; ~**s** *nmpl* (*burocracia*)
paperwork *sg*, procedures; (*JUR*)
proceedings.
tramo ['tramo] *nm* (*de tierra*) plot; (*de
escalera*) flight; (*de vía*) section.
tramoya [tra'moja] *nf* (*TEAT*) piece of
stage machinery; (*fig*) trick.
tramoyista [tramo'jista] *nm/f* scene
shifter; (*fig*) trickster.
trampa ['trampa] *nf* trap; (*en el suelo*)
trapdoor; (*prestidigitación*) conjuring
trick; (*engaño*) trick; (*fam*) fiddle; (*de
pantalón*) fly; **caer en la** ~ to fall into the
trap; **hacer** ~**s** (*hacer juegos de manos*) to
juggle, conjure; (*trampear*) to cheat.
trampear [trampe'ar] *vt, vi* to cheat.
trampilla [tram'piʎa] *nf* trap, hatchway.
trampolín [trampo'lin] *nm* trampoline; (*de
piscina etc*) diving board.
tramposo, a [tram'poso, a] *adj* crooked,
cheating ♦ *nm/f* crook, cheat.
tranca ['tranka] *nf* (*palo*) stick; (*viga*)
beam; (*de puerta, ventana*) bar;
(*borrachera*) binge; **a** ~**s y barrancas** with
great difficulty.
trancar [tran'kar] *vt* to bar ♦ *vi* to stride
along.
trancazo [tran'kaθo] *nm* (*golpe*) blow.
trance ['tranθe] *nm* (*momento difícil*)
difficult moment; (*situación crítica*)
critical situation; (*estado hipnotizado*)
trance; **estar en** ~ **de muerte** to be at
death's door.
tranco ['tranko] *nm* stride.
tranque ['tranke] *etc vb* V **trancar**.
tranquilamente [tranki'lamente] *adv* (*sin
preocupaciones: leer, trabajar*) peacefully;
(*sin enfadarse: hablar, discutir*) calmly.
tranquilice [tranki'liθe] *etc vb* V
tranquilizar.
tranquilidad [trankili'ðað] *nf* (*calma*)
calmness, stillness; (*paz*) peacefulness.
tranquilizador, a [trankiliθa'ðor, a] *adj*
(*música*) soothing; (*hecho*) reassuring.
tranquilizante [trankili'θante] *nm*
tranquillizer.
tranquilizar [trankili'θar] *vt* (*calmar*) to
calm (down); (*asegurar*) to reassure.
tranquilo, a [tran'kilo, a] *adj* (*calmado*)
calm; (*apacible*) peaceful; (*mar*) calm;
(*mente*) untroubled.
Trans. *abr* (*COM*) = **transferencia**.
transacción [transak'θjon] *nf* transaction.
transar [tran'sar] *vi* (*AM*) = **transigir**.
transatlántico, a [transat'lantiko, a] *adj*
transatlantic ♦ *nm* (ocean) liner.
transbordador [transβorða'ðor] *nm* ferry.
transbordar [transβor'ðar] *vt* to transfer;

~**se** *vr* to change.
transbordo [trans'ßorðo] *nm* transfer;
hacer ~ to change (trains).
transcender [transθen'der] *vt*
= **trascender**.
transcribir [transkri'ßir] *vt* to transcribe.
transcurrir [transku'rrir] *vi* (*tiempo*) to
pass; (*hecho*) to turn out.
transcurso [trans'kurso] *nm* passing,
lapse; **en el** ~ **de 8 días** in the course of
a week.
transeúnte [transe'unte] *adj* transient
♦ *nm/f* passer-by.
transexual [transe'kswal] *adj*, *nm/f*
transsexual.
transferencia [transfe'renθja] *nf*
transference; (*COM*) transfer; ~
bancaria banker's order; ~ **de crédito**
(*COM*) credit transfer; ~ **electrónica de
fondos** (*COM*) electronic funds transfer.
transferir [transfe'rir] *vt* to transfer;
(*aplazar*) to postpone.
transfiera [trans'fjera] *etc vb V* **transferir**.
transfigurar [transfiɣu'rar] *vt* to
transfigure.
transfiriendo [transfi'rjendo] *etc vb V*
transferir.
transformación [transforma'θjon] *nf*
transformation.
transformador [transforma'ðor] *nm*
transformer.
transformar [transfor'mar] *vt* to
transform; (*convertir*) to convert.
tránsfuga ['transfuɣa] *nm/f* (*MIL*) deserter;
(*POL*) turncoat.
transfusión [transfu'sjon] *nf* (*tb*: ~ **de
sangre**) (blood) transfusion.
transgredir [transɣre'dir] *vt* to transgress.
transgresión [transɣre'sjon] *nf*
transgression.
transición [transi'θjon] *nf* transition;
período de ~ transitional period.
transido, a [tran'siðo, a] *adj* overcome; ~
de angustia beset with anxiety; ~ **de
dolor** racked with pain.
transigir [transi'xir] *vi* to compromise;
(*ceder*) to make concessions.
transija [tran'sixa] *etc vb V* **transigir**.
Transilvania [transil'ßanja] *nf*
Transylvania.
transistor [transis'tor] *nm* transistor.
transitable [transi'taßle] *adj* (*camino*)
passable.
transitar [transi'tar] *vi* to go (from place to
place).
transitivo, a [transi'tißo, a] *adj* transitive.
tránsito ['transito] *nm* transit; (*AUTO*)
traffic; (*parada*) stop; **horas de máximo** ~

rush hours; "**se prohíbe el** ~" "no
thoroughfare."
transitorio, a [transi'torjo, a] *adj*
transitory.
transmisión [transmi'sjon] *nf* (*RADIO*, *TV*)
transmission, broadcast(ing);
(*transferencia*) transfer; ~ **en circuito**
hookup; ~ **en directo/exterior** live/
outside broadcast; ~ **de datos** (**en
paralelo/en serie**) (*INFORM*) (parallel/
serial) data transfer *o* transmission;
plena/media ~ **bidireccional** (*INFORM*)
full/half duplex.
transmitir [transmi'tir] *vt* to transmit;
(*RADIO*, *TV*) to broadcast; (*enfermedad*) to
give, pass on.
transparencia [transpa'renθja] *nf*
transparency; (*claridad*) clearness,
clarity; (*foto*) slide.
transparentar [transparen'tar] *vt* to reveal
♦ *vi* to be transparent.
transparente [transpa'rente] *adj*
transparent; (*aire*) clear; (*ligero*)
diaphanous ♦ *nm* curtain.
transpirar [transpi'rar] *vi* to perspire; (*fig*)
to transpire.
transpondré [transpon'dre] *etc vb V*
transponer.
transponer [transpo'ner] *vt* to transpose;
(*cambiar de sitio*) to move about ♦ *vi*
(*desaparecer*) to disappear; (*ir más allá*) to
go beyond; ~**se** *vr* to change places;
(*ocultarse*) to hide; (*sol*) to go down.
transponga [trans'ponga] *etc vb V*
transponer.
transportador [transporta'ðor] *nm*
(*MECÁNICA*): ~ **de correa** belt conveyor.
transportar [transpor'tar] *vt* to transport;
(*llevar*) to carry.
transporte [trans'porte] *nm* transport;
(*COM*) haulage; **Ministerio de T~s**
Ministry of Transport.
transpuesto [trans'pwesto], **transpuse**
[trans'puse] *etc vb V* **transponer**.
transversal [transßer'sal] *adj* transverse,
cross ♦ *nf* (*tb*: **calle** ~) cross street.
transversalmente [transßersal'mente] *adv*
obliquely.
tranvía [tram'bia] *nm* tram, streetcar (*US*).
trapecio [tra'peθjo] *nm* trapeze.
trapecista [trape'θista] *nm/f* trapeze artist.
trapero, a [tra'pero, a] *nm/f* ragman.
trapicheos [trapi'tʃeos] *nmpl* (*fam*)
schemes, fiddles.
trapisonda [trapi'sonda] *nf* (*jaleo*) row;
(*estafa*) swindle.
trapo ['trapo] *nm* (*tela*) rag; (*de cocina*)
cloth; ~**s** *nmpl* (*fam*: *de mujer*) clothes,

dresses; **a todo** ~ under full sail; **soltar el** ~ (*llorar*) to burst into tears.

tráquea ['trakea] *nf* trachea, windpipe.

traqueteo [trake'teo] *nm* (*crujido*) crack; (*golpeteo*) rattling.

tras [tras] *prep* (*detrás*) behind; (*después*) after; ~ **de** besides; **día** ~ **día** day after day; **uno** ~ **otro** one after the other.

trascendencia [trasθen'denθja] *nf* (*importancia*) importance; (*filosofía*) transcendence.

trascendental [trasθenden'tal] *adj* important; transcendental.

trascender [trasθen'der] *vi* (*oler*) to smell; (*noticias*) to come out, leak out; (*eventos, sentimientos*) to spread, have a wide effect; ~ **a** (*afectar*) to reach, have an effect on; (*oler a*) to smack of; **en su novela todo trasciende a romanticismo** everything in his novel smacks of romanticism.

trascienda [tras'θjenda] *etc vb V* **trascender**.

trasegar [trase'ɣar] *vt* (*mover*) to move about; (*vino*) to decant.

trasegué [trase'ɣe], **traseguemos** [trase'ɣemos] *etc vb V* **trasegar**.

trasero, a [tra'sero, a] *adj* back, rear ♦ *nm* (*ANAT*) bottom; ~**s** *nmpl* ancestors.

trasfondo [tras'fondo] *nm* background.

trasgo ['trasɣo] *nm* goblin.

trasgredir [trasɣre'ðir] *vt* to contravene.

trashumante [trasu'mante] *adj* migrating.

trasiego [tra'sjeɣo] *etc vb V* **trasegar** ♦ *nm* (*cambiar de sitio*) move, switch; (*de vino*) decanting; (*trastorno*) upset.

trasiegue [tra'sjeɣe] *etc vb V* **trasegar**.

trasladar [trasla'ðar] *vt* to move; (*persona*) to transfer; (*postergar*) to postpone; (*copiar*) to copy; (*interpretar*) to interpret; ~**se** *vr* (*irse*) to go; (*mudarse*) to move; ~**se a otro puesto** to move to a new job.

traslado [tras'laðo] *nm* move; (*mudanza*) move, removal; (*de persona*) transfer; (*copia*) copy; ~ **de bloque** (*INFORM*) block move, cut-and-paste.

traslucir [traslu'θir] *vt* to show; ~**se** *vr* to be translucent; (*fig*) to be revealed.

trasluz [tras'luθ] *nm* reflected light; **al** ~ against *o* up to the light.

trasluzca [tras'luθka] *etc vb V* **traslucir**.

trasmano [tras'mano]: **a** ~ *adv* (*fuera de alcance*) out of reach; (*apartado*) out of the way.

trasnochado, a [trasno'tʃaðo, a] *adj* dated.

trasnochador, a [trasnotʃa'ðor, a] *adj* given to staying up late ♦ *nm/f* (*fig*) night bird.

trasnochar [trasno'tʃar] *vi* (*acostarse tarde*) to stay up late; (*no dormir*) to have a sleepless night; (*pasar la noche*) to stay the night.

traspasar [traspa'sar] *vt* (*bala*) to pierce, go through; (*propiedad*) to sell, transfer; (*calle*) to cross over; (*límites*) to go beyond; (*ley*) to break; **"traspaso negocio"** "business for sale".

traspaso [tras'paso] *nm* transfer; (*fig*) anguish.

traspié [tras'pje], *pl* **traspiés** *nm* (*caída*) stumble; (*tropezón*) trip; (*fig*) blunder.

trasplantar [trasplan'tar] *vt* to transplant.

trasplante [tras'plante] *nm* transplant.

traspuesto, a [tras'pwesto, a] *adj*: **quedarse** ~ to doze off.

trastada [tras'taða] *nf* (*fam*) prank.

trastazo [tras'taθo] *nm* (*fam*) bump; **darse un** ~ (*persona*) to bump o.s.; (*en coche*) to have a bump.

traste ['traste] *nm* (*MUS*) fret; **dar al** ~ **con algo** to ruin sth; **ir al** ~ to fall through.

trastero [tras'tero] *nm* lumber room.

trastienda [tras'tjenda] *nf* backshop; **obtener algo por la** ~ to get sth by underhand means.

trasto ['trasto] *nm* (*mueble*) piece of furniture; (*tarro viejo*) old pot; (*pey: cosa*) piece of junk; (: *persona*) dead loss; ~**s** *nmpl* (*TEAT*) scenery *sg*; **tirar los** ~**s a la cabeza** to have a blazing row.

trastocar [trasto'kar] *vt* (*papeles*) to mix up.

trastornado, a [trastor'naðo, a] *adj* (*loco*) mad; (*agitado*) crazy.

trastornar [trastor'nar] *vt* to overturn, upset; (*fig: ideas*) to confuse; (: *nervios*) to shatter; (: *persona*) to drive crazy; ~**se** *vr* (*plan*) to fall through.

trastorno [tras'torno] *nm* (*acto*) overturning; (*confusión*) confusion; (*POL*) disturbance, upheaval; (*MED*) upset; ~ **estomacal** stomach upset; ~ **mental** mental disorder, breakdown.

trasunto [tra'sunto] *nm* copy.

trasvase [tras'βase] *nm* (*de río*) diversion.

tratable [tra'taβle] *adj* friendly.

tratado [tra'taðo] *nm* (*POL*) treaty; (*COM*) agreement; (*LITERATURA*) treatise.

tratamiento [trata'mjento] *nm* treatment; (*TEC*) processing; (*de problema*) handling; ~ **de datos** (*INFORM*) data processing; ~ **de gráficos** (*INFORM*) graphics; ~ **de márgenes** margin settings; ~ **de textos** (*INFORM*) word processing; ~ **por lotes** (*INFORM*) batch processing; ~ **de tú** familiar address.

tratante [tra'tante] *nm/f* dealer, merchandizer.

tratar [tra'tar] *vt* (*ocuparse de*) to treat; (*manejar, TEC*) to handle; (*INFORM*) to process; (*MED*) to treat; (*dirigirse a*: *persona*) to address ♦ *vi*: ~ **de** (*hablar sobre*) to deal with, be about; (*intentar*) to try to; ~ **con** (*COM*) to trade in; (*negociar*) to negotiate with; (*tener contactos*) to have dealings with; ~**se** *vr* to treat each other; **se trata de la nueva piscina** it's about the new pool; **¿de qué se trata?** what's it about?

trato ['trato] *nm* dealings *pl*; (*relaciones*) relationship; (*comportamiento*) manner; (*COM, JUR*) agreement, contract; (*título*) (form of) address; **de ~ agradable** pleasant; **de fácil ~** easy to get on with; ~ **equitativo** fair deal; **¡~ hecho!** it's a deal!; **malos ~s** ill-treatment *sg*.

trauma ['trauma] *nm* trauma.

traumático, a [trau'matiko, a] *adj* traumatic.

través [tra'ßes] *nm* (*contratiempo*) reverse; **al ~** across, crossways; **a ~ de** across; (*sobre*) over; (*por*) through; **de ~** across; (*de lado*) sideways.

travesaño [traße'saɲo] *nm* (*ARQ*) crossbeam; (*DEPORTE*) crossbar.

travesía [traße'sia] *nf* (*calle*) cross-street; (*NAUT*) crossing.

travesti [tra'ßesti] *nm/f* transvestite.

travesura [traße'sura] *nf* (*broma*) prank; (*ingenio*) wit.

travieso, a [tra'ßjeso, a] *adj* (*niño*) naughty; (*adulto*) restless; (*ingenioso*) witty ♦ *nf* crossing; (*ARQ*) crossbeam; (*FERRO*) sleeper.

trayecto [tra'jekto] *nm* (*ruta*) road, way; (*viaje*) journey; (*tramo*) stretch; (*curso*) course; **final del ~** end of the line.

trayectoria [trajek'torja] *nf* trajectory; (*desarrollo*) development, path; **la ~ actual del partido** the party's present line.

trayendo [tra'jendo] *etc vb V* **traer**.

traza ['traθa] *nf* (*ARQ*) plan, design; (*aspecto*) looks *pl*; (*señal*) sign; (*engaño*) trick; (*habilidad*) skill; (*INFORM*) trace.

trazado, a [tra'θaðo, a] *adj*: **bien ~** shapely, well-formed ♦ *nm* (*ARQ*) plan, design; (*fig*) outline; (*de carretera etc*) line, route.

trazador [traθa'ðor] *nm* plotter; ~ **plano** flatbed plotter.

trazar [tra'θar] *vt* (*ARQ*) to plan; (*ARTE*) to sketch; (*fig*) to trace; (*itinerario: hacer*) to plot; (*plan*) to follow.

trazo ['traθo] *nm* (*línea*) line; (*bosquejo*) sketch; ~**s** *nmpl* (*de cara*) lines, features.

TRB *abr* = **toneladas de registro bruto**.

trébol ['treßol] *nm* (*BOT*) clover; ~**es** *nmpl* (*NAIPES*) clubs.

trece ['treθe] *num* thirteen; **estar en sus ~** to stand firm.

trecho ['tretʃo] *nm* (*distancia*) distance; (*de tiempo*) while; (*fam*) piece; **de ~ en ~** at intervals.

tregua ['treɣwa] *nf* (*MIL*) truce; (*fig*) lull; **sin ~** without respite.

treinta ['treinta] *num* thirty.

treintena [trein'tena] *nf* (about) thirty.

tremendo, a [tre'mendo, a] *adj* (*terrible*) terrible; (*imponente: cosa*) imposing; (*fam: fabuloso*) tremendous; (*divertido*) entertaining.

trémulo, a ['tremulo, a] *adj* quivering; (*luz*) flickering.

tren [tren] *nm* (*FERRO*) train; ~ **de aterrizaje** undercarriage; ~ **directo/expreso/(de) mercancías/de pasajeros/suplementario** through/fast/goods *o* freight/passenger/ relief train; ~ **de vida** way of life.

trenca ['trenka] *nf* duffel coat.

trence ['trenθe] *etc vb V* **trenzar**.

trenza ['trenθa] *nf* (*de pelo*) plait.

trenzar [tren'θar] *vt* (*el pelo*) to plait ♦ *vi* (*en baile*) to weave in and out; ~**se** *vr* (*AM*) to become involved.

trepa ['trepa] *nf* (*subida*) climb; (*ardid*) trick.

trepador(a) [trepa'ðor(a)] *nm/f* (*fam*): **ser un(a) ~** to be on the make ♦ *nf* (*BOT*) climber.

trepar [tre'par] *vt, vi* to climb; (*TEC*) to drill.

trepidación [trepiða'θjon] *nf* shaking, vibration.

trepidar [trepi'ðar] *vi* to shake, vibrate.

tres [tres] *num* three; (*fecha*) third; **las ~** three o'clock.

trescientos, as [tres'θjentos, as] *num* three hundred.

tresillo [tre'siʎo] *nm* three-piece suite; (*MUS*) triplet.

treta ['treta] *nf* (*COM etc*) gimmick; (*fig*) trick.

tri... [tri] *pref* tri..., three-....

tríada ['triaða] *nf* triad.

triangular [trjangu'lar] *adj* triangular.

triángulo [tri'angulo] *nm* triangle.

tribal [tri'ßal] *adj* tribal.

tribu ['trißu] *nf* tribe.

tribuna [tri'ßuna] *nf* (*plataforma*) platform; (*DEPORTE*) stand; (*fig*) public speaking; ~ **de la prensa** press box; ~ **del acusado** (*JUR*) dock; ~ **del jurado** jury box.

tribunal [triβu'nal] *nm* (*juicio*) court; (*comisión*, *fig*) board; (*ESCOL: examinadores*) board of examiners; **T~ Supremo** High Court, (*US*) Supreme Court; **T~ de Justicia de las Comunidades Europeas** European Court of Justice.

tributar [triβu'tar] *vt* to pay; (*las gracias*) to give; (*cariño*) to show.

tributario, a [triβu'tarjo, a] *adj* (*GEO, POL*) tributary *cpd*; (*ECON*) tax *cpd*, taxation *cpd* ♦ *nm* (*GEO*) tributary ♦ *nm/f* (*COM*) taxpayer; **sistema ~** tax system.

tributo [tri'βuto] *nm* (*COM*) tax.

trice ['triθe] *etc vb V* **trizar**.

triciclo [tri'θiklo] *nm* tricycle.

tricornio [tri'kornjo] *nm* three-cornered hat.

tricota [tri'kota] *nf* (*AM*) knitted sweater.

tricotar [triko'tar] *vi* to knit.

tridimensional [triðimensjo'nal] *adj* three-dimensional.

trienal [trje'nal] *adj* three-year.

trifulca [tri'fulka] *nf* (*fam*) row, shindy.

trigal [tri'ɣal] *nm* wheat field.

trigésimo, a [tri'xesimo, a] *num* thirtieth.

trigo ['triɣo] *nm* wheat; **~s** *nmpl* wheat field(s) (*pl*).

trigueño, a [tri'ɣeɲo, a] *adj* (*pelo*) corn-coloured; (*piel*) olive-skinned.

trillado, a [tri'ʎaðo, a] *adj* threshed; (*fig*) trite, hackneyed.

trilladora [triʎa'ðora] *nf* threshing machine.

trillar [tri'ʎar] *vt* (*AGR*) to thresh; (*fig*) to frequent.

trillizos, as [tri'ʎiθos, as] *nmpl/nfpl* triplets.

trilogía [trilo'xia] *nf* triology.

trimestral [trimes'tral] *adj* quarterly; (*ESCOL*) termly.

trimestre [tri'mestre] *nm* (*ESCOL*) term; (*COM*) quarter, financial period; (: *pago*) quarterly payment.

trinar [tri'nar] *vi* (*MUS*) to trill; (*ave*) to sing, warble; **está que trina** he's hopping mad.

trincar [trin'kar] *vt* (*atar*) to tie up; (*NAUT*) to lash; (*agarrar*) to pinion.

trinchante [trin'tʃante] *nm* (*para cortar carne*) carving knife; (*tenedor*) meat fork.

trinchar [trin'tʃar] *vt* to carve.

trinchera [trin'tʃera] *nf* (*fosa*) trench; (*para vía*) cutting; (*impermeable*) trench-coat.

trineo [tri'neo] *nm* sledge.

trinidad [trini'ðað] *nf* trio; (*REL*): **la T~** the Trinity.

trino ['trino] *nm* trill.

trinque ['trinke] *etc vb V* **trincar**.

trinquete [trin'kete] *nm* (*TEC*) pawl; (*NAUT*) foremast.

trío ['trio] *nm* trio.

tripa ['tripa] *nf* (*ANAT*) intestine; (*fig, fam*) belly; **~s** *nfpl* (*ANAT*) insides; (*CULIN*) tripe *sg*; **tener mucha ~** to be fat; **me duelen las ~s** I have a stomach ache.

tripartito, a [tripar'tito, a] *adj* tripartite.

triple ['triple] *adj* triple; (*tres veces*) threefold.

triplicado, a [tripli'kaðo, a] *adj*: **por ~** in triplicate.

triplicar [tripli'kar] *vt* to treble.

triplo ['triplo] *adj* = **triple**.

trípode ['tripoðe] *nm* tripod.

Trípoli ['tripoli] *nm* Tripoli.

tríptico ['triptiko] *nm* (*ARTE*) triptych; (*documento*) three-part document.

tripulación [tripula'θjon] *nf* crew.

tripulante [tripu'lante] *nm/f* crewman/woman.

tripular [tripu'lar] *vt* (*barco*) to man; (*AUTO*) to drive.

triquiñuela [triki'ɲwela] *nf* trick.

tris [tris] *nm* crack; **en un ~** in an instant; **estar en un ~ de hacer algo** to be within an inch of doing sth.

triste ['triste] *adj* (*afligido*) sad; (*sombrío*) melancholy, gloomy; (*desolado*) desolate; (*lamentable*) sorry, miserable; (*viejo*) old; (*único*) single; **no queda sino un ~ penique** there's just one miserable penny left.

tristeza [tris'teθa] *nf* (*aflicción*) sadness; (*melancolía*) melancholy; (*de lugar*) desolation; (*pena*) misery.

tristón, ona [tris'ton, ona] *adj* sad, downhearted.

trituradora [tritura'ðora] *nf* shredder.

triturar [tritu'rar] *vt* (*moler*) to grind; (*mascar*) to chew; (*documentos*) to shred.

triunfador, a [triunfa'ðor, a] *adj* triumphant; (*ganador*) winning ♦ *nm/f* winner.

triunfal [triun'fal] *adj* triumphant; (*arco*) triumphal.

triunfante [triun'fante] *adj* triumphant; (*ganador*) winning.

triunfar [triun'far] *vi* (*tener éxito*) to triumph; (*ganar*) to win; (*NAIPES*) to be trumps; **triunfan corazones** hearts are trumps; **~ en la vida** to succeed in life.

triunfo [tri'unfo] *nm* triumph; (*NAIPES*) trump.

trivial [tri'βjal] *adj* trivial.

trivialice [triβja'liθe] *etc vb V* **trivializar**.

trivializar [triβjali'θar] *vt* to minimize, play

down.

triza ['triθa] *nf* bit, piece; **hacer algo ~s** to smash sth to bits; (*papel*) to tear sth to shreds.

trocar [tro'kar] *vt* (*COM*) to exchange; (*dinero, de lugar*) to change; (*palabras*) to exchange; (*confundir*) to confuse; (*vomitar*) to vomit; **~se** *vr* (*confundirse*) to get mixed up; (*transformarse*): **~se (en)** to change (into).

trocear [troθe'ar] *vt* to cut up.

trocha ['trotʃa] *nf* (*sendero*) by-path; (*atajo*) short cut.

troche ['trotʃe]: **a ~ y moche** *adv* helter-skelter, pell-mell.

trofeo [tro'feo] *nm* (*premio*) trophy; (*éxito*) success.

trola ['trola] *nf* (*fam*) fib.

tromba ['tromba] *nf* whirlwind; **~ de agua** cloudburst.

trombón [trom'bon] *nm* trombone.

trombosis [trom'bosis] *nf inv* thrombosis.

trompa ['trompa] *nf* (*MUS*) horn; (*de elefante*) trunk; (*trompo*) humming top; (*hocico*) snout; (*ANAT*) tube, duct ♦ *nm* (*MUS*) horn player; **~ de Falopio** Fallopian tube; **cogerse una ~** (*fam*) to get tight.

trompada [trom'paða] *nf*, **trompazo** [trom'paθo] *nm* (*choque*) bump, bang; (*puñetazo*) punch.

trompeta [trom'peta] *nf* trumpet; (*clarín*) bugle ♦ *nm* trumpeter.

trompetilla [trompe'tiʎa] *nf* ear trumpet.

trompicón [trompi'kon]: **a trompicones** *adv* in fits and starts.

trompo ['trompo] *nm* spinning top.

trompón [trom'pon] *nm* bump.

tronado, a [tro'naðo, a] *adj* broken-down.

tronar [tro'nar] *vt* (*AM*) to shoot, execute ♦ *vi* to thunder; (*fig*) to rage; (*fam*) to go broke.

tronchar [tron'tʃar] *vt* (*árbol*) to chop down; (*fig: vida*) to cut short; (*esperanza*) to shatter; (*persona*) to tire out; **~se** *vr* to fall down; **~se de risa** to split one's sides with laughter.

tronco ['tronko] *nm* (*de árbol, ANAT*) trunk; (*de planta*) stem; **estar hecho un ~** to be sound asleep.

tronera [tro'nera] *nf* (*MIL*) loophole; (*ARQ*) small window.

trono ['trono] *nm* throne.

tropa ['tropa] *nf* (*MIL*) troop; (*soldados*) soldiers *pl*; (*soldados rasos*) ranks *pl*; (*gentío*) mob.

tropecé [trope'θe], **tropecemos** [trope 'θemos] *etc vb V* **tropezar**.

tropel [tro'pel] *nm* (*muchedumbre*) crowd; (*prisa*) rush; (*montón*) throng; **acudir** *etc* **en ~** to come *etc* in a mad rush.

tropelía [trope'lia] *nm* outrage.

tropezar [trope'θar] *vi* to trip, stumble; (*fig*) to slip up; **~se** *vr* (*dos personas*) to run into each other; **~ con** (*encontrar*) to run into; (*topar con*) to bump into.

tropezón [trope'θon] *nm* trip; (*fig*) blunder; (*traspié*): **dar un ~** to trip.

tropical [tropi'kal] *adj* tropical.

trópico ['tropiko] *nm* tropic.

tropiece [tro'pjeθe] *etc vb V* **tropezar**.

tropiezo [tro'pjeθo] *etc vb V* **tropezar** ♦ *nm* (*error*) slip, blunder; (*desgracia*) misfortune; (*revés*) setback; (*obstáculo*) snag; (*discusión*) quarrel.

troqué [tro'ke], **troquemos** [tro'kemos] *etc vb V* **trocar**.

trotamundos [trota'mundos] *nm inv* globetrotter.

trotar [tro'tar] *vi* to trot; (*viajar*) to travel about.

trote ['trote] *nm* trot; (*fam*) travelling; **de mucho ~** hard-wearing.

Troya ['troja] *nf* Troy; **aquí fue ~** now there's nothing but ruins.

trozo ['troθo] *nm* bit, piece; (*LITERATURA, MUS*) passage; **a ~s** in bits.

trucha ['trutʃa] *nf* (*pez*) trout; (*TEC*) crane.

truco ['truko] *nm* (*habilidad*) knack; (*engaño*) trick; (*CINE*) trick effect *o* photography; **~s** *nmpl* billiards *sg*; **~ publicitario** advertising gimmick.

trueco ['trweko] *etc vb V* **trocar**.

trueno ['trweno] *etc vb V* **tronar** ♦ *nm* (*gen*) thunder; (*estampido*) boom; (*de arma*) bang.

trueque ['trweke] *etc vb V* **trocar** ♦ *nm* exchange; (*COM*) barter.

trufa ['trufa] *nf* (*BOT*) truffle; (*fig: fam*) fib.

truhán, ana [tru'an, ana] *nm/f* rogue.

truncado, a [trun'kaðo, a] *adj* truncated.

truncar [trun'kar] *vt* (*cortar*) to truncate; (*la vida etc*) to cut short; (*el desarrollo*) to stunt.

trunque ['trunke] *etc vb V* **truncar**.

tu [tu] *adj* your.

tú [tu] *pron* you.

tubérculo [tu'βerkulo] *nm* (*BOT*) tuber.

tuberculosis [tußerku'losis] *nf inv* tuberculosis.

tubería [tuße'ria] *nf* pipes *pl*, piping; (*conducto*) pipeline.

tubo ['tußo] *nm* tube, pipe; **~ de desagüe** drainpipe; **~ de ensayo** test-tube; **~ de escape** exhaust (pipe); **~ digestivo** alimentary canal.

tuerca ['twerka] *nf* (*TEC*) nut.
tuerce ['twerθe] *etc vb V* **torcer**.
tuerto, a ['twerto, a] *adj* (*torcido*) twisted; (*ciego*) blind in one eye ♦ *nm/f* one-eyed person ♦ *nm* (*ofensa*) wrong; **a tuertas** upside-down.
tuerza ['twerθa] *etc vb V* **torcer**.
tueste ['tweste] *etc vb V* **tostar**.
tuétano ['twetano] *nm* (*ANAT*: *médula*) marrow; (*BOT*) pith; **hasta los ~s** through and through, utterly.
tufo ['tufo] *nm* vapour; (*fig: pey*) stench.
tugurio [tu'ɣurjo] *nm* slum.
tul [tul] *nm* tulle.
tulipán [tuli'pan] *nm* tulip.
tullido, a [tu'ʎiðo, a] *adj* crippled; (*cansado*) exhausted.
tumba ['tumba] *nf* (*sepultura*) tomb; (*sacudida*) shake; (*voltereta*) somersault; **ser (como) una ~** to keep one's mouth shut.
tumbar [tum'bar] *vt* to knock down; (*doblar*) to knock over; (*fam: suj: olor*) to overpower ♦ *vi* to fall down; **~se** *vr* (*echarse*) to lie down; (*extenderse*) to stretch out.
tumbo ['tumbo] *nm* (*caída*) fall; (*de vehículo*) jolt; (*momento crítico*) critical moment.
tumbona [tum'bona] *nf* lounger.
tumefacción [tumefak'θjon] *nf* swelling.
tumor [tu'mor] *nm* tumour.
tumulto [tu'multo] *nm* turmoil; (*POL*: *motín*) riot.
tuna ['tuna] *nf* (*MUS*) student music group *V tb* **tuno**.

A **tuna** *is made up of university students, or quite often former students, who dress up in costumes from the* **Edad de Oro***, the Spanish Golden Age. These musical troupes go through the town playing their guitars, lutes and tambourines and serenade the young ladies in the halls of residence, or make impromptu appearances at weddings or parties singing traditional Spanish songs for a few* **pesetas***.*

---

tunante [tu'nante] *adj* rascally ♦ *nm* rogue, villain; **¡~!** you villain!
tunda ['tunda] *nf* (*de tela*) shearing; (*golpeo*) beating.
tundir [tun'dir] *vt* (*tela*) to shear; (*hierba*) to mow; (*fig*) to exhaust; (*fam: golpear*) to beat.
tunecino, a [tune'θino, a] *adj, nm/f* Tunisian.
túnel ['tunel] *nm* tunnel.

Túnez ['tuneθ] *nm* Tunis.
túnica ['tunika] *nf* tunic; (*vestido largo*) long dress; (*ANAT, BOT*) tunic.
Tunicia [tu'niθja] *nf* Tunisia.
tuno, a ['tuno, a] *nm/f* (*fam*) rogue ♦ *nm* (*MUS*) member of a "*tuna*".
tuntún [tun'tun]: **al ~** *adv* thoughtlessly.
tupamaro, a [tupa'maro, a] *adj, nm/f* (*AM*) urban guerrilla.
tupé [tu'pe] *nm* quiff.
tupí [tu'pi], **tupí-guaraní** [tupigwara'ni] *adj, nm/f* Tupi-Guarani.
tupido, a [tu'piðo, a] *adj* (*denso*) dense; (*fig: torpe*) dim; (*tela*) close-woven.
turba ['turßa] *nf* (*combustible*) turf; (*muchedumbre*) crowd.
turbación [turßa'θjon] *nf* (*molestia*) disturbance; (*preocupación*) worry.
turbado, a [tur'ßaðo, a] *adj* (*molesto*) disturbed; (*preocupado*) worried.
turbante [tur'ßante] *nm* turban.
turbar [tur'ßar] *vt* (*molestar*) to disturb; (*incomodar*) to upset; **~se** *vr* to be disturbed.
turbina [tur'ßina] *nf* turbine.
turbio, a ['turßjo, a] *adj* (*agua etc*) cloudy; (*vista*) dim, blurred; (*tema*) unclear, confused; (*negocio*) shady ♦ *adv* indistinctly.
turbión [tur'ßjon] *nf* downpour; (*fig*) shower, hail.
turbo ['turßo] *adj inv* turbo(-charged) ♦ *nm* (*tb coche*) turbo.
turbohélice [turßo'eliθe] *nm* turboprop.
turbulencia [turßu'lenθja] *nf* turbulence; (*fig*) restlessness.
turbulento, a [turßu'lento, a] *adj* turbulent; (*fig: intranquilo*) restless; (*: ruidoso*) noisy.
turco, a ['turko, a] *adj* Turkish ♦ *nm/f* Turk ♦ *nm* (*LING*) Turkish.
Turena [tu'rena] *nf* Touraine.
turgente [tur'xente], **túrgido, a** ['turxiðo, a] *adj* (*hinchado*) turgid, swollen.
Turín [tu'rin] *nm* Turin.
turismo [tu'rismo] *nm* tourism; (*coche*) saloon car; **hacer ~** to go travelling (abroad).
turista [tu'rista] *nm/f* tourist; (*vacacionista*) holidaymaker (*BRIT*), vacationer (*US*).
turístico, a [tu'ristiko, a] *adj* tourist *cpd*.
Turkmenistán [turkmeni'stan] *nm* Turkmenistan.
turnar [tur'nar] *vi*, **turnarse** *vr* to take (it in) turns.
turno ['turno] *nm* (*oportunidad, orden de prioridad*) opportunity; (*DEPORTE etc*) turn; **es su ~** it's his turn (next); **~ de**

día/de noche (*INDUSTRIA*) day/night shift.
turolense [turo'lense] *adj* of *o* from Teruel
♦ *nm/f* native *o* inhabitant of Teruel.
turquesa [tur'kesa] *nf* turquoise.
Turquía [tur'kia] *nf* Turkey.
turrón [tu'rron] *nm* (*dulce*) nougat; (*fam*)
sinecure, cushy job *o* number.
tute ['tute] *nm* (*NAIPES*) card game; **darse
un ~** to break one's back.
tutear [tute'ar] *vt* to address as familiar
"tú"; **~se** *vr* to be on familiar terms.
tutela [tu'tela] *nf* (*legal*) guardianship;
(*instrucción*) guidance; **estar bajo la ~ de**
(*fig*) to be under the protection of.
tutelar [tute'lar] *adj* tutelary ♦ *vt* to
protect.
tutor, a [tu'tor, a] *nm/f* (*legal*) guardian;
(*ESCOL*) tutor; **~ de curso** form master/
mistress.
tuve ['tuβe] *etc vb V* **tener.**
tuyo, a ['tujo, a] *adj* yours, of yours ♦ *pron*
yours; **los ~s** (*fam*) your relations, your
family.
TVE *nf abr* = *Televisión Española*.

U u

U, u [u] *nf* (*letra*) U, u; **viraje en U** U-turn; **U
de Ulises** U for Uncle.
u [u] *conj* or.
UAR [war] *nfpl abr* (*ESP*) = *Unidades
Antiterroristas Rurales*.
ubérrimo, a [u'βerrimo, a] *adj* very rich,
fertile.
ubicación [uβika'θjon] *nf* (*esp AM*) place,
position, location.
ubicado, a [uβi'kaðo, a] *adj* (*esp AM*)
situated.
ubicar [uβi'kar] *vt* (*esp AM*) to place,
situate; (: *fig*) to install in a post;
(: *encontrar*) to find; **~se** *vr* to be situated,
be located.
ubicuo, a [u'βikwo, a] *adj* ubiquitous.
ubique [u'βike] *etc vb V* **ubicar.**
ubre ['uβre] *nf* udder.
Ucrania [u'kranja] *nf* Ukraine.
ucraniano, a [ukra'njano, a] *adj, nm/f*
Ukrainian ♦ *nm* (*LING*) Ukrainian.
ucranio [u'kranjo] *nm* (*LING*) Ukrainian.
Ud(s) *abr* = **usted(es).**
UE *nf abr* (= *Unión Europea*) EU.

UEFA *nf abr* (= *Unión de Asociaciones de
Fútbol Europeo*) UEFA.
UEO *nf abr* (= *Unión Europea Occidental*)
WEU.
UEP *nf abr* = *Unión Europea de Pagos*.
uf [uf] *excl* (*cansancio*) phew!; (*repugnancia*)
ugh!
ufanarse [ufa'narse] *vr* to boast; **~ de** to
pride o.s. on.
ufano, a [u'fano, a] *adj* (*arrogante*)
arrogant; (*presumido*) conceited.
UGT *nf abr V* **Unión General de
Trabajadores.**
ujier [u'xjer] *nm* usher; (*portero*)
doorkeeper.
úlcera ['ulθera] *nf* ulcer.
ulcerar [ulθe'rar] *vt* to make sore; **~se** *vr* to
ulcerate.
ulterior [ulte'rjor] *adj* (*más allá*) farther,
further; (*subsecuente, siguiente*)
subsequent.
ulteriormente [ulterjor'mente] *adv* later,
subsequently.
últimamente ['ultimamente] *adv*
(*recientemente*) lately, recently;
(*finalmente*) finally; (*como último recurso*)
as a last resort.
ultimar [ulti'mar] *vt* to finish; (*finalizar*) to
finalize; (*AM: rematar*) to finish off,
murder.
ultimátum [ulti'matum] *nm, pl*
ultimátums ultimatum.
último, a ['ultimo, a] *adj* last; (*más reciente*)
latest, most recent; (*más bajo*) bottom;
(*más alto*) top; (*fig*) final, extreme; **en las
últimas** on one's last legs; **por ~** finally.
ultra ['ultra] *adj* ultra ♦ *nm/f* extreme
right-winger.
ultracongelar [ultrakonxe'lar] *vt* to deep-
freeze.
ultraderecha [ultraðe'retʃa] *nf* extreme
right (wing).
ultrajar [ultra'xar] *vt* (*escandalizar*) to
outrage; (*insultar*) to insult, abuse.
ultraje [ul'traxe] *nm* outrage; insult.
ultraligero [ultrali'xero] *nm* microlight
(*BRIT*), microlite (*US*).
ultramar [ultra'mar] *nm*: **de *o* en ~** abroad,
overseas; **los países de ~** the overseas
countries.
ultramarino, a [ultrama'rino, a] *adj*
overseas, foreign ♦ *nmpl*: **~s** groceries;
tienda de ~s grocer's (shop).
ultranza [ul'tranθa]: **a ~** *adv* to the death;
(*a todo trance*) at all costs; (*completo*)
outright; (*POL etc*) out-and-out, extreme;
un nacionalista a ~ a rabid nationalist.
ultrarrojo, a [ultra'rroxo, a] *adj*

= **infrarrojo, a.**

ultrasónico, a [ultra'soniko, a] *adj* ultrasonic.

ultratumba [ultra'tumba] *nf*: **la vida de ~** the next life; **una voz de ~** a ghostly voice.

ultravioleta [ultraßjo'leta] *adj inv* ultraviolet.

ulular [ulu'lar] *vi* to howl; (*búho*) to hoot.

umbilical [umbili'kal] *adj*: **cordón ~** umbilical cord.

umbral [um'bral] *nm* (*gen*) threshold; **~ de rentabilidad** (*COM*) break-even point.

umbrío, a [um'brio, a] *adj* shady.

================== *PALABRA CLAVE*

un, una [un, 'una] *art indef* a; (*antes de vocal*) an; **una mujer/naranja** a woman/an orange
♦ *adj* **1: unos (o unas): hay unos regalos para ti** there are some presents for you; **hay unas cervezas en la nevera** there are some beers in the fridge

2 (*enfático*): **¡hace un frío!** it's so cold!; **¡tiene una casa!** he's got some house!

U.N.A.M. ['unam] *nf abr* = *Universidad Nacional Autónoma de México.*

unánime [u'nanime] *adj* unanimous.

unanimidad [unanimi'ðað] *nf* unanimity; **por ~** unanimously.

unción [un'θjon] *nf* anointing.

uncir [un'θir] *vt* to yoke.

undécimo, a [un'deθimo, a] *adj, nm/f* eleventh.

UNED [u'ned] *nf abr* (*ESP UNIV*: = *Universidad Nacional de Enseñanza a Distancia*) ≈ Open University (*BRIT*).

ungir [un'xir] *vt* to rub with ointment; (*REL*) to anoint.

ungüento [un'gwento] *nm* ointment; (*fig*) salve, balm.

únicamente ['unikamente] *adv* solely; (*solamente*) only.

unicidad [uniθi'ðað] *nf* uniqueness.

único, a ['uniko, a] *adj* only; (*solo*) sole, single; (*sin par*) unique; **hijo ~** only child.

unidad [uni'ðað] *nf* unity; (*TEC*) unit; **~ móvil** (*TV*) mobile unit; (*INFORM*): **~ central** system unit, central processing unit; **~ de control** control unit; **~ de disco** disk drive; **~ de entrada/salida** input/output device; **~ de información** data item; **~ periférica** peripheral device; **~ de presentación visual** o **de visualización** visual display unit; **~ procesadora central** central processing unit.

unido, a [u'niðo, a] *adj* joined, linked; (*fig*) united.

unifamiliar [unifamil'jar] *adj*: **vivienda ~** single-family home.

unificar [unifi'kar] *vt* to unite, unify.

unifique [uni'fike] *etc vb V* **unificar.**

uniformado, a [unifor'maðo, a] *adj* uniformed, in uniform.

uniformar [unifor'mar] *vt* to make uniform; (*TEC*) to standardize.

uniforme [uni'forme] *adj* uniform, equal; (*superficie*) even ♦ *nm* uniform.

uniformidad [uniformi'ðað] *nf* uniformity; (*llaneza*) levelness, evenness.

unilateral [unilate'ral] *adj* unilateral.

unión [u'njon] *nf* (*gen*) union; (*acto*) uniting, joining; (*calidad*) unity; (*TEC*) joint; (*fig*) closeness, togetherness; **en ~ con** (together) with, accompanied by; **~ aduanera** customs union; **U~ General de Trabajadores (UGT)** (*ESP*) *Socialist Union Confederation;* **U~ Europea** European Union; **la U~ Soviética** the Soviet Union; **punto de ~** (*TEC*) junction.

unir [u'nir] *vt* (*juntar*) to join, unite; (*atar*) to tie, fasten; (*combinar*) to combine ♦ *vi* (*ingredientes*) to mix well; **~se** *vr* to join together, unite; (*empresas*) to merge; **les une una fuerte simpatía** they are bound by (a) strong affection; **~se en matrimonio** to marry.

unisex [uni'seks] *adj inv* unisex.

unísono [u'nisono] *nm*: **al ~** in unison.

unitario, a [uni'tarjo, a] *adj* unitary; (*REL*) Unitarian ♦ *nm/f* (*REL*) Unitarian.

universal [unißer'sal] *adj* universal; (*mundial*) world *cpd*; **historia ~** world history.

universidad [unißersi'ðað] *nf* university; **~ laboral** polytechnic, poly.

universitario, a [unißersi'tarjo, a] *adj* university *cpd* ♦ *nm/f* (*profesor*) lecturer; (*estudiante*) (university) student.

universo [uni'ßerso] *nm* universe.

unja ['unxa] *etc vb V* **ungir.**

================== *PALABRA CLAVE*

uno, a ['uno, a] *adj* one; **es todo ~** it's all one and the same; **~s pocos** a few; **~s cien** about a hundred
♦ *pron* **1** one; **quiero ~ solo** I only want one; **~ de ellos** one of them; **una de dos** either one or the other; **no doy una hoy** I can't do anything right today

2 (*alguien*) somebody, someone; **conozco a ~ que se te parece** I know somebody o someone who looks like you; **~s querían quedarse** some (people) wanted to stay

3 (*impersonal*) one; ~ **mismo** oneself; ~
nunca sabe qué hacer one never knows
what to do
4: ~**s** ... **otros** ... some ... others; **una y
otra son muy agradables** they're both
very nice; **(los)** ~**(s) a (los) otro(s)** each
other, one another
♦ *nf* one; **es la una** it's one o'clock
♦ *num* (number) one; **el día** ~ the first.

untar [un'tar] *vt* (*gen*) to rub; (*engrasar*) to
grease, oil; (*MED*) to rub (with
ointment); (*fig*) to bribe; ~**se** *vr* (*fig*) to be
crooked; ~ **el pan con mantequilla** to
spread butter on one's bread.
unto ['unto] *nm* animal fat; (*MED*)
ointment.
unza ['unθa] *etc vb V* **uncir**.
uña ['uɲa] *nf* (*ANAT*) nail; (*del pie*) toenail;
(*garra*) claw; (*casco*) hoof; (*arrancaclavos*)
claw; **ser** ~ **y carne** to be as thick as
thieves; **enseñar** *o* **mostrar** *o* **sacar las** ~**s**
to show one's claws.
UOE *nf abr* (*ESP MIL*) = *Unidad de
Operaciones Especiales*.
UPA *nf abr* = *Unión Panamericana*.
UPC *nf abr* (= *unidad procesadora central*)
CPU.
uperizado, a [uperi'θaðo, a] *adj*: **leche
uperizada** UHT milk.
Urales [u'rales] *nmpl* (*tb*: **Montes** ~) Urals.
uralita ® [ura'lita] *nf* corrugated asbestos
cement.
uranio [u'ranjo] *nm* uranium.
urbanidad [urßani'ðað] *nf* courtesy,
politeness.
urbanismo [urßa'nismo] *nm* town
planning.
urbanista [urßa'nista] *nm/f* town planner.
urbanización [urßaniθa'θjon] *nf* (*colonia,
barrio*) estate, housing scheme.
urbanizar [urßani'θar] *vt* to develop.
urbano, a [ur'ßano, a] *adj* (*de ciudad*)
urban, town *cpd*; (*cortés*) courteous,
polite.
urbe ['urße] *nf* large city, metropolis.
urdimbre [ur'ðimbre] *nf* (*de tejido*) warp;
(*intriga*) intrigue.
urdir [ur'ðir] *vt* to warp; (*fig*) to plot,
contrive.
urgencia [ur'xenθja] *nf* urgency; (*prisa*)
haste, rush; **salida de** ~ emergency exit;
servicios de ~ emergency services.
urgente [ur'xente] *adj* urgent; (*insistente*)
insistent; **carta** ~ registered (*BRIT*) *o*
special delivery (*US*) letter.
urgir [ur'xir] *vi* to be urgent; **me urge** I'm
in a hurry for it; **me urge terminarlo** I

must finish it as soon as I can.
urinario, a [uri'narjo, a] *adj* urinary ♦ *nm*
urinal, public lavatory, comfort station
(*US*).
urja ['urxa] *etc vb V* **urgir**.
urna ['urna] *nf* urn; (*POL*) ballot box; **acudir
a las** ~**s** (*fig*: *persona*) to (go and) vote;
(: *gobierno*) to go to the country.
urología [urolo'xia] *nf* urology.
urólogo, a [u'rolovo, a] *nm/f* urologist.
urraca [u'rraka] *nf* magpie.
URSS *nf abr* (= *Unión de Repúblicas
Socialistas Soviéticas*) USSR.
Uruguay [uru'ɣwai] *nm*: **El** ~ Uruguay.
uruguayo, a [uru'ɣwajo, a] *adj, nm/f*
Uruguayan.
usado, a [u'saðo, a] *adj* (*gen*) used; (*ropa
etc*) worn; **muy** ~ worn out.
usanza [u'sanθa] *nf* custom, usage.
usar [u'sar] *vt* to use; (*ropa*) to wear; (*tener
costumbre*) to be in the habit of ♦ *vi*: ~ **de**
to make use of; ~**se** *vr* to be used; (*ropa*)
to be worn *o* in fashion.
USO *nf abr* (*ESP*. = *Unión Sindical Obrera*)
workers' union.
uso ['uso] *nm* use; (*MECÁNICA etc*) wear;
(*costumbre*) usage, custom; (*moda*)
fashion; **al** ~ in keeping with custom; **al**
~ **de** in the style of; **de** ~ **externo** (*MED*)
for external application; **estar en el** ~ **de
la palabra** to be speaking, have the floor;
~ **y desgaste** (*COM*) wear and tear.
usted [us'teð] *pron* (*sg*: *abr* **Ud** *o* **Vd**: *formal*)
you *sg*; ~**es** (*pl*: *abr* **Uds** *o* **Vds**: *formal*)
you *pl*; (*AM*: *formal y fam*) you *pl*.
usual [u'swal] *adj* usual.
usuario, a [usw'arjo, a] *nm/f* user; ~ **final**
(*COM*) end user.
usufructo [usu'frukto] *nm* use; ~ **vitalicio
(de)** life interest (in).
usura [u'sura] *nf* usury.
usurero, a [usu'rero, a] *nm/f* usurer.
usurpar [usur'par] *vt* to usurp.
utensilio [uten'siljo] *nm* tool; (*CULIN*)
utensil.
útero ['utero] *nm* uterus, womb.
útil ['util] *adj* useful; (*servible*) usable,
serviceable ♦ *nm* tool; **día** ~ working
day, weekday; **es muy** ~ **tenerlo aquí
cerca** it's very handy having it here
close by.
utilice [uti'liθe] *etc vb V* **utilizar**.
utilidad [utili'ðað] *nf* usefulness, utility;
(*COM*) profit; ~**es líquidas** net profit *sg*.
utilitario [utili'tarjo] *nm* (*INFORM*) utility.
utilizar [utili'θar] *vt* to use, utilize;
(*explotar*) to harness.
utopía [uto'pia] *nf* Utopia.

utópico, a [u'topiko, a] *adj* Utopian.
uva ['uβa] *nf* grape; ~ **pasa** raisin; ~ **de
Corinto** currant; **estar de mala** ~ to be in
a bad mood.

In Spain **Las uvas** *play a big part on New
Years' Eve* **(Nochevieja)**, *when on the
stroke of midnight people from every part
of Spain, at home, in restaurants or in the*
plaza mayor *eat a grape for each stroke of
the clock of the* **Puerta del Sol** *in Madrid. It
is said to bring luck for the following year.*

---

uve ['uβe] *nf* name of the letter V; **en forma
de** ~ V-shaped; ~ **doble** name of the
letter W.
UVI ['uβi] *nf abr* (*ESP MED*: = *unidad de
vigilancia intensiva*) ICU.

V v

V, v [(*ESP*) 'uβe, (*AM*) be'lkorta, bet ∫ika] *nf*
(*letra*) V, v; **V de Valencia** V for Victor.
V. *abr* (= *visto*) approved, passed.
v. *abr* (= *voltio*) v.; (= *véase*) v.; (= *verso*) v.
va [ba] *vb* V **ir.**
V.A. *abr* = *Vuestra Alteza.*
vaca ['baka] *nf* (*animal*) cow; (*carne*) beef;
(*cuero*) cowhide; ~**s flacas/gordas** (*fig*)
bad/good times.
vacaciones [baka'θjones] *nfpl* holiday(s);
estar/irse *o* **marcharse de** ~ to be/go
(away) on holiday.
vacante [ba'kante] *adj* vacant, empty ♦ *nf*
vacancy.
vaciado, a [ba'θjaðo, a] *adj* (*hecho en
molde*) cast in a mould; (*hueco*) hollow
♦ *nm* cast, mould(ing).
vaciar [ba'θjar] *vt* to empty (out); (*ahuecar*)
to hollow out; (*moldear*) to cast; (*INFORM*)
to dump ♦ *vi* (*río*) to flow (*en* into); ~**se** *vr*
to empty; (*fig*) to blab, spill the beans.
vaciedad [baθje'ðað] *nf* emptiness.
vacilación [baθila'θjon] *nf* hesitation.
vacilante [baθi'lante] *adj* unsteady; (*habla*)
faltering; (*luz*) flickering; (*fig*) hesitant.
vacilar [baθi'lar] *vi* to be unsteady; to
falter; to flicker; to hesitate, waver;
(*persona*) to stagger, stumble; (*memoria*)
to fail; (*esp AM*: *divertirse*) to have a great
time.

vacilón [baθi'lon] *nm* (*esp AM*): **estar** *o* **ir de**
~ to have a great time.
vacío, a [ba'θio, a] *adj* empty; (*puesto*)
vacant; (*desocupado*) idle; (*vano*) vain;
(*charla etc*) light, superficial ♦ *nm*
emptiness; (*FÍSICA*) vacuum; (*un* ~)
(empty) space; **hacer el** ~ **a algn** to send
sb to Coventry.
vacuna [ba'kuna] *nf* vaccine.
vacunar [baku'nar] *vt* to vaccinate; ~**se** *vr*
to get vaccinated.
vacuno, a [ba'kuno, a] *adj* bovine.
vacuo, a ['bakwo, a] *adj* empty.
vadear [baðe'ar] *vt* (*río*) to ford; (*problema*)
to overcome; (*persona*) to sound out.
vado ['baðo] *nm* ford; (*solución*) solution;
(*descanso*) respite.
vagabundear [baɣabunde'ar] *vi* (*andar sin
rumbo*) to wander, roam; (*ser vago*) to be
a tramp *o* bum (*US*).
vagabundo, a [baɣa'βundo, a] *adj*
wandering; (*pey*) vagrant ♦ *nm/f* (*errante*)
wanderer; (*vago*) tramp, bum (*US*).
vagamente [baɣa'mente] *adv* vaguely.
vagancia [ba'ɣanθja] *nf* vagrancy.
vagar [ba'ɣar] *vi* to wander; (*pasear*) to
saunter up and down; (*no hacer nada*) to
idle ♦ *nm* leisure.
vagido [ba'xiðo] *nm* wail.
vagina [ba'xina] *nf* vagina.
vago, a ['baɣo, a] *adj* vague; (*perezoso*)
lazy; (*ambulante*) wandering ♦ *nm/f*
(*vagabundo*) tramp, bum (*US*); (*flojo*)
lazybones *sg*, idler.
vagón [ba'ɣon] *nm* (*de pasajeros*) carriage;
(*de mercancías*) wagon; ~ **cama/
restaurante** sleeping/dining car.
vague ['baɣe] *etc vb* V **vagar.**
vaguear [baɣe'ar] *vi* to laze around.
vaguedad [baɣe'ðað] *nf* vagueness.
vahído [ba'iðo] *nm* dizzy spell.
vaho ['bao] *nm* (*vapor*) vapour, steam;
(*olor*) smell; (*respiración*) breath; ~**s** *nmpl*
(*MED*) inhalation *sg*.
vaina ['baina] *nf* sheath ♦ *nm* (*AM*)
nuisance.
vainilla [bai'niʎa] *nf* vanilla.
vainita [bai'nita] *nf* (*AM*) green *o* French
bean.
vais [bais] *vb* V **ir.**
vaivén [bai'βen] *nm* to-and-fro movement;
(*de tránsito*) coming and going; **vaivenes**
nmpl (*fig*) ups and downs.
vajilla [ba'xiʎa] *nf* crockery, dishes *pl*; (*una
~*) service; ~ **de porcelana** chinaware.
val [bal], **valdré** [bal'dre] *etc vb* V **valer.**
vale ['bale] *nm* voucher; (*recibo*) receipt;
(*pagaré*) I.O.U.; ~ **de regalo** gift voucher

o token.
valedero, a [bale'ðero, a] *adj* valid.
valenciano, a [balen'θjano, a] *adj, nm/f*
Valencian ♦ *nm* (*LING*) Valencian.
valentía [balen'tia] *nf* courage, bravery;
(*pey*) boastfulness; (*acción*) heroic deed.
valentísimo, a [balen'tisimo, a] *adj* (*superl
de* **valiente**) very brave, courageous.
valentón, ona [balen'ton, ona] *adj*
blustering.
valer [ba'ler] *vt* to be worth; (*MAT*) to
equal; (*costar*) to cost; (*amparar*) to aid,
protect ♦ *vi* (*ser útil*) to be useful; (*ser
válido*) to be valid; ~**se** *vr* to defend o.s.
♦ *nm* worth, value; ~ **la pena** to be
worthwhile; **¿vale?** O.K.?; **¡vale!** (*¡basta!*)
that'll do!; **¡eso no vale!** that doesn't
count!; **no vale nada** it's no good;
(*mercancía*) it's worthless; (*argumento*)
it's no use; **no vale para nada** he's no
good at all; **más vale tarde que nunca**
better late than never; **más vale que nos
vayamos** we'd better go; ~**se de** to make
use of, take advantage of; ~**se por sí
mismo** to help *o* manage by o.s.
valga ['balɣa] *etc vb V* **valer**.
valía [ba'lia] *nf* worth; **de gran** ~ (*objeto*)
very valuable.
validar [bali'ðar] *vt* to validate; (*POL*) to
ratify.
validez [bali'ðeθ] *nf* validity; **dar** ~ **a** to
validate.
válido, a ['baliðo, a] *adj* valid.
valiente [ba'ljente] *adj* brave, valiant;
(*audaz*) bold; (*pey*) boastful; (*con ironía*)
fine, wonderful ♦ *nm/f* brave man/
woman.
valija [ba'lixa] *nf* case; (*AM*) suitcase;
(*mochila*) satchel; (*CORREOS*) mailbag; ~
diplomática diplomatic bag.
valioso, a [ba'ljoso, a] *adj* valuable; (*rico*)
wealthy.
valla ['baʎa] *nf* fence; (*DEPORTE*) hurdle;
(*fig*) barrier; ~ **publicitaria** billboard.
vallar [ba'ʎar] *vt* to fence in.
valle ['baʎe] *nm* valley, vale.
vallisoletano, a [baʎisole'tano, a] *adj* of *o*
from Valladolid ♦ *nm/f* native *o*
inhabitant of Valladolid.
valor [ba'lor] *nm* value, worth; (*precio*)
price; (*valentía*) valour, courage;
(*importancia*) importance; (*cara*) nerve,
cheek (*fam*); **sin** ~ worthless; ~
adquisitivo *o* **de compra** purchasing
power; **dar** ~ **a** to attach importance to;
quitar ~ **a** to minimize the importance
of; (*COM*): ~ **según balance** book value;
~ **comercial** *o* **de mercado** market value;

~ **contable/desglosado** asset/break-up
value; ~ **de escasez** scarcity value; ~
intrínseco intrinsic value; ~ **a la par** par
value; ~ **neto** net worth; ~ **de rescate/de
sustitución** surrender/replacement
value; *V tb* **valores**.
valoración [balora'θjon] *nf* valuation.
valorar [balo'rar] *vt* to value; (*tasar*) to
price; (*fig*) to assess.
valores [ba'lores] *nmpl* (*COM*) securities; ~
en cartera *o* **habidos** investments.
vals [bals] *nm* waltz.
válvula ['balβula] *nf* valve.
vamos ['bamos] *vb V* **ir**.
vampiro, iresa [bam'piro, i'resa] *nm/f*
vampire ♦ *nf* (*CINE*) vamp, femme fatale.
van [ban] *vb V* **ir**.
vanagloriarse [banaɣlo'rjarse] *vr* to boast.
vandalismo [banda'lismo] *nm* vandalism.
vándalo, a ['bandalo, a] *nm/f* vandal.
vanguardia [ban'gwardja] *nf* vanguard; **de**
~ (*ARTE*) avant-garde; **estar** *en o* **ir a la** ~
de (*fig*) to be in the forefront of.
vanguardista [bangwar'ðista] *adj* avant-
garde.
vanidad [bani'ðað] *nf* vanity; (*inutilidad*)
futility; (*irrealidad*) unreality.
vanidoso, a [bani'ðoso, a] *adj* vain,
conceited.
vano, a ['bano, a] *adj* (*irreal*) unreal;
(*irracional*) unreasonable; (*inútil*) vain,
useless; (*persona*) vain, conceited;
(*frívolo*) frivolous.
vapor [ba'por] *nm* vapour; (*vaho*) steam;
(*de gas*) fumes *pl*; (*neblina*) mist; ~**es**
nmpl (*MED*) hysterics; **al** ~ (*CULIN*)
steamed.
vaporice [bapo'riθe] *etc vb V* **vaporizar**.
vaporizador [baporiθa'ðor] *nm* (*perfume
etc*) spray.
vaporizar [bapori'θar] *vt* to vaporize;
(*perfume*) to spray.
vaporoso, a [bapo'roso, a] *adj* vaporous;
(*vahoso*) steamy; (*tela*) light, airy.
vapulear [bapule'ar] *vt* to thrash; (*fig*) to
slate.
vaque ['bake] *etc vb V* **vacar**.
vaquería [bake'ria] *nf* dairy.
vaquero, a [ba'kero, a] *adj* cattle *cpd* ♦ *nm*
cowboy; ~**s** *nmpl* jeans.
vaquilla [ba'kiʎa] *nf* heifer.
vara ['bara] *nf* stick, pole; (*TEC*) rod; ~
mágica magic wand.
varado, a [ba'raðo, a] *adj* (*NAUT*) stranded;
estar ~ to be aground.
varar [ba'rar] *vt* to beach ♦ *vi*, ~**se** *vr* to be
beached.
varear [bare'ar] *vt* to hit, beat; (*frutas*) to

knock down (with poles).
variable [ba'rjaßle] *adj, nf* variable (*tb
INFORM*).
variación [barja'θjon] *nf* variation; **sin** ~
unchanged.
variado, a [ba'rjaðo, a] *adj* varied; (*dulces,
galletas*) assorted; **entremeses** ~**s** a
selection of starters.
variante [ba'rjante] *adj* variant ♦ *nf*
(*alternativa*) alternative; (*AUTO*) bypass.
variar [ba'rjar] *vt* (*cambiar*) to change;
(*poner variedad*) to vary; (*modificar*) to
modify; (*cambiar de posición*) to switch
around ♦ *vi* to vary; ~ **de** to differ from;
~ **de opinión** to change one's mind; **para**
~ just for a change.
varicela [bari'θela] *nf* chicken pox.
varices [ba'riθes] *nfpl* varicose veins.
variedad [barje'ðað] *nf* variety.
varilla [ba'riʎa] *nf* stick; (*BOT*) twig; (*TEC*)
rod; (*de rueda*) spoke; ~ **mágica** magic
wand.
vario, a ['barjo, a] *adj* (*variado*) varied;
(*multicolor*) motley; (*cambiable*)
changeable; ~**s** various, several.
variopinto, a [barjo'pinto, a] *adj* diverse;
un público ~ a mixed audience.
varita [ba'rita] *nf*: ~ **mágica** magic wand.
varón [ba'ron] *nm* male, man.
varonil [baro'nil] *adj* manly.
Varsovia [bar'soßja] *nf* Warsaw.
vas [bas] *vb V* **ir**.
vasco, a ['basko, a], **vascongado, a**
[baskon'gaðo, a] *adj, nm/f* Basque ♦ *nm*
(*LING*) Basque ♦ *nfpl*: **las Vascongadas** the
Basque Country *sg o* Provinces.
vascuence [bas'kwenθe] *nm* (*LING*) Basque.
vasectomía [basekto'mia] *nf* vasectomy.
vaselina [base'lina] *nf* Vaseline ®.
vasija [ba'sixa] *nf* (earthenware) vessel.
vaso ['baso] *nm* glass, tumbler; (*ANAT*)
vessel; (*cantidad*) glass(ful); ~ **de vino**
glass of wine; ~ **para vino** wineglass.
vástago ['bastaɣo] *nm* (*BOT*) shoot; (*TEC*)
rod; (*fig*) offspring.
vasto, a ['basto, a] *adj* vast, huge.
váter ['bater] *nm* lavatory, W.C.
Vaticano [bati'kano] *nm*: **el** ~ the Vatican;
la Ciudad del ~ the Vatican City.
vaticinar [batiθi'nar] *vt* to prophesy,
predict.
vaticinio [bati'θinjo] *nm* prophecy.
vatio ['batjo] *nm* (*ELEC*) watt.
vaya ['baja] *etc vb V* **ir**.
Vda. *abr* = **viuda**.
Vd(s) *abr* = **usted(es)**.
ve [be] *vb V* **ir, ver**.
vea ['bea] *etc vb V* **ver**.

vecinal [beθi'nal] *adj* (*camino, impuesto etc*)
local.
vecindad [beθin'dað] *nf*, **vecindario**
[beθin'darjo] *nm* neighbourhood;
(*habitantes*) residents *pl*.
vecino, a [be'θino, a] *adj* neighbouring
♦ *nm/f* neighbour; (*residente*) resident;
somos ~**s** we live next door to one
another.
vector [bek'tor] *nm* vector.
veda ['beða] *nf* prohibition; (*temporada*)
close season.
vedado [be'ðaðo] *nm* preserve.
vedar [be'ðar] *vt* (*prohibir*) to ban, prohibit;
(*idea, plan*) to veto; (*impedir*) to stop,
prevent.
vedette [be'ðet] *nf* (*TEAT, CINE*) star(let).
vega ['beɣa] *nf* fertile plain *o* valley.
vegetación [bexeta'θjon] *nf* vegetation.
vegetal [bexe'tal] *adj, nm* vegetable.
vegetar [bexe'tar] *vi* to vegetate.
vegetariano, a [bexeta'rjano, a] *adj, nm/f*
vegetarian.
vegetativo, a [bexeta'tißo, a] *adj*
vegetative.
vehemencia [bee'menθja] *nf* (*insistencia*)
vehemence; (*pasión*) passion; (*fervor*)
fervour; (*violencia*) violence.
vehemente [bee'mente] *adj* vehement;
passionate; fervent; violent.
vehículo [be'ikulo] *nm* vehicle; (*MED*)
carrier; ~ **de servicio público** public
service vehicle; ~ **espacial** spacecraft.
veinte ['beinte] *num* twenty; (*orden, fecha*)
twentieth; **el siglo** ~ the twentieth
century.
veintena [bein'tena] *nf*: **una** ~ (about)
twenty, a score.
vejación [bexa'θjon] *nf* vexation;
(*humillación*) humiliation.
vejamen [be'xamen] *nm* satire.
vejar [be'xar] *vt* (*irritar*) to annoy, vex;
(*humillar*) to humiliate.
vejatorio, a [bexa'torjo, a] *adj* humiliating,
degrading.
vejez [be'xeθ] *nf* old age.
vejiga [be'xiɣa] *nf* (*ANAT*) bladder.
vela ['bela] *nf* (*de cera*) candle; (*NAUT*) sail;
(*insomnio*) sleeplessness; (*vigilia*) vigil;
(*MIL*) sentry duty; (*fam*) snot; **a toda** ~
(*NAUT*) under full sail; **estar a dos** ~**s**
(*fam*) to be skint; **pasar la noche en** ~ to
have a sleepless night.
velado, a [be'laðo, a] *adj* veiled; (*sonido*)
muffled; (*FOTO*) blurred ♦ *nf* soirée.
velador [bela'ðor] *nm* watchman;
(*candelero*) candlestick; (*AM*) bedside
table.

velar [be'lar] *vt* (*vigilar*) to keep watch over; (*cubrir*) to veil ♦ *vi* to stay awake; ~ **por** to watch over, look after.

velatorio [bela'torjo] *nm* (funeral) wake.

veleidad [belei'ðað] *nf* (*ligereza*) fickleness; (*capricho*) whim.

velero [be'lero] *nm* (*NAUT*) sailing ship; (*AVIAT*) glider.

veleta [be'leta] *nm/f* fickle person ♦ *nf* weather vane.

veliz [be'lis] *nm* (*AM*) suitcase.

vello ['beʎo] *nm* down, fuzz.

vellón [be'ʎon] *nm* fleece.

velloso, a [be'ʎoso, a] *adj* fuzzy.

velludo, a [be'ʎuðo, a] *adj* shaggy ♦ *nm* plush, velvet.

velo ['belo] *nm* veil; ~ **de paladar** (*ANAT*) soft palate.

velocidad [beloθi'ðað] *nf* speed; (*TEC*) rate, pace, velocity; (*MECÁNICA, AUTO*) gear; ¿**a qué** ~? how fast?; **de alta** ~ high-speed; **cobrar** ~ to pick up *o* gather speed; **meter la segunda** ~ to change into second gear; ~ **máxima de impresión** (*INFORM*) maximum print speed.

velocímetro [belo'θimetro] *nm* speedometer.

velódromo [be'loðromo] *nm* cycle track.

veloz [be'loθ] *adj* fast, swift.

ven [ben] *vb* V **venir**.

vena ['bena] *nf* vein; (*fig*) vein, disposition; (*GEO*) seam, vein.

venablo [be'naßlo] *nm* javelin.

venado [be'naðo] *nm* deer; (*CULIN*) venison.

venal [be'nal] *adj* (*ANAT*) venous; (*pey*) venal.

venalidad [benali'ðað] *nf* venality.

vencedor, a [benθe'ðor, a] *adj* victorious ♦ *nm/f* victor, winner.

vencer [ben'θer] *vt* (*dominar*) to defeat, beat; (*derrotar*) to vanquish; (*superar, controlar*) to overcome, master ♦ *vi* (*triunfar*) to win (through), triumph; (*pago*) to fall due; (*plazo*) to expire; **dejarse** ~ to yield, give in.

vencido, a [ben'θiðo, a] *adj* (*derrotado*) defeated, beaten; (*COM*) payable, due ♦ *adv*: **pagar** ~ to pay in arrears; **le pagan por meses** ~s he is paid at the end of the month; **darse por** ~ to give up.

vencimiento [benθi'mjento] *nm* collapse; (*COM: plazo*) expiration; **a su** ~ when it falls due.

venda ['benda] *nf* bandage.

vendaje [ben'daxe] *nm* bandage, dressing.

vendar [ben'dar] *vt* to bandage; ~ **los ojos** to blindfold.

vendaval [benda'ßal] *nm* (*viento*) gale; (*huracán*) hurricane.

vendedor, a [bende'ðor, a] *nm/f* seller; ~ **ambulante** hawker, pedlar (*BRIT*), peddler (*US*).

vender [ben'der] *vt* to sell; (*comerciar*) to market; (*traicionar*) to sell out, betray; ~**se** *vr* to be sold; ~ **al contado/al por mayor/al por menor/a plazos** to sell for cash/wholesale/retail/on credit; "**se vende**" "for sale"; "**véndese coche**" "car for sale"; ~ **al descubierto** to sell short.

vendimia [ben'dimja] *nf* grape harvest; **la** ~ **de 1973** the 1973 vintage.

vendimiar [bendi'mjar] *vi* to pick grapes.

vendré [ben'dre] *etc vb* V **venir**.

Venecia [be'neθja] *nf* Venice.

veneciano, a [bene'θjano, a] *adj, nm/f* Venetian.

veneno [be'neno] *nm* poison, venom.

venenoso, a [bene'noso, a] *adj* poisonous.

venerable [bene'raßle] *adj* venerable.

veneración [benera'θjon] *nf* veneration.

venerar [bene'rar] *vt* (*reconocer*) to venerate; (*adorar*) to worship.

venéreo, a [be'nereo, a] *adj* venereal.

venezolano, a [beneθo'lano, a] *adj, nm/f* Venezuelan.

Venezuela [bene'θwela] *nf* Venezuela.

venga ['benga] *etc vb* V **venir**.

vengador, a [benga'ðor, a] *adj* avenging ♦ *nm/f* avenger.

venganza [ben'ganθa] *nf* vengeance, revenge.

vengar [ben'gar] *vt* to avenge; ~**se** *vr* to take revenge.

vengativo, a [benga'tißo, a] *adj* (*persona*) vindictive.

vengue ['benge] *etc vb* V **vengar**.

venia ['benja] *nf* (*perdón*) pardon; (*permiso*) consent; **con su** ~ by your leave.

venial [be'njal] *adj* venial.

venida [be'niða] *nf* (*llegada*) arrival; (*regreso*) return; (*fig*) rashness.

venidero, a [beni'ðero, a] *adj* coming, future; **en lo** ~ in (the) future.

venir [be'nir] *vi* to come; (*llegar*) to arrive; (*ocurrir*) to happen; ~**se abajo** to collapse; ~ **a menos** (*persona*) to lose status; (*empresa*) to go downhill; ~ **bien** to be suitable, come just right; (*ropa, gusto*) to suit; ~ **mal** to be unsuitable *o* inconvenient, come awkwardly; **el año que viene** next year; ¡**ven acá!** come (over) here!; ¡**venga!** (*fam*) come on!

venta ['benta] *nf* (*COM*) sale; (*posada*) inn; ~ **a plazos** hire purchase; ~ **al contado/**

al por mayor/al por menor *o* **al detalle**
cash sale/wholesale/retail; ~ **a domicilio**
door-to-door selling; ~ **y arrendamiento**
al vendedor sale and lease back; ~ **de**
liquidación clearance sale; **estar de** *o* **en**
~ to be (up) for sale *o* on the market; ~**s**
brutas gross sales; ~**s a término**
forward sales.

ventaja [ben'taxa] *nf* advantage; **llevar la** ~
(*en carrera*) to be leading *o* ahead.

ventajoso, a [benta'xoso, a] *adj*
advantageous.

ventana [ben'tana] *nf* window; ~ **de**
guillotina/galería sash/bay window; ~ **de**
la nariz nostril.

ventanilla [venta'niʎa] *nf* (*de taquilla, tb*
INFORM) window.

ventearse [bente'arse] *vr* (*romperse*) to
crack; (*ANAT*) to break wind.

ventilación [bentila'θjon] *nf* ventilation;
(*corriente*) draught; (*fig*) airing.

ventilador [bentila'ðor] *nm* ventilator;
(*eléctrico*) fan.

ventilar [benti'lar] *vt* to ventilate; (*a secar*)
to put out to dry; (*fig*) to air, discuss.

ventisca [ben'tiska] *nf* blizzard.

ventisquero [bentis'kero] *nm* snowdrift.

ventolera [bento'lera] *nf* (*ráfaga*) gust of
wind; (*idea*) whim, wild idea; **le dio la** ~
de comprarlo he had a sudden notion to
buy it.

ventosear [bentose'ar] *vi* to break wind.

ventosidad [bentosi'ðað] *nf* flatulence.

ventoso, a [ben'toso, a] *adj* windy ♦ *nf*
(*ZOOL*) sucker; (*instrumento*) suction pad.

ventrículo [ben'trikulo] *nm* ventricle.

ventrílocuo, a [ben'trilokwo, a] *nm/f*
ventriloquist.

ventriloquia [bentri'lokja] *nf*
ventriloquism.

ventura [ben'tura] *nf* (*felicidad*) happiness;
(*buena suerte*) luck; (*destino*) fortune; **a la**
(**buena**) ~ at random.

venturoso, a [bentu'roso, a] *adj* happy;
(*afortunado*) lucky, fortunate.

venza ['benθa] *etc vb V* **vencer**.

ver [ber] *vt, vi* to see; (*mirar*) to look at,
watch; (*investigar*) to look into; (*entender*)
to see, understand; ~**se** *vr* (*encontrarse*)
to meet; (*dejarse* ~) to be seen; (*hallarse:*
en un apuro) to find o.s., be ♦ *nm* looks *pl*,
appearance; **a** ~ let's see; **a** ~ **si** ... I
wonder if ...; **por lo que veo** apparently;
dejarse ~ to become apparent; **no tener**
nada que ~ **con** to have nothing to do
with; **a mi modo de** ~ as I see it; **merece**
~**se** it's worth seeing; **no lo veo** I can't
see it; ¡**nos vemos!** see you (later)!;

¡**habráse visto!** did you ever! (*fam*);
¡**viera(n)** *o* **hubiera(n) visto qué casa!** (*AM*
fam) if only you'd seen the house!, what
a house!; **ya se ve que** ... it is obvious
that ...; **si te vi no me acuerdo** they *etc*
just don't want to know.

vera ['bera] *nf* edge, verge; (*de río*) bank; **a**
la ~ **de** near, next to.

veracidad [beraθi'ðað] *nf* truthfulness.

veraneante [berane'ante] *nm/f*
holidaymaker, (summer) vacationer
(*US*).

veranear [berane'ar] *vi* to spend the
summer.

veraneo [bera'neo] *nm*: **estar de** ~ to be
away on (one's summer) holiday; **lugar**
de ~ holiday resort.

veraniego, a [bera'njeɣo, a] *adj* summer
cpd.

verano [be'rano] *nm* summer.

veras ['beras] *nfpl* truth *sg*; **de** ~ really,
truly; **esto va de** ~ this is serious.

veraz [be'raθ] *adj* truthful.

verbal [ber'ßal] *adj* verbal; (*mensaje etc*)
oral.

verbena [ber'ßena] *nf* street party.

verbigracia [berßi'ɣraθja] *adv* for example.

verbo ['berßo] *nm* verb.

verborrea [berßo'rrea] *nf* verbosity, verbal
diarrhoea.

verboso, a [ber'ßoso, a] *adj* verbose.

verdad [ber'ðað] *nf* (*lo verídico*) truth;
(*fiabilidad*) reliability ♦ *adv* really; ¿~?,
¿**no es** ~? isn't it?, aren't you?, don't
you? *etc*; **de** ~ *adj* real, proper; **a decir** ~,
no quiero to tell (you) the truth, I don't
want to; **la pura** ~ the plain truth.

verdaderamente [berðaðera'mente] *adv*
really, indeed, truly.

verdadero, a [berða'ðero, a] *adj* (*veraz*)
true, truthful; (*fiable*) reliable; (*fig*) real.

verde ['berðe] *adj* green; (*fruta etc*) green,
unripe; (*chiste etc*) blue, smutty, dirty
♦ *nm* green; **viejo** ~ dirty old man; **poner**
~ **a algn** to give sb a dressing-down.

verdear [berðe'ar], **verdecer** [berðe'θer] *vi*
to turn green.

verdezca [ber'ðeθka] *etc vb V* **verdecer**.

verdor [ber'ðor] *nm* (*lo verde*) greenness;
(*BOT*) verdure; (*fig*) youthful vigour.

verdugo [ber'ðuɣo] *nm* executioner; (*BOT*)
shoot; (*cardenal*) weal.

verdulero, a [berðu'lero, a] *nm/f* green-
grocer.

verdura [ber'ðura] *nf* greenness; ~**s** *nfpl*
(*CULIN*) greens.

vereda [be'reða] *nf* path; (*AM*) pavement,
sidewalk (*US*); **meter a algn en** ~ to

bring sb into line.
veredicto [bere'ðikto] *nm* verdict.
vergel [ber'xel] *nm* lush garden.
vergonzoso, a [berɣon'θoso, a] *adj*
shameful; (*tímido*) timid, bashful.
vergüenza [ber'ɣwenθa] *nf* shame, sense
of shame; (*timidez*) bashfulness; (*pudor*)
modesty; **tener** ~ to be ashamed; **me da**
~ **decírselo** I feel too shy *o* it
embarrasses me to tell him; **¡qué ~!** (*de
situación*) what a disgrace!; (*a persona*)
shame on you!
vericueto [beri'kweto] *nm* rough track.
verídico, a [be'riðiko, a] *adj* true, truthful.
verificar [berifi'kar] *vt* to check; (*corroborar*) to verify (*tb INFORM*); (*testamento*) to
prove; (*llevar a cabo*) to carry out; ~**se** *vr*
to occur, happen; (*mitin etc*) to be held;
(*profecía etc*) to come *o* prove true.
verifique [beri'fike] *etc vb V* **verificar**.
verja ['berxa] *nf* iron gate; (*cerca*) railing(s)
(*pl*); (*rejado*) grating.
vermut [ber'mu], *pl* **vermuts** *nm*
vermouth ♦ *nf* (*esp AM*) matinée.
verosímil [bero'simil] *adj* likely, probable;
(*relato*) credible.
verosimilitud [berosimili'tuð] *nf* likeliness,
probability.
verruga [be'rruɣa] *nf* wart.
versado, a [ber'saðo, a] *adj*: ~ **en** versed
in.
Versalles [ber'saʎes] *nm* Versailles.
versar [ber'sar] *vi* to go round, turn; ~
sobre to deal with, be about.
versátil [ber'satil] *adj* versatile.
versículo [ber'sikulo] *nm* (*REL*) verse.
versión [ber'sjon] *nf* version; (*traducción*)
translation.
verso ['berso] *nm* (*gen*) verse; **un** ~ a line
of poetry; ~ **libre/suelto** free/blank
verse.
vértebra ['berteßra] *nf* vertebra.
vertebrado, a [berte'ßraðo, a] *adj, nm/f*
vertebrate.
vertebral [berte'ßral] *adj* vertebral;
columna ~ spine.
vertedero [berte'ðero] *nm* rubbish dump,
tip.
verter [ber'ter] *vt* (*vaciar*) to empty, pour
(out); (*tirar*) to dump ♦ *vi* to flow.
vertical [berti'kal] *adj* vertical; (*postura,
piano etc*) upright ♦ *nf* vertical.
vértice ['bertiθe] *nm* vertex, apex.
vertiente [ber'tjente] *nf* slope.
vertiginoso, a [bertixi'noso, a] *adj* giddy,
dizzy.
vértigo ['bertiɣo] *nm* vertigo; (*mareo*)
dizziness; (*actividad*) intense activity; **de**

~ (*fam: velocidad*) giddy; (: *ruido*)
tremendous; (: *talento*) fantastic.
vesícula [be'sikula] *nf* blister; ~ **biliar** gall
bladder.
vespa ® ['bespa] *nf* (motor) scooter.
vespertino, a [besper'tino, a] *adj* evening
cpd.
vespino ® [bes'pino] *nm o f* ≈ moped.
vestíbulo [bes'tißulo] *nm* hall; (*de teatro*)
foyer.
vestido [bes'tiðo] *nm* (*ropa*) clothes *pl*,
clothing; (*de mujer*) dress, frock.
vestigio [bes'tixjo] *nm* (*trazo*) trace; (*señal*)
sign; ~**s** *nmpl* remains.
vestimenta [besti'menta] *nf* clothing.
vestir [bes'tir] *vt* (*poner: ropa*) to put on;
(*llevar: ropa*) to wear; (*cubrir*) to clothe,
cover; (*pagar: la ropa*) to clothe, pay for
the clothing of; (*sastre*) to make clothes
for ♦ *vi* (*ponerse: ropa*) to dress; (*verse
bien*) to look good; ~**se** *vr* to get dressed,
dress o.s.; **traje de** ~ (*formal*) formal
suit; **estar vestido de** to be dressed *o*
clad in; (*como disfraz*) to be dressed as.
vestuario [bes'twarjo] *nm* clothes *pl*,
wardrobe; (*TEAT: para actores*) dressing
room; (: *para público*) cloakroom;
(*DEPORTE*) changing room.
Vesubio [be'sußjo] *nm* Vesuvius.
veta ['beta] *nf* (*vena*) vein, seam; (*raya*)
streak; (*de madera*) grain.
vetar [be'tar] *vt* to veto.
veterano, a [bete'rano, a] *adj, nm/f* veteran.
veterinario, a [beteri'narjo, a] *nm/f*
vet(erinary surgeon) ♦ *nf* veterinary
science.
veto ['beto] *nm* veto.
vetusto, a [be'tusto, a] *adj* ancient.
vez [beθ] *nf* time; (*turno*) turn; **a la** ~ **que** at
the same time as; **a su** ~ in its turn;
cada ~ **más/menos** more and more/less
and less; **una** ~ once; **dos veces** twice;
de una ~ in one go; **de una** ~ **para
siempre** once and for all; **en** ~ **de**
instead of; **a veces** sometimes; **otra** ~
again; **una y otra** ~ repeatedly; **pocas
veces** seldom; **de** ~ **en cuando** from
time to time; **7 veces 9** 7 times 9; **hacer
las veces de** to stand in for; **tal** ~
perhaps; **¿lo viste alguna** ~? did you
ever see it?; **¿cuántas veces?** how
often?; **érase una** ~ once upon a time
(there was).
v. g., v. gr. *abr* (= *verbigracia*) viz.
vía ['bia] *nf* (*calle*) road; (*ruta*) track, route;
(*FERRO*) line; (*fig*) way; (*ANAT*) passage,
tube ♦ *prep* via, by way of; **por** ~ **bucal**
orally; **por** ~ **judicial** by legal means; **por**

~ **oficial** through official channels; **por ~ de** by way of; **en ~s de** in the process of; **un país en ~s de desarrollo** a developing country; ~ **aérea** airway; **V~ Láctea** Milky Way; ~ **pública** public highway *o* thoroughfare; ~ **única** one-way street; **el tren está en la ~ 8** the train is (standing) at platform 8.

viable ['bjaßle] *adj* (*COM*) viable; (*plan etc*) feasible.

viaducto [bja'ðukto] *nm* viaduct.

viajante [bja'xante] *nm* commercial traveller, traveling salesman (*US*).

viajar [bja'xar] *vi* to travel, journey.

viaje ['bjaxe] *nm* journey; (*gira*) tour; (*NAUT*) voyage; (*COM: carga*) load; **los ~s** travel *sg*; **estar de ~** to be on a journey; ~ **de ida y vuelta** round trip; ~ **de novios** honeymoon.

viajero, a [bja'xero, a] *adj* travelling (*BRIT*), traveling (*US*); (*ZOOL*) migratory ♦ *nm/f* (*quien viaja*) traveller; (*pasajero*) passenger.

vial [bjal] *adj* road *cpd*, traffic *cpd*.

vianda ['bjanda] *nf* (*tb: ~s*) food.

viáticos ['bjatikos] *nmpl* (*COM*) travelling (*BRIT*) *o* traveling (*US*) expenses.

víbora ['bißora] *nf* viper.

vibración [bißra'θjon] *nf* vibration.

vibrador [bißra'ðor] *nm* vibrator.

vibrante [bi'ßrante] *adj* vibrant, vibrating.

vibrar [bi'ßrar] *vt* to vibrate ♦ *vi* to vibrate; (*pulsar*) to throb, beat, pulsate.

vicario [bi'karjo] *nm* curate.

vicecónsul [biθe'konsul] *nm* vice-consul.

vicegerente [biθexe'rente] *nm/f* assistant manager.

vicepresidente [biθepresi'ðente] *nm/f* vice president; (*de comité etc*) vice-chairman.

viceversa [biθe'ßersa] *adv* vice versa.

viciado, a [bi'θjaðo, a] *adj* (*corrompido*) corrupt; (*contaminado*) foul, contaminated.

viciar [bi'θjar] *vt* (*pervertir*) to pervert; (*adulterar*) to adulterate; (*falsificar*) to falsify; (*JUR*) to nullify; (*estropear*) to spoil; (*sentido*) to twist; ~**se** *vr* to become corrupted; (*aire, agua*) to be(come) polluted.

vicio ['biθjo] *nm* (*libertinaje*) vice; (*mala costumbre*) bad habit; (*mimo*) spoiling; (*alabeo*) warp, warping; **de** *o* **por ~** out of sheer habit.

vicioso, a [bi'θjoso, a] *adj* (*muy malo*) vicious; (*corrompido*) depraved; (*mimado*) spoiled ♦ *nm/f* depraved person; (*adicto*) addict.

vicisitud [biθisi'tuð] *nf* vicissitude.

víctima ['biktima] *nf* victim; (*de accidente etc*) casualty.

victimario [bikti'marjo] *nm* (*AM*) killer, murderer.

victoria [bik'torja] *nf* victory.

victorioso, a [bikto'rjoso, a] *adj* victorious.

vicuña [bi'kuɲa] *nf* vicuna.

vid [bið] *nf* vine.

vida ['biða] *nf* life; (*duración*) lifetime; (*modo de vivir*) way of life; ¡~!, ¡~ **mía!** (*saludo cariñoso*) my love!; **de por ~** for life; **de ~ airada** *o* **libre** loose-living; **en la/mi ~** never; **estar con ~** to be still alive; **ganarse la ~** to earn one's living; ¡**esto es ~!** this is the life!; **le va la ~ en esto** his life depends on it.

vidente [bi'ðente] *nm/f* (*adivino*) clairvoyant; (*no ciego*) sighted person.

vídeo ['biðeo] *nm* video; (*aparato*) video (recorder); **cinta de ~** videotape; **película de ~** videofilm; **grabar en ~** to record, (video)tape; ~ **compuesto/ inverso** (*INFORM*) composite/reverse video.

videocámara [biðeo'kamara] *nf* video camera; (*pequeña*) camcorder.

videocassette [biðeoka'set] *nm* video cassette.

videoclip [biðeo'klip] *nm* (music) video.

videoclub [biðeo'klub] *nm* video club; (*tienda*) video shop.

videodatos [biðeo'ðatos] *nmpl* (*COM*) viewdata.

videojuego [biðeo'xweɣo] *nm* video game.

videotex(o) [biðeo'teks(o)] *nm* Videotex ®.

vidriero, a [bi'ðrjero, a] *nm/f* glazier ♦ *nf* (*ventana*) stained-glass window; (*AM: de tienda*) shop window; (*puerta*) glass door.

vidrio ['biðrjo] *nm* glass; (*AM*) window; ~ **cilindrado/inastillable** plate/splinter-proof glass.

vidrioso, a [bi'ðrjoso, a] *adj* glassy; (*frágil*) fragile, brittle; (*resbaladizo*) slippery.

viejo, a ['bjexo, a] *adj* old ♦ *nm/f* old man/ woman; **mi ~/vieja** (*fam*) my old man/ woman; **hacerse** *o* **ponerse ~** to grow *o* get old.

Viena ['bjena] *nf* Vienna.

viene ['bjene] *etc vb V* **venir**.

vienés, esa [bje'nes, esa] *adj, nm/f* Viennese.

viento ['bjento] *nm* wind; (*olfato*) scent; **contra ~ y marea** at all costs; **ir ~ en popa** to go splendidly; (*negocio*) to prosper.

vientre ['bjentre] *nm* belly; (*matriz*) womb; **~s** *nmpl* bowels; **hacer de ~** to have a movement of the bowels.

vier. *abr* (= *viernes*) Fri.

viernes ['bjernes] *nm inv* Friday; **V~ Santo** Good Friday; *V tb* **Semana Santa**.

vierta ['bjerta] *etc vb V* **verter**.

Vietnam [bjet'nam] *nm*: **el ~** Vietnam.

vietnamita [bjetna'mita] *adj, nm/f* Vietnamese.

viga ['biɣa] *nf* beam, rafter; (*de metal*) girder.

vigencia [bi'xenθja] *nf* validity; (*de contrato etc*) term, life; **estar/entrar en ~** to be in/come into effect *o* force.

vigente [bi'xente] *adj* valid, in force; (*imperante*) prevailing.

vigésimo, a [bi'xesimo, a] *num* twentieth.

vigía [bi'xia] *nm* look-out ♦ *nf* (*atalaya*) watchtower; (*acción*) watching.

vigilancia [bixi'lanθja] *nf* vigilance.

vigilante [bixi'lante] *adj* vigilant ♦ *nm* caretaker; (*en cárcel*) warder; (*en almacén*) shopwalker (*BRIT*), floor-walker (*US*); **~ jurado** security guard (*licensed to carry a gun*); **~ nocturno** night watchman.

vigilar [bixi'lar] *vt* to watch over; (*cuidar*) to look after, keep an eye on ♦ *vi* to be vigilant; (*hacer guardia*) to keep watch.

vigilia [vi'xilja] *nf* wakefulness; (*REL*) fast; **comer de ~** to fast.

vigor [bi'ɣor] *nm* vigour, vitality; **en ~** in force; **entrar/poner en ~** to take/put into effect.

vigoroso, a [biɣo'roso, a] *adj* vigorous.

VIH *nm abr* (= *virus de inmunodeficiencia humana*) HIV.

vil [bil] *adj* vile, low.

vileza [bi'leθa] *nf* vileness; (*acto*) base deed.

vilipendiar [bilipen'djar] *vt* to vilify, revile.

villa ['biʎa] *nf* (*pueblo*) small town; (*municipalidad*) municipality; **la V~** (*ESP*) Madrid; **~ miseria** shanty town.

villancico [biʎan'θiko] *nm* (Christmas) carol.

villorrio [bi'ʎorrjo] *nm* one-horse town, dump; (*AM*: *barrio pobre*) shanty town.

vilo ['bilo]: **en ~** *adv* in the air, suspended; (*fig*) on tenterhooks, in suspense; **estar** *o* **quedar en ~** to be left in suspense.

vinagre [bi'naɣre] *nm* vinegar.

vinagrera [bina'ɣrera] *nf* vinegar bottle; **~s** *nfpl* cruet stand *sg*.

vinagreta [bina'ɣreta] *nf* French dressing.

vinatería [binate'ria] *nf* wine shop.

vinatero, a [bina'tero, a] *adj* wine *cpd* ♦ *nm* wine merchant.

vinculación [binkula'θjon] *nf* (*lazo*) link, bond; (*acción*) linking.

vincular [binku'lar] *vt* to link, bind.

vínculo ['binkulo] *nm* link, bond.

vindicar [bindi'kar] *vt* to vindicate; (*vengar*) to avenge; (*JUR*) to claim.

vinícola [bi'nikola] *adj* (*industria*) wine *cpd*; (*región*) wine-growing *cpd*.

vinicultura [binikul'tura] *nf* wine growing.

vino ['bino] *etc vb V* **venir** ♦ *nm* wine; **~ de solera/seco/tinto** vintage/dry/red wine; **~ de Jerez** sherry; **~ de Oporto** port (wine).

viña ['bina] *nf*, **viñedo** [bi'neðo] *nm* vineyard.

viñeta [bi'neta] *nf* (*en historieta*) cartoon.

viola ['bjola] *nf* viola.

violación [bjola'θjon] *nf* violation; (*JUR*) offence, infringement; (*estupro*): **~ (sexual)** rape; **~ de contrato** (*COM*) breach of contract.

violar [bjo'lar] *vt* to violate; (*JUR*) to infringe; (*cometer estupro*) to rape.

violencia [bjo'lenθja] *nf* (*fuerza*) violence, force; (*embarazo*) embarrassment; (*acto injusto*) unjust act.

violentar [bjolen'tar] *vt* to force; (*casa*) to break into; (*agredir*) to assault; (*violar*) to violate.

violento, a [bjo'lento, a] *adj* violent; (*furioso*) furious; (*situación*) embarrassing; (*acto*) forced, unnatural; (*difícil*) awkward; **me es muy ~** it goes against the grain with me.

violeta [bjo'leta] *nf* violet.

violín [bjo'lin] *nm* violin.

violón [bjo'lon] *nm* double bass.

violoncelo [bjolon'θelo] *nm* cello.

virador [bira'ðor] *nm* (*para fotocopiadora*) toner.

viraje [bi'raxe] *nm* turn; (*de vehículo*) swerve; (*de carretera*) bend; (*fig*) change of direction.

virar [bi'rar] *vi* to turn; to swerve; to change direction.

virgen ['birxen] *adj* virgin; (*cinta*) blank ♦ *nm/f* virgin; **la Santísima V~** (*REL*) the Blessed Virgin.

virginidad [birxini'ðað] *nf* virginity.

Virgo ['birɣo] *nm* Virgo.

viril [bi'ril] *adj* virile.

virilidad [birili'ðað] *nf* virility.

virrey [bi'rrei] *nm* viceroy.

virtual [bir'twal] *adj* (*real*) virtual; (*en potencia*) potential.

virtud [bir'tuð] *nf* virtue; **en ~ de** by virtue of.

virtuoso, a [bir'twoso, a] *adj* virtuous

voluminoso, a [bolumi'noso, a] *adj* voluminous; (*enorme*) massive.

voluntad [bolun'tað] *nf* will, willpower; (*deseo*) desire, wish; (*afecto*) fondness; **a ~ at will**; (*cantidad*) as much as one likes; **buena ~** goodwill; **mala ~** ill will, malice; **por causas ajenas a mi ~** for reasons beyond my control.

voluntario, a [bolun'tarjo, a] *adj* voluntary ♦ *nm/f* volunteer.

voluntarioso, a [bolunta'rjoso, a] *adj* headstrong.

voluptuoso, a [bolup'twoso, a] *adj* voluptuous.

volver [bol'ßer] *vt* to turn; (*boca abajo*) to turn (over); (*voltear*) to turn round, turn upside down; (*poner al revés*) to turn inside out; (*devolver*) to return; (*transformar*) to change, transform; (*manga*) to roll up ♦ *vi* to return, go/come back; **~se** *vr* to turn round; (*llegar a ser*) to become; **~ la espalda** to turn one's back; **~ bien por mal** to return good for evil; **~ a hacer** to do again; **~ en sí** to come to o round, regain consciousness; **~ la vista atrás** to look back; **~ loco a algn** to drive sb mad; **~se loco** to go mad.

vomitar [bomi'tar] *vt, vi* to vomit.

vómito ['bomito] *nm* (*acto*) vomiting; (*resultado*) vomit.

voracidad [boraθi'ðað] *nf* voracity.

vorágine [bo'raxine] *nf* whirlpool; (*fig*) maelstrom.

voraz [bo'raθ] *adj* voracious; (*fig*) fierce.

vórtice ['bortiθe] *nm* whirlpool; (*de aire*) whirlwind.

vos [bos] *pron* (*AM*) you.

voseo [bo'seo] *nm* (*AM*) addressing a person as "vos", *familiar usage*.

Vosgos ['bosɣos] *nmpl* Vosges.

vosotros, as [bo'sotros, as] *pron* you *pl*; (*reflexivo*) yourselves; **entre ~** among yourselves.

votación [bota'θjon] *nf* (*acto*) voting; (*voto*) vote; **~ a mano alzada** show of hands; **someter algo a ~** to put sth to the vote.

votar [bo'tar] *vt* (*POL: partido etc*) to vote for; (*proyecto: aprobar*) to pass; (*REL*) to vow ♦ *vi* to vote.

voto ['boto] *nm* vote; (*promesa*) vow; (*maldición*) oath, curse; **~s** *nmpl* (good) wishes; **~ de bloque/de grupo** block/card vote; **~ de censura/de (des)confianza/de gracias** vote of censure/(no) confidence/thanks; **dar su ~** to cast one's vote.

voy [boi] *vb* V **ir**.

voz [boθ] *nf* voice; (*grito*) shout; (*chisme*) rumour; (*LING: palabra*) word; (: *forma*) voice; **dar voces** to shout, yell; **llamar a algn a voces** to shout to sb; **llevar la ~ cantante** (*fig*) to be the boss; **tener la ~ tomada** to be hoarse; **tener ~ y voto** to have the right to speak; **a media ~** in a low voice; **a ~ en cuello** *o* **en grito** at the top of one's voice; **de viva ~** verbally; **en ~ alta** aloud; **~ de mando** command.

vozarrón [boθa'rron] *nm* booming voice.

vra., vro. *abr* = **vuestra, vuestro**.

Vto. *abr* (*COM*) = **vencimiento**.

vudú [bu'ðu] *nm* voodoo.

vuelco ['bwelko] *etc vb* V **volcar** ♦ *nm* spill, overturning; (*fig*) collapse; **mi corazón dio un ~** my heart missed a beat.

vuelo ['bwelo] *etc vb* V **volar** ♦ *nm* flight; (*encaje*) lace, frill; (*de falda etc*) loose part; (*fig*) importance; **de altos ~s** (*fig: plan*) grandiose; (: *persona*) ambitious; **alzar el ~** to take flight; (*fig*) to dash off; **coger al ~** to catch in flight; **~ en picado** dive; **~ libre** hang-gliding; **~ regular** scheduled flight; **falda de mucho ~** full *o* wide skirt.

vuelque ['bwelke] *etc vb* V **volcar**.

vuelta ['bwelta] *nf* turn; (*curva*) bend, curve; (*regreso*) return; (*revolución*) revolution; (*paseo*) stroll; (*circuito*) lap; (*de papel, tela*) reverse; (*de pantalón*) turn-up (*BRIT*), cuff (*US*); (*dinero*) change; **~ a empezar** back to square one; **~ al mundo** world trip; **V~ de Francia** Tour de France; **~ cerrada** hairpin bend; **a la ~** (*ESP*) on one's return; **a la ~ de la esquina, a la ~** (*AM*) round the corner; **a ~ de correo** by return of post; **dar ~s** to turn, revolve; **dar ~s a una idea** to turn over an idea (in one's mind); **dar una ~** to go for a walk; **dar media ~** (*AUTO*) to do a U-turn; (*fam*) to beat it; **estar de ~** (*fam*) to be back; **poner a algn de ~ y media** to heap abuse on sb; **no tiene ~ de hoja** there's no alternative.

vueltita [bwel'tita] *nf* (*esp AM fam*) (little) walk; (: *en coche*) (little) drive.

vuelto ['bwelto] *pp de* **volver** ♦ *nm* (*AM: moneda*) change.

vuelva ['bwelßa] *etc vb* V **volver**.

vuestro, a ['bwestro, a] *adj* your; (*después de n*) of yours ♦ *pron*: **el ~/la vuestra/los ~s/las vuestras** yours; **lo ~** (what is) yours; **un amigo ~** a friend of yours; **una idea vuestra** an idea of yours.

vulgar [bul'ɣar] *adj* (*ordinario*) vulgar; (*común*) common.

vulgarice [bulɣa'riθe] *etc vb* V **vulgarizar**.

vulgaridad [bulɣari'ðað] *nf* commonness; (*acto*) vulgarity; (*expresión*) coarse expression; **~es** *nfpl* banalities.
vulgarismo [bulɣa'rismo] *nm* popular form of a word.
vulgarizar [bulɣari'θar] *vt* to popularize.
vulgo ['bulɣo] *nm* common people.
vulnerable [bulne'raßle] *adj* vulnerable.
vulnerar [bulne'rar] *vt* to harm, damage; (*derechos*) to interfere with; (*JUR, COM*) to violate.
vulva ['bulßa] *nf* vulva.

Y y

Y, y [i'ɣrjeɣa] *nf* (*letra*) Y, y; **Y de Yegua** Y for Yellow (*BRIT*) *o* Yoke (*US*).
y [i] *conj* and; (*AM fam: pues*) well; ¿**~ eso?** why?, how so?; ¡**~ los demás?** what about the others?; **~ bueno, ...** (*AM*) well ...
ya [ja] *adv* (*gen*) already; (*ahora*) now; (*en seguida*) at once; (*pronto*) soon ♦ *excl* all right!; (*por supuesto*) of course! ♦ *conj* (*ahora que*) now that; **~ no** not any more, no longer; **~ lo sé** I know; **~ dice que sí, ~ dice que no** first he says yes, then he says no; ¡**~, ~!** yes, yes!; (*con impaciencia*) all right!, O.K.!; ¡**~ voy!** (*enfático: no se suele traducir*) coming!; **~ que** since.
yacer [ja'θer] *vi* to lie.
yacimiento [jaθi'mjento] *nm* bed, deposit; **~ petrolífero** oilfield.
Yakarta [ja'karta] *nf* Jakarta.
yanqui ['janki] *adj* Yankee ♦ *nm/f* Yank, Yankee.
yate ['jate] *nm* yacht.
yazca ['jaθka] *etc vb* V **yacer**.
yedra ['jeðra] *nf* ivy.
yegua ['jeɣwa] *nf* mare.
yema ['jema] *nf* (*del huevo*) yoke; (*BOT*) leaf bud; (*fig*) best part; **~ del dedo** fingertip.
Yemen ['jemen] *nm*: **el ~ del Norte** Yemen; **el ~ del Sur** Southern Yemen.
yemení [jeme'ni] *adj, nm/f* Yemeni.
yendo ['jendo] *vb* V **ir**.
yerba ['jerßa] *nf* = **hierba**.
yerbatero, a [jerßa'tero, a] *adj* (*AM*) maté ♦ *nm/f* (*AM*) herbal healer.
yerga ['jerɣa] *etc*, **yergue** ['jerɣe] *etc vb* V **erguir**.
yermo, a ['jermo, a] *adj* barren; (*de gente*) uninhabited ♦ *nm* waste land.
yerno ['jerno] *nm* son-in-law.
yerre ['jerre] *etc vb* V **errar**.
yerto, a ['jerto, a] *adj* stiff.
yesca ['jeska] *nf* tinder.
yeso ['jeso] *nm* (*GEO*) gypsum; (*ARQ*) plaster.
yo ['jo] *pron personal* I; **soy ~** it's me, it is I; **~ que tú/usted** if I were you.

W w

W, w ['uße'doßle, (*AM*) 'doßleße] *nf* (*letra*) W, w; **W de Washington** W for William.
walkie-talkie [walki'talki] *nm* walkie-talkie.
walkman ® ['wal(k)man] *nm* Walkman ®.
wáter ['bater] *nm* lavatory.
waterpolo [water'polo] *nm* waterpolo.
wátman ['watman] *adj inv* (*fam*) cool.
whisky ['wiski] *nm* whisky.
Winchester ['wintʃester] *nm* (*INFORM*): **disco ~** Winchester disk.
windsurf ['winsurf] *nm* windsurfing.

X x

X, x ['ekis] *nf* (*letra*) X, x; **X de Xiquena** X for Xmas.
xenofobia [seno'foßja] *nf* xenophobia.
xenófobo, a [se'nofoßo, a] *adj* xenophobic ♦ *nm/f* xenophobe.
xerografía [seroɣra'fia] *nf* xerography.
xilófono [si'lofono] *nm* xylophone.
Xunta ['shunta] *nf* (*tb* **~ de Galicia**) *regional government of Galicia*.

yodo ['joðo] *nm* iodine.
yoga ['joɣa] *nm* yoga.
yogur(t) [jo'ɣur(t)] *nm* yogurt.
yogurtera [joɣur'tera] *nf* yogurt maker.
yuca ['juka] *nf* yucca.
yudo ['juðo] *nm* judo.
yugo ['juɣo] *nm* yoke.
Yugoslavia [juɣos'laβja] *nf* Yugoslavia.
yugoslavo, a [juɣos'laβo, a] *adj*
Yugoslavian ♦ *nm/f* Yugoslav.
yugular [juɣu'lar] *adj* jugular.
yunque ['junke] *nm* anvil.
yunta ['junta] *nf* yoke.
yuntero [jun'tero] *nm* ploughman.
yute ['jute] *nm* jute.
yuxtapondré [jukstapond're] *etc vb* V
yuxtaponer.
yuxtaponer [jukstapo'ner] *vt* to juxtapose.
yuxtaponga [juksta'ponga] *etc vb* V
yuxtaponer.
yuxtaposición [jukstaposi'θjon] *nf*
juxtaposition.
yuxtapuesto [juksta'pwesto], **yuxtapuse**
[juksta'puse] *etc vb* V **yuxtaponer**.

Z z

Z, z ['θeta, (*esp AM*) 'seta] *nf* (*letra*) Z, z; **Z de**
Zaragoza Z for Zebra.
zafar [θa'far] *vt* (*soltar*) to untie; (*superficie*)
to clear; ~**se** *vr* (*escaparse*) to escape;
(*ocultarse*) to hide o.s. away; (*TEC*) to slip
off; ~**se de** (*persona*) to get away from.
zafio, a ['θafjo, a] *adj* coarse.
zafiro [θa'firo] *nm* sapphire.
zaga ['θaɣa] *nf* rear; **a la** ~ behind, in the
rear.
zagal [θa'ɣal] *nm* boy, lad.
zagala [θa'ɣala] *nf* girl, lass.
zaguán [θa'ɣwan] *nm* hallway.
zaherir [θae'rir] *vt* (*criticar*) to criticize; (*fig:*
herir) to wound.
zahiera *etc*, **zahiriendo** [θa'jera,
θai'rjendo] *etc vb* V **zaherir**.
zahorí [θao'ri] *nm* clairvoyant.
zaino, a ['θaino, a] *adj* (*color de caballo*)
chestnut; (*pérfido*) treacherous; (*animal*)
vicious.
zalamería [θalame'ria] *nf* flattery.
zalamero, a [θala'mero, a] *adj* flattering;
(*relamido*) suave.

zamarra [θa'marra] *nf* (*piel*) sheepskin;
(*saco*) sheepskin jacket.
Zambeze [θam'beθe] *nm* Zambezi.
zambo, a ['θambo, a] *adj* knock-kneed
♦ *nm/f* (*AM*) half-breed (*of Negro and*
Indian parentage); (*mulato*) mulatto ♦ *nf*
samba.
zambullida [θambu'ʎiða] *nf* dive, plunge.
zambullirse [θambu'ʎirse] *vr* to dive;
(*ocultarse*) to hide o.s.
zamorano, a [θamo'rano, a] *adj* of *o* from
Zamora ♦ *nm/f* native *o* inhabitant of
Zamora.
zampar [θam'par] *vt* (*esconder*) to hide *o*
put away (hurriedly); (*comer*) to gobble;
(*arrojar*) to hurl ♦ *vi* to eat voraciously;
~**se** *vr* (*chocar*) to bump; (*fig*) to
gatecrash.
zanahoria [θana'orja] *nf* carrot.
zancada [θan'kaða] *nf* stride.
zancadilla [θanka'ðiʎa] *nf* trip; (*fig*)
stratagem; **echar la** ~ **a algn** to trip sb up.
zancajo [θan'kaxo] *nm* (*ANAT*) heel; (*fig*)
dwarf.
zanco ['θanko] *nm* stilt.
zancudo, a [θan'kuðo, a] *adj* long-legged
♦ *nm* (*AM*) mosquito.
zángano ['θangano] *nm* drone; (*holgazán*)
idler, slacker.
zanja ['θanxa] *nf* (*fosa*) ditch; (*tumba*)
grave.
zanjar [θan'xar] *vt* (*fosa*) to ditch, trench;
(*problema*) to surmount; (*conflicto*) to
resolve.
zapapico [θapa'piko] *nm* pick, pickaxe.
zapata [θa'pata] *nf* half-boot; (*MECÁNICA*)
shoe.
zapateado [θapate'aðo] *nm* (flamenco) tap
dance.
zapatear [θapate'ar] *vt* (*tocar*) to tap with
one's foot; (*patear*) to kick; (*fam*) to ill-
treat ♦ *vi* to tap with one's feet.
zapatería [θapate'ria] *nf* (*oficio*)
shoemaking; (*tienda*) shoe-shop; (*fábrica*)
shoe factory.
zapatero, a [θapa'tero, a] *nm/f* shoemaker;
~ **remendón** cobbler.
zapatilla [θapa'tiʎa] *nf* slipper; (*TEC*)
washer; (*para deporte*) training shoe.
zapato [θa'pato] *nm* shoe.
zapear [θape'ar] *vi* to flick through the
channels.
zapping ['θapin] *nm* channel-hopping;
hacer ~ to channel-hop.
zar [θar] *nm* tsar, czar.
zarabanda [θara'βanda] *nf* saraband; (*fig*)
whirl.
Zaragoza [θara'ɣoθa] *nf* Saragossa.

zaragozano, a [θaraɤo'θano, a] *adj* of o from Saragossa ♦ *nm/f* native o inhabitant of Saragossa.

zaranda [θa'randa] *nf* sieve.

zarandear [θarande'ar] *vt* to sieve; (*fam*) to shake vigorously.

zarpa ['θarpa] *nf* (*garra*) claw, paw; **echar la ~ a** to claw at; (*fam*) to grab.

zarpar [θar'par] *vi* to weigh anchor.

zarpazo [θar'paθo] *nm*: **dar un ~** to claw.

zarza ['θarθa] *nf* (*BOT*) bramble.

zarzal [θar'θal] *nm* (*matorral*) bramble patch.

zarzamora [θarθa'mora] *nf* blackberry.

zarzuela [θar'θwela] *nf* Spanish light opera; **la Z~** *home of the Spanish Royal Family*.

zigzag [θiɤ'θaɤ] *adj* zigzag.

zigzaguear [θiɤθaɤe'ar] *vi* to zigzag.

zinc [θink] *nm* zinc.

zíper ['siper] *nm* (*AM*) zip, zipper (*US*).

zócalo ['θokalo] *nm* (*ARQ*) plinth, base; (*de pared*) skirting board.

zoco ['θoko] *nm* (Arab) market, souk.

zodíaco [θo'ðiako] *nm* zodiac; **signo del ~** star sign.

zona ['θona] *nf* zone; **~ fronteriza** border area; **~ del dólar** (*COM*) dollar area; **~ de fomento** o **de desarrollo** development area.

zonzo, a ['sonso, a] *adj* (*AM*) silly.

zoología [θoolo'xia] *nf* zoology.

zoológico, a [θoo'loxiko, a] *adj* zoological ♦ *nm* (*tb*: **parque ~**) zoo.

zoólogo, a [θo'oloɤo, a] *nm/f* zoologist.

zoom [θum] *nm* zoom lens.

zopenco, a [θo'penko, a] (*fam*) *adj* dull,

stupid ♦ *nm/f* clot, nitwit.

zopilote [sopi'lote] *nm* (*AM*) buzzard.

zoquete [θo'kete] *nm* (*madera*) block; (*pan*) crust; (*fam*) blockhead.

zorro, a ['θorro, a] *adj* crafty ♦ *nm/f* fox/ vixen ♦ *nf* (*fam*) whore, tart, hooker (*US*).

zote ['θote] (*fam*) *adj* dim, stupid ♦ *nm/f* dimwit.

zozobra [θo'θoßra] *nf* (*fig*) anxiety.

zozobrar [θoθo'ßrar] *vi* (*hundirse*) to capsize; (*fig*) to fail.

zueco ['θweko] *nm* clog.

zulo ['θulo] *nm* (*de armas*) cache.

zumbar [θum'bar] *vt* (*burlar*) to tease; (*golpear*) to hit ♦ *vi* to buzz; (*fam*) to be very close; **~se** *vr*: **~se de** to tease; **me zumban los oídos** I have a buzzing o ringing in my ears.

zumbido [θum'biðo] *nm* buzzing; (*fam*) punch; **~ de oídos** buzzing o ringing in the ears.

zumo ['θumo] *nm* juice; (*ganancia*) profit; **~ de naranja** (fresh) orange juice.

zurcir [θur'θir] *vt* (*coser*) to darn; (*fig*) to put together; **¡que las zurzan!** to blazes with them!

zurdo, a ['θurðo, a] *adj* (*mano*) left; (*persona*) left-handed.

zurrar [θu'rrar] *vt* (*TEC*) to dress; (*fam*: *pegar duro*) to wallop; (: *aplastar*) to flatten; (: *criticar*) to criticize harshly.

zurriagazo [θurrja'ɤaθo] *nm* lash, stroke; (*desgracia*) stroke of bad luck.

zurrón [θu'rron] *nm* pouch.

zurza ['θurθa] *etc vb V* **zurcir**.

zutano, a [θu'tano, a] *nm/f* so-and-so.

English-Spanish
Inglés-Español

Aa

A, a [eɪ] n (letter) A, a; (SCOL: mark) ≈
sobresaliente; (MUS): **A** la m; **A for
Andrew,** (US) **A for Able** A de Antonio; **A
road** n (BRIT AUT) ≈ carretera nacional; **A
shares** npl (BRIT STOCK EXCHANGE)
acciones fpl de clase A.

═══════════════════ KEYWORD

a [ə] indef art (before vowel or silent h: **an**) **1**
un(a); ~ **book** un libro; **an apple** una
manzana; **she's** ~ **nurse** (ella) es
enfermera; **I haven't got** ~ **car** no tengo
coche
2 (instead of the number "one") un(a); ~
year ago hace un año; ~ **hundred/
thousand pounds** cien/mil libras
3 (in expressing ratios, prices etc): **3** ~
day/week 3 al día/a la semana; **10 km an
hour** 10 km por hora; **£5** ~ **person** £5 por
persona; **30p** ~ **kilo** 30p el kilo; **3 times** ~
month 3 veces al mes.

a. abbr = **acre**.
AA n abbr (BRIT: = Automobile Association)
≈ RACE m (SP); (= Alcoholics Anonymous;
(US: = Associate in/of Arts) título
universitario; (= anti-aircraft) A.A.
AAA n abbr (= American Automobile
Association) ≈ RACE m (SP); ['θriː'eɪz]
(BRIT: = Amateur Athletics Association)
asociación de atletismo amateur.
A & R n abbr (MUS) (= artists and repertoire)
nuevos artistas y canciones; ~ **man**
descubridor de jóvenes talentos.
AAUP n abbr (= American Association of
University Professors) asociación de
profesores universitarios.
AB abbr (BRIT) = **able-bodied seaman**;

(Canada) = Alberta.
aback [ə'bæk] adv: **to be taken** ~ quedar(se)
desconcertado.
abandon [ə'bændən] vt abandonar;
(renounce) renunciar a ♦ n abandono;
(wild behaviour): **with** ~ con desenfreno;
to ~ **ship** abandonar el barco.
abandoned [ə'bændənd] adj (child, house
etc) abandonado; (unrestrained: manner)
desinhibido.
abase [ə'beɪs] vt: **to** ~ **o.s. (so far as to do
...)** rebajarse (hasta el punto de hacer ...).
abashed [ə'bæʃt] adj avergonzado.
abate [ə'beɪt] vi moderarse; (lessen)
disminuir; (calm down) calmarse.
abatement [ə'beɪtmənt] n (of pollution,
noise) disminución f.
abattoir ['æbətwɑː*] n (BRIT) matadero.
abbey ['æbɪ] n abadía.
abbot ['æbət] n abad m.
abbreviate [ə'briːvɪeɪt] vt abreviar.
abbreviation [əbriːvɪ'eɪʃən] n (short form)
abreviatura; (act) abreviación f.
ABC n abbr (= American Broadcasting
Company) cadena de televisión.
abdicate ['æbdɪkeɪt] vt, vi abdicar.
abdication [æbdɪ'keɪʃən] n abdicación f.
abdomen ['æbdəmən] n abdomen m.
abdominal [æb'dɔmɪnl] adj abdominal.
abduct [æb'dʌkt] vt raptar, secuestrar.
abductor [æb'dʌktə*] n raptor(a) m/f,
secuestrador(a) m/f.
abduction [æb'dʌkʃən] n rapto, secuestro.
Aberdonian [æbə'dəunɪən] adj de Aberdeen
♦ n nativo/a or habitante m/f de Aberdeen.
aberration [æbə'reɪʃən] n aberración f; **in a
moment of mental** ~ en un momento de
enajenación mental.

abet [ə'bɛt] *vt see* **aid**.
abeyance [ə'beɪəns] *n*: **in** ~ (*law*) en desuso; (*matter*) en suspenso.
abhor [əb'hɔː*] *vt* aborrecer, abominar (de).
abhorrent [əb'hɔrənt] *adj* aborrecible, detestable.
abide [ə'baɪd] *vt*: **I can't** ~ **it/him** no lo/le puedo ver *or* aguantar; **to** ~ **by** *vt fus* atenerse a.
abiding [ə'baɪdɪŋ] *adj* (*memory etc*) perdurable.
ability [ə'bɪlɪtɪ] *n* habilidad *f*, capacidad *f*; (*talent*) talento; **to the best of my** ~ lo mejor que pueda *etc*.
abject ['æbdʒɛkt] *adj* (*poverty*) sórdido; (*apology*) rastrero; (*coward*) vil.
ablaze [ə'bleɪz] *adj* en llamas, ardiendo.
able ['eɪbl] *adj* capaz; (*skilled*) hábil; **to be** ~ **to do sth** poder hacer algo.
able-bodied ['eɪbl'bɔdɪd] *adj* sano; ~ **seaman** marinero de primera.
ably ['eɪblɪ] *adv* hábilmente.
ABM *n abbr* = **anti-ballistic missile**.
abnormal [æb'nɔːməl] *adj* anormal.
abnormality [æbnɔː'mælɪtɪ] *n* (*condition*) anormalidad *f*; (*instance*) anomalía.
aboard [ə'bɔːd] *adv* a bordo ♦ *prep* a bordo de; ~ **the train** en el tren.
abode [ə'bəud] *n* (*old*) morada; (*LAW*) domicilio; **of no fixed** ~ sin domicilio fijo.
abolish [ə'bɔlɪʃ] *vt* suprimir, abolir.
abolition [æbəu'lɪʃən] *n* supresión *f*, abolición *f*.
abominable [ə'bɔmɪnəbl] *adj* abominable.
aborigine [æbə'rɪdʒɪnɪ] *n* aborigen *m/f*.
abort [ə'bɔːt] *vt* abortar; (*COMPUT*) interrumpir ♦ *vi* (*COMPUT*) interrumpir el programa.
abortion [ə'bɔːʃən] *n* aborto (provocado); **to have an** ~ abortar.
abortionist [ə'bɔːʃənɪst] *n* persona que practica abortos.
abortive [ə'bɔːtɪv] *adj* fracasado.
abound [ə'baund] *vi*: **to** ~ (**in** *or* **with**) abundar (de *or* en).

===== KEYWORD

about [ə'baut] *adv* **1** (*approximately*) más o menos, aproximadamente; ~ **a hundred/ thousand** *etc* unos(unas) *or* como cien/ mil *etc*; **it takes** ~ **10 hours** se tarda unas *or* más o menos 10 horas; **at** ~ **2 o'clock** sobre las dos; **I've just** ~ **finished** casi he terminado
2 (*referring to place*) por todas partes; **to leave things lying** ~ dejar las cosas (tiradas) por ahí; **to run** ~ correr por todas partes; **to walk** ~ pasearse, ir y venir; **is Paul** ~? ¿está por aquí Paul?; **it's the other way** ~ es al revés
3: **to be** ~ **to do sth** estar a punto de hacer algo; **I'm not** ~ **to do all that for nothing** no pienso hacer todo eso para nada
♦ *prep* **1** (*relating to*) de, sobre, acerca de; **a book** ~ **London** un libro sobre *or* acerca de Londres; **what is it** ~? (*book, film*) ¿de qué se trata?; **we talked** ~ **it** hablamos de eso *or* ello; **what** *or* **how** ~ **doing this?** ¿qué tal si hacemos esto?
2 (*referring to place*) por; **to walk** ~ **the town** caminar por la ciudad.

about face, about turn *n* (*MIL*) media vuelta; (*fig*) cambio radical.
above [ə'bʌv] *adv* encima, por encima, arriba ♦ *prep* encima de; **mentioned** ~ susodicho; ~ **all** sobre todo; **he's not** ~ **a bit of blackmail** es capaz hasta de hacer chantaje.
above board *adj* legítimo.
above-mentioned [əbʌv'mɛnʃnd] *adj* susodicho.
abrasion [ə'breɪʒən] *n* (*on skin*) abrasión *f*.
abrasive [ə'breɪzɪv] *adj* abrasivo.
abreast [ə'brɛst] *adv* uno al lado de otro; **to keep** ~ **of** mantenerse al corriente de.
abridge [ə'brɪdʒ] *vt* abreviar.
abroad [ə'brɔːd] *adv* (*to be*) en el extranjero; (*to go*) al extranjero; **there is a rumour** ~ **that** ... corre el rumor de que ...
abrupt [ə'brʌpt] *adj* (*sudden: departure*) repentino; (*manner*) brusco.
abruptly [ə'brʌptlɪ] *adv* (*leave*) repentinamente; (*speak*) bruscamente.
abscess ['æbsɪs] *n* absceso.
abscond [əb'skɔnd] *vi* fugarse.
absence ['æbsəns] *n* ausencia; **in the** ~ **of** (*person*) en ausencia de; (*thing*) a falta de.
absent ['æbsənt] *adj* ausente; ~ **without leave (AWOL)** ausente sin permiso.
absentee [æbsən'tiː] *n* ausente *m/f*.
absenteeism [æbsən'tiːɪzəm] *n* absentismo.
absent-minded [æbsənt'maɪndɪd] *adj* distraído.
absolute ['æbsəluːt] *adj* absoluto; ~ **monopoly** monopolio total.
absolutely [æbsə'luːtlɪ] *adv* totalmente; **oh yes,** ~! ¡claro *or* por supuesto que sí!
absolution [æbsə'luːʃən] *n* (*REL*) absolución *f*.
absolve [əb'zɔlv] *vt*: **to** ~ **sb (from)** absolver a alguien (de).
absorb [əb'zɔːb] *vt* absorber; **to be** ~**ed in a**

book estar enfrascado en un libro.
absorbent [əb'zɔːbənt] *adj* absorbente.
absorbent cotton *n* (*US*) algodón *m*
hidrófilo.
absorbing [əb'zɔːbɪŋ] *adj* absorbente; (*book*
etc) interesantísimo.
absorption [əb'zɔːpʃən] *n* absorción *f*.
abstain [əb'steɪn] *vi*: **to** ~ **(from)** abstenerse
(de).
abstemious [əb'stiːmɪəs] *adj* abstemio.
abstention [əb'stenʃən] *n* abstención *f*.
abstinence ['æbstɪnəns] *n* abstinencia.
abstract ['æbstrækt] *adj* abstracto.
abstruse [æb'struːs] *adj* abstruso, oscuro.
absurd [əb'sɔːd] *adj* absurdo.
absurdity [əb'sɔːdɪtɪ] *n* absurdo.
ABTA ['æbtə] *n abbr* = Association of British
Travel Agents.
abundance [ə'bʌndəns] *n* abundancia.
abundant [ə'bʌndənt] *adj* abundante.
abuse [ə'bjuːs] *n* (*insults*) insultos *mpl*,
improperios *mpl*; (*misuse*) abuso ♦ *vt*
[ə'bjuːz] (*ill-treat*) maltratar; (*take*
advantage of) abusar de; **open to** ~ sujeto
al abuso.
abusive [ə'bjuːsɪv] *adj* ofensivo.
abysmal [ə'bɪzməl] *adj* pésimo; (*ignorance*)
supino.
abyss [ə'bɪs] *n* abismo.
AC *abbr* (= *alternating current*) corriente *f*
alterna ♦ *n abbr* (*US*) = *athletic club*.
a/c *abbr* (*BANKING etc*) = *account, account*
current.
academic [ækə'dɛmɪk] *adj* académico,
universitario; (*pej: issue*) puramente
teórico ♦ *n* estudioso/a; (*lecturer*)
profesor(a) *m/f* universitario/a; ~ **year**
(*UNIV*) año académico.
academy [ə'kædəmɪ] *n* (*learned body*)
academia; (*school*) instituto, colegio; ~ **of**
music conservatorio.
ACAS ['eɪkæs] *n abbr* (*BRIT*: = *Advisory,*
Conciliation and Arbitration Service) ≈
Instituto de Mediación, Arbitraje y
Conciliación.
accede [æk'siːd] *vi*: **to** ~ **to** acceder a.
accelerate [æk'sɛləreɪt] *vt* acelerar ♦ *vi*
acelerarse.
acceleration [æksɛlə'reɪʃən] *n* aceleración *f*.
accelerator [æk'sɛləreɪtə*] *n* (*BRIT*)
acelerador *m*.
accent ['æksɛnt] *n* acento.
accentuate [æk'sɛntjueɪt] *vt* (*syllable*)
acentuar; (*need, difference etc*) recalcar,
subrayar.
accept [ək'sɛpt] *vt* aceptar; (*approve*)
aprobar; (*concede*) admitir.
acceptable [ək'sɛptəbl] *adj* aceptable;

admisible.
acceptance [ək'sɛptəns] *n* aceptación *f*;
aprobación *f*; **to meet with general** ~
recibir la aprobación general.
access ['æksɛs] *n* acceso ♦ *vt* (*COMPUT*)
acceder a; **the burglars gained** ~ **through**
a window los ladrones lograron entrar
por una ventana; **to have** ~ **to** tener
acceso a.
accessible [æk'sɛsəbl] *adj* accesible.
accession [æk'sɛʃən] (*of monarch*) subida,
ascenso; (*addition*) adquisición *f*.
accessory [æk'sɛsərɪ] *n* accesorio; **toilet**
accessories artículos *mpl* de tocador.
access road *n* carretera de acceso; (*to*
motorway) carril *m* de acceso.
access time *n* (*COMPUT*) tiempo de acceso.
accident ['æksɪdənt] *n* accidente *m*;
(*chance*) casualidad *f*; **by** ~
(*unintentionally*) sin querer; (*by*
coincidence) por casualidad; ~**s at work**
accidentes *mpl* de trabajo; **to meet with**
or **to have an** ~ tener *or* sufrir un
accidente.
accidental [æksɪ'dɛntl] *adj* accidental,
fortuito.
accidentally [æksɪ'dɛntəlɪ] *adv* sin querer;
por casualidad.
accident insurance *n* seguro contra
accidentes.
accident-prone ['æksɪdənt'prəun] *adj*
propenso a los accidentes.
acclaim [ə'kleɪm] *vt* aclamar, aplaudir ♦ *n*
aclamación *f*, aplausos *mpl*.
acclamation [æklə'meɪʃən] *n* (*approval*)
aclamación *f*; (*applause*) aplausos *mpl*; **by**
~ por aclamación.
acclimatize [ə'klaɪmətaɪz], (*US*) **acclimate**
[ə'klaɪmət] *vt*: **to become** ~**d** aclimatarse.
accolade ['ækəuleɪd] *n* (*prize*) premio;
(*praise*) alabanzas *fpl*, homenaje *m*.
accommodate [ə'kɔmədeɪt] *vt* alojar,
hospedar; (*oblige, help*) complacer; **this**
car ~**s 4 people comfortably** en este
coche caben 4 personas cómodamente.
accommodating [ə'kɔmədeɪtɪŋ] *adj*
servicial, complaciente.
accommodation *n*, (*US*)
accommodations *npl* [əkɔmə'deɪʃən(z)]
alojamiento; "~ **to let**" "se alquilan
habitaciones"; **seating** ~ asientos *mpl*.
accompaniment [ə'kʌmpənɪmənt] *n*
acompañamiento.
accompanist [ə'kʌmpənɪst] *n* (*MUS*)
acompañante *m/f*.
accompany [ə'kʌmpənɪ] *vt* acompañar.
accomplice [ə'kʌmplɪs] *n* cómplice *m/f*.
accomplish [ə'kʌmplɪʃ] *vt* (*finish*) acabar;

(*aim*) realizar; (*task*) llevar a cabo.
accomplished [ə'kʌmplɪʃt] *adj* experto,
hábil.
accomplishment [ə'kʌmplɪʃmənt] *n*
(*ending*) conclusión *f*; (*bringing about*)
realización *f*; (*skill*) talento.
accord [ə'kɔːd] *n* acuerdo ♦ *vt* conceder; **of**
his own ~ espontáneamente; **with one** ~
de *or* por común acuerdo.
accordance [ə'kɔːdəns] *n*: **in** ~ **with** de
acuerdo con.
according [ə'kɔːdɪŋ]: ~ **to** *prep* según; (*in*
accordance with) conforme a; **it went** ~ **to**
plan salió según lo previsto.
accordingly [ə'kɔːdɪŋlɪ] *adv* (*thus*) por
consiguiente.
accordion [ə'kɔːdɪən] *n* acordeón *m*.
accordionist [ə'kɔːdɪənɪst] *n* acordeonista
m/f.
accost [ə'kɔst] *vt* abordar, dirigirse a.
account [ə'kaunt] *n* (*COMM*) cuenta,
factura; (*report*) informe *m*; ~**s** *npl*
(*COMM*) cuentas *fpl*; "~ **payee only**"
"únicamente en cuenta del beneficiario";
your ~ **is still outstanding** su cuenta está
todavía pendiente; **of little** ~ de poca
importancia; **on** ~ a crédito; **to buy sth**
on ~ comprar algo a crédito; **on no** ~
bajo ningún concepto; **on** ~ **of** a causa
de, por motivo de; **to take into** ~, **take** ~
of tener en cuenta; **to keep an** ~ **of** llevar
la cuenta de; **to bring sb to** ~ **for sth/for**
having done sth pedirle cuentas a algn
por algo/por haber hecho algo.
▸**account for** *vt fus* (*explain*) explicar; **all**
the children were ~**ed for** no faltaba
ningún niño.
accountability [əkauntə'bɪlɪtɪ] *n*
responsabilidad *f*.
accountable [ə'kauntəbl] *adj*: ~ **(for)**
responsable (de).
accountancy [ə'kauntənsɪ] *n* contabilidad *f*.
accountant [ə'kauntənt] *n* contable *m/f*,
contador(a) *m/f* (*LAM*).
accounting [ə'kauntɪŋ] *n* contabilidad *f*.
accounting period *n* período contable,
ejercicio financiero.
account number *n* (*at bank etc*) número de
cuenta.
account payable *n* cuenta por pagar.
account receivable *n* cuenta por cobrar.
accoutrements [ə'kuːtrəmənts] *npl* equipo,
pertrechos *mpl*.
accredited [ə'kredɪtɪd] *adj* (*agent etc*)
autorizado, acreditado.
accretion [ə'kriːʃən] *n* acumulación *f*.
accrue [ə'kruː] *vi* (*mount up*) aumentar,
incrementarse; (*interest*) acumularse; **to**

~ **to** corresponder a; ~**d charges** gastos
mpl vencidos; ~**d interest** interés *m*
acumulado.
accumulate [ə'kjuːmjuleɪt] *vt* acumular ♦ *vi*
acumularse.
accumulation [əkjuːmju'leɪʃən] *n*
acumulación *f*.
accuracy ['ækjurəsɪ] *n* exactitud *f*,
precisión *f*.
accurate ['ækjurɪt] *adj* (*number*) exacto;
(*answer*) acertado; (*shot*) certero.
accurately ['ækjurɪtlɪ] *adv* (*count, shoot,*
answer) con precisión.
accursed [ə'kɜːst] *adj* maldito.
accusation [ækjuˈzeɪʃən] *n* acusación *f*.
accusative [ə'kjuːzətɪv] *n* acusativo.
accuse [ə'kjuːz] *vt* acusar; (*blame*) echar la
culpa a.
accused [ə'kjuːzd] *n* acusado/a.
accuser [ə'kjuːzə*] *n* acusador(a) *m/f*.
accustom [ə'kʌstəm] *vt* acostumbrar; **to** ~
o.s. to sth acostumbrarse a algo.
accustomed [ə'kʌstəmd] *adj*: ~ **to**
acostumbrado a.
AC/DC *abbr* = *alternating current/direct*
current.
ACE [eɪs] *n abbr* = *American Council on*
Education.
ace [eɪs] *n* as *m*.
acerbic [ə'səːbɪk] *adj* acerbo; (*fig*) mordaz.
acetate ['æsɪteɪt] *n* acetato.
ache [eɪk] *n* dolor *m* ♦ *vi* doler; (*yearn*): **to** ~
to do sth ansiar hacer algo; **I've got**
stomach ~ *or* (*US*) **a stomach** ~ tengo
dolor de estómago, me duele el
estómago; **my head** ~**s** me duele la
cabeza.
achieve [ə'tʃiːv] *vt* (*reach*) alcanzar; (*realize*)
realizar; (*victory, success*) lograr,
conseguir.
achievement [ə'tʃiːvmənt] *n* (*completion*)
realización *f*; (*success*) éxito.
Achilles heel [ə'kɪliːz-] *n* talón *m* de
Aquiles.
acid ['æsɪd] *adj* ácido; (*bitter*) agrio ♦ *n*
ácido.
acidity [ə'sɪdɪtɪ] *n* acidez *f*; (*MED*) acedía.
acid rain *n* lluvia ácida.
acid test *n* (*fig*) prueba de fuego.
acknowledge [ək'nɔlɪdʒ] *vt* (*letter: also:* ~
receipt of) acusar recibo de; (*fact*)
reconocer.
acknowledgement [ək'nɔlɪdʒmənt] *n*
acuse *m* de recibo; reconocimiento; ~**s** (*in*
book) agradecimientos *mpl*.
ACLU *n abbr* (= *American Civil Liberties*
Union) unión americana por libertades
civiles.

acme ['ækmɪ] n súmmum m.
acne ['æknɪ] n acné m.
acorn ['eɪkɔːn] n bellota.
acoustic [ə'kuːstɪk] adj acústico.
acoustic coupler [-'kʌplə*] n (COMPUT) acoplador m acústico.
acoustics [ə'kuːstɪks] n, npl acústica sg.
acquaint [ə'kweɪnt] vt: **to ~ sb with sth** (inform) poner a algn al corriente de algo; **to be ~ed with** (person) conocer; (fact) estar al corriente de.
acquaintance [ə'kweɪntəns] n conocimiento; (person) conocido/a; **to make sb's ~** conocer a algn.
acquiesce [ækwɪ'ɛs] vi (agree): **to ~ (in)** consentir (en), conformarse (con).
acquire [ə'kwaɪə*] vt adquirir.
acquired [ə'kwaɪəd] adj adquirido; **it's an ~ taste** es algo a lo que uno se aficiona poco a poco.
acquisition [ækwɪ'zɪʃən] n adquisición f.
acquisitive [ə'kwɪzɪtɪv] adj codicioso.
acquit [ə'kwɪt] vt absolver, exculpar; **to ~ o.s. well** defenderse bien.
acquittal [ə'kwɪtl] n absolución f, exculpación f.
acre ['eɪkə*] n acre m.
acreage ['eɪkərɪdʒ] n extensión f.
acrid ['ækrɪd] adj (smell) acre; (fig) mordaz, sarcástico.
acrimonious [ækrɪ'məunɪəs] adj (remark) mordaz; (argument) reñido.
acrobat ['ækrəbæt] n acróbata m/f.
acrobatic [ækrə'bætɪk] adj acrobático.
acrobatics [ækrə'bætɪks] npl acrobacias fpl.
acronym ['ækrənɪm] n siglas fpl.
across [ə'krɔs] prep (on the other side of) al otro lado de; (crosswise) a través de ♦ adv de un lado a otro, de una parte a otra; a través, al través; **to run/swim ~** atravesar corriendo/nadando; **~ from** enfrente de; **the lake is 12 km ~** el lago tiene 12 km de ancho; **to get sth ~ to sb** (fig) hacer comprender algo a algn.
acrylic [ə'krɪlɪk] adj acrílico.
act [ækt] n acto, acción f; (THEAT) acto; (in music-hall etc) número; (LAW) decreto, ley f ♦ vi (behave) comportarse; (take action) tomar medidas ♦ vt (part) hacer, representar; **~ of God** fuerza mayor; **it's only an ~** es cuento; **to catch sb in the ~** coger a algn in fraganti or con las manos en la masa; **to ~ Hamlet** hacer el papel de Hamlet; **to ~ as** actuar or hacer de; **~ing in my capacity as chairman, I ...** en mi calidad de presidente, yo ...; **it ~s as a deterrent** sirve para disuadir; **he's only ~ing** está

fingiendo nada más.
▶**act on** vt: **to ~ on sth** actuar or obrar sobre algo.
▶**act out** vt (event) representar; (fantasies) realizar.
acting ['æktɪŋ] adj suplente ♦ n: **to do some ~** hacer algo de teatro; **he is the ~ manager** es el gerente en funciones.
action ['ækʃən] n acción f, acto; (MIL) acción f; (LAW) proceso, demanda; **to put a plan into ~** poner un plan en acción or en marcha; **killed in ~** (MIL) muerto en acto de servicio or en combate; **out of ~** (person) fuera de combate; (thing) averiado, descompuesto; **to take ~** tomar medidas; **to bring an ~ against sb** entablar or presentar demanda contra algn.
action replay n (TV) repetición f.
activate ['æktɪveɪt] vt activar.
active ['æktɪv] adj activo, enérgico; (volcano) en actividad; **to play an ~ part in** colaborar activamente en; **~ file** (COMPUT) fichero activo.
active duty (AD) n (US MIL) servicio activo.
actively ['æktɪvlɪ] adv (participate) activamente; (discourage, dislike) enérgicamente.
active partner n (COMM) socio activo.
activist ['æktɪvɪst] n activista m/f.
activity [æk'tɪvɪtɪ] n actividad f.
actor ['æktə*] n actor m.
actress ['æktrɪs] n actriz f.
ACTT n abbr (BRIT: = Association of Cinematographic, Television and Allied Technicians) sindicato de técnicos de cine y televisión.
actual ['æktjuəl] adj verdadero, real.
actually ['æktjuəlɪ] adv realmente, en realidad.
actuary ['æktjuərɪ] n (COMM) actuario/a (de seguros).
actuate ['æktjueɪt] vt mover, impulsar.
acumen ['ækjumən] n perspicacia; **business ~** talento para los negocios.
acupuncture ['ækjupʌŋktʃə*] n acupuntura.
acute [ə'kjuːt] adj agudo.
acutely [ə'kjuːtlɪ] adv profundamente, extremadamente.
AD adv abbr (= Anno Domini) A.C. ♦ n abbr (US MIL) see **active duty**.
ad [æd] n abbr = **advertisement**.
adage ['ædɪdʒ] n refrán m, adagio.
Adam ['ædəm] n Adán; **~'s apple** n nuez f (de la garganta).
adamant ['ædəmənt] adj firme, inflexible.

adapt [ə'dæpt] *vt* adaptar; (*reconcile*) acomodar ♦ *vi*: **to ~ (to)** adaptarse (a), ajustarse (a).

adaptability [ədæptə'bɪlɪtɪ] *n* (*of person, device etc*) adaptabilidad *f*.

adaptable [ə'dæptəbl] *adj* (*device*) adaptable; (*person*) acomodadizo, que se adapta.

adaptation [ædæp'teɪʃən] *n* adaptación *f*.

adapter, adaptor [ə'dæptə*] *n* (*ELEC*) adaptador *m*.

ADC *n abbr* (*MIL*) = *aide-de-camp*; (*US*: = *Aid to Dependent Children*) *ayuda para niños dependientes*.

add [æd] *vt* añadir, agregar (*esp LAM*); (*figures: also*: ~ **up**) sumar ♦ *vi*: **to ~ to** (*increase*) aumentar, acrecentar.

► **add on** *vt* añadir.

► **add up** *vt* (*figures*) sumar ♦ *vi* (*fig*): **it doesn't ~ up** no tiene sentido; **it doesn't ~ up to much** es poca cosa, no tiene gran *or* mucha importancia.

addendum [ə'dɛndəm] *n* ad(d)enda *m or f*.

adder ['ædə*] *n* víbora.

addict ['ædɪkt] *n* (*to drugs etc*) adicto/a; (*enthusiast*) aficionado/a, entusiasta *m/f*; **heroin ~** heroinómano/a.

addicted [ə'dɪktɪd] *adj*: **to be ~ to** ser adicto a; ser aficionado a.

addiction [ə'dɪkʃən] *n* (*dependence*) hábito morboso; (*enthusiasm*) afición *f*.

addictive [ə'dɪktɪv] *adj* que causa adicción.

adding machine ['ædɪŋ-] *n* calculadora.

Addis Ababa ['ædɪs'æbəbə] *n* Addis Abeba *m*.

addition [ə'dɪʃən] *n* (*adding up*) adición *f*; (*thing added*) añadidura, añadido; **in ~** además, por añadidura; **in ~ to** además de.

additional [ə'dɪʃənl] *adj* adicional.

additive ['ædɪtɪv] *n* aditivo.

addled ['ædld] *adj* (*BRIT*: *rotten*) podrido; (: *fig*) confuso.

address [ə'drɛs] *n* dirección *f*, señas *fpl*; (*speech*) discurso; (*COMPUT*) dirección *f* ♦ *vt* (*letter*) dirigir; (*speak to*) dirigirse a, dirigir la palabra a; **form of ~** tratamiento; **absolute/relative ~** (*COMPUT*) dirección *f* absoluta/relativa; **to ~ o.s. to sth** (*issue, problem*) abordar.

address book *n* agenda (de direcciones).

addressee [ædrɛ'siː] *n* destinatario/a.

Aden ['eɪdn] *n* Adén *m*.

adenoids ['ædɪnɔɪdz] *npl* vegetaciones *fpl* (adenoideas).

adept ['ædɛpt] *adj*: **~ at** experto *or* ducho en.

adequacy ['ædɪkwəsɪ] *n* idoneidad *f*.

adequate ['ædɪkwɪt] *adj* (*satisfactory*) adecuado; (*enough*) suficiente; **to feel ~ to a task** sentirse con fuerzas para una tarea.

adequately ['ædɪkwɪtlɪ] *adv* adecuadamente.

adhere [əd'hɪə*] *vi*: **to ~ to** adherirse a; (*fig*: *abide by*) observar.

adherent [əd'hɪərənt] *n* partidario/a.

adhesion [əd'hiːʒən] *n* adherencia.

adhesive [əd'hiːzɪv] *adj, n* adhesivo.

adhesive tape *n* (*BRIT*) cinta adhesiva; (*US*: *MED*) esparadrapo.

ad hoc [æd'hɔk] *adj* (*decision*) ad hoc; (*committee*) formado con fines específicos ♦ *adv* ad hoc.

adieu [ə'djuː] *excl* ¡vaya con Dios!

ad inf [æd'ɪnf] *adv* hasta el infinito.

adjacent [ə'dʒeɪsənt] *adj*: **~ to** contiguo a, inmediato a.

adjective ['ædʒɛktɪv] *n* adjetivo.

adjoin [ə'dʒɔɪn] *vt* estar contiguo a; (*land*) lindar con.

adjoining [ə'dʒɔɪnɪŋ] *adj* contiguo, vecino.

adjourn [ə'dʒɜːn] *vt* aplazar; (*session*) suspender, levantar; (*US*: *end*) terminar ♦ *vi* suspenderse; **the meeting has been ~ed till next week** se ha levantado la sesión hasta la semana que viene; **they ~ed to the pub** (*col*) se trasladaron al bar.

adjournment [ə'dʒɜːnmənt] *n* (*period*) suspensión *f*; (*postponement*) aplazamiento.

Adjt. *abbr* = **adjutant**.

adjudicate [ə'dʒuːdɪkeɪt] *vi* sentenciar; (*contest*) hacer de árbitro en, juzgar; (*claim*) decidir.

adjudication [ədʒuːdɪ'keɪʃən] *n* fallo.

adjudicator [ə'dʒuːdɪkeɪtə*] *n* juez *m*, árbitro.

adjust [ə'dʒʌst] *vt* (*change*) modificar; (*arrange*) arreglar; (*machine*) ajustar ♦ *vi*: **to ~ (to)** adaptarse (a).

adjustable [ə'dʒʌstəbl] *adj* ajustable.

adjuster [ə'dʒʌstə*] *n see* **loss adjuster**.

adjustment [ə'dʒʌstmənt] *n* modificación *f*; arreglo; (*of prices, wages*) ajuste *m*.

adjutant ['ædʒətənt] *n* ayudante *m*.

ad-lib [æd'lɪb] *vt, vi* improvisar ♦ *adv*: **ad lib** a voluntad, a discreción.

adman ['ædmæn] *n* (*col*) publicista *m*.

admin ['ædmɪn] *n abbr* (*col*) = **administration**.

administer [əd'mɪnɪstə*] *vt* proporcionar; (*justice*) administrar.

administration [ædmɪnɪ'streɪʃən] *n* administración *f*; (*government*) gobierno;

the **A**~ (*US*) la Administración.
administrative [əd'mɪnɪstrətɪv] *adj*
administrativo.
administrator [əd'mɪnɪstreɪtə*] *n*
administrador(a) *m/f.*
admirable ['ædmərəbl] *adj* admirable.
admiral ['ædmərəl] *n* almirante *m.*
Admiralty ['ædmərəltɪ] *n* (*BRIT*) Ministerio
de Marina, Almirantazgo.
admiration [ædmə'reɪʃən] *n* admiración *f.*
admire [əd'maɪə*] *vt* admirar.
admirer [əd'maɪərə*] *n* admirador(a) *m/f*;
(*suitor*) pretendiente *m.*
admiring [əd'maɪərɪŋ] *adj* (*expression*) de
admiración.
admissible [əd'mɪsəbl] *adj* admisible.
admission [əd'mɪʃən] *n* (*exhibition,
nightclub*) entrada; (*enrolment*) ingreso;
(*confession*) confesión *f*; "~ free"
"entrada gratis *or* libre"; **by his own** ~ él
mismo reconoce que.
admit [əd'mɪt] *vt* dejar entrar, dar entrada
a; (*permit*) admitir; (*acknowledge*)
reconocer; "**this ticket** ~**s two**" "entrada
para 2 personas"; **children not** ~**ted** se
prohíbe la entrada a (los) menores de
edad; **I must** ~ **that** ... debo reconocer
que ...
▶**admit of** *vt fus* admitir, permitir.
▶**admit to** *vt fus* confesarse culpable de.
admittance [əd'mɪtəns] *n* entrada; "**no** ~"
"se prohíbe la entrada", "prohibida la
entrada".
admittedly [əd'mɪtədlɪ] *adv* de acuerdo
que.
admonish [əd'mɔnɪʃ] *vt* amonestar; (*advise*)
aconsejar.
ad nauseam [æd'nɔːsɪæm] *adv* hasta la
saciedad.
ado [ə'duː] *n*: **without (any) more** ~ sin más
(ni más).
adolescence [ædəu'lɛsns] *n* adolescencia.
adolescent [ædəu'lɛsnt] *adj, n* adolescente
m/f.
adopt [ə'dɔpt] *vt* adoptar.
adopted [ə'dɔptɪd] *adj* adoptivo.
adoption [ə'dɔpʃən] *n* adopción *f.*
adoptive [ə'dɔptɪv] *adj* adoptivo.
adorable [ə'dɔːrəbl] *adj* adorable.
adoration [ædə'reɪʃən] *n* adoración *f.*
adore [ə'dɔː*] *vt* adorar.
adoring [ə'dɔːrɪŋ] *adj*: **to his** ~ **public** a un
público que le adora *or* le adoraba *etc.*
adorn [ə'dɔːn] *vt* adornar.
adornment [ə'dɔːnmənt] *n* adorno.
ADP *n abbr see* **automatic data processing**.
adrenalin [ə'drɛnəlɪn] *n* adrenalina.
Adriatic [eɪdrɪ'ætɪk] *n*: **the** ~ **(Sea)** el (Mar)

Adriático.
adrift [ə'drɪft] *adv* a la deriva; **to come** ~
(*boat*) ir a la deriva, soltarse; (*wire, rope
etc*) soltarse.
adroit [ə'drɔɪt] *adj* diestro, hábil.
ADT *abbr* (*US*: = *Atlantic Daylight Time*) *hora
de verano de Nueva York*.
adulation [ædju'leɪʃən] *n* adulación *f.*
adult ['ædʌlt] *n* adulto/a ♦ *adj*: ~ **education**
educación *f* para adultos.
adulterate [ə'dʌltəreɪt] *vt* adulterar.
adulterer [ə'dʌltərə*] *n* adúltero.
adulteress [ə'dʌltrɪs] *n* adúltera.
adultery [ə'dʌltərɪ] *n* adulterio.
adulthood ['ædʌlthud] *n* edad *f* adulta.
advance [əd'vɑːns] *n* adelanto, progreso;
(*money*) anticipo; (*MIL*) avance *m* ♦ *vt*
avanzar, adelantar; (*money*) anticipar ♦ *vi*
avanzar, adelantarse; **in** ~ por
adelantado; (*book*) con antelación; **to
make** ~**s to sb** (*gen*) ponerse en contacto
con algn; (*amorously*) insinuarse a algn.
advanced *adj* avanzado; (*SCOL: studies*)
adelantado; ~ **in years** entrado en años.
advancement [əd'vɑːnsmənt] *n* progreso;
(*in rank*) ascenso.
advance notice *n* previo aviso.
advance payment *n* (*part sum*) anticipo.
advantage [əd'vɑːntɪdʒ] *n* (*also TENNIS*)
ventaja; **to take** ~ **of** aprovecharse de;
it's to our ~ es ventajoso para nosotros.
advantageous [ædvən'teɪdʒəs] *adj*
ventajoso, provechoso.
advent ['ædvənt] *n* advenimiento; **A**~
Adviento.
adventure [əd'vɛntʃə*] *n* aventura.
adventure playground *n* parque *m*
infantil.
adventurous [əd'vɛntʃərəs] *adj* aventurero;
(*bold*) arriesgado.
adverb ['ædvɔːb] *n* adverbio.
adversary ['ædvəsərɪ] *n* adversario,
contrario.
adverse ['ædvɔːs] *adj* adverso, contrario; ~
to adverso a.
adversity [əd'vɔːsɪtɪ] *n* infortunio.
advert ['ædvɔːt] *n abbr* (*BRIT*) =
advertisement.
advertise ['ædvətaɪz] *vi* hacer propaganda;
(*in newspaper etc*) poner un anuncio,
anunciarse; **to** ~ **for** (*staff*) buscar por
medio de anuncios ♦ *vt* anunciar.
advertisement [əd'vɔːtɪsmənt] *n* (*COMM*)
anuncio.
advertiser ['ædvətaɪzə*] *n* anunciante *m/f.*
advertising ['ædvətaɪzɪŋ] *n* publicidad *f*,
propaganda; anuncios *mpl.*
advertising agency *n* agencia de

♦ *pron* **1** todo; **I ate it ~, I ate ~ of it** me lo comí todo; **~ of them** todos (ellos); **~ of us** went fuimos todos; **~ the boys went** fueron todos los chicos; **is that ~?** ¿eso es todo?, ¿algo más?; (*in shop*) ¿algo más?, ¿alguna cosa más?
2 (*in phrases*): **above ~** sobre todo; por encima de todo; **after ~** después de todo; **at ~: anything at ~** lo que sea; **not at ~** (*in answer to question*) en absoluto; (*in answer to thanks*) ¡de nada!, ¡no hay de qué!; **I'm not at ~ tired** no estoy nada cansado/a; **anything at ~ will do** cualquier cosa viene bien; **~ in** a fin de cuentas
♦ *adv*: **~ alone** completamente solo/a; **to be/feel ~ in** estar rendido; **it's not as hard as ~ that** no es tan difícil como lo pintas; **~ the more/the better** tanto más/mejor; **~ but** casi; **the score is 2 ~** están empatados a 2.

all-around [ˈɔːləˈraund] *adj* (*US*) = **all-round.**
allay [əˈleɪ] *vt* (*fears*) aquietar; (*pain*) aliviar.
all clear *n* (*after attack etc*) fin *m* de la alerta; (*fig*) luz *f* verde.
allegation [ælɪˈɡeɪʃən] *n* alegato.
allege [əˈlɛdʒ] *vt* pretender; **he is ~d to have said ...** se afirma que él dijo ....
alleged [əˈlɛdʒd] *adj* supuesto, presunto.
allegedly [əˈlɛdʒɪdlɪ] *adv* supuestamente, según se afirma.
allegiance [əˈliːdʒəns] *n* lealtad *f.*
allegory [ˈælɪɡərɪ] *n* alegoría.
all-embracing [ˈɔːləmˈbreɪsɪŋ] *adj* universal.
allergic [əˈlɜːdʒɪk] *adj*: **~ to** alérgico a.
allergy [ˈælədʒɪ] *n* alergia.
alleviate [əˈliːvɪeɪt] *vt* aliviar.
alleviation [əliːvɪˈeɪʃən] *n* alivio.
alley [ˈælɪ] *n* (*street*) callejuela; (*in garden*) paseo.
alleyway [ˈælɪweɪ] *n* callejón *m.*
alliance [əˈlaɪəns] *n* alianza.
allied [ˈælaɪd] *adj* aliado; (*related*) relacionado.
alligator [ˈælɪɡeɪtə*] *n* caimán *m.*
all-important [ˈɔːlɪmˈpɔːtənt] *adj* de suma importancia.
all-in [ˈɔːlɪn] *adj* (*BRIT*) (*also adv: charge*) todo incluido.
all-in wrestling *n* lucha libre.
alliteration [əlɪtəˈreɪʃən] *n* aliteración *f.*
all-night [ˈɔːlˈnaɪt] *adj* (*café*) abierto toda la noche; (*party*) que dura toda la noche.
allocate [ˈæləkeɪt] *vt* (*share out*) repartir; (*devote*) asignar.
allocation [æləˈkeɪʃən] *n* (*of money*) ración

f, cuota; (*distribution*) reparto.
allot [əˈlɔt] *vt* asignar; **in the ~ted time** en el tiempo asignado.
allotment [əˈlɔtmənt] *n* porción *f*; (*garden*) parcela.
all-out [ˈɔːlaut] *adj* (*effort etc*) supremo ♦ *adv*: **all out** con todas las fuerzas, a fondo.
allow [əˈlau] *vt* (*permit*) permitir, dejar; (*a claim*) admitir; (*sum to spend, time estimated*) dar, conceder; (*concede*): **to ~ that** reconocer que; **to ~ sb to do** permitir a alguien hacer; **smoking is not ~ed** prohibido *or* se prohíbe fumar; **he is ~ed to ...** se le permite ...; **we must ~ 3 days for the journey** debemos dejar 3 días para el viaje.
►**allow for** *vt fus* tener en cuenta.
allowance [əˈlauəns] *n* concesión *f*; (*payment*) subvención *f*, pensión *f*; (*discount*) descuento, rebaja; **to make ~s for** (*person*) disculpar a; (*thing: take into account*) tener en cuenta.
alloy [ˈælɔɪ] *n* aleación *f.*
all right *adv* (*feel, work*) bien; (*as answer*) ¡de acuerdo!, ¡está bien!
all-round [ˈɔːlˈraund] *adj* completo; (*view*) amplio.
all-rounder [ˈɔːlˈraundə*] *n*: **to be a good ~** ser una persona que hace de todo.
allspice [ˈɔːlspaɪs] *n* pimienta inglesa *or* de Jamaica.
all-time [ˈɔːlˈtaɪm] *adj* (*record*) de todos los tiempos.
allude [əˈluːd] *vi*: **to ~ to** aludir a.
alluring [əˈljuərɪŋ] *adj* seductor(a), atractivo.
allusion [əˈluːʒən] *n* referencia, alusión *f.*
ally *n* [ˈælaɪ] aliado/a ♦ *vt* [əˈlaɪ]: **to ~ o.s. with** aliarse con.
almanac [ˈɔːlmənæk] *n* almanaque *m.*
almighty [ɔːlˈmaɪtɪ] *adj* todopoderoso.
almond [ˈɑːmənd] *n* (*fruit*) almendra; (*tree*) almendro.
almost [ˈɔːlməust] *adv* casi; **he ~ fell** casi *or* por poco se cae.
alms [ɑːmz] *npl* limosna *sg.*
aloft [əˈlɔft] *adv* arriba.
alone [əˈləun] *adj* solo ♦ *adv* sólo, solamente; **to leave sb ~** dejar a algn en paz; **to leave sth ~** no tocar algo; **let ~ ...** y mucho menos, y no digamos ...
along [əˈlɔŋ] *prep* a lo largo de, por ♦ *adv*: **is he coming ~ with us?** ¿viene con nosotros?; **he was limping ~** iba cojeando; **~ with** junto con; **all ~** (*all the time*) desde el principio.
alongside [əˈlɔŋˈsaɪd] *prep* al lado de ♦ *adv* (*NAUT*) de costado; **we brought our boat**

~ atracamos nuestro barco.
aloof [ə'luːf] *adj* distante ♦ *adv*: **to stand** ~ mantenerse a distancia.
aloud [ə'laud] *adv* en voz alta.
alphabet ['ælfəbɛt] *n* alfabeto.
alphabetical [ælfə'bɛtɪkəl] *adj* alfabético; **in** ~ **order** por orden alfabético.
alphanumeric [ælfənjuː'mɛrɪk] *adj* alfanumérico.
alpine ['ælpaɪn] *adj* alpino, alpestre.
Alps [ælps] *npl*: **the** ~ los Alpes.
already [ɔːl'rɛdɪ] *adv* ya.
alright ['ɔːl'raɪt] *adv* (*BRIT*) = **all right**.
Alsatian [æl'seɪʃən] *n* (*dog*) pastor *m* alemán.
also ['ɔːlsəu] *adv* también, además.
Alta. *abbr* (*Canada*) = *Alberta*.
altar ['ɔltə*] *n* altar *m*.
alter ['ɔltə*] *vt* cambiar, modificar ♦ *vi* cambiarse, modificarse.
alteration [ɔltə'reɪʃən] *n* cambio, modificación *f*; ~**s** *npl* (*ARCH*) reformas *fpl*; (*SEWING*) arreglos *mpl*; **timetable subject to** ~ el horario puede cambiar.
altercation [ɔltə'keɪʃən] *n* altercado.
alternate [ɔl'tə:nɪt] *adj* alterno ♦ *vi* ['ɔltəneɪt]: **to** ~ **(with)** alternar (con); **on** ~ **days** en días alternos.
alternately [ɔl'tə:nɪtlɪ] *adv* alternativamente, por turno.
alternating ['ɔltəneɪtɪŋ] *adj* (*current*) alterno.
alternative [ɔl'tə:nətɪv] *adj* alternativo ♦ *n* alternativa.
alternatively [ɔl'tə:nətɪvlɪ] *adv*: ~ **one could** ... por otra parte se podría....
alternative medicine *n* medicina alternativa.
alternator ['ɔltəneɪtə*] *n* (*AUT*) alternador *m*.
although [ɔːl'ðəu] *conj* aunque, si bien.
altitude ['æltɪtjuːd] *n* altitud *f*, altura.
altitude sickness *n* mal *m* de altura, soroche *m* (*LAM*).
alto ['æltəu] *n* (*female*) contralto *f*; (*male*) alto.
altogether [ɔːltə'gɛðə*] *adv* completamente, del todo; (*on the whole, in all*) en total, en conjunto; **how much is that** ~? ¿cuánto es todo *or* en total?
altruism ['æltruɪzəm] *n* altruismo.
altruistic [æltru'ɪstɪk] *adj* altruista.
aluminium [ælju'mɪnɪəm], (*US*) **aluminum** [ə'luːmɪnəm] *n* aluminio.
always ['ɔːlweɪz] *adv* siempre.
Alzheimer's ['æltshaɪməz] (*also*: ~ **disease**) enfermedad *f* de Alzheimer.
AM *abbr* = *amplitude modulation*.

am [æm] *vb see* **be**.
a.m. *adv abbr* (= *ante meridiem*) de la mañana.
AMA *n abbr* = *American Medical Association*.
amalgam [ə'mælgəm] *n* amalgama.
amalgamate [ə'mælgəmeɪt] *vi* amalgamarse ♦ *vt* amalgamar.
amalgamation [əmælgə'meɪʃən] *n* (*COMM*) fusión *f*.
amass [ə'mæs] *vt* amontonar, acumular.
amateur ['æmətə*] *n* aficionado/a, amateur *m/f*; ~ **dramatics** dramas *mpl* presentados por aficionados, representación *f* de aficionados.
amateurish ['æmətərɪʃ] *adj* (*pej*) torpe, inexperto.
amaze [ə'meɪz] *vt* asombrar, pasmar; **to be** ~**d (at)** asombrarse (de).
amazement [ə'meɪzmənt] *n* asombro, sorpresa; **to my** ~ para mi sorpresa.
amazing [ə'meɪzɪŋ] *adj* extraordinario, asombroso; (*bargain, offer*) increíble.
amazingly [ə'meɪzɪŋlɪ] *adv* extraordinariamente.
Amazon ['æməzən] *n* (*GEO*) Amazonas *m*; (*MYTHOLOGY*) amazona ♦ *cpd*: **the** ~ **basin/jungle** la cuenca/selva del Amazonas.
Amazonian [æmə'zəunɪən] *adj* amazónico.
ambassador [æm'bæsədə*] *n* embajador(a) *m/f*.
amber ['æmbə*] *n* ámbar *m*; **at** ~ (*BRIT AUT*) en amarillo.
ambidextrous [æmbɪ'dɛkstrəs] *adj* ambidextro.
ambience ['æmbɪəns] *n* ambiente *m*.
ambiguity [æmbɪ'gjuɪtɪ] *n* ambigüedad *f*; (*of meaning*) doble sentido.
ambiguous [æm'bɪgjuəs] *adj* ambiguo.
ambition [æm'bɪʃən] *n* ambición *f*; **to achieve one's** ~ realizar su ambición.
ambitious [æm'bɪʃəs] *adj* ambicioso; (*plan*) grandioso.
ambivalent [æm'bɪvələnt] *adj* ambivalente; (*pej*) equívoco.
amble ['æmbl] *vi* (*gen*: ~ **along**) deambular, andar sin prisa.
ambulance ['æmbjuləns] *n* ambulancia.
ambulanceman/woman ['æmbjulənsmən/wumən] *n* ambulanciero/a.
ambush ['æmbuʃ] *n* emboscada ♦ *vt* tender una emboscada a; (*fig*) coger (*SP*) *or* agarrar (*LAM*) por sorpresa.
ameba [ə'miːbə] *n* (*US*) = **amoeba**.
ameliorate [ə'miːlɪəreɪt] *vt* mejorar.
amelioration [əmiːlɪə'reɪʃən] *n* mejora.
amen [ɑː'mɛn] *excl* amén.
amenable [ə'miːnəbl] *adj*: ~ **to** (*advice etc*)

sensible a.

amend [ə'mɛnd] *vt* (*law, text*) enmendar; **to make ~s** (*apologize*) enmendarlo, dar cumplida satisfacción.

amendment [ə'mɛndmənt] *n* enmienda.

amenities [ə'mi:nɪtɪz] *npl* comodidades *fpl*.

amenity [ə'mi:nɪtɪ] *n* servicio.

America [ə'mɛrɪkə] *n* América (del Norte).

American [ə'mɛrɪkən] *adj, n* (norte)americano/a *m/f*, estadounidense *m/f*.

Americanism [ə'mɛrɪkənɪzəm] *n* americanismo.

americanize [ə'mɛrɪkənaɪz] *vt* americanizar.

Amerindian [æmər'ɪndɪən] *adj, n* amerindio/a.

amethyst ['æmɪθɪst] *n* amatista.

Amex ['æmɛks] *n abbr* = *American Stock Exchange*.

amiable ['eɪmɪəbl] *adj* (*kind*) amable, simpático.

amicable ['æmɪkəbl] *adj* amistoso, amigable.

amicably ['æmɪkəblɪ] *adv* amigablemente, amistosamente; **to part ~** separarse amistosamente.

amid(st) [ə'mɪd(st)] *prep* entre, en medio de.

amiss [ə'mɪs] *adv*: **to take sth ~** tomar algo a mal; **there's something ~** pasa algo.

ammo ['æməu] *n abbr* (*col*) = **ammunition**.

ammonia [ə'məunɪə] *n* amoníaco.

ammunition [æmju'nɪʃən] *n* municiones *fpl*; (*fig*) argumentos *mpl*.

ammunition dump *n* depósito de municiones.

amnesia [æm'ni:zɪə] *n* amnesia.

amnesty ['æmnɪstɪ] *n* amnistía; **to grant an ~ to** amnistiar (a); **A~ International** Amnistía Internacional.

amoeba, (*US*) **ameba** [ə'mi:bə] *n* amiba.

amok [ə'mɔk] *adv*: **to run ~** enloquecerse, desbocarse.

among(st) [ə'mʌŋ(st)] *prep* entre, en medio de.

amoral [æ'mɔrəl] *adj* amoral.

amorous ['æmərəs] *adj* cariñoso.

amorphous [ə'mɔːfəs] *adj* amorfo.

amortization [əmɔːtaɪ'zeɪʃən] *n* amortización *f*.

amount [ə'maunt] *n* (*gen*) cantidad *f*; (*of bill etc*) suma, importe *m* ♦ *vi*: **to ~ to** (*total*) sumar; (*be same as*) equivaler a, significar; **this ~s to a refusal** esto equivale a una negativa; **the total ~** (*of money*) la suma total.

amp(ère) ['æmp(ɛə*)] *n* amperio; **a 13 amp**

plug un enchufe de 13 amperios.

ampersand ['æmpəsænd] *n* signo &, "y" comercial.

amphetamine [æm'fɛtəmi:n] *n* anfetamina.

amphibian [æm'fɪbɪən] *n* anfibio.

amphibious [æm'fɪbɪəs] *adj* anfibio.

amphitheatre, (*US*) **amphitheater** ['æmfɪθɪətə*] *n* anfiteatro.

ample ['æmpl] *adj* (*spacious*) amplio; (*abundant*) abundante; **to have ~ time** tener tiempo de sobra.

amplifier ['æmplɪfaɪə*] *n* amplificador *m*.

amplify ['æmplɪfaɪ] *vt* amplificar, aumentar; (*explain*) explicar.

amply ['æmplɪ] *adv* ampliamente.

ampoule, (*US*) **ampule** ['æmpu:l] *n* (*MED*) ampolla.

amputate ['æmpjuteɪt] *vt* amputar.

amputee [æmpju'ti:] *n* persona que ha sufrido una amputación.

Amsterdam ['æmstədæm] *n* Amsterdam *m*.

amt *abbr* = **amount**.

amuck [ə'mʌk] *adv* = **amok**.

amuse [ə'mju:z] *vt* divertir; (*distract*) distraer, entretener; **to ~ o.s. with sth/ by doing sth** distraerse con algo/ haciendo algo; **he was ~d at the joke** le divirtió el chiste.

amusement [ə'mju:zmənt] *n* diversión *f*; (*pastime*) pasatiempo; (*laughter*) risa; **much to my ~** con gran regocijo mío.

amusement arcade *n* salón *m* de juegos.

amusement park *n* parque *m* de atracciones.

amusing [ə'mju:zɪŋ] *adj* divertido.

an [æn, ən, n] *indef art see* **a**.

ANA *n abbr* = *American Newspaper Association; American Nurses Association*.

anachronism [ə'nækrənɪzəm] *n* anacronismo.

anaemia [ə'ni:mɪə] *n* anemia.

anaemic [ə'ni:mɪk] *adj* anémico; (*fig*) flojo.

anaesthetic [ænɪs'θɛtɪk] *n* anestesia; **local/ general ~** anestesia local/general.

anaesthetist [æ'ni:sθɪtɪst] *n* anestesista *m/f*.

anagram ['ænəgræm] *n* anagrama *m*.

anal ['eɪnl] *adj* anal.

analgesic [ænæl'dʒi:sɪk] *adj, n* analgésico.

analogous [ə'næləgəs] *adj*: **~ to** *or* **with** análogo a.

analog(ue) ['ænəlɔg] *adj* (*computer, watch*) analógico.

analogy [ə'nælədʒɪ] *n* analogía; **to draw an ~ between** señalar la analogía entre.

analyse ['ænəlaɪz] *vt* (*BRIT*) analizar.

analysis, *pl* **analyses** [ə'næləsɪs, -si:z] *n* análisis *m inv*.

analyst ['ænəlɪst] *n* (*political ~*) analista *m/f*,

(*psycho~*) psicoanalista *m/f*.
analytic(al) [ænə'lɪtɪk(əl)] *adj* analítico.
analyze ['ænəlaɪz] *vt* (*US*) = **analyse**.
anarchic [æ'nɑːkɪk] *adj* anárquico.
anarchist ['ænəkɪst] *adj, n* anarquista *m/f*.
anarchy ['ænəkɪ] *n* anarquía, desorden *m*.
anathema [ə'næθɪmə] *n*: **that is ~ to him** eso es pecado para él.
anatomical [ænə'tɔmɪkəl] *adj* anatómico.
anatomy [ə'nætəmɪ] *n* anatomía.
ANC *n abbr* = *African National Congress*.
ancestor ['ænsɪstə*] *n* antepasado.
ancestral [æn'sɛstrəl] *adj* ancestral.
ancestry ['ænsɪstrɪ] *n* ascendencia, abolengo.
anchor ['æŋkə*] *n* ancla, áncora ♦ *vi* (*also*: **to drop ~**) anclar, echar el ancla ♦ *vt* (*fig*) sujetar, afianzar; **to weigh ~** levar anclas.
anchorage ['æŋkərɪdʒ] *n* ancladero.
anchor man, anchor woman *n* (*RADIO, TV*) presentador(a) *m/f*.
anchovy ['æntʃəvɪ] *n* anchoa.
ancient ['eɪnʃənt] *adj* antiguo; **~ monument** monumento histórico.
ancillary [æn'sɪlərɪ] *adj* (*worker, staff*) auxiliar.
and [ænd] *conj* y; (*before i, hi*) e; **~ so on** etcétera; **try ~ come** procure *or* intente venir; **better ~ better** cada vez mejor.
Andalusia [ændə'luːzɪə] *n* Andalucía.
Andean ['ændɪən] *adj* andino/a; **~ high plateau** altiplanicie *f*, altiplano (*LAM*).
Andes ['ændiːz] *npl*: **the ~** los Andes.
anecdote ['ænɪkdəʊt] *n* anécdota.
anemia [ə'niːmɪə] *n* (*US*) = **anaemia**.
anemic [ə'niːmɪk] *adj* (*US*) = **anaemic**.
anemone [ə'nɛmənɪ] *n* (*BOT*) anémone *f*; **sea ~** anémona.
anesthetic [ænɪs'θɛtɪk] *adj*, (*US*) = **anaesthetic**.
anesthetist [æ'niːsθɪtɪst] *n* (*US*) = **anaesthetist**.
anew [ə'njuː] *adv* de nuevo, otra vez.
angel ['eɪndʒəl] *n* ángel *m*.
angel dust *n* polvo de ángel.
angelic [æn'dʒɛlɪk] *adj* angélico.
anger ['æŋgə*] *n* ira, cólera, enojo (*LAM*) ♦ *vt* enojar, enfurecer.
angina [æn'dʒaɪnə] *n* angina (del pecho).
angle ['æŋgl] *n* ángulo; **from their ~** desde su punto de vista.
angler ['æŋglə*] *n* pescador(a) *m/f* (de caña).
Anglican ['æŋglɪkən] *adj, n* anglicano/a.
anglicize ['æŋglɪsaɪz] *vt* anglicanizar.
angling ['æŋglɪŋ] *n* pesca con caña.
Anglo- [æŋgləʊ] *pref* anglo... .

Angola [æŋ'gəʊlə] *n* Angola.
Angolan [æŋ'gəʊlən] *adj, n* angoleño/a *m/f*.
angrily ['æŋgrɪlɪ] *adv* enojado, enfadado.
angry ['æŋgrɪ] *adj* enfadado, enojado (*esp LAM*); **to be ~ with sb/at sth** estar enfadado con algn/por algo; **to get ~** enfadarse, enojarse (*esp LAM*).
anguish ['æŋgwɪʃ] *n* (*physical*) tormentos *mpl*; (*mental*) angustia.
anguished ['æŋgwɪʃt] *adj* angustioso.
angular ['æŋgjʊlə*] *adj* (*shape*) angular; (*features*) anguloso.
animal ['ænɪməl] *adj, n* animal *m*.
animal rights [-raɪts] *npl* derechos *mpl* de los animales.
animate ['ænɪmeɪt] *vt* (*enliven*) animar; (*encourage*) estimular, alentar ♦ ['ænɪmɪt] *adj* vivo, animado.
animated ['ænɪmeɪtɪd] *adj* vivo, animado.
animation [ænɪ'meɪʃən] *n* animación *f*.
animosity [ænɪ'mɔsɪtɪ] *n* animosidad *f*, rencor *m*.
aniseed ['ænɪsiːd] *n* anís *m*.
Ankara ['æŋkərə] *n* Ankara.
ankle ['æŋkl] *n* tobillo *m*.
ankle sock *n* calcetín *m*.
annex ['ænɛks] *n* (*also*: *Brit*: **annexe**) (*building*) edificio anexo ♦ *vt* [æ'nɛks] (*territory*) anexar.
annihilate [ə'naɪəleɪt] *vt* aniquilar.
annihilation [ənaɪə'leɪʃən] *n* aniquilación *f*.
anniversary [ænɪ'vɔːsərɪ] *n* aniversario.
annotate ['ænəʊteɪt] *vt* anotar.
announce [ə'naʊns] *vt* (*gen*) anunciar; (*inform*) comunicar; **he ~d that he wasn't going** declaró que no iba.
announcement [ə'naʊnsmənt] *n* (*gen*) anuncio; (*declaration*) declaración *f*; **I'd like to make an ~** quisiera anunciar algo.
announcer [ə'naʊnsə*] *n* (*RADIO, TV*) locutor(a) *m/f*.
annoy [ə'nɔɪ] *vt* molestar, fastidiar, fregar (*LAM*), embromar (*LAM*); **to be ~ed (at sth/with sb)** estar enfadado *or* molesto (por algo/con algn); **don't get ~ed!** ¡no se enfade!
annoyance [ə'nɔɪəns] *n* enojo; (*thing*) molestia.
annoying [ə'nɔɪɪŋ] *adj* molesto, fastidioso, fregado (*LAM*), embromado (*LAM*); (*person*) pesado.
annual ['ænjʊəl] *adj* anual ♦ *n* (*BOT*) anual *m*; (*book*) anuario.
annual general meeting (AGM) *n* junta general anual.
annually ['ænjʊəlɪ] *adv* anualmente, cada año.
annual report *n* informe *m or* memoria

anual.
annuity [ə'njuːɪtɪ] *n* renta *or* pensión *f* vitalicia.
annul [ə'nʌl] *vt* anular; (*law*) revocar.
annulment [ə'nʌlmənt] *n* anulación *f*.
annum ['ænəm] *n see* **per annum**.
Annunciation [ənʌnsɪ'eɪʃən] *n* Anunciación *f*.
anode ['ænəud] *n* ánodo.
anoint [ə'nɔɪnt] *vt* untar.
anomalous [ə'nɔmələs] *adj* anómalo.
anomaly [ə'nɔməlɪ] *n* anomalía.
anon. [ə'nɔn] *abbr* = **anonymous**.
anonymity [ænə'nɪmɪtɪ] *n* anonimato.
anonymous [ə'nɔnɪməs] *adj* anónimo; **to remain** ~ quedar en el anonimato.
anorak ['ænəræk] *n* anorak *m*.
anorexia [ænə'rɛksɪə] *n* (*MED*) anorexia.
anorexic [ænə'rɛksɪk] *adj*, *n* anoréxico/a *m/f*.
another [ə'nʌðə*] *adj*: ~ **book** otro libro; ~ **beer?** ¿(quieres) otra cerveza?; **in** ~ **5 years** en cinco años más ♦ *pron* otro; *see also* **one**.
ANSI *n abbr* (= *American National Standards Institution*) oficina de normalización de EEUU.
answer ['ɑːnsə*] *n* respuesta, contestación *f*; (*to problem*) solución *f* ♦ *vi* contestar, responder ♦ *vt* (*reply to*) contestar a, responder a; (*problem*) resolver; **to** ~ **the phone** contestar el teléfono; **in** ~ **to your letter** contestando *or* en contestación a su carta; **to** ~ **the bell** *or* **the door** abrir la puerta.
▶**answer back** *vi* replicar, ser respondón/ona.
▶**answer for** *vt fus* responder de *or* por.
▶**answer to** *vt fus* (*description*) corresponder a.
answerable ['ɑːnsərəbl] *adj*: ~ **to sb for sth** responsable ante algn de algo.
answering machine ['ɑːnsərɪŋ-] *n* contestador *m* automático.
ant [ænt] *n* hormiga.
ANTA *n abbr* = *American National Theater and Academy*.
antagonism [æn'tægənɪzəm] *n* antagonismo *m*.
antagonist [æn'tægənɪst] *n* antagonista *m/f*, adversario/a.
antagonistic [æntægə'nɪstɪk] *adj* antagónico; (*opposed*) contrario, opuesto.
antagonize [æn'tægənaɪz] *vt* provocar la enemistad de.
Antarctic [ænt'ɑːktɪk] *adj* antártico ♦ *n*: **the** ~ el Antártico.
Antarctica [ænt'ɑːktɪkə] *n* Antártida.
Antarctic Circle *n* Círculo Polar

Antártico.
Antarctic Ocean *n* Océano Antártico.
ante ['æntɪ] *n*: **to up the** ~ subir la apuesta.
ante... ['æntɪ] *pref* ante....
anteater ['æntiːtə*] *n* oso hormiguero.
antecedent [æntɪ'siːdənt] *n* antecedente *m*.
antechamber ['æntɪtʃeɪmbə*] *n* antecámara.
antelope ['æntɪləup] *n* antílope *m*.
antenatal [æntɪ'neɪtl] *adj* prenatal.
antenatal clinic *n* clínica prenatal.
antenna [æn'tɛnə], *pl* ~**e** [-niː] *n* antena.
anteroom ['æntɪrum] *n* antesala.
anthem ['ænθəm] *n*: **national** ~ himno nacional.
anthology [æn'θɔlədʒɪ] *n* antología.
anthropologist [ænθrə'pɔlədʒɪst] *n* antropólogo/a.
anthropology [ænθrə'pɔlədʒɪ] *n* antropología.
anti... [æntɪ] *pref* anti....
anti-aircraft ['æntɪ'ɛəkrɑːft] *adj* antiaéreo.
antiballistic [æntɪbə'lɪstɪk] *adj* antibalístico.
antibiotic [æntɪbaɪ'ɔtɪk] *adj*, *n* antibiótico.
antibody ['æntɪbɔdɪ] *n* anticuerpo.
anticipate [æn'tɪsɪpeɪt] *vt* (*foresee*) prever; (*expect*) esperar, contar con; (*forestall*) anticiparse a, adelantarse a; **this is worse than I** ~**d** esto es peor de lo que esperaba; **as** ~**d** según se esperaba.
anticipation [æntɪsɪ'peɪʃən] *n* previsión *f*; esperanza; anticipación *f*.
anticlimax [æntɪ'klaɪmæks] *n* decepción *f*.
anticlockwise [æntɪ'klɔkwaɪz] *adv* en dirección contraria a la de las agujas del reloj.
antics ['æntɪks] *npl* payasadas *fpl*.
anticyclone [æntɪ'saɪkləun] *n* anticiclón *m*.
antidote ['æntɪdəut] *n* antídoto.
antifreeze ['æntɪfriːz] *n* anticongelante *m*.
antihistamine [æntɪ'hɪstəmiːn] *n* antihistamínico.
Antilles [æn'tɪliːz] *npl*: **the** ~ las Antillas.
antipathy [æn'tɪpəθɪ] *n* (*between people*) antipatía; (*to person, thing*) aversión *f*.
antiperspirant ['æntɪpəːspɪrənt] *n* antitranspirante *m*.
Antipodean [æntɪpə'diːən] *adj* antípoda.
Antipodes [æn'tɪpədiːz] *npl*: **the** ~ las Antípodas.
antiquarian [æntɪ'kwɛərɪən] *n* anticuario/a.
antiquated ['æntɪkweɪtɪd] *adj* anticuado.
antique [æn'tiːk] *n* antigüedad *f* ♦ *adj* antiguo.
antique dealer *n* anticuario/a.
antique shop *n* tienda de antigüedades.
antiquity [æn'tɪkwɪtɪ] *n* antigüedad *f*.
anti-Semitic ['æntɪsɪ'mɪtɪk] *adj* antisemita.

anti-Semitism [æntɪ'sɛmɪtɪzəm] *n* antisemitismo.
antiseptic [æntɪ'sɛptɪk] *adj, n* antiséptico.
antisocial [æntɪ'səʊʃəl] *adj* antisocial.
antitank [æntɪ'tæŋk] *adj* antitanque.
antithesis, *pl* **antitheses** [æn'tɪθɪsɪs, -siːz] *n* antítesis *f inv*.
antitrust [æntɪ'trʌst] *adj*: ~ **legislation** legislación *f* antimonopolio.
antlers ['æntləz] *npl* cornamenta.
anus ['eɪnəs] *n* ano.
anvil ['ænvɪl] *n* yunque *m*.
anxiety [æŋ'zaɪətɪ] *n* (*worry*) inquietud *f*; (*eagerness*) ansia, anhelo.
anxious ['æŋkʃəs] *adj* (*worried*) inquieto; (*keen*) deseoso; **I'm very** ~ **about you** me tienes muy preocupado.
anxiously ['æŋkʃəslɪ] *adv* con inquietud, de manera angustiada.

══════════════════ *KEYWORD*

any ['ɛnɪ] *adj* **1** (*in questions etc*) algún/ alguna; **have you** ~ **butter/children?** ¿tienes mantequilla/hijos?; **if there are** ~ **tickets left** si quedan billetes, si queda algún billete
2 (*with negative*): **I haven't** ~ **money/ books** no tengo dinero/libros
3 (*no matter which*) cualquier; ~ **excuse will do** valdrá *or* servirá cualquier excusa; **choose** ~ **book you like** escoge el libro que quieras; ~ **teacher you ask will tell you** cualquier profesor al que preguntes te lo dirá
4 (*in phrases*): **in** ~ **case** de todas formas, en cualquier caso; ~ **day now** cualquier día (de estos); **at** ~ **moment** en cualquier momento, de un momento a otro; **at** ~ **rate** en todo caso; ~ **time: come (at)** ~ **time** ven cuando quieras; **he might come (at)** ~ **time** podría llegar de un momento a otro
♦ *pron* **1** (*in questions etc*): **have you got** ~? ¿tienes alguno/a?; **can** ~ **of you sing?** ¿sabe cantar alguno de vosotros/ustedes?
2 (*with negative*): **I haven't** ~ **(of them)** no tengo ninguno
3 (*no matter which one(s)*): **take** ~ **of those books (you like)** toma el libro que quieras de ésos
♦ *adv* **1** (*in questions etc*): **do you want** ~ **more soup/sandwiches?** ¿quieres más sopa/bocadillos?; **are you feeling** ~ **better?** ¿te sientes algo mejor?
2 (*with negative*): **I can't hear him** ~ **more** ya no le oigo; **don't wait** ~ **longer** no esperes más.

anybody ['ɛnɪbɔdɪ] *pron* cualquiera, cualquier persona; (*in interrogative sentences*) alguien; (*in negative sentences*): **I don't see** ~ no veo a nadie.
anyhow ['ɛnɪhaʊ] *adv* de todos modos, de todas maneras; (*carelessly*) de cualquier manera; (*haphazardly*) de cualquier modo; **I shall go** ~ iré de todas maneras.
anyone ['ɛnɪwʌn] = **anybody.**
anyplace ['ɛnɪpleɪs] *adv* (*US*) = **anywhere.**
anything ['ɛnɪθɪŋ] *pron* (*see* **anybody**) cualquier cosa; (*in interrogative sentences*) algo; (*in negative sentences*) nada; (*everything*) todo; ~ **else?** ¿algo más?; **it can cost** ~ **between £15 and £20** puede costar entre 15 y 20 libras.
anytime ['ɛnɪtaɪm] *adv* (*at any moment*) en cualquier momento, de un momento a otro; (*whenever*) no importa cuándo, cuando quiera.
anyway ['ɛnɪweɪ] *adv* de todas maneras; de cualquier modo.
anywhere ['ɛnɪwɛə*] *adv* (*see* **anybody**) dondequiera; (*interrogative*) en algún sitio; (*negative sense*) en ningún sitio; (*everywhere*) en *or* por todas partes; **I don't see him** ~ no le veo en ningún sitio; ~ **in the world** en cualquier parte del mundo.
Anzac ['ænzæk] *n abbr* (= *Australia-New Zealand Army Corps*).
apace [ə'peɪs] *adv* aprisa.
apart [ə'pɑːt] *adv* aparte, separadamente; **10 miles** ~ separados por 10 millas; **to take** ~ desmontar; ~ **from** *prep* aparte de.
apartheid [ə'pɑːteɪt] *n* apartheid *m*.
apartment [ə'pɑːtmənt] *n* (*US*) piso, departamento (*LAM*), apartamento; (*room*) cuarto.
apartment block *or* **building** (*US*) bloque *m* de pisos.
apathetic [æpə'θɛtɪk] *adj* apático, indiferente.
apathy ['æpəθɪ] *n* apatía, indiferencia.
APB *n abbr* (*US*: = *all points bulletin*) expresión usada por la policía que significa "descubrir y aprehender al sospechoso".
ape [eɪp] *n* mono ♦ *vt* imitar, remedar.
Apennines ['æpənaɪnz] *npl*: **the** ~ los Apeninos *mpl*.
aperitif [ə'pɛrɪtiːf] *n* aperitivo.
aperture ['æpətʃjuə*] *n* rendija, resquicio; (*PHOT*) abertura.
APEX ['eɪpɛks] *n abbr* (*AVIAT* = *advance purchase excursion*) APEX *m*.
apex ['eɪpɛks] *n* ápice *m*; (*fig*) cumbre *f*.
aphid ['eɪfɪd] *n* pulgón *m*.

aphorism ['æfərɪzəm] *n* aforismo.
aphrodisiac [æfrəu'dızıæk] *adj, n* afrodisíaco.
API *n abbr* = *American Press Institute.*
apiece [ə'piːs] *adv* cada uno.
aplomb [ə'plɔm] *n* aplomo, confianza.
APO *n abbr* (*US:* = *Army Post Office*) *servicio postal del ejército.*
Apocalypse [ə'pɔkəlɪps] *n* Apocalipsis *m.*
apocryphal [ə'pɔkrɪfəl] *adj* apócrifo.
apolitical [eɪpə'lɪtɪkl] *adj* apolítico.
apologetic [əpɔlə'dʒɛtɪk] *adj* (*look, remark*) de disculpa.
apologetically [əpɔlə'dʒɛtɪkəlɪ] *adv* con aire de disculpa, excusándose, disculpándose.
apologize [ə'pɔlədʒaɪz] *vi:* **to ~ (for sth to sb)** disculparse (con algn por algo).
apology [ə'pɔlədʒɪ] *n* disculpa, excusa; **please accept my apologies** le ruego me disculpe.
apoplectic [æpə'plɛktɪk] *adj* (*MED*) apoplético; (*col*): **~ with rage** furioso.
apoplexy ['æpəplɛksɪ] *n* apoplegía.
apostle [ə'pɔsl] *n* apóstol *m/f.*
apostrophe [ə'pɔstrəfɪ] *n* apóstrofo *m.*
appal [ə'pɔːl] *vt* horrorizar, espantar.
Appalachian Mountains [æpə'leɪʃən-] *npl:* **the ~** los (Montes) Apalaches.
appalling [ə'pɔːlɪŋ] *adj* espantoso; (*awful*) pésimo; **she's an ~ cook** es una cocinera malísima.
apparatus [æpə'reɪtəs] *n* aparato; (*in gymnasium*) aparatos *mpl.*
apparel [ə'pærl] *n* (*US*) indumentaria.
apparent [ə'pærənt] *adj* aparente; (*obvious*) manifiesto, evidente; **it is ~ that** está claro que.
apparently [ə'pærəntlɪ] *adv* por lo visto, al parecer, dizque (*LAM*).
apparition [æpə'rɪʃən] *n* aparición *f.*
appeal [ə'piːl] *vi* (*LAW*) apelar ♦ *n* (*LAW*) apelación *f*; (*request*) llamamiento, llamado (*LAM*); (*plea*) súplica; (*charm*) atractivo, encanto; **to ~ for** solicitar; **to ~ to** (*subj: person*) rogar a, suplicar a; (: *thing*) atraer, interesar; **to ~ to sb for mercy** rogarle misericordia a alguien; **it doesn't ~ to me** no me atrae, no me llama la atención; **right of ~** derecho de apelación.
appealing [ə'piːlɪŋ] *adj* (*nice*) atractivo; (*touching*) conmovedor(a), emocionante.
appear [ə'pɪə*] *vi* aparecer, presentarse; (*LAW*) comparecer; (*publication*) salir (a luz), publicarse; (*seem*) parecer; **it would ~ that** parecería que.
appearance [ə'pɪərəns] *n* aparición *f*; (*look, aspect*) apariencia, aspecto; **to keep up**

~s salvar las apariencias; **to all ~s** al parecer.
appease [ə'piːz] *vt* (*pacify*) apaciguar; (*satisfy*) satisfacer.
appeasement [ə'piːzmənt] *n* (*POL*) apaciguamiento.
append [ə'pɛnd] *vt* (*COMPUT*) añadir (al final).
appendage [ə'pɛndɪdʒ] *n* añadidura.
appendicitis [əpɛndɪ'saɪtɪs] *n* apendicitis *f.*
appendix, *pl* **appendices** [ə'pɛndɪks, -dɪsiːz] *n* apéndice *m*; **to have one's ~ out** operarse de apendicitis.
appetite ['æpɪtaɪt] *n* apetito; (*fig*) deseo, anhelo; **that walk has given me an ~** ese paseo me ha abierto el apetito.
appetizer ['æpɪtaɪzə*] *n* (*drink*) aperitivo; (*food*) tapas *fpl* (*SP*).
appetizing ['æpɪtaɪzɪŋ] *adj* apetitoso.
applaud [ə'plɔːd] *vt, vi* aplaudir.
applause [ə'plɔːz] *n* aplausos *mpl.*
apple ['æpl] *n* manzana.
apple tree *n* manzano.
appliance [ə'plaɪəns] *n* aparato; **electrical ~s** electrodomésticos *mpl.*
applicable [ə'plɪkəbl] *adj* aplicable, pertinente; **the law is ~ from January** la ley es aplicable *or* se pone en vigor a partir de enero; **to be ~ to** referirse a.
applicant ['æplɪkənt] *n* candidato/a; solicitante *m/f.*
application [æplɪ'keɪʃən] *n* aplicación *f*; (*for a job, a grant etc*) solicitud *f.*
application form *n* solicitud *f.*
applications package *n* (*COMPUT*) paquete *m* de programas de aplicación.
applied [ə'plaɪd] *adj* (*science, art*) aplicado.
apply [ə'plaɪ] *vt:* **to ~ (to)** aplicar (a); (*fig*) emplear (para) ♦ *vi:* **to ~ to** (*ask*) dirigirse a; (*be suitable for*) ser aplicable a; (*be relevant to*) tener que ver con; **to ~ for** (*permit, grant, job*) solicitar; **to ~ the brakes** echar el freno; **to ~ o.s. to** aplicarse a, dedicarse a.
appoint [ə'pɔɪnt] *vt* (*to post*) nombrar; (*date, place*) fijar, señalar.
appointee [əpɔɪn'tiː] *n* persona nombrada.
appointment [ə'pɔɪntmənt] *n* (*engagement*) cita; (*date*) compromiso; (*act*) nombramiento; (*post*) puesto; **to make an ~ (with)** (*doctor*) pedir hora (con); (*friend*) citarse (con); **"~s (vacant)"** "ofertas de trabajo"; **by ~** mediante cita.
apportion [ə'pɔːʃən] *vt* repartir.
appraisal [ə'preɪzl] *n* evaluación *f.*
appraise [ə'preɪz] *vt* (*value*) tasar, valorar; (*situation etc*) evaluar.
appreciable [ə'priːʃəbl] *adj* sensible.

appreciably [ə'priːʃəblɪ] *adv* sensiblemente, de manera apreciable.

appreciate [ə'priːʃɪeɪt] *vt* (*like*) apreciar, tener en mucho; (*be grateful for*) agradecer; (*be aware of*) comprender ♦ *vi* (*COMM*) aumentar en valor; **1 ~d your help** agradecí tu ayuda.

appreciation [əpriːʃɪ'eɪʃən] *n* aprecio; reconocimiento, agradecimiento; aumento en valor.

appreciative [ə'priːʃɪətɪv] *adj* agradecido.

apprehend [æprɪ'hɛnd] *vt* percibir; (*arrest*) detener.

apprehension [æprɪ'hɛnʃən] *n* (*fear*) aprensión *f*.

apprehensive [æprɪ'hɛnsɪv] *adj* aprensivo.

apprentice [ə'prɛntɪs] *n* aprendiz(a) *m/f* ♦ *vt*: **to be ~d to** estar de aprendiz con.

apprenticeship [ə'prɛntɪsʃɪp] *n* aprendizaje *m*; **to serve one's ~** hacer el aprendizaje.

appro. ['æprəʊ] *abbr* (*BRIT COMM: col*) = **approval**.

approach [ə'prəʊtʃ] *vi* acercarse ♦ *vt* acercarse a; (*be approximate*) aproximarse a; (*ask, apply to*) dirigirse a; (*problem*) abordar ♦ *n* acercamiento; aproximación *f*; (*access*) acceso; (*proposal*) proposición *f*; (*to problem etc*) enfoque *m*; **to ~ sb about sth** hablar con algn sobre algo.

approachable [ə'prəʊtʃəbl] *adj* (*person*) abordable; (*place*) accesible.

approach road *n* vía de acceso.

approbation [æprə'beɪʃən] *n* aprobación *f*.

appropriate [ə'prəʊprɪɪt] *adj* apropiado, conveniente ♦ *vt* [-rɪeɪt] (*take*) apropiarse de; (*allot*): **to ~ sth for** destinar algo a; **~ for** *or* **to** apropiado para; **it would not be ~ for me to comment** no estaría bien *or* sería pertinente que yo diera mi opinión.

appropriation [əprəʊprɪ'eɪʃən] *n* asignación *f*.

approval [ə'pruːvəl] *n* aprobación *f*, visto bueno; **on ~** (*COMM*) a prueba; **to meet with sb's ~** obtener la aprobación de algn.

approve [ə'pruːv] *vt* aprobar.
▶**approve of** *vt fus* aprobar.

approved school *n* (*BRIT*) correccional *m*.

approx. *abbr* (= *approximately*) aprox.

approximate [ə'prɔksɪmɪt] *adj* aproximado.

approximately [ə'prɔksɪmɪtlɪ] *adv* aproximadamente, más o menos.

approximation [əprɔksɪ'meɪʃən] *n* aproximación *f*.

Apr. *abbr* (= *April*) abr.

apr *n abbr* (= *annual percentage rate*) tasa de interés anual.

apricot ['eɪprɪkɔt] *n* albaricoque *m* (*SP*), damasco (*LAM*).

April ['eɪprəl] *n* abril *m*; **~ Fools' Day** *n* ≈ día *m* de los (Santos) Inocentes.

> El 1 de abril es **April Fools' Day** en la tradición anglosajona. Tal día se les gastan bromas a los más desprevenidos, quienes reciben la denominación de **April Fool** (≈ *inocente*), y tanto la prensa escrita como la televisión difunden alguna historia falsa con la que sumarse al espíritu del día.

apron ['eɪprən] *n* delantal *m*; (*AVIAT*) pista.

apse [æps] *n* (*ARCH*) ábside *m*.

APT *n abbr* (*BRIT*) = *advanced passenger train*.

Apt. *abbr* = *apartment*.

apt [æpt] *adj* (*to the point*) acertado, oportuno; (*appropriate*) apropiado; **~ to do** (*likely*) propenso a hacer.

aptitude ['æptɪtjuːd] *n* aptitud *f*, capacidad *f*.

aptitude test *n* prueba de aptitud.

aptly ['æptlɪ] *adj* acertadamente.

aqualung ['ækwəlʌŋ] *n* escafandra autónoma.

aquarium [ə'kwɛərɪəm] *n* acuario.

Aquarius [ə'kwɛərɪəs] *n* Acuario.

aquatic [ə'kwætɪk] *adj* acuático.

aqueduct ['ækwɪdʌkt] *n* acueducto.

AR *abbr* (*US*) = *Arkansas*.

ARA *n abbr* (*BRIT*)= *Associate of the Royal Academy*.

Arab ['ærəb] *adj*, *n* árabe *m/f*.

Arabia [ə'reɪbɪə] *n* Arabia.

Arabian [ə'reɪbɪən] *adj* árabe, arábigo.

Arabian Desert *n* Desierto de Arabia.

Arabian Sea *n* Mar *m* de Omán.

Arabic ['ærəbɪk] *adj* (*language, manuscripts*) árabe, arábigo ♦ *n* árabe *m*; **~ numerals** numeración *f* arábiga.

arable ['ærəbl] *adj* cultivable.

Aragon ['ærəɡən] *n* Aragón *m*.

ARAM *n abbr* (*BRIT*) = *Associate of the Royal Academy of Music*.

arbiter ['ɑːbɪtə*] *n* árbitro.

arbitrary ['ɑːbɪtrərɪ] *adj* arbitrario.

arbitrate ['ɑːbɪtreɪt] *vi* arbitrar.

arbitration [ɑːbɪ'treɪʃən] *n* arbitraje *m*; **the dispute went to ~** el conflicto laboral fue sometido al arbitraje.

arbitrator ['ɑːbɪtreɪtə*] *n* árbitro.

ARC *n abbr* = *American Red Cross*.

arc [ɑːk] *n* arco.

arcade [ɑː'keɪd] *n* (*ARCH*) arcada; (*round a square*) soportales *mpl*; (*shopping ~*) galería comercial.

arch [ɑːtʃ] *n* arco; (*vault*) bóveda; (*of foot*) empeine *m* ♦ *vt* arquear.
archaeological [ɑːkɪə'lɒdʒɪkl] *adj* arqueológico.
archaeologist [ɑːkɪ'ɒlədʒɪst] *n* arqueólogo/a.
archaeology [ɑːkɪ'ɒlədʒɪ] *n* arqueología.
archaic [ɑː'keɪɪk] *adj* arcaico.
archangel ['ɑːkeɪndʒəl] *n* arcángel *m*.
archbishop [ɑːtʃ'bɪʃəp] *n* arzobispo.
arched [ɑːtʃt] *adj* abovedado.
archenemy ['ɑːtʃ'enəmɪ] *n* enemigo jurado.
archeology [ɑːkɪ'ɒlədʒɪ] *etc* (*US*) = **archaeology** *etc*.
archer ['ɑːtʃə*] *n* arquero/a.
archery ['ɑːtʃərɪ] *n* tiro al arco.
archetypal ['ɑːkɪtaɪpəl] *adj* arquetípico.
archetype ['ɑːkɪtaɪp] *n* arquetipo.
archipelago [ɑːkɪ'pɛlɪgəu] *n* archipiélago.
architect ['ɑːkɪtɛkt] *n* arquitecto/a.
architectural [ɑːkɪ'tɛktʃərəl] *adj* arquitectónico.
architecture ['ɑːkɪtɛktʃə*] *n* arquitectura.
archive ['ɑːkaɪv] *n* (*often pl: also COMPUT*) archivo.
archive file *n* (*COMPUT*) fichero archivado.
archives ['ɑːkaɪvz] *npl* archivo *sg*.
archivist ['ɑːkɪvɪst] *n* archivero/a.
archway ['ɑːtʃweɪ] *n* arco, arcada.
ARCM *n abbr* (*BRIT*) = *Associate of the Royal College of Music.*
Arctic ['ɑːktɪk] *adj* ártico ♦ *n*: **the ~** el Ártico.
Arctic Circle *n* Círculo Polar Ártico.
Arctic Ocean *n* Océano (Glacial) Ártico.
ARD *n abbr* (*US MED*) = *acute respiratory disease.*
ardent ['ɑːdənt] *adj* (*desire*) ardiente; (*supporter, lover*) apasionado.
ardour, (*US*) **ardor** ['ɑːdə*] *n* ardor *m*, pasión *f*.
arduous ['ɑːdjuəs] *adj* (*gen*) arduo; (*journey*) penoso.
are [ɑː*] *vb see* **be**.
area ['ɛərɪə] *n* área; (*MATH etc*) superficie *f*, extensión *f*; (*zone*) región *f*, zona; **the London ~** la zona de Londres.
area code *n* (*US TEL*) prefijo.
arena [ə'riːnə] *n* arena; (*of circus*) pista; (*for bullfight*) plaza, ruedo.
aren't [ɑːnt] = **are not.**
Argentina [ɑːdʒən'tiːnə] *n* Argentina.
Argentinian [ɑːdʒən'tɪnɪən] *adj, n* argentino/a *m/f*.
arguable ['ɑːgjuəbl] *adj*: **it is ~ whether ...** es dudoso que + *subjun*.
arguably ['ɑːgjuəblɪ] *adv*: **it is ~ ...** es discutiblemente ....

argue ['ɑːgjuː] *vt* (*debate: case, matter*) mantener, argüir ♦ *vi* (*quarrel*) discutir; (*reason*) razonar, argumentar; **to ~ that** sostener que; **to ~ about sth (with sb)** pelearse (con algn) por algo.
argument ['ɑːgjumənt] *n* (*reasons*) argumento; (*quarrel*) discusión *f*; (*debate*) debate *m*; **~ for/against** argumento en pro/contra de.
argumentative [ɑːgju'mɛntətɪv] *adj* discutidor(a).
aria ['ɑːrɪə] *n* (*MUS*) aria.
ARIBA *n abbr* (*BRIT*) = *Associate of the Royal Institute of British Architects.*
arid ['ærɪd] *adj* árido.
aridity [ə'rɪdɪtɪ] *n* aridez *f*.
Aries ['ɛərɪz] *n* Aries *m*.
arise [ə'raɪz], *pt* **arose,** *pp* **arisen** [ə'rɪzn] *vi* (*rise up*) levantarse, alzarse; (*emerge*) surgir, presentarse; **to ~ from** derivar de; **should the need ~** si fuera necesario.
aristocracy [ærɪs'tɔkrəsɪ] *n* aristocracia.
aristocrat ['ærɪstəkræt] *n* aristócrata *m/f*.
aristocratic [ərɪstə'krætɪk] *adj* aristocrático.
arithmetic [ə'rɪθmətɪk] *n* aritmética.
arithmetical [ærɪθ'mɛtɪkl] *adj* aritmético.
Ariz. *abbr* (*US*) = *Arizona.*
Ark [ɑːk] *n*: Noah's **~** el Arca *f* de Noé.
Ark. *abbr* (*US*) = *Arkansas.*
arm [ɑːm] *n* (*ANAT*) brazo ♦ *vt* armar; **~ in ~** cogidos del brazo; *see also* **arms.**
armaments ['ɑːməmənts] *npl* (*weapons*) armamentos *mpl*.
armchair ['ɑːmtʃɛə*] *n* sillón *m*, butaca.
armed [ɑːmd] *adj* armado; **the ~ forces** las fuerzas armadas.
armed robbery *n* robo a mano armada.
Armenia [ɑː'miːnɪə] *n* Armenia.
Armenian [ɑː'miːnɪən] *adj* armenio ♦ *n* armenio/a; (*LING*) armenio.
armful ['ɑːmful] *n* brazada.
armistice ['ɑːmɪstɪs] *n* armisticio.
armour, (*US*) **armor** ['ɑːmə*] *n* armadura.
armo(u)red car *n* coche *m or* carro (*LAM*) blindado.
armo(u)ry ['ɑːmərɪ] *n* arsenal *m*.
armpit ['ɑːmpɪt] *n* sobaco, axila.
armrest ['ɑːmrɛst] *n* reposabrazos *m inv*, brazo.
arms [ɑːmz] *npl* (*weapons*) armas *fpl*; (*HERALDRY*) escudo *sg*.
arms control *n* control *m* de armamentos.
arms race *n* carrera de armamentos.
army ['ɑːmɪ] *n* ejército.
aroma [ə'rəumə] *n* aroma *m*, fragancia.
aromatherapy [ərəumə'θɛrəpɪ] *n* aromaterapia.

aromatic [ærə'mætɪk] *adj* aromático, fragante.

arose [ə'rəuz] *pt of* **arise**.

around [ə'raund] *adv* alrededor; (*in the area*) a la redonda ♦ *prep* alrededor de.

arousal [ə'rauzəl] *n* (*sexual*) excitación *f*; (*of feelings, interest*) despertar *m*.

arouse [ə'rauz] *vt* despertar.

arrange [ə'reɪndʒ] *vt* arreglar, ordenar; (*programme*) organizar ♦ *vi*: **we have ~d for a taxi to pick you up** hemos organizado todo para que le recoja un taxi; **to ~ to do sth** quedar en hacer algo; **it was ~d that ...** se quedó en que ....

arrangement [ə'reɪndʒmənt] *n* arreglo; (*agreement*) acuerdo; **~s** *npl* (*plans*) planes *mpl*, medidas *fpl*; (*preparations*) preparativos *mpl*; **to come to an ~ (with sb)** llegar a un acuerdo (con algn); **by ~ a** convenir; **I'll make ~s for you to be met** haré los preparativos para que le estén esperando.

arrant ['ærənt] *adj*: **~ nonsense** una verdadera tontería.

array [ə'reɪ] *n* (*COMPUT*) matriz *f*; **~ of** (*things*) serie *f or* colección *f* de; (*people*) conjunto de.

arrears [ə'rɪəz] *npl* atrasos *mpl*; **in ~** (*COMM*) en mora; **to be in ~ with one's rent** estar retrasado en el pago del alquiler.

arrest [ə'rɛst] *vt* detener; (*sb's attention*) llamar ♦ *n* detención *f*; **under ~** detenido.

arresting [ə'rɛstɪŋ] *adj* (*fig*) llamativo.

arrival [ə'raɪvəl] *n* llegada, arribo (*LAM*); **new ~** recién llegado/a.

arrive [ə'raɪv] *vi* llegar, arribar (*LAM*).

arrogance ['ærəgəns] *n* arrogancia, prepotencia (*LAM*).

arrogant ['ærəgənt] *adj* arrogante, prepotente (*LAM*).

arrow ['ærəu] *n* flecha.

arse [ɑːs] *n* (*BRIT col!*) culo, trasero.

arsenal ['ɑːsɪnl] *n* arsenal *m*.

arsenic ['ɑːsnɪk] *n* arsénico.

arson ['ɑːsn] *n* incendio provocado.

art [ɑːt] *n* arte *m*; (*skill*) destreza; (*technique*) técnica; **A~s** *npl* (*SCOL*) Letras *fpl*; **work of ~** obra de arte.

artefact ['ɑːtɪfækt] *n* artefacto.

arterial [ɑː'tɪərɪəl] *adj* (*ANAT*) arterial; (*road etc*) principal.

artery ['ɑːtərɪ] *n* (*MED, road etc*) arteria.

artful ['ɑːtful] *adj* (*cunning: person, trick*) mañoso.

art gallery *n* pinacoteca, museo de pintura; (*COMM*) galería de arte.

arthritis [ɑː'θraɪtɪs] *n* artritis *f*.

artichoke ['ɑːtɪtʃəuk] *n* alcachofa; **Jerusalem ~** aguaturma.

article ['ɑːtɪkl] *n* artículo, objeto, cosa; (*in newspaper*) artículo; (*BRIT LAW: training*): **~s** *npl* contrato *sg* de aprendizaje; **~s of clothing** prendas *fpl* de vestir.

articles of association *npl* (*COMM*) estatutos *mpl* sociales, escritura social.

articulate *adj* [ɑː'tɪkjulɪt] (*speech*) claro; (*person*) que se expresa bien ♦ *vi* [ɑː'tɪkjuleɪt] articular.

articulated lorry *n* (*BRIT*) trailer *m*.

artifice ['ɑːtɪfɪs] *n* artificio, truco.

artificial [ɑːtɪ'fɪʃəl] *adj* artificial; (*teeth etc*) postizo.

artificial insemination *n* inseminación *f* artificial.

artificial intelligence (A.I.) *n* inteligencia artificial (I.A.).

artificial respiration *n* respiración *f* artificial.

artillery [ɑː'tɪlərɪ] *n* artillería.

artisan ['ɑːtɪzæn] *n* artesano/a.

artist ['ɑːtɪst] *n* artista *m/f*; (*MUS*) intérprete *m/f*.

artistic [ɑː'tɪstɪk] *adj* artístico.

artistry ['ɑːtɪstrɪ] *n* arte *m*, habilidad *f* (artística).

artless ['ɑːtlɪs] *adj* (*innocent*) natural, sencillo; (*clumsy*) torpe.

art school *n* escuela de bellas artes.

artwork ['ɑːtwəːk] *n* material *m* gráfico.

arty ['ɑːtɪ] *adj* artistoide.

ARV *n abbr* (= *American Revised Version*) *traducción americana de la Biblia*.

AS *n abbr* (*US UNIV*: = *Associate in/of Science*) *título universitario* ♦ *abbr* (*US*) = *American Samoa*.

━━━━━━━━━━━━━━━━━━━ *KEYWORD*

as [æz] *conj* **1** (*referring to time: while*) mientras; (*: when*) cuando; **she wept ~ she told her story** lloraba mientras contaba lo que le ocurrió; **~ the years go by** a medida que pasan los años, con el paso de los años; **he came in ~ I was leaving** entró cuando me marchaba; **~ from tomorrow** a partir de *or* desde mañana

2 (*in comparisons*): **~ big ~** tan grande como; **twice ~ big ~** el doble de grande que; **~ much money/many books ~** tanto dinero/tantos libros como; **~ soon ~** en cuanto, no bien (*LAM*)

3 (*since, because*) como, ya que; **~ I don't**

speak German I can't understand him
como no hablo alemán no le entiendo, no
le entiendo ya que no hablo alemán
4 (*although*): **much ~ I like them,** ...
aunque me gustan, ...
5 (*referring to manner, way*): **do ~ you
wish** haz lo que quieras; **~ she said** como
dijo; **he gave it to me ~ a present** me lo
dio de regalo; **it's on the left ~ you go in**
según se entra, a la izquierda
6 (*concerning*): **~ for** *or* **to that** por *or* en
lo que respecta a eso
7: **~ if** *or* **though** como si; **he looked ~ if
he was ill** parecía como si estuviera
enfermo, tenía aspecto de enfermo; *see
also* **long; such; well**
♦ *prep* (*in the capacity of*): **he works ~ a
barman** trabaja de barman; **~ chairman
of the company, he** ... como presidente de
la compañía, ...

ASA *n abbr* (= *American Standards
Association*) *instituto de normalización*;
(*BRIT*: = *Advertising Standards Authority*)
*departamento de control de la
publicidad*; (: = *Amateur Swimming
Association*) *federación amateur de
natación*.
a.s.a.p. *abbr* (= *as soon as possible*) cuanto
antes, lo más pronto posible.
asbestos [æz'bɛstəs] *n* asbesto, amianto.
ascend [ə'sɛnd] *vt* subir, ascender.
ascendancy [ə'sɛndənsɪ] *n* ascendiente *m*,
dominio.
ascendant [ə'sɛndənt] *n*: **to be in the ~**
estar en auge, ir ganando predominio.
Ascension [ə'sɛnʃən] *n*: **the ~** la Ascensión.
Ascension Island *n* Isla Ascensión.
ascent [ə'sɛnt] *n* subida; (*slope*) cuesta,
pendiente *f*; (*of plane*) ascenso.
ascertain [æsə'teɪn] *vt* averiguar.
ascetic [ə'sɛtɪk] *adj* ascético.
asceticism [ə'sɛtɪsɪzəm] *n* ascetismo.
ASCII ['æskiː] *n abbr* (= *American Standard
Code for Information Interchange*) ASCII.
ascribe [ə'skraɪb] *vt*: **to ~ sth to** atribuir
algo a.
ASCU *n abbr* (*US*) = *Association of State
Colleges and Universities*.
ASE *n abbr* = *American Stock Exchange*.
ASH [æʃ] *n abbr* (*BRIT*: = *Action on Smoking
and Health*) *organización anti-tabaco*.
ash [æʃ] *n* ceniza; (*tree*) fresno.
ashamed [ə'ʃeɪmd] *adj* avergonzado; **to be
~ of** avergonzarse de.
ashcan ['æʃkæn] *n* (*US*) cubo *or* bote *m*
(*LAM*) de la basura.
ashen ['æʃn] *adj* pálido.

ashore [ə'ʃɔː*] *adv* en tierra.
ashtray ['æʃtreɪ] *n* cenicero.
Ash Wednesday *n* miércoles *m* de ceniza.
Asia ['eɪʃə] *n* Asia.
Asian ['eɪʃən], **Asiatic** [eɪsɪ'ætɪk] *adj*, *n*
asiático/a *m/f*.
aside [ə'saɪd] *adv* a un lado ♦ *n* aparte *m*; **~
from** *prep* (*as well as*) aparte *or* además de.
ask [ɑːsk] *vt* (*question*) preguntar; (*demand*)
pedir; (*invite*) invitar ♦ *vi*: **to ~ about sth**
preguntar acerca de algo; **to ~ sb sth/to
do sth** preguntar algo a algn/pedir a algn
que haga algo; **to ~ sb about sth**
preguntar algo a algn; **to ~ (sb) a
question** hacer una pregunta (a algn); **to
~ sb the time** preguntar la hora a algn;
to ~ sb out to dinner invitar a cenar a
algn.
▶**ask after** *vt fus* preguntar por.
▶**ask for** *vt fus* pedir; **it's just ~ing for
trouble** *or* **for it** es buscarse problemas.
askance [ə'skɑːns] *adv*: **to look ~ at sb**
mirar con recelo a algn.
askew [ə'skjuː] *adv* sesgado, ladeado.
asking price *n* (*COMM*) precio inicial.
asleep [ə'sliːp] *adj* dormido; **to fall ~**
dormirse, quedarse dormido.
ASLEF ['æzlɛf] *n abbr* (*BRIT*: = *Associated
Society of Locomotive Engineers and
Firemen*) *sindicato de ferroviarios*.
asp [æsp] *n* áspid *m*.
asparagus [əs'pærəgəs] *n* espárragos *mpl*.
ASPCA *n abbr* = *American Society for the
Prevention of Cruelty to Animals*.
aspect ['æspɛkt] *n* aspecto, apariencia;
(*direction in which a building etc faces*)
orientación *f*.
aspersions [əs'pəːʃənz] *npl*: **to cast ~ on**
difamar a, calumniar a.
asphalt ['æsfælt] *n* asfalto.
asphyxiate [æs'fɪksɪeɪt] *vt* asfixiar.
asphyxiation [æsfɪksɪ'eɪʃən] *n* asfixia.
aspirate ['æspəreɪt] *vt* aspirar ♦ *adj*
['æspərɪt] aspirado.
aspirations [æspə'reɪʃənz] *npl* aspiraciones
fpl; (*ambition*) ambición *f*.
aspire [əs'paɪə*] *vi*: **to ~ to** aspirar a,
ambicionar.
aspirin ['æsprɪn] *n* aspirina.
aspiring [əs'paɪərɪŋ] *adj*: **an ~ actor** un
aspirante a actor.
ass [æs] *n* asno, burro; (*col*) imbécil *m/f*; (*US
col!*) culo, trasero.
assailant [ə'seɪlənt] *n* agresor(a) *m/f*.
assassin [ə'sæsɪn] *n* asesino/a.
assassinate [ə'sæsɪneɪt] *vt* asesinar.
assassination [əsæsɪ'neɪʃən] *n* asesinato.
assault [ə'sɔːlt] *n* (*gen: attack*) asalto,

agresión *f* ♦ *vt* asaltar, agredir; (*sexually*) violar.

assemble [ə'sɛmbl] *vt* reunir, juntar; (*TECH*) montar ♦ *vi* reunirse, juntarse.

assembler [ə'sɛmblə*] *n* (*COMPUT*) ensamblador *m*.

assembly [ə'sɛmblɪ] *n* (*meeting*) reunión *f*, asamblea; (*construction*) montaje *m*.

assembly language *n* (*COMPUT*) lenguaje *m* ensamblador.

assembly line *n* cadena de montaje.

assent [ə'sɛnt] *n* asentimiento, aprobación *f* ♦ *vi* consentir, asentir; **to ~ (to sth)** consentir (en algo).

assert [ə'sə:t] *vt* afirmar; (*insist on*) hacer valer; **to ~ o.s.** imponerse.

assertion [ə'sə:ʃən] *n* afirmación *f*.

assertive [ə'sə:tɪv] *adj* enérgico, agresivo, perentorio.

assess [ə'sɛs] *vt* valorar, calcular; (*tax, damages*) fijar; (*property etc: for tax*) gravar.

assessment [ə'sɛsmənt] *n* valoración *f*; gravamen *m*; (*judgment*): **~ (of)** juicio (sobre).

assessor [ə'sɛsə*] *n* asesor(a) *m/f*; (*of tax*) tasador(a) *m/f*.

asset ['æsɛt] *n* posesión *f*; (*quality*) ventaja; **~s** *npl* (*funds*) activo *sg*, fondos *mpl*.

asset-stripping ['æsɛt'strɪpɪŋ] *n* (*COMM*) acaparamiento de activos.

assiduous [ə'sɪdjuəs] *adj* asiduo.

assign [ə'saɪn] *vt* (*date*) fijar; (*task*) asignar; (*resources*) destinar; (*property*) traspasar.

assignment [ə'saɪnmənt] *n* asignación *f*; (*task*) tarea.

assimilate [ə'sɪmɪleɪt] *vt* asimilar.

assimilation [əsɪmɪ'leɪʃən] *n* asimilación *f*.

assist [ə'sɪst] *vt* ayudar.

assistance [ə'sɪstəns] *n* ayuda, auxilio.

assistant [ə'sɪstənt] *n* ayudante *m/f*; (*BRIT: also:* **shop ~**) dependiente/a *m/f*.

assistant manager *n* subdirector(a) *m/f*.

assizes [ə'saɪzɪz] *npl* sesión *f* de un tribunal.

associate [ə'səuʃɪɪt] *adj* asociado ♦ *n* socio/a, colega *m/f*; (*in crime*) cómplice *m/f*; (*member*) miembro/a ♦ *vb* [ə'səuʃɪeɪt] *vt* asociar; (*ideas*) relacionar ♦ *vi*: **to ~ with sb** tratar con alguien; **~ director** subdirector/a *m/f*; **~d company** compañía afiliada.

association [əsəusɪ'eɪʃən] *n* asociación *f*; (*COMM*) sociedad *f*; **in ~ with** en asociación con.

association football *n* (*BRIT*) fútbol *m*.

assorted [ə'sɔ:tɪd] *adj* surtido, variado; **in ~ sizes** en distintos tamaños.

assortment [ə'sɔ:tmənt] *n* surtido.

Asst. *abbr* = **Assistant**.

assuage [ə'sweɪdʒ] *vt* mitigar.

assume [ə'sju:m] *vt* (*suppose*) suponer; (*responsibilities etc*) asumir; (*attitude, name*) adoptar, tomar.

assumed name *n* nombre *m* falso.

assumption [ə'sʌmpʃən] *n* (*supposition*) suposición *f*, presunción *f*; (*act*) asunción *f*; **on the ~ that** suponiendo que.

assurance [ə'ʃuərəns] *n* garantía, promesa; (*confidence*) confianza, aplomo; (*BRIT: insurance*) seguro; **I can give you no ~s** no puedo hacerle ninguna promesa.

assure [ə'ʃuə*] *vt* asegurar.

assured [ə'ʃuəd] *adj* seguro.

assuredly [ə'ʃuərɪdlɪ] *adv* indudablemente.

AST *n abbr* (= *Atlantic Standard Time*) hora oficial del este del Canadá.

asterisk ['æstərɪsk] *n* asterisco.

astern [ə'stə:n] *adv* a popa.

asteroid ['æstərɔɪd] *n* asteroide *m*.

asthma ['æsmə] *n* asma.

asthmatic [æs'mætɪk] *adj*, *n* asmático/a *m/f*.

astigmatism [ə'stɪgmətɪzəm] *n* astigmatismo.

astir [ə'stə:*] *adv* en acción.

astonish [ə'stɒnɪʃ] *vt* asombrar, pasmar.

astonishing [ə'stɒnɪʃɪŋ] *adj* asombroso, pasmoso; **I find it ~ that** ... me asombra *or* pasma que ....

astonishingly [ə'stɒnɪʃɪŋlɪ] *adv* increíblemente, asombrosamente.

astonishment [ə'stɒnɪʃmənt] *n* asombro, sorpresa; **to my ~** con gran sorpresa mía.

astound [ə'staund] *vt* asombrar, pasmar.

astounding [ə'staundɪŋ] *adj* asombroso.

astray [ə'streɪ] *adv*: **to go ~** extraviarse; **to lead ~** llevar por mal camino; **to go ~ in one's calculations** equivocarse en sus cálculos.

astride [ə'straɪd] *prep* a caballo *or* horcajadas sobre.

astringent [əs'trɪndʒənt] *adj*, *n* astringente *m*.

astrologer [əs'trɒlədʒə*] *n* astrólogo/a.

astrology [əs'trɒlədʒɪ] *n* astrología.

astronaut ['æstrənɔ:t] *n* astronauta *m/f*.

astronomer [əs'trɒnəmə*] *n* astrónomo/a.

astronomical [æstrə'nɒmɪkəl] *adj* astronómico.

astronomy [əs'trɒnəmɪ] *n* astronomía.

astrophysics ['æstrəu'fɪzɪks] *n* astrofísica.

astute [əs'tju:t] *adj* astuto.

asunder [ə'sʌndə*] *adv*: **to tear ~** hacer pedazos.

ASV *n abbr* (= *American Standard Version*) traducción americana de la Biblia.

promotor(a) *m/f*.
backfire [bæk'faɪə*] *vi* (*AUT*) petardear;
(*plans*) fallar, salir mal.
backgammon ['bækgæmən] *n*
backgammon *m*.
background ['bækgraund] *n* fondo; (*of
events*) antecedentes *mpl*; (*basic
knowledge*) bases *fpl*; (*experience*)
conocimientos *mpl*, educación *f* ♦ *cpd*
(*noise, music*) de fondo; (*COMPUT*)
secundario; ~ **reading** lectura de
preparación; **family** ~ origen *m*,
antecedentes *mpl* familiares.
backhand ['bækhænd] *n* (*TENNIS: also:* ~
stroke) revés *m*.
backhanded ['bæk'hændɪd] *adj* (*fig*)
ambiguo, equívoco.
backhander ['bæk'hændə*] *n* (*BRIT: bribe*)
soborno.
backing ['bækɪŋ] *n* (*fig*) apoyo, respaldo;
(*COMM*) respaldo financiero; (*MUS*)
acompañamiento.
backlash ['bæklæʃ] *n* reacción *f* (en contra).
backlog ['bæklɔg] *n*: ~ **of work** trabajo
atrasado.
back number *n* (*of magazine etc*) número
atrasado.
backpack ['bækpæk] *n* mochila.
backpacker ['bækpækə*] *n* mochilero/a.
back pay *n* atrasos *mpl*.
backpedal ['bækpɛdl] *vi* (*fig*) volverse/
echarse atrás.
backseat driver ['bæksiːt-] *n* pasajero que
se empeña en aconsejar al conductor.
backside ['bæksaɪd] *n* (*col*) trasero.
backslash ['bækslæʃ] *n* pleca, barra
inversa.
backslide ['bækslaɪd] *vi* reincidir, recaer.
backspace ['bækspeɪs] *vi* (*in typing*)
retroceder.
backstage [bæk'steɪdʒ] *adv* entre
bastidores.
back-street ['bækstriːt] *adj* de barrio; ~
abortionist persona que practica abortos
clandestinos.
backstroke ['bækstrəuk] *n* espalda.
backtrack ['bæktræk] *vi* (*fig*) = **backpedal**.
backup ['bækʌp] *adj* (*train, plane*)
suplementario; (*COMPUT: disk, file*) de
reserva ♦ *n* (*support*) apoyo; (*also:* ~ **file**)
copia de reserva; (*US: congestion*)
embotellamiento, retención *f*.
back-up lights *npl* (*US*) luces *fpl* de marcha
atrás.
backward ['bækwəd] *adj* (*movement*) hacia
atrás; (*person, country*) atrasado; (*shy*)
tímido.
backwardness ['bækwədnɪs] *n* atraso.

backwards ['bækwədz] *adv* (*move, go*)
hacia atrás; (*read a list*) al revés; (*fall*) de
espaldas; **to know sth** ~ *or* (*US*) ~ **and
forwards** (*col*) saberse algo al dedillo.
backwater ['bækwɔːtə*] *n* (*fig*) lugar *m*
atrasado *or* apartado.
backyard [bæk'jɑːd] *n* patio trasero.
bacon ['beɪkən] *n* tocino, bacon *m*, beicon
m.
bacteria [bæk'tɪərɪə] *npl* bacterias *fpl*.
bacteriology [bæktɪərɪ'ɔlədʒɪ] *n*
bacteriología.
bad [bæd] *adj* malo; (*serious*) grave; (*meat,
food*) podrido, pasado; **to go** ~ pasarse;
to have a ~ **time of it** pasarlo mal; **I feel** ~
about it (*guilty*) me siento culpable; ~
debt (*COMM*) cuenta incobrable; **in** ~ **faith**
de mala fe.
baddie, baddy ['bædɪ] *n* (*col: CINE etc*)
malo/a.
bade [bæd, beɪd] *pt of* **bid**.
badge [bædʒ] *n* insignia; (*metal* ~) chapa;
(*of policeman*) placa; (*stick-on*) pegatina.
badger ['bædʒə*] *n* tejón *m*.
badly ['bædlɪ] *adv* (*work, dress etc*) mal; ~
wounded gravemente herido; **he needs it**
~ le hace mucha falta; **to be** ~ **off (for
money)** andar mal de dinero; **things are
going** ~ las cosas van muy mal.
bad-mannered ['bæd'mænəd] *adj* mal
educado.
badminton ['bædmɪntən] *n* bádminton *m*.
bad-tempered ['bæd'tɛmpəd] *adj* de mal
genio *or* carácter; (*temporary*) de mal
humor.
baffle ['bæfl] *vt* desconcertar, confundir.
baffling ['bæflɪŋ] *adj* incomprensible.
bag [bæg] *n* bolsa; (*handbag*) bolso; (*satchel*)
mochila; (*case*) maleta; (*of hunter*) caza
♦ *vt* (*col: take*) coger (*SP*), agarrar (*LAM*),
pescar; ~**s of** (*col: lots of*) un montón de;
to pack one's ~**s** hacer las maletas.
bagful ['bægful] *n* saco (lleno).
baggage ['bægɪdʒ] *n* equipaje *m*.
baggage claim *n* recogida de equipajes.
baggy ['bægɪ] *adj* (*trousers*) ancho, holgado.
Baghdad [bæg'dæd] *n* Bagdad *m*.
bag lady *n* (*col*) mujer *sin* hogar cargada
de bolsas.
bagpipes ['bægpaɪps] *npl* gaita *sg*.
bag-snatcher ['bægsnætʃə*] *n* (*BRIT*)
ladrón/ona *m/f* de bolsos.
bag-snatching ['bægsnætʃɪŋ] *n* (*BRIT*) tirón
m (de bolsos).
Bahamas [bə'hɑːməz] *npl*: **the** ~ las (Islas)
Bahama.
Bahrain [bɑː'reɪn] *n* Bahrein *m*.
bail [beɪl] *n* fianza ♦ *vt* (*prisoner: also: grant*

~ **to**) poner en libertad bajo fianza; (*boat*: *also*: ~ **out**) achicar; **on** ~ (*prisoner*) bajo fianza; **to be released on** ~ ser puesto en libertad bajo fianza; **to** ~ **sb out** pagar la fianza de algn; *see also* **bale**.

bailiff [ˈbeɪlɪf] *n* alguacil *m*.

bait [beɪt] *n* cebo ♦ *vt* poner el cebo en.

bake [beɪk] *vt* cocer (al horno) ♦ *vi* (*cook*) cocerse; (*be hot*) hacer un calor terrible.

baked beans *npl* judías *fpl* en salsa de tomate.

baker [ˈbeɪkə*] *n* panadero/a.

baker's dozen *n* docena del fraile.

bakery [ˈbeɪkərɪ] *n* (*for bread*) panadería; (*for cakes*) pastelería.

baking [ˈbeɪkɪŋ] *n* (*act*) cocción *f*; (*batch*) hornada.

baking powder *n* levadura (en polvo).

baking tin *n* molde *m* (para horno).

balaclava [bæləˈklɑːvə] *n* (*also*: ~ **helmet**) pasamontañas *m inv*.

balance [ˈbæləns] *n* equilibrio; (*COMM*: *sum*) balance *m*; (*remainder*) resto; (*scales*) balanza ♦ *vt* equilibrar; (*budget*) nivelar; (*account*) saldar; (*compensate*) compensar; ~ **of trade/payments** balanza de comercio/pagos; ~ **carried forward** balance *m* pasado a cuenta nueva; ~ **brought forward** saldo de hoja anterior; **to** ~ **the books** hacer el balance.

balanced [ˈbælənst] *adj* (*personality, diet*) equilibrado.

balance sheet *n* balance *m*.

balcony [ˈbælkənɪ] *n* (*open*) balcón *m*; (*closed*) galería.

bald [bɔːld] *adj* calvo; (*tyre*) liso.

baldness [ˈbɔːldnɪs] *n* calvicie *f*.

bale [beɪl] *n* (*AGR*) paca, fardo.

►**bale out** *vi* (*of a plane*) lanzarse en paracaídas ♦ *vt* (*NAUT*) achicar; **to** ~ **sb out of a difficulty** sacar a algn de un apuro.

Balearic Islands [bælɪˈærɪk-] *npl*: **the** ~ **las** (Islas) Baleares.

baleful [ˈbeɪlful] *adj* (*look*) triste; (*sinister*) funesto, siniestro.

balk [bɔːk] *vi*: **to** ~ (**at**) resistirse (a); (*horse*) plantarse (ante).

Balkan [ˈbɔːlkən] *adj* balcánico ♦ *n*: **the ~s** los Balcanes.

ball [bɔːl] *n* (*sphere*) bola; (*football*) balón *m*; (*for tennis, golf etc*) pelota; (*dance*) baile *m*; **to be on the** ~ (*fig*: *competent*) ser un enterado; (: *alert*) estar al tanto; **to play** ~ (**with sb**) jugar a la pelota (con algn); (*fig*) cooperar; **to start the** ~ **rolling** (*fig*) empezar; **the** ~ **is in your court** (*fig*) le toca a usted.

ballad [ˈbæləd] *n* balada, romance *m*.

ballast [ˈbæləst] *n* lastre *m*.

ball bearing *n* cojinete *m* de bolas.

ballcock [ˈbɔːlkɔk] *n* llave *f* de bola *or* de flotador.

ballerina [bæləˈriːnə] *n* bailarina.

ballet [ˈbæleɪ] *n* ballet *m*.

ballet dancer *n* bailarín/ina *m/f* (de ballet).

ballistic [bəˈlɪstɪk] *adj* balístico; **intercontinental** ~ **missile** misil *m* balístico intercontinental.

ballistics [bəˈlɪstɪks] *n* balística.

balloon [bəˈluːn] *n* globo; (*in comic strip*) bocadillo ♦ *vi* dispararse.

balloonist [bəˈluːnɪst] *n* aeróstata *m/f*.

ballot [ˈbælət] *n* votación *f*.

ballot box *n* urna (electoral).

ballot paper *n* papeleta.

ballpark [ˈbɔːlpɑːk] *n* (*US*) estadio de béisbol.

ball-point pen [ˈbɔːlpɔɪnt-] *n* bolígrafo.

ballroom [ˈbɔːlrum] *n* salón *m* de baile.

balm [bɑːm] *n* (*also fig*) bálsamo.

balmy [ˈbɑːmɪ] *adj* (*breeze, air*) suave; (*col*) = **barmy**.

BALPA [ˈbælpə] *n abbr* (= *British Airline Pilots' Association*) sindicato de pilotos de líneas aéreas.

balsa (wood) [ˈbɔːlsə-] *n* (madera de) balsa.

Baltic [ˈbɔːltɪk] *adj* báltico ♦ *n*: **the** ~ (**Sea**) el (Mar) Báltico.

balustrade [bæləstreɪd] *n* barandilla.

bamboo [bæmˈbuː] *n* bambú *m*.

bamboozle [bæmˈbuːzl] *vt* (*col*) embaucar, engatusar.

ban [bæn] *n* prohibición *f* ♦ *vt* prohibir; (*exclude*) excluir; **he was ~ned from driving** le retiraron el carnet de conducir.

banal [bəˈnɑːl] *adj* banal, vulgar.

banana [bəˈnɑːnə] *n* plátano, banana (*LAM*).

band [bænd] *n* (*group*) banda; (*gang*) pandilla; (*strip*) faja, tira; (*at a dance*) orquesta; (*MIL*) banda; (*rock* ~) grupo.

►**band together** *vi* juntarse, asociarse.

bandage [ˈbændɪdʒ] *n* venda, vendaje *m* ♦ *vt* vendar.

Band-Aid ® [ˈbændeɪd] *n* (*US*) tirita, curita (*LAM*).

bandit [ˈbændɪt] *n* bandido; **one-armed** ~ máquina tragaperras.

bandstand [ˈbændstænd] *n* quiosco de música.

bandwagon [ˈbændwægən] *n*: **to jump on the** ~ (*fig*) subirse al carro.

bandy [ˈbændɪ] *vt* (*jokes, insults*) intercambiar.

bandy-legged ['bændɪ'lɛgd] *adj* patizambo.
bane [beɪn] *n*: **it** (*or* **he** *etc*) **is the ~ of my life** me amarga la vida.
bang [bæŋ] *n* estallido; (*of door*) portazo; (*blow*) golpe *m* ♦ *vt* golpear ♦ *vi* estallar ♦ *adv*: **to be ~ on time** (*col*) llegar en punto; **to ~ the door** dar un portazo; **to ~ into sth** chocar con algo, golpearse contra algo; *see also* **bangs**.
banger ['bæŋə*] *n* (*BRIT: car: also*: **old ~**) armatoste *m*, cacharro; (*BRIT col: sausage*) salchicha; (*firework*) petardo.
Bangkok [bæŋ'kɔk] *n* Bangkok *m*.
Bangladesh [bæŋɡlə'dɛʃ] *n* Bangladesh *f*.
bangle ['bæŋɡl] *n* brazalete *m*, ajorca.
bangs [bæŋz] *npl* (*US*) flequillo *sg*.
banish ['bænɪʃ] *vt* desterrar.
banister(s) ['bænɪstə(z)] *n(pl)* barandilla *f*, pasamanos *m inv*.
banjo, *pl* **~es** *or* **~s** ['bændʒəu] *n* banjo.
bank [bæŋk] *n* (*COMM*) banco; (*of river, lake*) ribera, orilla; (*of earth*) terraplén *m* ♦ *vi* (*AVIAT*) ladearse; (*COMM*): **to ~ with** tener la cuenta en.
▶**bank on** *vt fus* contar con.
bank account *n* cuenta bancaria.
bank balance *n* saldo.
bank card *n* = **banker's card**.
bank charges *npl* comisión *fsg*.
bank draft *n* letra de cambio.
banker ['bæŋkə*] *n* banquero; **~'s card** (*BRIT*) tarjeta bancaria; **~'s order** orden *f* bancaria.
bank giro *n* giro bancario.
bank holiday *n* (*BRIT*) día *m* festivo *or* de fiesta.

El término **bank holiday** *se aplica en el Reino Unido a todo día festivo oficial en el que cierran bancos y comercios. Los más destacados coinciden con Navidad, Semana Santa, finales de mayo y finales de agosto. Al contrario que en los países de tradición católica, no se celebran las festividades dedicadas a los santos.*

---

banking ['bæŋkɪŋ] *n* banca.
bank loan *n* préstamo bancario.
bank manager *n* director(a) *m/f* (de sucursal) de banco.
banknote ['bæŋknəut] *n* billete *m* de banco.
bank rate *n* tipo de interés bancario.
bankrupt ['bæŋkrʌpt] *n* quebrado/a ♦ *adj* quebrado, insolvente; **to go ~** quebrar, hacer bancarrota; **to be ~** estar en quiebra.
bankruptcy ['bæŋkrʌptsɪ] *n* quiebra, bancarrota.

bank statement *n* extracto de cuenta.
banner ['bænə*] *n* bandera; (*in demonstration*) pancarta.
banns [bænz] *npl* amonestaciones *fpl*.
banquet ['bæŋkwɪt] *n* banquete *m*.
banter ['bæntə*] *n* guasa, bromas *fpl*.
BAOR *n abbr* (= *British Army of the Rhine*) *fuerzas británicas en Alemania*.
baptism ['bæptɪzəm] *n* bautismo; (*act*) bautizo.
baptize [bæp'taɪz] *vt* bautizar.
bar [bɑ:*] *n* barra; (*on door*) tranca; (*of window, cage*) reja; (*of soap*) pastilla; (*fig: hindrance*) obstáculo; (*prohibition*) prohibición *f*; (*pub*) bar *m*, cantina (*esp LAM*); (*counter: in pub*) barra, mostrador *m*; (*MUS*) barra ♦ *vt* (*road*) obstruir; (*window, door*) atrancar; (*person*) excluir; (*activity*) prohibir; **behind ~s** entre rejas; **the B~** (*LAW: profession*) la abogacía; (: *people*) el cuerpo de abogados; **~ none** sin excepción.
Barbados [bɑ:'beɪdɔs] *n* Barbados *m*.
barbarian [bɑ:'beərɪən] *n* bárbaro/a.
barbaric [bɑ:'bærɪk] *adj* bárbaro.
barbarity [bɑ:'bærɪtɪ] *n* barbaridad *f*.
barbarous ['bɑ:bərəs] *adj* bárbaro.
barbecue ['bɑ:bɪkju:] *n* barbacoa, asado (*LAM*).
barbed wire ['bɑ:bd-] *n* alambre *m* de espino.
barber ['bɑ:bə*] *n* peluquero, barbero.
barbiturate [bɑ:'bɪtjurɪt] *n* barbitúrico.
Barcelona [bɑ:sɪ'ləunə] *n* Barcelona.
bar chart *n* gráfico de barras.
bar code *n* código de barras.
bare [bɛə*] *adj* desnudo; (*head*) descubierto ♦ *vt* desnudar; **to ~ one's teeth** enseñar los dientes.
bareback ['bɛəbæk] *adv* a pelo.
barefaced ['bɛəfeɪst] *adj* descarado.
barefoot ['bɛəfut] *adj*, *adv* descalzo.
bareheaded [bɛə'hɛdɪd] *adj* descubierto, sin sombrero.
barely ['bɛəlɪ] *adv* apenas.
bareness ['bɛənɪs] *n* desnudez *f*.
Barents Sea ['bærənts-] *n*: **the ~** el Mar de Barents.
bargain ['bɑ:ɡɪn] *n* pacto; (*transaction*) negocio; (*good buy*) ganga ♦ *vi* negociar; (*haggle*) regatear; **into the ~** además, por añadidura.
▶**bargain for** *vt fus* (*col*): **he got more than he ~ed for** le resultó peor de lo que esperaba.
bargaining ['bɑ:ɡənɪŋ] *n* negociación *f*; regateo; **~ table** mesa de negociaciones.
bargaining position *n*: **to be in a strong/**

weak ~ estar/no estar en una posición de fuerza para negociar.

barge [bɑːdʒ] n barcaza.

▶**barge in** vi irrumpir; (*conversation*) entrometerse.

▶**barge into** vt fus dar contra.

baritone ['bærɪtəun] n barítono.

barium meal ['bɛərɪəm-] n (*MED*) sulfato de bario.

bark [bɑːk] n (*of tree*) corteza; (*of dog*) ladrido ♦ vi ladrar.

barley ['bɑːlɪ] n cebada.

barley sugar n azúcar m cande.

barmaid ['bɑːmeɪd] n camarera.

barman ['bɑːmən] n camarero, barman m.

barmy ['bɑːmɪ] adj (*col*) chiflado, chalado.

barn [bɑːn] n granero; (*for animals*) cuadra.

barnacle ['bɑːnəkl] n percebe m.

barn owl n lechuza.

barometer [bə'rɔmɪtə*] n barómetro.

baron ['bærən] n barón m; (*fig*) magnate m; **the press ~s** los magnates de la prensa.

baroness ['bærənɪs] n baronesa.

baroque [bə'rɔk] adj barroco.

barrack ['bærək] vt (*BRIT*) abuchear.

barracking ['bærəkɪŋ] n: **to give sb a ~** (*BRIT*) abuchear a algn.

barracks ['bærəks] npl cuartel msg.

barrage ['bærɑːʒ] n (*MIL*) cortina de fuego; (*dam*) presa; (*fig: of criticism etc*) lluvia, aluvión m; **a ~ of questions** una lluvia de preguntas.

barrel ['bærəl] n barril m; (*of wine*) tonel m, cuba; (*of gun*) cañón m.

barren ['bærən] adj estéril.

barricade [bærɪ'keɪd] n barricada ♦ vt cerrar con barricadas.

barrier ['bærɪə*] n barrera; (*crash* ~) barrera.

barrier cream n crema protectora.

barring ['bɑːrɪŋ] prep excepto, salvo.

barrister ['bærɪstə*] n (*BRIT*) abogado/a.

En el sistema legal inglés **barrister** es el abogado que se ocupa de defender los casos de sus clientes en los tribunales superiores. El equivalente escocés es **advocate**. Normalmente actúan según instrucciones de un **solicitor**, abogado de despacho que no toma parte activa en los juicios de dichos tribunales. El título de **barrister** lo otorga el órgano colegiado correspondiente, **the Inns of Court**.

barrow ['bærəu] n (*cart*) carretilla.

barstool ['bɑːstuːl] n taburete m (de bar).

Bart. abbr (*BRIT*) = baronet.

bartender ['bɑːtɛndə*] n (*US*) camarero,

barman m.

barter ['bɑːtə*] vt: **to ~ sth for sth** trocar algo por algo.

base [beɪs] n base f ♦ vt: **to ~ sth on** basar or fundar algo en ♦ adj bajo, infame; **to ~ at** (*troops*) estacionar en; **I'm ~d in London** (*work*) trabajo en Londres.

baseball ['beɪsbɔːl] n béisbol m.

base camp n campamento base.

Basel ['bɑːzəl] n Basilea.

baseless ['beɪslɪs] adj infundado.

baseline ['beɪslaɪn] n (*TENNIS*) línea de fondo.

basement ['beɪsmənt] n sótano.

base rate n tipo base.

bases ['beɪsiːz] npl of **basis**; ['beɪsɪz] npl of **base**.

bash [bæʃ] n: **I'll have a ~ (at it)** lo intentaré ♦ vt (*col*) golpear.

▶**bash up** vt (*col: car*) destrozar; (: *person*) aporrear, vapulear.

bashful ['bæʃful] adj tímido, vergonzoso.

bashing ['bæʃɪŋ] n (*col*) paliza; **to go Paki-/queer-~** ir a dar una paliza a los paquistaníes/a los maricas.

BASIC ['beɪsɪk] n BASIC m.

basic ['beɪsɪk] adj (*salary etc*) básico; (*elementary: principles*) fundamental.

basically ['beɪsɪklɪ] adv fundamentalmente, en el fondo.

basic rate n (*of tax*) base f mínima imponible.

basil ['bæzl] n albahaca.

basin ['beɪsn] n (*vessel*) cuenco, tazón m; (*GEO*) cuenca; (*also:* **wash~**) palangana, jofaina; (*in bathroom*) lavabo.

basis ['beɪsɪs], pl **-ses** [-siːz] n base f; **on the ~ of what you've said** en base a lo que has dicho.

bask [bɑːsk] vi: **to ~ in the sun** tomar el sol.

basket ['bɑːskɪt] n cesta, cesto.

basketball ['bɑːskɪtbɔːl] n baloncesto.

basketball player n jugador(a) m/f de baloncesto.

basketwork ['bɑːskɪtwəːk] n cestería.

Basle [bɑːl] n Basilea.

basmati rice [bəz'mætɪ-] n arroz m basmati.

Basque [bæsk] adj, n vasco/a m/f.

Basque Country n Euskadi m, País m Vasco.

bass [beɪs] n (*MUS*) bajo.

bass clef n clave f de fa.

bassoon [bə'suːn] n fagot m.

bastard ['bɑːstəd] n bastardo/a; (*col!*) cabrón m, hijo de puta (*!*).

baste [beɪst] vt (*CULIN*) rociar (con su salsa).

bastion ['bæstɪən] *n* bastión *m*, baluarte *m*.
bat [bæt] *n* (ZOOL) murciélago; (for ball games) palo; (for cricket, baseball) bate *m*; (BRIT: for table tennis) pala; **he didn't ~ an eyelid** ni pestañeó, ni se inmutó.
batch [bætʃ] *n* lote *m*, remesa; (of bread) hornada.
batch processing *n* (COMPUT) proceso por lotes.
bated ['beɪtɪd] *adj*: **with ~ breath** sin respirar.
bath [bɑːθ, *pl* bɑːðz] *n* (action) baño; (~tub) bañera, tina (esp LAM) ♦ *vt* bañar; **to have a ~** bañarse, darse un baño; *see also* **baths**.
bathchair ['bɑːθtʃɛə*] *n* silla de ruedas.
bathe [beɪð] *vi* bañarse; (US) darse un baño, bañarse ♦ *vt* (wound etc) lavar; (US) bañar, dar un baño a.
bather ['beɪðə*] *n* bañista *m/f*.
bathing ['beɪðɪŋ] *n* baño.
bathing cap *n* gorro de baño.
bathing costume, (US) **bathing suit** *n* bañador *m*, traje *m* de baño.
bathing trunks *npl* bañador *m* *msg*.
bathmat ['bɑːθmæt] *n* alfombrilla de baño.
bathrobe ['bɑːθrəub] *n* albornoz *m*.
bathroom ['bɑːθrum] *n* (cuarto de) baño.
baths [bɑːðz] *npl* piscina *sg*.
bath towel *n* toalla de baño.
bathtub ['bɑːθtʌb] *n* bañera.
batman ['bætmən] *n* (BRIT) ordenanza *m*.
baton ['bætən] *n* (MUS) batuta.
battalion [bə'tælɪən] *n* batallón *m*.
batten ['bætn] *n* (CARPENTRY) listón *m*; (NAUT) junquillo, sable *m*.
▶**batten down** *vt* (NAUT): **to ~ down the hatches** atrancar las escotillas.
batter ['bætə*] *vt* maltratar, apalear; (subj: wind, rain) azotar ♦ *n* batido.
battered ['bætəd] *adj* (hat, pan) estropeado.
battery ['bætərɪ] *n* batería; (of torch) pila.
battery charger *n* cargador de baterías.
battery farming *n* cría intensiva.
battle ['bætl] *n* batalla; (fig) lucha ♦ *vi* luchar; **that's half the ~** (col) ya hay medio camino andado; **to fight a losing ~** (fig) luchar por una causa perdida.
battlefield ['bætlfiːld] *n* campo *m* de batalla.
battlements ['bætlmənts] *npl* almenas *fpl*.
battleship ['bætlʃɪp] *n* acorazado.
batty ['bætɪ] *adj* (col: person) chiflado; (: idea) de chiflado.
bauble ['bɔːbl] *n* chuchería.
baud [bɔːd] *n* (COMPUT) baudio.
baud rate *n* (COMPUT) velocidad *f* (de transmisión) en baudios.
bauxite ['bɔːksaɪt] *n* bauxita.

Bavaria [bə'vɛərɪə] *n* Baviera.
Bavarian [bə'vɛərɪən] *adj*, *n* bávaro/a *m/f*.
bawdy ['bɔːdɪ] *adj* indecente; (joke) verde.
bawl [bɔːl] *vi* chillar, gritar.
bay [beɪ] *n* (GEO) bahía; (for parking) parking *m*, estacionamiento; (loading ~) patio de carga; (BOT) laurel *m* ♦ *vi* aullar; **to hold sb at ~** mantener a alguien a raya.
bay leaf *n* (hoja de) laurel *m*.
bayonet ['beɪənɪt] *n* bayoneta.
bay window *n* ventana salediza.
bazaar [bə'zɑː*] *n* bazar *m*.
bazooka [bə'zuːkə] *n* bazuca.
BB *n abbr* (BRIT: = Boys' Brigade) organización juvenil para chicos.
B. & B. *n abbr* = **bed and breakfast**.
BBB *n abbr* (US: = Better Business Bureau) organismo para la defensa del consumidor.
BBC *n abbr* (= British Broadcasting Corporation) BBC *f*.

*La **BBC** es el organismo público británico de radio y televisión, autónomo en cuanto a su política de programas pero regulado por un estatuto (**BBC charter**) que ha de aprobar el Parlamento. Tiene dos cadenas nacionales de televisión (**BBC1** y **BBC2**) y un servicio mundial de televisión (**World Service TV**), así como cinco cadenas de radio nacional, numerosas de radio local y una mundial (**World Service**), en varios idiomas. A no tener publicidad, se financia a través de operaciones comerciales paralelas y del cobro de una licencia anual obligatoria (**TV licence**) para los que tienen aparato de televisión.*

BC *ad abbr* (= before Christ) a. de J.C. ♦ *abbr* (Canada) = British Columbia.
BCG *n abbr* (= Bacillus Calmette-Guérin) vacuna de la tuberculosis.
BD *n abbr* (= Bachelor of Divinity) Licenciado/a en Teología.
B/D *abbr* = **bank draft**.
BDS *n abbr* (= Bachelor of Dental Surgery) título universitario.

═══════════════════════ *KEYWORD*

be [biː] (*pt* **was, were**, *pp* **been**) *aux vb* **1** (with present participle: forming continuous tenses): **what are you doing?** ¿qué estás haciendo?, ¿qué haces?; **they're coming tomorrow** vienen mañana; **I've been waiting for you for hours** llevo horas esperándote

2 (with pp: forming passives) ser (but often

replaced by active or reflexive constructions);
to ~ murdered ser asesinado; **the box
had been opened** habían abierto la caja;
the thief was nowhere to ~ seen no se
veía al ladrón por ninguna parte
3 (in tag questions): **it was fun, wasn't it?**
fue divertido, ¿no? or ¿verdad?; **he's
good-looking, isn't he?** es guapo, ¿no te
parece?; **she's back again, is she?**
entonces, ¿ha vuelto?
4 (+to +infin): **the house is to ~ sold**
(necessity) hay que vender la casa;
(future) van a vender la casa; **he's not to
open it** no tiene que abrirlo; **he was to
have come yesterday** debía de haber
venido ayer; **am I to understand that ...?**
¿debo entender que ...?
♦ vb +complement **1** (with n or num
complement) ser; **he's a doctor** es médico;
2 and 2 are 4 2 y 2 son 4
2 (with adj complement: expressing
permanent or inherent quality) ser;
(: expressing state seen as temporary or
reversible) estar; **I'm English** soy inglés/
esa; **she's tall/pretty** es alta/bonita; **he's
young** es joven; ~ **careful/good/quiet** ten
cuidado/pórtate bien/cállate; **I'm tired**
estoy cansado/a; **I'm warm** tengo calor;
it's dirty está sucio/a
3 (of health) estar; **how are you?** ¿cómo
estás?; **he's very ill** está muy enfermo;
I'm better now ya estoy mejor
4 (of age) tener; **how old are you?**
¿cuántos años tienes?; **I'm sixteen (years
old)** tengo dieciséis años
5 (cost) costar; ser; **how much was the
meal?** ¿cuánto fue or costó la comida?;
that'll ~ £5.75, please son £5.75, por
favor; **this shirt is £17** esta camisa cuesta
£17
♦ vi **1** (exist, occur etc) existir, haber; **the
best singer that ever was** el mejor
cantante que existió jamás; **is there a
God?** ¿hay un Dios?, ¿existe Dios?; ~
that as it may sea como sea; **so ~ it** así
sea
2 (referring to place) estar; **I won't ~ here
tomorrow** no estaré aquí mañana
3 (referring to movement): **where have you
been?** ¿dónde has estado?
♦ impers vb **1** (referring to time): **it's 5
o'clock** son las 5; **it's the 28th of April**
estamos a 28 de abril
2 (referring to distance): **it's 10 km to the
village** el pueblo está a 10 km
3 (referring to the weather): **it's too hot/
cold** hace demasiado calor/frío; **it's
windy today** hace viento hoy

4 (emphatic): **it's me** soy yo; **it was Maria
who paid the bill** fue María la que pagó la
cuenta.

B/E abbr = **bill of exchange.**
beach [biːtʃ] n playa ♦ vt varar.
beach buggy [-bʌgɪ] n buggy m.
beachcomber ['biːtʃkəumə*] n raquero/a.
beachwear ['biːtʃwɛə*] n ropa de playa.
beacon ['biːkən] n (lighthouse) faro;
(marker) guía; (radio ~) radiofaro.
bead [biːd] n cuenta, abalorio; (of dew,
sweat) gota; ~**s** npl (necklace) collar m.
beady ['biːdɪ] adj (eyes) pequeño y
brillante.
beagle ['biːgl] n sabueso pequeño, beagle
m.
beak [biːk] n pico.
beaker ['biːkə*] n vaso.
beam [biːm] n (ARCH) viga; (of light) rayo,
haz m de luz; (RADIO) rayo ♦ vi brillar;
(smile) sonreír; **to drive on full** or **main** ~
conducir con las luces largas.
beaming ['biːmɪŋ] adj (sun, smile) radiante.
bean [biːn] n judía, fríjol/frijol m (esp LAM);
runner/broad ~ habichuela/haba; **coffee**
~ grano de café.
beanpole ['biːnpəul] n (col) espárrago.
beansprouts ['biːnsprauts] npl brotes mpl
de soja.
bear [bɛə*] n oso; (STOCK EXCHANGE) bajista
m ♦ (vb: pt **bore**, pp **borne**) vt (weight etc)
llevar; (cost) pagar; (responsibility) tener;
(traces, signs) mostrar; (produce: fruit) dar;
(COMM: interest) devengar; (endure)
soportar, aguantar; (stand up to) resistir
a; (children) tener, dar a luz ♦ vi: **to ~
right/left** torcer a la derecha/izquierda; **I
can't ~ him** no le puedo ver, no lo
soporto; **to bring pressure to ~ on sb**
ejercer presión sobre algn.
▶**bear on** vt fus tener que ver con,
referirse a.
▶**bear out** vt fus (suspicions) corroborar,
confirmar; (person) confirmar lo dicho
por.
▶**bear up** vi (cheer up) animarse; **he bore
up well under the strain** resistió bien la
presión.
▶**bear with** vt fus (sb's moods, temper)
tener paciencia con.
bearable ['bɛərəbl] adj soportable,
aguantable.
beard [bɪəd] n barba.
bearded ['bɪədɪd] adj con barba.
bearer ['bɛərə*] n (of news, cheque)
portador(a) m/f; (of passport) titular m/f.
bearing ['bɛərɪŋ] n porte m; (connection)

relación *f*; **(ball)** ~**s** *npl* cojinetes *mpl* a
bolas; **to take a** ~ marcarse; **to find one's**
~**s** orientarse.
bearskin ['bɛəskɪn] *n* (*MIL*) gorro militar
(*de piel de oso*).
beast [biːst] *n* bestia; (*col*) bruto, salvaje *m*.
beastly ['biːstlɪ] *adj* bestial; (*awful*)
horrible.
beat [biːt] *n* (*of heart*) latido; (*MUS*) ritmo,
compás *m*; (*of policeman*) ronda ♦ (*vb*: *pt*
beat, *pp* **beaten**) *vt* (*hit*) golpear; (*eggs*)
batir; (*defeat*) vencer, derrotar; (*better*)
sobrepasar; (*drum*) tocar; (*rhythm*)
marcar ♦ *vi* (*heart*) latir; **off the** ~**en track**
aislado; **to** ~ **about the bush** andarse con
rodeos; **to** ~ **it** largarse; **that** ~**s**
everything! (*col*) ¡eso es el colmo!; **to** ~
on a door dar golpes en una puerta.
▶**beat down** *vt* (*door*) derribar a golpes;
(*price*) conseguir rebajar, regatear;
(*seller*) hacer rebajar el precio ♦ *vi* (*rain*)
llover a cántaros; (*sun*) caer de plomo.
▶**beat off** *vt* rechazar.
▶**beat up** *vt* (*col*: *person*) dar una paliza a.
beater ['biːtə*] *n* (*for eggs, cream*) batidora.
beating ['biːtɪŋ] *n* paliza, golpiza (*LAM*); **to**
take a ~ recibir una paliza.
beat-up ['biːt'ʌp] *adj* (*col*) destartalado.
beautiful ['bjuːtɪful] *adj* hermoso, bello,
lindo (*esp LAM*).
beautifully ['bjuːtɪfəlɪ] *adv* de maravilla.
beautify ['bjuːtɪfaɪ] *vt* embellecer.
beauty ['bjuːtɪ] *n* belleza, hermosura;
(*concept, person*) belleza; **the** ~ **of it is**
that ... lo mejor de esto es que ....
beauty contest *n* concurso de belleza.
beauty queen *n* reina de la belleza.
beauty salon *n* salón *m* de belleza.
beauty sleep *n*: **to get one's** ~ *no perder*
horas de sueño.
beauty spot *n* lunar *m* postizo; (*BRIT*:
TOURISM) lugar *m* pintoresco.
beaver ['biːvə*] *n* castor *m*.
becalmed [bɪ'kɑːmd] *adj* encalmado.
became [bɪ'keɪm] *pt of* **become**.
because [bɪ'kɔz] *conj* porque; ~ **of** *prep*
debido a, a causa de.
beck [bɛk] *n*: **to be at the** ~ **and call of** estar
a disposición de.
beckon ['bɛkən] *vt* (*also*: ~ **to**) llamar con
señas.
become [bɪ'kʌm] (*irreg*: *like* **come**) *vi*
(+ *noun*) hacerse, llegar a ser; (+ *adj*)
ponerse, volverse ♦ *vt* (*suit*) favorecer,
sentar bien a; **to** ~ **fat** engordar; **to** ~
angry enfadarse; **it became known that** ...
se descubrió que ....
becoming [bɪ'kʌmɪŋ] *adj* (*behaviour*)

decoroso; (*clothes*) favorecedor(a).
becquerel [bɛkə'rɛl] *n* becquerelio.
BECTU *n abbr* (*BRIT*) = *Broadcasting*
Entertainment Cinematographic and Theatre
Union.
BEd *n abbr* (= *Bachelor of Education*) *título*
universitario; see also **Bachelor's Degree.**
bed [bɛd] *n* cama; (*of flowers*) macizo; (*of*
sea, lake) fondo; (*of coal, clay*) capa; **to go**
to ~ acostarse.
▶**bed down** *vi* acostarse.
bed and breakfast (B & B) *n* ≈ pensión *f*.

> *Se llama* **Bed and Breakfast** *a la casa de*
> *hospedaje particular, o granja si es en el*
> *campo, que ofrece cama y desayuno a*
> *tarifas inferiores a las de un hotel. El*
> *servicio se suele anunciar con carteles*
> *colocados en las ventanas del*
> *establecimiento, en el jardín o en la*
> *carretera y en ellos aparece a menudo*
> *únicamente el símbolo* **B & B.**

bedbug ['bɛdbʌg] *n* chinche *f*.
bedclothes ['bɛdkləuðz] *npl* ropa de cama.
bedding ['bɛdɪŋ] *n* ropa de cama.
bedeck [bɪ'dɛk] *vt* engalanar, adornar.
bedevil [bɪ'dɛvl] *vt* (*dog*) acosar; (*trouble*)
fastidiar.
bedfellow ['bɛdfɛləu] *n*: **they are strange**
~**s** (*fig*) hacen una pareja rara.
bedlam ['bɛdləm] *n* confusión *f*.
bedpan ['bɛdpæn] *n* cuña.
bedraggled [bɪ'drægld] *adj* desastrado.
bedridden ['bɛdrɪdn] *adj* postrado (en
cama).
bedrock ['bɛdrɔk] *n* (*GEO*) roca firme; (*fig*)
pilar *m*.
bedroom ['bɛdrum] *n* dormitorio, alcoba.
Beds *abbr* (*BRIT*) = *Bedfordshire.*
bed settee *n* sofá-cama *m*.
bedside ['bɛdsaɪd] *n*: **at sb's** ~ a la
cabecera de alguien.
bedside lamp *n* lámpara de noche.
bedsit(ter) ['bɛdsɪt(ə*)] *n* (*BRIT*) estudio.
bedspread ['bɛdsprɛd] *n* cubrecama *m*,
colcha.
bedtime ['bɛdtaɪm] *n* hora de acostarse;
it's ~ es hora de acostarse *or* de irse a la
cama.
bee [biː] *n* abeja; **to have a** ~ **in one's**
bonnet (about sth) tener una idea fija (de
algo).
beech [biːtʃ] *n* haya.
beef [biːf] *n* carne *f* de vaca; **roast** ~ rosbif
m.
▶**beef up** *vt* (*col*) reforzar.
beefburger ['biːfbəːgə*] *n* hamburguesa.

beefeater ['biːfiːtə*] *n alabardero de la Torre de Londres.*
beehive ['biːhaɪv] *n* colmena.
bee-keeping ['biːkiːpɪŋ] *n* apicultura.
beeline ['biːlaɪn] *n*: **to make a ~ for** ir derecho a.
been [biːn] *pp of* **be.**
beep [biːp] *n* pitido ♦ *vi* pitar.
beeper ['biːpə*] *n* (*of doctor etc*) busca *m inv.*
beer [bɪə*] *n* cerveza.
beer belly *n* (*col*) barriga (*de bebedor de cerveza*).
beer can *n* bote *m or* lata de cerveza.
beet [biːt] *n* (*US*) remolacha.
beetle ['biːtl] *n* escarabajo.
beetroot ['biːtruːt] *n* (*BRIT*) remolacha.
befall [bɪ'fɔːl] *vi* (*vt*) (*irreg: like* **fall**) acontecer (a).
befit [bɪ'fɪt] *vt* convenir a, corresponder a.
before [bɪ'fɔː*] *prep* (*of time*) antes de; (*of space*) delante de ♦ *conj* antes (de) que ♦ *adv* (*time*) antes; (*space*) delante, adelante; **~ going** antes de marcharse; **~ she goes** antes de que se vaya; **the week ~** la semana anterior; **I've never seen it ~** no lo he visto nunca.
beforehand [bɪ'fɔːhænd] *adv* de antemano, con anticipación.
befriend [bɪ'frɛnd] *vt* ofrecer amistad a.
befuddled [bɪ'fʌdld] *adj* aturdido, atontado.
beg [bɛg] *vi* pedir limosna, mendigar ♦ *vt* pedir, rogar; (*entreat*) suplicar; **I ~ your pardon** (*apologising*) perdóneme; (*not hearing*) ¿perdón?
began [bɪ'gæn] *pt of* **begin.**
beggar ['bɛgə*] *n* mendigo/a.
begin, *pt* **began,** *pp* **begun** [bɪ'gɪn, -gæn, -gʌn] *vt, vi* empezar, comenzar; **to ~ doing** *or* **to do sth** empezar a hacer algo; **I can't ~ to thank you** no encuentro palabras para agradecerle; **to ~ with,** **I'd like to know ...** en primer lugar, quisiera saber ...; **~ning from Monday** a partir del lunes.
beginner [bɪ'gɪnə*] *n* principiante *m/f.*
beginning [bɪ'gɪnɪŋ] *n* principio, comienzo; **right from the ~** desde el principio.
begrudge [bɪ'grʌdʒ] *vt*: **to ~ sb sth** tenerle envidia a alguien por algo.
beguile [bɪ'gaɪl] *vt* (*enchant*) seducir.
beguiling [bɪ'gaɪlɪŋ] *adj* seductor(a), atractivo.
begun [bɪ'gʌn] *pp of* **begin.**
behalf [bɪ'hɑːf] *n*: **on ~ of,** (*US*) **in ~ of** en nombre de; (*for benefit of*) por.
behave [bɪ'heɪv] *vi* (*person*) portarse, comportarse; (*thing*) funcionar; (*well: also:* **~ o.s.**) portarse bien.
behaviour, (*US*) **behavior** [bɪ'heɪvjə*] *n*

comportamiento, conducta.
behead [bɪ'hɛd] *vt* decapitar.
beheld [bɪ'hɛld] *pt, pp of* **behold.**
behind [bɪ'haɪnd] *prep* detrás de ♦ *adv* detrás, por detrás, atrás ♦ *n* trasero; **to be ~ (schedule)** ir retrasado; **~ the scenes** (*fig*) entre bastidores; **we're ~ them in technology** (*fig*) nos dejan atrás en tecnología; **to leave sth ~** olvidar *or* dejar algo; **to be ~ with sth** estar atrasado en algo; **to be ~ with payments (on sth)** estar atrasado en el pago (de algo).
behold [bɪ'həuld] (*irreg: like* **hold**) *vt* contemplar.
beige [beɪʒ] *adj* (*color*) beige.
being ['biːɪŋ] *n* ser *m*; **to come into ~** nacer, aparecer.
Beirut [beɪ'ruːt] *n* Beirut *m.*
Belarus [bɛlə'rus] *n* Bielorrusia.
Belarussian [bɛlə'rʌʃən] *adj, n* bielorruso/a ♦ *n* (*LING*) bielorruso.
belated [bɪ'leɪtɪd] *adj* atrasado, tardío.
belch [bɛltʃ] *vi* eructar ♦ *vt* (*also:* **~ out:** *smoke etc*) vomitar, arrojar.
beleaguered [bɪ'liːgəd] *adj* asediado.
Belfast ['bɛlfɑːst] *n* Belfast *m.*
belfry ['bɛlfrɪ] *n* campanario.
Belgian ['bɛldʒən] *adj, n* belga *m/f.*
Belgium ['bɛldʒəm] *n* Bélgica.
Belgrade [bɛl'greɪd] *n* Belgrado.
belie [bɪ'laɪ] *vt* (*give false impression of*) desmentir, contradecir.
belief [bɪ'liːf] *n* (*opinion*) opinión *f*; (*trust, faith*) fe *f*; (*acceptance as true*) creencia; **it's beyond ~** es increíble; **in the ~ that** creyendo que.
believable [bɪ'liːvəbl] *adj* creíble.
believe [bɪ'liːv] *vt, vi* creer; **to ~ (that)** creer (que); **to ~ in** (*God, ghosts*) creer en; (*method*) ser partidario de; **he is ~d to be abroad** se cree que está en el extranjero; **I don't ~ in corporal punishment** no soy partidario del castigo corporal.
believer [bɪ'liːvə*] *n* (*in idea, activity*) partidario/a; (*REL*) creyente *m/f*, fiel *m/f.*
belittle [bɪ'lɪtl] *vt* despreciar.
Belize [bɛ'liːz] *n* Belice *f.*
bell [bɛl] *n* campana; (*small*) campanilla; (*on door*) timbre *m*; (*animal's*) cencerro; (*on toy etc*) cascabel *m*; **that rings a ~** (*fig*) eso me suena.
bellboy ['bɛlbɔɪ] *n*, (*US*) **bellhop** ['bɛlhɔp] *n* botones *m inv.*
belligerent [bɪ'lɪdʒərənt] *adj* (*at war*) beligerante; (*fig*) agresivo.

bellow ['bɛləu] vi bramar; (person) rugir
♦ vt (orders) gritar.
bellows ['bɛləuz] npl fuelle msg.
bell push n pulsador m de timbre.
belly ['bɛlɪ] n barriga, panza.
bellyache ['bɛlɪeɪk] n dolor m de barriga or
de tripa ♦ vi (col) gruñir.
bellyful ['bɛlɪful] n: **to have had a ~ of ...**
(col) estar más que harto de ....
belong [bɪ'lɒŋ] vi: **to ~ to** pertenecer a;
(club etc) ser socio de; **this book ~s here**
este libro va aquí.
belongings [bɪ'lɒŋɪŋz] npl: **personal ~**
pertenencias fpl.
Belorussia [bɛləu'rʌʃə] n Bielorrusia.
Belorussian [bɛləu'rʌʃən] adj, n =
Belarussian.
beloved [bɪ'lʌvɪd] adj, n querido/a m/f,
amado/a m/f.
below [bɪ'ləu] prep bajo, debajo de ♦ adv
abajo, (por) debajo; **see ~** véase más
abajo.
belt [bɛlt] n cinturón m; (TECH) correa,
cinta ♦ vt (thrash) golpear con correa;
industrial ~ cinturón industrial.
►**belt out** vt (song) cantar a voz en grito or
a grito pelado.
►**belt up** vi (AUT) ponerse el cinturón de
seguridad; (fig, col) cerrar el pico.
beltway ['bɛltweɪ] n (US AUT) carretera de
circunvalación.
bemoan [bɪ'məun] vt lamentar.
bemused [bɪ'mju:zd] adj perplejo.
bench [bɛntʃ] n banco; **the B~** (LAW) el
tribunal; (people) la judicatura.
bench mark n punto de referencia.
bend [bɛnd] vb (pt, pp **bent** [bɛnt]) vt doblar;
(body, head) inclinar ♦ vi inclinarse; (road)
curvarse ♦ n (BRIT: in road, river) recodo;
(in pipe) codo; see also **bends.**
►**bend down** vi inclinarse, doblarse.
►**bend over** vi inclinarse.
bends [bɛndz] npl (MED) apoplejía por
cambios bruscos de presión.
beneath [bɪ'ni:θ] prep bajo, debajo de;
(unworthy of) indigno de ♦ adv abajo, (por)
debajo.
benefactor ['bɛnɪfæktə*] n bienhechor m.
benefactress ['bɛnɪfæktrɪs] n bienhechora.
beneficial [bɛnɪ'fɪʃəl] adj: **~ to** beneficioso
para.
beneficiary [bɛnɪ'fɪʃərɪ] n (LAW)
beneficiario/a.
benefit ['bɛnɪfɪt] n beneficio, provecho;
(allowance of money) subsidio ♦ vt
beneficiar ♦ vi: **he'll ~ from it** le sacará
provecho; **unemployment ~** subsidio de
desempleo.

Benelux ['bɛnɪlʌks] n Benelux m.
benevolence [bɪ'nɛvələns] n benevolencia.
benevolent [bɪ'nɛvələnt] adj benévolo.
BEng n abbr (= Bachelor of Engineering)
título universitario.
benign [bɪ'naɪn] adj (person, MED) benigno;
(smile) afable.
bent [bɛnt] pt, pp of **bend** ♦ n inclinación f
♦ adj (wire, pipe) doblado, torcido; **to be**
~ on estar empeñado en.
bequeath [bɪ'kwi:ð] vt legar.
bequest [bɪ'kwɛst] n legado.
bereaved [bɪ'ri:vd] adj afligido ♦ n: **the ~**
los afligidos mpl.
bereavement [bɪ'ri:vmənt] n aflicción f.
beret ['bɛreɪ] n boina.
Bering Sea ['bɛərɪŋ-] n: **the ~** el Mar de
Bering.
berk [bə:k] n (BRIT col) capullo/a (!).
Berks abbr (BRIT) = Berkshire.
Berlin [bə:'lɪn] n Berlín m; **East/West ~**
Berlín del Este/Oeste.
berm [bə:m] n (US AUT) arcén m.
Bermuda [bə:'mju:də] n las (Islas)
Bermudas.
Bermuda shorts npl bermudas mpl or fpl.
Bern [bə:n] n Berna.
berry ['bɛrɪ] n baya.
berserk [bə'sə:k] adj: **to go ~** perder los
estribos.
berth [bə:θ] n (bed) litera; (cabin) camarote
m; (for ship) amarradero ♦ vi atracar,
amarrar; **to give sb a wide ~** (fig) evitar
encontrarse con algn.
beseech, pt, pp **besought** [bɪ'si:tʃ, -'sɔ:t] vt
suplicar.
beset, pt, pp **beset** [bɪ'sɛt] vt (person) acosar
♦ adj: **a policy ~ with dangers** una política
rodeada de peligros.
besetting [bɪ'sɛtɪŋ] adj: **his ~ sin** su
principal falta.
beside [bɪ'saɪd] prep junto a, al lado de;
(compared with) comparado con; **to be ~**
o.s. with anger estar fuera de sí; **that's ~**
the point eso no tiene nada que ver con
el asunto.
besides [bɪ'saɪdz] adv además ♦ prep (as well
as) además de; (except) excepto.
besiege [bɪ'si:dʒ] vt (town) sitiar; (fig)
asediar.
besmirch [bɪ'smə:tʃ] vt (fig) manchar,
mancillar.
besotted [bɪ'sɒtɪd] adj: **~ with** chiflado por.
bespoke [bɪ'spəuk] adj (garment) hecho a la
medida; **~ tailor** sastre m que
confecciona a la medida.
best [bɛst] adj (el/la) mejor ♦ adv (lo) mejor;
the ~ part of (quantity) la mayor parte de;